—

IPSWICH BOROUGH ARCHIVES

1255–1835

A CATALOGUE

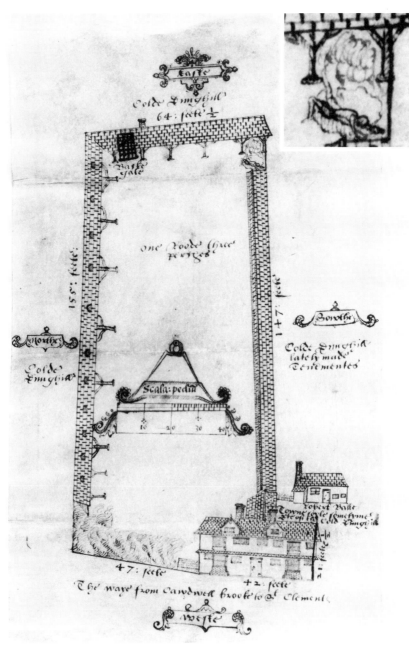

Frontispiece. Bird's-eye view from a grant by the Bailiffs, burgesses and commonalty, to Hugh Sheale of Ipswich, gunpowder maker, of a piece of common soil, lately part of the Cold Dunghill in St Clement's and St Margaret's parishes, in consideration of 200 lb gunpowder, 18 September 1593. In the south-east corner a man seems to have been flung to the ground in an explosion (detail inset). (C/3/8/4/31)

IPSWICH BOROUGH ARCHIVES

1255–1835

A CATALOGUE

Compiled by

DAVID ALLEN

with introductory essays on
the Governance of the Borough
by
GEOFFREY MARTIN and FRANK GRACE

THE BOYDELL PRESS

Published on 29 June 2000
to celebrate the 800th Anniversary
of the reception of King John's Charter
by the Burgesses
by the
SUFFOLK RECORDS SOCIETY
with the support of
THE BRITISH LIBRARY
and the town and county bodies listed

VOLUME XLIII

A Suffolk Records Society publication
with the support of
the British Library
and the town and county bodies listed opposite
First published 2000
The Boydell Press, Woodbridge

ISBN 0 85115 772 6

Issued to subscribing members for the year 1999–2000

The Boydell Press is an imprint of Boydell & Brewer Ltd
PO Box 9, Woodbridge, Suffolk IP12 3DF, UK
and of Boydell & Brewer Inc.
PO Box 41026, Rochester, NY 14604–4126, USA
website: http://www.boydell.co.uk

A catalogue record for this book is available
from the British Library

This publication is printed on acid-free paper

Printed in Great Britain by
St Edmundsbury Press Ltd, Bury St Edmunds, Suffolk

This catalogue is dedicated to the memory of
KATHRYN PATRICIA WOODGATE (1947–1993)
Archivist in the Suffolk Record Office
who knew and cared for the collection well

Contents

List of Illustrations

Preface

Each year since 1993, on Charter Day, 29 June, there has been a colourful procession from the churchyard of St Mary le Tower to the Cornhill, where translated excerpts of John's Charter have been read in public. In October 1995, James Hehir, the borough Chief Executive, began seriously to lay plans for the special events of the year 2000. In a letter inviting ideas, he wrote 'one of the prime needs is to mark the anniversary of the granting of the Royal Charter to the Borough'. The Charter Day procession in 2000, I replied, could recreate the annual feast day celebrations of the gild of Corpus Christi which between 1325 and 1547 brought together the whole community of medieval Ipswich. I also mentioned two possibly relevant 'strays' formerly in the borough archives: John Bale's play *King Johan*, and a 15th-century minstrels' book, now in Bodley. Admittedly, the Bard's seldom performed *King John* would be better entertainment than Bale's Protestant tract, and Ipswich (with Oxford) only receives mention in his *Henry VIII*.

The most important suggestion, however, concerned the archives of the borough, as fine a set as any in the country, never adequately catalogued, still less made more accessible by the best examples being illustrated. That there was general encouragement for a new catalogue appears from the large number of town and county bodies, and our patrons, who have supported the work; to them we are very grateful. If proof of the permanent value of the work were needed, the British Library grant, the largest they are able to give, and the support of the Marc Fitch Fund for selected illustrations are prime evidence. We are especially grateful to those private patrons and trusts who gave at the outset, for they enabled the word-processing of the text, with exemplary attention to detail, by Nicky Hogan.

It only remains for me to thank the members of the small working party who helped at crucial stages, setting out the classification to be adopted and giving expert advice from time to time. We have been fortunate to have been able to call on Geoffrey Martin and Frank Grace for essays illuminating the governance of the borough before and after the time of Richard Percyvale. Professor Martin also generously permitted full use of his work, published and unpublished, in the introductions to sections of the catalogue. The County Director of Libraries and Heritage, Amanda Arrowsmith, Gwyn Thomas and David Jones of the Suffolk Record Office, and Bill Serjeant, retired County Archivist, complete the list of those who supported David Allen's work on the project over two years. Finally, Richard Barber's enthusiasm at Boydell, and Pru Harrison's skill in setting the text ensured that the volume would be worthy to take its place as the Suffolk Records Society's forty-third.

John Blatchly
Project Director
August 1999

Editor's Introduction

Though Ipswich received its first charter from King John in 1200, the earliest record of the borough's administration now surviving is the Portmanmote Roll for 1255–56. The theft of the earlier court rolls (probably no very great quantity), together with the original custumal ('le Domesday'), by John le Blake the ex-Common Clerk in 1272 is discussed in the introduction to section two of this catalogue, JUSTICE AND THE COURTS (p. 41). John's charter itself is not heard of after 1696, in which year its presence in the town treasury was recorded by the Clavigers, the custodians of the muniments and Common Seal.

Despite these losses, the surviving archive now in the Suffolk Record Office in Ipswich nevertheless contains evidence from John's reign. Even the text of the missing charter survives, recited in full in the Charter of Confirmation issued by his grandson Edward I in 1291, and repeated in most successive charters down to that of Elizabeth I. Moreover, le Blake's theft led the borough authorities to appoint a panel of the best-advised burgesses to re-state the borough customs in the so-called 'Little Domesday', the surviving versions of which include an account, perhaps unique in England, of the procedure followed for settling the borough's constitution and electing its first municipal officers at a series of public meetings in the summer of 1200, following the reception of John's charter.

The survival of the 1255–56 Portmanmote Roll places the Ipswich borough archive among the earliest of such accumulations extant in England. The Roll is antedated by the Gild Rolls of Leicester and Shrewsbury (beginning in 1196 and 1209 respectively); by the Taxation Rolls (from 1227) and Burghmoot Rolls (from 1231–32) of Wallingford; by the rolls of London's Hustings Court, on which deeds were enrolled from 1252; and by the Anglo-Norman custumal of Exeter, begun *c.* 1240. Ipswich's Portmanmote Roll is, however, 'the earliest comprehensive court roll that can be shown to be the parent of later specialised records' (Martin 1961, 149). The evolution of Ipswich's other medieval courts and their records from the Portmanmote and its rolls is traced in detail in the introductory notes to section two and its various sub-divisions. The working of the borough's administrative institutions in the medieval and post-medieval periods is discussed at length in the essays by Geoffrey Martin and Frank Grace.

In 1654 the town's Recorder, Nathaniel Bacon, grandson of Elizabeth I's Lord Keeper Sir Nicholas, completed his *Annalls of Ipswiche*, the manuscript of which is preserved in the borough archive. Bacon's compilation made extensive use of the records of the medieval courts, and comparison of his sources with the surviving archive proves that very few early records have been lost since he wrote. Most losses of medieval material therefore occurred comparatively early in the history of the Corporation (Martin 1956, 87). The Clavigers' inventory of 1696, referred to above, provides evidence of careful administration at the end of the 17th century.

By the 19th century, however, the town was less fortunate in the custodians of its historic records. Documents were purloined by William Batley, a long-serving Town Clerk with a proprietorial interest in the borough's affairs and records, and there was extensive looting by, or on behalf of, his collector friends John Wodderspoon and the notorious William Stevenson Fitch (on whose activities, *see* Freeman 1997). In 1953 and 1955 two important groups of stray 16th- and 17th-century correspondence from the archive were purchased back by the then Ipswich and East Suffolk Record Office through a local antiquarian bookseller; this material is listed in detail as Appendix I to the catalogue. Other stray items have found their way into the Suffolk Record Office by diverse routes (*see* Appendix II); while yet others have passed irretrievably to the British Library (*see* Appendix III).

Other records strayed temporarily for more legitimate reasons, having been retained accidentally by a local firm of solicitors, one of whose 19th-century members, S. A. Notcutt, was a distinguished Town Clerk of Ipswich. Documents were returned to the Town Hall by this firm at intervals from 1891, and were re-united with the archive. Following this precedent, a substantial accumulation of deeds and manorial records relating to the estates of the town's various charities, from the same source, placed in the Record Office in the 1950s, has now been restored to the borough archive and listed for the first time in this catalogue.

Among the archive's areas of greatest strength are the series of records of the medieval courts, most notably perhaps the rolls of the Petty Court or Court of Petty Pleas, whose cases touched almost every aspect of the life of the town, and which in time became the borough's principal judicial agency. The rolls of the Petty Court of Recognizances, in effect a register of deeds (which from 1307 includes also enrolled testaments), furnish a detailed and invaluable record of transactions involving burgage tenements; the practice of enrolling deeds survived the demise of the old Corporation in 1835 and continued into the 20th century. The records of the borough's Justices of the Peace sitting in their General Sessions begin in 1440, and are thus considerably earlier in date than the corresponding archive of Suffolk's county Quarter Sessions, which contains nothing from before the middle of the 17th century (though a stray county Mainprize Roll covering the period 1431–1447 is unaccountably preserved in the Ipswich borough archive: *see* C/2/12/3).

The records of the town's principal financial officers, the Treasurer and Chamberlains, are particularly rich and detailed for the Elizabethan and Stuart periods. Also of great interest are the records, dating back to the early 17th century, of the relatively sophisticated water supply provided, literally 'on tap' (through a cock 'of the bigness of a swan's quill and no bigger') to the houses of those inhabitants prepared to pay to lease it. Much social history is contained in the administrative and financial records of the various town charities for the 16th to 19th centuries, many of which were examined in detail apparently for the first time during the compilation of this catalogue. To give but one example, many of the bundles of payment vouchers of the Renterwardens and Receivers of Tooley's and Smart's charities for the 18th century contain annual itemized apothecary's accounts for the medicines prescribed for the almspeople, which should be of particular interest to medical historians.

Perhaps the most disappointing aspect of the archive – especially when contrasted with the fullness of the medieval court rolls – is the almost total absence of financial records for the medieval period. There are no formal accounts, and the activities of the Chamberlains as revenue officers at this time are represented only by a handful of counter-rolls of the Portmanmote, Petty Court, Court of Recognizances and Leet, maintained as a safeguard against peculation by the Bailiffs.

Also disappointing is the almost complete lack of correspondence, either in the form of original letters or of letter-books. The stray letters purloined in the 19th century, recovered in the 1950s and catalogued in Appendix I indicate that it was formerly the practice to retain at least some in-letters. But at what point such documents ceased to be placed in the archive for safe custody, what proportion of what was formerly retained is represented by the recovered material, and how much of what is lost was deliberately pilfered or simply discarded, are questions that cannot now be answered.

A new catalogue of this most important archive is long overdue. The existing finding-aid was highly idiosyncratic in its arrangement. Its first main section was headed 'Groups of miscellaneous documents', with sub-sections such as 'Curious and choice', 'Curious certificates' and 'Rushring specimens', apparently derived from the examination made by J. Cordy Jeaffreson, the compiler of the 1883 Historical Manuscript Commission report on the archive. The second main section was entitled 'Groups awaiting classification', and contained many obvious strays from main series, unaccountably never incorporated into their proper sequence. Records such as the rolls of the medieval courts had no individual listing, the rolls of all the courts for a particular reign being merely placed together in one or more boxes with a single catalogue entry. Many charity records were attributed to the wrong charity, their catalogue entries having apparently been taken from the labels of the brown-paper parcels in which Jeaffreson had left them in the 19th century (and which appeared not to have been untied since). By contrast, other sections of the old catalogue, such as the calendar of grants of common soil, were sufficiently detailed to form the basis of the present work. A further major disadvantage of the old catalogue was the lack, for most record series, of introductory matter to indicate the kind of information to be found in them. Taken overall, it was a finding-aid which Record Office staff and researchers alike found extremely difficult to use.

Its fourteen main sections have now been reduced to six, the outlines of which were decided by the steering committee of the Ipswich 800 Project before work began, and the detailed structure of which emerged as cataloguing progressed. Purists may perhaps take exception to some of the decisions taken. For instance, though the records of the Land, Window and other Assessed Taxes are, strictly speaking, records of the Clerk of the Peace, and might therefore be expected to be found in section two, JUSTICE AND THE COURTS, with the records of the General Sessions, they have, for convenience, been placed with the few other surviving taxation records in section one, treated as an 'external obligation' on the borough. This arrangement had the added advantage of reducing the degree of sub-numbering required in catalogue references which were in danger of becoming too unwieldy. Similarly, a case could be made for separating the various records relating to the water supply. The financial records for the period in which the water rents were the responsibility of the Chamberlains, and those of the later Collectors of the water rents, could properly have formed two sub-sections of 'Finance and Town Property', and the deeds of the Quay Water Works could have been grouped with the evidences of title to other Corporation properties. But for convenience all these records, with the leases of the water supply to individual householders, have been placed together in section five, treated as a 'town responsibility and service'. A conscious attempt has been made to strike a balance between strict archival theory and the convenience of the user. It is believed that the present arrangement will make for greater ease of reference.

Because of considerations of space and cost, the *former* reference numbers have not been cited alongside the new references in the published version of the catalogue. (In any case, as mentioned above, some record series were not fully referenced in the superseded list.) However, it is intended that, in due course, a version of the catalogue will be available on-line *via* the CALM 2000 (Collection Management for Archives,

Libraries and Museums) system, where those users familiar with the old numbers will find them perpetuated for purposes of cross-reference.

The re-cataloguing of the archive has revealed much that was previously unknown except, perhaps, to the handful of scholars who have made extensive use of the records. It has rectified much (particularly among the charity records) that was incorrectly attributed, and assigned individual numbers for the first time to record series (such as the rolls of the various medieval courts) which were previously difficult to identify. Many documents are here listed for the first time. It is hoped that the appearance of this catalogue on the 800th anniversary of the reception of the first charter will stimulate much new research into many aspects of Ipswich's past, leading eventually to the publication of that full-scale history of the town, based on original source material, which at present it so conspicuously lacks.

David Allen
June 1999

The Governance of Ipswich

I. *From its origins to c.1550*

by Geoffrey Martin

The last year of the second Millennium, AD 2000, has a special significance for Ipswich, as the 800th anniversary of the borough's first charter of liberties, granted by King John. Yet when the burgesses gathered in St Mary le Tower churchyard on 29 June 1200 to celebrate the occasion their town was already several centuries old. There has been a settlement, originally called Gipeswic, at the head of the Orwell estuary at least since the 7th century AD, and Ipswich has been a focus of trade and industry and communications for more than 1300 years.

The community which negotiated and paid for a royal charter in 1200 received the document ceremoniously and immediately made a record, unique for its time, of its proceedings. That was the beginning of a rich archival heritage of which their successors in the town are rightly proud. The modern borough of Ipswich would seem strange to the earliest inhabitants of Gipeswic, but more familiar to the burgesses of the Middle Ages, who would recognize at least some of its churches and the names and even the lines of some of its streets. Both groups, however, and others from the intervening centuries, would readily understand the functions and interests of Ipswich today, as the town enters the third Millennium of its experience.

The earliest documents of English history are the names of places. The oldest known form of Ipswich, uttered long before it was written down, is Gipeswic, transmuted over the centuries through Gepeswiz and Gyppeswyche to Yepeswich. There are two elements in the name, and the second, wic, marks it as a place of trade. The first element may represent an otherwise unknown personal name, Gip or Gipe, or it may be related to gap and gape, and refer to the wide opening of the Orwell estuary. The earliest references to the place occur in the 10th century. Theodred, bishop of London and East Anglia, bought a *haga* or messuage in Ipswich and bequeathed it in his will *c*. 950.[1] The Anglo-Saxon chronicle says that the Danes sailed to Ipswich from Kent in 991, and raided the surrounding countryside. It was during that campaign that Byrhtnoth, ealdorman of Essex, challenged them on the Blackwater, and died in the battle celebrated in the Song of Maldon. The Danish fleet returned in 1010, and landed at Ipswich when they harried and occupied East Anglia.

It was always implicit in that sparse relation that Ipswich was a place of trade. Bishop Theodred's property was a town house rather than a farm. The Danes sought loot and combat rather than solitude, and though they valued the Orwell as an anchorage it was reasonable to suppose that they found something more than a signboard when they arrived there. In the 1950s, however, archaeological studies revealed that not only had there been a settlement at Ipswich from the 7th century onwards, but that it was characterized by the manufacture of a wheel-turned pottery which was widely distributed on the east coast.[2]

The implications of a traffic in the vessels known as Ipswich ware are more impressive than the remains of the pots themselves or, for that matter, the traces of the

---

[1] *See* Whitelock 1930, 4–5.
[2] *See* Hurst and West 1957, 29–60.

hutments in which they were made. There is no indication of any formal planning on the site, and some evidence that individual houses had their own defensive ditches as late as the middle of the 10th century.[3] On the other hand, the continuity of occupation and manufacture suggests that the wic was not merely a seasonal settlement. Its position at the head of the tidal water gave it a strategic importance, and countered its remoteness from the Roman road from Colchester through Baylham to Caistor. The obscurity of its nature is matched by the tribal organization of the rest of East Anglia, of which we still know very little.

Yet evidence of some civic identity follows soon after. In the course of a transaction 'before the whole city of Cambridge', c.1000, the men of Cambridge claimed that titles to land established in their presence required no further proof of their validity, and that they shared that privileged status with Ipswich, Norwich, and Thetford.[4] The claim may have been exaggerated, but it accords with the evidence of Domesday Book that Ipswich had both a distinctive urban character and some formal urban status before the Conquest.

When in the 10th century the West Saxons, under Alfred's successors, assimilated the territories which they recovered from the Danes, they divided them into shires, each with a court over which the king's reeve, the sheriff, presided. The shires were subdivided into hundreds, units with a name that looked back to some older tribal system, each of which also had a court. The central meeting place of the shire was generally a fortified town, which housed a licensed market and a mint, and had a court of its own, as well as housing the shire court. Such a town might be referred to indifferently as a *burh*, in respect of its fortifications, or a *poort*, meaning a place of trade, but *burh* has prevailed in modern English, as borough, to signify a community with a civic stamp upon it.

Some of those boroughs, like Ipswich and Colchester, ranked as hundreds or half-hundreds in themselves. Their courts were therefore the equivalent of hundred courts, but as we have seen they might also have privileges of their own.

Domesday Book is a valuable source of information about both town and countryside. The returns for Essex, Norfolk, and Suffolk are fuller than those for most other counties, but in respect of the towns they lack one element which is notable elsewhere.[5] The questions which the king's commissioners asked were entirely directed to assessing the agrarian sources of wealth, and made no reference to trade or the resources of towns. In many places, therefore, including Cambridge and Colchester, the assembled townsmen offered material which was important to them because it defined their relations with the king, but which could not be assimilated to the general plan of the survey. It was probably for that reason that the description of the chief town in the county is usually prefixed to the main text in Domesday, which describes and assesses the holdings of the king and his tenants in chief.[6]

It seems that the material collected in the eastern counties took longer to arrange than that from the rest of the country, and that when work on the survey was abandoned what now constitutes Little Domesday was left in an unfinished state. As it happens the description of Ipswich is fragmented, with the principal entry an item in

---

[3] *See* West *et al.* 1964, 233–303. A *haga* or haw was originally a dwelling enclosed by a hedge, but it came to mean what was subsequently called a burgage. The word survives in the name of Den Haag, in the Netherlands.

[4] *See* Blake 1962, xvi, 100; and Tait 1936, 41–43.

[5] On the character and content of Little Domesday, *see* Galbraith 1961; Finn 1964; and Darby 1952.

[6] *See further* Martin 1986, 143–63; and the discussion of evidence from York in Pallister 1990.

the survey of the royal demesne. Other references are scattered which might elsewhere have been gathered under a single heading. The king's lands were under the sheriff's management, and it may be that the townsmen were given no opportunity to make their own representations. What is clear is that the community had suffered catastrophic losses since the Conquest. Instead of the 538 burgesses who paid dues to King Edward, in 1086 there were only 110, and another 100 so poor that they could pay only a capitation tax. The sum is completed by 328 houses which lay waste. Some of them were probably levelled to clear a site for a castle, on the west side of the town, but others may have been destroyed in raids or in the aftermath of Earl Ralph's rebellion in 1075–6. The annual sum for which the sheriff answered had been reduced, and although the moneyers' dues had been greatly increased since 1066, they too had been moderated in recent years.

The reference to the moneyers, however, like those to a total of twelve churches in the town, are reminders that the community was not a simple one. The material damage which it suffered, though severe, had neither abolished its functions nor exhausted its resources. It was a meeting place, with political as well as commercial business in hand. It merited, though it can hardly have welcomed, a castle. It was a characteristic of the shire-boroughs to number tenants of rural manors amongst their burgesses. They were there for a variety of reasons, but chiefly because they gave their lords a stake in the affairs of the town. Those in Ipswich included a tenant of the manor of Moze, across the Stour in Essex. His presence shows the wide expanse of the haven rather as an extension of the town than as its southern boundary.

In 1125 the Orwell was a meeting-place for Henry I's counsellors and ship-masters when the law of the sea was codified.[7] Later customs accounts show a vigorous trade with the Rhineland and the Low Countries, and the security of its harbour goes far to explain the growth of Ipswich during the long decline of Dunwich. Two of the churches mentioned in Domesday Book were newly-endowed and staffed with Augustinian canons in the 12th century: St Peter and St Paul on the south side of the town, before the end of Henry I's reign, and Holy Trinity to the north-east.[8] A new parish church, St Clement's, was founded before 1136, as tenements spread eastwards along the quays. Those developments occurred at a time when the whole population of Europe was growing, and there was an unprecedented demand for foodstuffs and other goods and services. In Ipswich as elsewhere the physical expansion of the town was accompanied by a new confidence in the community.

Domesday Book, which was intensively consulted in the 12th century, had probably drawn the attention of the king and his advisers to the wealth and the potential of the towns. Kings could and did levy arbitrary taxes, known as tallage, on their estates, but towns were valuable enough to warrant a little diplomacy. Henry II (1154–89) bargained long and made only sparing concessions, but his sons Richard I (1189–99) and John (1199–1216) needed money more urgently. What the townsmen wanted was to exclude the sheriff from their affairs, and they achieved it by offering to pay more to the king than the sheriff customarily rendered. Ipswich began to negotiate with Richard I, probably in 1196. The talks themselves cost money, but the prize was enticing and experience is its own reward. Their charter was granted by John, in Normandy, at Orival (Seine Maritime), on 25 May 1200.

[7]   *See* Twiss 1871–76, i, 62–64.
[8]   On St Peter's *see VCH Suffolk* ii, 102–03; and on Holy Trinity, *ibid*, 103–04. The two houses in a short while acquired thirteen of the town's fifteen churches.

The charter probably gave John's burgesses of the borough of Ipswich all that they had asked for, and quite as much as they had expected. We have evidence that towns conferred one with another about the terms of their charters, and the king's ministers would have their own views at any particular time about what it was appropriate to grant. Ipswich was granted to its burgesses and their heirs to hold for ever of the king and his heirs, in return for an increase of five pounds above the sum customarily due. They were granted freedom of toll throughout John's lands, which was a more spacious concession in 1200 than it would be a few years later. They could have a gild merchant and hanse, a protective trade association, and they were exempted from billeting and other impositions by royal officers. They were not to be impleaded outside the borough in respect of their tenements there, nor for debts contracted within the town. They could enjoy their own free customs, and could choose their own magistrates; two Bailiffs, and four Coroners to keep, that is to say to identify and reserve, the pleas of the crown, and to ensure that the Bailiffs did justice to rich and poor alike.

The main provisions in the charter are to be found in grants made to other towns, but what followed upon its reception produced a record of exceptional interest.[9] On 29 June the townsmen assembled in St Mary le Tower churchyard to hear the charter read, and to celebrate their new status by electing Bailiffs and Coroners and making some ordinances. In a series of four further meetings, ending on 12 October 1200, they went on to elect twelve Chief Portmen, chosen by panels representing each parish of the town, to govern the borough and preserve its liberties. They also elected two Beadles, or Serjeants, approved the making of a common seal, and ordered that the charter be sent to be read in the county courts of Suffolk, a little way down the road, and Norfolk. They appointed an alderman of the newly licensed gild merchant, with four associates, and granted the meadow called Odenholm, now under Portman Road, to sustain the Chief Portmen's horses. Finally they resolved to write down the laws and customs of the town in a roll to be called Domesday, and the ordinances of the gild in another roll.[10] There must have been many similar scenes elsewhere, but they are documented only in Ipswich. With the narrative of those proceedings the records of the borough of Ipswich begin.

The first thing to say about the narrative is that it has come down to us in a later copy, indeed in a series of later copies. The second is that there is no reason to doubt its authenticity. The original text seems to have been lost at some time between the early 14th century and the middle of the 16th century, and probably sooner rather than later.[11] It was copied c.1310 into a parchment volume, now C/4/1/1, known as the Black Domeday Book of Ipswich, together with the text of the customs, which by that time had been reconstituted. Any text which survives only in copies is naturally suspect, but here we have a document which is internally consistent, contains no manifest anachronisms, and serves no perceptible ulterior purpose. That is to say that it asserts nothing which could be uniquely adduced to support some later political practice, argument, or innovation. It would be ungrateful not to take it at its face value.

---

[9] The text is published in full in Gross 1890, ii, 114–32.
[10] 'As is the practice in other cities and boroughs where there is a gild merchant'. *See further* Martin 1963, 129–34.
[11] There is a passage in c.17 of the narrative which appears only in Percyvale's Domesday (see below, p. xxvii–xxviii). It gives the alderman of the gild a monopoly of the trade in millstones and other stones in the town. It is most probably, but cannot be proved to be, a late interpolation, rather than a passage omitted from the earlier copies.

Although the narrative describes only the events of 1200, it bears in an interesting way upon what had gone before. The townsmen negotiated as a body with the crown, but it is certain that both the risks and the rewards of that undertaking would have fallen to the most substantial members of the community. Their leaders were presumably John fitz Norman and Robert Belines, who became the first Bailiffs of the chartered borough. They were also named as two of the four Coroners, with Philip de Porta and Roger Lew as their colleagues, and as all four were named first among the twelve Portmen it seems likely that they were the weightiest part, if they were not in fact the whole, of the group who had negotiated with the king's officers.

There may be a further clue in the narrative as to what they had sought, or to what beyond the new status of the town they most prized. There are several references, when the Portmen are elected, and when the gild roll is ordained, to practice in other boroughs. They are of a reassuring kind, and are meant to show that everything was done with due regard to the well-being and honour of the town. The statement of the laws and free customs, in contrast, speaks for itself. The ancient usages of the town, which are specifically mentioned in the charter, are distinguished from the beginning from the liberties which the king had newly granted.[12] The roll which contains them is to be known as the Domesday roll, an invocation of the most impressive act of royal authority that the popular memory encompassed.

The text of the Ipswich Domesday is a record which is deservedly prominent both in the history of Ipswich and of the English town at large. It is one of the very earliest and certainly the most wide-ranging of such custumals, and it links the municipality of later centuries with the community and its assembly adduced at Cambridge in 1000.

What changed in 1200, as the tone of the narrative shows, is that the townsmen now enjoyed a degree of autonomy and were conscious of its responsibilities. The town court was the focus of administration as well as a tribunal, and the distinctive customs of their community continued after the event as before. It is unlikely that they could have negotiated their liberties successfully without an organization substantially the same as that which they decreed under licence in 1200. The difference lies in their self-consciousness, their sense of success, and their determination to maintain an explicit record of their rights and their actions.

As it happens, the first records of the new borough are the memoranda of the gild, and their chief concern is with the admission of those from outside the town, including both lords and clergy, who wished to share in its privileges. No record of the borough court survives before 1255, and there is then a gap until the last years of Henry III's reign. The reason for that paucity, however, lies in the well-known perfidy of John Black, the Common Clerk who fled the town in 1272. Black carried off the Domesday roll, and a number of court rolls, probably because he had been accused of making false entries in them. Whatsoever the reason for his flight, it compelled the townsmen to take stock of their records. Their efforts to repair their loss opened a new phase of the town's history.

The survival of the roll for 1255–56 is fortunate, because it shows us the portmoot, as the chief court of the borough was called, at work in the middle of the century. There is nothing about the record to suggest that it was an innovation, and it is still a comprehensive register of transactions.[13] There are few indications that the court had begun to differentiate its business in the way that was formalized, and impressively

---

[12] *See* Gross 1890, 118.
[13] On the development of court and other records, *see* Martin 1997, 122–24.

documented, by the end of the century.[14] We can certainly suppose that it had functioned in much the same way since 1200, and that it was not only the gild that had kept records in that time. The records need not have been very extensive, but it is remarkable that anything has survived at all.

John Black is likely to have removed only the more recent court rolls, but at least we are sure that he did not decamp with all that there was to take. One impulse to systematic recording came in 1256, when the town received a charter from Henry III granting it the right, or imposing the duty, of returning writs directly to the royal chancery without the intervention of the sheriff. The innovation was a revenue-raising device imposed by the crown, but it furthered the autonomy of the court, and so of the town.

In 1283 there was a riot in Ipswich in which seamen disrupted a session of the county court, and Edward I took the town into his own hands. Its liberties were not restored until 1291 when the townsmen were rewarded for their contrite behaviour by receiving, and having to pay for, a new charter. Thereupon they appointed a panel of twenty-four of the most experienced burgesses to prepare a new statement of the free customs, saying that the loss of the old Domesday roll had caused uncertainty and contention over procedures. The work was undertaken at a time of intense activity in the borough, and in the common law courts at large. In describing the business of the borough courts the panel seems, and not unnaturally, to be dignifying some current practices with the stamp of antiquity. Nevertheless both the general tone of the customs and the detail are consonant with a serious effort to preserve what could be recollected of ancient usage.

It appears that the text of the new Domesday, like the old, was entered upon a roll. If so, like the original it was subsequently lost, though not before it had been copied for safety. Indeed it may be that it was the survival of multiple copies that led to the second roll being put aside and sooner or later abandoned. The earliest copy of its text that we have is in a parchment volume, now Additional MS 25,012 in the British Library.

The manuscript is a very plain one, written without ornament about 1312. The text is French, which is almost certainly the language used in 1291, though it is possible that the roll of 1200 was in Latin.[15] The customs are preceded by an index to their contents. The volume also contains the rules of porterage in the town, some extracts from the Portmanmote rolls of 1255–56 and 1270–72, a note of the constituents of the farm of the town, that is to say the annual dues which the burgesses paid to the exchequer, lists of knights' fees in neighbouring honours, the boundaries of the town leets, and an account of the election of the Chief Portmen in 1309.

There is one amendment to the text of the customs which is repeated in all the later copies of the custumal – the substitution of 'rent' for 'services' in the clause discussing the circumstances in which a landlord might distrain a tenant. Property in towns was let for cash, and was indeed the only secure form of investment available to a medieval merchant. In the free air of towns, too, a rent discharged in money constituted a less emotive contract than a tenure which depended upon service, with its hierarchic overtones. As it happens, however, although the amended text was duly copied in later versions, the entry in the index to the customs refers to the subject of the clause as the default of services, a point which escaped the reviser and all subsequent copyists.

---

[14] *See further* Martin 1954, 26–29.
[15] The text of the customs is printed in Twiss 1871–76, ii, 16–207.

The chief interest of the earliest Custumal is that it is a codex, a stitched and bound book, made at a time when all the administrative records of the town were rolls. A roll was well suited to keeping a cumulative record, which could readily be extended by adding membranes, either fastened head to tail (which is known as chancery style) or tied at the head (exchequer style).[16] The larger it grew, however, the less convenient it was to consult. The Great Court and the Petty Plea Rolls of Edward I's reign were beginning to pose such problems, but beyond a general prevalence of the exchequer style, which allows the reader to hold the roll at the head and turn the membranes like the pages of a book,[17] rolls held their own in court for more than another century.

For the customs, however, the codex set a pattern. The unadorned text of the first version of the Custumal was followed, within some fifteen years, by two more elaborate volumes, and by at least another two by the middle of the century. The contents and incidence of those books deserve particular attention.

Besides the customs, the earliest Custumal contains an exceptional note of the election of the Chief Portmen. There may have been other and even routine elections, but no record of them survives. No explanation of the event is offered, but over the next twelve years the office of Bailiff was filled by only five men, two of whom, Thomas Stacey and Thomas le Rente, almost monopolized the post. They were Bailiffs together from 1307 to 1311, and in 1318–20, and one or the other singly in 1312, 1313, 1314, and 1316. In those years the court records show nothing but an orderly round of events, and the grant of a new charter, from Edward II in 1317, seems a mark of earnest endeavour. The charter confirms and enlarges earlier grants, reduces the number of Coroners from four to two, and protects the burgesses' monopoly of trade. Two years later, however, there are signs of strife and change, which come in significant part from the custumals.

The second and third copies of the Custumal are the volumes known from their bindings as the Black Domesday and the White Domesday (Ipswich C/4/1/1 and C/4/1/2). The Black Domeday is the older of the two. Its text begins with the charter of 1317, and runs on through the customs and all the other material in the earliest Custumal except the Portmens' election. It adds to them the narrative of the proceedings in 1200, the oldest copy we have of that text, and an account of an inquest in 1200 into the privileges of religious houses seeking to market the produce of their estates in the town. The following records of the admission of what are called forinsic, i.e., foreign or external burgesses, including local lords and clerics, show that they became contributory to the farm of the borough, but also contributed to the hanse or fund of the gild, thus becoming gildsmen by virtue of becoming burgesses or *vice versa*.

That corpus of historical and constitutional material is filled out with the text of a remarkable set of ordinances, made in December 1320. They begin with a greeting from the Alderman, Bailiffs, and burgesses of the town, which makes them in effect a joint product of the gild and the borough, and they go on to decree that all merchandise should be freely offered for sale in the town, without abuse of contracts by denizens or forinsic merchants, and that while strangers are bound by the good usages of the town they also deserve protection. They also say in more or less detail that the Bailiffs should be freely and openly elected, that there should be financial officers, Chamberlains, to collect and account for the income of the town, and that the

---

[16] A codex can also be enlarged, by adding gatherings, up to the time when it is bound, but there is little advantage in keeping loose fascicules, and binding adds security to ease of handling.

[17] Though less conveniently, unless the text runs head to foot on the face and foot to head on the dorse of each membrane. Even so, rolled parchment has a strong propensity to curl, and often to snap shut.

admission of postulants to the freedom of the borough should be open and on strictly defined occasions, and not turned to the private profit of the Bailiffs.

Those were the commonplaces of reform in an age when everyone knew well enough what had been said and done, and the written word was set down to edify posterity. Although there is no explicit recrimination in the text, beyond the observation that it would be to the discredit and disadvantage of the town if such rules were not observed, we can readily deduce from it the recent course of events.[18] When we add the fact that Stacey and le Rente began the year as Bailiffs and were replaced in the course of it, and that the records of chancery refer to disturbances in the town continuing to 1324, in which year Thomas le Rente died, we can marvel at the writer's restraint.

For our present purposes, however, the effect of those events on the archives is of more consequence than the fortunes and misfortunes of individuals. The making of a security copy early in the reign of Stacey and le Rente was rounded off with a note of the election of Portmen, which was presumably a constitutional marker of some kind, and a small number of other items, not all associated with the Domesday roll. A decade later a new version of the Custumal provided an opportunity to publicize and preserve the instrument by which the administration had been reformed, and to associate it with all the historical material that the archives contained. The resulting emphasis upon the gild would have served to underline the standing of the Alderman, who presumably owed his prominence in the ordinances to the fact that he was not strictly speaking an officer of the borough.

Within a few years the customs were copied again, this time without the ordinances, into the White Domesday Book. In both volumes the text is carefully presented, with rubricized capitals and paragraph marks, to make a dignified work of reference. The omission of the ordinances from the White Domesday may reflect a desire to bury the dissensions of the early 1320s. The other material was presented in much the same order as in the Black Domesday, and the volume attracted civic memoranda, including oaths of office, for some two centuries. Two further copies were made in the middle years of the century. One is now British Library MS Egerton 2,788, which belonged to Paul de Roos, Common Clerk of Ipswich in the 1340s. The other (Ipswich C/4/1/3) is the most elaborately and handsomely decorated of the whole series, which is probably why it found its way into the hands of Sir John Maynard, of the Middle Temple, in the mid-17th century, and subsequently into the library of Sir Thomas Phillipps (1792–1872). It was returned to the town in 1973. The Custumal evidently had a talismanic quality in the Middle Ages, a reminder that the traditional lore of the town had its place in the world of written texts and the burgeoning intricacy of the common law.

Though the ordinances of 1320 figured only briefly in the Custumal, they had a striking effect on the records of the courts. Although almost all the medieval Chamberlains' accounts have been lost, it is clear that the injunction to keep records of receipts and duplicate records of the principal transactions of the courts, including recognizances of free tenement, was taken seriously in the 1320s.[19] The rolls themselves are set out from that time in a more orderly fashion, and generally establish a pattern which carries them through and beyond the acute crises of the middle of the

---

[18] For a lively account of the municipal politics, *see* Alsford 1984, 105–15; and for the text and a discussion of the ordinances, Martin 1955, 58–82 and Appendix 1.

[19] On recognizances of free-tenement, which registered a title to burgages in the town, and on the development of the Court of Recognizances, *see* Martin 1973, 9–19.

century. A further measure of the abundance of the archives by the 1330s, and of the importance attached to them, is the existence of an inventory of rolls, with notes on the date, contents and place of storage, compiled *c.*1333.[20]

During the 14th century Ipswich continued with an administrative system of its own contriving, under the authority of the charter granted by John. Its heart was still the Portmanmote, a legacy of pre-Conquest England, now known as the Great Court. The gild merchant, important during the borough's formative years, and evidently useful during the political imbroglio of the 1320s, was effectively recast as a devotional gild of Corpus Christi in 1325. It was a comparatively early manifestation of a cult which became ubiquitous in England after the Black Death.[21] The impulse to the change appears to have come from the priors of Holy Trinity and SS Peter and Paul, and the gild was supported by the clergy of the town, but it remained closely identified with the municipality, and all burgesses were members. The leading townsmen used it as a social club, and kept a close hand on crafts in the town by organizing their contributions to the pageants of the Corpus Christi day processions.

The borough received five further charters during the century: a confirmation of liberties from Edward III in 1338, two from Richard II, one in 1378, with a grant of wider jurisdiction, and a further confirmation in 1380. Richard's second charter was confirmed by Henry IV in December 1399, when he had been on the throne for three months, and the burgesses may have felt in need of reassurance.[22] John's charter had granted Ipswich to the burgesses of Ipswich and their heirs for ever, but recipients of royal grants were, advisedly, never wholly sure that their title could not be improved, or that powers that had not been recently used might not be challenged.

Ipswich had been briefly in the King's hands again in 1344–45, when the sheriff's deputy had presided over the courts. The town was severely affected by the bubonic plague in 1349, but although there were some interruptions, business continued and market and other dues were regularly collected. After the first onset of the plague, however, the Great Court seems to have fallen into a dormant, or at least a fitfully active state. From the middle of the century admissions to the freedom were recorded in the Court of Recognizances, and it is likely that other business was also transacted there. The attraction of the court was probably the regularity of its sessions and the consequent reliability of its records. The detailed process of change is obscured by gaps in the series and a consistent absence of explanatory comment, but while the Great Court declined both the Recognizance Court and Petty Court which heard personal and mixed pleas were continuously busy. There is a single Great Court roll in 1393–94, but it is not an impressive document, and records only two discontinued actions begun on writ of right. Administrative business seems to have passed then or soon afterwards to an assembly called the General Court, the first surviving register of which dates from *c.*1430.[23] In the meantime duplicate records of recognizances from 1405 to 1413 had been kept in a paper book, the first use of paper in the borough court, and also the first use of a book, in this instance a mere fascicule, for an administrative record.

General and Petty Courts continued into the 16th century, with their business recorded sometimes on rolls and sometimes in books. The registration of deeds and

---

[20] The inventory is C/4/7/1/1. *See below*, p. 431; and Martin 1954, 29–31 and 42.

[21] *See* Rubin 1991; and Westlake 1919, 21–22.

[22] Henry had granted two mills to the burgesses in October 1399, in enhancement of their revenues (*see below*, p. xxvii, n.28). The grant had presumably been negotiated before his usurpation in September.

[23] Now British Library Additional MS 30,158.

proof of testaments continued to be entered on rolls into Elizabeth's reign (1558–1603), with a conscious conservatism that attests the respect in which the record was held.

There are late echoes of those experiments and expedients in the early 19th century, on the eve of municipal reform. The Great Court was then a formal assembly, meeting chiefly to admit burgesses and convened for particular occasions, including the election of Members of Parliament. The Portmanmote, known as a court formerly held to hear common recoveries, was summoned by one of the Bailiffs to pass the estate of a married woman.[24] A Court of Small Pleas heard all actions, real, personal, and mixed, whilst a Petty Court could be called by both Bailiffs to pass the estate of a minor, whose competence so to act was originally prescribed in the medieval custumal. The distribution of the original powers of the Portmanmote, which was a sign of administrative vigour in the 13th and 14th centuries, was now dimly reflected in rituals about to be swept away as antiquarian lumber.[25]

The changes made in the 15th century, uncertain as they may seem, are symptomatic of much larger movements. In earlier centuries, towns such as Ipswich were islands of commercial life, in which the peculiar interests of merchants and manufacturers were protected by local usages attuned to the practices of a wider mercantile community. The chief features of such customs were the ready exchange and free devise of real property, which was a form of capital, and a concern with credit, debt, and contract. Outside the towns the law, largely tribal before the Conquest and martial afterwards, had little regard for such refinements. By the 14th century, however, the growth of the common law afforded a broader and more accommodating expertise for the protection of trade. Ipswich carefully reclaimed cases from the royal courts which ought to have been heard in the borough court, but like other towns it retained attorneys at Westminster for all kinds of general business.

The development of Parliament, in which the towns were directly represented, enabled individuals and communities to petition the crown over their own concerns, and also produced statute law binding upon the whole kingdom. From the 1330s there was a national system of taxation based on local assessment, and although the subsidies thus raised were never paid joyfully, the king's ministers had to ask the assembled commons for their assent, and at least to endure what the knights of Suffolk and other shires, and the burgesses of Ipswich and other boroughs had then to say. In that fashion the exigencies of the long wars with France created something like a national political community.

Some of the deepest changes came from the effects of the bubonic plague, which was itself the latest and most severe of a series of shocks to the economy. The losses of population produced a shortage of labour, which the government tried to control by repression.[26] Wages and prices nevertheless rose, and most employers paid what they were asked. The ordinary apparatus of justice was inadequate to the task of enforcement, and special commissions were issued to justices of the statute of labourers. Their ministrations stoked the bitter discontents that in 1381 flared in rebellion.[27]

---

[24] It was a distinctive feature of borough courts that a married woman could there debar her claim to dower in a property which she alienated jointly with her husband. *See* Martin 1971, 151–73.

[25] *See* Clarke 1830, 429–31.

[26] *See further* Ormrod 1986, 178–80. An employer who paid above the statutory (pre-plague) rates was fined, a workman who took more was imprisoned; neither was deterred.

[27] *See* e.g. Dobson 1970.

From that unrewarding exercise in social control, however, there emerged the more useful device of a permanent commission of the peace. When Ipswich received a new charter in 1446 the borough was formally incorporated. Its powers remained much as before, but royal officials were excluded from the liberties, and the office of Escheator, who accounted for estates which lapsed to the crown, was conferred on one of the Bailiffs. The chief innovation was that the Bailiffs were made Justices of the Peace *ex officio*, together with four of the Chief Portmen, and the fines which they levied were assigned to the common funds. Incorporation gave the town power to sue and be sued at law without exposing its officers to personal liability for communal actions, and also enabled it to hold real property in perpetuity.[28] The commission of the peace proclaimed the borough's parity with the county as a whole.

The townsmen resolved as early as 1451 to apply for a further charter, though by the time they secured it, in 1463, the Yorkist Edward IV was on the throne. It looked back over Henry VI's charter to confirm Richard II's, then effectively regranted Henry VI's provisions without referring to him. It further granted cognizance of all pleas to the borough's courts, and the powers of the admiralty to the Bailiffs. Ipswich had long contested control of the Orwell estuary with Harwich. The struggle was by no means over, but the town had won a significant advantage.

In the course of the 15th century Ipswich was a prosperous place, though it complained of the burdens of taxation. The growth of the cloth industry in East Anglia benefited trade at large. There were clothworkers in the town, but Ipswich was a focus rather than a centre of industry. Some cloth passed through the port, both to its traditional markets in the Low Countries, which it had long supplied with wool, but also to more distant ports in Scandinavia and Iceland.[29] Imports ranging from salt fish to wine supplied both the town's markets and the hinterland. Almost every one of the old parish churches, most notably St Clement's and St Margaret's, bear marks of extension or rebuilding. Little is left of the merchants' houses of the period, but inventories show them to have been well appointed, and even sumptuously furnished. The Corpus Christi gild flourished, set above the many others in the town, and its annual procession brought the clergy and the municipal authorities together in an imposing display of piety and harmony.

Late medieval Ipswich, with its gilds and its ocean voyages, would serve as the very type of its time. It was fittingly the birthplace of Thomas Wolsey, reformer and pluralist, a patron of the new learning who was also the enemy of the free-ranging inquiries which it inspired. Wolsey raised his great foundation Cardinal College in Oxford to outshine King's College in Cambridge, and chose Ipswich as the seat of the school, in the Cardinal's College of St Mary, which was to supply a transformed Oxford with pupils. In suppressing a string of small religious houses to endow his colleges, including SS Peter and Paul in Ipswich, he provided an example which his protegé Thomas Cromwell and his vengeful master Henry VIII took to its logical ends. In the meantime his own foundations could not survive his fall.

A contemporary of Wolsey's, Richard Percyvale, a Chief Portman of the borough, left his own memorial in the imposing version of the Custumal known as Percyvale's

---

[28] It remained subject to the restrictions of the Statute of Mortmain, which forbade religious houses, incorporate boroughs, and the like to hold property without royal licence. Being immortal, they deprived the king of the benefits of wardship and the payments due from heirs on succession. The Letters Patent of 1399 (above, p. xxv) licensed the burgesses to hold the two mills. *See further* Raban 1982.

[29] The trade with Iceland dwindled in the middle of the century, but subsequently revived. *See* Warner 1926, 41 and n.; and, on the revival, Webb 1962.

Domesday (Ipswich C/4/1/4). Completed in 1520, it presents an English text of the customs with a full range of historical and constitutional material from the earlier volumes, including a careful account of the Corpus Christi gild. It ends with the town's latest charters, from Henry VIII, to which Wolsey may have lent assistance. One was a general confirmation, made in 1512, and the other, of 1519, a further confirmation, together with a full grant of the powers of admiralty, extending the borough's jurisdiction to Paul's Head Sands, off Felixstowe.

The customs had been translated into English some eighty years earlier, at a time when English had emerged, for the first time since the Conquest, as the language of politics and administration. That text is in a volume now in the British Library (Add. MS 25,011).[30] It is accompanied by some ancillary material from the other copies of the Custumal, and shows some faint glimmers of an antiquarian sense. Percyvale's Domesday, however, though conscious of an historical purpose, is meant as a practical guide to the government of the town, and stayed in use for three centuries as an oath book and text for ceremonial uses. Yet it stands, like Wolsey's career, between two worlds. In particular the gild, to which Percyvale pays such careful attention, was dissolved within a generation in 1547.

Contention over religion was only one discordancy. There were intimations of economic trouble in the 1520s when the cloth industry's markets were shaken by war, and there were alarming demonstrations in London and in East Anglia.[31] The first serious crisis came in the middle of the century when over-production and a necessary but drastic reform of the coinage brought the traditional export trade to ruin.[32] Salvation lay in the development of what were called the new draperies, but in the meantime the East Anglian towns had the novel problems of industrial unemployment and structural destitution on their hands. Troubles usually congregate, and the dislocation of industry was aggravated by agrarian change and by the upheaval that followed the dissolution of the monasteries, and a huge redistribution of their estates. As in the 14th century, the government thought in terms of exhortation and repression. The towns reacted more positively. Colchester, Ipswich, and Norwich conferred together, and in 1556–57 began programmes of poor relief based not simply on alms and private charity, though there were charitable foundations in all three towns, but on the compulsory rating of property.[33] Their schemes remained tentative for some decades, but Ipswich acquired the site of the former Dominican friary in 1569, and established a foundation called Christ's Hospital, chartered in 1572. The renovated buildings provided an infirmary, almshouse, and house of correction which served the town for two and a half centuries, and provided, incidentally, a rich archival source which is still only partially explored.

By the time that the Hospital was functioning the day-to-day administration of the town was under the view of the borough Assembly, and the Assembly books, together with the Chamberlains' and Treasurer's accounts, run through to the age of municipal reform. There are some gaps in the records in the middle decades of the 16th century. Some of them, such as the absence of external correspondence, are probably the work of predatory collectors.[34] However, from the later 15th century, the clerks had a habit of making up bundles, called dogget rolls, of each year's rolls. Numbers of them

[30] The customs are printed in Twiss 1871–76, ii, 16–207.
[31] See VCH Suffolk, ii, 257.
[32] See the lucid account in Bindoff 1950, 140–44.
[33] See Webb, S and B., 1927–29, i; and Webb, J., 1966, 17–19.
[34] See further Freeman 1997, which does not display the whole of its admirable contents in its title.

survive, but others may well have fallen to the periodic need to clear a shelf or a chest. The dogget roll is not a device for ready reference, and may reflect new modes of working with current memoranda, often informal, which the ready availability of paper afforded in the 16th century. If so, even the gaps become eloquent.

II. c.*1550–1835*[35]

by Frank Grace

The Growth of Oligarchical Government c.*1550–1660*

By the mid-16th century the evolution of the constitutional and governmental struc-ture of Ipswich under the Charter of incorporation of 1200 and its succeeding late-medieval confirmations, was largely complete, as was the elaboration of the instruments by which the judicial, financial and economic order of the town was to be maintained. The Charters and, since the 13th century, the representation of Ipswich in Parliament, guaranteed its autonomy and status in relation to outside authority and shaped the nature of the civic governors' authority over the inhabitants. During the period *c*.1550–*c*.1660 the autonomy of the borough was in large part maintained, despite the increasing pressures and demands of central government and the crisis of civil war and revolution after 1640. At the same time a range of new responsibilities and powers placed greater demands on the Bailiffs and chief officers; new institutions increased the complexity of administration and added to the numbers of those involved. This growth of government is largely to be understood within the context of the unprecedented social and economic trends of the period: increasing population, the problem of poverty, and migration into the town created problems that required action if political and social order was to be maintained. Greater involvement in the religious life of the town is another important characteristic of borough government, particularly evident after 1600 when Ipswich became dominated by a godly Puritan elite. The additional responsibilities of the Bailiffs, Portmen and common council-men in the Assembly, as well as the external pressures on the borough, increased a tendency towards government by oligarchy which is apparent throughout the period.

The widening role of the Corporation in the social order of the town is exemplified most clearly in the establishment of the Tooley Foundation. Henry Tooley's bequest in 1551 of much of his substantial fortune for the foundation of an institution for the poor of the town led, by 1556, to the creation of a governing body, appointed each Michaelmas, of four officers as Wardens, two from the Portmen and two from the Twenty Four. One of these was to be Renter-warden – effectively the foundation's treasurer. The Renter-warden not only supervised day to day expenditure on the poor and the maintenance of the buildings in Foundation Street but also had to oversee the considerable estates Tooley had left, including the farm and rents of Ulveston Hall and farms in Whitton, Akenham, Claydon and Otley, to which was added, in 1599, part of William Smart's legacy, including property in Falkenham and moneys which

---

[35] Unless otherwise stated, all MSS cited are from the Ipswich Borough Archive in the Ipswich Branch of the Suffolk Record Office.

were to be used to purchase land in Creeting and elsewhere. By the mid-17th century, the annual receipts from these amounted to nearly £500. The management, annual audit of the accounts, and five-yearly inspection of the institution became, then, a major responsibility, but Tooley's Foundation was insufficient in itself to deal with the problem of poverty in the town at large. Vagrancy, begging and the consequences of epidemic outbreaks, in addition to the provision for the town's own deserving poor, all become a permanent concern of the town's governors from the 1550s. In 1568 the Great Court agreed to the purchase of the site and buildings of the former Black Friars priory and its adaptation as a municipal house for the poor. Under the Charter granted in 1572 this institution, Christ's Hospital, was to be governed by a committee, annually appointed, of one Portman, two of the Twenty Four and one freeman Burgess, and a number of inferior officers was created, including the Guider, a Clerk, a Schoolmaster and a Beadle.[36]

The oversight of Tooley's bequest and of Christ's Hospital was not the only such social duty that the officers of the town took on at this time. Indeed, from the 1570s until late in the 17th century, considerable sums of money, amounting to over £1,500, were left to the town by philanthropic benefactors for charitable uses. These came to constitute the town's Lending Cash for distribution to needy and deserving individuals – handicraftsmen, clothiers, shearmen, grocers, 'godly' tradesmen or poor persons and occupiers. Some of these bequests, like that of John Burroughs in 1613, Richard Martin in 1621 and John Crane in 1658, were for the purchase of estates whose revenues would then be lent out to young men, to those imprisoned for debt, to old women and others, usually provided they were the 'honest, godliest men'. Martin's bequest was of a farm in Westerfield in trust to the town for the support of two scholars of the Free School at Cambridge. A number of these charities, such as Tyler's, Martin's, Osmond's and Phillips', each had its own treasurer, appointed annually by the Assembly.[37]

It was the Assembly, too, that was responsible for the management of the Grammar School under a renewed and enlarged Charter of 1566. The Assembly had authority, under the bishop of Norwich, to appoint the Master and Usher, and to oversee the regulations, statutes and ordinances for the government of the school and choose scholars for the grant of scholarships left as legacies, such as Mopted's of 1558 to Trinity Hall, Scrivener's of 1598 and most famously Smart's Fellowship and two scholarships to Pembroke Hall of the same date, as well as Martin's mentioned above.

As well as its increasing responsibility for the oversight of the social welfare and educational provision of the townspeople, the Corporation acquired important new regulatory and fiscal powers. The costs of managing the poor necessitated the introduction of a poor rate, probably first raised at the local level in the late 1550s and then under the Act of 1572, which laid down a system for compulsory assessment of the inhabitants by the Bailiffs and Justices of the Peace at the Sessions. Population increase, poverty and epidemic disease brought the question of public health to the fore at the same time, and the Corporation, no doubt after an order of the Great Court for cleaning the streets had proved ineffective, acquired a parliamentary Statute of 1571 empowering them to raise rates for paving the streets of the town. 'At the assignment or appointment of the Bailiffs', all landlords, owners or tenants were to ensure that the road before their property was paved. The Headboroughs (the Leet officers

---

[36] Webb 1966, *passim*; Canning 1747 (2nd edn Ipswich, 1819),17–28, 53–61; Assembly Book C/4/3/1/3 ff.47–48, 54; Tooley Foundation Accounts, 1655–56, C/5/1/1/6/55.
[37] Canning 1747, 73–94.

for the four wards of the town) were to oversee this and had powers to fine those who neglected their duty, and lessees were given the right to deduct their costs out of their rents. This extended the existing authority of the Headboroughs to fine those who left refuse in or encroached on the streets. Outbreaks of plague, a regular occurrence throughout this period, necessitated the elaboration of a whole range of emergency powers by the Bailiffs and justices. During 1603–4, for instance, orders for stopping waggons by road and hoys by sea from entering the town, the appointment of keepers of the sickhouses, of searchers-out of infected strangers, of watch and ward to stop migrants, and an order for paling and gating the ramparts, were all necessitated. Strong measures were taken for fining those who refused to pay the emergency rates, for the double-rating of Portmen and Twenty Four men who neglected their duties at such a time, and for fining Headboroughs who left the town during the outbreak. Disputes over the use of these emergency powers had then to be resolved. In all these ways the authority of the town's chief officers expanded and bore more directly on the lives and the pockets of the inhabitants.[38]

Greater powers for the supervision of the social order are paralleled by an increasing concern of the magistracy for the ordering of the religious and moral lives of the inhabitants, indicative of the tendency towards greater lay involvement in post-Reformation England. Of greatest importance here was the decision by the Assembly in 1560 to appoint a Town Preacher, initially provided with wages of £20 per annum, a sum which increased to over £100 by the mid-17th century, as well as a house maintained by the Corporation. The godly preachers of the Word were to play an integral role alongside an increasingly godly magistracy in their efforts to discipline the community, especially with the appointment on 1 November 1605 of Samuel Ward, the father figure of Ipswich Puritanism for the following thirty years. An indication of the importance of the role that such a man had in the eyes of the town's leaders is evident in 1622–3. The outspoken Ward was silenced by ecclesiastical authority for publishing an anti-papal cartoon at a time of delicate diplomatic relations with Catholic Spain, but the townsmen were prepared to spend very large sums of money to send representatives to London and to the bishop of Norwich on his behalf. Again, in 1636 after Ward had been tried and silenced by the ecclesiastical court of High Commission, the town continued to pay his wages, and after his death in 1640, maintained his family. In 1641, when the Puritan-dominated leadership was again able to appoint a preacher, the matter was treated then and on later occasions with great seriousness and urgency.[39]

Secular involvement in the religious and moral lives of the inhabitants is also evident in the curious addendum to the paving statute of 1571 which gave the Corporation powers to raise a rate for supplementing the maintenance of parish ministers in the town and for the reparation of the fabric of the churches, and in the fearsome Sabbatarian orders passed in the Great Court in 1592 and again in 1606 and 1644. The evidence of the Sessions Books from the late-Elizabethan period to the 1650s also strongly suggests an intensification of measures to punish Sabbath breaking, absence

---

[38] Gray and Potter 1950, ch. 4; Canning 1747 (1819 edn), 101–14; Richardson 1884, 287, 290, 292; Rate Assessments, Enrolments of Apprenticeship, etc., C/3/2/2/2 ff.11v–12 and *passim*; Statutes of the Realm 13 Eliz. cap. 24 (*see* abstract in Canning 1747 (1819 edn), 240); Webb 1966, 110–18; Assembly Book, C4/3/1/3, ff.160–193v, *passim*.

[39] Wodderspoon 1850, 366–77; *DNB*, s.v. Samuel Ward; Treasurers' Accounts, C/3/4/1/46 (1622–3); Assembly Book, C/4/3/1/5, ff. 288, 319, 322–23, 327v, 337v; C/4/3/1/6, ff.9, 10, 25–26, 32, 36, 178, 179, 180, 185–88; Grace 1996a, 23–26.

from Church, swearing and fornication, as well as to suppress scandalous houses, bowling and other unlawful games. The public shaming of men and women for immorality by carting and the pillory is evidence of the magistrates' determination to impose moral order in the town in their drive to create a godly Ipswich.[40]

As a consequence of the increasing range of duties demanded of the town's governors, the role of the bureaucratic officers, in particular the Town Clerk and the Treasurer, became more centrally important. The duties of the Town Clerk were re-defined in the 1570s, and in addition, the administrative oversight of a range of new institutions and responsibilities swelled the numbers of office holders. By the early 17th century, the annual appointment of overseers, the setting of the rates and the taking in of the accounts of the various treasurers were done in Easter Week, adding to the calendar of business. As the number of the various legacies left in trust to the town increased, it was ordered that they be formally recorded, whilst a lengthy survey of the Town Lands between 1566 and 1572 became necessary as management of the estates became more complex. The growth of corporate business largely explains a parallel growth in size of the archival record during this period. When Nathaniel Bacon, the Town Recorder in the 1640s and 1650s, compiled his 'Annalls', he commented on the absence of any Great Court Books before the reign of Henry VI, and the negligence of the Clerk and the Clavigers thereafter in keeping the records, which 'lay buried up, as it were in a heape of rubbish'. From the beginning of Elizabeth I's reign, however, there is improvement. The Assembly Books and Great Court Books become, if not complete in every sense, continuous, and by the early 17th century the record of both the agenda and of attendance is formally copied. The record relating to the charitable institutions added significantly to the books, constitutions and other archives in the town treasury. The Treasurer's and Chamberlains' Accounts become increasingly more detailed and meticulous. Government was becoming more bureaucratic.[41]

As the arm of the Corporation's authority extended, legal disputes inevitably became more frequent: the contention in Star Chamber with Sir Edmund Withipoll of Christchurch Mansion over the rights to St Margaret's Fair in the later 1560s; the long dispute with the master of the Grammar School after his dismissal for supposed 'evil behaviour' in 1604 which involved attendance before the Bishop of Norwich, the Archbishop of Canterbury and the Bishop of London, as well as at the Assizes and the Privy Council; disputes with individual merchants and tradesmen about Foreign Fine abuses in the Court of Common Pleas; the challenge to the Charter presented by the Letters Patent granted by James I in 1606 to the tailors and clothworkers to form an 'under Corporation', thus undermining the Bailiffs' powers under the Charter to oversee economic activity in the town – these typify the often lengthy and complex cases that necessitated the Town Clerk's frequent attendance at courts in London and elsewhere. In 1574 the borough sought to resolve this by requiring the Clerk to remain resident, appointing a new legal officer in the hierarchy of the town's government, the Recorder, whose function was 'to solicit all causes of the town and

---

[40] *See* Canning 1747 (1819 edn), 187–88; Great Court Books, C/2/2/2/1, f. 256v; C/2/2/2/2 ff. 9v–10; Assembly Book, C/4/3/1/3, f. 25v; Sessions Books, C/2/9/1/1/8/7–8, *passim.* The Treasurers' Accounts frequently refer to forms of punishment.

[41] For the frequent surveys of properties and committees set up to oversee charities, *see* Richardson 1884, 273–87 *passim*; for the increasing complexity of borough finances, *see* Webb 1996 [on p.11, Webb notes a 'steady decline' in efficiency in the 17th century, but there is little evidence of this until after 1660]; Richardson 1884, i–ii.

aid the Bailiffs in all causes of judgment', and re-defining the conduct of legal business in the town.[42]

It was not only domestic matters that added to the burdens of the chief officers of the town. The demands of the state for taxes, for ships of war in the 1590s and again in the 1620s, for forced loans in 1627, for Ship Money in the mid-1630s – an issue which led to prolonged dispute over assessment of the town's contribution – and for soldiers in the Bishops' Wars of 1639–40, were persistent. *Quo Warranto* proceedings challenged the town's rights under the Charter on more than one occasion in the 1630s. Particularly serious, since it brought the town into direct dispute with Charles I, were the long proceedings during 1632–35 which arose out of the King's arbitrary seizure of the town lands at Ulveston in 1632, presumably on the basis of a claim that the lands were either held *in capite* of the King or that they were worth more than £100 per annum, stipulations that had been laid down in the Letters Patent of November 1556 when the Tooley bequest was being formalised. It was religion, though, more than any other factor, which brought the town into direct and dangerous confrontation with ecclesiastical authority and with the Crown. A Puritan cohort became increasingly dominant in the town's leadership during the 1620s, and the silencing, trial and imprisonment of their town preacher, Samuel Ward, in 1634–35, the metropolitan visitation by Archbishop Laud's vicar-general in 1634, and the inquisitorial visitation of the bishop of Norwich, Matthew Wren, in 1636, led to widespread riot in the town. The consequences of the events of 1636 were serious: Wren filed a bill in Star Chamber the preamble of which accused the town's governors of responsibility for the riots saying that they did 'Combine and Confederate how to resist and oppose all authority', having 'for divers years past endeavoured to vilify his Majesty's government'. Had the collapse of Charles I's government in 1640 not intervened, Ipswich might well have been in danger of having its Charter revoked. It was as a result of this experience in the 1630s that the borough became directly and actively involved in the wider political and religious life of the country: the godly Puritan town staunchly supported Parliament in the civil war that broke out in 1642, and thereafter its governance and constitution were continuously affected by factors outside its ancient liberties, and its autonomy and its political order were eventually undermined.[43]

The administrative elaboration and legal complexity of government had political and constitutional consequences within the arena of borough government as well. The sheer scale of business, often requiring immediate executive decisions, placed the burden of responsibility more appropriately in the hands of the Bailiffs and chief officers in the Assembly than in those of the whole body of Free Burgesses in the Great Court. The latter was the superior in legislative matters, and its mandate had to be sought and its members politically managed by the Bailiffs and Portmen, but by the late 16th century the Assembly framed the agendas for Great Court meetings and called it, apart from the formal occasion of the election of officers on 8 September and the 'new elects' assuming office on 29 September, only when it was felt necessary. In

[42] For the Withipoll suit, *see* C/1/6/4/1–14 and C/1/6/5/1–5. For the matter of the Grammar School Master, Leman, *see* Gray and Potter 1950, 54–56; Great Court Book, C/2/2/2/1, ff. 264, 269; Assembly Books, C/4/3/1/4, ff. 206v, 223v; C/4/3/1/5, ff.3–4v, 9–13, 15, 21r and v, 66, 75, 78; for Foreign Fines *see* Grace 1996b, 28–36; for the tailors and clothworkers issue *see* P.R.O. *Acts of the Privy Council 1619–21*, 122, 147–49, 209; State Papers Domestic, SP 14/112; Great Court Book, C/2/2/2/1, ff. 310, 313–14; Assembly Book, C/4/3/1/5, ff. 3, 9; for the Town Clerk , the Recorder and town properties *see* Richardson 1884, 277, 279, 283–84, 287, 290, 295–97, 301, 304.
[43] *See* the Assembly Books, C/4/3/1/3 and C/4/3/1/5. For the *Quo Warranto* case over Ulveston Hall, *see* C/4/3/1/5, ff. 202–43 *passim*; for the riots against Wren and their context *see* Grace 1996c, 97–120.

this respect the Great Court was inferior, effectively having little more than a freedom to assent to agendas put before it. This trend towards the oligarchical power of the Assembly in the town's affairs is clear from the formal record: between 1560 and 1600 there were on average a dozen meetings of the Assembly each year, whilst from 1600 to 1640 the average was over thirty and in three years over forty, and remained at over twenty up to 1660. The Assembly in the early 17th century became a permanent standing executive committee. This being the case, nonetheless the Great Court remained fundamental to the workings of the constitution and the voice of the free burgesses in it was becoming stronger, particularly from 1620 to 1660. The record of those freemen attending the Great Court on 8 September each year at the time of elections to office shows a noticeable increase. Before 1620, an average of fifty attended; between 1620 and 1640 some seventy, and over eighty after 1640. Notably, on the occasion of parliamentary elections in the borough in 1627, twice in 1640, in 1646 and in 1654, over a hundred attended. Both the 'popular' voice in the Great Court and the parallel rise of an oligarchical Assembly were to produce tensions within the body politic which arose from a weakness in the constitution that successive charters had not clarified.

In 1520, Richard Percyvale had sought to codify all laws, customs and other writings relating to the borough's constitution and the town's chartered rights in his Great Domesday. The concern of the Bailiffs and other officers for the correct workings of government are reflected in three extracts to which Nathaniel Bacon significantly drew attention in his 'Annalls' of 1654. He noted an order of 1552 which required all new elected and sitting officers to assemble at 8.00 a.m. every Monday and Wednesday between 8 and 29 September to read the Orders and Constitutions in the Domesday. A second extract, from 1554, orders that the Ordinances for the Commonwealth of the Town are to be hung up in the Moot Hall and read each Michaelmas Day, and the third, from 1561, refers to a decision of the Bailiffs to head a committee to 'set forth the office and duties of every officer within the said town for the better execution of the same'. Bacon clearly doubted how far in the intervening century these aims had been achieved, for he commented that 'few or none of the inhabitants of this town were acquainted with the trew nature of the government'. The relationship between the Great Court and the Assembly in terms of their legislative, executive and judicial powers raised for him the fundamental question of the true source of constitutional legitimacy. The question had come to the fore by the time Bacon wrote and had important long term consequences for good government and the political order. Bacon argued that the origins of the problem were to be found at the time of the first creation of Bailiffs and of Portmen. The choice, or election, of the former belonged 'to the people', but the latter, too, were chosen 'from the people'. But, whereas the Bailiffs were still formally elected in the Great Court by all the free burgesses on 8 September, the Portmen had evolved into a self-perpetuating body. This, Bacon said, had led to 'government concealed within the breasts of so few' that it had become 'cautelous to the people', and that the introduction of the Twenty Four common councilmen into the Assembly had been a device to resolve the issue. However, the Twenty Four itself had become self-perpetuating: hence the emergence of an oligarchy at the head of government.[44]

The friction within the body politic which might thus occur as a consequence of these trends in government and thus bring the constitution into question, can be

---

[44] C/4/1/4, Percyvale, R., 'Great Domesday of Ipswich' (1521); Richardson 1884, ii-v, 237, 243, 260.

illustrated by events in 1601–03. On 5 October 1601, the Great Court discharged the Town Clerk, Mr Walton, against whom there had been 'great complaints' and a suit in Star Chamber, and elected Thomas Rich in his place. Walton petitioned the Lord Treasurer, who called the Portmen to answer to the issues, but nothing was resolved. A year later, Edmund Deye, a burgess, came to the Assembly as a representative of the body of freemen and demanded that 'they might have the election'. The Bailiff, Ralph Scrivener, refused, saying that their right had been given away in Edward IV's reign and that the Lord Chief Justice had agreed, quoting the precedent of the city of Bristol. Deye was supported by one of the Twenty Four, Richard Bateman, who said that Ipswich's case was no more like that of Bristol than 'an apple is like an oyster', but when pressed on his presumptuous challenge to the highest legal authority he backed down. Walton was restored, but only after costly recourse to the Lord Treasurer, the Lord Chief Justice and the Attorney General. Months later, in April 1603, two burgesses and one of the Clavigers were in gaol for disputing this decision, George Raymer for factious speeches in Great Court, saying that 'Mr Walton was lawfully put out of office [by the Court] and he came in again he knoweth not how'. In June, the Assembly asserted its authority, stating that if 'the voice of the commons in displacing the town clerk or any other privilege which the commons claim' was made again, the matter would be arbitrated by the Attorney General and by any six men chosen by the commons, and then put to the 'umperage' of the Lord Treasurer. However, the matter had also divided the Assembly, the Twenty Four initially taking the part of the burgesses, but then splitting over whether to accept the arbitration offer.[45]

Constitutional tensions are most significant during the bitterly divisive period 1640–42 at the end of Charles I's personal rule and the ensuing First Civil War. Popular agitation was widespread at this time, and in Ipswich was to lead to an assertion of power by the Great Court between 1643 and 1647. The elections on two occasions in 1640 of the town's Members of Parliament had seen the first recorded contest and poll, and on the eve of war in May 1642, there was, and had been, 'great disorder in the Great Court . . . by many persons speaking together in a tumultuous manner'. The Royalist inclined Recorder, John Lany, was discharged from office by the Great Court, which then, in March 1643, directly challenged the right of Portmen to elect their own replacements, probably for political reasons because the man who had been chosen, Nicholas Phillips, had refused to subscribe to the parliamentary cause: the Court at the same time agreed the election of another burgess who actively supported Parliament. Phillips was discharged, and it was entered that the matter was not to be referred outside the Court. Indeed, on election day in 1644 there was an order entered (which was repeated in 1654) excluding all nominees for office from the Court until the elections were over. More importantly, the choosing and electing of both Portmen and Twenty Four men for the next four years took place in the Great Court. In the heightened political atmosphere of the time, a constitutional revolution seemed imminent whereby the free burgesses would seize control of their own affairs from the governing elite. Then, on 23 September 1647, 'after reading the ancient constitutions', a reversal took place and an order that Portmen and Twenty Four men 'ought' to choose their own replacements was entered in the Great Court book. On 30 September, however, the Court declared that the votes that had been cast the week before were null and void, and confusion was worse confounded the next day when an

---

[45] Assembly Book, C/4/3/1/3, ff.141v–142; Richardson 1884, 408–15 *passim*.

extraordinary compromise is recorded: that all elections of Portmen by Portmen *and* all elections of Portmen and Twenty Four men by the Great Court were legal. The motion that the dispute should be referred to Parliament was rejected after a division. Until after the Restoration, power in the borough was in uneasy balance between the oligarchy in the Assembly and the commons in Great Court.[46]

Despite these pressures both from central government in State and Church and from the commons in the Great Court, as well as the emergencies and exigencies of civil war and revolution between 1640 and 1660, the dominance of the Assembly in the government of the town seems to have been sustained. The persistent demands of Parliament for men and money, liaison with the Committee of Suffolk and with the Eastern Association of counties, gave the governing elite, many of whom actively served the parliamentary cause, additional executive powers. Popular unrest or Royalist plots did not disturb the town as was the case in Norwich, Bury St Edmunds, Yarmouth or Colchester during and after the Second Civil War in 1648. Above all, a dominant group of Puritans maintained control, and the town's militia, or parliamentary regiments, were on hand should it be necessary, although the town avoided being garrisoned. The books of the Assembly and the Great Court, as well as the accounts of the Treasurer and the Chamberlains, suggest that the government and administration and the finances of the borough were maintained efficiently under the magisterial and watchful eye of its Recorder, Nathaniel Bacon, and the Town Clerk, Thomas Dey, even if by the 1650s the keeping of the records was not as ordered and comprehensive as before. The ancient 'laws and constitutions' of the borough remained in place.

Dissolution and Decay: the Chartered Borough in Decline 1660–1835

The Restoration of 1660 was a turning point in the history of the government of the town. Ever since 1200, the rights and liberties granted to Ipswich and the order and authority of its organs of government and administration had given the town a status as great as any other chartered borough: 'Ipswich (the onely eie) of this Shire . . . might worthily haue borne the title of a Citie . . . whose trade, circuite, and seat, dothe equall most places of the Land' the historian John Speed declared in the description accompanying his map of Suffolk, published in 1610.[47]

The weakening of that status, and the disintegration of its order and governance over the period from 1660 to the Municipal Corporations Act of 1835 was a long process. It was political changes in the relationship between the borough and the monarchy and, more decisively, the effects of the rise of party in English politics in the late 17th century that brought the town inevitably out of its local context and into the national political arena. The political/religious divisions of the period 1640–1660 had, of course, begun this process and left their legacy after 1660. The borough was exposed, on the one hand, to the attempts of Charles II and James II to manipulate and control the town through the imposition of new charters and on the other, to the rise of Whigs and Tories – to the 'rage of party'. As a consequence the autonomy that had maintained control of the town in the hands of the resident freemen and their officers begins to be undermined.

The fact that the town was dominated by a strongly Puritan elite before 1660, and had, if not always with total enthusiasm, supported the republican regimes of the 1650s, made its loyalty to the restored monarchy suspect. Over the winter of 1662–63

---

[46] Great Court Book, C/2/2/2/2, ff. 301v–2, 305, 314–15; C/2/2/2/3, ff. 3, 4, 12v, 32, 34, 36.
[47] Speed 1611, ff. 33–34.

the consequences, particularly for the constitutional liberties of the borough, were made dramatically clear. Royal commissioners, acting under the Corporations Act of 1662, arrived in the town on 20 October. The Act required that all office holders and all freemen were to renounce the Puritan Covenant and acknowledge acceptance of the re-established episcopal government of the Church. Over the next three months six of the Portmen and twelve of the Twenty Four refused to compromise their strong consciences and were consequently purged – half, that is, of the Assembly. After these men had been replaced, in January 1663, 'whereas the Antient government and order of this towne hath been in these late distracted times much broken & altered', the right of the Portmen and the Twenty Four to co-opt new members was re-stated, and eventually Charles II was prepared to renew the charter in 1665. The Crown had the prerogative right to intervene in this way, but the purge of 1662–63 was an indication of a loss of liberty, and borough affairs throughout the decade afterwards were disturbed by disputes concerning men who sought to take up their freedoms or to assume office. The King, however, must have felt that convenient powers for 'the due correction and amendment of Evils and Inconveniences' having been exercised, 'the good regimen and government of the town' had been restored.[48]

Far more damaging to the constitution and liberties of the borough was another use of the royal prerogative in mid-1684, indicative of the reaction of the King to the Exclusion Crisis and the opposition of the Whigs. Charles II, in the closing years of his reign, made a concerted attack on borough charters in an attempt to bend their parliamentary political influence to his will. The Ipswich Charter was called in and arbitrarily replaced by a very different one, which named those who were to replace five of the Portmen who were purged, removed ten of the Twenty Four, and added four new named members. The consequences of this were ominous for the future of government in the town. For the first time in its history these Portmen who were imposed on it, including one of the Bailiffs, were not townsmen but county gentry. A new Town Clerk and Recorder were also outside appointments. At the same time, the Twenty Four were reduced to an Eighteen and the rights and liberties of the Freemen to participate in borough government were totally abrogated. Here was a deliberate attempt to create a closed Corporation which could be managed easily for political purposes. The effect on the town was to produce a chaotic situation, and the short calamitous years of James II's reign made matters worse. By the August of 1687, it was recognized that the oversight of the finances, the management of properties and the choosing of auditors of accounts, Clavigers and other inferior officers had been left legally in the hands of the Great Court, but that since 1685 decisions about such matters had been taken by the Assembly, which was declared to be 'contrary to the ancient constitutions of this town'. The Great Court had virtually ceased to exist and there were clearly concerns amongst some of the Eighteen as to the legality of their position, since there were large numbers of absentees from its meetings. Then, in the politically charged atmosphere of April–May 1688, James II gave orders in the Privy Council for another Charter, again with the desperate intention of securing a pliant borough in his interest, and four Portmen, six of the Eighteen and the Town Clerk were removed. The previous charter of 1684–85, however, was not annulled until 17 October, and the consequence was confusion. Men who had been purged in 1684, their replacements, and James II's new nominees all appeared at meetings of the Assembly or in the Great Court. By June, meetings of the former were called, but no

[48] Suffolk Record Office, Ipswich, X1/8/1; Assembly Book, C/4/3/1/6, ff. 285, 310, 316; Great Court Book, C/2/2/2/2, ff. 143, 153, 156–57, 160, 162, 169; Canning 1754, 30–48.

business was recorded; by October, as James's reign disintegrated, it becomes impossible from the records to be clear who was in or out of office. The townsmen appear to have agreed, by proclamation in the Great Court, to restore the old constitution in that month, but on one occasion in December forty-one names were recorded at an Assembly meeting – five more than was constitutionally possible. It was not until the change of monarchy occurred early in 1689 that those who had been in office before mid-1684 were finally re-instated.[49]

The Crown's attempts to manipulate the Charters, and the 'present troubles and distractions' of the Revolution of 1688–89, had left the town's government and constitution in disarray. It is possible to outline the long-term consequences. The dominance of the oligarchs in the Assembly before 1660 is still apparent and its role as a standing committee demonstrated by its continuing to be called on average more than once a month until 1689. The 1690s seem from the statistics to be crucial here: from the beginning of the decade the number of recorded meetings falls to about six a year, and no business is entered in the books for 64 of the 111 meetings. Attendance is frequently not registered, and very long gaps of as much as eleven months occur between meetings. On many occasions only one Bailiff attended, and only twice, in 1690 and 1694, did the Assembly meet on 8 September to prepare the agenda for elections, a function which before then it had invariably carried out. Between 1700 and the early 1720s, when the populist and manipulative Bailiff, Cooper Gravenor, used the Great Court more or less as a popular power base and largely ignored the Assembly, attendance at it plummeted. A sample from the years 1708–22 shows on average only three Portmen and seven of the Twenty Four on the register. Attempts by the Assembly to assert its authority and challenge the legality of proceedings in the Great Court were ineffective, or cynically over-ruled, as happened in 1711 when six Portmen and seventeen of the Twenty Four, having got a vote of censure passed, found that as soon as they had left the meeting the vote was reversed. After this, it was only at moments of political crisis in the town's affairs that members seem to have actively fulfilled their roles. Even during the period 1729–53, when it seems that the Assembly regained the initiative over the Great Court, the former only rarely met more than once a year. After the Assembly had split because of party political manoeuvring in the late 1740s and early 1750s and a majority of the Portmen were ousted in 1755, disintegration set in: between 1755 and 1767, only one Portman attended meetings, and from 1760 to 1766, none of the Twenty Four. The Portmen failed or refused to replace discharged or deceased members, and thus in 1782 only three remained. Had not new members been added then the Charter itself could legally have been revoked. By 1790 there were again five vacancies and, in 1824, the same situation recurred and the Charter was in danger again. Over the whole of the century from 1702 the Assembly met on average less than twice a year. It had effectively ceased to function as the executive head of the town's government well before the damning report of the Municipal Corporations Commissioners of 1834–35.

During the same period the Great Court, which had been effectively declared redundant in 1684, comes to play the central role in the politics of the town. In 1691, it resumed its control over those authorities and trusts that had been arrogated by the Assembly during the constitutional impasse of 1684–89. It disputed the mechanism by which Portmen and the Twenty Four were appointed. It attempted to discipline wayward Town Clerks and to bring the Treasurer under stricter control. It began to

[49] Canning 1754, 48–68, 68–74; Great Court Book, C/2/2/2/3, ff. 24–26; Assembly Book, C/4/3/1/7, ff. 45–46, 47, 110, 137–38, 143, 164.

meet more frequently than the Assembly, which, since it was traditionally the latter that summoned the former, suggests a shift in the balance of power within the structures of government. As this shift took place, however, the nature and function of the Great Court changed significantly: whereas formerly it had been the legislative body formally overseeing the governance of the town and the voice of the resident free burgesses, it became an arena in which the party political contests of the late-Stuart and Georgian period took place. Both parliamentary and municipal electioneering predominated over concerns for good government of the kind that Nathaniel Bacon hoped for in the 1650s. Whig and Tory interests outside penetrate the body politic and unscrupulous or self-seeking men in the town use and are used by them. G.R. Clarke, surveying the records in the 1820s, appropriately pinpointed the early 1700s as the period when 'confusion' and 'broils' begin to corrupt the town's affairs: as one participant in that process put it, 'party rage' had produced 'all the mischiefs we now complain of'.[50]

The device that more than anything else laid the borough open to this invasion of its self-governing status concerned the offering of the freedom for purchase by 'out-sitters', or granting honorary freedoms to aristocrats, knights, baronets and the clergy and gentry of Suffolk and farther afield in order to secure votes in both parliamentary and municipal elections. Direct political influence from outside in parliamentary elections was, of course, not unknown before the late 17th century, and Charles II in 1684 imposed county gentry on the Portmen, but from the 1690s the practice becomes endemic. The immediate aftermath of the Revolution of 1688–89 saw, for the first recorded time, a poll for the election of Bailiffs on 8 September 1690, at which six candidates were put forward, a precursor of the frequent, divisive and often tumultuous electioneering of the following century. The sale of freedoms is apparent in the 1690s despite attempts by the Assembly to restrict them by imposing a purchase price of £10 in 1698 and of £25 in 1702. The Assembly itself was divided politically by 1701, and it declared that to prevent 'heates and disturbances' at the next election, and to restore 'peace and union' in the town, the Portmen and Twenty Four would 'equally' choose the rival candidates, but to no avail. During Cooper Gravenor's succeeding period in power it was said that he 'procured great numbers of worthy gents to be made free'. In 1703 he got an order passed in Great Court that fines for freedoms were now to be dealt with at its pleasure, and between 1703 and 1710 'many gentlemen in town *and neighbourhood*', including on one occasion thirty-seven baronets, were made free. By 1710, honorary and non-resident freemen were beginning to swamp elections, despite protest from a majority of the Portmen, who had secured an order from the House of Commons Committee of Privileges. The order was ignored by the Great Court the following year when it offered a further fifty-two freedoms. At the parliamentary election of 1713, the issue was used as a political football, one pair of candidates declaring against the recent grants, the other condemning honorary freedoms *per se*. Both Whigs and Tories thereafter attempted to manipulate elections in this way, as in 1722, when sixty-eight freemen were admitted just prior to an election of the Bailiffs, and both tried to dispute the others' lists, as happened in 1731, 1753 and 1755. The latter occasion saw the peak of this phenomenon when 127 freedoms were sold for £5 each. The legal battle over this last

---

[50] Great Court Books, C/2/2/2/3, ff. 71v, 79, 88v, 93, 109, 163, 192–93; C/2/2/2/7, ff. 60–90 *passim*; Assembly Book, C/4/3/1/7, f.190; C/4/3/1/8, 29 Sep. 1755; Clarke 1830, 88; Suffolk Record Office, Ipswich, HD 490/1/3.

case dragged on for years until, in 1773, the Court of King's Bench finally declared their illegality. Nevertheless, the same device re-appeared at the election in 1822. By this time, too, even minor offices in the town's government, such as that of Town Crier, the Guider of Christ's Hospital, and the town lecturer, were bitterly contested.[51]

The increasing presence of 'out-sitter' voters in the affairs of the town at elections for borough offices and at the meetings of the Great Court had important consequences: disputes constantly disrupted the business of the Court, and the inability of the Assembly to control the affairs of the town became more apparent as the Portmen and the Twenty Four split into two warring factions by the middle of the 18th century. Most significant is the apparent debasement of the resident freemen's role in the Great Court. Gravenor, again, was probably the first to use populist appeals and 'treating' as a means of securing support in the town; the numbers of freemen attending Great Court from the mid-1720s declined steeply from about eighty previously to an average of thirty and forty thereafter, and those who were resident did not clearly predominate – it has been estimated that only 10 per cent of them actually participated in the town's affairs, and at elections had largely become an unruly mob to be manipulated by political interests. The non-resident freemen, brought on occasion from as far away as France and Holland to vote, outnumbered them by more than two to one by the 1830s.[52]

Parallel with this process of institutional decay and, indeed, a consequence of it, were what Clarke was to call the damagingly costly 'mazes of litigation' surrounding the struggles for power that are so evident during this period. Probably the earliest of these was a result of the attack on Charles Whittaker, the Recorder, and in 1701, Member of Parliament for the borough, mounted by Cooper Gravenor in the Great Court. Having failed to hand in the records and books – which included Bacon's 'Annalls' – that he had removed from the Treasury, he was charged with opposing the Bailiffs and was discharged. Thereupon, in 1704, he took out a writ of *Mandamus* against the Corporation, along with the Town Clerk, Richard Puplett, who had also been ousted. Whittaker was legally restored in 1707, but the Great Court overturned the decision. Gravenor had borrowed on the town property to further his case, and in 1705 had persuaded the Great Court to agree to give him 'full power under the seal' to hold and use the revenues from the Custom House, the town crane, the crane house at the quay and the Water Bailiffs' dues in order to fund the 'defence of the rights and liberties of the town' against Whittaker. This dubious manipulation of the burgesses was essential by then, since he had at least four other writs out against him, two of which were in the King's Bench. This was typical of other later costly cases that arose. In 1723, for instance, after his grip on the borough was removed, his opponents brought charges against him at the Assizes and he, in turn, took out writs in Chancery against the Corporation. A settlement was reached out of court at least over his debts to the town. At the time of another political overturning in 1754–55, another *Mandamus* was taken out against the previous Bailiffs for their attempt to stop the installation of their successors by refusing to attend at Great Court. The Bailiffs in their turn raised a *Quo Warranto* in King's Bench consisting of 'vexatious and malicious prosecutions' as their enemies claimed. These examples are representative of

[51] Great Court Books, C/2/2/2/3, ff. 53, 130, 132, 168, 174, 189, 195; C/2/2/2/4, ff. 210, 215, 249; C/2/2/2/5, ff. 3, 9, 31; C/2/2/2/6, f. 2; C/2/2/2/7, ff. 53–56; Assembly Book, C/4/3/1/7, f.221; B.L. Harleian MS 6,839; Clarke 1830, 72, 79–80, 119–20, 150–51.
[52] I am grateful to David Clemis for this information, and his help in sharing thoughts on the politics of this period from his work on the government of Ipswich in the 18th century.

the corrosive effects on the body politic of litigation, since they signified the mis-appropriation of the Corporation funds in the interests of factions.[53]

More fundamental and persistent from the Restoration onwards were the long-term consequences of debt and maladministration, if not corruption, for the town's finances and properties. The financial pressures of the Civil War and the continuing demands of the government during the Republic, the effects of the onset of the Dutch Wars in the 1650s, and the extraordinary expenditure and dislocation of economic life during the plague of 1665–66, when a separate 'Pest Account' was necessary, seem to have been cumulative. The period 1660–1834 is punctuated by recurrent crises, in 1691, 1697–98, 1704, 1743, 1786, 1806 and 1830. As early as 1660, the town had to borrow £250 on the security of the town marshes simply in order to provide for their gift to the newly restored king, and suits against those owing money as tenants of town property necessitated raising £300 with a Scot and Lot tax. In 1666, £300 was borrowed during the plague outbreak, and the first of a number of Committees to examine the emerging problem was appointed. Maiden's Grave, one of the town's properties, had to be sold in order to raise money. The debts remained, and an actuarially dubious attempt by the Treasurer on the order of the Great Court to clear them in 1675 resulted in over £500 being taken out of the Lending Cash at 4 per cent interest. The principal was never paid back and neither was the interest. The condition of town properties began to be of general concern at this time: the farms, the fabric of the Moot Hall and the town mills, the latter being in urgent need of repair. By 1690, both Handford Hall, the most valuable real estate, and the marshes, had been mort-gaged in order to pay back money borrowed from the Town Clerk, but this debt had not been cleared seven years later. At the same time, there is evidence of the maladministration of three farms belonging to the Tooley Foundation. The tenants at Whitton, Claydon and Otley were distrained for non-payment of rent, one since 1680, and the properties themselves were in bad disrepair, requiring over £350 to be spent on them. It is, perhaps, indicative of the trend in the town's financial affairs that, after 1660, the Treasurer's accounts were increasingly in deficit, as were those of the Chamberlains after 1673. The annual audit was not carried out regularly in the 1690s, and in 1691, 1697 and 1699 emergency Committees were appointed to try to rectify matters.[54]

The problem was never solved, indeed it intensified. By 1704 bankruptcy appeared to be imminent. Gravenor's litigation had drained the coffers, and a Scot and Lot to raise £600 was inadequate. A further £1,000 was then borrowed. This, however, had little effect; neither did attempts to call in bonds owing to the town and rent arrears. The dilapidation of the quays, the decay of bridges within the town's liberty and the continuing disrepair of the farm at Otley, as well as of the estate at Ulveston Hall are all recorded. Once again, money was raised by mortgaging Handford Hall for £1,000 at £50 interest, and then for £3,000. By 1720, an offer was even being considered for the sale of this prime asset for £3,600, though that disastrous course was not followed. Thereafter, the cycle of financial crisis came round constantly.[55]

[53] Great Court Books, C/2/2/2/4, ff. 9, 11, 38–39, 56, 73, 130, 132, 145; C/2/2/2/8, ff. 14, 18, 28, 43; C/2/2/2/7, ff.45, 60–90; Clarke 1830, 74.
[54] Great Court Books, C/2/2/2/2, ff. 187, 217, 219, 255; C/2/2/2/3, ff. 61, 73, 78v, 87v, 112, 131, 163; Assembly Book, C/4/3/1/6, ff. 247, 358, 391, 396, 402, 409; Tooley Foundation Accounts, C/5/1/1/6/90; Treasurer's Accounts, C/3/4/1/80–81; Canning 1747 (1819 edn), 85.
[55] Great Court Books, C/2/2/2/3, f. 188; C/2/2/2/4, ff.102, 132, 158, 170, 222; C/2/2/2/5, ff. 7, 50, 112–13, 118–19; C/2/2/2/6, f. 17; Clarke 1830, 77.

In the 1730s the maladministration of the town charities came sharply to light. The neglect of Christ's Hospital had been reported as early as 1706, and the Committee set up in the 1730s sat on and off for ten years. That the Portmen were opposed to it and tried to suppress its findings is suspicious, and when published privately in 1747 the evidence of jobbery and misappropriation was damning. The Tooley estates at Debenham were in a ruinous condition, the Foundation's finances were in deficit, the accounts missing and the Wardens non-resident. The Phillips Charity farm (part of the Christ's Hospital endowment) was tenantless, and there had been no new feoffment since 1720. The moneys deriving from gifts and legacies had been embezzled, and there was only some £80 of Lending Cash in the Clavigers' hands in 1744, and nearly £800 unaccounted for. Forfeited bonds amounting to nearly £600, some going back to the 1660s, had not been recovered. The Great Court had re-ordered the regulations for the management of Christ's Hospital, Tooley's Foundation, the Grammar School and the other charities in 1744, but the financial problem remained. In 1768, another report on the finances and charities spoke of 'misapplication' of funds over the previous fourteen years, whilst further mortgages taken out in the 1770s simply added to the debts. Another report, in 1785, stated that no officers had been appointed to oversee the estates and charities, the financial officers had not presented their accounts, the water rentals were in chaos and unrecoverable bonds for the Lending Cash were listed. It was discovered that there was only £132 to answer all expenses, whilst there were £440 of immediate demands on the town. The report's comment that strict economy was therefore necessary was all too obvious. One further example of the state of affairs by the end of the century must suffice. In 1794, the Corporation leased the site of the Shambles on the Cornhill, but the Rotunda that was built in its place as a speculative venture to improve Ipswich as a venue for social gatherings proved singularly unsuccessful. In 1810 the Corporation bought it back for £1,200, having in the interim received only £320 in rents over the whole period. £2,000 was then borrowed to replace the Rotunda with the town's first Corn Exchange, but that, too, was a failed venture. The corn merchants defaulted on the rents of stalls and only £42 a year on average was collected throughout the period to 1834, whilst the Corporation was paying £100 a year in interest on the loan.[56]

When the Municipal Corporations Commission reported on the state of the borough in 1834, they were, irrespective of their known political bias, in effect only recapitulating a state of affairs which had been developing for over a century and a half. The corruption of the government of the town had become endemic. In 1834, the Report found that the Treasurer's accounts were in disarray and many for the late 18th century missing. The Chamberlains were described as defunct due to the long neglect of their duties. No one knew what the assets and liabilities were. One witness stated that the normal annual revenue should have been £2,121 but that there was a shortfall of some £500. The accounts of the charities were unaudited; in the case of Tyler's Charity this had been the case from 1815 to 1826. The Corporation's responsibility for the conservation of the river had long been neglected, the silting up of the channels and the imminent collapse of the Common Quay being the result. The situation had become critical when in 1830 decisions were taken to borrow the enormous sum of £10,000 to pay off the debts, and to farm out the water

---

[56] Canning 1747 (1819 edn), 101–14; Clarke 1830, 95–96; Great Court Books, C/2/2/2/4, f. 102; C/2/2/2/6, ff. 135, 142–45, 152, 154; C/2/2/2/7, ff. 280, 318, 339; C/2/2/2/8, ff. 77–82; Assembly Book, C/4/3/1/8, 9 Dec. 1793, 26 Jul. 1810, 3 and 11 Jun. 1811.

rentals with an estimated loss of £1,300 a year as a consequence. The total estimated debts in 1834 were £14,300.[57]

This 'corruption' of the body politic and the decay of the central organs of government of the borough demonstrate that the old constitution was unable to adapt to the era of party politics. Divisions between the Portmen and the Twenty Four harden into factions as the involvement of the townsmen in the Great Court is diminished. Finance and administration cease to be efficient. After 1770, the bribery and corruption of partisan politics is more evident, especially with the emergence of political clubs in the town. These, the Yellows or Samaritans, and the Blues – the Wellington Club – were where patronage and influence determined office holding and where elections were organized. Like the growth of an electorate that was extra-mural and had little if any interest in the town, let alone knowledge of it, the political clubs were extra-constitutional.[58]

In the wider context of the community other influences and changes suggest that corporate legitimacy was gone and government under the Charter defunct by the close of the 18th century. Most indicative of this were the private Acts of Parliament that were secured by public organisation and action in order to improve the town's economic activity: the Paving and Lighting Act, the Stowmarket Navigation Act, both of 1793, and the Act of 1805 that created the River Commission. The Corporation opposed all three, in the latter case revealing its desperate attempt to maintain its monopoly of power. It first attempted to secure all places on the proposed Commission but the committee of subscribers, fearing the 'risk of Corporation politics', went ahead and, despite an attempt by some in the Corporation to disrupt their meetings, at one point by the use of the mob, achieved their ends and secured the Act. Complementing these examples of public agitation for change in the face of corporate supineness, the town's newspapers widened the discussion of matters of concern by their editorial comment, reports and letter columns. The proliferation of private charitable institutions from the 1780s served the needs of the community arguably better than the Corporation charities, and pamphlets and public meetings stimulated the discussion of reform.

The governance of Ipswich under the Charter had reached a high point of oligarchical order in the early 17th century, when the instruments of government, constitutional, administrative and financial appear to have served the interests of the townsmen efficiently. The Charter also served to ensure a very real degree of autonomy for the town in its relations with central government and the world beyond the boundary of its ancient liberties. From the Restoration, the undermining of that autonomy by royal manipulation of the Charters and later by the effects of national party politics, and the evidence of the corrosion of institutions, eventually left the borough's government in dissolution, the officers either corrupt or incompetent, 'enjoying neither the confidence nor the respect of the inhabitants'. The damning report of 1834, which variously described Ipswich as being ruled by 'a junto dictated to by a political club' and thus 'an ill-regulated republic' and 'an oligarchy of the worst description . . . now fast approaching a legal dissolution', was politically biased but in general accurately stated the facts.[59]

---

[57] *Municipal Corporations Report* 1835, *passim.*
[58] *Ibid.,* 2298–99, 2338–39; Clarke 1830, 121–23, 129; Atton 1979, 320ff.
[59] *Municipal Corporations Report* 1835, 2340.

When Nathaniel Bacon concluded his preface to the 'Annalls' of 1654, he wrote that his purpose had been to help establish 'a more perfect rule of a more righteous and peaceable government with truth within this Body'. Without that, he continued, 'righteousness and prosperity will get upon the wing and be gone and leave this place buried up in contempt'. His concern had, by 1835, proved all too prophetic.[60]

---

[60] Richardson 1884, vii.

Works Cited

Allen, D.H. (ed.), 1974. *Essex Quarter Sessions Order Book 1652–1661.* Chelmsford.

Allen, D.H., 1997. 'Daniel Browninge of Crowfield: a Little-Known High Sheriff of Suffolk and the Stowmarket Assizes of 1695', *Proc. Suffolk Inst. Archaeol.*, XXXIX, 28–47.

Alsford, S., 1982. 'Thomas le Rente: a Medieval Town Ruler', *Proc. Suffolk Inst. Archaeol.*, XXXV, 105–15.

Atton, K.J., 1979. 'Municipal and Parliamentary Politics in Ipswich, 1818–47' (unpublished Ph.D. thesis, University College, London).

Bindoff, S.T., 1950. *Tudor England.* Harmondsworth.

Blake, E.O. (ed.), 1962. *Liber Eliensis.* Royal Hist. Soc., Camden 3rd Ser., XCII.

Blatchly, J.M., 1989. *The Town Library of Ipswich Provided for the Use of the Town Preachers in 1599: a History and Catalogue.* Woodbridge.

Boynton, L., 1967. *The Elizabethan Militia 1558–1638.* London.

Canning, R., 1747. *An Account of the Gifts and Legacies that Have been Given and Bequeathed to Charitable Uses in the Town of Ipswich . . .* Ipswich.

[Canning, R.], 1754. *The Principal Charters which have been Granted to the Corporation of Ipswich in Suffolk.* London.

Clanchy, M.T., 1979. *From Memory to Written Record: England 1066–1307.* London.

Clarke, G.R., 1830. *The History and Description of the Town of Ipswich.* London.

Collier, J.P. (ed.), 1838. *Kynge Johan. A Play in Two Parts. By John Bale.* Camden Society, London.

Copinger, W.A., 1905–11. *The Manors of Suffolk*, 7 vols. London and Manchester.

Cross, R.L., 1968. *Justice in Ipswich 1200–1968.* Ipswich.

Darby, H.C., 1952. *The Domesday Geography of Eastern England.* Cambridge.

DNB. Dictionary of National Biography.

Dobson, R.B. (ed.), 1970. *The Peasants' Revolt of 1381.* London.

EANQ. East Anglian Notes and Queries.

Finn, R.W., 1964. *Domesday Studies: The Eastern Counties.* London.

Freeman, J.I., 1997. *The Postmaster of Ipswich: William Stevenson Fitch, Antiquary and Thief.* London.

Friar, S., 1991. *The Batsford Companion to Local History.* London.

Galbraith, V.H., 1961. *The Making of Domesday Book.* Oxford.

Gibson, J., Medlycott, M. and Mills, D., 1993. *Land and Window Tax Assessments.* Birmingham.

Glyde, J., 1850. *The Moral, Social and Religious Condition of Ipswich in the Middle of the Nineteenth Century.* Ipswich.

Grace, F., 1996a. 'The Appointment of Stephen Marshall as Town Preacher at Ipswich 1652–3', *Suffolk Review*, New Ser. 27, 23–26.

Grace, F., 1996b. 'Foreign Fines Disputes in Ipswich: Three Seventeenth-Century Cases', *Suffolk Review*, New Ser. 26, 28–36.

Grace, F., 1996c. 'Schismaticall and Factious Humours: Opposition in Ipswich to Laudian Church Government in the 1630s', *Religious Dissent in East Anglia III*, 97–120. University of East Anglia, Norwich.

Gray, I.E. and Potter, W.E., 1950. *Ipswich School 1400–1950*. Ipswich.

Grimsey, B.P., 1888. 'Armorial Insignia of the Borough of Ipswich', *Proc. Suffolk Inst. Archaeol.*, VI, 456–63.

Gross, C., 1890. *The Gild Merchant*, 2 vols. Oxford.

Harding, A., 1960. 'The Origins and Early History of the Keepers of the Peace', *Trans. Royal Hist. Soc.*, 5th Ser., X.

Harvey, P.D.A., 1984. *Manorial Records*. London.

HMC, 1883. *Ninth Report of the Royal Commission on Historical Manuscripts*. London.

Hurst, J.G. and West, S.E., 1957. 'Saxo-Norman Pottery in East Anglia, ii: Thetford Ware, with an Account of Middle-Saxon Ipswich Ware', *Proc. Cambridge Antiq. Soc.*, 1, 29–60.

Martin, G.H., 1954. *The Early Court Rolls of the Borough of Ipswich*. Leicester.

Martin, G.H., 1955. 'The Borough and the Merchant Community of Ipswich, 1317–1422' (unpublished D. Phil. thesis, University of Oxford).

Martin, G.H., 1956. 'The Records of the Borough of Ipswich, to 1422', *J. Soc. Archivists*, I, no. 4, 87–93.

Martin, G.H., 1961. 'The Origins of Borough Records', *J. Soc. Archivists*, II, no. 4, 147–53.

Martin, G.H., 1963. 'The English Borough in the Thirteenth Century', *Trans. Royal Hist. Soc.*, 5th Ser., XIII, 123–44.

Martin, G.H., 1971. 'The Registration of Deeds of Title in the Medieval Borough', in Bullough, D.A. and Storey, R.L. (eds), *The Study of Medieval Records: Essays in Honour of Kathleen Major*. Oxford.

Martin, G.H. (ed.), 1973. *The Ipswich Recognizance Rolls 1294–1327: a Calendar* (Suffolk Records Soc., XVI). Ipswich.

Martin, G.H., 1986. 'Domeday Book and the Boroughs', in Sawyer, P.H. (ed.), *Domesday Book: a Reassessment*. London.

Martin, G.H., 1997. 'English Town Records, 1200–1350', in Britnell, R. (ed.), *Pragmatic Literacy, East and West*, 119–30. Woodbridge.

Municipal Corporations Report, 1835. *Appendix to the First Report of the Commissioners on the Municipal Corporations (England and Wales), Part 4: Eastern and North Western Circuits*. London.

Ormrod, W.M., 1986. 'The English Government and the Black Death', in Ormrod, W.M. (ed.), *England in the Fourteenth Century*. Woodbridge.

Pafford, J.H.P. (ed.), 1931. *King Johan by John Bale*. Malone Society Reprints, Oxford.

Pallister, D.M., 1990. *Domesday York*. York.

Putnam, B.H., 1929. 'The Transformation of the Keepers of the Peace into the Justices of the Peace, 1327–1380', Trans. Royal Hist. Soc., 4th Ser., XII.

Raban, S., 1982. *Mortmain Legislation and the English Church, 1279–1500*. Cambridge.

Redstone, L.J., 1948. *Ipswich Through the Ages*. Ipswich.

Richardson, W.H. (ed.), 1884. *The Annalls of Ipswiche . . . by Nathaniel Bacon serving as Recorder and Town Clark . . . 1654.* Ipswich.

Rubin, M., 1991. *Corpus Christi: The Eucharist in Late Medieval Culture*. Cambridge.

Speed, J., 1611. *Theatre of the Empire of Great Britaine*. London.

Tait, J., 1936. *The Medieval English Borough*. Manchester.

Trustees, 1878. *A Short Account of the Municipal Charities of the Borough of Ipswich, prepared by direction of the Trustees*. Ipswich.

Twiss, T. (ed.), 1871–76. *The Black Book of the Admiralty*, 4 vols, Rolls Series, H.M.S.O., London.

VCH Suffolk, 1907. Victoria History of the Counties of England, *Suffolk*, II. London.

Warner, G. (ed.), 1926. *The Libelle of Englyshe Polycye: a Poem on the Use of Sea Power, 1436*. Oxford.

Webb, J., 1962. *Great Tooley of Ipswich: Portrait of an Early Tudor Merchant*. Ipswich.

Webb, J., 1966. *Poor Relief in Elizabethan Ipswich* (Suffolk Records Soc., IX). Ipswich.

Webb, J., 1996. *The Town Finances of Elizabethan Ipswich: Select Treasurers' and Chamberlains' Accounts* (Suffolk Records Soc., XXXVIII). Woodbridge.

Webb, S. and B., 1927–29. *English Poor Law History* (English Local Government, VII–IX), 3 vols. London.

Webb, S. and B., 1963. *The Manor and the Borough, Part I (English Local Government*, III), reprint. London.

West, S.E. *et al.*, 1964. 'Excavations at Cox Lane (1958) and at the Town Defences, Shire Hall Yard, Ipswich (1959)', *Proc. Suffolk Inst. Archaeol.*, XXIX, 223–303.

Westlake, H.F., 1919. *The Parish Gilds of Medieval England*. London.

Whitelock, D. (ed.), 1930. *Anglo-Saxon Wills*. Cambridge.

Wodderspoon, J., 1850. *Memorials of the Ancient Town of Ipswich*. Ipswich.

Abbreviations in the Catalogue

Throughout the catalogue the twelve ancient parishes of Ipswich and the three hamlets are abbreviated as follows:

CL	St Clement	MW	St Matthew
HL	St Helen	NI	St Nicholas
LW	St Lawrence	PE	St Peter
MG	St Margaret	ST	St Stephen
ME	St Mary Elms	BH	Brooks Hamlet*
MQ	St Mary at Quay	WB	Wix Bishop
MS	St Mary Stoke	WU	Wix Ufford
MT	St Mary le Tower		

* often referred to as Whitton cum Thurleston

List of Catalogue Contents

C/2 JUSTICE AND THE COURTS

C/3   FINANCE AND TOWN PROPERTY

C/4 TOWN GOVERNMENT

C/5   TOWN RESPONSIBILITIES AND SERVICES

C/6   ACCIDENTAL ACCUMULATIONS

APPENDICES

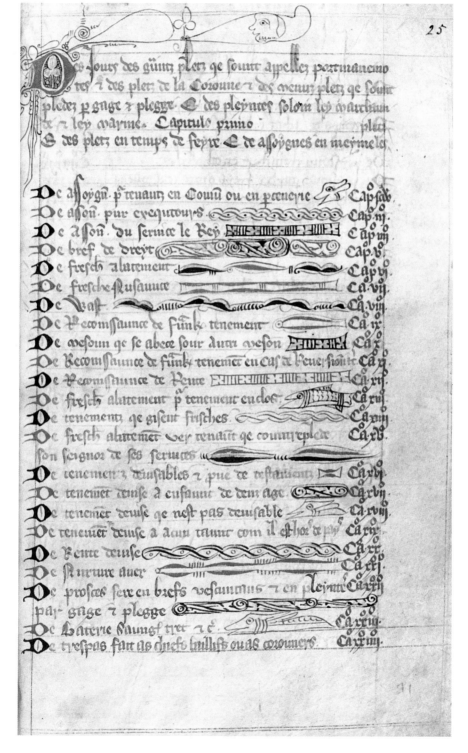

Pl. 1. Part of the index to the mid-14th-century *Custumale Gippovicense*, in Anglo-Norman French, rubricated and elaborately ornamented in red and blue. (C/4/1/3)

Pl. 2. The illuminated initial letter 'R' on the first Charter of Richard II, 1378, in gold leaf, red, blue and green depicting the King enthroned, bestowing a charter bearing the Lombardic letters 'RICARDUS DEI GRA...' on kneeling burgesses; similarly illuminated decoration with flowers and foliage extends along top and left-hand margins. (C/1/1/8)

Pl.3. Achievement of the Borough from the Confirmation of Grant by William Hervy, Clarenceux King of Arms, at his Visitation in 1561. (C/1/2/1)

Pl. 4. Detail from the manuscript map on vellum made in 1591 by the surveyor John Darby of an estate in Kirton and Falkenham, later part of Smart's bequest to the borough. The self-portrait is based on a figure in Peter Breughel's 'Aestas', 1568. (C/3/10/8/1/2)

C/1 STATUS, TITLE, EXTERNAL OBLIGATIONS

C/1/1 ROYAL CHARTERS AND LETTERS PATENT   1256–1688

The Charters and later Letters Patent (the solemn charter with its specific address and list of witnesses ceased to be issued by the royal Chancery in the 16th century) were the legal foundation – in a sense the title-deeds – of the unreformed borough's gradually increasing autonomy.

The earliest charter, for which the burgesses had begun negotiations before the end of Richard I's reign (Martin 1955, 18), was granted by King John and sealed on 25 May 1200. John's original charter is no longer extant. The last reference to its existence occurs in the inventory of the borough archive drawn up by the Clavigers in 1696 (C/4/7/1/2), at which time it was still in official custody in the Treasury chamber: 'Originall Charters of K. John Hen. 3^{d} Edw. I^{mi} and 2^{di} in a Black Box'. Much was purloined from the archive by 'collectors' in the earlier part of the 19th century; but while the whereabouts of many of these looted documents are known, and some 16th- and 17th-century correspondence has been recovered by purchase, the fate of John's charter remains a mystery. Its terms, however, are entered on the Charter Roll in the Public Record Office, and its text is recited in full in Edward I's *Inspeximus* of 1291 (C/1/1/2) and in most subsequent charters and Letters Patent down to Elizabeth I's confirmation of 1560.

The burgesses in 1200 were granted the borough with its liberties and free customs, to be held of the Crown for the customary farm and an additional 100s annually. They received exemption from a variety of tolls and customs dues throughout the kingdom, and from being obliged to plead in causes outside the borough, except where 'foreign' tenure was involved. A gild merchant and hanse were authorised. Burgage tenements were to be held according to the custom of Ipswich; pleas of debt and pledges contracted within the liberties were to be heard there; and the burgesses were empowered to choose two Bailiffs to head the town's government (subject to their presentation to the Chief Justice at the Exchequer on election), and four Coroners to keep the pleas of the Crown and act as a check on the power of the Bailiffs.

By Henry III's charter of 1256 the borough gained further governmental and trading rights, the most noteworthy of which was the return of writs. The borough's right of self-government suffered a setback in 1283 when the Sheriff, while presiding at a session of the County Court in Ipswich, was assaulted by a riotous mob; whereupon King Edward I seized the borough into his own hands and appointed his own officers to govern it. Autonomy was restored only in 1291, when Edward's 'Charter of Restitution' confirmed the charters of John and Henry III – for an increased fee-farm.

Thereafter, successive sovereigns confirmed the charters of their predecessors, and further privileges conferred from time to time gradually extended the borough's freedom from the intervention of officers of the Crown. In 1317 Edward II extended the right of the burgesses not to plead or be impleaded outside the borough, conceded that all assizes or inquisitions concerning internal affairs should be taken by burgesses, not by 'foreigners', and freed the town from the obligation of presenting newly-elected Bailiffs to the Chief Justice. The number of Coroners was reduced from four to two, in acknowledgement that two of the four positions had normally been occupied by the Bailiffs.

Edward III issued a confirmatory charter in July 1338, the immediate occasion for which seems to have been his revocation in June of his newly-granted charter to Harwich enabling the burgesses to collect dues on goods entering the 'port of Orwell pertaining to their town', which had infringed the rights of Ipswich (Redstone 1948, 55, 57, 142). There was a second brief loss of autonomy in 1344, when the Borough was again placed in the charge of the Sheriff, following an insult offered to the Assize Judge by an unruly mob of sailors.

By his charter of 1378 Richard II clarified disputed powers concerning the pleas to be determined in the borough courts. In 1380 his second charter confirmed all powers previously granted, even though they may not have been exercised in the past.

The next extension of powers came with Henry VI's charter of 1446 which constituted the Bailiffs and four of the Portmen Justices of the Peace for the borough, to the exclusion of the county Justices. The same charter marked Ipswich's success in the first stage of its bid to secure its much-prized Admiralty jurisdiction. The High Court of Admiralty, founded by Edward I and established as a civil court by Edward III in 1360, had as its original objects the prevention and punishment of piracy and the settlement of questions of prizes and wreck, though later Admirals of England, until restrained by statute in 1391, claimed jurisdiction over all contracts and pleas relating to maritime affairs. From Henry VI the borough now obtained the abolition of the Admiral's jurisdiction within the liberties. By Edward IV's charter of 18 March 1463 the Admiral's powers were specifically conferred upon the Bailiffs.

Edward IV's charter has not survived. Its text, however, is recited in the Letters Patent of *Inspeximus* of Richard III (1485), Henry VII (1488), Henry VIII (1512), Edward VI (1547) and Elizabeth (1560). In addition to its Admiralty provisions it reinforced the powers of the Bailiffs and Portmen as Justices of the Peace; granted to the borough all the profits of the Sessions of the Peace; and excluded the authority of the royal Escheator, Clerk of the Market and Steward and Marshal of the Household. The borough courts were given cognizance of all pleas, real, personal and mixed, to be determined before the Bailiffs, 'even though the said pleas . . . touch the King and his heirs'; and the Bailiffs and burgesses were granted exemption from service on juries and inquisitions, and from nomination to other offices outside the borough, without their consent.

Richard III in 1485 ratified the borough's Admiralty jurisdiction in perpetuity. In 1519 Henry VIII clarified the extent of this jurisdiction as including the whole length of the Orwell estuary as far as Polleshead, and included within it rights over the foreshore between the high and low tides, together with rights of wreck, flotsam and jetsam. The liberties were confirmed by Edward VI, Elizabeth and Charles I; for the text of Charles I's missing Letters Patent of 1635, *see* the 1653 book of precedents, C/4/2/1.

The next change in the borough's constitution was brought about by Charles II's first charter (Letters Patent) of 1665 which, while confirming the ancient privileges, converted the governing body into a 'close corporation' by empowering the twelve Portmen and twenty-four Common Councilmen to elect to vacancies in their own ranks, to the disfranchisement of the freemen at large. This charter also added the borough Recorder to the ranks of the magistracy.

Ipswich did not escape the wholesale surrender of municipal charters in the last years of Charles II's reign, following the failure of the Whig attempt to exclude James, Duke of York from the succession to the throne. Charles's second charter, issued in 1684 following the surrender, appointed royal nominees to all borough offices, reserving to the Crown power to remove any or all of them by Order in Council. James II's charter of 1688 was conceived in similar terms, though it was soon withdrawn by proclamation, in a vain attempt to recover his popularity before his flight abroad. Henceforth Ipswich was governed by the terms of Charles II's first charter of 1665 until the demise of the old Corporation in 1835.

The most significant charters are translated in Canning 1754. See also the *Calendars of the Charter Rolls*, II, 402; III, 344–45; IV, 449; V, 249, 263, 392; and VI, 54–55, 197–99; and the *Report of the Commissioners on the Municipal Corporations* (1835), Appendix, pp 2293–95. For translations of Henry VIII's Letters Patent of 1519 and James II's of 1688, *see* FORESHORE RIGHTS, C/1/7/2/2–3.

C/1/1/1   15 Apr. 1256
Charter of King Henry III
Burgesses to have return of all royal writs touching town and liberty; Bailiffs to account at Exchequer without intervention of Sheriff; burgesses to elect their own Coroners to make attachments of pleas of the Crown and answer before the Justices in Eyre; fish and other merchandise entering port by ship may be bought and sold freely by merchants without intervention of brokers
Witnesses: W[illiam] Bishop of Ely, W[alter] Bishop of Norwich, A[ymer] Bishop elect of Winchester, Roger le Bigot, Earl of Norfolk, Marshal of England, Humfrey de Bohun, Earl of Hereford and Essex, Peter de Sabaud, Guy de Leznman, William de Valencia, John Maunsell,

Provost of Beverley, William de Grey, Robert Waleraund, Nicholas de Sancto Mauro, Ralph de Bakepuz, Peter Everard, William Sancto Ermino and others. Given at Westminster
(21.5 cm × 22.5 cm, Latin, initial letter 'H' in blue with faded rubrication; fragment of Great Seal in green wax on red and green cords)

C/1/1/2   23 Jun. 1291
Charter (*Inspeximus*) of King Edward I [known as the 'Charter of Restitution']
Inspects and confirms King John's [missing] charter of 25 May 1200 which granted to burgesses: the borough with its liberties and free customs, to be held of Crown for accustomed farm and additional 100s annually; exemption from all toll, lastage, stallage, passage, pontage and other customs throughout land and seaports; exemption from pleading outside borough, except for pleas of foreign tenure; a merchant gild and hanse; no-one to be lodged within borough, and nothing to be taken by force; tenures and lands within borough to be held according to custom of Ipswich and other royal free boroughs; pleas to be held there of debts and pledges contracted and made within liberties; none to have judgment against him for money but according to laws of free boroughs; power to choose two lawful and discreet men [Bailiffs] (who are to be presented to Chief Justice at Exchequer) to keep government of borough and not to be removed except by common council so long as they behave well; power to choose four men [Coroners] to keep pleas of Crown and see that governors conduct themselves justly towards both poor and rich. Inspects and confirms also Henry III's charter of 15 Apr. 1256 (C/1/1/1). Restores borough to burgesses, following its seizure into King's hands for trespasses committed by them, to hold at annual fee farm of £60
Witnesses: R[obert] Bishop of Bath and Wells, Chancellor, Edmund our brother, Henry de Lacy, Earl of Lincoln, Robert Tibbetot, Walter de Bello Campo, William de Monte Reuell, Peter de Campania, Guy Ferre, Peter de Chaumpuent, Elias de Hanuill, Gilbert de Brideshale and others. Given at Berwick upon Tweed
(44.5 cm × 37 cm, Latin, initial letter 'E' omitted; Great Seal in green wax, incomplete, on red and green cords)

C/1/1/3   23 Jun. 1291
Duplicate of C/1/1/2
(44 cm × 37 cm, Latin, initial letter 'E' omitted; Great Seal in green wax, incomplete, on red and white/yellow cords)

C/1/1/4   20 May 1317
Charter (*Inspeximus*) of King Edward II
Inspects and confirms King John's charter of 25 May 1200 and Henry III's of 15 Apr. 1256. Grants further that no burgess shall plead or be impleaded outside borough, of any pleas, assizes or plaints, nor of lands and tenures within borough or suburbs, nor of any trespasses committed or contracts made within town liberty; all assizes or inquisitions taken *re* internal matters to be made by burgesses, not by foreigners, saving matters touching King or community of town; Bailiffs need no longer be presented at Exchequer on election; number of Coroners reduced from four to two; no-one indicted or arrested within borough or liberty to be imprisoned elsewhere than in King's prison in Ipswich, but kept there by Bailiffs until delivered according to law, unless removed on reasonable cause by special precept of King or Keeper of Forest, if charged with trespass of forest; burgesses to be quit of murage, pavage, picage, anchorage, strandage, and 'segeagio' [harbour dues] of all goods and merchandise throughout realm and through all seaports; no-one to meet merchants entering town with goods by land or sea to buy, before goods have been exposed for sale in market place; forestalling of such goods to be subject to heavy penalty to King.
Witnesses: W[alter] Archbishop of Canterbury, W[alter] Bishop of Exeter, Thomas, Earl of Norfolk, Marshal of England, Humfrey de Bohun, Earl of Hereford and Essex, Hugh le Despenser sen., John de Grey, William de Monte Acuto, Steward of the Household and others. Given at Westminster
(53.5 cm × 66 cm, Latin, initial letter 'E' depicting ship moored beside waterside building with

3

standing figure alongside, all uncoloured; fragment of Great Seal in green wax on red and green cords)

C/1/1/5   20 May 1317
Duplicate or copy of C/1/1/4
(55.5 cm × 65 cm, Latin, initial 'E' without ornament but other capitals of first line decorated with grotesque faces; prominent ruling, particularly of top, left- and right-hand margins, suggests that copy, though apparently contemporary, may be unofficial; red seal cords, with no other evidence of sealing)

C/1/1/6   30 [*sic*] May 1317
Duplicate or copy of C/1/1/4
(53.4 cm × 53.6 cm, Latin, initial 'E' without ornament; incorrectly dated; no turn-up at foot and no indication of attachment of seal)

C/1/1/7   1 Jul. 1338
Charter (*Inspeximus*) of King Edward III
Inspects and confirms Edward II's charter (C/1/1/4), inspecting and confirming in turn Edward I's charter of 23 Jun. 1291, which inspects and confirms John's charter of 25 May 1200 and Henry III's of 15 Apr. 1256
Witnesses: J[ohn] Archbishop of Canterbury, R[ichard] Bishop of Durham, R[obert] Bishop of Chichester, Chancellor, Henry de Lancastria, Earl of Derby, William de Bohun, Earl of Northampton, William de Monte Acuto, Earl of Salisbury, Henry de Ferariis, John Darcy, Steward of the Household and others. Given at Walton
(53.2 cm × 65.4 cm, Latin, illuminated initial letter 'E' in gold leaf, red, blue and pale purple depicting King enthroned, bestowing charter with pendant seal on kneeling burgesses; red and yellow seal cords, Great Seal missing)

C/1/1/8   10 Aug. 1378
Charter (*Inspeximus*) of King Richard II
Inspects and confirms Edward III's charter (C/1/1/7), inspecting and confirming in turn Edward II's charter of 20 May 1317, which inspects and confirms Edward I's charter of 23 Jun. 1291, which inspects and confirms John's charter of 25 May 1200 and Henry III's of 15 Apr. 1256. On petition of burgesses that, although by previous charters they have had cognizance of all pleas of lands, tenements and rents by writ of assize or other writs, and also cognizance of pleas of trespass, debt, account, contract and agreement, assizes of fresh force and all other pleas arising in town, dissensions have arisen and justice has been delayed because of uncertainty *re* such cognizance: further grant, on payment of 40s in hanaper, of cognizance of all such pleas
Witnesses: S[imon] Archbishop of Canterbury, W[illiam] Bishop of London, A[dam] Bishop of St David's, Chancellor, Thomas Bishop of Exeter, Treasurer, R[alph] Bishop of Salisbury, John, King of Arms to Duke of Lancaster, Edmund Earl of Cambridge, Thomas Earl of Buckingham, Richard le Scrope, Steward of the Household, John Fordham, Keeper of the Privy Seal and others. Given at Westminster
Turn-up inscribed with memorandum confirming powers granted in previous charters, even though they may not have been exercised, 26 Feb. 1380 [a copy of the final clause of Richard II's charter of that date, C/1/1/9]
(71 cm × 52.6 cm, Latin, illuminated initial letter 'R' in gold leaf, red, blue and green depicting King enthroned, bestowing charter on kneeling burgesses; similarly illuminated decoration with flowers and foliage extends along top and left-hand margins; fragment of Great Seal in green wax on red and green cords)

C/1/1/9   26 Feb. 1380
Charter (*Inspeximus*) of King Richard II
Inspects and confirms Richard II's first charter (C/1/1/8), with all earlier charters inspected and confirmed therein. Additional clause confirming to burgesses all powers previously granted, even though they may not have been exercised in the past

Witnesses: S[imon] Archbishop of Canterbury, Chancellor, W[illiam] Bishop of Winchester, Thomas Bishop of Exeter, Treasurer, Edmund, Earl of Cambridge, Thomas, Earl of Buckingham, William de Latymer, William de Bello Campo, Chamberlain, Hugh de Segrave, Steward of the Household, John de Fordham, Keeper of the Privy Seal and others. Given at Westminster
(71 cm × 54.3 cm, Latin, space left for large initial letter 'R' never added; Great Seal in green wax, almost complete, on red and green cords)

C/1/1/10   27 Jun. 1392
Letters Patent (*Inspeximus*) of King Richard II
Inspects and confirms indenture of feoffment from Geoffrey Starlyng and John Andreu, Bailiffs, and commonalty of Ipswich, to Gilbert de Boulge, William Gunnyld, Henry Walle and John Arnald, of piece of land of common soil, 320 ft × 120 ft on E. and 320 ft × 120 ft on W. side of causeway extending from Portbregge up to Stokebregge, with 'dammyng', 340 ft × 32 ft, extending from Stokebregge up to Stokemelledam, and watercourse there, for 6s 8d annual rent, 21 Aug. 1391. Given at Nottingham
(20.3 cm × 37 cm, Latin, large initial letter 'R' outlined for ornament never added; Great Seal in white wax, incomplete, on tag)

C/1/1/11   24 Oct. 1399
Letters Patent (*Inspeximus*) of King Henry IV
Inspects and confirms Letters Patent of Richard II, 6 Nov. 1377, inspecting and confirming charter of Edward I, 1 Feb. 1303, to foreign merchants trading in England, for their convenience and security and for precise exhibition of customs and dues to be paid by them. Inspects and confirms also, charter of Edward III, 14 Mar. 1327, inspecting and confirming charter of Edward II, 7 Dec. 1317 which confirms charter of Henry III to German merchants who have a house in London commonly called the Gildhall of the Teutons, promising to maintain them throughout realm in all liberties and free customs enjoyed by them in time of his ancestors. Given at Westminster
(83.1 cm × 56.3 cm, Latin, initial letter 'H' and some other capitals on first line omitted for insertion of ornament never added; slit for seal tag, Great Seal and tag missing)

C/1/1/12   28 Oct. 1399
Letters Patent of King Henry IV
After reciting grant of common soil [confirmed by Richard II in C/1/1/10], to the end that grantees should build two watermills on site, and that after repaying their cost of construction out of mill profits, mills should by royal licence be granted to Bailiffs and commonalty of Ipswich; and that mills were built, costs repaid and profits subsequently taken by Bailiffs and commonalty, who were found by inquisition before Roger Cavendissh, Escheator to Richard II, to have given site to grantees without royal licence, whereby mills were seized into King's hands: now Crown grants mills to Bailiffs and commonalty for ever, together with profits since time of above-mentioned inquisition. Given at Westminster
(49.4 cm × 28.2 cm, Latin, initial letter 'H' and exaggerated ascenders of other capitals on first line outlined for ornament never added; large fragment of Great Seal in green wax on green and purple cords)

C/1/1/13   11 Dec. 1399
Charter (*Inspeximus*) of King Henry IV
Inspects and confirms Richard II's second charter (C/1/1/9), with all earlier charters inspected and confirmed therein
Witnesses: Thomas Archbishop of Canterbury, R[ichard] Archbishop of York, R[obert] Bishop of London, J[ohn] Bishop of Ely, E[dmund] Bishop of Exeter, Edmund, Duke of York, Thomas, Earl Warr, Henry, Earl of Northumberland, Ralph, Earl of Westmorland, John de Scarle, Chancellor, John de Northbury, Treasurer, William Roos de Hamelak, William de Wyloghby, John de Cobham, Thomas de Erpyngham, Chamberlain, Thomas de Rempston,

5

Steward of the Household, Master Richard Clyfford, Keeper of the Privy Seal and others. Given at Westminster
(76 cm × 54.5 cm, Latin, initial letter 'H' and some other initial capitals on first line omitted for insertion of ornament never added; fragments of Great Seal in green wax on red and purple-cords)

C/1/1/14   28 Mar. 1446
Charter of King Henry VI
Granting to burgesses, in consideration that they are burdened by payment of annual farm: town to be free borough, corporate; burgesses to be one commonalty with perpetual succession, using common seal; liberty to choose two Bailiffs annually; Bailiffs and four other burgesses chosen by Bailiffs from among twelve Portmen to be Keepers and Justices of the Peace in town and liberty, to exclusion of Keepers and Justices in county of Suffolk; burgesses to have all fines, forfeited issues and amercements arising from office of Justice of the Peace, to be levied by their ministers in aid of farm and daily charges of town; and forfeiture of victuals by assize of bread, wine and ale; burgesses to choose one Bailiff to be King's Escheator for town, to exclusion of jurisdiction of any other Escheator; power in law to acquire lands, tenements and rents in town and elsewhere, notwithstanding Statute of Mortmain; Admiral of England, his lieutenant or deputy, and Steward, Marshal and Clerk of Market of King's Household, not to enter or sit within town and liberty, nor intermeddle therein, nor compel burgesses to plead outside it for any matter arising therein; burgesses to have all forfeited issues, fines and amercements arising before Escheator, and goods and chattels of residents outlawed in town, in aid of farm of town and its charges.
Witnesses: J[ohn] Archbishop of Canterbury, Chancellor, W[illiam] Bishop of Salisbury, A[dam] Bishop of Chichester, Keeper of the Privy Seal; W[alter] Bishop of Norwich, Humfrey, Duke of Gloucester, John, Duke of Exeter, Humfrey, Duke of Buckingham, Edmund, Marquess of Dorset, William, Marquess of Suffolk, William, Earl of Arundel, John, Earl of Shrewsbury, Sir Ralph Cromwell, Sir Ralph Boteler, Treasurer, and others. Given at Westminster
(62 cm × 38.7 cm, Latin; initial letter 'H' depicting King enthroned, crowned and holding sceptre and long-stemmed orb, the whole surmounted by a closed crown with four half-arches visible, its circlet inscribed 'Dieu et mon droit', in margin to left an angel supporting a blank shield, capitals on first line ornamented with delicate strapwork and arabesques, all uncoloured; Great Seal in green wax, incomplete, on red and green cords)

C/1/1/15   10 Jul. 1446
Letters Patent of King Henry VI
General pardon to the burgesses and commonalty of Ipswich, of offences committed before 9 April 1446, and of all fines and arrears of farms, etc. committed before 1 Sep. 1441; with proviso that such pardon shall not extend to Eleanor Cobham, daughter of Sir Reginald Cobham, kt, and other named felons, felonies and debts
(44 cm × 26 cm, Latin; Great Seal in white wax, incomplete, on tag)

C/1/1/16   16 Mar. 1485
Letters Patent (*Inspeximus*) of King Richard III
Inspects and confirms [missing] charter of Edward IV, 18 Mar. 1463 [for its provisions, see the introductory note to the charters], inspecting and confirming Richard II's charter of 26 Feb. 1380 (C/1/1/9) and all previous charters. Given at Westminster
(2 membranes, each 77 cm × 49.5 cm, Latin, initial letter 'R' and other capitals on first line omitted for insertion of ornament never added; Great Seal in green wax, almost complete, on red and blue cords)

C/1/1/17   20 Jan. 1488
Letters Patent (*Inspeximus*) of King Henry VII
Inspects and confirms [missing] charter of Edward IV, 18 Mar. 1463, inspecting and confirming Richard II's charter of 26 Feb. 1380 (C/1/1/9) and all previous charters. Given at Westminster

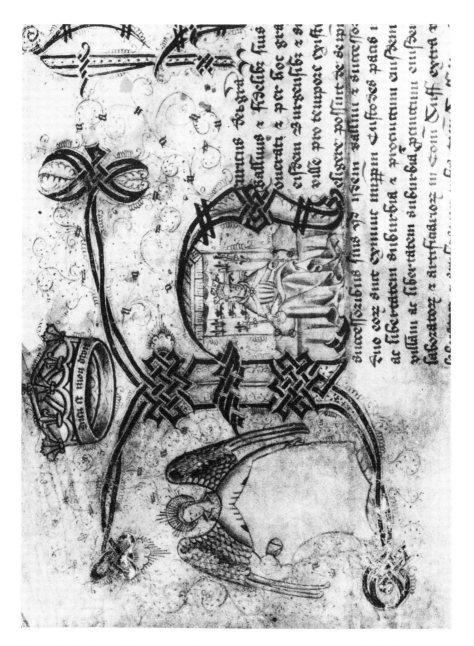

Fig. 1. Initial letter 'H' from the Charter granted to the Town in 1446 by Henry VI, depicting the King enthroned, crowned and holding sceptre and long-stemmed orb, the whole surmounted by a closed crown with four half-arches visible, its circlet inscribed 'Dieu et mon droit'. In the margin to the left an angel supporting a blank shield, capitals on first line ornamented with delicate strapwork and arabesques, all uncoloured. (C/1/1/14)

(2 membranes, each 76.5 cm × 49.8 cm, Latin, initial letter 'H' and other capitals on first line omitted for insertion of ornament never added; fragment of Great Seal in green wax, on red and white cords with gilt metallic threads)

C/1/1/18   25 Nov. 1511
Letters Patent of King Henry VIII
Granting to Bailiffs, burgesses and commonalty, licence to acquire and hold manors, lands, tenements, rents, reversions, services and hereditaments in Suffolk or elsewhere in England to yearly value of £50, notwithstanding the Statute of Mortmain. Given at Westminster
(45 cm × 26.4 cm, Latin, initial letter 'H' and other capitals on first line omitted for insertion of ornament never added; Great Seal in green wax, cracked but conserved, complete, on green and white cords with gilt metallic threads)

C/1/1/19   12 Mar. 1512
Letters Patent (*Inspeximus*) of King Henry VIII
Inspects and confirms Letters Patent of Henry VII, 20 Jan. 1488 (C/1/1/17), inspecting and confirming [missing] charter of Edward IV, 18 Mar. 1463, Richard II's charter of 26 Feb. 1380 (C/1/1/9) and all previous charters; also inspects and confirms Letters Patent, 25 Nov. 1511 (C/1/1/18). Given at Westminster
(2 membranes, each 85.5 cm × 57.5 cm, Latin, initial letter 'H' and other capitals on first line omitted for insertion of ornament never added; fragment of Great Seal in green wax, on green and white cords with gilt metallic threads)

C/1/1/20   3 Mar. 1519
Letters Patent of King Henry VIII
Confirms Edward IV's grant [by missing charter of 18 Mar. 1463] of Admiralty jurisdiction within liberty, and that such jurisdiction extends as far as Polleshead and includes foreshore between high and low tides; grants that Bailiffs for time being shall be Admirals for town and liberty; that town shall have all wrecks, flotsam and jetsam, goods washed ashore within liberty, goods of suicides, and deodands; that no foreigner and no-one not a free burgess shall buy goods within liberty for resale either in gross or by retail, under penalty of forfeiture; and that Bailiffs and burgesses shall have power to amend ordinances for town government. Given at Hampton Court
(85.8 cm × 50 cm, Latin, initial letter 'H' and other capitals on first line ornamented with Tudor rose, grotesque human face, arabesques and strapwork, all uncoloured; Great Seal in green wax, incomplete, on green and white cords with gilt metallic threads)

C/1/1/21   7 Feb. 1522
Letters Patent (*Inspeximus*) of King Henry VIII
Inspects and confirms Letters Patent of Henry VIII, 21 Nov. 1520, appointing John, Abbot of Bury St Edmunds, Robert Curson, kt, Robert Drury, kt, Richard Wentworth, kt, Philip Tylney, kt, Lionel Talmage and John Sulyard, commissioners to ascertain bounds of liberties of town of Ipswich; and sworn inquisition returned into Chancery by commissioners, 17 Sep. 1521, setting out bounds in precise detail. Given at Westminster
(61.8 cm × 37.7 cm, Latin and English; fragments (conserved) of Great Seal in white wax, on tag)

C/1/1/22   8 Jul. 1547
Letters Patent (*Inspeximus*) of King Edward VI
Inspects and confirms Henry VIII's Letters Patent of 3 Mar. 1519 (C1/1/20), 12 Mar. 1512 (C1/1/19) inspecting and confirming charters of previous reigns, and 25 Nov. 1511 (C/1/1/18). Given at Westminster
(3 membranes, 83.4 cm × 57 cm, 83.4 cm × 55 cm and 83.4 cm × 51.4 cm, Latin, initial letter 'E' depicting King enthroned and crowned, holding sceptre and orb, letters of first line ornamented with strapwork, royal arms and supporters, royal heraldic badges and arabesques, all uncoloured; green and white seal cords; Great Seal missing)

C/1/1/23   23 Sep. 1560
Letters Patent (*Inspeximus*) of Queen Elizabeth I

Inspects and confirms Letters Patent of Edward VI, 8 Jul. 1547 (C/1/1/22), inspecting and confirming charters of previous reigns. Given at Westminster
(3 membranes, 75.2 cm × 50.5 cm, 75 cm × 44.5 cm and 75.4 cm × 43 cm, Latin, initial letter 'E' depicting Queen enthroned and crowned, holding sceptre and orb, letters of first line ornamented with strapwork, royal heraldic badges and arabesques, all uncoloured and badly faded; green and purple seal cords, Great Seal missing)

C/1/1/24   16 May 1610
Letters Patent (*Inspeximus*) of King James I
Inspects and exemplifies under Exchequer Seal, record in Exchequer Court, 14 May 1610, of appointment, inquisition and return of commission charged to take order for equitable assessment of proportions of Fifteenths and Tenths due from town for Lay Subsidy, upon the various parishes and hamlets. Given at Westminster
(71.5 cm × 44.5 cm, Latin and English; Exchequer Seal missing from tag)

C/1/1/25   17 Feb. 1665
Letters Patent of King Charles II
Confirms all previous liberties, privileges and customs; confirms in office present High Steward, Bailiffs, Portmen, Twenty-four and Coroners (all by name); grants that Portmen and Twenty-four may elect to vacancies in their respective bodies; Recorder and Common Clerk may be appointed; Common Council empowered to fine those refusing to accept municipal office; Recorder as well as Bailiffs and four of Portmen to be a Justice of the Peace; confirms Holy Rood Fair on 14–16 Sep. annually; compels all municipal officers to take Oaths of Allegiance and Supremacy. Given at Westminster
(4 membranes, each 79 cm × 64 cm, Latin, first membrane with printed ornament including initial letter 'C' containing King's half-length portrait, royal arms and royal crests for England and Scotland; fragments of Great Seal in green wax, now conserved and detached from red and white cords)

C/1/1/26   8 Jul. 1684
Letters Patent of King Charles II
[Following enforced surrender of previous charters], 'Willing that for the future there may and shall be, within the . . . borough, one certain and indubitable method for keeping the peace . . . for the terror of evil men': grants that Bailiffs, burgesses and commonalty shall be a body corporate with perpetual succession; Bailiffs to be chosen annually from among Portmen; twelve Portmen, eighteen Chief Constables, Recorder, Deputy Recorder and two Coroners to remain in office during good behaviour; royal nominees appointed to all above offices; vacancies in number of Portmen to be filled by remainder from ranks of Chief Constables; vacancies among Chief Constables to be filled by Common Council; elections of Recorder, Common Clerk, Coroners and other officers to be made by Common Council, which is to consist of Bailiffs, Portmen and Chief Constables; Common Council to have power to make ordinances for town government, and to fine those refusing to take office; Bailiffs, Recorder and four senior Portmen to be Justices of the Peace; power reserved to Crown to remove Bailiffs and other officers by Order in Council; any person, resident or non-resident, may be admitted freeman on taking Oaths of Allegiance and Supremacy; two fairs to be held annually, on 7–8 May and 11–12 Aug. Given at Westminster
(4 membranes, 75.5 cm × 63 cm, 75.5 cm × 62 cm, 75.5 cm × 61.5 cm, 75.5 cm × 57 cm, Latin, initial letter 'C' containing King's head-and-shoulders portrait, all four membranes with printed ornament in top, left and right margins, including royal arms, separate shields for England, France, Scotland and Ireland, heraldic and other beasts, wild men and foliage; fragments of Great Seal in green wax, now conserved, on red and white cords)

C/1/1/27   15 Sep. 1688
Letters Patent of King James II
In similar terms to Charles II's Letters Patent of 8 Jul. 1684 (C/1/1/26), and appointing James's nominees to the Corporation. Given at Westminster
(4 membranes, each 73.5 cm × 63 cm, Latin, first membrane with printed ornament including

initial letter 'J' containing King's half-length portrait, royal arms and supporters, Tudor roses, foliage and arabesques; fragment of Great Seal in green wax, on red and white cords)

C/1/2   ARMORIAL BEARINGS   1561

C/1/2/1   20 Aug. 1561
Confirmation of borough arms and grant of helm, crest and supporters
William Harvey, Clarenceux King of Arms, confirms to Bailiffs and burgesses of Ipswich their ancient arms, 'partye par pale gulz and azure in the firste a Lyon rampant regardant golde armyd and langued azure, in the second thre demy botes of the thirde'; and grants to them a helm, for crest 'a demy lyon golde supportinge a shyppe sables on a wreathe argent and sables manteled gulz dobled argent', and for supporters 'two horses of the sea argent commonlye called neptunus horsses manyed and Fynned golde'
(71 cm × 51.5 cm, English, ornamented in colour: initial letter containing full-length portrait of Clarenceux; arms, crest and supporters of Ipswich emblazoned in left-hand margin with, below, royal chained portcullis badge within wreath; in top margin, royal arms flanked by Tudor rose and fleur-de-lis within wreaths; in right-hand margin, royal cypher and arms of Clarenceux within wreaths; top and right-hand margins with floral decoration; all ornament now much discoloured. Seals and tags missing. N.B., though the lion in the arms is described in the blazon as 'regardant', it is emblazoned guardant in the margin; it appears as guardant in the MSS of the College of Arms (*see* Grimsey 1888, 456).)

C/1/3   ACTS OF PARLIAMENT   1793–1846

C/1/3/1   1793
'An Act for paving, lighting, cleansing, and otherwise improving the town of Ipswich, in the county of Suffolk; and for removing and preventing encroachments, obstructions and annoyances therein'
(printed)

C/1/3/2   1797
'An Act for amending and rendering more effectual an Act passed in the thirty-third year of the reign of His present Majesty, for paving, lighting, cleansing, and otherwise improving the town of Ipswich, in the county of Suffolk; and for removing and preventing encroachments, obstructions and annoyances therein'
(printed)

C/1/3/3   2 May 1815
'An Act for amending and enlarging the powers of two Acts of His present Majesty, for paving, lighting, cleansing, and otherwise improving the town of Ipswich, in the county of Suffolk; and for removing and preventing encroachments, obstructions and annoyances therein; and for watching the said town'
(printed)

C/1/3/4   28 May 1821
'An Act for lighting with gas the town and borough of Ipswich, in the county of Suffolk'
(printed)

C/1/3/5   29 Mar. 1833
'An Act for more effectually repairing and improving the roads from Ipswich to Helmingham and to Debenham, and from Helmingham to Otley Bottom, in the county of Suffolk'
(printed)

C/1/3/6   28 Aug. 1833
'An Act to render valid indentures of apprenticeship allowed only by two Justices acting for the
county in which the parish from which such apprentices shall be bound, and for the county in
which the parish into which such apprentices shall be bound, shall be situated; and also for
remedying defective executions of indentures by corporations'
(printed)

C/1/3/7   1790–1846
'Ipswich Corporation: Stowmarket Navigation Acts'
Includes:
— 'An Act for making and maintaining a navigable communication between Stowmarket and
Ipswich, in the county of Suffolk' (30 Geo. III, cap. 57), 1790
— 'An Act for effectually carrying into execution an Act of Parliament of the thirtieth year
of His present Majesty, for making and maintaining a navigable communication between
Stowmarket and Ipswich . . .' (33 Geo. III, cap. 20), 1793
— 'An Act for amending an Act passed in the thirtieth year of . . . King George III . . . so as to
enable the Trustees of such Act to lease the said Navigation . . .' (9 and 10 Vic., cap. 106), 1846
(bound into 1 vol., stamped 'Town Clerk's Office Ipswich')

C/1/4   PARLIAMENTARY REPRESENTATION   1640–1832

C/1/4/1   POLL BOOKS   1806–1826

These are the original MS books. They record the names and towns of residence of the voters
(freemen), with the candidates for whom their votes were cast. The books for the 1826 election
contain in addition details of the voters' occupations. Many of the freemen were non-resident,
and travelled from as far afield as London, Deptford and Greenwich to cast their votes. (For poll
books in municipal elections, *see* C/4/4/7)

C/1/4/1/1   29 Oct. 1806
Votes recorded for each of the four candidates, who are identified only by the initial letters of
their surnames
(1 vol.)

C/1/4/1/2   12–17 Jun. 1826
Book 1, recording only those electors who voted for William Haldimand and Robert Torrens.
At end: note of total number of votes cast for all four candidates
(1 vol.)

C/1/4/1/3   12–17 Jun. 1826
Book 2, recording only those electors who voted for Charles Mackinnon and Robert Adam
Dundas
(1 vol.)

C/1/4/2   ELECTION INDENTURES   1640–1826

Counterparts, signed and sealed by the Sheriff of Suffolk, of indentures between the Sheriff and
the Bailiffs, burgesses and commonalty of Ipswich, for certification of the return of Members
of Parliament for the borough. The Bailiffs are not named, except in the 1640 and 1733
indentures.

C/1/4/2/1   26 Oct. 1640
For election of William Cage, gent. and John Gurdon, esq.; Sir Simonds D'Ewes, kt, Sheriff,
William Cage and John Smithier, gents, Bailiffs
(seal missing)

11

C/1/4/2/2   21 Nov. 1707
For election of Major William Churchill in the place of Henry Pooley, esq., deceased; Thomas
Macro, esq., Sheriff

C/1/4/2/3   6 May 1708
For election of Major William Churchill and Sir William Barker, bart; John Fuller, esq., Sheriff

C/1/4/2/4   30 May 1726
For election of Sir William Thomson, kt; Thomas Driver, esq., Sheriff

C/1/4/2/5   27 Jan. 1730
For election of Philip Broke, esq; Tobias Blosse, esq., Sheriff

C/1/4/2/6   29 Jan. 1733
For election of William Wollaston, esq. in the place of Francis Negus, esq., deceased; George
Dashwood, esq., Sheriff, John Marlow and Thomas Starling, Bailiffs

C/1/4/2/7   8 May 1741
For election of Edward Vernon, esq., Vice-Admiral of the Blue, and Samuel Kent, esq.; Samuel
Lucas, Sheriff

C/1/4/2/8   29 Jun. 1747
For election of the Hon. Edward Vernon, esq. and Samuel Kent, esq.; Robert Edgar, esq.,
Sheriff

C/1/4/2/9   7 Dec. 1757
For election of Thomas Staunton, esq.; Henry Moore, esq., Sheriff

C/1/4/2/10   20 Nov. 1759
For election of George Montgomerie, esq.; Sir John Rous, bart., Sheriff

C/1/4/2/11   27 Mar. 1761
For election of Thomas Staunton, esq. and Francis Vernon, esq.; Thomas Moseley, esq., Sheriff

C/1/4/2/12   27 Dec. 1762
For election of Francis [Vernon], Lord Orwell, he having resigned on acceptance of office as a
Commissioner for Trade and Plantations; Shadrach Brise, esq., Sheriff

C/1/4/2/13   3 Apr. 1784
For election of John Cator, esq. and William Middleton, esq.; John Wenyeve, esq., Sheriff

C/1/4/2/14   18 Jun. 1790
For election of Charles Alexander Crickitt, esq. and Sir John Hadley D'Oyly, bart; Miles
Barne, esq., Sheriff. With pencilled alterations indicating use as draft for election of Sir Home
Popham, kt and Robert Alexander Crickitt, esq.; Thomas Mills, esq., Sheriff, 5 May 47 Geo. III
(1807)

C/1/4/2/15   28 May 1796
For election of Charles Alexander Crickitt, esq. and Sir Andrew Snape Hamond, bart; John
Clayton, esq., Sheriff

C/1/4/2/16   5 Jul. 1802
For election of Charles Alexander Crickitt, esq. and Sir Andrew Snape Hamond, bart; Thomas
Cocksedge, esq., Sheriff

C/1/4/2/17   8 Feb. 1803
For election of William Middleton, esq. in the place of Charles Alexander Crickitt, esq.,
deceased; Thomas Cocksedge, esq., Sheriff

C/1/4/2/18   29 Oct. 1806
For election of the Hon. Robert Stopford and Richard Wilson, esq.; Michael William Leheup,
esq., Sheriff

C/1/4/2/19   5 Oct. 1812
For election of Robert Alexander Crickitt, esq. and John Round jun., esq.; Richard Moore, esq.,
Sheriff

C/1/4/2/20   17 Jun. 1826
For election of William Haldimans, esq. and Robert Torrens, esq.; John Payne Elwes, esq.,
Sheriff

C/1/4/3   MISCELLANEA   1761–1832

C/1/4/3/1   27 Mar. 1761
Certificate of oath taken by John Gravenor and John Trapnell, Bailiffs, as returning officers
That they have neither directly nor indirectly received any money or other inducement to make
any return at that day's election

C/1/4/3/2   Jun. 1832
Petition of Ipswich electors to Rigby Wason, esq., M.P.
Requesting him to stand as parliamentary candidate for the borough at forthcoming election, in
gratitude for 'the firm and persevering advocacy you have given to the great measure of
Reform'
Signatures of c.500 electors
(paper roll; wrapper endorsed, 'Presented by his grandson, Mr Rigby Wason, 9 Feb. 1944')

C/1/5   BOUNDARIES   c.1721–1815

In order that there should be no ambiguity regarding the extent of the borough's jurisdiction, its
boundaries had been perambulated periodically from medieval times. The preface to the 1815
account of the perambulations (C/1/5/4) records that 'upon searching the records of the
Corporation, no traces could be found of any perambulation of its boundaries having been performed since the year 1674 [see however C/1/5/1]; it was therefore determined that such a pro-
ceeding should be adopted, in order that its extent might be precisely ascertained, and distinctly
marked out: and on the 17th September 1812 it took place accordingly. The boundaries by
water had been gone in the preceding year. The great lapse of time since the boundary by land
was gone, having rendered much previous inquiry and laborious research necessary for setting
out the limits with accuracy, the Corporation, at a General Assembly, on the 29th of September
1812, came to a resolution, in order to prevent the occurrence of similar difficulties, to cause a
Survey to be taken, and Maps to be printed, pointing out the limits of the jurisdiction both by
land and water.' The bounds of the Admiralty jurisdiction were perambulated on 23 July 1827;
see TREASURER'S VOUCHERS for 1826–1827, C/3/4/4/91.

C/1/5/1   n.d. [c.1721]
'The Preambulation [sic] of the Town of Ipswich'
With note that the bounds were perambulated in Sep. 1674, Sep. 1694, and on 22 May 1721
(1 paper fol.)

C/1/5/2   17 Sep. 1812
'Description of the boundaries of the Corporation of Ipswich by land as the same stood at the
perambulation thereof on the seventeenth day of September one thousand eight hundred and
twelve and corresponding with the annexed plan'
Certified by William Batley, Bailiff (Robert Trotman, the other Bailiff, having died before the
instrument was prepared), three Portmen, eight Common Councilmen and John Bransby,
Surveyor
(4 parchment fols; the plan referred to is missing; for other copies, see C/1/5/3)

C/1/5/3   1812
The Liberties of Ipswich
Printed map by John Bransby, at scale of 2½ furlongs to 1 inch
'A map of the Liberties of Ipswich, in the county of Suffolk, as ascertained by a perambulation
performed by the Bailiffs and other members of the Corporation, September 17th 1812'
Includes churches, barracks and other public buildings, windmills, watermills, brewery, ship-
yards, streets, turnpike and other roads, tollgates, watercourses, bridges
(10 copies; uncoloured; paper. *See* TREASURER'S VOUCHERS for 1823–1824, C/3/4/4/89)

C/1/5/4   1815
'Ancient and Modern Perambulations; and Extracts from Charters, Trials and other Records,
relative to the Liberties of Ipswich by Land and Water, intended as a Companion to the Maps of
those Jurisdictions'
Texts of perambulations of 1351, 1522 and 1812; extracts from charters of Edward IV and
Henry VIII and from a commission of enquiry of 1340; and from various documents relating to
'processions for ascertaining the boundaries of the Admiralty jurisdiction', 1432–1814
(pamphlet, printed and sold by John Bransby [surveyor]; 13 copies. For the map referred to, *see*
C/1/5/3.)

C/1/6   LITIGATION CONCERNING THE LIBERTIES   1533–*c*.1800

(see also C/1/7, FORESHORE RIGHTS)

C/1/6/1   n.d. [1533]
Depositions of witnesses in suit brought by the Bailiffs, burgesses and commonalty against
Richard Cavendish [? of Trimley], in the Star Chamber
The case concerned a weir or fishgarth established by Cavendish against his marshes and in the
salt water and river, which was held to be an infringement of the Corporation's right to the foreshore of the Orwell and prejudicial to the liberties of the town; the court upheld the plaintiff's
view and ordered the weir to be demolished (*see* Richardson 1884, 206–07).
(11 fols, stitched together at the head)

C/1/6/2   n.d. [19c]
Transcript of C/1/6/1
N.B.: contains numerous inaccuracies
(4 fols)

C/1/6/3   n.d. [between 1554 and 1558]
Contemporary copy petition of Matthew Goodyng, Edmond Leche and William Barbor,
churchwardens of MG, to the Privy Council
Re matters in dispute between parishioners and Edmund Withypoll, esq., who on 19 Mar. 1554
was ordered by Council to pay to parishioners 10 years' arrears of £4 p.a., to permit them to
enjoy churchyard without interruption, and to rebuild churchyard wall which he had broken
down; Withypoll is further alleged to have pulled down priest's house and taken the ground; to
have seized stone, iron and glass from E. window of chancel, blown down by a storm of wind
(leaving window boarded up); and to be witholding Hollybrede Close from parish without just
title.
N.B., while not strictly concerned with the liberties of the borough as a whole, this dispute may
be understood as an aspect of the more general hostility between Withypoll and the Corporation
regarding its liberties: *see* C/1/6/4–6, below.

C/1/6/4   1567–1568
Case papers in suit brought by Edmund Withypoll, esq., owner of the Christchurch estate, *v* the
Bailiffs, burgesses and commonalty, in the Star Chamber

The case concerned the right of the Bailiffs and other officers of the Corporation to enter the Holy Rood Fair (held annually on 14 September and the two following days) preceded by their maces, to check weights and measures and ensure the keeping of the peace. Withypoll claimed the fair as successor in title to the Priors of Holy Trinity (Christchurch) who had obtained a grant by charter from the Crown, and maintained that it was held within the precincts of the Priory and was therefore outside the liberties of the town. He claimed further that before the Dissolution the town maces had been surrendered to the Prior on the eve of the fair, as an indication that the Corporation had no jurisdiction over it.

The Bailiffs, while not disputing Withypoll's title to the fair, claimed that they had exercised the office of Clerk of the Market at the fair, and had been responsible for keeping the peace there, from time immemorial. They denied that they or their predecessors had ever surrendered their maces to the Prior before the Dissolution, and brought a counter bill of complaint against Withypoll.

The immediate cause of the action was Withypoll's attempt in September 1567 to prevent the Bailiffs from exercising the powers they claimed at the fair, which resulted in a breach of the peace. The evidence shows that the fair was held partly on St Margaret's Green and partly on a piece of ground called the Lute, off the Westerfield road, the latter area being within the precincts of the dissolved Priory and used for the cattle and horse fair. The encounter between Withypoll and the Bailiffs took place between these two points, near the Conduit Head. The outcome of the case is unknown.

See also 'A note of those thinges that Edmund Wythipoll demaundeth of the towne of Ipswyche', n.d. (Iveagh MSS, Ipswich Record Office, HD 1538/271/20).

C/1/6/4/1   n.d. [1567]
Draft case papers
Includes:
— bill of complaint by Withypoll (11 fols)
— answers of Jeffrey Gylberd and John More, late Bailiffs, Robert Barker, William Smarte, Robert Sparrowe, John Barker and Stephen Baxter, defendants, to the bill of complaint (18 fols)
— replication of Withypoll to the defendants' answers (6 fols)
— rejoinder by the defendants to Withypoll's replication (7 fols)
(4 docs, filed together on a parchment thong)

C/1/6/4/2   n.d. [1567]
Interrogatories to be administered to Withypoll on behalf of the Bailiffs, burgesses and commonalty
(13 fols, stitched together at the head)

C/1/6/4/3   n.d. [1567]
Duplicate of C/1/6/4/2
(in a different hand; 14 fols, stitched together at the head)

C/1/6/4/4   20 Nov. 1567
Deposition by Withypoll to the interrogatories on behalf of the Bailiffs and burgesses
(56 fols, attached by parchment thongs)

C/1/6/4/5   27 Nov. 1567
Answers of the Bailiffs and burgesses to the interrogatories on behalf of Withypoll
(42 fols, attached by parchment thongs)

C/1/6/4/6   14 Mar. 1568
Depositions of witnesses on behalf of the Bailiffs, burgesses and commonalty
Taken at Ipswich before Sir Thomas Cornwallis, kt, John Blenerheysett, esq. and Robert Gurdon, esq.
(97 fols, attached by a parchment thong)

C/1/6/4/7   [14 Mar. 1568]
Partial fair copy of C/1/6/4/6
(ff. 1–20, 25–31, 41–46, 53–57, 70 *et seq* missing; parts of some others destroyed by damp; 31 fols, attached by a parchment thong)

C/1/6/4/8   17 Mar. 1568
Depositions of witnesses on behalf of both parties
Taken at Ipswich before Sir Thomas Cornwallis, kt, John Blenerhaset, esq. and Robert Gurdon, esq. by virtue of the Queen's writ of commission
(22 fols, attached by a parchment thong)

C/1/6/4/9   19 May 1568
Examinations of witnesses upon the interrogatories on behalf of the Bailiffs and burgesses
(50 fols, attached by parchment thongs)

C/1/6/4/10   20 May 1568
Examinations of witnesses upon the interrogatories on behalf of the Bailiffs and burgesses
(21 fols, attached by parchment thongs)

C/1/6/4/11   n.d. [1568]
Draft interrogatories to be administered to Withypoll on behalf of the Bailiffs, burgesses and commonalty
(5 fols, pinned together)

C/1/6/4/12   n.d. [1568]
Fair copy of C/1/6/4/11
(10 fols, stitched together at the head)

C/1/6/4/13   n.d. [1568]
Interrogatories to be administered to John Dyer and William Bloys on behalf of Withypoll
(4 fols, attached by parchment thongs)

C/1/6/4/14   n.d. [1568]
Case papers *re* counter bill of complaint brought by the Bailiffs, burgesses and commonalty against Withypoll and his servants
Includes:
— answer of Withypoll to the bill of complaint (10 fols)
— answers of William Meadowe, Roger Colthurst, Richard Langfild, John Thomson and Thomas Leyton, defendants (household servants to Withypoll), to the bill of complaint (4 fols)
— replication of the Bailiffs, burgesses and commonalty to Withypoll's answers (10 fols)
— replication of the Bailiffs, burgesses and commonalty to the answers of Withypoll's servants (4 fols)
— rejoinder of Withypoll to the Bailiffs' replication (3 fols)
— rejoinder of Withypoll's servants to the Bailiffs' replication (2 fols)
(6 docs, filed together on a parchment thong)

C/1/6/5   [1567–]1568
Case papers in suit brought by the Bailiffs and Commonalty *v* Edmund Withypoll, esq., owner of the Christchurch estate, in the Star Chamber
The case concerned numerous alleged injuries done by Withypoll to the town of Ipswich, including: stopping up or encroaching upon Dairy Lane, the Ipswich–Westerfield road, the Ipswich–Woodbridge road and the road to Claydon; enclosing and altering the Conduit Head; failure to send his servants to attend the Leet; refusal to pay tax except upon distress; pulling down the wall of St Margaret's churchyard and, when ordered to rebuild it, doing so in such a way as to encroach upon the churchyard; enclosing highways across Bolton Field; enclosing a field used as a shooting ground by the townspeople; making new ponds and allowing them to flood the street with filth; fishing unlawfully in the river; and obtaining citations in the Court of Arches against townspeople for payment of herbage and tithes. The outcome of the case is unknown.

16

C/1/6/5/1   n.d. [1567 or 1568]
Schedule of 'injuries and wronges done by Master Wythepolle within the towne of Ipswich to
the Bayliffs, Burgesses and Commonaltie of the said towne'
(3 fols)

C/1/6/5/2   n.d. [1567 or 1568]
Draft case papers
Includes:
— articles of alleged injuries committed by Withypoll (4 fols)
— answer of Withypoll to the articles (9 fols)
— replication of the Bailiffs, burgesses and commonalty to Withypoll's answer (10 fols)
(3 docs, filed together on a parchment thong)

C/1/6/5/3   n.d. [1567 or 1568]
Fair copy of C/1/6/5/2
(28 fols, attached by a parchment thong; damaged by rodent activity, text incomplete)

C/1/6/5/4   n.d. [1567 or 1568]
Interrogatories to be put on behalf of the Bailiffs, burgesses and commonalty
(11 fols, attached by a parchment thong)

C/1/6/5/5   19 May 1568
Examinations of witnesses upon the interrogatories, on behalf of the Bailiffs and burgesses
(80 fols, attached by parchment thongs)

C/1/6/6   18 Nov. 1567
Account of expenses incurred in riding to and from London to answer Edmund Withypoll, esq.
in Star Chamber
Submitted by William Smarte on behalf of himself, Mr Gilberte, Mr Moore, Robert Sparrowe,
John Barker, Steven Baxster, Richard Croft and 2 servants; presumably relates to suits
described in C/1/6/4–5
(1 vol.)

C/1/6/7   6 Jun. 1603
Letters Patent (*Inspeximus*) of King James I
Inspects and exemplifies under Exchequer Seal, record in Exchequer Court, 26 May 1603, of
proceedings upon bill of complaint by Bailiffs, burgesses and commonalty of Ipswich *v*
Thomas Eliott *alias* Collen, Nicholas Allen, John Wheler, John Lane, John Dedwall, Edward
Wicks, William Nobbes, Robert Paddy, Samuel Duncon, Simon Rosier, Richard Parkyns and
John Colman, for selling hides and skins in secret, not in open market, to injury and loss of commonalty; and court decree that every butcher, not being a free burgess, pay to Corporation 2*d*
for every raw hide of every great beast whose flesh be sold in town, and 2*d* for every dozen
calf-skins and sheep-skins. Given at Westminster
(69 cm × 54.4 cm, Latin and English; fragment of Exchequer Seal on tag)

C/1/6/8   1637 and n.d.
Case papers in suit brought by the Attorney General against the Bailiffs and 20 other
townspeople [in the Star Chamber]
The case concerned riots which took place in Ipswich in August 1636, in opposition to the royal
commissioners for enquiring into the value of the town's benefices and for settling measures to
provide adequate incomes for the parochial clergy and for maintaining the fabric of the
churches. *See* Richardson 1884, 515–16.

C/1/6/8/1   May-Jun. 1637 and n.d.
Case papers
Includes:
— brief of Attorney General's bill of complaint, filed 15 May 1637 (5 fols)
— defendants' answers to the bill of complaint, n.d. [Jun. 1637; *see* Richardson 1884, 515–16]
(3 fols)

— examinations of defendants, n.d. (19 fols)
(3 docs, stitched together)

C/1/6/8/2   n.d. [1637]
Charges against William Cage, one of the defendants, with depositions of witnesses
(10 fols, stitched together)

C/1/6/8/3   n.d. [1637]
Copy case papers
Includes:
— petition of Bailiffs, Portmen and chief burgesses to the King, against the practice of reading
prayers at the communion table in the chancel, n.d. [Aug. 1637]
— deposition concerning insult offered to Dr Goade, one of royal commissioners, on 8 Apr.
1636, n.d. [1637]
— remonstrance of Bailiffs, Portmen and chief burgesses in defence of their conduct during the
riots, n.d. [post Aug. 1637]
(28 fols, stitched together; ff. 1–2 missing; a note on f. 3 reads '2 sheets were taken away before
by the sollicitor')

C/1/6/8/4   n.d. [1637]
Draft of petition in C/1/6/8/3

C/1/6/9   [1640]
Copy petition of George Kirke and Henry Jermyn to King Charles I
On allegation that Bailiffs and others of Ipswich have usurped various franchises and unjustly
detained from Crown certain manors, lands and tenements formerly in possession of Cardinal
Wolsey, petitioners request powers to discover Crown's title and compound with tenants for
inheritance or fee-farm; and a grant of the property in return for 4th part of arrears of profits;
with note by Ralph Freman [Sir Ralph Freeman, Master of Requests 1618, Auditor of
Imprests and Master of the Mint 1629] of referral to Attorney General, dated at Oatlands,
31 Jul. 1640

C/1/6/10   n.d. [?1640]
Schedule of alleged 'privileges usurped' by the town of Ipswich
Apparently connected with the above petition (C/1/6/9)

C/1/6/11   1648
Case papers in suit brought by the Bailiffs, burgesses and commonalty against Edmund Clench,
Samuel Snelling, Ralph Noore and others unnamed, in the Exchequer Court in Trinity Term
The suit was brought for the recovery of dues on the import and export of grain by water,
payable, by the custom of the borough, by all merchants not being free burgesses; the defen-
dants allegedly having for some years 'confederated' in the trade and refused to pay.

C/1/6/11/1   1648
Case papers
Includes:
— brief of the plaintiffs' bill of complaint
— joint and several answers of Clench, Noore and Snelling
— replication general against Clench and Snelling, the other defendants having compounded
— depositions
(5 fols, stitched together)

C/1/6/11/2   1648
Duplicate of C/1/6/11/1
Last fol. annotated with scale of dues charged
(5 fols, stitched together)

C/1/6/12   n.d. [between 1654 and 1658]
Contemporary office copy of *quo warranto* proceedings by Andrew Broughton, Coroner and

Attorney of the Lord Protector, against the Bailiffs, burgesses and commonalty, in the Court of Upper Bench
Requiring the defendants to show by what authority they hold fairs annually on St George's Day (23 Apr.) and St James's Day (25 Jul.); proceedings dropped for lack of evidence
(9 fols, stitched together)

C/1/6/13   9 Nov. 1736
Writ of Mandamus out of Court of King's Bench
Commanding burgesses of Ipswich to assemble on 22 Nov. 1736 to elect a Bailiff, only one, John Sparrowe, having been elected on 8 Sep. 1736, to the obstruction of public justice

C/1/6/14   Jun. 1760 – Dec. 1765
Accounts and receipted bills for legal fees of Samuel Kilderbee [Town Clerk] and for witnesses' expenses in suit brought by the Bailiffs, burgesses and commonalty against [*blank*] Laston, at Bury Assizes
The case concerned the refusal of Laston and other merchants to pay the dues on imported coals to the Corporation.
(46 docs)

C/1/6/15   n.d. [*c.* 1800]
Notes *re* suit brought by the Bailiffs, burgesses and commonalty against [*blank*] Cobbold, court unnamed
The suit concerned an action for ejectment involving the Corporation's right to the foreshore or 'ooze' of the river Orwell.
(1 vol.)

C/1/7   FORESHORE RIGHTS   1304–*c.*1810

C/1/7/1   FORESHORE DEEDS   **1304–1609**

These seem originally to have formed part of the series of grants of common soil (*see* FINANCE AND TOWN PROPERTY, C/3/8), but appear to have been separated from it during searches arising out of litigation concerning the Corporation's right to the foreshore of the river Orwell.

C/1/7/1/1   ST CLEMENT PARISH   1398–1609

C/1/7/1/1/1   30 Sep. 1398
Piece of void ground (dimensions given) in suburb of Ipswich in CL
Grant from Bailiffs and commonalty to Thomas Edoun' of Ipswich and wife Masilia
Premises lie between grantee's tenement on W. and void piece of land next to town port on E., abutting S. on port and N. on highway; 6*d* annual rent; names of 5 witnesses including John Arnold and John Avelyne, Bailiffs
Latin; seal and tag missing

C/1/7/1/1/2   24 Apr. 1446
Piece of land (dimensions given) in CL
Demise from Thomas Denys and John Deken, Bailiffs, with assent of commonalty, to Richard Felawe of Ipswich, merchant and John Wytton of the same, grocer
Premises lie between highway called Clementstrete on N. and salt water on S., abutting E. on said way extending towards salt river bank and W. on tenement late of Thomas Edoun; 6*d* annual rent; names of 5 witnesses
Latin; grantee's seal on tag

19

C/1/7/1/1/3   26 Aug. 1499
Piece of land of common soil in CL
Grant from Thomas Baldry and Edmund Daundy, Bailiffs, and burgesses and commonalty, to
John Bramford of Ipswich
Premises lie between grantee's tenement on N. and salt water on S., abutting E. on common soil
in tenure of Thomas Alvard and W. on common soil in tenure of [*blank*], late of William Dewe;
dimensions given; 4*d* annual rent; 2*d* penalty for non-payment
Latin; grantee's seal on tag

C/1/7/1/1/4   26 Aug. 1499
Original of C/1/7/1/1/3
Latin; fragment of Common Seal on tag

C/1/7/1/1/5   26 Aug. 1499
Piece of land of common soil in CL
Grant (original) from Thomas Baldry and Edmund Daundy, Bailiffs, and burgesses and commonalty, to Thomas Alvard of Ipswich, merchant
Premises lie between grantee's tenement on N. and salt water on S., abutting E. on common soil
in tenure of John Lunt and W. on common soil in tenure of John Braunford; 4*d* annual rent; 2*d*
penalty for non-payment; Thomas Hall and William Stisted appointed attorneys to deliver
seisin
Latin; Common Seal (incomplete) on tag

C/1/7/1/1/6   26 Aug. 1499
Piece of common soil in CL which grantee has accroached to his tenement
Grant from Thomas Baldry and Edmund Daundy, Bailiffs, and burgesses and commonalty, to
John Lunt of Ipswich
Premises lie between grantee's tenement on N. and salt water on S., abutting E. on common soil
tenement of William Manser and William Sereue and W. on common soil in tenure of Thomas
Alvard; 14*d* annual rent; 4*d* penalty for non-payment
Latin; never slit for seal tag

C/1/7/1/1/7   26 Aug. 1499
Original of C/1/7/1/1/6
Latin; Common Seal (incomplete) on tag   .

C/1/7/1/1/8   26 Aug. 1499
Tenement on common soil in CL
Grant from Thomas Baldry and Edmund Daundy, Bailiffs, and burgesses and commonalty, to
William Harlewyn, merchant
Premises lie between common soil tenement in tenure of William Manser and William Shereve
on W. and common soil called le Wode on E., abutting N. on highway called Clementstrete and
S. on salt water; 12*d* annual rent; 4*d* penalty for non-payment
Latin; grantee's seal on tag

C/1/7/1/1/9   26 Aug. 1499
Tenement on common soil in CL
Grant from Thomas Baldry and Edmund Daundy, Bailiffs, and burgesses and commonalty, to
William Manser and William Shereue
Premises lie between common soil tenement in tenure of William Harlewyn on E. and tenement
of John Lunt on W., abutting N. on highway called Clemenestrete and S. on salt water; 4*d*
annual rent; 2*d* penalty for non-payment
Latin; fragments of 2 grantees' seals on 1 tag

C/1/7/1/1/10   18 May 1545
Piece of common soil in CL
Demise in fee farm from William Nottingham and John Allyn, Bailiffs, and burgesses and com-
monalty, to Robert Derhawe of Ipswich, gent

20

Premises extend from corner and principal post of grantee's messuage, sometime Thomas Cutler's, abutting N. on king's street called Clement; dimensions given; 2s annual rent; 4d penalty for non-payment; grantee to maintain gutter on E. part of ground whereby water and other filth may pass out of Clement strete and back lane coming from St Clement's church into common channel and salt water
English; no turn-up, slit, seal or tag; apparently not executed

C/1/7/1/1/11   18 May 1545
Counterpart of C/1/7/1/1/10
English; no slit, seal or tag; apparently not executed

C/1/7/1/1/12   [18 May 1545]
Copy of C/1/7/1/1/10, 11
English; incomplete; no turn-up, seal or tag; apparently not executed

C/1/7/1/1/13   10 Aug. 1570
Piece of land in CL
Feoffment from Robert Kynge and William Smarte, Bailiffs, and burgesses and commonalty, to Robert Cutler of Ipswich, merchant and Portman
Premises lie between land of Robert Andrewes on N. and salt water on S., abutting E. on common soil and W. on tenement of Joan Derhaughe, widow; dimensions given; 4d annual rent; 2d penalty for non-payment; to be void if alienated to lord of any manor within 4 miles of Ipswich; John Hawys and Henry Hannam appointed attorneys to deliver seisin
Latin

C/1/7/1/1/14   26 Sep. 1570
Tenement built on common soil, and 2 pieces of common soil, in CL
Feoffment from Robert Kynge and William Smarte, Bailiffs, and burgesses and commonalty, to Robert Cutler of Ipswich, burgess and Portman
Tenement lies between common soil called le Wode on E. and tenement of John Tye formerly of William Manser on W., abutting N. on common way called Clement Strete and S. on common soil lately salt water; first piece of common soil lies between said tenement on N. and salt water on S., abutting E. on salt water and W. on common soil, second piece lies between land of Robert Andrewes on N. and salt water on S., abutting E. on common soil and W. on tenement of Juliana Deraughe; dimensions given; 20d annual rent; 8d penalty for non-payment; to be void if alienated to lord of any manor within 4 miles of Ipswich; John Hawys and Henry Hannam appointed attorneys to deliver seisin
Latin

C/1/7/1/1/15   19 Dec. 1588
That part of common soil, parcel of the Old Quay, laid out from another part of Quay assigned to John Brennynge, in CL
Feoffment from Bailiffs, burgesses and commonalty to John Tye of Ipswich, merchant
Premises lie between part of Quay assigned to Brennynge on W. and quay or quay yard in tenure of William Wright and common way or waste soil on E., abutting N. on highway from St Clement's church to Nacton, and S. on salt water; dimensions given; £14 annual rent, to be extinguished on payment of £280

C/1/7/1/1/16   19 Dec. 1588
That part of common soil, parcel of the Old Quay, divided and laid out from the part of the Quay granted to John Tye, merchant, in CL
Feoffment from Bailiffs, burgesses and commonalty to John Brennynge of Ipswich, shipwright
Premises lie between messuage of Robert Cutler sen., Portman, on W. and residue of said Quay granted to John Tye on E., abutting [N.] on highway from St Clement's church to Nacton and S. on salt water; dimensions given; 2s 4d annual rent; grantee to fence premises against residue of Quay and maintain watercourse running through part of premises; John Hawys sen. appointed attorney to deliver seisin

C/1/7/1/1/17   4 Oct. 1609
Piece of void or common soil in CL with all messuages and buildings either anciently or newly
built thereon
Grant from Bailiffs, burgesses and commonalty to Margaret Bull of Ipswich, widow and
William Bull of Ipswich, ship carpenter
Premises lie between messuage late of John Tie lately built on common soil on W. and garden
of William Wright sen. on E., abutting S. on salt water and N. on highway; dimensions given;
John Lowe and Christopher Ballard appointed attorneys to deliver seisin
Latin

C/1/7/1/2   ST MARY AT QUAY PARISH   1499–1572

C/1/7/1/2/1   26 Aug. 1499
2 quays lying together in MQ
Grant from Thomas Baldry and Edmund Daundy, Bailiffs, and burgesses and commonalty, to
John Squyer, clerk
Premises lie between common soil in tenure of Margaret Gosse in 'le pale gardyn' on E. and
common quay on W., abutting N. on common way leading from common quay towards
Clementstrete and S. on salt water; 4d annual rent; 2d penalty for non-payment
Latin; grantee's seal on tag

C/1/7/1/2/2   26 Aug. 1499
Piece of common soil, in part built upon, in MQ
Grant from Thomas Baldry and Edmund Daundy, Bailiffs, and burgesses and commonalty, to
Thomas Herford
Premises lie between grantee's tenement on N. and salt water on S., abutting W. on tenement of
John Squyer, clerk and E. on common soil at le Comonkay; 4d annual rent; 2d penalty for
non-payment
Latin; grantee's amorial seal on tag

C/1/7/1/2/3   18 Jul. 1570
Messuage built on common soil, formerly Ratcliffes, formerly of Dame Anne Pargetor of
London, late of Roger Valentin, in MQ
Feoffment from Robert Kinge and William Smarte, Bailiffs, and burgesses and commonalty, to
Augustine Parker of Ipswich, merchant
Premises lie between land of Thomas Fuller on W. and tenement of John Harbottell gent., late
of Robert Pygott and before that of William Humfrey on E., abutting N. on Caiestrete and S. on
salt water; dimensions given; 2d annual rent; 2d penalty for non-payment; John Hawys and
Henry Hannam appointed attorneys to deliver seisin
Latin

C/1/7/1/2/4   17 Aug. 1570
2 pieces of common soil and quay of common soil called Kingeskey in MQ
Feoffment from Robert Kinge and William Smarte, Bailiffs, and burgesses and commonalty, to
Christopher Merell of Ipswich, merchant
First piece lies between soil late of William West *alias* Sebyn on E. and grantee's capital
tenement late of William West on W., abutting S. on salt water and N. on land of grantee;
second piece lies between grantee's tenement on S. and highway on N., abutting W. on
tenement of Richard Kynge late of William Wethereld and said highway, and E. on same way;
quay lies between common soil and quay in grantee's tenure on E. and common soil in tenure of
Richard Kynge on other side, abutting N. on said capital tenement and S. on salt water; 10d
annual rent; 4d penalty for non-payment; to be void if alienated to lord of any manor within
4 miles of Ipswich; John Hawys and Henry Hannam appointed attorneys to deliver seisin
Latin

22

C/1/7/1/2/5   18 Jul. 1572
Annual rent of 4*d* out of part of messuage called Brightyenes and Bremes and part of quay
opposite it, in MQ
Grant from John Carnaby of Ipswich, sailor, to Bailiffs, burgesses and commonalty, in consid-
eration of a feoffment from them to him of the property
Premises lie between common quay on W. and another part of said quay on E., abutting S. on
salt water and N. on way leading from common quay to Clementes Strete; formerly of Henry
Tolye of Ipswich, merchant, deceased
Latin

C/1/7/1/3   ST PETER PARISH   1416–1570

C/1/7/1/3/1   14 Oct. 1416
Piece of void land of common soil in PE
Demise to fee farm from John Starlyng and Hugh Hoo, Bailiffs, John Bernard and William
Stonham, Coroners, and commonalty, to John Spencer, esq., John Joye, vintner and William
Heylee of Ipswich
Premises lie between tenement of John Joye, late of Richard Crowlond, on N. and salt water on
S., abutting E. on common way called la Forthe and W. on said common soil; dimensions
given; 4*d* annual fee farm
Latin; 3 grantees' seals on 3 tags

C/1/7/1/3/2   14 Jan. 1424
2 pieces of land, one in PE, other in MQ
Grant from Thomas Asteleye and John Deken, Bailiffs, and commonalty, to William Phelipp,
kt, John Joye, vintner, William Whethereld and William Haylee of Ipswich
First piece lies in PE between tenement of John Joye called Crowlondes on S. and highway on
N., abutting W. on entry of gates of tenement of John Wade and E. on entry of gates of tenement
called Crowlondes; second piece lies in MQ between quay formerly of John Brightyf on W. and
salt water on E., abutting N. on common way and S. on salt water; dimensions given; 1*d* and 2*d*
annual fee farm; names of 6 witnesses including William Bury, one of Coroners
Latin; fragments of 3 grantees' seals on 3 tags, 4th seal missing from 4th tag

C/1/7/1/3/3   20 Dec. 1452
Piece of void land in PE
Grant from Richard Felawe and Robert Smyth, Bailiffs, and Portmen and commonalty, to
Richard Dallyng of Ipswich
Premises lie between highway on W. and salt water on E., abutting N. on tenement of Thomas
Barker and S. on 'le floodgates de le Newmelle' of Ipswich; dimensions given; 4*d* annual rent;
names of 5 witnesses
Latin; grantee's seal on tag

C/1/7/1/3/4   20 Dec. 1452
Piece of land of common soil late of Th . . . [*missing*], formerly of Henry Heywarde
Demise to fee farm from Richard Felawe and Robert Smyth, Bailiffs, and commonalty, to
William Wyntyr of Ipswich, pewterer
Premises lie between tenement formerly of Henry Heywarde on N. and salt water next to new
mill on [? S, *missing*]; dimensions given; 4*d* annual rent; names of 5 witnesses
Latin; grantee's seal on tongue

C/1/7/1/3/5   26 Jan. 1463
Piece of void land of common soil
Grant from Edmund Wynter and John Langcroft, Bailiffs, and burgesses and commonalty, to
William Wynter, pewterer
Premises lie between watergates of new mill on S., curtilage of John Bylys on N. and common

causeway on W.; to make a quay and enclose said land for his own use and use of farmer of new mill; dimensions given; 1*d* annual rent
Latin; grantee's seal on tongue

C/1/7/1/3/6   18 Sep. 1570
2 pieces of land of common soil in PE
Feoffment (original) from Robert Kinge and William Smarte, Bailiffs, and burgesses and commonalty, to John Nycolls of [*blank*], gent
First piece, late of Gilbert Debenham, lies between tenement formerly of John Crowland on N. and common soil lately salt water on S., abutting W. on residue of said piece in tenure of Walter Merrell and E. on common way called the Foorthe; second piece lies between first on N. and salt water on S., abutting similarly; dimensions given; 2*s* 6*d* annual rent; 6*d* penalty for non-payment; to be void if alienated to lord of any manor within 4 miles of Ipswich; John Hawys and Henry Hannam appointed attorneys to deliver seisin
Latin; Common Seal (incomplete) on tag; never filed

C/1/7/1/4   UNIDENTIFIED PARISH   1304

C/1/7/1/4/1   13 Feb. 1304
Piece of land in suburb of Ipswich
Grant from Bailiffs and commonalty to Peter Douneman, fellow burgess
Premises lie between salt water course on S. and highway extending before door of grantee's capital messuage on N.; dimensions given; grantee may construct quay, taking quayage according to custom of town; 4*d* annual rent; grantee not to build any house or 'Guyndatz' against will of commonalty, or hold any market to damage of town; names of 11 witnesses including Thomas Stace and Thomas le Rente, Bailiffs
Latin; incomplete; grantee's seal on tag

C/1/7/2   OTHER EVIDENCE   *c.*1806–*c.*1810

C/1/7/2/1   (1290–1738), *c.*1806
Extracts from Nathaniel Bacon's 'Annalls of Ipswiche' and from the Headboroughs' books
Containing evidence in support of the Corporation's claim to 'the ooze of the salt water river'
(9 fols; watermark dated 1806)

C/1/7/2/2   (3 Mar. 1519), *c.*1808
Copy and translation of Letters Patent of King Henry VIII (C/1/1/20)
(12 pp; prepared by Samuel Taylor for Pearson and Bunn [solicitors], apparently in connexion with a foreshore case; watermark dated 1808)

C/1/7/2/3   (15 Sep. 1688), *c.*1810
Translation of Letters Patent of King James II (C/1/1/27)
(16 pp; with note in hand of William Batley, Town Clerk, that 'it does not appear that the Corporation acted under the above Letters Patent, and the following Order of Council and proclamation annulled them, and soon after the King abdicated the Government and fled the Kingdom'; ? prepared in connexion with a foreshore case; watermark dated 1810)

C/1/7/2/4   (12 Nov. 1599), 19c
Extract from proceedings of Admiralty Court
Presentment of Nathaniel Ford for taking ballast at Greenwich Ness and Johns Ness below high water mark, on ground claimed by Broke family [of Nacton]: *see* Richardson 1884, 401

C/1/8   WAR AND DEFENCE   *c.* 1294–1643

See also the Borough correspondence (HD 36) in Appendix 1.

C/1/8/1   1294 or 1295

Compotus of John de Causton and John Lew, Bailiffs

For building a new galley and a barge for it, 'for the defence of the realm and the safety of the
seas against the enemies of King and kingdom, by the King's writ and by order of William de
Marchia, Bishop of Bath and Wells, the King's Treasurer, on behalf of the King in the 23rd year
[of his reign], under the supervision of and by the work of Philip Harneys and Thomas Aylred,
assigned to this work by the same writ'; and for repair of the galley, 'which was broken up and
split by the violence of the sea'

Latin; 1 membrane; full text printed in HMC 1883, 257–58

C/1/8/2   n.d. [mid 20c]

English translation of C/1/8/1
(2 pp., typescript)

C/1/8/3   20 May 1311

Acquittance

From John Irp, late master of ship 'le Mighel' of Ipswich, Nicholas de Orford, constable of
same ship, Henry Golding', Richard Roberd, John Lorkyn, Thomas son of Thomas le Maister,
William Fyn, Matthew Emme, Adam Fayrman, William Noreys, William Lyme, William
Fullere, Richard dil Ash and Gerard Petytcru, to the commonalty of Ipswich, on behalf of them-
selves and their fellow mariners, for their pay while on board the said ship on King's service in
Scotland from 8 Sep. – 12 Nov. 1310

Latin; 3 seals, incomplete, on tongue; seals from 2 other tongues missing

C/1/8/4   25 Aug. 1486

Counterpart indenture of agreement between King Henry VII and Bailiffs, burgesses and
commonalty

Borough authorities bind themselves to take sufficient surety from owner, master or purser of
every English ship in borough, in double the value of ship's tackle and victuals, that its mariners
while at sea shall keep the peace towards all King's subjects, allies and all others having safe
conduct; to endeavour to arrest every robber [pirate] at sea as soon as knowledge of an offence
reaches them; and to take further security if that already taken ceases to equal value of ship's
tackle and victuals

English; fragment of Common Seal on tongue

C/1/8/5   3 Jan. 1625

Letter from Matthew Brownrigg and John Sicklemore, Bailiffs and Deputy Lieutenants of
Ipswich, to Sir Thomas Middleton, kt and other Treasurers appointed to receive Subsidies

Certifying that, according to order of Council of War dated 3 Nov. 1624, William Clyatt, High
Collector of 2nd Subsidy in Ipswich, has disbursed to Capt. Gilbert Jenner £7 10*s* for conduct-
ing 25 soldiers from Ipswich to Dover and 25*s* for imprest money

C/1/8/6   8 Apr. 1643

Promissory note of Nicholas Phillips

To find 'two armes' and to pay two soldiers for defence of Associated Counties of Suffolk,
Norfolk, Essex, Cambridgeshire, Hertfordshire and Isle of Ely; to be entered in book of 'Mr
Dey' [? a Corporation officer]

C/1/9   TAXATION   ?1523–1807

C/1/9/1   LAY SUBSIDIES   ?1523, n.d.

Originating in the so-called 'Saladin Tithe' of 1181, the Lay Subsidy became the principal source of tax revenue in medieval England, being levied for specific purposes such as the financing of foreign wars. One-tenth of the value of a person's moveable goods was levied in towns and one-fifteenth in rural areas – hence the common designation of the tax as Tenths and Fifteenths. The Subsidy was last levied in 1623 (*see* Friar 1991, 218, 374–75).

C/1/9/1/1   n.d. [?1523–1524]
Borough assessment [for Lay Subsidy]
Names, valuations, and amounts assessed
(English, 4 paper fols attached 'Chancery' style, incomplete; discovered among MS collections in Ipswich Borough Library in 1943 and returned to the Town Clerk)

C/1/9/1/2   n.d. [16c]
Assessment [? for Lay Subsidy] of inhabitants of NI
Headed 'Ane Informassione of All the inhabitenttes of the pariss of St Neikkollas in Epssweche and ther parssinabelle Esstattes'
(1 vol., 12 unnumbered fols)

C/1/9/2   MILITIA ASSESSMENTS   1558

The Act of 1558 (4 and 5 Philip and Mary, cap. 2), which superseded earlier legislation on the same subject – Henry II's Assize of Arms of 1181, Edward I's 1285 Statute of Winchester, and their various re-enactments – decreed the weaponry which every man was obliged to provide for equipping the militia for national defence, in proportion to his wealth in landed property or goods, according to a set scale of charges (*see* Boynton 1967, 7–11).

C/1/9/2/1   1 May 1558
Table showing quantity of horses and arms to be provided [for militia service] in proportion to tax-payers' wealth in real property or goods, under Act of 4 and 5 Philip and Mary, cap. 2

C/1/9/3   PARLIAMENTARY ASSESSMENTS   1660

During the Civil War and Interregnum, Parliament made much use of the Assessment, a direct tax or rate on real and personal property, in which each locality had to raise a fixed sum and itself assess the contribution of each taxpayer. After the Restoration, this form of taxation was temporarily retained for the purpose of paying off the Cromwellian standing army.

C/1/9/3/1   n.d. [Oct. 1660]
Precept [of Bailiffs to Serjeants-at-Mace]
To warn 15 named persons for the 12 parishes and the hamlets of WB, WU and BH to appear at Moot Hall on 22 Oct. 1660, 'and then and there assesse the severall inhabitants of this towne for their personall estates towards the three mounths assessment nowe out by Act of Parliament'

C/1/9/4   LAND, WINDOW, AND OTHER ASSESSED TAXES   1721–1807

Though, for convenience, these records are listed here with the other surviving records of taxation as an 'external obligation' on the borough, they are, strictly speaking, records of the General Sessions. An Act of 1745 (18 Geo. II, cap. 18) provided for the deposit of Land Tax assessment duplicates with the Clerk of the Peace, and this requirement was re-enacted in 1780 by 20 Geo. III, cap. 17, s.3, which sought to lessen the number of disputes at parliamentary elections by providing that no person could vote unless assessed for the Land Tax.

All the records listed here relate to taxes levied on the so-called assessment principle, based on a fixed sum which the government wished to raise from the country as a whole. This gave the government the advantage of knowing in advance the theoretical yield of the tax (which was not the case with the old Subsidy, whereby so much in the pound was levied on personal wealth). Counties were allocated assessments, which were shared out among the hundreds; each hundred's assessment was further divided among its constituent parishes and townships (*see* Gibson *et al.* 1993, 4).

The records consist almost entirely of assessment duplicates for the twelve ancient parishes of Ipswich and the three hamlets of Brooks, Wix Bishop and Wix Ufford. All are represented in each annual or half-yearly bundle unless otherwise stated in the catalogue entry. Most of the duplicates relate to the Land Tax and Window Tax, though from 1778 duplicates for other assessed taxes survive, mostly because it became customary to record the assessments along with those for the Land and Window Taxes, in a single pre-printed parish volume. For some years duplicates survive for duties on Inhabited Houses, Retail Shops, Carriages, Carts and Wagons, Male Servants, Female Servants, and Horses.

The assessments for Brooks Hamlet (often referred to in the duplicates as Whitton-cum-Thurleston) always take the form of two lists, 'outsetters' and others, and those for Wix Ufford are generally in three parts – St Clement, Westerfield and Rushmere. Assessments by street came into frequent use in St Clement from 1727. This also became usual in St Peter and St Mary at Quay in the 1750s and in St Margaret slightly later. About the same time, however, an alphabetical arrangement came to be widely used; and in the period 1765–80 only St Mary at Quay and St Margaret habitually subdivided their assessments by using street names as headings. After 1780 the latter practice was revived in St Clement. It was used occasionally at various times by other parishes.

Where the dates written, presumably by the first custodian, on the dorse of the documents differ from those within, reliance in the arrangement of the assessments has been placed on the former. Most of the discrepancies in dating arose from the tendency for certain parishes etc. (notably Wix Bishop and Wix Ufford) to date their assessments for the period recently begun, instead of the preceding period for which the tax was actually being levied.

C/1/9/4/1   LAND TAX ASSESSMENT DUPLICATES, WITH   1721–1807
ASSOCIATED PAPERS

The Land Tax is generally considered to date from the Act of 1692 (4 William and Mary, cap. 1), which was designed to tax personal estate, public offices and land. For administrative convenience, local assessors tended to avoid assessing forms of wealth other than landed property, and the annual legislation from 1702 became known as the Land Tax Act (Gibson *et al.* 1993, 4).

The assessment duplicates listed here are annual bundles, the fiscal year running from Lady Day (25 March until 1752, 6 April according to the New Style Gregorian calendar thereafter).

From 1721 to 1767 there are separate returns for the Land Tax (though there is a nine-year gap in the surviving records from March 1747 to April 1756). From 1767 to 1790 the assessments, with one or two exceptions, are contained in composite parish volumes which also include the Window Tax and, in later years, other assessed taxes. These composite volumes are listed in a separate sequence: *see* C/1/9/4/3. From 1790 to 1807 the Land Tax assessments are again returned in separate volumes, though for this period the series is very incomplete, only three years being represented.

The assessments give the names of owners and occupiers, the valuation of the property and the amount payable. Certain properties, e.g. inns, are referred to by name. The names of the assessors and collectors are often given.

Many annual bundles include summaries, containing details of the proportional sum, sum collected and re-assessment for every parish and hamlet, useful to a limited extent where the

parochial duplicate has not survived. Many summaries include the names of the commissioners, assessors and collectors of the Tax. Until 1740 the bundles frequently contain warrants for
abatement, which normally state the reasons for granting tax relief.

C/1/9/4/1/1   1721
Assessed in 1722 for payment of arrears; LW, MS, MT missing
Includes:
— summary
(13 docs)

C/1/9/4/1/2   Mar. 1722– Mar. 1723
LW, MG, MS missing
Includes:
— summary
— 6 warrants for abatement
(18 docs)

C/1/9/4/1/3   1723–1724
LW, MT, NI missing
Includes:
— summary
— 25 warrants for abatement
— 3 misc. mem.
(41 docs)

C/1/9/4/1/4   1724–1725
LW, MT missing
Includes:
— 3 summaries
— 2 warrants for abatement
— 3 misc. mem.
(21 docs)

C/1/9/4/1/5   1725–1726
LW, MT, ST missing
Includes:
— summary
— account and summary of money due to the Receiver General in respect of the borough on
25 Mar. 1725
— 21 warrants for abatement
(36 docs)

C/1/9/4/1/6   1726–1727
HL only.
(1 doc.)

C/1/9/4/1/7   1727–1728
LW, MT missing
Includes:
— 5 warrants for abatement
(18 docs)

C/1/9/4/1/8   1728–1729
LW, MS, MT missing
Includes:
— summary
— 3 warrants for abatement
— revised assessments for HL, MW, NI, WB
(24 docs)

C/1/9/4/1/9   1729–1730
LW, MT missing
Includes:
— 11 warrants for abatement stitched to CL duplicate
— 2 warrants for abatement pinned to PE duplicate
(26 docs)

C/1/9/4/1/10   1730–1731
Includes:
— summary and related papers
— 20 warrants for abatement
(39 docs)

C/1/9/4/1/11   1731–1732
Includes:
— summary
— 18 warrants for abatement (2 attached to assessments by seal wafers)
(32 docs)

C/1/9/4/1/12   1732–1733
NI missing
Includes:
— summary
— 11 warrants for abatement (2 attached to assessments by seal wafers)
(24 docs)

C/1/9/4/1/13   1733–1734
MS missing
Includes:
— 2 acquittances for money paid in by collectors for MQ
(16 docs)

C/1/9/4/1/14   1734–1735
MW missing
Includes:
— summary
— 16 warrants for abatement (2 attached to assessments by seal wafers).
(29 docs)

C/1/9/4/1/15   1735–1736
Includes:
— summary
— 19 warrants for abatement (3 attached to assessments by seal wafers).
(32 docs)

C/1/9/4/1/16   1736–1737
MG missing
Includes:
— summary
— 24 warrants for abatement (6 attached to assessments by seal wafers)
(33 docs)

C/1/9/4/1/17   1737–1738
BH missing
Includes:
— summary
— 24 warrants for abatement (3 attached to assessments by seal wafers)
(36 docs)

C/1/9/4/1/18   1738–1739
Includes:
— summary
— writ to constable of NI, for distraint of goods of persons refusing to pay rate for repair of
Stoke Bridge, 23 May 1738 (incomplete; sealed, but lacking signatures of magistrates and
names of offenders)
— 44 warrants for abatement.
(60 docs)

C/1/9/4/1/19   1739–1740
MQ missing
Includes:
— summary
— calculation of sums paid by each parish to the Receiver General for the five years 1735–39,
with deficiencies
— 17 warrants for abatement (3 attached to assessments by seal wafers).
(30 docs)

C/1/9/4/1/20   1740–1741
MQ missing
Includes:
— summary and related papers
— additional assessment for arrears in ST
— account of Henry Bond, Receiver of the re-assessment for making good the deficiencies,
with 6 warrants to him from the Commissioners for payments to Collectors to make good the
deficiencies in their parishes
(22 docs)

C/1/9/4/1/21   1741–1742
Includes:
— summary
(16 docs)

C/1/9/4/1/22   1742–1743
Includes:
— summary
(16 docs)

C/1/9/4/1/23   1743–1744
MS missing
Includes:
— summary
(15 docs)

C/1/9/4/1/24   1744–1745
MG and ST only
(2 docs)

C/1/9/4/1/25   1745–1746
MW missing
Includes:
— summary
(15 docs)

C/1/9/4/1/26   1746–1747
Includes:
— summary
(16 docs)

C/1/9/4/1/27   1756–1757
ME and MQ missing
Includes:
— 2 lists of appeals
(15 docs)

C/1/9/4/1/28   1757–1758
Assessment for MT includes Window Tax assessment
Includes:
— list of assessors (Land and Window Tax)
— list of appeals (Land Tax)
(17 docs)

C/1/9/4/1/29   1758–1759
MT missing
Includes:
— list of appeals
— copy order of Commissioners for the Land Tax to Receiver General for town, for payment of
fees to Samuel Kilderbee, Town Clerk, for writing Assessors' and Collectors' warrants, 17 Jun.
1758
(16 docs)

C/1/9/4/1/30   1759–1760
Includes:
— summary
— list of appeals
(17 docs)

C/1/9/4/1/31   1760–1761
Includes:
— summary
— list of appeals
— copy list of appeals
(18 docs)

C/1/9/4/1/32   1761–1762
CL missing
Includes:
— summary
(15 docs)

C/1/9/4/1/33   1762–1763
BH, ME and ST missing. For MQ and WU, see Window Tax assessments, C/1/9/4/2/3/8
(9 docs)

C/1/9/4/1/34   1763–1764
NI missing. For MQ, MT, ST and WU, see Window Tax assessments, C/1/9/4/2/3/9
(10 docs)

C/1/9/4/1/35   1764–1765
MQ, MS, MT, NI, ST and WU missing
(9 docs)

C/1/9/4/1/36   1765–1766
MS and NI missing. For MQ, MT, PE, ST and WU, see Window Tax assessments,
C/1/9/4/2/3/10
(8 docs)

C/1/9/4/1/37   1766–1767
BH, LW, MG, MS, MW and WB only. For CL, HL, MT, PE, ST and WU, *see* Window Tax
assessments, C/1/9/4/2/3/11
(6 docs)

C/1/9/4/1/38   1787–1788
NI missing. For NI, *see* the composite volume for the same year, C/1/9/4/3/17
(10 vols, 4 docs)

C/1/9/4/1/39   1789–1790
NI and WU missing. For WU, *see* the composite volume for the same year,
C/1/9/4/3/18
(11 vols, 1 doc.)

C/1/9/4/1/40   1790–1791
NI missing
(11 vols, 3 docs)

C/1/9/4/1/41   1804–1805
ST only.
(1 vol.)

C/1/9/4/1/42   1806–1807
BH, MG, NI and WU missing
Includes:
— second copies for each parish/hamlet present, except ME, MW and ST
(15 vols, 4 docs)

C/1/9/4/2   WINDOW TAX ASSESSMENT DUPLICATES, WITH   1721–1785
ASSOCIATED PAPERS

The Window Tax was introduced in 1696 (7 and 8 William III, cap. 18). It was in fact two taxes
in one, the House Tax, assessed on the occupiers of inhabited dwellings liable to church and
poor rates, on which there was a flat-rate charge, to which was added in 1778 an additional
charge based on rateable values, and the Window Tax, for which there was a graduated scale of
bands on houses with more than a certain number of windows (Gibson *et al.*1993, 13).

The assessment duplicates listed here are six-monthly until 1746; from 1737 the two sets of
parish assessments for each Old Style calendar year are bundled together. There is a gap in the
surviving records from September 1746 to March 1755, following which annual assessments
were almost invariably made. From Lady Day 1767 these are contained in composite parish
volumes which also include the Land Tax and, in the later years, other assessed taxes. These
composite volumes are listed in a separate sequence: *see* C/1/9/4/3. (The six-monthly Window
Tax assessments for Michaelmas 1784 – Lady Day 1785 (C/1/9/4/2/3/13) are additional to the
composite series.)

The Window Tax assessments give the names of occupiers, including those excused as
'poor'; the number of windows ('lights'); notes of empty properties; and the amounts of old and
new duty. They sometimes include lists of abatements and the names of the collectors.

Many bundles include half-yearly (later annual) summaries for all parishes and hamlets,
useful where a parochial duplicate has not survived. These give the totals of old and new duties
for each parish/hamlet, and sometimes the names of assessors and collectors. Until 1755–1756
the bundles sometimes contain warrants for abatement, which normally state the reasons for
granting tax relief.

C/1/9/4/2/1   Half-yearly assessments   **1721–1737**

C/1/9/4/2/1/1   Sep. 1721–Mar. 1722
MQ missing
Includes:
— summary
(13 docs)

C/1/9/4/2/1/2   Mar.–Sep. 1722
MQ, MS and ST only
Includes:
— summary
— warrant for abatement of tax on Mr Isaac Alston's house in HL, which was empty for part of
last half year, 22 Oct. 1722
(5 docs)

C/1/9/4/2/1/3   Sep. 1722–Mar. 1723
BH, MS, MW, NI, PE and WU missing
(9 docs)

C/1/9/4/2/1/4   Mar.– Sep. 1723
HL, MQ, MS, NI and ST only
(5 docs)

C/1/9/4/2/1/5   Sep. 1723–Mar. 1724
MT missing
Includes:
— summary
— warrant for abatement
(15 docs)

C/1/9/4/2/1/6   Mar.–Sep. 1724
BH, MT, NI and WU missing
Includes:
— summary
— warrant for abatement
(13 docs)

C/1/9/4/2/1/7   Sep. 1724–Mar. 1725
MG, NI, WB, and WU missing
Includes:
— summary
— 2 warrants for abatement
— 2 lists of abatements
(16 docs)

C/1/9/4/2/1/8   Sep. 1725–Mar. 1726
Includes:
— summary
— 2 warrants for abatement
(18 docs)

C/1/9/4/2/1/9   Mar.–Sep. 1726
ME, MS and WB missing
Includes:
— 2 summaries
— 3 warrants for abatement
(17 docs)

C/1/9/4/2/1/10   Mar.–Sep. 1727
Includes:
— summary
— warrant for abatement
— memorandum *re* error in assessment
(18 docs)

C/1/9/4/2/1/11   Sep. 1727–Mar. 1728
Includes:
— summary
(16 docs)

C/1/9/4/2/1/12   Mar.–Sep. 1728
Includes:
— summary
— 5 warrants for abatement
(20 docs)

C/1/9/4/2/1/13   Sep. 1728–Mar. 1729
LW and NI missing
Includes:
— revised assessment for MQ
(14 docs. For NI *see* C/1/9/4/2/1/14)

C/1/9/4/2/1/14   Sep. 1728–Mar. 1729
NI only
(1 doc. Found with the coal meters' accounts for 1718–1719, C/3/5/1/103)

C/1/9/4/2/1/15   Mar.–Sep. 1729
BH, CL, MQ, MT, and WU missing
(10 docs)

C/1/9/4/2/1/16   Sep. 1729–Mar. 1730
(15 docs)

C/1/9/4/2/1/17   Mar.–Sep. 1730
BH, MQ, MS, MW and WU missing
(10 docs)

C/1/9/4/2/1/18   Sep. 1730–Mar. 1731
MS, MT, NI and PE missing
(11 docs)

C/1/9/4/2/1/19   Mar.–Sep. 1731
Includes:
— warrant for abatement
(16 docs)

C/1/9/4/2/1/20   Sep. 1731–Mar. 1732
BH missing
Includes:
— fair copy of duplicate for WU
— 11 warrants for abatement
(26 docs)

C/1/9/4/2/1/21   Mar.–Sep. 1732
MQ and WB missing
(13 docs)

C/1/9/4/2/1/22   Sep. 1732–Mar. 1733
BH missing
Includes:
— 4 warrants for abatement (1 attached to assessment by seal wafers)
(17 docs)

C/1/9/4/2/1/23   Mar.–Sep. 1733
MQ missing
Includes:
— revised assessment for WU
— summary
(16 docs)

C/1/9/4/2/1/24   Sep. 1733–Mar. 1734
BH and NI missing
Includes:
— summary
(14 docs)

C/1/9/4/2/1/25   Mar.–Sep. 1734
Includes:
— summary
(16 docs)

C/1/9/4/2/1/26   Sep. 1734–Mar. 1735
Includes:
— summary
(16 docs)

C/1/9/4/2/1/27   Mar.–Sep. 1735
Includes:
— summary
— 2 warrants for abatement (attached to assessments by seal wafers)
(16 docs)

C/1/9/4/2/1/28   Sep. 1735–Mar. 1736
Includes:
— summary
(16 docs)

C/1/9/4/2/1/29   Mar.–Sep. 1736
WU missing
Includes:
— summary
(15 docs)

C/1/9/4/2/1/30   Sep. 1736–Mar. 1737
Includes:
— summary
(16 docs)

C/1/9/4/2/2   Bundles covering a twelve-month period   **1737–1746**

From March 1737 until March 1746, the two sets of six-monthly assessment duplicates for each Old Style calendar year are bundled together. The first assessment in each bundle covers the half-year from Lady Day to Michaelmas (25 Mar.–29 Sep.), the second half-year from Michaelmas to Lady Day.

C/1/9/4/2/2/1   Mar. 1737–Mar. 1738
1st half-year: complete; 2nd half-year: CL, MG, ME and PE only
Includes:
— summary for both half-years
(20 docs)

C/1/9/4/2/2/2   Mar. 1738–Mar. 1739
1st half-year: complete; 2nd half-year: BH, CL, HL, LW, ME, MS, MT, WB and WU missing
Includes:
— summary for both half-years
(22 docs)

C/1/9/4/2/2/3   Mar. 1739–Mar. 1740
1st half-year: BH, MS, NI missing; 2nd half-year: BH, ME, MS, MT, MW and NI missing
Includes:
— summary for both half-years
(21 docs)

C/1/9/4/2/2/4   Mar. 1740–Mar. 1741
1st half-year: WU missing; 2nd half-year: BH, CL, LW, MQ, MS, MT, NI, PE, ST, WB and WU missing
Includes:
— summary for both half-years
— 2 warrants for abatement (attached to assessments by seal wafers)
(19 docs)

C/1/9/4/2/2/5   Mar. 1741–Mar. 1742
1st half-year: BH,MS and WB missing; 2nd half-year: ME, MS and MW missing
Includes:
— summary for both half-years
— 2 warrants for abatement for second half-year
(27 docs)

C/1/9/4/2/2/6   Mar. 1742–Mar. 1743
1st half-year: complete; 2nd half-year: MS missing
Includes:
— summary for both half-years
(30 docs)

C/1/9/4/2/2/7   Mar. 1743–Mar. 1744
Both half-years complete
Includes:
— summary for both half-years
(31 docs)

C/1/9/4/2/2/8   Mar. 1744–Mar. 1745
Both half-years complete
Includes:
— summary for both half-years
(31 docs)

C/1/9/4/2/2/9   Mar. 1745–Mar. 1746
Both half-years complete
Includes:
— summary for both half-years
— copy summary
(32 docs)

C/1/9/4/2/2/10   Mar.–Sep. 1746
(15 docs)

C/1/9/4/2/3   Annual assessments   **1755–1785**

C/1/9/4/2/3/1   1755–1756
MT missing
Includes:
— 3 lists of appeals
— 2 warrants for abatement
(19 docs)

C/1/9/4/2/3/2   1756–1757
CL, ME, NI and ST missing
(11 docs)

C/1/9/4/2/3/3   1757–1758
MQ and MT missing; for MT *see* Land Tax assessment, C/1/9/4/1/28
Includes:
— list of appeals
(14 docs)

C/1/9/4/2/3/4   1758–1759
WU missing
Includes:
– list of appeals
(16 docs)

C/1/9/4/2/3/5   1759–1760
Includes:
— summary, 18 Apr. 1761
— copy summary
— list of appeals
— 2 assessment tables (printed)
(20 docs)

C/1/9/4/2/3/6   1760–1761
Includes:
— summary
(16 docs)

C/1/9/4/2/3/7   1761–1762
Includes:
— summary
— list of appeals
(17 docs)

C/1/9/4/2/3/8   1762–1763
BH missing. Assessments for MQ and WU include Land Tax assessments
(14 docs)

C/1/9/4/2/3/9   1763–1764
NI missing. Assessments for MQ, MT, ST and WU include Land Tax assessments
(14 docs)

C/1/9/4/2/3/10   1765–1766
NI missing. Assessments for MQ, MT, PE, ST and WU include Land Tax assessments
(14 docs)

C/1/9/4/2/3/11   1766–1767
ME, MS and NI missing. Assessments for CL, HL, MT, PE, ST and WU include Land Tax
assessments
Includes:
— revised assessment for MG
(13 docs)

C/1/9/4/2/3/12   10 Oct. 1766–5 Apr. 1767
Half-year assessment only. MG and MQ missing
(13 docs)

C/1/9/4/2/3/13   10 Oct. 1784–5 Apr. 1785
Half-year assessment only. NI missing
(14 vols)

C/1/9/4/3   ASSESSMENT DUPLICATES FOR VARIOUS TAXES   1767–1790
(COMPOSITE VOLUMES)

Until 1777–1778, the assessments are for Land Tax and Window Tax only. Later volumes
include assessments for Inhabited House Duty (i.e., the additional charge based on rateable
value, added in 1778 to the flat-rate charge on occupiers of dwellings liable to church and poor
rates, which was collected with the Window Tax: *see* the introductory note to that Tax), Male
Servant Duty, Female Servant Duty, Retail Shop Duty, Carriage Duty, Wagon and Cart Duty
and Horse Duty. After 1784 the various taxes were consolidated and administered together,
although the full range of assessments is not always present in the records. The assessment
duplicates consist of annual bundles, the fiscal year running from Lady Day (6 April New
Style).

C/1/9/4/3/1   1767–1768
Land Tax and Window Tax only; NI missing; MG has Window Tax only
(14 vols)

C/1/9/4/3/2   1768–1769
Land Tax and Window Tax only; MS and NI missing; MG has separate books for each tax
(14 vols)

C/1/9/4/3/3   1769–1770
Land Tax and Window Tax only; NI missing
(14 vols)

C/1/9/4/3/4   1771–1772
Land Tax and Window Tax only
(15 vols)

C/1/9/4/3/5   1772–1773
Land Tax and Window Tax only
(15 vols)

C/1/9/4/3/6   1773–1774
Land Tax and Window Tax only; NI missing
(14 vols)

C/1/9/4/3/7   1775–1776
Land Tax and Window Tax only; NI missing
(14 vols)

C/1/9/4/3/8   1776–1777
Land Tax and Window Tax only; CL missing
(14 vols)

C/1/9/4/3/9   1777–1778
Land Tax and Window Tax only
(15 vols)

C/1/9/4/3/10   1778–1779
Land Tax and Window Tax; Inhabited House Duty for PE only; ME and NI missing
(14 vols)

C/1/9/4/3/11   1779–1780
Land Tax, Window Tax, Inhabited House Duty, Male Servant Duty (1778–1779)
(13 vols)

C/1/9/4/3/12   1780–1781
Land Tax, Window Tax, Inhabited House Duty, Male Servant Duty (1779–1780)
(15 vols)

C/1/9/4/3/13   1781–1782
Land Tax, Window Tax, Inhabited House Duty. NI missing. Male Servant Duty (1780–1781)
for BH, HL, MG, ME, MQ, MS, MT, MW and WB
(14 vols)

C/1/9/4/3/14   1782–1783
Land Tax, Window Tax, Inhabited House Duty. NI missing
Includes:
— 2nd copy for WU
(15 vols)

C/1/9/4/3/15   1783–1784
Land Tax, Window Tax, Inhabited House Duty. NI missing
(14 vols)

C/1/9/4/3/16   1784–1785
Land Tax, Window Tax, Inhabited House Duty. NI missing
(14 vols)

C/1/9/4/3/17   1787–1788
Land Tax, Window Tax, Inhabited House Duty, Retail Shop Duty, Male Servant Duty, Female
Servant Duty, Carriage Duty, Cart Duty, Wagon Duty, Horse Duty
(15 vols)

C/1/9/4/3/18   1788–1789
Land Tax, Window Tax, Inhabited House Duty, Retail Shop Duty, Male Servant Duty, Female
Servant Duty, Carriage Duty, Cart Duty, Horse Duty. NI missing
(14 vols)

C/1/9/4/3/19   1789–1790
Land Tax, Window Tax, Inhabited House Duty, Male Servant Duty, Female Servant Duty,
Carriage Duty, Cart Duty, Wagon Duty, Horse Duty. NI missing
Includes:
— 2nd copy for ST
(15 vols)

C/1/9/4/4   ASSESSMENT DUPLICATES FOR MALE SERVANT DUTY   1777–1778

Duty was payable by the employers of male servants under an Act of 17 George III (1777). The
assessments give the names of employers and servants, 'quality' (occupation) of servants, and
amount of yearly and quarterly charge.

C/1/9/4/4/1   5 Jul. 1777–Mar. 1778
For ¾ of a year. MT missing
(7 vols, 7 docs)

C/1/9/4/5 ASSESSMENT DUPLICATES FOR INHABITED HOUSE DUTY 1778–1780

The duty was payable under an Act of 18 George III (1778), and was an additional charge based on rateable values, over and above the flat-rate charge on occupiers of dwellings liable to church and poor rates which was collected with the Window Tax: *see* the introductory note to that Tax. The assessments give the valuation, name of occupier, ¾-year charge and quarterly charge.

C/1/9/4/5/1   5 Jul. 1778–Mar. 1779
For ¾ of a year. CL and PE missing
(9 vols, 5 docs)

C/1/9/4/5/2   5 Jul. 1779–[Dec. 1779]
For ¾ of a year. CL only
(1 vol.)

C/1/9/4/5/3   5 Jul. 1779–6 Apr. 1780
For ¾ of a year. MQ missing
(14 vols)

C/1/9/4/6 ASSESSMENT DUPLICATES FOR DUTY ON CARRIAGES AND HORSES   1789–1790

C/1/9/4/6/1   5 Jul. 1789–5 Apr. 1790
Additional duty for ¾ of a year. BH, CL and PE missing
(12 docs)

C/1/9/4/7 SCHEDULES FOR REDEMPTION OF LAND TAX UNDER THE ACT, 38 GEO. III, CAP. 60, SECTION 6; WITH ASSOCIATED PAPERS   1798–1803

The schedules, made by the property owners or their agents, give the name of owner and occupier, description of the property (e.g., messuage, warehouse) for which certificates of the amount of Land Tax are required, and the parish or hamlet of location.

C/1/9/4/7/1   28 Oct. 1798–23 Aug. 1799
Includes:
— 6 affidavits and one Quaker affirmation of ownership and agreement to advance redemption money, 1798
— 4 letters of request for redemption, 1799 and n.d.
(113 docs; originally filed on a lace, in approximate chronological order.)

C/1/9/4/7/2   14 Mar.–12 Sep. 1803
Includes:
— letter of request for redemption, 18 Apr. 1803
(7 docs; found loose with C/1/9/4/7/1)

C/1/9/5 UNIDENTIFIED   1699–1700

C/1/9/5/1   1699–1700
List of men and their wives
(1 parchment membrane, badly faded)

C/2   JUSTICE AND THE COURTS

In making use of the records of the borough courts, researchers should constantly bear in mind that although, for convenience, records of JUSTICE and TOWN GOVERNMENT have been separated in this catalogue (into sections C/2 and C/4 respectively), this division is to a great extent artificial. In the medieval period and beyond – indeed, in the case of the Sessions held by the Justices of the Peace, down to the local government reforms of the 19th century – the courts, both in the shires and in corporate towns, in addition to their judicial role, were responsible for much of the administration of local government.

The identification and classification of the medieval rolls of the various Ipswich courts owes much to the pioneering research carried out by Professor Geoffrey Martin in the 1950s. By Professor Martin's generous permission, this general introduction, as well as the introductory notes on the individual courts and their series of medieval records, is almost wholly derived from his published and unpublished works (Martin 1954, 1955, 1956, 1961 and 1973).

The evolution of the borough courts

Most of the Borough's judicial (and therefore also many of its administrative) institutions derive from the Portmanmote, which for most of the first century following the grant of King John's charter in 1200 was the borough's only court, whose jurisdiction was comprehensive. It took its name from the freemen of the *poort* (meaning a trading town, rather than a port in its modern, narrower sense), before whom all common business was transacted. The Portmanmote may even have predated the incorporation, for there are some grounds for believing that the meetings which took place between June and October 1200 to establish the town's system of self-government following receipt of the charter, and which appointed the senior (*capitales*) Portmen to assist the Bailiffs and render judgements, were not the first sessions of the Portmanmote, but rather the last appearance of a much more ancient institution, the folkmote, even at that time little more than a memory, specially revived for the great occasion (Martin 1954, 23).

The two earliest surviving Portmanmote Rolls – those for 39–40 and 54–56 Henry III (1255–56 and 1270–72) – are also the earliest surviving original records of the borough. The second roll (C/2/1/1/2) bears on its last membrane a note that on 19 September 1272 the former Common Clerk of the town, John le Blake, absconded in order to escape prosecution for unspecified felonies, taking with him in his flight a quantity of court rolls as well as the town's custumal, the roll called *le Domesday*. The likelihood is that his crimes had involved falsification of the records, and that the rolls (which were never recovered) were stolen to remove the evidence. The number purloined was probably not very great: not only was there a limit to what the fugitive would have been able to carry, but the written record only gradually supplanted oral tradition in England (Clanchy 1979), and it seems unlikely that the proceedings of the Portmanmote were formally recorded in the early years of the incorporation.

The business transacted in the Portmanmote and recorded on its rolls for 1255–56 and 1270–72 is comprehensive, indicative of that body's status at the time as the sole borough court. It includes the admission of free burgesses; 'real' actions (pleas involving land, later known as Great Pleas) initiated by royal writ (preceded by a transcript of the writ itself); pleas relating to free tenements, such as actions of waste; and actions of debt and trespass, probably begun by gage and pledge – i.e., initiated locally by formal complaint to the court – which came in time to be known as Petty Pleas. Also recorded are the property transactions known as recognizances of free tenement (from the grantor's formal acknowledgement of title – his avowal that the gift or sale was truly his act, and his wife's renunciation of her right to dower – that accompanied their enrolment).

41

The burgess, alone in the Middle Ages, had the right of transferring his tenement by devise, and from 1281 enrolments of testaments also appear on the Portmanmote Roll. From 1285 personal actions (Petty Pleas), which could be initiated by summary process before the Bailiffs, sitting more frequently than the alternate Thursdays on which the Portmanmote traditionally met, were enrolled separately. The maintenance of these Petty Plea Rolls encouraged the development of these Bailiffs' sessions into a separate court, the Court of Petty Pleas, or Petty Court, which was formalised during the 14th century. The development of the Petty Court is discussed more fully in the introductory note to the records of that court (C/2/3) below.

The Great Pleas (those touching real property, usually commenced by royal writ) remained the prerogative of the Portmanmote; indeed, common recoveries of burgage property continued to be suffered in the Portmanmote down to 1832, the year before the recovery was abolished by statute. The Great Pleas for a time gave the name of Great Court to the Portmanmote, though the Great (or General) Court proper, which emerged as a separate body from the Portmanmote in the 15th century, was a purely administrative body, shorn of judicial powers.

During the last decade of the 13th century the Common Clerk began to concentrate records of recognizances on a single membrane of the Portmanmote Roll, though not at first consistently. From 1294 the new record was detached from its parent and maintained as a separate series, the Recognizance Rolls, to which from 1307 were added the records of testaments proved. The Recognizance Rolls also took notice of land transactions recorded in the Court of Petty Pleas. By the mid-14th century a third formal court had evolved, called the Petty Court of Recognizances, which could if necessary be convened to witness a single transaction. (For further details, see the introductory notes to the Petty Court of Recognizances (C/2/4) and the Recognizance Rolls (C/2/4/1), below.)

Only one new class of entry appears on the Portmanmote/Great Court Rolls in Edward III's reign: the record, at the first court of the administrative year, of leases of some common sources of revenue – such as the markets, mills and quay – to individual burgesses for ready money. Such entries occur in 1334, 1339, 1340 and 1344–1350 inclusive. This addition apart, however, there are signs from early in the reign that the Portmanmote/Great Court was beginning to lose its pre-eminent position. Its importance had already been diminished by the capture of aspects of its business by the Court of Petty Pleas and the Petty Court of Recognizances, and between 1340 and 1346 there were months when the Portmanmote was suspended for lack of business. In the 1340s only the admission of new burgesses provided it with regular entries. The cause was doubtless the economic recession which affected the whole of Europe in the early 14th century and was at its worst in the plague years after 1348. After September 1351 there is no Portmanmote/Great Court Roll for more than forty years. From 1360 until 1394 the admission of burgesses is recorded on the Recognizance Rolls, a transfer which marked the end of the Portmanmote's position as the borough's chief assembly. From 1377, too, actions involving matters of public policy, which would once have been regarded as the exclusive preserve of the Portmanmote, are heard and determined by the Court of Petty Pleas, which by now had developed from an informal session of the Bailiffs dealing with personal actions, into an assembly with wide powers. The only kinds of business still beyond its competence seem to be the admission of burgesses, the election of officers and the hearing of real actions.

Early in the 15th century (the precise date cannot be established because there seems to have been a period of experiment in record-keeping which apparently led to confusion and loss) the Portmanmote/Great Court finally split into two distinct bodies. That which retained the name of Portmanmote preserved its jurisdiction in real actions, while a separate General Court – a purely administrative body, later to be known, confusingly, as the Great Court – assumed responsibility for the admission of burgesses and the election of officers. The General/Great Court, the assembly of all the free burgesses, also had the power to issue ordinances for the government of the borough, and was thus from this time onwards the supreme authority in non-judicial matters. It is first mentioned in 1432, though it must have been in existence earlier, since its earliest surviving register (B.L. Add. MS 30, 158), kept in volume form and drawn up c.1435, records the admissions of burgesses from 1415.

After Edward IV's charter of 1463 gave to the Court of Petty Pleas/Petty Court a comprehensive jurisdiction in all actions, real, personal and mixed, the Portmanmote's sphere of activity contracted still further; almost its sole remaining function was the hearing of actions of recovery. For the rest of its existence the Portmanmote apparently met only *ad hoc*, usually on receipt of royal writs for the commencement of actions. By the beginning of the 19th century it had however re-acquired one of its original functions – that of ratifying the transfer of a married woman's real property following her private examination before the Bailiffs – which it had cast off in the 14th century along with the recognizance business.

Because of the paucity of its surviving records, the origins of the Maritime Court, which determined disputes between strangers passing through the port, are obscure. But in view of the similarity of its business to that dealt with by the Petty Court, it seems likely that it originated as an off-shoot of that body, delegated to meet, when necessary, from tide to tide.

The Leet, as explained in more detail below in the introductory note to its records (C/2/8), was an even more ancient institution than the Portmanmote, having its origins in the Anglo-Saxon law-and-order system of Frankpledge. It was a jurisdiction delegated by the Crown to franchise-holders (whether manorial lords or corporate towns), and in Ipswich was presided over by the Bailiffs. It may from the beginning of the incorporation have been independent of the Portmanmote – as laid down in the custumal, it was held annually on the Tuesday in Whitsun week – but in the absence of any surviving Leet records earlier than the mid-14th century this must remain a matter for speculation. During the period for which records have survived, most of its business concerned the punishment of trading offences and the abatement of nuisances. In time, the latter came to supersede the former as the Leet's main *raison d'être*.

With the sole exception of the Leet, the Sessions of the Peace stood alone as the borough's only judicial institution which did not evolve from the Portmanmote. The Sessions were a Crown creation of the 15th century. Henry VI's charter of 28 March 1446 (C/1/1/14) constituted the Bailiffs and four of the twelve (capital) Portmen Justices of the Peace for the borough, with powers there as full as those enjoyed by the county Justices outside the liberties. This concession was confirmed by Edward IV's charter of 18 March 1463 (no longer extant: translation in Canning 1754, 11–21). The earliest surviving Sessions roll dates from 1440, before the court established its independence. From the time of its creation the court of General (Quarter) Sessions functioned as the criminal court of the borough, and from the 16th century onwards it was made responsible for an increasing number of administrative duties. Its functions are discussed in more detail in the introductory note to the records of the court (C/2/9) below.

C/2/1   PORTMANMOTE   1255–1823

The Portmanmote's original comprehensive jurisdiction as the borough's sole assembly, and the gradual loss of most of its functions, have been traced at length in the general introduction to JUSTICE AND THE COURTS, above.

The series of Portmanmote Rolls ends in 1394. Thereafter, minutes of Portmanmote proceedings may be found in the Composite Court Books (C/2/10/3) between 1488 and 1595, and in the Petty Court Books (C/2/3/7) from 1601 to 1832. Additionally, recoveries suffered in the Portmanmote in 1538 are entered in the Register of Enrolments (C/2/10/2). From 1575 to 1827 such proceedings of the Portmanmote as were deemed worthy of permanent enrolment were included in the resumed series of 'Dogget' Rolls and on the rolls of deeds acknowledged in the Petty Court which succeeded them in 1653 (C/2/10/1).

C/2/1/1   PORTMANMOTE ROLLS   1255–1394

For the changes in the classes of business recorded on the Portmanmote Rolls between 1255 and 1394, see the general introduction to JUSTICE AND THE COURTS, above.

The earliest rolls are composed of a number of parchment membranes stitched together 'Chancery' style (head-to-tail). This practice changed in 1289-90, and the Portmanmote Rolls from 17–18 Edward I onwards are made up 'Exchequer' style, with the membranes gathered and attached at the head for greater ease of reference. The 'Chancery' style rolls from Henry III's reign may have been made up during the course of compiling the record, but there is evidence at the end of the 13th century and during Edward III's reign that the practice then was to roll and endorse each membrane separately. Whether the bundles as they now exist were tied at the end of each administrative year (Michaelmas, when the incoming Bailiffs took office and their predecessors left for the Exchequer to account to the Crown for the farm of the borough), or were made at a later date, it is now impossible to say. The first course would represent good administrative practice, but the many endorsements made by Nathaniel Bacon, the 17th-century Recorder of the borough and compiler of the *Annalls of Ipswiche*, suggest that some of the rolls may owe their present form to him.

The Great Pleas recorded on the earliest surviving rolls are preceded by transcripts of the initiating royal writ. During Edward I's reign instances are found of the original writ, shorn of its seal and margins, being stitched to the margin of the roll. This practice does not become consistent until Edward III's reign, when the record of a process begins with a transcript of the writ and ends with the original sewn to the margin.

There are no surviving Portmanmote Rolls between September 1351 and December 1393. Those between 1351 and 1360 may be presumed lost, but the transference of the record of the admission of new burgesses to the Recognizance Rolls from 1360 suggests that after that date the Portmanmote Rolls simply ceased to be written up. How many were written after their brief re-appearance in 1393–94 it is impossible to say, but to judge from indications in the Petty Court Rolls they were probably very rare by the beginning of the 15th century; and the appearance then of the General Court and the pre-eminence of the Petty Court, relegating the Portmanmote to a restricted, minor role, marks the demise of its independent record (Martin 1955, 117–18).

The language of the Portmanmote Rolls is Latin throughout. The names of the Bailiffs, where they appear in the headings to the courts or in an endorsement, are given in the catalogue.

C/2/1/1/1   29 Apr. 1255–3 Aug. 1256
Silvester son of Wakelin, Thurston dil Cley, Bailiffs 1254–1255; Matthew de Porta, Hugh Leu, Bailiffs 1255–1256
37 courts for 39–40 Hen. III, described as the Pleas of Ipswich, *placita Gippewici*
(7 membranes; dorses of nos 1–3 and 7 blank; dorses of nos 4–5 contain only enrolments of admissions of forinsec burgesses in 39 and 40 Hen. III respectively, and that of no 6 *placita*; 1st (outer) membrane endorsed in a later hand, probably late 13c., 'Rotulus de magnis placitis G[ippewici] de anno regni regis Henrici filii regis Johannis xxxix° et eciam de anno xl° cum quodam rotulo huic rotulo enexo de forincecis burgensibus factis in diversis annis ut patet eodem rotulo', a misleading description which caused J.C. Jeaffreson, the compiler of the HMC Report on the borough records, to conclude, erroneously, that the division of Great and Petty Courts existed by the reign of Henry III)

C/2/1/1/2   17 Jul. 1270–22 Sep. 1272
H. Luy, R. Fader, Bailiffs 1269–1270; Matthew de Porta, Vivian son of Silvester, Bailiffs 1270–1271; R. de Orefford, Godfrey Davy, Bailiffs 1271–1272
48 courts for 54–56 Hen. III
The last entry on the dorse of the last membrane records the flight on 19 Sep. 1272 of John le Blake, late common clerk of the town, on being accused of various crimes, taking with him the custumal called the Domesday and many plea rolls: 'Sciendum est quod die Lune proxima post festum Exaltationis Sancte Crucis predicto Anno lvj° Johannes le Blake Clerk' qui nuper erat communis clericus ville Gippewici fugit extra eandem villam Gippewicum pro quod Indictatus fuit in prima de pluribus latrociniis Et asportavit secum quemdam Rotulum de legibus et consuetudinibus predicte ville qui vocabatur le domesday et alios plures rotulos de placitis eiusdem ville de tempore diversorum Balliorum.'
(10 membranes; dorses of nos 1–4 and 8 blank; dorses of nos 5–7 contain only enrolments of admissions of forinsec burgesses in 54–56 Hen. III respectively, and those of nos 9 and 10, *placita*)

44

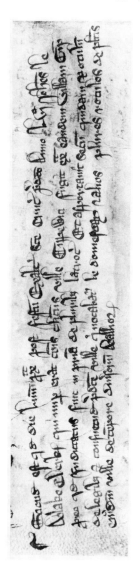

Fig. 2. Early vicissitudes of the archives.

(*Left*) Memorandum on the last membrane of the Portmanmote Roll for 1270–72
recording that on 19 September 1272 the former Common Clerk of the town, John
le Blake, absconded in order to escape prosecution for unspecified felonies, taking
with him in his flight a quantity of court rolls as well as the town's custumal, the
roll called *le Domesday*. (C/2/1/1/2)

(*Right*) Though John le Blake did not take the King John Charter, it was later lost
for a time, and recovered from Hadleigh in the early 17th century. 'It'm to Mr
Cardinall of Hadlie the 2 September 1610 for the Restoringe of the Charter w'ch
was first graunted to the towne and was missinge and not knowne where to be
found – five shillings.' (Fair copies of Treasurer's and Chamberlains' accounts,

C/2/1/1/3   20 Apr.–4 May 1273
Richard Fader, John Laurenz, Bailiffs
2 courts for 1 Edw. I
The single membrane has become detached from the rest of the roll for this regnal year (see C/2/1/1/4). The roll, which was still among the borough records when Bacon referred to it in his *Annalls* (p 10), was subsequently lost, and restored to the borough early in the 20th century. This membrane is now attached, with modern stitching, to 2 membranes (sewn 'Chancery' style) of a [Chamberlains'] petty rental, mostly for the occupation of common soil; an entry recording the payment of 4*d* by Roger Borham of Ipswich for a lease of a piece of void land in MT for 60 years from 1 Jul. 1 Hen. V appears to date the rental to 1415
(1 + 2 membranes; dorses of all 3 blank)

C/2/1/1/4   19 May–21 Sep. [1273]
10 courts for [1 Edw. I]
The 4 membranes have become detached from the 1st membrane of the roll (C/2/1/1/3). They are now attached, with modern stitching, to a single-membrane Abatement Roll (containing 3 actions) for 5–14 Apr. 1318 (11 Edw. II). The documents became separated from the borough records, and were purchased in London by V.B. Redstone in 1921 and restored to the custody of the Town Clerk
(4 + 1 membranes, sewn 'Chancery' style throughout; dorses of all 5 blank)

C/2/1/1/5   5 Oct. 1279–8 Aug. 1280
Richard Fader, Roger le Mestre, Bailiffs
23 courts for 7–8 Edw. I
(7 membranes; all dorses blank except that of no 2, which records only admissions of forinsec burgesses in 7 Edw. I)

C/2/1/1/6   3 Oct. 1280–18 Sep. 1281
Robert de Orford, Vivian son of Silvester, Bailiffs
26 courts for 8–9 Edw. I
With this roll the enrolment of testaments begins; brief notes of 3 testaments, Jan. 1281, are recorded on m. 1d.
(7 membranes; dorses of nos 2, 5 and 7 blank)

C/2/1/1/7   2 Oct. 1281–17 Sep. 1282
Robert de Orford, Vivian son of Silvester, Bailiffs
26 courts for 9–10 Edw. I
(7 membranes; dorses of nos 3–7 blank)

C/2/1/1/8   30 Sep. 1283–28 Sep. 1284
Thomas Aylred, Lawrence Horold, Bailiffs
26 courts for 11–12 Edw. I
(8 membranes; all dorses blank except for no 1, which records only admissions of forinsec burgesses in 11 Edw. I)

C/2/1/1/9   12 Oct. 1284–24 Oct. 1286
Vivian son of Silvester, John Clement, Bailiffs
52 courts for 12–14 Edw. I
The earliest Petty Plea (Petty Court) roll (19 Mar.–25 Jun. 1285) begins during the period covered by this roll
(8 membranes)

C/2/1/1/10   9 Oct. 1287–30 Jun. 1289
41 courts for 15–17 Edw. I
The date of the first entry, Thursday the feast of Denis (9 Oct.) *16* Edw. I, is a scribal error for *15* Edw. I, as subsequent entries make clear
(3 membranes)

C/2/1/1/11   14 Jul. 1289–10 Aug. 1290
28 courts for 17–18 Edw. I
(6 membranes; the first roll to be made up 'Exchequer' style: the chronological sequence of the
membranes may reflect a change of plan after the writing of the present 4th membrane, as the
order of a 'Chancery' style roll (recto, recto, dorso, dorso) is different from that of an
'Exchequer' roll (recto, dorso, recto, dorso); this roll's sequence of membranes is 5r, 6r, 4r, 2r,
2d, 3r, 3d, 1r, 1d; 6d and 4d record recognizances, 5d is blank. *See* Martin 1954, 42 note 4.)

C/2/1/1/12   24 Aug.–30 Nov. 1290
8 courts for 18–19 Edw. I
Another membrane from this roll, covering the dates 31 May–27 Sep. 19 Edw. I (1291) is
attached, as its 5th membrane, to the Portmanmote roll for 16–17 Edw. II, C/2/1/1/29
(1 membrane)

C/2/1/1/13   8 May–18 Sep. 1292
11 courts for 20 Edw. I
(1 membrane)

C/2/1/1/14   8 Oct. 1293–16 May 1297
John Leu, Thomas de Petra, Bailiffs 1293–1294; Lawrence Horald,Vivian Silvester, Bailiffs
1294–1295; Thomas Stace, Thomas le Mayster, Bailiffs, 1295–1297
84 courts for 21–25 Edw. I
The earliest separate Recognizance roll (16 Dec. 1294–22 Dec. 1300) begins during the period
covered by this roll
(9 membranes)

C/2/1/1/15   30 May 1297–2 Oct. 1298
Thomas Stace, Thomas le Rente, Bailiffs
36 courts for 25–26 Edw. I
(3 membranes)

C/2/1/1/16   16 Oct. 1298–13 Apr. 1301
Lawrence Cobbe, John de Whatefeld, Bailiffs 1298–1299; Thomas Stace, John le Mayster,
Bailiffs 1299–1301
64 courts for 26–29 Edw. I
(8 membranes)

C/2/1/1/17   12 Oct. 1301–26 Sep. 1303
John de Caustone, John Leu, Bailiffs 1301–1302; John Leu, Lawrence Cobbe, Bailiffs
1302–1303
50 courts for 29–31 Edw. I
Despite the appearance of the separate series of Recognizance rolls in 1294, recognizances for
the dates 11 Oct. 1302–23 May 1303 are nevertheless entered on the last membrane of this roll,
which is headed 'Rotulus de Recognicionibus de tenementis in Gippewico . . .'; this membrane
is printed in Martin 1973, 27–28
(8 membranes)

C/2/1/1/18   10 Oct. 1303–23 Sep. 1305
Thomas Stace, Thomas le Rente, Bailiffs
47 courts for 31–33 Edw. I
Recognizances for the dates 5 Dec. 1303–21 May 1305 are entered on the last membrane,
which is headed 'Rotulus de Recognicionibus liberi tenementi factis in Curia Gyppewici . . .';
this membrane is printed in Martin 1973, 28–31
(7 membranes)

C/2/1/1/19   7 Oct. 1305–7 Sep. 1307
Lawrence Cobbe, Thomas de Petra, Bailiffs
51 courts for 33–35 Edw. I and 1 Edw II
Recognizances for the dates 13 Jan. 1306–11 May 1307 are entered on the first membrane,

which is headed 'Rotulus de Recognicionibus liberi tenementi in Curia Gyppewici . . .'; this
membrane is printed in Martin 1973, 31–33
(6 membranes)

C/2/1/1/20   11 Apr. 1308–28 Sep. 1312
Thomas Stace, Thomas le Rente, Bailiffs
118 courts for 1–6 Edw. II
(12 membranes, attached in reverse chronological order)

C/2/1/1/21   12 Oct. 1312–27 Sep. 1313
Thomas Stace, Lawrence Cobbe, Bailiffs
24 courts for 6–7 Edw. II
(4 membranes, attached in reverse chronological order)

C/2/1/1/22   11 Oct. 1313–26 Sep. 1314
Richard Leu, Thomas de la Rente, Bailiffs
26 courts for 7–8 Edw. II
(6 membranes)

C/2/1/1/23   10 Oct. 1314–25 Sep. 1315
Thomas Stace, Alexander Margarete, Bailiffs
26 courts for 8–9 Edw. II
(5 membranes)

C/2/1/1/24   9 Oct. 1315–23 Sep. 1316
Lawrence Cobb, Gilbert Roberd, Bailiffs
26 courts for 9–10 Edw. II
(5 membranes, attached in reverse chronological order)

C/2/1/1/25   7 Oct. 1316–22 Sep. 1317
Thomas Stace, John de Whatefeld, Bailiffs
26 courts for 10–11 Edw. II
(5 membranes)

C/2/1/1/26   6 Oct. 1317–20 Sep. 1319
Lawrence Cobbe, Alexander Margarete, Bailiffs
52 courts for 11–13 Edw. II
(7 membranes)

C/2/1/1/27   21 Aug. 1320–17 Sep. 1321
26 courts for 14–15 Edw. II
(6 membranes)

C/2/1/1/28   1 Oct. 1321–16 Sep. 1322
Richard Lieu, Walter de Westhale, Bailiffs
26 courts for 15–16 Edw. II
(5 membranes)

C/2/1/1/29   30 Sep. 1322–29 Sep. 1323
John Harneys sen., William Malyn, Bailiffs; John de Prestone, Miles le Fenere, Chamberlains;
William de Kenebrok, clerk
27 courts for 16–17 Edw. II
Includes:
— (as 5th membrane), membrane from Portmanmote roll for 19 Edw. I, recording 6 courts,
31 May–27 Sep. 1291
(5 membranes)

C/2/1/1/30   13 Oct. 1323–27 Sep. 1324
Gilbert de Burgh, Edmund de Castelacre, Bailiffs; John Baude sen., John de Prestone, Coroners
28 courts for 17–18 Edw. II
(5 membranes)

C/2/1/1/31   11 Oct. 1324–26 Sep. 1325
John Irp, John de Prestone, Bailiffs; Gilbert Robert, John le Mayster, Coroners
26 courts for 18–19 Edw. II
(3 membranes)

C/2/1/1/32   11 Oct. 1324–26 Sep. 1325
Duplicate Portmanmote roll
23 courts for 18–19 Edw. II
This appears to be a Chamberlains' counter-roll, the maintenance of which was provided for by
the reforming ordinances of 1320. It omits the courts for 6 Jun., 4 Jul., 1 Aug. and 12 Sep. 1325
which appear on the original roll
Includes:
— (as m. 1r.) Abatement Roll for year beginning 29 Sep. 1324, containing 1 entry only, for
19 Aug. 1325
(7 membranes)

C/2/1/1/33   10 Oct. 1325–25 Sep. 1326
Gilbert de Burgh, John Harneys, Bailiffs; Gilbert Robert, John le Mayster, Coroners
25 courts for 19–20 Edw. II
(6 membranes)

C/2/1/1/34   9 Oct. 1326–16 Mar. 1327
Geoffrey Costyn, Geoffrey Stace, Bailiffs
13 courts for 20 Edw. II–1 Edw. III
(1 membrane)

C/2/1/1/35   9 Apr.–24 Sep. 1327
14 courts for 1 Edw. III
(2 loose membranes, presumably formerly attached to C/2/1/1/34)

C/2/1/1/36   8 Oct. 1327–22 Sep. 1328
John Irp, Richard de Leyham, Bailiffs
26 courts for 1–2 Edw. III, at 4 of which, 3 Mar–7 Apr. 1328, no business was transacted
(2 membranes)

C/2/1/1/37   6 Oct. 1328–21 Sep. 1329
26 courts for 2–3 Edw. III, at the last 3 of which, 24 Aug.–21 Sep. 1329, no business was transacted
(4 membranes)

C/2/1/1/38   11 Oct. 1330–26 Sep. 1331
Geoffrey Costyn, Thomas de Whatefeld, Bailiffs; John Irp, Walter de Caustone, Coroners
26 courts for 4–5 Edw. III, at the first 6 of which, 11 Oct.–20 Dec. 1330, no business was
transacted
(3 membranes)

C/2/1/1/39   10 Oct. 1331–24 Sep. 1332
Gilbert de Burgh, William le Smyth, Bailiffs
26 courts for 5–6 Edw. III
(6 membranes)

C/2/1/1/40   8 Oct. 1332–23 Sep. 1333
Geoffrey Costyn, Miles le Smyth, Bailiffs
26 courts for 6–7 Edw. III
(3 membranes)

C/2/1/1/41   7 Oct. 1333–22 Sep. 1334
Geoffrey Stace, William Ryngild, Bailiffs; John Irp, William Caustone, clerk, Coroners
26 courts for 7–8 Edw. III
(3 membranes, attached in reverse chronological order, all damaged by rodent action and incomplete)

C/2/1/1/42   6 Oct. 1334–21 Sep. 1335
John Irp, John Heued, Bailiffs; John Irp, William de Caustone, clerk, Coroners
26 courts for 8–9 Edw. III
(4 membranes)

C/2/1/1/43   5 Oct. 1335–19 Sep. 1336
John Lieu, Thomas le Cotiller, Bailiffs; John Irp, William de Caustone, clerk, Coroners
26 courts for 9–10 Edw. III
(5 membranes)

C/2/1/1/44   3 Oct. 1336–18 Sep. 1337
John de Prestone, John Irp, Bailiffs; William de Caustone, clerk, Coroner
27 courts for 10–11 Edw. III
Includes:
— continuations of pleas, 7 Aug.–13 Nov. 1337 (m. 6r.)
(7 membranes)

C/2/1/1/45   2 Oct. 1337–17 Sep. 1338
Gilbert de Burgh, Edmund Petygard, Bailiffs; John Irp, William de Caustone, Coroners
25 courts for 11–12 Edw. III
Neither the heading nor the proceedings of the court for 13 Nov. 1337 is entered on m. 1d.,
though the continuation of these proceedings appears on m. 6r. of the previous roll (C/2/1/1/44)
Includes:
— continuations of pleas, 9 Jul.–24 Dec. 1338 (m. 4r. and d.)
(6 membranes)

C/2/1/1/46   30 Sep. 1339–28 Sep. 1340
John Irp, John de Leyham, Bailiffs; John Irp, William de Caustone, clerk, Coroners
27 courts for 13–14 Edw. III
(5 membranes)

C/2/1/1/47   12 Oct. 1340–27 Sep. 1341
John de Prestone, Henry Brikoun, Bailiffs
28 courts for 14–15 Edw. III, at 20 of which, 4 Jan.–21 Jun., 26 Jul. and 2 Aug.–27 Sep. 1341,
no business was transacted; court of 5 Jul. 1341 records only the admission of 5 burgesses
(2 membranes)

C/2/1/1/48   11 Oct. 1341–26 Sep. 1342
Geoffrey Stace, William de Kenebrook, Bailiffs; John de Prestone, John Irp, Coroners
25 courts for 15–16 Edw. III, at 10 of which, 11 Oct.–13 Dec. 1341 and 10 Jan.–14 Mar. 1342,
no business was transacted; courts of 27 Dec. 1341 and 4 Jul. 1342 each record only the admission of 8 burgesses
(2 membranes; ascenders of letters of heading to court of 27 Dec. 1341 (m. 1r.) elaborately
decorated with grotesque human faces, oak leaves and acorns)

C/2/1/1/49   7 Oct. 1344–15 Sep. 1345
John de Prestone, John Irp, Bailiffs; William Ryngild, William de Kenebrook, Coroners
26 courts for 18–19 Edw. III, at 15 of which, 21 Oct. 1344–28 Apr. 1345, no business was transacted. Courts recorded on m. 2, 9 Dec. 1344–21 Jul. 1345, were held before Edmund Noon,
deputy to Sir John Howard, Sheriff of Norfolk and Suffolk, *Custos* of the town [which had been
taken into the King's hands following a riot by sailors, who had held a mock trial on the Assize

judge]. Courts recorded on m. 3d. are duplicates of those for 9 Dec. 1344–9 Jun. 1345 on m. 2r., and are struck through
(3 membranes)

C/2/1/1/50   29 Sep. 1345–14 Sep. 1346
John Lew, Edmund Petygard, Bailiffs; John de Prestone, William Ryngild, Coroners
26 courts for 19–20 Edw. III, at 6 of which, 24 Nov. 1345, 8 Dec. 1345, 8 Jun., 22 Jun., 20 Jul., 14 Sep 1346, no business was transacted; court of 6 Jul. 1346 records only the admission of 4 burgesses
(3 membranes)

C/2/1/1/51   5 Oct. 1346–20 Sep. 1347
John de Prestone, John Irp, Bailiffs
26 courts for 20–21 Edw. III, at 6 of which, 19 Oct.–30 Nov. 1346, 5–19 Apr. 1347, no business was transacted; court of 5 Oct. 1346 records only the admission of 2 burgesses
(5 membranes)

C/2/1/1/52   4 Oct. 1347–18 Sep. 1348
John de Prestone, Thomas Lew, Bailiffs; John de Prestone, William Ryngild, Coroners
26 courts for 21–22 Edw. III
(4 membranes)

C/2/1/1/53   2 Oct. 1348–24 Sep. 1349
John de Prestone, Thomas Lew, Bailiffs; John de Prestone, William Ryngeld, Coroners
23 courts for 22–23 Edw. III, at 10 of which, 18 Dec. 1348–18 Jun. 1349, no business was transacted
(2 membranes)

C/2/1/1/54   8 Oct. 1349–16 Sep. 1350
John de Prestone, John Cobet, Bailiffs; John de Prestone, William Ryngeld, Coroners
25 courts for 23–24 Edw. III, at 10 of which, 5 Nov.–31 Dec. 1349, 28 Jan.–25 Mar. 1350, no business was transacted; court of 9 Apr. 1349 records only the admission of 8 burgesses
(3 membranes)

C/2/1/1/55   Apr.–Jun. 1350
3 Courts for 29 Apr., 13 May, 27 May and 10 Jun. 1350
(1 membrane, pierced for attachment; foot including part of proceedings of court held 10 Jun. cut away; endorsed with memoranda apparently *re* work performed by various persons in Aug. 1381; apparently detached from C/2/1/1/54; found with Nathaniel Bacon's MS of his 'Annalls')

C/2/1/1/56   30 Sep. 1350–15 Sep. 1351
John de Prestone, John Cobet, Bailiffs; John [de Prestone], William Ryngeld, Coroners
24 courts for 24–25 Edw. III, at 2 of which, 1, 15 Sep. 1351, no business was transacted
(3 membranes)

C/2/1/1/57   18 Dec. 1393–27 Aug. 1394
Gilbert de Boulge, William dil Fen, Bailiffs
19 courts for 17–18 Ric. II. The heading describes the proceedings not as 'Placita Gippewici', as in earlier years, but as 'Placida de Portmanmot'
(1 membrane; scuffed and discoloured, in places legible only with difficulty)

C/2/1/2 ENGROSSMENTS OF RECOVERIES OF BURGAGE   1527–1544
TENEMENTS

Each engrossment is the record of a single action in the Portmanmote ['curia de Port-manmote'], initiated by royal Writ of Right directed to the Bailiffs. The text of the writ is always transcribed in the record, and in some cases the original writ, shorn of its seal and margins, is stitched to the left-hand margin of the engrossment, together with other related documents. The property concerned is described only in general terms, e.g. 'messuage', as with final concords and common recoveries in the central courts at Westminster. The proceedings were normally spread over two sessions of the court, at the first of which the writ was produced and enrolled, and the date set for the hearing of the action.

C/2/1/2/1   2–16 May 1527
Nicholas Hervy and Thomas Heyward *v.* Thomas Gosse, William Sebyn and wife Margaret
Annexed:
— fragment of writ (date missing)
— 2 memoranda of appointment of attorneys, n.d.
— Bailiffs' precept to serjeants to deliver seisin, 4 Jun. 1527
(1 membrane)

C/2/1/2/2   10 Jan.–7 Feb. 1538
William Gardenar *v.* Edmund Joly
(1 membrane)

C/2/1/2/3   2 Sep.–24 Oct. 1538
Thomas Petgrewe *v.* Christopher Lambard, wife Margaret and Thomas Purpet
(1 membrane; stitching in left-hand margin probably indicates former attachment of original writ)

C/2/1/2/4   23 Mar.–18 May 1542
Richard Harvy *v.* Symon Jacob
Annexed:
— fragment of writ, 1 Jul. 1541
(1 membrane)

C/2/1/2/5   10 Jan.–6 Mar. 1544
Augustine Byrd of Ipswich, gent. *v.* John Batte of Ipswich
Annexed:
— writ, 16 Nov. 1543
— Bailiffs' precept to serjeant to deliver seisin, 18 Apr. 1544
(1 membrane)

C/2/1/2/6   14–28 Aug. 1544
John Gawge, clerk *v.* William Fox
Annexed:
— writ, 26 Jun. 1544
— Bailiffs' precept to serjeant to deliver seisin, 20 Aug. 1544
(1 membrane)

C/2/1/2/7   14–28 Aug. 1544
William Style, clerk *v.* Edmund Leche
(1 membrane)

C/2/1/3   ENROLMENTS UNDER THE 1564 REFORMS   1565–1568

These probably resulted from the reforming ordinances of January 1564, which enjoined the Common Clerk, *inter alia*, to 'ingross in parchment all such matters as be reall accions, and such other accions as shall be tried by verdict . . . which doe amount to the summe of 5 li. or more'. From 1575 such enrolments of Portmanmote proceedings form part of the resumed series of 'Dogget' Rolls (*see* C/2/10/1 below).

C/2/1/3/1   1565–1568
Includes:
— Bailiffs' precept to serjeant to deliver seisin, 19 Jun. 1565 (incomplete), formerly stitched to margin
— Writ of Right, 31 May 1568, stitched to margin
— Writ of Right (fragment, date missing), formerly stitched to margin
(3 membranes)

C/2/1/4 EXEMPLIFICATIONS OF RECOVERIES   1562–1700

C/2/1/4/1   12 Sep. 1562
Garden and orchard in PE, George Coppyng *v.* Bartolomew Fenne and wife Joan
Latin; Common Seal, incomplete, on tag

C/2/1/4/2   21 Mar.–8 Apr. 1700
Messuage, garden and orchard in MG, Edward Pack and wife Elizabeth *v.* Francis Colman
(1 membrane. Though found stored with the 'Dogget' Rolls and enrolled deeds, this document differs in form from the usual enrolment of proceedings in the Portmanmote, the text commencing 'Omnibus Christi fidelibus ad quos hoc presens scriptum pervenerit certificamus quod ad Curia Domini Regis de Portmanimot . . .'.)

C/2/1/5 WRITS OF RIGHT PATENT   1800–1823

For the hearing of actions of recovery in the Portmanmote. Such writs were normally attached to the margins of the enrolments of Portmanmote proceedings. Bailiffs' precepts to the Serjeants-at-Mace to deliver seisin are annexed to the writs of 1822 and 1823.

C/2/1/5/1   20 Jan. 1800
In action of recovery, John King *v.* John Miller, of messuage, curtilage, yard and garden in CL

C/2/1/5/2   23 Apr. 1800
In action of recovery, Thomas Foster Notcutt, gent. *v.* Benjamin Brame jun., of 6 messuages in CL and MG

C/2/1/5/3   14 Oct. 1809
In action of recovery, Charles Gross *v.* John Milner, of 2 messuages, 2 tenements, 1 millhouse, 1 malt office, 2 outhouses, 3 curtilages, 3 yards and 3 gardens in MG and MQ

C/2/1/5/4   1 Nov. 1822
In action of recovery, John Ranson *v.* William Pearson, of 1 messuage, 2 curtilages, 2 orchards and 1 acre land in PE

C/2/1/5/5   11 Feb. 1823
In action of recovery, Henry Bunn *v.* Charles Smart, of 4th part of 1 messuage, 1 curtilage and 1 garden in LW

C/2/1/5/6   24 Jul. 1823
In action of recovery, John King *v.* William Batley, of 10 messuages, 20 cottages, 20 curtilages and 10 gardens in CL

C/2/1/6 PRECEDENTS   14c.

C/2/1/6/1   (1255–62), 14c.
Memoranda of legal precedents from Portmanmote Rolls for 39, 40, 44, 45 and 46 Hen. III
(Latin; 1 membrane)

C/2/2   GENERAL OR GREAT COURT   1470–1836

For the evolution of this Court and its separation from the Portmanmote early in the 15th century, see the general introduction to JUSTICE AND THE COURTS, above. Though commonly referred to as the Great Court, the headings to each session in the Court Books normally refer to it as the General Court until 1702, when the description Great Court becomes normal.

From the time of its formal separation from the Portmanmote the Great Court was a purely administrative body, although, puzzlingly, there are occasions between 1552 and 1600 when, according to minutes in the Composite Court Books (C/2/10/3) it apparently transacted Petty Court business; the reason for this is unknown. Though its function was otherwise non-judicial, its records are placed in this catalogue with those of JUSTICE rather than those of TOWN GOVERNMENT, both because of its status as a court and because of its origins and evolution.

The Great Court, an assembly of the freemen at large, remained the ultimate administrative authority in the borough down to 1835. The Assembly, composed of the twelve Capital Portmen and the twenty-four Common Councilmen, did not, at least in theory, act independently on behalf of the Corporation, but made recommendations to the Great Court. It was the Court which made administrative ordinances relating to all aspects of town government, elected the town's major officers at a session held annually on the feast of the Nativity of the Blessed Virgin (8 September), elected the members of Parliament for the borough, controlled the admission of freemen, and authorised mortgages of town property and grants or leases of the common soil. It also authorised the affixing of the Common Seal to exemplifications of recoveries suffered in the Portmanmote.

In addition to the Court Rolls (1470–1474), Court Books (1571–1836) and Minute Books (1582–1643 and 1778–1817), proceedings of the Great Court are enrolled on the 'Dogget' Rolls from 1438 to 1479 (C/2/10/1) and minutes are to be found in the Composite Court Books, 1486–1564 and 1600 (C/2/10/3).

C/2/2/1   COURT ROLLS   1470–1474

The business recorded consists chiefly of administrative orders, grants of common soil, elections of officers and admissions of burgesses. These membranes may perhaps have been intended for filing with the 'Dogget' Rolls.

C/2/2/1/1   1470–1474
Includes:
— (m. 2), ordinance, 17 Jul. 1472, requiring Thomas Busshop to release all town evidences and muniments to the Bailiffs by 8 Sep., and to account for the town rents
— (m. 3, 3d), ordinances, 25 Feb. 1474, *re* holding of Great Courts, election of officers, pledges for personal actions
(3 membranes; m. 3 perhaps originally attached to C/2/2/1/2, which also includes proceedings of the court of 25 Feb. 1474)

C/2/2/1/2   1472–1474
Includes:
— (m. 2) election of William Worsop, esq. and John Walworth jun. as burgesses to serve in Parliament, 2 Oct. 1472
— (m. 1) ordinances *re* use of town mills, 14 Oct. 1473
(3 membranes)

C/2/2/2   COURT BOOKS   1571–1836

The Court Book beginning *c*.30 Henry VIII (1538–1539), thought to have been the first in the series, is now missing. The main classes of Court business, reflected in the Court Books, are outlined in the introductory note to the GENERAL OR GREAT COURT. The session of 6 December 1571, the first recorded in the earliest surviving volume, gives a good indication of the variety of business covered. It issued ordinances for: the appointment of auditors for the Treasurer's and Chamberlains' accounts; the relief of Master Kelke, town preacher, from part of his duties on his election as Vice-Chancellor of Cambridge University; the prohibition of Sunday trading 'for the better order within this Towne and that the Churche be better frequented in preyer'; the remittance of part of a fine imposed for a brewing offence; the imposition of fines on one of the Coroners and various burgesses for infringing the liberties of the town; and the reimbursement to John Mynter of expenses incurred by the Queen's visit.

The language of the Court Books is English throughout, except for the Sessional headings, which are in Latin down to the 18th century, with the exception of the period April 1651–September 1660. The gap in the coverage of the Court Books between May 1633 and December 1642, during which period the record was apparently not engrossed, is filled by the Minute Book for 1609–1643 (C/2/2/3/3). The second and subsequent Court Books are less characteristically fair copies than the first, and are very similar in style to the Minute Books.

C/2/2/2/1   Dec. 1571–May 1633
(1 vol., 361 fols, ff 1–4, 361 blank, ff 349–60 defective with parts of text missing; marked 'No. 1' in an ? 18c. hand. Covers are of elaborately-tooled Morocco, which may not be strictly contemporary, since a double parchment folio of a late 13th-century theological text, in two columns, with glosses, rubricated and decorated in blue, bound into the front of the volume during conservation, may have formed part of the original cover.)

C/2/2/2/2   Dec. 1642–Aug. 1680
Includes:
— (at end) declaration that 'their lies noe Obligacion upon me or any other person from the Oath commonly called the Solem League and Covenant and that the same was in it selfe an unlawfull Oath and imposed uppon the subjects of this Realme against the knowne Lawes and liberties of the Kingdom', subscribed with signatures of Bailiffs and other officers, 1663–1667, 1679
(1 vol., 283 fols with near-contemporary foliation; front cover marked '4')

C/2/2/2/3   Sep. 1680–Sep. 1703
Includes:
— (at front) forms of Oath of Allegiance, oath abjuring papal authority, oath against taking arms against the King, and declaration against the Solem League and Covenant, the two last subscribed with signatures of Bailiffs or other officers, 1691–1719
(1 vol., 200 fols with near-contemporary foliation, ff 196, 197, 199, 200 blank; front cover marked '5')

C/2/2/2/4   Sep. 1703–Nov. 1710
(1 vol., foliated 1–248, ff 249–94 blank; front cover marked '6')

C/2/2/2/5   Mar. 1711–Apr. 1722
(1 vol., 133 fols, ff 132–33 blank; front cover marked '7')

C/2/2/2/6   Sep. 1722–Sep. 1750
(1 vol., 175 fols, ff 174–75 blank; front cover marked '8')

C/2/2/2/7   Sep. 1750–Mar. 1777
Includes:
— (pasted inside front cover) table of fees for admission of free burgesses by patrimony or servitude, purchase, and presentment
(1 vol., 343 fols; front cover marked 'No. 9')

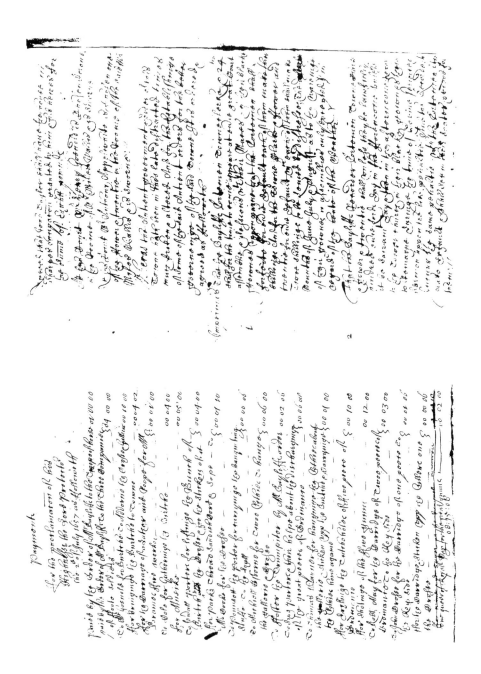

Fig. 3. (*Below*) Payments for the proclamation of His Highness the Lord Protector, 2 July 1657 (from Chamberlains' audited accounts, C/3/3/2/79)
(*Above*) Restoration of 'ancient order', 1663 (from Great Court Book 1642–1680, C/2/2/2/2)

C/2/2/2/8   May 1777–Mar. 1820
(1 vol., 362 pp, pp 262–362 unpaginated; front cover marked '10')

C/2/2/2/9   Mar. 1820–Dec. 1836
The last Great Court was held on 24 Jul. 1835, for the purpose of petitioning the House of Lords
to amend the Municipal Corporations Bill so as 'to preserve the rights, privileges and property
of your petitioners and all other municipal corporations as well as of all the individual Members
and Freemen of such corporations'. The remaining entry in the volume is a memorandum of the
election of (named) councillors to represent the various wards in the reformed borough under
the Municipal Corporations Act, on 26 Dec. 1836
(1 vol., 223 fols, ff 96–223 blank; front cover marked '11')

C/2/2/3 MINUTE BOOKS   1582–1817

These constitute the draft record of proceedings in the Great Court, from which the Court
Books were engrossed.

C/2/2/3/1   Dec. 1582–Oct. 1608
Includes:
— (ff 397–400) alphabetical list of names, apparently intended as index, though no folio
numbers are given
— (f 402v.) form of oath for Wardens of Tooley's Foundation
(1 vol., 404 fols with modern foliation, re-bound in 2 parts during conservation by PRO in
1938: Part 1 (Dec. 1582–Sep. 1594), ff 1–189; Part 2 (Oct. 1594–Oct. 1608), ff 190–404;
original front cover (bound with Part 1) inscribed in a 17c. hand, 'Minutes of Great Court
beginning 19° December 25° Eliza. finit. 6° Jac' and 'No. 2')

C/2/2/3/2   [Oct. or Nov.] 1609–Oct. [1643]
Down to May 1633 this volume formed the basis of the formal record engrossed in the Great
Court Book (C/2/2/2/1); from May 1633–Oct. 1643 it forms the sole record.
(1 vol., 322 fols with modern foliation; conserved and re-bound by PRO in 1939; ff 7, 320–22
blank, ff 1–10 defective with parts of text missing)

C/2/2/3/3   Feb. 1778–Mar. 1789
(1 vol., 46 fols, f 1 blank; front cover marked 'No. 1')

C/2/2/3/4   Sep. 1789–Jul. 1802
Enclosed:
— certificates of baptismal entries for William (1786) and Edward (1788), sons of William and
Sarah Franks, in Baylham parish registers, 1802
— note of names of Lionel Pepper, merchant and William Paxman, innkeeper as 'bondsmen for
Joseph Cooper for the Town's Money', n.d.
(1 vol., 43 unnumbered fols; front cover marked '2')

C/2/2/3/5   Sep. 1802–Sep. 1817
Includes:
— (f 1v) table of fees for admission of freemen by patrimony or servitude, purchase, and presentment, 8 Sep. 1805
(1 vol., 47 fols; front cover marked '3')

C/2/3   PETTY COURT   1285–1843

The evolution of the Court of Petty Pleas, or Petty Court, from the Portmanmote is discussed briefly in the general introduction to JUSTICE AND THE COURTS, above. A separate roll of Petty Pleas (*rotulus querelarum*) first appears in 1285, as the record of sessions held before the Bailiffs twice weekly to hear personal actions. At first these sessions enjoyed no great measure of prestige; in 1300, for instance, an action for wrongful distraint in Wix Bishop hamlet within the liberties of Ipswich moved the Bishop of Norwich's agent to claim his court, and the plea was therefore transferred to the Portmanmote; in a matter which touched the pretensions of the town, the new sessions were evidently not considered a proper setting for the argument (Martin 1955, 36–37). The Petty Plea Roll did however have some standing as a record: some recognizances of debt were entered upon it as early as 1285, and there is also evidence that Pleas of Abatement (the borough's version of the Assize of *Novel Disseisin*) were heard at these petty sessions (*ibid*).

All the Petty Plea Rolls for Edward II's reign have been lost, and there are only three survivors for the reign of his successor: those for 10–11 Edward III (1336–37) and 49–50 and 50–51 Edward III (1375–77). An inventory of the rolls for 1308–1333, drawn up during Edward III's reign (C/4/7/1/1) describes their distribution between 'John Preston's chest' (in which the records of Great Pleas, Recognizances and Testaments were stored) and 'the other' chest (to which the records of Petty Pleas were relegated, presumably as not being of such lasting importance). It seems likely that it was their separation from the other rolls that resulted in their loss (Martin 1954, 29–31, 43–44). The only records of Petty Pleas for Edward II's reign are two rolls listing the pleas commenced between 1322 and 1326 (C/2/3/2/1–2), which are probably Chamberlains' counter-rolls made in pursuance of the reforming ordinances of 1320.

It appears that during Edward II's reign the sessions for Petty Pleas developed into a fully-fledged court. By 1336, though the roll itself is still headed *rotulus querelarum*, the headings to the individual sessions describe them as *curia*.

By 1336 the Court seems to have suffered some loss of business. The Petty Plea Rolls of Edward I's reign were large; the first (13 Edward I) ran to sixteen membranes between March and November 1285, and the sessions were held twice a week. Some twenty-five to thirty pleas were held on these occasions and this quantity of business seems to have been maintained throughout the reign. In 1336 there are ten, or fewer, pleas to each court, and the courts are held once a week. The change must reflect some degree of economic depression, for the Petty Pleas are very largely pleas of debt, and after debt, pleas of contract and account, while at the end of the century the plea of *transgressio contra statutum* (i.e. the 1351 Statute of Labourers) is extensively used to enforce contracts of service.

As the pleas heard in the Petty Court touched almost every aspect of life in the town, their details make its rolls the most varied and interesting of the medieval records. After 1375, however, when the rolls re-appear, their interest is not confined to private actions, for there appears also a quantity of public business in entries that show the Petty Court discharging functions previously belonging to the Portmanmote. For example, in 1323, fines and bonds for good behaviour exacted from a number of offenders were recorded on the Portmanmote Roll; all the offences involved some defiance of authority – the Portmanmote was still the seat of authority where such matters were determined. But with the eclipse of the Portmanmote after 1351 the Petty Court is found in possession of such jurisdiction, showing that the Bailiffs' power was as fully represented in their sessions in the Court of Petty Pleas as it had originally been in the Portmanmote (Martin 1955, 130–33).

The headings for each of the two courts recorded on the latest Petty Court Roll surviving for the reign of Henry V (3 Dec. 1420 and 28 Jan. 1421) begin '*Curia domini regis tenta apud Gippewicum*', the first time that the Petty Court has been distinguished as *curia domini regis*. It is a proper acknowledgement of the importance that the court had assumed since the middle of the previous century, as the borough's principal judicial organ (Martin 1955, 147).

By virtue of Edward IV's charter of 1463 the court came to exercise a comprehensive jurisdiction in all actions, real, personal and mixed (Martin 1955, 111).

In the 18th century the Petty Court/Court of Petty Pleas became known as the Court of Small Pleas, and as such survived the municipal reform of 1835; its records exist down to 1882, although its final years lie outside the scope of this catalogue. By the 19th century another court, presumably an off-shoot of the Court of Small Pleas (and also known, confusingly, as the Petty Court), had emerged. It was held before the Bailiffs, for the sole purpose of passing the real estate of a minor. The estate had to be within the liberties, and the deed, which could be acknowledged at any age after fourteen, was enrolled by the Town Clerk (Cross 1968, 29). These sessions, at which the literacy and numeracy of the minors whose estates were to be conveyed were certified, are recorded in the Court Books of the Court of Small Pleas, though there is no indication in the headings that they formed the proceedings of a separate court.

The series of Rolls of the Petty Court/Court of Petty Pleas came to an end in 1444. For enrolments of proceedings in the Court from the mid-15th century onwards, see the 'Dogget' Rolls, 1438–1479 and 1575–1653 (C/2/10/1/1–8, 18–96) and the Extracts from Proceedings, 1472–1575 (C/2/3/6). For minutes of proceedings before the commencement of the Petty Court Books in 1601 (C/2/3/7), see the Composite Court Books, 1486–1601 (C/2/10/3).

C/2/3/1 PETTY COURT ROLLS   1285–1444

The content and progressively widening scope of these rolls is discussed at length in the introductory note to the Petty Court, above.

Until 1288 the membranes of the rolls are stitched together 'Chancery' style (head-to-tail). Thereafter they are made up 'Exchequer' style, gathered and attached at the heads. The language of the record is Latin throughout.

C/2/3/1/1   22 Mar.–25 Jun. 1285
24 courts for 13 Edw. I
(6 membranes)

C/2/3/1/2   28 Jun.–25 Oct. 1285
35 courts for 13 Edw. I
(10 membranes)

C/2/3/1/3   6 Nov. 1285–18 Mar. 1286
38 courts for 13–14 Edw. I
(9 membranes)

C/2/3/1/4   12 Dec. 1286–8 Sep. 1287
78 courts for 15 Edw. I
Includes:
— 1 court on m. 10 d. for 27 Apr. 18 Edw. I (1290)
(11 membranes)

C/2/3/1/5   29 Sep. 1287–3 Jul. 1288
71 courts for 15–16 Edw. I
(9 membranes)

C/2/3/1/6   3 Jul.–15 Oct. 1288
30 courts for 16 Edw. I
(4 membranes)

C/2/3/1/7   21 Oct.–9 Dec. 1288
7 courts for 16–17 Edw. I
(1 membrane)

C/2/3/1/8   19 Jan. 1289–6 Oct. 1290
210 courts for 17–18 Edw. I

(32 membranes; the first roll to be made up 'Exchequer' style; membranes attached in reverse chronological order)

C/2/3/1/9   28 Aug.–7 Sep. 1290
6 courts for 18 Edw. I
(1 membrane, presumably detached from C/2/3/1/8)

C/2/3/1/10   23 Oct. 1290–1 Oct. 1291
96 courts for 18–19 Edw. I
(13 detached membranes, 2 fragmentary)

C/2/3/1/11   1 Oct. 1291–28 Jul. 1292
86 courts for 19–20 Edw. I
(13 membranes, attached in reverse chronological order)

C/2/3/1/12   2 Oct. 1292–29 Sep. 1293
121 courts for 20–21 Edw. I
(21 membranes)

C/2/3/1/13   1 Oct. 1293–28 Sep. 1294
93 courts for 21–22 Edw. I
(12 membranes)

C/2/3/1/14   30 Sep. 1294–12 Sep. 1295
84 courts for 22–23 Edw. I
(10 membranes)

C/2/3/1/15   3 Oct. 1295–28 Sep. 1296
104 courts for 23–24 Edw. I
(12 membranes)

C/2/3/1/16   5 Oct. 1296–26 Sep. 1297
65 courts for 24–25 Edw. I
(7 membranes)

C/2/3/1/17   10 Oct. 1297–6 Oct. 1298
72 courts for 25–26 Edw. I
(9 membranes, attached in reverse chronological order)

C/2/3/1/18   9 Oct. 1298–28 Sep. 1299
102 courts for 26–27 Edw. I
(13 membranes)

C/2/3/1/19   1 Oct. 1299–20 Sep. 1300
90 courts for 27–28 Edw. I
(11 membranes, attached in reverse chronological order)

C/2/3/1/20   22 Sep. 1300–27 Sep. 1301
79 courts for 28–29 Edw. I
(13 membranes, attached in reverse chronological order)

C/2/3/1/21   2 Oct. 1301–27 Sep. 1302
90 courts for 29–30 Edw. I
(25 membranes)

C/2/3/1/22   8 Oct. 1302–26 Sep. 1303
96 courts for 30–31 Edw. I
(18 membranes)

C/2/3/1/23   4 Oct. 1303–22 Sep. 1304
75 courts for 31–32 Edw. I
(19 membranes, attached in approximate reverse chronological order)

C/2/3/1/24   8 Oct. 1304–4 Oct. 1305
65 courts for 32–33 Edw. I
(14 membranes, attached in reverse chronological order)

C/2/3/1/25   4 Oct. 1305–19 Sep. 1306
89 courts for 33–34 Edw. I
(17 membranes)

C/2/3/1/26   11 Oct. 1306–28 Sep. 1307
68 courts for 34 Edw. I–1 Edw. II
(14 membranes, attached in reverse chronological order)

C/2/3/1/27   4 Oct. 1336–24 Sep. 1337
40 courts for 10–11 Edw. III
(4 membranes, attached at the feet; the chronological sequence is m. 2, m. 1, m. 3, m. 4)

C/2/3/1/28   2 Oct. 1375–29 Sep. 1376
39 courts for 49–50 Edw. III
(5 membranes)

C/2/3/1/29   29 Sep. 1376–11 Jun. 1377
26 courts for 50–51 Edw. III
(3 membranes)

C/2/3/1/30   23 Jul. 1377–17 Feb. 1396
23 courts for 1, 16–17, 19 Ric. II
An artificial roll made up from three formerly separate rolls: 23 Jul.–29 Sep. 1377 (10 courts, 1 membrane); 7 Nov. 1392–29 Sep. 1393 (11 courts, 4 membranes); 25 Jan., 17 Feb. 1396 (2 courts, 1 membrane); the hand in which the regnal years are endorsed on the outer membrane suggests that the membranes were attached together in 16c or 17c
(6 membranes)

C/2/3/1/31   27 Nov. 1380–11 Aug. 1381
13 courts for 4–5 Ric. II
(3 membranes)

C/2/3/1/32   7 Oct. 1393–22 Sep. 1394
30 courts for 17–18 Ric. II
(9 membranes)

C/2/3/1/33   29 Sep. 1396–18 Sep. 1397
39 courts for 20–21 Ric. II
(12 membranes)

C/2/3/1/34   7 Oct.–21 Dec. 1400
16 courts for 2 Hen. IV
(6 membranes)

C/2/3/1/35   11 Jan.–29 Mar. 1401
20 courts for 2 Hen. IV
(5 membranes)

C/2/3/1/36   12 Apr.–23 Jun. 1401
18 courts for 2 Hen. IV
(4 membranes)

C/2/3/1/37   28 Jun.–29 Sep. 1401
12 courts for 2 Hen. IV
(3 membranes)

C/2/3/1/38   30 Sep. 1304–17 Sep. 1405
36 courts for 6 Hen. IV
(18 membranes)

C/2/3/1/39   25 Oct. 1405–28 Sep. 1406
41 courts for 7 Hen. IV
(17 membranes)

C/2/3/1/40   5 Oct. 1406–29 Sep. 1407
43 courts for 8 Hen. IV
(14 membranes)

C/2/3/1/41   4 Oct. 1407–25 Sep. 1408
33 courts for 9 Hen. IV
(8 membranes)

C/2/3/1/42   2 Oct. 1408–17 Sep. 1409
39 courts for 10 Hen. IV
(16 membranes)

C/2/3/1/43   1 Oct. 1409–25 Sep. 1410
37 courts for 11 Hen. IV
(16 membranes)

C/2/3/1/44   1 Oct. 1411–10 May 1412
23 courts for 13 Hen. IV
(8 membranes)

C/2/3/1/45   4 Oct. 1412–16 Mar. 1413
19 courts for 14 Hen. IV
(8 membranes)

C/2/3/1/46   30 Mar.–28 Sep. 1413
19 courts for 1 Hen. V
(8 membranes)

C/2/3/1/47   3 Oct. 1413–25 Sep. 1414
40 courts for 1–2 Hen. V
(17 membranes)

C/2/3/1/48   4 Oct. 1414–29 Sep. 1415
48 courts for 2–3 Hen. V
(18 membranes)

C/2/3/1/49   3 Oct. 1415–9 Apr. 1416
24 courts for 3–4 Hen. V
(10 membranes)

C/2/3/1/50   3 Dec. 1420, 28 Jan. 1421
2 courts for 8 Hen. V
The headings to both courts for the first time describe the Petty Court as 'Curia domini regis
tenta apud Gippewicum in Guihalda . . .', evidence that the Petty Court had by now superseded
the Portmanmote as the borough's principal judicial agency.
(2 detached membranes)

C/2/3/1/51   8 Jan. 1443–19 Nov. 1444
27 courts for 21–23 Hen. VI
(22 membranes)

C/2/3/2 COUNTER-ROLLS OF PETTY PLEAS   1322–1326

Each of these two rolls forms a continuous list of the pleas commenced during the administrative year. There are no headings for individual courts, and no dates are given for the commencement of any plea. Their function has not been positively determined, but the likelihood is that, since the earlier roll begins only two years after the reforming ordinances of 1320, they are Chamberlains' counter-rolls, made in pursuance of those reforms as part of the attempt to keep a continuous check on the power of the Bailiffs. They are the only surviving record of Petty Pleas for the period for which the Plea Rolls themselves have been lost.

C/2/3/2/1   1322–1323
(4 membranes, made up 'Exchequer' style, apparently in the wrong order: m. 2 bears the only heading, 'Querele Gippewici de Anno Regni Regis Edwardi xvj° incipientes a festo sancti Michaelis Arcangeli . . . tempore Johannis Harnays et W. Malyn tunc ballivorum . . .')

C/2/3/2/2   1325–1326
(4 membranes, made up 'Exchequer' style, m. 1 headed 'Rotulus Querelarum ville Gippewici tempore Gilberti de Burgh et Johannis Harneys', and all membranes endorsed with variants of the formula 'Rotulus querelarum de anno Regni Regis Edwardi xix°')

C/2/3/3 ESTREAT ROLLS   1467–1468

C/2/3/3/1   Sep. 1467–Sep. 1468
Names of parties to each plea; nature of plea; sums levied
(1 membrane, faded, some parts legible only under ultra-violet light)

C/2/3/4 RECORDS OF PLEAS REMITTED BY THE CENTRAL   1441–1445
COURTS

C/2/3/4/1   1441
Transcript of plea of trespass in Court of Common Pleas in Trinity Term
Stephen Denton *v* John, Prior of St Peter, Ipswich, Richard Waggestaft, his fellow-canon and Robert Fyssheman of Ipswich, bailiff; in which Bailiffs and burgesses of Ipswich claimed their court, and the case was ordered to be heard at Ipswich on 1 Aug. 1441
Annexed:
— writ to Sheriff of Suffolk to take security for appearance of plaintiff and defendants at Westminster in Michaelmas Term, 14 Sep. 1440
(Latin)

C/2/3/4/2   1445
Transcript of plea under Statute of Labourers in Court of Common Pleas in Easter Term
Gilbert Stonham *v* John Mansere of Ipswich, carpenter; in which Bailiffs and burgesses of Ipswich claimed their court, and the case was ordered to be heard at Ipswich on 20 May 1445
Annexed:
— writ to Sheriff of Suffolk to attach defendant for appearance at Westminster in Easter Term, 20 Jan. 1445
(Latin)

C/2/3/5 ENGROSSMENTS OF PETTY PLEAS   1474–1511

Each engrossment is the record of a single action in the Petty Court. The presence of royal writs, shorn of seals and margins, stitched to all except the first, suggests that it was the practice at this period to make such engrossments in cases where the central courts became involved.

The engrossments may perhaps have been intended for inclusion in the series of 'Dogget' rolls (see 'All Courts: Composite Enrolments', C/2/10/1 below).

C/2/3/5/1   3–10 Feb. 1474
Plea of debt on demand
John Byser *v* John Kent sen.
(1 membrane)

C/2/3/5/2   18 Apr.–7 Nov. 1475
Plea of debt on demand
Robert Casnell *v* Robert Deye of Ipswich
Annexed:
— Writ of Error removing case to the King's Bench, 24 Nov. 1475
(2 membranes, attached 'Chancery' style)

C/2/3/5/3   1 Apr.–10 Jun. 1477
Plea of trespass
John Hecham *v* Richard Cowpers
Annexed:
— jury list with 'guilty' verdict endorsed
— Writ of Error removing case to the King's Bench, 4 Nov. 1477
(1 membrane)

C/2/3/5/4   n.d.–6 Jun. 1508
Plea of debt
Robert Wright of Ipswich, carver, *v* Henry Man, executor of Angelus Bolton, late of Ipswich, shoemaker
Annexed:
— fragment of bond [3 Jul. 1502]
— writ instructing Bailiffs to determine the case, notwithstanding earlier writ for removing to Chancery the cause of the taking and detention of Henry Man, now in prison, 19 May 1509
(1 membrane)

C/2/3/5/5   29 Jul.–7 Oct. 1511
Plea of debt
Alexander Bramton *v* Robert Adle
Annexed:
— writ for appearance of defendant in the King's Bench at suit of John Middelton in plea of trespass, 22 Oct. 1511, with endorsement by Bailiffs that the cause of Adle's detention appears in schedule annexed to writ
(1 membrane)

C2/3/6   EXTRACTS OF PROCEEDINGS   1472–1575

Comparison with the Court Books which survive from 1486 (C/2/10/3) indicates that these enrolments are selective and, like the Composite Enrolments ('Dogget' Rolls) for the years 1438–1468 and 1478–1479 (C/2/10/1), do not constitute a complete record of proceedings. They may perhaps have been intended for inclusion in the series of 'Dogget' Rolls.

The main types of business recorded are: enrolment of deeds and wills, and occasionally of apprenticeship indentures, valuations of goods pledged, recognizances of debt and acceptance of arbitration (all of which are entered under dated court headings); and Petty Pleas of debt, trespass, covenant, detention of chattels and the like (all of which appear without heading or date, and many of which are incomplete).

C/2/3/6/1   1472–1478
Enrolments of deeds and wills only
(4 membranes)

C/2/3/6/2   1480–1481
Valuations of goods pledged, 1 enrolled deed, 1 recognizance of debt; Petty Pleas, mostly n.d.
Includes:
— (mm. 1–2) Petty Pleas, all incomplete, 1486–1487
(6 membranes)

C/2/3/6/3   1480–1481
1 enrolled deed; Petty Pleas, n.d.
(1 membrane; formerly part of C/2/3/6/2)

C/2/3/6/4   21 Jan.–18 Sep. 1483
2 recognizances of debt, 1 enrolled deed, 2 apprenticeship indentures
(1 membrane, numbered 5 in contemporary numeration but not pierced for attachment)

C/2/3/6/5   1486, 1489–1495
Recognizances of debt, to accept arbitration, etc; enrolled deeds
Includes:
— enrolment, 21 Apr. 1495, of Henry VII's charter, 30 Jan. 1486, exempting men and tenants
of manor of Blythburgh (of ancient demesne) from tolls and contributions to expenses of
knights of the shire in Parliament
(7 membranes, nos. 1–5 with contemporary numeration)

C/2/3/6/6   1495–1496
Recognizances of debt and to accept arbitration; recognizances before the Bailiffs, apparently
out of court
Includes:
— recognizance of debt taken before 1 Bailiff in St Clement's churchyard, 18 Dec. 1495
(1 membrane; ? formerly part of C/2/3/6/5)

C/2/3/6/7   1486–1487
Petty Pleas, all undated, all incomplete
(1 membrane, not pierced for attachment; dated by comparison with court book, C/2/10/3/1)

C/2/3/6/8   1486–1487
Petty Pleas, all undated, all incomplete
(1 membrane, not pierced for attachment; badly damaged by rodent action; dated by comparison with court book, C/2/10/3/1)

C/2/3/6/9   1486–1487
Enrolled deeds; Petty Pleas, all undated and most incomplete
(1 membrane, numbered 4, but not pierced for attachment; pleas dated by comparison with
court book, C/2/10/3/1)

C/2/3/6/10   1486–1487
Enrolled deeds; Petty Pleas, all undated and all incomplete
(1 membrane, numbered ? 2, but not pierced for attachment; pleas dated by comparison with
court book, C/2/10/3/1)

C/2/3/6/11   14 Apr.–16 May 1499
Lists of essoins, of licences to concord, of attachments and of fines for non-appearance; 3 pleas
of trespass (incomplete)
(1 membrane, not pierced for attachment; strip apparently cut from right-hand edge, and part of
text missing)

C/2/3/6/12   1509–1512
Petty Pleas (some incomplete), 1 recognizance of debt, 2 enrolled deeds
(5 membranes, with contemporary endorsement 'Rotule Record in i° & iij° H. viij°')

65

C/2/3/6/13   1 Oct.–6 Dec. 1537
4 enrolled wills
(1 membrane, not pierced for attachment)

C/2/3/6/14   1563–1568
Petty Pleas only
Dates of courts at which pleas commenced are omitted, but those of subsequent hearings are
normally given; some entries incomplete
(16 membranes)

C/2/3/6/15   1563–1568
1 Petty Plea only for 1563–1564; 1 Petty Plea and 1 recognizance of debt for 1567–1568
(2 detached membranes, rolled together, perhaps intended to form part of C/2/3/6/14)

C/2/3/6/16   1574–1575
Petty Pleas
Includes:
— Assize of Fresh Force, 1–20 Apr. 1574, in previous administrative year
(6 membranes; entries not in strict chronological sequence)

C/2/3/7   COURT BOOKS   1601–1843

The 17th- and 19th-century numeration of these volumes indicates that they are a continuation
(though obviously less comprehensive in their coverage) of the series of Composite Court
Books (C/2/10/3). Like that series, these volumes bear all the characteristics of minute books,
from which the formal enrolment of that select portion of the proceedings deemed worthy of
permanent retention was afterwards compiled. For the first half of the 17th century the proceedings tend to be very roughly entered, after which they become progressively neater and more
formal.

The most frequent business is judicial, the Petty Pleas themselves (mostly actions for debt
and trespass). There are brief entries for each plea, to which are added notes of process, together
with inventories and valuations of goods seized in execution in cases of debt. There are occasional transcripts of writs for removal of cases to the central courts or transfer of prisoners to
Westminster. Occasional assizes of Fresh Force (Novel Disseisin) occur in the 17th century.
Other Petty Court business recorded includes the swearing-in of the major officers of the
borough at Michaelmas following their election by the Great Court, and of lesser officers from
time to time during the year; the admission and discharge (for non-attendance or infirmity) of
court attorneys; the admission of freemen; and the enrolment of deeds.

The Court Books include minutes of recoveries of burgage tenements in the Portmanmote,
not always under Portmanmote headings. Very occasionally in the 18th century the initiating
Writ of Right was introduced in the Petty Court before the action of recovery commenced in the
next session of the Portmanmote. The last recovery in the Portmanmote was suffered in 1832.
The Portmanmote proceedings were recorded along with the Petty Pleas perhaps because the
latter, together with the recoveries, made up the whole of the civil litigation within the jurisdiction of the borough.

From June to September 1633, joint sessions of the Petty and Maritime Courts were held.
The pleas in both courts were of similar type.

The series of Court Books continues down to 1878, and the last two volumes are thus outside
the scope of this catalogue. After 1835, only pleas and memoranda of deeds enrolled (before the
Mayor and Coroners) are recorded. The last writ in a Petty Plea was issued on 14 August 1875;
subsequent entries refer only to the enrolment of deeds.

Except for the period April 1651–July 1660, when proceedings are in English, the language
of the record (except for some court orders and most inventories and valuations) is Latin down
to 1733.

C/2/3/7/1   Oct. 1601–Oct. 1606
Includes:
— ordinance *re* excessive court fees levied by Town Clerk, Attorney and Serjeants-at-Mace,
8 Oct. 1601
— (bound in following f. 100) parchment engrossment of plea of trespass, William Mathewe *v*
Rook Stott, n.d. (*post* 30 Apr. 1605)
(1 vol., 388 fols, front cover marked 'No. 26')

C/2/3/7/2   Oct. 1606–Sep. 1609
Includes:
— ordinance setting scale of fees for attorneys of the court, 28 Sep. 1608
— proceedings of Maritime Court, 3 Apr. 1609
(1 vol., 308 fols, ff 1–12 fragmentary, ff 295–306 blank; front cover marked 'No. 27')

C/2/3/7/3   Sep. 1609–Sep. 1611
Enclosed:
— engrossment of plea of debt, Henry Wright *v* William Ussett of Bramford, upholsterer, *post*
4 Jul. 1609
— interrogatories to witnesses in plea of trespass, Rauffe Norton *v* Robert Starlinge, n.d.
(1 vol., 316 unnumbered fols, 11 fols blank, 2 probably blank fols excised; front cover marked
(in a near-contemporary hand) 'No. 1' and (in a later hand) 'No. 28')

C/2/3/7/4   Sep. 1611–Sep. 1613
Enclosed:
— list of apprentices bound, with fees, Feb.–Apr., Sep. 1612
— original writ for production of Christopher Towlson, prisoner, at Westminster, 13 Jul. 1614
— account of free rents due to manor of Brokes Hall, many years in arrear, n.d.
(1 vol., 284 fols, nos 1–106 only numbered, 2 fols blank; front cover marked 'No. 2' and
'No. 29')

C/2/3/7/5   Sep. 1613–Feb. 1616
(1 vol., 404 fols; index of names A–C only; front cover marked 'No. 3' and 'No. 30')

C/2/3/7/6   Feb. 1616–Sep. 1619
(1 vol., 381 fols; title page inscribed in a contemporary hand 'The booke of small Pleaes'; front
cover marked 'No. 4' and 'No. 31')

C/2/3/7/7   Sep. 1619–Sep. 1623
(1 vol., 322 fols; front cover marked 'No. 5' and 'No. 32')

C/2/3/7/8   Sep. 1623–Apr. 1631
(1 vol., 451 fols; front cover marked 'No. 6' and 'No. 33')

C/2/3/7/9   Apr. 1631–Mar. 1637
Includes:
— joint sessions of Petty and Admiralty Courts (the formula of the headings is 'Curia [Domini
Regis] et Curia Admirall'), 14 Jun.–7 Sep. 1633
(1 vol., 430 unnumbered fols; front cover marked 'No. 7' and 'No. 34')

C/2/3/7/10   Apr. 1637–Mar. 1643
(1 vol., 283 unnumbered fols; 2 fols blank; front cover marked 'No. 8' and 'No. 35')

C/2/3/7/11   Mar. 1643–Sep. 1648
(1 vol., 280 unnumbered fols; 9 fols blank; front cover marked 'No. 9' and 'No. 36')

C/2/3/7/12   Sep. 1648–Mar. 1653
(1 vol., approx 284 unnumbered fols; 1st ?15 and last 4 fols fragmentary; badly damaged by
damp; Latin gives place to English from 16 Apr. 1651; front cover marked 'No. 10' and
'No. 37')

C/2/3/7/13   Mar. 1653–Mar. 1658
Includes:
— (at front) account of fees received by the court, 1653–1658
— memorandum of court's adjournment to Mr Bailiff Brandling's house in CL to enable him
to take his oath as Bailiff, he 'continewinge still sicke and weake and cannot come upp into the
Guild Hall', 9 Oct. 1655
(1 vol., 270 unnumbered fols; 14 fols blank; proceedings in English throughout, front cover
marked 'No. 11' and 'No. 38')

C/2/3/7/14   Apr. 1658–Oct. 1668
Includes:
— (at front) account of ? court fees received and sums laid out for proclamations etc.,
1659–1668
Enclosed:
— original writ for production of Robert Keble, prisoner, before the Justices at Westminster,
21 Jul. 1667
(1 vol., 439 unnumbered fols; 8 fols blank; proceedings revert to Latin from 3 Aug. 1660; front
cover marked 'No. 12' and 'No. 39')

C/2/3/7/15   Nov. 1668–Sep. 1676
Includes:
— (ff 1–4) account of ? court fees and expenses, 1668–1676
(1 vol., 290 fols, ff 5–8, 277–87 blank; front cover marked 'No. 13' and 'No. 40')

C/2/3/7/16   Sep. 1676–Jul. 1684
Includes:
— (at front) account of ? court fees and expenses, 1678–1684
— (at back) oath against taking arms against the King, and abjuring the Solemn League and
Covenant as an unlawful oath, with signatures of borough officers, 1677–1680
(1 vol., 255 unnumbered fols; front cover marked 'No. 14' and 'No. 41')

C/2/3/7/17   Jul. 1684–Oct. 1691
Includes:
– (ff 1–2) list of court sessions and adjournments, 1684–1688
– (ff 212–14) account of ? court fees, 1684–1688
(1 vol., 214 fols; front cover marked 'No. 15' and 'No. 42')

[*The volume covering the period Oct. 1691–Apr. 1701 and presumably marked 'No. 16' and
'No. 43' is missing.*]

C/2/3/7/18   Apr. 1701–Sep. 1713
Includes:
— (f. 1) form of oath of allegiance to Queen Anne and oath abjuring Papal authority, n.d.
— (ff 1v–2v) list of ? court fees, 1700–1705
— (f. 204) oath against taking arms against the Queen, with signatures of borough officers,
1703–1712
(1 vol., 205 fols; front cover marked 'No. 17' and 'No. 44')

[*The volume covering the period Sep. 1713–Nov. 1718 and presumably marked 'No. 18' and
'No. 45' is missing.*]

C/2/3/7/19   Nov. 1718–Mar. 1728
Includes:
— (at front) tables of fees payable to town officers for admission of freemen, recognizances of
deeds, water leases and recoveries, etc., and form of oath for Justices of the Peace
— (at back) list of water leases granted in time of Richard Love, Town Clerk, 1719–1720
(1 vol., 182 unnumbered fols; front cover marked 'No. 19' and 'No. 46')

C/2/3/7/20   Apr. 1728–Nov. 1745
(1 vol., 219 unnumbered fols; proceedings revert to English from 14 Apr. 1733; front cover
marked 'No. 20' and 'No. 47')

C/2/3/7/21   Nov. 1745–Sep. 1774
(1 vol., 310 fols; ff 1, 2, 306–310 blank; front cover marked 'No. 21' and 'No. 48')

C/2/3/7/22   Sep. 1774–Sep. 1804
(1 vol., 281 unnumbered fols)

C/2/3/7/23   Sep. 1804–Dec. 1834
The last recovery to be suffered in the Portmanmote took place 17–26 Sep. 1832
(1 vol., 286 unnumbered fols)

C/2/3/7/24   Jan. 1835–Sep. 1843
(1 vol., 272 unnumbered fols)

C/2/3/8 DEPOSITION BOOKS   1573–1651

These contain transcripts (not signed or sealed) of depositions made by, 'interrogatories' put to,
and answers given by witnesses, before the Bailiffs, in actions brought in the Petty Court. The
record is almost entirely in English throughout.

C/2/3/8/1   Feb. 1573–Feb. 1585
(1 vol., 610 pp)

C/2/3/8/2   Mar. 1584–Jan. 1651
(1 vol., 378 pp, pp 2–4, 204–18, 340, 347–78 blank; no entries recorded between 30 Sep. 1607
and 3 Feb. 1649; p 1 inscribed in a ? late 16c Secretary hand, among other pen-trials, 'I behaved
my selfe as though it hade bine my freind or my brother; I walked heavily as one that morneth
for his mother; I have bine younge but nowe ame old and yet never sawe the rightuous forsaken
nore his seede begginge their bread.')

C/2/3/9 VERDICT ROLLS   1586–1609

Except for C/2/3/9/1–2, each roll covers a single administrative year and is usually so endorsed.
Entries are in chronological order except in C/2/3/9/2 and C/2/3/9/8. The entry for each court
consists of lists of pleas (chiefly of debt and trespass), for which writs of *venire facias* or *habeas
corpus* were then returned, together with jury lists and verdicts. In the margins of some rolls are
notes of sums due for costs, in addition to the damages assessed by the jury. The proceedings
are in Latin throughout, except on the few occasions when extracts from English documents are
transcribed.

C/2/3/9/1   15 Mar. 1586
Verdict in one plea only
(2 membranes; endorsed in Nathaniel Bacon's hand, '28 El. Petticourt Trialls')

C/2/3/9/2   Jan.–Dec. 1590
Includes as wrapper:
— lease from Corporation to Nicholas Crane of Ipswich, tailor, of Cloth Hall under part of
Moot Hall, and farm of office of hallage and hall keeper, for 7 years at £8 2s 6d p.a. 25 Eliz.
(1582 or 1583)
(6 membranes; endorsed 'Verdicts Petty Court', and in Nathaniel Bacon's hand, 'Trials at the
Petty Court inrolled')

C/2/3/9/3   Dec. 1591–Oct. 1592
Includes as wrapper:

— apprenticeship indenture, John Wilbie, son of John Wilbie of Ipswich, weaver, to Nicholas Page of Ipswich, barber, 22 Eliz. (1579 or 1580)
— incomplete apprenticeship indenture, Hugh Burton, son of Thomas Burton, citizen and pewterer of London, to Robert Cutler jun., of Ipswich [*trade left blank*], n.d.
(10 membranes; endorsed in Nathaniel Bacon's hand, 'venire fac. 34 Eliz.')

C/2/3/9/4   Oct. 1593–Aug. 1594
Includes as wrapper:
— incomplete lease of watermill, [*blank*] Payne to Launcellott Harsted, for 21 years at £10 p.a., n.d. [16c.]
(5 membranes)

C/2/3/9/5   Oct. 1594–Sep. 1595
(3 membranes)

C/2/3/9/6   Oct. 1595–Sep. 1596
Includes as wrapper:
— record of plea of trespass upon the case, Henry Sharpe *v* Henry Fuller, 6 May–14 Aug. 1595 (membrane cut in 2 and incomplete: for the plea, see composite enrolments, C/2/10/1/41)
— fragment of manorial court roll with verdicts for Middleton, Kelsale, Knodishall and Buxlow, n.d. [16c.]
(7 membranes)

C/2/3/9/7   Dec. 1596–Sep. 1597
(4 membranes)

C/2/3/9/8   Dec. 1599–Sep. 1600
Includes as wrapper:
— incomplete apprenticeship indenture, Robert Kytson, son of Robert Kytson, to Richard Stannarde, tanner, n.d. [16c.]
— incomplete deed of bargain and sale of lands called Chapmans *alias* Barbaryes, Darbyes, Norrys, Buckes, Masons, Hamondes and Jurdons [*name of parish missing*], n.d. [16c.]
(6 membranes)

C/2/3/9/9   Oct. 1600–Sep. 1601
(4 membranes; endorsed in a 17c. hand, 'Verdicts')

C/2/3/9/10   Nov. 1602–Sep. 1603
(4 membranes; endorsed 'venire fac.')

C/2/3/9/11   Oct. 1603–Sep. 1604
(4 membranes)

C/2/3/9/12   Dec. 1604–Sep. 1605
Includes as outer detached wrapper (with endorsement indicating that it belonged originally to a roll for 3–4 Jac. I (1605–1606), now missing:
— apprenticeship indenture, Persivall Smythe of Ipswich, singleman, to John Feysie of Ipswich, sailcloth weaver, 1 Feb. 1588
(2 membranes)

C/2/3/9/13   Oct. 1608–Sep. 1609
(4 membranes)

C/2/3/10   BOOKS OF ACTIONS   **1760–1824**

Each folio is pre-embossed with stamps for duty payable, each entry being written in the space opposite a stamp.

C/2/3/10/1   Nov. 1760–Jun. 1776
Brief memoranda of debts sworn and amounts of damages awarded in pleas of trespass
(1 vol., 94 unnumbered fols; front cover inscribed in a contemporary hand, 'Ipswich Book of
Actions (No. 2)')

C/2/3/10/2   Jul. 1776–1824
Names of parties only
(1 vol., 228 unnumbered fols, 79 fols blank)

C/2/3/11   COURT FILES   1570–1591

The three surviving files, all dating from the Common Clerkship of John Hawys sen., contain
articles put to the juries in Petty Pleas, with details of verdicts, damages and costs added.
Between 1573 and 1576 a few jury lists also occur; from 1580 jury lists, together with lists of
pleas for which writs of *venire facias* and *habeas corpus* were returned, are usual. A few inventories of goods occur, and there are papers relating to pleas of Fresh Force and Dower between
June 1574 and October 1575. The files were apparently broken up at some stage, and refiled in
disorder. The language is mostly English. The Petty Court Verdict Rolls (C/2/3/9) contain fair
engrossments of similar records, including (C/2/3/9/1–2) those for courts of 15 Mar. 1586 and
20 Jan.–15 Dec. 1590 which are not recorded on these files.

C/2/3/11/1   Sep. 1570–Mar. 1584
Includes:
— (f 75v) draft of coroner's inquest on the body of Elizabeth Strutte, spinster, at Westerfield,
9 Nov. 1574
(136 docs, filed on string, in irregular chronological sequence)

C/2/3/11/2   Nov. 1584–Oct. 1588
(96 docs, filed on string)

C/2/3/11/3   Nov. 1579–Jul. 1591
(95 docs, filed on string)

C/2/3/12   COURT PAPERS   1456–1839

This series of papers in Petty Pleas in fact extends down to 1879, though its later years lie
outside the scope of this catalogue. Except for the two earliest documents, it includes throughout, plaintiffs' declarations setting out the circumstances of the plea. Plaintiffs' replications and
defendants' pleas and rejoinders also commonly occur, as do *Praecipes* for writs for the
appearance of defendants, affidavits of service, some writs, entries of appearance by or on
behalf of defendants, jury lists (sometimes giving verdicts), and bills of costs taxed by the
Common Clerk, with affidavits. For the period covered by the catalogue, bail bonds and bail
pieces (memoranda of recognizances on parchment) also occur (ceasing in 1838), together with
retainers for attorneys (ceasing 1842) and defendants' *cognovits* – confessions of plea (ceasing
1844). From 1800 onwards there are *Praecipes* for rules to plead, to enter judgement, etc. Until
1835 writs were tested by the Bailiffs, thereafter by the Recorder. Bail until 1835 was by bond
to the Bailiffs or bail piece made before a Bailiff; afterwards by bond to the Recorder or bail
piece before the Mayor.

C/2/3/12/1   10 Jul. 1456
Certificate of John Howard, esq., Robert Mannok, gent., Thomas Moleyns, gent., Robert
Rodyng, Thomas Wortham, John Hach, Thomas Chatrys, Robert Lunt, Hugh Smyth, Richard
Moor, John Barker and John Sergeant

That whereas George Page is impleaded in King's court in Ipswich before the Bailiffs in a plea
of debt upon demand of £18 at suit of John Howet of Stoke by Nayland, and it has been alleged
that Howet should disavow the suit since it was brought against his will, nevertheless Howet
will at all times avow whatever his attorney John Noreys shall do in the suit on his behalf
(English; 11 seals, 6 incomplete, on 4 tongues; 1 seal missing)

C/2/3/12/2   20 Oct. 1460
Certificate of Thomas Denys and William Rydout, Bailiffs
Of evidence taken before them in dispute between William Peke of Ipswich and Margaret
Kemp, widow, Thomas Kemp and Thomas Alvard of Woodbridge, executors of John Kemp of
Woodbridge, deceased, *re* payment of £50 due to Peke in exchange for lands and tenements to
the value of £100 with which he enfeoffed his sister Margaret, Kemp's wife, according to
agreement dated 12 Apr. 1454
(Latin; seal(s) and turn-up or tongue cut away)

C/2/3/12/3   28 Aug. 1599
Declaration in plea of trespass upon the case, Anthony Dove *v.* William Moyse
(1 doc)

C/2/3/12/4   Mar.–Sep. 1687
Declarations only
(11 docs)

C/2/3/12/5   25 Jun. 1687
Extract of proceedings in case of trespass upon the case, Samuel Fuller *v.* Robert Shuttleworth
(1 doc.)

C/2/3/12/6   1746–1758
(320 docs, formerly filed on a lace)

C/2/3/12/7   1781–1798
(749 docs, formerly filed on a lace; now stored in two parts, following conservation)

C/2/3/12/8   Sep. 1790–Sep. 1791
(102 docs, formerly filed on a lace)

C/2/3/12/9   Jul. 1790–Jan. 1794
(145 docs, formerly filed on a lace)

C/2/3/12/10   Nov. 1793–Mar. 1796
(61 docs, formerly filed on laces; some docs found with C/2/3/12/11 in 1950s and restored to
C/2/3/12/10 at that time)

C/2/3/12/11   Apr. 1799–Aug. 1807
Includes:
— sub-bundle of 18 plaintiffs' affidavits 'withdrawn', 27 May 1804–28 Nov. 1806
(260 docs)

C/2/3/12/12   Jul. 1804–Sep. 1810
(172 docs)

C/2/3/12/13   Jul. 1814–Oct. 1816
(160 docs)

C/2/3/12/14   Oct. 1820–Apr. 1822
(125 docs, filed on a string)

C/2/3/12/15   Nov. 1835–Aug. 1839
(470 docs)

C/2/3/13   BAIL BONDS   1822–1826

For appearance of defendants: taken before the Bailiffs

C/2/3/13/1   Jan. 1822–May 1826
(5 docs)

C/2/3/14   MINUTES OF PROCEEDINGS   1815

C/2/3/14/1   Feb.–Sep. 1815
Pleas and recognizance business (enrolment of deeds)
Includes:
— minutes of recovery in Portmanmote, George Vaux *v.* J.E. Sparrow, 23–25 Feb. 1815
(6 loose fols)

C/2/4   PETTY COURT OF RECOGNIZANCES   1294–1425

The record of recognizances of free tenement (transfers of real property, so-called from the grantor's formal acknowledgement of title – his avowal that the gift or sale was truly his act) comprises a register of titles to property within the liberties of the borough, which began in the last years of the 13th century and continued, in roll form until 1799 and thereafter, down to 1922, on parchment folios, many of which were (and the rest apparently intended to be) bound into volumes each covering several years. The general introduction to JUSTICE AND THE COURTS, above, has traced the evolution of the Recognizance Roll from the Portmanmote, and the subsequent development, by the middle of the 14th century, of this series of enrolments of documents produced in the Portmanmote and Petty Court into a separate Petty Court of Recognizances, which could be convened whenever required, even if only to witness a single transaction.

The series of Recognizance Rolls comes to an end in 1425. Thereafter, there are no surviving enrolments of deeds until 1438, when they are included on the 'Dogget' Rolls, which continue as a series of enrolled deeds down to the 20th century (*see* ALL COURTS: COMPOSITE ENROLMENTS, C/2/10/1 below). Minutes of recognizances may be found in the Composite Court Books, 1486–1549 (C/2/10/3) and the Petty Court Books, 1601–1843 (C/2/3/7). In the post-medieval period the Court Books show that the deeds were acknowledged and enrolled at ordinary sessions of the Court of Petty Pleas/Petty Court, along with such other court business as pleas of debt, trespass, etc. The independent existence of the Petty Court of Recognizances seems to have come to an end in the 15th century.

C/2/4/1   RECOGNIZANCE ROLLS   1294–1425

These consist primarily of transcripts of title deeds to burgage tenements granted or sold, the text of each deed accompanied by the memorandum of the grantor's recognizance or acknowledgement of title.

The first Recognizance Roll covers a period of six years, 1294–1300, and contains only six entries. Three of these are not straightforward recognizances, but compositions in Pleas of Abatement, the borough's version of the possessory assize of *Novel Disseisin*. The significance of these is discussed in the introductory note to the Abatement Rolls (C/2/4/2), below.

The last entry on the earliest Recognizance Roll also marks the first appearance of a very significant aspect of the record – the formal renunciation by a married woman of her title in the tenement that she and her husband have just conveyed or surrendered. A recognizance entered in that form in a borough court, secured by private examination before the magistrates (in Ipswich, the Bailiffs), was an absolute bar to any subsequent action of dower. The only other action offering the same assurance was the final concord levied before the King's justices at Westminster, and the registration of such disclaimers by married women was perhaps the most valuable of all the privileged customs of borough courts. Without that safeguard, or the expense of a final concord, the purchaser of a property had no defence against a married woman's subsequent allegation that she had acted under her husband's duress. As the result of a successful claim of dower by a widow was a life estate for herself in the property, followed perhaps by a life estate for a second husband, those who bought such property within a borough were well advised to secure a proper recognizance in the borough court (Martin 1973, 10).

From 1307 the Recognizance Rolls also attracted proofs of testaments (the first to be recorded on the Recognizance Roll was proved on 23 October that year), though both recognizances and testaments occasionally appear on the Portmanmote Roll for some years thereafter. Actions of Abatement also appear on the Recognizance Rolls between 1323 and 1332.

Though the Petty Plea Rolls for Edward II's reign are lost, it is plain that the Petty Court gradually came to produce a substantial portion of the business entered on the Recognizance Rolls. Though these rolls thus shared in the proceedings of both Portmanmote (Great Court) and Petty Court, the hearing of recognizances and proving of testaments was principally a function of the Petty Court by Edward III's reign.

In the 1340s, when lack of business in the Portmanmote sometimes produced on its roll a number of headings in the year with no business entered, the Recognizance Roll attracted the admissions of free burgesses also. From 1360 until 1394, during which period the Portmanmote Roll ceased to be maintained, this class of business is regularly recorded on the Recognizance Roll, which is by now the record of a distinct Petty Court of Recognizances.

Proceedings are in Latin throughout. The names of the presiding Bailiffs, which usually appear in the headings to the rolls, are only given in this catalogue for the years after the Portmanmote Roll (which also records their names) was discontinued.

C/2/4/1/1   16 Dec. 1294–22 Dec. 1300
For 23–29 Edw. I
Headed 'Rotulus de Recognicionibus liberi tenementi in Gypewyco . . .'; printed in Martin 1973, 15–27
(1 membrane, dorse blank; not pierced for attachment to Portmanmote/Great Court roll)

C/2/4/1/2   23 Oct. 1307–29 Aug. 1308
For 1–2 Edw. II
Printed in Martin 1973, 33–36
(2 membranes)

C/2/4/1/3   10 Oct. 1308–22 Jun. 1312
For 2–5 Edw. II
Printed in Martin 1973, 39–54
(6 membranes, attached in reverse chronological order)

C/2/4/1/4   27 Jul. 1312–27 Sep. 1313
For 6–7 Edw. II
Printed in Martin 1973, 54–57
(2 membranes; m. 2, containing 1 entry only, for 27 Jul. 1312, endorsed 'Rotuli de Recognicionibus liberi Tenementi et de Testamentis probatis Tempore Regis Edwardi filij Regis Edwardi de diversis Annis [ij° iij° iiij° v° *interlined*] Thoma Stace et Thoma le Rente Tunc Ballivis', indicating that it was formerly the outer membrane of C/2/4/1/3)

C/2/4/1/5   24 Oct. 1314–17 Jul. 1315
For 8–9 Edw. II
Printed in Martin 1973, 58–63
(2 membranes)

C/2/4/1/6   23 Oct. 1315–23 Sep. 1316
For 9–10 Edw. II
Printed in Martin 1973, 63–75
(5 membranes)

C/2/4/1/7   21 Oct. 1316–*post* 16 Dec. 1316
For 10 Edw. II
Printed in Martin 1973, 75–77
(1 membrane, badly damaged)

C/2/4/1/8   6 Oct. 1317–14 Sep. 1318
For 11–12 Edw. II
Printed in Martin 1973, 77–85
(3 membranes)

C/2/4/1/9   5 Oct. 1318–4 Oct. 1319
For 12–13 Edw. II
Printed in Martin 1973, 85–90
(2 membranes)

C/2/4/1/10   15 Nov. 1319–18 Sep. 1320
For 13–14 Edw. II
Printed in Martin 1973, 90–92
(1 membrane)

C/2/4/1/11   21 Oct. 1320–25 Jun. 1321
For 14–15 Edw. II
Printed in Martin 1973, 92–97
(2 membranes)

C/2/4/1/12   3 Dec. 1321–17 Sep. 1322
For 15–16 Edw. II
Printed in Martin 1973, 97–102
(2 membranes)

C/2/4/1/13   1 Oct. 1322–13 Jun. 1323
For 16–17 Edw. II
Printed in Martin 1973, 102–12
(3 membranes)

C/2/4/1/14   16 Nov. 1323–16 Aug. 1324
For 17–18 Edw. II
Printed (except for m. 3) in Martin 1973, 112–20
Includes:
— (as m. 3) Abatement Roll for year commencing Michaelmas 17 Edw. II (1323), recording
actions 7 Nov. 1323–4 Apr. 1324
(5 membranes)

C/2/4/1/15   9 Nov. 1324–27 Sep. 1325
For 18–19 Edw. II
Printed (except for m. 3r) in Martin 1973, 120–24
Includes:
— (as m. 3r) Abatement Roll for year commencing Michaelmas 18 Edw. II (1324), recording 1
action, 19 Aug. 1325; 1 testament entered on dorse, 27 Sep. 1325
(3 membranes)

C/2/4/1/16   10 Oct. 1325–19 Sep. 1326
For 19–20 Edw. II
Printed in Martin 1973, 125–29
(2 membranes)

C/2/4/1/17   6 Nov. 1326–4 Sep. 1327
For 20 Edw. II–1 Edw. III
Printed in Martin 1973, 129–32
(1 membrane)

C/2/4/1/18   27 Mar. 1327–23 Sep. 1327
For 1 Edw. III
Printed in Martin 1973, 132–37
(2 membranes)

C/2/4/1/19   14 Oct. 1327–28 Sep. 1328
For 1–2 Edw. III
(3 membranes, attached in reverse chronological order)

C/2/4/1/20   2 Nov. 1328–6 Aug. 1329
For 2–3 Edw. III
(3 membranes)

C/2/4/1/21   7 Nov. 1330–26 Sep. 1331
For 4–5 Edw. III
(3 membranes)

C/2/4/1/22   10 Oct. 1331–16 Sep. 1332
For 5–6 Edw. III
(4 membranes)

C/2/4/1/23   2 Oct. 1332–19 Sep. 1333
For 6–7 Edw. III
(4 membranes)

C/2/4/1/24   3 Jan.–31 Aug. 1334
For 7–8 Edw. III
(3 membranes, attached in reverse chronological order)

C/2/4/1/25   4 Oct. 1334–18 Apr. 1336
For 8–10 Edw. III
(3 membranes, attached out of chronological sequence, which is m. 2, m. 1, m. 3, m. 4)

C/2/4/1/26   23 Dec. 1337–7 Sep. 1338
For 11–12 Edw. III
(2 membranes)

C/2/4/1/27   27 Oct. 1338–22 Jul. 1339
For 12–13 Edw. III
(2 membranes)

C/2/4/1/28   27 Oct. 1339–29 Sep. 1340
For 13–14 Edw. III
(3 membranes)

C/2/4/1/29   6 Oct. 1340–26 Sep. 1341
For 14–15 Edw. III
(3 membranes)

C/2/4/1/30   10 Oct. 1341–25 Sep. 1342
For 15–16 Edw. III
(4 membranes; ascenders of letters of 1st line of heading to m. 1 elaborately decorated with grotesque human faces, oak leaves, etc.)

C/2/4/1/31   10 Oct. 1342–25 Sep. 1343
For 16–17 Edw. III
(3 membranes)

Fig. 4. Decorated headings, the ascenders of the letters embellished with grotesque human faces, oak leaves and acorns. (*Left*) The heading to the Recognizance Roll for 1341–42. (C/2/4/1/30). (*Right*) The heading to the court of 27 December 1341 in the Portmanmote Roll for 1341–42. (C/2/1/1/48).

C/2/4/1/32   22 Oct. 1343–29 Sep. 1344
For 17–18 Edw. III
(4 membranes)

C/2/4/1/33   3 Nov. 1344–21 Aug. 1345
For 18–19 Edw. III
Between 28 Feb. and 28 Jun. 1345, charters and testaments are enrolled before Edmund Noon
of Tilney (Norfolk), Deputy to Sir John Howard, Sheriff of Norfolk and Suffolk, *Custos* of the
town [which had been taken into the King's hands following a riot by sailors, who held a mock
trial on the Assize judge]
(3 membranes)

C/2/4/1/34   5 Oct. 1345–31 Mar. 1346
For 19–20 Edw. III
(1 membrane)

C/2/4/1/35   8 Jun.–28 Sep. 1346
For 20 Edw. III
(2 membranes; ? formerly attached to C/2/4/1/34)

C/2/4/1/36   2 Oct. 1346–18 Sep. 1347
For 20–21 Edw. III
(5 membranes)

C/2/4/1/37   19 Oct. 1347–23 Sep. 1348
For 21–22 Edw. III
(3 membranes)

C/2/4/1/38   20 Oct. 1348–27 Aug. 1349
For 22–23 Edw. III
The large number of testaments (52) proved during this period, which account for the unusual
bulk of the roll, reflect the high rate of mortality caused by the visitation of the Black Death
(9 membranes)

C/2/4/1/39   8 Jan.–19 Aug. 1350
For 23–24 Edw. III
(2 membranes)

C/2/4/1/40   11 Nov. 1350–15 Feb. 1351
For 24–25 Edw. III
(1 membrane)

C/2/4/1/41   13 Dec. 1351–26 Jul. 1359
John de Prestone, Walter Curteys, Bailiffs 1351–1352; John Cobet, Henry Rotoun, Bailiffs
1352–1353; John Cobet, Richard Haverynlond, Bailiffs 1353–1354; John Cobat, Thomas dil
Stoon, Bailiffs 1354–1355; Geoffrey Starlyng, Robert Tebrand, Bailiffs 1355–1356; Thomas
Mayster, Richard Haverynlond, Bailiffs 1356–1357; Walter Curteys, Henry Starlyng, Bailiffs
1357–1358; Thomas del Ston, Thomas de Eustone, Bailiffs 1358–1359
For 25–33 Edw. III
(13 membranes)

C/2/4/1/42   3 Mar.–30 Aug. 1360
Thomas le Mayster, Henry Starlyng, Bailiffs
For 34 Edw. III
The first Recognizance Roll to record (on 30 Aug.) the admission of burgesses, reflecting the
failure after Sep. 1351 to maintain the record of the Portmanmote/Great Court, on whose rolls
such admissions were previously recorded
(1 membrane)

C/2/4/1/43   22 Oct. 1361–25 Aug. 1362
Henry Starlyng, Walter Curteys, Bailiffs
For 35–36 Edw. III
(2 membranes, attached at the feet, in reverse chronological order)

C/2/4/1/44   25 Oct. 1362–22 Sep. 1363
Robert Thebaud, Thomas le Mayster, Bailiffs
For 36–37 Edw. III
(2 membranes, attached at the feet, in reverse chronological order)

C/2/4/1/45   6 Feb.–20 Sep. 1364
Henry Starlyng, Walter Curteys, Bailiffs
For 38 Edw. III
(1 membrane)

C/2/4/1/46   10 Oct. 1364–19 Sep. 1365
Thomas le Mayster, Robert de Prestone, Bailiffs
For 38–39 Edw. III
(2 membranes, attached at the feet, in reverse chronological order)

C/2/4/1/47   3 Oct. 1365–18 Sep. 1366
Robert Thebaud, Robert de Prestone, Bailiffs
For 39–40 Edw. III
(1 membrane)

C/2/4/1/48   21 Dec. 1366–8 Sep. 1367
Henry Starlyng, Robert Waleys, Bailiffs
For 40–41 Edw. III
(2 membranes, attached at the feet; entries not in chronological sequence)

C/2/4/1/49   2 Dec. 1367–31 May 1369
Hugh Lew, Robert Prestone, Bailiffs
For 41–43 Edw. III
(3 membranes, attached at the feet; the chronological sequence is m. 2, m. 1, m. 3)

C/2/4/1/50   6 Apr. 1370–26 Jun. 1371
John Cobat, Henry Starlyng, Bailiffs 1369–1370; Geoffrey Starlying, Robert de Prestone, Bailiffs 1370–1371
For 44–45 Edw. III
(2 membranes, attached at the feet, in reverse chronological order)

C/2/4/1/51   31 Dec. 1372–12 Feb. 1377
William le Maistre, Hugh Walle, Bailiffs 1372–1373; Henry Starlying, Robert Waleys, Bailiffs 1373–1374; Robert de Prestone, Hugh Walle, Bailiffs 1374–1375; Hugh Lew, Robert Waleys, Bailiffs 1375–1376; Geoffrey Starlying jun., Hugh Walle, Bailiffs 1376–1377
For 46–51 Edw. III
(5 membranes, attached in reverse chronological order)

C/2/4/1/52   29 Oct. 1377–12 Jun. 1380
Geoffrey Starlyng sen., Robert Waleys, Bailiffs 1377–1379; William le Maister, Roger Gosewold, Bailiffs 1379–1380
For 1–3 Ric. II
(4 membranes)

C/2/4/1/53   18 Jul. 1381–28 Mar. 1385
Geoffrey Starlyng jun., Hugh Walle, Bailiffs 1381–1384; Geoffrey Starlyng, Robert Waleys, Bailiffs 1384–1385
For 5–8 Ric. II
m. 6 is a duplicate of m. 4 (1 Oct. 1383–14 Jun. 1384), and m. 3 (21 Jun. 1384) a partial

duplicate of m. 7 (21 Jun.–8 Sep. 1384); the duplicates are rare survivals of the Chamberlains' counter-rolls
(7 membranes)

C/2/4/1/54   10 Nov. 1384–29 Sep. 1387
Geoffrey Starlyng, Robert Waleys, Bailiffs 1384–1386; John Andreu, William atte Fen, Bailiffs 1386–1387
For 8–11 Ric. II
m. 5 of C/2/4/1/53 (10 Nov. 1384–28 Mar. 1385) duplicates part of m. 1 (10 Nov. 1384–28 Sep. 1385) of this roll; the duplicate is a rare survival of the Chamberlains' counter-rolls
(3 membranes)

C/2/4/1/55   12 Dec. 1387–8 Sep. 1391
Geoffrey Starlyng, Robert Waleys, Bailiffs 1387–1389; Geoffrey Starlyng, John Andrewe, Bailiffs 1389–1391
For 11–15 Ric. II
(4 membranes)

C/2/4/1/56   6 May 1389–13 Jul. 1391
For 12–15 Ric. II
Duplicate [Chamberlains' counter-roll] of m. 2 and m. 4 of C/2/4/1/55
(2 membranes)

C/2/4/1/57   28 Nov. 1392–15 Jul. 1395
Geoffrey Starlyng, John Arnald, Bailiffs 1392–1393; Gilbert de Boulge, William dil Fen, Bailiffs 1393–1395
For 16–19 Ric. II
The last of the Recognizance Rolls to record the admission of burgesses, which they had done since 1360 following the demise of the Portmanmote/Great Court Roll. M. 3 (28 Nov. 1392–12 Jun. 1393) is a duplicate [Chamberlains' counter-roll] of m. 2
(6 membranes, not in strict chronological sequence)

C/2/4/1/58   9–23 Jul. 1394
For 18 Ric. II
Duplicate [Chamberlains' counter-roll] of m. 5 of C/2/4/1/57
(1 membrane)

C/2/4/1/59   22 Sep. 1394–16 Sep. 1399
Gilbert de Boulge, William dil Fen, Bailiffs 1394–1395; Geoffrey Starlyng, Robert Lucas, Bailiffs 1395–1396; John Bernard, John Avelyne, Bailiffs 1396–1397; John Arnald, Robert Lucas, Bailiffs 1397–1398; John Avelyne, John Arnald, Bailiffs 1398–1399
For 18–23 Ric. II
(6 membranes)

C/2/4/1/60   1 Jul. 1400–9 Sep. 1404
John Lew, John Parker, Bailiffs 1399–1400; John Lew, John Avelyne, John Horkeslee, Bailiffs 1400–1401; Richard Cherche, John Bernard, Bailiffs 1401–1402; John Horkeslee, William Debenham, Bailiffs 1402–1403; John Starlyng, John Avelyne, Bailiffs 1403–1404
For 1–5 Hen. IV
Includes:
— 1 admission of an heiress (Margery, daughter of John Howet) on proof of majority, 1 Feb. 1403
(3 loose membranes, rolled together, not pierced for attachment)

C/2/4/1/61   20 Jan. 1405–15 Nov. 1412
John Starlyng, Robert Lucas, Bailiffs 1404–1405; Robert Lucas, Thomas Andrew, Bailiffs 1405–1406; John Horkeslee, Thomas Andrew, Bailiffs 1406–1407; John Starlyng, John Kneppyng, Bailiffs 1407–1408; John Rous, Robert Lucas, Bailiffs 1408–1409; John

Horkeslee, John Kneppyng, Bailiffs 1409–1411; John Starlyng, Thomas Andrew, Bailiffs 1411–1413
For 6–14 Hen. IV
Includes, as wrapper:
— engrossment of plea of trespass in the Petty Court, John Warde v Ralph de Peyton, 18 Feb.–1 Mar. 1412
(10 + 1 membranes)

C/2/4/1/62   6 Jul. 1413–31 Mar. 1422
John Starlyng, Thomas Andrew, Bailiffs 1412–1413; John Horkeslee, John Kneppyng, Bailiffs 1413–1414; William Debenham, Hugh Hoo, Bailiffs 1414–1415; John Horkeslee, John Kneppyng, Bailiffs 1415–1416; John Starlyng, Hugh Hoo, Bailiffs 1416–1417; William Debenham, Robert Lucas, Bailiffs 1417–1420; John Kneppyng, John Joye, Bailiffs 1420–1422
For 1–10 Hen. V
(5 membranes)

C/2/4/1/63   20 Jan. 1405–24 Mar. 1422
[Chamberlains'] duplicate of Recognizance Rolls
For 6 Hen. IV–10 Hen. V
(Paper vol. of 18 fols (5 blank); parchment cover cut from membrane of [Chamberlains'] duplicate Recognizance Roll for 6 Hen. IV with enrolments 17 Mar.–24 Sep. 1405, whose mutilation apparently marks the abandonment of the roll format for the duplicate record; see Martin 1955, 122)

C/2/4/1/64   29 Sep. 1422–18 Jan. 1425
John Kneppyng, John Joye, Bailiffs 1421–1422; Thomas Asteley, John Dekene, Bailiffs 1422–1425
For 1–3 Hen. VI
(1 membrane, not pierced for attachment)

C/2/4/2   ABATEMENT ROLLS   1308–1329, 1443–1444

As mentioned briefly in the introductory note to the Recognizance Rolls (C/2/4/1), the earliest such roll, for 1294–1300, records three compositions in Pleas of Abatement, the borough's version of the possessory Assize of *Novel Disseisin* (more generally known in other boroughs, and also in Ipswich in the 15th and 16th centuries, as the Assize of Fresh Force). In a Plea of Abatement, the court was concerned only with the question of seisin, or validated occupation of a tenement, rather than with the absolute right to property. The issue to be judged was simply whether the plaintiff had been disseised; if disseisin was adjudged to have taken place by force and arms (*vi et armis*), the defendant was imprisoned. The action could thus be used to reinstate a tenant whose title was inferior to that of the ejector. Its great advantage over the solemn real action commenced by royal Writ of Right (in Ipswich, in the Portmanmote) was its speed: the plaintiff had to initiate the plea within forty days of the alleged offence (the tenement in question being meanwhile seized by the Bailiffs and viewed by a jury). No essoins (postponements of the hearing at the request of one or other party) were permitted, and the non-appearance of the defendant could at once be adjudged a default and judgement given for the plaintiff.

The successful prosecution of such an action, though it might restore a tenement to its rightful owner, did not bestow an absolute title, which could only be tested by a real action brought upon a Writ of Right. In practice, however, judgements in actions of Abatement in Ipswich seem very rarely to have been overturned. The earliest such actions recorded on the first Recognizance Roll were resolved by agreement between the parties, specifying the right of one of them, which in effect transformed a possessory into a real action, the record of which, entered on the court roll, confirmed absolute title. The successful party thus secured his estate by a much shorter process, and probably much more cheaply, than would have been possible by an action commenced by royal writ (Martin 1955, 40–41; Martin 1973, 10).

The Plea of Abatement seems to have been in fairly common use in Ipswich by the end of Edward I's reign. The Abatement Roll was the last class of record to emerge from the old composite roll of the Portmanmote, though it only briefly and uncertainly attained a separate existence, and never achieved the status of its own court. The compilation of the Abatement Rolls was almost certainly inspired by the emergence of the separate Recognizance Rolls, on which the earliest Pleas of Abatement appear, and they emerge immediately after them at the beginning of Edward II's reign, in 1308. Like the early Recognizance Rolls, they are simply a collection of one particular class of entry from the proceedings of an existing court, gathered together for convenience on one or more membranes.

Though the first four rolls, for the years 1308–1316, the roll for 1321–1322, and that for December 1329, all listed in this section, are separate records, others in the series were either never detached from the rolls of the parent court or (certainly in the case of the Abatement Roll for 1318) were wrongly attached at a later date. The Abatement Roll for April 1318 is now attached to part of the Portmanmote Roll for 1273 (C/2/1/1/4); that for November 1323–April 1324 to the Recognizance Roll for November 1323–August 1324 (C/2/4/1/14); and two rolls for 19 August 1325 to the duplicate Portmanmote Roll (Chamberlains' Counter-roll) for October 1324–September 1325 (C/2/1/1/32) and to the Recognizance Roll for November 1324–September 1325 (C/2/4/1/15) respectively. In addition, actions of Abatement, not gathered on to separate membranes, continue to be recorded on the Recognizance Rolls between 1325–1326 and 1331–1332.

The Abatement Roll for 3 Edward III, for December 1329, the latest surviving separate roll, was probably the last that had a separate existence, for after that time the number of such pleas diminished. The isolated single membrane for 1443–1444, containing what is by then described as a Plea of Fresh Force, is apparently detached from a Petty Court Roll.

In the later 16th century, enrolments of Pleas of Fresh Force are found occasionally among the Composite Enrolments: in 1572 (C/2/10/1/17), 1574 (C/2/10/1/22), 1580 (C/2/10/1/23), and 1583 (C/2/10/1/27).

C/2/4/2/1   13 Feb. 1308–29 Aug. 1309
12 actions for 1–3 Edw. II
(1 membrane)

C/2/4/2/2   13 Mar. 1310–21 Jul. 1312
7 actions for 3–6 Edw. II
(1 membrane)

C/2/4/2/3   *post* 29 Sep. 1312–24 Apr. 1313
2 actions for 6 Edw. II
(1 membrane)

C/2/4/2/4   16 Jan. 1315–14 Jul. 1316
10 actions for 8–10 Edw. II
(2 membranes, attached at the feet, in reverse chronological order)

C/2/4/2/5   *post* 29 Sep. 1321–1 Mar. 1322 and n.d.
3 actions for 15–16 Edw. II
(1 membrane)

C/2/4/2/6   20 Dec. 1329
1 action for 3 Edw. III
(1 membrane)

C/2/4/2/7   6 Aug. 1443–17 Sep. 1444
Assize of Fresh Force Roll
Plea, William Walworth and wife Margaret *v* William Debenham, *re 3s* annual rent out of free tenement in MT, Ipswich; continued from court to court
(1 membrane, apparently detached from a Petty Court roll)

C/2/5 MARITIME COURT

1434–post 1446

This court decided disputes concerning strangers passing through the port, and could therefore be adjourned from tide to tide. The pleas determined were similar in nature to those held in the Petty Court involving inhabitants of the borough. For proceedings of the Maritime Court in October 1464, see 'All Courts: Composite Enrolments' (C/2/10/1/2), and for proceedings at intervals between 1488 and 1507, see 'All Courts: Composite Court Books' (C/2/10/3/1,2,5,6).

C/2/5/1   COURT ROLLS

1434

C/2/5/1/1 30 Oct.–5 Nov. 1434
Pleas of account, debt and covenant
(Latin; 1 membrane; courts headed 'Curia ad legem maritinam' and held before the Bailiffs)

C/2/5/2   MISCELLANEA

post 1446

C/2/5/2/1 17 Apr. [post 1446]
Certificate of Thomas Denys and John Deken, Bailiffs, Robert Wade, William Walworth, William Wethereld, Peter Terry, Robert Smyth, John Drayell and Richard Felawe, Portmen, and commonalty of Ipswich
In dispute between John Caldewell of Ipswich and Hans Stendell of Danzig, merchants; certifying that Caldewell did not appoint Thomas Bradde his then apprentice to be his factor with power to act in matters of commercial credit; and that Bradde was proved during his apprenticeship to be in arrears in sum of £138 10s. to Caldewell and was committed to Ipswich gaol until he should give satisfaction.
(Latin; damaged by damp and incomplete; Common Seal, tag and turn-up cut away)

C/2/6 ADMIRALTY

1400–1440

The High Court of Admiralty was founded by Edward I for the prevention and punishment of piracy and the settlement of questions of prizes and wreck. It was established as a Civil Court by Edward III in 1360, and until 1391 claimed jurisdiction over all contracts and pleas relating to maritime affairs. By Henry VI's charter of 1446 the Admiral of England was deprived of jurisdiction within the liberties of Ipswich, and in 1463 Edward IV specifically conferred these powers on the Bailiffs. The town's Admiralty jurisdiction was ratified by Richard III's charter of 1485, and its extent clarified by Henry VIII in 1519. Though the documents listed here antedate the borough's grants of Admiralty jurisdiction, they are brought together for convenience under this heading.

C/2/6/1 21 May 1400
Inquisition taken before John Scardeburgh, esq. and William de Thorp of Harwich, deputies to Thomas Percy, Earl of Worcester, Admiral of England and Ireland, at Harwich [Essex], near the seashore
Re a case of piracy; the jurors found that John Frenssh, Robert Cobet, fuller, and Michael Dyster of Ipswich hired Robert Dysse and John Scholond of Fyssebane [sic], mariners, to sail Dysse's boat to Harwich, and that while in the Orwell, induced them to seize a vessel of William Fuller of Nacton, from which they took goods, a boy, and Sir John Brygge, a priest, whom they robbed of 2 purses containing 5 marks of gold and 5 marks of silver
(Latin; names of 18 jurors; seals, turn-up or tongues cut away)

C/2/6/2   29 Apr. 1438
Inquisition indented taken before Robert Wode and William Keche, Bailiffs, in the Wardmote
Re an attempt to defraud the royal customs; the jurors found that a cargo of wool and skins was
shipped to Ipswich by Joceus Cosyns of Utrecht on 21 Apr. 1438 and stored by William Horald
and Thomas Ingram of Ipswich in a house belonging to Thomas Cadon, and on the night of
26 Apr. was loaded by Horald and Ingram on to Ingram's boat to avoid customs and cocket
duty; following seizure by a Serjeant-at-Mace, boat and cargo were taken to Woolverstone by
Horald and Ingram, with intent to defraud the King
(Latin; names of 13 jurors and fragments of seals of 11 of them on 3 tongues)

C/2/6/3   24 Nov. 1440
Certificate of Robert Wode and Peter Terry, Bailiffs
Re testimony given by Matys Mathuesson and John Coteroke of Bargh' in Brabant, at instance
of Rumbald Herryesson, burgess of Ipswich, as to how, while on board Herryesson's ship 'le
Cogship', freighted on 21 May 1440 with cheese and other victuals, bound from port of Orwell
to Calais, they and their vessel were captured by 3 ships of Dieppe and Harflete and carried
towards Picardy, but regained possession of ship and cargo and brought them into port of
Sandwich [Kent]
(Latin; Common Seal and tag missing)

C/2/6/4   24 Nov. 1440
Draft certificate of Bailiffs, Portmen and commonalty
Re testimony given by Matys Mathuesson, John Coteroke and Peter Arnnoldesson, all of
Bargh' in Brabant, and John Mathu of Ipswich, late Serjeant, in case described in C/2/6/3
(Latin; unsealed)

C/2/7   CORONERS' SESSIONS   1329–1581

King John's charter empowered the burgesses to elect four Coroners to keep the Pleas of the
Crown within the liberties of Ipswich and to act as a check on the Bailiffs. In practice two
Coroners were elected annually, and sat alongside the Bailiffs to hear pleas in the borough
courts. Of the Coroners' more familiar function, that of holding inquests, the two rolls listed
below are the only ones to have survived. Original inquisitions may be found in the Sessions
Rolls (C/2/9/1/1/1) between 1722 and 1765, and in the Sessions Bundles (C/2/9/1/1/6) between
1799 and 1825.

C/2/7/1   CORONERS' ROLLS   **1329–1581**

C/2/7/1/1   6 Feb. 1329–*post* 25 Jan. 1340
John Irp, William de Causton, clerk, Coroners
31 inquisitions: 18 verdicts of murder, 'felonious slaying' or other deaths by violence (usually
by stabbing); 6 of accidental drowning; 1 death by lightning-strike; 3 of natural causes; and 3
records of confession following sanctuary, 2 resulting in the felon abjuring the realm.
(Latin; 3 membranes, attached 'Exchequer' style; last membrane faded and defective, and date
of last entry partly illegible; calendared in HMC 1883, 226–27)

C/2/7/1/2   17 Jan.–16 Jul. 1581
John Brenne, William Bloyse, Coroners
3 inquisitions: 2 verdicts of accidental death in the river, 1 of homicide
(Latin; 1 membrane)

C/2/7/2 MINUTES OF EVIDENCE   n.d.

C/2/7/2/1   [later 18c.]
Minutes of evidence given at inquest into death of unnamed seaman
(1 doc.)

C/2/8   THE LEET   1359–1789

The Leet had its origin in the Anglo-Saxon system known as Frankpledge, whereby the lay adult male population was divided into tithings of ten households, each tithing having a corporate responsibility for its members' conduct and for ensuring that alleged offenders appeared in court to answer the charge. In the shires, jurisdiction lay with the sheriff's tourn, but in franchises such as boroughs and manors the enforcement of Frankpledge was the responsibility of the Leet. Each tithing was administered by a tithingman (also known as borsholder, headborough or thirdborough).

By the late 13th century nothing was left of the tithing system except the formality of seeing that all men belonged, at least in theory, to a tithing-group (*decenna*); this was done by the View of Frankpledge, which from the later Middle Ages brought the Leet some profit from amercements on defaulters, but contributed little to the maintenance of law and order. The Leet did however retain a criminal jurisdiction over breaches of the King's peace involving wounding until the Act of 1 Edward IV cap. 2 (1461). Thereafter its chief functions were the upholding of the Assizes of Bread and Ale (i.e., ensuring that the produce of bakers and brewers met the required standards of quality and quantity), and the punishment of other trading offences and the wide and elastic class of offence denoted as a 'common nuisance'. The abatement of nuisances by the Leet was in fact the root from which sprang such services as the maintenance of highways, the drainage of towns, the paving, cleansing and lighting of streets, and the whole of what is now called 'Public Health'. The criminal jurisdiction of the Leet became the province of the Justices of the Peace in their sessions.

Procedure in the Leet was by presentment; the jury presented offenders out of their own knowledge, with no necessity to hear witnesses. The jury also indicated the appropriate amercement, and its presentment was then referred to 'Affeerors', officers appointed to assess the amercement, which was usually less than the maximum indicated.

In Ipswich an annual View of Frankpledge was prescribed in the custumal, to be held on the Tuesday in Whitsun week. This, together with the Leet, was held before the Bailiffs, and presentments were made by a jury of Capital Pledges or Headboroughs, three for each of the four Wards (North, South, East and West) of the town. When the borough Assembly, consisting of the twelve principal Portmen and twenty-four Capital Burgesses, emerged as an advisory body to the General or Great Court of the borough, the Headboroughs came to be chosen from among the Assembly's members.

On the Leet in general, see Harvey 1984, 46–47 and Webb 1963, 21–30.

C/2/8/1 LEET ROLLS   1359–1569

These comprise the presentments by the Capital Pledges ('capitales plegii', known as the Headboroughs once English had superseded Latin as the language of the record) for each Ward, made at the annual Leet held before the Bailiffs. They concern offences against the Assizes of Bread and Ale and other trading offences, public nuisances such as encroachments on the common soil and failure to remove filth from the highways, and (until the Leet's criminal jurisdiction was lost in 1461) cases of assault. The amounts of amercements are recorded in the left-hand margins and/or above the names of the persons amerced. Some of the 15th-century rolls include the names of the other tithingmen for each ward, in addition to the Capital Pledges;

and the names of the Affeerors are sometimes given following the presentments for the Ward, together with the total sum amerced in that Ward. The proceedings are in Latin throughout.

For Leet proceedings 1465–1468 and 1479, see 'All Courts: Composite Enrolments', C/2/10/1/3–7; for proceedings 1631–1765, see the Headboroughs' Verdict Books for those years, C/2/8/4/5–8.

C/2/8/1/1   11 Jun. 1359
South Ward only
Capital pledges: John Rever, Thomas [*illegible*] and [*illegible*]
(1 membrane, damp-stained and partly illegible)

C/2/8/1/2   21 May 1415
West and North Wards only
Capital pledges: William Rideout, Stephen Gosselyn, Edmund Bercok (West); Michael atte Hill, Thomas Brid, William Kech (North)
(2 membranes, not pierced for attachment)

C/2/8/1/3   9 Jun. 1416
East and North Wards only
Capital pledges: Thomas Wyseman, Thomas Butler, John Smyth (East); Michael Dexter, William Kech, Thomas Bryd (North)
(2 membranes, not pierced for attachment)

C/2/8/1/4   6 Jun. 1419
East and South Wards only
Capital pledges: Thomas Wysman, John Burch, Thomas Butler (East); Henry Heyward, Stephen Rolff, Simon Ty (South)
(2 membranes, not pierced for attachment)

C/2/8/1/5   13 May 1421
North, West, South and East Wards
Capital pledges: Michael Dexter, John Skirwhit, Thomas Brid (North); William Rideout, Edmund Bercok, Stephen Gosselyn (West); Simon Ty, Robert Brid, Robert Parmasay (South); Thomas Wysman, John Burch, Thomas Butler (East)
(4 membranes, attached at heads)

C/2/8/1/6   25 May 1423
North, East and West Wards only
Capital pledges: Richard Annot, Geoffrey Pipho, John Skirwhit (North); Thomas Wysman, John Burch, John Felawe (East); Stephen Gosselyn, Edmund Bercok, Walter Bonde (West)
(3 membranes, not pierced for attachment)

C/2/8/1/7   13 Jun. 1424
East, West and North Wards only
Capital pledges: Thomas Wysman, John Felawe, John Cole (East); Edmund Bercok, Walter Bonde, William Talifer (West); John Skirwhit, Richard Annot, Geoffrey Pipho (North)
(3 membranes, not pierced for attachment)

C/2/8/1/8   18 May 1434
South, East and North Wards only
Capital pledges: Robert Parmasey, John Fennyng, John Deve (South); Thomas Wysman, John Felawe, John Bole (East); John Skirwitt, Thomas Robert, William Pipho (North)
(3 membranes, m. 2 only pierced for attachment)

C/2/8/1/9   29 May 1436
West, [North] and East Wards only
Capital pledges: Edmund Bercok, William Talyfer, John Cole (West); John Skyrwitt, Thomas Robert, John Blampayn [North]; Thomas Wysman, Thomas Porteweye, Thomas Cadon (East)
(3 membranes, not pierced for attachment)

C/2/8/1/10   21 May 1437
South, North and East Wards only
Capital pledges: John Fennyng, Robert Parmasay, John Deve (South); John Skyrwit, Thomas
Robert, John Blanpayn (North); Thomas Portewey, John Franssh jun., Thomas Cadon (East)
(3 membranes, pierced but not attached)

C/2/8/1/11   3 Jun. 1438
North, South, East and West Wards
Capital pledges: John Blankpayn, John Frenssh sen., Robert Bryd (North); Robert Parmasey,
John Fennyng, John Deve (South); John Sudbury, John Frenssh jun., Thomas Porteweye
(East); Edmund Bercok, William Talyfere, John Cole (West)
(4 membranes, not pierced for attachment)

C/2/8/1/12   n.d. [1443 or 1455]
Ward unknown
Capital pledges: Thomas Cowman, John Creyk, John Lytyll
(1 membrane, not pierced for attachment; part of heading, with date, missing; Leet held before
Thomas Denys and John Ca[ldwell], who were Bailiffs in both 1443 and 1455)

C/2/8/1/13   4 Jun. 1471
West, East, North and South Wards
Capital pledges: William Wynter (Thomas Drayll *struck through*, William Sewale, Richard
Melys *substituted*) (West); Richard Machet, John Broun, John Osberne (East); Robert
Blomvile, John Litill, Thomas Wynter (North); twelve jurors named (South)
(4 membranes, formerly attached)

C/2/8/1/14   19 May 1472
South, West, East and North Wards
Capital pledges: Edmund Sharhowe, John Calwyn, Nicholas Wynter (South); William Wynter,
William Sewall, ——— [*missing*] [West]; ——[*missing*] Osbern, John Broun, William Wattes
(East); Thomas Wynter, John Lytill, Robert Blomfeld (North)
(2 membranes, m.2 fragmentary; attached at heads)

C/2/8/1/15   31 May 1474
West, North, South and East Wards
Capital pledges: William Wynter, William Sewall, Richard Melys (West); John Lytill, Robert
Blomfeld (North); Nicholas Wynter, Nicholas Purchet, Thomas Punttyng (South) Geoffrey
Osberne, William Wattis, John Broun (East)
(1 membrane, not pierced for attachment; proceedings for East Ward break off in mid-entry)

C/2/8/1/16   16 May 1475
West, East, South and North Wards
Capital pledges: William Wynter, William Sewall, Richard Melys (West); John Osberne,
William Wattes, John Broun (East); Nicholas Purchet, Nicholas Wynter (South); John Lytyll,
Robert Blomfeld, Thomas Wynter (North)
(1 membrane, not pierced for attachment)

C/2/8/1/17   12 Jun. 1481
West, South, East and North Wards
Capital pledges: Peter Powyll, Thomas Halle, John Kyrre (West); Nicholas Porchett, Thomas
Poortman, Thomas Bole (South); William Wattys, John Broun, William Pernell (East);
Thomas Skypper, William Gnatte, Richard Bayly (North)
(2 membranes, not pierced for attachment)

C/2/8/1/18   28 May 1482
East, South, North and West Wards
Capital pledges: Geoffrey Osbern, John Broun, William Pernell (East); Nicholas Porchet,
Thomas Portman, Thomas Bole (South); William Gnatte, Richard Bayly, Thomas Skypper

(North); John Kyrre, Peter Powyll, Thomas Cady (West)
(2 membranes, not pierced for attachment)

C/2/8/1/19   20 May 1483
South, West, East and North Wards
Capital pledges: Nicholas Porchet, Thomas Bole, James Kene (South); John Kyrre, Peter Powyll, Thomas Cady (West); Geoffrey Osberne, John Broun, William Pernell (East); William Gnatte, Richard Bayly, Thomas Skypper (North)
(2 membranes, not pierced for attachment)

C/2/8/1/20   8 Jun. 1484
South, North, West and East Wards
Capital pledges: Nicholas Porchet, James Kene, Thomas Bole (South); Thomas Skypper, Richard Bayly, William Gnatte (North); John Kyrre, Peter Powyll, Thomas Cady (West); Geoffrey Osbern, John Broun, William Pernell (East)
(2 membranes, m. 1 fragmentary at foot; not pierced for attachment)

C/2/8/1/21   5 Jun. 1487
East, South, West and North Wards
Capital pledges: William Pernell, Geoffrey Osberne, John Broun (East); Nicholas Porchet, Thomas Bole, James Kene (South); John Kyrre, William Manser, Thomas Smyth (West); Thomas Skypper, Richard Bayly, William Gnatte (North)
(2 membranes, not pierced for attachment)

C/2/8/1/22   27 May 1488
South, North, West and East Wards
Capital pledges: Nicholas Porchet, James Kene, Thomas Bole (South); Richard Bayly, William Ropkyn, John Poortman (North); William Manser, Thomas Smyth, Thomas Gardener (West); John Broun, William Pernell, Geoffrey Osberne (East)
(2 membranes, not pierced for attachment)

C/2/8/1/23   31 May 1569
East, West, North and South Wards
Capital pledges: Edmund Leche, Robert Sallows, Christopher Crane (East); Robert Sparrowe, George Coppyng, Sebastian Man (West); Richard Bynge, John Barker, Geoffrey Cage (South); names omitted (North)
(2 membranes, attached at heads)

C/2/8/2   LEET ESTREAT ROLLS   ? 1384–1737

These comprise, in abridged form, those entries from the Leet Rolls that gave rise to payments to be collected. The 17th- and 18th-century rolls are endorsed with the Bailiffs' precepts to the Chamberlains for levying the amercements on the goods of the respective offenders.

C/2/8/2/1   ? 31 May 1384
Apparently for all wards
(1 membrane, stained; regnal year indistinct, probably 7 Ric. II)

C/2/8/2/2   26 May 1461
West Ward only
Capital pledges: John Campyon, William Manser
(1 membrane, headed 'Mervyn' [? one of the serjeants], pierced for attachment

C/2/8/2/3   23 May 1469
West Ward only
(1 membrane, pierced for attachment)

C/2/8/2/4   19 May 1472
West Ward only
(1 membrane, pierced for attachment)

C/2/8/2/5   1 Jun. 1685
All wards
(2 membranes)

C/2/8/2/6   30 May 1732
All wards
(1 membrane)

C/2/8/2/7   28 Jun. 1732
Adjournment; all wards
(2 membranes)

C/2/8/2/8   10 Jul. 1736
Adjournment; all wards
(1 membrane)

C/2/8/2/9   18 Jun. 1737
Adjournment; all wards
(1 membrane)

C/2/8/2/10   n.d. [14c.]
List of names with sums of money recorded against each; possibly an estreat roll
(1 membrane; endorsed 'Extract' in Nathaniel Bacon's hand)

C/2/8/3 RECORDS OF THE VIEW OF FRANKPLEDGE   1508–1597

The View of Frankpledge formed part of the proceedings of the annual Leet. For Frankpledge
proceedings for the period 1631–1765, see the Headboroughs' Verdict Books, C/2/8/4/5–8.

C/2/8/3/1   13 Jun. 1508
Frankpledge Roll
Apparently for all four wards
Presentments by twelve jurors (presumably the three capital pledges for each ward), mostly for
prostitution and keeping disorderly houses
(1 membrane, headed 'Gippewicum: ad Curiam Visus Franchipleg' ibidem tentam'; in spite of
the heading, the type of business recorded is more akin to Leet presentments. Not pierced for
attachment)

C/2/8/3/2   Jun. 1565–May 1597
Headboroughs' Frankpledge Book
Lists of male inhabitants for each ward, headed by the constables, made at the views of
frankpledge held annually on Tuesday in Whitsun week; with sums of money against each
name, presumably amercements for default in appearance
(1 vol., 166 unnumbered fols, the last two gatherings now detached)

C/2/8/4 HEADBOROUGHS' VERDICT BOOKS   1553–1765

These are the record of the presentments or 'verdicts' of the twelve Headboroughs (three for
each ward), meeting for the whole town, relating to various market and other trading offences
and to common nuisances, with details of the sums amerced on offenders. The record includes
verdicts on special views of obstructions of the highway and similar matters on the order of the
Bailiffs or at the request of individual householders, and verdicts enforcing the borough
building regulations or giving permission for alterations to buildings in cases where the

highway might be subject to encroachment. There are also recommendations by the Head-boroughs for grants or leases of the common soil. The Headboroughs met at irregular intervals, but on average perhaps every two or three months. By the 18th century the abatement of nuisances rather than the punishment of trading offences accounted for most of the Headboroughs' business. From 1631 the books include the proceedings of the annual Leet and View of Frankpledge. The record is in English throughout.

C/2/8/4/1   Aug. 1553–Mar. 1574
(1 vol., 142 fols; covers formed from double fol. of an ecclesiastical MS, rubricated and decorated in blue, badly scuffed and partly illegible)

C/2/8/4/2   Mar. 1586–Jul. 1603
(1 vol., 298 fols; front cover marked 'No. 3' in an 18c or 19c hand)

C/2/8/4/3   Oct. 1603–Aug. 1611
(1 vol., 194 fols; front cover marked 'No. 4')

C/2/8/4/4   Nov. 1611–Oct. 1630
(1 vol., 355 unnumbered fols; front cover marked 'No. 5')

C/2/8/4/5   Jan. 1631–May 1654
Includes:
— annual leets and views of frankpledge
(1 vol., 320 unnumbered fols; front cover marked 'No. 6')

C/2/8/4/6   May 1654–Jun. 1677
Includes:
— annual leets and views of frankpledge
(1 vol., 360 fols; front cover marked 'No.7')

C/2/8/4/7   Feb. 1678–Dec. 1713
Includes:
— annual leets and views of frankpledge
(1 vol., 277 fols; front cover marked 'No.8')

C/2/8/4/8   Jun. 1715–May 1765
Includes:
— annual leets and views of frankpledge
(1 vol., 182 fols; front cover marked 'No.9')

C/2/8/5 HEADBOROUGHS' MINUTE BOOKS   1710–1789

Minutes of presentments and orders made on viewing alleged nuisances

C/2/8/5/1   Jun. 1710–Nov. 1723
(1 vol., 76 unnumbered fols; front cover marked 'A')

C/2/8/5/2   Oct. 1723–Jan. 1789
(1 vol., 89 unnumbered fols; front cover marked 'B' and 'Dirt Book')

C/2/8/6 HEADBOROUGHS' ORIGINAL VERDICTS   1737–1745

Orders or verdicts, bearing the original signatures of the Headboroughs, made on special views of alleged nuisances or encroachments on the highway.

C/2/8/6/1   Jan. 1737–Jun. 1745
(5 docs; found loose inside C/2/8/5/2)

C/2/9 SESSIONS   1440–1846

The office of Justice of the Peace had developed in the 14th century from that of the earlier *custos pacis* or Keeper of the Peace, which in turn had its origin in Archbishop Hubert Walter's edict of 1195, issued at a time of disorder occasioned by Richard I's absence from England, assigning knights to swear all men above the age of fifteen to keep the peace. (On the origin of the Keepers and their transformation into Justices of the Peace, see Putnam 1929, Harding 1960, and Allen 1974, ix–xiii.) By the late Middle Ages the Justices had replaced the Sheriff as the leading power in the county; in 1461 the Sheriff's right of awarding process upon indictments and presentments was transferred to the county Justices in their Sessions, while in 1495 the Justices were authorised to convict and punish extortionate Sheriffs and their subordinates.

Not unnaturally, municipal corporations, ever anxious to increase their autonomy, sought to obtain their own Sessions of the Peace to exclude the county authorities. As stated in the general introduction to JUSTICE AND THE COURTS, Ipswich secured from Henry VI in 1446 a charter which constituted the Bailiffs and four of the twelve (capital) Portmen Justices of the Peace for the borough.

Throughout the 16th century and beyond, the foremost duty of the Justices of the Peace remained, as their title implies, the enforcement of law and order. But if the essential nature of the office remained unchanged, the Tudor monarchs greatly added to the administrative duties of the Justices, giving them a pivotal role in carrying out much of the social and economic legislation of the period. Their administrative responsibilities continued to proliferate until the local government reforms of the 19th century.

While many of the Justices' statutory duties could be carried out by any two of their number (one being of the quorum), it was only when sitting as a body in their General Sessions of the Peace that the powers of the magistracy could be exercised in full. Special Sessions were also held, such as the annual Licensing Meetings for inns and alehouses (which in Ipswich took place in August). Additionally, Petty Sessions, with more limited powers than the General Sessions, were held at more frequent intervals.

C/2/9/1 GENERAL (QUARTER) SESSIONS   1440–1846

County General Sessions were held by statute (2 Hen. V, cap. 24) four times a year, in the weeks following the feasts of Epiphany, Easter, the Translation of St Thomas the Martyr, and St Michael; hence they became known as Quarter Sessions. In Ipswich, however, the borough General Sessions were rarely held more than twice a year before the 1830s. Indeed, the term 'Quarter Sessions' appears in the heading to the Sessions Roll for the first time in April 1834.

From their creation in the 15th century the borough's General Sessions were Ipswich's principal criminal court. In addition, the court dealt with such administrative matters as the supervision of repairs to highways and bridges and the oversight of the Poor Law – including rating appeals, adjudication of cases of disputed settlement, and the coercion of putative fathers to support their illegitimate offspring. It was responsible for the regulation of alehouses (a function closely allied to the Justices' original *raison d'être* of the maintenance of public order). The court was further empowered to levy special rates for charitable purposes such as the relief of wounded soldiers and sailors (particularly important in a port such as Ipswich, where servicemen disembarked on their return from Continental wars), and for the repair of bridges and buildings such as the borough gaol. In Ipswich all these charges were financed out of the Marshalsea rate. Some idea of the multiplicity of duties which came to be assigned to the Justices in General Sessions between the 16th and the 19th century may be gained from the introductory note on the contents of the Sessions Rolls (C/2/9/1/1/1) below.

Following the abolition of the old Corporation in 1835, Ipswich was granted a new court of Quarter Sessions by Letters Patent dated 4 March 1836. This court retained its independence until the general supercession of Quarter Sessions and Assizes by the Crown Courts in 1972.

C/2/9/1/1 THE COURT IN SESSION 1440–1846

C/2/9/1/1/1 Sessions Rolls **1440–1835**

The Sessions 'Rolls' are not, strictly speaking, rolls in the normal sense of a court roll (the formal enrolment of the record of proceedings of the court), but are more properly described as *rolled files*, made up of the original documents generated by the court and its officers or submitted to the court for action – in essence, the 'working papers' of the Sessions. At the end of the Session they were threaded on a file lace, and the file rolled for compactness of storage. All have now been flattened and guarded into board covers.

After 12 January 1544 there are no surviving Sessions Rolls until 19 March 1722, after which the series is continuous down to 1948, though the years after 1835 lie outside the scope of this catalogue. During the period for which the Rolls are missing, their lack is compensated for by information from the Sessions Books (C/2/9/1/1/8) from 1549 onwards, supplemented between 1576 and 1651 by the Sessions proceedings recorded in the Composite Enrolments of the borough courts (C/2/10/1) – 'court roll' material proper.

In the earlier period, 1440–1544, some of the Rolls are for Sessions of the Peace only and some are for separate Sessions of Gaol Delivery. While there might otherwise have been a case for their separation into separate archive series, this course was precluded by the conservation work referred to above; when the flattened rolls were guarded in the 1960s, several of them were sometimes guarded into a single binder, with the result that some Peace and Gaol Delivery Rolls, formerly separate, are now bound together. For practical reasons, to avoid disbinding, they are therefore treated here as a single series.

From the resumption of the series in 1722, all the Rolls relate to joint Sessions of the Peace and Gaol Delivery.

In the period 1440–1544, some of the surviving Rolls contain only indictments (usually all indictments made by one jury at one Session are on a single large membrane; until 1486 there are usually two juries, one for the town and the other for the four hamlets of Stoke, Brooks, Wix Bishop and Wix Ufford). Other Rolls for the period are more varied in content and include precepts, lists of officers (usually Coroners, Serjeants and hamlet Bailiffs, and sometimes the town Bailiffs and Justices of the Peace), jury lists, indictments and gaol calendars.

By the time the series resumes in 1722 the classes of document represented on the Rolls have become much more diverse. Those which are usual or frequent include: calendars of prisoners in the gaol, bridewell and house of correction (between 1722 and 1760, and also in 1768, 1773 and 1774); lists of constables and of the Grand and Crown Juries, 1727–1835; Coroners' inquisitions, 1722–1765; examinations of defendants and informations of witnesses, 1722–1742 and 1781–1806; indictments, 1722–1835; precepts to the Serjeants for the appearance of parish surveyors and others, 1722–1824, and for the appearance of juries, 1727–1835; presentments by the Grand Jury and Constables, 1722–1827, and by the Grand Jury alone, 1828–1835; Corn Return Certificates (1793–1807) and Dealers' Declarations (1794–1809) under the Act of 31 George III, cap. 30; and recognizances throughout the series. Types of document which occur more occasionally include: articles of the peace, 1765–1834; certificates of conviction out-of-Sessions, 1735–1835; Friendly Societies' regulations, 1823–1834; presentments of highways by the Justices, 1754–1832, and Justices' certificates of their repair, 1764–1819; engrossed indictments and verdicts, 1722–1775; oaths (of Allegiance, Abjuration and Supremacy), with sacrament certificates and declarations against transubstantiation, 1737–1738; oaths of returning officers and poll clerks for Parliamentary elections, 1730–1835; orders (mostly regarding bastardy cases and apprenticeship) 1729–1788; petitions for pensions for maimed soldiers, 1727–1733; and surveyors' presentments, 1723, 1725 and 1727.

The contents of the normally very slim Rolls for 1440–1544 are described in full in the individual catalogue entries. The entries for the often fuller and much more diverse Rolls for 1722–1835, a detailed indication of whose general contents is given above, note only the appearance of unusual items of special interest.

Almost all the documents are in Latin down to 1544. From 1722 to 1731 the majority are in English, and thereafter the language is English throughout.

C/2/9/1/1/1/1   1440–1451
Sessions of the Peace only
Sessions held 22 Dec. 1440, 17 Apr. 1441, 12 Sep. 1441, 20 Sep. 1451
Indictments only
Includes:
— (m. 2d.) list of court rolls t. Hen. III–Edw. VI, in the hand of Nathaniel Bacon
(7 membranes; mm. 3 and 4 probably added later to the original roll; now guarded with
C/2/9/1/1/1/2–4)

C/2/9/1/1/1/2   1446–1451
Sessions of the Peace only
Sessions held 17 Jun. 1446, 19 Jan. 1447, 3 Aug. 1447, 17 May 1448, 18 Sep. 1448, 7 Jan. 1449,
16 Mar. 1451
Indictments only
(11 membranes; part of m. 9 cut away; now guarded with C/2/9/1/1/1/1, 3 and 4)

C/2/9/1/1/1/3   1454–1455
Sessions of the Peace only
Sessions held 11 Dec. 1454, 28 Mar. 1455, 18 Jul. 1455, 28 Sep. 1455
Indictments only
(7 membranes; now guarded with C/2/9/1/1/1/1, 2 and 4)

C/2/9/1/1/1/4   11–19 Dec. 1455
Sessions of the Peace only
Sessions held 19 Dec. 1455
Includes:
— list of officers, with note that one Bailiff of Stoke is in mercy for default, n.d.
— 4 precepts to Sheriff for appearance of indicted persons, n.d.
— precept for appearance of jurors and officers, 11 Dec. 1455
— 2 appointments of attorneys (1 fragmentary), n.d.
— Grand Jury lists for town and hamlets, n.d.
— list of persons making fine, and their pledges, n.d.
(11 membranes; mm. 8–10 formerly sewn together; now guarded with C/2/9/1/1/1/1–3)

C/2/9/1/1/1/5   1458–1459
Sessions of the Peace only
Sessions held 6 Jul. 1458, 15 Dec. 1458, 6 Apr. 1459, 21 Dec. 1459
Indictments only
(7 membranes; now guarded with C/2/9/1/1/1/6–9)

C/2/9/1/1/1/6   20–23 Jul. 1461
Sessions of the Peace only
Sessions held 23 Jul. 1461
Includes:
— precept to Sheriff for appearance of jurors for town and hamlets, and officers, 20 Jul. 1461
— precepts to Bailiffs of BH, WB and WU for appearance of jurors, n.d.
(4 membranes; now guarded with C/2/9/1/1/1/5,7–9)

C/2/9/1/1/1/7   Sep.–Dec. 1467
Sessions of the Peace only
Sessions held 25 Sep., 18 Dec. 1467
Indictments only
(1 membrane; originally found with C/2/9/1/1/1/9; now guarded with C/2/9/1/1/1/5–6, 8–9)

C/2/9/1/1/1/8   6–24 Feb. 1468
Sessions of the Peace only
Sessions held 24 Feb. 1468

93

Includes:
— list of officers, n.d.
— precept to ministers of court for appearance of jurors for town and hamlets, and of officers, 6 Feb. 1468
— precepts to Bailiffs of BH, WB and WU for appearance of jurors, n.d.
— 2 precepts to Sheriff for appearance of trial juries, 6 Feb. 1468
— Grand Jury lists, hamlets and ? town (m. 6) n.d.
— Trial Jury list, n.d.
(10 membranes, found loose; now guarded with C/2/9/1/1/1/5–7, 9)

C/2/9/1/1/1/9   (26 Apr. 1468) n.d.
[Sessions of the Peace]
Indictment for affray, 26 Apr. 1468 (no heading; no jury named)
(1 membrane; now guarded with C/2/9/1/1/1/5–8)

C/2/9/1/1/1/10   1473–1478
Sessions of the Peace only
Sessions held 15 Dec. 1473, 30 Mar. 1474, 28 Jun. 1474, 24 Aug. 1474, 4 Sep. 1475, 12 Dec. 1475, 14 Mar. 1476, 25 Sep. 1476, 29 Jan. 1477, 18 Apr. 1477, 18 Feb. 1478
Includes:
— (mm. 1–5, 15 Dec. 1473) list of officers; Grand Jury lists; indictments
— (mm. 6–7, 30 Mar. 1474) Grand Jury list; indictments
— (mm. 8–10, 28 Jun. 1474) list of officers; Grand Jury list (hamlets); indictments
— (mm. 11–14, 24 Aug. 1474) 2 lists of officers; Grand Jury list (town); indictments
— (mm. 15–17, 4 Sep. 1475) list of officers; indictments
— (mm. 18–22, 30–31, 12 Dec. 1475) list of officers; precept to Serjeants for appearance of jurors and officers; Grand Jury lists (hamlets and town); indictments
— (mm. 23–29, 14 Mar. 1476) list of officers; precept to Serjeants for appearance of jurors and officers; Grand Jury lists (hamlets and town); indictments
— (mm. 49–51, 25 Sep. 1476) list of officers; Grand Jury list; indictments
— (mm. 36–37, 29 Jan. 1477) Grand Jury list (hamlets); indictment
— (mm. 45–48, 18 Apr. 1477) list of officers, Grand Jury lists (hamlets and town); indictments
— (mm. 52–54, 18 Feb. 1478) list of officers; Grand Jury list; indictments
— (mm. 39, 40, 42, 12 Feb. 1476) precepts to Serjeants for appearance of indicted persons at Session of 14 Mar. 1476
— (mm. 32–35, 41, 43, 44, 21 Nov. 1475–10 Oct. 1476) precepts to Bailiffs to supercede arrest of persons who have given security for appearance
— (m. 38, 28 Oct. 1476) writ of *supersedeas* to Justices for release of persons for whom security has been given for appearance in Chancery
(54 membranes; found filed together)

C/2/9/1/1/1/11   1478–1479
Sessions of the Peace only
Sessions held 16 Dec. 1478, 25 Jun. 1479, 14 Jul. 1479, 9 Sep. 1479
Indictments only
(4 membranes; originally found with C/2/9/1/1/1/12; now guarded with C/2/9/1/1/1/12–14)

C/2/9/1/1/1/12   1479–1480
Sessions of the Peace only
Sessions held 16 Dec. 1479, 19 Apr. 1480, 14 Jul. 1480
Indictments only
(2 membranes; now guarded with C/2/9/1/1/1/11, 13, 14)

C/2/9/1/1/1/13   1483–1486
Sessions of the Peace only
Sessions held 5 Feb. 1483, 10 Jun. 1483, 16 Jan. 1484, 4 Jun. 1484, 10 Sep. 1484, 10 Dec. 1484, 31 Dec. 1484, 18 Jan. 1485, 5 Dec. 1485, 2 Dec. 1486

Indictments only
(8 membranes; now guarded with C/2/9/1/1/1/11–12, 14)

C/2/9/1/1/1/14   1485–1487
[? Sessions of the Peace only]
Sessions held 5 Dec. 1485, 16 Mar. 1486, ? 15 Jun. 1486, 11 Sep. 1486, 2 Mar. 1487
Estreats only: sums due from William Cady, Bailiff of MS, for default in attendance
(1 membrane, indented; now guarded with C/2/9/1/1/1/11–13)

C/2/9/1/1/1/15   Mar.–Jul. 1488
Sessions of Gaol Delivery only
Sessions held 11 Mar. 1488 and (by adjournment) 17 Jul. 1488
Includes:
— commission, 10 Feb. 1488
— list of officers, with note of delivery of a prisoner by proclamation, n.d.
— precept to Bailiffs for appearance of indicted persons, 10 Jan. 1488
— Sheriff's precept to Serjeants to summon prisoners, etc., 4 Mar. 1488
— precept to Bailiffs for appearance of jurors and officers, 4 Mar. 1488
— precept to Bailiffs of BH and WB for appearance of constables and jurors, 4 Mar. 1488
— Grand Jury list, n.d.
— list of Constables, n.d.
— list of adjournments to 17 Jul. 1488, n.d.
— indictments made before Justices of the Peace, 5 Dec. 1487, 27 Jan. 1488, 20 Jun. 1488
(14 membranes; now guarded with C/2/9/1/1/1/16)

C/2/9/1/1/1/16   4 Dec. 1488
Sessions of the Peace only
Indictments, with 1 recognizance to accept arbitration in case of trespass
(1 membrane; now guarded with C/2/9/1/1/1/15)

C/2/9/1/1/1/17   Mar.–Aug. 1491
Sessions of the Peace and Gaol Delivery
Sessions held 21 Mar. 1491 (Peace), 15 Jun. 1491 (Peace), 19 Aug. 1491 (Gaol Delivery)
Includes for Sessions, 21 Mar. 1491 (mm. 13–19):
— precepts to hamlet Bailiffs for appearance of jurors, 10 Mar. 1491
— Grand Jury list, n.d.
— 3 precepts to Bailiffs to supercede arrest of persons who have given security for appearance,
etc., 24 Aug.–27 Nov. 1490
Includes for Sessions, 15 Jun. 1491 (mm. 20–24):
— precepts to hamlet Bailiffs for appearance of jurors, 10 Jun. 1491
— Grand Jury list, n.d.
— precept to supercede arrest, 17 Apr. 1491
Includes for Sessions, 19 Aug. 1491 (mm. 1–12, 25–30):
— commission, 11 Jul. 1491
— writ to Sheriff for production of prisoners, 11 Jul. 1491
— Sheriff's precept to Bailiffs for appearance of prisoners, officers and jurors, 8 Aug. 1491
— precepts to Bailiffs of WB and WU for appearance of Constables and jurors, 8 Aug. 1491
— list of officers, with note of adjournment to 2 Dec. 1491, n.d.
— list of Constables, n.d.
— 2 Grand Jury lists, n.d.
— inquisition before Coroners, 18 Mar. 1491
— indictments, 21 Mar. 1491, 19 Aug. 1491 and n.d.
— appeal of felony, 24 Apr. 1491
— 4 Trial Jury lists, n.d.
(30 membranes)

C/2/9/1/1/1/18   1504–1508
Sessions of Gaol Delivery only
Sessions held 26 Aug. 1506, n.d.
Includes:
— commission, 6 Jul. 1504
Includes for Sessions, 26 Aug. 1506:
— calendar of prisoners, reciting indictments before Justices of the Peace, and of persons taken
on suspicion of felony, with note of bailment of convict until next adjournment on 17 Apr. 1507
Includes for Sessions, n.d.:
— calendar of prisoners indicted for offences committed on 26 Dec. 1506, 20 May 1507
— indictments for offences committed on 20 Jan. 1508 and 12 Feb. 1508, with related Trial
Jury list, n.d.
— Grand Jury list, n.d.
(7 membranes)

C/2/9/1/1/1/19   1507–1508
Sessions of the Peace only
Sessions held 17 Dec. 1507
Indictments, with annexed writ of *certiorari* into Chancery, 25 Jan. 1508
(2 membranes; now guarded with C/2/9/1/1/1/20–21)

C/2/9/1/1/1/20   18 Aug. 1508
Sessions of the Peace only
Indictments only
(1 membrane; now guarded with C/2/9/1/1/1/19, 21)

C/2/9/1/1/1/21   1508–1510
Sessions of Gaol Delivery only
Sessions held 20 Jan. 1509, 9 Oct. 1510
Includes:
— indictment for felony committed 27 Apr. 1508, n.d.
Includes for Sessions, 20 Jan. 1509:
— indictments and calendar of persons taken on suspicion of felony
Includes for Sessions, 9 Oct. 1510:
— precept to Sheriff for appearance of prisoners, officers and jurors, 1 Oct. 1510
— calendar of prisoners indicted at Gaol Delivery, 14 Dec. 1509 and at Sessions of the Peace,
18 Sep. 1510, and of persons taken on suspicion of felony
— indictment at Sessions of the Peace, 18 Sep. 1510
— Trial Jury list, n.d.
(5 membranes; now guarded with C/2/9/1/1/1/19–20)

C/2/9/1/1/1/22   Nov.–Dec. 1509
Sessions of Gaol Delivery only
Sessions held 14 Dec. 1509
Includes:
— precept to Sheriff for appearance of prisoners, officers and jurors, 16 Nov. 1509
— indictments and calendar of persons taken on suspicion of felony, with notes of adjournment
to 30 Jul. 1511
(2 membranes, found detached, probably once attached to C/2/9/1/1/1/21)

C/2/9/1/1/1/23   1509–1510
Sessions of Gaol Delivery only
Sessions held 20 Jan. 1509, 9 Oct. 1510
Includes for Sessions, 20 Jan. 1509:
— jury list for trial of John Skynner, n.d.
Includes for Sessions, 9 Oct. 1510:
— indictments of Hugh Vaughan *alias* Howell Vaughan, weaver (marked 'Billa vera') and
Hugh Noone, lastmaker, for crimes committed 30 Jul. 1509, n.d.

— Grand Jury list, n.d.
(3 'stray' membranes, probably once attached to C/2/9/1/1/1/21)

C/2/9/1/1/1/24   1510–1511
Sessions of the Peace only
Sessions held 16 Aug. 1510, 27 Jun. 1511, 26 Sep. 1511, 19 Dec. 1511
Indictments only
(1 membrane)

C/2/9/1/1/1/25   1513–1515
Sessions of Gaol Delivery only
Sessions held 21 Jan. 1513, 9 Apr. 1513, 28 May 1513, 1 Oct. 1513, 7 Oct. 1513, 7 Oct. 1513,
29 Apr. 1514, 13 Oct. 1514, 28 Apr. 1515, 11 Jun. 1515
Includes:
— notes of adjournment for most Sessions
— calendar of persons taken on suspicion of felony and delivered by proclamation, 21 Jan.
1513
— calendar and list of officers, 7 Oct. 1513
— calendar and list of officers, 11 Jun. 1515
Annexed:
— file (8 docs) for Sessions, 21 Jan. 1513, comprising: commission, 26 Nov. 1512; writ to
Sheriff for production of prisoners, 26 Nov. 1512; precept to Sheriff for appearance of prisoners, officers and jurors, 12 Jan. 1513; Sheriff's appointment of deputies, 16 Jan. 1513; 2 Grand
Jury lists, n.d.; indictment, n.d.; Trial Jury list, n.d.
— file (4 docs) for Sessions, 7 Oct. 1513, comprising: Grand Jury list, indictments and Trial
Jury list, all n.d.
— file (5 docs) for Sessions, 11 Jun. 1515, comprising: Sheriff's appointment of deputies,
1 Dec. 1514; Grand Jury list, n.d.; indictments, n.d.; 2 Trial Jury lists, n.d.
(1 membrane with 3 files attached)

C/2/9/1/1/1/26   1517–1520
Sessions of Gaol Delivery only
Sessions held 23 Jun. 1517, 20 Jan. 1519, 25 Mar. 1520, 31 Aug. 1520
Includes:
— lists of officers and calendars of prisoners, 1517–1520
— notes of adjournment of sessions, 1517–1520
— (at Sessions, 25 Mar. 1520) Bishop of Norwich's commission to receive clerical prisoners,
dated at Ipswich, 4 Jun. 1517
(2 membranes)

C/2/9/1/1/1/27   1520–1523
Sessions of the Peace and Gaol Delivery
Sessions held 15 Jun. 1520 (Peace), 31 Mar. 1522 (Gaol Delivery)
Includes for Sessions, 15 Jun. 1520:
— list of officers, n.d.
— precepts to Sheriff for appearance of jurors, officers and indicted persons, 10 Jun. 1520
— precept to hamlet Bailiffs for appearance of jurors, 10 Jun. 1520
Includes for Sessions, 31 Mar. 1522:
— precepts to Bailiffs of BH and WB for appearance of jurors, 20 Mar. 1522
— Grand Jury list, n.d.
— indictments, n.d.
— list of verdicts, 31 Mar. 1522
— Trial Jury list, n.d.
— jury list, n.d.

Includes:
— (m. 14) precept from Bailiffs and Admirals to Serjeants for appearance of Peter de
Landaverda, a Spaniard, and others from ship 'le Thomas de Caunterbury' before Bailiffs at
10 a.m. on 31 Aug. next; 29 Aug. 1523
(17 membranes)

C/2/9/1/1/1/28   May–Jun. 1531
Sessions of Gaol Delivery only
Sessions held 2 Jun. 1531
Includes:
— precept to Sheriff for appearance of prisoners, jurors and officers, 15 May 1531
— precepts to hamlet Bailiffs for appearance of jurors, 15 May 1531
— Grand Jury list, n.d.
— indictments, n.d.
(8 membranes)

C/2/9/1/1/1/29   1533–1534
Sessions of Gaol Delivery only
Sessions held 20 Aug. 1533, 4 Aug. 1534
Includes for Sessions, 20 Aug. 1533:
— (m. 11) 'inquisition' before Justices, in which Jury declares that all (formerly) annexed bills
are true
Includes for Sessions, 4 Aug. 1534:
— Sheriff's appointment of deputies, 30 Jul. 1534
— precepts to hamlet Bailiffs for appearance of jurors, 1 Aug. 1534
— Grand Jury list, n.d.
— indictments, n.d.
— Trial Jury list, n.d.
(11 membranes; m. 11 formerly detached)

C/2/9/1/1/1/30   1534–1535
Sessions of Gaol Delivery only
Sessions held 15 Sep. 1535
Includes:
— commission, 12 Feb. 1534
— Sheriff's appointment of deputies, 12 Sep. 1535
— precepts to hamlet Bailiffs for appearance of jurors, 8 Sep. 1535
— Grand Jury list, n.d.
— indictments, n.d.
— list of presentments (in English), n.d.
— 'inquisition' in which Jury declares that all (formerly) annexed bills are true, 15 Sep. 1535,
with memorandum of adjournment of Sessions until 24 Apr. 1536
(15 membranes)

C/2/9/1/1/1/31   1536–[1537]
Sessions of Gaol Delivery only
Sessions held 19 Mar. 1537
Includes:
— Sheriff's appointment of deputies, 9 Oct. 1536
— precepts to hamlet Bailiffs for appearance of jurors, 9 Oct. 1536
— Grand Jury list, n.d.
(6 membranes)

C/2/9/1/1/1/32   29 Oct. 1540
Sessions of the Peace only
Includes:
— Grand Jury list, 29 Oct. 1540

— indictment (endorsed 'billa vera'), n.d.
(2 membranes)

C/2/9/1/1/1/33   1–31 Mar. 1542
Sessions of Gaol Delivery only
Sessions held 31 Mar. 1542
Includes:
— list of officers, n.d.
— 4 precepts to Sheriff for appearance of indicted persons, 1 Mar. 1542
— precept to Sheriff for appearance of jurors for town and hamlets, and of officers, 1 Mar. 1542
— 3 precepts to hamlet Bailiffs for appearance of jurors, n.d.
— Grand Jury lists for town and hamlets
(11 membranes)

C/2/9/1/1/1/34   Mar.–Apr. 1543
Sessions of Gaol Delivery only
Sessions held 5 Apr. 1543
Includes:
— commission, 2 Mar. 1543
— precepts to hamlet Bailiffs for appearance of jurors, 28 Mar. 1543
— Grand Jury list, n.d.
— list of presentments (in English), n.d.
— indictments, n.d.
— Trial Jury lists, n.d.
(12 membranes)

C/2/9/1/1/1/35   10–12 Jan. 1544
Sessions of Gaol Delivery only
Sessions held 12 Jan. 1544
Includes:
— precepts to hamlet Bailiffs for appearance of jurors, 10 Jan. 1544
— Grand Jury list, n.d.
— indictment, n.d.
— Trial Jury list, n.d.
(8 membranes)

C/2/9/1/1/1/36   Sep. 1721–Mar. 1722
Sessions held 19 Mar. 1722
(46 docs)

C/2/9/1/1/1/37   Feb. 1722–Jun. 1723
Sessions held 13 Dec. 1722
(47 docs)

C/2/9/1/1/1/38   Oct. 1722–Aug. 1723
Sessions held 7 Aug. 1723
(38 docs)

C/2/9/1/1/1/39   Jul.–Dec. 1723
Sessions held 18 Dec. 1723
(34 docs)

C/2/9/1/1/1/40   Dec. 1723–Dec. 1724
Sessions held 21 Dec. 1724
(47 docs)

C/2/9/1/1/1/41   Dec. 1724–May 1725
Sessions held 25 May 1725
(66 docs)

C/2/9/1/1/1/42   May 1725–Mar. 1726
Sessions held 28 Mar. 1726
(63 docs)

C/2/9/1/1/1/43   Mar. 1726–Mar. 1727
Sessions held 27 Mar. 1727
(69 docs)

C/2/9/1/1/1/44   Mar.–Aug 1727
Sessions held 10 Aug. 1727
(35 docs)

C/2/9/1/1/1/45   Aug. 1727–Jan. 1728
Sessions held 2 Jan. 1728
(39 docs; now guarded with C/2/9/1/1/1/46–50)

C/2/9/1/1/1/46   Jan.–Jun. 1728
Sessions held 13 Jun. 1728
(27 docs; now guarded with C/2/9/1/1/1/45, 47–50)

C/2/9/1/1/1/47   Jun. 1728–Mar. 1729
Sessions held 31 Mar. 1729
(38 docs; now guarded with C/2/9/1/1/1/45–46, 48–50)

C/2/9/1/1/1/48   Mar.–Aug. 1729
Sessions held 8 Aug. 1729
(21 docs; now guarded with C/2/9/1/1/1/45–47, 49–50)

C/2/9/1/1/1/49   Aug. 1729–Dec. 1730
Sessions held 15 Dec. 1730
(33 docs; now guarded with C/2/9/1/1/1/45–48, 50)

C/2/9/1/1/1/50   Dec. 1730–Jun. 1731
Sessions held 8 Jun. 1731
(33 docs; now guarded with C/2/9/1/1/1/45–49)

C/2/9/1/1/1/51   Jun.–Dec. 1731
Sessions held 27 Dec. 1731
Includes:
— Poor Rate assessment for BH for half-year ending Sep. 1731
(34 docs; now guarded with C/2/9/1/1/1/52–55)

C/2/9/1/1/1/52   Dec. 1731–Aug 1732
Sessions held 17 Aug. 1731
(26 docs; now guarded with C/2/9/1/1/1/51, 53–55)

C/2/9/1/1/1/53   Aug. 1732–Mar. 1733
Sessions held 16 Mar. 1733
(31 docs; now guarded with C/2/9/1/1/1/51–52, 54–55)

C/2/9/1/1/1/54   Mar.–Aug. 1733
Sessions held 6 Aug. 1733
(25 docs; now guarded with C/2/9/1/1/1/51–53, 55)

C/2/9/1/1/1/55   Aug. 1733–Aug. 1734
Sessions held 12 Aug. 1734
(57 docs; now guarded with C/2/9/1/1/1/51–54)

C/2/9/1/1/1/56   Aug. 1734–Aug. 1735
Sessions held 4 Aug. 1735
(49 docs; now guarded with C/2/9/1/1/1/57–60)

C/2/9/1/1/1/57   Aug. 1734–Mar. 1736
Sessions held 29 Mar. 1736
(41 docs; now guarded with C/2/9/1/1/1/56, 58–60)

C/2/9/1/1/1/58   Mar.–Sep. 1736
Sessions held 3 Sep. 1736
(33 docs; now guarded with C/2/9/1/1/1/56–57, 59–60)

C/2/9/1/1/1/59   Sep. 1736–Mar. 1737
Sessions held 18 Mar. 1737
(33 docs; now guarded with C/2/9/1/1/1/56–58, 60)

C/2/9/1/1/1/60   Jan.–Aug. 1737
Sessions held 15 Aug. 1737
(28 docs; now guarded with C/2/9/1/1/1/56–59)

C/2/9/1/1/1/61   Dec. 1733–Mar. 1738
Sessions held 27 Mar. 1738
Includes:
— debtors' petitions and related papers under Act for Relief of Insolvent Debtors (10 Geo. II
cap. 26), Feb. 1738
(93 docs; now guarded, out of sequence, with C/2/9/1/1/1/62–65)

C/2/9/1/1/1/62   Apr.–Aug. 1738
Sessions held 7 Aug. 1738
(18 docs; now guarded, out of sequence, with C/2/9/1/1/1/61, 63–65)

C/2/9/1/1/1/63   Aug. 1738–Apr. 1739
Sessions held 24 Apr. 1739
(37 docs; now guarded, out of sequence, with C/2/9/1/1/1/61–62, 64–65)

C/2/9/1/1/1/64   Apr.–Aug. 1739
Sessions held 20 Aug. 1739
(13 docs; now guarded, out of sequence, with C/2/9/1/1/1/61–63, 65)

C/2/9/1/1/1/65   Jun. 1739–Apr. 1740
Sessions held 3 Apr. 1740
(43 docs; now guarded, out of sequence, with C/2/9/1/1/1/61–64)

C/2/9/1/1/1/66   Feb.–Aug. 1740
Sessions held 28 Aug. 1740
(27 docs; now guarded with C/2/9/1/1/1/67–71)

C/2/9/1/1/1/67   Sep. 1740–Aug. 1741
Sessions held 12 Aug. 1741
(57 docs; now guarded with C/2/9/1/1/1/66, 68–71)

C/2/9/1/1/1/68   Aug. 1741–Jan. 1742
Sessions held 28 Dec. 1741
(22 docs; now guarded with C/2/9/1/1/1/66–67, 69–71)

C/2/9/1/1/1/69   Dec. 1741–Apr. 1742
Sessions held 21 Apr. 1742
(16 docs; now guarded with C/2/9/1/1/1/66–68, 70–71)

C/2/9/1/1/1/70   May–Aug. 1742
Sessions held 17 Aug. 1742
(20 docs; now guarded with C/2/9/1/1/1/66–69, 71)

C/2/9/1/1/1/71   Aug. 1742–Jan. 1743
Sessions held 3 Jan. 1743
(27 docs; now guarded with C/2/9/1/1/1/66–70)

C/2/9/1/1/1/72   Feb.–Aug. 1743
Sessions held 10 Aug. 1743
(18 docs; now guarded with C/2/9/1/1/1/73–75)

C/2/9/1/1/1/73   Aug. 1742–Jul. 1744
Sessions held 30 Jul. 1744
(32 docs; now guarded with C/2/9/1/1/1/72, 74–75)

C/2/9/1/1/1/74   Jul. 1751–Apr. 1752
Sessions held 6 Apr. 1752
(38 docs; now guarded with C/2/9/1/1/1/72–73, 75)

C/2/9/1/1/1/75   Sep. 1752–Apr. 1753
Sessions held 26 Apr. 1753
(56 docs; now guarded with C/2/9/1/1/1/72–74)

C/2/9/1/1/1/76   May 1753–Jul. 1754
Sessions held 9 Jul. 1754
(75 docs; now guarded with C/2/9/1/1/1/77–79)

C/2/9/1/1/1/77   Jul. 1754–Jul. 1755
Sessions held 2 Jul. 1755
Includes:
— certificate of Thomas Graves of Ipswich, cordwainer, an insolvent debtor, under 21 Geo. II
cap. 31, 2 Jul. 1755
(45 docs; now guarded with C/2/9/1/1/1/76, 78–79)

C/2/9/1/1/1/78   Jul. 1755–Jun. 1756
Sessions held 3 Jun. 1756
(37 docs; now guarded with C/2/9/1/1/1/76–77, 79)

C/2/9/1/1/1/79   Aug. 1756–Jul. 1757
Sessions held 21 Jul. 1757
(32 docs; now guarded with C/2/9/1/1/1/76–78)

C/2/9/1/1/1/80   Aug. 1757–Jun. 1758
Sessions held 21 Jun. 1758
(28 docs; now guarded with C/2/9/1/1/1/81–85)

C/2/9/1/1/1/81   Oct. 1758–Apr. 1759
Sessions held 17 Apr. 1759
(17 docs; now guarded with C/2/9/1/1/1/80, 82–85)

C/2/9/1/1/1/82   May 1759–Jun. 1760
Sessions held 2 Jun. 1760
Includes:
— order for Poor Rate assessment for town and hamlets, 2 Jun. 1760
(56 docs; now guarded with C/2/9/1/1/1/80–81, 83–85)

C/2/9/1/1/1/83   Jun. 1760–Jan. 1762
Sessions held 7 Jan. 1762
(55 docs; now guarded with C/2/9/1/1/1/80–82, 84–85)

C/2/9/1/1/1/84   21 Oct. 1762
Sessions held 4 Nov. 1762
Precepts to officers only
(11 docs; now guarded with C/2/9/1/1/1/80–83, 85)

C/2/9/1/1/1/85   Jan. 1762–May 1764
Sessions held 7 May 1764
(29 docs; now guarded with C/2/9/1/1/1/80–84)

C/2/9/1/1/1/86   May 1764–Jun. 1765
Sessions held 27 Jun. 1765
(12 docs; now guarded with C/2/9/1/1/1/87–96)

C/2/9/1/1/1/87   Jul. 1766–Jul. 1767
Sessions held 13 Jul. 1767
(28 docs; now guarded with C/2/9/1/1/1/86, 88–96)

C/2/9/1/1/1/88   7–12 Oct. 1767
Sessions held 12 Oct. 1767
(7 docs; now guarded with C/2/9/1/1/1/86–87, 89–96)

C/2/9/1/1/1/89   Oct. 1767–Jan. 1768
Sessions held 21 Jan. 1768
(11 docs; now guarded with C/2/9/1/1/1/86–88, 90–96)

C/2/9/1/1/1/90   Feb.–Apr. 1768
Sessions held 21 Apr. 1768
(12 docs; now guarded with C/2/9/1/1/1/86–89, 91–96)

C/2/9/1/1/1/91   Apr.–Jul. 1768
Sessions held 14 Jul. 1768
(13 docs; now guarded with C/2/9/1/1/1/86–90, 92–96)

C/2/9/1/1/1/92   Jul.–Oct. 1768
Sessions held 18 Oct. 1768
(33 docs; now guarded with C/2/9/1/1/1/86–91, 93–96)

C/2/9/1/1/1/93   Oct. 1768–Jan. 1769
Sessions held 6 Jan. 1769
(14 docs; now guarded with C/2/9/1/1/1/86–92, 94–96)

C/2/9/1/1/1/94   Jan.–Apr. 1769
Sessions held 25 Apr. 1769
(19 docs; now guarded with C/2/9/1/1/1/86–93, 95–96)

C/2/9/1/1/1/95   Aug.–Oct. 1769
Sessions held 20 Oct. 1769
(10 docs; now guarded with C/2/9/1/1/1/86–94, 96)

C/2/9/1/1/1/96   Dec. 1769–Mar. 1770
Sessions held 13 Mar. 1770
(14 docs; now guarded with C/2/9/1/1/1/86–95)

C/2/9/1/1/1/97   Mar.–Jul. 1770
Sessions held 2 Aug. 1770
(18 docs; now guarded with C/2/9/1/1/1/98–105)

C/2/9/1/1/1/98   Sep.–Nov. 1770
Sessions held 9 Nov. 1770
(15 docs; now guarded with C/2/9/1/1/1/97, 99–105)

C/2/9/1/1/1/99   Nov. 1770–Oct. 1771
Sessions held 1 Oct. 1771
(20 docs; now guarded with C/2/9/1/1/1/97–98, 99–105)

C/2/9/1/1/1/100   Dec. 1771–Jan. 1772
Sessions held 23 Jan. 1772
(16 docs; now guarded with C/2/9/1/1/1/97–99, 101–105)

C/2/9/1/1/1/101   Apr.–May 1772
Sessions held 2 May 1772
(10 docs; now guarded with C/2/9/1/1/1/97–100, 102–105)

C/2/9/1/1/1/102   Jul.–Sep. 1772
Sessions held 25 Sep. 1772
(16 docs; now guarded with C/2/9/1/1/1/97–101, 103–105)

C/2/9/1/1/1/103   Oct. 1772–Feb. 1773
Sessions held 25 Feb. 1773
(20 docs; now guarded with C/2/9/1/1/1/97–102, 104–105)

C/2/9/1/1/1/104   Sep. 1768–Jul. 1773
Sessions held 28 Jul. 1773
Includes:
— apprenticeship indenture, William Browne, son of William Browne of Ipswich, gardener,
bound to James Fraser of Ipswich, feltmaker, 8 Sep. 1768
(38 docs; now guarded with C/2/9/1/1/1/97–103, 105)

C/2/9/1/1/1/105   Aug.–Dec. 1773
Sessions held 20 Dec. 1773
(21 docs; now guarded with C/2/9/1/1/1/97–104)

C/2/9/1/1/1/106   Dec. 1773–Jul. 1774
Sessions held 25 Jul. 1774
(25 docs; now guarded with C/2/9/1/1/1/107–116)

C/2/9/1/1/1/107   Jul. 1774–Mar. 1775
Sessions held 17 Mar. 1775
(17 docs; now guarded with C/2/9/1/1/1/106, 108–116)

C/2/9/1/1/1/108   Jun.–Aug. 1775
Sessions held 7 Aug. 1775
(15 docs; now guarded with C/2/9/1/1/1/106–107, 109–116)

C/2/9/1/1/1/109   Oct. 1775–Mar. 1776
Sessions held 18 Mar. 1776
(13 docs; now guarded with C/2/9/1/1/1/106–108, 110–116)

C/2/9/1/1/1/110   Apr.–Jul. 1776
Sessions held 30 Jul. 1776
(11 docs; now guarded with C/2/9/1/1/1/106–109, 111–116)

C/2/9/1/1/1/111   Sep. 1776–Jul. 1777
Sessions held 11 Jul. 1777
(13 docs; now guarded with C/2/9/1/1/1/106–110, 112–116)

C/2/9/1/1/1/112   Nov. 1777–Jan. 1778
Sessions held 7 Jan. 1778
(11 docs; now guarded with C/2/9/1/1/1/106–111, 113–116)

C/2/9/1/1/1/113   May–Aug. 1778
Sessions held 3 Aug. 1778
(9 docs; now guarded with C/2/9/1/1/1/106–112, 114–116)

C/2/9/1/1/1/114   Aug. 1778–Mar. 1779
Sessions held 9 Mar. 1779
(21 docs; now guarded with C/2/9/1/1/1/106–113, 115–116)

C/2/9/1/1/1/115   Jun.–Jul. 1779
Sessions held 16 Jul. 1779
(7 docs; now guarded with C/2/9/1/1/1/106–114, 116)

C/2/9/1/1/1/116   Aug. 1779–Sep. 1780
Sessions held 15 Mar. 1780
(22 docs; now guarded with C/2/9/1/1/1/106–115)

C/2/9/1/1/1/117   Mar.–Jul. 1780
Sessions held 31 Jul. 1780
(22 docs; now guarded with C/2/9/1/1/1/118–125)

C/2/9/1/1/1/118   Sep. 1777–Mar. 1781
Sessions held 14 Mar. 1781
Includes:
— apprenticeship indenture, John Pallant bound by churchwardens and overseers of MG to
James Durrant of Ipswich, farrier, 11 Sep. 1777
(18 docs; now guarded with C/2/9/1/1/1/117, 119–125)

C/2/9/1/1/1/119   Mar.–Sep. 1781
Sessions held 19 Sep. 1781
(22 docs; now guarded with C/2/9/1/1/1/117–118, 120–125)

C/2/9/1/1/1/120   Nov. 1781–Mar. 1782
Sessions held 14 Mar. 1782
(20 docs; now guarded with C/2/9/1/1/1/117–119, 121–125)

C/2/9/1/1/1/121   10–22 May 1782
Sessions held 22 May 1782
(9 docs; now guarded with C/2/9/1/1/1/117–120, 122–125)

C/2/9/1/1/1/122   May–Sep. 1782
Sessions held 26 Sep. 1782
(16 docs; now guarded with C/2/9/1/1/1/117–121, 123–125)

C/2/9/1/1/1/123   Oct. 1782–Mar. 1783
Sessions held 12 Mar. 1783
(22 docs; now guarded with C/2/9/1/1/1/117–122, 124–125)

C/2/9/1/1/1/124   Mar.–Aug. 1783
Sessions held 13 Aug. 1783
(14 docs; now guarded with C/2/9/1/1/1/117–123, 125)

C/2/9/1/1/1/125   Sep. 1783–Mar. 1784
Sessions held 18 Mar. 1784
(21 docs; now guarded with C/2/9/1/1/1/118–124)

C/2/9/1/1/1/126   Apr.–Jul. 1784
Sessions held 30 Jul. 1784
(11 docs; now guarded with C/2/9/1/1/1/127–132)

C/2/9/1/1/1/127   Aug. 1784–Mar. 1785
Sessions held 16 Mar. 1785
(33 docs; now guarded with C/2/9/1/1/1/126, 128–132)

C/2/9/1/1/1/128   Oct. 1784–Jul. 1785
Sessions held 4 Jul. 1785
(113 docs; now guarded with C/2/9/1/1/1/126–127, 129–132)

C/2/9/1/1/1/129   Jul.–Nov. 1785
Sessions held 18 Nov. 1785
Includes:
— presentments of Grand Jury and Petty Constables at Sessions held 4 Jul. 1785, ? originally
filed with C/2/9/1/1/1/128
(21 docs; now guarded with C/2/9/1/1/1/126–128, 130–132)

C/2/9/1/1/1/130   Nov. 1785–Mar. 1786
Sessions held 17 Mar. 1786
Includes:
— copy resolution of County Sessions of the Peace held 22 Nov. 1785, *re* reception of Ipswich
prisoners into new County Gaol and appropriate compensation payable
(37 docs; now guarded with C/2/9/1/1/1/126–129, 131–132)

C/2/9/1/1/1/131   Mar.–Jul. 1786
Sessions held 28 Jul. 1786
(22 docs; now guarded with C/2/9/1/1/1/126–130, 132)

C/2/9/1/1/1/132   Jul. 1786–Mar. 1787
Sessions held 23 Mar. 1787
(54 docs; now guarded with C/2/9/1/1/1/126–131)

C/2/9/1/1/1/133   Mar.–Jul. 1787
Sessions held 20 Jul. 1787
(29 docs; now guarded with C/2/9/1/1/1/134–137)

C/2/9/1/1/1/134   Jul. 1787–Mar. 1788
Sessions held 17 Mar. 1788
(82 docs; now guarded with C/2/9/1/1/1/133, 135–137)

C/2/9/1/1/1/135   Apr. 1788–Mar. 1789
Sessions held 18 Mar. 1789
(50 docs; now guarded with C/2/9/1/1/1/133–134, 136–137)

C/2/9/1/1/1/136   Apr.–Sep. 1789
Sessions held 11 Sep. 1789
(21 docs; now guarded with C/2/9/1/1/1/133–135, 137)

C/2/9/1/1/1/137   Nov. 1789–Mar. 1790
Sessions held 15 Mar. 1790
(24 docs; now guarded with C/2/9/1/1/1/133–136)

C/2/9/1/1/1/138   Mar.–Jul. 1790
Sessions held 19 Jul. 1790
(27 docs; now guarded with C/2/9/1/1/1/139–144)

C/2/9/1/1/1/139   Mar. 1790–Mar. 1791
Sessions held 21 Mar. 1791
(44 docs; now guarded with C/2/9/1/1/1/138,140–144)

C/2/9/1/1/1/140   Apr. 1791–Mar. 1792
Sessions held 19 Mar. 1792
(21 docs; now guarded with C/2/9/1/1/1/138–139, 141–144)

C/2/9/1/1/1/141   Apr. 1792–Mar. 1793
Sessions held 25 Mar. 1793
(28 docs; now guarded with C/2/9/1/1/1/138–140, 142–144)

C/2/9/1/1/1/142   Apr. 1792–Mar. 1794
Sessions held 18 Mar. 1794
(29 docs; now guarded with C/2/9/1/1/1/138–141, 143–144)

C/2/9/1/1/1/143   Apr. 1794–Mar. 1795
Sessions held 23 Mar. 1795
(28 docs; now guarded with C/2/9/1/1/1/138–142, 144)

C/2/9/1/1/1/144   Mar. 1795–Mar. 1796
Sessions held 14 Mar. 1796
(28 docs; now guarded with C/2/9/1/1/1/138–143)

C/2/9/1/1/1/145   Mar. 1796–Mar. 1797
Sessions held 20 Mar. 1797
(39 docs; now guarded with C/2/9/1/1/1/146–149)

C/2/9/1/1/1/146   Mar.–Nov. 1797
Sessions held 20 Nov. 1797
(34 docs; now guarded with C/2/9/1/1/1/145, 147–149)

C/2/9/1/1/1/147   Dec. 1797–Mar. 1799
Sessions held 4 Mar. 1799
(45 docs; now guarded with C/2/9/1/1/1/145–146, 148–149)

C/2/9/1/1/1/148   Mar. 1799–Mar. 1800
Sessions held 17 Mar. 1800
(42 docs; now guarded with C/2/9/1/1/1/145–147, 149)

C/2/9/1/1/1/149   Aug. 1800–Mar. 1801
Sessions held 16 Mar. 1801
(59 docs; now guarded with C/2/9/1/1/1/145–148)

C/2/9/1/1/1/150   Mar.–Dec. 1801
Sessions held 21 Dec. 1801
(20 docs; now guarded with C/2/9/1/1/1/151–155)

C/2/9/1/1/1/151   Dec. 1801–Jul. 1802
Sessions held 26 Jul. 1802
(28 docs; now guarded with C/2/9/1/1/1/150, 152–155)

C/2/9/1/1/1/152   Aug. 1802–Mar. 1803
Sessions held 8 Mar. 1803
(40 docs; now guarded with C/2/9/1/1/1/150–151, 153–155)

C/2/9/1/1/1/153   May–Jul. 1803
Sessions held 20 Jul. 1803
(20 docs; now guarded with C/2/9/1/1/1/150–152, 154–155)

C/2/9/1/1/1/154   May 1803–Jan. 1804
Sessions held 19 Jan. 1804
(39 docs; now guarded with C/2/9/1/1/1/150–153, 155)

C/2/9/1/1/1/155   Jan.–Jul. 1804
Sessions held 12 Jul. 1804
(24 docs; now guarded with C/2/9/1/1/1/150–154)

C/2/9/1/1/1/156   Nov. 1798–Nov. 1804
Sessions held 29 Nov. 1804
(36 docs; now guarded with C/2/9/1/1/1/157–159)

C/2/9/1/1/1/157   Nov. 1804–Mar. 1805
Sessions held 6 Mar. 1805
(49 docs; now guarded with C/2/9/1/1/1/156, 158–159)

C/2/9/1/1/1/158   Mar. 1805–Feb. 1806
Sessions held 14 Feb. 1806
(77 docs; now guarded with C/2/9/1/1/1/156–157, 159)

C/2/9/1/1/1/159   Nov. 1805–Jul. 1806
Sessions held 11 Jul. 1806
(47 docs; now guarded with C/2/9/1/1/1/156–158)

C/2/9/1/1/1/160   Dec. 1805–Dec. 1806
Sessions held 9 Dec. 1806
(80 docs; now guarded with C/2/9/1/1/1/161–163)

C/2/9/1/1/1/161   Oct. 1806–Apr. 1807
Sessions held 3 Apr. 1807
(46 docs; now guarded with C/2/9/1/1/1/160, 162–163)

C/2/9/1/1/1/162   Oct. 1806–Feb. 1808
Sessions held 23 Feb. 1808
(35 docs; now guarded with C/2/9/1/1/1/160–161, 163)

C/2/9/1/1/1/163   Apr. 1807–Feb. 1809
Sessions held 20 Feb. 1809
(57 docs; now guarded with C/2/9/1/1/1/160–162)

C/2/9/1/1/1/164   Nov. 1808–Aug. 1809
Sessions held 15 Aug. 1809
(33 docs; now guarded with C/2/9/1/1/1/165–168)

C/2/9/1/1/1/165   Aug. 1809–Feb. 1810
Sessions held 20 Feb. 1810
(43 docs; now guarded with C/2/9/1/1/1/164, 166–168)

C/2/9/1/1/1/166   Mar.–Aug. 1810
Sessions held 2 Aug. 1810
(40 docs; now guarded with C/2/9/1/1/1/164–165, 167–168)

C/2/9/1/1/1/167   Aug. 1810–May 1811
Sessions held 19 Feb. 1811
(43 docs; now guarded with C/2/9/1/1/1/164–166, 168)

C/2/9/1/1/1/168   Mar.–Jul. 1811
Sessions held 30 Jul. 1811
(44 docs; now guarded with C/2/9/1/1/1/164–167)

C/2/9/1/1/1/169   Nov. 1811–Feb. 1812
Sessions held 17 Feb. 1812
(35 docs; now guarded with C/2/9/1/1/1/170–173)

C/2/9/1/1/1/170   Jul.–Sep. 1812
Sessions held 23 Sep. 1812
(21 docs; now guarded with C/2/9/1/1/1/169, 171–173)

C/2/9/1/1/1/171   Oct. 1812–Mar. 1813
Sessions held 4 Mar. 1813
(37 docs; now guarded with C/2/9/1/1/1/169–170, 172–173)

C/2/9/1/1/1/172   Mar.–Aug. 1813
Sessions held 4 Aug. 1813
(34 docs; now guarded with C/2/9/1/1/1/169–171, 173)

C/2/9/1/1/1/173   Oct. 1813–Feb. 1814
Sessions held 15 Feb. 1814
(47 docs; now guarded with C/2/9/1/1/1/169–172)

C/2/9/1/1/1/174   Feb.–Jul. 1814
Sessions held 28 Jul. 1814
(42 docs; now guarded with C/2/9/1/1/1/175–177)

C/2/9/1/1/1/175   Mar.–Jul. 1815
Sessions held 15 Jul. 1815
(31 docs; now guarded with C/2/9/1/1/1/174, 176–177)

C/2/9/1/1/1/176   Jul. 1815–Feb. 1816
Sessions held 26 Feb. 1816
(44 docs; now guarded with C/2/9/1/1/1/174–175, 177)

C/2/9/1/1/1/177   6–31 Jul. 1816
Sessions held 31 Jul. 1816
(11 docs; now guarded with C/2/9/1/1/1/174–176)

C/2/9/1/1/1/178   Aug. 1816–Mar. 1817
Sessions held 3 Mar. 1817
(66 docs; now guarded with C/2/9/1/1/1/179–181)

C/2/9/1/1/1/179   Apr.–Jul. 1817
Sessions held 23 Jul. 1817
(35 docs; now guarded with C/2/9/1/1/1/178, 180–181)

C/2/9/1/1/1/180   Aug. 1817–Mar. 1818
Sessions held 2 Mar. 1818
(74 docs; now guarded with C/2/9/1/1/1/178–179, 181)

C/2/9/1/1/1/181   Mar.–Aug. 1818
Sessions held 5 Aug. 1818
(64 docs; now guarded with C/2/9/1/1/1/178–180)

C/2/9/1/1/1/182   Aug. 1818–Mar. 1819
Sessions held 1 Mar. 1819
(72 docs; now guarded with C/2/9/1/1/1/183)

C/2/9/1/1/1/183   Mar.–Jul. 1819
Sessions held 29 Jul. 1819
(52 docs; now guarded with C/2/9/1/1/1/182)

C/2/9/1/1/1/184   Aug. 1819–Feb. 1820
Sessions held 28 Feb. 1820
(40 docs; now guarded with C/2/9/1/1/1/185–186)

C/2/9/1/1/1/185   Feb.–Aug. 1820
Sessions held 4 Aug. 1820
(45 docs; now guarded with C/2/9/1/1/1/184, 186)

C/2/9/1/1/1/186   Jun. 1820–Mar. 1821
Sessions held 6 Mar. 1821
(66 docs; now guarded with C/2/9/1/1/1/184–185)

C/2/9/1/1/1/187   Apr.–Jul. 1821
Sessions held 30 Jul. 1821
(40 docs; now guarded with C/2/9/1/1/1/188)

C/2/9/1/1/1/188   Aug. 1821–Mar. 1822
Sessions held 19 Mar. 1822
Includes:
— order by two Justices for division of responsibility for repair of Ipswich–Wherstead
highway in MS and PE, 30 Jan. 1822
— plan of above highway, by John Bransby, n.d. [c. 1822]
(93 docs; now guarded with C/2/9/1/1/1/187)

C/2/9/1/1/1/189   Apr.–Jul. 1822
Sessions held 12 Jul. 1822
(34 docs; now guarded with C/2/9/1/1/1/190)

C/2/9/1/1/1/190   Jan. 1822–Mar. 1823
Sessions held 11 Mar. 1823
Includes:
— plan of new road in MS, by John Bransby, 18 Dec. 1822
— order by two Justices for diversion of Ipswich–Belstead highway in MS, 8 Jan. 1823
(86 docs; now guarded with C/2/9/1/1/1/189)

C/2/9/1/1/1/191   Apr.–Jul. 1823
Sessions held 11 Jul. 1823
(33 docs; now guarded with C/2/9/1/1/1/192)

C/2/9/1/1/1/192   Jul.–Nov. 1823
Sessions held 17 Nov. 1823
Includes:
— 5 alehouse keepers' certificates, Oct.–Nov. 1823
— 6 alehouse keepers' recognizances, Oct.–Nov. 1823
— certificate of completion of diverted section of Ipswich–Belstead highway in MS, 13 Nov. 1823
— certificate of completion of diverted section of highway in NI, 15 Nov. 1823
(71 docs; now guarded with C/2/9/1/1/1/191)

C/2/9/1/1/1/193   Nov. 1823–Mar. 1824
Sessions held 15 Mar. 1824
(70 docs; now guarded with C/2/9/1/1/1/194)

C/2/9/1/1/1/194   Mar.–Aug. 1824
Sessions held 2 Aug. 1824
(53 docs; now guarded with C/2/9/1/1/1/193)

C/2/9/1/1/1/195   Aug. 1824–Mar. 1825
Sessions held 15 Mar. 1825
(117 docs; now guarded with C/2/9/1/1/1/196)

C/2/9/1/1/1/196   Dec. 1824–Jul. 1825
Sessions held 25 Jul. 1825
(48 docs; now guarded with C/2/9/1/1/1/195)

C/2/9/1/1/1/197   Apr. 1823–Mar. 1826
Sessions held 1 Mar. 1826
Includes:
— order by two Justices for division of responsibility for repair of part of Ipswich–Bucklesham highway in MG and CL, 14 Dec. 1825
— plan of above part of highway, by John Bransby, Jan. 1825
— order by two Justices for division of responsibility for highway from the Mount to Handford Bridge in MW and PE, 1 Feb. 1826
— plan of above highway, by John Bransby, Jan. 1825
(115 docs; now guarded with C/2/9/1/1/1/198)

C/2/9/1/1/1/198   Mar.–Jul. 1826
Sessions held 7 Jul. 1826
(122 docs; now guarded with C/2/9/1/1/1/197)

C/2/9/1/1/1/199   Jul. 1826–Mar. 1827
Sessions held 21 Mar. 1827
(88 docs; now guarded with C/2/9/1/1/1/200)

C/2/9/1/1/1/200   Mar.–Jul. 1827
Sessions held 24 Jul. 1827
(59 docs; now guarded with C/2/9/1/1/1/199)

C/2/9/1/1/1/201   Aug. 1827–Mar. 1828
Sessions held 12 Mar. 1828
(79 docs; now guarded with C/2/9/1/1/1/203)

C/2/9/1/1/1/202   n.d. [Mar. 1828]
[Sessions held 12 Mar. 1828]
Indictment of George Webb of MW, for libelling Robert Bowman by accusing him of concealing smuggled goods in Jun. 1827

110

(12 membranes, stitched together 'Chancery' style, the outer membrane endorsed 'True Bill'; never attached to C/2/9/1/1/1/201)

C/2/9/1/1/1/203   Mar.–Jul. 1828
Sessions held 23 Jul. 1828
(51 docs; now guarded with C/2/9/1/1/1/201)

C/2/9/1/1/1/204   Oct. 1828–Mar. 1829
Sessions held 23 Mar. 1829
Includes:
— rules and regulations for the Ipswich Provident Bank in MQ, certified 13 Dec. 1828
(76 docs; now guarded with C/2/9/1/1/1/205)

C/2/9/1/1/1/205   Apr.–Aug. 1829
Sessions held 3 Aug. 1829
(30 docs; now guarded with C/2/9/1/1/1/204)

C/2/9/1/1/1/206   Aug. 1829–Mar. 1830
Sessions held 22 Mar. 1830
(59 docs; now guarded with C/2/9/1/1/1/207–209)

C/2/9/1/1/1/207   Mar.–Sep. 1830
Sessions held 20 Sep. 1830
(28 docs; now guarded with C/2/9/1/1/1/206, 208–209)

C/2/9/1/1/1/208   Oct. 1830–Apr. 1831
Sessions held 11 Apr. 1831
(62 docs; now guarded with C/2/9/1/1/1/206–207, 209)

C/2/9/1/1/1/209   Sep. 1830–Jun. 1831
Sessions held 30 Jun. 1831
(31docs; now guarded with C/2/9/1/1/1/206–208)

C/2/9/1/1/1/210   Jul. 1831–Feb. 1832
Sessions held 16 Feb. 1832
(101 docs; now guarded with C/2/9/1/1/1/211)

C/2/9/1/1/1/211   Feb.–Jul. 1832
Sessions held 24 Jul. 1832
(37 docs; now guarded with C/2/9/1/1/1/210)

C/2/9/1/1/1/212   Aug. 1832–Mar. 1833
Sessions held 11 Mar. 1833
(74 docs; now guarded with C/2/9/1/1/1/213)

C/2/9/1/1/1/213   Feb.–Jul. 1833
Sessions held 15 Jul. 1833
(91 docs; now guarded with C/2/9/1/1/1/212)

C/2/9/1/1/1/214   Jul. 1833–Feb. 1834
Sessions held 12 Feb. 1834
(111 docs; now guarded with C/2/9/1/1/1/215–217)

C/2/9/1/1/1/215   Feb.–Apr. 1834
Sessions held 16 Apr. 1834; the first to be described as 'General Quarter Sessions' rather than simply 'General Sessions'
(13 docs; now guarded with C/2/9/1/1/1/216–217)

C/2/9/1/1/1/216   Apr.–Jun. 1834
Sessions held 30 Jun. 1834
(44 docs; now guarded with C/2/9/1/1/1/215, 217)

C/2/9/1/1/1/217   Jul.–Oct. 1834
Sessions held 30 Oct. 1834
Includes:
— notice by Mrs Mary Jane Williams, of intention to apply for licence for house in Church
Street, CL, as asylum for 6 insane female patients, 26 Sep. 1834
— certificate of fitness of above premises, by G. M. Williams, M.D., 11 Sep. 1834
— certificate of fitness of Robert King to keep private asylum, 30 Oct. 1834
(50 docs; now guarded with C/2/9/1/1/1/214–216)

C/2/9/1/1/1/218   Nov. 1834–Mar. 1835
Sessions held 9 Mar. 1835
(53 docs; now guarded with C/2/9/1/1/1/219–220)

C/2/9/1/1/1/219   Mar.–Jun. 1835
Sessions held 30 Jun. 1835
(52 docs; now guarded with C/2/9/1/1/1/218, 220)

C/2/9/1/1/1/220   Jul.–Oct. 1835
Sessions held 27 Oct. 1835
(44 docs; now guarded with C/2/9/1/1/1/218–219)

C/2/9/1/1/2   Presentments – Surveyors of the highways   1746–c.1810

Names of parishioners defaulting in work on the highways, with number of days in default,
financial penalties imposed, and reasons for abatement (e.g. 'poor', 'in the King's service',
'came late into the parish'). Most surviving presentments will be found on the Sessions Rolls.

C/2/9/1/1/2/1   24 Nov. 1746
MT; John Stannard and James Raymond, Surveyors
(1 doc.)

C/2/9/1/1/2/2   29 Nov. 1746
MG; Henry Betts, Surveyor
(1 vol.)

C/2/9/1/1/2/3   29 Nov. 1746
MW; William Alsse, James Bennet, Surveyors
(1 fol.)

C/2/9/1/1/2/4   24 Nov. 1746
NI; Robert Rivers, James Dobby, Surveyors
(1 fol.)

C/2/9/1/1/2/5   14 Dec. 1747
NI; Robert Rivers, James Dobby, Surveyors
(1 fol.)

C/2/9/1/1/2/6   c.1773–c.1810
Blank forms of presentments of highways out of repair
Includes:
— blank form of recognizance to keep the peace, n.d.
(11 docs)

C/2/9/1/1/3   Other presentments   c.1702

Most surviving presentments will be found on the Sessions Rolls.

C/2/9/1/1/3/1   n.d. [*c.*1702]
Contemporary copy presentment of Thomas Moody, late of Ipswich, gent., for digging sand and soil in Wash Lane, diverting the water from running there, and obstructing the highway with 10 loads of sand and dirt, on 13 Apr. 1702
With English translation
(2 docs)

C/2/9/1/1/4   Process Books of Indictments   1683–1687

Lists of names of persons indicted at General Sessions, with notes of process added

C/2/9/1/1/4/1   Jul. 1683–May 1687
(1 vol., 64 pp, 12 pp blank; with index of names)

C/2/9/1/1/5   Records of Process   1722–1832

Engrossments of proceedings in criminal cases

C/2/9/1/1/5/1   19 Mar. 1722
Attested copy
Against William Cooke, late of Ipswich, cooper, indicted for an assault on customs officers
Annexed:
— copy verdict and judgment in the cause, 19 Mar. 1722
(2 docs; Latin)

C/2/9/1/1/5/2   Dec. 1724–Aug. 1727
Copy
Against Sarah Browne, late of Ipswich, widow, indicted for following trade of linen draper without having served an apprenticeship
(22 pp; Latin)

C/2/9/1/1/5/3   17 Aug. 1832
Copy
Against John Pixley, late of Ipswich, labourer, indicted for assault on John Prigg, customs officer
(Latin)

C/2/9/1/1/6   Sessions Bundles   1799–1828

As found, these bundles were totally disarranged, each folder containing documents for several years, with overlapping covering dates. It seems probable that there was originally one bundle for each Sessions but, given the virtual impossibility of accurate reconstruction, one annual bundle has been made up for each calendar year.

From 1799 to 1811 the bundles consist entirely of Coroner's original inquisitions (by the Act of 25 Geo. II, cap. 29 (1752), Coroner's expenses were allowed by Quarter Sessions; other inquisitions may be found in the Sessions Rolls (C/2/9/1/1/1) between 1722 and 1765). From 1812, though inquisitions are present in every year down to 1825, the chief contents of the bundles are informations sworn before the Justices, with a smaller number of precepts to summon jurors and to produce prisoners in court or before individual justices.

C/2/9/1/1/6/1   Apr.–Dec. 1799
Coroner's inquisitions only, on: John Elliott, 5 Apr. 1799; Elizabeth Garwood, 13 Apr. 1799; Richard Fryatt, 3 May 1799; Peter Moy, 26 Jun. 1799; Mary Cunnold, 3 Jul. 1799; Mark Loom, 21 Jul. 1799; John Aldrich, 22 Dec. 1799
(7 docs)

C/2/9/1/1/6/2   May–Oct. 1800
Coroner's inquisitions only, on: Joseph Smith, 16 May 1800; John Levett, 19 Jun. 1800; Elizabeth Rogers, 1 Oct. 1800; John Hines, 15 Oct. 1800
(4 docs)

C/2/9/1/1/6/3   Feb.–Dec. 1801
Coroner's inquisitions only, on: James Butcher, 26 Feb. 1801; Joseph Gibbs, 1 Apr. 1801; William Parker, 9 Jun. 1801; Richard Wythe, 27 Nov. 1801; Henry Fist, 11 Dec. 1801
(5 docs)

C/2/9/1/1/6/4   Jan.–Dec. 1802
Coroner's inquisitions only, on: William Cook, infant, 12 Jan. 1802; Joseph Jackaman, 24 Feb. 1802; Mary Bocking, 30 Apr. 1802; Mary Bone, 1 Sep. 1802; Isaac Spooner, 3 Sep. 1802; John Gooding, 9 Dec. 1802; John Green Groves, 16 Dec. 1802
(7 docs)

C/2/9/1/1/6/5   Jan.–Apr. 1803
Coroner's inquisitions only, on: Susan Blacktop, 14 Jan. 1803; George Howard, 14 Mar. 1803; Joseph Plumb, 1 Apr. 1803; Isaac Beamish, 27 Apr. 1803
(4 docs)

C/2/9/1/1/6/6   Feb.–Jun. 1804
Coroner's inquisitions only, on: Edward Creed, 7 Feb. 1804; Sarah Smith, 2 Apr. 1804; Robert Christie, infant, 24 Jun. 1804
(3 docs)

C/2/9/1/1/6/7   Aug.–Nov. 1805
Coroner's inquisitions only, on: Robert Haxell, 30 Aug. 1805; Henry Fox, 24 Sep. 1805; Thomas Porter, 23 Nov. 1805
(3 docs)

C/2/9/1/1/6/8   Feb.–Oct. 1806
Coroner's inquisitions only, on: Richard Harris, 19 Feb. 1806; William Canham, 28 Mar. 1806; Robert Harding, 4 Jul. 1806; John Gooding, 14 Jun. 1806; Robert Pooley, 21 Jul. 1806; John Scarlett sen., 4 Aug. 1806; John Scarlett jun., 4 Aug. 1806
(7 docs)

C/2/9/1/1/6/9   Mar. 1807
Coroner's inquisition only, on: Zachariah Barker, 24 Mar. 1807
(1 doc)

C/2/9/1/1/6/10   Feb.–Dec. 1808
Coroner's inquisitions only, on: William Barbell, 7 Feb. 1808; Elizabeth Ashkettle, 9 Feb. 1808; Charles Rudding, 24 Apr. 1808; Solomon Bear, 25 Oct. 1808; Robert Roper, 7 Dec. 1808
(5 docs)

C/2/9/1/1/6/11   Feb.–Dec. 1809
Coroner's inquisitions only, on: John Watson, 26 Feb. 1809; David Debney, 3 Mar. 1809; Frederick Hanel, 11 May 1809; Robert Boyce, 3 Jun. 1809; Elizabeth Ellis, 31 Jul. 1809; Jemima Vincent, 25 Sep. 1809; James Read, 30 Nov. 1809; Robert Fox, 12 Dec. 1809 (with informations and examinations of witnesses)
(9 docs)

C/2/9/1/1/6/12   Feb.–Aug. 1810
Coroner's inquisitions only, on: a new-born male child, 14 Feb. 1810; Sarah, wife of William Cracknall, 24 Aug. 1810
(2 docs)

C/2/9/1/1/6/13   Jun.–Dec. 1811

Coroner's inquisitions only, on: Henry Hofmeyer, private in 3rd Regiment of German Hussars, 6 Jun. 1811; Thomas Bird, 15 Jun. 1811; Henry Jenkins, 9 Aug. 1811; Catherine Guess, infant, 15 Oct. 1811; Honor Howes, widow, 18 Nov. 1811; John Gowing, 26 Dec. 1811

(6 docs)

C/2/9/1/1/6/14   Mar.–Dec. 1812

Includes:

— Coroner's inquisitions on: Robert Cash Murphy, 10 Mar. 1812; Lucy Acton, infant, 24 Jun. 1812; Frederick Muller, 8 Jul. 1812; Van den Berg, 16 Jul. 1812; Gregory Riches, 4 Aug. 1812; Jeremiah Laws, 29 Aug. 1812; Charlotte Marshford, 26 Dec. 1812

(17 docs)

C/2/9/1/1/6/15   Jan.–Dec. 1813

Includes:

— Coroner's inquisitions on: James Wells, 27 Jan. 1813; John Grimwood, 30 Jan. 1813; William Ferritt, 24 Mar. 1813; John Head, 12 Apr. 1813; John Alecock, 18 Jun. 1813; Francis Favior, 8 Jul. 1813; William Bird, 29 Jul. 1813; Zaver Schonpflug, 11 Aug. 1813

(81 docs)

C/2/9/1/1/6/16   Jan.–Dec. 1814

Includes:

— Coroner's inquisitions on: Matthias Burrows, 31 Jan. 1814; Elizabeth Woolf, 16 Mar. 1814; a man unknown, 24 Mar. 1814; George Kerridge sen., 9 Apr. 1814; William Anderson, 12 Apr. 1814; John Robson, 12 Apr. 1814; John Simpson, 12 Apr. 1814; Thomas Ryder, 28 Jun. 1814; John Kerridge, 25 Jul. 1814; Dorothea Shultz, infant, 4 Sep. 1814; Martin Glaghern, 26 Dec. 1814

(66 docs)

C/2/9/1/1/6/17   Jan.–Dec. 1815

Includes:

— Coroner's inquisitions on: Ann Welham, 22 Jun. 1815; Henry Bird, 26 Jun. 1815; John Rushmore jun., 13 Jul. 1815; William Backhouse, 15 Nov. 1815

(46 docs)

C/2/9/1/1/6/18   Jan.–Dec. 1816

Includes:

— Coroner's inquisitions on: Edward Fisher, 18 Jan. 1816; Elizabeth Kent, 31 Jan. 1816; William Read, 17 Feb. 1816; a female infant, 2 Mar. 1816 (with informations of witnesses); Sarah Planten, 13 Apr. 1816; Jonathan Davy, 5 Jul. 1816; Jemima Fuller, 27 Aug. 1816; Thomas Hare, 6 Sep. 1816; Mary Payn, 6 Sep. 1816; Mary Daldy, 9 Nov. 1816; Susan Powell, 21 Dec. 1816

(47 docs)

C/2/9/1/1/6/19   Jan.–Dec. 1817

Includes:

— Coroner's inquisitions on: James Death sen., 10 Jan. 1817; Robert Groom, 18 Jan. 1817; William Williams, 7 Feb. 1817; Peter Dankers, 17 Mar. 1817; Eleanor Caston, infant aged 20 months, 24 Mar. 1817; Sarah Fosdike, 11 Apr. 1817; William Davis, 27 May 1817; William Corbould, 31 May 1817; Samuel Everingham, 21 Jun. 1817; James Widger, 24 Jun. 1817; a male infant unknown, 2 Sep. 1817; William Randall, 13 Sep. 1817; Absalom Bloomfield, 18 Oct. 1817; Charles Greaves, 3 Nov. 1817; Charlotte Smith, 18 Dec. 1817

(44 docs)

C/2/9/1/1/6/20   Jan.–Dec. 1818

Includes:

— Coroner's inquisitions on: William Cain, prisoner in House of Correction, 3 Feb. 1818; a male infant unknown, 24 Feb. 1818 (with informations of witnesses); John Osborn, 27 Apr.

1818 (with information of witness); Edward Stannard, 13 Jun. 1818; a man unknown, 9 Jul. 1818; William Reeve, 10 Jul. 1818 (with informations of witnesses); John Bird, 24 Sep. 1818 (with informations of witnesses); Harriet Taylor, 17 Oct. 1818; Susanna Rivers, infant aged 9 weeks, 22 Nov. 1818
(87 docs)

C/2/9/1/1/6/21   Jan.–Dec. 1819
Includes:
— Coroner's inquisitions on: Henry Scott, infant, 16 Jan. 1819; John Chaplin, 22 Jan. 1819; Abraham Gooding, 24 Jan. 1819; Ann Foxwell, widow, 25 Jan. 1819; Richard Bateman, 9 Feb. 1819; Charles Turner, 10 Mar. 1819; Ebenezer Powling, 12 Mar. 1819; Sarah, wife of William Kidman, 7 May 1819; Charles Scott, 15 Jul. 1819 (with informations of witnesses); Davison Nixon, 30 Jul. 1819; Jeffery Trigger, 25 Aug. 1819 (with information of witness); Foxhall Baldry, 21 Oct. 1819; Philip Weatherley, 17 Sep. 1819; James Dungate, 23 Nov. 1819 (with informations of witnesses); Henry Graystone, 27 Dec. 1819 (with informations of witnesses)
(82 docs)

C/2/9/1/1/6/22   Jan.–Dec. 1820
Includes:
— Coroner's inquisitions on: Edward Finch, 29 Feb. 1820; William Davy, 25 Jun. 1820; William Vernon Simpson, 24 Jul. 1820; Samuel Eastaugh, 24 Oct. 1820
— order for diversion of highway in NI and PE, 14 Aug. 1820, with annexed plan by John Bransby, 4 Aug. 1820
(78 docs)

C/2/9/1/1/6/23   Jan.–Dec. 1821
Includes:
— Coroner's inquisitions on: William Lawrance, aged 9 years, 19 Feb. 1821; a male infant unknown, 1 May 1821; Alexander Bird, 16 Aug. 1821; Jacob Lindsey Green, 25 Aug. 1821; William Harrington, 9 Sep. 1821; Charles Burrows, 29 Sep. 1821
— rules of Society of Brotherly Love held at the Maypole Inn, Whitton, established 1806, confirmed 30 Jul. 1821
— amendment to rules of Union Benefit Society held at the Waggon and Horses Inn, Ipswich, confirmed 6 Mar. 1821
— draft estreats of fines, Sep. 1820–Sep. 1821
(131 docs)

C/2/9/1/1/6/24   Jan.–Dec. 1822
Includes:
— Coroner's inquisitions on: William Day, 12 Jan. 1822; Elizabeth Clarke, widow, 25 Mar. 1822; Sarah Mudd, infant aged 4 months, 24 Apr. 1822; Eliza Welham, 30 Apr. 1822; John Peirson, 6 Jun. 1822; infant son of Samuel Abbott, 18 May 1822; James Crask, 6 Jul. 1822; Phoebe Hayward, 19 Aug. 1822; William Bird, 20 Oct. 1822; Richard Carr, 20 Oct. 1822; William Clarke, 20 Oct. 1822; Mary Selby, 27 Nov. 1822
— draft minutes of Sessions, 20 Oct. 1821–7 Sep. 1822
— draft estreats of fines, Sep. 1821–Sep. 1822
— accounts of bread supplied for gaol, Aug. 1821–Mar. 1822
(77 docs)

C/2/9/1/1/6/25   Feb.–Dec. 1823
Includes:
— Coroner's inquisitions on: Ann Hughes, aged 8 years, 23 Mar. 1823; John Boggis, 31 Mar. 1823; Robert Pain, 12 May 1823; Elizabeth Cotton, 8 Jun. 1823; James Barker, 27 Jun. 1823; John Locke, 23 Sep. 1823; Thomas Nichols, 25 Oct. 1823; John Wooby, 19 Nov. 1823; John Parker, 29 Nov. 1823; James Masters, 10 Dec. 1823
— draft minutes of Sessions, 11 Mar. 1823
— draft minutes of Sessions, 11 Jul. 1823

— draft estreats of fines, Sep. 1822–Sep. 1823
— copy verses from *London Chronicle* (7 May 1761), n.d. [? 1823]
(100 docs)

C/2/9/1/1/6/26   Feb.–Dec. 1824
Includes:
— Coroner's inquisitions on: infant male child of John Brighten and wife Martha, 7 Feb. 1824;
Samuel Hyem, 30 Mar. 1824; John Baker, 24 Apr. 1824; Thomas Dobson, 10 Jun. 1824;
Samuel Hamblin, 26 Jul. 1824; Richard Howard, 30 Jul. 1824; Samuel Crisp, 25 Aug. 1824;
Mary Walford *alias* Smith, 16 Oct. 1824; Ruth Nunn, 16 Oct. 1824; William Reeve, 16 Oct.
1824; James Perry, 2 Nov. 1824; male infant of Henry Page and wife Sarah, 8 Dec. 1824;
Bridget, wife of John Hare, 17 Dec. 1824
— 8 alehouse licences, Sep. 1824
— 7 alehouse keepers' recognizances, with parochial certificates annexed, Oct. 1824
(72 docs)

C/2/9/1/1/6/27   Jan.–Dec. 1825
Includes:
— Coroner's inquisitions on: James Dale, shipwright, 11 Jan. 1825; John Blake, 13 Jan. 1825;
Mary Humphrey, 7 Mar. 1825; Ambrose Emmerson, 19 Mar. 1825; newborn daughter of Sarah
Stannard, 19 Jul. 1825
— draft minutes of Sessions, 15 Mar. 1825
— draft minutes of Sessions, 25 Jul. 1825
— draft estreats of fines, Sep. 1824–Sep. 1825
(176 docs)

C/2/9/1/1/6/28   Jan.–Sep. 1826
Includes:
— 99 alehouse keepers' parochial certificates, 9–13 Sep. 1826
— draft minutes of Sessions, 1 Mar. 1826
— draft estreats of fines, Sep. 1825–Sep. 1826
(191 docs)

C/2/9/1/1/6/29   Jan.–Dec. 1827
Mostly bills and vouchers for payment by the Treasurer of the Marshalsea Rate
(91 docs)

C/2/9/1/1/6/30   Jan.–Jul. 1828
Mostly bills and vouchers for payment by the Treasurer of the Marshalsea Rate
(51 docs)

C/2/9/1/1/7   Insolvent debtors' accounts and papers   **1814–1846**

These records were left unclassified in the previous catalogue. They are now placed with the
records of the borough Sessions on the presumption that their presence in the borough archive
results from the provisions of the Insolvent Debtors Relief Act of 1748 (21 Geo. II, cap. 31,
subsequently re-enacted on a number of occasions), whereby gaolers were required to deliver
to Quarter Sessions a list of persons imprisoned for debt, and debtors to submit details of their
real and personal estate.

Since so many of the documents listed here bear the name of one Grimsey, attorney, it is
possible that they are instead part of the records of his law practice, in which case their presence
in the archive is accidental.

Most of the documents have been listed alphabetically by debtor; documents of unidentified
debtors have been placed at the end of the list, in alphabetical order of trade. To prevent anoma-
lies in numbering when listing the *post*-1835 records, those debtors whose records relate in
whole or in part to the 1840s, outside the normal scope of the published catalogue, have nevertheless been included.

C/2/9/1/1/7/1   James Abbott, hairdresser   1831–1837
Account books, all marked 'No. 51157. James Abbott . . . Boro' Gaol Ipswich. Grimsey Attorney'

C/2/9/1/1/7/1/1   1829–1831
(1 vol.)

C/2/9/1/1/7/1/2   1832–1837
(1 vol.)

C/2/9/1/1/7/1/3   1834–1837
(1 vol.)

C/2/9/1/1/7/2   John Bird, grocer   1836–1843
Account books

C/2/9/1/1/7/2/1   1836–1842
(1 vol.; front cover marked 'No. 63042. John Bird, Boro' Gaol Ipswich . . . Grimsey Attorney')

C/2/9/1/1/7/2/2   1841–1842
(1 vol.)

C/2/9/1/1/7/3   John Burrows of the 'White Hart', Saxmundham, innkeeper   1829–1840
and cattle dealer

C/2/9/1/1/7/3/1   1837–1839
Pass book, Gurney, Turner, Brightwen and Lloyd's Bank
(1 vol.; front cover marked 'No. 55424. John Burrows, Boro' Gaol Ipswich . . . Grimsey Attorney')

C/2/9/1/1/7/3/2   1837–1839
Cheque counterfoils
(106 docs)

C/2/9/1/1/7/3/3   1829–1840
Bills and associated creditors' correspondence
(61 docs)

C/2/9/1/1/7/4   John Delf of St Matthew's Street, Ipswich, general shopkeeper   1824–1841
Account books and associated papers, all marked 'No. 56698. John Delf, Boro' Gaol Ipswich
. . . Grimsey Attorney'

C/2/9/1/1/7/4/1   1824–1841
Account book
At front: cash account 1824–1841
At back: miscellaneous accounts 1824–1839
(1 vol.)

C/2/9/1/1/7/4/2   1831–1837
Account book
Includes (at back):
— various recipes
(1 vol.)

C/2/9/1/1/7/4/3   1838–1840
Account book
(1 vol.)

C/2/9/1/1/7/4/4   23 Mar. 1841
Household goods, furniture, stock in trade and effects
Deed of assignment by John Delf to James Haill of Ipswich, auctioneer, for benefit of creditors
(1 doc)

C/2/9/1/1/7/4/5   1 Apr. 1841
Sale catalogue
Household furniture, fixtures, stock in trade and effects of John Delf
(1 doc)

C/2/9/1/1/7/4/6   1 Apr. 1841
Auctioneer's account of proceeds of sale
(2 docs)

C/2/9/1/1/7/5   Richard Dodd, shoemaker and cobbler   1820–1837

C/2/9/1/1/7/5/1   1820–1822
Account book
(1 vol.; front cover marked 'No. 47747. Richard Dodd, County Gaol, Ipswich . . . Grimsey
Attorney')

C/2/9/1/1/7/5/2   May–Dec. 1825
Account book
(1 vol.)

C/2/9/1/1/7/5/3   1832–1837
Bills for shoe repairs
(9 docs, found loose inside C/2/9/1/1/7/5/2)

C/2/9/1/1/7/6   John Driver, general dealer   1829–1837
Account books, both marked 'No. 47750. John Driver, Boro' Gaol, Ipswich . . . Grimsey
Attorney', with miscellaneous papers

C/2/9/1/1/7/6/1   1831–1837
(1 vol.)

C/2/9/1/1/7/6/2   n.d.
(1 vol., blank)

C/2/9/1/1/7/6/3   Apr. 1829
Accounts of goods supplied
(3 docs, found loose inside C/2/9/1/1/7/6/2)

C/2/9/1/1/7/7   W. Fisk, jobbing builder   1835–1842
Day books

C/2/9/1/1/7/7/1   1835–1839
(1 vol.)

C/2/9/1/1/7/7/2   1840–1842
(1 vol.)

C/2/9/1/1/7/8   Stephen Stock Gower, surveyor and estate manager   1816–1842
Account books, both marked 'No. 65816. Stephen Stock Gower, Boro' Prison Ipswich . . .
Grimsey Attorney'

C/2/9/1/1/7/8/1   1816–1842
Ledger; estate unidentified
(1 vol.; no entries between Dec. 1817 and Jan. 1842)

C/2/9/1/1/7/8/2   1839–1842
Account book
Mainly *re* surveys undertaken
(1 vol.; with index of clients)

C/2/9/1/1/7/9   Henry Herbert of the 'Horse Shoes', Colchester (Essex), innkeeper   1836

119

C/2/9/1/1/7/9/1   1836
Account book of 'Debts as copied from the scoring boards by Mrs Herbert'
Each entry annotated 'bad' or 'good'
(1 vol.; front cover marked 'No. 17079. Henry Herbert, Borough Gaol Ipswich . . . Grimsey
Attorney, Ipswich')

C/2/9/1/1/7/10   John Hicks, butcher   1835–1838
Account books, all marked 'No. 47751. John Hicks, County Gaol Ipswich . . . Grimsey
Attorney'

C/2/9/1/1/7/10/1   1835–1838
(1 vol.)

C/2/9/1/1/7/10/2   1835–1838
(1 vol.)

C/2/9/1/1/7/10/3   1837–1838
(1 vol.)

C/2/9/1/1/7/11   George Hunt, jobbing builder   1814–1826

C/2/9/1/1/7/11/1   1815–1820
Day book
(1 vol.)

C/2/9/1/1/7/11/2   1821–1826
Day book
Includes (at end):
— accounts of expenses for service as constable of MG, charged to churchwardens and
overseers, 1823–1826
(1 vol.)

C/2/9/1/1/7/11/3   1814–1820
Account book
(1 vol.)

C/2/9/1/1/7/11/4   1823–1826
Account book
(1 vol.)

C/2/9/1/1/7/12   Edward Marshall, butcher   1838–1842
Account and day books, marked 'No. 60,199. Edmund Marshall, Boro' Gaol Ipswich . . .
Grimsey Attorney'

C/2/9/1/1/7/12/1   1838–1842
Account book
(1 vol.)

C/2/9/1/1/7/12/2   n.d.
Day book
(1 vol.; watermarks dated 1841)

C/2/9/1/1/7/12/3   (1785, 1837) 1842
Abstract of will, 1785, of John Marshall of Ipswich, butcher, and of mortgage, 1837, from
Edmund Marshall of Ipswich, butcher, to William Sparrow Sexton of Wherstead, farmer and
Josiah Wilkinson of Chancery Lane, London, gent
Re dwelling house and butcher's shop in MG, Ipswich
(1 doc)

C/2/9/1/1/7/13   Zachariah Ottywell, coachmaker   1838–1843
Account books etc., all marked 'No. 62973. Zachariah Ottywell, Borough Gaol Ipswich . . .
Grimsey Attorney'

C/2/9/1/1/7/13/1   1838–1841
Account book
Accounts with principal creditors, 1838–1840; wages account, 1840–1841
(1 vol.)

C/2/9/1/1/7/13/2   1842–1843
Wages account book
(1 vol.)

C/2/9/1/1/7/13/3   1842–1843
Weekly cash account book
(1 vol.)

C/2/9/1/1/7/13/4   Jan.–Dec. 1842
Day book
(1 vol.)

C/2/9/1/1/7/13/5   1842–1843
Rough credit ledger
Details of work done
(1 vol.)

C/2/9/1/1/7/13/6   [1842–1843]
Index to C/2/9/1/1/7/13/5
(1 vol.)

C/2/9/1/1/7/13/7   2 May 1843
Personal effects
Deed of assignment by Zachariah Ottywell and John Allen, both of Ipswich, coach makers and
co-partners, to Benjamin Colchester of Ipswich, auctioneer, for benefit of creditors
(1 doc)

C/2/9/1/1/7/14   — Parker, ? miller   1820–1824
Account books, labelled 'Mr Parker's Books'

C/2/9/1/1/7/14/1   1818–1819
(1 vol.)

C/2/9/1/1/7/14/2   1820–1821
(1 vol.)

C/2/9/1/1/7/14/3   1822–1824
(1 vol.)

C/2/9/1/1/7/15   Robert Paul, repairer of vehicles, harness and agricultural   1831–1836
implements
Account books, all marked 'No. 44538. Robert Paul, Boro' Gaol Ipswich . . . Grimsey
Attorney'

C/2/9/1/1/7/15/1   1831–1836
(1 vol.)

C/2/9/1/1/7/15/2   1835–1836
(1 vol.)

C/2/9/1/1/7/15/3   Jan.–Dec. 1836
(1 vol.)

C/2/9/1/1/7/16   William Paxman, private tutor   1826–1843
Account books for tuition and books and stationery supplied, both marked 'No. 63972. William
Paxman, Boro' Gaol Ipswich . . . Grimsey Attorney'

C/2/9/1/1/7/16/1   1826–1843
(1 vol.)

C/2/9/1/1/7/16/2   Jan.–Jun. 1843
(1 vol.)

C/2/9/1/1/7/17   John Peck of Tower Ditches, Ipswich, keeper of livery   1827–1840
stables and hire carriages
Account books etc. marked 'John Peck . . . Borough Gaol Ipswich. Grimsey Attorney'

C/2/9/1/1/7/17/1   1829–1839
Day book
(1 vol.)

C/2/9/1/1/7/17/2   1831–1835
Day book
(1 vol.)

C/2/9/1/1/7/17/3   1836–1837
Day book
(1 vol.)

C/2/9/1/1/7/17/4   1837–1838
Day book
(1 vol.)

C/2/9/1/1/7/17/5   1839–1840
Day book
(1 vol.)

C/2/9/1/1/7/17/6   1827–1830
Pass book, Alexander's Bank
(1 vol.)

C/2/9/1/1/7/17/7   1828–1833
Pass book, Bacon, Cobbold and Rodwell's Bank
(1 vol.)

C/2/9/1/1/7/17/8   1826–1833
Account book
Peck in account with John Smith, horse dealer
(1 vol.)

C/2/9/1/1/7/17/9   Jun.–Jul. 1837
Account book
re auction of Peck's effects
(1 vol.)

C/2/9/1/1/7/17/10   7 Jul. 1837
Sale particulars
Horses, ponies, harness, carriages and house contents
(1 doc.)

C/2/9/1/1/7/18   William Poulter jun., grocer and draper   1825–1829

C/2/9/1/1/7/18/1   1825–1829
Ledger
(1 vol.; front cover marked 'C. At the Suffolk Hotel Ipswich this 29th day of July 1834.
Exhibited to us under a Fiat in Bankruptcy against William Poulter the younger [signed] B
Brame, Jas Wenn, J Chevallier Cobbold')

C/2/9/1/1/7/19   William Pulfer, knacker and tanner   1832–1839
Account books, all marked 'No. 52647. William Pulfer . . . Borough Gaol Ipswich. Grimsey
Attorney'

C/2/9/1/1/7/19/1   1832–1839
(1 vol.)

C/2/9/1/1/7/19/2   1833–1835
In account with Webb and Sons for supply of hides, etc.
(1 vol.)

C/2/9/1/1/7/19/3   Mar. 1833–Jan. 1834
Stock and wages accounts
(1 vol.)

C/2/9/1/1/7/20   Mary Ann Roper, ? innkeeper   1821–1822

C/2/9/1/1/7/20/1   1821–1822
Day book
(1 vol.)

C/2/9/1/1/7/21   William Scopes, grocer   1839–1842
Account books, all marked 'No. 59593. Wm Scopes, Boro' Gaol, Ipswich . . . Grimsey
Attorney'

C/2/9/1/1/7/21/1   1839–1840
(1 vol.)

C/2/9/1/1/7/21/2   1840–1841
(1 vol.)

C/2/9/1/1/7/21/3   1841–1842
(1 vol.)

C/2/9/1/1/7/22   John J Smith of Ipswich, ? grocer   1827–1837
Account books, all marked 'No. 54628. Jno. J. Smith, Boro' Gaol Ipswich . . . Grimsey
Attorney'

C/2/9/1/1/7/22/1   1827
(1 vol.)

C/2/9/1/1/7/22/2   1833–1834
(1 vol.)

C/2/9/1/1/7/22/3   1837
(1 vol.)

C/2/9/1/1/7/23   Robert Smith, veterinary surgeon   1821–1839
Account books, both marked 'No. 55523. Robert Smith, Boro' Gaol Ipswich . . . Grimsey
Attorney'

C/2/9/1/1/7/23/1   1831–1836
Includes:
— notes on lectures delivered by Prof. Coleman on anatomy and pathology at the Veterinary
College, 1828–1829
(1 vol.)

C/2/9/1/1/7/23/2   1837–1839
(1 vol.)

C/2/9/1/1/7/24   James Spearman, ? draper   1836–1846
Account books

C/2/9/1/1/7/24/1   1836–1845
(1 vol.; front cover marked 'Mr Sampson Book'; formerly pinned to C/2/9/1/1/7/24/2)

C/2/9/1/1/7/24/2   1839–1846
(1 vol.; front cover marked '67919. James Spearman, Boro' Gaol . . . R.Galsworthy')

C/2/9/1/1/7/25   Henry Waller jun. of Claydon, miller   1840–1846
Accounts and related papers, all marked 'No. 68057. Henry Waller the younger, Boro' Gaol
Ipswich . . . Grimsey Attorney'

C/2/9/1/1/7/25/1   1840–1843
Account book
(1 vol.; with index)

C/2/9/1/1/7/25/2   13 May 1843
Household goods, furniture and stock-in-trade
Bill of sale by Henry Waller to John Lott Ensor of Ipswich, gent., for securing repayment of
debt

C/2/9/1/1/7/25/3   6 Apr. 1846
Receipted bill for goods supplied to Henry Waller by Henry Forsdick

C/2/9/1/1/7/26   Thomas Woollard, carpenter and repairer of vehicles, harness   1819–1835
and agricultural implements
Account books, both marked 'No. 44540. Thomas Woollard, Boro' Gaol Ipswich . . . Grimsey
Attorney'

C/2/9/1/1/7/26/1   1819–1834
(1 vol.)

C/2/9/1/1/7/26/2   1834–1835
(1 vol.)

C/2/9/1/1/7/27   Unidentified Debtors   1817–1842

C/2/9/1/1/7/27/1   1840–1841
Day book of unidentified baker
(1 vol.; front cover marked 'FEEK':? William Feek, Tavern St – Pigot's 1839 Directory)

C/2/9/1/1/7/27/2   1840–1841
Day book of unidentified baker
(1 vol.)

C/2/9/1/1/7/27/3   1841–1842
Day book of unidentified baker
(1 vol.)

C/2/9/1/1/7/27/4   1842
Day book of unidentified baker
(1 vol.)

C/2/9/1/1/7/27/5   1820–1825
Account book of unidentified butcher
(1 vol.)

C/2/9/1/1/7/27/6   1824–1826
Day book of unidentified butcher
(1 vol.)

C/2/9/1/1/7/27/7   1833–1841
Day book of unidentified butcher
(1 vol.)

C/2/9/1/1/7/27/8   1836–1841
Day book of unidentified greengrocer and market gardener
(1 vol.)

C/2/9/1/1/7/27/9   1841–1842
Order and day book of unidentified haberdasher
(1 vol.)

C/2/9/1/1/7/27/10   1817–1825
Account book of unidentified innkeeper and farmer
(1 vol.)

C/2/9/1/1/8   Sessions Books   **1509–1839**

The series extends down to 1844, though the last volume (for 1840–1844) is beyond the scope
of this catalogue. Though described on their covers as 'Sessions Books', these volumes are in
the nature of minute books, recording the proceedings of the court. Their nature is borne out by
the later series of Sessions Minute Books beginning in 1778 and continuous from 1841: with
the exception of the first two Minute Books (for 1778–1809 and March 1841–January 1845),
which appear to be drafts from which the Sessions Books were written up, the Minute Books
from January 1845 are virtually indistinguishable from the later Sessions Books, which they
supersede and continue as the main record of the court down to 1956.

Most of the courts in the earliest Sessions Book (for 1509–1515) are described as 'Sessions
of the Peace' only. Most subsequent Sessions are of the Peace and Gaol Delivery. Sessions of
the Peace alone still appear in books 2–6 (C/2/9/1/1/8/2–6) for 1549–1616, where the entries
are similar to those of the composite Sessions except that the gaol calendars are usually
omitted. Sessions of the Peace between January 1642 and October 1654 (C/2/9/1/1/8/7–8) deal
mainly (in very brief entries) with cases of riot. 'Special Sessions', October 1763–April 1775
(C/2/9/1/1/8/10) are for rating appeals only; and Sessions of the Peace, January 1819–
September 1822 (C/2/9/1/1/8/12) are for orders for the relief of imprisoned debtors, diversion
of highways and other administrative matters.

Most of the entries in the first volume consist merely of lists of officers and grand jurors, and
memoranda of recognizances for appearance or to keep the peace (the last rarely dated) made in
or out of Sessions. In subsequent volumes the usual contents are: recognizances; grand jury
lists; trial jury lists (1564–1815); calendars of prisoners with notes of process; and court orders
(including those for discharging apprentices, 1564–1585; for bridge rates, 1692–1741; for the
Marshalsea Treasurer's rates, 1741–1836; and for highway diversions from 1818). Lists of the
overseers and collectors of the twelve parishes appear annually, 1577–1589, and appointments
of the Treasurers for the Sick and Wounded, with orders to them, 1593–1783. Lists of coroners,
serjeants and bailiffs (or constables) of hamlets appear between 1549 and 1601, and occasionally 1601–1616. Badgers' licences appear occasionally, 1564–1720; and alehouse licences
occasionally, 1587–1616.

The language of the record is mostly Latin down to 1652, when English supersedes it until
1660. From the Restoration many entries are again in Latin until its abolition for legal purposes
in 1731.

From 1576 to 1651 the record of the Sessions Books is augmented by entries in the series of
composite enrolments of the borough courts (C/2/10/1) which, for those criminal cases considered worthy of permanent enrolment, recite the process in full following each indictment.

C/2/9/1/1/8/1   ? Jun. 1509–Sep. 1515
Includes documents, formerly loose inside vol., tipped in during conservation
— (fol. 5A) memorandum of taking of Howell Vaghan at Ipswich for felony, by pursuit of
Robert Wauhan and William Wylson of Herefordshire, 30 Jul. 1509
— (fol. 5B) memorandum of recognizance of Robert Johnson and John Hiat, both of Ipswich,
tailors, for appearance of Robert Wyndover of 'Halley' [? Haughley], labourer, at next Sessions
of Gaol Delivery, 3 Nov. 1509

— (fol. 5C) memorandum of recognizance of Margery Carles to keep the peace, n.d.

— (fol. 7A) partial enrolment of plea, Florence Claiston *v* Nicholas Hode, *re* recovery of goods, n.d.; *endorsed*: memoranda of recognizances for Joan Creek sen. and Joan Creek jun. to keep the peace, n.d.

— (fol. 17A) justice's precept to Bailiffs to supersede arrest of Simon Wightred of Ipswich, butcher, who has given security to keep the peace towards William Middleton of Ipswich, minstrel, and to appear at Sessions on 22 Mar. 1515

— (fol. 17B) justices' precept to John Barbour, Bailiff of WB, to summon jurors, 19 Mar. 1515

— (fol. 17C) justice's precept to town serjeants, reciting writ of *venire facias* for obtaining security from William Bullok not to harm William Baron, 6 Feb. 1515

— (fol. 17D) justice's precept to Bailiffs to supercede arrest of John Povey of Ipswich, glover, who has given security to keep the peace towards William Burwelle of Ipswich, glover, 20 Mar. 1515

— (fol. 18A) justices' precept to John Bateman, Bailiff of WU, to summon jurors, 23 Sep. 1511

— (fol. 18B) original writ recited on fol. 17C, 16 Jan. 1515

— (fol. 19A) [constables'] presentment of Skynner and wife at the Half Moon and Jacsson and wife, all for 'bawdry and yll rwle', n.d.

— (fol. 19B) precept of Sir H. Marney, kt., an Essex justice, to Keeper of Gaol at Ipswich, to deliver Robert Brigesman of Ramsey (Essex), smith, indicted of felony, to Sheriff of Essex, 1 Jun. 1514

— (fol. 19C) writ to Bailiffs and justices for release of Thomas Brian from his recognizance, he having given security of the peace in Chancery, 26 May 1514

— (fol. 19D) justice's precept to Bailiffs to supersede arrest of John Polet of Ipswich, shoe-maker, who has given security to keep the peace towards Alice Andrew of Ipswich, spinster, and to appear at next Sessions, 16 Jan. 1512

— (fol. 19E) justice's precept to serjeants and constables to supersede arrest of Hugh Beskett of Ipswich, surgeon, who has given security to keep the peace and to appear at next Sessions, 21 Mar. 1514

— (fol. 19F) writ to justices for release of Richard Barwyk and wife Elizabeth from their recognizances, they having given security of the peace in Chancery, 22 Nov. 1511

— (fol. 19G) justice's precept to Bailiffs to supersede arrest of William Bulle of Ipswich, labourer, who has given security to keep the peace towards Hugh Doun, clerk, and to appear at next Sessions, 3 Jun. 1511

— (fol. 19H) justices' precept to John Catermayn, Bailiff of WU, to summon jurors, 30 Dec. 1514

— (fol. 19I) [constables'] presentments of John Blackesale, Thomas Sponer, William Baker and [*blank*] Blogates, for trespass, and Alice Andrew, Richard ? Tove, Peter Smyth and Lamyt's wife for bawdry, n.d.

— (fol. 19J) justices' precept to John Barbour, Bailiff of WB, to summon jurors, 30 Dec. 1514

— (fol. 21A) indictment of Robert Norfolk of Ipswich, butcher, for trespass, 28 May 1513

— (fol. 21B) indictment of John Baker of Ipswich, barker, for felony, 16 Sep. 1513

— (fol. 21C) list of court cases, n.d. [16 Sep. 1513]

— (fol. 21D) jury presentments, n.d. [1513]

— (fol. 21E) jury list, n.d.

— (fol. 21F) jury list, n.d.

— (fol. 21G) [constables'] presentments of Thomas Kavyll and wife for affray; Bull's wife as a common scold; and 'Gret the Duche woman for a commyn harlot', n.d.

— (fol. 21H) [constables'] presentments of Matthew Boger and William Notyng for engrossing cheese and butter; and Jacson of PE for keeping ill rule, n.d.

— (fol. 21I) indictment of John Baker of Ipswich, barker, for felony (endorsed 'Billa vera'), 10 Jun. 1513

— (fol. 21J) memorandum of (? presentment) of William Waller of Ipswich, stringmaker, for receiving stolen goods, n.d.

— (fol 21K) jury list, n.d.

— (fol. 21L) writ of *venire facias* for obtaining security from Richard Parys not to harm John Coksale, 12 Apr. 1513

— (fol. 21M) writ of *venire facias* for obtaining security from Richard Walton not to harm Thomas Bedyll, 8 Jul. 1513

— (fol. 21N) [constables'] presentments of Robert Beerde and John Pette for demanding excessive wages, n.d.

— (fol. 21O) justices' precept to serjeants to summon jurors, . . . Apr. ? 1513

— (fol. 27A) [constables'] presentments of John Cleve and [*blank*] Garard for engrossing herring, and of John Benett 'for brekyng of Thomas Kavyll hed', n.d.

— (fol. 28A) jury presentments, 26 Jul., 22 Sep. and 10 Dec. 1512

— (fol. 29A) jury presentments, n.d.

— (fol. 30A) [constables'] presentments, n.d.

(1 vol., 27 fols, 3 fragmentary, made up of two paper books originally bound in folio from a late medieval service book with musical notation on four staves, rubricated and ornamented in blue)

C/2/9/1/1/8/2   Dec. 1549–Aug. 1564
Includes:
— recognizances from 5 Oct. 1549
Bound in during conservation:
— (fol. 10A) letter of John Holt, gent., Deputy Steward of the Liberty of Bury St Edmunds, to the Bailiffs, acknowledging receipt of John Walker at Bury gaol to answer for certain felonies, 13 Apr. 1551
(1 vol.; 61 fols, 13 fragmentary, originally bound in folio from a late medieval service book with musical notation on four staves, rubricated and profusely ornamented in gold, blue, red and green)

C/2/9/1/1/8/3   ? Dec. 1564–Sep. 1585
Includes:
— recognizances to 5 Apr. 1586
— (fol. 105v) copy letter of Edmund [Freke], Bishop of Norwich, appointing George Webbe, clerk, his commissary for Gaol Delivery at Ipswich [on 6 Aug. 1577], 12 Feb. 1577
(1 vol., 176 fols, 4 fragmentary; original cover (deed fragment) marked 'No. 4')

C/2/9/1/1/8/4   Jul. 1587–Sep. 1601
Includes:
— recognizances Jan. 1587–Oct. 1601
— (attached to p. 390) information against John Talle, 11 Jan. 1598
— (attached to p. 542) jury presentment of Thomas Sherman of Ipswich, grocer, for assault on Thomas Hall of Ipswich, gent, on 11 Jun. 1598
— (attached to p. 546) jury presentment of 17 named persons for playing bowls on 10 Jul. 1597 and other days
— (attached to p. 548) fragmentary note *re* search for sheep and skins, n.d.
— (attached to p. 555) note *re* prices and weights of loaves, 17 Oct. 1601
(1 vol., 556 pp., 53 pp. blank, 8 pp. excised; with index of names (incomplete) to proceedings Jun. 1587–Apr. 1599, at front and back; front cover marked 'No. 5')

C/2/9/1/1/8/5   Oct. 1601–Sep. 1604
Proceedings 29 Jul. 1602–2 Sep. 1603 and recognizances 13 Jul.–27 Aug. 1603 are derived from a briefer and rougher record in C/2/9/1/1/8/6, which contains additional recognizances 21 Nov. 1601–25 Apr. 1602 and 17 Jan.–7 Jun. 1604
Includes:
— recognizances to 14 Dec. 1604
(1 vol., 76 pp., 14 pp. blank, 2 pp. excised; apparently the first 4 gatherings of a larger book; cover marked 'No. 6')

C/2/9/1/1/8/6   Jul. 1602–Sep. 1616
See note under C/2/9/1/1/8/5

Includes:
— (attached to fol. 42) apprenticeship indenture, Richard Topliff, son of Thomas Topliff of Ipswich, clothworker, bound to Andrew Writt of Ipswich, clothworker, 7 Dec. 1607
— (attached to fol. 114) list of names, n.d.
(1 vol., 165 fols, fols 1, 161–165 fragmentary; crudely made up from 8 separate books of varying dimensions; original covers missing)

C/2/9/1/1/8/7   May 1618–Sep. 1650
Includes:
— (attached to p. 42) presentment of defaults by townsmen in work on highways, n.d. [Sessions 20 Sep. 1619]
— (attached to p. 135) bill for supply of barrels, Dec. 1622–Aug. 1623
— (attached to p. 448) bill for shoes for Mr Clark, Jan. 1662
(1 vol., 470 pp., 9 pp. blank, 8 pp. excised; front cover marked 'No. 8')

C/2/9/1/1/8/8   Jun. 1652–Aug. 1720
Additional entries (mainly orders) for 25 Sep. 1657–13 Sep. 1658, 19 Jan. 1659–14 Aug. 1662, 20 Aug. 1663, 18 Apr. and 20 Aug. 1666, 16 Aug. 1671, 7 Apr. 1675, 5 Jul. 1676, and 29 Aug. 1677 appear in irregular order on pp. 3, 4, 718–728
For lists of indictments, 19 Jul. 1683–19 May 1687, see indictment book, C/2/9/1/1/4/1
Includes:
— (p. 692) audited account of John Goldson as Treasurer for Sick and Wounded, 1696–1699 (audited 7 Jun. 1714)
— (p. 693) audited account of Keble Cross as Treasurer for Sick and Wounded, 1700–1705 (audited 7 Jun. 1714)
— (inside front and back covers) Clerk's miscellaneous memoranda, n.d.
(1 vol., 734 pp., 67 pp. blank, 6 pp. excised; front cover marked 'No. 9')

C/2/9/1/1/8/9   Jul. 1721–Aug. 1742
Includes:
— (pasted inside front cover) printed proclamation 'for the encouragement of piety and virtue, and for the preventing and punishing of vice, prophaneness, and immorality', 1714
(1 vol., 346 pp., 41 pp. blank; front cover marked 'No. 10')

C/2/9/1/1/8/10   Jan. 1743–Mar. 1776
Includes:
— (inside front cover) 'the proportions of the several parishes to raise £100, with the valuations of the same parishes' (2 versions), 15 Dec. 1772, 2 Sep. 1773
(1 vol., 442 pp., 9 pp. blank)

C/2/9/1/1/8/11   Jul. 1776–Mar. 1815
Includes:
— (inside front cover) 'proportions of the several parishes for a rate of £100 according to the valuation in 1781'
(1 vol., 568 pp., 5 pp. blank)

C/2/9/1/1/8/12   Jul. 1815–Mar. 1828
Includes:
— (loose inside back cover) printed calendar of prisoners for trial at Sessions of 20 Sep. 1830; with verdicts and sentences added in MS
(1 vol., 520 pp., 6 pp. blank)

C/2/9/1/1/8/13   Jul. 1828–Oct. 1839
Includes (attached by seal wafers inside back cover):
— certificate of John E Sparrow, Clerk of the Peace, of conviction of Eleanor, wife of Robert Austin, of felony (theft), at Sessions of 6 Mar. 1821; 22 Mar. 1830
— jury presentment of assault committed by William Pollard late of HL, labourer, on Robert Farman on 3 Dec. 1844
(1 vol., 460 pp., 15 pp. blank, 2 pp. excised)

C/2/9/1/1/9 Minute Books   1778–1809

The series extends down to 1956, though all but the earliest volume lie outside the scope of this catalogue. The first two volumes (for 1778–1809 and March 1841–January 1845) are drafts, from which the Sessions Books (C/2/9/1/1/8) were written up. The later Minute Books are virtually indistinguishable from the later Sessions Books, which they supersede and continue as the main record of the court.

The principal contents of the first volume are: lists, entered at each Sessions, of recognizances made since the previous Sessions; court orders; gaol calendars; memoranda of convictions and sentences; and lists of payments to be made by the Marshalsea Treasurer. Later volumes (not listed here) include also lists of convictions out of Sessions; lists of Coroner's inquisitions; memoranda of licensing of asylums and appointment of visitors; and lists of payments to be made by the Borough Treasurer.

C/2/9/1/1/9/1   Aug. 1778–Aug. 1809
(1 vol., 180 pp., unpaginated)

C/2/9/1/1/10 Engrossments of proceedings   1573–1586

The single roll represented here may have been intended for inclusion in the series of composite enrolments of proceedings in the borough courts (C/2/10/1). The presentments and indictments recorded are formal enrolments, rather than the original documents found on the rolled files known as the Sessions Rolls.

C/2/9/1/1/10/1   1573–1586
Sessions of the Peace
Courts 2 Apr. 1573–6 Aug. 1577 and 11 Apr.–5 Sep. 1586
Names of officers and jurors, jury presentments and indictments only
(14 membranes)

C/2/9/1/1/11 Miscellanea   16c.–1834

C/2/9/1/1/11/1   n.d. [? early 16c.]
Jury list
Names of 24 jurors, 12 marked as sworn
(1 membrane)

C/2/9/1/1/11/2   n.d. [? later 17c.]
List of auditors and accountants
(1 doc; originally found with Sessions Roll for 13 Aug. 1783, C/2/9/1/1/1/124)

C/2/9/1/1/11/3   Mar. 1725–Mar. 1726
Copy record of process at Bury St Edmunds Assizes
Against Moses Slyth, late of Ipswich, bricklayer, for taking William Holmes as his apprentice for 5 years only, contrary to statute
(20 pp.; Latin; found with rolls of Ipswich General Sessions)

C/2/9/1/1/11/4   23 Jan. 1761
Deposition of Mary Trumell of PE, before H. Rant, J.P. *Re* putative father of her unborn child
(Endorsed: 'for Edward Lavender's appearance at next Sessions . . .')

C/2/9/1/1/11/5   1–9 Apr. 1789
Papers *re* transportation of Susanna, wife of John Hunt
Susanna Hunt was convicted of grand larceny at the General Sessions of 17 Mar. 1788 and sentenced to 7 years' transportation
Includes:
— contract between Justices and William Richards jun. of Walworth (Surrey) gent. for her conveyance to Botany Bay, 1 Apr. 1789

— bond for performance of contract, 2 Apr. 1789
— warrant to master of 'Lady Juliana' transport, Woolwich, London, to receive prisoner on board, 4 Apr. 1789
— master's receipt for prisoner, 4 Apr. 1789
— letter from Richards to Keeper of Ipswich Gaol enclosing contract and bond, 9 Apr. 1789
(5 docs)

C/2/9/1/1/11/6   1825–1828
Miscellaneous court papers
Includes:
— deposition of Gilbert Brothers, overseer of the poor of MT, *re* default in payment of mainte-nance by Jonathan Mason of Ipswich, cordwainer, reputed father of bastard son of Frances Rudd, singlewoman, 24 May 1825
— settlement examination of Susan Burgess of MS, widow, 13 Oct. 1825
— settlement examination of Henry Piper, private in the 82nd Regiment of Foot, 27 Jun. 1826
— settlement examination of Francis Pallant, convict in the borough gaol, 10 Jul. 1826
— 2 orders of the Sessions to the Treasurer of the Marshalsea Rate for payment to the Town Clerk of his expenses in prosecuting criminals (names and offences given), 23 Jul. 1828
(6 docs)

C/2/9/1/1/11/7   1834
Brief for appellant
in appeal by Revd Mileson Gery Edgar against Churchwardens and Overseers of MG, *re* alleged over-rating of his mansion, pleasure grounds and outbuildings in the parish, at Easter Sessions
(endorsed: 'Court holds that it has no jurisdiction, the borough of Ipswich having more than six justices')

C/2/9/1/2   ADMINISTRATION AND FINANCE   1579–1835

C/2/9/1/2/1   Clerk of the Peace   **1820–1833**

C/2/9/1/2/1/1   Correspondence   *1820–1833*

Letters addressed to the Clerk of the Peace, or forwarded to him, for action, by the Bailiffs, Recorder and Gaoler; chiefly from the Home Office concerning returns of offenders, and from the War Office and Admiralty concerning deserters from the armed forces.

C/2/9/1/2/1/1/1   Feb.–Dec. 1820
(2 docs)

C/2/9/1/2/1/1/2   Jan.–Dec. 1821
Includes:
— return of persons tried or committed for trial for felony and misdemeanour in 1820
— return of persons committed for trial for grand and petty larceny in 1820
(16 docs)

C/2/9/1/2/1/1/3   Mar.–Dec. 1822
Includes:
— return of persons committed for trial for grand and petty larceny in 1821
— letters from the Home Office *re* conduct of Sir William Middleton [Bailiff] in leaving the Ipswich Court of General Sessions without adequate cause, whereby the court became dis-solved, thus rendering himself liable to indictment in the King's Bench, 23, 25 Jul. 1822
(22 docs)

C/2/9/1/2/1/1/4   Jan.–Nov. 1823
Includes:
— acquittance for Thomas Wilkinson, received on board the 'Justitia' hulk in the Thames from custody of the Bailiffs, under sentence of transportation for 7 years
(17 docs)

C/2/9/1/2/1/1/5   Jan.–Dec. 1824
(3 docs)

C/2/9/1/2/1/1/6   Jan.–Dec. 1825
(22 docs)

C/2/9/1/2/1/1/7   Jan.–Sep. 1826
(14 docs)

C/2/9/1/2/1/1/8   1830–1833
(5 docs)

C/2/9/1/2/1/2   Millers' and corn merchants' declarations   *1821–1822*

An Act of 1791 (31 Geo. III, cap. 30) for regulating the import and export of corn, continued by an Act of 1821 (1–2 Geo. IV, cap. 87, s. 19), rendered millers and corn merchants liable to a fine for purchasing corn for sale without first filing with the Clerk of the Peace, a declaration that their returns of prices would be true.

C/2/9/1/2/1/2/1   Aug.–Dec. 1821
(97 docs)

C/2/9/1/2/1/2 /2   Jan.–Apr. 1822
(18 docs)

C/2/9/1/2/1/3   Returns   *1825*

C/2/9/1/2/1/3/1   Mar.–Jul. 1825
Return of forfeitures levied by the Justices under Acts of Parliament for more effectual prevention of use of defective weights, unequal balances or false measures

C/2/9/1/2/2   Nominations for appointment of parish officers   1822–1826

Signed copies of minutes of Vestry meetings containing the nominations submitted for the approval of the Justices. The appointment of Overseers of the Poor had rested with the Justices of the Peace since 1598 (39 Eliz., cap. 3), and that of Surveyors of the Highways since 1691. Unless otherwise stated in the catalogue, the nominations dated March and April are for Overseers (proposed at the Easter Vestry), and those dated September for Surveyors. Nominations for other offices, and occasional nominations for members of the select Vestries, are mentioned where they occur.

C/2/9/1/2/2/1   Mar.–Apr. 1822
For CL (includes Vestry and Constables for parish and WB), HL, LW, MG (includes Vestry), ME, MQ, MS, MT (includes Constables), MW (Churchwardens and Constables only), NI, PE, ST, Westerfield and Whitton
(17 docs)

C/2/9/1/2/2/2   23 Sep. 1822
For CL, MG, ME, MS, MT, MW, NI, PE, ST and Whitton
(11 docs)

C/2/9/1/2/2/3   Mar.–Apr. 1823
For CL (includes Vestry and Constables), HL, LW, MG (includes Vestry and Constables), MQ,
MS, MT, MW, NI, PE, ST
(13 docs)

C/2/9/1/2/2/4   n.d.[? Mar.–Apr. 1824]
For LW, PE and Whitton
Includes:
— list of parishioners who have not served as Overseer in HL since 1810
(6 docs)

C/2/9/1/2/2/5   Sep.–Oct. 1824
For CL, MG, MQ, MS, MT, MW, PE and ST
(9 docs)

C/2/9/1/2/2/6   n.d.[? Sep. 1824]
For HL
(1 doc.)

C/2/9/1/2/2/7   Mar.–Apr. 1825
For CL (includes Vestry and Constables for parish and WB), HL, LW, MG (includes Vestry
and Constables), ME (includes Vestry), MQ (includes Constables), MS, MT, MW, ST and WU
(15 docs)

C/2/9/1/2/2/8   22 Sep. 1825
For CL, HL, MQ and ST
(4 docs)

C/2/9/1/2/2/9   Mar.–Apr. 1826
For CL (includes Vestry, Churchwardens and Constables for parish and WB), HL, MG
(includes Vestry, Constables and Assistant Overseer and Collector of parish rates), ME, MQ,
MS, MT, MW (includes Vestry), ST and Westerfield
(13 docs)

C/2/9/1/2/3   Highways   1630–1824

Following the Statute of Highways of 1555 (2 and 3 Philip and Mary, cap. 18), which ordered
the annual appointment of two Surveyors in each parish to enforce the statutory labour on the
highways (or its compounding by a money payment), the oversight of the system became a duty
of the Justices of the Peace.

C/2/9/1/2/3/1   1630
Surveyors' account: West Ward
William Tyler, Peter Fisher, Robert Clarke, Richard Sayer and [blank] Puckell, Surveyors
Names of inhabitants with sums collected from each; names of those who performed their
statutory labour; payments to labourers
(1 vol.)

C/2/9/1/2/3/2   1655–1656
Surveyors' audited account: ward unidentified
Surveyors unnamed
Receipts and payments
(1 vol.)

C/2/9/1/2/3/3   1761
Surveyors' summary accounts
For CL, HL, LW, MG, ME, MS, MT, MW, NI, PE, Westerfield and Whitton
(4 fols)

C/2/9/1/2/3/4   22 Sep. 1812
Lists of nominations submitted by the parish Vestries (MG missing) to the Justices, for Surveyors of the Highways for the coming year
(11 docs)

C/2/9/1/2/3/5   22 Sep. 1824
List of nominations submitted by HL Vestry to the Justices, for Surveyors of the Highways for the coming year
(1 doc)

C/2/9/1/2/4   Bridges   1669–1819

By the Statute of Bridges of 1531 (22 Hen. VIII, cap. 5), the Justices in Quarter Sessions were empowered to hear and determine 'all manner of annoyances of bridges broken in the highways', and to enforce their repair. If no other liability could be established, bridges within corporate towns became a municipal responsibility, and the Justices were empowered to levy a rate for the purpose of repair.

C/2/9/1/2/4/1   Rates   *1696–1722*

C/2/9/1/2/4/1/1   1696–1722
'A Book for the Entering of Bridge Rates 1696'
Rate assessments for the 12 parishes and the hamlets of WB and WU, for repair of the town's bridges, made at General Sessions of the Peace, Apr. 1696–Mar. 1710
Includes:
— accounts of ward collectors, giving totals charged on parishes and (sometimes) details of abatements, 1698–1716
— (p. 94) memorandum of agreement between the town and Mr John Acton *re* responsibility for making good future flood damage at Handford Bridge, 7 Jun. 1700
— (at front) minute of appointment of Surveyors of the Highways and Constables for parishes and wards at Special Sessions, 17 Jan. 1699
— (at back) list of 16 poor persons to whom butter confiscated from traders in the Butter Market for giving short weight was distributed, 10 Jul. 1697
— (at back) accounts of money due from soldiers of three companies of Sir Bevill Grenvile's Regiment of Foot to keepers of various inns (named) and others, Apr. 1696–May 1697
(1 vol., 373 pp., 224 pp. blank)

C/2/9/1/2/4/2   Agreements   *1579–1757*

C/2/9/1/2/4/2/1   1 Sep. 1579
Articles of agreement for repair of Bourne Bridge
Made between Sir Robert Wyngfeld of Letheringham, kt., Sir Phillip Parker of Erwarton, kt., Thomas Seckford of Ipswich, esq, and Philip Tylney of Shelley, esq. [county Justices]; Robert Cutler and John Knappe [Bailiffs], John Moore and John Barker [borough Justices], all of Ipswich, merchants; and John Knights of Balton [? Belton] and William Knights of Crowfield, free masons; the bridge, said to be 'gretely ruyned and decaied', to be repaired for £300, half to be paid by the county and half by the borough

C/2/9/1/2/4/2/2   16 Dec. 1609
Articles of agreement for repair of that part of Bourne Bridge lying within the town limits
Made by William Bloyse and Tobias Bloyse, Bailiffs, and Robert Cutler, Portman, with Thomas Reynberd of Stowmarket, free mason; the bridge to be repaired for £27 10*s*

C/2/9/1/2/4/2/3   28 Sep. 1757
Articles of agreement for repair of that part of Bourne Bridge lying within the town limits
Made by Thomas Richardson, William Truelove and John Gravenor, Justices, with Richard Slyth, James Slyth and James Scott, all of Ipswich, bricklayers; the bridge to be repaired for £160

C/2/9/1/2/4/3 Accounts and vouchers   *1669–1749*

C/2/9/1/2/4/3/1   1669–1671
Surveyors' audited accounts for repairs to Handford, Stoke and Bourne Bridges
John Sawyer, Jonathan Butter, Surveyors
(1 vol.)

C/2/9/1/2/4/3/2   Apr. 1747–Jun. 1749
Vouchers submitted by John and William Lane [? builders]
For materials supplied and work carried out by craftsmen and others contracted by them for
repairs to Stoke Bridge
(53 docs; presence of filing holes indicates that they were formerly filed on a lace)

C/2/9/1/2/4/4 Papers   *1779–1819*

C/2/9/1/2/4/4/1   Dec. 1779–May 1782
Papers *re* rebuilding of Handford Bridge and its approaches
Includes:
— minutes of meeting of principal inhabitants of Ipswich, 28 Dec. 1779
— minutes of meetings of bridge committee, Jan. 1780–May 1782
— petition of inhabitants to House of Commons for leave to bring in Bill to rebuild bridge, erect
causeway, and pave, light and cleanse town, n.d. [? 1780]
— plan 'for the reparation of the road near Handford Bridge without building another bridge'
n.d. [? 1780]
— estimate for road with 3 or 5 culverts, 1 Mar. 1780
— estimate for rebuilding present bridge, n.d. [? 1782]
— estimates for timber and brick bridges, 2 May 1782 and n.d.
— specification for brick bridge, n.d. [? May 1782]
(13 docs)

C/2/9/1/2/4/4/2   n.d.[*c.* 1800]
Estimate by Samuel Lane, bricklayer, for repairs to St Peter's Bridge

C/2/9/1/2/4/4/3   Apr. 1818–Jun. 1819
Papers *re* building of new Stoke Bridge
Includes:
— elevation drawing, n.d.
— minutes of meetings of Bailiffs and Justices, 13 Apr.–2 Jun. 1818
— draft notice *re* passage of vessels and barges through temporary floating bridge at St Peter's
Dock, 2 May 1818
— comparative estimates for iron and brick bridges, 11 May 1818
— reports by William Cubitt [civil engineer] to the magistrates on progress of the works,
20 Apr. 1818–28 Jun. 1819
— draft advertisement *re* opening of new bridge on 19 Jun. 1819, 11 Jun. 1819
(26 docs)

C/2/9/1/2/5 Gaol   **1800–1824**

C/2/9/1/2/5/1   Nov. 1800– Jan. 1824
Register of 'prisoners under confinement in the Town and Borough Gaol'
Details for each prisoner include name, age, trade, height, complexion, date of committal, name
of committing magistrate, length of sentence, crime of which indicted or convicted, and date of
discharge. A note inside front cover reads, 'John Flord Wilkinson made his escape from prison
the 27 of September 1811 and was retaken the same day'.
(1 vol., 132 unnumbered fols)

C/2/9/1/2/5/2   Mar. 1800–Mar. 1801
Account of bread supplied by Frederick Coe to prisoners in gaol and bridewell
(1 vol.)

C/2/9/1/2/5/3   Jul.–Nov. 1804
Account of bread supplied by Frederick Coe to prisoners in gaol and bridewell
(1 vol.)

C/2/9/1/2/5/4   Nov. 1804–Mar. 1805
Account of bread supplied by Frederick Coe to prisoners in gaol and bridewell
Prisoners named
(1 vol.)

C/2/9/1/2/6   Treasurer of the Marshalsea Rate   1632–1835

A statute of 1784 (24 Geo. III, cap. 54) empowered those municipal corporations possessing
their own courts of Quarter Sessions to levy a rate 'in the nature of a County Rate' to defray the
costs of the administration of justice. The further power to pay for the erection and maintenance
of gaols out of the rate was given in 1823 (4 Geo. IV, cap. 63). Long before this, however,
borough Justices sitting in their Quarter Sessions had arrogated to themselves the authority, in
imitation of the county Justices, to levy a rate on all householders to pay for the expenses of the
court, the conveyance of vagrants, the maintenance of the gaol and house of correction, the
repair of bridges and, especially in war time, the relief of wounded soldiers and sailors. It was
variously known as the County, Borough, Marshalsea or Gaol Rate. In Ipswich the term
Marshalsea Rate was usual, though in the 17th and early 18th century the Marshalsea Treasurer
was referred to as the Treasurer for Maimed Soldiers and Mariners, or for the Sick and
Wounded.

C/2/9/1/2/6/1   Accounts   1632–1835

For a detailed breakdown of the types of expenditure with which the office was concerned, see
the introductory notes to the Marshalsea Treasurer's vouchers and the militia vouchers
(C/2/9/1/2/6/2–3), below.

C/2/9/1/2/6/1/1   May 1632–Feb. 1633
Maimed soldiers' and mariners' account. Audited
(1 vol.; found with accounts of the Governors and Treasurer of Christ's Hospital)

C/2/9/1/2/6/1/2   Jun. 1633–May 1634
Joseph Pemberton, Treasurer 'for the maymed Souldgers and marynores'
(1 vol.)

C/2/9/1/2/6/1/3   1705–1718
Thomas Starling, Treasurer 'for Sick and Maimed Soldiers'. Audited
(1 vol.; found with audited accounts of town charities)

C/2/9/1/2/6/1/4   Mar. 1787–Jul. 1790
John Tyrrell, Treasurer. Audited
(1 vol.)

C/2/9/1/2/6/1/5   Jul. 1828–Dec. 1837
Marshalsea Treasurer Jul. 1828–Dec. 1835, continued by Borough Treasurer, Jan. 1836–Dec.
1837, and audited at General Sessions of the Peace
(1 vol.)

C/2/9/1/2/6/1/6   n.d. [? late 18c.]
Schedule of total sums disbursed by Treasurer of the Marshalsea to families of militiamen
serving for counties of Cambridgeshire, East Essex, Hertfordshire, East Norfolk, Northumberland, Oxfordshire, Somerset and West Suffolk
(1 fol., apparently removed from a vol.)

C/2/9/1/2/6/2   Vouchers: General Series   *1696–1832*

(For separate bundles relating to the payment of maintenance to militiamen's dependents, see C/2/9/1/2/6/3 below.)

From 1696 to 1714 the bundles consist chiefly of Justices' warrants for payment of relief to travellers and to wounded or discharged soldiers or sailors; warrants for payment of regular pensions; and bills from parish officers for passing vagrants and conveying paupers to their parishes of lawful settlement. The large number of vouchers for 1713 and 1714 is particularly noteworthy, reflecting the mass demobilization of the armed forces following the Peace of Utrecht. Payments for the relief of wounded soldiers and sailors feature prominently again during the French Revolutionary and Napoleonic Wars of the late 18th and early 19th centuries.

After 1714 there is a sixty-six-year break in the series. After its resumption in 1781 the contents of the bundles are much more varied. These later bundles include orders of Sessions, bills and vouchers relating to the expenses of the court and the administration of justice: payment of prosecution and witness expenses; the Town Clerk's charges for legal services; payments to the Coroners for holding inquests; the salaries of officers such as the recorder, gaoler, keeper of the bridewell, gaol surgeon, gaol chaplain and his clerk; the repair of the gaol and bridewell; and the welfare of the prisoners, including weekly subsistence payments, detailed accounts of bread supplied to each (named) prisoner, provision of clothing, shaving them and cutting their hair, and an annual Christmas dinner. There are occasional bills and orders for escorting convicted felons to the hulks to await transportation to the colonies.

Many vouchers relate to the billeting and transport of troops, and include payment of the billet-master's salary and the cost of searching for deserters and escorting them back to the military authorities. The inspection of weights and measures seems also to have been financed out of the Marshalsea Rate.

The presence of filing holes in almost all the documents indicates that they were formerly threaded on laces. A few bundles are still so filed.

C/2/9/1/2/6/2/1   Oct. 1696–Sep. 1697
John Goldson, Treasurer
(127 docs, filed on a lace)

C/2/9/1/2/6/2/2   Oct. 1697–Sep. 1698
John Goldson, Treasurer
(165 docs, filed on a lace)

C/2/9/1/2/6/2/3   Oct. 1698–Sep. 1699
John Goldson, Treasurer
(156 docs, filed on a lace)

C/2/9/1/2/6/2/4   Oct. 1699–Sep. 1700
John Goldson, Treasurer
(104 docs, filed on a lace)

C/2/9/1/2/6/2/5   Jan.–Sep. 1706
Thomas Starling, Treasurer
Includes as wrappers:
— account for repairs to Tooley's almshouses, n.d. (*c.*1560)
— memorandum by Richard Bryd, Tooley's executor, to the Bailiffs, *re* his expenses, 5 Jan. 1568
(48 docs)

C/2/9/1/2/6/2/6   Oct. 1707–Sep. 1708
Thomas Starling, Treasurer
(81 docs)

C/2/9/1/2/6/2/7   Oct. 1708–Sep. 1709
Thomas Starling, Treasurer
(123 docs; found among the annual bundles of vouchers of the Renterwardens of Tooley's and
Smart's Charities)

C/2/9/1/2/6/2/8   Oct. 1709–Oct. 1710
Thomas Starling, Treasurer
Includes:
— Treasurer's account, 1709–1710
(180 docs)

C/2/9/1/2/6/2/9   Oct. 1710–Sep. 1711
Thomas Starling, Treasurer
Includes:
— Treasurer's account, 1710–1711
(108 docs)

C/2/9/1/2/6/2/10   Oct. 1711–Sep. 1712
Thomas Starling, Treasurer
(143 docs)

C/2/9/1/2/6/2/11   Sep. 1712–Sep. 1713
Thomas Starling, Treasurer
Includes:
— Treasurer's account, 1712–1713
(189 docs)

C/2/9/1/2/6/2/12   Oct. 1713–Sep. 1714
Thomas Starling, Treasurer
(271 docs)

C/2/9/1/2/6/2/13   Apr. 1781–Jul. 1785
Richard Batley, Treasurer
Includes:
— estimation of damage done to lands of Thomas Waller at Handford Hall in MS, by building
of the new Handford Bridge, 7 Nov. 1782
(395 docs)

C/2/9/1/2/6/2/14   Aug. 1785–Apr. 1786
Richard Batley, Treasurer
Includes:
— Treasurer's audited account, Aug. 1785–Apr. 1786
(150 docs)

C/2/9/1/2/6/2/15   Mar.–Sep. 1786
Richard Batley, Treasurer
Includes:
— Treasurer's audited account, Apr.–Sep. 1786
(57 docs)

C/2/9/1/2/6/2/16   Sep. 1786–Mar. 1787
Richard Batley, Treasurer
Includes:
— Treasurer's audited account, Sep. 1786–Mar. 1787
— 'Shave and Jackson's complete list and performances of the horses etc. that are to run for His
Majesty's purse of one hundred guineas, on Ipswich Race Ground, on Tuesday, July 5, 1785'
(printed)
(123 docs)

C/2/9/1/2/6/2/17 Mar.–Sep. 1787
John Tyrrell, Treasurer
Includes:
— handbill advertising wholesale and retail sale of woollen cloths by J Smith of Yorkshire,
woollen manufacturer, at the 'Bull's Head', Ipswich, 21 Apr. 1787 (printed)
(163 docs)

C/2/9/1/2/6/2/18 Sep. 1787–May 1788
John Tyrrell, Treasurer
(84 docs, filed on a lace)

C/2/9/1/2/6/2/19 Mar.–Sep. 1788
John Tyrrell, Treasurer
(26 docs; found with the vouchers of the Treasurer of Christ's Hospital)

C/2/9/1/2/6/2/20 Sep. 1788–Mar. 1789
John Tyrrell, Treasurer
Includes:
— itemised account of medicines supplied to Daynes, a prisoner in the Bridewell, 18 Feb. 1788,
allowed 27 Sep. 1788
(49 docs)

C/2/9/1/2/6/2/21 Mar.–Sep. 1789
John Tyrrell, Treasurer
Includes:
— acquittance for £8 11s for transportation of Susanna Hunt to Botany Bay, 4 Apr.1789
(105 docs)

C/2/9/1/2/6/2/22 Sep. 1789–Mar. 1790
John Tyrrell, Treasurer
(71 docs, filed on a lace)

C/2/9/1/2/6/2/23 Mar.–Jul. 1790
John Tyrrell, Treasurer
(76 docs, filed on a lace)

C/2/9/1/2/6/2/24 Mar. 1791–Mar. 1792
John Tyrrell, Treasurer
Includes:
— letter from William Richards jun. of Walworth [London] to the Keeper of Ipswich gaol,
requesting payment of final instalment of money due for transportation of a female convict
from Ipswich on board the 'Lady Juliana' transport in Apr. 1789; 10 Oct. 1791
(78 docs)

C/2/9/1/2/6/2/25 Mar. 1792–Mar. 1793
John Tyrrell, Treasurer
Includes:
— handbill printed by order of William Batley, Town Clerk, re magistrates' intention to
enforce the laws against vagrancy, because of its recent great increase within the jurisdiction,
20 Jun. 1792, endorsed with order for payment of printing costs
(166 docs)

C/2/9/1/2/6/2/26 Mar. 1793–Mar. 1794
John Tyrrell, Treasurer
(151 docs)

Wherstead 29th June 1789
Recd of Thos. Hinsby Constable
of the Hamlett of Wix Bishop in
the Borough of Ipswich – the Body of
Amy Willby a Vagabond, by Pass
to Lawford in Essex
Rivers

Mr Tyrell
Pay the Bearer five shillings for
the above Thos. Norris Bailiff

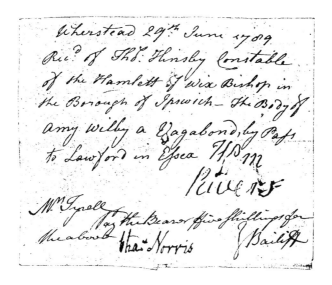

Fig. 5. Acquittance for passing a vagrant from Wix Bishop to Wherstead, *en route* to Lawford in Essex. (From a bundle of payment vouchers of the Treasurer of the Marshalsea Rate, March–September 1789, C/2/9/1/2/6/2/21)

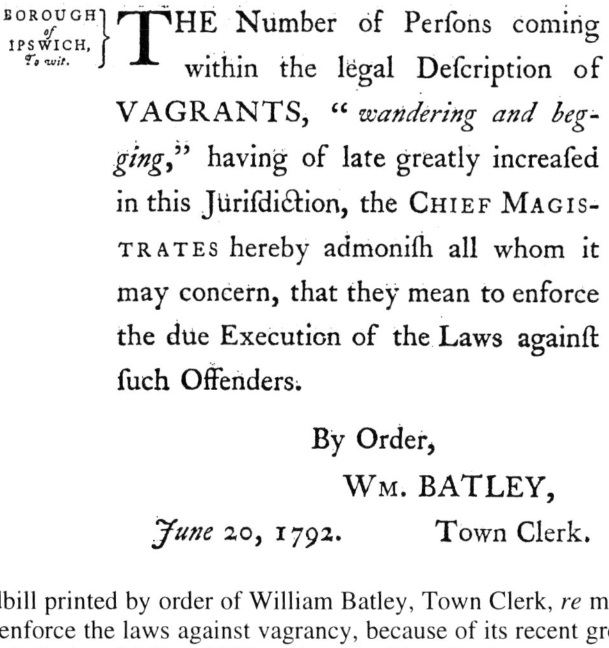

BOROUGH of IPSWICH, *To wit.*

THE Number of Perſons coming within the legal Deſcription of VAGRANTS, "*wandering and begging*," having of late greatly increaſed in this Juriſdiction, the CHIEF MAGISTRATES hereby admoniſh all whom it may concern, that they mean to enforce the due Execution of the Laws againſt ſuch Offenders.

By Order,

WM. BATLEY,

June 20, 1792. Town Clerk.

Fig. 6. Handbill printed by order of William Batley, Town Clerk, *re* magistrates' intention to enforce the laws against vagrancy, because of its recent great increase within the jurisdiction, 20 June 1792, endorsed with order for payment of printing costs. (From a bundle of payment vouchers of the Treasurer of the Marshalsea Rate, March 1792–March 1793, C/2/9/1/2/6/2/25)

C/2/9/1/2/6/2/27   Mar. 1794–Mar. 1795
John Tyrrell, Treasurer
Includes:
— order for payment 'for taking away the ice from the shore by the Quay, and in Brook Street
etc.' 24 Jan. 1795
(127 docs)

C/2/9/1/2/6/2/28   Mar.–Sep. 1796
John Tyrrell, Treasurer
(86 docs)

C/2/9/1/2/6/2/29   Sep. 1796–Mar. 1797
John Tyrrell, Treasurer
Includes:
— Treasurer's account book (unaudited), Mar. 1794–Mar. 1795 with, at end, account of
payments to militiamen's families, Apr. 1795–Dec. 1796
(107 docs)

C/2/9/1/2/6/2/30   Mar.–Nov. 1797
John Tyrrell, Treasurer
Includes:
— Treasurer's account book (including account of payments to militiamen's families), Mar.
1793–Mar. 1797
(149 docs)

C/2/9/1/2/6/2/31   Nov. 1797–Feb. 1799
John Tyrrell, Treasurer
Includes:
— letter by an unknown correspondent (signature torn away) at Harleston to Lord Rous, 4 Jul.
1798 *re* one Lone, 'who travels with a poppet-shew and shews slight of hand tricks [and] hath
lately spread about the smallpox in this neighbourhood'; Lone is now 'on his road to Ipswich
for the remainder of the races' and the Bailiffs should be warned. Endorsed with order for
payment of 5s to Robert Turner, special constable, 'for extra duty respecting this information',
31 Jul. 1798
(135 docs)

C/2/9/1/2/6/2/32   Mar. 1799–Jan. 1800
John Tyrrell, Treasurer
Includes:
— Treasurer's audited account, Feb. 1797–Jan. 1800, including account of allowances paid to
dependents of members of the East Suffolk Militia (giving name, rank, parish of residence,
number in family, number of weeks, dates and amounts paid), Mar. 1797–Jul. 1799
— schedule of payments to dependents of members of the East Suffolk Militia (details as
above, though number in family omitted), Dec. 1796–Oct. 1799
(173 docs)

C/2/9/1/2/6/2/33   Feb.–Dec. 1800
Samuel Howes, Treasurer
Includes:
— order for payment of 10s 6d to the Volunteers 'for expenses at the White Hart on Saturday
Sept. 13 1800 in consequence of the disturbance of the populace', n.d.
(65 docs)

C/2/9/1/2/6/2/34   Jan. 1800–Feb. 1801
Samuel Howes, Treasurer
For poor relief and vagrancy only
(241 docs)

C/2/9/1/2/6/2/35   Mar.–Dec. 1801
Samuel Howes, Treasurer
Includes:
— order of Sessions for payment of £2 12s 6d to William Norris, one of the chief constables,
'for returns issued under the late population act' [census], 16 Mar. 1801
(208 docs)

C/2/9/1/2/6/2/36   Dec. 1801–Jul. 1802
Samuel Howes, Treasurer
Includes:
— Bailiffs' order for payment of £1 18s constables' allowance 'for attending the proclaiming
of peace and attending the illumination at night', 3 May 1802
(209 docs)

C/2/9/1/2/6/2/37   Jul. 1802–Jan. 1803
Samuel Howes, Treasurer
(149 docs)

C/2/9/1/2/6/2/38   Mar.–Jul. 1803
Samuel Howes, Treasurer
(95 docs)

C/2/9/1/2/6/2/39   Jul. 1803–Jun. 1804
Samuel Howes, Treasurer
(131 docs)

C/2/9/1/2/6/2/40   Jul. 1803–Jun. 1804
Samuel Howes, Treasurer
(75 docs)

C/2/9/1/2/6/2/41   Mar. 1803–Jul. 1804
Samuel Howes, Treasurer
(24 docs)

C/2/9/1/2/6/2/42   Mar.–Nov. 1804
Samuel Howes, Treasurer
(78 docs)

C/2/9/1/2/6/2/43   Jul. 1804–Jan. 1806
Samuel Howes, Treasurer
Includes:
— Coroner's inquisitions on: John Stollery, 20 Jul. 1804; William Bent, 20 Sep. 1804; Elizabeth Theobald, widow, 19 Oct. 1804; William Farrer, 24 Nov. 1804
— handbill for grand lottery beginning 3 Feb. 1806, tickets on sale at Messrs Crickett and Co.'s
Bank, Ipswich (printed), n.d.; endorsed with order for payment of relief to unnamed bearer,
14 Dec. 1805
(266 docs)

C/2/9/1/2/6/2/44   Feb.–Jul. 1806
Samuel Howes, Treasurer
(93 docs)

C/2/9/1/2/6/2/45   Feb.–Dec. 1806
Samuel Howes, Treasurer
Includes:
— Justices' authorization to Treasurer to borrow up to £200 for 3 months, to be applied towards
the purposes of the Marshalsea rates, 21 Apr. 1806
(104 docs)

Grand Lottery,

Begins February 3, 1806.

SCHEME.

3	Prizes of	£20,000	are	£60,000
3	------	10,000	------	30,000
3	------	5,000	------	15,000
3	------	2,000	------	6,000
8	------	1,000	------	8,000
20	------	500	------	10,000
50	------	100	------	5,000
120	------	50	------	6,000
5,000	First-drawn Tickets 22 each		--	110,000
25,000	Tickets			£250,000

Part of the above Capitals;

First-drawn Ticket	1st Day	£10,000
Ditto	.... 4th Day	20,000
Ditto	.... 6th Day	20,000
Ditto	.... 8th Day	5,000
Ditto	...; ....10th Day	2,000

DAYS OF DRAWING;

1st Monday, ...	Feb. 3	6th Thursday,....Feb.	27
2d Friday, ...	Feb. 7	7th Saturday, ...March	1
3d Thursday,......	Feb. 13	8th Wednesday,..March	5
4th Tuesday, ...	Feb. 18	9th Friday,......March	7
5th Saturday, ...	Feb. 22	10th Monday, ...March	10

Tickets and Shares are on Sale by

JAMES SMYTH,

(At Messrs. CRICKETT & Co's Bank,)

IPSWICH,

AGENT TO

HAZARD, BURNE and Co.

LONDON.

†+† Observe, the first 5,000 Ticket are entitled to £22 each, besides the usual Chance for the CAPITALS.

Evans & Ruffy, (Commercial-Press) Budge Row, London.

Fig. 7. Handbill for grand lottery beginning 3 February 1806, tickets on sale at Messrs Crickett and Co.'s Bank, Ipswich; endorsed with order for payment of relief to unnamed bearer, 14 December 1805. (From a bundle of payment vouchers of the Treasurer of the Marshalsea Rate, July 1804–January 1806, C/2/9/1/2/6/2/43)

C/2/9/1/2/6/2/46   Dec. 1806–Jul. 1807
Samuel Howes, Treasurer
(80 docs)

C/2/9/1/2/6/2/47   Dec. 1806–Feb. 1808
Benjamin Brame sen., Treasurer
(49 docs, found loose; a note in the previous catalogue indicates that the original wrapper was
endorsed 'Allowed at Sessions 23 Feb. 1808')

C/2/9/1/2/6/2/48   Dec. 1806–Feb. 1808
Benjamin Brame sen., Treasurer
(35 docs, filed on a string)

C/2/9/1/2/6/2/49   Apr. 1807–Feb. 1808
Benjamin Brame sen., Treasurer
(20 docs, filed on a string)

C/2/9/1/2/6/2/50   May 1807–Feb. 1808
Benjamin Brame sen., Treasurer
(44 docs, filed on a string)

C/2/9/1/2/6/2/51   Aug. 1809–Jul. 1810
Benjamin Brame jun., Treasurer
Includes:
— account of disbursements to families of NCOs in East Suffolk Regiment of Militia for the
Beccles, Woodbridge and Ipswich Divisions, by John Spooner, Treasurer of the Ipswich
Division, Apr. 1809–Feb. 1810
(155 docs; a note in the previous catalogue indicates that the original wrapper was endorsed
'Allowed at Sessions 2 Aug. 1810')

C/2/9/1/2/6/2/52   Feb. 1810–Feb. 1811
Benjamin Brame jun., Treasurer
(265 docs)

C/2/9/1/2/6/2/53   Feb. 1811–Apr. 1812
Benjamin Brame, Treasurer
Includes:
— account of disbursements to families of sergeants, corporals and drummers in East Suffolk
Regiment of Militia for the Beccles, Woodbridge and Ipswich Divisions, by John Spooner,
Treasurer of the Ipswich Division, May 1810–Feb. 1811
(274 docs)

C/2/9/1/2/6/2/54   Jul. 1812–Aug. 1813
Benjamin Brame, Treasurer
Includes:
— Justices' warrant for payment of £1 12s 6d to 13 constables 'for attending the public streets
during the illumination on 20th Augst 1812 in honour of Marquis Wellington's victory', 7 Sep.
1812 [Wellington entered Madrid on 12 Aug.]
— account of disbursements to families of NCOs in East Suffolk Regiment of Militia for the
Beccles and Woodbridge Divisions, Jan. 1811–Jan. 1812
— similar account, Jun. 1811–Jan. 1813
(245 docs)

C/2/9/1/2/6/2/55   Aug. 1813–Feb. 1814
Benjamin Brame, Treasurer
Includes:
— order of [Henry Addington, Viscount] Sidmouth [Home Secretary] for removal of 5 named
convicts, sentenced to transportation, from Ipswich gaol to the hulks on the Medway, on their
being certified free from 'any putrid or infectious distemper', 16 Jul. 1813; endorsed with

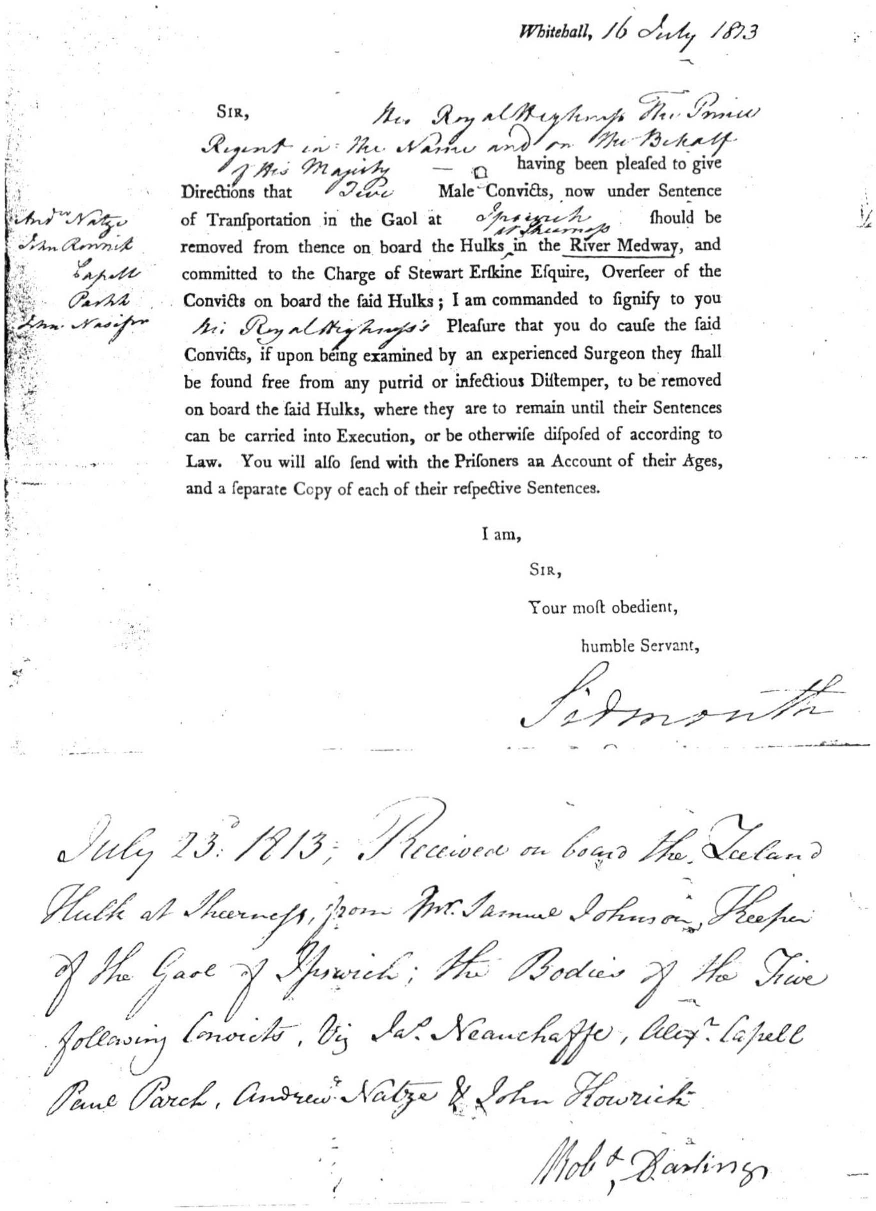

Whitehall, 16 July 1813

SIR,

His Royal Highness The Prince Regent in the Name and on the Behalf of His Majesty — having been pleaſed to give Directions that Five Male Convicts, now under Sentence of Tranſportation in the Gaol at Ipswich ſhould be removed from thence on board the Hulks at Sheerness in the River Medway, and committed to the Charge of Stewart Erſkine Eſquire, Overſeer of the Convicts on board the ſaid Hulks; I am commanded to ſignify to you His Royal Highness's Pleaſure that you do cauſe the ſaid Convicts, if upon being examined by an experienced Surgeon they ſhall be found free from any putrid or infectious Diſtemper, to be removed on board the ſaid Hulks, where they are to remain until their Sentences can be carried into Execution, or be otherwiſe diſpoſed of according to Law. You will alſo ſend with the Priſoners an Account of their Ages, and a ſeparate Copy of each of their reſpective Sentences.

Andw Natze
John Ronnick
Capell
Parch
Jam. Neasifer

I am,

SIR,

Your moſt obedient,

humble Servant,

Sidmouth

July 23d 1813; Received on board the Zeeland Hulk at Sheerness, from Mr. Samuel Johnson, Keeper of the Gaol of Ipswich; the Bodies of the Five following Convicts, Viz Jas. Neauchaffe, Alexr. Capell Paul Parch, Andrew Natze & John Howrick

Robt Darling

Fig. 8. Transportation from Ipswich Gaol, July 1813. The Home Secretary's order for removal of five named convicts, sentenced to transportation, from Ipswich Gaol to the hulks on the Medway, on their being certified free from 'any putrid or infectious distemper', 16 July 1813; endorsed with Gaoler's acquittance on receipt of prisoners on board the 'Zeeland' hulk at Sheerness (Kent), 23 July 1813. (From a bundle of payment vouchers of the Treasurer of the Marshalsea Rate, August 1813–February 1814, C/2/9/1/2/6/2/55)

Gaoler's acquittance on receipt of prisoners on board the 'Zeeland' hulk at Sheerness [Kent], 23 Jul. 1813
(87 docs; wrapper endorsed 'Bills and vouchers allowed at Sessions 15th February 1814')

C/2/9/1/2/6/2/56   Feb.–Jul. 1814
Benjamin Brame, Treasurer
Includes:
— account of disbursements to families of NCOs in East Suffolk Regiment of Militia for the Beccles, Woodbridge and Ipswich Divisions, Mar. 1813–Mar. 1814
(108 docs; a note in the previous catalogue indicates that the original wrapper was endorsed 'Allowed at Sessions 28 Jul. 1814')

C/2/9/1/2/6/2/57   Jul. 1814–Mar. 1815
Benjamin Brame, Treasurer
Includes:
— schedule of names of persons convicted of grand larceny at Ipswich Sessions, Feb. 1811–Jul. 1814, with annexed Justices' order for payment of Town Clerk's fees, 28 Jul. 1814
(102 docs; a note in the previous catalogue indicates that the original wrapper was endorsed 'Allowed at Sessions Mar. 1815')

C/2/9/1/2/6/2/58   Mar.–Jul. 1815
Benjamin Brame, Treasurer
Includes:
— 2 Justice's orders to Collectors of Land Tax for payment of £1 to John Spratbury, drum major in 1st Surrey Militia, for apprehending 2 deserters, Moses Lucas and William Rich, both drummers in the Regiment, 30 Nov. 1812
(131 docs; a note in the previous catalogue indicates that the original wrapper was endorsed 'Allowed at Sessions Jul. 1815')

C/2/9/1/2/6/2/59   Mar. 1815–Mar. 1816
Benjamin Brame, Treasurer
(104 docs)

C/2/9/1/2/6/2/60   Jul. 1815–Jul. 1816
Benjamin Brame, Treasurer
(81 docs)

C/2/9/1/2/6/2/61   Jul. 1816–Mar. 1817
Benjamin Brame, Treasurer
(123 docs)

C/2/9/1/2/6/2/62   Mar.–Jul. 1817
Benjamin Brame, Treasurer
(103 docs)

C/2/9/1/2/6/2/63   Jul. 1817–Feb. 1818
Benjamin Brame, Treasurer
(94 docs)

C/2/9/1/2/6/2/64   Mar.–Aug. 1818
Benjamin Brame, Treasurer
(163 docs)

C/2/9/1/2/6/2/65   Aug. 1818–Feb. 1819
Benjamin Brame, Treasurer
(136 docs)

C/2/9/1/2/6/2/66   Mar.–Jul. 1819
Benjamin Brame, Treasurer
(134 docs)

C/2/9/1/2/6/2/67   Jul. 1819–Feb. 1820
Benjamin Brame, Treasurer
Includes:
— Justices' order for payment of £3 12*s* to 2 constables 'for attending the banks of the river to
prevent persons from bathing and improperly exposing themselves . . . 49 days 1818'
(119 docs; a note in the previous catalogue indicates that the original wrapper was endorsed
'Allowed at Sessions 28 Feb. 1820')

C/2/9/1/2/6/2/68   Feb.–Jul. 1820
Benjamin Brame, Treasurer
(83 docs; a note in the previous catalogue indicates that the original wrapper was endorsed
'Allowed at Sessions 4 Aug. 1820')

C/2/9/1/2/6/2/69   Aug. 1820–Feb. 1821
Benjamin Brame, Treasurer
(133 docs)

C/2/9/1/2/6/2/70   Mar.–Jul. 1821
[Benjamin Brame, Treasurer]
(100 docs)

C/2/9/1/2/6/2/71   Jul. 1821–Mar. 1822
Benjamin Brame, Treasurer
(89 docs)

C/2/9/1/2/6/2/72   Mar.–Jun. 1822
Benjamin Brame, Treasurer
(50 docs)

C/2/9/1/2/6/2/73   Mar. 1822–Apr. 1823
Benjamin Brame, Treasurer
Includes:
— mortgage by Bailiffs, Recorder and Justices at General Sessions, of county rates to
Benjamin Brame, esq., for repayment of £400 advanced by him towards cost of building Stoke
Bridge, 1 Mar. 1819
— similar mortgage to Henry Seekamp, esq., for repayment of £800, 1 Mar. 1819
— similar mortgage to William Barnard Clarke, esq., for repayment of £500, 29 Jul. 1819
(198 docs)

C/2/9/1/2/6/2/74   Jul.–Dec. 1823
Benjamin Brame, Treasurer
(107 docs)

C/2/9/1/2/6/2/75   Mar.–Jun. 1824
Benjamin Brame, Treasurer
(108 docs)

C/2/9/1/2/6/2/76   Jul. 1824–Feb. 1825
Benjamin Brame, Treasurer
(104 docs)

C/2/9/1/2/6/2/77   Mar.–Jul. 1825
Benjamin Brame, Treasurer
(94 docs)

C/2/9/1/2/6/2/78   Jul. 1825–Feb. 1826
Benjamin Brame, Treasurer
(80 docs; a note in the previous catalogue indicates that the original wrapper was endorsed
'Allowed at Sessions 1 Mar. 1826')

The Bailiff & Justices of the Town & Borough of Ipswich to Jn Green & Wm Brest Constables for attending the Banks of the River to prevent persons from Bathing & improperly exposing themselves by order of the Magistrate 49 Days 1818

£ 3. 12. 0.

Fig. 9. (*Above*) Justices' order for payment of £3 12*s* to two constables 'for attending the banks of the river to prevent persons from bathing and improperly exposing themselves . . . 49 days 1818' (from a bundle of payment vouchers of the Treasurer of the Marshalsea Rate, July 1819–February 1820, C/2/9/1/2/6/2/67). (*Below*) Watch and clockmaker's trade card used as a 'stop' for the file lace of Samuel Thorndike's payment vouchers as Town Treasurer, 1813–14. In the 1798 Directory his premises were in the Buttermarket. (C/3/4/4/82)

C/2/9/1/2/6/2/79   Mar.–Jul. 1826
Benjamin Brame, Treasurer
(94 docs; a note in the previous catalogue indicates that the original wrapper was endorsed 'Allowed at Sessions 7 Jul. 1826')

C/2/9/1/2/6/2/80   Jul. 1826–Mar. 1827
Benjamin Brame, Treasurer
Includes:
— 2 mortgages by Bailiffs, Recorder and Justices at General Sessions, of county (Marshalsea) rates to William Barnard Clarke, esq., for repayment of 2 sums of £100 advanced by him towards cost of purchasing, rebuilding and enlarging new gaol, 11 Mar. 1823; both endorsed with acquittances on repayment, Jul. 1825–Mar. 1827
(121 docs)

C/2/9/1/2/6/2/81   Mar.–Jul. 1827
Benjamin Brame, Treasurer
(137 docs)

C/2/9/1/2/6/2/82   Jul. 1828–Mar. 1829
Benjamin Brame, Treasurer
(108 docs)

C/2/9/1/2/6/2/83   Mar.–Jul. 1829
Benjamin Brame, Treasurer
(120 docs)

C/2/9/1/2/6/2/84   Mar. 1831–Jul. 1832
Samuel Alexander, Treasurer
(141 docs)

C/2/9/1/2/6/3 Vouchers: Militia   *1782–1808*

By the Militia Act of 1758 (31 Geo. II, cap. 26, s. 28), parish Overseers of the Poor were required to pay weekly allowances, which could be authorised by any one Justice of the Peace, to the dependants of serving militiamen. Such allowances were to be reimbursed by the County Treasurer out of the county stock. Within the borough of Ipswich, reimbursement was made by the Treasurer of the Marshalsea Rate.

 The documents listed here consist chiefly of bills for maintenance provided to the families of named militiamen, submitted by the officers of the various Ipswich parishes to the Marshalsea Treasurer and allowed by Justices of the Peace; and printed Justices' warrants to the Treasurer for reimbursement to the parishes. Testimonials from militia officers and orders for relief addressed by them to the parish officers are also sometimes included. Vouchers for maintenance of dependants of those serving as substitutes in the militia regiments of counties other than Suffolk usually give also the name and parish of residence of the person whose service is being performed by the substitute. Many of the documents are initialled 'W.B.' [William Batley, Clerk of the Peace], indicating his scrutiny.

 Until 1802 the vouchers were bundled by regiment; from 1803 onwards they were always arranged by parish. A note in the previous catalogue states that the five bundles for St Nicholas parish for the year 1805 (C/2/9/1/2/6/3/77–81) were originally found attached to each other, as were the three bundles for St Mary Elms for the same year (C/2/9/1/2/6/3/65–67). This practice has formed the basis for the arrangement of the *post*-1802 bundles in the present list, in that all the bundles for a given parish for the same calendar year have been listed consecutively. The presence of filing holes indicates that most of the documents were formerly threaded on laces; a few bundles are still so filed.

C/2/9/1/2/6/3/1   Jun. 1782–Dec. 1784
East Suffolk Regiment

Includes:
— list of disbursements to dependants of named militiamen in NI, with summary of ? disbursements in all Ipswich parishes and hamlets, n.d.
— letter from [*signature illegible*], Norwich, to Richard Batley [Marshalsea Treasurer], *re* default in payment by 'that scoundrel Finch', 14 Dec. 1784
(7 docs)

C/2/9/1/2/6/3/2   Dec. 1792–Feb. 1794
East Suffolk Regiment
Includes:
— account of John Tyrrell, Treasurer, of money disbursed to militiamen's dependants, Dec. 1792–Aug. 1793
(31 docs)

C/2/9/1/2/6/3/3   Feb.–Dec. 1795
East Suffolk Regiment
(24 docs)

C/2/9/1/2/6/3/4   Jan.–Dec. 1796
East Suffolk Regiment
(28 docs)

C/2/9/1/2/6/3/5   7–10 Jan. 1797
East Suffolk Regiment
(4 docs)

C/2/9/1/2/6/3/6   Mar.–Oct. 1797
East Suffolk Regiment
(17 docs)

C/2/9/1/2/6/3/7   Jan.–Aug. 1798
East Suffolk Regiment
(16 docs)

C/2/9/1/2/6/3/8   Oct.–Nov. 1798
East Suffolk Regiment
(6 docs)

C/2/9/1/2/6/3/9   Dec. 1798–Jan. 1799
East Suffolk Regiment
(8 docs)

C/2/9/1/2/6/3/10   Mar.–Nov. 1799
East Suffolk Regiment
(22 docs)

C/2/9/1/2/6/3/11   Mar. 1797–Jan. 1799
Hertfordshire Regiment
(29 docs, filed on lace)

C/2/9/1/2/6/3/12   Apr. 1797–Jan. 1799
Cambridgeshire Regiment
(13 docs)

C/2/9/1/2/6/3/13   Apr. 1797–Jan. 1799
East Essex Regiment
(34 docs)

C/2/9/1/2/6/3/14   May 1797–Jan. 1799
West Suffolk Regiment
(33 docs, filed on lace)

C/2/9/1/2/6/3/15 Northumberland Regiment (7 docs)	Jul. 1797–Jan. 1799
C/2/9/1/2/6/3/16 East Norfolk Regiment (6 docs)	Jul. 1797–Jan. 1799
C/2/9/1/2/6/3/17 Somerset Regiment (9 docs, filed on lace)	Mar. 1798–Jan. 1799
C/2/9/1/2/6/3/18 Oxfordshire Regiment (4 docs)	Aug.–Dec. 1798
C/2/9/1/2/6/3/19 East Norfolk Regiment (1 doc)	26 Sep. 1800
C/2/9/1/2/6/3/20 East Suffolk Regiment (19 docs)	Jan.–Dec. 1800
C/2/9/1/2/6/3/21 East Essex Regiment (9 docs)	Apr.–Dec. 1800
C/2/9/1/2/6/3/22 West Suffolk Regiment (3 docs)	Apr.–Dec. 1800
C/2/9/1/2/6/3/23 Northumberland Regiment (1 doc)	1 Dec. 1800
C/2/9/1/2/6/3/24 West Suffolk Regiment (3 docs)	Mar.–Apr. 1801
C/2/9/1/2/6/3/25 Oxfordshire Regiment (3 docs)	Apr.–Sep. 1801
C/2/9/1/2/6/3/26 East Essex Regiment (8 docs)	Jan.–Dec. 1801
C/2/9/1/2/6/3/27 East Suffolk Regiment (23 docs)	Mar.–Dec. 1801
C/2/9/1/2/6/3/28 Leicestershire Regiment (38 docs)	Jul.–Dec. 1801
C/2/9/1/2/6/3/29 Warwickshire Regiment (15 docs)	Jul.–Dec. 1801
C/2/9/1/2/6/3/30 Cambridgeshire Regiment (37 docs)	Jul. 1801–May 1802

C/2/9/1/2/6/3/31
Leicestershire Regiment
(14 docs)   Feb.–May 1802

C/2/9/1/2/6/3/32
Warwickshire Regiment
(6 docs)   Feb.–May 1802

C/2/9/1/2/6/3/33
East Suffolk Regiment
(2 docs)   Apr.–May 1802

C/2/9/1/2/6/3/34
East Essex Regiment
(2 docs)   7 May 1802

C/2/9/1/2/6/3/35
Oxfordshire Regiment
(1 doc)   7 May 1802

C/2/9/1/2/6/3/36
PE (1 doc)   29 Sep. 1803

C/2/9/1/2/6/3/37
LW (4 docs)   Sep. 1803–Jan. 1804

C/2/9/1/2/6/3/38
HL (3 docs)   Sep. 1803–Mar. 1804

C/2/9/1/2/6/3/39
ST (4 docs)   Sep. 1803–Jun. 1804

C/2/9/1/2/6/3/40
MG (11 docs)   Nov. 1803–Apr. 1804

C/2/9/1/2/6/3/41
CL (12 docs)   Nov. 1803–May 1804

C/2/9/1/2/6/3/42
MG (7 docs)   6 Jul. 1804

C/2/9/1/2/6/3/43
CL (4 docs)   20–31 Aug. 1804

C/2/9/1/2/6/3/44
CL (11 docs)   28 Sep. 1804

C/2/9/1/2/6/3/45
HL (2 docs)   Jun.–Sep. 1804

C/2/9/1/2/6/3/46
MG (29 docs, filed on thread)   Jun.–Oct. 1804

C/2/9/1/2/6/3/47
MQ (4 docs)   Oct. 1803–Mar. 1804

C/2/9/1/2/6/3/48
MQ (17 docs)   Jun.–Oct. 1804

C/2/9/1/2/6/3/49
MT (6 docs)   6 Nov. 1804

C/2/9/1/2/6/3/50
MW: vouchers only (9 docs)   Oct.–Nov. 1804

C/2/9/1/2/6/3/51   Jun.–Dec. 1804
MW: orders for relief only (20 docs)

C/2/9/1/2/6/3/52   12 Apr. 1804
NI (3 docs)

C/2/9/1/2/6/3/53   24 Sep. 1804
NI (9 docs)

C/2/9/1/2/6/3/54   26 Mar. 1804
PE (1 doc)

C/2/9/1/2/6/3/55   14 Jan. 1805
CL (13 docs)

C/2/9/1/2/6/3/56   23 Apr. 1805
CL (10 docs)

C/2/9/1/2/6/3/57   15–22 Jul. 1805
CL (10 docs)

C/2/9/1/2/6/3/58   26 Oct. 1805
CL (11 docs)

C/2/9/1/2/6/3/59   28 Dec. 1805
CL (10 docs)

C/2/9/1/2/6/3/60   Sep.–Dec. 1805
HL (5 docs)

C/2/9/1/2/6/3/61   9 Jan. 1805
MG (17 docs)

C/2/9/1/2/6/3/62   8 Apr. 1805
MG (18 docs)

C/2/9/1/2/6/3/63   19 Jul. 1805
MG (11 docs)

C/2/9/1/2/6/3/64   18 Oct. 1805
MG (12 docs)

C/2/9/1/2/6/3/65   Sep. 1804–Mar. 1805
ME (6 docs)

C/2/9/1/2/6/3/66   10 Oct. 1805
ME (3 docs)

C/2/9/1/2/6/3/67   30 Dec. 1805
ME (3 docs)

C/2/9/1/2/6/3/68   26 Mar. 1805
MQ (3 docs)

C/2/9/1/2/6/3/69   24 Jun. 1805
MQ (7 docs)

C/2/9/1/2/6/3/70   24 Sep. 1805
MQ (4 docs)

C/2/9/1/2/6/3/71   27 Dec. 1805
MQ (3 docs)

C/2/9/1/2/6/3/72   18 Feb. 1805
MT (7 docs)

C/2/9/1/2/6/3/73 MT (7 docs)	30 May 1805
C/2/9/1/2/6/3/74 MT (8 docs)	28–29 Nov. 1805
C/2/9/1/2/6/3/75 MT (4 docs)	30 Dec. 1805
C/2/9/1/2/6/3/76 MW (3 docs)	20 Sep. 1805
C/2/9/1/2/6/3/77 NI (7 docs)	18 Feb. 1805
C/2/9/1/2/6/3/78 NI (7 docs)	2 Apr. 1805
C/2/9/1/2/6/3/79 NI (7 docs)	22 Jun. 1805
C/2/9/1/2/6/3/80 NI (6 docs)	2 Oct. 1805
C/2/9/1/2/6/3/81 NI (6 docs)	21 Dec. 1805
C/2/9/1/2/6/3/82 PE (10 docs)	May–Dec. 1805
C/2/9/1/2/6/3/83 ST (1 doc)	25 Feb. 1805
C/2/9/1/2/6/3/84 CL (13 docs)	1–4 Apr. 1806
C/2/9/1/2/6/3/85 CL (13 docs)	Jun.–Jul. 1806
C/2/9/1/2/6/3/86 CL (15 docs)	30 Oct. 1806
C/2/9/1/2/6/3/87 HL (4 docs)	6 Jan. 1806
C/2/9/1/2/6/3/88 HL (4 docs)	31 Mar. 1806
C/2/9/1/2/6/3/89 HL (4 docs)	26 Jun. 1806
C/2/9/1/2/6/3/90 HL (3 docs)	Mar.–Sep. 1806
C/2/9/1/2/6/3/91 HL (4 docs)	1 Oct. 1806
C/2/9/1/2/6/3/92 HL (5 docs)	26 Dec. 1806
C/2/9/1/2/6/3/93 MG (10 docs)	1 Jan. 1806
C/2/9/1/2/6/3/94 MG (10 docs)	4 Apr. 1806

C/2/9/1/2/6/3/95 MG (10 docs)	7 Jul. 1806
C/2/9/1/2/6/3/96 MG (11 docs)	13 Oct. 1806
C/2/9/1/2/6/3/97 ME (3 docs)	10 Apr. 1806
C/2/9/1/2/6/3/98 ME (4 docs)	4 Jul. 1806
C/2/9/1/2/6/3/99 ME (4 docs)	28 Nov. 1806
C/2/9/1/2/6/3/100 ME (4 docs)	29–30 Dec. 1806
C/2/9/1/2/6/3/101 MQ (7 docs)	25 Mar. 1806
C/2/9/1/2/6/3/102 MQ (4 docs)	26 Jun. 1806
C/2/9/1/2/6/3/103 MQ (6 docs)	30 Sep. 1806
C/2/9/1/2/6/3/104 MQ (7 docs)	29 Dec. 1806
C/2/9/1/2/6/3/105 MQ (10 docs)	29 Dec. 1806
C/2/9/1/2/6/3/106 MT (3 docs)	31 Mar. 1806
C/2/9/1/2/6/3/107 MT (3 docs)	1 Jul. 1806
C/2/9/1/2/6/3/108 MT (2 docs)	30 Sep. 1806
C/2/9/1/2/6/3/109 MT (2 docs)	29 Dec. 1806
C/2/9/1/2/6/3/110 MW (8 docs)	1 Jan. 1806
C/2/9/1/2/6/3/111 MW (7 docs)	18 Apr. 1806
C/2/9/1/2/6/3/112 MW (7 docs)	4 Jul. 1806
C/2/9/1/2/6/3/113 MW (8 docs)	27 Sep. 1806
C/2/9/1/2/6/3/114 NI (9 docs)	29 Mar. 1806
C/2/9/1/2/6/3/115 NI (9 docs)	28 Jun. 1806
C/2/9/1/2/6/3/116 NI (9 docs)	23 Sep. 1806

C/2/9/1/2/6/3/117 NI (9 docs)	22 Dec. 1806
C/2/9/1/2/6/3/118 PE (3 docs)	Apr.–Nov. 1806
C/2/9/1/2/6/3/119 ST (2 docs)	Sep.–Dec. 1806
C/2/9/1/2/6/3/120 CL (36 docs)	1 Jan. 1807
C/2/9/1/2/6/3/121 CL (14 docs)	6 Apr. 1807
C/2/9/1/2/6/3/122 HL (6 docs)	30 Mar. 1807
C/2/9/1/2/6/3/123 MG (9 docs)	5 Jan. 1807
C/2/9/1/2/6/3/124 MG (9 docs)	30–31 Mar. 1807
C/2/9/1/2/6/3/125 ME (4 docs)	31 Mar. 1807
C/2/9/1/2/6/3/126 MQ (6 docs)	30 Mar. 1807
C/2/9/1/2/6/3/127 MT (2 docs)	31 Mar. 1807
C/2/9/1/2/6/3/128 MW (8 docs)	9 Jan. 1807
C/2/9/1/2/6/3/129 MW (6 docs)	1 Apr. 1807
C/2/9/1/2/6/3/130 NI (7 docs)	20 Mar. 1807
C/2/9/1/2/6/3/131 PE (3 docs)	Jan.–Mar. 1807
C/2/9/1/2/6/3/132 ST (1 doc.)	4 Mar. 1807
C/2/9/1/2/6/3/133 MG; arrears for period Sep. 1803–Mar. 1804 (1 doc.)	10 Apr. 1808

C/2/9/1/2/7   Weights and measures   1792

C/2/9/1/2/7/1   13 Nov. 1792
Acknowledgement of receipt
From Samuel Turner of London, gent, to Lords Commissioners of Treasury, for 1 brass bushel
measure for delivery to Bailiffs of Ipswich for town's use
(indented)

C/2/9/2 PETTY SESSIONS   1835

C/2/9/2/1 DRAFT MINUTES   1835

C/2/9/2/1/1   May–Nov. 1835
Draft minutes
Proceedings before the Justices: chiefly examinations of defendants and witnesses, and notes of
committal for trial [at Quarter Sessions]; with initials of presiding Justices
(1 vol.)

C/2/9/3 LICENSING SESSIONS   1736–1835

Alehouses had been subject to control by the Justices of the Peace since the Act of 5–6 Edw. VI,
cap. 25 (1552), which required alehouse keepers to be licensed by the Justices in Quarter
Sessions, or by two Justices out of court. Recognizances for good behaviour were also to be
taken before two Justices, who were to 'certify the same at the next Quarter Session . . . there to
remain of record'. In 1619 a royal proclamation ordered that licences should be issued annually
at special licensing ('Brewster') sessions, a provision which received statutory force in 1729.
An Act of 1753, which clarified the licensing laws, also required new applicants for licences to
produce certificates of good character signed by the ministers, churchwardens and leading
inhabitants of the parish.

C/2/9/3/1 ALEHOUSEKEEPERS' LICENCES   1810–1835

Licences, granted at the General Annual Licensing Meeting ('Brewster Sessions') held in
August, and at intervening Special Licensing Meetings, to keep an alehouse and sell victuals
and 'all such exciseable liquors as shall be licensed and empowered to be sold under the
authority . . . of any excise licence which shall be duly granted by the Commissioners of Excise
. . . or by any Collector or Supervisor of Excise . . .'. Printed forms, naming the licensee,
alehouse and parish.

C/2/9/3/1/1   15 Oct. 1810
(56 docs)

C/2/9/3/1/2   Aug.–Nov. 1811
(34 docs)

C/2/9/3/1/3   11 Oct. 1819
(82 docs)

C/2/9/3/1/4   21 Sep. 1825
With annexed certificates of good conduct, signed by parish minister, churchwardens, overseers and 'reputable and substantial inhabitants'
(210 docs)

C/2/9/3/1/5   4 Sep. 1834
(3 docs)

C/2/9/3/1/6   27 Aug. 1835
(56 docs)

C/2/9/3/2 ALEHOUSEKEEPERS' EXCISE LICENCES   1810–1811

Issued by the Collector of Excise for Suffolk and the Supervisor of Excise for Ipswich District,
to retail beer, ale, cider and perry under the Act of 48. Geo III

C/2/9/3/2/1	2–5 Nov. 1810
(19 docs)	
C/2/9/3/2/2	16 Oct. 1811
(6 docs)	

C/2/9/3/3   ALEHOUSEKEEPERS' PAROCHIAL CERTIFICATES   1811–1835

Certificates of good conduct and fitness to keep an alehouse, signed by the minister, church-wardens, overseers and principal inhabitants of the parish; without which the Justices' licence was not granted

C/2/9/3/3/1	Jul.–Oct. 1811
(88 docs)	
C/2/9/3/3/2	8–19 Oct. 1812
(5 docs)	
C/2/9/3/3/3	Oct.–Nov. 1820
(92 docs; mostly printed forms)	
C/2/9/3/3/4	15–18 Aug. 1835
(95 docs)	

C/2/9/3/4   ALEHOUSEKEEPERS' RECOGNIZANCES   1824

C/2/9/3/4/1   20 Sep. 1824
Each recognizance with annexed parochial certificate of fitness
(196 docs; wrapper endorsed: 'Alehouse recognizances and licences [*sic*] September 1824. Filed pursuant to the Stat. 3 Geo. IV cap. 77')

C/2/9/3/5   WINE LICENCE BONDS   1736

C/2/9/3/5/1   24 Aug. 1736
John Ellett of Ipswich, vintner, bound to Bailiffs in £50 for payment of £5 p.a. for wine licence for 'Queen's Head' in MT

C/2/9/3/5/2   24 Aug. 1736
Elizabeth Smith of Ipswich, widow, bound to Bailiffs in £30 for payment of £5 p.a. for wine licence for 'White Horse' in MT

C/2/10   ALL COURTS: COMPOSITE RECORDS   1438–1835

The ancient series of court rolls of the medieval borough, those of the Portmanmote/Great Court, Petty Court, and Petty Court of Recognizances, came to an end in the late 14th and early 15th centuries. There followed an interval of apparent confusion, and the emergence of the series of Composite Enrolments and Composite Court Books listed below seems to mark a new stage in a prolonged period of experiment in record-keeping, of which not much earlier evidence has survived, apart from the General Court Register drawn up *c.*1435 and recording, *inter alia*, the admission of free burgesses from 1415 (B.L. Add. MS 30,158). Though the series of Court Books now begins only in 1486, Nathaniel Bacon's 'Annalls of Ipswiche' furnish evidence that he had access to other volumes for the period 1431–1486 which are no longer extant.

157

C/2/10/1 COMPOSITE ENROLMENTS   1438–1835

In 1438 the practice was introduced of entering on a single roll the significant business of all the courts except the Sessions. These composite enrolments may owe their origin, at least in part, to the belief that, though records were now beginning to be maintained in book form, the traditional roll format possessed a special dignity and solemnity which rendered it alone appropriate for matter deemed worthy of permanent record.

The first roll, covering the period 1438–1460, relates mostly to the clerkship (1439–1464) of Thomas Bushop. Its arrangement is haphazard: the entries are not in strict chronological sequence, nor are those on each membrane confined to one administrative year. Four membranes are headed as Recognizance Rolls, though Recognizance and General Court business are intermingled. That the roll is not a complete record of General Court proceedings is proved by entries in Bacon's 'Annalls' which are omitted from the enrolments; Bacon evidently had access, not only to the surviving General Court Register (B.L. Add. MS. 30, 158), but also, as already mentioned, to the now lost Court Books, 1431–c.1486.

Bushop's practice was refined by John Balhed (Clerk 1464–1470 and again 1478–1496), who between Michaelmas 1464 and 1468 made up a composite roll for each administrative year. These are the documents described in the HMC Report on the borough records as 'Dogget' (i.e. 'docket': abstract or digest) Rolls, from the headings ('Dogett Johannis Balhed Clerici . . .') on their index membranes.

The composite rolls were discontinued after 1468, and re-introduced briefly in 1478–1479. As in Bushop's time, the entries are often indiscriminately mixed and out of chronological sequence. It seems to have been the practice to fair-copy a number of entries on to the roll at once, leaving space for business not complete. Once again, comparison with Bacon's 'Annalls' shows that the rolls are not a complete record.

In the 15th century the main types of business enrolled for the General Court are administrative ordinances, the election of officers, admissions of free burgesses, grants of common soil and leases of town property. Petty Pleas are enrolled plea by plea; the dates of courts are rarely given. The numbers of pleas enrolled vary from year to year, suggesting that only a small proportion of them was so recorded. Recognizance business is normally given under the headings of the 'Curia de Minutis Placitis', suggesting that the independent existence of the Petty Court of Recognizances had come to an end. The proceedings of the Leet and Piepowder Courts are also occasionally enrolled.

No enrolments exist for the years 1480–1567. It is likely that they simply ceased to be compiled, for the reforming ordinances of 17 January 1564 enjoined the newly appointed Common Clerk, John Hawes, *inter alia*, to 'ingross in parchement all suche matters as be reall accions, and suche other accions as shall be tried by verdict, within the liberties . . . which doe amount to the summe of 5 li. or more' – a requirement analogous to the earlier reform of 1320 which had led to the introduction of the Chamberlains' Counter-roll as a check on revenue and fraud.

Enrolments of deeds and wills now exist from 1567, and in 1575 the series regains its composite nature as 'Dogget' Rolls, each annual roll (for the administrative year commencing at Michaelmas) containing all business transacted before the borough's courts (except the by now solely administrative General or Great Court) which was considered worthy of permanent record.

The resumed series of 'Dogget' Rolls includes Sessions business, Petty Pleas, the proceedings of the Portmanmote, recognizances of deeds, and occasional enrolments of wills. Most Sessions entries are for 'Sessions of the Peace and Gaol Delivery', at which there were important criminal cases, and include lists of justices, coroners, serjeants and the grand jury, together with indictments for felonies and petty larceny corresponding with the gaol calendars in the Court Books, the subsequent process being recited in full after each indictment. Until 1598 only, there occur other indictments for lesser offences, which do not correspond to entries in the Court Books. Entries for 'Sessions of the Peace', usually for petty matters such as vagrancy and licensing offences, with some recognizances, occur occasionally down to 1595, after which they are not normally enrolled. The enrolment of Sessions business ceased in 1651.

Petty Pleas are normally enrolled under the heading 'Curia Domini Regis' ('Curia Burgi et Ville Gippewici' during the Interregnum), and are enrolled plea by plea; they are only a selection of the pleas recorded in the Court Books. Their enrolment was discontinued after 1563.

Actions in the Portmanmote are by now limited almost entirely to recoveries of burgage tenements; the attachment of the original initiating royal Writ of Right Patent (sometimes still sealed on the tongue with the *pes sigilli*) to the margins of the Portmanmote enrolments adds force to the view that it was the traditional roll form, rather than the Court Books, that was regarded as the formal and authentic (if incomplete) record of the borough courts. The enrolments of deeds and occasional wills continue to be headed 'Curia de Minutis Placitis'.

After 1653 the enrolments lose their composite nature. The deeds continue to be enrolled down to 1922, on annual parchment rolls until Michaelmas 1799, and thereafter on parchment folios, many of which were (and the rest apparently intended to be) bound into volumes each covering several years. The custom of entering an annual heading at Michaelmas, with the names of the incoming Bailiffs, was usually observed until 1830. Until the end of the series the deeds continue to be enrolled under Petty Court headings (in later years as 'Enrolments of deeds in the Court of Small Pleas'). Recoveries in the Portmanmote, normally not more than one or two a year, continue to be enrolled with the deeds down to 1827, probably because an exemplification of a recovery was itself a form of title deed. (The enrolments from 1835 to 1922 are outside the scope of this catalogue.)

C/2/10/1/1   1438–1460
General Courts, Petty Courts, recognizances
(11 membranes)

C/2/10/1/2   1464–1465
General Courts, Petty Courts, 1 Maritime Court 1–2 Oct. 1464, 1 Leet 16 Apr. 1465
(17 membranes with contemporary numeration; 2 are blank, 1 is an index headed 'Gippewicum: Dogett Johannis Balhed Clerici eiusdem de Recordis Curiarum tentarum ibidem . . .')

C/2/10/1/3   1465–1466
General Courts, Petty Courts, 1 Leet (N, E and S wards only) 27 May 1466
General Court, 31 Mar. 1466 (m. 3) includes admission of William Sewale of Ipswich as burgess on condition that he provide a new footbridge at 'le greyffrerysbregge' within 1 year
(13 membranes, including index; contemporary numeration)

C/2/10/1/4   1466–1467
General Courts, Petty Courts, 1 Leet 19 May 1467
General Court, 13 May 1467 (m. 3d) includes election of John Wymondham, esq. and James Hoberd as burgesses to serve in Parliament
(10 membranes including incomplete index; contemporary numeration)

C/2/10/1/5   1467–1468
Petty Courts (enrolments of deeds only); 1 Leet (W ward only) 19 Apr. 1468 (for remainder of Leet proceedings, *see* C/2/10/1/6)
Includes:
— (m. 5) General Court, 8 May 1470, recording ordinance barring John Newport, sub-bailiff, from all borough offices for life, for his 'iniurijs et decepcionibus' against the Corporation
(5 membranes, 2 with contemporary numeration)

C/2/10/1/6   19 Apr. 1468
Leet (S, E and N wards)
(3 membranes with contemporary numeration; formerly part of C/2/10/1/5)

C/2/10/1/7   1478–1479
1 General Court 17 Sep. 1479, Petty Courts, 1 Leet 1 Jun. 1479, Piepowder Courts
Piepowder Court, 29 Dec. 1478 (m. 2) includes enrolment of Letters of Protection to William Lakford of Bury St Edmunds, panterer, in company of Henry, Lord Grey, Deputy Lieutenant in Ireland

Includes:
— (mm. 16, 17, 18, 18d) estreats collected by serjeants at Petty Courts, Leet and Sessions of the Peace
— (m. 3) compotus of William Sewale and John Poortman, Wardens of Corpus Christi Guild, 14 Jun. 1479
(19 membranes including index; contemporary numeration 1–20, mm. 8, 9 missing and not indexed; for m. 7, *see* C/2/10/1/8)

C/2/10/1/8   [1478–1479]
Petty Pleas, all undated, most incomplete
(1 membrane, numbered 7; formerly part of C/2/10/1/7)

C/2/10/1/9   1567–1568
John Smythe *alias* Dyer, Robert Barker, Bailiffs
Deeds only
(6 membranes)

C/2/10/1/10   1568–1569
William Whetcroft, Robert Cutler, Bailiffs
Deeds and wills only
(7 membranes)

C/2/10/1/11   1569–1570
Robert King, William Smarte, Bailiffs
Deeds only
(3 membranes)

C/2/10/1/12   1570–1571
John Gardner, John Barker, Bailiffs
Deeds and wills only
(5 membranes)

C/2/10/1/13   1571–1572
Geoffrey Gilbard, Richard King, Bailiffs
Deeds and wills only
(5 membranes)

C/2/10/1/14   1572–1573
John Moore, Robert Sparrowe, Bailiffs
Deeds and wills only
Includes:
— 1 deed enrolled 29 Jul. 1572, in previous administrative year
(11 membranes)

C/2/10/1/15   1573–1574
Robert Cutler, Ralph Scryvener, Bailiffs
Deeds and 1 will only
Annexed:
— Petty Plea Roll, 1572–1574
(Deeds 5 membranes; Pleas 9 membranes; made up and attached as two distinct rolls and subsequently joined at the heads by a single parchment tie)

C/2/10/1/16   1574–1575
Robert King, John Tye, Bailiffs
Deeds
Includes:
— 1 bond
— 1 deed enrolled 23 Sep. 1574, in previous administrative year
(7 membranes)

C/2/10/1/17   1574–1575
Robert King, John Tye, Bailiffs
Deeds
Includes:
— Assize of Fresh Force, 2 Oct. 1572
(4 detached membranes, formerly pinned together)

C/2/10/1/18   1575–1576
William Smarte, Edward Goodynge, Bailiffs
Sessions omitted
Includes:
— will, Robert Hall of MG, clothier, 11 Oct. 1575
— will, Katheryn Dyer *alias* Smythe, widow, 21 Jan. 1576
— 1 recognizance of debt
(14 membranes including index)

C/2/10/1/19   1575–1577
John Barker, Augustine Parker, Bailiffs
Includes:
— will, Thomas Bobbett, innholder, 20 Oct. 1576
— will, Thomas Wynde, glazier, 24 Sep. 1577
— Headboroughs' verdicts and charges
(16 membranes including index)

C/2/10/1/20   1577–1578
John Moore, Robert Sparrowe, Bailiffs
Includes:
— will, Thomas Bell of PE, glover, 13 May 1578
— Plea of Dower, 1 Sep. 1573, in a previous administrative year
(12 membranes including index)

C/2/10/1/21   14 Oct. 1577–18 Jul. 1580
Headboroughs' verdicts and charges only
(8 membranes, 2 detached)

C/2/10/1/22   1578–1579
Robert Cutler, John Knappe, Bailiffs
Includes:
— will, Robert Braye, 15 Dec. 1578
— deposition *re* alteration to will of George Coppinge, fishmonger, 6 Mar. 1579
— Assize of Fresh Force, 1–20 Apr. 1574
(12 membranes including index)

C/2/10/1/23   1579–1580
Ralph Scryvener, John Tye, Bailiffs
Includes:
— will, Jeffrey Gylbert, goldsmith, 21 Jan. 1580
— Assize of Fresh Force, 11 Dec. 1578–20 Jan. 1580
— Petty Plea, 6 Oct. 1580, in following administrative year
(22 membranes including index)

C/2/10/1/24   1579–1580
Petty Pleas only
(2 detached membranes, perhaps intended for attachment to C/2/10/1/23, but not listed in index
to that roll)

C/2/10/1/25   1580–1581
William Smarte, Thomas Blosse, Robert Lymmer, Bailiffs

161

Includes:
— will, William Whetcroft, gent., 3 May 1581
— Petty Plea, 5 May 1573, partly enrolled on same membrane as Plea of 6 Sep. 1580
(13 membranes including index)

C/2/10/1/26   1581–1582
John Barker, Edward Gooding, Bailiffs
Includes:
— Petty Plea, 12 Sep. 1581, in previous administrative year
— 1 membrane of enrolled deeds, Apr.–May 1588
(7 membranes including index)

C/2/10/1/27   1582–1583
Augustine Parker, Christopher Crane, Bailiffs
Includes:
— Assize of Fresh Force, 8–15 Jan. 1583
(11 membranes including index)

C/2/10/1/28   1583–1584
Robert Cutler, William Bloyse, Bailiffs
(12 membranes including index)

C/2/10/1/29   1584–1585
John Moore, John Knappe, Bailiffs
(17 membranes including index)

C/2/10/1/30   1585–1586
Ralph Scryvener, Stephen Baxter, Bailiffs
Petty Pleas and Sessions omitted
Includes:
— will, William Limefield, innholder, 29 Mar. 1586
(8 membranes including index)

C/2/10/1/31   1586–1587
William Smarte, Robert Lymmer, Bailiffs
Deeds only
(5 membranes)

C/2/10/1/32   22 Nov. 1586
1 Petty Plea only
(2 membranes)

C/2/10/1/33   1587–1588
John Barker, Edward Goodyng, Bailiffs
Sessions omitted
(12 membranes including index)

C/2/10/1/34   1588–1589
Christopher Crane and William Mydnall, Bailiffs
Portmanmote and Sessions omitted
Includes:
— will, Aggas Dawson of MG, mariner, 13 Aug. 1589
— will, Steven Baxter, merchant (date of probate not given)
— will, Thomas Kenyngton sen. (date of probate not given)
(15 membranes; no index)

C/2/10/1/35   1589–1590
Robert Cutler, Robert Snellynge, Bailiffs
Sessions and Petty Pleas omitted

162

Includes:
— will, Thomas Celye, merchant, 9 Oct. 1589
(11 membranes; no index)

C/2/10/1/36   1590–1591
William Bloyse, Robert Barker, Bailiffs
Sessions and Petty Pleas omitted
(5 membranes; no index)

C/2/10/1/37   1591–1592
John Knappe, Robert Cutler jun., Bailiffs
Includes as wrapper:
— fragment of deed of property in Barham, Henley and Hemingstone, stitched to fragment of
will, John Armiger of Clopton, both n.d. [16c.]
(8 membranes; no index)

C/2/10/1/38   1592–1593
Ralph Scryvener, Edward Cage, Bailiffs
Includes as wrapper:
— fragment of deed of property in Sproughton, Washbrook and Copdock, 1585, stitched to
fragment of deed of property in Shotley, n.d. [16c.]
(12 membranes including index)

C/2/10/1/39   1593–1594
William Smarte, Robert Lymmer, Bailiffs
Portmanmote omitted
Includes as wrapper:
— deed of assignment of lease of messuage in MW, John Purpett of Newbourn, gent. to
Humfry Seckforde of Ipswich, esq., 17 Jul. 1591
(14 membranes including index)

C/2/10/1/40   1594–1595
Edward Goodinge, William Midnall, Bailiffs
Includes:
— will, Sebastian Man sen., grocer, 20 Mar. 1595
— as wrapper: lease of parsonage of Capel, Timothy Fitzallen, parson, to John Hawys jun. of
Ipswich, gent., 17 Oct. 1587 (cut in two and stitched together end to end)
(12 membranes including index)

C/2/10/1/41   1595–1596
Robert Cutler, Robert Snellinge, William Midnall, Bailiffs
Includes:
— will, Robert Cutler, merchant, 8 Jun. 1596
— will, William Jeffrey, clothier, 27 Jul. 1596
— Plea of dower in Portmanmote, Anne Peppercorne, widow v. Andrew Sorrell and wife Alice,
16 Sep. 1595
— as wrapper: lease of lands in MS, Thomas Ungle of Ipswich, merchant to William Hawys of
Ipswich, gent., 27 Jun. 1596
(21 membranes including index)

C/2/10/1/42   1596–1597
William Bloyse, Robert Barker, Bailiffs
Portmanmote omitted
Includes:
— will, Thomas Whytman, proved in Suffolk Archdeaconry Court, 24 Feb., enrolled 24 Oct.
1596
(22 membranes including index)

C/2/10/1/43   1597–1598
John Knappe, Robert Cutler, Bailiffs
Portmanmote omitted
Includes:
— writ, 5 Feb. 1599 forbidding Ipswich JPs to molest Merable Cason, spinster, who has been
pardoned of felony by the Crown; stitched to enrolment of Sessions of the Peace, 6 Mar. 1598
(16 membranes including index)

C/2/10/1/44   1598–1599
Ralph Scryvener, Edward Cage, Bailiffs
Portmanmote omitted
Includes:
— writ, 12 Jun. 1599, forbidding Ipswich JPs to molest Margaret Powell, who has been
pardoned of felony by the Crown; stitched to enrolment of Sessions of the Peace, 11 Jan. 1599
— as wrapper: fragment of assignment of lease of the New Mills in Ipswich, Robert Noothe to
Edmund Newbye, both of Ipswich, millers, 1 Aug. 1588
(9 membranes including index)

C/2/10/1/45   1599–1600
Edward Goodinge, William Sparrowe, Bailiffs
Portmanmote and Petty Pleas omitted
Includes:
— writ, 18 Nov. 1600, forbidding Ipswich JPs to molest Nicholas Garth, yeoman, who has been
pardoned of felony by the Crown; stitched to enrolment of Sessions of the Peace, 23 Jun. 1600
— as wrapper: lease of messuage in Shotley, Edward Kynneslonde and wife Joan to Christopher
Hubberde, all of Shotley, 30 Nov. 1587 (cut in two and stitched together end to end)
(9 membranes including index)

C/2/10/1/46   1600–1601
William Midnall, Anthony Bull, Bailiffs
Portmanmote, Petty Pleas and Sessions omitted
Includes as wrapper:
— assignment of lease of lands in Holbrook, Freston and Harkstead, Richard Kynge of
Ipswich, merchant to John Clenche, Justice of the Queen's Bench, 15 Jan. 1589
(5 membranes including index)

C/2/10/1/47   1601–1602
John Knappe, Robert Snellinge, William Bloyse, Bailiffs
Petty Pleas omitted; Sessions incomplete
Includes as wrapper:
— exemplification of depositions of Simon Sutton, clerk, Matthew Wynde, glazier and Christopher Brooke, tailor, all of Ipswich, *re* valuation of goods in possession of Richard Frythe and
Daniel Felton, n.d.; stitched to fragment of deed of property copyhold of manor of Claydon,
n.d. [? late 16c.]
(4 membranes including index)

C/2/10/1/48   1602–1603
Robert Cutler, Thomas Sicklemore, Bailiffs
Portmanmote and Petty Pleas omitted; Sessions incomplete
Includes:
— will, Eme Man, widow, 12 Apr. 1603
— as wrapper: lease of garden in Tankard Street, Ipswich, Corporation to Matthew Wynde of
Ipswich, glazier, 3 May 1583; stitched to fragment of lease of messuage, Corporation to
Thomas Kenyngton of Ipswich, surgeon, 3 May 1583
(9 membranes including index)

C/2/10/1/49   1603–1604
Ralph Scryvener, Thomas Sherman, Bailiffs
Petty Pleas omitted
Includes:
— Plea of Dower [? in Portmanmote], Alice Wilde *alias* Wyles, widow *v.* John Wilde,
8–13 Mar. 1604
— Plea of Dower [? in Portmanmote], Margery Fennynge, widow *v.* Thomasine Nicholas,
2–11 Aug. 1604
— as wrapper: fragment of tripartite indenture *re* lands in Little Bealings and Playford,
between George — [*missing*] of Bealings, gent., Francis Willard of Woodbridge, and Robert
Clarke, gent. and Anthony Wade, maltster, both of Ipswich, Mar. 1675
(11 membranes including index)

C/2/10/1/50   1604–1605
Edward Goodinge, William Bloyse jun., Bailiffs
Portmanmote and Petty Pleas omitted
Includes as wrapper:
— feoffment of tenement in PE, copyhold of manor of Weylonds, John Knappe of Ipswich,
merchant to John Dicklie of Ipswich, gent., 13 Oct. 1578; stitched to apprenticeship indenture,
James Shearman, son of John Shearman of Ipswich, innholder, bound to Peter Raye of Ipswich,
tailor, 10 Mar. 1579; endorsed with brief scriptural texts
(7 membranes including index)

C/2/10/1/51   1605–1606
William Sparrowe, Matthew Brownrigge, Bailiffs
Includes as wrapper:
— mutilated lease of cottage, lately hayhouse, in Freston, Francis Stanton of Barking (Essex),
gent. to John Goffe of Freston, husbandman, 14 Sep. 1586
(8 membranes including index)

C/2/10/1/52   1606–1607
Robert Cutler, John Humfrie, Bailiffs
Portmanmote and Petty Pleas omitted
Includes as wrapper:
— apprenticeship indenture, Robert Whitman, son of Thomas Whitman of Ipswich, deceased,
bound to Henry Deale of Ipswich, yeoman, to learn craft of mariner, 28 Mar. 1563; stitched to
apprenticeship indenture, John Grymbell, son of John Grymbell of Ipswich, mariner, bound to
Henry Deale of Ipswich, mariner, 20 Jan. 1590; stitched to fragment of deed, n.d.
(6 membranes including index)

C/2/10/1/53   1607–1608
Richard Marten, Robert Snellinge, Bailiffs
Portmanmote and Petty Pleas omitted
Includes:
— will, Matthew Wynde, glazier, 24 Oct. 1607
— as wrapper: feoffment of land (14 a.) in Ipswich (names of parties erased), 13 Oct. 1608
(10 membranes including index)

C/2/10/1/54   1608–1609
Thomas Sicklemore, William Acton, Bailiffs
Petty Pleas omitted
(11 membranes including index)

C/2/10/1/55   1609–1610
William Bloyse, Tobias Blosse, Bailiffs
Portmanmote omitted

Includes as wrapper:
— fragments of 2 deeds of property in Bramford and Claydon and in Coddenham, Creeting All Saints, Creeting St Mary and Creeting St Olave respectively, n.d.
(8 membranes including index)

C/2/10/1/56   1610–1611
William Sparrowe, William Cage, Bailiffs
Includes as wrapper:
— fragments of 2 deeds of property in Bramford and in Darmsden, Baylham and Hemingstone respectively, n.d.
(10 membranes including index)

C/2/10/1/57   1611–1612
Robert Cutler, Matthew Brownerigge, Bailiffs
Portmanmote omitted
(12 membranes including index)

C/2/10/1/58   1612–1613
Richard Marten, Richard Cocke, Bailiffs
Includes as wrapper:
— Bailiffs' certificate intended to be attached to writ in proof of compliance with its direction at Sessions of the Peace 14 Jun. 1613; stitched to fragment of lease of lands in Whitton and Bramford, Corporation to Susan Cardinall, n.d.
(12 membranes including index)

C/2/10/1/59   1613–1614
Robert Snellinge, Robert Goodinge, Bailiffs
Petty Pleas omitted
Includes as wrapper:
— exemplification of depositions *re* sale of cloth, in which Robert Jacob of Needham and Walter Merrell and James Bere, both of Ipswich, merchants were concerned, 30 May 1614 (deponents' names erased); stitched to Bailiffs' certificate of compliance with writ of *venire facias* in plea of debt, John Cole *v.* John Sparrowe of Needham, clothier, 25 Jun. 1614 (incomplete)
(8 membranes including index)

C/2/10/1/60   1614–1615
Tobias Blosse, Michael Goodere, Bailiffs
Petty Pleas omitted
Includes as wrapper:
—— mutilated lease of lands belonging to Tooley's Foundation in Whitton, Akenham and Claydon, Corporation to Leonard Gates of Akenham, yeoman, 22 Jan. 1602
(9 membranes including index)

C/2/10/1/61   1615–1616
Thomas Sicklemore, Thomas Johnson, Bailiffs
Petty Pleas omitted
Includes as wrapper:
— mutilated lease of office of water bailiff and town house on Common Quay, Corporation to Robert Harvie, vintner (whose name is struck out and that of John Blomfeld substituted), Mar. 1613 or 1614
(8 membranes including index)

C/2/10/1/62   1616–1617
William Bloyse, William Cage, Bailiffs
Includes as wrapper:
— feoffment of tenement in MW, Edward Bliethe of Hempstead (Essex), wife Mary, son William, Robert Laye of Layham, wheelwright and wife Dorcas to [*blank*], 18 Jul. 1617;

stitched to unexecuted deed of moiety of same property and fragment of another deed, n.d.
(11 membranes including index)

C/2/10/1/63   1617–1618
Robert Cutler, Richard Martin, Bailiffs
Includes as wrapper:
— fragment of lease of lands in Bramford and Whitton, Corporation to Christopher Lawrence,
n.d. [17c]
(8 membranes including index)

C/2/10/1/64   1618–1619
Matthew Brownrigg, Richard Cocke, Bailiffs
Petty Pleas and Sessions omitted, left-hand half of Portmanmote membrane torn away and
missing
(5 membranes; fragment only of index)

C/2/10/1/65   1619–1620
Robert Snellinge, George Acton, Bailiffs
Includes as wrapper:
— lease of lands in Rushmere, Katherine Dameron of Rushmere, widow to Thomas Tame of
Ipswich, yeoman, 16 Feb. 1605; stitched to fragment of deed of sale of one-eighth of barque
'Phillipp and Jane' of Ipswich, Phillip Gardner of Ipswich, shipwright to John Bloyse of
Trimley St Martin, yeoman, n.d. [17c]
(9 membranes including index)

C/2/10/1/66   1620–1621
Robert Goodinge, Samuel Cutler, Bailiffs
Includes as wrapper:
— fragment of lease of lands in MG, John Tye of Ipswich to Anthony Bull, gent., William
Bloyce, mercer, Richard Lewes and Richard Bateman, draper, all of Ipswich, 1 May 1604;
stitched to fragment of conveyance of messuage in LW, John Hawys to Phillip Newton of
Ipswich, grocer, 11 Nov. 1574; and fragment of grant of rent charge out of lands in Barking,
Ringshall and Willisham, John Hawys of Barking to Thomas Johnson, 25 Apr. 1559
(7 membranes including index)

C/2/10/1/67   1621–1622
Tobias Blosse, Thomas Eldred, Bailiffs
Petty Pleas omitted
Includes as wrapper:
— fragments of bargain and sale of lands in Ufford, Richard Margetts, yeoman to William
Pemberton of Rendlesham, clerk, 20 Sep. 1597; formerly stitched to (detached) fragment of
deed of sale of one-eighth of ship 'Dilligent' of Ipswich (150 tons), Anne Chaplen of Ipswich,
widow to John Chaplen of Capel, clerk, 10 Mar. 1617
(8 membranes including index)

C/2/10/1/68   1622–1623
Michael Goodere, Robert Sparrowe, Bailiffs
Includes:
— Plea of Dower in Petty Court, Emma Goodinge, widow v. Henry Goodinge, 16 Oct. 1622,
with Writ of Right annexed, 28 Sep. 1622
— as wrapper: incomplete deed of bargain and sale of lands in Grundisburgh, John Bloyse of
Trimley St Martin, yeoman to Robert Finche of Little Bealings, yeoman, 10 May 1612; stitched
to fragment of another deed, n.d.
(12 membranes including index)

C/2/10/1/69   1623–1624
William Cage, Robert Benham, Bailiffs
Portmanmote omitted

Includes:
— plea of debt on demand in Petty Court, Samuel Ward [Town Preacher] *v.* Gregory Tailor, commenced 9 Oct. 1623
— as wrapper: fragment of deed of assignment of goods between Robert Benham and William Bloyse, executors of Augustine Parker deceased, n.d.; stitched to fragment of deed, 26 Feb. 1614
(8 membranes including index)

C/2/10/1/70   1624–1625
Matthew Brownerigge, John Sicklemore, Bailiffs
Portmanmote and Petty Pleas omitted
Includes as wrapper:
— feoffment of messuage in MS, William Dade of Tannington, gent. and Anne Dade of Crowfield, widow to Jeronna Catelinge of Ipswich, clerk, 15 Nov. 1623; stitched to incomplete lease and counterpart of royalty of fishing and fowling in river belonging to manor of Sproughton, Henry Felton of Shotley, esq. to Thomas Cutler of Sproughton, esq., John Turner of Sproughton, gent. and Stephen Gardiner of Ipswich, yeoman, 4 Apr. 1620
(5 membranes including index)

C/2/10/1/71   1625–1626
Richard Cocke, Christopher Aldgate, Bailiffs
Portmanmote omitted
(5 membranes including index)

C/2/10/1/72   1626–1627
Robert Snellinge, William Moysey, Bailiffs
Includes as wrapper:
— bond of indemnity *re* lands in Barking and Ringshall, Thomas Johnson of Norwich, grocer to John Hawys of Ipswich, 6 Oct. 1557
(9 membranes including index)

C/2/10/1/73   1627–1628
George Acton, Edmund Keene, Bailiffs
Includes as wrapper:
— apprenticeship indenture, Richard Rusten, son of Thomas Rusten of Elmham (Norfolk), deceased, to Gregory Briden of Bury St Edmunds, bowyer, 31 Dec. 1580; lease of watermill in Belstead, William Hawys of Ipswich, yeoman to William Bell of Great Saling (Essex), miller, 20 Jun. 1599; bond of indemnity *re* messuage in MG, 4 Apr. 1590; all stitched together
(7 membranes including index)

C/2/10/1/74   1629–1630
Robert Goodinge, Robert Sparrowe, Matthew Brownerigge, Bailiffs
Portmanmote omitted
Includes as wrapper:
— deed of assignment of close in Newbourn, Margaret Fynch, widow and John Fynch, yeoman, both of Playford, to William Fynch of Waldringfield, 16 Jan. 1615; stitched to fragment of record of plea of debt, Richard Dawtrey, gent. *v.* Robert Starlinge, 1606 or 1607
(7 membranes including index)

C/2/10/1/75   1630–1631
William Cage, James Tillott, Bailiffs
Portmanmote omitted
Index endorsed on fragment of lease of messuage in MT, in occupation of Samuel Warde, B.D. [Town Preacher] and Thomas Cleeve, from Matthew Brownerigge, merchant to William Cage, James Tillott, George Acton, Robert Sparrowe, John Sicklemore, Christopher Aldgate, William Moysey and Edmund Keene, aldermen of Ipswich, n.d.

Includes as wrapper (now detached):
— lease of water supply, Corporation to Anne Jermie of Worlingworth, widow, for house in NI, 19 Aug. 1620
(6 membranes including index)

C/2/10/1/76   1631–1632
John Sicklemore, Richard Puplett, Bailiffs
Portmanmote omitted
Index endorsed on certificate [incomplete] of John Hawys, Town Clerk, of his scale of fees, for return to Commissioners of Inquiry into exacted fees and new-erected offices, n.d. [c.1630]
Includes as wrapper:
— mortgage of messuage called the Swan in MT, Simon Burton of Ipswich, weaver to John Hawys of Ipswich, gent., 20 Nov. 1627; stitched to fragments of 2 other deeds
(7 membranes including index)

C/2/10/1/77   1632–1633
William Moysey, John Barbor, Bailiffs
Portmanmote and Petty Pleas missing
Includes as wrapper:
— apprenticeship indenture, Thomas Bull, son of Peter Bull of Ipswich, to George Balles jun. of Ipswich, bladesmith and miller, 8 Apr. 1602; stitched to fragment of deed re offences committed by William Savell of Ipswich, vintner, in selling wine, n.d. [later 16c.]
(7 membranes including index)

C/2/10/1/78   1633–1634
Matthew Brownerigge, John Aldus, Bailiffs
Portmanmote omitted
Includes as wrapper:
— copy court roll of admission of John Campe jun. to tenement called Kendalles, copyhold of manor of Broughtons in Stonham Aspal, 30 Aug. 1563; bond for production of deeds to tenement in LW, Thomas Howsyng alias Laster to William Lymefelde, innholder, 1570; precept to town serjeants to arrest [blank] for refusing to serve in his craft of turner, 27 Jun. 1590; all stitched together
(6 membranes including index)

C/2/10/1/79   1634–1635
Edmund Kene, Thomas Selie, Bailiffs
Petty Pleas omitted
Includes:
— Plea of Dower in Petty Court, Susan Meadowe, widow v. John Meadowe, 30 Mar. 1635, with Writ of Right, 24 Apr. 1635, precept and return annexed
— as wrapper: draft certificate of Bailiffs to a Justice of Common Pleas in chambers re detention of John Knapp of Ipswich, clothier, for debt, 1620 or 1621; stitched to fragment of lease of manor of Ulveston Hall in Debenham, Corporation to William Buckenham of Debenham, 27 Sep. 1622
(8 membranes including index)

C/2/10/1/80   1635–1636
Robert Sparrowe, Edmund Humfrie, Bailiffs
Includes:
— Plea of Dower in Petty Court, Frances Tye, widow v. Humfrey Atkins, 29 Apr. 1636, with Writ of Right, 19 Apr. 1636, precept and return annexed
— presentment at Sessions of the Peace, 19 Aug. 1636, of ten ship's carpenters for riot in PE on 11 Aug.
— as wrapper: mutilated lease of lands in Whitton, Corporation to Samuel Hadlock, 18 Dec. 1613
(11 membranes including index)

C/2/10/1/81   1636–1637
William Cage, William Tyler, Bailiffs
(12 membranes including index)

C/2/10/1/82   1637–1638
John Sicklemore, William Sparrowe, Bailiffs
Portmanmote omitted
Includes as wrapper:
— fragment of lease of site of manor of Ulveston Hall in Debenham, Corporation to Edward
Sheppard of Debenham, yeoman, 6 May 1578
(6 membranes including index)

C/2/10/1/83   1638–1639
William Moysey, John Barbor, Bailiffs
Portmanmote omitted
(9 membranes including index)

C/2/10/1/84   1639–1640
Richard Purplett, John Aldus, Bailiffs
Portmanmote omitted
Includes as wrapper:
— fragment of record of unidentified Petty Plea, ? 1621
(6 membranes including index)

C/2/10/1/85   1641–1642
Edmund Humfrie, John Brandlinge, Bailiffs
Portmanmote and Petty Pleas omitted
Includes as wrapper:
— deed of bargain and sale of tenement lately called the Gryffin in MT, Thomas Elmes of
Ipswich, yeoman to Richard Sherman of Ipswich, doctor of physick, 22 Mar. 1581; stitched to
bond for repayment of loan from Alice Scrivener's Charity (unexecuted and incomplete), n.d.
(4 membranes including index)

C/2/10/1/86   1642–1643
William Tyler, John Brandlinge, Bailiffs
Deeds only
(4 membranes)

C/2/10/1/87   1643–1644
Peter Fisher, Robert Dunckon, Bailiffs
Deeds only
Includes as wrapper:
— deed of bargain and sale of messuage in NI, Robert Aylmer of Wherstead to William
Tranham and wife Mary (incomplete), 1639
(4 membranes; no index)

C/2/10/1/88   1644–1645
Richard Pupplett, Joseph Pemberton, Bailiffs
Deeds only
(2 membranes)

C/2/10/1/89   1645–1646
William Sparrowe, Richard Hoyle, Bailiffs
Portmanmote and Sessions omitted
Includes as wrapper:
— fragment of ? deed of partnership between Henry Dancke of Aldeburgh, Matthew Figgett,
John Wells and William Dancke re trade in pitch, tar, iron and timber, n.d. [17c]
(6 membranes; no index)

C/2/10/1/90   1646–1647
John Barbur, Nicholas Philipps, Bailiffs
Deeds only
Includes as wrapper:
— another fragment of the deed similarly employed for C/2/10/1/89
(6 membranes; no index)

C/2/10/1/91   1647–1648
John Alldus, Manuel Sorrell, Bailiffs
Deeds only
(4 membranes; no index)

C/2/10/1/92   1648–1649
Edmund Humfrey, John Smythier, Bailiffs
Deeds only
Includes as wrapper:
— fragment of deed *re* delivery of (named) prisoners in custody of late Sheriff of Suffolk to Sir
Calthropp Parker, kt, High Sheriff, 1611 or 1612
(4 membranes; no index)

C/2/10/1/93   1649–1650
John Brandlinge, Jacob Caley, Bailiffs
Portmanmote omitted
Includes as wrapper and dorse of index:
— 3 substantial fragments of record of plea of Trespass in Petty Court, Richard Hylle *v.* Isabella
Payne, ? 1643
(7 membranes including index)

C/2/10/1/94   1650–1651
Peter Fisher, Robert Donckon, Bailiffs
Deeds only
(2 membranes; no index)

C/2/10/1/95   1650–1651
Peter Fisher, Robert Donckon, Bailiffs
Petty Pleas and Sessions only; 1 Petty Plea is continued in C/2/10/1/96; after this year the enrol-
ment of Sessions proceedings was discontinued
(2 detached membranes, not pierced for attachment but presumably intended to be filed with
C/2/10/1/94; no index)

C/2/10/1/96   22 Aug. 1651–25 Jul. 1653
Richard Hayles, Richard Jennings, Bailiffs 1651–1652; Richard Puplet, Nicholas Phillipps,
Bailiffs 1652–1653
After 1652–1653 the enrolment of the record of Petty Pleas was discontinued
(19 membranes including index to deeds only)

C/2/10/1/97   Mar. 1653–Mar. 1654
Richard Pupplett, Nicholas Phillipps, Bailiffs 1652–1653; John Aldus, Manuell Sorrell, Bailiffs
1653–1654
Deeds and Portmanmote only
(12 membranes including index)

C/2/10/1/98   Mar. 1654–Mar. 1655
John Aldus, Manuell Sorrell, Bailiffs 1653–1654; John Smythier, Henry Whiting, Bailiffs
1654–1655
Deeds and Portmanmote only
(15 membranes; detached paper index)

C/2/10/1/99   Mar. 1655–Sep. 1656
John Smythier, Henry Whiting, Bailiffs 1654–1655; John Brandlinge, Peter Fisher, Bailiffs
1655–1656
Deeds and Portmanmote only
(14 membranes including index)

C/2/10/1/100   1656–1657
Peter Fisher, Robert Dunkon, Bailiffs
Enrolled deeds only
(11 membranes including index)

C/2/10/1/101   1657–1658
Richard Hayles, Richard Jenninges, Bailiffs
Deeds and Portmanmote only
Includes:
— 2 membranes of enrolled deeds for 1656–1657, presumably intended for attachment to
C/2/10/1/100
(9 membranes including index)

C/2/10/1/102   23 Jun.–7 Jul. 1658
Richard Hayles, Richard Jenninges, Bailiffs
Portmanmote only
(1 membrane; included in index to C/2/10/1/101 and probably formerly attached thereto)

C/2/10/1/103   1658–1659
Nicholas Phillipps, Robert Sparrowe, Bailiffs
Deeds, Portmanmote and 1 will
Includes:
— will, Thomas Cleere, gent., 22 Jul. 1659
— Portmanmote proceedings (1 membrane), 23 Nov.–2 Dec. 1659, in following administrative
year
(20 membranes including index)

C/2/10/1/104   1659–1660
Manuell Sorrell, Thomas Wright, Bailiffs
Deeds only
(7 membranes including index)

C/2/10/1/105   1660–1661
John Smyther, Henry Whitinge, Bailiffs
Deeds only
(7 membranes including index)

C/2/10/1/106   1661–1662
Luke Jowers, Bailiff
Deeds only
(11 membranes including index)

C/2/10/1/107   1662–1663
Richard Hayes, Thomas Burrough, Bailiffs
Deeds only
Includes:
— attached membrane for 1652–1653, with will of Barnaby Frier, linen weaver, proved and
enrolled 26 Jan. 1653
(9 membranes including index)

C/2/10/1/108   1663–1664
Nicholas Phillips, John Robinson, Bailiffs
Deeds only

Includes as wrapper:
— incomplete lease of messuage called the Three Feathers in MW, John Burton of Rushmere, yeoman to John Scales of Ipswich, shipwright, 18 Dec. 1647
(7 membranes including index)

C/2/10/1/109   1664–1665
Robert Sparrowe, John Wright, Bailiffs
Deeds only
(7 membranes including index)

C/2/10/1/110   1665–1666
Sir Manuel Sorrell, kt, Gilbert Lindfield, Bailiffs
Deeds only
(5 membranes including index)

C/2/10/1/111   1666–1667
Luke Jowers, Miles Wallis, Bailiffs
Deeds only
(8 membranes including index)

C/2/10/1/112   1667–1668
Andrew Sorrell, Henry Gosnold, Bailiffs
Deeds only
(11 membranes including index)

C/2/10/1/113   1668–1669
Nicholas Phillips, Thomas Reeve, Bailiffs
Deeds and ? Portmanmote/Petty Court
Includes:
— Plea of Dower, ? in Portmanmote, Susan Richman, widow *v.* Samuel Richman, Leonard Goodburne, Thomas Burradge and William Haile, 22 Jul. 1668, in previous administrative year (the heading to this membrane, 'Curia Domini Regis burgi et ville Gippewici', is that used for sessions of the Petty Court until the Interregnum)
(11 membranes including index)

C/2/10/1/114   Sep. 1669–Feb. 1671
Robert Sparrowe, William Cullum, Bailiffs 1669–1670; John Wright, Charles Wright, Bailiffs 1670–1671
Deeds only
(8 membranes including index)

C/2/10/1/115   Apr. 1671–Aug. 1672
John Wright, Charles Wright, Bailiffs 1670–1671; Gilbert Lindfild, John Pemberton, Bailiffs 1671–1672
Deeds only
Includes on dorse of index:
— fragment of lease of sheepwalk in Sutton, Bromeswell and Eyke, William Ferneley of Sutton, gent. to Sir Nicholas Bacon, n.d. [17c]
(6 membranes including index)

C/2/10/1/116   1672–1673
Luke Jours, Miles Wallis, Bailiffs
Deeds only
(4 membranes including index)

C/2/10/1/117   1673–1674
Andrew Sorrell, Laurence Stisted, Bailiffs
Deeds only
(5 membranes including index)

C/2/10/1/118   1674–1675
Henry Gosnold, Richard Philips, Bailiffs
Deeds only
(4 membranes including index)

C/2/10/1/119   1675–1676
William Cullum, Edward Renoldes, Bailiffs
Deeds only
(5 membranes; no index)

C/2/10/1/120   1676–1677
John Wright, John Burrough, Bailiffs
Deeds only
(3 membranes; no index)

C/2/10/1/121   1677–1678
Charles Wright, Richard Sparrowe, Bailiffs
Deeds only
(5 membranes including index)

C/2/10/1/122   1678–1679
Gilbert Lindfild, William Neave, Bailiffs
Deeds only
(9 membranes including index)

C/2/10/1/123   1679–1680
John Pemberton, William Sayer, Bailiffs
Deeds only
(5 membranes)

C/2/10/1/124   1680–1681
Henry Gosnold, Laurence Stistead, Bailiffs
Deeds only
(5 membranes including index)

C/2/10/1/125   6–24 Apr. 1681
Henry Gosnold, Laurence Stistead, Bailiffs
Portmanmote only
(1 membrane; presumably intended for attachment to C/2/10/1/124)

C/2/10/1/126   1681–1682
Richard Phillips, William Browne, Bailiffs
Deeds only
(8 membranes; no index)

C/2/10/1/127   1682–1683
Edward Rennolds, John Blomfield, Bailiffs
Deeds
Includes:
— Portmanmote, 1–4 Mar. 1684, for following administrative year
Deeds only
(5 membranes; no index)

C/2/10/1/128   17 Feb.–2 Mar. 1683
Edward Rennolds, John Blomfield, Bailiffs
Portmanmote only
(1 membrane, presumably intended for attachment to C/2/10/1/127)

174

C/2/10/1/129   1683–1684
Sir Henry Felton, bart., John Burrough, Bailiffs
Deeds only; for Portmanmote *see* C/2/10/1/127
(3 membranes; no index)

C/2/10/1/130   1684–1685
Sir John Barker, bart., William Neave, Bailiffs
Deeds only
(5 membranes including index)

C/2/10/1/131   6 Dec. 1684
Sir John Barker, bart., William Neave, Bailiffs
1 deed only
(1 membrane; presumably intended for attachment to C/2/10/1/130)

C/2/10/1/132   1685–1686
Sir Robert Broke, bart., John Pemberton, Bailiffs
Deeds only
(6 membranes including index)

C/2/10/1/133   1686–1687
Sir Nicholas Bacon, KB, Laurence Stisted, Bailiffs
Deeds only
(6 membranes including index)

C/2/10/1/134   1687–1688
Richard Phillips, Miles Wallis, Bailiffs
Deeds only
(4 membranes, not pierced for attachment; no index)

C/2/10/1/135   1688–1689
Charles Wright, John Wade, Bailiffs
Deeds only
(6 membranes including index)

C/2/10/1/136   1689–1690
William Browne, Henry Sparrowe, Bailiffs
Deeds only
(7 membranes including index)

C/2/10/1/137   1690–1691
Richard Pupplett, Robert Manning, Bailiffs
Deeds and Portmanmote
(7 membranes including index)

C/2/10/1/138   1691–1692
Charles Wright, William Browne, Bailiffs
Deeds and Portmanmote
(7 membranes including index)

C/2/10/1/139   1692–1693
William Browne, Henry Sparrowe, Bailiffs
Deeds only
(7 membranes; no index)

C/2/10/1/140   1693–1694
John Wade, Thomas Bowle, Bailiffs
Deeds only
(4 membranes including index)

C/2/10/1/141   1694–1695
Richard Phillipps, Samuel Reynolds, Bailiffs
Deeds and Portmanmote
(8 membranes; no index)

C/2/10/1/142   1695–1697
Lawrence Stysted, Thomas Bright, Bailiffs 1695–1696; Charles Wright, Edward Melsupp,
Bailiffs 1696–1697
Deeds only
(10 membranes; no index)

C/2/10/1/143   1697–1698
William Neave, Henry Hill, Bailiffs
Deeds only
(5 membranes; no index)

C/2/10/1/144   1698–1699
Henry Sparrow, Henry Skynner, Bailiffs
Deeds only
(6 membranes; no index)

C/2/10/1/145   1699–1700
Lawrence Stisted, Jacob Hudson, Bailiffs
Deeds only
(6 membranes; no index)

C/2/10/1/146   1700–1701
Samuel Reynolds, John Goldson, Bailiffs
Deeds only
(8 membranes including index)

C/2/10/1/147   1701–1702
Thomas Bowell, Henry Hill, Bailiffs
Deeds only
(6 membranes including index)

C/2/10/1/148   1702–1703
Richard Philips, Cooper Gravenor, Bailiffs
Deeds only
(2 membranes; with detached index)

C/2/10/1/149   12 Jun. 1704–30 Dec. 1709
Deeds only
(27 membranes; no index)

C/2/10/1/150   30 Jun. 1710–23 Sep. 1712
Deeds only
(20 membranes; no index; first entry incomplete and at least one membrane therefore missing)

C/2/10/1/151   18 Nov. 1712–6 Nov. 1714
Deeds only
(21 membranes; no index)

C/2/10/1/152   1 Dec. 1714–4 Jan. 1717
Deeds only
(16 membranes; no index)

C/2/10/1/153   18 Jan. 1717–11 Jan. 1718
Deeds only
(7 membranes; no index)

C/2/10/1/154   1718–1719
Cooper Gravenor, Thomas Starling, Bailiffs
Deeds and Portmanmote
(13 membranes including index)

C/2/10/1/155   1719–1720
John Goldson, George Scott, Bailiffs
Deeds
Includes:
— enrolled apprenticeship indentures, 22 Jan. 1717–23 Mar. 1719 (1 detached membrane, not
pierced for attachment, but included in index to roll for 1719–1720)
(12 membranes including index)

C/2/10/1/156   1720–1721
Cooper Gravenor, Thomas Starling, Bailiffs
Deeds and Portmanmote
(12 membranes including index)

C/2/10/1/157   1721–1722
John Marlow, John Steward, Bailiffs
Deeds only
(10 membranes including index)

C/2/10/1/158   1722–1723
John Cornelius, John Sparrowe, Bailiffs
Deeds only
(12 membranes; index endorsed)

C/2/10/1/159   1723–1724
George Scott, Edward Bowell, Bailiffs
Deeds only
(11 membranes; index endorsed)

C/2/10/1/160   1724–1725
John Cornelius, John Sparrowe, Bailiffs
Deeds only
(9 membranes; index endorsed)

C/2/10/1/161   1725–1726
Henry Hill, Henry Nash, Bailiffs
Deeds only
(9 membranes; index endorsed)

C/2/10/1/162   1726–1727
Francis Colman, Thomas Starling, Bailiffs
Deeds and Portmanmote
(11 membranes; index endorsed)

C/2/10/1/163   1727–1728
John Cornelius, John Steward, Bailiffs
Deeds only
(9 membranes; index endorsed)

C/2/10/1/164   1728–1729
John Marlow, John Sparrow, Bailiffs
Deeds and Portmanmote
(15 membranes; index endorsed)

C/2/10/1/165   1729–1730
Henry Hill, Edward Bowell, Bailiffs
Deeds only
(10 membranes; index endorsed)

C/2/10/1/166   1730–1731
Francis Negus, John Cornelius, Bailiffs
Deeds and Portmanmote
(10 membranes; index endorsed)

C/2/10/1/167   1731–1732
Francis Colman, John Sparrowe, Bailiffs
Deeds only
(7 membranes; index endorsed)

C/2/10/1/168   1732–1733
John Marlow, Thomas Starling, Bailiffs
Deeds only
(10 membranes; index endorsed)

C/2/10/1/169   1733–1734
John Cornelius, Nathaniel Cole, Bailiffs
Deeds only
(9 membranes; index endorsed)

C/2/10/1/170   1734–1735
John Steward, John Sparrowe, Bailiffs
Deeds only
(3 membranes; index endorsed)

C/2/10/1/171   1735–1736
John Cornelius, Nathaniel Cole, Bailiffs
Deeds only
(5 membranes; index endorsed)

C/2/10/1/172   1736–1737
John Sparrowe, Edward Lynch, Bailiffs
Deeds and Portmanmote
(6 membranes; index endorsed)

C/2/10/1/173   1737–1738
John Cornelius, Robert Marston, Bailiffs
Deeds and Portmanmote
(9 membranes; index endorsed)

C/2/10/1/174   1738–1739
John Sparrowe, Richard Lloyd, Bailiffs
Deeds and Portmanmote
(6 membranes; index endorsed)

C/2/10/1/175   1739–1740
John Cornelius, Nathaniel Cole, Bailiffs
Deeds only
(5 membranes; index endorsed)

C/2/10/1/176   1740–1741
John Sparrowe, John Margerum, Bailiffs
Deeds only
(6 membranes; index endorsed)

C/2/10/1/177   1741–1742
John Cornelius, Nathaniel Cole, Bailiffs
Deeds only
(8 membranes; index endorsed)

C/2/10/1/178   1742–1743
John Sparrowe, Robert Marston, Bailiffs
Deeds and Portmanmote
(8 membranes; index endorsed)

C/2/10/1/179   1743–1744
John Cornelius, John Margerum, Bailiffs
Deeds only
(6 membranes; index endorsed)

C/2/10/1/180   1744–1745
John Sparrowe, Henry Skynner, Bailiffs
Deeds only
(6 membranes, the last blank except for index endorsed)

C/2/10/1/181   1745–1746
John Cornelius, Humphry Rant, Bailiffs
Deeds and Portmanmote
(9 membranes; index endorsed)

C/2/10/1/182   1746–1747
John Margerum, Henry Skynner, Bailiffs
Deeds only
(5 membranes; index endorsed)

C/2/10/1/183   1747–1748
John Cornelius, Nathaniel Cole, Bailiffs
Deeds only
(8 membranes; index endorsed)

C/2/10/1/184   1748–1749
John Sparrowe, Humphry Rant, Bailiffs
Deeds only
(9 membranes; index endorsed)

C/2/10/1/185   1749–1750
John Margerum, Michael Thirkle, Bailiffs
Deeds only
(8 membranes; index endorsed)

C/2/10/1/186   1750–1751
John Sparrowe, Goodchild Clarke, Bailiffs
Deeds only
(14 membranes; index endorsed)

C/2/10/1/187   1752–1753
Humphry Rant, Goodchild Clarke, Bailiffs
Deeds and Portmanmote
(9 membranes; no index)

C/2/10/1/188   12 Apr.–6 Oct. 1755
Deeds only
(3 membranes; first entry incomplete, last entry continued in C/2/10/1/189; endorsed index
headed 'Ipswich Roll from Michaelmas 1755 to Michaelmas 1756' and annotated in the same
hand 'Part of the Roll No. 9 concluded in the next. (Wanting Rolls No. 1, 2, 3 & 4)')

C/2/10/1/189   6 Oct. 1755–19 Oct. 1757
Lark Tarver, Thomas Bowell, Bailiffs 1755–1756; Thomas Richardson, William Truelove,
Bailiffs 1756–1757
Deeds; Portmanmote for administrative year 1756–1757
(18 membranes; endorsed index headed 'Ipswich Roll from Michaelmas 1756 to Michaelmas
1757')

C/2/10/1/190   1757–1758
John Gravenor, John Dade, Bailiffs
Deeds only
(7 membranes; index endorsed)

C/2/10/1/191   1758–1759
Thomas Richardson, Samuel Hamblin, Bailiffs
Deeds and Portmanmote
(5 membranes; index endorsed)

C/2/10/1/192   1759–1760
William Truelove, Richard Lockwood, Bailiffs
Deeds only
(8 membranes; index endorsed)

C/2/10/1/193   1760–1761
John Gravenor, John Trapnell, Bailiffs
Deeds and Portmanmote
(9 membranes; index endorsed)

C/2/10/1/194   1761–1762
William Truelove, Samuel Hamblin, Bailiffs
Deeds and Portmanmote
(14 membranes; index endorsed)

C/2/10/1/195   1762–1763
John Gravenor, Richard Lockwood, Bailiffs
Deeds only
Includes:
— 1 entry for 6 Oct. 1763, in next administrative year, also entered in index
(8 membranes; index endorsed)

C/2/10/1/196   1763–1764
William Truelove, John Trapnell, Bailiffs
Deeds and Portmanmote
(9 membranes; index endorsed)

C/2/10/1/197   1764–1765
John Gravenor, Samuel Hamblin, Bailiffs
Deeds and Portmanmote
(12 membranes; index endorsed)

C/2/10/1/198   1765–1766
Richard Lockwood, Charles Norris, Bailiffs
Deeds and Portmanmote
(12 membranes; index endorsed)

C/2/10/1/199   1766–1767
John Trapnell, William Truelove, Bailiffs
Deeds only
(16 membranes including detached index forming wrapper)

C/2/10/1/200   1767–1768
Humphry Rant, Miles Wallis, Bailiffs
Deeds only
(15 membranes; index endorsed)

C/2/10/1/201   1768–1769
William Hammond, William Wollaston, Bailiffs
Deeds only
(13 membranes; index endorsed)

C/2/10/1/202   1769–1770
Miles Wallis, Peter Clarke, Bailiffs
Deeds and Portmanmote
(19 membranes; index endorsed)

C/2/10/1/203   1770–1771
William Hammond, Thomas Staunton, Bailiffs
Deeds and Portmanmote
(21 membranes; index endorsed)

C/2/10/1/204   1771–1772
Miles Wallis, William Clarke, Bailiffs
Deeds only
(12 membranes; index endorsed)

C/2/10/1/205   1772–1773
Humfrey Rant, William Wollaston, Bailiffs
Deeds only
Includes:
— 1 entry for 5 Oct. 1773, in next administrative year, also entered in index
(15 membranes; index endorsed)

C/2/10/1/206   1773–1774
Miles Wallis, William Clarke, Bailiffs
Deeds and Portmanmote
(14 membranes; index endorsed)

C/2/10/1/207   1774–1775
Humphry Rant, Thomas Hallum, Bailiffs
Deeds only
(22 membranes; index endorsed)

C/2/10/1/208   1775–1776
William Wollaston, William Clarke, Bailiffs
Deeds only
(8 membranes; index endorsed)

C/2/10/1/209   1776–1777
Peter Clarke, Thomas Hallum, Bailiffs
Deeds only
Includes:
— 1 entry for 17 Sep. 1776, in previous administrative year, also entered in index
(10 membranes; index endorsed)

C/2/10/1/210   1777–1778
William Wollaston, Joseph Clarke, Bailiffs
Deeds only
(8 membranes; index endorsed)

C/2/10/1/211   1778–1779
Thomas Staunton, Peter Clarke, Bailiffs
Deeds only
(5 membranes; index endorsed)

C/2/10/1/212   1779–1780
Joseph Clarke, William Clarke, Bailiffs
Deeds and Portmanmote
(7 membranes; index endorsed)

C/2/10/1/213   1780–1781
Peter Clarke, Thomas Hallum, Bailiffs
Deeds and Portmanmote
(6 membranes; index endorsed)

C/2/10/1/214   1781–1782
William Clarke, Samuel Wollaston, Bailiffs
Deeds only
(5 membranes; index endorsed)

C/2/10/1/215   1782–1784
Thomas Hallum, Henry Seekamp, Bailiffs 1782–1783; Peter Clarke, John Spooner, Bailiffs 1783–1784
Deeds and Portmanmote
(16 membranes; index endorsed)

C/2/10/1/216   1784–1787
William Truelove, Charles Stisted, Bailiffs 1784–1785; Charles Norris, William Middleton, Bailiffs 1785–1786; Robert Trotman, Charles Squire, Bailiffs 1786–1787
Deeds and Portmanmote
(27 membranes including index membrane)

C/2/10/1/217   1787–1788
William Truelove, John Kerridge, Bailiffs
Deeds only
(14 membranes; index endorsed)

C/2/10/1/218   1788–1789
Charles Norris, William Lynch, Bailiffs
Deeds and Portmanmote
(4 membranes; index endorsed)

C/2/10/1/219   1789–1790
William Truelove, Robert Trotman, Bailiffs
Deeds and Portmanmote
(11 membranes; index endorsed)

C/2/10/1/220   1790–1791
Henry Seekamp, John Spooner, Bailiffs
Deeds only
(7 membranes; index endorsed)

C/2/10/1/221   1791–1792
William Truelove, John Kerridge, Bailiffs
Deeds and Portmanmote
(13 membranes; index endorsed)

C/2/10/1/222   1792–1793
Charles Stisted, William Lynch, Bailiffs
Deeds and Portmanmote
(16 membranes; index endorsed)

C/2/10/1/223   1793–1794
John Kerridge, William Norris, Bailiffs
Deeds and Portmanmote
(10 membranes; index endorsed)

C/2/10/1/224   1794–1795
Robert Trotman, John Walford, Bailiffs
Deeds and Portmanmote
(22 membranes; index endorsed)

C/2/10/1/225   1795–1796
John Kerridge, Samuel Thorndike, Bailiffs
Deeds and Portmanmote
(18 membranes; index endorsed)

C/2/10/1/226   1796–1797
William Norris, Samuel Howes, Bailiffs
Deeds only
(5 detached membranes; index endorsed)

C/2/10/1/227   1797–1798
John Kerridge, Robert Trotman, Bailiffs
Deeds and Portmanmote
(10 membranes; index endorsed)

C/2/10/1/228   1798–1799
Thomas Hallum, Samuel Thorndike, Bailiffs
Deeds and Portmanmote
(7 membranes; index endorsed)

C/2/10/1/229   1799–1806
Deeds and Portmanmote
(1 vol., 314 pp.; includes separate indexes for 1799–1800, 1800–1802 and 1802–1806)

C/2/10/1/230   1806–1810
Deeds and Portmanmote
(1 vol., 205 pp., with index)

C/2/10/1/231   29 Sep.–24 Dec. 1810
Deeds only
(1 vol., paginated 1–16; no index; interrupted text continues in next vol.)

C/2/10/1/232   24 Dec. 1810–22 Jun. 1811
Deeds only
(1 vol., paginated 17–32; no index; interrupted text continues in next vol.)

C/2/10/1/233   22 Jun.–22 Oct. 1811
Deeds only
(1 vol., paginated 33–48; no index; interrupted text continues in next vol.)

C/2/10/1/234   22 Oct. 1811–29 Apr. 1812
Deeds and Portmanmote
(1 vol., paginated 49–64; no index; interrupted text continues in next vol.)

C/2/10/1/235   29 Apr. 1812
Deeds only
(1 vol., paginated 65–80; no index; interrupted text continues in next vol.)

C/2/10/1/236   29 Apr.–30 Jul. 1812
Deeds only
(1 vol., paginated 81–96; no index; interrupted text continues in next vol.)

C/2/10/1/237   30 Jul.–22 Oct. 1812
Deeds only
(1 vol., paginated 97–112; no index; interrupted text continues in next vol.)

C/2/10/1/238   22 Oct. 1812–13 May 1813
Deeds and Portmanmote
(1 vol., 16 pp., unpaginated; no index; interrupted text continues in next vol.)

C/2/10/1/239   13 May–16 Jun. 1813
Deeds only
(1 vol., 16 pp., unpaginated; no index; interrupted text continues in next vol.)

C/2/10/1/240   16 Jun. 1813–6 Jan. 1814
Deeds only
(1 vol., 16 pp., unpaginated; no index; interrupted text continues in next vol.)

C/2/10/1/241   6 Jan.–15 Jun. 1814
Deeds only
(1 vol., 16 pp., unpaginated; no index; interrupted text continues in next vol.)

C/2/10/1/242   15 Jun.–21 Nov. 1814
Deeds only
(1 vol., 16 pp., unpaginated; no index; interrupted text continues in next vol.)

C/2/10/1/243   29 Nov. 1814–24 Feb. 1815
Deeds and Portmanmote
(1 vol., 16 pp., unpaginated; no index; interrupted text continues in next vol.)

C/2/10/1/244   24 Feb.–6 May 1815
Deeds and Portmanmote
(1 vol., 16 pp., unpaginated; no index; interrupted text continues in next vol.)

C/2/10/1/245   6 May 1815
Deeds only
(1 vol., 16 pp., unpaginated; no index; interrupted text continues in next vol.)

C/2/10/1/246   6 May–29 Jun. 1815
Deeds only
(1 vol., 16 pp., unpaginated; no index; interrupted text continues in next vol.)

C/2/10/1/247   29 Jun.–21 Oct. 1815
Deeds only
(1 vol., 16 pp., unpaginated; no index)

C/2/10/1/248   10 Nov. 1815–4 Apr. 1816
Deeds only
(1 vol., 16 pp., unpaginated; no index)

C/2/10/1/249   22 Jul. 1816–21 Jan. 1817
Deeds only
(1 vol., 16 pp., unpaginated; no index; interrupted text continues in next vol.)

C/2/10/1/250   21 Jan.–3 May 1817
Deeds only
(1 vol., 16 pp., unpaginated; no index; interrupted text continues in next vol.)

C/2/10/1/251   3 May–12 Jul. 1817
Deeds only
(1 vol., 16 pp., unpaginated; no index; interrupted text continues in next vol.)

C/2/10/1/252   12 Jul.–17 Sep. 1817
Deeds only
(1 vol., 16 pp., unpaginated; no index)

C/2/10/1/253   11 Oct. 1817–31 Mar. 1818
Deeds only
(1 vol., 16 pp., unpaginated; no index; interrupted text continues in next vol.)

C/2/10/1/254   31 Mar.–4 Sep. 1818
Deeds only
(1 vol., 16 pp., unpaginated; no index; interrupted text continues in next vol.)

C/2/10/1/255   4 Sep.–24 Oct. 1818
Deeds only
(1 vol., 16 pp., unpaginated; no index; interrupted text continues in next vol.)

C/2/10/1/256   24 Oct. 1818–27 Feb. 1819
Deeds only
(1 vol., 16 pp., unpaginated; no index; interrupted text continues in next vol.)

C/2/10/1/257   27 Feb.–29 Oct. 1819
Deeds only
(1 vol., 16 pp., unpaginated; no index; interrupted text continues in next vol.)

C/2/10/1/258   29 Oct. 1819–6 May 1820
Deeds only
(1 vol., 16 pp., unpaginated; no index; interrupted text continues in next vol.)

C/2/10/1/259   6 May–8 Jul. 1820
Deeds only
(1 vol., 16 pp., unpaginated; no index; interrupted text continues in next vol.)

C/2/10/1/260   8 Jul.–22 Aug. 1820
Deeds and Portmanmote
(1 vol., 16 pp., unpaginated; no index; interrupted text continues in next vol.)

C/2/10/1/261   22 Aug.–27 Sep. 1820
Deeds only
(1 vol., 22 pp., unpaginated; no index)

C/2/10/1/262   29 Sep.–23 Dec. 1820
Deeds only
(1 vol., paginated 1–16; no index; interrupted text continues in next vol.)

C/2/10/1/263   23 Dec. 1820–30 Jun. 1821
Deeds only
(1 vol., paginated 17–32; no index; interrupted text continues in next vol.)

C/2/10/1/264   30 Jun. 1821–27 Apr. 1822
Deeds only
(1 vol., paginated 33–48; no index; interrupted text continues in next vol.)

C/2/10/1/265   27 Apr.–11 Oct. 1822
Deeds only
(1 vol., paginated 49–64; no index; interrupted text continues in next vol.)

C/2/10/1/266   11 Oct. 1822–1 Jan. 1823
Deeds only
(1 vol., paginated 65–80; no index; interrupted text continues in next vol.)

C/2/10/1/267   1 Jan.–23 Apr. 1823
Deeds only
(1 vol., paginated 81–96; no index)

C/2/10/1/268   2 Jul.–9 Aug. 1823
Includes:
— Recovery in Portmanmote, 8–11 Nov. 1822, and beginning of another, 19 Feb. 1823
(1 vol., paginated 97–104; no index; interrupted text continues in next vol.)

C/2/10/1/269   19 Feb.–9 Aug. 1823
Portmanmote only
(1 vol., paginated 105–112; no index; with note that 'Mr Jackaman was Town Clerk from Sept.
1823 to Sept. 1824, therefore those enrolments are in his custody')

C/2/10/1/270   11 Nov. 1823–27 May 1824
Deeds only
(1 vol., 28pp., unpaginated; no index; interrupted text continues in next vol.)

C/2/10/1/271   27 May–28 Sep. 1824
Deeds only
(1 vol., 16 pp., unpaginated; no index)

C/2/10/1/272   12 Oct. 1824–3 Jan. 1825
Deeds only
(1 vol., 28 pp., paginated 113–140; no index)

C/2/10/1/273   3 Jan.–29 Apr. 1825
Deeds only
(1 vol., 36 pp., paginated 141–176; no index)

C/2/10/1/274   25 May–8 Aug. 1825
Deeds only
(1 vol., 24 pp., paginated 177–200; no index)

C/2/10/1/275   8 Oct.–9 Nov. 1825
Deeds only
(1 vol., 24 pp., paginated 201–224; no index)

C/2/10/1/276   6 Dec. 1825–8 Mar. 1826
Deeds only
(1 vol., 28 pp., paginated 225–252; no index; interrupted text continues in next vol.)

C/2/10/1/277   8 Mar.–8 Apr. 1826
Deeds only
(1 vol., 8 pp., paginated 253–260; no index; interrupted text continues in next vol.)

C/2/10/1/278   8–22 Apr. 1826
Deeds only
(1 vol., 8 pp., paginated 261–268; no index)

C/2/10/1/279   19 May–29 Jul. 1826
Deeds only
(1 vol., 16 pp., paginated 269–284; no index; interrupted text continues in next vol.)

C/2/10/1/280   29 Jul.–19 Sep. 1826
Deeds only
(1 vol., 8 pp., paginated 285–292; no index; interrupted text continues in next vol.)

C/2/10/1/281   19 Sep.–13 Dec. 1826
Deeds and Portmanmote
(1 vol., 12 pp., paginated 293–304; no index)

C/2/10/1/282   28 Oct. 1826–5 May 1827
Deeds only
(1 vol., 40 pp., unpaginated; no index; interrupted text continues in next vol.)

C/2/10/1/283   5 May–28 Sep. 1827
Deeds only
(1 vol., 34 pp., unpaginated; no index)

C/2/10/1/284   11 Oct. 1827–16 Jan. 1828
Deeds and Portmanmote; the last Portmanmote enrolment is a recovery, 19–20 Dec. 1827
(1 vol., 24 pp., unpaginated; no index; interrupted text continues in next vol.)

C/2/10/1/285   16 Jan.–12 Jul. 1828
Deeds only
(1 vol., 20 pp., unpaginated; no index; interrupted text continues in next vol.)

C/2/10/1/286   12 Jul.–26 Aug. 1828
Deeds
Includes:
— memorandum of enrolment of deed, with enquiry into age of a minor, 29 Jul. 1828
(1 vol., 34 pp., unpaginated; no index)

C/2/10/1/287   22 Nov. 1828–11 May 1829
Deeds only
(1 vol., 48 pp., unpaginated; no index; interrupted text continues in next vol.)

C/2/10/1/288   11 May 1829–3 Apr. 1830
Deeds only
(1 vol., 48 pp., unpaginated; no index; interrupted text continues in next vol.)

C/2/10/1/289   3 Apr. 1830–21 Jan. 1831
Deeds only
(1 vol., 46 pp., unpaginated; no index; interrupted text continues in next vol.)

C/2/10/1/290   21 Jan. 1831–15 Feb. 1832
Deeds only
(1 vol., 54 pp., unpaginated; no index)

C/2/10/1/291   5 Jan. 1832–30 May 1833
Deeds only
(1 vol., 46 pp., unpaginated; no index)

C/2/10/1/292   10 Apr. 1833–24 Feb. 1834
Deeds only
(1 vol., 44 pp., unpaginated; no index)

C/2/10/1/293   28 Feb. 1834–9 Jan. 1835
Deeds only
(1 vol., 46 pp., unpaginated; no index)

C/2/10/1/294   26 Jun.–7 Dec. 1835
Deeds only
Includes as covers:
— Coroner's inquisition at Laxfield on body of Amos Webber, 31 Jan. 1794
— Coroner's inquisition at Chediston on body of William Wincopp, 31 Aug. 1791 (incomplete)
(1 vol., 24 pp., 16 blank, unpaginated; no index)

C/2/10/2 REGISTERS OF ENROLMENTS   1537–1561

C/2/10/2/1   Oct. 1537–Oct.1561
This volume appears to represent another, short-lived, experiment in record-keeping. There is
no evidence that it ever formed part of a series. The headings entered for each administrative

year between September 1549 and September 1558 describe the contents as follows: 'He sunt carte et alia scripta que irrotulantur in tempore [*names of Bailiffs*] . . . a festo Sancti Michaelis Archangeli . . .'; the volume is in effect a register of enrolled deeds and wills. Also entered are some depositions made before the Bailiffs, mostly relating to the documents enrolled. Includes:
— (ff. 15–16) enrolment of recoveries suffered in the Portmanmote, 10 Jan.–7 Feb., 5 Sep.– 24 Oct. 1538
— (f. 62) arbitration award of goods and chattels of Robert Hill of Nacton, deceased, 27 Dec. 1548
— (f. 87) memoranda of proceedings in the Petty Court for committal of apprentices to new masters, usually by the Bailiffs and one of the constables, 15 Sep. 1551–19 Jan. 1552
— (*passim*) memoranda *re* committal of children and others to masters, usually by the Bailiffs and a constable, 16 May 1548–5 Mar. 1560
(1 vol., 192 fols, f. 192 blank; entries not always in strict order or strictly under the relevant administrative year. Some deeds and apprenticeship indentures recorded among the Petty Court business in the composite court book for 1540–1549 (C/2/10/3/10) are not included in the register.)

C/2/10/3   COMPOSITE COURT BOOKS   1486–1601

This series of volumes is believed to have begun in the ninth year of King Henry VI (1430–1431); the early volumes are now missing. The volume for 5–12 Henry VIII (1513– 1520), marked 'No. 8', is in the British Library (Add.MS. 24,435, described in the catalogue as a register of courts held by the Bailiffs, containing chiefly pleas of debt and trespass, with copies of deeds enrolled and lists of justices of the peace, coroners and other officers). Though always referred to as court books, the volumes bear all the characteristics of rough minute books, from which the formal record of that select portion of the proceedings of the various courts deemed worthy of permanent retention was afterwards enrolled in detail (*see* the series of composite enrolments, C/2/10/1).

By far the greater part of the entries consists of proceedings of the Petty Court, by now well established as the principal borough court. Petty Court business occurs throughout the series, containing brief entries for each plea (most frequently of debt, trespass and detention of chattels), to which were added notes of process, together with valuations and inventories of goods in cases of debt. The oaths of lesser officers are also recorded throughout. The first nine volumes also include enrolled deeds or memoranda of their enrolment, and the oaths of burgesses on admission. The later volumes include enrolled apprenticeship indentures (C/2/10/3/10, 13–15, 21, 22); memoranda *re* the binding of (? pauper) apprentices (C/2/10/3/11–22); depositions – occasionally made out of court before the Bailiffs – (C/2/10/3/10–14, 21); regulations *re* court fees and procedure (C/2/10/3/13–22); oaths of principal officers installed at Michaelmas (C/2/10/3/13–22); returns made by the serjeants-at-mace to court precepts (C/2/10/3/15–20); lists of litigants' costs (C/2/10/3/16–22); copies of writs relating to proceedings in the Court (C/2/10/3/21–22); and cases of dower (generally commenced by Writ of Right) and novel disseisin (C/2/10/3/12–22).

Minutes of the proceedings of the General or Great Court are entered most frequently in C/2/10/3/1–9, the proceedings at that time including the appointments of officers (other than those appointed annually on 8 September (the feast of the Nativity of the Blessed Virgin) to serve for the administrative year beginning at Michaelmas – *see below*); appointments of tax assessors and collectors; elections of burgesses to serve in Parliament; admissions and oaths of burgesses; administrative ordinances; grants of common soil; and sometimes lists of burgesses present in court. The sessions of the General Court held specifically for the election of the principal officers on 8 September are minuted in C/2/10/3/1–12. Courts headed as General Courts but apparently dealing with Petty Court business appear in C/2/10/3/11–13 (the separate series of Great Court books now beginning in 1572 is believed to have been instituted *c*.1538).

Portmanmote proceedings contain incomplete records of actions of (common) recovery commenced by Writ of Right, and occasional Petty Pleas including cases of dower and novel disseisin (fresh force).

Assize of Bread proceedings consist of lists of defaults and fines imposed. Proceedings of the Maritime and Piepowder Courts consist of minutes of pleas similar to those in the Petty Court.

Most entries were made in chronological sequence; in the following list, therefore, page numbers are cited only in cases of departure from this practice or where attention is drawn to untypical business. The language of the record is Latin throughout.

C/2/10/3/1   1486–1491
Petty Courts Sep. 1486–Sep. 1491; General Courts Nov. 1486–Sep. 1491; Assizes of Bread Oct. 1486–Sep. 1491; Piepowder Courts (pp. 180–81) Apr. 1488–Aug. 1491; Portmanmotes (pp. 133–34; dates only – general dates on which Petty Courts were held – except for plea of waste, 24 Jul. 1488) Jul.–Dec. 1488; Maritime Courts (pp. 107, 230) Mar. 1488–Jul. 1490
Includes:
— (p. 1) memorandum of recognizance for appearance to answer for assault and blood draught (incomplete), 1486 or 1487
— (p. 1) list of contributors (with sums given) for furnishing 6 'valetti' for King's service, 1488 or 1489
— (p. 142) resolution of General Court for grant of 10 marks to Master of Grammar School to celebrate for Guild of Corpus Christi for year beginning next Michaelmas, 19 Sep. 1488
(1 vol., 300 pp., pp. 63–66 excised; front cover marked 'No. 1', back cover 'Recognizances of debt')

C/2/10/3/2   1491–1493
Petty Courts Sep. 1491–Sep. 1493; General Courts Oct. 1491–Sep. 1493; Assizes of Bread Oct. 1491–Aug. 1493; Maritime Court (p. 130) 30 Jul. 1493
(1 vol., 155 pp., 20 pp. blank, 14 unused pages excised; front cover marked 'No. 2')

C/2/10/3/3   1493–1496
Petty Courts Sep. 1493–Sep. 1496; General Courts Oct. 1493–Sep. 1496; Assizes of Bread Nov. 1493–Sep. 1496 and (p. 171) n.d.; Piepowder Court (p. 87) 1 Jun. 1495
Includes:
— (p. 1) list of persons selling fish in market, n.d.
— (p. 76) minutes of meeting of Bailiffs, Portmen and Twenty-four, with list of persons to provide 10 men and horses for service of King and Earl of Oxford, 13 Mar. 1495
— (pp. 106, 107) list of contributions for repair of Stoke Bridge, n.d.
— (p. 166) list of persons to provide harness and horses, n.d. [? 1496]
— (p. 168) list of estreats collected by serjeants, and their liveries and wages, n.d. [? 1496]
— (p. 169) list of indentures [? grants of common soil] delivered by Thomas Hall [Common Clerk], n.d.
— (p. 170) list of charters delivered by Hall and Richard Bayly and William Revet [Bailiffs] 4 Dec. 1501
Enclosed:
— list of crafts and named persons [? re Corpus Christi procession], with endorsed list of contributions for food and drink
— jury lists, n.d.
— list of Portmen and burgesses at 'colloquium' in St Mary le Tower church, 7 Jan. –
(1 vol., 172 pp., 6 pp. blank; front cover marked 'No. 3')

C/2/10/3/4   1496–1497
Petty Courts Jan.–Apr. 1497; General Courts 15, 21 Apr. 1497; deeds enrolled 30 Dec. 1496; Assize of Bread 31 Dec. 1496
Includes:
— text of letter from Earl of Oxford requiring provision of 20 armed men for King's service in army to be raised 'for the repressing the presumpsion and malys of the Kyng of Scottes', 27 Mar. 1497, entered in Great Court, 15 Apr. 1497, with names of those responsible for providing weaponry and money

(Gathering of 16 pp., formerly part of C/2/10/3/3; entries not in strict chronological sequence; recovered from private custody in 1957)

C/2/10/3/5   1497–1505
Petty Courts Sep. 1497–1504; General Courts Dec. 1497–Sep. 1498, Sep. 1501–Dec. 1504; Assizes of Bread Oct. 1497–Jan. 1505; Piepowder Courts Jun. 1498–Jul. 1502; Portmanmotes (p. 20, heading only, 12 Oct. 1497; p. 545, action initiated by Writ of Right resulting in final concord, 21 Nov. 1504); Maritime Courts (pp. 119, 120, 398, 399) 9–15 Jan. 1499, 8–11 Oct. 1502; Sessions (pp. 198, 282, 286–288, 484, memoranda of recognizances for keeping the peace) 5–8 Dec. 1499, 16 Hen. VII (1500 or 1501), 24 Jan. 1504
Includes:
— (pp. 390, 531) memoranda of delivery of prisoners to incoming Bailiffs, Sep. 1502 and Sep. 1504
Enclosed:
— Writ of Error into King's Bench, 30 Mar. 1500
— Writ of Habeas Corpus from King's Bench, 6 Feb. 1500
— Writ of Procedendo *re* a prisoner, 25 Apr. 1502
— Writ of Procedendo *re* a plea of debt, 7 May 1502
— fragmentary enrolment of a plea, 19 Hen. VII (1503 or 1504)
— fragmentary list of pleas, n.d.
— inventory and valuation of clothing, n.d.
Stitched to margins:
— (p. 228) draft enrolment of a deed, n.d. (deed dated 22 Sep. 1500)
— (pp. 466, 473) Assizes of Bread, 24 Oct. 1503 and n.d.
(1 vol., 590 pp.; pp. 251–254, 267, 268, 307, 308, 319, 320, 577–590 excised; pp. 557–576 mutilated and partly illegible; front cover marked 'No. 4')

C/2/10/3/6   1505–1507
Petty Courts Sep. 1505–Sep. 1507; General Courts Mar. 1506–Sep. 1507; Assizes of Bread Sep. 1505–Sep. 1507; Admiralty and Maritime Court (p. 140, 1 plea of debt only) 11 Mar. 1507; Sessions (pp. 173, 175–78, mainly lists of officers and memoranda of recognizances) Dec. 1505–Sep. 1507 and n.d.; Leet (p. 74, list of officers for each ward and list of persons presented in East Ward) 2 Jun. 1506
Includes:
— (p. 74) copy Signet Writ to Corporation for discharge of William Spencer, Customer of Ipswich, from office of Bailiff, 6 Mar. 1506
— (p. 90) copy letter from Master General of the Order of Carmelite Friars to Corporation, *re* convent at Ipswich (incomplete), n.d.
— (p. 145) copy Signet letter to Corporation *re* divisions in the town because of 'diverse Reteyndours'; inhabitants shall henceforth be 'holy Reteyned unto us without any separacion', Secretary to be certified as to names and numbers of men to be provided for King's service, 12 Mar. 1507
(1 vol., 178 pp., 8 pp. blank; front cover marked 'No. 5')

C/2/10/3/7   1507, 1508, 1531–1532
At front: Petty Courts (pp. 5–13) *pre* 4 Nov.–Dec. 1507; (pp. 20–24) Jan.–Feb. 1508; (pp. 1–4) ? Feb.–Mar. 1508; (pp. 25–26) ? 21–28 Mar. 1508; Assizes of Bread (p. 19) Jan., Mar. 1508; Admiralty Court (p. 18, jury list only) 17 Dec. 1507; Sessions (pp. 14, 16, memoranda of recognizances for appearance and to keep the peace) 17 Dec. 1507 and n.d.
In middle: Petty Courts Jan. 1531–Jun. 1532; General Courts Feb. 1531–Apr. 1532
At back: Petty Courts Jul.–Sep. 1532; General Courts 8, 23 Sep. 1532
(1 vol., consisting of 3 books bound together, now paginated separately; first (32 pp., 5 pp. blank) made up of detached folios pasted together in wrong order; second (80 pp.); third (14 pp. marked 'No. 10' on first page)

C/2/10/3/8   1508–1513
Petty Courts Mar. 1508–Sep. 1513; General Courts May 1508–Sep. 1513; Assizes of Bread
(pp. 21, 24, 214, 215, 210, 211, 341) n.d. [? Aug. 1508], Aug. 1509–Aug. 1510, Dec. 1510–Sep.
1511, Jul. 1512; Admiralty Courts (pp. 391, 394, jury list and presentments only) 4 Aug., 7 Sep.
1513; Sessions (pp. 116–26, 130, memoranda of recognizances, lists of prisoners and officers)
Aug. 1508–Apr. 1509 and n.d.
Includes:
— (p. 220) copy letter from Bishop [Richard Nykke] of Norwich to Corporation, enjoining
them to advise townsmen heretically questioning the right of bishops to grant absolution to
reform themselves, 31 Mar. [?1510]
Enclosed:
— agreement between John Balles and William Bemonde for payment of £4 13s 4d, endorsed
with form of morning and evening prayers, n.d.
— inventory of furniture, n.d.
— writ for production of William Coteler at Westminster to answer Thomas Harford in plea of
trespass, 11 Jul. 1509; copied on p. 216
— Writ of Error into King's Bench in plea of debt between William Gilis and Alan Osborn,
11 Oct. 1512
— 3 lists of offenders, Assize of Bread, 13 Aug. 1512, ? 15 Oct. 1512–28 Sep. 1513
— Bailiffs' precept to serjeants in plea of detention of chattels, Richard Thurston and wife Joan
v. John Lambe and Richard Lambe, 16 Jan. 1513
(1 vol., 404 pp., 13 pp. blank; pp. 217–18 excised; front cover marked 'No. 7')

C/2/10/3/9   1520–1524, 1527–1531
Petty Courts Sep. 1520–Sep. 1524, Sep. 1527–Jan. 1531; General Courts Mar. 1521–Sep.
1524, May 1528–Sep. 1530; Assemblies (pp. 259, 315–316, 363) 30 Dec. 1528, 17, 19 Nov.
1529, 31 Oct. 1530
Includes:
— (p. 1) list of names of 9 soldiers for the town, n.d.
For entries for 1531–1532, see C/2/10/3/7 above
(1 vol., 368 pp., 10 pp. blank, pp. 175–80 excised; apparently made up from 4 books; front
cover marked 'No. 9')

C/2/10/3/10   1540–1549
Petty Courts pre –2 Oct. 1540–Sep. 1549; General Courts (sessions of 8 Sep. only) 1541–1549;
Portmanmotes Mar. 1542–Jul. 1544
Includes:
— (p. 546) undertaking for provision of 30 combs of malt to Bailiffs, 26 Sep. 1549
— (p. 547) recognizances for good behaviour and appearance before Bailiffs and Sir Thomas
Wentworth, kt., 6, 9 Jun. 1549
— (p. 548) miscellaneous memoranda
Enclosed:
— partial record of plea, Robert Williams v. Sankey Johnson, n.d.
(1 vol., 548 pp., 6 pp. blank, pp. 1, 2, 257, 258 excised; front cover marked 'No. 13')

C/2/10/3/11   1549–1557
Petty Courts Oct. 1549–? Apr. 1557; General Courts (sessions of 8 Sep. only) 1550–1556;
General Courts (dealing apparently with Petty Court business) Sep. 1552, May 1553–Mar.
1557
(1 vol., 488 pp., 5 pp. blank, pp. 459–466 fragmentary, pp. 1–8, 163, 164, 467–88 excised;
cover missing, though fragments attached to spine indicate that it consisted of a re-used MS,
rubricated and decorated in blue; front page marked 'No. 14')

C/2/10/3/12   1559–1564
Petty Courts Jan. 1559–Dec. 1564; General Courts (sessions of 8 Sep. only) 1559–1564;
General Courts (Petty Court business) Sep. 1559–Aug. 1562 and Sep. 1564; Portmanmotes
(pp. 145, 146, 153) 15, 29 Jun. 1559, 18 Dec. 1561; Maritime Court (p. 300) 22 Feb. 1564

(1 vol., 376 pp., 5 pp. blank, pp. 1–4, 369–76 fragmentary; pp. 135, 136, 201, 203, 233, 234, 295, 296, 315, 316 excised; modern re-binding following conservation; fragment of original binding consists of MS including list of saints, rubricated and decorated in blue, marked 'No. 15')

C/2/10/3/13   1565–1571
Petty Courts May 1565–Sep. 1570 (including oaths of officers at Michaelmas from 1566); General Court (list of officers sworn and Petty Court business) 29 Sep. 1565; Portmanmotes Dec. 1566–Apr. 1569; Maritime Courts Mar. 1568–Sep. 1570
Includes:
— (ff. 352–375) copies of depositions before the Bailiffs in various cases, Jul. 1570–Sep. 1571
(1 vol. with index of surnames for proceedings Sep. 1566–Sep. 1570 (incomplete), 379 fols, most with contemporary foliation; front cover marked 'No. 16')

C/2/10/3/14   1570–1575
Petty Courts Sep. 1570–Mar. 1575; Portmanmotes Mar.–Dec. 1571, Mar. 1573–Jun. 1574, ? Dec. 1574; Maritime Courts Oct. 1570–Jun. 1574
Includes:
— (pp. 131–33, 661–98) copies of depositions before the Bailiffs in Petty Court cases, 24 Jul. 1571, Nov. 1571–Feb. 1573
— (inside back cover) note by John Hawys [Common Clerk] that he was certified on 28 Jun. by Christopher Taylor re Richard, supposed child of — Cell, ostler at Lynnefeld's, n.d.
(1 vol. with index of surnames for proceedings Sep. 1570–Feb. 1573, 698 pp., 19 pp. blank, pp. 41–44 excised)

C/2/10/3/15   1575–1580
Petty Courts May 1575–Mar. 1580; Portmanmotes 12, 19 Apr. 1575; Maritime Courts Oct. 1575–Mar. 1580
Includes:
— (p. 130) memorandum of agreement to indemnify Bailiffs re appointment of Christopher Lawrence as collector of hallage of cloth until Michaelmas next, 15 Nov. 1575
— (p. 143) ordinance re payment for unbaited bulls, 13 Dec. 1575
— (p. 255) election of Governors of Christ's Hospital in Petty Court, 29 Sep. 1576
(1 vol. with index of surnames F–W for proceedings Apr. 1575–Sep. 1577, contemporary foliation, modern pagination, 928 pp., 10 pp. blank, pp. 1–12, 847–928 excised, pp. 805–16, 829–34 defective, covers missing; first page (p. 13) marked 'No. 18')

C/2/10/3/16   1581–1584
Petty Courts pre-19 Jan. 1581–Sep. 1584; Maritime Courts Jan. 1581–Sep. 1583
Includes:
— (pp. 477–84) alphabetical list of burgesses showing wards to which they belong, n.d.
(1 vol., partial contemporary foliation, modern pagination, 488 pp., 4 pp. blank, pp. 103, 104, 181–84, 461, 462, 485, 486 excised; first gathering (ff. 1–32) and front cover missing; first page marked 'No. 19')

C/2/10/3/17   1584–1586
Petty Courts Sep. 1584–Sep. 1586; Maritime Court (p. 126) 20 Jul. 1585
(1 vol., 380 pp., 16 pp. blank, pp. 3–8, 13–18 excised; front cover marked 'No. 20')

C/2/10/3/18   1586–1588
Petty Courts Sep. 1586–Mar. 1588; Portmanmotes (pp. 290, 300) 22 Dec., 16 Jan. 1588
(1 vol., 338 pp., 9 pp. blank, pp. 5–10 excised; front cover marked 'No. 21')

C/2/10/3/19   1588–1589
Petty Courts Apr. 1588–Sep. 1589; Portmanmotes Jul.–Sep. 1588
(1 vol., 288 pp., 8 pp. blank, pp. 3, 4, 7, 8, 31, 32, 59, 60, 233, 234, 237, 238 excised; front cover missing; first page marked 'No. 22')

C/2/10/3/20   1589–1591
Petty Courts Sep. 1589–Dec. 1591; Portmanmotes Feb.–Mar. 1590, May–Sep. 1591; Maritime
Court 18 Sep. 1590
(1 vol., 416 pp., 24 pp. blank, pp. 221, 222, 347, 348, 350, 351 excised; pp. 391–416 defective;
front cover marked 'No. 23')

C/2/10/3/21   1593–1596
Petty Courts Sep. 1593–Oct. 1596; Portmanmotes Aug.–Oct. 1595; Maritime Courts Aug.
1594–Jan. 1596
Includes:
— (p. 599) deposition of Elizabeth Robertson *re* a bastard child from North Walsham
(Norfolk), left in care of Elizabeth Cooke [of Ipswich], n.d.
— (pp. 599–601) Sessions memoranda, including recognizances to keep the peace and list of
constables, 1593–1596 and n.d.
(1 vol., 602 pp., 4 pp. blank, pp. 1–3, 413, 414 excised; front cover marked 'No. 24')

C/2/10/3/22   1596–1601
Petty Courts Oct. 1596–Sep. 1601; General Court (p. 779; Petty Court business only) 14 Oct.
1600
Includes:
— swearing in of officers at Petty Court, 29 Sep. 1598
— (pp. 941–944 and inside back cover) Sessions memoranda, including recognizances to keep
the peace and list of defaulters in providing themselves with arms, 1597–1601
— (inside front cover) note *re* sailors of ? Kirton, Wherstead, Trimley St Mary and Trimley St
Martin aged between 15 and 40 years, n.d.
(1 vol., 944 pp., 11 pp. blank, pp. 111, 112, 157, 158, 205, 206, 263, 264, 675, 676 excised; pp.
905–940 (1 gathering) found detached and replaced; front cover marked 'No. 25')

C/2/11   OFFICERS OF THE COURTS   1434–1675

C/2/11/1   TOWN SERJEANTS   **1434–1675**

Since the 13th century the Town Serjeants, or Serjeants-at-Mace, had acted as tipstaffs – the
Bailiffs' executive officers both in and out of court. Additionally, by the late 14th century they
had become prominent as subordinate collectors of revenue, assisting the Chamberlains. In the
17th century their chief function remained that of officers of the courts, in which capacity they
were required to enter into bonds to the Bailiffs for the diligent performance of their office.

C/2/11/1/1   ELECTIONS   1434

C/2/11/1/1/1   8 Sep. 1434
Memorandum of agreement for election of 4 Serjeants annually
Made in the Guildhall and 'acted and entred in the book of plees wher as alle materes of record
that be attained to fore the bailles of the said burgh for the tyme occupyeng be dependant and
remayne undir the custodie of the said bailles and the common Clerk'; for resolution of a
dispute as to whether 4 Serjeants, rather than the traditional 2, should be elected
78 witnesses named
Not sealed

C/2/11/1/2   BONDS   1667–1675

C/2/11/1/2/1   29 Sep. 1667
Thomas Boston of Ipswich, clothworker, serjeant; Thomas List, bricklayer and Thomas Cooke, maltster, both of Ipswich, sureties

C/2/11/1/2/2   19 Oct. 1670
John Taylor of Ipswich, cordwinder, serjeant; John Eaton and Robert Scot, both of Ipswich, mariners, sureties

C/2/11/1/2/3   29 Sep. 1675
Dionisius Smith of Ipswich, clothworker, serjeant; Thomas Searles, locksmith and Thomas Hardy, hosier, both of Ipswich, sureties

C/2/11/2   TOWN ATTORNEYS   **1625–1662**

C/2/11/2/1   ACCOUNTS   1625–1662

C/2/11/2/1/1   Oct. 1625–Jul. 1662
Account Book
Though the title page is inscribed 'A note of all such somes of money [that] are and shall growe dewe unto me for [or] by reason of my Attornishippe in Ipswich at Court with the tyme when everie Accion was entered', the main series of entries gives dates and names only, with no details of fees. 26 fols at the back of the volume record transactions for the period Feb. 1640–Aug. 1659 and include details of fees paid, together with memoranda of business transacted, mostly relating to sale or exchange of horses, including transactions by soldiers of the Parliamentary army.
(1 vol., 282 unnumbered fols, 10 fols blank)

C/2/12   EXTERNAL JURISDICTIONS   1388–1618

These miscellaneous documents are rare examples among the borough records of the jurisdiction of royal officers within the liberties.

C/2/12/1   31 Aug.–16 Nov. 1388
County Court (Suffolk) roll
4 courts, held at Ipswich, for 12 Ric. II
(Latin; 1 membrane)

C/2/12/2   (1411–1420), 1420
Gaol delivery roll for county of Suffolk
Includes:
— transcript of commission by Letters Patent of Henry V to Thomas Rolf, John Staverton, John Glemham, William Waller and John Grey, appointing them Justices to deliver prisoners in King's gaol of Ipswich, with precept to Sheriff of Suffolk to produce prisoners, 4 Feb. 1420
— transcripts of 15 indictments made before county Justices of the Peace at Henhowe [near Bury St Edmunds], Wickham Market, Dunwich, Blythburgh, Stowmarket and Eye, 22 Feb. 1411–22 Mar. 1420
(2 membranes; Latin; indictments not in chronological sequence)

C/2/12/3   1417–1447
Mainprise roll of Suffolk Sessions of the Peace
Proceedings before county Justices of the Peace at Beccles, Dunwich, Eye, Henhowe [near

Bury St Edmunds], Ipswich and Wickham Market for appearance of defendants and their manucaptors [sureties] at future Sessions, 1431–1447
Includes:
— (m. 9) record of proceedings before Justices of Gaol Delivery at Melton, by commission dated 18 Nov. 1417, against John Thedrych of Otley, wright, for felony, and his committal to the ordinary on claiming benefit of clergy
— (m. 5) record of proceedings before Justices of Gaol Delivery at Henhowe, resulting in acquittal of Robert East of Trimley, waterman, of homicide, 24 Jul. 1434
— (m. 8) record of proceedings against John Laborer, lately servant to Richard Tylere of Trimley, ploughman, for felony, mainprised from Sessions of the Peace at Henhowe to Court of King's Bench, Michaelmas term 1435
— (m. 7d) schedule of amercements at Wickham Market Sessions, 23 Sep. 1432
— (m. 1) schedule of debts owed to Robert Wode for his term as Bailiff of the Liberty of St Etheldreda, n.d.
(Latin; 9 membranes; ? an artificial roll, made up into its present form at a later date)

C/2/12/4   26 Jun. 1618
Licence
From Sir Henry Mountagu, kt, Chief Justice of King's Bench, and Sir John Dodderidge, kt, Justices of Assize for Suffolk, and Sir Giles Mompesson, kt and James Thurbarne, esq., Commissioners for licensing inns and hostelries, to Thomas Burrage of Ipswich, to keep an inn at the sign of the 'Three Coonyes' during lives of his wife Elizabeth, Edmund Greeneleafe of Ipswich and John Greeneleafe his son, and survivor of them, for £5 fine and 10s p.a.

C/3 FINANCE AND TOWN PROPERTY

With certain exceptions, such as some of the composite records and the accounts of subordinate collectors of certain special classes of revenue, notably the coal-meters of the port, the records of the town's finances and the administration of its communal property, listed here, are either those created by the Chamberlains and Treasurers or relate to matters (such as the leasing of the common soil) in which those financial officers had a direct interest.

The Bailiffs, as joint heads of the administration, responsible to the Crown for the annual farm of the borough, enjoyed, for more than a century following the grant of John's charter in 1200, full control over the town's revenues. The four men appointed in 1200 to assist them in revenue collection (Redstone 1948, 54) may have been the precursors of the town Chamberlains, but there is no evidence for the continuous existence of this office (Martin 1955, 72).

The reforming ordinances of 1320 clearly recognized the Bailiffs' opportunities for large-scale misappropriation of funds. They were accused, *inter alia,* of extorting salary-augmenting fees beyond those customarily assigned them, and of imposing inordinate dues and putting the money to personal use (Alsford 1982, 107). As a continuous check on their activities, therefore, a system of counter-rolls was devised, a duplicate record of all court business in which fines and amercements were levied. The counter-rolls were to be kept by two new officers, the Chamberlains, to whom the revenues were entrusted, and with whom the Bailiffs were now obliged to account by indentures and estreats.

No financial records (i.e., accounts) of this early period have survived. Only one complete Chamberlains' counter-roll of a Portmanmote roll is extant, duplicating the roll for 18–19 Edward II (C/2/1/1/32); and there are two presumed counter-rolls of Petty Pleas, 1322–1326 (C/2/3/2/1–2); but some odd membranes among the Recognizance rolls for Richard II's reign (C/2/4/1/53–54, 56–58) show that the practice was still kept up at the end of the 14th century. Moreover, the vigilance of the Chamberlains is attested by their numerous marginalia on the court rolls (Martin 1955, 78–81).

By Richard II's reign the Chamberlains, from their comparatively humble origin as a check on the Bailiffs' ambitions, had emerged as important fiscal officers of the borough, as shown by the fact that the Town Serjeants, in addition to their original function as tipstaffs – the Bailiffs' executive officers both in and out of court – are now equally prominent as collectors of revenue, in which capacity they act as the Chamberlains' subordinates (Martin 1955, 140). The actions in which the Chamberlains pleaded in the borough courts show that they had now assumed responsibility for the care and leasing of common assets, such as the plots of 'common soil' and the town mills. For instance, in 1396, when the water wheel of the New Mill was broken, it was the Chamberlains, in their own names, who sued the miller – and who lost the action and were amerced when the jury found that the wheel had been broken *per infortuniam* (Martin 1955, 141).

What is not clear, in the 14th and 15th centuries, is whether the Chamberlains were inferior in authority to the Treasurers, or even whether the two offices were then identical. The Treasurers, whose origins are obscure, appear only once in the records of the period, in 1415 (Martin 1955, 140, citing the Petty Court roll for 3–4 Henry V, C/2/3/1/49, m. 10d), and there is no other evidence for their existence at this time, while the Chamberlains appear to exercise an untrammelled authority.

From the 1540s, however, either one or two Treasurers were elected annually by the Great Court on 8 September, to serve for the financial year beginning at Michaelmas, and from 1563 it became the standard practice to elect a single Treasurer (Richardson 1884, *passim*). The office had by now emerged as both separate from, and senior (at least in status) to, that of the Chamberlains. The Treasurers were always substantial burgesses, normally members of the Twenty-four, and some went on to serve as Bailiffs. The Chamberlains were chosen from the ranks of the 'inferior' burgesses, though they were usually elected to the Twenty-four soon after completing their term of office (Webb 1996, 1–2).

It must be emphasised that, in practice, there was considerable overlap between the spheres of activity of the two offices. In general, however, the main revenues administered by the Treasurer were the rents from certain property, mostly land and mostly outside the borough, such as the Handford Hall estate and lands in Bramford and Whitton. Within the town they received the income from various tenements, fines for the admission of 'foreign' freemen, and penalties imposed at meetings of the Great Court and Assembly. They also received the proceeds of special collections such as those for scot and lot, plague relief, and the maintenance of the Town Preacher. Out of these receipts the Treasurer normally paid the salaries of the more important officers such as the High Steward, Recorder and Members of Parliament. He usually paid for repairs to public buildings, bridges and the water supply, and laid out many smaller sums for such purposes as supplementary poor relief.

The Chamberlains' main receipts were from rents (mainly from buildings, such as the Town House, Custom House, butchers' stalls and mills, rather than from land); minor fines imposed by the law courts, profits of the Admiralty Court, 'foreign' fines and penalties levied by the Headboroughs. They were responsible for the many small payments essential for the day-to-day running of the town. (For further details of the respective responsibilities of the Treasurer and Chamberlains, *see* Webb 1996, 1–6, on which the two foregoing paragraphs are substantially based.)

Between the 16th and the 19th centuries there were continual fluctuations in the boundaries between those responsibilities. Studies of the accounts and vouchers of Treasurers and Chamberlains reveal that, in practice, much was done on an *ad hoc* basis.

C/3/1   RECORDS OF THE BAILIFFS   1396–1759

The Bailiffs, as joint heads of the borough administration, were legally responsible to the Crown for the farm of the borough. Indeed, King John's charter of 1200 made their free election by the burgesses conditional upon their being presented to the Chief Justice at the Exchequer, a requirement relaxed by Edward II in his charter of 1317. It was to the Bailiffs that the Pipe Office issued the annual *quietus* for the farm.

C/3/1/1   QUIETUS ROLLS   1554–1759

Most of the rolls are for the fee-farm of the borough and/or judicial profits. With the farm are generally coupled payments for what appear to be Crown tenements (though the tenants named are often long deceased). From 1678 onwards the location of the tenement is often given, and sometimes the size. The dates at the head of each entry in this list are those of the Exchequer accounting year (which ran from Michaelmas to Michaelmas); the date when the Pipe Office drew up the *quietus* is added where given. At some stage the rotulets for the reigns of Philip and Mary and Elizabeth I were made up into a single roll for each reign, including a small number of accounts of fees paid into the Exchequer; the rotulets from the reign of James I onwards have been merely rolled into bundles of convenient size. In this list, a separate number has been assigned to each individual *quietus*. In the Marian and Elizabethan rolls, where the order is not strictly chronological, the rotulets have been numbered in the order in which they were filed when the rolls were made up.

C/3/1/1/1   1553–1554
Richard Byrde, Richard Skynner, Bailiffs

C/3/1/1/2   1554–1555
Robert Daundy, John Gardyners, Bailiffs

Includes payments from:
— Richard Lorde, King's Searcher
— Robert Scirrope, Collector of Customs and Subsidies

C/3/1/1/3   1558–1559
Richard Smarte, Matthew Goodynge, Bailiffs

C/3/1/1/4   1557–1558
John Smith *alias* Dyer, Thomas Goddinge, Bailiffs

C/3/1/1/5   1557–1558
Bailiffs unnamed; for debts relating to the second year of the late King Edward VI (? due at Michaelmas 1549)

C/3/1/1/6   1559–1560
Richard Byrde, Robert Kinge, Bailiffs

C/3/1/1/7   1560–1561
John Gardener, Geoffrey Gilbert, Bailiffs

C/3/1/1/8   1561–1562
John Dyer, Thomas Goodyng, Bailiffs

C/3/1/1/9   1562–1563
Richard Bryde *alias* Byrd, Robert Bray, Bailiffs

C/3/1/1/10   1563–1564
Robert Barker, William Whetecrofte, Bailiffs

C/3/1/1/11   1564–1565
Robert Kynge, William Barbour, Bailiffs (for various fines)

C/3/1/1/12   1564–1565
Robert Kynge, William Barbour, Bailiffs (for the farm)

C/3/1/1/13   1565–1566
John Gardyner, Thomas Goodwyn, Bailiffs

C/3/1/1/14   1566–1567
Geoffrey Gilberd, John More, Bailiffs

C/3/1/1/15   1567–1568
John Smyth *alias* Dyer, Robert Barker, Bailiffs
Includes:
— list of issues of the Court of Common Pleas

C/3/1/1/16   1568–1569
William Wheatcrofte, Robert Cutler, Bailiffs

C/3/1/1/17   1570–1571
John Baker, John Gardener, Bailiffs

C/3/1/1/18   1571–1572
Geoffrey Gylberd, Richard Kynge, Bailiffs

C/3/1/1/19   1572–1573
John More, Robert Sparrowe, Bailiffs (for the farm)

C/3/1/1/20   1572–1573
John More, Robert Sparrowe, Bailiffs (for various issues and amercements)

C/3/1/1/21   1573–1574
Robert Cutler, Ralph Scryvener, Bailiffs

C/3/1/1/22   1574–1575
Robert Kynge, John Tye, Bailiffs

C/3/1/1/23   1575–1576
William Smarte, Edward Goodynge, Bailiffs

C/3/1/1/24   1576–1577
John Barker, Augustine Parker, Bailiffs

C/3/1/1/25   1576–?1577
Richard Goltye, Collector of Subsidies paid into Exchequer on 6 Jul. 1576

C/3/1/1/26   1577–1578
Geoffrey Gilbard, John More, Bailiffs

C/3/1/1/27   1578–1579
Robert Cutler, John Knappe, Bailiffs

C/3/1/1/28   1579–1580
Ralph Scrivener, John Tye, Bailiffs

C/3/1/1/29   1580–1581
William Smarte, Robert Limber, Bailiffs

C/3/1/1/30   1581–1582
John Barker, Edward Goodinge, Bailiffs

C/3/1/1/31   1581–1582
Account of fees paid in the Exchequer for Barker and Goodinge at Michaelmas 24 Eliz.

C/3/1/1/32   1583–1584
Account of fees paid in the Exchequer for Mr Cutler and Mr Bloyes, late Bailiffs, due at
Michaelmas 26 Eliz.

C/3/1/1/33   1583–1584
Robert Cutler, William Bloyes, Bailiffs

C/3/1/1/34   1584–1585
John More, John Knappe, Bailiffs

C/3/1/1/35   1585–1586
Ralph Scryvener, Stephen Baxster, Bailiffs

C/3/1/1/36   1586–1587
William Smarte, Robert Limber, Bailiffs

C/3/1/1/37   1586–1587
Account of fees and expenses paid in the Exchequer for the late Bailiffs, due at Michaelmas
1587

C/3/1/1/38   1587–1588
John Barker, Edward Goodwin, Bailiffs

C/3/1/1/39   1587–1588
Account of fees paid in the Exchequer for Mr Barker and Mr Goodwin, late Bailiffs, due at
Michaelmas 30 Eliz.

C/3/1/1/40   1588–1589
Christopher Crane, William Midnall, Bailiffs

C/3/1/1/41   1589–1590
Robert Cutler, Robert Snellinge, Bailiffs

C/3/1/1/42   1591–1592
John Knappe, Robert Cutler, Bailiffs

C/3/1/1/43   1592–1593
Ralph Scrivener, Edward Cage, Bailiffs

C/3/1/1/44   1593–1594
William Smarte, Robert Lymber, Bailiffs

C/3/1/1/45   1593–1594
Account of fees paid in the Exchequer for William Smarte and Robert Limber, late Bailiffs, due
at Michaelmas 1594

C/3/1/1/46   1594–1595
Edward Goodinge, William Midnall, Bailiffs

C/3/1/1/47   1595–1596
Robert Cutler sen., William Midnall, Robert Snellinge, Bailiffs

C/3/1/1/48   1596–1597
William Bloyes, Robert Barker, Bailiffs

C/3/1/1/49   1598–1599
John Knappe, Robert Cutler, Bailiffs

C/3/1/1/50   1590–1591
For £7 for moiety of 7 woollen cloths seized for the Queen's use by Nicholas Crane and Robert
Scarlett

C/3/1/1/51   1605–1606
William Sparrowe, Matthew Brownrigge, Bailiffs

C/3/1/1/52   1625–1626
Richard Cocke, Christopher Aldgate, Bailiffs

C/3/1/1/53   1628–1629
Tobias Blosse, William Cliatte, Bailiffs

C/3/1/1/54   1645–1646
William Sparrowe, Richard Hoile [Haill], Bailiffs

C/3/1/1/55   1677–1678
William Hambry, Geoffrey .... [missing], Bailiffs

C/3/1/1/56   1681–1682
Richard Phillipps, William Browne, Bailiffs, 21 Feb. 1683

C/3/1/1/57   1685–1686
Richard Phillipps, Miles Wallis, Bailiffs, 26 Jul. 1689

C/3/1/1/58   1689–1690
William Browne, Henry Sparowe, Bailiffs, 12 Jun. 1691

C/3/1/1/59   1690–1691
Richard Pupplett, Robert Maning, Bailiffs, 18 Dec. 1691

C/3/1/1/60   1694–1695
Richard Phillipps, Samuel Reynolds, Bailiffs, 20 Jan. 1696

C/3/1/1/61   1705–1706
Cooper Gravener, William Tye, Bailiffs, 19 Feb. 1707

C/3/1/1/62   1715–1716
Henry Hill, Henry Nash, Bailiffs, 7 Jan. 1719

C/3/1/1/63   1717–1718
Francis Coleman, George Scott, Bailiffs, 30 Apr. 1719

C/3/1/1/64	1718–1719
Cooper Gravenor, Thomas Starling, Bailiffs, 5 Mar. 1720	
C/3/1/1/65	1722–1723
John Cornelius, John Sparrowe, Bailiffs, 21 May 1724	
C/3/1/1/66	1724–1725
John Cornelius, John Sparrowe, Bailiffs, 18 Feb. 1726	
C/3/1/1/67	1728–1729
John Marlow, John Sparrowe, Bailiffs, 4 May 1730	
C/3/1/1/68	1729–1730
Henry Hill, Edward Boswell, Bailiffs, 19 Feb. 1731	
C/3/1/1/69	1732–1733
John Marlow, Thomas Starling, Bailiffs, 10 Oct. 1734	
C/3/1/1/70	1733–1734
John Cornelius, Nathaniel Cole, Bailiffs, 7 Apr. 1736	
C/3/1/1/71	1734–1735
John Sparrow, John Steward, Bailiffs, 22 Apr. 1736	
C/3/1/1/72	1736–1737
John Sparrow, Edward Lynch, Bailiffs, 6 Feb. 1739	
C/3/1/1/73	1737–1738
John Cornelius, Robert Marston, Bailiffs, 16 Feb. 1739	
C/3/1/1/74	1738–1739
John Sparowe, Richard Loyd, Bailiffs, 2 Feb. 1741	
C/3/1/1/75	1742–1743
John Sparowe, Robert Marston, Bailiffs, 10 Dec. 1746	
C/3/1/1/76	1744–1745
John Sparowe, Henry Skinner, Bailiffs, 16 Dec. 1746	
C/3/1/1/77	1749–1751
John Sparowe, Goodchild Clark, Bailiffs, 22 May 1753	
C/3/1/1/78	1751–1752
Michael Thirkle jun., William Hammond, Bailiffs, 22 May 1753	
C/3/1/1/79	1752–1753
H. Rant, Good[child] Clarke, Bailiffs, 3 Feb. 1755	
C/3/1/1/80	1754–1755
Thomas Richardson, J. Gravenor, Bailiffs, 7 Feb. 1756	
C/3/1/1/81	1755–1756
Lark Tarver, Thomas Bowell, Bailiffs, 7 Nov. 1758	
C/3/1/1/82	1756–1757
Thomas Rechardson, W. Truelove, Bailiffs, 27 May 1759	

C/3/1/2   OTHER ACCOUNTS   1396–1752

C/3/1/2/1   29 Sep. 1396–29 Sep. 1397
Account of John Avelyn and John Bernard, Bailiffs, for the farm of the town
Includes, annexed:
— petitions of Avelyn and John Stathe [*sic*], lately Bailiffs, in Exchequer, for allowances

against the accounts of Thomas Curson and William Rees, lately Sheriffs of Norfolk and Suffolk, Sep. 1397
(Latin; 2 membranes)

C/3/1/2/2   1752–1754
Account of Michael Thirkle, esq. [Bailiff 1753–1754], of disposal of money received by him from James Blythe [Town Treasurer], for the income of the Portmen's Marshes; and of expenses of rebuilding Handford Mill and house
Audited 21 Oct 177 . . ., and balance agreed in favour of Thirkle's executors
(1 vol; found with Treasurer's vouchers)

C/3/2   COMPOSITE FINANCIAL RECORDS   1559–1835

C/3/2/1   FAIR COPIES OF THE TREASURERS' AND   1559–1642
CHAMBERLAINS' ANNUAL AUDITED ACCOUNTS, KEPT IN
VOLUME FORM FOR EASE OF REFERENCE

Some words are spelt differently, sub-totals are not always included, the layout often varies slightly, and there are occasional trivial errors and slips of the pen. On the whole, however, these are faithful copies of the originals, made by a contemporary who was able to decipher, and if necessary query, the many amendments made at the audit, which so often disfigure parts of the original texts. They also include some accounts, the originals of which have been lost. *See* Webb 1996, 9–10, 15–17.

C/3/2/1/1   1559–1588
Treasurers' and Chamberlains' accounts and other memoranda
(The years given below indicate the calendar years in which the relevant financial years ended.)
Includes:
— Treasurers' accounts
   – (ff. 32r–v) 1560 (incomplete)
   – (ff. 4r–6r) 1565
   – (ff. 164v–168r) 1567
   – (ff. 40r–43r) 1571
   – (ff. 210v–216v) 1580
   – (ff. 183r–190v) 1581
— Chamberlains' accounts
   – (f. 2(a)–(e)) [1559]
   – (ff.7r–9r) 1565
   – (ff. 13r–18r) 1567
   – (ff. 18v–24r) 1568
   – (ff. 24v–31r) 1569
   – (ff. 219r–225r) 1580
   – (ff. 192r–198r) 1581
— Treasurers' and Chamberlains' accounts, arranged by years
   – (ff. 169r–174v) 1572–1579 (Chamberlains', 1577, incomplete)
   – (ff. 225v–318r) 1582–1588 (Treasurers', 1587, omitted)
   – (ff. 325v–327r) Scot and Lot assessments for suits between the town and Edmund Withipoll, esq. and other expenses, 1568
   – (ff. 327v–329r) arrears of Scot and Lot committed to the collection of various persons at the audit, 1568
   – (f. 329v) list of names, 1572
   – (ff. 318v–323r) Scot and Lot assessment, 1573
   – (ff. 230v–231r) account of Edward Goodyng, Bailiff (preachers' wages, conveying harlots and other disbursements), 1582

– (f. 330r) memorandum *re* payment of legacy of Roger Barney, deceased, to poor scholars of Ipswich, 1582
– (f. 330v) order of Bailiffs and Portmen for assistance of Samuel Goodyer, MA of St John's College, Cambridge, from Barney legacy, 1585
The Chamberlains' account for 1559 is original, presumably included when the book was rebound in 1939.
(1 vol., 335 fols)

C/3/2/1/2   1593–1642
Treasurers' and Chamberlains' accounts
Entered together by years. The Treasurer's account for 1600 is omitted; the Treasurer's account for 1624 and the Chamberlains' for 1593 are incomplete.
(1 vol., 477 fols. It cost 13s 4d when bought in 1596, when it was described as 'a book to enter the accomptes of the treasorer and chamberlens' C/3/4/1/26/1)

C/3/2/2   REVENUE MEMORANDA BOOKS   1565–1685

C/3/2/2/1   1565–1668
Memorandum book of Corporation revenues
Estreats from Sessions of the Peace and other courts, rentals and auditors' memoranda relating to the Treasurers' and Chamberlains' accounts 1565–1616, and lists of Foreign Fines 1565–1668. Until 1590 the clerks tended to enter all items for each year together; later they devoted sections of the book to entries of each particular type. A single section was consistently devoted to auditors' memoranda. The years given below indicate the calendar years in which the relevant financial years ended. Some or all of the Foreign Fines dated 1580–1618 may in fact belong to the financial years immediately following those indicated here. Persons paying Petty Rents are listed by parishes; persons paying Foreign Fines by wards, their occupations generally being given and sometimes from 1622 notes about their apprentices. The lists giving the fixed rents to be received by the officers and the other sources of their receipts may have been precedents to be followed in the drawing up of accounts.
Includes:
— rentals and estreats (including Foreign Fines) relating to the Chamberlains, 1565–1590:
    – (ff. 59r–66r) Petty Rental and Foreign Fines, 1565
    – (ff. 66v–67r) fines (Sessions) and Forfeitures only, ?1566
    – (ff. 79v–82r) Foreign Fines only, 1568
    – (ff. 82v–87r) 1569
    – (ff. 88r–91r) Foreign Fines only, 1571
    – (ff. 91v–99r) Foreign Fines and Petty Rental only, 1572
    – (ff. 99v–104r) 1573
    – (ff. 104v–109r) with Chamberlains' rental, 1574
    – (ff. 109v–113v) 1575
    – (ff. 114r–116r, 182r–184r) 1576
    – (ff. 184v–245r) 1577–1590
— Foreign Fines, 1594–1668
    – (ff. 67v–79r) 1594–1598, 1600, 1602
    – (ff. 251v–252v) 1603–1614
    – (ff. 36v–58r) 1615–1616
    – (ff. 23r–26v) 1618 (2 versions)
    – (ff. 326r–331v) 1620–1623
    – (ff. 304v–313r) 1624–1629
    – (ff. 320r–324v) 1630–1633
    – (ff. 331v–332 v) 1634
    – (ff. 245v–249r) 1635–1636
    – (ff. 9v–14v) 1637–1639

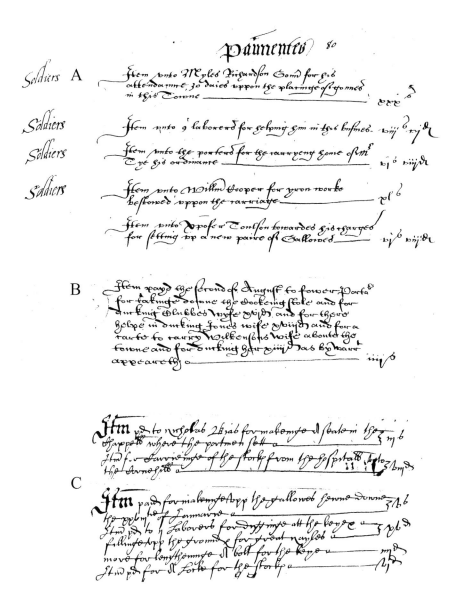

Fig. 10. Defence and punishment: A. ordnance and gallows in 1596, (fol. 40v.);
B. ducking in 1597, (fol. 50v); and C. stocks and gallows in 1607–08. (All from
Treasurer's audited accounts, 1593–1642, C/3/2/1/2)

 – (ff. 21v–22v) 1640
 – (ff. 117r–179v) 1641–1668
— fines (Sessions), 1595–1616; fines (Assize of Bread), 1595, 1597, 1600, 1601:
 – (ff. 248v–265) 1595–1611
 – (ff. 315v–319v) 1612–1616
— (ff. 19v–21v) lists of rents and fines and of the other sources of Chamberlains' receipts, with lists of Chamberlains' payments, 1595
 – (ff.31r–35v) Petty Rental 1595
— rentals and memoranda relating to the Treasurer
 – (ff. 3r–4v, 17r –v) lists of rents and other sources of receipts, 1565
 – (ff. 313v–315r) inventories (5) of forfeited weights, goods pertaining to the Town House, chains etc. at the gaol and goods in custody of the Treasurer, 1565–1583
 – (f.84r) list of fines and profits of Great Courts, 1569
 – (f.5r) list of rents to be received, 1570
 – (f.18v) list of rents and other sources of Treasurers' receipts, 1595
 – (f.21r) list of Treasurers' payments, 1595
— auditors' memoranda
 – (ff. 265v–268r, 269v–270v) 1565–1568
 – (ff. 271r–304r) 1568–1597
 – (f.268v) abstract of will of Margery Wild, widow, containing legacies for repair of highways and Bourne Bridge, enrolled 1549
 – (f.269r) memorandum of legacies by Thomas Dameron of Rushmere to the poor of Ipswich and Rushmere, 1540
— (bound in following f. 263) list of householders and inns for quartering two troops of horse, 1650
(1 vol., 333 fols)

C/3/2/2/2   1571–1651
Rate assessment and memorandum book
This is apparently the paper book ordered to be kept by the clause in the Paving Act (18 Eliz., cap. 24) allowing rates to be made for the maintenance of the town churches and their incumbents. It soon came to be used also for assessments for rates to maintain the Town Preachers; as the book required for entering poor rate assessments under 14 Eliz., cap. 5; for memoranda mostly relating to the administration of poor relief and the food supply; for a paving rate; and for a rate for providing powder and matches. Also included are enrolments of apprenticeship indentures, which were probably entered to provide a record of persons entitled to become freemen. (There is in the Local Studies Library in the Ipswich Record Office, under the reference S Ips. 929.4, a MS calendar by John Glyde of the apprenticeship indentures, rate assessments and certain other material from the volume, together with an index of persons.)
Includes:
— church rate assessments made under 18 Eliz. cap. 24 for all parishes except CL and MS, 1571–1638
 – (f.1r) NI, 12 Dec. 1571
 – (f.3r) MW, 22 Feb. 1572
 – (f.5r) MT, 27 May 1572
 – (f.7r) LW, 9 Oct. 1573
 – (f.8r) MQ, 22 Feb. 1574
 – (f.10r) MT, 3 Apr. 1578
 – (f.13r) HL, 9 Oct. 1584
 – (f.15v) NI, 21 Dec. 1597
 – (f.19v) ME, 25 Feb. 1607
 – (f.20v) MT, 28 Sep. 1608
 – (f.22r) NI, 15 Dec. 1609
 – (f.27v) LW, 1 Nov. 1608
 – (f.29v) NI, 26 Sep. 1612

- (f.32v) NI, 26 Sep. 1613
- (f.34v) MT, 8 Jul. 1634
- (f.36v) LW, 10 May 1637
- (f.39v) NI, 10 May 1637
- (f.44v) MT, 26 May 1637
- (f.48v) MQ, 26 May 1637
- (f.51r) ME, 10 Jun. 1637
- (f.53r) ST, 23 Jun. 1637
- (f.55r) PE, 23 Jun. 1637
- (f.60v) MG, 18 Sep. 1637
- (f.69r) MG, 16 Feb. 1638

— rate assessments for Town Preachers' wages, by order of the Great Court, 1574–1585
- (ff. 400v–405r) by wards, 12 Mar. 1574
- (ff. 373v–374r) MT only, 1576
- (ff. 405v–411r) by parish (MS omitted), 21 Jun. 1577
- (ff. 243r–251r) by parishes, 1583
- (ff. 251v–256r) by parishes, 15 Dec. 1585

— poor rate assessments, 1573–1590
- (ff. 391r–397v) 30 Dec. 1573 with later additions (includes list of poor for all parishes except ST, and of aldermen and constables)
- (ff. 382v–388r) 25 Aug. 1574 (MS omitted; includes lists of poor, except for MS, MQ and LW)
- (ff. 363r–368r) 30 Eliz. (1577 or 1578)
- (ff. 289v–297r) 24 Aug. 1581, renewed 23 Aug. 1582 (includes lists of poor)
- (ff. 278v–289r) 19 Aug. 1583, with later alterations, renewed 21 Aug. 1584 (includes lists of poor)
- (ff. 101r–107r) 23 Aug. 1590, renewed 23 Aug. 1591 (MS omitted; includes lists of poor, except for PE and MS)

— other entries *re* poor relief, 1580–1583 and n.d.
- (f.397v) list of sums of money for each ward (? weekly payments to poor), and parishes appointed to each ward, n.d.
- (f.398v) list of persons, by parish, maintained by other parishes, n.d.
- (f.399r) list of poor in Hospital at Frysell's charge (? showing weekly cost of maintenance), n.d.
- (ff. 326v–346v) rate assessment, 1580 (exceptional rate taken in time of plague; *see* Richardson 1884, 323; MS omitted)
- (ff. 233r–242r) assessments 'towards the setting of the poor on work', 16 Sep. 1583
- (f.242v) lists of 'Governors of the Poor' and 'Collectors of the Stock', 1583
- (ff. 297v–302r) assessment by wards and hamlets, by authority of Privy Council and order of Great Court, towards cost of the 'stey of the Infeccion' by plague (*see* Richardson 1884, 344) Oct. 1585
- (ff. 303v–311r) copy certificate for first part of subsidy of 26 Eliz., 1585

— other rates, 1578–1586
- (ff. 11v–12r) assessment by virtue of 18 Eliz. cap. 24 for paving against St Mary at Quay churchyard, 13 Jul. 1578
- (ff. 268v–273r) assessment by wards for money to be lent towards powder and matches, 10 Jan. 1587

— apprenticeship indentures, 1596–1651
- (ff. 108v–167r) 1596–1611
- (ff. 170v–233r) 1611–1635
- (ff. 256v–268r) 1634–1639
- (ff.273v–278r) 1639–1641
- (ff. 311r–326r) 1641–1651

— miscellaneous memoranda, 1574–1590
- (ff. 98v–100v) copy Letters Patent for monopoly of manufacture of sail cloths called

'mydrene and polledavis' for 21 years, manufacture to be confined to Ipswich and Woodbridge and three miles around each town, 1574

- – (ff. 415v–418r) copy orders *re* killing and eating of flesh in Lent, with covering letter [? from Privy Council], 1587
- – (ff. 418v–420v) lists of persons licensed to eat flesh in Lent, n.d. [?1586, 1587]
- – (ff. 167v–169v) copy Privy Council order in restraint of killing and eating flesh in Lent, with form of certificate for licence to eat flesh, 1590

(1 vol., 420 fols)

C/3/2/2/3   1634–1685
Account book: Treasurers, Chamberlains and Town Charities
Draft accounts and rentals of the Treasurers and Chamberlains, and accounts relating to Ipswich charities. The volume appears to have been used originally for private trading, since the first 11 pages consist of accounts, 1622–1624, apparently of an Ipswich merchant dealing principally in cloth and containing references to various clothiers and merchants. It is possible that some entries for 1677 and later dates were intended as precedents for drawing up future accounts.
Includes:
— Treasurer's records
  – (pp. 77–81) rental with list of receipts from licensed alehouses and list of regular payments, ?1684–1685 (incomplete draft account)
  – (pp. 82, 83) list of payments taken from previous accounts, with related memoranda, ?1685
— Chamberlains' records
  – (pp. 22–37) lists of receipts and payments, 1633–1634
  – (pp. 51–54) water rental, 1683–1684 (HL, MG, LW, MT, NI and MW) with memorandum by Thomas Broke *re* arrival of new charter and his becoming Town Clerk
  – (pp. 65–73) Petty Rental, 1683–1684 (13 parishes including Whitton)
  – (pp. 57–60) Chamberlains' rental, 1684–1685 (marshes, shops and important properties), with list of other sources of receipts and payments (incomplete draft account)
— Tooley's Foundation and Smarte's Gift
  – (pp. 39–49) Renterwarden's account with lists of recipients of these charities, 1646–1647
  – (pp. 85–87) draft Renterwarden's account, 1677–1678 (incomplete)
— Other charities
  – (p. 13) lists of clothing distributed on St Thomas's Day and out of Mr Martyn's Gift, 1684
  – (pp. 95–96) draft account of Receiver of Martyn's Gift, for benefit of scholars in Cambridge and clothing the poor, ?1683–1684 (incomplete)
  – (p. 91) draft account of Treasurer of Christ's Hospital, 1683–1684 (incomplete)
(1 vol., 106 fols, paginated up to p. 96, all subsequent leaves blank. Cover marked 'No. 3', 1633–1684)

C/3/2/3   AUDIT BOOKS   1695–1835

Memoranda made at audits by the various accountants; usually signed by the auditors, with a statement of the balance and orders relating to its disposal
NB, accounts covering several years were sometimes audited at one session.

C/3/2/3/1   1695–1819
Memoranda for the following accountants and dates:
— Chamberlains, 1718–1814
— Town Treasurer, 1719–1818
— Collector of Water Rents, ?1719–1818
— Collector of Coal Dues, ?1750–1819
— Receiver of Tyler's Charity, 1704–1819
— Receiver of Martin's Charity, 1713–1818

— Treasurer of Christ's Hospital, 1720–1817
— Renterwarden of Tooley's Foundation, ?1720–1816
— Treasurer of Smart's Charity, ?1720–1816 (Tooley's and Smart's accounts were apparently combined until the audit of 15 Nov. 1762)
— Receiver of Osmond's Charity, ?1722–1813
— Clavigers, 1756–1816
and:
— Crane's Charity, accounts and distribution lists, 1700–1804 (account of rents due Lady Day 1693 and 1698; disbursements 1700, list of distributions 1788–1804)
— Cutler's Charity, list of distributions of rent received from Handford Hall Farm, 1810
— Lending Cash Charity, memoranda, 1695–1713
— original receipt by Edmund Beeston for sums paid to him as Lecturer by the Chamberlains, 15 Feb. 1727 (bound in)
(1 vol., 182 unnumbered fols)

C/3/2/3/2   1813–1835
Memoranda for the following accountants, entered at audits 2 Feb. 1820–24 Dec. 1835:
— Town Treasurer, 1818–1835
— Collector of Water Rents, 1818–1820
— Collector of Coal Dues, 1820–1832
— Receiver of Tyler's Charity, 1813–1835
— Receiver of Osmond's Charity, 1813–1830
— Renterwarden of Tooley's Foundation, 1816–1835
— Receiver of Smart's Charity, 1816–1835
— Treasurer of Christ's Hospital, 1817–1834
— Treasurer of Martin's Charity, 1818–1834
(1 vol., 180 unnumbered fols, of which only the first 29 are used)

C/3/3   RECORDS OF THE CHAMBERLAINS   1446–1813

On the origin and functions of the office of Chamberlain, *see* the general introductory note to FINANCE AND TOWN PROPERTY. The few surviving medieval Chamberlains' counter-rolls are listed under JUSTICE AND THE COURTS: for the sole counter-roll of the Portmanmote, for 1324–1325, *see* C/2/1/1/32; for counter-rolls of Petty Pleas, 1322–1326, *see* C/2/3/2/1–2; and for counter-rolls of Recognizance Rolls, 1383–1384 and 1389–1391, *see* C/2/4/1/53–54, 56–58. The Chamberlains' Leet Estreat Rolls, 1384–1472 and 1685–1737 are listed with the Leet records (C/2/8/2/1–9). For convenience, the Chamberlains' financial records relating to the town's water supply have been placed with those of the later Collector of the Water Rents under TOWN RESPONSIBILITIES AND SERVICES (C/5/5).

C/3/3/1   COMPOTUS ROLLS   1446–1531

Accounts of annual receipts and payments. Receipts include income from property rentals, fees for the use of the crane on the Common Quay, profits of the Leet and other courts, and profits from fairs. Payments include the borough fee-farm to the Crown, property repairs, and fees of the Bailiffs, Town Clerk and other officers.

C/3/3/1/1   1446–1447
Roger Tough, John James, Chamberlains
(Latin; 4 parchment membranes, stitched together 'Chancery' style)

C/3/3/1/2   n.d. [1463–1464]
John Hastyng, Edmund Sherawe, Chamberlains

Includes:
— payment of £3 13s 4d for 'owr charter' [Edward IV's charter of 1463]
Acquired by Ipswich Borough Library at an unknown date and restored to the borough archive
in 1943. For published extracts, see EANQ, New Ser. I (1885–86), 119–21.
(English, 5 paper fols, pasted (formerly stitched) together 'Chancery' style)

C/3/3/1/3   n.d. [1530–1531]
Thomas Cutler, Jefry Gylbert, Chamberlains
Includes:
— payments to 'Mr Brandon the Kynges Jugler' and to 'mynstrelles pleyers and bere wardes'
(English; 9 paper fols stitched together 'Chancery' style)

C/3/3/2   AUDITED ACCOUNTS   1554–1813

These usually include rents received for certain larger properties, frequently rents for stalls and
shops, and occasionally receipts from Great Courts, Sessions, the Assize of Bread and less
important sources. Petty Court receipts, Foreign Fines, Headboroughs' fines, water rents and
petty rents are represented by totals. Until c. 1785, disbursements include details of payments
to borough officers, the Exchequer, and for Corporation business (generally excepting that
within the Treasurer's special province). The later accounts are summary in nature, dealing
only with receipts such as collections in the markets, water rents and Sessions fines. For the
period 1731–1791, see also the Chamberlains' vouchers (C/3/3/3).

C/3/3/2/1   1553–1554
John Golding, Richard Cely, Chamberlains
(1 vol.)

C/3/3/2/2   1555–1556
Robert Sparowe, Jafferrey Carre, Chamberlains
Includes:
— various payments 'for the excicusion of the ij women whiche ware burnede' [Agnes Potten
and Joan Trunchfield, burnt at the stake on the Cornhill early in 1556]
(1 vol.)

C/3/3/2/3   1556–1557
Robert Sallowes, Thomas Madok, Chamberlains
(front cover only)

C/3/3/2/4   1557–1558
Robert Nottingham, William Harvy, Chamberlains
(1 vol.)

C/3/3/2/5   1561–1562
Richard Kynge, Steven Baxster, Chamberlains
(1 vol.)

C/3/3/2/6   1562–1563
John Barker, Robert Andrew, Chamberlains
(1 vol.)

C/3/3/2/7   1563–1564
William Bucknam, George Wildes, Chamberlains
(1 vol.)

C/3/3/2/8   1566–1567
Richard Gadge, Thomas Blosse, Chamberlains
(1 vol.)

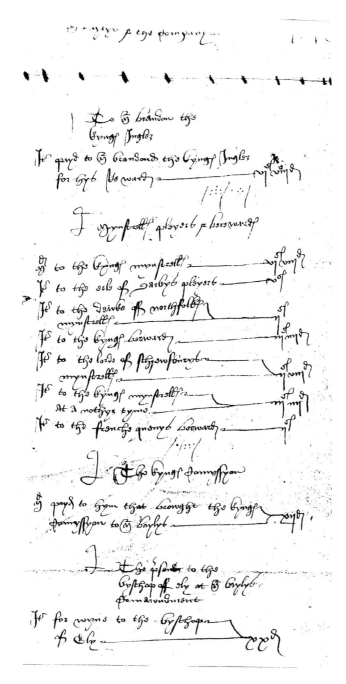

Fig. 11. Costs of hiring Mr Brandon the Kyngs Jugler, mynstrells, pleyers and berewards, for the entertainment of Thomas Lord Wentworth, and presents from the Bailiffs for the Bishop of Ely. Chamberlains' compotus roll [stitching visible; note the small dots used to assist the auditors], 1530–1531. (C/3/3/1/3)

211

C/3/3/2/9   1568–1569
Christopher Alderman, John Cole, Chamberlains
(1 vol.)

C/3/3/2/10   1569–1570
James Bedingfelde, Augustin Parkar, Chamberlains
(1 vol.)

C/3/3/2/11   1570–1571
[Robert Martin, William Cuttler, Chamberlains]
(1 vol.)

C/3/3/2/12   1571–1572
Edmund Flicke, Laurence Troste, Chamberlains
(1 vol., bound in 2 fols of MS with glossed text, possibly canon law, decorated in red and blue:
see Webb 1996, 12)

C/3/3/2/13   1572–1573
Oliver Cowper, William Jeffery, Chamberlains
(1 vol.)

C/3/3/2/14   1575–1576
John Knape, Robert Barker, Chamberlains
(1 vol.)

C/3/3/2/15   1576–1577
Thomas Gleade, Robert Snellinge, Chamberlains
(1 vol.)

C/3/3/2/16   1577–1578
Richard Goltye, Thomas Knappe, Chamberlains
(1 vol., bound in 1 fol. of MS, rubricated and decorated in red and blue)

C/3/3/2/17   1578–1579
Godfrey Woolnale, Edward Revett, Chamberlains
(1 vol., bound in 2 fols of MS, 1 incomplete, with musical notation, rubricated and decorated in
red and blue, and containing sections of the *Officium Defunctorum: In primo nocturno* with
plainsong, including the antiphon *Dirige Domine Deus meus* through the *Qui Lazarum* and
Libera me with readings interspersed: *see* Webb 1996, 12)

C/3/3/2/18   1579–1580
Nicholas Crane, John Carnabye, Chamberlains
(1 vol., bound in 2 fols of MS, probably of 15c. date, decorated in red and blue)

C/3/3/2/19   1580–1581
Samuel Smith and Thomas Eldred, Chamberlains
(1 vol.)

C/3/3/2/20   1582–1583
Thomas Sherman, Edward Cage, Chamberlains
Includes:
— memorandum of lease by Chamberlains of part of Great Marsh *alias* Leyham Marsh held of
manor of Stoke, following seizure from previous lessee, William Webb, merchant, an outlaw
(1 vol., apparently at one time sewn together with C/3/3/2/5–7, 9–19)

C/3/3/2/21   1583–1584
Robert Cutler, William Acton, Chamberlains
(1 vol., stitched together with C/3/3/2/22–25)

C/3/3/2/22   1584–1585
Robert Knapp, John Raynberd, Chamberlains
(1 vol., stitched together with C/3/3/2/21, 23–25)

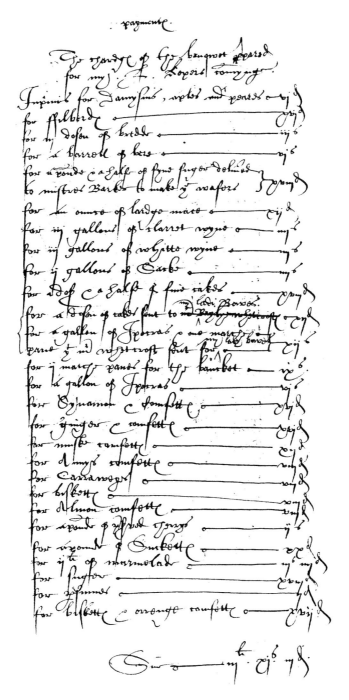

Fig. 12. 'The chardges of the banqwet prepared for my L[ord] Keper's commynge'
(From the Chamberlain's accounts for 1568–1569, C/3/3/2/9). Transcript in Webb
1996, 92.

C/3/3/2/23   1585–1586
Luke Melton, John Humfrey, Chamberlains
Includes:
— loose account of expenses of Mr Hawis, Edmond Flyck and Thomas Gleed in 'Rydyng to
London abowt the townes Busynes', reimbursed 27 May 1586
(1 vol., stitched togeher with C/3/3/2/21–22, 24–25)

C/3/3/2/24   1586–1587
Thomas Celie, Robert Halie, Chamberlains
(1 vol., stitched together with C/3/3/2/21–23, 25)

C/3/3/2/25   1587–1588
[William Sparrow, Christopher Laurence, Chamberlains]
(1 vol., stitched together with C/3/3/2/21–24)

C/3/3/2/26   1588–1589
John Sturgeon, John Ward, Chamberlains
Includes:
— payment of 5d for 'conters for the Awdett', a reference to the use of a 'counter table' and
counters, kept in the Treasury and used in compiling and auditing the accounts
(1 vol.)

C/3/3/2/27   1589–1590
Edward Huntynge, Richard Marten, Chamberlains
(1 vol., stitched to C/3/3/2/28)

C/3/3/2/28   1590–1591
John Toplyffe, George Parkhurst, Chamberlains
(1 vol., stitched to C/3/3/2/27)

C/3/3/2/29   1591–1592
William Cock, Richard Cornelles, Chamberlains
(1 vol.)

C/3/3/2/30   1592–1593
John Fairewether, Henry Ashly, Chamberlains
(1 vol.)

C/3/3/2/31   1598–1599
Thurston Ashley, Robert Scarlett, Chamberlains
(1 vol.)

C/3/3/2/32   1599–1600
Nicholas Groome, Richard Bateman, Chamberlains
(1 vol.)

C/3/3/2/33   1600–1601
John Boore, Phillip Dod, Chamberlains
Includes:
— inventories of recovered stolen property
(1 vol.)

C/3/3/2/34   1601–1602
Robert Nooth, Robert Cole, Chamberlains
Includes:
— entries (struck out, but fully legible) for 'presse mony given unto Souldiers' when men were
enlisted, probably for service in Ireland. Apparently some at least of the recruits had been prisoners freed from the town gaol. The costs involved were met from a local tax which was
ordered to be raised in Aug. 1602 from those inhabitants whose names were in the Subsidy
Book: see Assembly Book, C/4/3/1/3, ff. 98v, 124r, and Webb 1996, 146.
(1 vol.)

C/3/3/2/35   1603–1604
James Tyllott, Francis Crowe, Chamberlains
(1 vol.)

C/3/3/2/36   1604–1605
Owen Candler, Robert Benham, Chamberlains
(1 vol.)

C/3/3/2/37   1605–1606
John Manhoode, Richard Cocke, Chamberlains
(1 vol.)

C/3/3/2/38   1606–1607
William Cage, Edmond Daye, Chamberlains
(1 vol.)

C/3/3/2/39   1607–1608
Robert Goodinge, George Acton, Chamberlains
(1 vol.)

C/3/3/2/40   1608–1609
George Reymond, Thomas Johnson, Chamberlains
Includes:
— account of John Butler, meter, 1608–1609 and (on loose page) details of his 'chardges payd'
— receipt for 'charitable benevolence' collected in Ipswich for people of Bury St Edmunds 'for
their losses there lately susteyned by casualty of Fier' (loose page, pinned in)
(1 vol.)

C/3/3/2/41   1609–1610
Henry Buckenham, Thomas Hailes, Chamberlains
(1 vol.)

C/3/3/2/42   1610–1611
Thomas Woodgat, Christopher Alldgat, Chamberlains
(1 vol.)

C/3/3/2/43   1611–1612
John Randes, William Brydoun, Chamberlains
(1 vol.)

C/3/3/2/44   1612–1613
William Moysey, Benjamin Osmonde, Chamberlains
(1 vol.)

C/3/3/2/45   1614–1615
Edmund Keene, Joseph Parkhurst, Chamberlains
Includes:
— account of distribution to 8 parishes of £10 received from Bailiffs of Colchester (Essex) 'For
the gifte of Mr Hunt to be distributed amongst the poore in Ipswich'
(1 vol.)

C/3/3/2/46   1616–1617
Peter Cole, Thomas Ellett, Chamberlains
(1 vol.)

C/3/3/2/47   1617–1618
Thomas Selie, Henry Humfry, Chamberlains
Includes:
— account of money raised from wards and hamlets for maintenance of soldiers
(1 vol.)

C/3/3/2/48   1618–1619
John Blomefeild, Richard Pupplett, Chamberlains
(1 vol.)

C/3/3/2/49   1619–1620
John Barbur, Nicholas Freman, Chamberlains
(1 vol.)

C/3/3/2/50   1620
John Barbur, Nicholas Fremen, Chamberlains
Receipts and payments 'since the Audyte ended at Chrystmas 1620'
(1 vol.)

C/3/3/2/51   1620–1621
John Aldus, Edmond Humfry, Chamberlains
(1 vol., incomplete)

C/3/3/2/52   1623–1624
Richard Jeninges, Peter Alldus, Chamberlains
Includes:
— account of fines on brewers 'for laieinge in beere to unlicensed victellers', laid out for poor
relief
(1 vol.)

C/3/3/2/53   1624–1625
Edward Laverake, Robert Pinson [or Pinswayne], Chamberlains
(1 vol.)

C/3/3/2/54   1625–1626
John Alderman, Richard Herne, Chamberlains
(1 vol.)

C/3/3/2/55   1626–1627
Peter Fisher, Barnaby Burroughe, Chamberlains
Includes:
— schedule of sums outstanding in the account (loose page)
(1 vol.)

C/3/3/2/56   1627–1628
Edmund Allen, William Doggitt, Chamberlains
(1 vol.)

C/3/3/2/57   1629–1630
William Bull, William Sparrowe, Chamberlains
(1 vol.)

C/3/3/2/58   1630–1631
Nicholas Fillipes, Joseph Pemberton, Chamberlains
(1 vol.)

C/3/3/2/59   1631–1632
Robert Howe, John Blomfield, Chamberlains
(1 vol.)

C/3/3/2/60   1632–1633
William Markham, Robert Harvy, Chamberlains
Includes:
— memorandum *re* fines levied on brewers for delivering beer to unlicensed alehouse keepers,
and laid out in poor relief
(1 vol.)

C/3/3/2/61   1633–1634
John Smythier, John Blythe, Chamberlains
(1 vol.)

C/3/3/2/62   1634–1635
Thomas Knapp, Robert Dunkon, Chamberlains
(1 vol.)

C/3/3/2/63   1636–1637
Samuel Duncon, Henry Chapline, Chamberlains
Includes:
— memorandum as in C/3/3/2/60
— account of moneys to be abated out of the account (loose page)
(1 vol.)

C/3/3/2/64   1637–1638
Robert Clarke, Ellis Colman, Chamberlains
(1 vol.)

C/3/3/2/65   1638–1639
William Carewe *alias* Cooke, Mannuell Sorrell, Chamberlains
Includes:
— inventory of Mr Collett's [? a suicide] goods left in his house upon Mrs Collett's promise to
produce them to Bailiffs (loose page)
(1 vol.)

C/3/3/2/66   1639–1640
John Cole, Jonathan Fulcher, Chamberlains
(1 vol.)

C/3/3/2/67   1641–1642
Thomas Wright, Henry Parkhurst, Chamberlains
Payments such as 7s 4d 'for mendinge the windowes where the powder lies at the hospitall',
10s 5d for hooping the powder and match barrels, and 3s 4d to 'Browne the Cutler for making
cleane of swords' reflect the outbreak of the Civil War.
(1 vol.)

C/3/3/2/68   1644–1645
Richard Girlinge, Luke Jowers, Chamberlains
(1 vol.)

C/3/3/2/69   1645–1646
Robert Turner, Thomas [Newton], Chamberlains
(1 vol.)

C/3/3/2/70   1646–1647
John Raymond, Thomas Carter, Chamberlains
(1 vol.)

C/3/3/2/71   1647–1648
Robert Daines, Richard Sheppard, Chamberlains
(1 vol.)

C/3/3/2/72   1648–1649
Symond Cumberland, Isaac Daye, Chamberlains
Includes:
— memorandum *re* fines [? on brewers] laid out in poor relief
— valuation of anchor and cable on board the hoy 'Margett', taken in Feb. 1648 by Alexander
Stote, master of 'Premirose', 21 Dec. 1648 (loose page)
— list of allowances to Chamberlains on their account (loose page)
(1 vol.)

C/3/3/2/73   1649–1650
Samuel Carnabye, William Hawys, Chamberlains
(1 vol.)

C/3/3/2/74   1650–1651
Nicholas Sicklemore, Thomas Griggs, Chamberlains
(1 vol.)

C/3/3/2/75   1651–1652
Robert Sparham, Matthew Windes, Chamberlains
(1 vol.)

C/3/3/2/76   1652–1653
George Copping, Gilbert Lindfild, Chamberlains
(1 vol.)

C/3/3/2/77   1654–1655
William Feast, Edward Keene, Chamberlains
(1 vol.)

C/3/3/2/78   1655–1656
Richard Pemberton, John Denton, Chamberlains
(1 vol.)

C/3/3/2/79   1656–1657
William Weekly, Richard Clopton , Chamberlains
Includes:
— detailed accounts of payments 'For the proclamacion of his Highnesse the Lord Protector',
2 Jul. 1657
(1 vol.)

C/3/3/2/80   1657–1658
Charles Wright, John Pemberton, Chamberlains
(1 vol.)

C/3/3/2/81   1658–1659
William Cooke, Titus Camplaine, Chamberlains
(1 vol.)

C/3/3/2/82   1659–1660
Joseph Haymer, Thomas Wright, Chamberlains
Includes:
— detailed accounts of payments 'uppon the Proclemacion day of our Soveraigne Lord King
Charles the Second', 12 May 1660
(1 vol.)

C/3/3/2/83   1660–1661
John Sawyer, Richard Sparrow, Chamberlains
(1 vol.)

C/3/3/2/84   1661–1662
Robert Alldus, Edward Gaell, Chamberlains
(1 vol.)

C/3/3/2/85   1662–1663
John Jolley, James Storey, Chamberlains
(1 vol.)

C/3/3/2/86   1663–1664
Robert Hornigold, John Reeve, Chamberlains

Includes on loose pages:
— list of water rents
— petition for discharge for uncollected petty rents
— Treasurer's receipt for rents
(1 vol.)

C/3/3/2/87 James Harwell, Samuel Male, Chamberlains (1 vol.)	1664–1665
C/3/3/2/88 William Neave, William Sayer, Chamberlains (1 vol.)	1665–1666
C/3/3/2/89 Rowland Scofeild, Thomas Sidny, Chamberlains (1 vol.)	1666–1667
C/3/3/2/90 Thomas Bright, John Gibbon, Chamberlains (1 vol.)	1667–1668
C/3/3/2/91 John Wade, Richard Beaumond, Chamberlains (1 vol.)	1669–1670
C/3/3/2/92 George Girlinge, Robert Cockrell, Chamberlains (1 vol.)	1670–1671
C/3/3/2/93 Christopher Fincham, John Blomfeild, Chamberlains (1 vol.)	1671–1672
C/3/3/2/94 Thomas Bantoft, Robert Hovel *alias* Smith, Chamberlains (1 vol.)	1673–1674
C/3/3/2/95 John Sayer, John Hovall *alias* Smyth, Chamberlains (1 vol.)	1674–1675
C/3/3/2/96 Robert Small, Richard Thurston, Chamberlains (1 vol.)	1675–1676
C/3/3/2/97 William Cole, John Jeffery, Chamberlains (1 vol.)	1677–1678
C/3/3/2/98 James Page, Benjamin Beaumont, Chamberlains (1 vol.)	1678–1679
C/3/3/2/99 Charles Rederish, Eleazer Duncon, Chamberlains (1 vol.)	1682–1683
C/3/3/2/100 Keble Crosse, Israell Barrell, Chamberlains (1 vol.)	1683–1684

C/3/3/2/101   1684–1685
James Phillips, Stephen Searson, Chamberlains
Includes:
— payments 'for things layd in against the Assizes' [though the Assizes in this period were
usually held at Bury St Edmunds, the court did occasionally meet in Ipswich; on this occasion
Lord Chief Justice Jeffreys presided: *see* Redstone 1948, 102, and Allen 1997, 37–38.]
(1 vol.)

C/3/3/2/102   1685–1686
Henry Hill, Henry Bond, Chamberlains
Includes:
— payment of 7s 6d to William Tydeman 'for Ringinge uppon the news of taking Buda'
[Charles of Lorraine captured Buda for the Habsburg Monarchy on 22 Sep. 1686, ending 145
years of Turkish rule.]
(1 vol.)

C/3/3/2/103   1686–1687
John Gulson, Samuel Rudkin, Chamberlains
(1 vol.)

C/3/3/2/104   1687–1688
Thomas Jeffery, Joseph Colman, Chamberlains
(1 vol.)

C/3/3/2/105   1688–1689
Cooper Gravenor, Jonathan Quintin, Chamberlains
Includes:
— payments for expenses of proclamation of William III and Mary II, and of their Coronation
(1 vol.)

C/3/3/2/106   1689–1690
Thomas Searles, Thomas King, Chamberlains
(1 vol.)

C/3/3/2/107   1690–1691
Robert Newton, Edward Melsupp, Chamberlains
(1 vol.)

C/3/3/2/108   1691–1692
John Long, Jacob Hudson, Chamberlains
(1 vol.)

C/3/3/2/109   1692–1693
Thomas Gall, Thomas May, Chamberlains
(1 vol.)

C/3/3/2/110   1693–1694
Salter Burrage, John Canting, Chamberlains
(1 vol.)

C/3/3/2/111   1695–1696
Peter Butcher, John Norris, Chamberlains
(1 vol.)

C/3/3/2/112   1696–1697
Samuel Hambling, John Choate, Chamberlains
(1 vol.)

C/3/3/2/113   1696–1697
Samuel Hambling, John Choate, Chamberlains
(1 vol.; another copy, incomplete)

Fig.13. (*Above*) Suppression of Conventicles: John Langston 'keepinge an unlawful Conventicle in his house 1 Feb [16]83' (General Sessions 19 July 1684 in Process Book of Indictments 1683–87, C/2/9/1/1/4/1)
(*Below*) Laid out when King William came to towne ['to' altered to 'thorrow']
(from Chamberlains' audited accounts, 1692–93, C/3/3/2/109)

221

C/3/3/2/114   1697–1698
Thomas Burwell, Henry Smyth, Chamberlains
(1 vol.)

C/3/3/2/115   1698–1699
John Groome, John Jolly, Chamberlains
(1 vol.)

C/3/3/2/116   1699–1700
John Browne, Nicholas Cooke, Chamberlains
(1 vol.)

C/3/3/2/117   1700–1701
Henry Nash, Samuel Smith, Chamberlains
(1 vol.)

C/3/3/2/118   1701–1702
Matthew Goodwin, Lionel Ward, Chamberlains
(1 vol.)

C/3/3/2/119   1702–1703
George Girling, John Clarke, Chamberlains
(1 vol.)

C/3/3/2/120   1704–1705
David Sare, James Cole, Chamberlains
(1 vol.)

C/3/3/2/121   1705–1706
James Southgeat, Robert Marston, Chamberlains
(1 vol.)

C/3/3/2/122   1706–1707
John Buck, Christopher Thorne, Chamberlains
(1 vol.)

C/3/3/2/123   1707–1708
John Holbrough, John Prige, Chamberlains
(1 vol.)

C/3/3/2/124   1708–1709
John Richer, Charles Nuthall, Chamberlains
(1 vol.)

C/3/3/2/125   1709–1710
Edward Hubbard, John Fowle, Chamberlains
(1 vol.)

C/3/3/2/126   1711–1712
Matthew Wealy, William Clark, Chamberlains
(1 vol.)

C/3/3/2/127   1712–1713
Richard Smartt, Daniel Heckford, Chamberlains
(1 vol.)

C/3/3/2/128   1713–1714
Samuel Hamblin, Thomas May, Chamberlains
(1 vol.)

C/3/3/2/129   1714–1715
Edward Syer, Thomas Grimwood, Chamberlains
(1 vol.)

C/3/3/2/130   1715–1716
John May, Tobias Searson, Chamberlains
(1 vol.)

C/3/3/2/131   1716–1717
William Scott, Edward Duck, Chamberlains
(1 vol.)

C/3/3/2/132   1717–1718
Samuel Parker, John Chaplin, Chamberlains
(1 vol.)

C/3/3/2/133   1718–1719
Hugh Wright, Thomas Wilder, Chamberlains
(1 vol.)

C/3/3/2/134   1719–1720
Nathaniel Parsey, Thomas Foulser, Chamberlains
(1 vol.)

C/3/3/2/135   1720–1721
Daniel Bond, James Betts, Chamberlains
(1 vol.)

C/3/3/2/136   1721–1722
Thomas Booth, John Plaice, Chamberlains
(1 vol.)

C/3/3/2/137   1722–1723
Joseph Rand, John Boore, Chamberlains
(1 vol.)

C/3/3/2/138   1723–1724
John Jermyn, Edward Clarke, Chamberlains
(1 vol.)

C/3/3/2/139   1725–1726
Roger Goodchild, Benjamin Freshfield, Chamberlains
(1 vol.)

C/3/3/2/140   1727–1728
Thomas Driver, William Leman, Chamberlains
(1 vol.)

C/3/3/2/141   1728–1729
John Bumpsted, Henry Bond, Chamberlains
(1 vol.)

C/3/3/2/142   1729–1730
William Hallum, Christopher Mallet, Chamberlains
(1 vol.)

C/3/3/2/143   1730–1731
Jonathan Bradstreet, Edward Clarke, Chamberlains
(1 vol.)

C/3/3/2/144   1731–1732
Michael Thurkle, John Blythe, Chamberlains
(1 vol.)

C/3/3/2/145   1733–1734
Samuel Goldsbury, Isaac Carneby, Chamberlains; the name of Thomas Golding is associated
with them on the front cover.
(1 vol.)

C/3/3/2/146   1734–1735
Cooper Gravenor, Cornelius Goldsbury, Chamberlains
(1 vol.)

C/3/3/2/147   1735–1736
John Thorndike, Benjamin Rowning, Chamberlains
(1 vol.)

C/3/3/2/148   1736–1737
Samuel Stead, Joseph Clarke, Chamberlains
(1 vol.)

C/3/3/2/149   1737–1738
James Grant, William Wade, Chamberlains
(1 vol.)

C/3/3/2/150   1738–1739
Edward Bacon, John Plummer, Chamberlains
(1 vol.)

C/3/3/2/151   1738–1739
Edward Bacon, John Plummer, Chamberlains
(1 vol.; duplicate)

C/3/3/2/152   1739–1740
John Elliston, William Usher, Chamberlains
(1 vol.)

C/3/3/2/153   1740–1741
William Bedwell, James Raimond, Chamberlains
(1 vol.)

C/3/3/2/154   1741–1742
Richard Batley, Robert Castons, Chamberlains
(1 vol.)

C/3/3/2/155   1742–1743
John Savage, Edward Duck jun., Chamberlains
(1 vol.)

C/3/3/2/156   1744–1745
Thomas Crick, Samuel Lane, Chamberlains
(1 vol.)

C/3/3/2/157   1745–1746
Charles Norris, John Garrod, Chamberlains
(1 vol.)

C/3/3/2/158   1746–1747
Jacob Rix, James Blythe, Chamberlains
(1 vol.)

C/3/3/2/159   1747–1748
William Wade, William Tye, Chamberlains
(1 vol.)

C/3/3/2/160   1748–1749
John Hammond, Joseph Clarke jun, Chamberlains
(1 vol.)

C/3/3/2/161   1749–1750
Joseph Frost, Christopher Skidmore, Chamberlains
(1 vol.)

C/3/3/2/162   1750–1751
William Robinson, Robert Robinson, Chamberlains
(1 vol.)

C/3/3/2/163   1751–1752
John Levers, Israel Murton, Chamberlains
(1 vol.)

C/3/3/2/164   1752–1753
Othniel Frost, John Boardman, Chamberlains
(1 vol.)

C/3/3/2/165   1753–1754
Robert Manning, Edward Bets, Chamberlains
(1 vol.)

C/3/3/2/166   1754–1755
William Blichenden, John Forsett, Chamberlains
(1 vol.)

C/3/3/2/167   1755–1756
Henry Boyzard, John Thorndike jun, Chamberlains
(1 vol.)

C/3/3/2/168   1756–1757
John Clarke, Thomas Nuttol, Chamberlains
(1 vol.)

C/3/3/2/169   1757–1758
John Tyrrell, Samuel Thorndike, Chamberlains
(1 vol.)

C/3/3/2/170   1758–1759
William Norris, Samuel Howes, Chamberlains
(1 vol.)

C/3/3/2/171   1759–1760
Edward Bacon, William Keeble, Chamberlains
(1 vol.)

C/3/3/2/172   1759–1760
Edward Bacon, William Keeble, Chamberlains
(1 vol.; incomplete duplicate)

C/3/3/2/173   1760–1761
Edmund Wade, Robert Thorndike, Chamberlains
(1 vol.)

C/3/3/2/174   1763–1764
Richard Slythe, Edward Martin, Chamberlains
(1 vol.)

C/3/3/2/175   1764–1765
Edward Bond, John Gooding, Chamberlains
(1 vol.)

C/3/3/2/176   1765–1766
George Brame, John Denny, Chamberlains
(1 vol.)

C/3/3/2/177   1767–1768
Joseph Cole, Miles Lane, Chamberlains
(1 vol.)

C/3/3/2/178   1768–1769
Samuel Harrison, John Young, Chamberlains
(1 vol.)

C/3/3/2/179   1769–1770
John Howes, Thomas Read, Chamberlains
(1 vol.)

C/3/3/2/180   1770–1771
James Coe jun., Rix Clarke, Chamberlains
(1 vol.)

C/3/3/2/181   1771–1772
Benjamin Brame, William Goodchild, Chamberlains
(1 vol.)

C/3/3/2/182   1774–1775
Edward Hayward, George Durrant, Chamberlains
(1 vol.)

C/3/3/2/183   1775–1776
Robert Manning, John Brook, Chamberlains
(1 vol.)

C/3/3/2/184   1776–1777
John Spooner, Robert Garwood, Chamberlains
(1 vol.)

C/3/3/2/185   1776–1777
John Spooner, Robert Garwood, Chamberlains
(1 vol.; duplicate)

C/3/3/2/186   1770–1780
Benjamin Parkhurst, Edward Wiles, Chamberlains
(1 vol.)

C/3/3/2/187   1780–1781
John Harrison, Robert Small, Chamberlains
(1 vol.)

C/3/3/2/188   1781–1782
Thomas Lane, John Chaplin, Chamberlains
(1 vol.)

C/3/3/2/189   1782–1783
Thomas Willson, Thomas Frost, Chamberlains
(1 vol.)

C/3/3/2/190   1783–1784
Robert Battley, Joseph Pooley, Chamberlains
(1 vol.)

C/3/3/2/191   1784–1785
Stephen Bumstead, Barnaby Sheppard, Chamberlains
(1 vol.)

C/3/3/2/192   1786–1787
Samuel Thorndike, Benjamin Catt, Chamberlains
(1 vol.)

C/3/3/2/193   1787–1788
James Garrod, Chamberlain; for 29 Sep. 1787–25 Mar. 1788 only
(1 vol.)

C/3/3/2/194   1788
John Gooding, Chamberlain; for 25 Mar.–29 Sep. 1788 only
(1 vol.)

C/3/3/2/195   1788–1789
George Durrant, Chamberlain; for 29 Sep. 1788–25 Mar. 1789 only
(1 vol.)

C/3/3/2/196   1788–1789
Barlee Garwood, Chamberlain (with G. Durrant)
(1 vol.)

C/3/3/2/197   1790–1791
John Forsett, Chamberlain; for 29 Sep. 1790–25 Mar. 1791
(1 vol.)

C/3/3/2/198   1791
Robert Chaplin, Chamberlain; for 25 Mar.–29 Sep. 1791
(1 vol.)

C/3/3/2/199   1791–1792
Daniel Simpson, Chamberlain
(1 vol.)

C/3/3/2/200   1791–1792
John Finch, Chamberlain; for 29 Sep. 1791–25 Mar. 1792
(1 vol.)

C/3/3/2/201   1792–1793
William Downs, Chamberlain
(1 vol.)

C/3/3/2/202   1792–1793
D Raymond, Chamberlain
(1 vol.)

C/3/3/2/203   1794–1795
Benjamin Channing, Benjamin Palmer Green, Chamberlains
(1 vol.)

C/3/3/2/204   1795–1796
Charles Batley, William Norris jun, Chamberlains
(1 vol.)

C/3/3/2/205   1796–1797
Samuel Bagley, James Gooding, Chamberlains
(1 vol.)

C/3/3/2/206   1797–1798
William Chaplin, Richard Bruce, Chamberlains
(1 vol.)

C/3/3/2/207   1811–1812
William Callum, Robert Scarlott, Chamberlains
(1 vol.)

C/3/3/2/208   1812–1813
John Lamb, John Finch, Chamberlains
(1 vol.)

C/3/3/3   VOUCHERS AND RELATED PAPERS   **1730–1791**

Annual bundles, the documents formerly filed on a lace; some include parchment rentals
(usually those for shops and certain of the more important Corporation properties such as Stoke
and Handford Mills, the Town House, Custom House and crane, and the Corporation marshes),
which were originally wrapped around the bundles to form covers. Petty rentals, water rentals
and other accounts also occur in some bundles. Regular payments include those for Land Tax,
provision of charity bread, wine for Corporation hospitality, use of the pulpit and desk in
St Mary le Tower church for the Town Preacher or Lecturer, salaries of officers including the
Serjeants-at-Mace, Master and Usher of the Grammar School, Town Preacher, Town Crier
(whose duties also included 'setting the psalm'), Clerk of St Mary le Tower, and Flesh Warden,
fees to the bell-ringers on royal anniversaries and occasions, and expenses in connexion with
the town races.

C/3/3/3/1   1730–1731
[Edward] Clarke and [Jonathan] Breadstreet, Chamberlains
Includes:
— rental
— vouchers for repair and furniture of town boat
(100 docs)

C/3/3/3/2   1731–1732
Includes:
— Foreign Fines assessment for N, S, E and W wards
— voucher for payment for use of cart 'when Lee was whipped by order of Sessions'
— voucher for broad ribbon for the 'town musick'
— voucher for hire of coach to Bury Assizes for Corporation witnesses
(99 docs)

C/3/3/3/3   1732–1733
(90 docs)

C/3/3/3/4   1733–1734
Samuel Goldsbury, [Thomas] Golding, Chamberlains
Includes:
— rental
— voucher for repairs to both Bailiffs' maces
— voucher for 'ribbands for the Town Musick'
(83 docs)

C/3/3/3/5   1734–1735
Cooper Gravenor, Cornelius Goldsbury, Chamberlains
Includes:
— rental
(78 docs)

C/3/3/3/6   1735–1736
John Thorndike, Benjamin Rowning, Chamberlains
Includes:
— rental
(83 docs)

C/3/3/3/7   1736–1737
Samuel Stead, Joseph Clarke, Chamberlains
Includes:
— rental (incomplete)
(83 docs)

C/3/3/3/8   1737–1738
William Wade, James Grant, Chamberlains
Includes:
— rental (incomplete)
(69 docs)

C/3/3/3/9   1738–1739
John Plummer, Edward Bacon, Chamberlains
Includes:
— rental
(86 docs)

C/3/3/3/10   1740–1741
William Bedwell, James Raymond, Chamberlains
Includes:
— rental (butchers' shops only)
— voucher for supply of fireworks (sky rockets, Catherine wheels and 'sarpons' [serpents])
(90 docs)

C/3/3/3/11   1741–1742
Richard Batley, Robert Caston, Chamberlains
Includes:
— voucher for supply of fireworks (sky rockets, Catherine wheels, serpents and line runners)
(90 docs)

C/3/3/3/12   1742–1743
Edward Duck, John Savage, Chamberlains
(84 docs)

C/3/3/3/13   1743–1744
John Lane, Samuel Howes, Chamberlains
(75 docs)

C/3/3/3/14   1744–1745
Samuel Lane, Thomas Crick, Chamberlains
Includes:
— rental
— voucher for carpentry including construction of guard room under the 'Mutt Hoal' [Moot
Hall]
(86 docs)

C/3/3/3/15   1745–1746
Charles Norris, John Garrod, Chamberlains
Includes:
— voucher for overhauling [fire] engine
(78 docs)

C/3/3/3/16   1746–1747
Jacob Rix, James Blythe jun., Chamberlains
(89 docs)

C/3/3/3/17   1747–1748
William Wade, William Tye, Chamberlains
(78 docs)

C/3/3/3/18   1748–1749
Joseph Clarke jun., John Hammond, Chamberlains
Includes:
— agreement between Bailiffs and Benjamin Smith, tenant of Handford Mill, for Smith to
repair tiling and ruinous 'lean-to' of mill, in return for rent reduction, 31 Jul. 1749
(99 docs)

C/3/3/3/19   1749–1750
Joseph Frost, Christopher Skidmore, Chamberlains
Includes:
— 'A bill of charges for the highwayman's horse'
(86 docs)

C/3/3/3/20   1750–1751
William Robinson, Robert Robinson, Chamberlains
Includes:
— voucher 'For binding the maps of the estates belonging to the Corporation of Ipswich',
5 Mar. 1751
(93 docs)

C/3/3/3/21   1751–1752
John Lever, Israel Murton, Chamberlains
(96 docs)

C/3/3/3/22   1752–1753
John Bordman, Otheniel Frost, Chamberlains
(85 docs)

C/3/3/3/23   1753–1754
Robert Manning, Edward Betts, Chamberlains
Includes:
— list of freemen (107 in number), 1754
(79 docs)

C/3/3/3/24   1754–1755
John Forsett, William Blickenden, Chamberlains
(81 docs)

C/3/3/3/25   1755–1756
Henry Boyzard, John Thorndike jun., Chamberlains
Includes:
— bond from Corporation to Benjamin Smith, tenant of Handford Mill, for payment of debt of
£106 with interest, in annual instalments of £10, 10 May 1751
(88 docs)

C/3/3/3/26   1756–1757
John Clarke, Thomas Nuthall, Chamberlains
(98 docs)

C/3/3/3/27   1757–1758
John Tyrrell, Samuel Thorndike, Chamberlains
Includes:
— voucher for payment to constables 'for their trouble in going about the town to prevent the
pernicious practice of throwing at cocks', 6 Feb. 1758
(98 docs)

C/3/3/3/28   1758–1759
William Norris, Samuel Howes, Chamberlains
(103 docs)

C/3/3/3/29   1759–1760
William Keeble, Edward Bacon, Chamberlains
(116 docs)

C/3/3/3/30   1761–1762
Benjamin Chenery, Samuel Rudland, Chamberlains
Includes:
— voucher for 'wine at the declaration of war against Spain', 15 Jan. 1762
— voucher 'for ringing on account of the news of the whole island of Martinico [Martinique]
having surrendered', 3 Apr. 1762
— printed bill-head detailing articles manufactured at Nacton Workhouse and sold by the
Guardians there and at their warehouse at Mr William Truelove's in the Butter Market,
Ipswich, 5 Dec. 1761
(112 docs)

C/3/3/3/31   1762–1763
Miles Wallis, William Clarke, Chamberlains
(100 docs)

C/3/3/3/32   1763–1764
Richard Slythe, Edward Martin, Chamberlains
(97 docs)

C/3/3/3/33   1764–1765
John Gooding, Edward Bond, Chamberlains
(84 docs)

C/3/3/3/34   1765–1766
George Brame, John Denny, Chamberlains
(106 docs)

C/3/3/3/35   1766–1767
Cornelius Goldsbury, Christopher Rolfe, Chamberlains
(101 docs)

C/3/3/3/36   1767–1768
Miles Lane, Joseph Cole, Chamberlains
Includes:
— rental
(96 docs)

C/3/3/3/37   1768–1769
John Young, [Samuel] Harrison, Chamberlains
(101 docs)

C/3/3/3/38   1769–1770
John Howes, Thomas Read jun., Chamberlains
Includes:
— rental
(102 docs)

C/3/3/3/39   1770–1771
James Coe jun., Rix Clarke, Chamberlains
Includes:
— rental
— petty rental
— water rental
(110 docs)

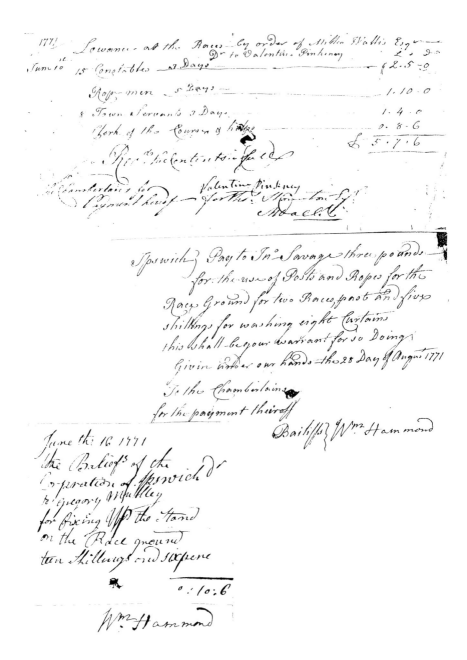

Fig. 14. Expenses of Ipswich Races, 1771. (From Chamberlains' vouchers, C/3/3/3/39)

C/3/3/3/40   1771–1772
Benjamin Brame, William Goodchild, Chamberlains
Includes:
— rental
(97 docs)

C/3/3/3/41   1773–1774
William Lane, Pearl Betts, Chamberlains
(82 docs)

C/3/3/3/42   1774–1775
George Durrant, Edmund Hayward, Chamberlains
Includes:
— detailed bills for repair work to town water supply, 1774–1776
(78 docs)

C/3/3/3/43   1775–1776
Robert Manning jun., John Brooke Dorkin, Chamberlains
(85 docs)

C/3/3/3/44   1776–1777
John Spooner, Robert Garwood (Garrod/Garrard) jun., Chamberlains
Includes:
— detailed bill for repair work to town water supply, 1777
(83 docs)

C/3/3/3/45   1777–1778
Samuel Hamblin, John Savage, Chamberlains
Includes:
— rental
— cash account book including list of defaulters on water rent roll
— water rental (vol.)
(80 docs)

C/3/3/3/46   1778–1779
William Hayward, Samuel Marchant, Chamberlains
Includes:
— rental
— cash account book including list of rents unpaid upon the water rent roll
— water rental (vol.)
(84 docs)

C/3/3/3/47   1779–1780
Benjamin Parkhurst, Edward Wiles, Chamberlains
Includes:
— rental
(81 docs)

C/3/3/3/48   1780–1781
John Harrison, Robert Small, Chamberlains
Includes:
— rental
— detailed bills for repair work to town water supply, 1781
(80 docs)

C/3/3/3/49   1781–1782
John Chaplin, Thomas Lane, Chamberlains
Includes:
— rental

— trade card of Taylor and Co. for the Ipswich and Norwich New Coach, with details of route, times and fares, n.d. (endorsed with receipt, 28 Nov. 1782)
(95 docs)

C/3/3/3/50   1782–1783
Thomas Frost, Thomas Wilson, Chamberlains
(76 docs)

C/3/3/3/51   1783–1784
Robert Batley, Joseph Pooley, Chamberlains
(100 docs)

C/3/3/3/52   1784–1785
Steven Bumpstead, B. Sheppard, Chamberlains
Includes the following documents relating to the year of office of Robert Graves and Samuel
Howes jun, Chamberlains for 1785–1786:
— rental, 1785–1786
— water rental, 1785–1786
— cash account book including list of rents unpaid on the water rent roll, 1785–1786, the cover
formed from printed 'Proposals for the Ipswich Subscription Concerts for the Year 1786'
(87 docs)

C/3/3/3/53   1785–1786
Robert Graves, Samuel Howes jun., Chamberlains
For the rental, water rental and cash account book for their year of office, *see* C/3/3/3/52
(93 docs)

C/3/3/3/54   1790–1791
  Robert Chaplin, John Forsett, Chamberlains
(34 docs; found among the records of the Collector of the Water Rents)

C/3/3/4 PETTY RENTALS   1499–1792

(The earliest Petty Rental now surviving (apparently for 1415) is stitched to the first membrane
(C/2/1/1/3) of the Portmanmote roll for 1 Edw. I (1273). The two documents were united at a
time when they were out of official custody: the stitching is modern.)
    C/3/3/4/1–2, which are in book form, apparently record petty rents due for pieces of common
soil within the twelve urban parishes. The properties are arranged by wards, and apparently in
topographical order, with the abuttals given. Details include later alterations in the names of
tenants and marginal notes *re* tenants' evidences of title. C/3/3/4/3–37 are in the form of parchment rolls, made up 'Exchequer' style (except those for the years 1765–1775, which are in the
form of paper books). They record the rents due from properties in the twelve urban parishes
and Whitton. For other similar rentals, *see* the Chamberlains' vouchers, C/3/3/3.

C/3/3/4/1   26 Aug. 1499, 20 Jan. 1542
Includes:
— (f. 8) memorandum of agreement at a General Court, between Thomas Baldry and John
Forgon, for sharing payment of accustomed rent for piece of land lately of John Lunte, 1514
— (enclosed between ff. 13 and 14) indented inventory of goods in the Town House delivered
by 'Father Hoye' to Arthur Butler, n.d. [16c.]
— (enclosed between ff. 45 and 46) memorandum of 2 grants by the Headboroughs, to be
entered, n.d.
— (f. 55v) memorandum of tenements held of the Corporation in Bramford by Robert Cook,
husbandman, Joan Kenton, widow and Thomas Carter, smith, all of Bramford, by indentures of
8 Jul. 1548
— (f. 57) memorandum of sums due to town by will of Mr Ropkyn, by will of Mistress Wyldes
for repair of Bourne Bridge, and from John Alen, 'somtyme Collectour of this town'
(2 rentals, bound together in parchment covers, with a single sequence of modern foliation)

C/3/3/4/2   n.d. [? 1570]
Formerly considered to date from the 17th century, but comparison with briefer Petty Rentals
in the memorandum book of Corporation revenues, 1565–1668 (C/3/2/2/1) suggests an earlier
date. Internal evidence suggests that the rental was made as a result of the order of 6 Mar. 1570
that the Bailiffs should settle the rents to be paid by tenants of common soil (*see* Richardson
1884, 285).
(1 vol.)

C/3/3/4/3   1637
(1 roll of 3 membranes)

C/3/3/4/4   1642
(1 roll of 2 membranes)

C/3/3/4/5   1654
(1 roll of 4 membranes)

C/3/3/4/6   1668
(1 roll of 8 membranes)

C/3/3/4/7   1672
(1 roll of 2 membranes)

C/3/3/4/8   1720
(1 roll of 3 membranes)

C/3/3/4/9   1722
Endorsed: 'Memorand' to make mencon on the mergeant and sett downe the present tenents
names of all the houses in this rentall least the towne should hereafter be ignorant how to find
out the houses and so loose the rents.'
(1 roll of 2 membranes)

C/3/3/4/10   1730
(1 roll of 2 membranes)

C/3/3/4/11   1731
(1 roll of 2 membranes)

C/3/3/4/12   1732
(1 roll of 2 membranes)

C/3/3/4/13   1733
(1 roll of 2 membranes)

C/3/3/4/14   1734
(1 roll of 2 membranes)

C/3/3/4/15   1735
(1 roll of 2 membranes)

C/3/3/4/16   1736
(1 roll of 2 membranes)

C/3/3/4/17   1737
(1 roll of 3 membranes)

C/3/3/4/18   1738
(1 roll of 2 membranes)

C/3/3/4/19   1744
(1 roll of 2 membranes)

C/3/3/4/20   1745
(1 roll of 2 membranes)

C/3/3/4/21   1748
(1 roll of 2 membranes)

C/3/3/4/22   1751
(1 roll of 2 membranes)

C/3/3/4/23   1752
(1 roll of 2 membranes)

C/3/3/4/24   1753
(1 roll of 2 membranes)

C/3/3/4/25   1754
(1 roll of 2 membranes)

C/3/3/4/26   1757
(1 roll of 2 membranes)

C/3/3/4/27   n.d. [?1758]
(1 roll of 2 membranes)

C/3/3/4/28   1759
(1 roll of 2 membranes)

C/3/3/4/29   1765
(1 vol.)

C/3/3/4/30   1768
(1 vol.)

C/3/3/4/31   1769
(1 vol.)

C/3/3/4/32   1774
(1 vol., incomplete: ME and Whitton parishes missing)

C/3/3/4/33   1775
(1 vol.)

C/3/3/4/34   1785
(1 roll of 1 membrane; found with Chamberlains' account for 1783–1784)

C/3/3/4/35   1789
(1 double fol.; found with Chamberlains' accounts)

C/3/3/4/36   1791
(1 roll of 1 membrane; found with the water rent accounts)

C/3/3/4/37   1792
Includes:
— annexed account of dues collected in the butter and fruit market, Mar.–Aug. 1792
(2 docs)

C/3/3/5   RENTALS FOR THE MAJOR PROPERTIES   1732–1758

These properties, separated from the Petty Rentals, include Stoke Mill, Handford Mill, the
Town House, Leather Hall, Custom House, crane (on the Common Quay), town marshes and
butchers' shops.

C/3/3/5/1   1732
(1 roll of 1 membrane)

C/3/3/5/2   1756
(1 roll of 1 membrane)

C/3/3/5/3   1758
(1 roll of 1 membrane)

C/3/3/6   MISCELLANEA   n.d.

C/3/3/6/1   n.d. [? *c.* 1774]
Chamberlains' draft receipts
For fee-farm rent from Robert Edgar, esq.; salary from royal grant to Master of Grammar
School; and salary from royal grant to Usher of Grammar School; all for 1740–1774
(1 doc.)

C/3/4   RECORDS OF THE TREASURER   1558–1836

On the origin and functions of the office of Treasurer, *see* the general introductory note to
FINANCE AND TOWN PROPERTY.

C/3/4/1   AUDITED ACCOUNTS   1558–1836

Most bear the signatures and many the alterations of the auditors. The receipts sometimes
include the names of those paying fines (including 'Freedom' fines and fines to be excused
office), or making payments for 'the growndage of mylne stones that come to the towne', in
addition to those who pay rents for certain larger properties and who are regularly named.
Details of payments for alehouse licences are common after 1650. In addition to the wages,
liveries and fees of officers, the payments generally contain details of expenditure on public
works, the financing of which seems to have been the Treasurer's responsibility, although
examination of the Chamberlains' accounts and vouchers indicates that the areas of responsibility were far from being rigidly demarcated in practice.

   Unless otherwise stated, the accounts are for a period of 1 year, from Michaelmas (29 Sep.)
to Michaelmas. Similar accounts, filed with the Treasurers' vouchers, may be found in that
series (C/3/4/4).

C/3/4/1/1   1557–1558
John Dyer, Treasurer (and Bailiff)
Includes:
— detailed payments for repair and provisioning of the ship 'James of Orwell' and for arming
and equipping soldiers
(1 vol.)

C/3/4/1/2   11 Dec. 1559–9 Dec. 1560
Robert Fyske and Edmund Leche, Treasurers
Includes:
— account of a rate on 'foreigners' (named), for providing soldiers to serve in Scotland
— account of scot and lot collected from freemen (named), living out of the town
— detailed payments for arming and equipping 40 (named) soldiers
(1 vol. Bound in folio from a liturgical text, rubricated, with ornamental capitals in blue)

C/3/4/1/3   Dec. 1562–13 Dec. 1563
Edmund Leche and Robert Sparrowe, Treasurers

Includes:
— detailed payments for arming and equipping 20 soldiers, Jun. 1563
(1 vol.)

C/3/4/1/4   1564–1565
Robert Sallowes, Treasurer
(1 vol.)

C/3/4/1/5   1565–1566
Robert Sallowes, Treasurer
(1 vol.)

C/3/4/1/6   Dec. 1567–12 Dec. 1568
Robert Sallowes, Treasurer
(1 vol.)

C/3/4/1/7   [1573–1574]
[Christopher Ward, Treasurer]
(1 vol.)

C/3/4/1/8   1574–1575
Christopher Ward, Treasurer
(1 vol.)

C/3/4/1/9   1575–1576
Christopher Ward, Treasurer
(1 vol.)

C/3/4/1/10   1576–1577
Henry Hannam, Treasurer
(1 vol., bound in 2 fols of a 15th-century legal text)

C/3/4/1/11   1577–1578
Henry Hannam, Treasurer
Includes:
— payments for repairs to the gaol 'uppon the breche thereof bi certen prisoners', Nov. 1577
— payments for repairs to the butchers' stalls 'after certen of there shoppes were broken up and robbed', Nov. 1577
(1 vol., bound in 2 fols of MS, rubricated, with capitals decorated in gold leaf and blue; apparently from the same volume as the covers to C/3/4/1/12 and 13)

C/3/4/1/12   1578–1579
Henry Hannam, Treasurer
Includes:
— inventory of town goods (including arms) delivered by Hannam to his successor William Mydnall at the audit, Dec. 1579
(1 vol., bound as C/3/4/1/11)

C/3/4/1/13   1579–1580
William Mydnall, Treasurer
Includes:
— inventory of furniture and 'nesseasareres' of the town (including arms) in Mydnall's custody
— inventory of necessaries belonging to the gaol in the Gaoler's custody
(1 vol., bound as C/3/4/1/11)

C/3/4/1/14   1580–1581
William Mydnall, Treasurer
Includes:
— inventory of furniture and goods (including arms) of the town in the Treasurer's custody

— inventory of necessaries belonging to the gaol in the Gaoler's custody
(1 vol., bound in 2 fols of a theological text, ?*c.* 1300)

C/3/4/1/15   1581–1582
William Mydnall, Treasurer
Includes:
— Treasurer's account book for 1616, shown to Richard Crowe upon his examination to the
11th interrogatory on the plaintiff's part, 6 Apr. 1654
(2 vols in 1 cover formed from 2 fols of a theological text, rubricated, with capitals decorated in
blue, n.d.)

C/3/4/1/16   1582–1583
William Mydnall, Treasurer
Includes:
— list of bonds in the Treasurer's custody
(1 vol., bound in 2 fols of a theological text, rubricated, with capitals alternately in blue and red,
n.d.)

C/3/4/1/17   1583–1586
Accounts for 3 years, sewn together

C/3/4/1/17/1   1583–1584
William Mydnall, Treasurer
(1 vol., bound in 2 fols of a theological text, rubricated, with capitals decorated in blue)

C/3/4/1/17/2   1584–1585
William Mydnall, Treasurer
Includes:
— account of expenditure on 'the poore, sycke and infected persons'
— account of 'charges bestowed at the sycke howse'
— account for arming and equipping 6 (named) soldiers
(1 vol.)

C/3/4/1/17/3   1585–1586
William Mydnall, Treasurer
Includes:
— account of expenditure on 'poore and infected persons'
— inventory of goods (including arms) in Treasurer's custody
— inventory of weights and measures in Clerk of the Market's custody
— inventory of goods in Beadle's custody
— inventory of contents of gaol in Gaoler's custody
(1 vol.)

C/3/4/1/18   1586–1587
Thomas Gleed, Treasurer
(1 vol.)

C/3/4/1/19   1588–1589
Edward Cage, Treasurer
Includes:
— memorandum by Cage *re* disposition of money received by him by order of the Sessions, for
the use of the poor in [Christ's] Hospital, Sep. 1589
(1 vol.)

C/3/4/1/20   1589–1590
Edward Cage, Treasurer
Includes:
— memorandum on the same subject as that in C/3/4/1/19
(1 vol.)

C/3/4/1/21   1590–1591
Thomas Sicklemore, Treasurer
(1 vol., bound in part of deed of assignment of lease of moiety of the New Mills in Ipswich from
John Pavis *alias* Deye to Robert Noothe, miller, n.d. [16c.])

C/3/4/1/22   1591–1592
Thomas Sicklemore, Treasurer
Includes:
— detailed inventory of town goods delivered by Sicklemore to his successor Thomas Sherman,
1592
(1 vol.)

C/3/4/1/23   1593–1594
Thomas Sherman, Treasurer
(1 vol., bound in the lower part of a double folio of a liturgical text, rubricated, with capitals
decorated in blue and red, and musical notation)

C/3/4/1/24   1595
Abstract of accounts of William Mydnall for the cost of equipping 2 warships for the Queen's
service at Calais
(1 vol.)

C/3/4/1/25   1594–1595
Thomas Sherman, Treasurer
(1 vol., bound in part of a notarial instrument, with notary's mark of Francis Moundeforde,
Ll.B., *re* matrimonial cause between William Sidaye and Alice Herberde, 8 Apr. 1593)

C/3/4/1/26   1594–1596
Seven books, sewn together

C/3/4/1/26/1   25 Mar.–29 Sep. 1596
Treasurer's account for the half–year
Thomas Sherman, Treasurer
Includes:
— account of William Sparrow, Treasurer, for half-year 29 Sep. 1595–25 Mar. 1596, said to
have omitted 'all manner of receiptes and paymentes'
(1 vol., bound in lower part of a double folio from a liturgical text, rubricated, with capitals
decorated in gold leaf and blue and red, and musical notation)

C/3/4/1/26/2   1594
Thomas Sherman's account of receipts and payments 'for the makyng of the Towne Bredges',
with accounts of money disbursed for repairing decayed bridges by William Jefferye,
Christopher Lawrence, Robert Haly and John Carnaby
(1 vol.)

C/3/4/1/26/3   29 Sep.–25 Dec. 1596
Treasurer's account
William Acton, Treasurer
(1 vol.)

C/3/4/1/26/4   n.d. [late 16c.]
Census of the poor in NI
Giving, in tabular form, name, details of dependents, whether 'able' or 'impotent', age, trade,
relief, and requirements
(1 vol., bound in 2 fols of a theological text, ? *c.*1100)

C/3/4/1/26/5   n.d. [late 16c.]
Similar census for MW and ME
(1 vol., bound in 2 fols of the same text)

C/3/4/1/26/6   n.d. [late 16c.]
Similar census for MT, LW and ST
(1 vol., bound in 2 fols of the same text)

C/3/4/1/26/7   n.d. [late 16c.]
Similar census for CL, MQ and MS
(1 vol., bound in 2 fols of the same text)

C/3/4/1/27   1599–1600
John Warde, Treasurer
(1 vol.; cover inscribed with memoranda that the book was shown to John Screvener, esq. and
Thomas Corbould, gent., on their examinations to the 11th interrogatory on the plaintiff's part,
6 Apr. 1654)

C/3/4/1/28   1600–1601
Richard Martin, Treasurer
(1 vol.; cover inscribed with similar memoranda to that of C/3/4/1/27)

C/3/4/1/29   1601–1602
Richard Martin, Treasurer
(1 vol.; cover inscribed with similar memoranda to that of C/3/4/1/27)

C/3/4/1/30   1602–1603
Richard Martin, Treasurer
Includes:
— account of John Goodwyn, of receipts and payments relating to a lawsuit concerning the
butchers in Easter term 1603, 16 Dec. 1603
(1 vol.; cover inscribed with similar memoranda to that of C/3/4/1/27)

C/3/4/1/31   1603–1604
Richard Martin, Treasurer
(1 vol.; cover inscribed with similar memoranda to that of C/3/4/1/27)

C/3/4/1/32   1606–1607
Richard Cornelius *alias* Joyner, Treasurer
(1 vol.)

C/3/4/1/33   1607–1608
Richard Cornelius *alias* Joyner, Treasurer
(1 vol.)

C/3/4/1/34   1608–1609
Robert Cole, Treasurer
(1 vol.; damaged by damp and rodents; a small amount of text missing)

C/3/4/1/35   1609–1610
Robert Cole, Treasurer
Payments for maintenance of town water supply include 6*s* 8*d* for posts and rails 'to keepe of
horses from treadinge the pipes', 14 Feb. 1610
(1 vol.)

C/3/4/1/36   1610–1611
Robert Goodinge, Treasurer
(1 vol.)

C/3/4/1/37   1611–1612
John Flicke, Treasurer
(1 vol.)

C/3/4/1/38   1612–1613
John Flicke, Treasurer
Includes:
— repayment of money laid out in defending a suit brought by Mr Colleye and Christopher Warde 'concerninge a rate made for mynisters wadges'
Enclosure:
— account of money still owed to the Treasurer, n.d.
(1 vol.)

C/3/4/1/39   1613–1614
Thomas Eldred, Treasurer
(1 vol.)

C/3/4/1/40   1614–1615
Thomas Eldred, Treasurer
(1 vol.)

For the account for 1615–1616, bound with that for 1581–1582, *see* C/3/4/1/15.

C/3/4/1/41   n.d. [? 1618–1619]
[? Francis Crowe, Treasurer]
Found with the Chamberlains' accounts, but identified from internal evidence as a Treasurer's account
(1 vol., inscribed with memorandum that it was shown to Richard Crowe on his examination to the 11th interrogatory on the plaintiff's part, 6 Apr. 1654)

C/3/4/1/42   1619–1620
Francis Crowe, Treasurer
(1 vol.; inscribed with similar memorandum to that of C/3/4/1/41)

C/3/4/1/43   1620–1621
Francis Crowe, Treasurer
(1 vol., incomplete; cover inscribed with memoranda that the book was shown to Richard Crowe on his examination to the 12th interrogatory, 12 Oct. 1652, and to Thomas Corbould, gent., on his examination to the 11th interrogatory on the plaintiff's part, 8 Apr. 1654

C/3/4/1/44   1621–1622
Francis Crowe, Treasurer
(1 vol.; inscribed with memoranda that it was shown to Richard Crowe on his examination to the 12th and 11th interrogatories on 11 Oct. 1652 and 6 Apr. 1654, and to Thomas Corbould, gent. on his examination to the 11th interrogatory, 8 Apr. 1654

C/3/4/1/45   1621–1622
Copy of C/3/4/1/44
(1 vol., incomplete and unaudited; cover inscribed 'Mr Crowes last accompt')

C/3/4/1/46   1622–1623
Christopher Aldgate, Treasurer
(1 vol.)

C/3/4/1/47   1624–1625
William Ingelthorpe, Treasurer
Enclosure:
— statement of balance of account, 7 Jan. 1628/9
(1 vol.)

C/3/4/1/48   1625–1626
Thomas Seelye, Treasurer
Includes:
— payment outstanding 'for pressinge marryners for the lord Duke' [? of Buckingham]
(1 vol.)

SAMUEL WARD TOWN PREACHER 1605–1640

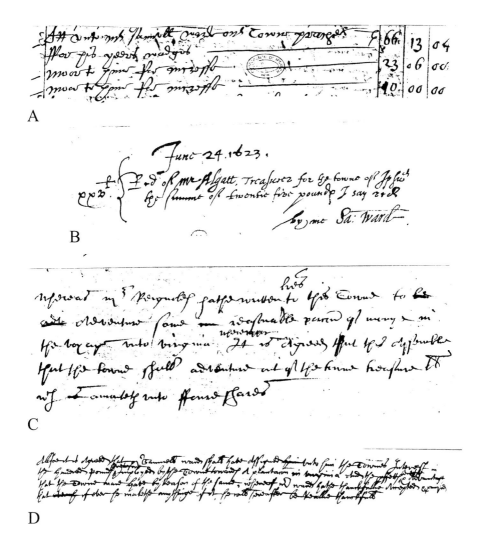

Fig. 15. Remuneration of Samuel Ward, Town Preacher: A. his salary, with two increases, 1622–23 (Treasurer's audited accounts, C/3/4/1/46); B. acquittance to (Christopher) Algatt, Town Treasurer, for £25, 24 June 1623 (HD 36/A/99); C. one hundred pounds invested in the Virginia Plantation project, 1610 (Assembly Book, C/4/3/1/4 fol. 37v); D. Mr Ward 'hathe thankfully accepted' the interest on the Virginia plantation money, 1631 (Assembly Book, C/4/3/1/5 p. 196)

C/3/4/1/49   1628–1629
Robert Knapp, Treasurer
(1 vol.)

C/3/4/1/50   1630–1631
William Tyler, Treasurer
(1 vol.; inscribed with memoranda that it was shown to Gilbert Lindfeild on his examination to
the 12th interrogatory, 11 Oct. 1652, and to Lindfeild and Samuel Tovell on their examinations
to the 11th interrogatory on the plaintiff's part, 10 Apr. 1654)

C/3/4/1/51   1631–1632
William Tyler, Treasurer
(1 vol.; inscribed with similar memoranda to those in C/3/4/1/50)

C/3/4/1/52   1633–1634
Isaac Day, Treasurer
(1 vol.; inscribed with memorandum that it was shown to Isaac Day sen., gent., on his examination to the 11th interrogatory on the plaintiff's part, 8 Apr. 1654)

C/3/4/1/53   1634–1635
Isaac Day, Treasurer
(1 vol.; inscribed with similar memorandum to that in C/3/4/1/52)

C/3/4/1/54   1635–1636
Richard Jeninges, Treasurer
(1 vol.; inscribed with memorandum that it was shown to Richard Jeninges, gent., on his examination to the 11th interrogatory on the plaintiff's part, 8 Apr. 1654)

C/3/4/1/55   1636–1637
Richard Jeninges, Treasurer
Enclosure:
— account of money outstanding on the account of Isaac Daye [the previous Treasurer]
(1 vol.)

C/3/4/1/56   1637–1638
Thomas Ives, Treasurer
(1 vol.)

C/3/4/1/57   1639–1640
Peter Fisher, Treasurer
(1 vol.)

C/3/4/1/58   1640–1641
Peter Fisher, Treasurer
(1 vol.)

C/3/4/1/59   1641–1642
Peter Fisher, Treasurer
(1 vol.; cover inscribed with memoranda that it was shown to Richard Crowe on his examination to the 12th interrogatory, 11 Oct. 1652, and to Thomas Corbould, gent., on his examination
to the 11th interrogatory on the plaintiff's part, 8 Apr. 1654)

C/3/4/1/60   1642–1643
Peter Fisher, Treasurer
Includes:
— 'chardges about the fortifications'
— payment for 'making the gibbett at the peper mill to carry the chaine and setting the post'
Annexed:
— 2 small books, stitched together, containing respectively the accounts of Fisher and of
Joseph Pemberton, of receipts and payments for the fortifications
(3 vols)

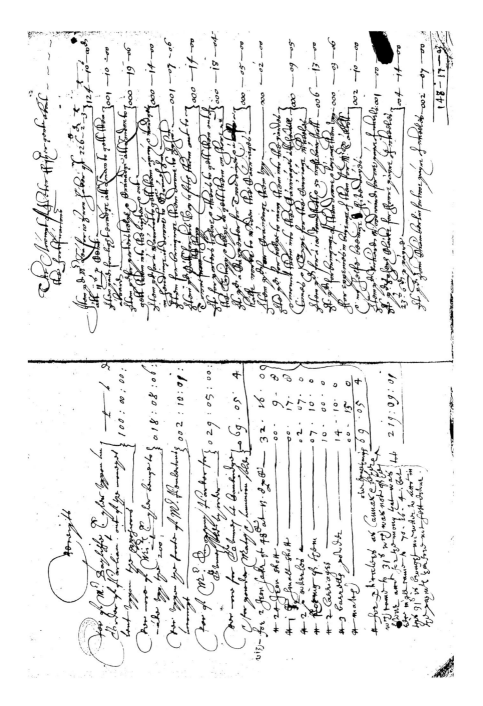

Fig. 16. Account of Peter Fisher, Town Treasurer, for fortifications, 1642–43
(C/3/4/1/60)

C/3/4/1/61 Mannuell Sorrell, Treasurer (1 vol.)	1644–1645
C/3/4/1/62 John Blomfeild, Treasurer (1 vol.)	1645–1646
C/3/4/1/63 John Blackborne, Treasurer (1 vol.)	1646–1647
C/3/4/1/64 John Blackborne, Treasurer (1 vol.)	1648–1649
C/3/4/1/65 Thomas Wright, Treasurer (1 vol.)	1649–1650
C/3/4/1/66 Thomas Wright, Treasurer (1 vol.)	1650–1651
C/3/4/1/67 Richard Girling, Treasurer (1 vol.)	1651–1652
C/3/4/1/68 Benjamin Butter, Treasurer (1 vol.)	1652–1653
C/3/4/1/69 Benjamin Butter, Treasurer (1 vol.)	1653–1654
C/3/4/1/70 Benjamin Butter, Treasurer (1 vol.)	1654–1655
C/3/4/1/71 Luke Jower, Treasurer (1 vol.)	1655–1656
C/3/4/1/72 Draft (unaudited) of C/3/4/1/71 Luke Jower, Treasurer (1 vol.)	1655–1656
C/3/4/1/73 Draft (unaudited) Luke Jower, Treasurer (1 vol.)	1656–1657
C/3/4/1/74 Luke Jower, Treasurer (1 vol.)	1657–1658
C/3/4/1/75 Thomas Burrough, Treasurer (1 vol.)	1659–1660

C/3/4/1/76   1660–1661
Simon Cumberland, Treasurer
(1 vol.)

C/3/4/1/77   1662–1663
Henry Gosnold, Treasurer
Includes:
— payments (totalling £84 5s 7d) for 2 new maces for the Corporation
— inventory of town property in the Lecturer's house, Apr. 1663
— inventory of town property in the gaol, n.d.
— inventory of town property in the school house, c. 25 Mar. 1663
(1 vol.)

C/3/4/1/78   1663–1664
Henry Gosnold, Treasurer
Includes:
— payments 'upon the trayneinge accoumpt' [for the militia muster], 27 Mar. 1664
— inventory of town property in the Lecturer's house, Apr. 1663
— inventory of town property in the gaol, 1663
— inventory of town property in the school house, c. 25 Mar. 1663
(1 vol.)

C/3/4/1/79   1664–1665
Henry Gosnold, Treasurer
(1 vol.)

C/3/4/1/80   1665–1666
Henry Gosnold, Treasurer
Includes:
— payments (totalling £217 6s) for renewing the borough charter
(1 vol.)

C/3/4/1/81   1667–1677
'The Accoumpt of Henry Gosnold, of money dew to him from the Towne of Ipswich from the
yeare 1666 to the yeare 1677', for his 4 years' Treasurership
Includes:
— gratuity which Gosnold was promised by the Assembly 'for his trouble, paynes and hazard
of his life in the Pest time, which he leaves to the townes consideracion'
(1 vol.)

C/3/4/1/82   1666–1667
Henry Cosin, Treasurer
(1 vol.)

C/3/4/1/83   1667–1668
John Pemberton, Treasurer
(1 vol.)

C/3/4/1/84   1668–1669
John Pemberton, Treasurer
(1 vol.)

C/3/4/1/85   1669–1670
John Sawyer, Treasurer
Includes:
— under 'Work done about the Crosse', payments to Truth Norris for 'takinge doune the old
Justice and setting up the new and the use of his staginge'; to Edward Baddison 'for
lengtheninge the beame and wyringe the scales' and 'for fittinge the sword'; and to John Brame
'for paintinge the Figure'
(1 vol.)

C/3/4/1/86   1671–1672
Samuel Colman, Treasurer
(1 vol.)

C/3/4/1/87   1672–1673
Samuel Colman, Treasurer
(1 vol.)

C/3/4/1/88   1674–1675
John Furman, Treasurer
(1 vol.)

C/3/4/1/89   1679–1680
William Browne, Treasurer
(1 vol.)

C/3/4/1/90   1680–1681
William Browne, Treasurer
(1 vol.)

C/3/4/1/91   1681–1682
Thomas Bright, Treasurer
(1 vol.)

C/3/4/1/92   1682–1683
Thomas Bright, Treasurer
(1 vol.)

C/3/4/1/93   1684–1685
John Reeve, Treasurer
Enclosures:
— Chamberlain's voucher for quit-rents for manor of Wix Ufford, 1689
— Chamberlain's voucher for 25s 6d 'being the value of an horse, cart and three baskets of
apples of John Pullam of Woodbridg Haston [Hasketon] being found by the Jury as Deodand
for the killinge of John Kirke', 1690
(1 vol.)

C/3/4/1/94   1686–1687
John Camplin, Treasurer
(1 vol.)

C/3/4/1/95   1688–1689
William Tye, Treasurer
(1 vol.; inscribed with memorandum that the book was shown to George Girling, Cooper
Gravenor, Jonathan Quintin and John Norris, gents., on their examinations to the 5th interrogatory on the complainant's part in the case of William Tye, gent. v. the Bailiffs, burgesses and
commonalty of Ipswich, in Chancery, 16 Apr. 1729)

C/3/4/1/96   1689–1690
William Tye, Treasurer
(1 vol.; inscribed with similar memorandum to that of C/3/4/1/95)

C/3/4/1/97   1690–1691
John Gibbon, Treasurer
Includes:
— payment for 'work done at the Maggazine by Jn⁰ Mellsuppe ... for removeing all the
Powder and shott and setting all other Ammunicon to right in the Maggazine'
(1 vol.)

C/3/4/1/98   1696–1697
Robert Snelling, Treasurer

Includes:
— receipts for 'Lycences to draw beere' from 65 named alehouse keepers for named alehouses
— payments for the ducking chair
(1 vol.)

C/3/4/1/99   1697–1698
Robert Snelling, Treasurer
Includes:
— receipts for 'Lycences to draw beere' from 74 named alehouse keepers for named alehouses
(1 vol.)

C/3/4/1/100   1698–1699
Robert Snelling, Treasurer
Includes:
— receipts for 'Lycences to draw beere' from 73 named alehouse keepers for named alehouses
— list of debts outstanding to the town
(1 vol.)

C/3/4/1/101   1699–1700
Samuel Rudkin, Treasurer
Includes:
— names of alehouse keepers and alehouses
(1 vol.)

C/3/4/1/102   1700–1701
Edward Veron, Treasurer
Includes:
— names of alehouse keepers and alehouses
(1 vol.)

C/3/4/1/103   1701–1702
John Pemberton, Treasurer
Includes:
— names of alehouse keepers and alehouses
(1 vol.)

C/3/4/1/104   1702–1703
Keeble Cross, Treasurer
Includes:
— names of alehouse keepers and alehouses
(1 vol.)

C/3/4/1/105   1703–1704
Keeble Cross, Treasurer
Includes:
— names of alehouse keepers and alehouses
(1 vol.)

C/3/4/1/106   1704–1705
Keeble Cross, Treasurer
Includes:
— names of alehouse keepers and alehouses
(1 vol.)

C/3/4/1/107   1705–1706
Henry Bond, Treasurer
Includes:
— names of alehouse keepers and alehouses
(1 vol.)

C/3/4/1/108   1706–1707
George Girling, Treasurer
Includes:
— names of alehouse keepers and alehouses
(1 vol.)

C/3/4/1/109   1707–1708
George Girling, Treasurer
Includes:
— names of alehouse keepers and alehouses
(1 vol.)

C/3/4/1/110   1708–1709
Henry Nash, Treasurer
Includes:
— names of alehouse keepers and alehouses
(1 vol.)

C/3/4/1/111   1714–1716
John Steward, Treasurer
Includes:
— names of alehouse keepers and alehouses
(1 vol.)

C/3/4/1/112   1716–1717
Thomas Osborn, Treasurer
Includes:
— names of victuallers and alehouses
(1 vol.)

C/3/4/1/113   1717–1719
Isaac Sutton, Treasurer
Includes:
— names of victuallers and alehouses
(1 vol.)

C/3/4/1/114   1719–1721
Thomas Grimwood, Treasurer
Includes:
— names of victuallers and alehouses
(1 vol.)

C/3/4/1/115   1721–1722
Tobias Searson, Treasurer
Includes:
— names of victuallers and alehouses
(1 vol.)

C/3/4/1/116   1722–1723
Robert Marston, Treasurer
(1 vol.)

C/3/4/1/117   1723–1724
Robert Marston, Treasurer
(1 vol.)

C/3/4/1/118   1724–1725
Robert Marston, Treasurer
(1 vol.)

C/3/4/1/119   1766–1767
Charles Norris, Treasurer
Includes:
— account of payments up to 7 Mar. 1770
(1 vol.)

C/3/4/1/120   1790–1791
Peter Clarke, Treasurer
(1 vol.)

C/3/4/1/121–123   1785–1836
These volumes, though each contains the accounts of several treasurerships, are a continuation
of the main series of audited accounts

C/3/4/1/121   1785–1794
William Norris, Treasurer, for the accounting years:
1785–1786; 1786–1787; 1787–1788; 1788–1789; 1789–1790; 1790–1791; 1791–1792; 1792–
1793
R. Small, Treasurer, 1793–1794
(1 vol., cover marked 'No. 1', 171 fols, 92 blank)

C/3/4/1/122   1806–1819
William Hammond, Treasurer, 1806–1807 (copy); S. Thorndike, Treasurer, 1807–1808 (copy);
James Thorndike, Treasurer, 1808–1809 (copy); Samuel Thorndike, Treasurer, 1809–1810;
James Thorndike, Treasurer, 1810–1811; James Thorndike, Treasurer, 1811–1812; James
Thorndike, Treasurer, 1812–1813; Samuel Thorndike, Treasurer, 1813–1814; James Thorndike,
Treasurer, 1814–1815; John Denny, Treasurer, 1815–1816; James Thorndike, Treasurer,
1816–1817; James Thorndike, Treasurer, 1817–1818; James Thorndike, Treasurer, 1818–1819
Includes:
— note signed by Henry Clarke, of return of the book to custody of Bailiffs, having been acci-
dentally found in a closet among his late father's papers, 1834
For original audited account for 1807–1808, see the Treasurer's vouchers for that year,
C/3/4/4/75.
(1 vol., cover marked 'No. 2', 89 fols)

C/3/4/1/123   1819–1836
Samuel Thorndike, Treasurer, 29 Sep. 1819–5 Apr. 1820; Edward Ablitt, Treasurer, 5 Apr.–
29 Sep. 1820; F. F. Seckamp, Treasurer, 1820–1821; William Barnard Clarke, Treasurer,
1821–1822; William Barnard Clarke, Treasurer, 1822–1823; John E. Sparrow, Treasurer,
1823–1824; H. Alexander, Treasurer, 1824–1825; William Hammond, Treasurer, 1825–1826;
F. F. Seekamp, Treasurer, 1826–1827; Robert Denham, Treasurer, 1827–1828; John Denny,
Treasurer, 1828–1829; Charles Tovell, Treasurer, 1829–1830, 1830–1831; William Calver,
Treasurer, 1831–1832
T. Duningham, Treasurer, 1832–1833; Richard William Porter, Treasurer, 1833–1834;
James Thorndike, Treasurer, 1834–1835, 1835–1836 (incomplete)
Includes, following the accounts for 1830–1831:
— account of money borrowed by the Corporation from Col. Clarke's trustees, 1830–1834
— account of the Corporation with B. B. Catt for rent of his marshes, 1828–1834
(1 vol., cover marked 'No. 3', 135 fols)

C/3/4/2   COPY ACCOUNTS   1802–1834

These are contemporary copies of the Treasurer's audited accounts in account books Nos. 2 and
3 (C/3/4/1/122–123), probably made after the audit.

C/3/4/2/1   1802–1826
For the financial years 1802–1803 and from 1806–1807 to 1824–1825, with a partial account
for 1825–1826
The accounts for 1806–1807, 1807–1808 and 1809–1810 follow those for 1818–1819; otherwise the order is chronological
(1 vol.; cover marked 'No. 5', 123 fols)

C/3/4/2/2   1825–1834
For the financial years 1825–1826 to 1833–1834; the account for 1825–1826 is a continuation
of that begun at the end of C/3/4/2/1
Includes, following the accounts for 1830–1831:
— additional accounts as in C/3/4/1/123
— voucher for payments to constables and town servants, n.d.
(1 vol., cover marked 'No. 4', 129 fols, 66 blank)

C/3/4/2/3   1820–1823
For the financial years 1820–1821, 1821–1822 and 1822–1823
(25 fols, stitched together)

C/3/4/3   LEDGERS   **1826–1834**

C/3/4/3/1   1826–1834
Disbursements and receipts in respect of the following Corporation properties:
Handford Hall, Water and Water Head Meadow, farm at Whitton, Town Hall, Corn Exchange,
Grammar School, quay and crane, warehouse on quay, Custom House, Handford Mill, Stoke
Mill, conduit house, Shire Hall, and marshes
Also accounts of salaries to town servants, ringers and the Town Music, charity bread for
churches, the Sessions, freemen and Great Courts, coal dues, petty rents, law expenses, the
races, Tower Church, and sundry annual expenses
(1 vol., cover labelled 'Corporation Accounts', 220 fols, 130 blank)

C/3/4/4   VOUCHERS AND RELATED PAPERS: GENERAL SERIES   **1720–1835**

Annual bundles, the documents originally filed on a lace. They consist for the most part of bills
paid by the Treasurer on behalf of the Corporation, Bailiffs' warrants for disbursements, and
acquittances for moneys received. The majority of the disbursements are for the maintenance of
Corporation property, including the water supply; other payments include officials' salaries
and the relief of vagrants. Comparison with the Chamberlains' vouchers reveals many similari-
ties in the types of expenditure and underlines the fact that the areas of responsibility of the two
offices were far from being rigidly demarcated in practice.
    Some bundles include original Treasurer's accounts, formerly used as wrappers; these and
other non-standard items are noted where they occur.

C/3/4/4/1   1720–1721
Thomas Grimwood, Treasurer
(101 docs)

C/3/4/4/2   1721–1722
Tobias Searson, Treasurer
Includes:
— account for purchase of 4 vols of the Statutes at Large from 1 Anne to 7 George I, 18 Jan.
1722
(106 docs)

C/3/4/4/3   1724–1725
Robert Marston, Treasurer
(36 docs)

C/3/4/4/4   1724–1725
Robert Marston, Treasurer
Originally found with warrants to the Treasurer for Sick and Wounded, 1705–1706
(37 docs)

C/3/4/4/5   1733–1735
John Sparrow, Treasurer (and Bailiff)
For the financial years 1733–1734 and 1734–1735
Includes:
— Bailiffs' warrant for payment of 15s to Anthony Capon 'for casting brass assizes of oysters
for the use of the Corporacion', 23 Nov. 1733
(181 docs)

C/3/4/4/6   1735–1736
John Sparrow, Treasurer (and Bailiff)
(114 docs)

C/3/4/4/7   1736–1737
John Sparrow, Treasurer (and Bailiff)
Includes:
— bill 'for carrying stones from the Old Chapple to Fryars Bridge, 2 days'
(108 docs)

C/3/4/4/8   1737–1738
John Sparrow, Treasurer
(110 docs, guarded into 2 vols following conservation)

C/3/4/4/9   1738–1739
John Sparrow, Treasurer
Includes:
— bill 'for 13 Flamboys to light his Magesty into Ipswich', 15 Jan. 1737
(107 docs)

C/3/4/4/10   1739–1740
John Sparrow, Treasurer
(101 docs)

C/3/4/4/11   1740–1741
William Artis, Treasurer
(126 docs)

C/3/4/4/12   1741–1742
Henry Bond, Treasurer
Includes:
— Treasurer's own bill for 'new leathering and cork for the engine after the fire at Mr Thirkels'
and for 'cleaning it and looking after it 3 years and playing it divers times', paid 13 Feb. 1744
(104 docs)

C/3/4/4/13   1742–1743
John Firmin, Treasurer
(104 docs)

C/3/4/4/14   1743–1744
John Firmin, Treasurer
(121 docs)

C/3/4/4/15   1744–1745
John Blythe, Treasurer
(42 docs)

C/3/4/4/16   1744–1746
John Blythe, Treasurer
Mostly for the financial year 1744–1745, with a few vouchers for the year 1745–1746
(60 docs)

C/3/4/4/17   1745–1746
John Blythe, Treasurer
(96 docs)

C/3/4/4/18   1746–1748
John Blythe, Treasurer
For the financial years 1746–1747 and 1747–1748
(79 docs)

C/3/4/4/19   1747–1749
John Blythe, Treasurer
For the financial years 1747–1748 and 1748–1749
Includes:
— bill detailing repairs carried out to Corporation fire engine, 28 Jan. 1748
(128 docs)

C/3/4/4/20   1748–1749
John Blythe, Treasurer
(71 docs)

C/3/4/4/21   1749–1750
John Blythe, Treasurer
(65 docs)

C/3/4/4/22   1750–1751
John Blythe, Treasurer
(59 docs)

C/3/4/4/23   1751–1752
John Blythe, Treasurer
(67 docs)

C/3/4/4/24   1752–1754
John Blythe, Treasurer (1752–1753)
Charles Norris, Treasurer (1753–1754)
For the financial years 1752–1753 and 1753–1754
(169 docs)

C/3/4/4/25   1754–1756
Charles Norris, Treasurer (1754–1755)
Samuel Hamblin, Treasurer (1755–1756)
For the financial years 1754–1755 and 1755–1756
Includes:
— bill of Joshua Kirby and Co. for cleaning, painting, gilding and varnishing the scales of the
figure of Justice on the Market Cross, 24 Apr. 1756, receipted by his assistant and later partner,
Andrew Baldrey
(140 docs)

C/3/4/4/26   1756–1760
Thomas Burrell *alias* Burwell, Treasurer (1756–1759)
For the financial years 1756–1757, 1757–1758, 1758–1759 and 1759–1760. The few vouchers
for 1759–1760 relate to outstanding payments from Burrell's term of office.
(129 docs)

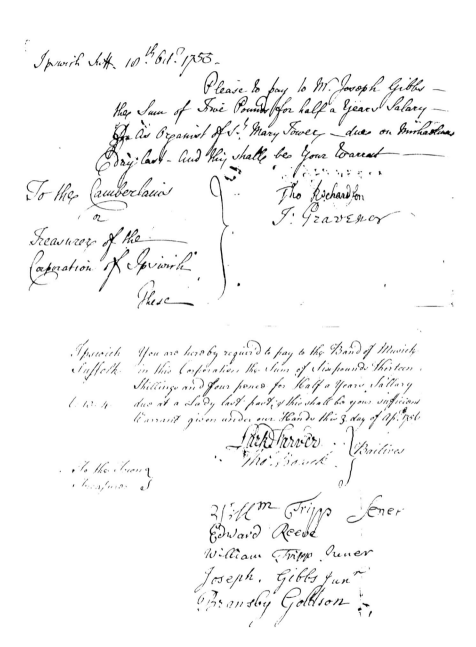

Fig. 17. Payments to Joseph Gibbs, Tower church organist, October 1755, and to the Band of Musick April 1756. (Treasurer's vouchers, 1754–56, C/3/4/4/25)

255

C/3/4/4/27   1756–1759
Thomas Burrell *alias* Burwell, Treasurer
For the financial years 1756–1757, 1757–1758 and 1758–1759
Includes:
— 1 voucher for 1767
(21 docs; found wrapped with C/3/4/4/26)

C/3/4/4/28   1759–1760
Thomas Richardson, Treasurer
Includes:
— voucher for payment to Capt. Richard Lockwood for flags, flag-bearers, gunners, gunpowder and carriage of the guns, for the proclamation of King George III, 15 Dec. 1760
(68 docs)

C/3/4/4/29   1760–1761
Thomas Richardson, Treasurer
Includes:
— certificate by J. Whitehead, British Consul at Oporto, Portugal, that Hannah Spinder, a felon, having been taken by the French and carried into Vigo on board the 'Hercules' of Bristol, in which she was going to H.M. plantations in America, came to Oporto and is now embarked in the 'Bedford', whose Master is requested to deliver her at the first opportunity to any Justice of the Peace; dated 19 May 1761; inscribed with the Bailiffs' warrant to the Treasurer for payment to the gaoler for keeping her for 8 days, 10 Sep. 1761
(77 docs)

C/3/4/4/30   1761–1762
Thomas Richardson, Treasurer
Includes:
— order of the Great Court, 12 Aug. 1761, for payment of £10 3s 6d to Peter Clarke in full settlement of his bill, on condition that he deliver to the Town Clerk 'all books, papers, parchments and writings belonging to this Corporation'
(59 docs)

C/3/4/4/31   1762–1763
William Truelove sen., Treasurer
(67 docs)

C/3/4/4/32   1763–1765
William Truelove jun., Treasurer
For the financial years 1763–1764 and 1764–1765
(123 docs)

C/3/4/4/33   1764–1766
William Truelove jun., Treasurer
For the financial years 1764–1765 and 1765–1766
(85 docs)

C/3/4/4/34   1765–1766
William Truelove jun., Treasurer
(57 docs)

C/3/4/4/35   1766–1767
Charles Norris, Treasurer
(174 docs)

C/3/4/4/36   1767–1768
William Clarke, Treasurer
Includes:
— bill for payment to 6 men for assisting to handcuff and secure a prisoner attempting to break out on 2 occasions, 31 May 1768

— bill for supplying bread to prisoners in the gaol, naming 14 prisoners with dates of committal, discharge and, in the case of Martha Green, execution; authorised for payment on 29 Sep. 1768
(86 docs)

C/3/4/4/37   1768–1769
William Clarke, Treasurer
(92 docs, guarded into 4 files following conservation)

C/3/4/4/38   1769–1770
William Clarke, Treasurer
(66 docs)

C/3/4/4/39   1770–1771
William Clarke, Treasurer
Includes:
— 2 justice's precepts, by order of the Secretary at War, to impress carriages and drivers for conveyance of arms, clothing and accoutrements of the 3rd Regiment of Dragoon Guards to Eye and of the 3rd Regiment of Horse to Stowmarket, 18 Dec. 1770 and 27 Mar. 1771
(94 docs)

C/3/4/4/40   1771–1772
William Clarke, Treasurer
Includes:
— 5 justice's precepts, by order of the Secretary at War, to impress carriages and drivers for conveyance of arms, clothing and accoutrements of the 10th Regiment of Dragoons and of the 2nd Regiment of Horse from Ipswich to Colchester and Sudbury, 10 Apr.–18 Aug. 1772
(108 docs)

C/3/4/4/41   1772–1773
William Clarke, Treasurer
Includes:
— 3 vouchers for 1768, 1769 and 1770
— 4 justice's precepts, by order of the Secretary at War, to impress carriages and drivers for conveyance of arms, clothing and accoutrements of the 2nd Regiment of Horse to Colchester and Stowmarket, and of arms etc. of the 2nd Regiment of Dragoons to Woodbridge and Diss, 16 Apr., 6 Jun., 13 Jun. and 20 Sep. 1773
(89 docs)

C/3/4/4/42   1773–1774
William Clarke, Treasurer
Includes:
— 5 vouchers for 1771–1772
— 2 justice's precepts, by order of the Secretary at War, to impress carriages and drivers for conveyance of arms, clothing and accoutrements of the 2nd Regiment of Horse from Ipswich to Diss and from Ipswich to Colchester, 28 Mar. and 3 Apr. 1774
(84 docs)

C/3/4/4/43   1774–1775
William Clarke, Treasurer
Includes:
— bill for 'a copper oar washd with silver for the use of the water Bayliff', 16 Mar. 1775
(86 docs)

C/3/4/4/44   1775–1776
William Clarke, Treasurer
Includes:
— acquittance by Robert Chaplin, William Ide, William Keyes and Samuel Sharman for

payment 'for 16 nights watching and apprehending diverse vagrants that secreted themselves at several cinder ovens within this Borough', 20 Feb. 1776
(88 docs)

C/3/4/4/45   1776–1777
William Clarke, Treasurer
Includes:
— bond of the Corporation to Edmund Sparrow of Kettleburgh, gent., in £532 10s 6d for payment of £266 5s 3d, 17 Mar. 1763, endorsed with memorandum by Sparrow that the money secured to him is in trust for Samuel Kilderbee of Ipswich, gent.
— assignment of bond by Sparrow and Kilderbee to Peter Clarke of Ipswich, gent., 10 Jun. 1771
(149 docs)

C/3/4/4/46   1777–1778
Peter Clarke, Treasurer
Includes:
— Treasurer's audited accounts, 1777–1778 and 1778–1779
(80 docs)

C/3/4/4/47   1778–1779
Peter Clarke, Treasurer
(105 docs)

C/3/4/4/48   1779–1780
Peter Clarke, Treasurer
Includes:
— Treasurer's audited account, 1779–1780
(120 docs)

C/3/4/4/49   1780–1781
Henry Seekamp jun., Treasurer
Includes:
— Treasurer's audited account (vol.), 1780–1781
— account of dues on coals received by order of the Bailiffs and Portmen by Thomas Folkard, Surveyor of the Customs of the port of Ipswich, 6 Jun.–29 Sep. 1781 (giving date of payment, name of ship and master, home port, port where voyage originated, quantity of coal delivered and sum received)
(129 docs)

C/3/4/4/50   1781–1782
Henry Seekamp jun., Treasurer
Includes:
— accounts of dues on coals received by order of the Bailiffs and Portmen by Thomas Folkard, Surveyor of the Customs of the port of Ipswich, 29 Sep. 1781–25 Mar. 1782 and 25 Mar.–29 Sep. 1782 (giving date of payment, name of ship and master, home port, port where voyage originated, quantity of coal delivered and sum received)
(122 docs)

C/3/4/4/51   1782–1783
Henry Seekamp jun., Treasurer
Includes:
— Treasurer's audited account (vol.), 1782–1783 (marked 'N 3', i.e. for his 3rd term of office)
(99 docs)

C/3/4/4/52   1783–1784
Henry Seekamp jun., Treasurer
Includes:
— Treasurer's audited account (vol.), 1783–1784 (marked 'N 4', i.e. for his 4th term of office)

— bill of Andrew Baldrey for making 2 staffs for the town Beadles, Dec. 1783
— printed advertisement card for Nicholson's Academy for boys in Cotherstone, Yorkshire, giving as character reference Mr Crawley of St Peter's Street, Ipswich, n.d. (used as a 'stop' for the lace on which the vouchers were originally filed)
(102 docs)

C/3/4/4/53   1784–1785
Henry Seekamp jun., Treasurer
Includes:
— Treasurer's audited account (vol.), 1784–1785 (marked 'N 5', i.e. for his 5th term of office)
— printed cheque drawn by the Treasurer on Messrs Alexander, Cornwell, Alexander and Spooner of Ipswich and Needham Market, bankers, 31 May 1785 (apparently the first recorded payment by cheque by the Town Treasurer)
(51 docs)

C/3/4/4/54   1785–1786
William Norris, Treasurer
Includes:
— valuation for repair of town barge, 8 Aug. 1785
(131 docs. Bundle endorsed 'Mr W. Norris Town Treasurer vouchers for 1 year and half ending Mich. 1786')

C/3/4/4/55   1786–1787
William Norris, Treasurer
(221 docs)

C/3/4/4/56   1787–1788
William Norris, Treasurer
(224 docs)

C/3/4/4/57   1788–1789
William Norris, Treasurer
(248 docs)

C/3/4/4/58   1791–1792
William Norris, Treasurer
(191 docs)

C/3/4/4/59   1792–1793
William Norris, Treasurer
Includes:
— 2 letters from Arthur Benson, House of Commons, to William Batley, Town Clerk, *re* payment of fees due on the Corporation's petition against the Ipswich Paving Bill, 22 May, 14 Jun. 1793
— Bailiff's warrant for payment of 10*s* to the Beadles for weighing the jockeys on the 1st day's races, 1793
(191 docs)

C/3/4/4/60   1793–1794
Robert Small, Treasurer
Includes:
— Bailiff's warrants for payment of £1 6*s* 8*d* each to Joseph Gibbs and Thomas Channing, 'as a survivor of the heretofore Town Band . . . being one fifth part of the old Sallery, to Lady 1794' [for many years previously the Treasurer's accounts and vouchers had included regular payments to 'the Town Musick' or 'the town Band of Musick']
(184 docs)

C/3/4/4/61   Sep. 1794–May 1795
Robert Small, Treasurer
(72 docs)

C/3/4/4/62   May 1795–Sep. 1795
Robert Small, Treasurer
(49 docs)

C/3/4/4/63   Sep. 1795
Robert Small, Treasurer
(35 docs)

C/3/4/4/64   1795–1796
John Walford, Treasurer
Includes:
— Treasurer's audited account, 1795–1796
— Bailiff's warrant for payment of 10s to Joseph Gibbs, 'a survivor of the old Town Band',
29 Sep. 1796
(208 docs)

C/3/4/4/65   1796–1797
John Walford, Treasurer
Includes:
— Treasurer's audited account, 1796–1797
(213 docs)

C/3/4/4/66   1797–1798
John Walford, Treasurer
Includes:
— Treasurer's audited account, 1797–1798
(187 docs)

C/3/4/4/67   1798–1799
John Walford, Treasurer
Includes:
— Treasurer's audited account, 1798–1799
— bill of William Burrell for printing 500 copies of a catalogue of the books in the Town
Library, 28 Sep. 1799
(202 docs)

C/3/4/4/68   1799–1800
John Walford, Treasurer
Includes:
— Treasurer's audited account, 1799–1800
— 'Town Barge Book' containing accounts for weekly payments to the bargemen and inven-
tories of equipment, 1793–1800, with (enclosed) 10 vouchers for repairs to barge, 1799–1800
(182 docs)

C/3/4/4/69   1800–1801
John Walford, Treasurer
Includes:
— Treasurer's audited account, 1800–1801
— Bailiff's warrant for payment to the ringers for ringing the bells of St Lawrence, 16 Apr.
1801, 'for the victory over the Danish fleet' [battle of Copenhagen, 2 Apr.]
— Bailiff's warrant for payment 'for ringing the bells in consequence of the glorious news from
Egypt this day', 1 May 1801 [? the repulse of the French at Aboukir on 21 Mar., followed by the
Anglo-Turkish capture of Rosetta]
(187 docs)

C/3/4/4/70   1801–1802
John Walford, Treasurer
Includes:
— Treasurer's audited account, 1801–1802

— bill for 7s 6d to Andrew Baldrey who 'painted a plan on Church wall over the Bailiffs seat and wrote an inscription on ditto in black–very troublesome', 23 Oct. 1801

— undertaking by Thomas Burrage, newly appointed Clerk of the Markets, to pay 1 guinea *per annum* for use of the 'stall stuff' lately purchased by the Corporation from the previous Clerk Joseph Prigg, and to keep it in good repair, in exchange for the usual fees and perquisites of the office, 1 Apr. 1802; with, annexed, inventory of the 'stall stuff', 22 Feb. 1802, and Bailiff's warrant for payment of £15 18s 6d to Prigg for it, 1 Apr. 1802
(199 docs)

C/3/4/4/71   1802–1803
James Thorndike, Treasurer
Includes:
— Treasurer's audited account, 1802–1803
(177 docs)

C/3/4/4/72   1803–1804
John Walford, Treasurer
Includes:
— Treasurer's audited account, 1803–1804
(198 docs)

C/3/4/4/73   1804–1805
John Walford, Treasurer
Includes:
— Treasurer's audited account, 1804–1805
— bill of charges of William Batley [Town Clerk] in connexion with the Ipswich Port Bill, 1805
(188 docs)

C/3/4/4/74   1805–1806
John Walford, Treasurer
Includes:
— Treasurer's audited account, 1805–1806
— Coroners' inquisition into the death of Sarah Nunn, an infant, killed while crossing the highway in MG on 27 Sep. 1805, by a horse ridden by the wife of Major Paston of the West Suffolk Militia, 30 Sep. 1805; signed by the Coroners William Norris and Samuel Thorndike, and with signatures or marks of the jurors, and endorsed with amount of deodand paid; with, enclosed, deposition of John Cook of Ipswich, carpenter, a witness, 30 Sep. 1805
— Bailiff's warrant for payment of £1 16s to Thomas Blythe 'for tolling the bells at the different parishes in Ipswich upon the day of the funeral of Lord Nelson', 11 Jan. 1806
(268 docs)

C/3/4/4/75   1807–1808
Samuel Thorndike, Treasurer
Includes:
— Treasurer's audited account, 1807–1808
— card printed in support of candidacy of Simon Jackaman and Edward Bacon for Bailiffs and [William] Batley for Town Clerk, in the 'True Blue Interest', n.d. (used as a 'stop' for the lace on which the vouchers were originally filed)
(237 docs)

C/3/4/4/76   1808–1809
James Thorndike, Treasurer
Includes:
— list of names of 44 constables, including those for the races, 4 Jul. 1809
— bill for S. Jackaman's legal fees in taking action against 12 persons 'for having dredged in the River Orwell and taken away the oyster spat', authorised for payment 7 Dec. 1809
(198 docs)

C/3/4/4/77   1808–1809
James Thorndike, Treasurer
(51 docs; found with C/3/4/4/76, but filed on a separate lace)

C/3/4/4/78   1809–1810
Samuel Thorndike, Treasurer
(207 docs; the 'stop' for the file lace formed from a white-enamelled watch dial and a trade card
for Frost and Goward, coppersmiths, braziers, tinplate workers and furnishing ironmongers of
Orwell Place, Ipswich, n.d.)

C/3/4/4/79   1810–1811
James Thorndike, Treasurer
(200 docs)

C/3/4/4/80   1811–1812
James Thorndike, Treasurer
Includes:
— Bailiff's warrant for payment to the ringers on the reported peace with America, 19 Sep.
1812
(210 docs)

C/3/4/4/81   1812–1813
James Thorndike, Treasurer
Includes:
— estimate of damage done to the Corporation marshes in occupation of Henry Ellis 'in consequence of the inundation occasioned by the sluice gates being broke down', 27 May 1812
(255 docs)

C/3/4/4/82   1813–1814
Samuel Thorndike, Treasurer
Includes:
— Bailiff's warrants for payments to the ringers on the Prince Regent's visit to Ipswich, 29 and
30 Oct. 1813; 'on the joyful news of the Dutch freeing themselves from French tyranny and
oppression', 23 Nov. 1813; and 'on the capture of Paris by the Allied armies', 11 Apr. 1814
— trade card for Thorndike, watch and clock maker and goldsmith, Brook Street, Ipswich, n.d.,
used as a 'stop' for the file lace
(190 docs)

C/3/4/4/83   1814–1815
James Thorndike, Treasurer
Includes:
— Bailiff's warrant for payment to Messrs Wenn and Duningham [solicitors] of fees for con-
vening a meeting of the inhabitants 'to consider of the propriety of petitioning Parliament
against the continuance or renewal of the Property Tax' and engrossing the subsequent petition,
10 Mar. 1815
— bill of John Bransby, cartographer, for surveying and drawing plans of the Liberty of
Ipswich, and for surveying the river Orwell and its shores, pointing out the Admiralty jurisdiction, 1812–1814, authorised for payment 9 Jun. 1815
— warrant for payment to the ringers on 23 Jun. 'on account of the total defeat of Buonaparte's
army by the Duke of Wellington [at Waterloo] on the 18th inst.', 24 Jun. 1815
— warrant for payment to the ringers on 22 Jul. on the news of Napoleon's surrender, 25 Jul.
1815
(204 docs)

C/3/4/4/84   1815–1816
John Denny, Treasurer
(213 docs)

C/3/4/4/85   1816–1817
James Thorndike, Treasurer
Includes:
— list of 166 freemen, 29 Oct. 1816
— Bailiff's warrant for payment to the ringers 'for their very extraordinary performance on
Monday last, ringing five thousand and eighty eight changes on the bells of St Mary Tower', 14
May 1817
(258 docs)

C/3/4/4/86   1817–1818
James Thorndike, Treasurer
Mostly relating to payment of interest on mortgage of Corn Exchange
Includes:
— statement of account of interest on shares of the Corn Exchange, with names and signatures
of 12 persons who have advanced money, 30 Sep. 1819
(27 docs)

C/3/4/4/87   1821–1822
William Barnard Clarke, Treasurer
(199 docs)

C/3/4/4/88   1822–1823
William Barnard Clarke, Treasurer
Includes:
— payment for 'cleaning and scouring water closet pewter', 10 Oct. 1822, indicating that this
convenience was installed in the Town Hall by this date
(180 docs)

C/3/4/4/89   1823–1824
John Eddowes Sparrow, Treasurer
Includes:
— account of John Bransby, Jan. 1815, for engraving 2 large copper plates, printing and colour-
ing 110 maps of the Liberties of Ipswich and 110 maps of the river Orwell, with paper for the
maps, advertising and other expenses, and 300 pamphlets of the ancient and modern perambulations; with note that on 28 Sep. 1824 Bransby delivered into the care of the Clavigers the 2
copper plates, 50 [unsold] maps of the Liberties, 50 maps of the Orwell and 219 copies of the
perambulations
— account of John Bransby for surveying and planning on vellum the Town Marshes, and surveying and planning Waterhead Meadow, authorised for payment 28 Sep. 1824
— various repair bills indicating that wooden water pipes were still in use in HL at this date
(227 docs)

C/3/4/4/90   1824–1825
Henry Alexander, Treasurer (182 docs)

C/3/4/4/91   1826–1827
Frederick Francis Seekamp, Treasurer
Includes:
— Agreement between John Osboldstone of Ipswich, plumber, and Sir William Middleton,
bart. and Frederick Francis Seekamp, Bailiffs, to lay a lead water main along Dove Lane, Rope
Lane and Long Lane to the bottom of New Street, for £132, 5 Jan. 1822
— Deed of assignment from Osboldstone to William Mason of Ipswich, cheese and butter
factor, of payment and interest due under above agreement, for £110, 1 Jun. 1822
— rental, 29 Sep. 1826
— account of Frederick Parish for 'attendance of Town Band perambulating the Admiralty
jurisdiction bounds July 23rd 1827'
(215 docs)

C/3/4/4/92   1827–1828
Robert Denham, Treasurer
(227 docs)

C/3/4/4/93   1829–1830
Charles Tovell, Treasurer
Includes:
— account of Thomas Gray for advertising postponement of Ipswich Races in the *Suffolk Chronicle, Ipswich Journal* and *Racing Calendar* on account of death of King George IV, 20 Jul. 1830
— card requesting support for candidature of Mr Mackinnon and Mr Dundas in the parliamentary election for the borough, n.d.
(205 docs)

C/3/4/4/94   1830–1831
[Charles Tovell, Treasurer]
(187 docs)

C/3/4/4/95   1832–1833
Thomas Duningham, Treasurer
Includes:
— Bailiff's warrant for payment to Thomas Crowe for 'cleaning the model of the Royal George on the Town Hall', 27 Apr. 1833
— account of Thomas Crowe 'for rigging, repairing and painting the old ship Porto Bello belonging to the Town Hall' [a model], 19 Jul. 1833
(224 docs)

C/3/4/4/96   1834–1835
Treasurer not named
Includes:
— account of John Bransby [surveyor and cartographer] for calculating quantity of land within the Liberties, and surveying the Town Hall chambers and drawing plans on deeds, 1832, and for 6 large skins of parchment made into a book and a plan of the Corporation marshes, 1834
(241 docs)

C/3/4/4/97   1834–1836
William Fisk, Treasurer
(107 docs)

C/3/4/4/98   Sep.–Dec. 1835
Treasurer not named
(42 docs)

C/3/4/5   VOUCHERS: SPECIAL PAYMENTS   **1734–1773**

C/3/4/5/1   1744–1755
Vouchers for maintenance of Common Quay and Town House thereon, and Land Tax on Town House
Preserved separately from main series of annual vouchers, and found with vouchers of the Treasurer of the Marshalsea Rate
(117 docs)

C/3/4/5/2   1754–1755
Vouchers for the rebuilding of Handford Mill and Mill House
Includes:
— valuation of work done and materials used, by Samuel Anderson and John Lane, 24 Feb. 1755 (vol.), with (annexed), agreement by William Scarlett and John Denton, bricklayers, and

Thomas Howes and John Howes, carpenters, all of Ipswich, to abide by the measurement and valuation, 11 Feb. 1755
Work commissioned, and most of bills paid by, Michael Thirkle, Bailiff
(33 docs)

C/3/4/5/3   1734–1765
Vouchers for payments in connexion with Ipswich races
(14 docs, apparently extracted from the main series of bundles of Treasurer's vouchers; guarded into volume)

C/3/4/5/4   1772–1773
Vouchers for work carried out by order of William Greenleaf on the charity farm at Whitton [William Clarke, Treasurer]
(32 docs)

C/3/4/6   LOANS   17c.

C/3/4/6/1   n.d. [17c.]
Note that 'Goodman Micklesope doth ofer as suertys for the twenty nobles that the towen hath lent him, Thomas Packle, shomaker [and] Samewell Swan, baker'

C/3/5   RECORDS OF THE COAL METERS   1615–1758

It was the responsibility of these officers to assess and levy the duty payable by the registered owners of ships on cargoes landed at the port. Freemen of Ipswich were exempt; when they were part-owners of vessels, their 'foreign' partners paid only the amount of duty proportional to their shares.

C/3/5/1   ACCOUNTS   1615–1748

These accounts, usually kept in small notebooks, normally include the name of the meter, ship, master and home port, the quantity of goods (normally coal, but also including oats, rye, French or Spanish salt, fuller's earth, etc.) measured, what proportion is 'free' or 'foreign', and amount of meterage paid. In the earlier accounts, certain items of expenditure by the meters are also recorded. Many of the 17th-century accounts bear the signatures of the auditors. The accounting year ran from Michaelmas (29 September) to Michaelmas, although for a time in the 1670s and 1680s the account books begin and end in December. Some of the later accounts cover less than a full year. For the period 1748/9 to 1757/8, *see* the abstracts of accounts submitted for the annual audit, C/3/5/2/31–39).

C/3/5/1/1   1615–1616
John Butler, meter
(1 vol.)

C/3/5/1/2   1621–1622
[Edmund Pepper], meter
(1 vol.)

C/3/5/1/3   1621–1622
Giles Barber, meter
(1 vol.)

C/3/5/1/4   1621–1622
Lawrence Hutcherson, meter
(1 vol.)

C/3/5/1/5   1622–1623
Edmund Pepper, meter
(1 vol.)

C/3/5/1/6   1622–1623
Giles Barber, meter
(1 vol.)

C/3/5/1/7   1622–1623
Lawrence Hutcherson, meter
(1 vol.)

C/3/5/1/8   1623–1624
Edmund Pepper, meter
(1 vol.)

C/3/5/1/9   1623–1624
Giles Barber, meter
(1 vol.)

C/3/5/1/10   1624–1625
Edmund Pepper, meter
(1 vol.)

C/3/5/1/11   1625–1626
Giles Barber, meter
(1 vol.)

C/3/5/1/12   1625–1626
Lawrence Hutcherson, meter
(1 vol.)

C/3/5/1/13   1628–1629
Giles Barber, Lawrence Hutcherson and Edmund Pepper, meters
(3 vols, sewn together)

C/3/5/1/14   1630–1631
Giles Barber, meter
(1 vol.)

C/3/5/1/15   1630–1631
Lawrence Huchenson, meter
(1 vol.)

C/3/5/1/16   1631–1632
Giles Barber, meter
(1 vol.)

C/3/5/1/17   1631–1632
Edmund Pepper, meter
(1 vol.)

C/3/5/1/18   1635–1636
Giles Barber, meter
Note on front cover gives totals collected by Barber, Edmund Pepper and Martyn Hutchinson
(1 vol.)

C/3/5/1/19   1641–1642
Edmund Pepper, meter
(1 vol.)

C/3/5/1/20   1643–1644
Edmund Pepper, meter
(1 vol.)

C/3/5/1/21   1644–1645
Giles Barber, meter
(1 vol.)

C/3/5/1/22   1645–1646
Giles Barber, meter
(1 vol.)

C/3/5/1/23   1646–1647
Giles Barber, meter
(1 vol.)

C/3/5/1/24   1647–1648
Edmund Pepper, meter
(1 vol.)

C/3/5/1/25   1648–1649
Gyles Barber, meter
(1 vol.; found among the records of the Ipswich charities)

C/3/5/1/26   1648–1649
Nathaniel Munpresse, meter
(1 vol., incomplete, badly damaged by damp and barely legible)

C/3/5/1/27   1650–1651
Edmund Pepper, meter
(1 vol.)

C/3/5/1/28   1652–1653
Edmund Pepper, meter
(1 vol.)

C/3/5/1/29   1654–1655
Thomas Randall, meter
(1 vol.)

C/3/5/1/30   [1655]–1656
Thomas Barker, meter
(1 vol.)

C/3/5/1/31   1656–1657
Nathaniel Munpresse, meter
(1 vol.)

C/3/5/1/32   [1657]–1658
Daniel Chrismes, meter
(1 vol.)

C/3/5/1/33   [1658]–1659
Nathaniel Mimpris, meter
(1 vol.)

C/3/5/1/34 Nathaniel Mimpris, meter (1 vol.)	1659–[1660]
C/3/5/1/35 Thomas Barker, meter (1 vol.)	Jan.–Sep. 1660
C/3/5/1/36 Thomas Barker, meter (1 vol.)	1660–1661
C/3/5/1/37 Nathaniel Mimpris, meter (1 vol.)	1660–1661
C/3/5/1/38 Nathaniel Mimpris, meter (1 vol.)	1661–1662
C/3/5/1/39 Nathaniel Mimpris, meter (1 vol.)	1664–1665
C/3/5/1/40 Edward Marston, meter (1 vol., found among the records of the Ipswich charities)	26 Mar.–29 Sep. 1665
C/3/5/1/41 Edward Marston, meter (1 vol.)	1666–1667
C/3/5/1/42 Robert Parkhurst, meter (1 vol.)	1666–1667
C/3/5/1/43 Edward Marston, meter (1 vol.)	1667–1668
C/3/5/1/44 Henry ? Fryer, meter (1 vol.)	1668–1669
C/3/5/1/45 Robert Parkhurst, meter (1 vol.)	1668–1669
C/3/5/1/46 Robert Parkhurst, meter (1 vol.)	1669–1670
C/3/5/1/47 John Burrage, meter (1 vol.)	Mar.–Sep. 1670
C/3/5/1/48 Edward Marston, meter (1 vol.)	Feb. 1670–Jan. 1671

C/3/5/1/49   Jan.–Nov. 1671
John Burradge, meter
(1 vol.)

C/3/5/1/50   Jan.–Oct. 1671
Robert Parkhurst, meter
(1 vol.)

C/3/5/1/51   Mar.–Nov. 1671
Thomas Allard, meter
(1 vol.)

C/3/5/1/52   Jan.–Nov. 1672
Thomas Allard, meter
(1 vol.)

C/3/5/1/53   Feb.–Nov. 1672
Thomas Burradge, meter
(1 vol.)

C/3/5/1/54   Nov. 1671–Oct. 1672
Robert Parkhurst, meter
(1 vol.)

C/3/5/1/55   Dec. 1672–Nov. 1673
Thomas Burradge, meter
(1 vol.)

C/3/5/1/56   Dec. 1673–Dec. 1674
Robert Parkhurst, meter
(1 vol.)

C/3/5/1/57   Dec. 1673–Dec. 1674
John Burridge, meter
(1 vol.)

C/3/5/1/58   Dec. 1673–Dec. 1674
[Thomas] Alward, meter
(1 vol.)

C/3/5/1/59   Dec. 1674–Dec. 1675
Robert Parkhurst, meter
(1 vol.)

C/3/5/1/60   Dec. 1674–Dec. 1675
John Burridge, meter
(1 vol.)

C/3/5/1/61   Dec. 1674–Dec. 1675
Thomas Alward, meter
(1 vol.)

C/3/5/1/62   Dec. 1675–Dec. 1676
Robert Parkhurst, meter
(1 vol.)

C/3/5/1/63   Dec. 1675–Dec. 1676
John Burrage, meter
(1 vol.)

C/3/5/1/64   Dec. 1675–Dec. 1676
Francis Rednall, meter
(1 vol.)

C/3/5/1/65   Dec. 1676–Dec. 1677
John Burrage, meter
(1 vol.)

C/3/5/1/66   Dec. 1676–Dec. 1677
Robert Parkis, meter
(1 vol.)

C/3/5/1/67   Dec. 1677–Dec. 1678
John Burrage, meter
(1 vol.)

C/3/5/1/68   Dec. 1677–Dec. 1678
Robert Parker, meter
(1 vol.)

C/3/5/1/69   Dec. 1677–Dec. 1678
Francis Rednall, meter
(1 vol.)

C/3/5/1/70   Dec. 1678–Dec. 1679
Robert Parkhurst, meter
(1 vol.)

C/3/5/1/71   Dec. 1678–Dec. 1679
Francis Rednall/Rednold, meter
(1 vol.)

C/3/5/1/72   Dec. 1679–Dec. 1680
Daniel Christmas, meter
(1 vol.)

C/3/5/1/73   Dec. 1679–Nov. 1680
Francis Rydnold, meter
(1 vol.)

C/3/5/1/74   Jan.–Dec. 1681
Daniel Christmas, meter
(1 vol.)

C/3/5/1/75   Dec. 1681–Dec. 1682
Daniel Christmas, meter
(1 vol.)

C/3/5/1/76   Nov. 1681–Dec. 1682
Meter unnamed
(1 vol.)

C/3/5/1/77   Feb.–Nov. 1683
Daniel Christmas, meter
(1 vol.)

C/3/5/1/78   Mar.–? Dec. 1683
Samuel Warner, meter
(1 vol.)

C/3/5/1/79   Mar.–Dec. 1683
John Stanard, meter
(1 vol.)

C/3/5/1/80   Mar.–? Dec. 1684
Samuel Warner, meter
(1 vol.)

C/3/5/1/81   Mar.–Oct. 1684
John Stannard, meter
(1 vol.)

C/3/5/1/82   Nov. 1684–Aug. 1685
Daniel Christmas, meter
(1 vol.)

C/3/5/1/83   Nov. 1684–Sep. 1685
John Stannard, meter
(1 vol.)

C/3/5/1/84   Oct. 1685–Sep. 1686
Daniel Christmas, meter
(1 vol.)

C/3/5/1/85   Oct. 1685–Nov. 1686
Samuel Warner, meter
(1 vol.)

C/3/5/1/86   Oct. 1686–Sep. 1687
Daniel Christmas, meter
(1 vol.)

C/3/5/1/87   Oct. 1686–Sep. 1687
John Heath, meter
(1 vol.)

C/3/5/1/88   [? Oct. 1686–? Sep.] 1687
Samuel Warner, meter
(1 vol.)

C/3/5/1/89   Oct. 1687–Sep. 1688
Daniel Christmas, meter
(1 vol.)

C/3/5/1/90   Oct. 1687–Sep. 1688
John Heath, meter
(1 vol.)

C/3/5/1/91   29 Sep. 1687–27 Sep. 1688
Samuel Warner, meter
(1 vol.)

C/3/5/1/92   Dec. 1688–Sep. 1689
Daniel Christmas, meter
(1 vol.)

C/3/5/1/93   Nov. 1689–Jul. 1690
John Heath, meter
(1 vol.)

C/3/5/1/94   Nov. 1689–Nov. 1690
John Heath, meter
(1 vol.)

C/3/5/1/95   Feb.–Oct. 1690
Daniel Christmas, meter (to 25 Jun.), Henry Kinge (from 5 Jul.)
(1 vol.)

C/3/5/1/96   Feb.–Sep. 1691
Francis Ridnell, meter
(1 vol.)

C/3/5/1/97   Mar.–Sep. 1691
Meter unnamed
(1 vol.)

C/3/5/1/98   Oct. 1691–Sep. 1692
John Heath, meter
(1 vol.)

C/3/5/1/99   Oct. 1691–Sep. 1692
Samuel Warner, meter
(1 vol.)

C/3/5/1/100   Oct. 1692–Nov. 1693
John Heath, meter
(1 vol.)

C/3/5/1/101   Nov. 1692–Oct. 1693
Francis Ridnell, meter
(1 vol.)

C/3/5/1/102   Oct. 1692–Jan. 1693
Samuel Warner, meter
(1 vol.)

C/3/5/1/103   Oct. 1718–Sep. 1719
Edward Bell, meter
(1 vol.)

C/3/5/1/104   Oct. 1718–Sep. 1719
John Blechenden, meter
(1 vol.)

C/3/5/1/105   Oct. 1718–Sep. 1719
Thomas Blythe, meter
(1 vol.)

C/3/5/1/106   Nov. 1718–Sep. 1719
William Coe, meter
(1 vol.)

C/3/5/1/107   Oct. 1718–Sep. 1719
Robert Harper, meter
(1 vol.)

C/3/5/1/108   Feb.–Dec. 1719
Francis Ridnell, meter
(1 vol.)

C/3/5/1/109   Jan.–Sep. 1720
Edward Bell, meter
(1 vol.)

C/3/5/1/110   Oct. 1719–Sep. 1720
John Blechenden, meter
(1 vol.)

C/3/5/1/111   Oct. 1719–Aug. 1720
Thomas Blythe, meter
(1 vol.)

C/3/5/1/112   Dec. 1719–Sep. 1720
William Coe, meter
(1 vol.)

C/3/5/1/113   Jan.–Sep. 1720
Francis Ridnell, meter
(1 vol.)

C/3/5/1/114   Oct. 1720–Sep. 1721
Edward Bell, meter
(1 vol.)

C/3/5/1/115   Oct. 1720–Sep. 1721
John Blechenden, meter
(1 vol.)

C/3/5/1/116   Sep. 1720–Sep. 1721
Thomas Blythe, meter
(1 vol.)

C/3/5/1/117   Oct. 1720–Sep. 1721
William Coe, meter
(1 vol.)

C/3/5/1/118   Dec. 1720–Sep. 1721
Robert Harper, meter
(1 vol.)

C/3/5/1/119   Oct. 1720–Sep. 1721
Francis Ridnell, meter
(1 vol.)

C/3/5/1/120   Oct. 1721–Aug. 1722
Edward Bell, meter
(1 vol.)

C/3/5/1/121   Oct. 1721–Sep. 1722
John Blechenden, meter
(1 vol.)

C/3/5/1/122   Oct. 1721–Sep. 1722
Thomas Blythe, meter
(1 vol.)

C/3/5/1/123   Oct. 1721–Sep. 1722
William Coe, meter
(1 vol.)

C/3/5/1/124   Oct. 1721–Sep. 1722
Robert Harper, meter
(1 vol.)

C/3/5/1/125   Oct. 1721–Sep. 1722
Francis Ridnell, meter
(1 vol.)

C/3/5/1/126   Oct. 1722–Sep. 1723
Edward Bell, meter
(1 vol.)

C/3/5/1/127   Oct. 1722–Sep. 1723
John Blechenden, meter
(1 vol.)

C/3/5/1/128   Oct. 1722–Sep. 1723
Thomas Blythe, meter
(1 vol.)

C/3/5/1/129   Oct. 1722–Sep. 1723
William Coe, meter
(1 vol.)

C/3/5/1/130   Oct. 1722–Sep. 1723
Francis Ridnell, meter
(1 vol.)

C/3/5/1/131   Oct. 1723–Sep. 1724
Edward Bell, meter
(1 vol.)

C/3/5/1/132   Oct. 1723–Sep. 1724
John Blechenden, meter
(1 vol.)

C/3/5/1/133   Oct. 1723–Sep. 1724
Thomas Blythe, meter
(1 vol.)

C/3/5/1/134   Oct. 1723–Sep. 1724
William Coe, meter
(1 vol.)

C/3/5/1/135   Oct. 1723–Sep. 1724
Jacob Keyes, meter
(1 vol.)

C/3/5/1/136   Oct. 1723–Sep. 1724
Meter unnamed [Francis Ridnell]
(1 vol.)

C/3/5/1/137   Dec. 1724–Sep. 1725
Edward Bell, meter
(1 vol.)

C/3/5/1/138   Oct. 1724–Sep. 1725
John Blechenden, meter
(1 vol.)

C/3/5/1/139 Thomas Blythe, meter (1 vol.)	Sep. 1724–Sep. 1725
C/3/5/1/140 William Coe, meter (1 vol.)	Nov. 1724–Sep. 1725
C/3/5/1/141 Jacob Keyes, meter (1 vol.)	Oct. 1724–Sep. 1725
C/3/5/1/142 Francis Ridnell, meter (1 vol.)	Nov. 1724–Sep. 1725
C/3/5/1/143 Edward Bell, meter (1 vol.)	Oct. 1725–Sep. 1726
C/3/5/1/144 John Blechenden, meter (1 vol.)	Nov. 1725–Sep. 1726
C/3/5/1/145 Thomas Blythe, meter (1 vol.)	Nov. 1725–Sep. 1726
C/3/5/1/146 William Coe, meter (1 vol.)	Oct. 1725–Sep. 1726
C/3/5/1/147 Jacob Keyes, meter (1 vol.)	Nov. 1725–Aug. 1726
C/3/5/1/148 Francis Ridnell, meter (1 vol.)	Nov. 1725–Sep. 1726
C/3/5/1/149 Edward Bell, meter (1 vol.)	Oct. 1726–Sep. 1727
C/3/5/1/150 John Blechenden, meter (1 vol.)	Sep. 1726–Sep. 1727
C/3/5/1/151 Thomas Blythe, meter (1 vol.)	Oct. 1726–Sep. 1727
C/3/5/1/152 William Coe, meter (1 vol.)	Oct. 1726–Sep. 1727
C/3/5/1/153 Jacob Keyes, meter (1 vol.)	Apr.–Dec. 1727

C/3/5/1/154   Oct. 1726–Sep. 1727
Francis Ridnell, meter
(1 vol.)

C/3/5/1/155   Oct. 1727–Sep. 1728
Edward Bell, meter
(1 vol.)

C/3/5/1/156   Oct. 1727–Sep. 1728
John Blechenden, meter
(1 vol.)

C/3/5/1/157   Dec. 1727–Sep. 1728
Thomas Blythe, meter
(1 vol.)

C/3/5/1/158   Oct. 1727–Sep. 1728
William Coe, meter
(1 vol.)

C/3/5/1/159   Oct. 1727–Sep. 1728
Jacob Keyes, meter
(1 vol.)

C/3/5/1/160   Oct. 1727–Sep. 1728
Francis Ridnell, meter
(1 vol.)

C/3/5/1/161   Oct. 1728–Sep. 1729
Edward Bell, meter
(1 vol.)

C/3/5/1/162   Oct. 1728–Sep. 1729
John Blechenden sen., 'James Bridges to apear for him'
(1 vol.)

C/3/5/1/163   Oct. 1728–Sep. 1729
Thomas Blythe, meter
(1 vol.)

C/3/5/1/164   Oct. 1728–Sep. 1729
William Coe, meter
(1 vol.)

C/3/5/1/165   Oct. 1728–Aug. 1729
Jacob Keyes, meter
(1 vol.)

C/3/5/1/166   Oct. 1728–Sep. 1729
Francis Ridnell, meter
(1 vol.)

C/3/5/1/167   Oct. 1729–Sep. 1730
Edward Bell, meter
(1 vol.)

C/3/5/1/168   Dec. 1729–Sep. 1730
[John] Blechenden, meter
(1 vol.)

C/3/5/1/169   Sep. 1729–Aug. 1730
Thomas Blythe, meter
(1 vol.)

C/3/5/1/170   Oct. 1729–Sep. 1730
William Coe, meter
(1 vol.)

C/3/5/1/171   Oct. 1729–Sep. 1730
Jacob Keyes, meter
(1 vol.)

C/3/5/1/172   Oct. 1729–Sep. 1730
Francis Ridnell, meter
(1 vol.)

C/3/5/1/173   Oct. 1730–Sep. 1731
Thomas Blythe, meter
(1 vol.)

C/3/5/1/174   Nov. 1730–Sep. 1731
Habakkuk Bowell, meter
(1 vol.)

C/3/5/1/175   Nov. 1730–Sep. 1731
[Anthony] Dorkins, meter
(1 vol.)

C/3/5/1/176   Oct. 1730–Sep. 1731
John Brame, meter
(1 vol.)

C/3/5/1/177   Nov. 1730–Sep. 1731
John Cooper, meter
(1 vol.)

C/3/5/1/178   Oct. 1730–Sep. 1731
Jacob Keyes, meter
(1 vol.)

C/3/5/1/179   [1731]–1732
Thomas Blythe, meter
(1 vol.)

C/3/5/1/180   Oct. 1731–Sep. 1732
Habakkuk Bowell, meter
(1 vol.)

C/3/5/1/181   Oct. 1731–Sep. 1732
John Brame, meter
(1 vol.)

C/3/5/1/182   Oct. 1731–Sep. 1732
Anthony Docken [sic], meter
(1 vol.)

C/3/5/1/183   Oct. 1731–Sep. 1732
Jacob Keyes, meter
(1 vol.)

C/3/5/1/184
Thomas Blythe, meter
(1 vol.)

Oct. 1732–Sep. 1733

C/3/5/1/185
John Brame, meter
(1 vol.)

Oct. 1732–Sep. 1733

C/3/5/1/186
John Cooper, meter
(2 loose leaves)

Nov. 1732–Sep. 1733

C/3/5/1/187
Anthony Dorkings, meter
(1 vol.)

Nov. 1732–Sep. 1733

C/3/5/1/188
Meter unnamed [? Habakkuk Bowell]
(1 vol.)

Sep. 1732–Sep. 1733

C/3/5/1/189
Thomas Blythe, meter
(1 vol.)

Oct. 1733–Sep. 1734

C/3/5/1/190
Habakkuk Bowell, meter
(1 vol.)

Oct. 1733–Aug. 1734

C/3/5/1/191
John Brame, meter
(1 vol.)

Oct. 1733–Aug. 1734

C/3/5/1/192
John Cooper, meter
(1 loose leaf)

Oct. 1733–Sep. 1734

C/3/5/1/193
Anthony Dorkin, meter
(1 vol.)

Oct. 1733–Sep. 1734

C/3/5/1/194
Isaac Richardson, meter
(1 vol.)

Dec. 1733–Sep. 1734

C/3/5/1/195
Thomas Blythe, meter
(1 vol.)

Nov. 1734–Sep. 1735

C/3/5/1/196
Habakkuk Bowell, meter
(1 vol.)

Oct. 1734–Sep. 1735

C/3/5/1/197
John Brame, meter
(1 vol.)

Oct. 1734–Sep. 1735

C/3/5/1/198
John Cooper, meter
(1 double folio)

Dec. 1734–Sep. 1735

C/3/5/1/199 Anthony Dorkin, meter (1 vol.)	Nov. 1734–Sep. 1735
C/3/5/1/200 Isaac Richardson, meter (1 vol.)	Oct. 1734–Sep. 1735
C/3/5/1/201 Thomas Blythe, meter (1 vol.)	Oct. 1735–Sep. 1736
C/3/5/1/202 Habakkuk Bowell, meter (1 vol.)	Sep. 1735–Sep. 1736
C/3/5/1/203 John Brame, meter (1 vol.)	Sep. 1735–Sep. 1736
C/3/5/1/204 John Cooper, meter (1 double folio)	Sep. 1735–Sep. 1736
C/3/5/1/205 Anthony Dorkins, meter (1 vol.)	Oct. 1735–Sep. 1736
C/3/5/1/206 Isaac Richardson, meter (1 vol.)	Sep. 1735–Sep. 1736
C/3/5/1/207 Thomas Blythe, meter (1 vol.)	Nov. 1736–Aug. 1737
C/3/5/1/208 Habakkuk Bowell, meter (1 vol.)	Oct. 1736–Sep. 1737
C/3/5/1/209 John Brame, meter (1 double folio)	Sep. 1736–Sep. 1737
C/3/5/1/210 John Cooper, meter (1 folio)	Sep. 1736–Sep. 1737
C/3/5/1/211 Anthony Dorkin, meter (1 vol.)	Oct. 1736–Sep. 1737
C/3/5/1/212 Isaac Richardson, meter (1 vol.)	Sep. 1736–Sep. 1737
C/3/5/1/213 Thomas Blythe, meter (1 vol.)	Oct. 1737–Sep. 1738

C/3/5/1/214 Habakkuk Bowell, meter (1 vol.)	Oct. 1737–Sep. 1738
C/3/5/1/215 John Brame, meter (1 vol.)	Oct. 1737–Sep. 1738
C/3/5/1/216 John Cooper, meter (1 double folio)	Sep. 1737–Sep. 1738
C/3/5/1/217 Anthony Dorking, meter (1 vol.)	Oct. 1737–Sep. 1738
C/3/5/1/218 Isaac Richardson, meter (1 vol.)	Nov. 1737–Sep. 1738
C/3/5/1/219 Thomas Blythe, meter (1 vol.)	Oct. 1738–Sep. 1739
C/3/5/1/220 Habakkuk Bowell, meter (1 vol.)	Nov. 1738–Sep. 1739
C/3/5/1/221 John Brame, meter (1 vol.)	Oct. 1738–Sep. 1739
C/3/5/1/222 John Cooper, meter (1 double folio)	Sep. 1738–Sep. 1739
C/3/5/1/223 Anthony Dorkin, meter (1 vol.)	Sep. 1738–Sep. 1739
C/3/5/1/224 Isaac Richardson, meter (1 vol.)	Oct. 1738–Sep. 1739
C/3/5/1/225 Thomas Blythe, meter (1 vol.)	Oct. 1739–Sep. 1740
C/3/5/1/226 Habakkuk Bowell, meter (1 vol.)	Nov. 1739–Sep. 1740
C/3/5/1/227 John Brame, meter (1 vol.)	Oct. 1739–Sep. 1740
C/3/5/1/228 John Cooper, meter (1 double folio)	Oct. 1739–Sep. 1740

C/3/5/1/229   Oct. 1739–Sep. 1740
Anthony Dorkin, meter
(1 vol.)

C/3/5/1/230   Oct. 1739–Sep. 1740
Isaac Richardson, meter
(1 vol.)

C/3/5/1/231   Oct. 1740–Sep. 1741
Thomas Blythe, meter
(1 vol.)

C/3/5/1/232   Sep. 1740–Sep. 1741
Habakkuk Bowell, meter
(1 vol.)

C/3/5/1/233   Oct. 1740–Sep. 1741
John Brame, meter
(1 vol.)

C/3/5/1/234   Sep. 1740–Sep. 1741
John Cooper, meter
(1 double folio)

C/3/5/1/235   Oct. 1740–Sep. 1741
Isaac Richardson, meter
(1 vol.)

C/3/5/1/236   Oct. 1741–Aug. 1742
Thomas Blythe, meter
(1 vol.)

C/3/5/1/237   Oct. 1741–Aug. 1742
Habakkuk Bowell, meter
(1 vol.)

C/3/5/1/238   Sep. 1741–Sep. 1742
John Brame, meter
(1 vol.)

C/3/5/1/239   Sep. 1741–Sep. 1742
John Cooper, meter
(1 vol.)

C/3/5/1/240   [Sep. 1741–Sep. 1742]
Isaac Richardson, meter
(1 double folio)

C/3/5/1/241   Jun.–Sep. 1742
William Usher, meter
(1 vol.)

C/3/5/1/242   May–Sep. 1742
Daniel Wade, meter
(1 vol.)

C/3/5/1/243   Oct. 1742–Aug. 1743
Henry Blythe, meter
(1 vol.)

C/3/5/1/244 Thomas Blythe, meter (1 vol.)	Nov. 1742–Aug. 1743
C/3/5/1/245 Habakkuk Bowell, meter (1 vol.)	Oct. 1742–Sep. 1743
C/3/5/1/246 John Brame, meter (1 vol.)	Sep. 1742–Aug. 1743
C/3/5/1/247 John Cooper, meter (1 double folio)	Sep. 1742–Sep. 1743
C/3/5/1/248 William Usher, meter (1 vol.)	Oct. 1742–Aug. 1743
C/3/5/1/249 Daniel Wade, meter (1 vol.)	Sep. 1742–Aug. 1743
C/3/5/1/250 Henry Blythe, meter (1 vol.)	Oct. 1743–Sep. 1744
C/3/5/1/251 Habakkuk Bowell, meter (1 vol.)	Nov. 1743–Aug. 1744
C/3/5/1/252 John Brame, meter (1 vol.)	Nov. 1743–Sep. 1744
C/3/5/1/253 Archibald Broun, meter (1 vol.)	Jun.–Sep. 1744
C/3/5/1/254 John Cooper, meter (1 folio, incomplete)	Sep. 1743–Sep. 1744
C/3/5/1/255 William Usher, meter (1 vol.)	Nov. 1743–Sep. 1744
C/3/5/1/256 Henry Blythe, meter (1 vol.)	Oct. 1744–Sep. 1745
C/3/5/1/257 Habakkuk Bowell, meter (1 vol.)	Oct. 1744–Sep. 1745
C/3/5/1/258 John Brame, meter (1 vol.)	Oct. 1744–Sep. 1745

C/3/5/1/259   Oct. 1744–Sep. 1745
Archibald Browne, meter
(1 vol.)

C/3/5/1/260   Sep. 1744–Sep. 1745
John Cooper, meter
(1 folio)

C/3/5/1/261   Oct. 1744–Sep. 1745
William Usher, meter
(1 vol.)

C/3/5/1/262   Oct. 1744–Sep. 1745
Daniel Wade, meter
(1 vol.)

C/3/5/1/263   Oct. 1745–Sep. 1746
Habakkuk Bowell, meter
(1 vol.)

C/3/5/1/264   Oct. 1745–Sep. 1746
John Brame, meter
(1 vol.)

C/3/5/1/265   Oct. 1747–Sep. 1748
Habakkuk Bowell, meter
(1 vol.)

C/3/5/2   ABSTRACTS OF ACCOUNTS   1719–1758

The dates given in the three earliest abstracts, and the audit certificates found with some of the later ones, indicate that it was the practice to submit them for audit at the Moot Hall on the Monday following the feast of St Nicholas (6 December). They normally give the quantity of goods metered, the rate of meterage per chaldron or other measure, and the total meterage paid, and sometimes state whether goods are 'free' or 'foreign'. Ships and masters are not usually named, and dates of landing are not usually given. The bundles for some years include abstracts for meters whose original accounts have not survived.

C/3/5/2/1   7 Dec. 1719
Abstracts for Thomas Blythe, Edward Bell and [Francis] Rednall; summary totals of meterage for all 6 meters
(1 doc.)

C/3/5/2/2   12 Dec. 1720
Abstracts for John Blitchenden [sic], Thomas Blythe, Edward Bell and Robert Harper; summary totals of meterage for all 6 meters
(1 doc.)

C/3/5/2/3   11 Dec. 1721
Abstracts for Edward Bell, Francis Rednell and Thomas Blythe; summary totals of meterage for all 6 meters
(2 docs)

C/3/5/2/4   10 Dec. 1722
Abstracts for [Francis] Ridnell and [Edward] Bell; summary totals of meterage for all 6 meters
(3 docs)

C/3/5/2/5   [1722–1723]
Abstracts for John Blechenden and Francis Rednell
(2 docs)

C/3/5/2/6   [1723]–1724
Abstracts for Thomas Blythe, John Blechenden, William Coe, Jacob Keys and Francis Ridnell
(4 docs)

C/3/5/2/7   13 Dec. 1725
Abstracts for John Blechenden, Thomas Blythe, William Coe and Jacob Keyes
(4 docs)

C/3/5/2/8   [1725]–1726
Abstracts for William Coe, Jacob Keyes and Francis Ridnell
(3 docs)

C/3/5/2/9   [1726]–1727
Summary totals of meterage only, for all 6 meters
(1 doc.)

C/3/5/2/10   [1727]–1728
Summary totals of meterage only, for all 6 meters
(1 doc.)

C/3/5/2/11   [1728]–1729
Abstract for Jacob Keyes; summary totals of meterage only, for all 6 meters
(1 doc.)

C/3/5/2/12   1729–1730
Abstracts for Blessingham [sic], Thomas Blythe, [Jacob] Keyes, Edward Bell, William Coe
and Francis Ridnell; summary totals of meterage only, for all 6 meters
(4 docs)

C/3/5/2/13   [1730–1731]
Abstracts for Thomas Blythe, Habakkuk Bowell, John Brame, [John] Cooper and [Anthony]
Dorkin
(6 docs)

C/3/5/2/14   1731–1732
Abstracts for Thomas Blythe, John Brame, Anthony Dorkin, Jacob Keyes and 1 unnamed
meter
(5 docs)

C/3/5/2/15   1732–1733
Abstracts for Thomas Blythe, Habakkuk Bowell, John Brame, John Cooper and Anthony
Dorkin
(5 docs)

C/3/5/2/16   1733–1734
Abstracts for Thomas Blythe, Habakkuk Bowell, John Brame, John Cooper, Anthony Dorkin
and Isaac Richardson
(6 docs)

C/3/5/2/17   1734–1735
Abstracts for Thomas Blythe, Habakkuk Bowell, John Brame, John Cooper, Anthony Dorkin
and Isaac Richardson
(6 docs)

C/3/5/2/18   1735–1736
Abstracts for Thomas Blythe, John Brame, Anthony Dorkin and Isaac Richardson
(4 docs)

C/3/5/2/19   [1735]–1736
Abstract for Habakkuk Bowell; summary totals of meterage for all 6 meters
(1 doc.; found with meters' accounts for 1729–1730, C/3/5/1/167–172)

C/3/5/2/20   1736–1737
Abstracts for Thomas Blythe, John Brame, John Cooper, Isaac Richardson and 1 unnamed meter; with summary totals of meterage for all 6 meters
(5 docs)

C/3/5/2/21   1737–1738
Abstracts for Thomas Blythe, Habakkuk Bowell, [John Brame], John Cooper, Anthony Dorking and Isaac Richardson; with summary totals of meterage for all 6 meters
(6 docs)

C/3/5/2/22   1738–1739
Abstracts for Thomas Blythe, Habakkuk Bowell, John Brame, John Cooper, Anthony Dorking and Isaac Richardson
(6 docs)

C/3/5/2/23   1739–1740
Abstracts for Thomas Blythe, Habakkuk Bowell, John Brame, John Cooper, Anthony Dorkins and Isaac Richardson; with summary totals of meterage for all 6 meters
(6 docs)

C/3/5/2/24   1740–1741
Abstracts for Thomas Blythe, Habakkuk Bowell, John Brame, John Cooper and Isaac Richardson
(5 docs)

C/3/5/2/25   1741–1742
Abstracts for Henry Blythe, Thomas Blythe, Habakkuk Bowell, John Brame, John Cooper, William Usher, Daniel Wade and Isaac Richardson
(9 docs)

C/3/5/2/26   1742–1743
Abstracts for Henry Blythe, Thomas Blythe, Habakkuk Bowell, John Brame, John Cooper, William Usher and Daniel Wade
(8 docs)

C/3/5/2/27   1743–1744
Abstracts for Henry Blythe, Habakkuk Bowell, Archibald Broom, William Usher, Benjamin Wade and Daniel Wade
(9 docs)

C/3/5/2/28   1744–1745
Abstracts for Henry Blythe, Habakkuk Bowell, John Brame, Archibald Brown, John Cooper, William Usher, Benjamin Wade and Daniel Wade
(9 docs)

C/3/5/2/29   1745–1746
Abstracts for Henry Blythe, Habakkuk Bowell, John Brame, [Archibald] Brown, Thomas Cuthbert, William Usher and Daniel Wade
(9 docs)

C/3/5/2/30   1747–1748
Abstracts for Henry Blythe, Thomas Cuthbert, John Smith, William Usher, Benjamin Wade and Daniel Wade; with auditors' certificate, 12 Dec. 1748
(7 docs)

C/3/5/2/31   1748–1749
Abstracts for Henry Blythe, Habakkuk Bowell, John Brame, Thomas Cuthbert, William Elliston, John Smith, William Usher, Benjamin Wade and Daniel Wade; with auditors' certificate, 11 Dec. 1749
(10 docs)

C/3/5/2/32   1749–1750
Abstracts for Henry Blythe, Habakkuk Bowell, Thomas Cuthbert, William Elliston, John Smith, William Usher, Benjamin Wade and Daniel Wade; with auditors' certificate, 10 Dec. 1750
(10 docs)

C/3/5/2/33   1750–1751
Abstracts for Habakkuk Bowell, Thomas Cuthbert, William Elliston, John Smith, William Usher, Benjamin Wade and Daniel Wade; with auditors' certificate, 9 Dec. 1750
(9 docs)

C/3/5/2/34   1751–1752
Abstracts for Richard Blythe, Habakkuk Bowell, Thomas Cuthbert, William Elliston, John Smith, William Usher, Benjamin Wade and Daniel Wade; with auditors' certificate, 11 Dec. 1752
(9 docs)

C/3/5/2/35   1752–1753
Abstracts for Richard Blythe, Habakkuk Bowell, Thomas Cuthbert, William Elliston, John Smith, William Usher, Benjamin Wade and Daniel Wade; with auditors' certificate, 11 Dec. 1753
(9 docs)

C/3/5/2/36   1753–1754
Abstracts for Richard Blythe, Habakkuk Bowell, Thomas Cuthbert, William Elliston, John Smith, William Usher, Benjamin Wade and Daniel Wade; with auditors' certificate, 9 Dec. 1754
(9 docs)

C/3/5/2/37   1754–1755
Abstracts for Richard Blythe, Habakkuk Bowell, Thomas Cuthbert, William Elliston, John Smith, William Usher, Benjamin Wade and Daniel Wade
(8 docs)

C/3/5/2/38   1755–1756
Abstracts for Richard Blythe, Habakkuk Bowell, Thomas Cuthbert, William Elliston, John Smith, William Usher, Benjamin Wade and Daniel Wade
(9 docs)

C/3/5/2/39   1757–1758
Abstracts for Richard Blythe, Habakkuk Bowell, Thomas Cuthbert, William Elliston, Joseph Parkhurst, William Usher, Benjamin Wade and Daniel Wade
(10 docs)

C/3/6   OTHER FINANCIAL RECORDS   1553–1755

C/3/6/1   18 Aug. 1553
Audited accounts of Rauf Goodwyn and William ? Debbyn, merchants and Portmen, of all their receipts and payments on behalf of the town 'from the beginning of the world' to the date of audit.

    Although there are references to money received by the Chamberlains and remaining in their hands, these appear to be neither Chamberlains' nor Treasurers' accounts; neither office was held by Goodwyn or ? Debbyn that year, and the format differs markedly from that of those officers' accounts. The receipts are arranged by parish, covering all twelve ancient parishes, and give only the names of the contributors and amounts paid, with some occupations. Most payments record only the name of the recipient and the sum paid; a very few mention the

purpose, e.g. 'work on the dikes' 'costs to London' and 'Lent at the setting forthe of the sowdyers to Bulleyn' [Boulogne]. Though found with the parochial account books for poor relief (C/5/3/2), these accounts are apparently unrelated. The audit statement records that the accounts were delivered together with 'oon peyer of Chaleys of sylver broke in iiij^{or} peces wayeing xj ownces & di' [11½ ounces].
(1 vol.)

C/3/6/2   n.d. [later 17c.]
Schedule of rents
Giving, in tabular form, by parish, names of owners and occupiers, present annual rent, fine, rent per annum and rack rent
For HL, MG, LW, MT, NI and MW only
(purpose and provenance unknown; 10 fols, attached at heads)

C/3/6/3   Sep. 1744–Sep. 1755
Audited accounts of Messrs John Scott, Robert Scott and William Westhorp [as farmers or lessees of the Common Quay]
(1 vol.)

C/3/7   FINANCE COMMITTEE   1785–19c.

C/3/7/1   1785–1787
Minutes of the Committee appointed to inquire into the state of the accounts, property and revenues of the Corporation
Committee established by order of the Great Court, 8 Sep. 1785, copied into the front of the volume. The minutes usually refer to the body as 'the Committee to inquire into the state of the Corporation and its charities'.
Includes:
— numerous references to the town barge and the dredging of the Orwell
(1 vol., mostly blank)

C/3/7/2   n.d. [early 19c.]
Letter from John Chevallier Cobbold to J. E. Sparrowe *re* state of Corporation finances, and proposal to establish a sinking fund

C/3/8   GRANTS OF COMMON SOIL   1315–1697

An order on the Patent Roll in 1335 for an inquest on the extent of the port of Ipswich records that the burgesses had requested licence to build on the King's waste places in the town, and to receive the farms and profits arising from them for their own use. Their petition appears to have received no direct answer (though the inquest on the port was held in 1340), yet the Portmanmote Rolls record that some pieces of common soil upon the ramparts had been leased as long ago as 1303, presumably without formal licence, and more were leased during the course of the 14th century. By 1335 the waste was clearly regarded as a desirable and necessary addition to the community's resources if it was to command a freely disposable revenue. If the burgesses' petition *did* receive an answer it must have been a favourable one; if not, 'need and opportunity provided the warrant' (Martin 1955, 93–97).

The presence of filing holes in most of the documents, together with the evidence of endorsements, suggests that the counterparts sealed by the recipients of the grants, and perhaps some originals, were kept on parochial files; the originals have fewer holes than the counterparts, presumably indicating that they were not filed until a new grant was made. All documents which can be identified by reference to the Petty Rentals of 1499, 1541/2 and ?1570 (C/3/3/4/1–2) and to a calendar of grants contained in the Book of Benefactors *t*. Car. II (C/3/10/1/1/1) have been arranged by parishes. A few documents have numbering on the seal tags. The 'foreshore deeds' (C/1/7/1) seem originally to have been part of this series, but were presumably separated from it during searches arising out of litigation concerning the Corporation's foreshore rights.

C/3/8/1   GRANTS IN ST CLEMENT'S PARISH   1479–1585

C/3/8/1/1   4 Dec. 1479
Piece of land of common soil (1½ a)
Demise from Benedict Caldewell and John Gosse, Bailiffs, and Portmen and burgesses, to Richard Felawe of Ipswich, merchant
Premises lie next to Meredyck within grantee's close, part of tenement of Pondys on W. and highway from Ipswich to Nacton; 4*d* annual rent
Latin; seal missing from tag; endorsed with memorandum of cancellation because of surrender to use of town

C/3/8/1/2   3 Jul. 1570
Piece of land of common soil in Sherehouse pettes, in part built upon, in CL
Feoffment from Robert Kynge and William Smarte, Bailiffs, and burgesses and commonalty, to Henry Asshelye of Ipswich, clothier
Dimensions given; 4*d* annual rent; 2*d* penalty for non-payment; to be void if alienated to lord of any manor within 4 miles of Ipswich; John Hawys and John Hannam appointed attorneys to deliver seisin
Latin; grantee's seal on tag

C/3/8/1/3   3 Jul. 1570
Original of C/3/8/1/2
Latin; Common Seal (incomplete) on tag

C/3/8/1/4   27 Jul. 1570
Piece of common soil late of Thomas Boyse, previously granted to John Bramforde, in CL
Feoffment from Robert Kynge and William Smarte, Bailiffs, and burgesses and commonalty, to Alice Huggett of Ipswich, widow
Premises lie between feoffee's tenement on N. and salt water on S., abutting E. on land of William Raynbald late of Thomas Alvarde and W. on common soil late of William Dowe; dimensions given; 4*d* annual rent; 2*d* penalty for non-payment; to be void if alienated to lord of any manor within 4 miles of Ipswich; John Hawys and John Hannam appointed attorneys to deliver seisin
Latin; grantee's seal on tag

C/3/8/1/5   3 Sep. 1583
Piece of void land of common soil in CL
Feoffment from Bailiffs, burgesses and commonalty to Richard Boyse of Ipswich, mariner
Premises lie between Clement Strete on W. and common way from church gate to Warwycke Pyttes on E., abutting N. on garden late of Robert Braye, deceased, and S. on said common way; dimensions given; for 10*s*., 2*s* annual rent and 12*d* penalty for non-payment; to be void if alienated to lord of any manor within 4 miles of Ipswich; John Hawys and Edward Cage appointed attorneys to deliver seisin
Latin; grantee's seal on tag

C/3/8/1/6   29 Jul. 1585
Piece of void land of common soil, partly newly built upon by feoffee, in CL
Feoffment from Bailiffs, burgesses and commonalty to Lambert Rogman of Ipswich, tailor and wife Thebia
Premises lie on N. side of highway leading from Warrwyck Pettes of Ipswich, by St Clement's

churchyard to 'the olde keye', between highway on S. and close of John Purpett, gent. on N.; dimensions given; 6*d* annual rent; 12*d* penalty for non-payment; to be void if alienated to lord of any manor within 4 miles of Ipswich; John Hawys and Edward Cage appointed attorneys to deliver seisin
Latin; seal on tongue torn away

C/3/8/1/7   29 Jul. 1585
Piece of void land of common soil, partly newly built upon by feoffee, in CL
Feoffment from Bailiffs, burgesses and commonalty to John Ingram of Ipswich, mariner and wife Rachel
Premises lie on N. side of highway leading from lez Warrwyck Pettes, by St Clement's church-yard to le old keye, between highway on S. and close of John Purpett, gent. on N.; dimensions given; 6*d* annual rent; 12*d* penalty for non-payment; to be void if alienated to lord of any manor within 4 miles of Ipswich; John Hawys and Edward Cage appointed attorneys to deliver seisin
Latin; grantees' 2 seals on tags

C/3/8/1/8   31 Oct. 1585
Piece of ground of common soil, lately void, now partly built upon by inhabitants of CL, as severally enclosed
Feoffment from Bailiffs, burgesses and commonalty to John Jermye, gent., Thomas Pratt, gent., Godfrey Wolnall, William Serles, John Umfrye, John Tye sen., Thomas Glascocke sen., John Chapman, William Cock, Robert Wardall, Thomas Rounketle, John Brunnynge, John Deresly, Robert Flycke, Robert Braye, John Umfrye jun., John Tye jun., Christopher Wolnall, John Umfry jun. [*sic*] and Thomas Glascock jun., inhabitants of CL
Premises lie between highway leading from Warwyck Pettes, by St Clement's churchyard to Old Key on S. and close of John Purpett, gent. on N., abutting E. on messuage of John Ingram and W. on messuage of Lambert Rogman; 4*d* annual rent; 8*d* penalty for non-payment; to place therein honest poor persons born in parish; to be void if alienated to lord of any manor within 4 miles of Ipswich; John Hawys and Edward Cage appointed attorneys to deliver seisin
English; 22 seals (2 incomplete) on 6 tags

C/3/8/2   GRANTS IN ST HELEN'S AND ST STEPHEN'S PARISHES   1448–1516

C/3/8/2/1   20 Oct. 1448
Piece of land of common soil in ST
Grant from John Caldewell and Richard Felawe, Bailiffs, and Portmen and commonalty, to John Wytton of Ipswich
Premises lie between St Stephen's lane on E. and walls of Carmelite friars on W., abutting N. on common soil and S. on garden of Stephen Benton; dimensions given; 5*d* annual rent; names of 5 witnesses
Latin; grantee's seal on tag

C/3/8/2/2   14 Jun. 1475
Piece of land of common soil in ST
Demise from John Walworth and Richard Felawe, Bailiffs, and burgesses and commonalty, to Roger Stannard
Premises lie between Sentsteuenes lane on E. and walls of friars of Mount Carmel on W., abutting S. on garden late of Stephen Benton and N. on common soil; dimensions given; 6*d* annual rent
Latin; grantee's seal on tag

C/3/8/2/3   20 Jun. 1516
Cottage built on common soil in HL
Grant from Bailiffs, burgesses and commonalty to William Legy, wheelwright
Premises lie between grantee's messuage [on E. *missing*] and messuage of John Manne on W., abutting S. on curtilage of John Manne and N. on highway; dimensions given; 2*s* annual rent;

4*d* penalty for non-payment; William Notyngham and Robert Bray appointed attorneys to deliver seisin
Latin; fragment of grantee's seal on tag

C/3/8/3 GRANTS IN ST LAWRENCE PARISH   1395–1570

C/3/8/3/1   2 Nov. 1395
Void piece of land
Grant from Bailiffs and commonalty to Robert Lucas, fellow burgess
Premises lie next to St Lawrence churchyard on N. and highway leading from fish market to Brokestrete on S., abutting E. on lane from said market to le condewyte and W. on shop formerly of John Leu; dimensions given; 8*d* annual rent; names of 6 witnesses including Geoffrey Sterling, Bailiff
Latin; grantee's seal (incomplete) on tag; endorsed with memorandum of new grant to John Bedfeld and wife Matilda, 15 Hen. VII, for 10*d* annual rent

C/3/8/3/2   16 May 1426
Shop formerly of John Gerard of Ipswich, mercer, lately of Stephen Benton, with 8 other shops adjoining on either side
Quitclaim from Bailiffs and commonalty to Stephen Benton and wife Alice, of 10*d* out of 12*d* annual rent due for premises
Premises lie on corner of fish market and street called Cokerowe, near St Lawrence churchyard
Latin; grantee's seals (1 incomplete) on 2 tags

C/3/8/3/3   1 Aug. 1448
3 stalls in LW
Grant from William Walworth and Robert Smyth, Bailiffs, with consent of whole commonalty, to Matthew Stabeler of Ipswich
Premises lie together between stall of Stephen Benton on W. and S. gate of St Lawrence churchyard on E., abutting S. on highway and N. on shops of John Malton formerly of Hugh Lew; dimensions given; 3*s* annual rent; names of 7 witnesses
Latin; seal and tag missing; endorsed with memorandum of re-grant to William Baker, notary, for same rent, n.d.

C/3/8/3/4   20 Jan ?1483
Messuage with adjoining curtilage in LW
Demise from [Benedict] Caldewell and Thomas Drayll, Bailiffs, and burgesses and commonalty, to John Bedfeeld and wife Matilda
Premises lie between tenement of William Gamyn on N. and tenement of Hugh Lowys on S., abutting E. on curtilage –[*missing*] and W. on highway; dimensions given; 4*s* 8*d* annual rent
Latin; incomplete; 2 grantees' seals on tags

C/3/8/3/5   20 Sep. 1486
3 stalls in fish market in LW
Grant from Roger Tympyrley and Nicholas Wynter, Bailiffs, and Portmen, burgesses and commonalty, to William Baker and wife Katherine, John Algore, William Wymbyll and Thomas Drayll
Premises lie between shops of William Baker on N. and highway on S., abutting E. on entrance from highway to St Lawrence churchyard and W. on stall of Thomas Skyppe; dimensions given; 3*s* annual rent; in case of default in payment, power to distrain on 2 shops between churchyard on N. and said stalls on S.
Latin; 2 grantees' seals on tags, 2 others missing

C/3/8/3/6   24 Feb. 1498
Piece of land of common soil in LW
Demise from Thomas Draill, Bailiff, and burgesses and commonalty, to William Baker

Premises lie between grantee's shop in which [*blank*] Grey dwells on E. and entrance from fish market to St Lawrence churchyard on W.; dimensions given; 2*d* annual rent
Latin; grantee's seal on tag; endorsed 'off ye voyde growm betwene ye howsys yn ye fyssh market'

C/3/8/3/7   26 Aug. 1499
Tenement built on common soil in LW, with adjoining piece of common soil
Grant from Thomas Baldrey and Edmund Daundy, Bailiffs, and burgesses and commonalty, to John Bedfeld and wife Matilda
Premises lie between fish market on S. and St Lawrence churchyard on N., abutting E. on highway from fish market to water conduit and W. on fish market, shop of William Baker, notary, formerly Liewes, and churchyard; dimensions given; 10*d* annual rent; 2*d* penalty for non-payment
Latin; grantee's seal on tag

C/3/8/3/8   21 Sep. 1570
5 shops under 1 roof, formerly of William Baker, notary, in LW; and piece of waste soil formerly of Lawrence Stisted, before that of John Wytten, in ST
Grant from Robert Kynge and William Smarte, Bailiffs, and burgesses and commonalty, to Elizabeth Cooke of Ipswich, widow of John Cooke
Shops lie between St Lawrence churchyard on N. and 4 stalls of grantee, late of William Baker, notary, on S., abutting E. on entrance to churchyard; waste soil lies between way on E. and grantee's garden on W., abutting S. on garden of Robert Cooke and N. on cottage of Robert Cooke; dimensions given; 12*d* annual rent; 4*d* penalty for non-payment; to be void if alienated to lord of any manor within 4 miles of Ipswich; John Hawys and Henry Hannam appointed attorneys to deliver seisin
Latin; grantee's seal on tag

C/3/8/4   GRANTS IN ST MARGARET'S PARISH   1344–1697

C/3/8/4/1   8 Jan. 1344
Piece of land in MG in suburbs
Demise in fee-farm from Bailiffs and commonalty to John son of James Le Clerk of Stratford
Premises lie between great ditches of town and highway from Thingstede towards Caldewalle strete, 1 head abutting on tenement formerly of Sir Thomas Breed, perpetual vicar of church of Preston by Lavenham, other head on said highway and great ditches; 6*d* annual fee-farm; names of 15 witnesses including John de Preston and John Irp, Bailiffs
Latin; grantee's seal on tag; tag numbered xiiij

C/3/8/4/2   30 Sep. 1392
Piece of land on common ditches at E. end of town
Lease from Bailiffs (not named) burgesses and commonalty to Richard Skyrwyt, burgess of Ipswich
Dimensions given; to make a tenter-yard; common way there not to be damaged or obstructed; for 50 years at 16*d* annual rent
Latin; fragment of grantee's seal on tag

C/3/8/4/3   28 Jan. 1406
Piece of land of common soil in MG
Demise from Robert Lucas and Thomas Andrew, Bailiffs, and commonalty, to William Fuller of Ipswich and wife Alice
Premises lie between remembered town ditches on S. and highway on N., abutting W. on common soil and E. on tenement of William Wryght; dimensions given; 8*d* annual rent; ditches to be maintained; names of 7 witnesses including John Bernard and John Kneppyng, Coroners
Latin; armorial seal on tag numbered viij; 2nd seal missing from tag

C/3/8/4/4   24 May 1419
Piece of void land of common soil in MG
Demise to fee-farm from William Debenham and Robert Lucas, Bailiffs, John Bernard and
William Stonham, Coroners, and commonalty, to John Dekene of Ipswich
Premises lie between town walls on S. and common way on N., abutting E. on curtilage of John
Leme and ditch of same wall and W. on common soil; dimensions given; 12d annual fee-farm
Latin; grantee's seal on tag, tag numbered xvij

C/3/8/4/5   14 Jun. 1475
Piece of land of common soil in MG
Demise to fee-farm from John Walworth and Richard Felawe, Bailiffs, and burgesses and com-
monalty, to Roger Stannard
Premises lie between town ditches on S. and highway on N.; abutting E. on highway and W. on
tenement of John Lytill lately common soil; dimensions given; 20d annual rent
Latin; grantee's seal (incomplete) on tag

C/3/8/4/6   14 Jun. 1475
Original of C/3/8/4/5
Latin; cancelled by mutilation; Common Seal and tag missing

C/3/8/4/7   18 Aug. 1480
Piece of land in MG
Demise to fee-farm from Benedict Caldewell and John Gosse, Bailiffs, and Portmen and bur-
gesses, to John Halle, dyer
Premises lie next to town ditch on E.; dimensions given; 8d annual fee-farm
Latin; seal missing from tag

C/3/8/4/8   25 Sep. 1482
Piece of land of common soil
Demise from John Hastyng and Robert Blomvyle, Bailiffs, and Portmen and burgesses, to
Thomas Fastolff, esq., Alexander Bussh and wife Matilda
Premises lie between common ditch of town on W. and highway from tenement formerly John
Joye's to town quay on E.; dimensions given; 4d annual rent
Latin; grantees' 3 seals on tags

C/3/8/4/9   25 Sep. 1482
Piece of land of common soil in MG
Demise from John Hastyng and Robert Blomvyle, Bailiffs, and burgesses and commonalty, to
Richard Osborne of Ipswich
Premises lie between highway on E. and common ditch of town on W., abutting N. on curtilage
of John Halle and S. on common soil; dimensions given; 6d annual rent
Latin; grantee's seal on tag

C/3/8/4/10   26 Sep. 1482
Piece of land of the ditches
Demise from John Hastyng and Robert Blomvyle, Bailiffs, and Portmen, burgesses and com-
monalty, to William Gnatte of Ipswich, barker
Premises lie between land of Richard Baily on N. and land of John Halle on S.; dimensions
given; 6d annual rent
Latin; grantee's seal on tag

C/3/8/4/11   19 Jul. 1484
Piece of land of common soil in MG
Demise to fee-farm from Richard Hawkyswade and William Sewale, Bailiffs, and Portmen and
commonalty, to Thomas Fastolff, esq.
Premises lie between grantee's close on W. and town ditch on E.; dimensions given; 2d annual
rent
Latin; fragment of grantee's seal on tag

C/3/8/4/12   30 May 1488
Piece of land of common soil in MG
Demise to fee-farm from Thomas Drayll and Robert Blomvyle, Bailiffs, and Portmen and com-
monalty, to Margaret Lytyll of Ipswich, widow
Premises lie between grantee's tenements on N. and top of town ditch on S.; dimensions given;
18d annual rent
Latin; grantee's seal on tag

C/3/8/4/13   30 May 1488
Original of C/3/8/4/12
Latin; cancelled by mutilation; Common Seal cut from tag

C/3/8/4/14   26 Aug. 1499
Tenement upon common soil, parcel of piece of common soil formerly granted to William
Fuller in MG
Grant from Thomas Baldry and Edmund Daundy, Bailiffs, and burgesses and commonalty, to
Juliana Jent
Premises lie between piece of common soil in tenure of Robert Elys on S. and common way on
N., abutting W. on piece of common soil in tenure of William Manser and E. on tenement of
Robert Elys built on common soil; dimensions given; 4d annual rent; 2d penalty for non-
payment
Latin; grantee's seal on tag; endorsed 'North ward'

C/3/8/4/15   26 Aug. 1499
2 tenements lying together upon common soil in MG
Grant from Thomas Baldry and Edmund Daundy, Bailiffs, and burgesses and commonalty, to
Robert Elys
Premises lie between tenement of William Manser late of John Litill on E. and tenement of
common soil which Juliana Jent holds and common soil in tenure of William Manser on W.;
abutting N. on common way towards Thingstede and S. on common soil in tenure of William
Manser; dimensions given; 2s annual rent; 4d penalty for non-payment
Latin; grantee's seal on tag

C/3/8/4/16   26 Aug. 1499
Piece of land of common soil with 'le Shedde' thereon in MG
Grant from Thomas Baldry and Edmund Daundy, Bailiffs, and burgesses and commonalty, to
Robert Fox of Ipswich, butcher
Premises lie between grantee's tenement late of John Brown on W. and common ditches of
town on E., abutting N. on common soil in tenure of Thomas Fastolff, esq. and S. on common
soil; dimensions given; 6d annual rent; 2d penalty for non-payment
Latin; grantee's seal on tag

C/3/8/4/17   26 Aug. 1499
Tenement with garden upon common soil in MG
Grant from Thomas Baldry and Edmund Daundi, Bailiffs, and burgesses and commonalty, to
John Bole and wife Elizabeth, lately wife of Robert Curdi
Premises lie between common ditches of town on S. and common way on N., abutting W. on
common soil tenement of Alice Calton and E. on common soil in tenure of William Manser;
dimensions given; 2s 6d annual rent; 4d penalty for non-payment
Latin; 2 seals of grantees (1 incomplete) on tags; endorsed 'North ward'

C/3/8/4/18   26 Aug. 1499
Common soil in MG
Grant from Thomas Baldry and Edmund Daundy, Bailiffs, and burgesses and commonalty, to
William Manser of Ipswich
Premises lie between top of town ditches and bottom of those ditches on S., and highway from
Thingsted to Caldewell, grantee's tenement late of John Litill, common soil in tenure of Robert
Elys and common way on N., abutting W. on common soil in tenure of John Bole and grantee's

tenement, and E. on common soil in tenure of Alexander Hert, Juliana Jent and Robert Elys; dimensions not inserted; 4s annual rent; 4d penalty for non-payment
Latin; grantee's seal (incomplete) on tag

C/3/8/4/19   26 Aug. 1499
Garden of common soil in MG
Grant from Thomas Baldry and Edmund Daundi, Bailiffs, and burgesses and commonalty, to Alexander Hert
Premises lie between highway from Thingstede to Caldewell on N. and town ditches on S., abutting W. on common soil in tenure of William Manser and E. on highway; dimensions given; lately granted to Roger Stanurd and re-entered for non-payment of rent; 2s annual rent; 4d penalty for non-payment
Latin; grantee's seal on tag; endorsed 'North ward'

C/3/8/4/20   26 Aug. 1499
Piece of common soil in MG
Grant from Thomas Baldry and Edmund Daundy, Bailiffs, and burgesses and commonalty, to William Ropkyn and John Portman
Premises lie between common ditches of town on W. and common way on E., abutting N. on common soil and S. on common soil in tenure of John Halle, dyer; dimensions given; to perform last will of John Gnatte, deceased; 8d annual rent; 2d penalty for non-payment
Latin; fragment of grantee's seal on tag

C/3/8/4/21   26 Aug. 1499
Tenement built on common soil with garden annexed in MG
Grant from Thomas Baldry and Edmund Daundy, Bailiffs, and burgesses and commonalty, to Alice Calton, lately wife of [Richard] Calton, and Thomas Calton her son
Premises lie between common way on N. and common ditches of town on S., abutting W. on void common soil next to Northgate and E. on common soil tenement of John Bole; dimensions given; 20d annual rent; 4d penalty for non-payment
Latin; 2 tags, both seals missing

C/3/8/4/22   26 Aug. 1499
Original of C/3/8/4/21
Latin; Common Seal (incomplete) on tag

C/3/8/4/23   20 Jan. 1535
Parcel of void ground of common soil in MG and parcel of wall dykes of town
Demise in fee-farm from Nicholas Harvy and Thomas Manser, Bailiffs, and burgesses and commonalty, to Thomas Bele of Tuddenham, tailor
Premises lie between residue of wall dykes on S. and piece of land which Bele has of an old grant on N., abutting E. on curtilage of William Curdy and on 'waldykes' and W. on common soil; dimensions given; 8d annual rent; 2d penalty for non-payment
English; grantee's seal on tag

C/3/8/4/24   — Jul. 1570
Tenement built on common soil in MG, and parcel of common soil ditches of town, both late in farm of Thomas Beale
Original grant from Robert Kinge and William Smarte, Bailiffs, and burgesses and commonalty, to John Smithe of Ipswich, bladesmith
Premises lie between void parcel of common ditches on S. and common street on N., abutting W. on common soil at Olde Barregates and E. on common soil in tenure of Robert Bacon; dimensions given; 2s 4d annual rent; penalty for non-payment not inserted; to be void if alienated to lord of any manor within 4 miles of Ipswich; John Hawys and Henry Hannam appointed attorneys to deliver seisin
Latin; Common Seal (incomplete) on tag

C/3/8/4/25   4 Jul. 1570
2 pieces of common soil in MG
Grant from Robert Kinge and William Smarte, Bailiffs, and burgesses and commonalty, to
Robert Hall of Ipswich, clothier
1st piece lies on N. side of lane anciently called Cretinges Lane which used to lead from
Caldewell Brooke to Clementes Strete, between grantee's tenement on W. and close late of
Robert Riche, kt, Lord Riche, on E., abutting S. on waste soil called Warwicks Pittes and N. on
common way at Caldwell Brooke; dimensions given; 3s 4d annual rent; 16d penalty for
non-payment; 2nd piece, now parcel of grantee's close, lies between Caldwell Brooke on S.
and parcel of grantee's close on N., abutting E. on tenement of John Medowe and W. on land
late of grantee; dimensions given; 4d annual rent; 4d penalty; to be void if alienated to lord of
any manor within 4 miles of Ipswich; John Hawys and Henry Hannam appointed attorneys to
deliver seisin
Latin; grantee's seal on tag

C/3/8/4/26   10 Aug. 1570
Piece of common soil with shed now built thereon in MG, and piece of common soil in ST,
parcel of tenement newly built by grantee
Grant from Robert Kinge and William Smarte, Bailiffs, and burgesses and commonalty, to
Christopher Crane of Ipswich, clothier
1st piece lies between grantee's tenement on W. and town land called Gramerscole land on E.,
abutting N. on Tankard Strete and S. on grantee's land; 2nd piece lies between Tankard Strete
on N. and grantee's tenement on S., abutting W. on Tankard Strete and E. on grantee's
tenement; with liberty to take water from water running in Brookestrett; dimensions given; 7d
annual rent; 3d penalty for non-payment; to be void if alienated to lord of any manor within 4
miles of Ipswich; John Hawys and Henry Hannam appointed attorneys to deliver seisin
Latin; grantee's seal on tag

C/3/8/4/27   10 Aug. 1570
Piece of common soil in MG, part of tenement formerly Stavelers and before that Skyrwyttes
Grant from Robert Kinge and William Smarte, Bailiffs, and burgesses and commonalty, to
Robert Hall, clothier
Premises lie opposite place where cross formerly stood, extending along highway from that
place to the quay; 4d annual rent; 2d penalty for non-payment; to be void if alienated to lord of
any manor within 4 miles of Ipswich; John Hawys and Henry Hannam appointed attorneys to
deliver seisin
Latin; grantee's seal on tag

C/3/8/4/28   27 Sep. 1576
Piece of land of town ditches, and enclosed garden, in MG
Grant from William Smarte and Edward Goodynge, Bailiffs, and burgesses and commonalty,
to Thomas Selye of Ipswich, mercer
Land lies between common way at the Barregates on E. and garden of Luke Melton parcel of
ditches on W., abutting N. on common way and S. on highway or town waste; garden lies at the
Olde Barregates on top of the Walldiches, abutting W. on gates and E. on waste soil in tenure of
John Smythe; reserving right of entry and exit to repair conduit pipe; dimensions given; 8d
annual rent; 4d penalty for non-payment; to be void if alienated to lord of any manor within 4
miles of Ipswich; John Hawys and Henry Hannam appointed attorneys to deliver seisin
Latin; grantee's seal on tag

C/3/8/4/29   8 Jul. 1589
Piece of common soil late parcel of the Colldongehill, lately built anew by grantee, in MG
Grant from Bailiffs, burgesses and commonalty, to Edmund Burroughe of Ipswich, capper
Premises lie between highway on S. and another parcel of le Colhill on N., abutting W. on
another parcel of le Colhill lately granted to Robert Baylye, and E. on another parcel of le
Collhill late of John Smyth; dimensions given; 16d annual rent; 8d penalty for non-payment; to

be void if alienated to lord of any manor within 4 miles of Ipswich; John Hawys and Edward Cage appointed attorneys to deliver seisin; grantee to maintain common way
Latin; seal missing from tag

C/3/8/4/30   8 Jul. 1589
Piece of common soil, late parcel of the Colldongehill, lately in part built anew by grantee, in MG
Grant from Bailiffs, burgesses and commonalty, to Robert Baylye of Ipswich, tailor
Premises lie between highway on S. and another parcel of le Coledongehill on N., abutting W. on another parcel and E. on parcel lately granted to Edmund Burroughe; dimensions given; 12d annual rent; 6d penalty for non-payment; to be void if alienated to lord of any manor within 4 miles of Ipswich; John Hawys and Edward Cage appointed attorneys to deliver seisin; grantee to maintain common way
Latin; grantee's seal on tag

C/3/8/4/31   18 Sep. 1593
Piece of common soil late parcel of the Coldonghill, now in part built upon, in CL and MG
Grant from Bailiffs, burgesses and commonalty, to Hugh Sheale of Ipswich, gunpowder maker, in consideration of 200 lb gunpowder
Premises lie between the Coldonghill on N. and tenements in occupation of Robert Balie, Edmund Burroughe, Laurence Hulinge and Jane Whitfilde now or late common soil on S., abutting W. on highway from Cawdewell Broke to St Clement's church and E. on Coldonghill; dimensions given; 20s annual rent; 20s penalty for non-payment; to be void if alienated to lord of any manor within 4 miles of Ipswich; Thomas Sherman and William Sparrowe appointed attorneys to deliver seisin
Latin; plan of gunpowder works annexed (see frontispiece); grantee's seal on tag

C/3/8/4/32   27 Sep. 1596
Piece of common soil in part newly built upon, parcel of the Coldonghill in CL and MG
Grant from William Bloyse and Robert Barker, Bailiffs, and burgesses and commonalty, to John Upson of Ipswich, husbandsman
Premises lie between parcels of the Coldonghill on N., S. and E., abutting W. on highway from Caldwell Brooke to CL; dimensions given; 12d annual rent; 6d penalty for non-payment; to be void if alienated to lord of any manor within 4 miles of Ipswich; William Hawys and Samuel Smithe appointed attorneys to deliver seisin
Latin; grantee's seal on tag

C/3/8/4/33   28 Sep. 1599
Piece of common soil, parcel of the Coldonghill, now partly built upon by grantee
Grant from Bailiffs, burgesses and commonalty, to John Cole of Ipswich, labourer, and wife Thomasina
Premises lie near common park of town called the town pound; dimensions given; 8d annual rent; 8d penalty for non-payment; to be void if alienated to lord of any manor within 4 miles of Ipswich; William Hawys appointed attorney to deliver seisin
Latin; 1 seal (incomplete), 2nd missing from tag

C/3/8/4/34   15 Feb. 1622
Piece of land of common wall ditch in MG, in grantee's occupation
Demise to fee-farm from Bailiffs, burgesses and commonalty, to Richard Marten, gent., Portman
Premises abut E. on Caldwell Brooke from yard of Edward Wetherell to house of Moses Sheild, W. on piece of ground called the Saffron panne, N. on houses of grantee and S. on ground in occupation of Robert Barbor; with licence to take water out of Caldwell Brooke; 4d annual rent; property having come to grantee from various persons, but some of deeds being so ancient as to be barely legible and much impaired
English; grantee's seal on tag; never filed

C/3/8/4/35   28 Sep. 1657

Tenements in MG, held of the town in free burgage

Conveyance by bargain and sale from Bailiffs, burgesses and commonalty, to Richard Wilkinson of Ipswich, carpenter, for £130

Premises lie between common street on E. and house and ground of Allen Day and yard in occupation of Robert Woodsid on W., abutting N. on common street and S. on timber yard of house in occupation of Thomas Lettis; 1*d* annual rent; Robert Clarke of Ipswich, gent., appointed attorney to deliver seisin

English; grantee's seal on tag; never filed

C/3/8/4/36   1 Jun. 1663

Piece of ground now paled in, formerly part of the Colddunghill in MG

Lease from Bailiffs, burgesses and commonalty to John Greene of Ipswich, bricklayer, for 1,000 years, for £25 and 12*d* annual rent

English; seal missing from tag; never filed

C/3/8/4/37   1 Oct. 1663

Piece of ground now paled in, formerly part of the Coldunghill in MG

Lease from Bailiffs, burgesses and commonalty to Tymothy Hawkins of Ipswich, carpenter, for 1,000 years, for £20 and 12*d* annual rent

English; lessee's seal on tag

C/3/8/4/38   19 Apr. 1697

Piece of the town ditches in MG

Lease from Bailiffs, burgesses and commonalty to John Greetum of Ipswich, wheelwright, for 900 years, for £9 15*s* and 20*d* annual rent

English; lessee's applied seal; never filed

C/3/8/5   GRANTS IN ST MARY ELMS PARISH   1344–1655

C/3/8/5/1   13 Jun. 1344

Place on town walls in ME, to build dye works

Demise from commonalty to Roger le Norice of Ipswich, dyer

Premises lie on S. of way leading from St Mary Elms church to Horswade Mill; dimensions given; 8*d* annual rent; grantee to maintain wall; names of 11 witnesses including John de Preston and John Irp, Bailiffs

Latin; grantee's seal on tag

C/3/8/5/2   19 Feb. 1456

Piece of land of common soil

Demise from Bailiffs, burgesses and commonalty to John Sharpe of Ipswich, glover

Premises lie below close of Prior of St Peter, between that close on N. and common soil on S., abutting E. on common way and W. on common bank; dimensions given; 12*d* annual rent

Original, Latin, cancelled by mutilation; Common Seal and tag missing

C/3/8/5/3   5 May 1474

Piece of land of common soil

Demise from Benedict Caldewell and John Hastyngs, Bailiffs, and burgesses and commonalty, to Thomas Punttyng of Ipswich

Premises lie between common way on E. and river bank on W., abutting S. on common soil and N. on Mandolffeslane; dimensions given; 14*d* annual rent

Latin; grantee's seal on tag; endorsed with memorandum of re-grant to Aveline, wife of John Deer, formerly wife of Thomas Puntyng, for 20*d* rent, 15 Hen. VII

C/3/8/5/4   5 May 1474

Original of C/3/8/5/3

Latin; cancelled by mutilation; Common Seal and tag missing

C/3/8/5/5   5 Nov. 1490
Piece of town ditches in ME
Demise from Roger Tymperley and William Harlewyn, Bailiffs, and burgesses and common-
alty, to Thomas Gardyner
Premises lie on S. side of way leading from St Mary Elms church to Horswade Mylle; dimen-
sions given; 12d annual rent; grantee to repair lane called le Watyrlane up to common bank
from highway
Latin; grantee's seal (incomplete) on tag

C/3/8/5/6   12 Mar. 1492
Piece of land of town ditches
Demise from Thomas Drayll and William Baker, Bailiffs, and burgesses and commonalty, to
Thomas Myxser of Ipswich, barker
Premises lie on S. side of le Wodehows and land of Thomas Gardyner; dimensions given; 8d
annual rent
Latin; marginal note in English that 'this woodhowse was John Coles and now the tenementes
of Elizabeth Cole vid. at Mr Acton his backside'; grantee's seal and tag missing

C/3/8/5/7   26 Aug. 1499
Cottage with curtilage of common soil
Grant from Thomas Baldry and Edmund Daundy, Bailiffs, and burgesses and commonalty, to
Hugh Lowes and wife Alice
Premises lie between close of Prior of St Peter on N. and Mandolfes lane on S., abutting E. on
common way and W. on common bank; dimensions given; 20d annual rent; 4d penalty for
non-payment; grantees to scour river for length of property
Latin; grantee's seal (incomplete) on tag, 2nd seal missing

C/3/8/5/8   26 Aug. 1499
Piece of land of common soil
Grant from Thomas Baldry and Edmund Daundy, Bailiffs, and burgesses and commonalty, to
Thomas Gardener of Ipswich
Premises lie between grantee's tenement on E. and common soil below town ditches on W.,
abutting N. on tenement of John Mey and S. on common soil newly granted to John Reynolds;
2d annual rent; 2d penalty for non-payment
Latin; grantee's seal missing from tag

C/3/8/5/9   13 Mar. 1503
Piece of common soil
Grant from Thomas Baldry and William Ropkyn, Bailiffs, and burgesses and commonalty, to
Thomas Gardiner
Premises lie between grantee's messuage late of John Cassenell on E. and common soil in
tenure of John Reynolds on W., abutting S. on common soil in tenure of Thomas Cady and N.
on common way; dimensions given; 6d annual rent; 2d penalty for non-payment; Edmund
Gelgelt and Henry Valantyn appointed attorneys to deliver seisin
Latin; grantee's seal (incomplete) on tag

C/3/8/5/10   20 Sep. 1521
Piece of land of common soil
Grant from Bailiffs, burgesses and commonalty, to Thomas Crickemer
Premises lie between Manfeldes lane on N. and garden of John Smyth 'ortchalmaker'
[? maker of orchil, a red or violet dye prepared from certain lichens] on S., abutting W. on bank
and E. on common way; dimensions given; 12d annual rent; 2d penalty for non-payment;
Christopher Heiward and Robert Bray appointed attorneys to deliver seisin
Latin; grantee's seal missing from tag; endorsed 'St Mary Elmes'

C/3/8/5/11   10 Sep. 1523
Piece of land of common soil
Grant from Bailiffs, burgesses and commonalty to John Smyth

Premises lie between lands of Christopher Heiward on S. and land of Thomas Crickemer on N., abutting E. on common way and W. on common bank; dimensions given; 12*d* annual rent; 2*d* penalty for non-payment; Robert Bray and John Pypho appointed attorneys to deliver seisin
Latin; grantee's seal missing from tag; endorsed 'St Mary Elmes'

C/3/8/5/12   16 Nov. 1542
Piece of land of common soil in ME
Grant from Henry Toley and William Raynbald, Bailiffs, and burgesses and commonalty, to John Archer, weaver
Premises lie between common soil garden in tenure of widow of Christopher Heyward on S. and common soil in tenure of widow Crykmere on N., abutting E. on common lane and W. on common fresh stream; dimensions given; 20*d* annual rent; 4*d* penalty for non-payment; Richard Bryd appointed attorney to deliver seisin
Latin; grantee's seal missing from tag

C/3/8/5/13   31 Jul. 1570
Piece of common soil formerly of Thomas Cuttynge in ME
Grant from Bailiffs, burgesses and commonalty to Arthur Butler of Ipswich, yeoman
Premises abut N. on land late of John Warde, formerly of Alexander Sparhawke, and S. on soil of Edmund Gardner late of [*blank*] Heywarde; dimensions given; 6*d* annual rent; 2*d* penalty for non-payment; to be void if alienated to lord of any manor within 4 miles of Ipswich; John Hawys and Henry Hannam appointed attorneys to deliver seisin
Latin; grantee's seal on tag

C/3/8/5/14   15 Aug. 1570
Piece of common soil, now a garden, with barn built thereon in NI; piece of common soil in NI; and piece of common soil in ME
Grant from Robert Kinge and William Smarte, Bailiffs, and burgesses and commonalty, to Thomas Bobbett of Ipswich, innholder
1st piece lies between garden of Richard Cornelius *alias* Joyner on E. and common soil in tenure of Christopher Alderman on W., abutting N. on common way and S. on garden of Walter Burne; 2nd piece between grantee's messuage on S. and common way on N., abutting E. on common soil of Christopher Alderman and W. on common way from Borne bredge to le Corne hill; 3rd piece by common soil garden late of relict of Christopher Heyward on S. and common soil of widow Kryckmere on N., abutting E. on common lane and W. on common fresh stream; dimensions given; 2*s* 5*d* annual rent; 7*d* penalty for non-payment; to be void if alienated to lord of any manor within 4 miles of Ipswich; John Hawys and Henry Hannam appointed attorneys to deliver seisin
Latin; grantee's seal on tag

C/3/8/5/15   5 Jul. 1586
Piece of common soil in ME or MW, newly built upon by lessees
Lease from Bailiffs, burgesses and commonalty to Johane Hopton of Ipswich, widow and son Henry Rycarde of Ipswich, labourer
Premises lie between highway leading from St Mary Elms church to Horsswade Mill on N. and close of George Wyld late common soil on S., both heads abutting on highway; for 1,000 years; 4*d* annual rent; 8*d* penalty for non-payment; not to be alienated without licence
English, 2 seals of grantees on tags

C/3/8/5/16   19 Jan. 1655
Capital messuage with malthouses in occupation of John Burrage, built on town soil and held in free burgage, in ME
Feoffment from Bailiffs, burgesses and commonalty to William Russell of Ipswich, maltster
Premises escheated to town after execution of George Wilde for felony; consideration of £150; 8*d* annual rent; Benjamin Butler appointed attorney to deliver seisin
English; grantee's seal missing from tag; never filed

C/3/8/6   GRANTS IN ST MARY AT QUAY PARISH   1419–1599

C/3/8/6/1   27 Sep. 1419
Piece of void land in MQ
Demise to fee-farm from William Debenham and Robert Lucas, Bailiffs, John Bernard and
William Stonham, Coroners, and commonalty, to John Tyler of Ipswich
Premises lie between common ditches on W. and highway on E., abutting N. and S. on common
soil; dimensions given; 8d annual rent
Latin; grantee's seal on tag; endorsed with memorandum of re-grant to William Carre for 12d
rent, 15 Hen. VII

C/3/8/6/2   27 Sep. 1419
Original of C/3/8/6/1
Latin; cancelled by mutilation; turn-up, Common Seal and tag cut away

C/3/8/6/3   26 Aug. 1434
Piece of land of common soil for building, and parcel of town walls in MQ
Demise from William Debenham and Thomas Denys, Bailiffs, and commonalty, to Richard
Doket, John Deken, William Whethereld, John Caldewell, Peter Terry, John Geet and Thomas
Dounham
Premises abut S. on common way from messuage late of William Snowe, now of John Tyndale
to town quay, and N. on said walls; dimensions given; 3d annual rent; names of 7 witnesses
Latin; 4 seals, 3 incomplete, on 3 tags

C/3/8/6/4   5 Feb. 1439
Piece of void land of common soil, late parcel of town walls, in MQ
Demise from John Dekene and William Whethereld, Bailiffs, and commonalty, to Richard
Doket, John Caldewall, Peter Terry, William Rydout, John Geet and Thomas Downham
Premises lie between tenement of John Tyler on E. and way leading towards house of Friars
Preachers on W., abutting S. on tenement of John Dekene and N. on Friars' garden; dimensions
given; 1d annual rent; names of 7 witnesses
Latin; 5 seals, 2 fragmentary

C/3/8/6/5   5 Feb. 1439
Original of C/3/8/6/4
Latin; fragment of Common Seal on tag

C/3/8/6/6   5 Feb. 1439
Piece of void land of common soil in MQ
Demise from John Dekene and William Whethereld, Bailiffs, and commonalty, to William
Debenham, Thomas Denys, Thomas Fastolf, Thomas Cowman, John Drayll and John
Caldewalle
Premises lie between tenement late of William Walworth and wife Margaret called langa[m]
domu[m] tegulat[am] (? the long tiled house) on W. and highway from le Caystrete to le
Frerysbryge on E., abutting S. on le Caystrete and N. on tenement of John Tyler; dimensions
given; 2s annual rent; names of 7 witnesses
Latin; seals of 4 grantees on 2 tags, 2 seals missing

C/3/8/6/7   24 Apr. 1446
Piece of void land in MQ
Grant from Thomas Denys and John Deken, Bailiffs, and commonalty, to Richard Gowty of
Ipswich
Premises lie between walls of Friars Preachers on W. and common way next to great pit called
le Sherhoushill on E., abutting S. on common latrine and common soil of town and N. on bridge
called le Frerysbrigge and on common soil of town; dimensions given; 12d annual rent; names
of 5 witnesses
Latin; fragment of grantee's seal on tag

C/3/8/6/8   24 Apr. 1446
Piece of void land of common soil in MQ
Grant from Thomas Denys and John Deken, Bailiffs, and commonalty, to William Baldry of
Ipswich, merchant
Premises lie between highway on N. and grantee's tenement formerly of Thomas Andrew on
S., abutting W. on tenement of William Whethereld formerly of Thomas Astelee and on
highway, and E. on said highway; dimensions given; 2*d* annual rent; names of 5 witnesses
Latin; grantee's seal on tag

C/3/8/6/9   [1448]
Piece of void land in MQ
Original grant from William Walworth and Robert [Smyth] [Bailiffs] . . . to John Gee . . .
[? Geete]
Latin; fragment only, cancelled by mutilation

C/3/8/6/10   27 Sep. 1453
Piece of void land of common soil
Demise from Richard Felawe and Robert Smyth, Bailiffs, and burgesses and commonalty, to
Thomas Denys of Ipswich
Premises lie in le Sherehous pettys, between garden formerly of Robert Wode and tenement of
Richard Felawe on E. and common soil called le Sherehous pettys on W., abutting N. on said
common soil and S. on way leading from Clement Strete to common latrines of town; dimen-
sions given; 4*d* annual rent
Latin; grantee's seal on tag

C/3/8/6/11   24 Mar. 1462
Piece of land of common soil
Demise in fee-farm from Roger Stannard, Bailiff, and burgesses and commonalty, to Richard
Felawe of Ipswich
Premises lie between garden of John Gosse on N. and tenements of Richard Felawe and Walter
Whytlok on S., abutting E. on tenement of Thomas Denys and W. on highway; 4*d* annual rent
Latin; grantee's seal on tag

C/3/8/6/12   31 Mar. 1466
2 pieces of land of common soil in MQ
Grant from Richard Felawe and Roger Stannard, Bailiffs, and commonalty, to John Gosse of
Ipswich
1st piece lies between walls of Friars Preachers on W. and common way next to le Sherehowse
hyll on E., abutting S. on common latrine and common soil of town and N. towards bridge
called le Frerysbregge on common soil there; 2nd piece between land of Nicholas Swan and
land late of William Keche and John Osberne, abutting W. on common way and E. on land of
Thomas Vyrdon; dimensions given; 8*d* annual rent; names of 5 witnesses
Latin; grantee's seal on tag

C/3/8/6/13   20 Apr. 1479
Piece of land of common soil
Demise from John Rever and Thomas Drayll, Bailiffs, and Portmen, burgesses and common-
alty, to John Pekerell
Premises lie between brook flowing from Caldwell to quay of Ipswich on E. and walls of Friars
Preachers on W., abutting S. on curtilage of Richard Barbour, barker; 4*d* annual rent
Latin; fragment of grantee's armorial seal on tag

C/3/8/6/14   20 Apr. 1479
Piece of land of common soil
Demise from John Rever and Thomas Drayll, Bailiffs, and Portmen, burgesses and common-
alty, to John Tymperley sen. of Ipswich, esq.
Premises lie on E. side of grantee's tenement; dimensions given; 4*d* annual rent
Latin; grantee's armorial seal (fine impression) on tag

C/3/8/6/15   20 Aug. 1482
Piece of land of common soil with moiety of curtilage late of William Wattys in MQ; lately seized for non-payment of rent
Demise from John Hastyngs and Robert Blomvyle, Bailiffs, and Portmen, burgesses and commonalty, to John Tymperley sen., esq., wife Alice and son Roger
Premises lie between tenement formerly of William Snowe on W. and way leading from gate of Friars Preachers to common way on E., abutting N. on other part of said curtilage and S. on said common way; dimensions given; 6d annual rent
Latin; grantees' 3 seals on tags; endorsed with memorandum of re-grant to Margaret Gosse for 12d, 15 Hen. VII

C/3/8/6/16   26 Jun. 1487
Piece of land of common soil
Demise from John Walworth and William Bakere, Bailiffs, and burgesses and commonalty, to John Squyer, clerk
Premises lie below walls of Friars Preachers on E. and N.; dimensions given; annual rent of 3s 4d and 1 red rose; grantee to erect on said land a latrine for the grammar school boys
Latin; seal missing from tag; endorsed 'St Marie Key'

C/3/8/6/17   26 Aug. 1499
Piece of land of common soil
Grant from Thomas Baldry and Edmund Daundy, Bailiffs, and burgesses and commonalty, to William Bole
Premises lie between walls of Friars Preachers on W. and common way on E., abutting N. on common soil in tenure of Margaret Yole and S. on common soil in tenure of Margaret Johnson; dimensions given; 4d annual rent; 2d penalty for non-payment
Latin; grantee's seal missing from tongue; endorsed 'Seynt Mary Keye'

C/3/8/6/18   26 Aug. 1499
Piece of land of common soil
Grant from Thomas Baldry and Edmund Daundy, Bailiffs, and burgesses and commonalty, to Margaret Johnson, widow
Premises lie between walls of Friars Preachers on W. and common way on E., abutting N. on common soil in tenure of William Bole and S. on common soil in tenure of Margaret Gosse; dimensions given; 8d annual rent; 2d penalty for non-payment
Latin; fragment of grantee's seal on tag; endorsed 'St Mary Key'

C/3/8/6/19   26 Aug. 1499
Piece of land of common soil
Grant from Thomas Baldry and Edmund Daundy, Bailiffs, and burgesses and commonalty, to John Forgon of Ipswich
Premises lie between walls of Friars Preachers on W. and highway on E., abutting N. on common soil and S. on common soil in tenure of Peter Joye; dimensions given; 4d annual rent; 2d penalty for non-payment
Latin; grantee's seal on tag

C/3/8/6/20   26 Aug. 1499
Piece of land of common soil
Grant from Thomas Baldry and Edmund Daundy, Bailiffs, and burgesses and commonalty, to Peter Joye of Ipswich, roper
Premises lie between walls of Friars Preachers on W. and common way on E., abutting N. on common soil in tenure of John Forgon and S. on common soil in tenure of Ralph Stonham; dimensions given; 4d annual rent; 2d penalty for non-payment
Latin; grantee's seal (incomplete) on tag

C/3/8/6/21   26 Aug. 1499
Piece of land of common soil

Grant from Thomas Baldry and Edmund Daundy, Bailiffs, and burgesses and commonalty, to Ralph Stonham of Ipswich

Premises lie between walls of Friars Preachers on W. and common way on E., abutting N. on common soil in tenure of Peter Joye and S. on common soil in tenure of John Forgon; dimensions given; 3d annual rent; 2d penalty for non-payment

Latin; grantee's seal (incomplete) on tag

C/3/8/6/22   26 Aug. 1499

Piece of land of common soil

Grant from Bailiffs, burgesses and commonalty to John Forgon

Premises lie between walls of Friars Preachers on W. and [*missing*] on E., abutting N. on common soil in tenure of Ralph Stonham and S. on common soil in tenure of [*missing*] chaplain; dimensions given; 8d annual rent; 2d penalty for non-payment

Latin; grantee's seal on tag

C/3/8/6/23   26 Aug. 1499

Piece of land of common soil in 2 gardens

Grant from Thomas Baldry and Edmund Daundy, Bailiffs, and burgesses and commonalty, to John Squyer, clerk

Premises lie between garden which Margaret Gosse, widow, holds of common soil in lez Shirehouspittes on N. and garden which Richard Haxwarde held lately of common soil and common soil which is entrance from highway into tenement late of Richard Haxwade on S., abutting W. on highway and E. on common soil late in tenure of Geoffrey Osbern and said garden late of Richard Haxwade; dimensions given; 4d annual rent; 2d penalty for non-payment

Latin; grantee's seal on tag

C/3/8/6/24   26 Aug. 1499

Piece of land of common soil

Grant from Thomas Baldry and Edmund Daundi, Bailiffs, and burgesses and commonalty, to John Squyer, clerk

Premises lie between walls of Friars Preachers on W. and common way and common latrines on E., abutting N. on common soil, said latrines, and common soil in tenure of Margaret Gosse, and S. on common soil in tenure of William Carre late of Nicholas Wilkynson; dimensions given; 2d annual rent; 2d penalty for non-payment

Latin; grantee's seal on tag

C/3/8/6/25   26 Aug. 1499

Piece of land of common soil in 2 gardens

Grant from Thomas Baldry and Edmund Daundy, Bailiffs, and burgesses and commonalty, to Margaret Yole, widow

Premises lie between walls of Friars Preachers on W. and highway on E., abutting N. on common soil in tenure of William Lyster, chaplain and S. on common soil in tenure of William Cole; dimensions given; 4d annual rent; 2d penalty for non-payment

Latin; grantee's seal on tag

C/3/8/6/26   26 Aug. 1499

Tenement with garden and curtilage on common soil in MQ

Grant from Thomas Baldry and Edmund Daundy, Bailiffs, and burgesses and commonalty, to William Carre of Ipswich

Premises lie between walls of Friars Preachers of common soil and common soil in tenure of Thomas Alvard on W. and highway on E., abutting N. on common soil in tenure of John Squyer, clerk and S. on common soil in tenure of Thomas Alvard; dimensions given; 12d annual rent; 4d penalty for non-payment

Latin; grantee's seal (incomplete) on tag

C/3/8/6/27   10 Aug. 1518

Piece of land of common soil

Grant from Bailiffs, burgesses and commonalty to John Forgon of Ipswich, tanner
Premises lie between walls of Friars Preachers on W. and common way on E., abutting N. on common soil late in tenure of Peter Joye and S. on common soil in tenure of grantee; dimensions given; 3*d* annual rent; 2*d* penalty for non-payment; Nicholas Hervy and Robert Bray appointed attorneys to deliver seisin
Latin; seal and tag missing

C/3/8/6/28   18 Mar. 1553
Piece of land of common soil
Grant from John Hollond and Matthew Goodyng, Bailiffs, and burgesses and commonalty, to William Whetcroft, gent., Town Clerk
Premises lie at le Backgate of grantee, where he throws 'his horse mucke'; dimensions given; 2*d* annual rent; 1*d* penalty for non-payment
Latin; grantee's seal on tag; endorsed 'St Mary Key'

C/3/8/6/29   30 Mar. 1570
Piece of land of common soil in MQ, formerly in tenure of William Lyster, clerk
Grant from Robert Kinge and William Smarte, Bailiffs, and burgesses and commonalty, to Henry Charles of Ipswich, yeoman
Premises lie between common way on E. and wall of house late of Friars Preachers on W., abutting N. on common soil granted to Edmund Talbott and S. on common soil in tenure of Thomas Baylye; dimensions given; 4*d* annual rent; 2*d* penalty for non-payment; to be void if alienated to lord of any manor within 4 miles of Ipswich; John Hawys and Henry Hannam appointed attorneys to deliver seisin
Latin; grantee's seal on tag

C/3/8/6/30   30 Mar. 1570
Piece of land of common soil with 'le woodhouse' built thereon in MQ
Grant from Robert Kinge and William Smarte, Bailiffs, and burgesses and commonalty, to Henry Asshely of Ipswich, clothier
Premises lie between common way on E. and wall of house of Friars Preachers on W., abutting N. on common soil of town; dimensions given; with right to take sufficient water flowing beneath 'le woodhouse' for necessary use; dimensions given; 6*d* annual rent; 2*d* penalty for non-payment; to be void if alienated to lord of any manor within 4 miles of Ipswich; John Hawys and Henry Hannam appointed attorneys to deliver seisin
Latin; grantee's seal on tag

C/3/8/6/31   30 Mar. 1570
Piece of land of common soil, formerly in tenure of William Lyster, clerk, in MQ
Grant from Robert Kynge and William Smarte, Bailiffs, and burgesses and commonalty, to Edmund Talbott of Ipswich, sailor
Premises lie between common way on E. and wall late of Friars Preachers on W., abutting N. on common soil called le lyme yard; dimensions given; 4*d* annual rent; 2*d* penalty for non-payment; to be void if alienated to lord of any manor within 4 miles of Ipswich; John Hawys and Henry Hannam appointed attorneys to deliver seisin
Latin; grantee's seal on tongue

C/3/8/6/32   25 Sep. 1571
2 pieces of common soil and quay of common soil called Kinges Key in MQ
Grant from John Gardener and John Barker, Bailiffs, and burgesses and commonalty, to Christopher Merrell of Ipswich, merchant
1st piece lies between soil late of James Aldham on E. and capital tenement of grantee on W., abutting S. on salt water and N. on land of grantee; 2nd piece between grantee's tenement on S. and highway on N., abutting W. on tenement of Richard Kinge and said highway and E. on same way; quay between common soil in grantee's tenure on E. and common soil in tenure of Richard Kinge on other side, abutting N. on his capital tenement and S. on salt water; 10*d* annual rent; 4*d* penalty for non-payment; to be void if alienated to lord of any manor within

4 miles of Ipswich; John Hawys and Henry Hannam appointed attorneys to deliver seisin
Latin; grantee's seal on tag

C/3/8/6/33   28 Sep. 1599
Piece of land of common soil on which grantee has lately built new house
Grant from Bailiffs, burgesses and commonalty to John Carnabie of Ipswich, mariner
Premises lie near common quay; dimensions given; 12*d* annual rent; 12*d* penalty for non-payment; to be void if alienated to lord of any manor within 4 miles of Ipswich; William Hawys appointed attorney to deliver seisin
Latin; fragment of grantee's seal on tag

C/3/8/7   GRANTS IN ST MARY LE TOWER PARISH   1479–1581

C/3/8/7/1   17 Sep. 1479
Piece of land of common soil
Demise from John Rever and Thomas Drayll, Bailiffs, and Portmen and burgesses, to Roger Tymperley sen. of Ipswich
Premises lie next to wall ditches, opposite and near le Deyerylane; dimensions given; 2*d* annual rent
Latin; grantee's seal on tag

C/3/8/7/2   25 Sep. 1482
Piece of land of town ditch
Demise from John Hastyngs and Robert Blomvyle, Bailiffs, and Portmen, burgesses and commonalty, to Roger Tymperley sen. of Ipswich
Dimensions given; 1*d* annual rent
Latin; grantee's seal on tag

C/3/8/7/3   25 Sep. 1482
Original of C/3/8/7/2
Latin; cancelled by mutilation and incomplete; Common Seal and tag missing

C/3/8/7/4   25 Oct. 1485
Piece of land of common soil, built upon
Demise from Roger Tymperley and Nicholas Wynter, Bailiffs, and burgesses and commonalty, to Robert Kyrkehous
Premises lie on N. side of tenement of Archdeacon of Suffolk; dimensions given; 6*d* annual fee-farm
Latin; fragment of grantee's seal on tag

C/3/8/7/5   26 Jun. 1487
Piece of land of common soil
Demise from John Walworth and William Baker, Bailiffs, and Portmen and burgesses, to Master William Pekenham, Archdeacon of Suffolk
Premises lie on N. of grantee's tenement, extending 75 ft in length from Richard Dallyng's curtilage and 8 ft in width from stone wall of tenement; 2*d* annual rent
Latin; grantee's seal on tag

C/3/8/7/6   26 Aug. 1499
Piece of land of common soil
Grant from Thomas Baldry and Edmund Daundy, Bailiffs, and burgesses and commonalty, to William Baker, notary
Premises lie between tenement of Archdeacon of Suffolk on S. and common way on N., abutting W. on common soil in tenure of Henry Stannard and E. on highway; dimensions given; 2*d* annual rent; 2*d* penalty for non-payment; Thomas Hall and William Stisted appointed attorneys to deliver seisin
Latin; not slit for seal tag and apparently unexecuted

C/3/8/7/7   26 Aug. 1499
Piece of land of common soil late in tenure of Roger Tymperley
Grant from Thomas Baldry and Edmund Daundy, Bailiffs, and burgesses and commonalty, to
Robert Joury
Premises lie between town ditch on S. and highway called Cleystrete on N., abutting E. on
garden late of Roger Tymperley and common soil, and W. on common soil; dimensions given;
4d annual rent; 2d penalty for non-payment
Latin; fragment of grantee's seal on tag

C/3/8/7/8   20 Sep. 1513
Piece of land of common soil
Grant from Bailiffs (not named), burgesses and commonalty, to Richard Lenaker
Premises lie between highway leading from St Margaret's church to chapel of St Mary of Grace
on N. and common ditch of town on S., abutting E. on garden of John Melys and W. on pond;
dimensions given; 4d annual rent; 2d penalty for non-payment; Richard Roppekyn and Robert
Bray appointed attorneys to deliver seisin
Latin; grantee's seal on tongue

C/3/8/7/9   [19 Mar.] 1535
Piece of land of common soil
Grant from Nicholas Harvy and Thomas Manser, Bailiffs, and burgesses and commonalty, to
William Barone, clerk
Premises lie between capital ditch of town on S. and highway called Cleystrett on N., abutting
E. on garden of Thomas Manser and W. on garden of John Aleyn; dimensions given; 4d annual
rent; 2d penalty for non-payment
Latin; grantee's seal on tag

C/3/8/7/10   26 May 1536
Piece of land of common soil in MT
Grant to fee-farm from Robert Bray and John Pypho, Bailiffs, and burgesses and commonalty,
to John Aleyn of Ipswich, cordwainer
Premises lie between grantee's garden, formerly Richard Lynaker's on E. and common soil on
W., abutting S. on upper part of town ditch called le Waldykes and N. on common way from Holy
Trinity Priory to St Mary's chapel called Our Lady of Grace; dimensions given; 2d annual rent
Latin; grantee's seal on tag

C/3/8/7/11   4 Jul. 1548
Garden at le Walle Dytches
Grant from John Gardyner and Richard Byrde, Bailiffs, and burgesses and commonalty, to
William Candeler of Ipswich, tailor
Premises abut E. on little lane leading from le Walle Dytches to le Whoode house of Robert
Daundi of Ipswich, merchant, and W. on common soil; dimensions given; 6d annual rent; 4d
penalty for non-payment; Richard Byrde, cooper, appointed attorney to deliver seisin
Latin, grantee's seal on tag

C/3/8/7/12   1 Mar. 1552
Piece of land of common soil in MT
Grant from John Smith *alias* Dyer and Richard Smarte, Bailiffs, and burgesses and common-
alty, to Richard Bloyes of Ipswich, mercer
Premises lie near common soil garden in tenure of William Notingham sen.; dimensions given;
2s annual rent; 4d penalty for non-payment; grantee to maintain town wall against his land;
William Whetcrofte, gent., Common Clerk, appointed attorney to deliver seisin
Latin, grantee's seal on tag

C/3/8/7/13   20 Sep. 1552
Piece of land of common soil
Grant from John Smythe *alias* Dyer and Richard Smarte, Bailiffs, and burgesses and common-
alty, to Philip Wyllyams *alias* Foteman of Ipswich

Premises lie near common soil garden in tenure of Roger Heywarde on W.; dimensions given; 16*d* annual rent; 4*d* penalty for non-payment; grantee to maintain town wall against his land
Latin; incomplete and badly damp-stained; seal missing from tag

C/3/8/7/14   27 Jul. 1570
Piece of land, now a garden, in MT
Grant from Robert Kinge and William Smarte, Bailiffs, and burgesses and commonalty, to William Draper of Ipswich, fletcher
Premises abut W. on tenement of Robert Rooke and E. on barn of John Braye; dimensions given; 2*d* annual rent; 1*d* penalty for non-payment; to be void if alienated to lord of any manor within 4 miles of Ipswich; John Hawys and Henry Hannam appointed attorneys to deliver seisin
Latin, grantee's seal on tag

C/3/8/7/15   10 Aug. 1570
2 pieces of common soil, formerly in tenure of Anthony Cabo, in MT
Grant from Robert Kinge and William Smarte, Bailiffs, and burgesses and commonalty, to Henry Bodnam of Ipswich, pewterer
Premises lie, 1 piece between garden late of Thomas Manser, afterwards of [*blank*] Branston on W. and garden of Thomas Selye on E., abutting N. on Cleyestrete and S. on piece of void soil in common ditches lately granted to Anthony Cabo; 2nd piece [abutting] S. on common ditches, N. on garden late of Thomas Manser, E. on garden of Thomas Selye and W. on garden of Elizabeth Bennett; 4*d* annual rent; 2*d* penalty for non-payment; to be void if alienated to lord of any manor within 4 miles of Ipswich; John Hawys and Henry Hannam appointed attorneys to deliver seisin
Latin, grantee's seal on tag

C/3/8/7/16   10 Aug. 1570
Piece of common soil partly built upon, formerly of Robert Kyrkhouse, in MT
Grant from Robert Kinge and William Smarte, Bailiffs, and burgesses and commonalty, to Robert Rooke of Ipswich, labourer
Premises lie between Archdeacon of Suffolk's garden or orchard on S. and highway on N., abutting E. on John Bery's barn and W. on highway; dimensions given; 2*d* annual rent; 1*d* penalty for non-payment; to be void if alienated to lord of any manor within 4 miles of Ipswich; John Hawys and Henry Hannam appointed attorneys to deliver seisin
Latin, grantee's seal on tag

C/3/8/7/17   10 Aug. 1570
Original of C/3/8/7/16
Latin; fragment of Common Seal on tag; never filed

C/3/8/7/18   4 Apr. 1581
Piece of common soil partly built upon, formerly granted to Robert Roke, in MT
Grant from William Smarte and Robert Lymner, Bailiffs, and burgesses and commonalty, to Richard Goltie of Ipswich, yeoman
Premises lie between Archdeacon of Suffolk's garden or orchard on S. and highway on N., abutting E. on barn late of John Berrye and W. on highway; dimensions given; 2*d* annual rent; 1*d* penalty for non-payment; to be void if alienated to lord of any manor within 4 miles of Ipswich; John Hawys and Edward Cage appointed attorneys to deliver seisin
Latin, grantee's seal on tag

C/3/8/8   GRANTS IN ST MATTHEW'S PARISH   **1315–1597**

C/3/8/8/1   25 Sep. 1315
Void piece of land in MW
Demise from Thomas Stace and Alexander Margarete, Bailiffs, with assent of Richard Leeu, Thomas le Rente and Elias le Keu, Coroners, John de Whatefeld, Walter de Wessthale,

Laurence Cobbe, Gilberd Roberd, Henry le Rotoun, John le Mayster, William Schakelok, Roger Bonde, Clement le Spicer, John de Akenham and other good men, to Peter le Lokyer
Premises lie between Peter's messuage and messuage formerly of Robert le Chamberleyn on S. and common ditch of town on N.; grantee and heirs to maintain that part of ditch
Latin; seal missing

C/3/8/8/2   14 Jun. 1475
Pightle of common soil
Demise from John Walworth and Richard Felawe, Bailiffs, and Portmen and burgesses, to Robert Blomvyle of Ipswich
Premises lie next to Hanford Bregge, between meadow of Prior of Holy Trinity on N. and highway on S., E. head abutting on highway and W. head on common river bank; 2s 4d annual rent
Latin; grantee's seal on tag

C/3/8/8/3   2 Oct. 1476
Piece of common soil in MW
Demise to fee-farm from Benedict Caldewell and Edmund Wynter, Bailiffs, and burgesses and commonalty, to Walter Heryng of Ipswich
Premises lie next to lez Barregatis, between town ditch on E. and highway on W., abutting N. on highway and S. on common soil; dimensions given; 2d annual rent
Latin; grantee's seal on tag

C/3/8/8/4   2 Oct. 1476
Original of C/3/8/8/3
Latin; cancelled by mutilation; Common Seal and tag missing

C/3/8/8/5   17 Sep. 1479
Piece of land of town ditch
Demise from John Rever and Thomas Drayll, Bailiffs, and Portmen and burgesses, to Walter Heryng of Ipswich, merchant
Premises lie on N. of his tenement, lengthways from elm next to lez Buttys; dimensions given; 6d annual rent
Latin; grantee's seal (cracked) on tag

C/3/8/8/6   17 Sep. 1479
Original of C/3/8/8/5
Latin; cancelled by mutilation; Common Seal and tag missing

C/3/8/8/7   17 Sep. 1479
Piece of land of town ditch
Demise from John Rever and Thomas Drayll, Bailiffs, and Portmen and burgesses, to Walter Cowpere of Ipswich, labourer
Premises lie 100 ft lengthways from curtilage of Walter Heryng; dimensions given; 4d annual rent
Latin; grantee's seal on tag

C/3/8/8/8   17 Sep. 1479
Original of C/3/8/8/7
Latin; cancelled by mutilation; Common Seal and tag missing

C/3/8/8/9   19 Jun. 1483
Piece of common soil in MW
Demise from Benedict Caldewell and Thomas Drayll, Bailiffs, and burgesses and commonalty, to John Parker of Ipswich, carpenter
Premises lie between highway on N. and curtilage of Nicholas Pecok and town pasture called le pounde on S., abutting E. on common soil and W. on highway; dimensions given; 4d annual rent
Latin; grantee's seal on tag

C/3/8/8/10   26 Jun. 1487
Piece of common soil
Demise from John Walworth and William Baker, Bailiffs, and burgesses and commonalty, to
Calixtus Clerk and wife Emma
Premises lie between garden of Robert Dunche on N. and common soil on S.; dimensions
given; 2d annual rent
Latin; fragment of 1 seal on tag, 2nd seal missing

C/3/8/8/11   26 Jun. 1487
Original of C/3/8/8/10
Latin; cancelled by mutilation; Common Seal and tag missing

C/3/8/8/12   5 Feb. 1490
Piece of common soil in MW
Demise from John Hastyng and John Halle, Bailiffs, and Portmen and commonalty, to Robert
Fuller of Ipswich and wife Margaret, William Manser, Geoffrey Osborne, Robert Benne and
Robert Hardyng
Premises lie between Robert Fuller's tenement on W. and common way on E., abutting N. on
common way; dimensions given; 1d annual rent
Latin; 5 seals on tags, 6th seal missing; endorsed with memorandum of agreement that Robert
Fuller and his feoffees will forfeit 2d for every default in payment of rent

C/3/8/8/13   7 Jun. 1490
Piece of common soil with draw-well in MW
Demise from John Hastyng and John Halle, Bailiffs, and burgesses and commonalty, to
Thomas Cuttyng of Ipswich, mason
Premises lie on W. side of Robert Smyth's garden; dimensions given; 2d annual rent
Latin; seal missing from tag

C/3/8/8/14   7 Jun. 1490
Original of C/3/8/8/13
Latin; cancelled by mutilation; Common Seal and tag missing

C/3/8/8/15   11 Jul. 1491
Piece of land of common soil with piece of land previously granted to John Parker
Demise from Roger Tymperley and William Harlewyn, Bailiffs, and burgesses and common-
alty, to John Bryggys, chaplain
Premises lie between highway on N. and curtilage of Nicholas Pecok and wall of Ipswich Gaol
on S.; dimensions given; 6d annual rent; wardens of Corpus Christi Gild to have option of
buying land for 40s or to have 40s from any sale of land after grantee's death
Latin; grantee's seal (incomplete) on tag

C/3/8/8/16   21 Jul. 1497
Piece of land of common soil
Demise from Thomas Draill and William Baker, Bailiffs, and burgesses and commonalty, to
John Brigges, chaplain
Premises lie opposite grantee's chamber which he has newly built on another piece of common
soil granted to him shortly before; dimensions given; 2d annual rent
Latin; grantee's seal (incomplete) on tag

C/3/8/8/17   26 Aug. 1499
Tenement on common soil in MW
Grant from Thomas Baldry and Edmund Daundy, Bailiffs, and burgesses and commonalty, to
Margery who was wife of John Meye, deceased, Thomas Cady of Stoke, Thomas Gardener and
William Scarp
Premises lie between lane called Burstallane on E. and common ditch of town on W., abutting
N. on highway and S. on tenement of Thomas Gardener formerly of William Rydout; to hold to
use of last will of John Meye; 8d annual rent; 2d penalty for non-payment
Latin; 4 seals on tags; endorsed 'West Ward, Saint Mathues parissh'

C/3/8/8/18   26 Aug. 1499
Piece of common soil formerly of town ditch, and another piece of land of common soil, in MW
Grant from Thomas Balldry and Edmund Daundy, Bailiffs, and burgesses and commonalty, to
William Scarp
Premises lie, 1st piece between common soil held by Agnes Gosse on W. and lane leading from
highway to Clystrete on E., abutting S. on grantee's tenement and N. on Clystrete, 2nd piece
between said tenement on W. and lane on E., abutting N. on said tenement and S. on highway;
dimensions given; 4s annual rent; 4d penalty for non-payment
Latin; grantee's seal on tag; endorsed 'St Mathewe West Ward'

C/3/8/8/19   26 Aug. 1499
Piece of land of common soil in MW
Grant from Thomas Baldry and Edmund Daundy, Bailiffs, and burgesses and commonalty, to
Katherine Hill of Ipswich, widow
Premises lie between common soil held by Peter Lambe on W. and common soil held by Agnes
Gosse on E., abutting N. on Cleystrete and S. on grantee's tenement; dimensions given; 2s
annual rent; 4d penalty for non-payment
Latin; grantee's seal on tag; endorsed 'St Mathew West Ward'

C/3/8/8/20   26 Aug. 1499
Piece of land of common soil partly built upon in MW
Grant from Thomas Baldry and Edmund Daundy, Bailiffs, and burgesses and commonalty, to
Agnes Gosse, lately wife of Walter Heryng
Premises adjoin grantee's tenement, lying between common soil held by Katherine Hill on W.
and common soil held by William Scarp on E., abutting N. on Cleystrete; of which John Broke,
merchant, formerly held part for 6d annual rent; dimensions given; 3s 4d annual rent; 4d
penalty for non-payment
Latin; grantee's seal on tag; endorsed 'St Mathewe West Ward'

C/3/8/8/21   26 Aug. 1499
Tenement built on common soil in MW
Grant from Thomas Baldry and Edmund Daundy, Bailiffs, and burgesses and commonalty, to
Peter Lambe of Ipswich
Premises lie between tenement of Nicholas Pekocke which is of common soil on W. and
tenement and common soil garden of Katherine Hill on E., abutting S. on highway and N. on
highway called Cleye strete; 16s annual rent; 4d penalty for non-payment
Latin; grantee's seal on tag; endorsed 'St Mathewe'

C/3/8/8/22   26 Aug. 1499
Tenement on common soil, with garden, in MW
Grant from Thomas Baldry and Edmund Daundy, Bailiffs, and burgesses and commonalty, to
Nicholas Pecok and wife Margaret
Premises lie between highway on S. and common soil in tenure of John Brigges, chaplain on N.,
abutting E. on common soil tenement of Peter Lambe and W. on town gates; 12d annual rent;
2d penalty for non-payment
Latin; 2 seals of grantees on tags; endorsed 'St Mathew'

C/3/8/8/23   26 Aug. 1499
Tenement on piece of land of common soil in MW
Grant from Thomas Baldry and Edmund Daundy, Bailiffs, and burgesses and commonalty, to
Agnes Gosse, widow, lately wife of Walter Heryng
Premises lie between west gates of town on E. and common way on W., abutting S. on common
soil garden held by William Brakested and N. on highway; dimensions given; formerly granted
to Walter Heryng; 6d annual rent; 2d penalty for non-payment
Latin; fragment of grantee's seal on tag; endorsed 'St Mathewe West Ward'

C/3/8/8/24   26 Aug. 1499
Piece of land of common soil in MW

Grant from Thomas Baldry and Edmund Daundy, Bailiffs, and burgesses and commonalty, to Thomas Cuttyng
Premises lie between Robert Smyth's garden on E. and common way leading from Horswade towards highway leading from Ipswich towards Typtotes Crosse on W., abutting N. on same highway; dimensions given; 4d annual rent; 2d penalty for non-payment
Latin; grantee's seal on tag

C/3/8/8/25   26 Aug. 1499
Piece of land of common soil
Grant from Thomas Baldry and Edmund Daundy, Bailiffs, and burgesses and commonalty, to John Pitte sen.
Premises lie on W. of highway called Seynt Georges Lane in which a cross was lately placed, between garden and cottage of Thomas Drayll on N. and cottage of Prior of Holy Trinity on S., abutting W. on grantee's land; dimensions given; 4d annual rent; 2d penalty for non-payment
Latin; seal missing

C/3/8/8/26   26 Aug. 1499
Piece of land of common soil in MW
Grant from Thomas Baldry and Edmund Daundy, Bailiffs, and burgesses and commonalty, to William Braksted
Premises lie between town ditch on E. and common way on W., abutting S. on common soil garden held by Calixtus Clerk and N. on common soil curtilage held by Agnes Gosse; dimensions given; 8d annual rent; 2d penalty for non-payment
Latin; fragment of grantee's seal; endorsed 'Seynt Mathes West Ward'

C/3/8/8/27   30 Sep. 1499
Piece of land of common soil in MW
Grant from Thomas Baldry and Edmund Daundy, Bailiffs, and burgesses and commonalty, to Calixtus Clerk and wife Emma
Premises lie between town ditch on E. and common way on W., abutting N. on common soil garden of William Braksted and S. on common soil; dimensions given; 4d annual rent; 2d penalty for non-payment
Latin; 2 seals, both incomplete, on tags; endorsed 'St Mathewe West Ward'

C/3/8/8/28   20 Apr. 1517
Piece of land of common soil in MW
Grant from Henry Stannard and William Stisted, Bailiffs, and burgesses and commonalty, to Alexander Sparhauk
Premises lie between town ditch on E. and common way on W., abutting N. on common soil garden lately in tenure of Calixtus Clerk and S. on common soil curtilage held by Agnes Gosse; dimensions given; 8d annual rent; 2d penalty for non-payment
Latin; grantee's seal on tag

C/3/8/8/29   20 Apr. 1517
Original of C/3/8/8/28
Latin; Common Seal on tag; never filed

C/3/8/8/30   2 Aug. 1518
Piece of land of common soil with newly-built shop thereon in MW
Grant from Bailiffs (not named), burgesses and commonalty to John Peerson, haberdasher
Premises lie between messuage of William Barker, cooper, on E. and high street on W., abutting S. and N. on common soil; dimensions given; 8d annual rent; 2d penalty for non-payment
Latin; seal missing from tag

C/3/8/8/31   20 May 1521
Small piece of land of common soil in MW
Grant from Bailiffs (not named), burgesses and commonalty to John Wilde of Ipswich, mercer

311

Premises lie at W. end of grantee's tenement; dimensions given; 2d annual rent; 1d penalty for non-payment; Christopher Heiward and Robert Bray appointed attorneys to deliver seisin
Latin; grantee's seal (incomplete) on tag

C/3/8/8/32   10 Nov. 1523
Small piece of land of common soil
Grant from Bailiffs (not named), burgesses and commonalty to John Pipho
Premises lie at E. end of chapel of St Mildred the Virgin of Ipswich; dimensions given; 20d annual rent; 4d penalty for non-payment; Alexander Sparhawk and Robert Bray appointed attorneys to deliver seisin
Latin; grantee's seal on tag

C/3/8/8/33   2 Sep. 1538
Easement with horse and cart in lane on W. side of grantee's messuage, of old time called the Mille Waye and on piece of ground on W. of grantee's broad gate
Demise to fee-farm from Robert Joyne and Lawrence Stysted, Bailiffs, and burgesses and commonalty, to Margaret Pykerell, widow; 1d annual rent; 1d penalty for non-payment
English; grantee's seal on tag

C/3/8/8/34   14 Mar. 1547
Piece of ground of common soil
Demise to fee farm from John Holland and John Dier, Bailiffs, and burgesses and commonalty, to William Notingham sen., merchant
Premises lie on N. side of wall dykes towards S. and common way leading from St Matthew's church to St Margaret's church on N., abutting W. on messuage sometime John Heyron's and E. on residue of common soil; dimensions given; 2s annual rent; 6d penalty for non-payment; Richard Brid alias Byrd, Town Clerk appointed attorney to deliver seisin
English; grantee's seal on tag

C/3/8/8/35   20 Sep. 1552
Piece of land of common soil
Grant from John Smythe alias Dyar and Richard Smarte, Bailiffs, and burgesses and commonalty, to John Rewarde alias Harrys of Ipswich, sawyer
Premises lie on W. of St George's Lane between garden and cottage of [blank] Reynborough on N. and cottage in grantee's tenure on S., abutting W. on land of John Smithe alias Dyer; dimensions given; 4d annual rent; 2d penalty for non-payment
Latin; seal missing from tag

C/3/8/8/36   30 Mar. 1570
Piece of common soil on which part of grantee's capital messuage is now built, in MW
Grant from Robert Kinge and William Smarte, Bailiffs, and burgesses and commonalty, to Christopher Lawrence of Ipswich, clothier
Premises lie between residue of grantee's tenement on W. and common way at well there on E., abutting N. on highway; dimensions given; 1d annual rent; 1d penalty for non-payment; John Hawys and Henry Hannam appointed attorneys to deliver seisin; to be void if alienated to lord of any manor within 4 miles of Ipswich
Latin; grantee's seal on tongue

C/3/8/8/37   4 Jul. 1570
Piece of land of common soil with tenement and draw-well lately built thereon, in MW
Grant from Robert Kinge and William Smarte, Bailiffs, and burgesses and commonalty, to Thomas Bateman of Ipswich, blacksmith
Premises lie between lane from Horswade Mill to Typtotts Cross on W. and garden late of John Curtis on E., abutting N. on highway; dimensions given; 4d annual rent; 2d penalty for non-payment; John Hawys and Henry Hannam appointed attorneys to deliver seisin; to be void if alienated to lord of any manor within 4 miles of Ipswich
Latin; grantee's seal on tongue

C/3/8/8/38   27 Jul. 1570
Piece of land of common soil in MW
Grant from Robert Kinge and William Smarte, Bailiffs, and burgesses and commonalty, to
James Nottingham of Ipswich, grocer
Premises lie between town ditch on S. and common way leading from St Matthew's church to
St Margaret's church on N., abutting W. on lane next to messuage formerly John Heyron's and
E. on common soil; dimensions given; 2s annual rent; 6d penalty for non-payment; John Hawis
and Henry Hannam appointed attorneys to deliver seisin; to be void if alienated to lord of any
manor within 4 miles of Ipswich
Latin; grantee's seal (incomplete) on tag

C/3/8/8/39   27 Sep. 1581
Piece of land of common soil, lately newly built upon in part, in MW
Grant (original) from William Smarte and Robert Lymner, Bailiffs, and burgesses and commonalty, to Geoffrey Moose of Ipswich, labourer
Premises lie in suburbs, between highway on S. and close in occupation of William Dyer on N.,
abutting E. on land in tenure of John Gilham and W. on said highway; dimensions given; 2d
annual rent; 1d penalty for non-payment; to be void if alienated to lord of any manor within
4 miles of Ipswich; John Hawys and Edward Cage appointed attorneys to deliver seisin
Latin; Common Seal (incomplete) on tag

C/3/8/8/40   19 Feb. 1596
Piece of land of common soil, now newly built upon in part, in MW
Grant from Bailiffs (not named), burgesses and commonalty to John Mose *alias* Bower of
Ipswich, ropemaker
Premises lie by the Butts, between common way from Ipswich to Bramford on N. and close of
Edmund Withepoll, esq. in occupation of John Murton on S.; dimensions given; 12d annual
rent; 6d penalty for non-payment; to be void if alienated to lord of any manor within 4 miles of
Ipswich; Christopher Ballard and William Hawys appointed attorneys to deliver seisin
Latin; grantee's seal on tag

C/3/8/8/41   30 Jan. 1597
Piece of land of common soil, now newly built upon in part, in MW
Grant from William Sparrowe and John Brownerigge, Bailiffs, and burgesses and commonalty
to William Webster of Ipswich, carpenter
Premises lie against cross called Stoninge Crosse, between highway from Ipswich to Sproughton
on N. and land of Tobias Blosse in occupation of William Nobbes on S.; dimensions given; 4d
annual rent; 3d penalty for non-payment; to be void if alienated to lord of any manor within
4 miles of Ipswich; William Hawys, gent. appointed attorney to deliver seisin
Latin; grantee's seal (incomplete) on tag; never filed

C/3/8/9   GRANTS IN ST NICHOLAS PARISH   **1332–1663**

C/3/8/9/1   7 Jul. 1332
Piece of land in NI
Grant from Bailiffs and commonalty to Roger de Croxtone, fellow burgess of Ipswich
Premises lie at le Colhull, between highway next to Carmelite friars on N. and tenement
formerly of Geoffrey Stonylynere on S., abutting W. on grantee's garden formerly purchased
from Gilbert Waleys and wife Gundred and E. on said highway; dimensions given; 2d annual
rent towards town farm; names of 10 witnesses including Gilbert de Burgh and William Smyth,
Bailiffs
Latin; grantee's seal on tag

C/3/8/9/2   29 Apr. 1378
Piece of land of common soil in NI

Grant from Geoffrey Starlyng sen. and Robert Waleys, Bailiffs, and commonalty, to George de Filbrigge and Richard de Martlesham
Premises lie between house of friars of St Mary of Mount Carmel and highway leading towards Stokebregge, abutting N. on said house and S. on messuage formerly of Richard Ryngeld; dimensions given; 2d annual rent; names of 5 witnesses
Latin; 2 seals on tags, 1 armorial and 1 (cracked) equestrian

C/3/8/9/3   14 Sep. 1417
Piece of land of common soil in NI
Demise to fee-farm from John Starling and Hugh Hoo, Bailiffs, John Bernard and William Stonham, Coroners, and commonalty, to Robert Parmasay of Ipswich
Premises lie between common way on E. and [river] bank running from Horswademell towards new mill on W., abutting S. on common way called la Forthe and N. on common soil; dimensions given; 8d annual rent
Latin; grantee's seal on tag; endorsed with memorandum of regrant to Thomas Bole for 3s annual rent, 15 Hen. VII

C/3/8/9/4   14 Sep. 1417
Original of C/3/8/9/3
Latin; cancelled by mutilation; Common Seal and tag missing

C/3/8/9/5   14 Sep. 1417
Piece of land of common soil in NI
Demise to fee-farm from John Starlyng and Hugh [Hoo], Bailiffs, John [Bernard and William] Stonham, Coroners, and commonalty, to Robert Parmasay
Premises lie between common way called [missing] on N. and garden of [Friars] Minor on S., abutting E. on common way and [W. on river] bank; 8d annual rent
Latin; incomplete; grantee's seal on tag; endorsed with memorandum of regrant to Agnes Kene for 12d annual rent, 15 Hen. VII

C/3/8/9/6   12 Aug. 1421
Piece of land of common soil in NI
Demise to fee-farm from John Kneppyng and John Joye, Bailiffs, John Wode and Robert Bikleswade, Coroners, and commonalty, to Richard Chamberleyn of Chelmyngton [?Chelmondiston], Thomas Denys, Michael Dexter, Thomas Wysman, Thomas Chamberleyn of Ipswich and wife Alice
Premises lie between messuage of grantees on S. and tenement of John Soty on N., abutting W. on highway leading from Stokebrigge towards le Cornhill; dimensions given; 2d annual rent
Latin; 6 seals on 6 tags; endorsed with memorandum of regrant to Walter Quyntyn for same rent, 15 Hen. VII

C/3/8/9/7   7 Mar. 1437
2 pieces of common soil, in NI and CL
Demise to fee-farm from William Walworth and Robert Drye, Bailiffs, and commonalty, to William Debenham, John Deken, William Wethereld, John Caldewell, John Blankpayn, William Rydout, Robert Parmasey and John Frenssh jun.
1st piece in NI lies next to messuage of John Frenssh on S. and common way on N.; 2nd piece in CL lies next to highway on W., opposite messuage of John Frenssh on E.; dimensions given; 4d and 2d annual rent
Latin; 8 seals on 4 tags; endorsed with memorandum of regrant of 1st piece to John Mason for 8d annual rent, 15 Hen. VII, and that 2nd piece lies in highway

C/3/8/9/8   4 Apr. 1443
Void piece of land of common soil
Demise from Thomas Denys and John Caldewall, Bailiffs, and commonalty, to Robert Parmasay
Premises lie between common river bank on W. and highway on E., abutting S. on grantee's common soil garden and [N.] on common spring; dimensions given; 4d annual rent

Latin; grantee's seal on tag; endorsed with memorandum of regrant to Thomas Bole for 3s rent, 15 Hen VII

C/3/8/9/9   13 Feb. 1483
Common soil called le Colehyll
Demise from Benedict Caldwell and Thomas Drayll, Bailiffs, and Portmen, burgesses and commonalty, to William Baker, notary
Premises lie between grantee's curtilage on E. and curtilage late of Richard Bramston on W., abutting N. on common way and S. on soil of Prior of St Peter; 4d annual rent
Latin; grantee's seal on tag

C/3/8/9/10   15 Mar. 1493
Piece of land of common soil
Demise from Richard Haxwade and William Sewale, Bailiffs, and burgesses and commonalty, to Hugh Lavys and wife Alice
Premises lie near le Colhyll, between garden late of Nicholas Bramston on S. and common soil on N.; dimensions given; 2d annual rent
Latin; fragment of 1 grantee's seal on tag, the other missing

C/3/8/9/11   26 Aug. 1499
Part of tenement once of Thomas Chambirleyn, i.e. the part on common soil, in NI
Grant from Thomas Baldry and Edmund Daundy, Bailiffs, and burgesses and commonalty, to Walter Quyntyn, clerk, John Resshbroke, John Lane and Richard Faryngton
Premises lie between grantee's messuage formerly of Thomas Chambirleyn on S. and tenement of John Stey now of William Baker, notary on N., abutting E. on highway; dimensions given; 2d annual rent; 2d penalty for non-payment
Latin; 1 seal and fragments of 3 others on 2 tags; endorsed 'South ward'

C/3/8/9/12   26 Aug. 1499
Piece of land of common soil in NI
Grant from Thomas Baldry and Edmund Daundy, Bailiffs, and burgesses and commonalty, to Thomas Cady of Stoke
Premises lie near le Colehyll, between grantee's garden on W. and common soil on E., 58½ ft long from garden of Hugh Lowes to S.; other dimensions given; 2d annual rent; 2d penalty for non-payment
Latin; grantee's seal on tag

C/3/8/9/13   (26 Aug. 1499) [t. Eliz I]
Piece of land of common soil in NI
Grant from Thomas Baldry and Edmund Daundy, Bailiffs, and burgesses and commonalty, to Agnes Kene, widow
Premises lie between walls of Friars Minor on S. and common way called le Forthe on N., abutting E. on common soil in common way and W. on common stream; dimensions given; 12d annual rent; 4d penalty for non-payment; Thomas Hall and William Stysted appointed attorneys to deliver seisin
Latin; later re-issue; seal missing from tag

C/3/8/9/14   26 Aug. 1499
Original of C/3/8/9/13
Latin; never filed; fragment of Common Seal on tag

C/3/8/9/15   10 Oct. 1511
Piece of land of common soil
Grant from Bailiffs, burgesses and commonalty to Thomas Bole, barker
Premises lie between common river bank leading to Horswade Mill on W. and common way on E., abutting N. on common soil in tenure of Avelina wife of John Dier and S. on common way and le Forthe; dimensions given; 3s annual rent; 4d penalty for non-payment; grantee to repair bank; John Barbor and Robert Bray appointed attorneys to deliver seisin
Latin; seal missing from tag; endorsed 'Seynt Nycholas'

C/3/8/9/16   27 May 1536
Piece of land of common soil in NI
Demise to fee-farm from Robert Bary and John Pypho, Bailiffs, and burgesses and common-
alty, to Robert Bobet sen. of Ipswich, mercer
Premises lie between and below stone wall of Friars Minor on N. and garden of Thomas Clere
of Colchester on S., abutting W. on fresh stream and E. on entrance to garden of Thomas Clere
called 'a karte waye'; dimensions given; 2s annual rent
Latin; seal missing from tag

C/3/8/9/17   1 Sep. 1547
Piece of waste ground
Demise to fee-farm from John Holland and John Dier, Bailiffs, and burgesses and commonalty,
to John Butler of Ipswich, grocer
Premises lie by way from White Friars' back gate to back gate of late College to W. and by
garden of grantee to E., abutting S. on residue of soil called Cothill and N. on common soil;
dimensions given; 2d annual rent; 1d penalty for non-payment; Richard Brid *alias* Bird
appointed attorney to deliver seisin
English: fragment of grantee's seal on tag

C/3/8/9/18   22 Apr. 1567
Piece of common soil in NI
Grant from Geoffrey Gylberte and John Moore, Bailiffs, and burgesses and commonalty, to
Christopher Alderman of Ipswich, clothier
Premises lie opposite St Nicholas's churchyard at W. end of his garden; dimensions given;
grantee to allow common way 24 ft wide on N. of said piece; 12d annual rent, or 2s if not paid
on Monday after Michaelmas; Robert Hall appointed attorney to deliver seisin
Latin; grantee's seal on tag

C/3/8/9/19   10 Aug. 1570
Piece of common soil newly built upon in NI
Feoffment from Robert Kynge and William Smarte, Bailiffs, and burgesses and commonalty,
to John Gardner of Ipswich, clothier, one of the Portmen of Ipswich
Premises lie between garden of William Barbor on S. and common path near le Forthe on N.,
abutting W. on garden late of Thomas Maddocke and E. on said common path; dimensions
given; 1d annual rent, 1d penalty for non-payment; to be void if alienated to lord of any manor
within 4 miles of Ipswich; John Hawys and Henry Hannam appointed attorneys to deliver
seisin
Latin; grantee's seal on tag

C/3/8/9/20   18 Sep. 1570
Various pieces of common soil in NI, late Beamondes
Feoffment from Robert Kynge and William Smarte, Bailiffs, and burgesses and commonalty,
to Christopher Alderman of Ipswich, clothier
Premises lie between garden late of Thomas Sotye on S. and common lane on N., abutting E. on
garden of Thomas Bobbett; and another piece formerly of William Baker, notary, lies between
last piece on E. and tenement and land late of Robert Bobbett on W., abutting N. on said
common land and S. on curtilage of grantee, late of William Baker, formerly of Thomas Sotye;
5d annual rent; 2d penalty for non-payment; to be void if alienated to lord of any manor within 4
miles of Ipswich; John Hawys and Henry Hannam appointed attorneys to deliver seisin
Latin; grantee's seal on tag

C/3/8/9/21   21 Sep. 1570
Garden, parcel of piece of land of common soil formerly of Roger Croxton in NI
Feoffment from Robert Kynge and William Smarte, Bailiffs, and burgesses and commonalty,
to Richard Cornelius *alias* Joyner of Ipswich, joiner
Premises lie between common soil late of John Boyston on E. and common soil garden and
barn of Thomas Bobbett on W., abutting N. on common way next to late Carmelite Friars and S.

on garden of Walter Hunne late of Geoffrey Stovelyn; dimensions given; 1*d* annual rent; 1*d* penalty for non-payment; to be void if alienated to lord of any manor within 4 miles of Ipswich; John Hawys and Henry Hannam appointed attorneys to deliver seisin
Latin; grantee's seal on tag

C/3/8/9/22   4 Apr. 1581
Piece of land, in part lately called a lane, part of common soil
Feoffment from William Smarte and Robert Lymner, Bailiffs, and burgesses and commonalty, to John Hawys of Ipswich, gent.
Premises lie between garden of capital messuage of Bishop of Norwich, late of Lord Curson, garden of almshouses of NI, and garden late of William Hawys, deceased, on W., and garden held by copy of court roll of lords of St Peter late in tenure of Thomas Whytinge, garden late of George Coppinge, deceased, and garden late of Bartholomew Fenn in right of his deceased wife on E., abutting S. on common soil garden late in tenure of George Coppinge and N. on common way; 6*d* annual rent; 3*d* penalty for non-payment; to be void if alienated to lord of any manor within 4 miles of Ipswich; Edward Cage and Peter Astbrooke appointed attorneys to deliver seisin
Latin; seal missing from tag

C/3/8/9/23   29 Jul. 1585
Triangular piece of void soil, in part newly built upon, in NI
Feoffment from Bailiffs, burgesses and commonalty to Richard Glede of Ipswich, mason
Premises lie on E. side of highway leading from St Nicholas church to orchard or garden of John Pavys *alias* Daye, late Jennyngs, near wall of William Webbe; dimensions given; 6*d* annual rent; 12*d* penalty for non-payment; to be void if alienated to lord of any manor within 4 miles of Ipswich; John Hawys sen. and Edward Cage appointed attorneys to deliver seisin
Latin; seal and tag torn away

C/3/8/9/24   1 Oct. 1663
Little piece of ground sometime occupied with several poor houses of the town, with house built on part thereof in occupation of John Deering sen., with well and pump, in NI
Demise for 1,000 years from Bailiffs, burgesses and commonalty to John Deering jun. of Ipswich, baker
Premises lie between house and ground of John Deering and orchard belonging to Cursome House; dimensions given; 2*s* annual rent, 2*s* 6*d* penalty for non-payment
English; grantee's seal on tag; never filed

C/3/8/10   GRANTS IN ST PETER'S PARISH   1416–1567

C/3/8/10/1   12 Sep. 1416
Void piece of land of common soil in PE
Demise to fee-farm from John Kneppyng and Hugh Hoo, Bailiffs, William Chamb'r, 1 of Coroners, and commonalty, to John Chestan, Robert Lucas, William Piers, William Heylee and Edmund Carleton
Premises lie between tenement of Edmund Carleton on W. and highway on E., abutting S. on highway called Brookstrete and N. on entrance through great gates from said highway to Edmund's tenement; dimensions given; 4*d* annual rent
Latin; 5 grantees' seals on 5 tags; endorsed 'St Mary Key' [*sic*]

C/3/8/10/2   23 May 1426
Piece of void land of common soil in PE
Demise to fee-farm from John Joye and John Caldewell, Bailiffs, John Kneppyng and William Whedereld, Coroners, and commonalty, to Geoffrey Pape of Ipswich
Premises lie next to grantee's messuage on E. and common way leading from bridge called Stokebrigge towards St Peter's church; dimensions given; 4*d* annual rent
Latin; grantee's seal on tag

C/3/8/10/3   4 Oct. 1473
Piece of land of common soil in PE
Demise from Benedict Caldewell and John Hastyng, Bailiffs, and commonalty, to Nicholas
Wynter
Premises lie between pond of new mill on S. and common way on N., abutting W. on garden of
John Braunston and E. on tenement of John Heynys; dimensions given; 4*d* annual rent
Latin; grantee's seal on tag

C/3/8/10/4   n.d. [1499]
Piece of void land of common soil now built upon, parcel of grantee's tenement, lately granted
to Geoffrey Pape
Grant from Thomas Baldry and Edmund Daundy, Bailiffs, and burgesses and commonalty, to
Edmund Steward
Premises lie between grantee's tenement on E. and common way leading beyond le Stokebregge
on W.; dimensions given; 4*d* annual rent; 2*d* penalty for non-payment
Latin; grantee's seal on tag; endorsed 'Southward'

C/3/8/10/5   26 Aug. 1499
Piece of land of common soil which grantee has accroached to his tenement
Grant from Thomas Baldry and Edmund Daundy, Bailiffs, and burgesses and commonalty, to
William Spenser of Ipswich
Premises lie between grantee's tenement on S., abutting E. on common soil lately in tenure of
Richard Haxwade; 2*s* annual rent
Latin; grantee's seal incomplete; endorsed 'Sencte Peter'

C/3/8/10/6   31 Jul. 1509
Licence to build 'pictorium vocatum a tentour' [? a dye works] on common soil called le Shete;
with free entry and exit
Grant from Thomas Drayll and William Spencer, Bailiffs, and burgesses and commonalty, to
Robert Goodwyn
Premises lie on S. side of new mill; 6*d* annual rent
Latin; grantee's seal and most of tag missing

C/3/8/10/7   30 Jun. 1513
Piece of land of common soil called le Shete, on which is newly built 'unum pictorium vocatum
a Teyntour' [? a dye works], with free entry and exit by gate between great bridge on S. end of
watermill house
Grant from Bailiffs, burgesses and commonalty to Robert Goodwyn
6*d* annual rent; 2*d* penalty for non-payment; grantee to repair all stonework and timber work of
quay of le Shete of said mill up to E. end of le Shete, and from E. end to great bridge; Richard
Ropkyn and Robert Bray appointed attorneys to deliver seisin
Latin; seal and tag missing

C/3/8/10/8   10 Sep. 1514
Piece of land of common soil
Grant from Bailiffs, burgesses and commonalty to Robert Kene of Ipswich, tailor
Premises lie between pond of watermill on S. and highway leading from Friars Minor to town
quay, abutting E. on garden of Robert Goodwyn and W. on garden of Nicholas Wynter; dimensions given; 4*d* annual rent; 2*d* penalty for non-payment; Thomas Wymbill and Robert Bray
appointed attorneys to deliver seisin; grantee to open land whenever grantors flood and scour
mill pond of 'le Newe millis'
Latin; grantee's seal on tongue

C/3/8/10/9   1 Mar. 1515
Piece of land of common soil
Grant from Bailiffs, burgesses and commonalty to Thomas Reynold of Ipswich, tailor
Premises lie between grantee's curtilage on E. and piece of common soil late in tenure of
William Baker, notary, parcel of le Colehill, now lying void, on W., abutting S. on garden of

318

John Botteler and N. on highway; dimensions given; 4d annual rent; 2d penalty for non-payment; Robert Bray and Thomas Bloyse appointed attorneys to deliver seisin
Latin; fragment of grantee's seal on tongue; endorsed 'Sent Peters'

C/3/8/10/10   22 Apr. 1567
Piece of land of common soil in PE
Feoffment from Geoffrey Gylbert and John Moore, Bailiffs, and burgesses and commonalty, to Robert Hall of Ipswich, clothier
Premises lie on either side of common soil now granted to Christopher Alderman, up to W. end of grantee's garden; dimensions given; 12d annual rent, or 2s if not paid by Monday after Michaelmas; Christopher Alderman of Ipswich, clothier, appointed attorney to deliver seisin
Latin; grantee's seal on tag

C/3/8/11   GRANTS IN UNIDENTIFIED PARISHES   1341–1499

C/3/8/11/1   23 Nov. 1341
Place on the great walls of Ipswich
Demise for life, from Bailiffs and commonalty to Peter Casteleyn of Ipswich
Premises lie opposite Peter's tenement on E.; to build dye works 40 ells long; 6d annual rent, grantee to maintain wall opposite; names of 16 witnesses including Geoffrey Stace and William de Kenebrook, Bailiffs
Latin; seal missing

C/3/8/11/2   23 May 1344
Place on the walls of Ipswich
Demise from commonalty to William de Ipre
Premises lie opposite le Shirehoushes next to S. gates of Friars Preachers; for dye works, 40 ells long, to be newly built by grantee; grantee to repair wall opposite; 10d annual rent; names of 13 witnesses including John de Prestone and John Irp, Bailiffs
Latin; grantee's seal on tag

C/3/8/11/3   16 Feb. 1349
Place of land adjoining the place of the Friars Preachers
Grant in free alms from Bailiffs and commonalty to Prior and Convent of Friars Preachers of Ipswich
Premises lie between Friars' curtilage on N. and common place on S., abutting W. on curtilage and E. on middle of ditch of common wall; Friars to maintain wall opposite and 2 great gates at N. and S. ends of their court; commonalty to have access through gates for defence of town; 6d annual rent; names of 12 witnesses including John de Prestone and Thomas Lew, Bailiffs
Latin; ascenders of letters ornamented with grotesque faces; seal missing

C/3/8/11/4   13 Apr. 1368
Empty place (24 ft square) in timber market
Demise from Bailiffs and commonalty to Henry Starlying
To build upon; annual rent of 12d to the farm of the town
Latin; grantee's seal on tag

C/3/8/11/5   21 Aug. 1391
Piece of land of the common soil
Grant from Godfrey Starlying and John Andreu, Bailiffs, and commonalty, to Gilbert de Boulge, William Gunnyed, Henry Walle and John Arnald
Premises lie on either side of causeway from Portbregge to Stokebregge, with 'dammying' extending from Stokebregge towards Stokemelledam; 6s annual rent
Latin; 4 seals, 1 armorial, 1 incomplete

C/3/8/11/6   21 Aug. 1391
Original of C/3/8/11/5
Common Seal, almost complete, on tag

C/3/8/11/7   31 Mar. 1468
Parcel of town ditch, with sluice
Demise from Robert Halle and William Style, Bailiffs, and commonalty, to John Walworth of
Ipswich, gent
Premises lie opposite grantee's curtilage; 4d annual rent
Latin; endorsed with memorandum of voidance for non-payment; fragment of seal on tag

C/3/8/11/8   17 Sep. 1479
Parcel of common soil
Demise from John Rever and Thomas Drayll, Bailiffs, and Portmen and burgesses, to Peter
Joye of Ipswich, roper
Premises lie next to town ditch, opposite highway leading from round cross to Blakfryysbregge;
8d annual rent
Latin; endorsed with memorandum of grant to Richard Osberne; incomplete seal on tag
[property in East Ward, 15 Hen. VII]

C/3/8/11/9   26 Aug. 1499
Tenement on common soil
Grant from Thomas Baldrey and Edmund Daundy, Bailiffs, and commonalty, to Matthew
Wood of Ipswich, butcher
Premises lay on S. side of butcher's house in le Tinbirmerket formerly granted to Henry Sterlyng
and afterwards in occupation of William Keche; 12d annual rent
Latin; fragment of seal on tag
[property in West Ward, 15 Hen. VII; became fleshstalls]

C/3/9   TOWN ESTATE   1312–1833

C/3/9/1   EVIDENCES OF TITLE   **1388–1814**

C/3/9/1/1   OLD BOROUGH GAOL   1388–1636

C/3/9/1/1/1   1388–1636
Two messuages in MW and/or ME
Evidences of title for purchase by Edmond Kene, John Aldus, William Tyler, William
Sparrowe, gents, Peter Fisher, mercer, Thomas Knappe, merchant, Richard Dennye sen.,
haberdasher and William Doggett, mercer, all of Ipswich [on behalf of Ipswich Corporation],
from Christopher Tollson of Ipswich, haberdasher, wife Margaret, and Anne Tollson, widow,
10 Sep. 1636
First messuage lay in MW between messuage in occupation of Francis Goodinge and James
Greve and way from New Barrgates to Stoke Bridge on W. and tenement late of John Cole on
E., abutting N. on St Matthew's Street and S. on garden late of John Cole, land late of Sir Robert
Hitcham, kt, and second messuage; second messuage lay in MW or ME, between yard in occu-
pation of William Moysey on S. and messuage in occupation of Goodinge and Greve on N.,
abutting W. on way from Barrgates and E. on first messuage
(Rolled file of 19 docs, threaded on a lace and endorsed: 'The Conveyances for the Gaole late
Tollsons, perused 29 May [16]85')

C/3/9/1/1/2   30 Sep., 7 Nov. 1636
[Property as in C/3/9/1/1/1]
Acquittances by Christopher Toulson for instalments of purchase money for house 'latelie
assured by me and my mother to the townes use and late my fathers'
(2 acquittances on 1 fol.)

C/3/9/1/1/3   22 Nov. 1636
[Property as in C/3/9/1/1/1]
Acquittance by Christopher Toulson for final instalment of purchase money for house 'nowe
used for the Towne Gaole' and adjoining tenement

C/3/9/1/2   ST CLEMENT'S WORKHOUSE   1444–1636

C/3/9/1/2/1   1444–1636
2 messuages in CL
Evidences of title for mortgage of one messuage from Henry Ashley of Hasketon, sailor to
Henry Leake of Hasketon, husbandman, 19 Sep. 1617; and for purchase of second messuage by
Daniel Snow of Ipswich, salt refiner, from Peter Fisher of Ipswich, mercer, 10 Apr. 1633
Includes:
— copy will of John Purpett of Paglesham (Essex), 1569
— copy will of Henry Ashley of Ipswich, dyer, 1602
(34 docs; bundle labelled 'Deeds relating to houses now St Clement's Workhouse formerly
Purpetts, Ashley, Snow and Fishers')

C/3/9/1/3   OTHER PROPERTIES   1521–1814

C/3/9/1/3/1   7 Oct. 1521
Triangular piece of meadow (1a) in Stoke by Ipswich
Feoffment from Andrew Sulyerd, esq. to Bailiffs, burgesses and commonalty, the property,
which was in dispute, having been the subject of arbitration by Humphrey Wyngfeld, esq.
Premises lay between Portmanysmedowe *alias* Odenholme on S. and common river flowing
towards Horswadmylle on N., abutting E. on meadow of William Stisted and common marsh

C/3/9/1/3/2   4 Mar. 1567
Acquittance
From Thomas Sowthwell to Bailiffs, burgesses and commonalty, for arrears of rent on lands in
Claydon granted by him to the town

C/3/9/1/3/3   14 Sep. 1574
3 pieces of meadow and pasture (3½a) in Ipswich, Stoke by Ipswich and Whitton
Lease from Christopher Crane of Ipswich, clothier, to Bailiffs, burgesses and commonalty, for
2,000 years, rent free
2 pieces adjoin river and Portman's Meadow; third piece adjoins highway from Ipswich to
Norwich
Endorsed 'Exchange betwene the towne and Cristofer Crane'

C/3/9/1/3/4   23 Sep. 1574
2 pieces of land (7a 2r 1p) in MS
Counterpart feoffment indented from Bailiffs, burgesses and commonalty to Christopher Crane
of Ipswich, clothier

C/3/9/1/3/5   1754–1814
Handford Meadow (4a 1r 30p) in MS
Evidences of title for conveyance from Dykes Alexander, esq. to Samuel Alexander, esq., both
of Ipswich, in trust for Bailiffs, burgesses and commonalty of Ipswich, 11 Oct. 1814
Includes:
— copy will of Nathaniel Turner of Ipswich, esq., 1791
(22 docs)

C/3/9/2 MORTGAGES   1614–1833

All the properties were mortgaged in the name of the Bailiffs, burgesses and commonalty.

C/3/9/2/1   15 Sep. 1614
Portmans Meadow (11a) in occupation of Richard Cocke in Ipswich and Stoke by Ipswich
Mortgage to William Bloyse, Thomas Blosse and Richard Marten, all of Ipswich, gents, for
£200
Latin; cancelled by mutilation; fragment of Common Seal on tag

C/3/9/2/2   15 Sep. 1614
Counterpart of C/3/9/2/1
Latin, damaged by rodent action, text incomplete

C/3/9/2/3   6 Dec. 1616
Portmans Meadow (11a) lately in occupation of Richard Cocke in Ipswich and Stoke by
Ipswich
Mortgage to Robert Benham, mercer, Augustine Parker, merchant and John Acton, gent., all of
Ipswich, for £200
Latin; cancelled by mutilation; Common Seal, incomplete, on tag

C/3/9/2/4   1 Jul. 1737
Bond
Bailiffs, burgesses and commonalty bound in £360 to Edward Leeds of Ipswich, clerk, for
repayment of loan of £180 16s 8d with interest within 5 years
Endorsed with acquittances for repayment of instalments, Dec. 1738–May 1744

C/3/9/2/5   23 Nov. 1811
18th share of newly-built Corn Exchange on site of former Rotunda in MT
Mortgage to John Head of Ipswich, grocer and tea dealer, for £100
Endorsed with acknowledgement by Jeremiah Head, son and executor of mortgagee, that principal and interest are property of Benjamin Brame of Ipswich, gent., 16 Feb. 1821; and with
memorandum of redemption and cancellation, 1823

C/3/9/2/6   4 Jan. 1812
18th share of newly-built Corn Exchange
Mortgage to William Brown of Ipswich, timber merchant, for £100
Endorsed with acquittance, 15 Jun. 1821, and memorandum of redemption and cancellation,
1823

C/3/9/2/7   10, 29 Jul. 1833
Farm in Whitton cum Thurleston and Bramford, except those parts held in trust for Tooley's,
Smart's and Felaw's Charities
Mortgage by lease and release to Isaac Currie of Cornhill, London, esq., Charles Purvis of
Darsham, esq. and John Commelin of Dumfries (Scotland), banker, trustees of marriage settle-
ment of Alexander Kennedy Clark, Lt. Col., 7th Dragoon Guards, and wife Harriet Rebeckah,
for securing repayment of £1,500 at 4 per cent interest
Endorsed: reconveyance, 11 Jan. 1859
(3 docs)

C/3/9/3 LEASES AND ASSOCIATED PAPERS   1312–1833

Unless otherwise stated, all the leases were granted in the name of the Bailiffs, burgesses and
commonalty. From the 14th century the Chamberlains, as shown in the introductory note to
FINANCE AND TOWN PROPERTY (C/3), had assumed responsibility for the leasing of
communal property, which formed an important source of the borough's revenue.

C/3/9/3/1 MILLS   1312–1809

C/3/9/3/1/1   25 Sep. 1312
Horsewade Mill with its profits
Counterpart lease to John de Whatefeld, Thomas Stace, Thomas dil la Rente and Gilbert
Roberd, burgesses of Ipswich, for 10 years, in consideration of payment of £32 to the common-
alty 'ad ardua negotia sua' and unspecified annual services
Covenants for maintenance of premises
Latin; all 3 seals and 2 tags missing

C/3/9/3/1/2   20 Nov. 1336
Horsewade Mill with waters and pond, and meadow called Odenholm
Counterpart lease from Bailiffs, burgesses and commonalty to John, son of Richard Haltebe,
for 8 years, for one red rose p.a.
Preamble states that 'molendinum . . . casu fortuno nuper erat omnino combustum', and that
lessee has agreed to rebuild it at his own expense
Latin; lessee's seal on tag

C/3/9/3/1/3   25 Sep. 1399
Horsewade Mill
Agreement between James Andrew of Stoke by Ipswich and Bailiffs and commonalty, for
improvement of the mill
Anglo-Norman French; cancelled by mutilation; Common Seal, fine impression but incom-
plete, on tag

C/3/9/3/1/4   31 May 1632
Horsewade Mill
Letter of attorney from Bailiffs, burgesses and commonalty to Robert Howe and John
Blomefeild, Chamberlains, to repossess premises from Henry Churche of Ipswich, miller (to
whom they were leased on 1 Feb. 1628), for default in payment of rent
Fragment of Common Seal on tag

C/3/9/3/1/5   4 Jan. 1553
Two watermills used as grist mills, called the New Mills, mill houses, mill dam and pasture
called Mill Marsh, with use of salt and fresh water
Counterpart lease to Robert Fyske, clothmaker and Jeffery Gylbard, goldsmith, both of
Ipswich, for 20 years at £32 p.a.

C/3/9/3/1/6   20 Nov. 1809
Report on proposed covenants in draft lease of Stoke Mill, by G. Constable of East Bergholt

C/3/9/3/2 CLOTH HALL   1583–1589

This room, which lay under part of the Moot Hall, was 'used for the discharge, laying and
bestowing of woollen cloths brought to the . . . town to be sold in gross'; the leases included the
farm of the office of Hallage and Hall Keeper, with its hallages, amercements, fines, forfeitures
and profits.

C/3/9/3/2/1   3 May 1583
Counterpart lease to Nicholas Crane of Ipswich, tailor, for 7 years at £8 2s 6d p.a.

C/3/9/3/2/2   8 Jul. 1589
Lease to William Jeffery of Ipswich, clothier, for 1 year at £8
Fragment of Common Seal on tag

C/3/9/3/2/3   8 Jul. 1589
Counterpart of C/3/9/3/2/2

323

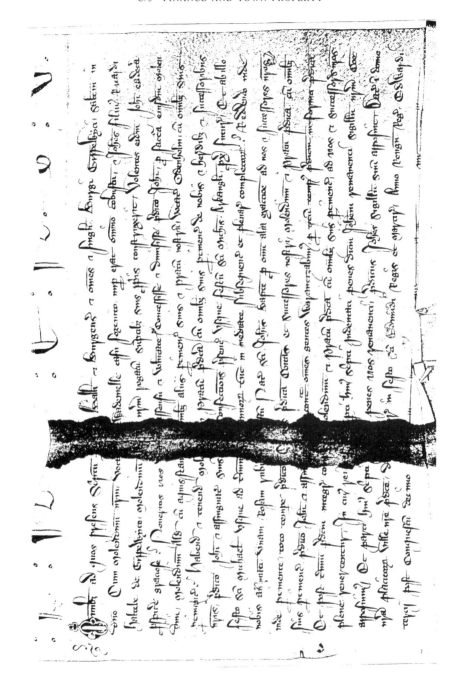

Fig. 18. Lease of Horsewade Mill dated 20 November 1336 from the Bailiffs and burgesses of Ipswich to John, son of Richard Haltebe, for eight years, at the nominal rent of one red rose annually on the feast of the Nativity of St John the Baptist. At the town's request, Haltebe has agreed to rebuild the mill at his own expense after its accidental destruction by fire. (C/3/9/3/1/2)

C/3/9/3/3   OTHER BUILDINGS   1511–1832

C/3/9/3/3/1   10 Sep. 1511
Flesh house with stalls therein, customs of carcases of beasts sold therein, common marsh, pasture called the Harpe *alias* the Hope in MS, customs of horses and cattle; except flesh house cellars
Lease to John Cowper of Ipswich, butcher, for 7 years at £20 1*s* 4*d* p.a.

C/3/9/3/3/2   2 Dec. 1551
Conduit house in LW
Lease to Edmond Jolly of Ipswich, tailor, for 10 years at 6*s* 8*d* p.a.

C/3/9/3/3/3   24 Jan. 1613
Piece of ground with little house thereon, formerly used as house of easement, in MQ
Lease to Augustine Parker of Ipswich, merchant, for 300 years at 5*s* p.a.
Common Seal missing from tag

C/3/9/3/3/4   24 Jan. 1613
Counterpart of C/3/9/3/3/3

C/3/9/3/3/5   28 Nov. 1625
Messuage in lessee's occupation in ME
Counterpart lease to Joseph Pemberton of Ipswich, maltster, for 7 years at £5 p.a.

C/3/9/3/3/6   8 Apr. 1637
House lately used as stable, with yard and well, sometime in occupation of Thomas Seckforde, esq., deceased, in MW
Counterpart lease to William Moysey of Ipswich, gent., for 38 years at 40*s* p.a.

C/3/9/3/3/7   6 Oct. 1763
Cottage and shop in occupation of Thomas Calver in LW
Lease to Philip Coleman of Ipswich, esq., for 21 years at £2 5*s* p.a.

C/3/9/3/3/8   29 Sep. 1763
Stable lately N. part of messuage called Felaws House, with yard, in Foundation Street in MQ
Lease to Richard Canning, clerk, for 15 years at £3 p.a.

C/3/9/3/3/9   1 Nov. 1776
Stable lately N. part of messuage called Felaws House, with yard, in Foundation Street in MQ
Counterpart lease to Revd Jarvis Holmes of Ipswich, clerk, for 12 years at £3 p.a.

C/3/9/3/3/10   30 May 1832
Second floor of Ipswich Moot Hall
Lease to Revd William Aldrich, clerk, Revd Francis Cobbold, clerk, Andrew Wood Baird, M.D., Jeremiah Head, esq., George Bullen, surgeon, William May, merchant and George Josselyn, gent., all of Ipswich, by consent of Edward Bacon, esq., mortgagee, for use by the Ipswich Literary Institution, for 42 years at 20*s* p.a.
(with plan)

C/3/9/3/4   TOWN MARSHES AND MEADOWS   1486–1833

C/3/9/3/4/1   20 May 1486
Meadow called Portmann Medue *alias* Odynholme
Counterpart lease from Roger Tymperley and Nicholas Wynter, Bailiffs, and John Walworth sen., Thomas Drayll, Richard Hawkyswade, John Gosse, John Hastyng, William Sewale, Robert Blomvyle and William Baker notary, Portmen, to Thomas Baldry, Portman, for 12 years at one red rose p.a.
Latin; seal on tongue

C/3/9/3/4/2   4 Feb. 1533
Marshes called the Common Marsh, the Hopper and the Harpe, Bailiffs Meadow, Portmans
Meadow, meadow newly dyked by lessee, and meadow in occupation of Matthew Woode,
butcher, all in Ipswich and Stoke by Ipswich
Counterpart lease to Robert Goodwyn, Portman of Ipswich, for 20 years at £6 13s 4d p.a.
Each Portman to have a load of hay yearly from Portmans Meadow; Bailiffs to have first crop
of Bailiffs Meadow

C/3/9/3/4/3   23 Jun. 1591
Doled meadow (2a ½r) and land (1a ½r) in lessee's occupation, with liberty of passage and
chase, in Ipswich and Stoke by Ipswich
Counterpart lease to George Wylde of Ipswich, clothier, for 21 years at 53s 6d p.a.
Lessee to keep a horse at Ipswich; not to pasture swine or sheep on premises; nor to sub-let to
any butcher, innholder, tippler, taverner, carter, pedder, kidder or foreigner, or to any burgess
who is farmer or occupier of part of town marsh

C/3/9/3/4/4   15 Mar. 1637
Marsh (2½a) part of town marsh and adjoining land (1½a) lately leased to William Acton,
deceased, in Ipswich and Stoke by Ipswich
Counterpart lease to William Cage of Ipswich, gent., for 21 years, for £32 fine, £4 annual rent,
and 30s annually per acre ploughed without licence

C/3/9/3/4/5   Mar.–Jun. 1819
2 marshes (6½a) in MS and MW
Lease to Robert Skitter of Ipswich, innholder, for 11 years at £25 p.a., 1 Mar. 1819; with assignment to Frederick Francis Seekamp of Ipswich, gent., 23 Jun. 1819
(2 docs)

C/3/9/3/4/6   21 Feb. 1833
Letter from Leaper Robert Wells of Ipswich, gent., to the Assembly
Requesting grant of lease of 2 marshes, formerly Klopfers, in his possession as sub-tenant

C/3/9/3/5   OTHER LANDS   1519–1833

C/3/9/3/5/1   10 Jul. 1519
Common heath on Caldewellehethe in Ipswich, except piece lying in close of Richard Brook,
serjeant-at-law, pertaining to his tenement called Pondis
Counterpart lease to John Ussherwoodde of Rushmere, yeoman, for 30 years at 20s p.a.

C/3/9/3/5/2   1 Aug. 1766
Land on which Grammar School formerly stood in Foundation Street, Ipswich
Counterpart lease to John Gravenor of Ipswich, gent., for 10 years at £2 10s p.a.

C/3/9/3/5/3   31 Aug. 1785
Bond
From Robert Finch of Ipswich, yeoman, to Bailiffs, burgesses and commonalty, in £23, to
perform covenants in lease of unspecified property

C/3/9/3/5/4   20 Apr. 1833
Letter from C. Gross of Ipswich, attorney, to Bailiffs
Requesting grant of lease of hardway at Pin Mill in Chelmondiston, to high water mark, to
William Cornell jun. of Chelmondiston, merchant
Annotated with resolution of grant of 21-year lease at 10s p.a.

C/3/9/4 SURVEYS AND VALUATIONS 1804–c.1827

C/3/9/4/1 25 Jan. 1804
'Valuation of the buildings upon the estates belonging to the Corporation of Ipswich and its charities', surveyed by William Brown
Buildings include:
— Town Hall, Custom House, Upper Foundation, Lower Foundation, farmhouses and buildings at Handford Hall, Otley, Debenham, Kirton, Whitton, Akenham, Claydon, Creeting St Peter and Westerfield

C/3/9/4/2 n.d. [c. 1808]
Account of John Josselyn jun. for surveying town and charity estates, 1805–1808

C/3/9/4/3 28 Sep. 1809
Valuation of Stoke Mill, in occupation of Messrs Reeve, Rainbird and Cook, by G. Constable and John Peecock

C/3/9/4/4 23 Sep. 1824
Valuation of Corporation Marsh in PE, in occupation of Messrs Cook and Calver, by John Edwards

C/3/9/4/5 n.d. [c.1827]
'Corporation rents and Charities'
Schedule of leases of Corporation and Charity properties, authorised by the Great Court, giving names of tenants, date of commencement, length of term, description of property, and amount of rent and outgoings
(1 vol.; watermark dated 1827)

C/3/10 CHARITY ESTATES later 13c.–1851

Details of the origins and objects of the various town charities for which administrative records have survived may be found in the introductory notes to the records of their administration: *see* TOWN RESPONSIBILITIES AND SERVICES – CORPORATION CHARITIES (C/5/1). While the administration of the charitable institutions and the application of their funds (the revenues of the estates) was, subject to audit by the Corporation, the responsibility of the Wardens and other officers of the respective charities, the estates themselves were vested in the Corporation as a whole, by the name of 'the Bailiffs, burgesses and commonalty of Ipswich' – the Bailiffs, for instance (as joint heads of the Corporation), rather than the Wardens of Tooley's Foundation, being *ex-officio* lords of the Tooley manors in Debenham. Though the revenues were separately applied, the estates appear to have been managed as a single asset. For these reasons, and also because some of the estates were purchased jointly with funds from the endowments of two or more charities, the estate records have been arranged by function – evidences of title, manorial administration, etc. – rather than by charity.

C/3/10/1 RECORDS OF FOUNDATION AND ENDOWMENT 1521–19c.

C/3/10/1/1 GENERAL SURVEYS AND MEMORANDA c.1672–19c.

C/3/10/1/1/1 c.1672–c.1695
'The Book of Benefactors and Benefactions of Ipswich'
List of benefactors, with texts of relevant clauses of their wills or deeds of gift, to which are added notes on where the various properties lie, to what uses the revenues are put, whether houses have been demolished, etc.

The list is prefixed (on f. 7) by the statement that 'in the writing of this I intend to set forth the severall benifactors of lands, houses and monies given to the towne of Ipswich . . . with the liberties and some of the previlidges belonginge to the said towne together with some usages and customes there practised'

Includes:

— copy decree in Corporation suit *re* butchers' duties, 1603

— order of Justices of the Peace that inhabitants of HL be rated towards relief of poor of NI, n.d.

— table of Town Clerk's fees, n.d.

— table of Attorney's fees, n.d.

— table of charges for suffering Recoveries in the borough court, n.d.

— articles of enquiry in the Court of Admiralty, n.d.

— forms of acquittance for salaries of Master and Usher of Grammar School, n.d.

— memorandum *re* early history, bounds and constitution of Ipswich, n.d.

— (ff. 52–53) perambulation of Ipswich

— (f. 54) extracts from records in London's Guildhall *re* exemption of Ipswich burgesses from duties on merchandise bought or sold in London, n.d.

— (f. 57v) account of King Charles II's visit to Lord Hereford at Christchurch, and of ceremonial observed by Corporation, 5 Oct. 1668

— (f. 59ff) customs of the borough and fees due to various office-holders, n.d.

— (f. 78ff) forms of oaths of office-holders, n.d.

— ff. 85v ff) details of annual receipts and payments by Treasurers, Chamberlains and Treasurer of Christ's Hospital, n.d.

— (f. 88v ff) list of grants of common soil, arranged by parish

— (f. 110v ff) translation of Charles II's charter to the borough, 1684

— (f. 115 ff) text [Latin] of Elizabeth I's charter for the Free School, 1566

— (f. 117v) population figures (male and female) for each parish and hamlet in accordance with Act of Parliament, 1695

— (f. 118) translation of Commission to enquire into Ipswich Haven, 1340

— (f. 119 ff) Latin text of above Commission, 1340

— (f. 121) text of Commission of inquiry and Inquisition into extent of port of Ipswich, 1379

— (f. 122) grant of Admiralty jurisdiction by Thomas, Earl of Surrey, Great Admiral of England, to the Corporation, 1520

— (f. 123ff) estreats of water rents, 1680

— (f. 125) account of annual rent of town marshes, 1657

— (f. 126) lease from the Corporation to John Felawe, of 2 mills, moot hall, town houses, common quay, customs, court leet fines and other duties, 1439

— (f. 127v ff) schedule of rates of duty to be paid by 'foreigners' on goods brought into or transported from the town by water, and of weekly charges for such goods housed in the Town House, n.d.

— (f. 131v) customary tithe payments to MS for town marshes, n.d.

— (f. 131v) butchers' customary payments for hides and skins, n.d.

— (f. 134) text of grant of freedom to the Duke of Albemarle, 1681

— (f. 134v) text of instrument of surrender of the borough charter, 1684

— (f. 135) table of dues for meterage of coals, groundage of stones, anchorage and other port dues, n.d.

— (f. 135v) form of warrant for appointment of Serjeant of Admiralty, n.d.

(1 vol., with index of benefactors. The greater part apparently in the hand of Robert Clarke, Town Clerk. On the inside of the front cover, 'liber Roberti Barnard', in a 17th-century hand, has been struck through. The first page bears the signatures 'Hen. Nash' and 'Wm Stevenson Fitch, given me by my friend Mr Henry Clarke June 28 1833'; the book was thus at one time out of official custody.)

C/3/10/1/1/2   n.d. [? later 17c.]
'Ipswich Gifts and Miscellaneous Memoranda Book'
List of benefactors, with texts of, or extracts from, their wills or deeds of gift

Includes:
— (at front) 'Observations respecting holding Great Courts etc', n.d.
— perambulation of the town, 1674
— statement *re* exemption of Ipswich burgesses from various dues throughout the kingdom, 1587
— account of visit by King Charles II to Lord Hereford at Christchurch, 1668
— account of customs of the town, n.d.
— account of business to be done on Michaelmas Day, n.d.
— forms of oaths of office-holders
(1 vol.)

C/3/10/1/1/3   1718
'A Memorandum of Gifts to the Town of Ipswich with an account of some of their customs and constitutions as also the several oaths administered to the several officers belonging to the said town'
List of benefactors, with texts of, or extracts from, their wills or deeds of gift
Includes:
— (pp. 42–44) customs of the town
— (pp. 46–52) forms of oaths of officers
— (pp. 54–56) schedule of sums for each Gift to remain in cash for interest-free loans, and account of sums borrowed by the town for various purposes
— (p. 58) schedule of officers' salaries
(1 vol.; with index)

C/3/10/1/1/4   1725
'A Booke or Memorandum of all the Charyties, together with copies of the severall uses, wills or clauses of wills and such other perticulars as could be recovered and collected to this time or year'
(1 vol., with index. A memorandum on the title page explains that only those gifts are included which are administered by the Corporation, gifts to individual parishes being omitted.)

C/3/10/1/1/5   n.d. [19c.]
'An Account of the Estates, Gifts and Legacies directed to be applied to charitable purposes, and of the present Charitable Institutions in Ipswich', compiled by William Batley
Details of the foundation and estates of the town charities, gifts to individual parishes, and 19th-century philanthropic organisations
Original documents pasted in, covering the years 1569–1833, include:
— petitions, warrants for payment, letters and press-cuttings
— plan of the Tooley Foundation, Christ's Hospital and Grammar School, n.d.
— orders of service for charity sermons, 1816, 1819
— annual reports of the Ipswich Education Society, 1814–1816
— rules of the Ipswich Friendly Society, 1810
— list of subscribers to the Ipswich Public Dispensary, 1797, amended to 1816
— rules of the same, 1817
— rules of the Ipswich Provident Bank for the savings of the Poor, 1816
— rules of the Ipswich and Suffolk Savings Bank, 1816
(1 vol.; some pages with watermark dated 1814)

C/3/10/1/2 TOOLEY'S FOUNDATION   1521–1568

C/3/10/1/2/1 Records of Henry Tooley and his executors   **1521–1568**

C/3/10/1/2/1/1   1521–1551
Merchant's account book of Henry Tooley
For the most part relating to the period after 1534, when there is much information *re* Tooley's overseas trade, but more particularly the local trade which he carried on from Ipswich,

329

Fig. 19. Portraits of King Philip and Queen Mary from their Letters Patent of 30 November 1556 granting licence to John Southwell, esq., Robert Daundy, William Daundy and Richard Bride, executors of will of Henry Tooley of Ipswich, merchant, deceased, to establish an almshouse in Ipswich and to alienate to the Bailiffs, burgesses and commonalty, for its endowment, manors, messuages and lands worth £100 p.a., notwithstanding the Statute of Mortmain. (C/3/10/1/2/2/2)

primarily a record of his distributive operations. For a detailed account of the volume and its significance, *see* Webb 1962, Appendix B, pp. 165–67.
(1 vol. First 86 fols missing, and about one-third of the remaining 156 blank. For the most part the entries are in Tooley's own hand, though several other hands may be distinguished. Repaired by the Public Record Office in 1937, retaining the surviving parts of the contemporary leather binding stamped with a pattern of roses and lozenges, some of the latter bearing the crowned double-headed eagle of the Holy Roman Empire and others a castle with four towers. Preserved by Tooley's executors presumably for its evidence of his debtors, and presumably kept with the evidences of title to Tooley's properties bequeathed for the benefit of the poor of Ipswich.)

C/3/10/1/2/1/2   c.1550–1568
Papers of Henry Tooley's executors John Sowthwell, Richard Skynner, Richard Byrde, Robert Daundy and William Daundy, *re* administration of his estate, litigation arising out of his will, and the establishment of the Tooley Foundation
Includes:
— copy will of Henry Tooley (4 Nov. 1550), n.d.
— executors' accounts, 1562 and n.d.
— schedule of lands in Akenham, Claydon, Thurleston and Whitton, endorsed 'thes be the peces of londes and medow exchanged betwixt John Hyll and Barnard', n.d.
— sketch plan of lands bounded by lands of manor of Brokes Hall [in Ipswich, Bramford, Whitton, Thurleston and Westerfield], n.d.
— accounts of the executors for administration of the Foundation, delivered to the Bailiffs of Ipswich 'accordynge unto an order . . . set forthe by Sir Nycholas Bacon, knyghte, Lorde Keper of the greate Seale of Ingland', for year ending 29 Sep. 1563
— legal papers (interrogatories, responses, copy of appeal, statement of effect of sentence), 1564 and n.d.
— account of repairs carried out by William Shanckford by order of the Bailiffs of Ipswich on farmhouse leased to him by the town, Aug.–Dec. 1568
(19 docs)

C/3/10/1/2/2 Deeds of endowment   1552–1563

C/3/10/1/2/2/1   17 Aug. 1552
Manor of Ulveston Hall and messuages, lands and tenements in Debenham, Pettaugh, Aspall, Mickfield and Stonham
Feoffment from Henry Tooley of Ipswich, merchant, to John Southwell, esq., Robert Daundy, William Daundy and Richard Brid *alias* Byrd, his executors, to use of Tooley for life, then in trust to use profits for maintenance of 10 poor persons dwelling within the former house of Carmelite friars in Ipswich
Latin

C/3/10/1/2/2/2   30 Nov. 1556
Letters Patent of King Philip and Queen Mary
Grants licence to John Southwell, esq., Robert Daundy, William Daundy and Richard Bride, executors of will of Henry Tooley of Ipswich, merchant, deceased, to establish almshouse in Ipswich and to alienate to Bailiffs, burgesses and commonalty, for its endowment, manors, messuages and lands worth £100 p.a., notwithstanding Statute of Mortmain
Latin; initial letter 'P' depicting monarchs enthroned; capitals on first line ornamented with delicate strapwork and foliage, pomegranate, crowned Tudor rose, lion sejant with banner, and fleur-de-lis; Great Seal missing from green and white cords

C/3/10/1/2/2/3   16 Jul. 1562
Manors of Ulveston Hall and Sackvilles in Debenham and all lands late of Henry Tooley in Ipswich, Debenham, Akenham, Whitton and Claydon
Deed of covenant between John [Parkhurst], Bishop of Norwich; John Southwell, esq., Richard

Bride and William Daundy, executors of will of Henry Tooley of Ipswich, merchant, deceased; and Bailiffs, burgesses and commonalty of Ipswich
For making true inventory and terrier of estates, to be registered together with title deeds which are to be sorted, boxed and kept in Town Treasury with 5 locks, keys to be held by Bailiffs and executors; for conveyance of property from executors to town; for establishment and permanent maintenance of almshouse to be known as 'the howse of the poore of Maister Toolyes Foundacion'; and laying down detailed rules for its governance
Seals of Bishop and executors on tags

C/3/10/1/2/2/4   28 Apr. 1563
Manors of Ulveston Hall and Sackvilles, 60 messuages, 60 curtilages, 60 gardens, 1,000 acres land, 200 acres meadow, 1,000 acres pasture, 100 acres wood, £20 rent in Debenham, Winston, Pettaugh, Ashfield, Ipswich, Whitton, Akenham, Claydon, Great Blakenham, Bramford and Thurleston
Exemplification of final concord, Hillary Term 1563, Bailiffs, burgesses and commonalty of Ipswich, plaintiffs, and John Southwell, esq., Richard Bryde, gent. and William Daundy (executors of will of Henry Tooley of Ipswich, merchant, deceased) deforciants
Latin

C/3/10/1/3   SMART'S CHARITY   [1599]

C/3/10/1/3/1   n.d. [1599]
Draft of William Smart's instructions for the administration of his bequest
This is a draft of the schedule annexed to Smart's 1,000-year lease, dated 15 Sep. 1599, to Thomas Walton, Ralph Scrivener and Leonard Caston, of all his lands in Kirton and Falkenham, in trust to convey them to the Bailiffs and commonalty of Ipswich, to the uses expressed in his will dated 8 Jan. 1599 (see C/3/10/2/4/1/12 below, and Canning 1747, 31–43).
(7 fols, stitched together, 4 blank)

C/3/10/1/4   CHRIST'S HOSPITAL   1576–1683

C/3/10/1/4/1   Kelke's bequest   **1576**

C/3/10/1/4/1/1   10 Jan. 1576
Probate copy will of Roger Kelke, Master of Magdalene College, Cambridge [and Town Preacher of Ipswich] (Prerogative Court of Canterbury)
Bequeathes surplus of estate, if any after payment of other legacies, to 'the Hospitall in Ipswich'
Signed, 12 Dec. 1575

C/3/10/1/4/2   Robinson's gift   **1683**

In 1683 Mrs Elizabeth Robinson of Ipswich, widow, gave £100 to the Bailiffs, burgesses and commonalty, to maintain two poor boys in Christ's Hospital, filling up each vacancy when it occurred. In 1705 it was ordered that the interest of £7 10s should be paid annually by the Town Treasurer to the Treasurer of the Hospital (see Canning 1747, 65).

C/3/10/1/4/2/1   13 Sep. 1683
Deed poll
The Bailiffs, burgesses and commonalty acknowledge receipt of £100 from Elizabeth Robinson, widow, and undertake to comply with the terms of her gift
Common Seal on tag

C/3/10/1/5   CRANE'S CHARITY   1656

C/3/10/1/5/1   (1651), 1656
Copy of will of John Crane, with legal queries and opinion of John Glanvill, serjeant-at-law, *re* Crane's Charity lands in Lincolnshire
(1 doc)

C/3/10/1/6   HUNWICK'S CHARITY   1595

C/3/10/1/6/1   Deeds of covenant   **1595**

C/3/10/1/6/1/1   18 Aug. 1595
Bailiffs and commonalty of Colchester (Essex) covenant with Bailiffs, burgesses and commonalty of Ipswich for annual distribution of John Hunwick's gift to poor of Colchester; for production of accounts for audit every fifth year; and for payment of £10 every fifth year for use of poor of Ipswich, Maldon (Essex) and Sudbury
Cancelled by mutilation; Common Seal of Colchester missing

C/3/10/1/6/1/2   25 Aug. 1595
In similar terms to C/3/10/1/6/1/1; Common Seal of Colchester missing

C/3/10/1/7   GARDENER'S GIFT   1601

This was a parochial benefaction to the poor of St Mary Elms. As such, the presence of the document in the borough archive is anomalous, but for convenience it is listed here, rather than under ACCIDENTAL ACCUMULATIONS, C/6.

C/3/10/1/7/1   19 Dec. 1601
Attested copy will of John Gardyner of Ipswich, clothier (Norwich Consistory Court)
Includes:
— bequest of 20*s* to the poor of ME
Signed, 10 Aug. 1598

C/3/10/2   EVIDENCES OF TITLE   **later 13c.–1851**

N.B.: the strict chronological order of the calendared medieval deeds has necessarily been interrupted in the case of certain small groups of deeds which were found tied together at their seal-tags or filed on near-contemporary parchment thongs.

C/3/10/2/1   DAUNDY'S CHARITY   1573–1589

By his will dated 2 May 1515, Edmund Daundy, Portman, bequeathed certain lands to the Bailiffs, burgesses and commonalty of Ipswich, charged with payment of 13*s* 4*d* annually on the feast of St John *ante portam latinam* (6 May) to each Ipswich friary to keep the obits of the testator and his family, and with provision of 100 faggots of firewood annually to the testator's almshouses in Lady Lane. The lands were sold by the Corporation to John Clenche (Recorder of Ipswich, 1574, Justice of the Queen's Bench, 1584) in 1588 (*see* Canning 1747, 163–64, and Richardson 1884, 287n., 301, 347, 348, 354, 356).

C/3/10/2/1/1   22 Jan. 1573
Lands and tenements in Holbrook and Harkstead
Deed of attornment by Edmund Leche of Ipswich, yeoman, and widow Goslyn, to William Smarte and Christopher Crane, according to terms of feoffment made by the Bailiffs, burgesses

and commonalty of Ipswich to Smarte and Crane dated 21 Jan. 1573, *re* property leased from the Corporation

C/3/10/2/1/2   4–13 Jan. 1589
Messuages and lands called Carres, Mores and Bartillmewes in Holbrook, Freston and Harkstead
Evidences of title for purchase by John Clenche, Justice of Queen's Bench, from Bailiffs, bur-
gesses and commonalty, William Smart of Ipswich, merchant and Christopher Crane of
Ipswich, clothier, 13 Jan. 1589
(2 docs)

C/3/10/2/2   CADEY'S CHARITY   1593

By his will dated 18 April 1531, Thomas Cadey of St Mary Stoke, Ipswich, bequeathed three
tenements 'for almshouses for poor couples for ever to dwell in, that be old, impotent and lame
persons, to pray for my soul and all Christian souls'. By 1747 the site of the almshouses was
unknown (*see* Canning 1747, 162).

C/3/10/2/2/1   18 Sep. 1593
Messuages, yards and gardens called Cadies almshouses in NI
Quitclaim from Robert Dawbnye of Ipswich, carpenter, to the Bailiffs, burgesses and
commonalty

C/3/10/2/3   TOOLEY'S FOUNDATION   later 13c.–1797

C/3/10/2/3/1   Ulveston family purchases in Debenham, Pettaugh and   later 13c.–1487
Stonham Aspall

C/3/10/2/3/1/1   n.d. [? later 13c.]
Land (1a 3r) in Debenham
Feoffment from John, son of Hervey de Wlueston, to Matthew de Kent, for 26*s* fine and 6*d*
annual rent
Premises lie between lands of feoffor and Roger Tuffin; names of 7 witnesses
Latin; seal missing from tag

C/3/10/2/3/1/2   n.d. [? later 13c.]
Piece of land (2a) in Debenham
Feoffment from William Spornefluid of Debenham to Robert his brother and legitimate heirs of
his body, with remainder, in default of such issue, to Robert's sister Catherine
Premises lie in field formerly called Rumleye, between lands of Gilbert Baylcheyn and feoffor,
1 head abutting on lands of Stephen de Ulveston and James his brother; names of 8 witnesses
Latin; seal missing from tag

C/3/10/2/3/1/3   n.d. [? later 13c.]
Arable land (1a) [in Debenham]
Feoffment from Robert Spornefluit of Debenham and sister Katherine to John de Ulvestone
Premises lie in field called Romeleye, between feoffors' land and land of Gilbert de la Haye,
abutting on lands of Alice de Ulvestone and Stephen de Ulvestone; names of 7 witnesses
Latin; both seals missing from tags

C/3/10/2/3/1/4   n.d. [? later 13c.]
Lands and tenements in Debenham
Feoffment from Robert Hervi, chaplain of Debenham, to John de Ulveston, for 15 marks fine
and 1 peppercorn annually
Names of 12 witnesses
Latin; seal on tag

C/3/10/2/3/1/5   n.d. [? later 13c.]
Piece of land in Debenham
Feoffment from Jocelin de Debenham, clerk, to John de Ulveston, for 7 marks fine and 3*d*
annually
Premises lie between lands of Prior and convent of Butley and of feoffee, abutting on feoffee's
land and on his pasture called le Chapelbroch; names of 11 witnesses
Latin; seal, incomplete, on tag

C/3/10/2/3/1/6   n.d. [? later 13c.]
Piece of land in Debenham
Feoffment from John de Ulveston to Richard del Haye, rector of Brettenham church, for 11*s*
fine, 2*d* annually, and 1*d* in 20*s* scutage when levied
Premises lie between lands of feoffee and of Gilbert Fukelot, 1 head abutting on croft of Gilbert
Nel, the other on land of feoffee and of Stephen Beylone; names of 12 witnesses
Latin; seal, incomplete, on tag

C/3/10/2/3/1/7   12 Jan. 1271
Suit of King's court and tenement in market place of Debenham
Quitclaim from Gilbert de Colevile of Aspall to Roger Caulyeladel, cobbler
Names of 10 witnesses
Latin; armorial seal on tag

C/3/10/2/3/1/8   1 Jan. 1276
Piece of meadow in Debenham
Feoffment from Peter Fukelot of Debenham to John de Ulvestone, for 5*s* fine and 1 clove
annually
Premises lie between meadows of Isabel le Hond and William Pilerok, abutting on lands of
John son of Osbert and heir of late Hervey Multer; names of 7 witnesses
Latin; seal missing from tag

C/3/10/2/3/1/9   n.d. [? later 13c.]
Piece of meadow in exchange for piece of land, both in Debenham
Feoffment from William, son of Hervey Michel of Debenham, to John de Ulvestone
Meadow lies between meadow of John Greg and land of Gilbert de Colevile, abutting on
meadows of John Greg and Isabel le Hund; land lies between land of Robert Geffrey and dower
land of Lady Ida de Ulvestone, abutting on land of Robert Geffrey and on common way; names
of 11 witnesses
Chirograph; Latin; seal, incomplete, on tag by which tied to C/3/10/2/3/1/10–11

C/3/10/2/3/1/10   15 Jan. 1276
Piece of meadow in Debenham
Feoffment from Walter, son of Gilbert de Debenham, to John de Ulvestone, for 8*s* fine and 1
clove annually
Premises lie between meadows of feoffee and Philip Multer, abutting on land of William de
Norhamtone and meadow formerly of Hervey Multer; names of 7 witnesses
Latin; seal on tag by which tied to C/3/10/2/3/1/9 and 11

C/3/10/2/3/1/11   1284 or 1285
Piece of meadow in Debenham, in exchange for another
Feoffment from Hervey the smith of Debenham to John ...... [*missing*]
Names of 7 witnesses
Chirograph; Latin; badly damaged by rodent action, much of text missing, date (13 Edw. I)
incomplete; seal missing from tag by which tied to C/3/10/2/3/1/9–10

C/3/10/2/3/1/12   6 Apr. 1310
House in Debenham
Feoffment from John de Wortham sen. to Nicholas de Schotford and John Costard

Premises lie between curtilage of Ingreda Cage and way called le Newestrete, both heads abutting on Ingreda's tenement; names of 8 witnesses
Latin; seal missing from tag

C/3/10/2/3/1/13   11 Oct. 1311
Piece of land in Debenham
Grant for life from William le Buteler of Wemme [? Wem, Shropshire], kt, wife Ela and Isabel de Hylles, to Peter Dunning of Debenham, chaplain, for 2s p.a.
Premises lie between land of John de Ulveston and way leading to Debenham church, abutting on meadow of John de Ulveston and land formerly of William Hervy; names of 6 witnesses
Latin; 1 seal, 2 seals missing from tags

C/3/10/2/3/1/14   22 Sep. 1312
Tenement with messuages, houses, arable lands and pastures in Debenham, except land called Brantestoft purchased from Richard del Haghe
Feoffment from Ingreda Cage of Debenham to Stephen de Ulveston
Names of 9 witnesses
Latin; seal on tag

C/3/10/2/3/1/15   25 Oct. 1314
Piece of land with fences and ditches in Debenham
Quitclaim from Robert de Capele jun. of Debenham to Stephen de Ulveston
Premises are those which Stephen had by gift of William, son of William Spornefluit and which Robert lately challenged; names of 7 witnesses
Latin; seal missing from tag

C/3/10/2/3/1/16   20 Feb. 1315
Piece of land called Mayheuscroft in Debenham
Feoffment from John Mayheu of Wetheringsett to John de Ulveston sen., John his son, and Joan wife of John the son
Premises lie next to way called Luttyngeshaghe Weye; names of 9 witnesses
Latin; fragment of seal on tag by which tied to C/3/10/2/3/1/17

C/3/10/2/3/1/17   23 Feb. 1315
Piece of land called Maiheuscroft in Debenham
Quitclaim from John Maiheu of Wetheringsett to John de Ulveston sen., son John, and Joan wife of John the son
Premises are bounded as in C/3/10/2/3/1/16; names of 9 witnesses
Latin; seal on tag by which tied to C/3/10/2/3/1/16

C/3/10/2/3/1/18   28 Jan. 1316
Portion of piece of land [in Debenham]
Feoffment from Wymark, daughter of late William Huy of Debenham, to John de Ulveston sen. and John de Ulveston jun. his son and heir
Premises are feoffor's portion of land which she and sisters Alice and Agnes had jointly by feoffment of their father; names of 8 witnesses
Latin; seal missing from tag

C/3/10/2/3/1/19   11 Feb. 1327
Piece of land in Debenham
Feoffment from Robert del Hawe to Stephen de Ulvestone of Debenham
Premises lie between lands of Gilbert Hamd and Robert le Taillur, abutting on land formerly of John Poysoun and on common way; names of 7 witnesses
Latin; seal missing from tag

C/3/10/2/3/1/20   4 Jun. 1329
Piece of land with adjoining piece of meadow in Stonham Antegan [Stonham Aspal]
Feoffment from Richard Leu, kt, to John de Ulveston

Premises lie between lands of Sir Robert de Aspale and feoffee; names of 6 witnesses
Latin; armorial seal on tag

C/3/10/2/3/1/21   29 Sep. 1326
Messuage with houses, buildings and fences in Pettaugh
Feoffment from Agnes, daughter of late Walter Hosgoth of Mendham, to John de Ulveston
Premises are those which feoffor purchased of Nicholas de Scotford, and lie between Nicho-
las's close and Pettaugh Green, abutting on way from Ipswich to Debenham, and on land of Sir
Albert de Leyston; names of 5 witnesses
Latin; seal missing from tag by which tied to C/3/10/2/3/1/22

C/3/10/2/3/1/22   1 Sep. 1332
Piece of land in Pettaugh
Feoffment from Emma Rolph of Pettaugh to John de Ulveston and son Leonard
Premises lie between lands of Abbot and convent of Leiston and Roger Wulniston, abutting on
way called le Lange Lond Weye; names of 5 witnesses
Latin; seal missing from tag by which tied to C/3/10/2/3/1/21

C/3/10/2/3/1/23   3 Nov. 1332
Piece of land in Pettaugh in exchange for 3 acres there
Feoffment from John de Calston' of Pettaugh to John de Ulveston; remainder to Leonard, son
of John de Ulveston and legitimate heirs of his body, or in default of such issue, to right heirs of
John de Ulveston
Premises lie between lands of John de Ulveston and Lady Emma, widow of Sir Richard Leeu, 1
head abutting on John de Ulveston's land called le Suterescroft; names of 5 witnesses
Latin; seal missing from tag

C/3/10/2/3/1/24   29 Apr. 1333
Close called Hayiscroft in Stonham Antegan [Stonham Aspal]
Quitclaim from William Bacun, parson of Ringshall church, and Roger Bacun, to Robert, son
of John de Stanham, chaplain
Premises abut E. on tenement of Ralph Olive and W. on land of Geoffrey Thurhout; names of 7
witnesses
Latin; 1 seal, incomplete, on tag, second seal missing

C/3/10/2/3/1/25   30 Jun. 1333
Piece of meadow in Debenham
Feoffment from Thomas de le Wynchil to John de Ulveston
Premises lie between feoffee's lands on both sides, abutting on meadow of William Lenegor
and land of Peter Hert; names of 5 witnesses
Latin; seal missing from tag

C/3/10/2/3/1/26   31 Mar. 1354
1 rose annual rent out of lands and tenements which were Richard de Ulveston's in Debenham
Counterpart grant from John, son of Thomas de Ulveston, to William Bavent and wife Katherine, for greater security of certain lands and tenements which he lately granted them by charter;
if they are expelled, they are to have 2 marks annual rent out of premises
Chirograph; Latin; seal fragment on tag, second seal missing

C/3/10/2/3/1/27   24 Aug. 1326
Piece of land called le Blakelond in Debenham
Quitclaim from Joan, widow of William Kyng of Debenham, to John, son of John de Ulveston
Premises are those which John de Ulveston the father formerly purchased from Thomas, Joan's
father, and abut W. on John's land; names of 5 witnesses
Latin; seal missing from tag by which tied to C/3/10/2/3/1/28–29

C/3/10/2/3/1/28   6 Oct. 1354
Land (7a 1r) in Debenham
Feoffment conditional from John, son of Thomas de Ulveston of Debenham, to John de

337

Westwode of Mickfield, son Richard, and legitimate heirs of their bodies, with reversion, in default of such issue, to feoffor and heirs; for 40¼d annual rent
Premises lie between way belonging to Ivo, son of John de Kenton and land formerly of Walter Pod, abutting on land of John de Ulveston called Blakelond and on common way; names of 5 witnesses
Chirograph; Latin; seal missing from tag by which tied to C/3/10/2/3/1/27 and 29

C/3/10/2/3/1/29   14 Sep. 1360
Piece of land called Blakelond in Debenham
Feoffment from Thomas Hay of Debenham to John de Ulveston, wife Joan and son Richard
Premises are those which feoffor formerly purchased from Walter Wysman, and lie lengthwise between land of John Priur and feoffor's pasture, 1 head abutting on land of Sir Roger de Aspale; names of 6 witnesses
Latin; seal on tag by which tied to C/3/10/2/3/1/27–28

C/3/10/2/3/1/30   10 Jun. 1395
Messuage with croft in Shaderukesfeld in Debenham
Quitclaim from John Bradwey of Pettaugh to Thomas More and Robert Gryges, clerks, Robert Asshefeld, William de Thurtone, and their successors as feoffees of manor of Debenham, formerly of John de Ulvestone, kt and Thomas de Ulvestone his son; with release of all actions for debt or trespass to Nicholas Blunvyle and Richard de Lyng, executors of Sir John de Ulvestone's will
Premises lie next to land of manor, abutting N. on highway called Shaderokesweye
Latin; seal on tag

C/3/10/2/3/1/31   7 Jun. 1411
Way called Douneweye [in Debenham]
Quitclaim from Robert Multer, late of Debenham, to Robert Heydon and William Grenehod
Way extends from Robert Massingham's tenement to meadow called Sclademedewe; names of 5 witnesses
Latin; seal on tag

C/3/10/2/3/1/32   23 Jun. 1415
Tenement in Debenham
Counterpart lease from Thomas Ulveston to John Dallyng, both of Debenham, for 7 years at 16s p.a.
Premises lie between tenement of John Gurdon on S. and tenement formerly of Thomas de Wode on N., abutting E. on town cemetery and W. on common way
Latin; lessee's seal on tag

C/3/10/2/3/1/33   30 Nov. 1465
Field called Stonhamfeld in Debenham and Stonham Aspal
Counterpart lease from Elizabeth, widow of John Ulvestone, esq. and Richard Ulvestone, son of John, to William Jerald of Debenham, for 12 years at 53s 4d p.a.
Latin; lessee's seal on tag

C/3/10/2/3/1/34   25 Dec. 1469
Close with pightle and little lane between, in Debenham
Quitclaim from Lady Margaret Bedyngfeld, widow, to Edmund Bedyngfeld, esq., son of Thomas Bedyngfeld, esq., her son
Close lies between highway and close of Robert Cheke formerly called Baggysclos, abutting N. on close of manor of Kenton and close of Prior of Butley called le Hoper, in tenure of Robert Cheke, and S. on said land leading from close of Robert Cheke to pightle of manor of Kenton in tenure of John Talmage; pightle lies between highway on one side and closes of Prior and John Talmage on the other, abutting N. on lane and S. on close of Prior called Calstoncroft, in tenure of John Talmage
Latin; fine armorial seal on tag

338

C/3/10/2/3/1/35   12 Oct. 1471
Close called le Cete and piece of land abutting thereon in Debenham
Feoffment from Robert Boys, Robert Cheke, John Goslen and John Edwards, to Edward
Grymston, esq., John Page sen. and John Buk sen.
Premises are those which feoffors lately had, among other lands and tenements, jointly with
Thomas Ganokyr, now deceased, by feoffment of Richard Jerald, clerk; close lies between land
called Poysuns on W. and land late of John Northagh on E., abutting S. on highway and N. on
Poysuns and said piece of land; which lies between Poysuns on W. and land of manor of Aspal
Stonham and of John Page on E., abutting S. on le Cete and land late of John Northagh, and N.
on land of manor of Ulveston Hall; names of 5 witnesses
Latin; 4 seals on 2 tags

C/3/10/2/3/1/36   12 Jul. 1487
Piece of land in Debenham
Feoffment from John Page sen. lately called John Page jun., John Blogat sen., John Stogy and
John Buke sen., to John Nicoll, Robert Love, clerk, John Nonne, John Cooke and Richard
Ponchard
Premises are those which feoffors lately had by feoffment of Lawrence Fydeon and Roger
Curwyn, and lie between land of John Nicoll late of Robert Boys on W. and field called
Prikysfeld on E., abutting N. on land of manor of Stonham Aspal and of John Nicoll, and S. on
John Cheke's grove called Shatherokkesgrove; names of 5 witnesses
Latin; 4 seals on tags

C/3/10/2/3/2   Manor of Ulveston Hall in Debenham   1332–1509

C/3/10/2/3/2/1   29 Mar. 1332
Manor of Ulveston with lands and tenements in Debenham, Mickfield, Stonham, Wetheringsett
and Aspall
Quitclaim from Thomas de Bavent, kt, to Richard de Biskele and John de Hoxne
Premises are those which Thomas lately acquired, jointly with Richard, John, and Stephen de
Thweyt and Ellis le Chapman, chaplain, from John de Ulveston
Latin; armorial seal on tag by which tied to C/3/10/2/3/2/2

C/3/10/2/3/2/2   21 Jun. 1332
3 messuages, land (116a 1r), meadow (11a), wood (6a ½r), rent (29s 6d) and third part of mill,
in Debenham, Stonham, Mickfield, Aspall and Wetheringsett
Acknowledgement by John de Ulveston that he holds premises on behalf of his son Thomas and
Thomas's wife Clemence (who had them from Richard de Biskelee and John de Hoxne by fine
levied in King's Court), in exchange for maintenance for themselves and their household while
they choose to remain with him at his manor of Ulveston; property to be given up if they choose
to live elsewhere
Anglo-Norman French; seal missing from tag by which tied to C/3/10/2/3/2/1

C/3/10/2/3/2/3   21 Jun. 1355
Manor of Ulveston with lands and tenements in Debenham, Mickfield, Stonham, Wetheringsett
and Aspall
Feoffment from John de Ulvestone to Roger de Weskele, parson of Frostenden church, John
Jernegan, Walter Hert, chaplain and Adam Gardener, chaplain
Names of 7 witnesses
Latin; seal missing from tag

C/3/10/2/3/2/4   17 Apr. 1358
Manor of Ulveston with lands and tenements in Debenham, Mickfield, Stonham, Wetheringsett
and Aspall
Feoffment from Roger de Biskele, parson of Frostenden church, John Jernegan, Walter Hert,
chaplain and Adam le Gardener, chaplain, to John de Ulveston

Names of 7 witnesses
Latin; 4 seals, 1 armorial, on tags

C/3/10/2/3/2/5   28 Sep. 1362
Manor of Ulveston [in Debenham] with 50s annual rent of Pettaugh and various chattels
Counterpart lease from John Dargentem, kt, Alexander Broseyerd parson of Barsham church,
Edmund Man of Mutford and John Botild of Stoven, to Walter Fraunceys, for 4 years at
£25 13s 4d p.a.
Latin; lessee's seal on tag

C/3/10/2/3/2/6   11 Nov. 1399
Manor of Ulveston in Debenham with appurtenances in Stonham, Aspall, Mickfield, Kenton
and Wetheringsett
Release from Thomas Moor, clerk, Robert Asshefeld and William de Thurtone to Thomas de
Ulvestone, provided they are not held to warranty
Premises were lately acquired jointly with Roger Boys and John de Wyngefeld, kts and John de
Pishale, Guy Crokedok and Robert Grygge, clerks, from Richard Dautres and John Botyld of
'Burgh iuxta Hengham' [sic]; names of 7 witnesses
Latin; 3 armorial seals on tags

C/3/10/2/3/2/7   13 Sep. 1400
Manor of Ulveston in Debenham with its members in Stonham, Aspall, Mickfield, Kenton and
Wetheringsett
Feoffment from Thomas Ulvestone to William de Snetesham, Thomas Crafue, William
Bernham, clerk, John Thornham and Roger Prat
Premises were lately acquired from Thomas Moor, clerk, Robert Asshefeld and William de
Thurtone; names of 7 witnesses
Latin; armorial seal on tag

C/3/10/2/3/2/8   14 Sep. 1400
Manor of Ulveston in Debenham
Letter of attorney from Thomas Ulvestone to John Gurdon of Debenham and Henry Bocher of
Wetheringsett to deliver seisin to William Snetesham, Thomas Crafue, William Bernham,
clerk, John Thornham and Roger Prat
Latin; armorial seal on tag

C/3/10/2/3/2/9   16 Sep. 1400
Manor of Ulveston in Debenham with appurtenances in Stonham, Aspall, Mickfield, Kenton
and Wetheringsett
Quitclaim from Roger Prat of Norwich [Norfolk] to William Snetesham, Thomas Crafue,
William Bernham, clerk and John Thornham
Latin; seal on tag

C/3/10/2/3/2/10   26 Jun. 1412
Manor of Ulveston Hall in Debenham with lands and tenements in Debenham, Stonham,
Aspall, Mickfield, Kenton and Wetheringsett
Grant from Robert Hedon, vicar of Debenham church, and William Grenehood of Mickfield, to
Thomas Ulveston and wife Isabel, for life of grantees, with reversion to Thomas Crane [recte
Cravene], John Framelyngham, John Thornham, Robert Suffeld of Norwich [Norfolk] and
Robert Reve of Beccles, chaplain
Premises are those which grantors lately had by grant of Thomas Crane, William de Snetisham,
William Bernham, clerk, John Thornham and Roger Prat
Latin; 2 seals on tags

C/3/10/2/3/2/11   26 Jun. 1412
Counterpart of C/3/10/2/3/2/10
Latin; 2 seals (with same devices as those attached to C/3/10/2/3/2/10) on tags

340

C/3/10/2/3/2/12   23 Aug. 1417
Manor of Ulveston Hall in Debenham with lands and tenements in Debenham, Stonham,
Aspall, Mickfield, Kenton and Wetheringsett
Quitclaim from Thomas Cravene to John Framlyngham, John Thornham, Robert Suffeld of
Norwich and Robert Reve of Beccles, chaplain
Latin; armorial seal on tag

C/3/10/2/3/2/13   23 Apr. 1422
Manor of Ulveston Hall in Debenham
Grant for life from Isabel Ulveston of Wangford, widow, to Simon Fylbrygge, William Phelyip
and John Hefnyngham, kts, William Mannyng, William Mekefelde, James Jose, William
Wallere, John Brasyer perpetual vicar of Debenham, William Brasyer perpetual vicar of
Reydon, Richard Banyard, Robert Crane, Robert Banyard, Geoffrey de Weston, Roger Boorhed,
Thomas Lestere and Richard Jerald; with remainder, after her death, to John Ulveston her son;
names of 6 witnesses
Latin; seal on tag

C/3/10/2/3/2/14   23 Apr. 1422
Manor of Ulveston Hall in Debenham
Letter of attorney from Isabel Ulveston, widow, to William Fullere of Wetheringsett, to deliver
seisin to Simon Fylbrygge, kt, John Brasyer perpetual vicar of Debenham, and their fellows, for
her lifetime
Latin; seal on tongue

C/3/10/2/3/2/15   1503–1509
Manor of Ulveston Hall in Debenham
Evidences of title for purchase by Christopher Thwaytes, gent., merchant of the Staple at
Calais, from John Ulveston of Ely (Cambridgeshire), esq., for £466 13s 4d, 27 Apr. 1506, with
covenant for marriage between William, eldest son of Christopher Thwaytes, and Margaret,
daughter of John Ulveston
(24 docs)

C/3/10/2/3/3   Manors of Ulveston Hall and Sackvilles in Debenham   **1406–1549**

C/3/10/2/3/3/1   1406–1531
Manor of Sackvilles in Debenham, Kenton, Aspall, Wetheringsett and Winston
Evidences of title for purchase by William Thwaytes of Manningtree (Essex), esq., from Robert
Crane of Chilton, esq., 1 Jul. 1530
Includes:
— letter of attorney with armorial seal of Thomas Sackville, esq., 1406
(11 docs)

C/3/10/2/3/3/2   1512–1549
Manor of Ulveston Hall and reversion of manor of Sackvilles, in Debenham, Aspall, Winston,
Wetheringsett, Earl Stonham, Stonham Aspal, Little Stonham and Mickfield
Evidences of title for purchase by Henry Tooley of Ipswich, merchant, from Christopher
Thwaytes, son and heir of William Thwaytes of Debenham, esq., deceased, for £526 13s 4d,
1548; N.B. the main purchase deed is not present.
Includes:
— schedule of deeds, n.d. [?1548], listing documents 13c.–31 Hen. VIII (1539 or 1540)
(16 docs)

C/3/10/2/3/4   Tooley estate in Whitton, Akenham, Great Blakenham,   **later 13c.–1797**
Little Blakenham, Bramford and Claydon

The great majority of the medieval deeds are believed to relate to the properties called Kents
and Holme Place, purchased by Henry Tooley from Simon Hill of East Bergholt in 1546 and

1547 respectively (*see* C/3/10/2/3/4/104 below) and later known as Walnut Tree Farm. It is possible, however, that some may relate to the Street Farm in Whitton and Bramford, owned jointly by Tooley's Foundation, Smart's Charity and Christ's Hospital.

C/3/10/2/3/4/1   n.d. [? later 13c.]
2 pieces of land in Akenham
Feoffment from Richard, son and heir of William le Ry of Akenham, to William Perachat and Roger his brother, for ½ mark
Premises lie between land of Sir Richard de Breuse on E., and land of Adam Algor on W., with land of Alan the smith in the middle, abutting N. on land of Margery de Pole and S. on land of William Algor; names of 8 witnesses
Latin; seal missing from tag

C/3/10/2/3/4/2   n.d. [? later 13c.]
Land with houses, buildings and pastures in Barham and Claydon
Feoffment from Stephen Chiuath to Juliana Litewyne, both of Barham, for 40s.
Names of 10 witnesses
Latin; seal on tag

C/3/10/2/3/4/3   n.d. [? later 13c.]
Land (½a) in Whitton
Feoffment from Roger Henri of Rubroc [*sic*] to Augustine Quinting of Akenham, for 8s.
Premises lie in Roger's croft, between his land and land of Peter son of William de Bosco, abutting on Roger's land towards messuage of William Vincent, and on land of Edina de Marisco; names of 8 witnesses
Latin; seal (incomplete) on tag

C/3/10/2/3/4/4   29 May 1297
Piece of land called Wlfalle in Barham
Quitclaim from Matilda, widow of Reginald de Houtoun, to John Aunsys of Barham
Premises lie between land of Geoffrey del Hoo on W. and way called Lanedio ... on E., abutting S. on ... and N. on Wodeweye; names of 6 witnesses
Latin; damaged by rodent action and incomplete; seal missing from tag

C/3/10/2/3/4/5   20 Jul. 1301
Land (1a) in Akenham
Feoffment from William Pachet and Roger Pachet, both of Ipswich, merchants, to John the merchant of Akenham, wife Katherine and son Robert, for 2 marks
Premises lie between land of Lescia Kede on E. and land of Arnulph Hereward on W., abutting N. on land of William de Bossco of Akenham and S. on land of William Algor; names of 8 witnesses
Latin; both seals missing from tags

C/3/10/2/3/4/6   20 Nov. 1316
Piece of land in Whitton
Feoffment from John Doket to Sir Martin de le Wode, chaplain, both of Whitton
Premises lie between way from Whitton to Bramford on N. and feoffor's land on S., abutting E. on feoffor's messuage and W. on land of John le Knyg; names of 7 witnesses
Latin; seal missing from tag

C/3/10/2/3/4/7   21 Aug. 1322
Piece of land in Bramford
Feoffment from Walter Aylild of Bramford to Master Geoffrey de Horwod, rector of Bramford, and John le Neuman of Bramford
Premises lie between lands of feoffees on both sides, abutting N. on land of Reginald Tokon and S. on pasture of Thomas de la Grene; names of 7 witnesses
Latin; seal missing from tag

C/3/10/2/3/4/8   26 Dec. 1328
Messuage enclosed with fences and ditches, with 2 adjoining pieces of land, in Whitton
Grant for life from Robert de Bosco, kt, to Sir Martin de Bosco of Whitton, chaplain, for 2s
annual rent
Premises are those which Roger de Bosco formerly held in villeinage from grantor's predeces-
sors; names of 6 witnesses
Latin; seal and tag missing

C/3/10/2/3/4/9   27 Aug. 1329
6s 8d annual rent out of land called Baldewyneslond in Whitton
Bond from William Lolt of Whitton, chaplain to Sir Godfrey Lumkyn, chaplain, for payment of
rent for ever
Premises lie between land of Sir Nigel de Kentone, kt on S. and land of William Malyn on N.;
names of 5 witnesses
Latin; seal missing from tongue

C/3/10/2/3/4/10   12 Jan. 1330
Third part of messuage with buildings, adjoining curtilage and 3 pieces of arable land in
Whitton and Claydon; with all goods and chattels therein
Feoffment and grant from John de Tremeleie of Whitton to John Dekes of Claydon and wife
Cecily
Messuage and curtilage lie between messuage of William Lolt, chaplain, on N. and feoffor's
messuage on S., abutting E. on land formerly of Ralph Lolt and W. on highway from Ipswich to
Norwich; first piece of land lies between feoffor's land on N. and messuage of William Heued
on S., abutting E. on land formerly of Ralph Lolt and W. on highway; second piece between
land of William de Bosco on S. and feoffor's land on N., abutting W. on pasture of William de
Bosco and E. on land of William Donne; third piece between feoffor's land on S. and land
formerly of John Prede on N., abutting E. on highway and W. on land formerly of Walter de
Westhale; names of 7 witnesses
Latin; seal missing from tag

C/3/10/2/3/4/11   3 Jun. 1330
Two pieces of arable land in Whitton
Feoffment from William de Schrubelund of Coddenham and wife Agnes to John de Stonham,
cutter
Premises lie in furlong called Coupotteshill; first piece between land of William Bovus on N.
and land of Peter le Thacchere of Stradbroke, formerly of Hervey Lolt on S., abutting E. on land
of Geoffrey Stace and W. on highway from Bramford to Akenham; second piece between
land of Peter le Thacchere on E. and W., abutting N. on land formerly of Hervey Lolt and S. on
land of Richard Lolt; names of 7 witnesses
Latin; both seals missing from tags

C/3/10/2/3/4/12   6 Oct. 1331
Piece of land called le Windmelnehul in Whitton
Indenture declaring that feoffment of same date from Richard Lolt, son of late Robert Lolt of
Whitton, to Sir Martin de Bosco, chaplain, was by way of mortgage for 13s, to be repaid at
following Michaelmas
Names of 7 witnesses
Latin; seal missing from tag

C/3/10/2/3/4/13   22 Dec. 1331
Lands and tenements in Whitton
Grant of reversion from William de Schrybelound of Coddenham and wife Agnes to Roger de
Aula of Rushmere, after death of Matilda Lolt, widow of Hervey Lolt, who holds premises in
dower
Names of 6 witnesses
Latin; seal missing from tag

C/3/10/2/3/4/14   22 Dec. 1331
Lands and tenements in Whitton
Bond from William de Schribbelound of Coddenham to Roger de Aula of Rushmere, pledging
all his lands in Coddenham as warranty for premises
Premises are those which Matilda Lolt, widow of Hervey Lolt, holds in dower; names of 7 wit-
nesses
Latin; seal missing from tag

C/3/10/2/3/4/15   21 Mar. 1332
Messuage in Whitton
Feoffment from Matilda called le Clerk to Sir Godfrey Lumbekyn of Bramford, rector of
Tattingstone church
Premises were purchased from Sir William Lolt of Whitton, chaplain, and lie between
messuage of John Deykes on S. and way from Roubrok Cross to Whitton church on N., abutting
E. on garden of John de Ayessch, chaplain, purchased from feoffor, and W. on highway from
Ipswich to Norwich; names of 8 witnesses
Latin; seal missing from tag

C/3/10/2/3/4/16   24 Jan. 1333
2 pieces of arable land in Whitton
Quitclaim from John, son of Walter Lolt of Whitton, to Sir Godfrey Lumkyn of Bramford,
rector of Rendlesham church
Premises were lately conveyed by feoffment from John Lolt to Sir Godfrey; names of
8 witnesses
Latin; seal missing from tag

C/3/10/2/3/4/17   25 Apr. 1333
Lands and tenements in Whitton, Thurleston and Claydon
Quitclaim from Tristram de Eston to Roger de Aula of Rushmere; names of 5 witnesses
Latin; seal missing from tag

C/3/10/2/3/4/18   9 May 1333
Piece of land in Bramford
Feoffment from Hugh de la Grene of Bramford to William Bruges of Ipswich
Premises lie between land formerly of Thomas Wydie and way leading from house formerly of
Thomas de Spina towards field called Hoberwe, abutting on land once of Peter de la Ty and
land of John Aylild; names of 5 witnesses
Latin; seal, incomplete, on tag

C/3/10/2/3/4/19   13 Jan. 1334
Piece of arable land with way adjoining it lengthwise in Whitton
Feoffment from John Lolt of Whitton to Sir Godfrey Lumkyn of Bramford, rector of Rendlesham
church, and sister Margaret
Premises lie between land of John Kyng on N. and lands of Sir Godfrey Lumkyn and John de
Stonham, cutter, on S., abutting E. on lands of William Kymbel and W. on feoffor's messuage;
names of 7 witnesses
Latin; seal on tag

C/3/10/2/3/4/20   22 Jan. 1334
Messuage with buildings, garden and curtilage in Whitton
Feoffment from John Lolt of Whitton to Sir Godfrey Lumkyn of Bramford, rector of Rendlesham
Premises lie between land of Roger de Aula on N. and way leading from cross called
Roubrokescruch to Whitton church on S., abutting E. on land of Sir Godfrey and sister Margery
and W. on highway; names of 7 witnesses
Latin; seal missing from tag

C/3/10/2/3/4/21   29 Sep. 1335
Lands and tenements in Whitton, Bramford, Little Blakenham and Thurleston, except solar in messuage in Whitton
Lease from Sir Martin de Bosco of Whitton, chaplain, to Roger de Braumforde his brother, for 4 years at 40s p.a.
Names of 6 witnesses
Latin; seal missing from tag

C/3/10/2/3/4/22   9 Oct. 1335
Piece of land in Whitton
Feoffment from John Kyng of Bramford to Sir Godfrey Lumkyn of Bramford, parson of Rendlesham church
Premises lie between land of Sir Godfrey and land of Roger de Halle, abutting S. on land of Roger de Halle and N. on land formerly of Walter de Westhale; names of 9 witnesses
Latin; seal missing from tag

C/3/10/2/3/4/23   20 Sep. 1337
2s annual rent out of piece of land called le Marelond [in Whitton]
Grant from Gundred, widow of John le Chapman of Whitton, and son Roger, to John Lumkyn of Ipswich
Names of 5 witnesses
Latin; seal missing from tag

C/3/10/2/3/4/24   1 Feb. 1338
Built messuage in Barham
Feoffment from Roger Bele of Barham to William de Okenhille of Barham
Premises lie between messuage of Thomas Lumbard and pightle of William de Okenhille, abutting on highway and marsh of John the clerk; names of 7 witnesses
Latin; seal missing from tag

C/3/10/2/3/4/25   7 Mar. 1342
Piece of land in Whitton
Feoffment from Roger de Halle of Whitton and wife Alice to Miles Wynter of Stratford
Premises lie between land of John Lumbekyn on S. and land of Gundred Lolt on N., abutting W. on highway and E. on land of Robert de Beverlee; names of 8 witnesses
Latin; 1 seal on tag, second seal missing

C/3/10/2/3/4/26   15 Jun. 1343
Piece of land in Whitton
Feoffment from Henry Bretoun of Ipswich, wife Sayeva, and John, son of late Roger le Barker of Ipswich and said Sayeva, to John Coleman sen. of Ipswich
Premises lie between land formerly of Sir Robert de Bosco, kt and land of feoffee, abutting S. on land of Sir Robert and N. on land formerly of Augustine Cotewene, chaplain; names of 7 witnesses
Latin; 3 seals, 1 armorial, on tags

C/3/10/2/3/4/27   20 Nov. 1343
Land (3a) held of manor of Bramford [in Bramford]
Copy of court roll recording plea of land between Robert Sperwe of Bramford and wife Dionisia, plaintiffs, and Thomas de Bruges of Ipswich, defendant; resolved by compromise
Latin

C/3/10/2/3/4/28   3 Jul. 1344
Land in [? Bramford]
Conveyance, apparently between Peter .... [*missing*] and Thomas, son of William de Bruges of Ipswich
Fragment only; Latin; seal missing from tag

C/3/10/2/3/4/29   31 Jan. 1345
Messuage with buildings, fences and ditches in Whitton
Quitclaim from Joan, daughter of Tristan Markaunt of Easton, to John de Coggishale and wife
Clemence
Premises lie between messuage of Sir Godfrey Lumkyn and land of Gundred Loult, abutting on
highway from Ipswich to Norwich and land of Roger de Halle; names of 5 witnesses
Latin; seal missing from tag

C/3/10/2/3/4/30   3 Feb. 1345
Piece of land in Whitton
Feoffment from Roger de Aula to Walter Weylond, both of Whitton
Premises lie between land of rector of Whitton church on E. and land of William del Wode on
W., both heads abutting on land of William del Wode; names of 6 witnesses
Latin; seal missing from tag

C/3/10/2/3/4/31   29 May 1345
Piece of arable land in Whitton
Feoffment from Roger, son of William Sorel of Blakenham, to Robert Brid of Thurleston
Premises lie between land of Sir Godfrey Lumbekyn on N. and land of Robert Hayy on S.,
abutting W. on highway and E. on land of Martin de Wode, chaplain; names of 7 witnesses
Latin; seal on tag

C/3/10/2/3/4/32   30 May 1345
Piece of land in Whitton
Quitclaim from Roger, son of William Sorel of Blakenham, to Robert Brid of Thurleston
Premises descended to Roger on death of Katherine his mother, and are bounded as described
in C/3/10/2/3/4/31; names of 7 witnesses
Latin; seal on tag

C/3/10/2/3/4/33   25 Jun. 1345
2 parts of piece of land and reversion of third part, in Whitton
Feoffment and grant from Robert Brid of Thurleston to Godfrey Lumkyn, parson of Rendlesham
church, and Robert his brother, chaplain
Premises are bounded as described in C/3/10/2/3/4/31; names of 7 witnesses
Latin; seal missing from tag

C/3/10/2/3/4/34   24 Aug. 1345
Piece of land in Whitton
Feoffment from Roger de Aula of Whitton and wife Alice to Baldwin de le Dale, son of Thomas
de le Dale of Thurleston
Premises lie between land of Christina Dogat on S. and land of Gundred Lolt on N., abutting W.
on pasture of William de Bossco and E. on land of William Donne; names of 6 witnesses
Latin; seal missing from tag

C/3/10/2/3/4/35   28 Oct. 1347
2 pieces of land in Bramford
Feoffment from Robert, son of late William de Bruges of Ipswich, to Thomas his brother
First piece lies between land of John de Prestone on W. and land formerly of John Vynion on E.,
abutting S. on land of John de Prestone and N. on Sampsones Weye; second piece between land
of Sir John Brese on E. and land of John le Cartere, carpenter, on W., abutting N. on land of Sir
John Brese and S. on lane leading from house formerly of John Vynion to Bramford church;
names of 8 witnesses
Latin; seal and tag missing

C/3/10/2/3/4/36   10 Dec. 1347
Piece of land in Caluecroft in Barham
Feoffment from John dil Grene of Barham to daughter Christina

Premises lie between land of Nicholas del Lane and land formerly of Adam Myle, abutting on land of Simon Malyn and feoffor's land; names of 7 witnesses
Latin; seal on tag

C/3/10/2/3/4/37   23 Dec. 1347
20s annual rent out of lands and tenements in Ipswich and its suburbs, Bramford and elsewhere in Suffolk
Grant from Thomas, son of late William de Bruges of Ipswich, to Thomas Struttyng and Roger Loy, chaplain, both of Ipswich
Names of 11 witnesses
Latin; seal on tag

C/3/10/2/3/4/38   4 Jan. 1349
Piece of land in Whitton
Feoffment from Robert, son of William dil Wode of Akenham, chaplain, to Walter Weylond, smith
Premises lie between land of feoffee and land of John, son and heir of late Roger de Halle, abutting on close of Richard le Seriaunt and common called le Fremersh; names of 7 witnesses
Latin; seal, incomplete, on tag

C/3/10/2/3/4/39   16 Mar. 1349
Lands and tenements in Whitton
Feoffment from William, parson of Whitton church, to John Dogat of Whitton and wife Alice
Premises are those which feoffor lately purchased from feoffee; names of 5 witnesses
Latin; seal missing from tag

C/3/10/2/3/4/40   21 Sep. 1349
Built curtilage [in Akenham]
Feoffment and quitclaim from John Sporoun, chaplain, to Thomas, son of Joan Dameroun, both of Akenham
Premises are those with which Thomas previously enfeoffed John; names of 4 witnesses
Latin; seal missing from tag

C/3/10/2/3/4/41   14 Mar. 1350
Cottage in Whitton
Feoffment from John le Shepherde to Nicholas le Chapman, both of Whitton
Premises lie between messuage of Robert Lumkyn, parson of Horham church, on E. and land of John de Halle on W.; names of 5 witnesses
Latin; seal missing from tag

C/3/10/2/3/4/42   3 Jun. 1350
Land (½a) in Claydon
Feoffment from Rose, Alice and Constance Ayston, cousins and heirs of Sir John Ayston, chaplain, to Roger de Pikston of Otley and wife Sarah
Names of 5 witnesses
Latin; 3 seals on tags

C/3/10/2/3/4/43   3 Oct. 1350
Messuage in Whitton
Feoffment from Robert Lumkyn, parson of Horham church, to Nicholas le Chapman
Premises were formerly John Lolt's and lie between le Chercheweye on S. and land of John de Halle on N., abutting W. on highway; names of 5 witnesses
Latin; seal on tag

C/3/10/2/3/4/44   27 Dec. 1351
Lands and tenements in Akenham
Quitclaim from John, son of Eustace Hilt of Little Blakenham to Margaret Martyn of Akenham

347

Premises are John's part of property formerly of Nicholas Kede of Akenham, which descended to him on death of his mother Alice; names of 5 witnesses
Latin; seal on tag

C/3/10/2/3/4/45   13 Oct. 1352
Part of messuage with curtilage in Whitton
Feoffment from Christina, daughter of late Peter Chaumpayn of Stradbroke, to John de Halle of Whitton and wife Margery
Premises are that part which descended to feoffor by inheritance after death of Margaret her mother, and lie between tenements of feoffee on both sides, abutting E. on tenement of feoffee and W. on highway from Ipswich to Claydon; names of 7 witnesses
Latin; seal missing from tag

C/3/10/2/3/4/46   8 Jan. 1354
Lands and tenements with meadows, grazing lands and pastures in Whitton
Feoffment from Martin dil Wode, chaplain, to John Poulyn, both of Whitton
Names of 6 witnesses
Latin; seal missing from tag

C/3/10/2/3/4/47   8 Nov. 1355
Lands and tenements in Akenham, Whitton, Claydon, Barham and Coddenham, except tenement called Brademedwes
Feoffment from Robert dil Wode, parson of Sproughton church, to Gilbert Debenham, Roger de Wolferstone, John Deneys, William de Boytone, Thomas Deneys and Philip Deneys
Latin; seal, almost complete, on tag

C/3/10/2/3/4/48   14 Jul. 1349
House with adjoining curtilage in Akenham
Feoffment from Emma Tolle to Thomas Dameroun of Akenham
Premises lie between land of heirs of Richard Martyn on E. and messuage of John Spigurnel on W., abutting S. on way from tenement of John Colevile to Akenham church and N. on tenement formerly of Simon Ficat; names of 5 witnesses
Latin; seal on tag by which tied to C/3/10/2/3/4/49–51

C/3/10/2/3/4/49   15 Feb. 1356
Messuage in Akenham
Feoffment from Robert Fiket to Thomas Dameroun, both of Akenham
Premises descended to feoffor on death of father, Simon Fyket, and lie between land formerly of Richard Martyn on E. and highway on W., abutting S. on feoffee's tenement and N. on highway; names of 5 witnesses
Latin; seal missing from tag by which tied to C/3/10/2/3/4/48, 50 and 51

C/3/10/2/3/4/50   4 Jun. 1357
Tenement with buildings and curtilage in Akenham
Feoffment from Thomas Dameroun to John Medwe, both of Akenham
Tenement was formerly of Simon Fykat of Akenham and lies between land formerly of Sir Richard Martyn on E. and highway from Ipswich to Debenham on W., abutting S. on common way from tenement of Margaret Martyn to Akenham church and N. on land formerly of Sir Richard Martyn; curtilage was lately purchased by feoffor from Lenota Heyward and lies between curtilage of John Spygurnel on N. and tenement called Herewards on S., abutting E. on tenement of John Spygurnel and W. on highway; names of 5 witnesses
Latin; seal on tag by which tied to C/3/10/2/3/4/48, 49 and 51

C/3/10/2/3/4/51   23 Jul. 1357
Messuage in Akenham
Quitclaim from Robert Fyket to Thomas Dameroun, both of Akenham

Premises were formerly of Simon Fyket, Robert's father, and are bounded as in C/3/10/2/3/4/49; names of 5 witnesses
Latin; seal missing from tag by which tied to C/3/10/2/3/4/48–50

C/3/10/2/3/4/52   18 Feb. 1358
Lands and tenements in Whitton and Bramford
Feoffment from John Poulyn of Whitton to John Turry of Whitton and Stephen le Bacster of Ipswich
Premises are those which feoffor formerly purchased from Martin de Wode, chaplain; names of 5 witnesses
Latin; seal, incomplete, on tag

C/3/10/2/3/4/53   29 Sep. 1359
Piece of pasture in Whitton
Quitclaim from Philip Justus of Thurleston to John Halle of Whitton
Premises lie between land of Whitton church and land formerly of John Brademedwe, abutting on church land and land formerly of John Brademedwe; names of 5 witnesses
Latin; seal missing from tag

C/3/10/2/3/4/54   8 Jun. 1360
Piece of arable land with way adjoining it lengthwise in Whitton
Feoffment from Margery, daughter of late Roger Lumbekyn of Bramford, to Nicholas Schapman of Whitton and wife Margery
Premises lie between land of heir of William de Hel and land of feoffees, abutting on messuage of feoffees and lands of Robert Lumbekyn and Hugh Aylemer; names of 5 witnesses
Latin; seal missing from tag

C/3/10/2/3/4/55   13 Oct. 1361
Piece of arable land in Whitton
Feoffment from John Reynold, rector of Somerleyton church, William Hel, chaplain and Margery Lumbekyn, sister of late Robert, rector of Horham church, to Nicholas Schapman of Whitton
Premises lie between land of Christina Jai and land formerly of John Poulyn, abutting on highway called Roubrokstrete and land formerly of John Poulyn; names of 5 witnesses
Latin; 1 seal incomplete, second missing from tag, third seal and tag missing

C/3/10/2/3/4/56   13 Oct. 1361
Piece of meadow in Westmede in Whitton
Quitclaim from John .... [illegible] to Nicholas Schapman, both of Whitton
Premises lie between meadows of William Smith of Akenham on both sides; names of 3 witnesses
Latin; damp-stained and partly illegible; seal missing from tag

C/3/10/2/3/4/57   6 Jun. 1362
Tenement in Whitton
Feoffment from William atte Hel, chaplain and Margery, sister of late Robert Lumbekyn, rector of Horham church, to William Rynggedale of Whitton
Premises lie between tenement of John Deykys and common way from Bramford to Whitton church, abutting E. on land of John atte Hil and W. on highway; names of 5 witnesses
Latin; 2 seals on tags

C/3/10/2/3/4/58   4 May 1363
Lands and tenements in Whitton
Feoffment from John Doo of Whitton to Matthew Bernard
Premises are those which feoffor formerly purchased from Hugh Aylmer; names of 5 witnesses
Latin; seal on tag

C/3/10/2/3/4/59   22 May 1363
Piece of meadow in Whitton
Quitclaim from John Dogat of Whitton to Robert Waleys of Ipswich
Premises lie between land formerly of Richard de Leyham on N. and pasture of Sir Robert
Lumbekyn on S., abutting E. on tenement of John Poulyn and W. on land formerly of Richard
de Leyham; names of 5 witnesses
Latin; seal missing from tag

C/3/10/2/3/4/60   26 Jun. 1363
Lands and tenements in Whitton and Bramford
Feoffment from Alice, widow of Stephen Ablot of Ipswich, baxter, to Adam de Brandiston of
Ipswich, clerk
Premises were formerly purchased from John Turry of Witnesham; names of 6 witnesses
Latin; seal on tag

C/3/10/2/3/4/61   28 Aug. 1363
Lands and tenements in Whitton and Bramford
Feoffment from Adam de Brandiston of Ipswich to Robert Waleys of Ipswich and wife Alice
Premises are those which feoffor had by gift of Alice, widow of Stephen Ablot of Ipswich,
baxter; names of 6 witnesses
Latin; 1 seal, second missing from tag

C/3/10/2/3/4/62   16 Jan. 1365
Lands and tenements in Whitton
Feoffment from Philip Justous, William Pyntene of Thurleston and Matthew Bernard of
Akenham to John Halle of Whitton
Premises are those which feoffors lately purchased from feoffee; names of 4 witnesses
Latin; all 3 seals missing from tags

C/3/10/2/3/4/63   17 Jan. 1367
Piece of arable land in Whitton
Feoffment from Matthew Bernard of Akenham to John Doget of Whitton
Premises lie between land of Nicholas Lolt on both sides, abutting on common way from
Whitton to Westerfield and on land of Robert Waleys; names of 3 witnesses
Latin; seal and tag missing

C/3/10/2/3/4/64   5 Apr. 1367
Lands and tenements in Akenham, Whitton, Claydon, Barham and Coddenham
Feoffment from John Deneys, Roger de Wolferstone, Thomas Deneys and Philip Deneys to
John de Kent and wife Katherine
Premises were received by feoffors from Robert dil Wode, formerly parson of Sproughton
church
French; 1 seal on tag, second seal missing

C/3/10/2/3/4/65   23 Jul. 1367
Piece of arable land in Whitton
Feoffment from John Doget to Nicholas Lolt, both of Whitton
Premises lie between land of feoffee on both sides, abutting S. on land of Robert Waleys and N.
on way from feoffee's house to Whitton church; names of 5 witnesses
Latin; seal missing from tag

C/3/10/2/3/4/66   31 Dec. 1368
Lands and tenements in Whitton, Thurleston, Akenham, Claydon and Coddenham
Quitclaim from Philip Deneys to John de Kent of Akenham and wife Katherine
Premises are those which Deneys lately purchased from Robert dil Wode, parson of Sproughton
church; names of 3 witnesses
Latin; seal missing from tag

C/3/10/2/3/4/67   18 Oct. 1369
Part of tenement called Kedys and meadow called Sporunismedwe in Akenham and 2 pieces of
land in Thurleston
Feoffment from Edmund, parson of Whatfield church, William Pyntone, parson of Akenham
church, David Wyth, chaplain of Bedfield and John Turry of Witnesham to Robert Sewyne of
Bramford and wife Mariota
Meadow lies between Gosele Wode and land of Akenham rectory; first piece of land between
land of Sir John Brewse, kt and land formerly of Philip Justous; and second piece between land
formerly of Philip Justous and way from Thurleston church to Goselemedwe; names of
5 witnesses
Latin; all 4 seals missing from tags

C/3/10/2/3/4/68   3 Feb. 1370
Messuage with adjoining croft in Whitton and 2 pieces of arable land with adjoining way in
Bramford and Whitton
Feoffment from William Randolf and Adam Hefd and wife Joan to Walter Weylond of Whitton
and wife Beatrice
Messuage and croft lie in Whitton between messuage and land of Robert Alman on both sides,
abutting on highway and land of Nicholas Lolt; first piece of land lies in Bramford between
land of William Pertre and said way; second piece in Whitton between land of Lovetotis Hall
and said way; and way lies between parishes of Bramford and Whitton, lengthwise from
highway from Whitton Street to Carbonnellhel; names of 7 witnesses
Latin; 1 seal, 2 others missing from tags

C/3/10/2/3/4/69   3 Oct. 1371
Piece of arable land in Whitton
Quitclaim from Ralph, parson of Whitton church, to Robert Alman of Whitton
Premises were formerly purchased from John Deykys and lie next to free land of Whitton
church, abutting on highway from Ipswich to Claydon
Latin; seal missing from tag

C/3/10/2/3/4/70   6 Nov. 1371
Piece of arable land in Whitton
Feoffment from John Doket of Whitton to John de Kent of Akenham
Names of 5 witnesses
Latin; on paper; 1 seal

C/3/10/2/3/4/71   1 May 1372
Piece of land in Whitton
Feoffment from Nicholas Lolt of Whitton to John Halle and wife Margery
Premises lie between land of John Kent on N. and land of feoffee on S., abutting E. on land of
William Fyke and wife Agnes and W. on common way from Akenham to Whitton; names of
5 witnesses
Latin; seal missing from tag

C/3/10/2/3/4/72   1 Aug. 1372
Lands and tenements [in Akenham]
Feoffment from John Kent of Akenham to Robert Sewyne of Akenham and wife Mariota
Premises are that portion of property formerly of Nicholas Kede of Akenham which feoffor
lately purchased from William Parys of Little Blakenham; names of 5 witnesses
Latin; seal missing from tag

C/3/10/2/3/4/73   28 Nov. 1376
Messuage as enclosed with fences and ditches in Whitton
Feoffment from William Pyntone, rector of Akenham church, to Nicholas Lolth of Whitton and
wife Margaret
Premises are those which feoffor lately purchased from feoffees, and lie between land of

feoffees on E. and highway on W., abutting S. on church way and N. on land of feoffees; names
of 5 witnesses
Latin; seal on tag

C/3/10/2/3/4/74   12 Dec. 1383
Lands and tenements in Akenham and Thurleston
Feoffment from Edmund, son of John Medwe of Akenham, to William Smyth of Akenham and
son John, with grant of reversion of any part of premises after death of Robert Got
Names of 6 witnesses
Latin; seal missing from tag

C/3/10/2/3/4/75   3 Dec. 1386
Lands and tenements in Akenham
Feoffment from Robert Sewyne of Akenham and wife Mariota to son Robert, chaplain
Names of 5 witnesses
Latin; 2 seals on tags

C/3/10/2/3/4/76   12 Jun. 1391
Messuage in Barham
Feoffment from John Dunys and John Borham, both of Claydon, to John Pykot sen. of Barham
and wife Margery, formerly wife of William Rynggedale of Whitton
Premises are those which feoffors lately had by feoffment of John Pykot, and lie between
highway from Ipswich to Norwich on E. and marsh of John Chese sen. on W., abutting N. on
messuage of John Chese sen. and S. on Barham rectory; names of 5 witnesses
Latin; both seals missing from tags

C/3/10/2/3/4/77   28 Mar. 1404
12 pieces of arable land in the fields of Claydon
Feoffment from John ? Sygor of Claydon to John Kent of Akenham
Latin; badly stained by damp and partly illegible; seal missing

C/3/10/2/3/4/78   27 May 1414
Lands and tenements (no details) in Little Blakenham, Great Blakenham and Bramford
Quitclaim from James Draper to Robert, rector of Gimingham [Norfolk], John Siglemere and
Nicholas Fiket
Premises are those which James, Robert and Nicholas had by feoffment from John Hayl of
Little Blakenham; names of 7 witnesses
Latin; seal on tag

C/3/10/2/3/4/79   10 Oct. 1417
Lands and tenements (no details) in Little Blakenham, Great Blakenham, Bramford and
Claydon
Feoffment from Thomas Godeston of Colchester [Essex], James Draper, John Justise, John
Sorel and Nicholas Hayl, son of John Hayl of Little Blakenham, to Robert Aldewyk of
Rattlesden, John his son, and John Bilhagh of Wetheringsett, for £46 13s 4d
Premises are those which feoffors lately had by feoffment of Sir Robert Stratton, rector of
Gimingham [Norfolk], John Siglemere and Nicholas Fiket; names of 5 witnesses
Latin; 3 seals on tags

C/3/10/2/3/4/80   1 Aug. 1430
Lands and tenements in Akenham, Whitton, Bramford, Claydon, Great Blakenham, Coddenham
and Barham
Feoffment from John Kent of Akenham to John Lacforthe of Ipswich
Names of 5 witnesses
Latin; seal on tag by which tied to C/3/10/2/3/4/81

C/3/10/2/3/4/81   25 Feb. 1431
Lands and tenements in Akenham, Whitton, Bramford, Claydon, Great Blakenham, Coddenham
and Barham

Feoffment from John Lacforthe of Ipswich to John Kent of Akenham, Stephen Benton, John Priowr and John Felawe of Ipswich
Premises are those which feoffor lately had by feoffment of John Kent; names of 5 witnesses
Latin; seal on tag by which tied to C/3/10/2/3/4/80

C/3/10/2/3/4/82   20 Feb. 1435
Lands and tenements in Akenham, Thurleston and Westerfield, except lands called Fullereslondes in Thurleston
Feoffment from John Smyth sen. of Akenham to Robert Crane and Thomas Dounham of Ipswich and Robert Fennyng, Thomas Vyncent and John Smyth, son of feoffor, of Akenham
Names of 7 witnesses
Latin; seal on tag

C/3/10/2/3/4/83   5 Sep. 1439
Lands and tenements in Little Blakenham, Great Blakenham, Bramford and Claydon
Demise from Sir Robert Wetheryngsete, Archdeacon of Ely, Stephen Wetheryngsete, John Sumpter, chaplain and John Bronewyn of Wetheringsett to Thomas Curson, esq. and wife Margaret, Roger Spice, George Sekford and Clement Spice, esqs, Richard Doket, John Curson, Robert Curson, Robert Kempe, clerk, John Bacon and William Pilbergh
Demisors had premises, formerly of Nicholas Hayll, jointly with Robert Hamond, esq., John Bilhagh and William Rowdham, all now deceased, by grant of John Rikkys, clerk, Robert Havell of Creeting, Thomas Wade of Needham Market, John Wodeward of Wetheringsett, John Sewell of Bramford, Richard Lymbrennere of Claydon and John Grymeprest of Wetheringsett; names of 7 witnesses
Latin; 11 seal tags, all seals missing

C/3/10/2/3/4/84   14 Sep. 1439
Lands and tenements in Little Blakenham, Great Blakenham, Bramford and Claydon
Quitclaim from Thomas Mosell, John Andrewe, William Curson, Robert Morwhile and Alice, widow of Richard Talmage of Sproughton, to Thomas Curson, esq. and wife Dame Margaret
Latin; 2 seals on tongue, second tongue with seals torn away

C/3/10/2/3/4/85   5 Apr. 1443
Close [in Akenham]
Acquittance for purchase price of 26s 8d, from John Smyth sen. of Akenham to Richard Dalyng of Ipswich
Latin; seal missing from tongue

C/3/10/2/3/4/86   20 Oct. 1443
Lands and tenements (no details) in Little Blakenham, Great Blakenham, Claydon and Bramford
Quitclaim from George Sekford, esq. to Thomas Brewes, esq., Robert Crane, Thomas Denys, Robert Cook, Nicholas Rose and John Hill
Premises are those which George lately had jointly with Thomas Curson, esq., Dame Margaret his wife, Roger Spyce, esq., Clement Spyce, esq., Richard Doket, John Curson, Robert Curson, Robert Kempe, clerk, John Bacon and William Pilbergh, by feoffment of Robert Wetheryngsete Archdeacon of Ely, Stephen Wetheryngsete, John Sumpter, chaplain and John Bronewene of Wetheringsett, and were formerly Nicholas Haill's; names of 5 witnesses
Latin; seal on tag

C/3/10/2/3/4/87   15 May 1459
Pightle (3r) between Blakenham churchyard on N., Mylneweye on S., lord's pasture on E. and highway on W., copyhold of manor of Blakenham
Copy court roll recording lord's grant to Canon William Ficher, rector of Blakenham, and successors
Latin

C/3/10/2/3/4/88   20 Sep. 1461
40s legal money of England

Letter of attorney from Richard Dallyng late of Ipswich and William Lynde of Greenwich by London (Kent), gent., to Benedict Caldwell, to receive the money from John de Hill of Claydon, yeoman and Geoffrey de Hill of Blakenham de Hill [Little Blakenham], husbandman, his son
Latin; 2 seals

C/3/10/2/3/4/89   25 Aug. 1474
Piece of land (14a) in Greteclos and moiety of meadow (2a) called Bysshoppysbrigge, held of the manor of Bramford
Copy court roll recording lord's grant to William Lynde for 40 years at 18s 8d annual rent
Latin

C/3/10/2/3/4/90   23 Oct. 1480
Lands and tenements in Akenham, Whitton, Bramford, Claydon, Coddenham, Great Blakenham and Barham
Quitclaim from Richard Felawe, son and heir of John Felawe, to John Hyll of Claydon
Premises are those which John Felawe lately had jointly with John Kent, Stephen Benton and John Pryour by feoffment of John Lakford of Ipswich
Latin; seal on tag

C/3/10/2/3/4/91   26 Oct. 1480
Lands and tenements called Kentes and Powlyns in Akenham, Whitton, Bramford, Claydon, Coddenham, Great Blakenham and Barham
Feoffment from John Hyll of Claydon to Nicholas Hyll his son, Margaret Forde, widow of Robert Forde of Hadleigh, James Hobart, William Forde, Stephen Furmage and Nicholas Furmage, to use of Nicholas Hyll and heirs of his body
Premises are those which feoffor lately had jointly with William Whethered, Thomas Denys, John Tangham, Thomas Maunsell and Nicholas Rose, all now deceased, by feoffment of John Kent and release of Richard Felawe, son and heir of John Felawe; names of 5 witnesses
Latin; seal on tag

C/3/10/2/3/4/92   26 Oct. 1480
Counterpart of C/3/10/2/3/4/91
Latin; seal on tag

C/3/10/2/3/4/93   5 Jan. 1486
Watermill called Crakeforth Mille with all meadow and pasture belonging to it in Claydon, as formerly let out to farm, copyhold of manor of Akenham
Copy court roll recording admission of Geoffrey at Hill and Robert and Thomas his sons, on surrender of John Hyll, deceased; for 33s 4d annual rent
Latin

C/3/10/2/3/4/94   14 Sep. 1486
Messuage with adjoining alder carr and lands and tenements in Barham and Claydon
Feoffment from Geoffrey Hyll, son and heir of John Hyll of Claydon, to John Kech of Ipswich and Robert Hill, John Sorell and John Cruet, all of Claydon
Premises are those which descended to feoffor by inheritance on death of his father, and were formerly Matilda Jurdon's; names of 3 witnesses
Latin; seal missing from tag

C/3/10/2/3/4/95   5 Jan. 1487
Cottage and land (1a 1r) in Claydon, copyhold of manor of Akenham
Copy court roll recording surrender by John Hardy to the use of John Hart and John Keche
Latin

C/3/10/2/3/4/96   14 Jun. 1487
Pieces of meadow and pasture west of Creykemelle and in Hunteriscroft in Baylham, copyhold of manor of Barham

Copy court roll recording admission of Thomas Hill following surrender by his father Geoffrey Hill before his death
Latin

C/3/10/2/3/4/97   27 May 1498
Lands and tenements called Haylys in Blakenham and Bramford
Feoffment from James Hobert to William Hyll
Latin; seal on tag

C/3/10/2/3/4/98   16 Jan. 1505
Messuage, lands and tenements in Barham and Claydon, and messuage called Cokes tenement in Claydon
Feoffment from Richard Sorrell of Henley, clerk, to William Bernard of Akenham, gent., Thomas Ward of Akenham, clerk, and Nicholas Hyll, John Sorrell, James Meltam and wife Isabel and John Cruett, all of Claydon
Latin; equestrian seal on tag

C/3/10/2/3/4/99   10 Jun. 1506
Lands and tenements in Aldham, Elmsett, Whatfield, Claydon, Akenham, Whitton, Thurleston, Little Blakenham, Great Blakenham, Bramford and Wetheringsett
Quitclaim from Robert Hyll, son and heir of William Hyll, son and heir of Geoffrey Hyll, son and heir of John Hyll late of Claydon, to William Hyll of East Bergholt
Latin; seal missing from tag

C/3/10/2/3/4/100   28 Feb. 1508
Piece of land in Barham field and close called Jordonysclose in Claydon
Feoffment from William Barnarde, gent. and Thomas Warde, clerk, both of Akenham, Nicholas Hyll of Claydon, James Meltam, wife Isabel and John Ornett, to William Hyll of Bergholt, merchant, Nicholas Hylle and Philip Hyll, sons of William, Edmund Daundy and John Regnold of Ipswich
Premises are those which feoffors had, with John Sorell now deceased, by feoffment of Richard Sorell of Henley, clerk, dated 16 Jan. 1505; piece of land lies between land called Ryderys meer on S. and land of Barham Hall on N., abutting E. on land of Barham Hall and W. on land of John Deer; close abuts W. on river flowing towards Bramford and E. on Norwich Wey
Latin; all 6 seals missing from tags

C/3/10/2/3/4/101   30 Mar. 1508
Tenement called Bernuys (1a) in Barham and Claydon
Feoffment from Edmund atte Hylle of Barham and William atte Hylle his brother to William Hylle of Bergholt, merchant, Nicholas Hylle and Philip Hylle his sons, and John Regnold of Ipswich
Premises are those which feoffors had jointly with Robert atte Hylle, son of Geoffrey atte Hylle of Great Blakenham, now deceased, by feoffment of Adam atte Hylle of Barham; and abut W. on highway from Ipswich to Norwich and E. on way from Claydon Street to Barham church
Latin; 1 seal on tag, second seal missing

C/3/10/2/3/4/102   Jan. 1519
6 acres land, 6 acres pasture in Barham and Claydon
Final concord, William Hylle, gent., Philip Hylle, Simon Hylle and Humfrey Hylle, pls; James Melcham and wife Isabella, defs

C/3/10/2/3/4/103   Jan. 1519
Counterpart of C/3/10/2/3/4/102

C/3/10/2/3/4/104   1505–1563
Messuage and land called Kents, and reversion of messuage and lands called Holme Place, in Akenham, Whitton, Bramford, Claydon, Thurleston and Coddenham
Evidences of title for purchase by Henry Tooley of Ipswich, merchant, from Simon Hill of East Bergholt, gent., 30 Sep. 1546 and 22 Sep. 1547, with subsequent licences from lords of manors

of Lovetofts, Claydon and Brokes Hall to Tooley's surviving executors to alienate to Tooley Foundation, property held of their respective manors, 8 Oct. 1562 and 5 Apr. 1563 (28 docs)

C/3/10/2/3/4/105   11 Mar. 1650
Copyhold land (½a) on the Cliff in Claydon
Conveyance by bargain and sale from John Harwell of Bramford, gent, executor of Marie Lytell of Bramford, widow, deceased, to Henry Whitinge, linen draper, Richard Sheppard, linen draper, Samuel Brandlinge, esq., John Smithier jun., gent. and William Haile, gent., all of Ipswich, in trust for the poor of Tooley's Foundation

C/3/10/2/3/4/106   26 May 1797
Land in Whitton, part of waste of manor of Lovetofts in Bramford
Grant from George Thomas, lord of manor, of premises enclosed without licence as part of Walnut Tree Farm, in trust for Wardens of Tooley's Foundation

C/3/10/2/3/5   The Lime Kiln Farm in Claydon   later 13c.–1474

C/3/10/2/3/5/1   n.d. [? later 13c.]
3 pieces of land in Claydon and piece of meadow in Blakenham
Feoffment from Hervey de Claidun, chaplain to Robert the chaplain, his son, for 40s
First piece of land lies between land of Roger de Staplesford and lands of Nicholas the smith and Richard son of Robert, messuage of Robert the miller and lands of other men, abutting on way to Claydon church and land of Sawin de Scarweston; second piece between tenement of Ernald Longi and free land of Claydon church, abutting on land of Ernald Longi and little wood; third piece at Walleslade between free land of Claydon church and land of Roger de Staplesford, abutting on way to Hertesford called Witelond and on free land of Barham church; and meadow in Blakenham abuts on Holuwescroft and on pond of Middelmelne; names of 12 witnesses
Latin; seal and tag missing

C/3/10/2/3/5/2   n.d. [? later 13c.]
11d annual rent in Claydon
Grant from Jordan le Waleys to Richard, son of William de Holebrok, for 9s fine and 1 clove annually
Rent is payable by Bartholomew de Cruce and heirs for tenement held of grantor in Claydon; names of 9 witnesses
Latin; seal missing from tag

C/3/10/2/3/5/3   n.d. [? later 13c.]
Piece of land in Claydon
Feoffment from Robert Hinoon to John Ode, both of Claydon, for 5s fine and ¼d annually
Premises lie between land of Augustine Hinoon le Cuppere and land of Adam de Cruce, both heads abutting on land of William de Aula of Claydon; names of 10 witnesses
Latin; seal missing from tag

C/3/10/2/3/5/4   n.d. [? later 13c.]
Piece of land in Claydon
Feoffment from Robert de Hahe to Ailmar de Templo, for 5s 4d fine and 2d annually
Premises lie in field called Hyaxhahe between feoffee's lands, abutting on land of Walter Gudheie and land which William de Castre held of the land of Pawel, which widow Alice held of feoffor's fee; names of 13 witnesses
Latin; seal missing from tag

C/3/10/2/3/5/5   n.d. [? later 13c.]
Land (1a) in Claydon
Feoffment from Robert de Haghe to William, son of William de Kenebroc, for 8s fine, ½d annual rent and ½d castleguard

Premises lie in field called Mickelefeld, between free land of Hakeham [? Akenham] church and feoffor's demesne, abutting on highway; names of 10 witnesses
Latin; seal missing from tag

C/3/10/2/3/5/6   n.d. [? later 13c.]
Land (4r) in Claydon
Feoffment from John Warin to Simon de Stapelford, for 8s fine and annual services to chief lords of fee: 2d to John de Lunetot, 1 clove to Everard le Poter and ½d to Geoffrey Gekeiman
½a lies between land of Agnes de Hertesforde, abutting on way from Barham to Ipswich and on lane from Claydon to Barham; 1r lies between said ½a and land of Simon Sigor, abutting on highway from Barham to Ipswich and on lane from Barham church to Claydon; 1r lies between land of Richard Long and land of Robert Alfild; names of 10 witnesses
Latin; seal missing from tag

C/3/10/2/3/5/7   7 Jan. 1291
Tenements with messuages, buildings, lands, pastures, ways, paths and commons in Claydon
Grant of remainder, after her death, from Alice Sygor of Claydon to Roger Homond of Pilecok Thornham [sic], in free marriage with Katherine Sygor her daughter
Names of 7 witnesses
Latin; seal missing from tag

C/3/10/2/3/5/8   30 Nov. 1292
2 pieces of land in Claydon
Feoffment from John Malin of Barham to Henry le Taylur of Claydon and wife Alice, for 17s fine and 3½d annually to chief lords of fee
First piece lies between land of Roger Moy on S. and feoffee's land on N.; second piece between land of William de Aula on N. and land of William de Aula and James Cocus on S.; names of 7 witnesses
Latin; seal missing from tag

C/3/10/2/3/5/9   6 May 1295
Piece of land in Claydon
Feoffment from William Sigor of Claydon to Roger Knotte of Wingfield, for 14s fine and 1d annually to chief lords of fee; remainder, in default of issue, to Isabel, Roger's sister
Premises lie between lands of Roger Mayi on W. and E., abutting N. on land of William de Cleydon and S. on highway; names of 12 witnesses
Latin; damaged by rodent action, text incomplete; seal, incomplete, on tag

C/3/10/2/3/5/10   8 Sep. 1304
2 pieces of land in Claydon
Quitclaim from John de Hertisford of Claydon to William Wodekoc of Holbrook and Juliana, John's sister
First piece lies between dower land of Juliana de Aula of Claydon and land of Sir Richard le Langge, chaplain; second piece between [sic] land of Isabel de Crakeford on one side, abutting N. on land of Sir Richard le Langge and S. on land of William de Aula of Claydon; names of 8 witnesses
Latin; seal missing from tongue

C/3/10/2/3/5/11   14 Sep. 1304
5 pieces of land in Claydon
Quitclaim from Katherine de Hertisford, widow of John Hertisford of Claydon, to William Wodecok of Holbrook and Juliana, Katherine's daughter
Premises are those which Katherine holds as dower; names of 8 witnesses
Latin; seal, incomplete, on tag

C/3/10/2/3/5/12   19 Feb. 1306
Piece of land (3r) in Claydon

357

Grant from William Sygor of Claydon to John Lumbard and wife Alice for life, with remainder to Thomas de Westone, wife Joan and legitimate heirs of their bodies
Premises lie between lands of John Lumbard on both sides, abutting N. on his land and S. on way called Wytelondeweye; names of 6 witnesses
Latin; seal missing from tag

C/3/10/2/3/5/13   11 Jan. 1308
3 pieces of land in Claydon
Feoffment from William de Cracford to Adam Ayston and wife Rose, all of Claydon, for Rose's lifetime, then to heirs of Adam
First piece lies in field called Wytelondhyl between land of John Chevat and land of William Sygor, abutting on land of John Lumbard; second piece in same field between land of John Lumbard and land of John Chevat, abutting on little way from Claydon to Barham Hall; third piece between land formerly of John Hertisford and land of William Sygor, abutting on said little way and on highway from Ipswich to Norwich; names of 9 witnesses
Latin; seal on tag

C/3/10/2/3/5/14   21 Mar. 1309
Piece of meadow in Claydon
Feoffment from William de Culfo to John Coleman of Ipswich and [? wife] Emma
Premises lie between river and meadow which was William Wolmer's, abutting S. on ....
and N. on land of Reginald the miller and ....; names of 9 witnesses
Latin; damaged by rodent action, text incomplete; seal, incomplete, on tag

C/3/10/2/3/5/15   12 Jul. 1309
Piece of land in Claydon
Feoffment from Thomas Bryd of Bucklesham to William de Cleydone
Premises lie between foeffee's land on E. and land of William Sygor on W., abutting S. on messuage formerly of Richard le Cuylter; names of 6 witnesses
Latin; seal missing from tag

C/3/10/2/3/5/16   17 Oct. 1311
Pightle marked by boundaries in Claydon
Feoffment from John Martyn of Claydon to Roger, son of Martin Panecake of Barham
Premises lie between feoffor's messuage and feoffee's land on E. and land of John Farnham and Thomas son of Geoffrey Oteley on W., abutting S. on highway from house of Hubert Densy to Prachelmerys and N. on land of John Aylmer; names of 9 witnesses
Latin; seal on tag

C/3/10/2/3/5/17   4 Jan. 1312
Piece of land in Claydon
Feoffment from Roger Moy of Ipswich to Robert le Colewyle of Helmingham and nephew Robert, son of Walter Demel of Stonham
Premises lie between land of feoffees and land formerly of John de Hertesforde, abutting on highway and on way from Barham Hall to Crakeford; names of 5 witnesses
Latin; seal on tag

C/3/10/2/3/5/18   14 Mar. 1316
Piece of land in Claydon
Feoffment from William Wodekoc of Tattingstone and wife Juliana, daughter of late John de Hertisford, to Alice, daughter of Adam Ayston of Claydon
Premises lie between land of Alice le Taulour on N. and land of John Lumbard on S., abutting E. on land of Adam Ayston and [N.] on way from Claydon to Barham; names of 8 witnesses
Latin; both seals missing from tags

C/3/10/2/3/5/19   31 Oct. 1316
Messuage with piece of land abutting thereon in Claydon
Feoffment from Thomas, son of late Adam Langstaf, to William le Kyng, both of Claydon

Premises lie between land of Sir William de Cleydone and tenement of Martin Gulle, one head abutting on highway, the other on land of Sir William de Cleydone and Alan Ode; names of 7 witnesses
Latin; seal missing from tag

C/3/10/2/3/5/20   7 Feb. 1317
Piece of land in Claydon
Feoffment from William de Cleydone, kt to Robert, son of William Sygor of Claydon
Premises lie between lands of John Chevat on both sides, abutting on land of John Lumbard and land of Agnes Lumbard; names of 7 witnesses
Latin; seal missing from tag

C/3/10/2/3/5/21   11 Nov. 1320
5 pieces of land in Claydon
Quitclaim from William Wodekoc of Tattingstone and wife Juliana to Matilda and Joan, daughters of Adam Ayston jun.
First piece lies in field called le Rede between land of William Tastard, abutting on land formerly of John Cratun; second piece in same field between land formerly of Robert the smith, abutting on land formerly of said Robert; third piece in same field between land of Claydon church, abutting on land of Sir William de Cleydone, kt; fourth piece in same field between land of John Cratun, abutting on land of Sir William de Cleydone and land of William Tastard; fifth piece between lands of Claydon church, abutting on lands of Sir William de Cleydone; names of 7 witnesses
Latin; both seals missing from tags

C/3/10/2/3/5/22   27 Sep. 1321
Messuage with houses built thereon and adjoining piece of land in Claydon
Quitclaim from Thomas, son of Adam Bangstam of Claydon to Robert le Meller of Claydon
Premises lie between messuage of Martin Gulle and land of Sir William de Cleydone, kt, abutting W. on highway from Claydon to Ipswich and E. on land formerly of Adam Ode; names of 7 witnesses
Latin; seal, incomplete, on tag

C/3/10/2/3/5/23   25 Apr. 1322
Piece of meadow enclosed with ditches in Claydon
Feoffment from John Coleman of Ipswich to Hugh Sory of Claydon
Premises lie between land of Reginald the miller and meadow formerly of Fabian Kent, abutting E. on meadow formerly of Alan Ode and W. on river bank from Middelmelle to Crakefordmelle; names of 7 witnesses
Latin; seal on tag

C/3/10/2/3/5/24   14 Jun. 1323
Piece of land in Claydon
Feoffment from John ? Abraham of Ipswich to John the chaplain, son of Adam Ayston of Claydon
Premises lie between land of Robert Martin on N. and land of John Lumbard on S., abutting E. on land of Adam Ayston and [W.] on way from Claydon to Barham church; names of 7 witnesses
Latin; seal, incomplete, on tag

C/3/10/2/3/5/25   7 Oct. 1326
Land called Smethislond and Lepereslond (20a) [in Claydon]
Quitclaim from Stephen Sporoun of Sandon [Essex], son and heir of Ralph Sporoun, to Sir William de Cleydone and wife Eleanor
Premises lie between highway leading towards Chelmsford [Essex] on E. and land of Sir William de Cleydone, formerly of Sir William de Hanygfeld on W.; names of 5 witnesses
Latin; seal missing from tag

359

C/3/10/2/3/5/26   3 Feb. 1328
2 pieces of land and part of messuage in Claydon
Feoffment from John Pride and wife Catherine to Roger Brion, all of Claydon
First piece lies between lands of Thomas Cratun on both sides, abutting on highway and land
called Sucrofit; second piece between lands of Adam Martin and Thomas Cratun; names of
6 witnesses
Latin; seal missing from tag

C/3/10/2/3/5/27   13 Oct. 1332
Piece of land in Claydon
Feoffment from Robert Martyn of Claydon to Roger Goldyng of Hemingstone
Premises lie between land of Richard Sygor and feoffor's land, abutting on land of John de
Cleydone and on way from Barham church to house of Henry le Cook; names of 5 witnesses
Latin; seal missing from tag

C/3/10/2/3/5/28   27 Jan. 1317
Piece of land in Claydon
Feoffment from William Wodekoc of Tattingstone to Robert Denyel of Barham
Premises lie between feoffee's land and land of Adam Ayston, abutting on highway from
Barham to Ipswich and on way from Barham church to house of Henry le Couk; names of
7 witnesses
Latin; seal missing from tag by which tied to C/3/10/2/3/5/29

C/3/10/2/3/5/29   30 Jan. 1335
Piece of land in Claydon
Quitclaim from Roger Golding of Hemingstone to John Ayston of Claydon, chaplain
Premises are those which Roger lately purchased from Robert Martin of Claydon, and lie
between land of Richard Sygor and land of John Ayston, abutting on land formerly of Sir
William de Cleydone, kt and way from Barham church to house of Richard le Cok; names of
8 witnesses
Latin; seal missing from tag by which tied to C/3/10/2/3/5/28

C/3/10/2/3/5/30   5 Oct. 1335
Piece of land in Claydon
Feoffment from Robert Martyn to John Ayston, chaplain, both of Claydon
Premises lie between land of Richard Sygor and feoffee's land, abutting on land formerly of Sir
William de Cleydone and on way from Barham church to house of Richard le Cok; names of 8
witnesses
Latin; seal on tag

C/3/10/2/3/5/31   20 Jul. 1338
Piece of land in Claydon
Feoffment from John de Cruce of Coddenham, chaplain, to Thomas Lumbard of Barham
Premises lie between feoffee's lands on both sides, abutting on land of John de Beylham and
way called Witlond Weye; names of 7 witnesses
Latin; seal missing from tag

C/3/10/2/3/5/32   ? 2 Nov. 1343
Piece of land in Claydon
Feoffment from Isabel, widow of Adam Ode of Claydon, to John Ode, her son
Premises are those which feoffor holds as dower, and lie between land of Adam Martyn and
land of John Ode, both heads abutting on lands of John Cok; names of 8 witnesses
Latin; badly discoloured by damp and much of text almost illegible; seal and tag missing

C/3/10/2/3/5/33   8 Sep. 1346
7 pieces of arable land, chamber and kiln called le lym kelne in Claydon
Lease from Thomas Cratoun of Ipswich and wife Isabel to John Martin of Claydon and wife

Rose, for 7 years, paying 1 quarter of corn, 2 quarters of barley, 2 bushels of peas and 8*d* annually for land, and 2 quarters of lime weekly for kiln; names of 6 witnesses
Latin; both seals missing from tags

C/3/10/2/3/5/34   14 Sep. 1346
Messuage with houses built thereon in Claydon street
Feoffment from Thomas Cratoun of Ipswich to Adam Martin of Claydon
Premises lie between feoffor's messuage and messuage called le Smythe formerly of Sir
William de Cleydone, abutting on highway from Ipswich to Norwich and land formerly of Sir
William de Cleydone; names of 7 witnesses
Latin; seal missing from tag

C/3/10/2/3/5/35   21 Jan. 1352
Messuage in Claydon
Feoffment from Thomas dil Cok of Barham to Robert Gulle of Claydon and wife Alice
Premises lie between way from Claydon church to house of Adam Martyn, and messuage of
Thomas Hardel formerly called le Hepworth, abutting on highway from Ipswich to Norwich;
names of 8 witnesses
Latin; seal missing from tag

C/3/10/2/3/5/36   1 Oct. 1343
6*s* annual rent in Claydon
Bond for payment, from John Wyldefer to Robert Sigor, both of Claydon, on security of
messuage in Claydon
Messuage lies between messuage of Richard le Cook and messuage of Robert Sigor; names of
5 witnesses
Latin; seal on tag by which tied to C/3/10/2/3/5/37

C/3/10/2/3/5/37   11 Mar. 1356
6*s* annual rent payable out of messuage in Claydon
Grant from Reginald Lacy of Thorneye and Ralph Lolt of Claydon to Thomas de Bergham,
Gilbert de Debenham and Robert del Wode, parson of Sproughton church
Messuage is that which John Wyldefier of Claydon lately held in fee and pledged for payment;
names of 5 witnesses
Latin; seal on tag by which tied to C/3/10/2/3/5/36

C/3/10/2/3/5/38   11 Oct. 1356
Messuage in Claydon
Feoffment from Felicia Sigor to William Schet, both of Claydon
Premises lie between messuage formerly of John Wyldefer and curtilage of Alan Stel on one
side and messuage of John Pekot on the other, abutting on highway from Ipswich to Norwich
and way from Claydon to Barham church; names of 5 witnesses
Latin; seal on tag

C/3/10/2/3/5/39   25 Apr. 1357
Messuage with buildings in Claydon
Feoffment from Adam Martyn to Adam ate Cros and wife Margaret, all of Claydon, and grant
of reversion of that part of premises which Isabel, widow of Thomas Cratoun of Claydon, holds
as dower
Premises are those which feoffor formerly purchased of Thomas Cratoun, and lie between
tenement formerly of Sir William de Cleydone, kt on N. and tenement formerly of Petronilla
Cratoun on S., abutting E. on land formerly of Sir William de Cleydone and W. on highway
from Ipswich to Norwich; names of 7 witnesses
Latin; seal missing from tag

C/3/10/2/3/5/40   21 Aug. 1361
2 messuages in Claydon
Feoffment from William Skete to Adam Martyn, Alan Stel, John Seymour, John de Kent and
Robert Gulle

One messuage lies next to highway on one side and way from Barham church to Claydon street on the other, abutting on messuage of John Picot and messuage formerly of John Masoun; other messuage next to highway on one side and land formerly of Ralph Lolte on the other, abutting on land of Ralph Lolte and curtilage called Newebys; names of 5 witnesses
Latin; endorsed 'Johanni Kent' in late medieval hand; seal on tag

C/3/10/2/3/5/41   21 Jan. 1364
Curtilage with house built thereon in Claydon
Feoffment from John Pykot of Claydon to John Martyn of Claydon, wife Rose and daughter Rose
Premises lie between messuage of John Schaldeford and messuage of John Seymour, abutting E. on highway and W. on pasture of Claydon Hall; names of 5 witnesses
Latin; fragment of seal on tag

C/3/10/2/3/5/42   5 Aug. 1375
Lands and tenements in Claydon and Great Blakenham, lands and tenements in Chattisham and Hintlesham, and 10d rent in Washbrook
Feoffment and grant from John Cratoun, vicar of Hintlesham church, to Henry Launche of Hintlesham, Thomas de Mundeford and Walter atte Heel of Hintlesham
Premises in Claydon and Great Blakenham are those formerly of Thomas Craton; rent was purchased from Richard, son of William de Mundeford; names of 5 witnesses
Latin; seal on tag

C/3/10/2/3/5/43   4 Oct. 1377
Lands and tenements in Claydon
Feoffment from Alice Gulle of Claydon, widow, to Thomas Boteler, rector of Claydon church, and Robert Selwyn, chaplain
Names of 5 witnesses
Latin; seal, incomplete, on tag

C/3/10/2/3/5/44   3 Jun. 1378
Piece of land in Claydon
Feoffment from Thomas Boteler, parson of Claydon church, and Robert Sewyn, to John Seymour of Claydon and wife Marion
Premises are those which feoffors formerly purchased from Alice, widow of Robert Gulle, and lie at le lymkill between lands formerly of Adam Martyn on both sides, abutting E. on land formerly of John Cratoun, chaplain and W. on highway from Ipswich to Norwich; names of 5 witnesses
Latin; both seals missing from tags

C/3/10/2/3/5/45   4 Jul. 1389
Lands and tenements in Claydon
Remise from Alexander, rector of Helmingham church, John, rector of Claydon church, John Wodeward, John Taverner, Stephen de Tangham and John Smyth to John Seymour and wife Mariota for life, with remainder to Thomas, son of John Coupere of Helmingham, and wife Eleanor
Premises are those which remitters formerly had by feoffment of John Seymour; names of 5 witnesses
Latin; 2 seals on tags, third seal missing

C/3/10/2/3/5/46   14 Apr. 1392
Lands and tenements in Claydon
Feoffment from Alice Gulle to John Aystoun, both of Claydon
Names of 5 witnesses
Latin; seal fragment on tag

C/3/10/2/3/5/47   24 Jul. 1394
Messuage [in Claydon]

Quitclaim from John Swanlonde, rector of Claydon church, John Seymour and John Boroun of Claydon, to Robert Canoun of Claydon
Premises are those which Swanlonde, Seymour and Boroun formerly had by feoffment of Rose Martyn of Claydon
Latin; 3 seals, 2 incomplete, on tags

C/3/10/2/3/5/48   30 Apr. 1402
Piece of land with orchard annexed called Aldirmanyscroft or Pekyscroft [in Claydon]
Feoffment from John Seymour of Claydon to John Gryssent of Baylham, Robert Lolt, John Pycot and John Amys of Claydon
Premises lie next to Chalkhel on E. and way from Claydon to Bramford, abutting on land of Hervey Lolt and common pasture called Fremersche; names of 5 witnesses
Latin; seal, incomplete, on tag

C/3/10/2/3/5/49   8 May 1391
Messuage with adjoining curtilage in Claydon
Feoffment from Richard de Bregge of Ipswich and wife Lettice to Robert Canoun of Raydon
Premises lie between land of manor of Claydon and highway from Ipswich to Norwich, both heads abutting on land of manor of Claydon; names of 5 witnesses
Latin; 2 seals, one incomplete, on tags by which tied to C/3/10/2/3/5/50

C/3/10/2/3/5/50   10 Dec. 1402
Messuage with adjoining curtilage in Claydon
Feoffment from Robert Kanoun of Claydon to John Weylond of Whitton
Premises lie between land of manor of Claydon and highway from Ipswich to Norwich; names of 5 witnesses
Latin; seal on tag by which tied to C/3/10/2/3/5/49

C/3/10/2/3/5/51   4 Dec. 1407
Piece of land with orchard annexed called Aldyrmancroft or Pekyscroft in Claydon
Quitclaim from Thomas Belyaunt of Barham to John Dinys of Claydon
Premises lie next to Chalkhel on E. and way from Claydon to Bramford, abutting on land formerly of Hervey Lolt and common pasture; names of 5 witnesses
Latin; seal on tag

C/3/10/2/3/5/52   4 Dec. 1407
Piece of land with orchard annexed called Aldirmancroft or Pekiscroft in Claydon
Quitclaim from John Gryssente of Baylham and Robert Lolt of Claydon to John Dinys of Claydon
Premises are those which John and Robert lately had by feoffment of John Seymour of Claydon
Latin; 1 seal on tag, second seal missing

C/3/10/2/3/5/53   21 May 1439
50s in respect of lands and tenements [in Claydon]
Acquittance from John Felawe and Stephen Bentone, both of Ipswich, to John Hill of Claydon, by hand of John Lakforde of Ipswich, executor of John de Kent of Akenham, deceased
Payment due for last Easter term for property sold to Hill by Felawe, Bentone and Kent
Latin; seal on tongue

C/3/10/2/3/5/54   17 Mar. 1440
Messuage with adjoining alder carr, lands and tenements in Barham and Claydon
Quitclaim from Margery Clerk of Rattlesden, widow, daughter of John Jordon sometime of Barham, to John Hill of Claydon, Nicholas Rose of Little Blakenham, Geoffrey Hill of Barham and John Fax of Claydon
Premises were lately John Jordon's; first piece of land lies in Barham field between lands of Thomas Deer and Alice Jordon, abutting E. on land of John Bouwell and W. on highway; second in same field between land of John Bouwell on N. and way to Barham church on S., abutting E. on land formerly of John Jordon and W. on highway; third in same field next to

chapel of St Peter of Barham; and five pieces in Claydon field: first between lands of Robert Pegot and John Lolt, abutting N. on land of John Bouwell and S. on way from Walkesslade to Claydon; second between lands of John Lolt and Robert Pegot, abutting W. on land of John Lolt and E. on land of Robert Pegot; third between land of John Lolt and highway called Greneweye, both ends abutting on land of Barham rectory; fourth called Stonyhalfacre between lands of John Lolt and Robert Pegot, abutting E. on land of Robert Pegot and W. on land of John Lolt; fifth between Stonhill and land of Barham rectory, abutting W. on land of John Lolt and E. on Norwychweye; piece of land called Fowrestechis in Barham field between lands of Robert Pegot and John Lolt, abutting W. on highway and E. on land of John Lolt; and 3 pieces of land lying divided in same field in close called Jordonysclos; names of 5 witnesses
Latin; seal, incomplete, on tag

C/3/10/2/3/5/55   3 Feb. 1454
Lands and tenements in Claydon and Barham
Feoffment from Nicholas Rose, Matthew Passhemere and John Cruet, all of Claydon, to John Attehill, Geoffrey Attehill, Walter Bowbrook and Adam Attehill
Premises are those which feoffors lately had by grant of Walter Brenn of Claydon; names of 5 witnesses
Latin; 3 seals on tags

C/3/10/2/3/5/56   23 Dec. 1469
General release of all actions, personal quarrels and demands
From Margaret, widow of Edmund Bedyngfelde, esq., to John Hill of Claydon
Latin; endorsed 'Claydon' in 17c. hand; seal missing from tongue

C/3/10/2/3/5/57   6 May 1474
2 pieces of land in Claydon
Feoffment from John Lolt to John Hill, both of Claydon; Alan Cowper of Whitton attorney to deliver seisin
First piece lies lengthwise next to le Stonicrouch and highway from Norwich to Ipswich on one side and land late of John Amys on S., abutting W. on land late of John Weylond; second piece abutting S. on highway; names of 4 witnesses
Latin; seal fragment on tag

C/3/10/2/3/6   Property in St Clement, Ipswich   1464–1527

C/3/10/2/3/6/1   5 Aug. 1464
3 messuages with curtilages in CL and close in St John of Caldewell, in the suburbs of Ipswich
Letter of attorney from John Drayll to Geoffrey Hyll to deliver seisin to John Howard, kt, John Sulyard, James Hobart and John Hyll
Latin; seal with no discernible impression

C/3/10/2/3/6/2   20 Jan. 1527
Warehouses, 'teinitries' [dye works], quay, crane, curtilages and gardens called the Palis Yard *alias* Gossis Yard in CL, abutting S. on the salt river
Bargain and sale from William Hille of East Bergholt, gent., Thomas Gosse of Colchester (Essex), mercer (son and heir of Richard Gosse of Ipswich, merchant, deceased, son and heir of John Gosse of Ipswich, merchant, deceased), William West *alias* Sebyn of Ipswich, vintner and wife Margaret (daughter and heiress of William Gosse jun. of Ipswich, merchant, deceased, son of John Gosse), to Robert Bray of Ipswich, gent., for £50

C/3/10/2/3/7   Property in St Helen, Ipswich   1545

C/3/10/2/3/7/1   1 Jul. 1545
2 tenements with woodhouse and 3 adjoining pieces of land in HL
Feoffment from Matthew Goodyng and wife Joan to Henry Tooley
Latin

C/3/10/2/3/8 Property in St Mary at Quay, Ipswich 1518–1567

C/3/10/2/3/8/1 31 Mar. 1518
Messuage with curtilage in MQ, abutting N. on high street and S. on salt water
Feoffment from William Courtnall and Robert Bray, both of Ipswich, to Henry Toley of
Ipswich, merchant, William Stisted of Ipswich, mercer and Portman, William Rede of Beccles,
merchant, Thomas Manser of Ipswich, clothmaker, Robert Daundy of Beccles, merchant,
Thomas Purpet of Ipswich, wax chandler and Nicholas Hervy of Ipswich, merchant
Latin

C/3/10/2/3/8/2 16 Oct. 1534
Garden (½a 6p 9ft) next to gate of House of Friars Preachers in Ipswich leading from church of
St Mary at Quay to said house
Lease from Prior Edmund and Convent of Friars Preachers to Henry Toley of Ipswich,
merchant, for 80 years 2*d* p.a.
(found among the Corporation water leases)

C/3/10/2/3/8/3 16 Oct. 1534
Counterpart of C/3/10/2/3/8/2

C/3/10/2/3/8/4 16 Dec. 1534
Garden in MQ
Quitclaim from Prior Edmund Hythe and convent of Friars Preachers of Ipswich to Henry
Tooley of Ipswich, merchant and wife Alice
Premises had previously been leased to Tooley by Prior and convent
Latin; Priory seal missing from tag

C/3/10/2/3/8/5 14 Sep. 1535
Garden next to gate of House of Friars Preachers of Ipswich going from MQ parish to said
house
Counterpart lease from Prior Edmund and convent of Friars Preachers to Henry Toley of
Ipswich, merchant and wife Alys, for 40 years at 2*d* annual rent

C/3/10/2/3/8/6 6 Sep. 1537
Garden in MQ
Feoffment from Prior Edmund Hythe and convent of Friars Preachers of Ipswich to Henry
Tooley and wife Alice
Latin; Priory seal (poor impression) on tag

C/3/10/2/3/8/7 28 Nov. 1542
Brewhouse with curtilage late in occupation of Symond Fuller, with quay yard and easement of
crane, except long cellar or vault and house entering into cellar, in MQ
Counterpart lease from Henry Toley of Ipswich, merchant, to John Rogman of Ipswich, beer
brewer, for 12 years at £7 p.a.

C/3/10/2/3/8/8 17 Sep. 1567
Messuages, tenements, lands and gardens lately of Henry Tolye of Ipswich, merchant, deceased
and wife Alice, in MQ
Quitclaim from John Purpett of Paglesham (Essex), gent., to Bailiffs, burgesses and common-
alty of Ipswich
Latin

C/3/10/2/3/9 Property in St Peter, Ipswich 1524–1534

C/3/10/2/3/9/1 1524–1534
Capital messuage with curtilage, garden, entry and upper solar; and tenement with curtilage; all
in PE

Evidences of title for purchase by Henry Tooley, merchant, from George Reveley, clothmaker, both of Ipswich, 28 Sep. 1534, and conveyance to feoffees to Tooley's use, 1 Oct. 1534
Premises adjoin pond of New Mills on S.
(4 docs)

C/3/10/2/4   SMART'S CHARITY   later 13c.–1764

C/3/10/2/4/1 Coles and Coningtons in Falkenham and Kirton   later 13c.–1607

C/3/10/2/4/1/1   n.d. [later 13c.]
Part of croft in Falkenham, with reversion of moiety of tenement which grantor's mother Agnes holds as dower
Feoffment from Alice Gunter to son John
Premises lie between lands of Walter le Melle; names of 10 witnesses
Latin; seal missing from tag

C/3/10/2/4/1/2   16 May 1297
Piece of land in Falkenham
Feoffment from Adam de Pertenhale and wife Alice Gunter of Falkenham to Robert Bast of Guchestone [*sic*] and wife Alice, for ½ mark
Premises lie in field called Oselockessach, between land of John Sax on N. and land of Andrew the miller on S., abutting E. on Chercheweye and W. on Michelecroft; names of 12 witnesses
Latin; both seals missing from tags

C/3/10/2/4/1/3   19 Feb. 1302
Messuage with buildings, meadows, curtilages, ditches, hedges, gardens, alder carrs and trees in Stratton hamlet in Kirton, and 8 pieces of arable land in Croxton [? Norfolk]
Feoffment from Thomas le Scriveyn of Kirton, chaplain, to Roger de Croxston, for 20 marks
Kirton premises lie between messuage of Peter del Walle and messuage of Walter Alwynee, abutting E. on highway; names of 12 witnesses
Latin; seal missing from tag

C/3/10/2/4/1/4   19 Feb. 1302
Counterpart of C/3/10/2/4/1/3
Latin; seal missing from tag

C/3/10/2/4/1/5   7 Sep. 1309
Piece of land in Falkenham
Feoffment from Edmund Gunter of Falkenham to John Bacon of Kirton, wife Margery and son John, for 3s
Premises lie between land which was William de Bruera's and land of Margaret Horin, abutting on lands of Edmund Robekyn and John Norkyn; names of 7 witnesses
Latin; seal missing from tag

C/3/10/2/4/1/6   8 Feb. 1310
Lands and tenements in Falkenham
Demise from John dil Wode and sister Isabella to their mother Alice Gunter for her lifetime, for 100s
Premises are those which John and Isabella purchased from Alice; names of 3 witnesses
Latin; both seals missing from tongues

C/3/10/2/4/1/7   21 Jan. 1323
Piece of meadow called Gunteresmedue in Kirton
Feoffment from Alan de Kerketon, chaplain, to Robert son of Augustine de Kenebrockes and wife Isabella
Premises lie between meadow of John Ryver on N. and messuage of John Surcote on S.,

abutting E. on land of Peter Doweman and W. on land formerly William Est's; names of 10 witnesses
Latin; seal missing from tag

C/3/10/2/4/1/8   16 Sep. 1323
Piece of land in Kirton
Feoffment from Alan de Kyrketone, chaplain, to Robert de Kenebrok and wife Isabella
Premises lie between land of John Baldewyne and land of John Croucheman, abutting S. on land of John Sax and N. on land of Robert de Kenebrok; names of 5 witnesses
Latin; seal and tag missing

C/3/10/2/4/1/9   4 Dec. 1329
Moiety of croft and 3 pieces of land in Falkenham
Feoffment from Alan de Kirketone, chaplain and Robert son of Alexander dil Medue of Falkenham, to Alice Gunter of Falkenham and son Walter
Croft lies on E. of croft which Alan and Robert had by feoffment of Alice, within close of messuage formerly William Gunter's, Alice's father, between lands of William le Mellere; and 3 pieces lie in field called Planych; names of 7 witnesses
Latin; both seals missing from tags

C/3/10/2/4/1/10   4 Dec. 1329
Lands and tenements, moiety of croft, and 3 pieces of land, in Falkenham
Feoffment from Alan de Kirketone, chaplain and Robert son of Alexander dil Medwe of Falkenham, to Alice Gunter of Falkenham and daughter Isabella
Lands and tenements are those which Alan and Robert lately had by feoffment of Alice; croft is E. part of croft lying within close of capital messuage formerly William Gunter's, Alice's father, between lands of William le Mellere; 3 pieces lie in field called Planych; names of 7 witnesses
Latin; both seals missing from tags

C/3/10/2/4/1/11   8 Sep. 1385
Messuage with houses, trees, pastures and common of pasture [in Falkenham or Kirton]
Feoffment from Robert Bateman of Falkenham to John Wode of Falkenham and Robert Toke of Kirton
Names of 3 witnesses
Latin; seal missing from tag

C/3/10/2/4/1/12   1523–1607
Freehold messuages, lands, pastures and marshes called Coles and Coningtons in Falkenham and Kirton
Evidences of title for conveyance from Thomas Walton of Hadleigh, esq. and Leonard Caston of Ipswich, gent., to Bailiffs, burgesses and commonalty of Ipswich, in performance of will of William Smart of Ipswich, deceased, 10 Dec. 1607
(55 docs; bundle labelled 'Smart's Charity . . .')

C/3/10/2/4/2   Foxe's in Falkenham and Kirton   1284–1636

These documents, as found, were contained in a linen bag inscribed in a 17th-century hand 'The writinges of Foxes Londes in Falkenham', with a 19th-century label reading 'Smart's Charity'.

C/3/10/2/4/2/1   Mar. 1284
2 pieces of land in Newbourne
Feoffment from William, son of late Peter de Bossco of Newbourne, to Walter, son of Alan del Ker, for 20s fine and ½d annually; on condition of maintaining 2 lamps in chancel of Newbourne to burn daily at all services for ever, and on 13 nights a year, i.e. nights of: Circumcision; Epiphany; Conception, Purification, Annunciation, Assumption and Nativity of BVM; Easter; Pentecost; Nativity of St John the Baptist; SS Peter and Paul; and All Saints
First piece of land lies between land of Walter Herman and land formerly of Agnes of the

Church, abutting on land formerly of Gilbert de Bossco and on land of William de Fonte; second piece upon Blolond between land formerly of Roger Syward and land of Hugh de Ponte, abutting on land formerly of Gilbert de Bossco and on land of Richard de Carelton; names of 7 witnesses
Latin; seal missing from tag

C/3/10/2/4/2/2   May 1296
Land (1r) in Kirton
Feoffment from John Toke to Alexander Nog, for 6s fine and ¼d annually
Premises lie between lands of Norman Bast and John Sax, abutting E. on feoffor's land and W. on way called Snauergateweye; names of 6 witnesses
Latin; seal missing from tag

C/3/10/2/4/2/3   28 Apr. 1332
Piece of land in Falkenham
Feoffment from Isabel, daughter of Alice Gunter, to William le Mellere and wife Juliana, all of Falkenham
Premises lie between land of Alexander ..... [missing] on S. and land of William le Mellere on N.; names of 5 witnesses
Latin; surface of parchment flaking and some of text missing; seal and tag missing

C/3/10/2/4/2/4   1 Apr. 1359
Piece of arable land in Falkenham
Feoffment from John Harding of Kirton to Robert Batemant of Falkenham
Premises lie in field called Langelond, between lands of feoffee and of John Reveyt of 'Struestone' [? Stratton Hall], abutting on highway to Falkenham and on field called Ramheye; names of 5 witnesses
Latin; seal missing from tag

C/3/10/2/4/2/5   14 Nov. 1428
7 pieces of land in Falkenham and Kirton
Feoffment from John Dysse and John Gounnore of Kirton to William Randulf of Falkenham
First piece lies in field called Northlasach, between feoffee's land on S. and land late of John Markaunt on N., abutting E. on way called Snaregateweye and W. on close of William Holton; second and third pieces in field called Colemannysdole, between lands late of Robert Toke on W. and E., abutting S. on land late of Roger Sax and N. on way called Hardynggysweye; fourth piece in close called Langgelondtoft, between lands of William Willy on S. and N., abutting E. on field called Langgelond and W. on way called Aldeth; fifth piece in field called Greynecomb, between land of John Pavy on E. and land late of Roger Sax on W., abutting S. on Greynecomb and N. on land late of Thomas Wode; sixth piece in Greynecomb, between land late of Roger Sax on E. and land of Roger Sax on W., abutting S. on land late of Roger Sax and N. on land of John Pavy; seventh piece in close called Hardynggys, late of Robert Toke of Kirton; names of 5 witnesses
Latin; fragments of 2 seals on tags

C/3/10/2/4/2/6   1 Feb. 1439
Lands and tenements in Falkenham and Kirton or elsewhere in Colneis Hundred
Feoffment from Matilda Randulff, widow of Robert Randulff of Falkenham, to William Randulff of Falkenham, her son
Premises were those which descended to feoffor by right of inheritance from her father, Thomas Wode, and which formerly belonged to Stephen, son of William Gunter; names of 5 witnesses
Latin; seal, incomplete, on tag

C/3/10/2/4/2/7   1 Feb. 1439
Lands and tenements in Falkenham and Kirton

Letter of attorney from Matilda Randulff, widow of Robert Randulff of Falkenham, to William Holton of Kirton, to deliver seisin to William Randulff her son
Latin; seal, incomplete, on tongue

C/3/10/2/4/2/8   21 Dec. 1441
Land and tenements in Colneis Hundred
Quitclaim from Juliana de Wode, daughter of John de Wode of Thorpe, to John Feltewelle and Thomas Smyth of Trimley
Names of 4 witnesses
Latin; filed on parchment thong with C/3/10/2/4/2/9–11; seal on tag

C/3/10/2/4/2/9   31 Jan. 1445
Probate copy will of Laurence Cole of Falkenham (Consistory Court of Norwich)
Signed, 18 Nov. 1444
Latin; filed on parchment thong with C/3/10/2/4/2/8, 10 and 11; fragment of seal on tongue

C/3/10/2/4/2/10   30 Dec. 1452
Piece of land in Falkenham
Feoffment from John Sax and John Scot to Henry Smyth and wife Christian, all of Falkenham
Premises are those which feoffors lately had by feoffment of Margery Halk, and lie between land of Prior of Dodnash on N. and highway to Ipswich on S., abutting E. on land of Prior of Dodnash and W. on messuage of John Hore; names of 5 witnesses
Latin; filed on parchment thong with C/3/10/2/4/2/8, 9 and 11; armorial seal on tag, second seal missing

C/3/10/2/4/2/11   8 Jun. 1461
Piece of arable land in Kirton
Feoffment from John Fen sen. of Kirton to John Conyngton sen. of Falkenham; 1*d* to be paid annually to Kirton parish church
Premises were formerly Isabel de Muston's, and lie in field called Lytelhond, between land late of Laurence Cole on W. and land of William Randulph on E., abutting N. on feoffee's land and S. on pasture called Wodebrok; names of 5 witnesses
Latin; filed on parchment thong with C/3/10/2/4/2/8–10; seal on tag

C/3/10/2/4/2/12   12 Mar. 1358
Land (3½a) in Kirton, copyhold of manor of Walton
Copy of court roll for admission of John atte Wod on surrender of John Burrych
Latin; filed on parchment thong with C/3/10/2/4/2/13–17

C/3/10/2/4/2/13   10 Jun. 1368
Lands (3r) in Kirton, copyhold of manor of Walton
Copy of court roll for admission of John atte Wode on surrender of Mabel and Alice Howe
Latin; filed on parchment thong with C/3/10/2/4/2/12, 14–17

C/3/10/2/4/2/14   30 Jun. 1433
Land (6a 1½r 10p) on which rent is paid (*molondi*), of tenement Constables in Kirton, copyhold of manor of Walton
Copy of court roll for admission of John Conyngton on death of his mother Isabel
Latin; filed on parchment thong with C/3/10/2/4/2/12, 13, 15–17

C/3/10/2/4/2/15   11 Jun. 1433
Lands in Falkenham and Kirton, copyhold of manor of Walton
Copy of court roll for admission of Edmund Sax on death of his father John Sax; his surrender to the use of John Sax and wife Agnes; their admission; and quitclaim by Ellen, widow of John Sax the father
Property comprises moiety of: land (3a) newly brought under cultivation; land on which rent is paid (21a 1r 32p), of tenements Bunter, Sax, John Sax and John Syward, John Revet, John Norkyn and Robert Byldo; messuage and customary land (23a) of tenement Saxe's; and customary land (1½r) of tenement Robbyn
Latin; filed on parchment thong with C/3/10/2/4/2/12–14, 16 and 17

C/3/10/2/4/2/16   30 Nov. 1454
Tenement in Falkenham
Copy of court roll of manor of Walton, recording acknowledgement by John Dale of his deten-
tion from John Hore of 14*d*, being 2 years' arrears of rent, which is to be levied to Hore's use
Latin; filed on parchment thong with C/3/10/2/4/2/12–15 and 17

C/3/10/2/4/2/17   30 Nov. 1454
Duplicate of C/3/10/2/4/2/16
Latin; filed on parchment thong with C/3/10/2/4/2/12–16

C/3/10/2/4/2/18   n.d. [later 15c.]
Lands and tenements [in Falkenham]
Feoffment from John Conyngton late of Harwich [Essex], son and heir of John Conyngton of
Falkenham, deceased, to John Conyngton, wife Margery, William Cole, Richard Scroton son
of John Scroton of Walton, and John Scroton jun. at le Thorn
Premises were formerly of William Conyngton of Falkenham and descended to feoffor on
death of his father; names of 9 witnesses
Latin; filed on parchment thong with C/3/10/2/4/2/19–28; seal on tag

C/3/10/2/4/2/19   10 May 1487
Piece of land in Falkenham
Feoffment from Alexander Ropken of Kirton to John Cole of Falkenham
Premises lie in Cleyhell between lands of feoffee on either side, abutting S. on land of William
Scroton and N. on common way; names of 3 witnesses
Latin; filed on parchment thong with C/3/10/2/4/2/18, 20–28; seal on tag

C/3/10/2/4/2/20   20 Apr. 1499
Piece of arable land in Kirton
Feoffment from John Conyngton of Falkenham to John Cole, Thomas Cole his son, William
Scrotoun jun., John Holton and William Randolf; 1*d* to be paid annually to Kirton parish church
Premises lie in field called Litilhound, formerly of Isabel de Muston, between land late of
Laurence Cole on W. and land of William Randolf on E., abutting N. on feoffor's land and S. on
common pasture called Wodebrok; names of 3 witnesses
Latin; filed on parchment thong with C/3/10/2/4/2/18, 19, 21–28; seal on tag

C/3/10/2/4/2/21   6 Nov. 1499
5 pieces of land in Falkenham
Feoffment from William Randolf, son and heir of John Randolf late of Falkenham, son and heir
of William Randolf, to Thomas Cole
First piece of land lies in field called Langelond, between lands of John Cole and William
Benne; second piece in Colmansdole, next to land of William Benne on E.; third piece in
Colmansdole between lands of William Benne on either side; fourth piece in Noggis, between
lands of John Martyn on either side, one head abutting on way called le Comounweye; fifth
piece in close called Guntertoft between Falkenham common on W. and land of John Martyn
on E., abutting S. and N. on lands of John Martyn; names of 5 witnesses
Latin; filed on parchment thong with C/3/10/2/4/2/18–20, 22–28; seal on tag

C/3/10/2/4/2/22   10 Oct. 1500
2 pieces of land [in Falkenham]
Feoffment from John Conyngton of Falkenham, son and heir of John Conyngton late of
Falkenham, and wife Margaret, daughter and heiress of Mariot, daughter and one of heiresses
of Walter Gunter formerly of Falkenham, deceased, to John Cole of Falkenham
First piece of land lies in Grencombe, between land of feoffee on E. and land late of William
Bren on W., abutting N. and S. on lands of feoffee; second piece in Litilhounde, between lands
of feoffee on either side, abutting N. on land of feoffor and S. on Falkenham common; names of
5 witnesses
Latin; filed on parchment thong with C/3/10/2/4/2/18–21, 23–28; seal on tag

370

C/3/10/2/4/2/23   10 Oct. 1500
3 pieces of land in Falkenham
Feoffment from John Conyngton of Falkenham, son and heir of John Conyngton late of
Falkenham, and wife Margaret, daughter and heiress of Mariot, daughter and one of heiresses
of Walter Gunter formerly of Falkenham, deceased, to John Cole of Falkenham
Premises lie in field called Planych, first piece between lands late of John Randolf on either
side, abutting E. on common marsh and W. on land of feoffee; second piece between lands late
of John Randolf and late of John Fen, both heads abutting as with previous piece; third piece
between land late of John Randolf on N. and land of feoffee on S., both heads abutting as with
first and second pieces; names of 5 witnesses
Latin; filed on parchment thong with C/3/10/2/4/2/18–22, 24–28; seal on tag

C/3/10/2/4/2/24   10 Jul. 1501
Piece of land in Falkenham
Feoffment from William Conyngton to John Coole, both of Falkenham
Premises descended to feoffor on death of his father John Conyngton, and lie in furlong called
Clerkisallond, between lands of feoffee on either side, abutting N. on land of feoffee and S. on
land of John Holton; names of 3 witnesses
Latin; filed on parchment thong with C/3/10/2/4/2/18–23, 25–28; seal on tag

C/3/10/2/4/2/25   20 Sep. 1504
Piece of land in Falkenham
Feoffment from William Conyngton to John Cole, both of Falkenham
Premises descended to feoffor on death of his father John Conyngton, and lie in le Slade,
between land of feoffee on W. and land of William Randolf, late of John Randolf on E.,
abutting N. on land of William Randolf and S. on brook called Woodebrook; names of
3 witnesses
Latin; filed on parchment thong with C/3/10/2/4/2/18–24, 26–28; seal on tag

C/3/10/2/4/2/26   27 Sep. 1504
Piece of land [in Falkenham]
Feoffment from William Randolf of Falkenham to William Hendy of Trimley St Martin
Premises descended to feoffor on death of his father John Randolf, and lie in le Slade, between
land of John Coole, late of William Conyngton on W. and land of John Holton on E., abutting
N. on land of feoffor and S. on brook called Woodebrook; names of 3 witnesses
Latin; filed on parchment thong with C/3/10/2/4/2/18–25, 27 and 28; seal on tag

C/3/10/2/4/2/27   29 Sep. 1504
Piece of land in Falkenham
Feoffment from William Hendy of Trimley St Martin to John Coole of Falkenham
Premises are those which feoffor lately had by gift of William Randolf dated 27 Sep. 1504, and
lie in le Slade, bounded as stated in C/3/10/2/4/2/26; names of 3 witnesses
Latin; filed on parchment thong with C/3/10/2/4/2/18–26 and 28; seal on tag

C/3/10/2/4/2/28   29 Sep. 1504
5 pieces of land in Falkenham
Feoffment from Richard Coone and wife Joan to John Cole of Falkenham
Premises are those which were bequeathed to Joan by will of her late husband Thomas Cole;
first piece of land lies in field called Langlond, between lands of feoffee and of William Benne;
second piece in Colmandole, next to land of William Benne on E.; third piece in Colmandole
between lands of William Benne on either side; fourth piece in Noggis, between lands of John
Martyn on either side, one head abutting on le Comounweye; fifth piece called Cranetoft,
between Falkenham common on W. and land of John Martyn on E., abutting S. and N. on lands
of John Martyn; names of 3 witnesses
Latin; filed on parchment thong with C/3/10/2/4/2/18–27; 2 seals on tags

C/3/10/2/4/2/29   29 Nov. 1504
3 pieces of land (2a 16p) in Falkenham, copyhold of manor of Walton with Trimley

Copy of court roll for admission of John Cole and Margaret Laurence, widow, on surrender of
John Grenman, now deceased; premises to be sold for profit of Falkenham church in accor-
dance with Grenman's will
Latin

C/3/10/2/4/2/30   1551–1636
Messuage and lands late Thomas Randolfe's in Falkenham and Kirton
Evidences of title for purchase by Bailiffs, Portmen and burgesses of Ipswich from Roger Foxe
of Falkenham, husbandman and wife Mary, daughter and heir of Thomas Randolfe of Levington,
yeoman, deceased, for £160 and life annuity of £10, 26 Mar. 1625
Includes:
— will of John Randall of Falkenham, 1551
— will of Thomas Randell of Levington, husbandman, 1606
(7 docs)

C/3/10/2/4/3   Property in Falkenham, Kirton, Trimley, Walton and   1614–1681
Felixstowe

C/3/10/2/4/3/1   1614–1641
3 pieces of land and pasture in Walton, Trimley St Mary, Trimley St Martin, Felixstowe, Kirton
and Falkenham
Evidences of title for purchase by Simon Rosyer, tanner, from Samuel Wightman, clothier,
both of Needham Market, 28 Jun. 1641
(5 docs)

C/3/10/2/4/3/2   14 Mar. 1681
Marsh (25a) in Falkenham and Kirton, allegedly copyhold of manors of Walton cum Trimley
and Felixstowe
Deed of enfranchisement from Sir John Barker, bart, lord of the manors, to Bailiffs, burgesses
and commonalty of Ipswich, for determination of all disputes
Mutilated; part of text missing

C/3/10/2/4/4   Mollonds in Bramford   1633–1700

C/3/10/2/4/4/1   1633–1700
Close called Mollonds *alias* Mellands (8½a) copyhold of manor of Lovetofts in Bramford
Evidences of title for purchase by Bailiffs, burgesses and commonalty of Ipswich from Robert
Withe and wife Beatrice, for use of the poor, 23 Sep. 1646, and for admissions of successive
feoffees
(5 docs; bundle endorsed with memorandum of purchase with part of Mr Smart's money)

C/3/10/2/4/5   Property in Ipswich   1697–1764

C/3/10/2/4/5/1   19 Apr. 1697
Decayed messuage with yards and gardens in PE
Counterpart demise from Bailiffs, burgesses and commonalty to John Jolley of Ipswich, brick-
layer, for 900 years for £10 at peppercorn rental
Endorsed: '. . . the house in St Peter . . . called Wincall. N.B. this house is given to Charity and
ought not to have been sold. J.H.'

C/3/10/2/4/5/2   9, 10 Nov. 1764
'Ipswich Arms' public house in Foundation Street in MQ, part of property of Christ's Hospital
Conveyance by lease and release from Bailiffs, burgesses and commonalty to Samuel Pickering
of Ipswich, gent., to use of Smart's Charity, for £120 out of Smart's revenues
(2 docs)

C/3/10/2/5   CHRIST'S HOSPITAL   1390–1851

C/3/10/2/5/1   Hospital site   **1536–1575**

C/3/10/2/5/1/1   1536–1569
Site of dissolved house of Friars Preachers (Blackfriars) in MQ
Evidences of title for purchase by Bailiffs, burgesses and commonalty from John Southwell of
Barham, esq., for £126 13s 4d and £106 offset against a judgment against John Southwell his
late father, 6 Aug. 1569
Includes:
— Letters Patent of Henry VIII to Elizabeth Davers, widow, licensing alienation of premises,
2 Mar. 1545 (Great Seal fragmentary)
(6 docs)

C/3/10/2/5/1/2   1 Sep. 1575
Garden in MQ
Feoffment from William Whetcrofte of Ipswich, gent. and wife Alice to John Barker, merchant,
Richard Kinge, merchant and Christopher Crane, clothier, all of Ipswich, for £5 6s 8d, to use of
poor residing in Christ's Hospital

C/3/10/2/5/2   Snow's house in St Clement, Ipswich   **1631–1633**

George Snow's house was sold for £280, and the money put towards the purchase of part
of Gardner's Farm in Creeting from Joseph Crane in 1657 (*see* Canning 1747, 69, and
C/3/10/2/6/1/14 below).

C/3/10/2/5/2/1   11 Oct. 1631
Messuage called the Waggon in LW, abutting W. on messuage of Robert Sparrowe [the
Ancient House] , N. on Butter Market and S. on St Stephen's churchyard; messuage in CL,
abutting W. on St Clement's Street and E. on way from Cole Dunghill to St Clement's Church;
8 messuages lying together in MS; messuage in MT abutting N. on street leading from common
conduit towards Market Cross; and messuage called the Falcon in NI
Deed to lead the uses of a common recovery, Samuel Lane of Ipswich, yeoman to Richard
Nitingale and Robert Clarke, both of Ipswich, gents, Peter Fysher of Ipswich demandant ; to the
use of Samuel Lane

C/3/10/2/5/2/2   10 Apr. 1632
Messuage abutting W. on St Clement's Street and E. on way leading from the Cole Dunghills
towards St Clement's church in CL
Feoffment from Samuel Lane of Ipswich, yeoman to Peter Fysher of Ipswich, mercer, for
£280

C/3/10/2/5/2/3   10 Apr. 1633
Messuage in which John Benjamin dwelt, now in occupation of Thomas Nutman, with little
yard or garden belonging thereto, adjoining tenement in occupation of Bittrice Bacon, widow,
John Boyce and [*blank*] Gleede, widow, in CL
Feoffment from Peter Fisher of Ipswich, mercer, wife Elizabeth, and Samuel Lane of Ipswich,
yeoman, to Daniel Snow of Ipswich, saltfyner

C/3/10/2/5/3   Other Ipswich property   **1544–1841**

C/3/10/2/5/3/1   1544–1722
Messuage with adjoining close (10a) in PE and close (5a) in PE and MS
Evidences of title for purchase by Bailiffs and Portmen from Francis Colman and Henry Nash,
both of Ipswich, gents., executors of will of Richard Pupplett of Ipswich, esq., deceased, for
£340, 12 May 1722; in trust that part of revenues be used to keep 2 poor children of MW in
Christ's Hospital in accordance with will, 1698, of Thomas Bright of MW, gent., deceased, and

part for upkeep of Christ's Hospital in accordance with will, 1719, of Richard Philipps of Ipswich, esq., deceased
Includes:
— will of John Purpett of Ipswich, merchant, 1544 (apparently a stray item)
(28 docs; main purchase deed endorsed '. . . bought with money given by Mr Richard Philipps and Mr Thomas Bright . . .')

C/3/10/2/5/3/2   1819–1841
Piece of marshland (4a) in MS
Evidences of title for purchase by Bailiffs, burgesses and commonalty, by direction of Governors of Christ's Hospital School, from John Wood of Melton, gent. and Benjamin Colchester of Ipswich, gent., devisees in trust for sale under will of Robert Fulcher of Ipswich, timber merchant, deceased, for £250, 27 Sep. 1819; and for subsequent mortgage and assignments
(5 docs)

C/3/10/2/5/4   Kersey's Farm in Debenham   1390–1851

The bequest of this property by Nicholas Phillips, Portman of Ipswich, in 1670, may be considered as the foundation of the school in Christ's Hospital (see Canning 1747, 63–65).

C/3/10/2/5/4/1   20 Dec. 1390
Lands and tenements in Debenham
Feoffment from John Buk to John Gurdon, Robert Kenton and John Brun, all of Debenham
Names of 7 witnesses
Latin; seal on tag

C/3/10/2/5/4/2   29 Apr. 1413
Piece of land in Debenham
Feoffment from John Calston of 'Herlawe' [? Harlow (Essex)] to Richard Talmage, Thomas Deye of Mickfield, Richard Moyse of Winston and Thomas Talmage of Debenham
Premises lie between lands of John de Framlyngham on either side, abutting on tenement called Salmanis and land of Thomas Talmage; names of 5 witnesses
Latin; seal on tag

C/3/10/2/5/4/3   1558–1593
Meadow (2a) in Debenham, copyhold of manor of Debenham Butley
Copies of court roll for admission of George Phillips on surrender of Edward Shepparde, 3 May 1593
(3 docs)

C/3/10/2/5/4/4   1487–1619
2 pieces of meadow (3r) in Debenham, copyhold of manor of Debenham Butley
Copies of court roll for admission of James Phillips on surrender of William Styles, 20 Jan. 1619
(5 docs, stitched together)

C/3/10/2/5/4/5   1533–1625
Tenement and lands (10a) in Debenham, part freehold and part copyhold of manor of Crow's Hall with Woodwards
Evidences of title for purchase by George Phillips of Debenham, pewterer, from Robert Fryer of Kelsale, yeoman, 30 Oct. 1594, and subsequent conveyance to his son Nicholas Phillips of Ipswich, grocer, 20 Oct. 1625
(10 docs)

C/3/10/2/5/4/6   1558–1625
2 closes of pasture (9a) called Dawlinges and Cawstons in Debenham
Evidences of title for purchase by George Phillips of Debenham, yeoman, from Thomas

Sherman of Ipswich, gent., 16 Dec. 1608, and subsequent quitclaim to his son Nicholas Phillips
of Ipswich, grocer, 7 Oct. 1625
(8 docs)

C/3/10/2/5/4/7   1544–1649
Closes (24a) called le Hoopper *alias* Wheateclose and Pyescloses, and wasted cottage called
Calstons with adjoining pightle (2½a), in Debenham, copyhold of manor of Debenham Butley
Copies of court roll for admission of James Phillips of Debenham on surrender of Charles
Gibson and quitclaim of Barnaby Gibson, 31 Oct. 1633, and subsequent admission of James
Phillips sen. on surrender of his son James, 3 Jan. 1649
(14 docs)

C/3/10/2/5/4/8   1596–1651
Freehold portion of meadow (6a) called East Meadow in Debenham
Evidences of title for purchase by Nicholas Phillips of Ipswich, merchant, from his brother
James Phillips of Debenham, yeoman, for £300, 1 May 1651
(7 docs)

C/3/10/2/5/4/9   1526–1654
Tenement called Buckes and lands called Millfield and Scaldings in Debenham
Evidences of title for purchase by Nicholas Phillips of Ipswich, gent., from Barnaby Gibson of
Little Stonham, gent., for £540, 25 and 26 Aug. 1654
(53 docs)

C/3/10/2/5/4/10   1650, 1654
Lands and tenements [in Debenham], copyhold of manor of Debenham Butley
Copies of court roll for successive surrenders by Nicholas Phillips, gent., to the use of his last
will and testament, 15 Oct. 1650 and 27 Oct. 1654
(2 docs)

C/3/10/2/5/4/11   n.d. [1670]
Extract from will of [Nicholas Phillips of Ipswich, gent.]
Devising to his executors Richard Phillips jun. and Richard Phillips sen., all his freehold and
copyhold lands in Debenham, to be amortised and secured to the Bailiffs, burgesses and commonalty of Ipswich, the revenues to be employed towards the teaching of poor children of the
town, their maintenance, and 'for providing a convenient house for the said children to be
taught in'

C/3/10/2/5/4/12   31 May 1676
Freehold and copyhold lands and tenements in Debenham [Kersey's Farm]
Conveyance by bargain and sale from Richard Phillips sen. and Richard Phillips jun., both of
Ipswich, merchants, executors of Nicholas Phillips of Ipswich, merchant, deceased, to John
Wright, Luke Jours, Gilbert Lindfield, Miles Wallis, Henry Gosnold, William Cullum, Charles
Wright, John Pemberton, Lawrence Stistead, Edward Rennolds and John Burrough, all of
Ipswich, Portmen, in performance of Nicholas Phillips's will, in trust to employ annual profits
'towards the learninge and teachinge of poor children belonginge to the towne of Ipswich and
providinge bookes, inke, paper, convenient apparrell, bindinge of them out of apprentices, and
for the providinge of flax, hemp or woole or such other needfull thinges as well for the settinge
such children on worke as for the releife of them, and alsoe for the providinge . . . of beddinge
convenient and necessary for such children, and alsoe for the providinge [of a] convenient
house for the said children to bee educated and taught in . . .'

C/3/10/2/5/4/13   3 Apr. 1782
Lands called Salmons, copyhold of manor of Scotnetts with the Haugh in Debenham
Copy court roll for admission of Charles Cornwallis, jun., clerk, Thomas Hallum, clerk,
Thomas Foster Notcutt, gent. and William Barnard Clarke, gent., all of Ipswich, as trustees for
purposes declared by will of Nicholas Phillips, following death of last surviving trustee, Robert
Edgar, esq.

C/3/10/2/5/4/14   1720–1851
Lands and tenements in Debenham, copyhold of manors of Crow's Hall with Woodwards,
Debenham Butley, Kenton with Suddon Hall, and Scotnetts with the Haugh
Copies of court roll for admissions of successive trustees, to the purposes expressed in the will
of Nicholas Phillips
(7 docs)

C/3/10/2/6   JOINTLY OWNED ESTATES   later 13c.–1749

**C/3/10/2/6/1   Creeting and Earl Stonham estate (Smart's, Christ's   1316–1687
Hospital and Tyler's Charities)**

Though the income from this estate was applied in equal portions to Smart's and Tyler's
Charities and Christ's Hospital (see Trustees 1878, 12, 16, 30), the main purchase deed of
10 July 1649 makes clear that the estate was bought with money from the Smart and Tyler
funds only; Christ's Hospital benefited only because of irregularities in administration (see
Canning 1747, 69).

C/3/10/2/6/1/1   13 Jun. 1316
Curtilage surrounded by fences and ditches in Little Stonham, and piece of land in Stonham
Aspal, with right of chase
Feoffment from Alexander le Whyte of Earl Stonham to Walter le Whyte, his brother
Curtilage abuts W. on feoffee's land and E. on highway called le Rode; land lies between lands
of Ralph de Bakepol and Henry de Bakepol, abutting N. on pasture of John le Whyte and S. on
his land; names of 13 witnesses
Latin; seal missing from tag

C/3/10/2/6/1/2   8 Jul. 1335
Tenement in Steeple Creeting [? Creeting St Peter]
Feoffment from Ralph le Slaghtere of Creeting St Mary and Ralph le Schepherde of Steeple
Creeting, to Robert le Talyour of Steeple Creeting and wife Agnes for life, with remainder to
Ralph their son
Premises are those which feoffors had by feoffment of Robert, and comprise: messuage lying
between common way called Holbakwaye on one side and land called Sponereslond and close
formerly Sponere's on the other, upper head abutting on high street called le Rodeweye; and 2
pieces of arable land and piece of meadow, first piece of land called le Dounelond lying
between lands formerly of Felicia le Cyrsy on both sides, lower head abutting on said meadow,
which lies next to meadow formerly of John de Cretyng, kt; and second piece of land lying
between lands of Ralph le Slaghtere on both sides, abutting on pasture formerly of Felicia le
Cyrsy and on Holbakstrete; names of 8 witnesses
Latin; seal on tag, second seal missing

C/3/10/2/6/1/3   25 May 1348
Piece of land in Earl Stonham
Feoffment from Walter le Whyte of Stonham Aspal to Hugh the Chaplain, his son
Premises lie between lands of William de Hendley and Robert Morwyle, abutting N. on land of
parson of Little Stonham and S. on meadow of Robert le Pynkeney; names of 5 witnesses
Latin; seal missing from tag

C/3/10/2/6/1/4   22 Sep. 1355
Garden with adjoining piece of land called Sponeris in Earl Stonham
Feoffment from William de Seynt Clou to Thomas le White, for 2d annually; proviso for
distraint in case of default in payment
Premises lie between messuage and land of feoffee and garden and croft of Ralph Dounyng;
names of 5 witnesses
Chirograph; Latin; seal on tag

C/3/10/2/6/1/5   12 Jun. 1371
Lands and tenements in Creeting All Saints and Creeting St Olave
Feoffment from Ralph le Cook to Hugh Bugg, Thomas le Whyte and William Crispyn, all of
Creeting All Saints
Names of 5 witnesses
Latin; seal, incomplete, on tag

C/3/10/2/6/1/6   28 Apr. 1417
Lands and tenements in Creeting All Saints, Creeting St Mary, Creeting St Olave and Earl
Stonham
Feoffment from Nicholas Hwyte of Creeting All Saints to Thomas Baude of Creeting, John ate
Thorn of Earl Stonham and John Schytte of Creeting All Saints
Names of 5 witnesses
Latin; seal on tag

C/3/10/2/6/1/7   16 Aug. 1417
Cottage abutting on Peekhamstrete in Creeting St Mary
Feoffment from Matilda, widow of Walter Bachham, to Bartholomew Leton of Creeting All
Saints and Thomas Bawde of Creeting St Peter
Names of 5 witnesses
Latin; seal, incomplete

C/3/10/2/6/1/8   23 Dec. 1465
Lands and tenements in Creeting All Saints
Release from William Leton of Creeting St Mary and John Smyth, son of late John Smyth of
Creeting All Saints, to Thomas Cook of Creeting All Saints, son of William Cook, Robert
Thorn of 'Bakpool' and John Skot of 'Holbak'
Premises are those which Leton and Smyth lately had jointly with Robert Turnor of Creeting,
now deceased, by feoffment of William Strotyl of Creeting; names of 7 witnesses
Latin; 2 seals on tags

C/3/10/2/6/1/9   30 Sep. 1467
Lands and tenements in Creeting All Saints, Creeting St Mary, Creeting St Olave and Earl
Stonham
Feoffment from William Cook of Creeting St Peter, wife Joan, and John Baldre of Creeting All
Saints, to Thomas Hunne and William Baldewyn, both of Coddenham, and Thomas Cook of
Creeting
Premises are those which feoffors lately had jointly by gift of John Cook of Creeting All Saints;
names of 3 witnesses
Latin; 2 seals on tags

C/3/10/2/6/1/10   20 Dec. 1477
Tenement called Slowgh in Creeting All Saints and Creeting St Mary
Feoffment from John Coke of Coddenham, son of late John Coke sen. of Creeting All Saints,
and wife Agnes, to Thomas Coke, wife Margaret and John Baldrye, all of Creeting All Saints,
and John Scott of Creeting St Olave
Premises are those which feoffors lately had by feoffment of late John Coke sen., and lie next to
land formerly of Robert Merssh, now of John Crane on S. and land of Thomas Bugg on N.,
abutting E. on land of Gilbert Debenham and W. on highway called le Rode; names of
5 witnesses
Latin; 2 seals on tags

C/3/10/2/6/1/11   17 Jan. 1480
Messuages, lands, tenements and cottages in Creeting All Saints and Creeting St Mary, and 3
pieces of land in Creeting All Saints and Creeting St Olave
Feoffment from William Havell of Needham Market and Hugh Crispyn of Creeting All Saints
to Thomas Cook, Thomas Hunne, Robert Cook, John Scott and John Baldrye
Premises in Creeting All Saints and Creeting St Mary are those which feoffors lately had jointly

with Bartholomew Leton, now deceased, by grant of Robert Wynde, clerk, dated 1 Jul. 1472; premises in Creeting All Saints and Creeting St Olave are those which they lately had jointly with Bartholomew Leton and John Leton his son, now deceased, by feoffment of William Leton of Creeting St Mary, dated 11 Aug. 1468; first piece of land lying between land formerly of Thomas Dunche and land of rectory of Creeting All Saints, abutting on land of manor of Creeting St Mary and pasture or land of Wonhalle; second piece at Wolronnesmere, between land formerly of Thomas Dunche and third piece, abutting on lands of manor of Creeting St Mary and on land of John Baldrye; third piece between second piece and land of Wonhalle; names of 5 witnesses
Latin; 2 seals, 1 fragmentary, on tags

C/3/10/2/6/1/12   20 Oct. 1564
Lands, meadows, marshes and woods in Creeting All Saints, West Creeting [Creeting St Peter] and Earl Stonham
Quitclaim by John Clenche of Creeting All Saints, gent., executor of will of Thomas Almot, gent., deceased, to James Ryvett of West Creeting, gent.

C/3/10/2/6/1/13   1564–1652
Closes called Watts, Warrens and Longland (62a) in Creeting St Peter, Stowmarket, Creeting All Saints and Earl Stonham
Evidences of title for gift from Anne Sothebie of Earl Stonham, widow, to Joseph Crane of Earl Stonham, gent., her son and heir, 8 Dec. 1652
(12 docs, in near-contemporary leather box lined with pages from a printed psalter with musical notation)

C/3/10/2/6/1/14   30 Oct. 1657
Closes called Watts, Warrandes and Longland with adjoining grove (62a) in Creeting St Peter, Stowmarket, Creeting All Saints and Earl Stonham
Conveyance by bargain and sale from Joseph Crane of Earl Stonham, gent. and wife Martha, to Bailiffs, burgesses and commonalty of Ipswich, for £440

C/3/10/2/6/1/15   1480–1687
Capital messuage called Stedds in Creeting St Peter, with land (75½a) in Creeting St Peter and Earl Stonham; and messuage called Stedds Hill with lands in Creeting St Peter
Evidences of title for purchase by Bailiffs, burgesses and commonalty of Ipswich from Miles Fernelie of Sutton, esq., Edmund Fernelie of Creeting St Peter, esq. and Elinor Tyers of Shottisham, widow, 10 Jul. 1649, for £585 (£300 from William Tyler's bequest, residue from William Smart's bequest); property to be held by Peter Fysher, Robert Donckon, Richard Harle, Jacob Caley, Henry Whitinge, George Boldero, Robert Turnor and Richard Sheppard, all of Ipswich, gents, in trust to pay annually out of revenues, £18 for purposes appointed in Tyler's will, and residue for purposes appointed in Smart's will
Includes:
— will of Edmund Rozer of Needham Market, tanner, 1601
— account of admission fees and arrears of rent for copyholds, 1687
(35 docs; wrapper labelled 'Deeds relating to the Creeting estate late Crane's')

C/3/10/2/6/2 The Street Farm in Whitton and Bramford (Tooley's, 1378–1626
Smart's and Christ's Hospital Charities)

C/3/10/2/6/2/1   10 Jul. 1378
Lands, tenements and buildings in Bramford
Quitclaim from Everard de Flete, chaplain in Ipswich, to Alice, widow of William Watton of Ipswich
Premises are those which Everard had by feoffment of John Brugge of Ipswich
Latin; seal on tongue

C/3/10/2/6/2/2   12 Jun. 1380
Lands and tenements in Bramford
Quitclaim from John Brugges, son of late Adam Brugges of Bramford, to Alice, widow of
William de Watton
Premises were formerly of Thomas Brugges, and descended to John his son, and are those
which Thomas Maistre of Ipswich had by feoffment of John, son of Thomas Brugges which
John son of Adam purchased from Thomas Maistre; names of 5 witnesses
Latin; seal on tag

C/3/10/2/6/2/3   21 Mar. 1381
Lands and tenements in Bramford
Feoffment from John Brugges, son and heir of Thomas Brugges of Ipswich, to Bartholomew
Andrew, John Bakoun and Thomas Bardy, all of Bramford
Premises are those which accrued to feoffor by inheritance on death of father and uncle Robert
Brugges; names of 5 witnesses
Latin; seal, incomplete, on tag

C/3/10/2/6/2/4   15 Jul. 1381
Lands and tenements in Bramford, except messuage with garden, 2 crofts lying together and
meadow and pasture in Alnesmersch
Feoffment from Bartholomew Andrew, Thomas Bardy and John Bakoun, all of Bramford, to
Thomas le Hert of London, mercer and wife Alice for life, with remainder to Margaret,
daughter of William Watton and said Alice, and heirs of her body, or in default of issue, to
Thomas, son of Roger le Hert, and wife Alice, daughter of Thomas le Maystyr of Ipswich, and
heirs of their bodies, or in default of issue, to right heirs of Thomas le Maystyr
Premises are those which feoffors formerly purchased from John Bruges, son and heir of
Thomas le Bruges of Ipswich; names of 7 witnesses
Latin; 3 seals on tags

C/3/10/2/6/2/5   16 Jul. 1381
Lands and tenements in Bramford
Quitclaim from John, son of Adam le Bruges of Bramford, to Thomas Hert of London, mercer
and wife Alice for life, Margaret, daughter of William Watton, and heirs of her body, Thomas,
son of Roger le Hert, wife Alice and heirs of their bodies, and right heirs of Thomas le Maystyr
of Ipswich
Premises are those which Thomas Hert and wife lately purchased from Bartholomew Andrew,
Thomas Bardy and John Bakoun, all of Bramford
Latin; seal on tag

C/3/10/2/6/2/6   24 Jun. 1387
Piece of land in Bramford
Feoffment from John de Westone to Simon dil Brook, both of Ipswich
Premises lie between highway from Sproughton to Ipswich on S. and land called le Belleroplond
on N., abutting E. on feoffee's messuage and W. on land called Gardenerescroft; names of
5 witnesses
Latin; endorsed 'Pese lond'; seal on tag

C/3/10/2/6/2/7   15 May 1391
2 pieces of land in Bramford
Feoffment from John Doget and Matthew Bernard to John Kene of Akenham
Premises are those which feoffors lately purchased from William Ryngedale of Whitton and
were formerly of Thomas de Wynbooysham, and lie between lands of Sir Robert Lumbekyn,
formerly parson of Horham church, and land formerly of Richard de Leyham; names of 5
witnesses
Latin; both seals missing from tags

C/3/10/2/6/2/8   27 Dec. 1391
Lands and tenements in Bramford

Feoffment from John Parmeteer of Bramford and wife Beatrix to John Kyng of Bramford, chaplain and Robert de Neketone of Higham
Names of 5 witnesses
Latin; one seal, incomplete, on tag, second seal missing

C/3/10/2/6/2/9   10 Jun. 1395
2 pieces of meadow in Bramford and Claydon
Lease from Alice, widow of William Watton of Ipswich, to William Mayster of Ipswich, until next feast of St Mary Magdalene (22 Jul.) and then for 10 years at 3s 4d p.a.
One piece was formerly of Sir Alexander Baroun, the other formerly of Sir Godfrey Lumkyn
Latin; seal missing from tag

C/3/10/2/6/2/10   (12 Mar. 1400), n.d. [15c.]
Lands, tenements, rents and services in Stoke by Ipswich, 2 messuages called Baldries in CL and MT, toft in MG, and lands, tenements, rents and services in Whitton
Copy grant of reversion by Alice, widow of Simon de Wynchecombe, citizen and armourer of London, and daughter and heir of Thomas le Mayster of Ipswich, to William Enotte, citizen and weaver of London and wife Margaret, daughter of Alice de Wynchecombe; with memorandum of recognizance in Chancery, 15 Apr. 1400
Names of 7 witnesses
Latin; unsealed

C/3/10/2/6/2/11   4 Jul. 1412
Tenement called le Wattonslond in Bramford
Lease from Alice Wynchecombe, widow to Roger Sukley of Bramford, for 10 years from previous Michaelmas, at 30s p.a.
Latin; fragment of seal on tag

C/3/10/2/6/2/12   15 May 1451
Tenement in Bramford
Lease from Richard Montgomery to John Cook of Bramford, for 7 years at 13s 4d p.a.
Premises are those which Robert Cook, John's father, leased from Richard Montgomery
Latin; seal missing from tongue

C/3/10/2/6/2/13   8 Sep. 1467
Lands and tenements called Wattones in Bramford, except piece of meadow and pasture (1a) lately leased to John Cook of Bramford
Lease from Roger Tymperley and wife Katherine to William Sorell and John Gardenere, both of Bramford, for 7 years at 29s, 1 bushel of barley and 1 bushel of corn p.a.
Latin; 2 seals, both incomplete, on tongue

C/3/10/2/6/2/14   9 Oct. 1475
Tenement called Dogetts in Bramford
Feoffment from William Bernard, cousin and heir of John Bernard sen., late of Akenham, to Margaret Webbe, wife of William Webbe and daughter of late Margaret More of Tattingstone
Names of 5 witnesses
Latin; seal, incomplete, on tag

C/3/10/2/6/2/15   2 Jul. 1485
3 pieces of land in Bramford and Whitton
Feoffment from John Lee of Ipswich and John Brook late of Debenham to Henry Wentworth, kt, John Barnaby, gent., Roger Tymperley, gent., John Balhed and John Bernard
First piece lies in Whitton between land late of John Hyll on E. and land of Alan Cowpere on W., abutting N. on land of Alan Cowpere and S. on land late of John Hyll; second piece in Whitton between land of John Hyll on S. and land late of Robert Halle on N., abutting E. and W. on land late of John Hyll; third piece in Bramford between land of Roger Tymperley on E. and land of John Hyll on W., abutting N. on land of William Webbe and S. on land of Roger Tymperley; names of 5 witnesses
Latin; one seal on tag, second seal missing

C/3/10/2/6/2/16   20 May 1524
Lands (36a) held of manor of Kentons in Bramford
Mortgage from Thomas Russhe, esq. to Thomas Baldry, merchant, both of Ipswich, for £50

C/3/10/2/6/2/17   22 Jan. 1573
Lands and tenements in Bramford, Whitton, Holbrook and Harkstead
Quitclaim from William Bloyse of Ipswich, mercer, John Hawys of Ipswich, gent., William
Dawndy of Ipswich, merchant, Bartholomew Hall of Wherstead, gent., William Reynbald of
Ipswich, merchant, Christopher Goodwyn of Ipswich, draper, William Stysted of Ipswich,
gent., Augustine Burde, gent., William Sebyn *alias* West, Thomas Barber, Richard Heyward
and Robert Pypho to William Smarte of Ipswich, draper and Christopher Crane of Ipswich,
clothier
Latin

C/3/10/2/6/2/18   17 Sep. 1604
Piece of pasture (3a) in Bramford
Counterpart grant in perpetuity from Bailiffs, burgesses and commonalty of Ipswich to John
Carter of Bramford, clerk, for 15s p.a.

C/3/10/2/6/2/19   8 Dec. 1626
Piece of ground called Mullings in Bramford
Bond of Richard Bateman of Ipswich, draper, in £20 for surrender of premises to Robert Steffe
of Tuddenham, clerk

**C/3/10/2/6/3   Kersey's Farm in Otley (Tooley's, Smart's and Christ's   later 13c.–1749
Hospital Charities)**

C/3/10/2/6/3/1   n.d. [? later 13c.]
Piece of land [in Otley]
Feoffment from Seman Weston to Henry the smith, for 10s fine and 3d annually
Premises lie between lands of feoffor and of Gunnora Curde, abutting on land of Sir John the
chaplain and land which was Walter de Brademedue's; names of 12 witnesses
Latin; seal missing from tag

C/3/10/2/6/3/2   n.d. [? later 13c.]
Piece of land in Otley
Feoffment from John Wyn of Otley to Richard the carpenter and wife Ida, for 18s fine and 1½d
annually
Premises lie between feoffee's messuage and land of Robert Wym, abutting on messuages of
Thomas son of Walter and Robert Wym; names of 9 witnesses
Latin; seal missing from tag

C/3/10/2/6/3/3   n.d. [? later 13c.]
Piece of meadow in Otley
Feoffment from Nicholas de Vinscole to Peter, son of Sir Arnold de Otheleya, for 3s fine and 1d
annually
Premises lie lengthwise between land of Luke de Otheleya and feoffee's land; names of
10 witnesses
Latin; seal missing from tag

C/3/10/2/6/3/4   n.d. [? later 13c.]
Piece of land with pasture pertaining to it in Otley
Feoffment from Andrew del Wyndscole to Sir William Faukes of Otley, chaplain, and daughter
Alice, for 8s fine and 1d annually
Premises lie between lands of Alice and of Ward dille Wyndschele, abutting N. on highway and
S. on messuage formerly of Nicholas dil Wyndscole; names of 9 witnesses
Latin; seal on tag

C/3/10/2/6/3/5   n.d. [? later 13c.]
Piece of land in Otley
Feoffment from William Faukes of Otley, chaplain, to Robert Ynggold of Helmingham, in free marriage with William's daughter Alice
Premises lie lengthwise between land of John le Gardiner on E. and land of Robert Page on W., abutting S. on messuage of John le Gardiner and N. on land of Walter the miller; names of 6 witnesses
Latin; seal missing from tag

C/3/10/2/6/3/6   n.d. [? later 13c.]
Piece of land in Otley
Feoffment from John, son of Luke de Otteleya, to Alan Lewekin, for 10s fine and 2d annually
Premises lie between lands of Hervey le Waleys and Gerard Medus, abutting on lands of Alexander Cocston and Thomas, son of Walter de Brademeduwe; names of 9 witnesses
Latin; seal, incomplete, on tag

C/3/10/2/6/3/7   n.d. [? later 13c.]
Piece of land called Tortebrege in Alduluestun [? in Otley]
Feoffment from Ralph, son of Gerard Meduz of Grundisburgh, to William le Gardener of Otley, for 10s fine, 8d annually to Sir Richard de Breeus, 1 ginger root annually to feoffor, ½d towards castleguard of Lancaster, and ½d in £1 scutage when levied
Premises lie between lands of Alan Leuekin and of Sir Robert the chaplain, abutting N. on land of Thomas son of Walter and S. on land of Ralph Thurde; names of 10 witnesses
Latin; seal missing from tag

C/3/10/2/6/3/8   22 Jun. 1293
Enclosed pightle in Otley
Feoffment from John Cunpost, son of Julian Cunpost of Clopton, and wife Catherine, to Alice, daughter of Geoffrey de Bukessale of Otley
Premises lie between messuage of Robert Ingold on either side, abutting N. on messuage of feoffee and sister Joan; names of 6 witnesses
Latin; both seals missing from tags

C/3/10/2/6/3/9   25 Jul. 1305
Piece of land in Otley
Feoffment from John Lucas of Otley to Gilbert le Erl and wife Amicia
Premises are those which feoffor's father Robert acquired from Robert Thwyn jun. of Otley, and lie between feoffor's land and land which he holds at fee farm from Sir John Faynel, abutting S. on common way and N. on feoffor's meadow; names of 7 witnesses
Latin; seal missing from tag

C/3/10/2/6/3/10   19 May 1309
13d annual rent, 1d annual wardship, and lands and tenements [in Otley]
Quitclaim from Joan de le Wynchole to Robert Yngold and wife Alice, all of Otley
Payments are those which Robert used to pay for his tenement held of Joan, and premises those which Robert and Alice acquired by Joan's gift; names of 7 witnesses
Latin; seal missing from tag

C/3/10/2/6/3/11   8 Jul. 1317
Piece of land in Otley
Feoffment from Richard Puston to Richard le Porter, both of Otley
Premises lie between land of Thomas le Herl on E. and boundary called Swynlonderowe on S., abutting on land of Prioress of Wix [Essex] and on way leading to grange formerly of Simon Ayston; names of 7 witnesses
Latin; seal missing from tag

C/3/10/2/6/3/12   7 Jan. 1318
Piece of land in Otley

Feoffment from Robert Ingold of Otley to John Burrich of Clopton
Premises are divided by boundaries made between feoffor and feoffee, and abut N. on common
way called le Stanstrete and S. on land of Richard le Smeth, lying between feoffee's messuage
on E. and feoffor's land on W.; names of 7 witnesses
Latin; seal and tag missing

C/3/10/2/6/3/13   8 May 1321
Piece of land called ? Cattebreche in Otley
Feoffment from Robert Ingold of Otley to John Archer of Grundisburgh and Matilda, Robert's
daughter
Premises lie between land of Thomas Gardeyn on one side and lands of Jurdan le Chaumberlayn
and Robert the smith on the other, abutting on lands of William Archer and Thomas Gardeyn;
names of 7 witnesses
Latin; discoloured by damp; seal on tag

C/3/10/2/6/3/14   1 Oct. 1330
Tenement in Otley
Feoffment from Alice, widow of Jordan le Chaumberlayn of Grundisburgh, and John her son,
to Sir Robert Ingold of Otley, chaplain
Names of 7 witnesses
Latin; both seals missing from tags

C/3/10/2/6/3/15   25 Jun. 1284
Close with house built thereon in Otley
Quitclaim from William son of Thomas son of Walter of Otley to John his younger brother
Premises are those which William, John and Edmund their brother acquired from Thomas their
father; names of 9 witnesses
Latin; seal missing from tag by which tied to C/3/10/2/6/3/16–18

C/3/10/2/6/3/16   27 Feb. 1329
Tenements in Otley
Feoffment from John le Fyz Water of Otley to John de Ardeleye of Swilland
Names of 8 witnesses
Latin; seal on tag by which tied to C/3/10/2/6/3/15, 17 and 18

C/3/10/2/6/3/17   5 Jan. 1333
Lands and tenements in Otley
Feoffment by way of exchange, from John Herdeleye of Swilland to John Archer sen. and wife
Mabel
Premises are those which feoffor formerly purchased from John fitz Water; premises received
in exchange are not described; names of 7 witnesses
Latin; seal missing from tag by which tied to C/3/10/2/6/3/15, 16 and 18

C/3/10/2/6/3/18   5 Jan. 1333
Duplicate of C/3/10/2/6/3/17
In a different hand; Latin; seal missing from tag by which tied to C/3/10/2/6/3/15–17

C/3/10/2/6/3/19   14 May 1360
2 marks rent with wardships, reliefs and escheats out of piece of land called Olmerislond in
Otley
Quitclaim from William le Wodeward of Helmingham and John le Reve of Otley to Edmund
Ingold of Otley
Names of 6 witnesses
Latin; 2 seals on tags

C/3/10/2/6/3/20   28 Oct. 1360
2 pieces of land in Otley
Feoffment from Alice le Chapman of Swilland to John de Ordeleye of Swilland and Edmund
Ingold of Otley

One piece lies in rood called Mollerislond, the other between land of Edmund Ingold and way called le Melleweye, one head abutting on said way; names of 5 witnesses
Latin; seal missing from tag

C/3/10/2/6/3/21   22 Mar. 1366
3 pieces of land in Otley
Feoffment from Robert Page of Otley to Edmund Ingold of Otley and son Robert
First piece lies between lands of Edmund Archer and of Edmund Ingold, abutting on way to Ipswich and land of Edmund Ingold; second piece next to land of Edmund Ingold, abutting on his land and on land of Walter Cressener; third piece between lands of Edmund Ingold on both sides, one head abutting on his land; names of 5 witnesses
Latin; seal and tag missing

C/3/10/2/6/3/22   9 Sep. 1369
Messuages in Otley and Grundisburgh
Feoffment from Edmund Ingold of Otley to Walter de Wytnisham, John Pers of Otley, Robert Wryte, Robert Fich, John Holm and John Burgeys
Names of 5 witnesses
Latin; seal, incomplete, on tag

C/3/10/2/6/3/23   1 Dec. 1407
Piece of land [in Otley]
Feoffment from John Gardener to Robert Ingold, both of Otley
Premises are those which feoffor lately had by feoffment of Edmund Archer, deceased, and lie between feoffee's lands on both sides, abutting E. on land formerly of Edmund Archer and W. on feoffee's garden; names of 5 witnesses
Latin; seal on tag

C/3/10/2/6/3/24   3 Nov. 1409
Lands and tenements in Otley
Feoffment from John Skynnere of Marlesford and wife Joan to Robert Ingold of Otley and son Edmund
Premises are those which were Edmund Archer's by inheritance from John Archer his father, and descended to Joan on death of Edmund, her father; names of 5 witnesses
Latin; both seals missing from tags by which tied to C/3/10/2/6/3/25–27

C/3/10/2/6/3/25   16 Nov. 1409
Lands and tenements in Otley
Quitclaim from John Gardener sen. to Robert Ingold and son Edmund, all of Otley
Premises descended as stated in C/3/10/2/6/3/24
Latin; seal on tag by which tied to C/3/10/2/6/3/24, 26 and 27

C/3/10/2/6/3/26   26 Jun. 1410
Lands and tenements in Marlesford, Hacheston and Campsea Ashe
Release from William Alred, rector of Huntingfield church, Nicholas Blounvill and Robert Wode, to Robert Ingold of Otley and son Edmund; to be void provided that Robert and Edmund are not disseised of property in Otley which they had by feoffment of John Skynnere of Marlesford and wife Joan, through any claim, whether of dower or otherwise
Chirograph; Latin; 4 seals, 1 armorial, almost complete, on tags by which tied to C/3/10/2/6/3/24, 25 and 27

C/3/10/2/6/3/27   4 Jul. 1426
Lands and tenements in Otley
Quitclaim from Joan, daughter of Edmund Archer and widow of John Skynnere of Marlesford, to Robert Ingold and John Gardener, both of Otley, Robert Smyth of Saxmundham and Thomas Smyth his brother
Premises descended as stated in C/3/10/2/6/3/24
Latin; fragment of seal on tag by which tied to C/3/10/2/6/3/24–26

C/3/10/2/6/3/28   1 May 1431
Piece of land in field called le Berugh in Otley
Letter of attorney from Robert Ingold of Otley to Nicholas Peyntour, perpetual vicar of
Ashbocking, to deliver seisin to his son Edmund Ingold, William Gardener, William Walle and
Richard Armeiard, all of Otley
Premises are those which Robert lately had jointly with John Gardener of Otley by feoffment of
John Cautel and John Glaunvyle of Clopton
Latin; seal, incomplete, on tongue

C/3/10/2/6/3/29   2 Oct. 1456
Chamber with solar built over it, at back of hall of grantor's tenement in Otley, and 40s annual
pension out of all grantor's lands and tenements in Otley, Grundisburgh, Clopton and Swilland
Grant for life, from Robert Ingold, son and heir of Edmund Ingold late of Otley, to Joan Ingold
his mother
Chirograph; Latin; seal on tag by which tied to C/3/10/2/6/3/30

C/3/10/2/6/3/30   2 Oct. 1456
Counterpart of C/3/10/2/6/3/29
Seal on tag

C/3/10/2/6/3/31   8 Nov. 1423
Lands and tenements in Otley, Grundisburgh, Clopton and Swilland
Feoffment from Robert Ingold of Otley to Edmund Ingold his son and wife Joan
Names of 3 witnesses
Latin; seal on tag by which tied to C/3/10/2/6/3/32 and 33

C/3/10/2/6/3/32   19 Jun. 1456
Lands and tenements in Otley, Grundisburgh, Clopton and Swilland
Feoffment from Joan, widow of Edmund Ingold, to Robert Ingold her son
Names of 5 witnesses
Latin; seal on tag by which tied to C/3/10/2/6/3/31 and 33

C/3/10/2/6/3/33   4 Oct. 1456
Lands and tenements in Otley, Grundisburgh, Clopton and Swilland
Feoffment from Robert Ingold, son of Edmund Ingold, to Robert Wysdam and Edmund Ingold
Names of 5 witnesses
Latin; seal on tag by which tied to C/3/10/2/6/3/31 and 32

C/3/10/2/6/3/34   1532–1587
Messuage and land in Otley
Evidences of title for purchase by Edward Gooddinge of Ipswich, gent., from Thomas Baxter
of Rainthorpe Hall (Norfolk), gent., 23 Jan. 1585
(11 docs)

C/3/10/2/6/3/35   1575–1599
Capital messuage and land in Otley
Evidences of title for purchase by Robert Cutler sen., William Smarte, Ralph Scrivener, John
Knappe, Robert Lymmer, William Bloyse, William Midnall, Robert Barker, Robert Snellinge,
Robert Cutler jun. and Edward Cage, Portmen of Ipswich, from Edward Goodinge of Ipswich,
gent., 20 Dec. 1593, and release to Bailiffs, burgesses and commonalty, 30 Aug. 1599
(3 docs)

C/3/10/2/6/3/36   (1631, 1632), 1674
Extract from will and codicil of Jeffrey Pleasance of Hitcham, gent.
Charging orchard and adjoining piece of ground in Otley with annuity for use of poor of Otley

C/3/10/2/6/3/37   21 Sep. 1660
Messuage and land (38a) in Otley and Swilland

Mortgage from Thomas Pleasance of Stanton, gent., to Edmund Frost of Langham, gent., for
£300
Seal missing from tag

C/3/10/2/6/3/38   20 Jun. 1664
Tenement and land (12a) called Collyns Atfeild in Otley, copyhold of manor of Otley
Copy court roll recording regrant to Robert Sparrowe, John Wright, Gilbert Linefeild, Robert
Clarke and Edward Keene, following seizure for failure to claim property on death of last sur-
viving trustee

C/3/10/2/6/3/39   1502–1674
Capital messuage and land (40a) in Otley
Evidences of title for purchase by William Drane of Otley, yeoman, from Jeffery Wincoll,
7 Oct. 1661, and for subsequent mortgages (N.B. the main purchase deed is not present)
Includes:
— will of Thomas Smyth of Otley, 1552
— schedule of deeds, c.1670, listing deeds 1491–1661
(41 docs)

C/3/10/2/6/3/40   1661–1749
Messuage and 4 closes (40a) in Otley
Evidences of title for purchase by Richard Philips jun., Lawrence Stisted jun., Edward
Renoldes, John Wright jun., William Neave, Samuel Colman, William Vesey, Robert Clarke
jun., Gilbert Lindfild jun. and Anthony Gosnold, all of Ipswich, gents., from William Drane
sen., yeoman and wife Joyce and William Drane jun. and wife Anne, all of Otley, in trust for
Bailiffs, burgesses and commonalty of Ipswich, 9 Nov. 1674; and for admission of subsequent
borough officers as tenants to copyhold portion of premises
(13 docs)

C/3/10/2/7   OSMOND'S CHARITY   1558–1628

C/3/10/2/7/1   10 Dec. 1558
Piece of common soil, partly built upon, in MW
Feoffment from William Pytman of Woodbridge, son of Geoffrey Pytman late of Ipswich, hus-
bandman, to John Pytman his brother
Premises lie between town ditches on E. and common way on W., abutting S. on common soil
garden lately in tenure of Calixtus Clarke and N. on common soil curtilage which Agnes Gosse
lately held
Latin

C/3/10/2/7/2   12 Dec. 1558
Piece of land of common soil (119ft x 32ft), in MW
Feoffment from John Pytman of Ipswich, singleman to William Pytman of Woodbridge, his
brother
Premises lie between town ditch on E. and common way on W., abutting S. on garden late in
tenure of Calixtus Clarke and N. on garden late in tenure of Agnes Gosse
Latin

C/3/10/2/7/3   1581–1628
Newly-built tenements in MW
Evidences of title for purchase by William Cage, Robert Sparrowe, John Sicklemore and
William Moysey, all of Ipswich, gents [as trustees], from Abraham Commyn, yeoman, wife
Margaret, and Frances Lord, widow, all of Woolverstone, 1 Nov. 1628
[Premises lay in St Matthew's Street, next to 'Fleece' inn]
(rolled file of 22 docs, attached by parchment thong and labelled 'Osmonds Writings . . .')

C/3/10/2/8   CRANE'S CHARITY   1617–1726

C/3/10/2/8/1   (10 Nov. 1658), n.d. [17c.]
Copy letter from Thomas Rant of Thorpe Market (Norfolk) [executor of will of John Crane of
Cambridge] to Nathaniel Bacon, Master of Requests, Guybon Goddard, Thomas Buck and
Henry Ferrour [Trustees of Crane's Charity]
Re conveyance of charity estates in Lincolnshire to trustees in pursuance of decree in Chancery
[dated 28 Jun. 1658]

C/3/10/2/8/2   (1617–1726), n.d. [18c.]
Land (97a) in Fleet (Lincolnshire)
Office copies of evidences of title for purchase by Thomas Rant of Gray's Inn (Middlesex),
gent. [executor of will of John Crane of Cambridge] from Reuben Parke of Lutton (Lincolnshire), gent. and Richard Parke his son, 17 Oct. 1656, and for subsequent leases to tenants
(11 docs)

C/3/10/2/9   MARTIN'S AND BURROUGHS'S GIFTS   1508–1764

C/3/10/2/9/1   1508–1622
Messuages and lands purchased from John Man of MS, 1 Jun. 1615; lands called Church Croft
and Swan's Nest purchased from George Wynnyffe and others, 23 Mar. 1619; and close called
Great Maungers purchased from Anthony Brooke and wife Dorothie, 15 Feb. 1620; all in
Westerfield, Rushmere and Tuddenham
Evidences of title for purchase of parts of property by the Bailiffs, burgesses and commonalty
from Richard Martin, gent., Portman of Ipswich, 29 Nov. 1621, with £100 bequeathed by John
Burroughs of London, gent., deceased, the income to be distributed annually on Good Friday to
the poor of LW; and for gift of parts of property by Martin to the Bailiffs, burgesses and commonalty, 18 Feb. 1622, in trust to pay, out of profits: in first year after deaths of feoffor and wife
Anne, £20 apiece to Nathaniel and Deborah, children of Samuel Ward, public preacher of
Ipswich, and residue equally to Robert Snelling and Edward Lany, son of John Lany, Recorder
of Ipswich; annually after first year, £10 for life to Thomas Martin and Sarah Fluellyn, £20 to 2
students at Cambridge University, former scholars of Ipswich Free School, to be nominated by
the Bailiffs and majority of Portmen (one to be B.A. and to receive £14, the other to receive £6),
and £10 to be distributed in clothing to the town's poor (those of MG to receive 40s worth);
after cessation of life annuities, surplus profits to be lent on good security to poor clothiers and
shearmen for terms not exceeding 7 years, preference being given to kinsmen of feoffor and wife.
(37 docs)

C/3/10/2/9/2   20 Dec. 1621
Close called Great Maungers (24a) and piece of meadow (2a) parcel of meadow called
Swannes Neast, in Westerfield, Rushmere and Tuddenham, lately sold by Richard Martin,
gent., Portman of Ipswich, to the Bailiffs, burgesses and commonalty
Counterpart lease from the Bailiffs, burgesses and commonalty to Richard Martin and wife
Anne, for 100 years at £5 p.a.

C/3/10/2/9/3   1 Aug. 1632
Messuages, lands and tenements in Westerfield and Ipswich granted by Richard Martin, gent.,
Portman of Ipswich, deceased, to the Bailiffs and Portmen, 18 Feb. 1622
Conveyance to new feoffees: Matthew Brownerigge, William Cage and George Acton, Portmen
of Ipswich, to John Sicklemore and Richard Pupplett, Bailiffs, and Robert Sparrowe, William
Moysey, Edmond Kene, James Tyllott, John Barbor, Roger Cutler and John Aldus, Portmen of
Ipswich

C/3/10/2/9/4   13 Apr. 1635
2 pieces of land (2a) in Tuddenham, copyhold of manor of Tuddenham Hall
Copy court roll recording admission of William Cage and George Acton, surviving parties to

indenture dated 18 Feb. 1622 between Richard Martyn, gent. and the then Bailiffs and Portmen of Ipswich

C/3/10/2/9/5   10 Apr. 1640
Messuages, lands and tenements in Westerfield and Ipswich granted by Richard Martin, gent., Portman of Ipswich, deceased, to the Bailiffs and Portmen, 18 Feb. 1622
Conveyance to new feoffees: William Cage, gent., Portman, to Richard Pupplett and John Aldus, Bailiffs, and Robert Sparrowe, John Sicklemore, William Moysey, Edmond Keene, John Barbor, Edmond Humfrie, William Tyler and William Sparrowe, Portmen of Ipswich

C/3/10/2/9/6   28 May 1657
Messuages, lands and tenements in Westerfield and Ipswich granted by Richard Martin, gent., Portman of Ipswich, deceased, to the Bailiffs and Portmen, 18 Feb. 1622
Conveyance to new feoffees: Richard Pupplett and John Aldus, Portmen, to Peter Fisher and Robert Dunkon, Bailiffs, and John Smythier, John Brandlinge, Nicholas Phillipps, Richard Hayle, Manuell Sorrell, Jacob Caley, Richard Jennings and Henry Whitinge, Portmen of Ipswich

C/3/10/2/9/7   24 Jul. 1764
2 pieces of land (2a) in Tuddenham, copyhold of manor of Tuddenham Hall
Copy court roll recording re-grant to Thomas Trapnell jun., gent., Samuel Kilderbee jun., gent., William Hamblin, plumber and William Truelove jun., following seizure for failure to claim property on death of last surviving trustee

C/3/10/2/10   SCRIVENER'S GIFT   1319–1609

C/3/10/2/10/1   13 Oct. 1319
Piece of land in [Little] Blakenham and piece of meadow in Bramford
Feoffment from Thomas de Ros of Little Blakenham to William his brother
Blakenham premises lie between land of Ralph Ponkel and land of rector; Bramford premises between land of Walter Oliver and meadow of Thomas de Ver; names of 7 witnesses
Latin; seal missing from tag

C/3/10/2/10/2   24 Mar. 1381
Piece of land abutting S. on Mondone Lane and W. on highway from Bramford to Needham [? in Great Blakenham]
Feoffment from Walter Fullere, son of Seman Fullere of Blakenham on the Water [Great Blakenham], to Robert Chanteby of Blakenham on the Water
Names of 5 witnesses
Latin; seal missing

C/3/10/2/10/3   28 Oct. 1430
Lands and tenements in Great Blakenham
Feoffment from Joan Soreel of Great Blakenham, widow of Thomas Soreel, to Hugh Sparke of Great Blakenham, Thomas Bryd, clerk and Nicholas Rose of Claydon
Names of 5 witnesses
Latin; seal, incomplete, on tag

C/3/10/2/10/4   1590–1609
Annuity of £26 13s 4d [the 'Brooks Annuity'] out of messuage and land (120a) in Ipswich and Bramford
Evidences of title for purchase, 19 Jun. 1609, by Bailiffs, burgesses and commonalty from John Scrivener of Ipswich, esq., to use of poor of Ipswich, for £280 and sale to him of £7 annuity granted by Ralph Scrivener, deceased, to the town out of messuage and land called Thornes in Bramford and lands called Phillipps in Great Blakenham and Baylham
Includes:
— schedule of lands (Brookes, Saffron Panes, Lome Pytts, Brookes Hall Fyldes, Little

Bradmere, Great Bradmere, Over Bradmere and Bramford Fyldes in Ipswich and Bramford)
out of which 40 marks annuity is payable, n.d. [c.1609]
(7 docs; bundle labelled 'Brooks Annuity £26 13s 4d in Bramford and St Matthews')

C/3/10/2/11   ALLEN'S GIFT   1570

C/3/10/2/11/1   12 Sep. 1570
£4 10s annual rent out of: capital messuage [the Bull Inn] and garden, messuage and tenement
in MQ; lands and tenements called Reymes and lands and tenements late of Richard Goldinge
in Wherstead; and messuage and land in Witnesham
Grant from William Whetcrofte of Ipswich, gent., to the Bailiffs, burgesses and commonalty of
Ipswich, to be paid for relief of the poor of Ipswich in satisfaction for legacy of shirts and
smocks to be distributed annually under will of John Allen, Portman, deceased

C/3/10/2/12   CUTLER'S CHARITY   c.1284–1479

By his will dated 24 January 1621, William Cutler, merchant, bequeathed £100 to the Bailiffs,
burgesses and commonalty, on trust to purchase lands to the annual value of £6, the profits to be
employed for the maintenance of three poor persons, each of them to receive 40s p.a. The
property purchased was a meadow in St Mary Stoke, between Handford Road and the river.
(See Canning 1747, 161–62, and Trustees 1878, 32.)

C/3/10/2/12/1   n.d.[1284–1291]
Piece of meadow in Stoke [by Ipswich]
Feoffment from Richard Tholle, son of late Adam Tholle of Ipswich, to John Baldewin of
Ipswich and wife Juliana, for 20s fine and 1 clove annually
Premises lie between meadows of Reginald Roland and John Roland, abutting N. on river bank
and S. on land of John Baldewin; names of 12 witnesses, including Geoffrey Kempe 'tunc
custode Gyppewic' [the town being in the King's hands between 1284 and 1291]
Latin; endorsed 'Rodlonds' in 17c. hand; seal on tag

C/3/10/2/12/2   21 Jan. 1308
Arable land (3r) [? in MS]
Feoffment from John Rodlond of Asschewelle and wife Hawys to John Pikenot of Asschewelle
½a lies at Gossemere next to land of Geoffrey Jeppoun, abutting against le Watewey; 1r near
the same, next to Geoffrey's land, abutting on said way; names of 7 witnesses
Latin; 1 seal on tag; second seal missing

C/3/10/2/12/3   9 Sep. 1330
Lands and tenements in Handford hamlet in MS
Feoffment from Peter, son of late Reginald Rudlond, to John, son of late John Rudlond, both of
Handford hamlet next Ipswich
Names of 6 witnesses
Latin; seal missing from tag

C/3/10/2/12/4   15 Nov. 1336
All lands and tenements formerly of John, son of William Goldyng of Ipswich, in Ipswich, its
suburbs, Stoke by Ipswich, and hamlets of Haveford, WU and WB
Quitclaim by Thomas, son of Thomas de Westone of Ipswich, to John, son of John Rodlond of
Ipswich, his brother [sic]
Names of 9 witnesses
Latin; seal on tag

C/3/10/2/12/5   6 Oct. 1337
Property as in C/3/10/2/12/4

Quitclaim by John, son of Thomas de Westone of Ipswich, to John, son of John Rodlond of Ipswich, his brother [*sic*]
Names of 8 witnesses
Latin; seal on tag

C/3/10/2/12/6   16 Nov. 1340
Built cottage with adjoining piece of land of fee of Prior and convent of Alnesbourn, in CL
Feoffment from Nicholas de Burgate and wife Mabel, to Thomas le Mayster sen. of Ipswich
Premises lay between land of William Baldry on E. and land of feoffee on W., abutting S. on Siwardeslond and N. on river bank of Granewich; names of 6 witnesses
Latin; both seals missing from tags

C/3/10/2/12/7   28 Jul. 1361
Lands and tenements in Handford hamlet in Ipswich and in Stoke by Ipswich
Feoffment from Henry Rodlond, burgess of Ipswich, to Thomas le Maister of Ipswich and Amyas Baldry
Names of 6 witnesses
Latin; seal fragment on tag

C/3/10/2/12/8   9 Jul. 1362
Lands, tenements, rents and services (no details) in Ipswich and suburbs, Bramford and Stoke by Ipswich
Bond in £80 from Henry Rodlond to Thomas le Maister of Ipswich for levying fine of premises to Thomas le Maister, Thomas le Spicer and William dil Fen, either in court of Prior of Ely for manor of Stoke, or in King's court
Latin; seal and tongue missing

C/3/10/2/12/9   30 Sep. 1362
Lands and tenements (parish unnamed), and messuages in CL
Quitclaim from Henry Rodlond and wife Margery to Thomas le Mayster of Ipswich
Property in unnamed parish was acquired by Thomas le Mayster from Robert dil Wode, parson of Sproughton, who purchased it from Margery Baldry; property in CL formerly belonged to William Baldry
Names of 7 witnesses
Latin; one seal, second missing from tag

C/3/10/2/12/10   24 Apr. 1368
Lands and tenements in MS
Feoffment from Robert Oseloks and wife Joan to Roger Oseloks, all of Ipswich
Names of 7 witnesses
Latin; badly damp-stained; both seals missing from tags

C/3/10/2/12/11   2 Oct. 1373
Lands and tenements (no details) in Ipswich and suburbs and in fees of WU, WB, Stoke by Ipswich, Greenwich, Bramford, Claydon, Whitton or elsewhere; except tavern formerly of William Smyth
Feoffment from Eborard de Flete, chaplain and William Fen of Ipswich, to Thomas le Maister of Ipswich
Premises were lately acquired from Thomas le Maister; names of 7 witnesses
Latin; 2 seals, incomplete, on tags

C/3/10/2/12/12   20 Mar. 1400
Lands and tenements called Rodlondes in Stoke by Ipswich, 2 messuages called Baldries in CL and MT, and toft in MG
Lease from William Enote, citizen and draper of London, and wife Margaret, to Alice, widow of Simon de Wynchecombe, citizen and armourer of London, for lives of lessors, for 1 rose p.a.
Names of 7 witnesses
Latin; badly damp-stained and partly illegible; seal missing from tag

C/3/10/2/12/13   12 Feb. 1401
Lands and tenements called Rodlondes, lands and tenements formerly Robert Rodlond's, and
lands and tenements formerly of Miles, heir of Roger de Crokkeston, all in Stoke by Ipswich; 2
messuages called Baldries in CL and MT, and toft in St Mary [*recte* MG], Ipswich
Grant of reversion of property in Stoke, and lease for life of other property, from William Enot
and wife Margaret to Alice, widow of Simon de Wynchecombe
Names of 7 witnesses
Latin; both seals missing from tags

C/3/10/2/12/14   30 Jan. 1466
Lands, tenements, rents, reversions and services in Ipswich and other towns in Suffolk
Feoffment from Thomas Beaufitz, clerk and John Craneley to Richard Bothe, esq., Roger
Tymperley and wife Katherine, Richard Felawe, Roger Stannard and John Pyt
Premises were lately acquired from Richard Bothe, Roger Tymperley and wife, and were
formerly of Richard Moungomery late of Ipswich; names of 5 witnesses
Latin; 2 seals on tags

C/3/10/2/12/15   31 Oct. 1479
Lands and tenements, rents and reversions in Ipswich and elsewhere in Suffolk
Feoffment from Roger Tymperley, wife Katherine, Richard Felawe and John Pytte to John
Austyn, clerk and John Cappe, chaplain
Premises are those which feoffors lately had jointly, together with Richard Boche, esq., and
Roger Stannard, both now deceased, by grant of Thomas Beaufitz and John Craneley, clerks;
names of 8 witnesses
Latin; 4 seals, 1 fragmentary, on tags

C/3/10/2/13   BEAUMONT'S GIFT   1599

This was a parochial charity for the benefit of the poor of St Nicholas. As such, the document's
presence in the borough archive is anomalous, but for convenience it is listed here, rather than
under ACCIDENTAL ACCUMULATIONS, C/6.

C/3/10/2/13/1   11 Feb. 1599
Cottage called Tylers *alias* the Almys Howse with adjoining garden and land in NI
Feoffment from Richard Beamonte of Ipswich, yeoman, son of William Beamonte of Ipswich,
clothmaker, deceased, to Ralph Scryvener, gent., William Bloyse sen., mercer, Robert Cutler,
merchant, Edward Cage, gent., William Bloyse jun., mercer, Edward Huntyng, merchant,
Samuel Cutler, merchant, William Cage, gent., William Buck, merchant, Isaac Grenwyche,
clothier, Thomas Hayles, clothier, Peter Scryvener, son of Ralph Scryvener, Thomas Cutler,
son of Robert Cutler, and Stephen Grenwyche, son of Isaac Grenwyche; in performance of his
father's will; premises to be used to house one or more old or impotent poor persons of NI
for ever
Latin

C/3/10/2/14   UNIDENTIFIED CHARITIES   1349–1553

C/3/10/2/14/1   10 Dec. 1349
Two messuages in MQ, 3 pieces of land, 1 called Colliscroftes, in Thurleston, 10 pieces of land
in Whitton and BH, piece of land in Bramford, 2 pieces of land in Hallowtree and Alnesbourn,
and 2 pieces of meadow in Stoke by Ipswich
Grant for life from William Malyn sen. of Ipswich to Emma, former wife of William Malyn
jun. of Ipswich, for 100s p.a.; remainder to John, son of William Malyn jun., and lawful issue
Names of 10 witnesses
Latin; seal missing from tag

C/3/10/2/14/2 (10 Dec. 1349), n.d. [15c.]
Copy of C/3/10/2/14/1

C/3/10/2/14/3 17 Jan. 1354
Annual autumn bond labour (*opus autumpnalis*) of Richard Sexteyn and his heirs in Capel
Grant from John Waryn to John de Breccles; names of 5 witnesses
Latin; seal on tag

C/3/10/2/14/4 15 Aug. 1398
Lands and tenements (no details) in Capel and Great Wenham
Feoffment from John Gryth of Stratford and John Corton of [East] Bergholt to Gilbert
Debenham and John atte Hel of Hintlesham
Premises are those which feoffors had jointly with Thomas Gryth, William Snellyng and Roger
Gilberd, all now deceased, by feoffment of Nicholas Gryth of Capel; names of 5 witnesses
Latin; 2 seals on tags

C/3/10/2/14/5 27 Oct. 1513
Lands and tenements sometime Richard Mongomerey's in Ipswich, Sproughton, Whitton and
Bramford
Conveyance by bargain and sale from Robert Fourthe jun. of Hadleigh, merchant, John Flegge
of Needham Market, yeoman, John Stannard and wife Alice, Rauff Warner and wife Julian,
Robert Smyth and wife Alice, and William Stile, to Bailiffs, burgesses and commonalty of
Ipswich, for £266 13s 4d
Fragment of Common Seal on tag

C/3/10/2/14/6 4 Oct. 1553
Messuage with curtilage in LW and MT
Conveyance by bargain and sale from Robert Baron of Ipswich, tailor, to Thomas Elyot of
Stonham Aspal, husbandman, for £65
Premises lie between messuage late of Thomas Eylles on E. and tenement of Thomas Judgeas
on W., abutting S. on high street and N. on churchyard of St Mary le Tower and tenement late of
Thomas Eylles

C/3/10/3 LITIGATION CONCERNING TITLE 1634–1655

C/3/10/3/1 n.d. [1634]
Case papers in suit brought by Sir Robert Hitcham, kt, King's Serjeant, against the Bailiffs, burgesses and commonalty, in Chancery
The suit was brought by Hitcham as Crown lessee of the manor of Walton cum Trimley, and
concerned the Corporation's title to the town lands in Falkenham and Kirton given by William
Smart for the endowment of his charity, and to a copyhold tenement on Bygottes Quay in PE,
devised by will of John Nicholls for the upkeep of Christ's Hospital: *see* Richardson 1884,
507n.
Includes
— defendants' answer to plaintiff's bill of complaint, n.d.
— memoranda *re* lands in Falkenham, n.d.
(2 docs; a reference in the text of the answer to Queen Anne's [consort of James I] death 15
years earlier dates these documents to 1634)

C/3/10/3/2 22 Oct. 1641
Certain closes of land and pasture belonging to Ulveston Hall [in Debenham]
Letter of attorney from the Bailiffs, burgesses and commonalty of Ipswich to Joseph Pemberton
and Edmond Morgan, to take possession of the property unlawfully entered by Nicholas
Garnishe, gent.
Endorsed with memorandum of repossession, 17 Nov. 1641

C/3/10/3/3/1–11   1652–1653
Case papers in suit brought by the Bailiffs, burgesses and commonalty against John Curtis *alias*
Courthois, esq. and wife Gertrude, in Chancery
The suit was brought for the establishment of the Corporation's title to, and precise location of,
lands in Bramford, and the recovery of ten years' rent arrears thereon. The lands were granted
by the Corporation to Thomas Bacon of Bramford (with whose own lands they were intermingled) on long-term lease in 1598. Gertrude Curtis having become possessed of the estate in her
own right, the defendants allegedly demolished the boundary marks and refused payment of the
rent. Judgment was given in favour of the Corporation.

C/3/10/3/3/1   n.d. [9 Feb. 1652]
Plaintiffs' bill of complaint
(12 fols, stitched together)

C/3/10/3/3/2   n.d. [9 Feb. 1652]
Brief of the plaintiffs' bill of complaint, defendants' answer and proofs on behalf of the
plaintiffs
(3 copies, each 1 fol.)

C/3/10/3/3/3   (9 Feb. 1652), n.d.
Contemporary copy decree
Ordering payment of rent to Corporation, and appointment of impartial commissioners to
determine disputed boundaries
(2 fols)

C/3/10/3/3/4   28 May 1652
Joint and several answers of the defendants to the bill of complaint
(11 fols, stitched together)

C/3/10/3/3/5   20 Sep. 1652
Depositions of witnesses for the plaintiffs
Taken at the 'King's Head' in Ipswich before William Bloys sen., esq. and Henry Parker, esq.
(53 fols, stitched together)

C/3/10/3/3/6   5 Feb. 1653
Memorandum of agreement between Nathaniel Bacon [Recorder of Ipswich] and John
Curtis
On appointment of a commission to set out the disputed lands, and on its terms of reference
(1 fol.)

C/3/10/3/3/7   9 Feb. 1653
Order in Chancery
Requiring the defendant to pay the rent with arrears, and ordering the appointment by the Six
Clerks of indifferent commissioners to set out and bound the disputed lands
Endorsed:
— memorandum of nomination of commissioners, 21 Feb. 1653
(1 fol.)

C/3/10/3/3/8   n.d. [? Mar. 1653]
Copy certificate of Edmund Ferneley, Thomas Vesey and Ralph Meadowe, commissioners
appointed by C/3/10/3/3/7
Setting out the lands (intermingled with those of the defendants) belonging to the plaintiffs, and
the defendants' refusal to accept arbitration
Annexed:
— copy of the commission, 28 Feb. 1653
(13 fols, stitched together)

C/3/10/3/3/9   n.d. [? Mar. 1653]
Copy certificate, as C/3/10/3/3/8

Annexed:
— report on commissioners' findings, n.d. [? Mar. 1653]
(4 fols, stitched together)

C/3/10/3/3/10   28 May 1653
Copy decree in Chancery in favour of the plaintiffs
(35 fols, stitched together)

C/3/10/3/3/11   26 Nov. 1653
Exemplification of the Chancery decree of 28 May 1653
(2 membranes; Great Seal of the Keepers of the Liberty of England, poor impression, incomplete)

C/3/10/3/4/1–3   1654–1655
Case papers in suit brought by the Bailiffs, burgesses and commonalty against John Weston, in Chancery
The suit was brought for the establishment of the boundaries of, and recovery of arrears of rent on, lands lying in Ducklemore Field and elsewhere in Bramford, which were granted by the Corporation in 1598 to Ralph Scrivener (with whose own lands they were intermingled) for an annual fee-farm rent. The premises were subsequently conveyed privately to the defendant, who refused payment of the rent.

C/3/10/3/4/1   6 Apr. 1654
Depositions of witnesses on behalf of the plaintiffs
Taken at Sibton before John Hawys and John Harwell, gents.
(37 fols, stitched together)

C/3/10/3/4/2   n.d. [? Apr. 1654]
Depositions of witnesses on behalf of the defendant
Taken at Sibton before John Hawys and John Harwell, gents.
(25 fols, stitched together)

C/3/10/3/4/3   n.d. [? Jan. 1655]
Brief of plaintiffs' bill of complaint, defendant's answer and depositions of witnesses on behalf of the plaintiffs, for hearing on 29 Jan. 1655
(3 copies, 1 each for the Attorney General, Solicitor General and Serjeant Keble; each 3 fols)

C/3/10/4 MANORIAL ADMINISTRATION   1316–1675

The manors of Sackville's and Ulveston Hall in Debenham were purchased by Henry Tooley from Christopher Thwaytes in 1548 (*see* C/3/10/2/3/3/2), and subsequently formed part of the original endowment of Tooley's Foundation.

C/3/10/4/1   MANOR OF SACKVILLE'S   1428–1675

Related records in the Ipswich Record Office include: court rolls 1626–1708 (HD 1480/15–16), court books 1685–1936 (HD 1480/17, 19–20), surveys 1568–1569 and 1594 (HD 1480/22–23), and rentals 1801–1839 (HD 1480/24–25).

C/3/10/4/1/1   Court Rolls   1428–1622

C/3/10/4/1/1/1   1428–1455
Courts held 22 Sep. 1428, 4 Dec. 1437, 9 Feb. 1439, 10 or 24 Jul. 1439, 25 Nov. 1444 and 24 Oct. 1455 only; those of 22 Sep. 1428, 4 Dec. 1437 and 24 Oct. 1455 include market courts (*'curia fori'*) for Debenham in addition to the manor court (*'curia campi'*)
(3 membranes, not in chronological order)

C/3/10/4/1/1/2   1491–1508
Courts held 16 May 1491, 4 Jun. 1499, 3 Oct. 1504, 14 May 1505, 3 Jun. 1506, 2 Oct. 1507 and 13 Nov. 1508
(5 membranes; the last 3, containing the court proceedings for 1505–1508, appear from the script to be later transcripts, in an early 17c. hand)

C/3/10/4/1/1/3   1509–1552
Courts held 12 Nov. 1509, 14 May 1512, 8 Nov. 1513, 2 Dec. 1519, 14 May 1521, 9 May 1522, 4 Aug. 1530, 18 Mar. 1532, 4 Jun. 1532, 5 Aug. 1534, 22 Jul. 1536, 26 Apr. 1538, 25 Nov. 1540, 21 Jul. 1545, 17 Mar. 1546, 4 Jun. 1549, 4 Mar. 1550, 16 Jun. 1551, 21 Dec. 1552
(5 membranes, in reverse chronological order; those for 12 Nov. 1509 and 9 May 1522 appear from the script to be later transcripts, in an early 17c. hand, and a similar partial transcript of the court of 21 Dec. 1552 is included next to the original)

C/3/10/4/1/1/4   1553–1554
Courts held 20 Nov. 1553 and 17 Jul. 1554
(2 membranes)

C/3/10/4/1/1/5   1559–1602
No courts held in 1560, 1561, 1568, 1570, 1571, 1575, 1579, 1580, 1584 or 1600; otherwise one court each year except 1559, 1565, 1588 (2 courts each) and 1576 (3 courts)
(27 membranes)

C/3/10/4/1/1/6   1603–1622
One court for each year except 1619 and 1621
(11 membranes)

C/3/10/4/1/2   Draft Court Books   **1563–1579**

C/3/10/4/1/2/1   Sep. 1563–Feb. 1573
(1 vol.)

C/3/10/4/1/2/2   Apr.–Dec. 1576
(1 vol.)

C/3/10/4/1/2/3   21 Jul. 1578
(1 vol.)

C/3/10/4/1/2/4   Feb. 1577–Jul. 1579
(1 vol.)

C/3/10/4/1/3   Minutes of Courts   **1505–1590**

C/3/10/4/1/3/1   May 1505–Mar. 1546
(17 unattached fols)

C/3/10/4/1/3/2   Jun. 1549–May 1562
(13 unattached fols)

C/3/10/4/1/3/3   Aug. 1588–Sep. 1590
(8 unattached fols)

C/3/10/4/1/4   Rentals   **1594–1614**

C/3/10/4/1/4/1   29 Sep. 1594
For year ending at Michaelmas
(2 membranes, stitched together 'Exchequer' style)

C/3/10/4/1/4/2   29 Sep. 1614
Renewed at Michaelmas, for 1 year
(2 membranes, stitched together 'Exchequer' style)

C/3/10/4/1/5   Steward's Papers   1591–1675

Chiefly presentments or verdicts of the homage and memoranda of out-of-court surrenders

C/3/10/4/1/5/1   1591–1624
(10 docs)

C/3/10/4/1/5/2   1614–1624
(9 docs)

C/3/10/4/1/5/3   1626–1641
Includes:
— 1 memorandum for manor of Ulveston Hall, 19 Jun. 1627
(38 docs, filed on parchment thong)

C/3/10/4/1/5/4   1640–1653
(30 docs, filed on parchment thong)

C/3/10/4/1/5/5   1651–1661
(21 docs)

C/3/10/4/1/5/6   1649–1675
Includes:
— fragment of court roll for 30 Jul. 1650
— copy will of George Phillipps of Debenham, singleman, 15 Jun. 1653
— copy will of Nicholas Sherman of Debenham, yeoman, 18 Jul. 1662
(14 docs)

C/3/10/4/2   MANOR OF ULVESTON HALL   1316–1673

Related records in the Ipswich Record Office include: court rolls 1318–1361 and 1703–1708 (HD 1480/1–14, 16), court books 1685–1850 (HD 1480/17–18), extent mid-16c. (HD 1480/21), surveys 1568–1569 and 1594 (HD 1480/22–23), and rentals 1801–1839 (HD 1480/24–25).

C/3/10/4/2/1   Court Rolls   1459–1622

C/3/10/4/2/1/1   1 Oct. 1459
(1 membrane)

C/3/10/4/2/1/2   1476–1480
Courts held 25 Sep. 1476, 9 Oct. 1477, 17 Nov. 1479, 17 May 1480 and 24 Oct. 1480. Heading for first court states that it is held in the name of Elizabeth, widow of John Ulveston, in whom the manor is vested for life, with remainder to John Ulveston, son and heir of Richard Ulveston (5 membranes)

C/3/10/4/2/1/3   1486–1509
Courts held 23 Nov. 1486, 2 Oct. 1488, 18 Jun. 1489, 3 Aug. 1507 and 15 Apr. 1509 only (4 membranes)

C/3/10/4/2/1/4   1516–1538
Courts held 30 Sep. 1516, 14 Apr. 1519, 21 Mar. 1532, 29 Jul. 1534, 22 Jul. 1536 and 25 Apr. 1538 only
(5 membranes)

C/3/10/4/2/1/5   1548–1555
Courts held 5 Apr. 1548, 19 Jun. 1550, 18 Jul. 1554 and 2 Dec. 1555 only. Court of 19 Jun. 1550
is the first of Henry Tooley of Ipswich, merchant (with attornment); court of 18 Jul. 1554 is the
first of John Southewell, esq., Robert Daundy, merchant, Richard Bird, gent. and William
Daundy, merchant, Tooley's executors
(3 membranes, not in chronological order)

C/3/10/4/2/1/6   1558–1602
No courts in 1559–1563, 1565–1567, 1572–1573, 1575, 1577, 1579, 1590, 1600; otherwise 1
court each year except 1569 (2 courts) and 1576 (3 courts); the headings usually give the names
of the Bailiffs of Ipswich for the year, as *ex officio* lords of the manor
(23 membranes)

C/3/10/4/2/1/7   1603–1622
One court for each year except 1619 and 1621
(10 membranes)

C/3/10/4/2/2   Draft Court Books   **1564–1582**

C/3/10/4/2/2/1   Sep. 1564–Feb. 1582
No entries between 4 Sep. 1570 and 26 Feb. 1582
(1 vol.)

C/3/10/4/2/3   Minutes of Courts   **1476–1590**

C/3/10/4/2/3/1   Sep. 1476–Oct. 1480
(6 fols, stitched together)

C/3/10/4/2/3/2   Mar. 1532–Apr. 1539
(6 unattached fols)

C/3/10/4/2/3/3   Oct. 1541–Oct. 1554
(14 fols, stitched together)

C/3/10/4/2/3/4   9 Dec. 1555
(2 fols)

C/3/10/4/2/3/5   Nov. 1570–Sep. 1590
(19 unattached fols)

C/3/10/4/2/4   Estreats   **1521–1578**

C/3/10/4/2/4/1   5 Apr. 1521
Includes:
— entries for Market Court and manor of Crow's Hall
(1 membrane)

C/3/10/4/2/4/2   – Aug. 1566
(1 fol.; part of heading missing)

C/3/10/4/2/4/3   21 Jul. 1578
Includes:
— entries for manor of Sackvilles
(1 fol.)

C/3/10/4/2/5   Rentals   **1355–1617**

C/3/10/4/2/5/1   6 Nov. 1355
(1 membrane)

C/3/10/4/2/5/2   1388 *or* 1389
Dated only by regnal year, 12 Ric. II
(2 membranes, stitched together 'Chancery' style)

C/3/10/4/2/5/3   [early 15c.]
Dated only as 'tempore Elizabethe nuper uxoris Johannis Ulveston filij Thome Ulveston
armigeri'
(2 membranes, stitched together 'Chancery' style)

C/3/10/4/2/5/4   29 Sep. 1564
For half-year ending at Michaelmas
(1 membrane)

C/3/10/4/2/5/5   29 Sep. 1569
For year ending at Michaelmas
(1 membrane)

C/3/10/4/2/5/6   29 Sep. 1569
Duplicate
(1 membrane)

C/3/10/4/2/5/7   29 Sep. 1594
For year ending at Michaelmas
(2 membranes, stitched together 'Exchequer' style)

C/3/10/4/2/5/8   25 Mar. 1617
Renewed at Lady Day, for 1 year
(2 membranes, stitched together 'Exchequer' style)

C/3/10/4/2/6 Compoti   **1438–1469**

C/3/10/4/2/6/1   Sep. 1438–Sep. 1439
Richard Wysman, collector
(1 doc.)

C/3/10/4/2/6/2   Sep. 1468–Sep. 1469
Lawrence Fedyon, Bailiff and Receiver
(2 fols, stitched together 'Chancery' style)

C/3/10/4/2/7 Surveys   **1564**

C/3/10/4/2/7/1   4 Sep. 1564
Draft
(1 vol.)

C/3/10/4/2/8 Steward's Papers   **1316–1673**

With the exception of the three earliest items, these consist chiefly of presentments and verdicts
of the homage and memoranda of out-of-court surrenders.

C/3/10/4/2/8/1   29 Sep. 1316
List of the free tenants of John de Ulveston of Debenham who owe scutage, annual rent and
other services
Tenants' names, details of land held and rents payable
(1 membrane)

C/3/10/4/2/8/2   n.d. [later 16c.]
Schedule of rents and fines payable by the writer's son James to the lords of the manor

C/3/10/4/2/8/3   14 Apr. 1607
Little lane leading from highway from Debenham to Kenton and various pieces of land and
pasture next to Howndemedowe, copyhold of manor of Ulveston [Hall] in Debenham
Copy court roll recording admission of James Harrison on the death of his father George Harrison

C/3/10/4/2/8/4   1613–1624
(12 docs)

C/3/10/4/2/8/5   1625–1641
(22 docs, filed on parchment thong)

C/3/10/4/2/8/6   1643–1653
(41 docs, filed on parchment thong)

C/3/10/4/2/8/7   1651–1673
Includes:
— inventory of house contents, n.d. [17c.]
(58 docs)

C/3/10/4/3   MANORS OF SACKVILLE'S AND ULVESTON HALL: 1574–1671
COMPOSITE RECORDS

C/3/10/4/3/1   Draft Court Books   **1581–1619**

C/3/10/4/3/1/1   Aug. 1581–Sep. 1619
(1 vol.; some entries out of chronological sequence)

C/3/10/4/3/2   Estreats   **1574–1576**

C/3/10/4/3/2/1   2 Sep. 1574
(1 membrane)

C/3/10/4/3/2/2   18 Dec. 1576
(2 fols)

C/3/10/4/3/3   Rentals   **? late 16c.–1671**

C/3/10/4/3/3/1   n.d. [? late 16c.]

C/3/10/4/3/3/2   n.d. [? early 17c.]
(1 membrane)

C/3/10/4/3/3/3   25 Mar. 1652
(1 membrane)

C/3/10/4/3/3/4   25 Mar. 1671
(1 membrane)

C/3/10/5   LEASES AND ASSOCIATED PAPERS   **1548–1808**

All the leases are granted in the names of the Bailiffs, burgesses and commonalty of Ipswich.

C/3/10/5/1   DAUNDY'S CHARITY   1550

C/3/10/5/1/1   4 Jan. 1550
Messuage with lands, meadows and pastures in lessee's occupation in Holbrook
Counterpart lease to Richard Gosselyn of Holbrook, husbandman, for 25 years at 42*s* p.a.

C/3/10/5/1/2   12 Aug. 1550
Lands and tenements in Holbrook and Harkstead in occupation of Nicholas Smyth, George
Heyward, John Lockwoode, Osmund Rolff, Thomas Rolff and Robert Kenderly, except
messuage and lands in occupation of Richard Gosselyn of Holbrook, husbandman
Counterpart lease to Edmund Leche of Ipswich, yeoman, for 10 years at 57s 6d p.a.
Endorsement indicates subsequent use as wrapper for Great Court Rolls of the reign of
Edward II

C/3/10/5/2   TOOLEY'S FOUNDATION   1548–1779

C/3/10/5/2/1   Ulveston Hall estate in Debenham   **1589**

C/3/10/5/2/1/1   26 Jun. 1589
Site of manor of Ulveston Hall with lands in Debenham, Mickfield and Wetheringsett
Counterpart lease, by consent of Wardens of Tooley's Foundation, to Lionel Kenyngall of
Debenham, yeoman, for 11 years at £90 p.a.
Annexed: bond for performance of covenants (2 docs)

C/3/10/5/2/2   Kents (Walnut Tree Farm) in Whitton, Akenham and   **1567–1761**
Claydon

C/3/10/5/2/2/1   20 Apr. 1567
Counterpart lease to Matthew Goodynge of Ipswich, clothier, for 11 years at £13 6s 8d p.a.

C/3/10/5/2/2/2   1 Apr. 1592
Counterpart lease to Leonard Gates of Somersham, yeoman, for 11 years at £38 p.a.

C/3/10/5/2/2/3   19 Feb. 1761
Surrender by William Wright of Akenham, yeoman, of Corporation lease dated 25 Jan. 1753,
for £122

C/3/10/5/2/3   Taylor's Farm in Whitton, Bramford and Thurleston   **1570–1589**
C/3/10/5/2/3/1   21 Aug. 1570
Counterpart lease to Robert Style of Whitton, husbandman, for 11 years at £13 6s 8d p.a.

C/3/10/5/2/3/2   8 Jul. 1589
Counterpart lease to Thomas Mynter of Thurleston, yeoman, for 11 years at £28 p.a.

C/3/10/5/2/4   Properties in Bramford   **1548–1594**

C/3/10/5/2/4/1   8 Jul. 1548
Pieces of land and pasture (20a) lately in occupation of John Cooke, deceased, in Bramford
Counterpart lease to Richard Cardynall of Bramford, yeoman, for 10 years at 34s annual rent
Latin

C/3/10/5/2/4/2   8 Jul. 1548
Two pieces of land (6a) in lessee's occupation in Bramford
Counterpart lease to Joan Kenton of Bramford, widow, for 10 years at 6s annual rent
Latin

C/3/10/5/2/4/3   20 Sep. 1594
Messuage and 13 pieces of land (53a) in Bramford
Counterpart lease to Thomas Galston of Whitton, husbandman, for 11 years at £50 p.a.

C/3/10/5/2/5   The Lime Kiln Farm in Claydon   1592–1779

C/3/10/5/2/5/1   1 Apr. 1592
Messuage, lands and limekiln in Claydon, parcel of lands of Tooley's Foundation
Counterpart lease to Oliver Jollie of Claydon, husbandman, for 11 years at £28 p.a.

C/3/10/5/2/5/2   10 Nov. 1779
Bond
Thomas Cooper of Claydon, farmer, bound in £200 to Ipswich Corporation for performance of
terms of lease of unspecified property

C/3/10/5/2/6   Properties in Whitton   1556–1760

C/3/10/5/2/6/1   12 Aug. 1556
Lands, meadows and pastures in Whitton, in lessee's occupation
Lease to Robert Style of Whitton, husbandman, for 10 years at £4 6s 8d p.a.

C/3/10/5/2/6/2   28 Feb. 1573
Messuage and lands in Whitton
Counterpart lease to Richard Battell of Ipswich, for 11 years at £3 6s 8d p.a.

C/3/10/5/2/6/3   8 Jul. 1612
3 pieces of land, meadow and pasture (9a) in Whitton and Bramford
Counterpart lease to Edward Huntinge of Ipswich, merchant and wife Joan, for 21 years at
40s p.a.

C/3/10/5/2/6/4   3 Apr. 1760
Messuage and land in Whitton
Lease to John Orford jun. of Whitton, yeoman, for 11 years at £125 p.a.

C/3/10/5/2/7   Properties in Ipswich   1568

C/3/10/5/2/7/1   4 May 1568
Messuage late of Henry Tooley, with curtilage, tiled buildings, yards and gardens, and orchard
next to tenement of Richard Goltye, in HL
Lease to Robert Smart of Ipswich, clothier, with assent of Richard Bride *alias* Byrde, William
Smarte, Edmond Leche and George Coppynge, Wardens of the lands etc. of the late Henry
Tooley appointed by order of the Lord Keeper, for 100 years at 56s 8d p.a.

C/3/10/5/2/7/2   4 May 1568
7 adjoining houses with orchard in HL
Counterpart lease with assent of Richard Bride, William Smart, Edmund Leche and George
Coppynge, the Wardens appointed by order of the Lord Keeper for disposition of Henry
Tooley's lands, to Robert Smarte of Ipswich, clothier, for 100 years at 56s 8d p.a.

C/3/10/5/2/7/3   4 May 1568
Messuage late of Henry Tooley, with 4 adjoining houses and wellhouse in PE
Lease to John Barker of Ipswich, merchant, for 100 years at 40s p.a.

C/3/10/5/3   CHRIST'S HOSPITAL   1551–1808

C/3/10/5/3/1   The 'Grammar School Lands' in Whitton   1551–1573

C/3/10/5/3/1/1   6 Mar. 1551
Close (8a), parcel of 3 closes sometime called the Grammer Skoll Landes in Whitton
Counterpart lease to Robert Kyng of Ipswich, mercer, for 21 years at 14s p.a.

C/3/10/5/3/1/2   4 Jan. 1553
2 pieces of ground, pasture and meadow lately leased to James Leman in BH
Counterpart lease to John Gardyner, clothmaker and Portman of Ipswich, for 20 years, for 20s
fine and 22s 8d p.a.

C/3/10/5/3/1/3   8 Jan. 1558
Three closes of arable and pasture called the Grammar School Lands in Brooks Hall [sic]
hamlet and Whitton
Counterpart lease to John Smyth *alias* Dyer, Alderman [sic] of Ipswich, for life, at 43s 4d p.a.

C/3/10/5/3/1/4   28 Feb. 1573
Two closes of land and pasture in Whitton
Counterpart lease to William Jeffrye of Ipswich, clothier, for 11 years at £8 p.a.

C/3/10/5/3/2   Properties in Ipswich   **1591–1763**

C/3/10/5/3/2/1   11 May 1591
Solar called Taylers Hall, now severed by itself, parcel of Christ's Hospital in Ipswich
Counterpart lease to William Cope and Phillip Dod of Ipswich, tailors, Wardens of the
Company of Tailors in Ipswich, for 11 years at 13s 4d p.a.

C/3/10/5/3/2/2   24 Feb. 1725
Piece of ground (9 rods x 2 rods) abutting W. on Shire House yard, fronting the backside of the
Shire House, in MQ
Counterpart lease to Jonathan Quintin, for 99 years at 1s p.a.
Cancelled by mutilation; incomplete

C/3/10/5/3/2/3   29 Sep. 1763
Stable lately N. part of messuage called Felaw's House, with yard, abutting E. on Foundation
Street in MQ
Counterpart lease to Richard Canning of Ipswich, clerk, for 15 years at £3 p.a., the first 8 years
rent-free in consideration of building conversion carried out by lessee

C/3/10/5/4   JOINTLY OWNED ESTATES   1559–1808

C/3/10/5/4/1   The Street Farm in Whitton and Bramford (Tooley's,   **1559–1808**
Smart's and Christ's Hospital Charities)

C/3/10/5/4/1/1   12 Apr. 1559
Six pieces of land in lessee's occupation in Bramford
Counterpart lease to Robert Cocke of Bramford, husbandman, for 10 years at 16s annual rent
Latin

C/3/10/5/4/1/2   16 Mar. 1752
Farm (91a) in lessee's occupation in Whitton and Bramford
Counterpart lease to William Blomfield of Whitton, yeoman, for 11 years at £35 p.a.

C/3/10/5/4/1/3   28 Sep. 1763
Farm in occupation of William Tye in Whitton
Lease to Luke Taylor of Bramford, yeoman, for 11 years at £63 p.a.

C/3/10/5/4/1/4   28 Sep. 1763
Counterpart of C/3/10/5/4/1/3
Annexed:
— bond for performance of covenants
(2 docs)

C/3/10/5/4/1/5   10 Nov. 1774
Farm in lessee's occupation in Whitton
Counterpart lease to William Greenleafe of Ipswich, yeoman, for 11 years at £63 p.a.

C/3/10/5/4/1/6   1 Sep. 1808
Farm in Whitton and Bramford
Lease to Simon Jackaman of Ipswich, gent. and Isaac Jackaman of Whitton, farmer, for 11 years at £110 p.a.

C/3/10/5/4/2   Kersey's Farm in Otley (Tooley's, Smart's and Christ's Hospital   1807 Charities)

C/3/10/5/4/2/1   29 Dec. 1807
Bond
Robert Burcham of Ipswich, butcher and James King of Otley, farmer, bound in £300 to Ipswich Corporation for performance of terms of lease of unspecified property

C/3/10/5/5   MARTIN'S CHARITY   1635–1646

C/3/10/5/5/1   3 Oct. 1635
Messuage and lands in Westerfield
Counterpart lease to Edward Garrett of Henley, yeoman, for 11 years, for £20 entry fine and £30 p.a.

C/3/10/5/5/2   10 Oct. 1646
Messuage and lands in Westerfield
Counterpart lease to Edmond Ketteridge of Witnesham, yeoman, for 11 years at £30 p.a.

C/3/10/6   SURVEYS AND VALUATIONS   ? early 16c.–1824

C/3/10/6/1   TOOLEY'S FOUNDATION   ? early 16c.–1809

C/3/10/6/1/1   Ulveston Hall estate in Debenham   1798–1809

C/3/10/6/1/1/1   28, 29 Jun. 1798
Valuation; with covering letter by the valuer, John Josselyn of Belstead

C/3/10/6/1/1/2   13, 20 Mar. 1809
Valuation; with covering letter by the valuer, John Josselyn jun. of Belstead

C/3/10/6/1/2   Walnut Tree Farm in Whitton etc.   ? early 16c.–1697

C/3/10/6/1/2/1   n.d. [? early–mid 16c.]
Terrier of lands in Claydon, Whitton and Bramford
(Latin, 1 vol.)

C/3/10/6/1/2/2   n.d. [? mid 16c.]
Extent of lands in Whitton
Compiled in part from a rental of the manor of Bramford, Jul. 1505, and a court roll of the manor of Akenham for 2 Edw. VI (1548 or 1549)
(roll of 5 paper fols, 2 blank)

C/3/10/6/1/2/3   n.d. [later 16c.]
Terrier of lands and tenements of Ipswich Corporation in Thurleston, Whitton and Bramford

C/3/10/6/1/2/4   21 Sep. 1697
Terrier of Kents Farm [in Akenham, Whitton, Bramford, Thurleston and Coddenham]

C/3/10/6/2   CHRIST'S HOSPITAL   1808–1818

C/3/10/6/2/1   Property in Debenham and Ipswich   **1808–1818**

C/3/10/6/2/1/1   Mar. 1808
Valuation of estates in Debenham and PE, in respective occupations of the widow Worledge
and Robert Burcham, by John Josselyn of Belstead

C/3/10/6/2/1/2   7 Dec. 1818
Valuation of estate in Debenham, in occupation of Brownin Worledge, by John Josselyn of
Sproughton

C/3/10/6/2/1/3   6 Aug. 1818
Estimate of annual value of an estate in PE and MS in occupation of John King

C/3/10/6/3   JOINTLY OWNED ESTATES   1697–1824

**C/3/10/6/3/1   Creeting and Earl Stonham estate (Smart's, Christ's Hospital and   1824
Tyler's Charities)**

C/3/10/6/3/1/1   4 Feb. 1824
Valuation of farm in Creeting St Peter, Creeting All Saints and Earl Stonham, in occupation of
James Tydeman, by John Edwards of Bramford

**C/3/10/6/3/2   The Street Farm in Whitton and Bramford (Tooley's,   1697–1785
Smart's and Christ's Hospital Charities)**

C/3/10/6/3/2/1   21 Sep. 1697
Terrier of farm in Whitton belonging to Ipswich Corporation, in occupation of Edward Aldus

C/3/10/6/3/2/2   21 Jan. 1785
Valuation of farm in Whitton, in occupation of Edward Mayhew, by John Josselyn of Belstead

**C/3/10/6/3/3   Kersey's Farm in Otley (Tooley's, Smart's and Christ's   1784–1807
Hospital Charities)**

C/3/10/6/3/3/1   3 Dec. 1784
Valuation of farm in Otley, in occupation of Charles and Robert Burchams, by John Josselyn of
Belstead

C/3/10/6/3/3/2   Apr. 1807
Valuation of estate in Otley, in occupation of Robert Burcham, by John Josselyn of Belstead

**C/3/10/6/3/4   Property in Ipswich and Whitton (Tooley's, Smart's and   1806–1818
Christ's Hospital Charities)**

C/3/10/6/3/4/1   23–26 Sep. 1806
Valuation of marshes in PE and MS, and of a farm in Whitton in occupation of J. Jackaman;
with covering letter by the valuer, John Josselyn jun. of Belstead

C/3/10/6/3/4/2   Mar. 1818
Valuation of marsh and pasture in MS, PE, and HL, by John Josselyn of Sproughton

C/3/10/6/4   JOINT SURVEYS   1803

C/3/10/6/4/1   Tooley's and Smart's Charities estates   1803

C/3/10/6/4/1/1   Nov., 3 Dec. 1803
Valuation of farm in Falkenham and Kirton [Smart's Charity] in occupation of George Cook,
and farm in Whitton and Akenham [Tooley's Foundation] in occupation of Thomas Cooper
jun.; with covering letter by the valuer, John Josselyn jun. of Belstead

C/3/10/7   TRIMLEY, KIRTON AND NACTON INCLOSURE   1805–1808

These papers relate to the Smart's Charity estate in Kirton.

C/3/10/7/1   9 Sep. 1805
Notice of objection
From Samuel Kilderbee of Ipswich, gent., to the elder Warden of Smart's Charity, *re* the
Wardens' claim to right of common in Kirton

C/3/10/7/2   1805
State of claims
(printed)

C/3/10/7/3   13 Nov. 1807
Extracts from Inclosure Award
(printed)

C/3/10/7/4   13 Nov. 1807
Extract of Award to Wardens of Smart's Charity
Annexed:
— receipt for expenses of Inclosure Act, 20 Jan. 1808

C/3/10/8   MAPS AND PLANS   **1591–c. mid 19c.**

Most of the following maps and plans have been bound into two volumes. It has therefore been
necessary to list here the very few bound maps that do not relate to charity property. For convenience, four miscellaneous maps have also been placed under this heading.

C/3/10/8/1   VOLUME I   1591–1731

A rough pen-and-ink sketch of the borough arms on the front cover, dated 1833, indicates that
the maps had been bound by that date. The volume is probably the one bound in 1751: *see*
Chamberlains' vouchers 1750–1751 (C/3/3/3/20).

C/3/10/8/1/1   n.d. [*c.*1723]
Farm in [? MW and Bramford]
Manuscript map by [Richard Tallemach], at scale of 3 chains to 1 inch
Includes field names, acreages, buildings, trees, fences, roads, adjacent owners
(ink and watercolour on parchment)

C/3/10/8/1/2   1591
[Smart's Charity] estate in Kirton and Falkenham
Manuscript map by [John Darby], at scale of 20 perches to 1 inch
'A trewe description of a mesuage, and of certeyne landes, meadowes and pastures sometyme
Coles, scituate, lyinge and beinge in Kirton and Faltenham [*sic*] in the county of Suffolk and
late occupied together with other grounds by one Nicholas Byles deceased'

Includes field names, buildings, trees, fences, road, drawing of surveyor with instruments and miniature animals
(ink and watercolour on parchment)

C/3/10/8/1/3   Jul. 1723
[Christ's Hospital] estate in Debenham
Manuscript map by Robert Wade, at scale of 16 perches to 1 inch
'A map of lands belonging to the Corporation of Ipswich, scituated in Debenham Suffolk in the occupation of George Kersey, survey'd by the order of John Cornelius Esqr and John Sparrow Gent., Bailiffs of the Corporation'
Includes field names, acreages, arable and pasture, buildings, trees, responsibility for fences, roads, adjacent owners
(ink and watercolour on parchment)

C/3/10/8/1/4   n.d. [1723]
[Tooley's Foundation] estate in Whitton, Akenham, Claydon, Bramford and Coddenham
Manuscript map by [Robert Wade], at scale of ? 16 perches to 1 inch
'A map of Kents Farme belonging to the Corporation of Ipswich in the occupation of Fynn Aldus: scituated in Whitton, Akenham, Claydon, Bramford and Coddenham, survey'd by the order of John Cornelius Esqr and John Sparrow Gent., Bailiffs of the Corporation'
Includes field names, acreages, buildings, roads, adjacent owners
(ink and watercolour on parchment)

C/3/10/8/1/5   n.d. [1723]
[Tooley's Foundation] estate in Claydon
Manuscript map by [Robert Wade], at scale of 16 perches to 1 inch
'A map of the Lime-Kell Farme scituated in Claydon, in the occupation of Robert Rudland: belonging to the Corporation of Ipswich: surveyed by the order of John Cornelius Esqr and John Sparrow Gent., Bailiffs of the Corporation'
Includes field names, acreages, buildings including limekiln, glebe land, waste land, roads, adjacent owners
(ink and watercolour on parchment)

C/3/10/8/1/6   1723
[Tyler's, Smart's and Christ's Hospital Charities] estate in Creeting St Peter
Manuscript map by Richard Tallemach, at scale of 3 chains to 1 inch
'A map of an estate given by Mr Wm Tyler and Mr Snow for charitable uses for the Corporation of Ipswich, whereof Mr Tyler gave three hundred pounds and with the mony Mr Snow's houses were sold for this estate was bought, lying in West Creeting and Creeting St Peters in Suffolk and now in the occupation of Mr Samuel Pratt and surveyed by the order of John Cornelius Esqr and John Sparrow Gentleman present Bailiffs of the Corporation of Ipswich . . .'
Includes field names, acreages, buildings, woodland, roads, adjacent owners
(ink and watercolour on parchment)

C/3/10/8/1/7   1723
Tooley's Foundation estate in Otley
Manuscript map by Richard Tallemach, at scale of 3 chains to 1 inch
'A map of an estate given by Mr Henry Tooley, merchant, to charitable uses for the Corporation of Ipswich, lying in Otley in Suffolk and now in the occupation of Richard Cearsey, surveyed by the order of John Cornelius Esqr and John Sparrow Gent., Bailiffs of the Corporation . . .'
Includes field names, acreages, arable and pasture, buildings, trees (mostly pollard oaks), roads, ownership of fences, adjacent owners
(ink and watercolour on parchment)

C/3/10/8/1/8   Jul. 1723
[Tooley's Foundation] estate in Debenham, Wetheringsett and Mickfield
Manuscript map by Robert Wade, at scale of 16 perches to 1 inch
'A map of Ulverstone Hall scituated in Debenham, Wethersett [sic] and Mickfield, in the

occupation of Thomas Kersey, belonging to the Corporation of Ipswich, survey'd by the order of John Cornelius Esqr and John Sparrow Gent., Bailiffs of the Corporation'
Includes field names, acreages, arable and pasture, buildings, roads, responsibility for fences, adjacent owners
(ink and watercolour on parchment)

C/3/10/8/1/9   n.d. [1723]
[Smart's and Christ's Hospital Charities] estate in Whitton and Bramford
Manuscript map by [Robert Wade], at scale of 16 perches to 1 inch
'A map of lands belonging to the Corporation of Ipswich, in the occupation of Willm Blomfield, scituated in Whitton and Bramford, surveyed by the order of John Cornelius Esqr and John Sparrow Gent., Bailiffs of the Corporation'
Includes field names, acreages, woodland, buildings, roads, adjacent owners
(ink and watercolour on parchment)

C/3/10/8/1/10   n.d. [1723]
[Tooley's Foundation, Smart's and Christ's Hospital Charities] estates in Whitton, Ipswich and Bramford
Manuscript map by [Robert Wade], at scale of 16 perches to 1 inch
'A map of lands belonging to the Corporation of Ipswich, in the occupation of Peter Day, scituated in Whitton, Ipswich and Bramford, survey'd by the order of John Cornelius Esqr and John Sparrow Gent., Bailiffs of the Corporation'
Includes field names, acreages, woodland, buildings, roads, adjacent owners
(ink and watercolour on parchment)

C/3/10/8/1/11   n.d. [c.1723]
[Corporation marshes/meadows in PE]
Manuscript map by [Richard Tallemach], at scale of 3 chains to 1 inch
Includes acreages, names of lessees, buildings including Handford Mill, Stoke Mill and marsh house, drainage channels, freshwater river, salt river, Stoke Bridge, Friars Bridge, rights of way including Portmans Walk
(ink and watercolour on parchment)

C/3/10/8/1/12   1723
Martin's Charity estate in Westerfield
Manuscript map by Richard Tallemach, at scale of 3 [chains] to 1 inch
'A mapp of an estate given by Mr Martin, one of the Portmen of the Corporation of Ipswich, for charitable uses, being in Westerfield in Suffolk and now in the occupation of Mr Francis Brook (taken by the order of John Cornelius Esquire and John Sparrow Gentleman, present Bailiffs of the said Corporation) . . .'
Includes field names, acreages, buildings, roads, field gates, adjacent owners
(ink and watercolour on parchment)

C/3/10/8/1/13   1731
[Smart's Charity] estate in Kirton
Manuscript map by Anthony Sallows, at scale of 4 chains to 1 inch
'A mapp of an estate belonging to the Corporation of Ipswich lying in Kirton in the county of Suffolk and now in the occupation of Tyrell Bird, surveyed by the order of Francis Negus and John Cornelius Esqrs, Bailiffs of the abovesaid Corporation'
Includes field names, acreages, arable and pasture, buildings, trees, roads, driftways, water-courses, ponds, saltings, field gates, adjacent owners
(ink and watercolour on parchment)

C/3/10/8/2   VOLUME II   1799–c. mid 19c.

The volume was made up in this form in the then Ipswich and East Suffolk Record Office, probably in the 1950s.

C/3/10/8/2/1   1799
Martin's Charity estate in Westerfield
Manuscript map by John Bransby, at scale of 22 rods to 1 inch
'The map of an estate in Westerfield given by Mr Martin to the Corporation of Ipswich,
surveyed, 1799, by order of Thomas Hallum, Esq. and Samuel Thorndike, Gent., Bailiffs'
Includes field names, acreages, arable and pasture, buildings including blacksmith's shop and
Swan Inn, field gates, roads, rights of way, ponds, [gravel pit], adjacent owners
(ink and watercolour on parchment)

C/3/10/8/2/2   1809
Martin's Charity estate in Westerfield
Manuscript map by John Bransby, at scale of 16 rods to 1 inch
'Plan of an estate in Westerfield, given by Mr Martin to the Corporation of Ipswich, surveyed
1809 by order of Saml Thorndike and Wm Batley, Esqs, Bailiffs'
Includes field names, acreages, arable and pasture, details of lands exchanged, buildings, roads,
driftway, ponds, gravel pit, adjacent owners
(ink and watercolour on parchment)

C/3/10/8/2/3   1813
[Tyler's, Smart's and Christ's Hospital Charities] estate in Creeting St Peter, Creeting All
Saints and Earl Stonham
Manuscript map by John Bransby, at scale of 16 rods to 1 inch
'Plan of an estate in Creeting and Stonham, the property of the Corporation of Ipswich, in the
occupation of Mr James Tydeman . . . surveyed . . . by order of Mr Saml Thorndike, Renter
Warden'
Includes field names, acreages, arable and pasture, buildings, roads, ponds, parish boundaries,
adjacent owners; annotated in pencil to show crops grown in each field in 1838
(ink and watercolour on parchment)

C/3/10/8/2/4   1813
Smart's Charity estate in Kirton and Falkenham
Manuscript map by John Bransby, at scale of 27 rods to 1 inch
'Plan of an estate in Kirton and Falkenham, the property of the Corporation of Ipswich, and
applied to the purposes of Smart's Charity . . . Mr George Cook, tenant, surveyed . . . by order of
Mr Samuel Thorndike, Renter Warden'
Includes field names, acreages, arable and pasture, buildings, ponds, saltings, river walls, river
Deben, hardway, marshes, adjacent owners
(ink and watercolour on parchment)

C/3/10/8/2/5   1814
Charity and other Corporation buildings in Ipswich
Manuscript map by John Bransby, at scale of 22 yards to 1 inch
'Plan of Christ's Hospital, Tooley's and Smart's Foundations, the Shire Hall, Bridewell,
Grammar School, etc., Ipswich'
Includes buildings, yards, gardens, streets, rights of way, adjacent owners including MQ
workhouse
(ink and watercolour on paper)

C/3/10/8/2/6   1818
Waterhead Meadow in HL, the property of the Corporation
Manuscript plan by John Bransby, at scale of 8 rods to 1 inch
Includes acreage, pond, ? conduit heads, Watery Lane, adjacent owners
(ink and watercolour on paper)

C/3/10/8/2/7   1818
[Tooley's Foundation and Christ's Hospital Charities] estate in Otley
Manuscript map by John Bransby, at scale of 16 rods to 1 inch

'Plan of an estate in Otley, Suffolk, the property of the Corporation of Ipswich, Mr James King, tenant, Edward Bacon, Esq., John E. Sparrow, Esq., Bailiffs'
Includes field names, acreages, arable and pasture, buildings, roads, drift, ponds, adjacent owners
(ink and watercolour on parchment)

C/3/10/8/2/8   17 Sep. 1819
[Christ's Hospital] estate in Debenham
Manuscript map by John Bransby, at scale of 16 rods to 1 inch
'Plan of an estate [Camp Green Farm] in Debenham, Suffolk, the property of the Corporation of Ipswich, and in the occupation of Mr Bronwin Worledge . . . William Batley and John Denny, Esqrs, Bailiffs'
Includes field names, acreages, arable and pasture, buildings, roads, toll gate, ponds, watercourse, adjacent owners
(ink and watercolour on parchment)

C/3/10/8/2/9   1820
Corporation marshes in PE and MS
Manuscript map by John Bransby, at scale of 16 rods to 1 inch
'Plan of the marshes in the parishes of St Peter and St Mary Stoke, belonging to the Corporation of Ipswich, James Thorndike and John Eddowes Sparrow, Esquires, Bailiffs'
Includes occupiers' names, acreages, parish boundary, buildings, rivers Orwell and Gipping, Stoke Bridge, Friars Bridge, carriage roads, footpaths, towing paths
(ink and watercolour on parchment)

C/3/10/8/2/10   n.d. [c. mid 19c.]
[Martin's Charity] estate in Westerfield
Manuscript map by an unnamed surveyor; no scale given
'Westerfield Farm'
Includes field names, acreages, arable and pasture distinguished by colour, buildings, roads, ponds, [gravel pit], adjacent owners
(ink and watercolour on paper)

C/3/10/8/2/11   n.d. [c. mid 19c.]
[Tooley's Foundation, Smart's and Christ's Hospital Charities] estate in Whitton, MW and Bramford
Manuscript map by an unnamed surveyor; no scale given
'T Kersey's Farm at Whitton' (endorsement)
Includes field names, acreages, arable and pasture distinguished by colour, buildings, exchanged glebe, roads, parish boundaries, adjacent owners
(ink and watercolour on paper)

C/3/10/8/2/12   n.d. [c. mid 19c.]
Tooley's Foundation, [Smart's and] Christ's Hospital Charities estate in Whitton, MW and Bramford
Manuscript map by an unnamed surveyor; no scale given
'Plan of farm in the parish of Whitton belonging to Tooley's Charity and Christ's Hospital Charity and the Corporation of Ipswich'
Includes field names, acreages, arable and pasture distinguished by colour, buildings, roads, parish boundaries, adjacent owners
(ink and watercolour on paper)

C/3/10/8/2/13   n.d. [c. mid 19c.]
Christ's Hospital estate in Debenham
Manuscript map by an unnamed surveyor, at scale of 6 chains to 1 inch
'Plan of Camp Green Farm in the parish of Debenham, belonging to Christ's Hospital Charity in Ipswich'

Includes field names, acreages, arable and pasture distinguished by colour, buildings, roads, ponds, watercourses, adjacent owners
(ink and watercolour on paper)

C/3/10/8/2/14   n.d. [c. mid 19c.]
Tooley's Foundation estate in Debenham, Wetheringsett and Mickfield
Manuscript map by an unnamed surveyor, at scale of 6 chains to 1 inch
'Plan of Ulverston Hall Farm in the parishes of Debenham, Wetheringsett and Mickfield belonging to Tooley's Charity'
Includes field names, acreages, arable and pasture distinguished by colour, buildings, roads, rights of way, moat, ponds, watercourses, parish boundaries, adjacent owners
(ink and watercolour on paper)

C/3/10/8/3   UNBOUND MAPS OF CHARITY LANDS   early 19c.–1833

C/3/10/8/3/1   (1723) [early 19c.]
[Smart's and Christ's Hospital Charities] estate in Whitton and Bramford
Manuscript map copied from the original by [Robert Wade] (C/3/10/8/1/9), at scale of 16 perches to 1 inch
'Copy of a map of lands belonging to the Corporation of Ipswich, in the occupation of Willm Blomfield, scituated in Whitton and Bramford . . . in 1722 [sic]'
(ink and watercolour on paper)
Annexed:
— letter from J. Hallum to John Chevallier Cobbold, confirming that plan corresponds with present state of farm, 9 Jan. 1833
(2 docs)

C/3/10/8/3/2   1 Oct. 1833
Charity land in Ipswich
Manuscript sketch map by 'E.C.', at scale of 1 inch to 50 feet
'Plan of the Charity land affected by the new river channel, shewing by the red colour boundary the portion required for the purposes of the Ipswich Dock'
(ink on paper)

C/3/10/8/4   MISCELLANEOUS MAPS AND PLANS   1676–1814

C/3/10/8/4/1   (1610) [1676]
Suffolk
Printed county map by John Speed, at scale of 3 miles to 1 inch
'Suffolke described and divided into Hundreds, the situation of the fayre towne Ipswich shewed, with the armes of the most noble families that have bene either Dukes or Earles both of that Countie as also of Clare'
Includes royal arms and inset plan of Ipswich with its churches and other principal buildings; [1676] edition with arms of John Holles, Earl of Clare added, to be sold by Thomas Bassett in Fleet Street and Richard Chiswell in St Paul's Churchyard
(hand-coloured; paper)

C/3/10/8/4/2   1686
Coastal waters between Walton on the Naze (Essex) and Hollesley
Printed navigational chart by Capt. Greenvil Collins, Hydrographer to the King, at scale of ⅔ mile to 1 inch
'Harwich, Woodbridge and Handfordwater, with the sands from the Nazeland to Hosely Bay'

Includes navigation hazards, soundings, landmarks; dedication to Samuel Pepys, Secretary to the Admiralty, President of the Royal Society and Master of Trinity House
(uncoloured; paper)

C/3/10/8/4/3   (1753) [?1785]
Suffolk
Printed county map by Emanuel Bowen, Geographer to His Majesty, at scale of 2¼ common miles or 2½ statute miles to 1 inch
'An accurate map of the county of Suffolk divided into its Hundreds, drawn from surveys, with various additional improvements, illustrated with historical extracts relative to its trade, manufactures, natural produce etc.'
Includes churches distinguishing rectories and vicarages, boroughs and other towns, water mills, former religious houses, modern charity schools, ruined churches and chapels, roads with distances in miles and furlongs, market days; dedication to Charles, Duke of Grafton, K.G., Lord Lieutenant and Custos Rotulorum; printed for Carington Bowles in St Paul's Churchyard, Robert Wilkinson in Cornhill and Robert Sayer in Fleet Street; ? 1785 edition
(partially hand-coloured; paper)

C/3/10/8/4/4   1814
Halifax Shipyard and other premises in MS
Manuscript plan by John Bransby, at scale of 8 rods to 1 inch
Includes main river channel, high water mark, Bourn Bridge, buildings, quantities of land of various owners, with quantity claimed by the Corporation from each
(ink and watercolour on paper)

Fig. 20. Tudor blind-stamping of front board of the early 14th-century Black Domesday, the earliest version of the Custumal now remaining in the town. (C/4/1/1)

C/4   TOWN GOVERNMENT

It should be borne in mind that, both during the medieval period and beyond, much of local government, both in the shires and in corporate towns, was curial in nature, with the courts responsible for much administrative, as well as legal, business. Much information relating to town government will, therefore, be found in Section 2 of this catalogue, JUSTICE AND THE COURTS. For details of the Borough's constitution, *see* the essays by Geoffrey Martin and Frank Grace.

C/4/1   CUSTUMALS   *c.*1320–19c.

Six medieval versions of the Ipswich Custumal (known locally as the 'Little Domesday' to distinguish it from Richard Percyvale's greatly extended 16th-century recension known as the 'Great Domesday') have survived. Of these, three (including the earliest) are now in the British Library, two have remained in unbroken custody in the Ipswich borough archive, and one was re-united with this archive in 1973 after having strayed at least as long ago as the mid-17th century.

Except for the version known as the *Custumale Gippovicense*, which was unavailable when he wrote, the comparative dating of the various medieval texts was carried out in the early 1950s by Professor Geoffrey Martin, on whose works (especially Martin 1954 and Martin 1955 chapter II) the following note is substantially based, by kind permission.

Following receipt of the first charter from King John in 1200, a series of public meetings was held in the churchyard of St Mary le Tower to settle the form of the town government. A detailed account of these meetings, copied from a roll said to have been in the common chest of the town and perhaps still extant in Percyvale's time (Martin 1954, 12–13), is included in all but the earliest version of the Little Domesday. It relates that the last meeting, held on 12 October, ordered the compilation of a roll of the free customs of the borough, to be called the Domesday Roll.

The first Custumal has not survived. Its loss can be pinpointed with total accuracy, for the Portmanmote roll for 54–56 Henry III records on its last membrane the theft of the Domesday and a quantity of court rolls by John le Blake, the former Common Clerk, on 19 September 1272, when he fled the town to escape prosecution for felony (see the introduction to section C/2 of this catalogue). The loss was not made good for twenty years, presumably because from 1284 to 1291 the borough was in the King's hands. Immediately upon the restoration of autonomy by Edward I's charter of 1291, however, the customs were restated by a panel of the best-advised men of the town, and a new Domesday roll was made. This also has failed to survive, but before its loss various copies were made in codex form in the 14th and 15th centuries; and it is in these third- and fourth-hand versions that the text of the customs has survived.

The borough's bitter experience with le Blake may well have suggested the wisdom of having a second copy of the Custumal, and the codex form was presumably considered more convenient for ready reference than the roll. Even the earliest codex began to attract other material, including an account of various tolls levied in the town, a list of knights' fees and tenants of three feudal honours in Suffolk, and an account of the election of the Capital Portmen in 1309. Subsequent recensions contain a variety of interesting fragments.

The earliest extant version of the Custumal is B.L. Add. MS 25,012. (Together with a later version, Add. MS 25,011, it was misguidedly lent by Ipswich Corporation to the eminent historian and Deputy Keeper of the Public Records, Sir Francis Palgrave, for examination, and on his death in 1861 both MSS were sold by his executors. The texts of both versions are printed in Twiss 1873.) Add. MS 25,012 is written in a hand closely resembling, if not identical with, that of the borough court rolls for 1307–09, and may be roughly dated by the inclusion in it of the borough ordinances of 1309. It is the only surviving text whose capitals are not rubricated, its plainness suggesting that it was intended as a working copy. Some of its contents are also unique, for the tenants of two of the three honours (Lancaster and Leicester) and the 1309 election do not feature in any other copy, while additional material incorporated in the next version to be compiled has been copied into subsequent volumes (Martin 1955, 48).

The so-called 'Black Domesday' in the borough archive (C/4/1/1) seems to have originated at about the same time, for both versions have preserved an archaic French spelling, rationalized in later copies (Martin 1954, 10). Its rubrication and other ornament suggest that it was probably intended as the formal record. It seems to have been compiled over a number of years, for to the transcript of the customs were added the text of Edward II's charter of 1317, the borough ordinances of 1320, and other early matter, 'a deliberate and thorough collection of material . . . that was clearly considered to be of historical interest – evidence that the town ought to preserve' (Martin 1955, 51). The two later working copies (the 'White Domesday' in the borough archive (C/4/1/2) and B.L. Egerton MS 2,788), the second formal, ornamented text in Ipswich (the *Custumale Gippovicense,* C/4/1/3), and the 15th-century English version (B.L. Add. MS 25,011) were all derived from the 'Black Domesday'.

The 'White Domesday' and Egerton MS 2,788 are by the same copyist and therefore almost, if not quite, contemporary. The 'White Domesday' was probably in process of compilation before 1338, the year in which Edward III granted his charter of confirmation, for while the copyist transcribed into it the text of Edward II's charter of 1317 (as being presumably the instrument then currently in force), he appended to that charter the final, confirmatory clauses of Edward III's new grant. Egerton MS 2,788 includes a note that 'Iste liber constat Paulo de Roos': de Roos was the borough's Common Clerk from *c.*1336 until his death in 1349 (Martin 1955, 83).

The version (unavailable to Professor Martin when he wrote) known, from the 19th-century inscription by Sir Thomas Phillipps on fol. 1, reproduced on the spine of its 1827 binding, as the *Custumale Gippovicense* (C/4/1/3), represents another formal copy of the Custumal, its rubrication and ornament indeed making it the most elaborate version of all. It appears to be slightly later in date than the White and Egerton Domesdays, for while the charter transcribed is still that of Edward II and lacks the appended clauses of that of Edward III, it contains a list of Bailiffs, all in the same hand, down to 1344. In addition to the Latin text of the Assize of Bread contained in the White (but not in the Black) Domesday, the *Custumale* also includes a contemporary English translation. It had strayed from the borough archive at least as early as 1646, in which year, as recorded by a contemporary inscription on its last folio, it was in the possession of John Maynard of the Middle Temple. It was acquired by Sir Thomas Phillipps (becoming Phillipps MS 3,099) from the library of Sir Gregory Page Turner, bart in 1827, in which year it was rebound, and re-acquired for the borough archive in 1973.

The remaining medieval version of the Custumal (B.L. Add. MS 25,011) is a 15th-century English text. Though previously accorded little respect, as a late version and a translation, it is of real interest as a new edition. The compiler, despite some errors in the numbering of the customs, has marshalled the additional material in an attempt to rationalize the constitutional evidence. He associates some ordinances of 1429 with the account of the original appointment of the Portmen in 1200, and has added to the first list of burgesses admitted up to 1204, a decree of 1351 which attempted to devote the admission fees to particular funds. In this respect, Add. MS 25,011 may be regarded as the forebear of Percyvale's 'Great Domesday' (C/4/1/4), in which the customs occupy only one section out of seven (Martin, 1954, 40).

All the extant versions of the Little Domesday, following their compilation, continued to attract later memoranda on their blank folios, in some cases down to the 16th century.

The 'Great Domesday', compiled by Richard Percyvale, one of the Portmen, was completed, according to its 'prologue' or preface, in September 1520. It stands apart from its medieval predecessors: divided into seven 'books' with the record texts presented with a minimum of connecting commentary, it is as much the first history of the town as the last of its Custumals

(Martin 1956, 87). The prologue explains that the work was undertaken because, though it was necessary for all Bailiffs and burgesses to be acquainted with their ancient grants, liberties, ordinances, laws and constitutions, 'many of the same . . . be wretyn in Frenche', and the town's governors no longer had 'the perfyte understondyng of the Frenche tonge lyke as they have had in old tyme past be cause the said Frenche tong ys not now so comonly usyd in this Realme'. Percyvale therefore translated the French text of the actual borough customs into English (though, strangely, a few additional French documents which he included in his compilation were transcribed in their original language). Material in Latin, a language then still in current use for legal purposes and thus not regarded as posing a problem to the administrators of his day, was similarly merely transcribed. Of particular interest are some ordinances (ff. 85r–86r) for the more efficient performance of the religious services and celebrations of the merchants' (Corpus Christi) gild, which no longer survive in any earlier source.

About the middle of the 16th century a transcript of the 'Great Domesday' was undertaken, though by whom, by what authority, or for what purpose, has not been established. A fragment (twelve detached paper folios) of this transcript, which may perhaps never have been completed, was acquired for the borough archive from a Sussex clergyman in 1920 (C/4/1/5). A more substantial fragment of the same work is still in private ownership and was placed on deposit in the Ipswich Record Office in 1951 as HD 115/1/1. It consists of eighteen paper folios, in poor condition, containing Edward I's 'charter of restitution' of 1291, the account of the compilation of the second Domesday roll in 1290–91, and chapters 55–103 only of the customs (all from Book Two of the 'Great Domesday'); the Assize of Weighing of Bread (from Book Three); and two documents of 1425 and 1513 relating to Horsewade Mill (both from Book Four).

Early in the 19th century the Corporation commissioned a full English translation of the medieval Custumal from William Illingworth, then Deputy Keeper of the [Public] Records. The version from which Illingworth worked was the 'Black Domesday', and his translation, which was placed in the borough archive (C/4/1/6), was completed in 1812.

C/4/1/1   n.d. [c.1320]
'Little Domesday' ('Black Domesday')
— (ff. 1r–5v) Edward II's charter of 30 [sic] May 1317 (Latin)
— (f. 6r) blank
— (ff. 6v–7v) names of the Kings of England after the coming of St Augustine, down to Henry VII (Latin; added in an early 16c. hand)
— (f. 8r) blank
— (f. 8v) names of the Cinque Ports (English, added in an early 16c. hand)
— (ff. 9r–11v) index to the borough customs (French)
— (ff. 12r–59v) the customs, with preamble explaining the background to the compilation of the second Domesday roll in 1290–1291 (French)
— (ff. 60r–62r) rules for common porterage at the quay (French)
— (ff. 62r–68v) customs pertaining to the farm of the town (French)
— (ff. 68v–69r) list of knights' fees of the honours of Lancaster and Leicester in Suffolk (Latin)
— (ff. 69r–70r) list of tenants of the honour of Richmond in Samford Hundred (Latin)
— (ff. 70r–70v) extent of the four leets (wards) of Ipswich (French)
— (f. 71r) precedents from Portmanmote rolls for 39–40 and 54–56 Hen. III (Latin)
— (ff. 71v–76v) ordinances of 1320 (French)
— (ff. 76v–81Ar) account of meetings in St Mary le Tower churchyard, Jun.–Oct. 1200, to settle the government of the town following receipt of John's charter, transcribed from a roll remaining in the Common Chest (Latin)
— (ff. 81Ar–81Bv) inquisition upon election of 'foreign' burgesses, Oct. 1200 (Latin)
— (ff. 81Bv–83r) account of 'foreign' burgesses admitted during John's reign (Latin)
— (f. 83r) note on making of the town's great ditches in 1203 (Latin)
— (ff. 83v–87v) account of 'foreign' burgesses admitted, 18–56 Hen. III (Latin)
— (f. 87v) note on the flight of John le Blake, late Common Clerk, with the roll called 'le Domesday' and other rolls of pleas in 1272 (Latin)

— (f. 88r) ordinance on admission of 'foreign' burgesses, 18 Oct. 1274 (Latin)
— (ff. 88r–91v) account of 'foreign' burgesses admitted in reign of Edward I (Latin)
— (ff. 92–94) blank
(1 vol., 22 cm × 15 cm × 3 cm, 95 vellum fols, mostly in a single 14c. hand, with early 16c. additions, rubricated and with other ornamentation in red and blue; bound in dark brown (the 'black' of its popular title) leathered boards with remains of two metal clasps, the front and back covers blocked with the Tudor royal arms with dragon and greyhound supporters, and with a Tudor rose with angel supporters)

C/4/1/2   n.d. [c.1338]
'Little Domesday' ('White Domesday')
— (f. 1r) order of Corpus Christi procession (English; added in an early 16c. hand)
— (f. 1v) inventory of 'irons' belonging to the gaol (English, early 16c.)
— (ff. 2r–3r) list of rents to be reserved annually by the Town Treasurer (English, early 16c.)
— (f 3v) list of rents of farms in Holbrook, Freston and Tattingstone given by Edmund Daundy (English, post-1515)
— (ff. 4–7) blank
— (ff. 8r–9r) list of burgesses, some marked as 'mort' (Latin, ? early 16c.)
— (ff. 9v–10r) memoranda re payment of the farm of the borough, and of Henry IV's Letters Patent to Archbishop, Prior and Convent of Canterbury and their tenants, granting exemption from market tolls throughout the kingdom, 14 Oct. 1399 (Latin, 15c.)
— (ff. 10r–11r) memoranda re the borough farm, 1285–1436 (Latin, 15c.)
— (f. 11v) blank
— (f. 12) excised
— (f. 13r–14v) forms of oaths of Bailiffs, Chamberlains, Serjeants, Portmen, Twenty-four, and Common Clerk (French and English, 15c. and 16c.)
— (f. 15r) ordinance on admission of 'foreign' burgesses, 1274, and note on the flight of John le Blake, 1272 (Latin, 15c.)
— (f. 15v) blank
— (f. 16r) ordinance for reform of weights and measures, 28 Dec. 1523 (English)
— (f. 16v) blank
— (f. 17r) memorandum re the farm of Ipswich from the 'great roll' of 10 Ric. I (1198–99), 1536 (Latin)
— (ff. 17v–19v) ordinances made 20 Oct. 1429 (Latin, 15c. or early 16c.)
— (ff. 20r–21r) index to the borough customs (French)
— (ff 21v–49r) the customs, with preamble (French)
— (ff 49r–50r) rules for common porterage at the quay (French)
— (ff. 50v–54r) customs pertaining to the farm of the town (French)
— (f. 54v) list of knights' fees of the honours of Lancaster and Leicester in Suffolk (Latin)
— (ff. 55r–55v) list of tenants of the honour of Richmond in Samford Hundred (Latin)
— (ff. 55v–56r) extent of the four leets (wards) of Ipswich (French)
— (ff. 56v–58v) Assize of Bread (Latin)
— (ff. 58v–62r) Edward II's charter of 30 [sic] May 1317 with, appended, final confirmatory clauses of Edward III's charter of 1 Jul. 1338 (Latin)
— (ff. 62r–64r) account of the meetings in St Mary le Tower churchyard, Jun.–Oct. 1200 (Latin)
— (ff. 64v–65v) inquisition upon election of 'foreign' burgesses, Oct. 1200 (Latin)
— (ff. 65v–66r) account of 'foreign' burgesses admitted during John's reign (Latin)
— (f. 66v) ordinances made at court held 8 Sep. 1378 (Latin; added in a ? 15c. hand)
— (f. 67r) view of frankpledge (French, 15c.)
— (f. 67v) note re weights and measures (Latin) and form of oath of Serjeants (French) (15c.)
— (f. 68) excised
— (f. 69r) form of oath of burgess (English, 15c.)
— (f. 69v) memorandum of arbitration by John, Duke of Norfolk, re election of Serjeants-at-Mace of Ipswich, 15 Hen. VI (1436 or 1437) (Latin, 15c.)

— (f. 70r) list of rents etc. granted by the Crown in Ipswich and note on making of the town's great ditches in 1203 (Latin, 15c.)
— (f. 70v) agreement between Prior and Canons of Woodbridge and burgesses of Ipswich, in resolution of dispute *re* weekly market at Woodbridge, 18 Nov. 18 King Henry [*sic*] (Latin; 15c.)
— (f. 71r) blank
— (f. 71v) memorandum that the liberties of Ipswich were allowed by the King's Justices in Michaelmas term 1323 (Latin, 15c.)
— (f. 72r–v) 'lez pagentz': order of the Corpus Christi procession (Latin and English, 15c.)
— (f. 73r) list of Kings of England from Harold to Henry III (Latin, 15c.)
— (f. 73v) list of Bailiffs, Portmen and burgesses (Latin, 15c.)
— (ff. 74r–77v) ordinances made on 5 Mar. 1473 (Latin, 15c.)
— (ff. 78–92) blank
(1 vol., 24.5 cm × 15 cm × 3.4 cm, 93 vellum fols, the main text in a single 14c. hand, with additions in a variety of 15c. and 16c. hands; main text only rubricated and with other ornamentation in red and blue; bound in white leathered boards (hence its popular title) with leather strap and metal clasps)

C/4/1/3   n.d. [? mid 14c.]
'Little Domesday' ('*Custumale Gippovicense*')
— (ff. 2r–6r) Edward II's charter of 30 [*sic*] May 1317 (French translation)
— (ff. 6v–7v) blank
— (ff. 8r–11v) Edward II's charter of 1317 (Latin text)
— (ff. 12r–14r) blank
— (f. 14v) note that following 'privilegia' (f. 15r) were exhibited in the town court ('in domo placitorum ville Gippewici') before the Bailiffs, 1 Oct. 1378, and written 'in registro nostro' for perpetual memory (Latin, late 14c.)
— (f. 15r) Letters Patent of Richard II, 20 Aug. 1378, confirming Edward III's grant of exemption from custom dues to merchants of Bayonne, 4 Feb. 1350 (Latin, late 14c.)
— (f. 15v) blank
— (f. 16r) account of farm paid by Norwich, Bury St Edmunds, Great Yarmouth and Ipswich (Latin)
— (f. 16v) memorandum *re* resolution of dispute between Exchequer clerks at Shrewsbury and the Bailiffs of Ipswich (present to respond to the account of the Sheriff of Norfolk touching the liberties of Ipswich), concerning collation to be provided by the Bailiffs, 5 Edw. [? III, *c.*1331]; and memorandum that the men of Ipswich made no payment of their farm at the Exchequer because it was assigned to Isabella and Philippa, Queens of England, n.d. (Latin)
— (f. 17) blank
— (ff. 18r–v) list of Bailiffs, 1307–1344 (Latin)
— (f. 19) blank
— (ff. 20r–22v) account of meetings in St Mary le Tower churchyard, Jun.–Oct. 1200 (Latin)
— (ff. 23–24) blank
— (ff. 25r–26v) index to the borough customs (French)
— (f. 26v) precedents from Portmanmote rolls for 39–40 and 54–56 Hen. III (Latin)
— (ff. 27r–60v) the customs, with preamble (French)
— (ff. 61r–65v) Assize of Bread (Latin, with English translation)
— (f. 66) blank
— (ff. 67r–72v) customs pertaining to the farm of the town (French)
— (f. 73) blank
(1 vol., 25.5 cm × 17 cm × 2.25 cm, 73 vellum fols, mostly in a single 14c. hand, with a very few late 14c. additions (ff. 14v–15r), rubricated and with other elaborate ornamentation in red and blue; f. 73v inscribed in a 17c. hand 'Liber Johannis Maynard de medio Templo London 2° Julij 1646'; f. 1r inscribed in a 19c. hand 'Custumale Gippovicense. Liber Thoma Phillipps, ex Bibliotheca D. Gregorii Page Turner, Barti. 1827'; bound in brown calf, 1827; formerly Phillipps MS 3099; purchased by the then Ipswich and East Suffolk Record Office from Alan Thomas, esq. in April 1974.)

C/4/1/4   18 Sep. 1520
'Great Domesday' ('Percyvale's Domesday')
Compiled by Richard Percyvale, Portman. For substantial published extracts, *see* HMC 1883,
Appendix, pp. 243–48.
— (ff. 1–5) blank
— (ff. 6r–7r) prologue on the purposes of the compilation (English)
Liber primus
— (ff. 7r–9r) table of contents (English)
— (ff. 9r–10r) King John's charter of 25 May 1200 (Latin)
— (ff. 10r–15r) account of meetings in St Mary le Tower churchyard, Jun.–Oct. 1200, to settle
the government of the town (Latin)
— (ff. 15r–16v) inquisition upon election of 'foreign' burgesses, Oct. 1200 (Latin)
— (ff. 16v–18r) account of 'foreign' burgesses admitted during John's reign (Latin)
— (f. 18r) note on making of the town's great ditches in 1203 (Latin)
— (ff. 18r–23r) account of 'foreign' burgesses admitted 18–56 Hen. III (Latin)
— (f. 23r) note on the flight of John le Blake with 'le Domesday' and other rolls in 1272 (Latin)
— (ff. 23r–v) ordinance on admission of 'foreign' burgesses, 18 Oct. 1274 (Latin)
— (ff. 23v–25v) account of 'foreign' burgesses admitted in reign of Edward I (Latin)
— (f. 25v) memorandum of seizure of the borough into the King's hands in 1284, and of
Edward I's restoration of autonomy by charter of 23 Jun. 1291 (Latin)
— (ff. 26r–v) extent of the four wards of Ipswich (English)
— (f. 27) blank
Liber secundus
— (ff. 28r–29v) Edward I's charter of 23 Jun. 1291 (Latin)
— (ff. 30r–84v) the customs, with preamble explaining the background to the compilation of
the second Domesday roll in 1290–1291 (English and Latin)
— (ff. 85r–86r) ordinances for more efficient performance of religious services and celebrations of the merchants' (Corpus Christi) gild (Latin)
— (ff. 86v–102v) blank)
Liber tercius
— (ff. 103r–104v) rules for common porterage at the quay (English)
— (ff. 105r–110v) customs pertaining to the fee farm of the town (English)
— (ff. 110v–116v) the Assize of Weighing of Bread after the Statute of Winchester (English)
— (ff. 117r–v) the Assize for Brewers (Latin)
— (f. 118) blank
Liber quartus
— (ff. 119r–122r) constitution for the Corpus Christi procession and for the Maundy (Latin)
— (ff. 122v–124r) extracts concerning Ipswich from the 'magno domusday de Scaccario'
(Latin)
— (ff. 124r–v) extracts concerning Ipswich from the 'libro Feodorum de Scaccario in Suffolcia
qui vocatur le Domysday' (Latin)
— (ff. 124v–125v) extracts concerning Ipswich from the 'Magno Rotulo' of 6 Ric. I in Norfolk,
'Magno Rotulo' of 7 Ric. I in Norfolk and dorse of 'Magno Rotulo' of 10 Ric. I in Norfolk and
Suffolk (Latin)
— (ff. 125v–126r) extracts concerning Ipswich from the 'Magno Rotulo' of 14 Edw. I (Latin)
— (ff. 126r–v) agreement between the Prior and canons of Woodbridge and burgesses of
Ipswich, in resolution of dispute *re* weekly market at Woodbridge, 18 Nov. 18 King Henry [*sic*]
(Latin)
— (ff. 126v–127r) acquittance by executors of Lord Robert Tebetoth [Tiptoft] to burgesses of
Ipswich, *re* certain tuns of wine, 1305 (French)
— (f. 127r) memorandum that the liberties of Ipswich were allowed by the King's Justices in
Michaelmas term 1323 (Latin)
— (f. 127v) general pardon by Thomas of Brotherton to burgesses of Ipswich, 20 May 1336
(Latin)
— (ff. 127v–128r) memorandum *re* value of a talent of gold, 1347 (Latin)

— (ff. 128r–130r) deed of exchange of lands in St Mildred's and St Margaret's parishes, between Prior and convent of Holy Trinity [Christchurch] and Bailiffs and commonalty, 5 Dec. 1393 (Latin)

— (ff. 130r–133r) deed of covenant between James Andrewe of Stoke and Bailiffs and commonalty re Horsewade Mill, 25 Sep. 1399 (French)

— (ff. 133v–134r) enrolment of Richard II's inspeximus of Edward III's Letters Patent of 12 Aug. 1342 in confirmation of Edward II's Letters Patent of 19 Jul. 1324 in favour of Harwich, 20 Mar. 1378 (Latin)

— (ff. 134r–140v) Exchequer enrolment of Edward III's inspeximus of 21 Feb. 1338 confirming the liberties of the Bishop of Norwich, 1343 (Latin)

— (ff. 140v–141r) memorandum of Henry IV's Letters Patent to Archbishop, Prior and convent of Canterbury and their tenants, granting exemption from market tolls, 14 Oct. 1399 (Latin)

— (ff. 141r–v) grant by Bailiffs and burgesses to Abbot and convent of Albemarle, of exemption from toll in Belstead, 28 Jun. 1255 (Latin)

— (ff. 142r–v) acquittance by executors of Lord Robert Tybbotoht [Tiptoft] to the men of Ipswich on their recognizance, 19 Apr. 1305 (French)

— (f. 142v) general acquittance by Payne Tybbototh to the burgesses of Ipswich, of all offences, 22 Apr. 1314 (Latin)

— (ff. 143r–v) memorandum of arbitration by John, Duke of Norfolk, re election of Serjeants-at-Mace of Ipswich, 15 Hen. VI (1436 or 1437) (Latin)

— (ff. 143v–144r) table of statutory weights and measures (Latin)

— (f. 144r) extent of the common heath of Ipswich (Latin)

— (ff. 144r–145r) extract from will of Richard Felawe re School House and Hospital, 1482 (English)

— (ff. 145r–162r) Exchequer enrolment of Henry VII's inspeximus confirming the liberties of the Bishop of Ely and convent of St Etheldreda, 16 Nov. 1485 (Latin and Anglo-Saxon)

— (ff. 162r–164v) Exchequer record re liberty of Ipswich in the matter of an arrest in Whitton church, 1491 (Latin)

— (ff. 164v–166r) lease from the Prior and convent of Ely to Bailiffs and commonalty, of Stoke Mill and adjacent pastures, 20 Jun. 1491 (Latin)

— (ff. 166r–167r) memorandum of exhibition of borough charter to Henry VII in case involving goods alleged to be forfeit to the town, 1492 (Latin)

— (ff. 167r–v) account of seizure of an outlaw's goods to the town's use, 25 Sep. 1508 (Latin)

— (ff. 167r–168v) precedents for exemption of burgesses of Ipswich from tolls in London, from records in London's Guildhall, 1318 and 1512 (Latin)

— (ff. 168v–171r) indenture of agreement between Prior and convent of Holy Trinity, Ipswich, Bailiffs and commonalty, and executors of Thomas Draile, for performance of Draile's bequest for easing Ipswich residents of tolls, 27 Oct. 1509 (English)

— (ff. 171r–172r) grant by Bailiffs and commonalty to James Andrewe, of 20s annual rent for life in lieu of rent for Horsewade Mill, 23 Apr. 1425 (Latin)

— (ff. 172r–v) lease from Bailiffs and commonalty to Robert Goodwyn, of Horsewade Mill, 10 Sep. 1513 (English)

— (ff. 173r–v) extract from will of Edmund Daundy, Portman, re bequest of lands in Holbrook, 2 May 1515 (English)

— (ff. 173v–175v) articles for regulation of Edmund Daundy's chantry in St Lawrence's church, 30 Nov. 1514 (Latin)

— (ff. 175v–176v) lease from Bailiffs and commonalty to John Ussherwoode of Rushmere, yeoman, of common heath, 10 Jul. 1519 (English)

— (ff. 176r–177v) grant by Andrew Sulyard, esq. to Bailiffs and commonalty, following arbitration, of meadow adjoining Portman's Meadow in Stoke hamlet, 7 Oct. 1521 (Latin)

— (f. 178r) extract from will of Richard Oke of Ipswich, porter, devising remainder in house in Brook Street to the use of the poor of Ipswich, 26 May 1522 (English)

— (ff. 178v–179r) lease from Thomas Russhe of Ipswich, esq. to Thomas Pacard, rector of St Stephen's, of parsonage garden, 6 May 1518 (Latin, in a different hand)

— (ff. 179r–180r) feoffment by Henry Tooley of Ipswich, merchant, to his executors, of manor of Ulveston Hall and lands in Debenham, Pettaugh, Aspall, Mickfield and Stonham, 17 Aug. 1552 (Latin, in a later hand)

— (f. 183r) extract from will of Thomas Cady of Stoke, yeoman, *re* bequest of almshouses, 4 Oct. 1531 (English, in a later hand)

— (f. 183v) memorandum of gift of Sir Thomas White, citizen and alderman of London, to Ipswich and other towns, for maintenance of poor clothiers, n.d. (English, in a later hand)

— (f. 184r) memoranda of writ of *quo titulo* awarded in Exchequer *v.* Bailiffs and commonalty *re* the New Mills, 1587, and of seizure of goods of William Randall on his conviction of felony for conjuration and invocation, 1579 (English, in a later hand)

— (ff. 184v–186r) agreement for repair of Bourne Bridge, 1 Sep. 1579 (English, in a later hand)

— (ff. 186v–187r) lease from Bailiffs and commonalty to John Manser and William Manser, butchers, John Smyth, tailor and William Ropkyn, barker, all of Ipswich, of the flesh stalls and customs on hides, etc., 20 Nov. 1486 (English, in a later hand)

— (ff. 187v–188r) grant by Rose Bloyze, widow, to Bailiffs and commonalty, of £20 for loans to poor young tradesmen, 13 Sep. 1579 (English, in a later hand)

— (f. 188v) blank

— (f. 189r) extract from will of Thomas Goodynge of Freston, gent., bequeathing £60 for use of the poor of Ipswich, 10 Apr. 1595 (English, in a later hand)

— (ff. 189r–v) extract from will of Katherine Baxter of Ipswich, widow, bequeathing 20 marks for use of the poor of Ipswich and £30 towards the stock for maintenance of the poor in Christ's Hospital, 8 Dec. 1595 (English, in a later hand)

— (ff. 189v–192r) agreement between Bailiffs and commonalties of Ipswich and Colchester *re* distribution of John Hunwick's bequest, 25 Aug. 1595 (English, in a later hand)

— (ff. 192v–193v) will of William Smarte of Ipswich, 8 Jan. 1599 (English, in a later hand)

— (ff. 193v–196v) 1,000 year lease from William Smarte to Thomas Walton, esq., Ralph Scryvener, gent. and Leonard Cason, gent., all of Ipswich, of salt marshes in Falkenham and Kirton, in trust for Bailiffs and commonalty, to the uses of Smarte's will, 15 Sep. 1599, with assignment of lease to Portmen and others, 19 Sep. 1599 (English, in a later hand)

— (ff. 197–199r) blank

— (ff. 199v–201r) forms of oaths of borough officers (English, in a later hand)

Liber quintus

— (ff. 201v–207r) forms of oaths of borough officers (English)

— (ff. 207r–211r) articles to be observed and proclaimed by Bailiffs, mostly for regulation of various trades (English)

— (ff. 211v–212v) inquisition into the liberties of Ipswich by water, 10 Nov. 1379 (Latin)

— (ff. 212v–220r) perambulation of the liberties of Ipswich by land (English), with confirmation by exemplification under the Great Seal, 7 Feb. 1522 (Latin and English) following dispute between the borough and Philip Bernard of Akenham, escheator for Suffolk and Norfolk, in 11 Hen. VIII (1519 or 1520)

— (ff. 220v–222v) blank

Liber sextus

— (ff. 223r–235v) table of royal taxes paid by Suffolk towns, arranged by hundreds (Latin)

— (ff. 235v–236v) blazons of arms of European monarchs (English)

— (ff. 237r–237v) list of knights' fees of the honours of Lancaster and Leicester in Suffolk (Latin)

— (ff. 237v–239v) verses on the Kings of England from William I to Henry VI [? by John Lydgate] (English)

— (ff. 240r–242v) blank

Liber septimus

— (ff. 243r–256r) Henry VIII's 'charter' (Letters Patent) of *inspeximus*, 12 Mar. 1512 (Latin)

— (ff. 256r–260r) Henry VIII's Letters Patent clarifying the extent of Ipswich's Admiralty jurisdiction, 3 Mar. 1519 (Latin)

— (ff. 260r–261v) confirmation by Thomas, Earl of Surrey, Admiral of England, requiring his officers to acknowledge Ipswich's Admiralty jurisdiction, 17 Feb. 1520 (English)

— (ff. 262–270) blank

420

(1 vol., 41 cm × 29 cm × 10 cm, 270 vellum fols, written throughout (with the exception of some later 16c. insertions at the end of *Liber quartus* between ff. 178v and 201r) in a uniform, bold and clearly legible hand, partly rubricated, bound in brown tooled leather boards)

C/4/1/5   n.d. [? mid 16c.]
Fragment of a transcript of the 'Great Domesday'
Includes:
— index (English) to borough customs (*see* 'Great Domesday', ff. 31r–34v)
— memorandum of exhibition of borough charter to Henry VII in a case involving goods alleged to be forfeit to the town, 1492 (ff. 166r–167v)
— account of proof of right of Ipswich in the matter of an arrest in Whitton church, 1491 (ff. 162r–164v)
— lease from Prior and convent of Ely to Bailiffs and commonalty of Ipswich, of Stoke Mill and adjacent pastures, 20 Jun. 1491 (ff. 164v–166r)
Assize of Brewers (ff. 117r–v)
— Henry VIII's Letters Patent of Inspeximus, 12 Mar. 1512 (ff. 243r–256r)
— Henry VIII's Letters Patent clarifying extent of Admiralty jurisdiction, 3 Mar. 1519 (ff. 256r–260r)
— confirmation by Thomas, Earl of Surrey, of Ipswich's Admiralty jurisdiction (ff. 260r–261v)
(12 detached, unnumbered paper fols, each 35.5 cm × 24 cm after conservation; mostly Latin, with English headings. For another fragment of the same transcript, in private ownership, *see* Ipswich Record Office, HD115/1/1.)

C/4/1/6   1812
'Translation of the Domesday of Ipswich containing the antient Laws Usages and Constitutions of that Borough . . . by W[illiam] Illingworth F.S.A., Deputy Keeper of His Majesty's Records in the Tower'
The order of the entries, and marginal references to the foliation of the original, indicate that this MS is a translation of the whole of the 'Black' Domesday (C/4/1/1), omitting only the later insertions on ff. 6v–8v of that volume. The original order is followed, with the single exception that Edward II's 1317 charter (ff. 1r–5v in the Black Domesday) is inserted on ff. 130–142, between the precedents from the Portmanmote rolls of Henry III and the ordinances of 1320.
(1 vol., 24.8 cm × 20 cm × 4.5 cm, 202 paper fols each written on the *recto* only, 43 fols blank; with, as frontispiece, a fine ink and wash drawing by S. Cossart, of the royal arms and Tudor rose blocking on the covers of the Black Domesday)

C/4/1/7   n.d. [19c.]
Transcript of the Prologue, *Liber primus* and *Liber secundus* of Percyvale's 'Great Domesday' (C/4/1/4)
(1 vol., 32 cm × 20.5 cm × 1.8 cm, 111 unnumbered fols, 27 fols blank; bound in paper-covered boards)

C/4/2   OTHER COMPILATIONS OF PRECEDENTS   1653–19c.
(*see also* C/1/7, FORESHORE RIGHTS)

C/4/2/1   1653
Book of precedents
Includes:
— table of contents to King Charles I's Letters Patent, 11 Mar. 1635
— copy of King Edward IV's Letters Patent of Inspeximus to Holy Trinity Priory, Ipswich, 1 Feb. 1465, from a certified copy taken from the Patent Roll in 1607
— extracts from court rolls of manor of Wix Ufford, n.d., apparently relating to leet jurisdiction
— extract of proceedings in Court of Common Pleas, the Bailiffs *v.* George Crosby *alias*

Gawdey, tailor, a 'foreigner', for selling wares within the liberty without licence, Michaelmas term 1644
— copy of King Charles I's Letters Patent of Inspeximus to the borough, 11 Mar. 1635
— copy legal opinion on rights of 'foreigners' trading in the borough, arising out of case of Bailiffs *v.* Crosby alias Gawdey, 1644
— extract of proceedings ? in Court of Common Bench, Crosby *alias* Gawdey *v.* the Chamberlains of Ipswich, for trespass, Easter term 1653
— extract of proceedings ? in Court of Common Bench, Thomas Partridge *v.* Gilbert Lyndfeild [Chamberlain], *re* distraint of goods, Michaelmas term 1653
— petition of Bailiffs, burgesses and commonalty to Barons of the Exchequer *re* 'foreign' butchers, Michaelmas term 1653
(1 vol., 48 fols; front cover inscribed 'The Charter of the Towne of Ipswich 1653')

C/4/2/2   1654
'The Annalls of Ipsw^che. The Lawes Customes and Govern^mt of the same Collected out of the Records Books and writings of that Towne by Nath^ll Bacon serving as Recorder and Town Clark in that Towne Ann. Dom. 1654'
MS extracts from the medieval rolls and later court books, 'of remarkable accuracy, and . . . as useful a guide to these materials as are many modern editions of borough records to the documents on which they are based' (Martin 1955, 7), and forming in effect a history of the borough; compiled by Nathaniel Bacon (1593–1660, grandson of Lord Keeper Bacon; Recorder of Ipswich 1642, Town Clerk and Clerk of the Peace 1651, Claviger 1653 and MP 1654, all of which offices he held until his death). His preface ('To the Reader') stated that 'my ayme is principally to recollect those auncient memorialls remaining in scattered writings and records whereof noe recollection hath been formerly made and therby lay buried up as it were in a heape of rubbish and to adjoine therto all the later orders and ordinances and acts concerning the governm^t and order of the people or Town lands as things of greatest observacion for the future managem^t of affaires; and these onely in a summary way, referring the reader to those Court bookes concerning the literall composure of the same'. For the published text, *see* Richardson 1884.
(1 vol., 39.5 cm × 26 cm × 7.5 cm, paper, 866 numbered pp., 45 unnumbered pp. (appendices and index) and 59 blank unnumbered pp., bound in brown leathered boards, clasps missing)

C/4/2/3   n.d. [*c.* mid 18c.]
Transcript of preface to Nathaniel Bacon's 'Annalls'
(2 fols; in the hand of Thomas Martin of Palgrave (1697–1771), attorney and antiquary)

C/4/2/4   [9 May 1562] 17c.
Transcript of Letters Patent (Inspeximus) of Queen Elizabeth I to the city of London
Confirming charters and Letters Patent of her predecessors back to William I
(incomplete; 126 fols, fol. 1 headed 'Prima pars: a folio primo usque fol. cxxviij')

C/4/2/5   n.d. [early 19c.]
'Extracts from Charters and Records of the Corporation of Ipswich respecting the Trade and Merchandize formerly carried on in the Town, the Usages and Customs in respect thereof and of the Markets and Fairs held within the same', compiled by William Batley [Town Clerk]
Includes:
— a number of original payment vouchers, bills etc. and press-cuttings, 1575–1815, pasted in
(1 vol., 159 pp., some wrongly paginated and some unpaginated, 35 pp. blank; bound in half-leathered boards)

C/4/2/6   (5 Oct. 1478), early 19c.
Transcript of heading to General [Great] Court Roll

C/4/3   ASSEMBLY   1563–1835

The Assembly first appears in the records in the 16th century, as a check on the General or Great Court of all the freemen, which had separated from the Portmanmote in the 15th century to become the town's supreme authority in non-judicial matters. Presided over by the Bailiffs, the Assembly was composed of the twelve Portmen and Twenty-four Common Councilmen. It became in course of time a self-perpetuating body, with each of its two constituent parts filling up vacancies in its own ranks by co-option.

Constitutionally it was merely a deliberative body, a standing advisory council both to the Bailiffs and to the Great Court, with no authority to act independently on behalf of the Corporation; its resolutions had the status of recommendations to the Great Court as the ultimate authority, though those recommendations took precedence on the agenda of that body. In reality, however, the Assembly was a committee with wide powers – in the 17th century, for instance, it was active in taking measures to combat plague and in instituting legal proceedings in defence of the town's privileges – and in practice it frequently assumed and exercised the powers of a governing body.

The Assembly also served, in effect, as a panel, from whose members alone the freemen assembled in the Great Court annually elected the Bailiffs, Coroners and other principal officers on whom the government of the town in reality depended. In addition, it functioned as an audit committee for the borough finances.

C/4/3/1   ASSEMBLY BOOKS   1563–1835

These contain the formal record of proceedings in the Assembly. The earlier volumes have the characteristics of rough minutes; the record becomes more formal and more neatly kept from the later 17th century onwards.

The most usual types of business recorded are the leasing of Corporation lands and buildings; repairs to town property; appointments of officers such as the Headmaster and Usher of the Grammar School and the Wardens and Receivers of the various Corporation charities; and the admission of scholars to the Grammar School on Smart's and Tyler's Foundations.

The Assembly Books also contain the minutes of meetings of the majority of the Twenty-four Common Councilmen for filling vacancies in their own number; and of meetings of the Bailiffs and the majority of the Portmen for awarding Cambridge University exhibitions under the terms of Martin's Charity.

Except for the Latin headings to the sessions, the record is in English throughout.

C/4/3/1/1   Dec. 1563–Sep. 1577
In irregular order of entry:
— (ff. 1–62) 4 Dec. 1563–5 Jan. 1570
— (f. 62A) 13 Dec. 1568
— (ff. 63–71) 21 Feb. 1570–7 Aug. 1572
— (ff. 72–73) 8 Jan.–3 May 1571
— (ff. 74–75) 4, 9 Dec. 1572
— (ff. 76–80) 10 Apr. 1571–29 Sep. 1572
— (ff. 81–89v) 29 Sep. 1569–27 Sep. 1570
— (ff. 90–111v) 30 Sep. 1572–27 Sep. 1574
— (ff. 112–151v) ? Sep. 1574–17 Sep. 1577
(1 vol., 151 fols; marked 'No. 1')

C/4/3/1/2   Dec. 1577–Apr. 1589
(1 vol., 122 fols; marked 'No. 2')

C/4/3/1/3   May 1589–May 1608
In irregular order of entry:

— (ff. 1–228v) 14 Jul. 1589–9 May 1608
— (ff. 229, 229v) 7 Oct. 1602: apparently a draft of proceedings entered on ff. 127–128
— (f. 230) 29 Mar. 1597
— (f. 231) 29 May 1589
— (f. 231v) 27 May 1589
(1 vol., 231 fols; front cover marked '3')

C/4/3/1/4   Oct. 1608–May 1619
(1 vol., 250 fols; marked 'No. 4')

C/4/3/1/5   Jan. 1620–Jan. 1644
Includes:
— (f. 2) form of oath of Wardens of [Tooley's] Foundation, 29 Sep. 162[? 0]
(1 vol., 176 fols; front cover marked '5')

C/4/3/1/6   Jan. 1644–Aug. 1680
Includes:
— (p. 561) depositions *re* purchase of a parcel of iron by John Woodward of Bramford from Mr Acton, 18 Jan. 1649
— (p. 562) minutes of meeting *re* allocation of places in almshouses, 16 Jul. 1645, and of meeting *re* billeting of troops, 6 Mar. 1648
(1 vol., 563 pp; front cover marked '6')

C/4/3/1/7   Sep. 1680–Mar. 1724
Includes:
— (p. 287) names of Portmen and Common Councilmen sworn in, 24 Jul. 1684
(1 vol., 290 pp; front cover marked '7')

C/4/3/1/8   Sep. 1724–Sep. 1831
Includes:
— (at front) names of Portmen and Common Councilmen elected, with name of predecessor of each, 1763–1820
— (tipped in, following proceedings, 24 Feb. 1803) letter from Collector and Comptroller of Customs, Ipswich, to Bailiffs, as to whether Corporation is willing to build and let a new custom house, 29 Apr. 1803
— (loose, following proceedings, 26 Aug. 1831) proceedings of meeting of Bailiffs, senior Portman and Town Clerk, *re* nomination to vacant rectory of Gedding, 22 Sep. 1831
(1 vol., 217 unnumbered fols)

C/4/3/1/9   Nov. 1831–Sep. 1835
Includes:
— (at front) names of Portmen and Common Councilmen elected, with name of predecessor of each, 1791–1833
(1 vol.; only the first 20 fols used)

C/4/3/2   ASSEMBLY MINUTE BOOKS   **1834–1835**

The draft minutes from which the formal record in the Assembly Book was compiled.

C/4/3/2/1   Dec. 1834–Sep. 1835
(1 vol.; only the first 5 fols used)

C/4/3/3   DRAFT MINUTES   **Jan.–Oct. 1833**

C/4/3/3/1   17 Jan.–6 Jun. 1833
(2 fols)

C/4/3/3/2   15 Oct. 1833
(2 fols)

C/4/3/4 RESOLUTIONS   **1755**

C/4/3/4/1   18 Sep. 1755
Nominating and electing Samuel Tuffnell of Waltham (Essex), esq. and John Jolliffe Tuffnell,
esq., MP for Beverley (Yorkshire), Portmen in the places of 2 deceased Portmen; with signed
protest by James Wilder against election of non-residents, and also on the grounds that J. J.
Tuffnell's election increases the number of Portmen to more than that permitted by the charters
Original signatures of 7 Portmen

C/4/3/5 MISCELLANEA   **1793–1834**

C/4/3/5/1   27 Feb. 1793
Resolution to the Bailiffs
From meeting called at instance of William Causton of PE to view alleged damage caused to his
gardens by raising of water level of river for working of Frederick Penning's mill
(1 fol.)

C/4/3/5/2   Jan. 1834
Broadsheet
Resolution of special Assembly of Norwich city Corporation, protesting against findings of
Municipal Corporation Commissioners; with annexed letter proposing a meeting of deputa-
tions from other municipal corporations 'to oppose any and every measure of aggression and
spoliation that may be attempted against them', 9 Jan. 1834; sent by post to J. E. Sparrowe, esq.,
Ipswich, 10 Jan.
(printed; 2 fols)

C/4/4 THE FRANCHISE   1653–1826

The freemen of the unreformed borough were alone eligible for all the Corporation offices
except those of Recorder and (honorary) High Steward. They alone made up the Great Court
which elected the borough's senior officers, sanctioned all corporate acts and regulations, and
formed in post-medieval times the borough's supreme authority in non-judicial matters. Until
the 1832 Reform Act freemen alone enjoyed the vote in Parliamentary elections.

The personal privileges enjoyed by freemen included exemption from payment both of the
town dues and of customary tolls throughout the kingdom; exemption from jury service outside
the borough; an exclusive right to land their goods free of toll at the Common Quay; and (certainly in medieval times) a monopoly of trade in the town.

The freedom, conferred from the 15th century onwards by the Great Court, could be acquired
by patrimony, servitude (apprenticeship), purchase or gift. All the sons of a freeman, if born
after their father's admission, were entitled to the franchise, even if born outside the liberties.
Apprentices of freemen were likewise admitted after seven years' service within or outside the
town. From medieval times 'foreigners' could become freemen on payment of the appropriate
fees ('foreign fines'), and honorary freedom by gift was normally conferred upon the High
Steward, Recorder, and Members of Parliament for the borough.

C/4/4/1   FREEMEN'S STAMP BOOKS   1764–1807

These contain the names of the freemen with the dates of their election, on pages embossed with stamps for payment of duty on each admission.

C/4/4/1/1   1764–1773
(1 vol.)

C/4/4/1/2   1773–1807
(1 vol.)

C/4/4/2   FREEMEN'S CERTIFICATES OF ADMISSION   1719–1826

Each document gives the name of the freeman with the date of his election and/or swearing. Most specify election by right of patrimony, servitude or presentment; for those admitted by patrimony or servitude the name of the father or master is usually given. Until the mid-18th century the names of sons and apprentices of freemen admitted are also frequently given, and the certificates show that in the same period many of the freemen were sworn in the Petty rather than the Great Court. All the certificates were stamped for payment of duty. Until 1764 they are on parchment; from 1784 on paper. Those for the period 1719–1784 were found filed on laces.

C/4/4/2/1   Sep. 1719–Aug. 1740
(451 docs, filed on a lace)

C/4/4/2/2   Sep. 1740–Sep. 1746
(141 docs, filed on a lace)

C/4/4/2/3   Jun.–Sep. 1755
(84 docs, filed on a lace)

C/4/4/2/4   Sep. 1755–Jun. 1764
(103 docs, filed on a lace)

C/4/4/2/5   3 Apr. 1784
(35 docs, filed on a lace)

C/4/4/2/6   Mar.–Sep. 1811
(6 docs)

C/4/4/2/7   Sep.–Oct. 1812
(40 docs)

C/4/4/2/8   8–29 Sep. 1813
(10 docs)

C/4/4/2/9   Mar.–Sep. 1814
(9 docs)

C/4/4/2/10   Sep.–Nov. 1815
(14 docs)

C/4/4/2/11   24 Apr. 1816
(2 docs)

C/4/4/2/12   8–29 Sep. 1821
(16 docs)

C/4/4/2/13   8–29 Sep. 1822
(33 docs)

C/4/4/2/14   8 Sep. 1823
(41 docs)

C/4/4/2/15   7–29 Sep. 1825
(67 docs)

C/4/4/2/16   10–17 Jun. 1826
(50 docs)

C/4/4/3   FREEMEN'S ADMISSION LISTS   **1722–1822**

C/4/4/3/1   1722–1822
Alphabetical list of freemen admitted
Apparently abstracted from the Great Court Books. Distinguishes admissions by birth, apprenticeship and purchase; names of fathers and masters are given, together with dates of admission and of taking freeman's oath
(1 vol.; signatures of John Spooner, B.B. Brame and Stephen A. Notcutt inside front cover)

C/4/4/4   WRITS OF MANDAMUS   **1820**

Issued by the Court of King's Bench, requiring the Bailiffs, burgesses and commonalty to admit as freemen persons who are so qualified by servitude

C/4/4/4/1   3 Jun. 1820
For admission of Robert Keeble Balam, painter and glazier

C/4/4/4/2   21 Jun. 1820
For admission of Crispin Snelling, cordwainer

C/4/4/5   LISTS OF 'FOREIGN' TRADESMEN   **1653–1666 and n.d.**

Until the 18th century, all 'foreigners' carrying on trade in the town were required to purchase their freedom by the payment of a fine, which varied in its amount according to the station and circumstances of the trader. The lists were apparently drawn up by assessors appointed by a 'committee of foreigners', which made an annual report. The last committee for this purpose was appointed in 1737 (*see Municipal Corporations Report* 1835, 2305). Many of the names in the lists have sums of money noted against them, and many names have been struck through.

C/4/4/5/1   1653
North Ward
(1 doc.)

C/4/4/5/2   1656
North and East Wards
(2 docs)

C/4/4/5/3   1657
North, East and West Wards
(3 docs)

C/4/4/5/4   1666
Ward unidentified
(1 doc.)

C/4/4/5/5   n.d. [later 17c.]
North Ward
(4 docs)

C/4/4/5/6   n.d. [later 17c.]
South Ward
(1 doc.)

C/4/4/5/7   n.d. [later 17c.]
East Ward
(7 docs)

C/4/4/5/8   n.d. [later 17c.]
West Ward
(4 docs)

C/4/4/5/9   n.d. [later 17c.]
Wards unidentified
(6 docs)

C/4/4/6   FOREIGN FINES   **1668–1733**

C/4/4/6/1   1668–1733
Register of Foreign Fines
Annual assessments of the fines levied by the Corporation on 'foreigners' for their 'severall
tradings, traffekings and openinges of their shopps' in the town
Names and occupations of traders, arranged by wards, with amount of fine payable. Assessments, 1688–1723, include prohibition against 'foreigners' taking apprentices except town-born
children without consent of Bailiffs
Includes, at end:
— list of traders to whom Bailiffs and Treasurer have agreed to let butchers' shops, with rents
payable, 1697
(1 vol.)

C/4/4/7   POLL BOOKS (MUNICIPAL ELECTIONS)   **1821–1826**

The major Corporation offices were subject to annual election by the whole body of freemen
who constituted the Great Court, which during the 18th century had split irretrievably into the
'Blue' and 'Yellow' factions. The volumes listed here are the original MS poll books. They
record the names, occupations and towns of residence of the freemen (many were non-resident
in Ipswich or even Suffolk), with the candidates for whom their votes were cast.
(For poll books in Parliamentary elections, *see* C/1/4/1)

C/4/4/7/1   8 Sep. 1821
Poll for election of High Steward, Bailiffs and Town Clerk: 'Blue' faction book
Candidates:
— for High Steward: Sir Robert Harland, bart (elected) and the Duke of Wellington
— for Bailiffs: Sir William Middleton, bart. and Frederick Francis Seekamp (elected); William
Batley and John Eddowes Sparrow
— for Town Clerk: S. A. Notcutt (elected) and Simon Jackaman
(1 vol.)

C/4/4/7/2   8 Sep. 1821
Poll for election of High Steward, Bailiffs and Town Clerk: 'Orange' [*sic*] faction book
Candidates as above
(1 vol.)

C/4/4/7/3   29 Sep. 1821
Poll for election to unspecified offices: 'Blue' faction book
Candidates identified only by initial letters of surnames
(1 vol.)

C/4/4/7/4   29 Sep. 1821
Poll for election to unspecified offices: 'Yellow' faction book
Candidates identified only by initial letters of surnames
(1 vol.)

C/4/4/7/5   8 Sep. 1823
Poll for election of Bailiffs and Town Clerk: 'Blue' faction book
Candidates:
— for Bailiffs: William Batley and John Aldrich (elected); William Pearson and Richard
Crawley
— for Town Clerk: Simon Jackaman (elected) and S.A. Notcutt
(1 vol.)

C/4/4/7/6   8 Sep. 1823
Poll for election of Bailiffs and Town Clerk: 'Orange' [sic] faction book
Candidates as above
(1 vol.)

C/4/4/7/7   8 Sep. 1825
Poll for election of Bailiffs and Town Clerk: 'Blue' faction book
Candidates:
— for Bailiffs: Frederick Francis Seekamp and Charles Chambers Hammond (elected);
Edward Bacon and John C. Cobbold
— for Town Clerk: S.A. Notcutt (elected) and Simon Jackaman
(1 vol.)

C/4/4/7/8   8 Sep. 1825
Poll for election of Bailiffs and Town Clerk: 'Orange' [sic] faction book
Candidates as above
(1 vol.)

C/4/4/7/9   8 Sep. 1826
Poll for election of Bailiffs and Town Clerk: [votes of both factions]
Candidates:
— for Bailiffs: John Chevallier Cobbold and William Lane (elected); William Hammond and
William Batley
— for Town Clerk: Charles Gross (elected), Stephen Abbott Notcutt and Simon Jackaman
(1 vol.)

C/4/4/7/10   n. d. [19c.]
Poll for election to unspecified offices [apparently recording votes of both factions]
Candidates identified only by initial letters of surnames
(1 vol.)

C/4/4/8   MISCELLANEA   mid-17c.–1811

C/4/4/8/1   n.d. [mid-17c.]
Petition of John Jellians to the Bailiffs
Having a speech impediment he requests time to speak to them, 'the reson is that I keepe open
shop winders in this toune, I am free by an ordinance of the Lord Protector and his Councell and
I am a maimed soulder and have receved severall wounds in the states sarves'

C/4/4/8/2   22 Dec. 1664
Petition of William Willoby to the Bailiffs, Justices and 'the reste of the Ceasers of farrin fines'
For reduction of fine imposed on him 'laste sitting'

C/4/4/8/3   n.d. [later 17c.]
Statement re irregular trading activities of Goodman Weilby, a 'foreign' glover

C/4/4/8/4   24 Mar. 1731
Engrossment of order or by-law of Great Court, 19 Feb. 1730
Prohibiting 'foreigners' from keeping shops within the liberties without licence; sealed by Lord
Chancellor and Lord Chief Justice of Common Pleas, in accordance with Act of 19 Hen. VII

C/4/4/8/5   4 Jan. 1763
Account of fees paid by Lord Orwell on being sworn a Freeman
(1 doc.)

C/4/4/8/6   8 Aug. 1811
Certificate under Common Seal
Bailiffs certify acceptance of surrender of franchise by Henry Seekamp, William Batley,
Robert Dewey, Benjamin Parkhurst, William Sharpe, Thomas Stone, Nathaniel Baker, Ezekiel
Deacon, John Prentice, Joseph Jobson, Charles Jobson, Edward Caston and William White-
head, previously agreed by order of Great Court

C/4/5   QUALIFICATION FOR OFFICE   1662

C/4/5/1   31 Dec. 1662
Instrument under seals of William Devereux, Henry Felton, Robert Broke, B. Cutler and John
Sicklemore, Commissioners appointed under 1661 Corporation Act
Confirming as Portman Sir Manuell Sorrell on his taking the oath renouncing the Solemn
League and Covenant; removing other Portmen and members of the Twenty-four for refusal;
and appointing others in their places
Annexed:
— form of oath with subscribers' signatures
(2 docs)

C/4/6   REGULATION OF TRADE   1594

C/4/6/1   27 Aug. 1594
Grant of constitution to the Drapers', Tailors' and Hosiers' Company of Ipswich
Made by order of Great Court dated 19 Jul. 1594, on petition of members of the respective
trades; preamble states that the Company is established because 'foreigners' of various trades
have established themselves in the town, whereby burgesses have been driven out and scot and
lot cannot easily be collected
(Common Seal missing from purple and yellow silk cords; endorsed in a 17c. hand: 'A Charter
from the Greate Court to the Merchant Taylors &c.')

C/4/7   TOWN OFFICERS   *c.* 1333–1832

C/4/7/1 CLAVIGERS   *c.* 1333–1832

The Clavigers' duties, as defined in their oath of office, consisted in ensuring the safe custody
of the charters and other muniments in the Treasury, together with the Common Seal. They
were to prevent the sealing of any documents save in the presence of the Bailiffs by order of
the Great Court. They also had charge of the debtors' bonds of the Lending Cash Charity.
Three guardians of the Common Seal had been appointed in 1200, but on that occasion they
were the Bailiffs and one of the Coroners. The Clavigers are first mentioned, along with the

Chamberlains, in the reforming ordinances of 1320; both offices were apparently intended as part of the same plan for a continuous check on the opportunities of the Bailiffs to misappropriate corporate funds and property (Martin 1955, 72).

C/4/7/1/1   n.d. [c. 1333]
Inventory of the borough court rolls
Listing the rolls 1308–1333 and describing their distribution between 2 chests: the Portmanmote/ Great Court Rolls, Recognizance and Testament Rolls and Abatement Rolls in 'John Preston's chest', the Petty Plea Rolls in 'the other' chest. The separation of the Petty Plea Rolls, presumably considered as of less permanent value, probably explains the loss of all of them for the reign of Edward II. For a full commentary on this document, see Martin 1954, 29–31, 43–44.
(Latin; 1 membrane, badly faded, parts legible only under ultra-violet light)

C/4/7/1/2   1696
Inventory of the borough records
Compiled by Henry Hill, Samuel Rudkin and John Copeman, Clavigers, this document has been described (Martin 1955, 9) as 'the first modern survey of the records'. Though it omits any reference to the medieval court rolls (presumably no longer considered of value for administrative purposes), it is of particular interest as containing the latest evidence for the survival of King John's original charter of 1200, still in official custody in a black box in the Treasury Chamber
(1 vol.)

C/4/7/1/3   n.d. [post 1778]
'Table of references to the Writeings in the Treasury, Ipswich'
Inventory of borough archives, with details of numbered drawers, cupboards and chests in which stored
(1 vol.)

C/4/7/1/4   n.d. [post 1778]
'Table of references to the Writings in the Treasury'
(1 vol.)

C/4/7/1/5   Oct. 1754–Jan. 1756
Clavigers' Memorandum Book
Includes:
— form of Clavigers' oath
— court orders relating to Clavigers, Oct. 1754–Jan. 1756
— notes of leases, letters of attorney, etc. sealed, Jun.–Nov. 1755
(1 vol.)

C/4/7/1/6   Jun. 1755–Oct. 1757
Audited account
Thomas Pulford, Jonathan Mallen and William Truelove jun., Clavigers
For fines paid by newly-sworn freemen
(1 vol.)

C/4/7/1/7   13 Oct. 1832
Receipt given by Sir Francis Palgrave to the Corporation for loan of 3 vols from the borough archive
2 of the 3 were versions of the 'Little Domesday', which were sold by Palgrave's executors and acquired by the British Museum: see the introductory note to CUSTUMALS, C/4/1 above.

C/4/7/2   OTHER OFFICERS   1572–1794

C/4/7/2/1   26 Sep. 1572
Letter of attorney

From Bailiffs, burgesses and commonalty to William Whetcrofte, Ralph Scryvener and John Hawys, gents, Christopher Crane, Thomas Blosse, Thomas Bennett, Augustine Parker and William Cutler, to appear in courts before judges, justices and stewards in matters touching Corporation manors, lands and tenements, and to receive or distrain for Corporation rents
Latin; Common Seal, incomplete, on tag

C/4/7/2/2   3 Oct. 1628
Letter of attorney
From Bailiffs, burgesses and commonalty to Richard Dennyesen and John Warner, to receive rents and forfeitures, and to distrain in case of non-payment
Latin; Common Seal, incomplete, on tag

C/4/7/2/3   20 Apr. 1601
Grant of office of High Steward of borough
From Bailiffs, burgesses and commonalty to Thomas, Lord Buckhurst, Lord Treasurer of England, with fee of £10 p.a. and power to distrain on manor of Handford Hall in case of non-payment [Thomas Sackville, Baron Buckhurst, created Earl of Dorset 1604, was elected High Steward on conviction of his predecessor, the Earl of Essex, of high treason, and held the office until his death on 25 Feb. 1609, when he was succeeded by Robert Cecil, Earl of Salisbury: *see* Richardson 1884, 406, 435]
Latin; Common Seal, incomplete, on tag

C/4/7/2/4   26 Apr. 1726
Counterpart acquittance
From Bailiffs, burgesses and commonalty to Cooper Gravenor, Portman, for resolution of differences between them: Corporation quitclaim all actions against Gravenor and bind themselves in £1,000 to indemnify him against demands on account of his receiving Corporation dues for merchandize exported or imported during his term as Water Bailiff and occupier of Town House and Quay under leases which have been adjudged void

C/4/7/2/5   30 Sep. 1782
Bond
Benjamin Parkhurst, customs officer, John Spooner, banker and Thomas Foster Notcutt, gent., all of Ipswich, bound to Bailiffs, burgesses and commonalty in £200 for due performance of office of Collector of Coal Dues for the port by Parkhurst, to which office he was appointed for life by the Great Court, 29 Sep. 1782, having purchased it for £84

C/4/7/2/6   1794
'The Oaths of Office of the Chief Magistrates, Subordinate Officers and Free Burgesses of the Corporation of Ipswich'
(printed pamphlet, 28 copies)

C/5 TOWN RESPONSIBILITIES AND SERVICES

C/5/1   CORPORATION CHARITIES   1565–1836

The poor of Ipswich were fortunate in both the number and variety of the charities endowed for their welfare from the mid-16th century onwards. The charities whose surviving administrative and financial records are listed here are those which were for the benefit of the disadvantaged of the whole town and which were administered by officers elected by the Corporation. There were in addition numerous parochial charities, whose administration was not the borough's concern. The Corporation charities retained separate officers until the Municipal Corporations Act of 1835. Thereafter a single board of Trustees was established to provide a unified administration for all the Ipswich Municipal Charities.

The surviving title deeds to the various charity estates, with related property surveys, maps and valuations and the court records of the Debenham manors which formed part of Henry Tooley's Charity, will be found listed in section C/3/10, FINANCE AND TOWN PROPERTY: CHARITY ESTATES.

C/5/1/1   TOOLEY'S FOUNDATION AND SMART'S CHARITY   1565–1836

On his death in 1551 Henry Tooley, the richest merchant of Tudor Ipswich, left the bulk of his estate to the poor of the town. After a decade of legal wrangling involving Tooley's relatives and executors and Ipswich Corporation, which long prevented the effective administration of the bequest, Lord Keeper Bacon's order of 1562 formally established Tooley's Foundation as an efficient institution for the welfare of Ipswich's poor. For the first few years of its existence, control of the Foundation remained with the surviving executors, but from 1566 the borough's Assembly elected annually at Michaelmas four Wardens (two Portmen and two members of the Twenty-Four), one of whom was appointed Renterwarden to take charge of the Foundation's finances for the year.

Most of the income was devoted to maintaining the almshouse which, despite the long-running litigation, seems already to have been built by the late 1550s on a site in what is now Foundation Street, not far from Tooley's burial place in the parish church of St Mary at Quay. It originally consisted of five separate lodgings, each to accommodate two people, though it was early recognised that, after the deaths of Tooley's widow Alice and Alice Thwaytes, both of whom received pensions out of the endowment, more almspeople could be maintained.

From 1569, when the Corporation established Christ's Hospital on the nearby site of the former Dominican Priory (*see* the introductory note to the records of that charity, C/5/1/2, below), there was close co-operation between the two institutions. Shortly after the founding of the Hospital the numbers of Tooley's almspeople were increased, and it was agreed that, rather than extending the almshouses, the additional persons should be placed in spare Hospital accommodation in the Blackfriars buildings. In 1583 part of these premises was apparently bought by the Foundation's Wardens. By the mid-1580s, therefore, the Tooley Foundation had come to consist of two equally important sets of neighbouring lodgings (known in later years as the Upper and Lower Foundations) housing over forty inmates.

The main sources of the Foundation's income were: Tooley's manors of Ulveston Hall and Sackville's in Debenham; Walnut Tree Farm in Whitton, Bramford, Claydon and Akenham; the Lime Kiln Farm in Claydon; part of the Street Farm in Whitton and Bramford; and two-thirds of a farm in Otley.

In 1599 William Smart, Portman, bequeathed a farm and lands called Coles and Coningtons in Kirton and Falkenham, after the death of his wife Alice, to Ipswich Corporation, the rents to be applied for the various charitable purposes detailed in his will. He directed that the bequest should be administered by the Wardens of Tooley's Foundation, and in practice the income was applied to the same purposes and in the same manner as that of the Foundation. Subsequent purchases of land (some of them made jointly with other Ipswich charities) were added to Smart's original endowment. These included a farm in Creeting St Peter, Creeting All Saints and Earl Stonham (owned jointly with Christ's Hospital and Tyler's Charity), part of the Street Farm in Whitton and Bramford; and the ground rent of three cottages in St Peter's, Ipswich.

For further details, *see* Webb 1962, 154–60, and Webb 1966, 11–18 (on which this note is substantially based); Canning 1747, 1–51; and Trustees 1878, 6–12.

C/5/1/1/1 ORDER BOOKS OF THE WARDENS   1565–1835

These contain orders setting and increasing the weekly allowances to named poor persons; for payments to the churchwardens of St Mary at Quay towards the minister's wages, provision of stools for the poor in the church, and the funerals of those residents of Foundation houses who shall die during the year; for provision of clothing; and for the placing of named poor persons in Foundation houses.

C/5/1/1/1/1   1565–1622
For Tooley's Foundation only
There are no entries between 28 Sep. 1567 and 29 Sep. 1574
Includes:
— memoranda of election of Wardens
(1 vol. Front cover marked 'No. 5'. Title page inscribed: 'The book or legyer concernyng the Election of Wardeyns of the rentes and revenues of the howse of the poore of Henrye Toolye and also concernyng the grauntyng of leases and other orders for the placeyng displacyng and releefe of the poore of the sayd Foundacion accordyng to an order yn that behaulff devysed by the ryght honorable Syr Nycholas Bacon knyght, Lord Keper of the greate Seale of Englond 1575')

C/5/1/1/1/2   20 Sep. 1634–30 Jul. 1635
For Tooley's Foundation only
Includes:
— 'payrolls' for 2 half-years beginning Sep. 1634 and Apr. 1635
(1 vol.)

C/5/1/1/1/3   1738–1797
Tooley's Foundation and Smart's Charity
At or about Michaelmas each year are entered the names of all persons who are to receive a weekly allowance during the coming year, with the amount to be paid to each
(1 vol. Front cover marked 'No. 7'. Orders for Tooley at front, orders for Smart at back)

C/5/1/1/1/4   1798–1835
Tooley's Foundation and Smart's Charity
Includes, on end-paper at back of vol.:
— declaration by Edward Bacon: 'Having as a Warden of Tooley's Foundation taken the usual solemn oath that I will see the Rules and Regulations appertaining to that charity are complied with by all persons who are admitted thereon, and with the view to prevent the recurrence of those abuses which have hitherto crept into it, to the almost subversion of the benevolent donor's intentions, as described and settled in the Indentures tripartite, and particularly that of absenting themselves from Church on the Sabbath Day; I feel it my duty to protest and do now protest against the future admission of any person or persons who do not either produce a certificate from the Minister of the parish that they are Regular Communicants of the Established Church, or give satisfactory assurance to the Wardens that they will regularly attend it', 5 Oct. 1811
(1 vol. Orders for Tooley at front, orders for Smart at back)

C/5/1/1/2   PRECEDENTS   ? late 16c.–early 19c.

C/5/1/1/2/1   n.d. [early 19c.]
Precedent and memorandum book
Contents include: notes and extracts, 1566–1806, from legal proceedings relating to the boundaries and rights of the manor of Ulveston Hall in Debenham, and from orders of the borough
Assembly relating to the election and powers of the Wardens and Renterwarden, method of
auditing accounts, placing of and payments to the Foundation poor, medical assistance, abatement or suspension of payments, discharge and punishment of Foundationers, instruction of the
poor in religion, church attendance, burial of Foundationers, coal, wood and clothing allowances, officers' appointments and salaries, death or departure from the town of serving
Renterwardens, and particulars of the Charity estates
(1 vol.)

C/5/1/1/2/2   n.d. [? late 16c. – ? early 19c.]
Miscellaneous papers
Includes:
— form of prayer for use of inmates of Tooley's Foundation, with schedule of household
goods, n.d. [? late 16c.]
— notes in an unidentified form of shorthand, n.d. [?early 19c.]
(3 docs, found loose inside C/5/1/1/2/1)

C/5/1/1/3   ADMISSIONS   1569–1597

C/5/1/1/3/1   1569–1597
Register of Admissions to Tooley's Foundation
Contains names of those admitted, including those admitted first to Christ's Hospital and afterwards transferred to the Foundation; dates of admission or transfer, discharge or death; name of
officer authorising admission; some entries include details of age and amount of weekly allowance granted, reason for admission (e.g. 'beyng blynd') or discharge (e.g. 'went with Peverell
the sawer to worke into the countrye'), and place of burial. The Bailiffs for each year are
named, and sometimes the Wardens of the Foundation
(1 vol., indexed; front cover marked 'No. 8' and inscribed with verse from Psalm 41: 'Blessed
is the man that providethe for the sicke and poore: the Lorde shall delyver hym yn the daye of
trowble.'; back cover inscribed with verse from the Book of Proverbs: 'Hee that oppressethe
the poore reprovethe Hym that made hym, but hee honorethe Hym, that hathe mercy on the
poore.')

C/5/1/1/4   'PAYROLLS' OF THE TOOLEY AND SMART ALMSPEOPLE   1761–?1824

These give the names and the weekly payments to each person throughout the year. Deaths are
noted. Most of the surviving payrolls are to be found in the annual files of Renterwarden's and
Receiver's vouchers (C/5/1/1/8), of which they usually formed the wrappers.

C/5/1/1/4/1   1761–1762
Endorsed with summary of weekly expenditure

C/5/1/1/4/2   1774–1775

C/5/1/1/4/3   1791–1792

C/5/1/1/4/4   1793–1794

C/5/1/1/4/5   1794–1795

C/5/1/1/4/6   ?1823–?1824
Undated, but records deaths in 1823 and 1824
(1 vol.)

C/5/1/1/4/7   n.d. [? early 19c.]
(1 vol.)

C/5/1/1/4/8   n.d. [? early 19c.]
List of inmates of the Upper and Lower Foundations (Tooley's Charity), the Shire Hall Yard
and Stoke Foundation (Smart's Charity), and of Tooley and Smart out-pensioners, with sums of
money paid or payable to each
(1 doc.)

C/5/1/1/5   LEGAL PAPERS   1814 and n.d.

C/5/1/1/5/1   (16, 17 Dec. 1814) n.d.
Copies of counsel's opinions by Sir Arthur Piggott of Lincoln's Inn
Re the respective rights of the Bailiffs of Ipswich and the Wardens of Tooley's and Smart's
Foundation to nominate poor persons to the almshouses (for the cases on which these opinions
were given, *see* the precedent book, C/5/1/1/2/1, pp. 12–15)

C/5/1/1/6   AUDITED ACCOUNTS OF THE RENTERWARDEN OF   1611–1836
TOOLEY'S FOUNDATION AND THE RECEIVER OF RENTS OF
SMART'S CHARITY

It appears that, for the whole period covered by these accounts (though because of gaps in the
series it is not absolutely certain) the same person was appointed both Renterwarden of
Tooley's Foundation and Receiver of Rents of Smart's Charity for the year. Many of the
accounts for the Tooley Foundation were submitted for audit in the names of all four Wardens,
of whom the Renterwarden was almost invariably one; the Smart's accounts are almost always
in the name of the Receiver only. Usually a separate account book was kept for each charity,
and the two books for the accounting year (Michaelmas to Michaelmas) were frequently
stitched together, perhaps at the time of the annual audit. Most accounts bear the signatures of
the auditors, but in some the evidence of audit consists merely of their annotations.
    Most of the cash receipts for both charities derive from property rents, with occasional
income from other sources such as the felling of timber. Tooley Foundation payments are regularly made to the poor 'within the House' and 'out of House' (details are given of the names of
recipients, weekly and annual rates, periods of sickness); for nursing; burials; clothing;
firewood; coal; and repairs to the Foundation buildings and other charity-owned property.
Smart's Charity payments to the sick are also specified. Part of the salaries of the Master and
Usher of the Grammar School was also paid from Smart's funds, together with exhibitions and
payments for clothing for scholars of the School on Smart's Foundation.
    For the annual accounts for the financial years 1765–1766, 1777–1778 to 1781–1782,
1785–1786, 1787–1788, 1785–1786, 1787–1788, 1788–1789, 1794–1795 to 1808–1809,
1813–1814 and 1815–1816, *see* the Renterwarden's and Receiver's voucher files for the years
in question (C/5/1/1/8).

C/5/1/1/6/1   1611–1612
Richard Cock, Thomas Suclemore, Robert Snelling and Thomas Eldred, Wardens, Richard
Cock Renterwarden
Tooley's Foundation only
(1 vol.)

C/5/1/1/6/2   1612–1613
Thomas Sickellmore, Tobias Blosse, Robert Gooding and Thomas Eldred, Wardens, Tobias
Blosse Renterwarden
Tooley's Foundation only
(1 vol.)

C/5/1/1/6/3   1612–1613
Tobias Blosse, Receiver
Smart's Charity only
(1 vol.)

C/5/1/1/6/4   1613–1614
Tobias Blosse, William Sparrowe, Christopher Ballarde and Francis Crowe, Wardens
Tooley's Foundation only
(1 vol.)

C/5/1/1/6/5   1613–1614
Christopher Ballarde, Receiver
Smart's Charity only
(1 vol.)

C/5/1/1/6/6   1614–1615
Richard Martyn, William Cage, John Flick and Christopher Algate, Wardens, William Cage
Renterwarden
Tooley's Foundation only
(1 vol.)

C/5/1/1/6/7   1615–1616
William Cage, Robert Gooding, John Flicke and Christopher Aldgate, Wardens of Tooley's
Foundation, John Flicke Renterwarden and Receiver
Only the Tooley accounts are audited
(1 vol. covering both charities)

C/5/1/1/6/8   1616–1617
Richard Cocke, Robert Gooding, George Acton and Christopher Allgate, Wardens, Richard
Cocke Renterwarden
Tooley's Foundation only
(1 vol.)

C/5/1/1/6/9   1616–1617
Richard Cocke, Receiver
Smart's Charity only
(1 vol.)

C/5/1/1/6/10   1617–1618
George Acton, Receiver
Smart's Charity only
(1 vol.)

C/5/1/1/6/11   1618–1619
Robert Goodinge, Michael Goodere, Henry Buckenham and John Rands, Wardens of Tooley's
Foundation, Michael Goodere Renterwarden and Receiver
(2 vols, stitched together)

C/5/1/1/6/12   1619–1620
William Bloyse, Michael Goodere, Henry Buckenham and Peter Coale, Wardens of Tooley's
Foundation, Peter Coale Renterwarden and Receiver
(2 vols, stitched together)

C/5/1/1/6/13   1620–1621
William Bloyse, George Acton, Thomas Hailes and Peter Cole, Wardens of Tooley's Foundation, George Acton Renterwarden and Receiver
Only the Smart accounts are audited
(2 vols, stitched together)

C/5/1/1/6/14   1621–1622
George Acton, Samuel Cutler, John Carnoby and Thomas Hailes, Wardens of Tooley's Foundation, Thomas Hailes Renterwarden and Receiver
(2 vols, stitched together)

C/5/1/1/6/15   1622–1623
Samuel Cutler, Thomas Eldred, Robert Benham and John Canebey, Wardens, Thomas Eldred Renterwarden
Tooley's Foundation only
(1 vol.)

C/5/1/1/6/16   1622–1623
Thomas Eldred, Receiver
Smart's Charity only
(1 vol.)

C/5/1/1/6/17   1623–1624
Tobias Blosse, Thomas Eldred, Joseph Parkust and Richard Hayle, Wardens of Tooley's Foundation, Richard Hayle Renterwarden and Receiver
(2 vols, stitched together)

C/5/1/1/6/18   1624–1625
Tobias Blosse, Robert Sparrow, William Moyse and Joseph Parkhurst, Wardens of Tooley's Foundation, Robert Sparrow Renterwarden and Receiver
(2 vols, stitched together)

C/5/1/1/6/19   1625–1626
Robert Gooding, Robert Sparrow, William Moysey and Isaac Greenwich, Wardens of Tooley's Foundation, William Moysey Renterwarden and Receiver
(2 vols, stitched together)

C/5/1/1/6/20   1626–1627
Robert Goodinge, John Sicklemor, Isaac Grenwedge and Richard Pupplett, Wardens of Tooley's Foundation, John Sicklemor Renterwarden and Receiver
(2 vols, stitched together)

C/5/1/1/6/21   1626–1627
Robert Goodinge, John Sicklemor, Isaac Grenwedge and Richard Pupplett, Wardens, John Sicklemor Renterwarden
Tooley's Foundation only
(1 vol.)

C/5/1/1/6/22   1626–1627
John Sicklemor, Receiver
Smart's Charity only; not audited
(1 vol.)

C/5/1/1/6/23   1627–1628
William Cage, John Sicklemor, Robert Knapp and Richard Pupplett, Wardens, Richard Pupplett Renterwarden
Tooley's Foundation only
(1 vol.)

C/5/1/1/6/24   1627–1628
Richard Pupplett, Receiver
Smart's Charity only; not audited
(1 vol.)

C/5/1/1/6/25   1628–1629
William Cage, Christopher Aldgate, Robert Knappe and William Inglethorpe, Wardens, Christopher Aldgate Renterwarden
Tooley's Foundation only; not audited
(1 vol.)

C/5/1/1/6/26   1628–1629
Christopher Aldgate, Receiver
Smart's Charity only; not audited
(1 vol.)

C/5/1/1/6/27   1628–1629
Copy of C/5/1/1/6/25–26
(1 vol.)

C/5/1/1/6/28   1629–1630
George Acton, Christopher Aldgate, William Inglethorpe and Richard Herne, Wardens, William
Inglethorpe Renterwarden
Tooley's Foundation only; not audited
(1 vol.)

C/5/1/1/6/29   1630–1631
George Acton, William Moysey, Richard Herne and Richard Jennings, Wardens, William
Moysey Renterwarden
Tooley's Foundation only
(1 vol.)

C/5/1/1/6/30   1630–1631
William Moysey, Receiver
Smart's Charity only
(1 vol.)

C/5/1/1/6/31   1631–1632
Robert Sparrowe, William Moysey, Richard Jennings and Richard Dennye, Wardens of
Tooley's Foundation, Richard Jennings Renterwarden and Receiver
(2 vols, stitched together)

C/5/1/1/6/32   1632–1633
Robert Sparrowe, Edmund Keene, Edmund Humphry and Richard Denny, Wardens of Tooley's
Foundation, Edmund Keene Renterwarden, Keene and Robert Sparrow Receivers
(2 vols, stitched together)

C/5/1/1/6/33   1633–1634
John Sicklemore, Edmund Keene, Edmund Humfrey and William Sparrow, Wardens of
Tooley's Foundation, Edmund Humfrey Renterwarden and Receiver
(2 vols, stitched together)

C/5/1/1/6/34   1634–1635
John Sicklemore, James Tillott, William Tiler and William Sparrowe, Wardens of Tooley's
Foundation, James Tillott Renterwarden and Receiver
(2 vols, stitched together)

C/5/1/1/6/35   1635–1636
William Moysey, James Tyllott, William Tyler and William Doggett, Wardens of Tooley's
Foundation, William Tyler Renterwarden and Receiver
(2 vols, stitched together)

C/5/1/1/6/36   1636–1637
William Moyse, Richard Pupplett, Robert Cooper and William Dogett, Wardens of Tooley's
Foundation, Richard Pupplett Renterwarden and Receiver
(2 vols, stitched together)

C/5/1/1/6/37   1637–1638
Richard Puplet, Edmund Keene, Robert Cowper and John Blyth, Trustees of Tooley's Foundation and Smart's lands, Robert Cowper Renterwarden and Receiver
(2 vols, stitched together)

C/5/1/1/6/38   1638–1639
Edmund Keene, John Aldus, John Bliethe and Thomas Knappe, Wardens of Tooley's Foundation, John Aldus Renterwarden and Receiver
(2 vols, stitched together)

C/5/1/1/6/39   1639–1640
William Cage, John Aldus, Thomas Knapp and Samuel Knapp, Wardens of Tooley's Foundation, Thomas Knapp Renterwarden and Receiver
(2 vols, stitched together)

C/5/1/1/6/40   1641–1642
John Sicklemore, John Barbur, Joseph Pemberton and Samuel Knapp, Wardens of Tooley's
Foundation 'and soe Receivers of the rents belonginge to Mr Smart's gifte', Joseph Pemberton
Renterwarden
(2 vols, stitched together)

C/5/1/1/6/41   1642–1643
John Sickellmor, Edmund Humfrey, Edmund Morgayne and Robert Donckone, Wardens of
Tooley's Foundation, Edmund Humfrey Renterwarden and Receiver
(2 vols, stitched together)

C/5/1/1/6/42   1643–1644
Edmund Humfrey, Robert Dunkon, Joseph Pemberton and John Bloomfield, Wardens of
Tooley's Foundation and Receivers of Smart's Gift, Joseph Pemberton Renterwarden
(2 vols, stitched together)

C/5/1/1/6/43   1644–1645
John Barbur, William Sparowe, John Blomefeild and Henry Chapline, Wardens of Tooley's
Foundation, William Sparowe Renterwarden
Tooley's Foundation only
(1 vol.)

C/5/1/1/6/44   1644–1645
William Sparrowe, Receiver
Smart's Charity only
(1 vol.)

C/5/1/1/6/45   1644–1645
Copies of C/5/1/1/6/43–44
(2 vols, stitched together)

C/5/1/1/6/46   1645–1646
Henry Chapline, Renterwarden and Receiver
Not audited
(2 vols, stitched together)

C/5/1/1/6/47   1646–1647
John Aldus, John Smythier, Thomas Ives and William Greene, Wardens of Tooley's Foundation, John Smythier Renterwarden [and Receiver]
(2 vols, stitched together)

C/5/1/1/6/48   1647–1648
Edmund Humfre, John Smether, Thomas Ives and Thomas Wright, Wardens of Tooley's Foundation, Thomas Ives Renterwarden and Receiver
(2 vols, stitched together)

C/5/1/1/6/49   1648–1649
John Brandlinge, Renterwarden and Receiver
Includes:
— Brandlinge's audited account of money received 'uppon any accomptes concerning the
Towen of Ipswitch', including purchase of Mr Fearnlye's land, 1649–1650
(3 vols, stitched together)

C/5/1/1/6/50   1649–1650
John Smythier, John Brandlinge, Henry Whitinge and Benjamin Butter, Wardens of Tooley's
Foundation, Henry Whitinge Renterwarden and Receiver
(2 vols, stitched together)

C/5/1/1/6/51   1650–1651
John Smythier, Richard Hayles, Benjamin Wade and William Cooke, Wardens of Tooley's
Foundation, Richard Hayles Renterwarden and Receiver
(2 vols, stitched together)

C/5/1/1/6/52   1652–1653
John Barbur, Peter Fisher, William Cooke and Robert Turner, Wardens of Tooley's Foundation
and Receivers of Smart's Gift, Peter Fisher Renterwarden
(2 vols, stitched together)

C/5/1/1/6/53   1653–1654
Richard Purpplett, Peter Fisher, Robert Turner and Robert Deines, Wardens of Tooley's Foundation, Robert Turner Renterwarden and Receiver
(2 vols, stitched together; front cover of Smart vol. annotated 'This the first acct of Creeting
Lands Smart vid: the value')

C/5/1/1/6/54   1654–1655
Nicholas Philips, John Aldus, Robert Daynes and Miles Wallis, Wardens of Tooley's Foundation, Nicholas Philips Renterwarden and Receiver
(2 vols, stitched together; title page of Smart vol. annotated 'Theese Bookes are to be given in
to the Towne of Ipswich and discharges to be made in the said Bookes by the Baliffs signing
them – and the Assembly.')

C/5/1/1/6/55   1655–1656
Miles Wallis, John Aldus, Nicholas Philips and Robert Manning, Wardens of Tooley's Foundation, Miles Wallis Renterwarden and Receiver
(2 vols, stitched together; title page of Smart vol. annotated similarly to C/5/1/1/6/54)

C/5/1/1/6/56   1656–1657
John Smyther, Manuell Sorrell, Thomas Burroughes and Robert Manning, Wardens of Tooley's
Foundation, Manuell Sorrell Renterwarden and Receiver
(2 vols, stitched together)

C/5/1/1/6/57   1657–1658
Thomas Burrough, John Smyther, Manuell Sorrell and John Blomfeild, Wardens of Tooley's
Foundation, Thomas Burrough Renterwarden and Receiver
(2 vols, stitched together)

C/5/1/1/6/58   1658–1659
John Brandling, Robert Dunkon, John Bloumfeild and Simon Cumberland, Wardens of
Tooley's Foundation, Robert Dunkon Renterwarden and Receiver
(2 vols, stitched together)

C/5/1/1/6/59   1660–1661
Richard Hayle, Robert Sparowe, Robert Daynes and Henry Cosine, Wardens of Tooley's
Foundation, Robert Sparowe Renterwarden and Receiver
(2 vols, stitched together)

C/5/1/1/6/60   1661–1662
Henry Whitinge, Robert Sparrowe, Robert Daines and Thomas Griggs, Wardens of Tooley's
Foundation, Robert Daines Renterwarden and Receiver
(2 vols, stitched together)

C/5/1/1/6/61   29 Sep. 1662–25 Mar. 1663
Thomas Wright, Sir Manuell Sorrell, Miles Wallis and Henry Gosnold, Wardens of Tooley's
Foundation, Thomas Wright Renterwarden and Receiver
Half-year only
(2 vols, stitched together)

C/5/1/1/6/62   29 Sep. 1662–25 Mar. 1663
Unaudited draft or copy of C/5/1/1/6/61
(2 vols, stitched together)

C/5/1/1/6/63   25 Mar.–29 Sep. 1663
Thomas Wright, Sir Manuell Sorrell, Miles Wallis and Henry Gosnold, Wardens of Tooley's
Foundation, Thomas Wright Renterwarden and Receiver
Half-year only
(2 vols, stitched together)

C/5/1/1/6/64   1663–1664
Thomas Reeve, Renterwarden and Receiver
(2 vols, stitched together)

C/5/1/1/6/65   1664–1665
Gilbert Lindfeild, Renterwarden and Receiver
(2 vols, stitched together)

C/5/1/1/6/66   1666–1667
Andrew Sorrell, John Wright, Robert Rednall and Charles Wright, Wardens of Tooley's
Foundation, Andrew Sorrell Renterwarden and Receiver
(2 vols, stitched together)

C/5/1/1/6/67   1667–1668
Nicholas Phillips, John Wright, Charles Wright and Robert Rednall, Wardens of Tooley's
Foundation, Nicholas Phillips Renterwarden, Robert Rednall Receiver
(2 vols, stitched together)

C/5/1/1/6/68   1668–1669
Luke Jower, Gilbert Lindfild, William Feast and Jonathan Butter, Wardens of Tooley's
Foundation, Luke Jower Renterwarden and Receiver
(2 vols, stitched together)

C/5/1/1/6/69   1669–1670
William Feast, Renterwarden and Receiver
(2 vols, stitched together)

C/5/1/1/6/70   1670–1671
William Cullum, Gilbert Linfeild, Jonathan Butter and John Camplin, Wardens of Tooley's
Foundation, William Cullum Renterwarden and Receiver
(2 vols, stitched together)

C/5/1/1/6/71   1671–1672
Luke Jowers, William Cullum, Benjamin Butter and John Campling, Wardens of Tooley's
Foundation, John Burrough Renterwarden and Receiver
(2 vols, stitched together)

C/5/1/1/6/72   1672–1673
Henry Gosnold, John Wright, Thomas Reeve and Richard Clopton, Wardens of Tooley's Foundation, Henry Gosnold Renterwarden and Receiver
(2 vols, stitched together)

C/5/1/1/6/73   1673–1674
Edward Reynolds, Renterwarden and Receiver
(2 vols, stitched together)

C/5/1/1/6/74   1674–1675
Charles Wright, Renterwarden and Receiver
(2 vols, stitched together)

C/5/1/1/6/75   1675–1676
John Sawyer, Renterwarden and Receiver
(2 vols, stitched together)

C/5/1/1/6/76   1676–1677
John Pemberton, Renterwarden
Tooley's Foundation only
(1 vol.)

C/5/1/1/6/77   1676–1677
John Pemberton, Receiver
Smart's Charity only; apparently not audited
(1 vol.)

C/5/1/1/6/78   1677–1678
John Firmyn, Renterwarden and Receiver
(2 vols, stitched together)

C/5/1/1/6/79   1679–1680
John Reeve, Renterwarden
Tooley vol. produced in Chancery suit, William Tye, gent. *v.* Ipswich Corporation, 16 Apr.
1729
(2 vols, stitched together)

C/5/1/1/6/80   1680–1681
Richard Philips, Renterwarden and Receiver
(2 vols, stitched together)

C/5/1/1/6/81   1681–1682
John Blomfeild, Renterwarden and Receiver
(2 vols, stitched together)

C/5/1/1/6/82   1682–1683
John Burrough, Renterwarden and Receiver
(2 vols, stitched together; Tooley vol. annotated with memorandum of its production to Robert
Marston, Confectioner and John Sparowe, esq., on their examinations to the 11th interrogatory
on the part of the defendant, in Chancery cause, William Tye *v.* the Bailiffs, burgesses and commonalty of Ipswich, 16 Apr. 1729)

C/5/1/1/6/83   1683–1684
John Pemberton, John Burrough, Thomas Bright and John Wade, Wardens of Tooley's Foundation, Thomas Bright Renterwarden and Receiver
(2 vols, stitched together)

C/5/1/1/6/84   1684–1685
William Browne, John Lambe, John Wade and Miles Wallis, Wardens of Tooley's Foundation,
William Browne Renterwarden and Receiver
(2 vols, stitched together)

C/5/1/1/6/85   1685–1686
John Wade, William Neave, William Browne and William Tye, Wardens of Tooley's Foundation, John Wade Renterwarden and Receiver
(2 vols, stitched together)

C/5/1/1/6/86   1686–1687
William Neave, Renterwarden and Receiver
(2 vols, stitched together)

C/5/1/1/6/87   1688–1689
Edward Reynolds, Richard Phillips, John Firman and Nathaniel Bateman, Wardens, Edward
Reynolds Renterwarden
Tooley's Foundation only
(1 vol.)

C/5/1/1/6/88   1688–1689
Edward Reynolds, Receiver
Smart's Charity only
(1 vol.)

C/5/1/1/6/89   1689–1690
John Gibbon, Richard Phillips, Edward Reynolds and Truth Norris, Wardens of Tooley's
Foundation, John Gibbon Renterwarden and Receiver
(2 vols, stitched together)

C/5/1/1/6/90   1690–1691
Henry Sparrow, Renterwarden and Receiver
Annexed:
— 'apprisement' (inventory and valuation) of goods, chattels and cattle of Richard Howell of
Claydon, distrained for rent by the Bailiffs, burgesses and commonalty, 25 Aug. 1691, with
account of goods sold and money received, 2 Sep. 1691, account of corn sold at market prices,
27 Oct. 1691–25 Feb. 1692, and account of his goods sold to Robert Rudland [the new]
tenant, n.d.
— 'apprisement' of goods, chattels and cattle of William Drane of Otley, distrained for rent,
18 Sep. 1691, with account of goods sold, 22 Sep. 1691, and account of 'what [household]
goods given to Wm. Drane and his wife by order of Great Court after apprised', n.d.
(4 vols, stitched together)

C/5/1/1/6/91   1691–1692
Nicholas Philips, Renterwarden and Receiver
(2 vols, stitched together)

C/5/1/1/6/92   1692–1693
Nicholas Philips, Renterwarden and Receiver
(2 vols, stitched together)

C/5/1/1/6/93   1693–1694
Charles Wright, Nicholas Phillips and Nathaniel Bateman, Wardens of Tooley's Foundation,
Nathaniel Bateman Renterwarden and Receiver
(2 vols, stitched together)

C/5/1/1/6/94   1694–1695
Henry Sparrow, Renterwarden and Receiver
(1 vol. covering both charities)

C/5/1/1/6/95 1695–1696
Henry Sparrow, Renterwarden and Receiver
(2 vols, stitched together)

C/5/1/1/6/96 1698–1699
Thomas Bowle, Samuel Reynolds, Truth Norris and Keeble Cross, Wardens of Tooley's
Foundation, Thomas Bowle Renterwarden and Receiver
(2 vols, stitched together)

C/5/1/1/6/97 1699–1700
John Goldson, Renterwarden
Tooley's Foundation only
(1 vol.)

C/5/1/1/6/98 1699–1700
John Goldson, Receiver
Smart's Charity only
(1 vol.)

C/5/1/1/6/99 1700–1701
Isaac Sutton, John Goldson, Robert Newton and Francis Coleman, Wardens, Isaac Sutton
Renterwarden
Tooley's Foundation only; apparently not audited
(1 vol.)

C/5/1/1/6/100 1700–1701
Isaac Sutton, Receiver
Smart's Charity only; apparently not audited
(1 vol.)

C/5/1/1/6/101 1701–1702
Isaac Sutton, John Goldson, Robert Newton and Francis Coleman, Wardens, Isaac Sutton
Renterwarden
Tooley's Foundation only
(1 vol.)

C/5/1/1/6/102 1701–1702
Isaac Sutton, Receiver
Smart's Charity only; apparently not audited
(1 vol.)

C/5/1/1/6/103 1703–1704
Henry Capon, Receiver
Smart's Charity only
(1 vol.)

C/5/1/1/6/104 1704–1705
Thomas Day, John Clarke, Stephen Searson and Cooper Gravenor, Wardens, Cooper Gravenor
Renterwarden
Tooley's Foundation only
(1 vol.)

C/5/1/1/6/105 1705–1706
Stephen Searson, Renterwarden
Tooley's Foundation only
(1 vol.)

C/5/1/1/6/106   1705–1706
Stephen Searson, Receiver
Smart's Charity only; not audited
(1 vol.)

C/5/1/1/6/107   1706–1707
Jonathan Quintin, Stephen Searson and John Norris, Wardens, Thomas Day Renterwarden
Tooley's Foundation only
(1 vol.)

C/5/1/1/6/108   1706–1707
Thomas Day, Receiver
Smart's Charity only
(1 vol.)

C/5/1/1/6/109   1709–1710
Cooper Gravenor, Keeble Cross, George Girling and Thomas Osborn, Wardens, Thomas
Osborn Renterwarden
Tooley's Foundation only
(1 vol.)

C/5/1/1/6/110   1709–1710
Thomas Osborn, Renterwarden [sic]
Smart's Charity only; apparently not audited
(1 vol.)

C/5/1/1/6/111   1710–1711
Cooper Gravenor, Francis Colman, George Scott and Thomas Osborn, Wardens, Thomas
Osborn Renterwarden
Tooley's Foundation only
(1 vol.)

C/5/1/1/6/112   1710–1711
Thomas Osborn, Renterwarden
Smart's Charity only; not audited
(1 vol.)

C/5/1/1/6/113   1711–1712
Francis Coleman, Thomas Hallum and John Jolly, Wardens, George Scott Renterwarden
Tooley's Foundation only
(1 vol.)

C/5/1/1/6/114   1711–1712
George Scott, Receiver
Smart's Charity only
(1 vol.)

C/5/1/1/6/115   1712–1713
Thomas Bowell, Cooper Gravenor, John Pew and George Scott, Wardens, Cooper Gravenor
Renterwarden
Tooley's Foundation only
(1 vol.)

C/5/1/1/6/116   1712–1713
Cooper Gravenor, Renterwarden [sic]
Smart's Charity only
(1 vol.)

C/5/1/1/6/117   1713–1714
[Cooper] Gravenor, [blank] Quintton, and [blank] Starling, Wardens, George Girling
Renterwarden
Tooley's Foundation only
(1 vol.)

C/5/1/1/6/118   1713–1714
George Girling, Receiver
Smart's Charity only
(1 vol.)

C/5/1/1/6/119   1715–1716
John Jolly sen., Renterwarden
Tooley's Foundation only
(1 vol.)

C/5/1/1/6/120   1715–1716
John Jolly sen., Receiver
Smart's Charity only; apparently not audited
(1 vol.)

C/5/1/1/6/121   1717–1718
Cooper Gravenor, George Scott, Edward Seyer and George Girling, Wardens, Cooper Gravenor
Renterwarden
Tooley's Foundation only
(1 vol.)

C/5/1/1/6/122   1718–1719
John Marlow, Cooper Gravenor, George Girling and Edward Hubbard, Wardens, John Marlow
Renterwarden
Tooley's Foundation only
(1 vol.)

C/5/1/1/6/123   1719–1720
John Marlow, Thomas Starling, John Steward and Edward Hubbard, Wardens, Edward Hubbard
Renterwarden
Tooley's Foundation only
(1 vol.)

C/5/1/1/6/124   1719–1720
Edward Hubbard, Renterwarden [sic]
Smart's Charity only; apparently not audited
(1 vol.)

C/5/1/1/6/125   1720–1721
John Goldson, Edward Hubbard, John Steward and Thomas Starling, Wardens of Tooley's
Foundation, Thomas Starling Renterwarden and Receiver
(2 vols, stitched together)

C/5/1/1/6/126   1721–1722
Francis Collman, Hugh Wright, Matthew Wines and Thomas Starling, Wardens, Thomas
Starling Renterwarden
Tooley's Foundation only
(1 vol.)

C/5/1/1/6/127   1724–1725
Richard Smart, Henry Nash, Edward Bowell and Daniel Hickford, Wardens, Richard Smart
Renterwarden
Tooley's Foundation only
(1 vol.)

C/5/1/1/6/128   1725–1726
Edward Bowell, John Sparowe, Robert Marston and Richard Smartt, Wardens of Tooley's foundation, Edward Bowell Renterwarden and Receiver
(2 vols, stitched together)

C/5/1/1/6/129   1726–1727
John Cornelius, Edward Bowell, Tobias Searson and Edward Syer, Wardens of Tooley's Foundation, Edward Syer Renterwarden and Receiver
(1 vol. covering both charities)

C/5/1/1/6/130   1727–1728
John Cornelius, John Steward, Edward Syer and Hugh Wright, Wardens of Tooley's Foundation, John Cornelius Renterwarden and Receiver
(1 vol. covering both charities)

C/5/1/1/6/131   1728–1729
John Cornelius, John Marlow, John Sparowe and Hugh Wright, Wardens of Tooley's Foundation, Isaac Sutton Renterwarden and Receiver
(2 vols, stitched together)

C/5/1/1/6/132   1729–1730
John Sparowe, Renterwarden and Receiver
(1 vol. covering both charities)

C/5/1/1/6/133   1730–1731
John Gouldston, John Sparowe, Christopher Thorne and Edward Duck, Wardens of Tooley's Foundation, Edward Duck Renterwarden and Receiver
(2 vols, stitched together)

C/5/1/1/6/134   1731–1732
Robert Marston, Edward Duck and Tobias Searson, Wardens of Tooley's Foundation, Robert Marston Renterwarden and Receiver
(1 vol. covering both charities)

C/5/1/1/6/135   1732–1733
John Marlow, Robert Marston, Samuel Hamblin and Michael Beaumont, Wardens of Tooley's Foundation, Michael Beaumont Renterwarden and Receiver
(1 vol. covering both charities)

C/5/1/1/6/136   1733–1734
John Marlow, Nathaniel Cole, Michael Beaumont and Philip Turner, Wardens of Tooley's Foundation, John Marlow Renterwarden and Receiver
(2 vols, stitched together)

C/5/1/1/6/137   1735–1736
Henry Hill, Nathaniel Cole, Hugh Wright and William Truelove, Wardens of Tooley's Foundation, Nathaniel Cole Renterwarden and Receiver
(1 vol. covering both charities)

C/5/1/1/6/138   1736–1737
John Cornelius, Nathaniel Cole, Henry Bond and William Artis, Wardens of Tooley's Foundation, William Artis Renterwarden and Receiver
(1 vol. covering both charities)

C/5/1/1/6/139   1737–1738
John Cornelius, Edward Lynch, John Ferman and William Artis, Wardens of Tooley's Foundation, John Cornelius Renterwarden and Receiver
(1 vol. covering both charities)

C/5/1/1/6/140   1738–1739
John Cornelius, John Margerum, John Day and William Truelove, Wardens of Tooley's Foundation, William Truelove Renterwarden and Receiver
(1 vol. covering both charities)

C/5/1/1/6/141   1739–1740
William Truelove, Richard Lloyd, William Hallum and John Margerum, Wardens of Tooley's Foundation, John Margerum Renterwarden and Receiver
(1 vol. covering both charities)

C/5/1/1/6/142   1741–1742
Richard Lloyd, Robert Marston, Samuel Hamblin and Thomas Pulford, Wardens of Tooley's Foundation, Richard Lloyd Renterwarden and Receiver
(1 vol. covering both charities)

C/5/1/1/6/143   1743–1744
Humphry Rant, Henry Skinner, Lark Tarver and Thomas Pulford, Wardens of Tooley's Foundation, Humphry Rant Renterwarden and Receiver
(1 vol. covering both charities)

C/5/1/1/6/144   1744–1745
Thomas Pulford, Humphry Rant, Henry Skynner and Lark Tarver, Wardens of Tooley's Foundation, Thomas Pulford Renterwarden and Receiver
(1 vol. covering both charities)

C/5/1/1/6/145   1745–1746
Henry Skynner, Goodchild Clarke, Thomas Pulford and John Gravenor, Wardens of Tooley's Foundation, Henry Skynner Renterwarden and Receiver
(1 vol. covering both charities)

C/5/1/1/6/146   1746–1747
Nathaniel Cole, Henry Skynner, Lark Tarver and John Firmin, Wardens of Tooley's Foundation, John Firmin Renterwarden and Receiver
(2 vols, stitched together)

C/5/1/1/6/147   1747–1748
Goodchild Clarke, Renterwarden and Receiver
(1 vol. covering both charities)

C/5/1/1/6/148   1748–1749
John Cornelius, Goodchild Clarke and William Hammond, Wardens of Tooley's Foundation, Thomas Burwell Renterwarden and Receiver
(1 vol. covering both charities)

C/5/1/1/6/149   1749–1750
[blank] Margerum, Renterwarden and Receiver
(1 double folio, covering both charities)

C/5/1/1/6/150   1750–1751
Michael Thirkle, William Hammond, Thomas Bowell and Charles Norris, Wardens, Charles Norris Renterwarden
Tooley's Foundation only
(1 vol.)

C/5/1/1/6/151   1750–1751
Charles Norris, Receiver
Smart's Charity only
(1 vol.)

C/5/1/1/6/152   1751–1752
Michael Thirkle, Renterwarden and Receiver
(1 vol.)

C/5/1/1/6/153   1752–1753
Michael Thirkle, James Wilder, William Truelove and William Truelove jun., Wardens,
William Truelove Renterwarden
Tooley's Foundation only
(1 vol.)

C/5/1/1/6/154   1752–1753
William Truelove, Receiver
Smart's Charity only
(1 vol.)

C/5/1/1/6/155   1753–1754
William Hammond, Renterwarden and Receiver
(2 vols, stitched together)

C/5/1/1/6/156   1754–1755
Thomas Bowell, Renterwarden and Receiver
(2 vols, stitched together)

C/5/1/1/6/157   1758–1759
Richard Batley, Renterwarden and Receiver
(1 vol. covering both charities)

C/5/1/1/6/158   1758–1759
Richard Batley, Renterwarden and Receiver
Not audited
(1 doc.)

C/5/1/1/6/159   1759–1760
Michael Thirkle, Renterwarden and Receiver
(1 vol. covering both charities)

C/5/1/1/6/160   1762–1763
John Forsett, Renterwarden and Receiver
(1 vol. covering both charities)

C/5/1/1/6/161   1766–1767
John Sharp, Renterwarden and Receiver
(1 vol. covering both charities)

C/5/1/1/6/162   1768–1769
John Trapnell, Renterwarden and Receiver
(1 vol. covering both charities)

C/5/1/1/6/163   1771–1772
Peter Clarke, Renterwarden and Receiver
(1 vol. covering both charities)

C/5/1/1/6/164   1772–1773
Robert Goodwin, Renterwarden
Tooley's Foundation only
(1 vol.)

C/5/1/1/6/165   1773–1774
William Clarke, Renterwarden and Receiver
(1 vol. covering both charities)

C/5/1/1/6/166   1774–1775
Robert Manning, Senior Renterwarden
(1 vol. covering both charities)

C/5/1/1/6/167   1775–1776
Miles Wallis and William Clarke, Renterwardens and Receivers
(1 vol. covering both charities)

C/5/1/1/6/168   1776–1777
Thomas Hallum, Renterwarden and Receiver
(1 vol. covering both charities)

C/5/1/1/6/169   1777–1778
Thomas Hallum, Renterwarden and Receiver
Includes:
— Hallum's audited account as Treasurer of Christ's Hospital, 1777–1778
— Thomas Notcutt's audited accounts as Treasurer of Christ's Hospital, 1778–1779 and
1779–1780
(1 vol.)

C/5/1/1/6/170   1782–1783
Charles Norris, Renterwarden and Receiver
(1 doc. covering both charities)

C/5/1/1/6/171   1783–1784
Samuel Wollaston, Renterwarden and Receiver
(1 vol. covering both charities)

C/5/1/1/6/172   1784–1785
Edward Bacon, Renterwarden and Receiver
(1 vol. covering both charities)

C/5/1/1/6/173   1786–1787
Christopher Rolfe, Renterwarden and Receiver
(1 vol. covering both charities)

C/5/1/1/6/174   1791–1792
H. Seekamp, Renterwarden
Tooley's Foundation only
(1 vol.)

C/5/1/1/6/175   1791–1792
H. Seekamp, Receiver
Smart's Charity only
(1 vol.)

C/5/1/1/6/176   1793–1794
Thomas Hallum, Renterwarden
Tooley's Foundation only
(1 vol.)

C/5/1/1/6/177   1793–1794
Thomas Hallum, Receiver
Smart's Charity only
(1 vol.)

C/5/1/1/6/178   ?1803–1804
(1 doc. Badly damaged by rodents; incomplete)

C/5/1/1/6/179   1809–1836
Like the earlier annual volumes, these are the original accounts, bearing the signatures of the
auditors. A note following the latest account for Tooley's Foundation reads: 'The account for
this Charity will now be found in a book, procured for that purpose, by the direction of the
Trustees of the Ipswich Charities'.
(1 vol. Accounts for Tooley at front, accounts for Smart at back)

C/5/1/1/7   COPIES OF THE RENTERWARDEN'S ACCOUNTS   1595–1695
(TOOLEY'S FOUNDATION ONLY)

These appear to be fair copies of the annual audited accounts, for they include the auditors'
names (which are not original signatures).

C/5/1/1/7/1   1595–1695
(1 vol; front cover marked 'No 2')

C/5/1/1/8   PAYMENT VOUCHERS OF THE RENTERWARDEN OF   1720–1836
TOOLEY'S FOUNDATION AND THE RECEIVER OF RENTS FOR
SMART'S CHARITY

These are chiefly annual bundles (or, more properly, files, the documents for most years originally being filed on laces). Unless otherwise stated, each file contains the vouchers for both
charities for the year. Also unless otherwise stated, each file down to 1803–1804 includes a
parchment 'paybill' or 'payroll'– a list of the Tooley and Smart almspeople with details of the
weekly payments due to each for the whole year, usually used as a wrapper in which the filed
documents were rolled. From 1803–1804 the payroll is in the form of a paper volume.
    Regular payments are for clothing, shoes, firewood and coal for the almspeople; funeral
charges; repairs to the almshouses and to buildings on the charity estates; expenses of holding
courts of the manor of Ulveston Hall in Debenham; sums due annually to the Master and Usher
of the Grammar School by Smart's bequest; and (named) boys' exhibitions to the School. Until
almost the end of the 18th century, most files include itemised apothecary's bills for the various
kinds of medicines supplied to (named) almspeople throughout the year.

C/5/1/1/8/1   1720–1721
Thomas Starling, Receiver
Smart's Charity only
(55 docs)

C/5/1/1/8/2   1721–1722
Thomas Starling, gent., Renterwarden and Receiver
(44 docs)

C/5/1/1/8/3   1726–1727
Henry Nash, Renterwarden and Receiver
Includes:
— some vouchers for 1728–1730
(120 docs)

C/5/1/1/8/4   1727–1728
John Cornelius, Renterwarden and Receiver
(51 docs)

C/5/1/1/8/5   1728–1729
Isaac Sutton, Renterwarden and Receiver
(50 docs)

C/5/1/1/8/6   1729–1730
John Sparowe, Renterwarden and Receiver
(57 docs)

C/5/1/1/8/7   1733–1734
John Marlow, Renterwarden and Receiver
(41 docs)

C/5/1/1/8/8   1734–1735
Hugh Wright, Renterwarden and Receiver
(50 docs)

C/5/1/1/8/9   1735–1736
Nathaniel Cole, Renterwarden and Receiver
(36 docs)

C/5/1/1/8/10   1736–1738
For 2 financial years
William Artis, Renterwarden and Receiver, 1736–1737
John Cornelius, Renterwarden and Receiver, 1737–1738
'Payroll' for 1736–1737 only
(107 docs)

C/5/1/1/8/11   1738–1739
William Truelove, Renterwarden and Receiver
(47 docs)

C/5/1/1/8/12   1739–1740
Capt John Margerum, Renterwarden and Receiver
(51 docs)

C/5/1/1/8/13   1740–1741
Samuel Hamblin, Renterwarden and Receiver
(59 docs)

C/5/1/1/8/14   1742–1743
John Day, Renterwarden and Receiver
(41 docs)

C/5/1/1/8/15   1744–1745
Thomas Pulford, Renterwarden and Receiver
(59 docs)

C/5/1/1/8/16   1745–1746
Henry Skinner, Renterwarden and Receiver
(79 docs)

C/5/1/1/8/17   1746–1748
For 2 financial years
John Firmin, Renterwarden and Receiver, 1746–1747
Goodchild Clarke, Renterwarden and Receiver, 1747–1748
'Payroll' not present for either year
Includes:
— Chamberlains' rental, 1759–1760 used as wrapper
(160 docs)

C/5/1/1/8/18   1748–1749
Thomas Burwell, Renterwarden and Receiver
(55 docs)

C/5/1/1/8/19   1749–1750
John Margerum, Renterwarden and Receiver (died in office)
Jacob Rix, Deputy Renterwarden
(42 docs)

C/5/1/1/8/20   1750–1751
Charles Norris, Renterwarden and Receiver
(86 docs)

C/5/1/1/8/21   1751–1752
Michael Thirkle, Renterwarden and Receiver
(48 docs)

C/5/1/1/8/22   1752–1754
For 2 financial years
William Truelove, Renterwarden and Receiver
'Payrolls' present for both years
(55 docs)

C/5/1/1/8/23   1753–1755
For 2 financial years
William Hammond, Renterwarden and Receiver
'Payroll' present for 1754–1755 only
(52 docs)

C/5/1/1/8/24   1754–1756
For 2 financial years
Thomas Bowell, Renterwarden and Receiver
'Payroll' present for 1755–1756 only
(73 docs)

C/5/1/1/8/25   1755–1756
James Wilder, Renterwarden and Receiver
'Payroll' for the year not present
Includes:
— 'payroll' for 1756–1757
(63 docs)

C/5/1/1/8/26   1756–1758
For 2 financial years
William Truelove jun., Renterwarden and Receiver, 1756–1757
James Wilder, Renterwarden and Receiver, 1757–1758
'Payroll' present for 1757–1758 only
Includes:
— bill of Thomas Singleton 'for a Portland stone with Mr Tooley's arms engraved and fixed at
the Lower Foundation House, £2.2.0', 11 Jun. 1757
(150 docs)

C/5/1/1/8/27   1758–1759
Richard Batley, Renterwarden and Receiver
(68 docs)

C/5/1/1/8/28   1759–1760
Michael Thirkle, Renterwarden and Receiver
(55 docs)

C/5/1/1/8/29   1760–1761
Capt Richard Lockwood, Renterwarden and Receiver
(86 docs)

C/5/1/1/8/30   1761–1762
James Wilder, Renterwarden and Receiver
'Payroll' not present
(46 docs)

C/5/1/1/8/31   1762
James Wilder, Receiver
Smart's Charity only
Payments of exhibitions to Grammar School boys, Oct. 1762 and to Robert Hingeston, Master
of the Grammar School, May and Sep. 1762 only
(10 docs)

C/5/1/1/8/32   1762–1763
James Wilder, Renterwarden and Receiver
For 'Payroll' see C/5/1/1/8/33
(20 docs)

C/5/1/1/8/33   1762–1763
John Forsett, Renterwarden
Tooley Foundation only
(48 docs)

C/5/1/1/8/34   1763–1764
James Wilder, Renterwarden and Receiver
'Payroll' not present
(124 docs)

C/5/1/1/8/35   1764–1765
John Gravenor, Renterwarden and Receiver
'Payroll' not present
(87 docs)

C/5/1/1/8/36   1765–1766
Michael Thirkle, Renterwarden
Tooley Foundation only
Includes:
— Renterwarden's audited account (vol.) 1765–1766
(48 docs)

C/5/1/1/8/37   1765–1766
Michael Thirkle, Receiver
Smart's Charity only
For 'payroll', see C/5/1/1/8/36
Includes:
— Renterwarden's audited account (vol.), 1765–1766
(15 docs)

C/5/1/1/8/38   1766–1767
John Sharp, Renterwarden and Receiver
'Payroll' not present
(103 docs)

C/5/1/1/8/39   1767–1768
William Hammond, Receiver
Smart's Charity only
'Payroll' not present
(43 docs)

C/5/1/1/8/40   1768–1769
Capt John Trapnell, Renterwarden and Receiver
Includes:
— survey (vol.) of oak timber at Mr Darson's of Kirton, by Robert Bond, Jun. 1769
(68 docs)

C/5/1/1/8/41   1771–1772
Peter Clarke, Renterwarden and Receiver
(76 docs)

C/5/1/1/8/42   1772–1773
Robert Goodwin, Renterwarden and Receiver
(83 docs)

C/5/1/1/8/43   1773–1774
William Clarke, Renterwarden and Receiver
(110 docs)

C/5/1/1/8/44   1774–1775
Robert Manning sen., Renterwarden
Tooley Foundation only
'Payroll' not present
(58 docs)

C/5/1/1/8/45   1774–1775
Robert Manning sen., Receiver
Smart's Charity only
'Payroll' not present
(16 docs)

C/5/1/1/8/46   1775–1776
Miles Wallis, Renterwarden and Receiver
'Payroll' is for 1773–1774, duplicating that in C/5/1/1/8/43
(72 docs)

C/5/1/1/8/47   1776–1777
Edward Betts, Renterwarden and Receiver
(73 docs)

C/5/1/1/8/48   1777–1778
Capt Thomas Hallum, Renterwarden and Receiver
Includes:
— Renterwarden's audited account (Tooley) (vol.), 1777–1778
— Receiver's audited account (Smart) (vol.), 1777–1778
(83 docs)

C/5/1/1/8/49   1778–1779
Thomas Nuthall, Renterwarden
Tooley Foundation only
'Payroll' not present
Includes:
— Renterwarden's and Receiver's audited account (Tooley and Smart) (vol.), 1778–1779
(92 docs)

C/5/1/1/8/50   1778–1779
Thomas Nuthall, Receiver
Smart's Charity only
'Payroll' not present
(42 docs)

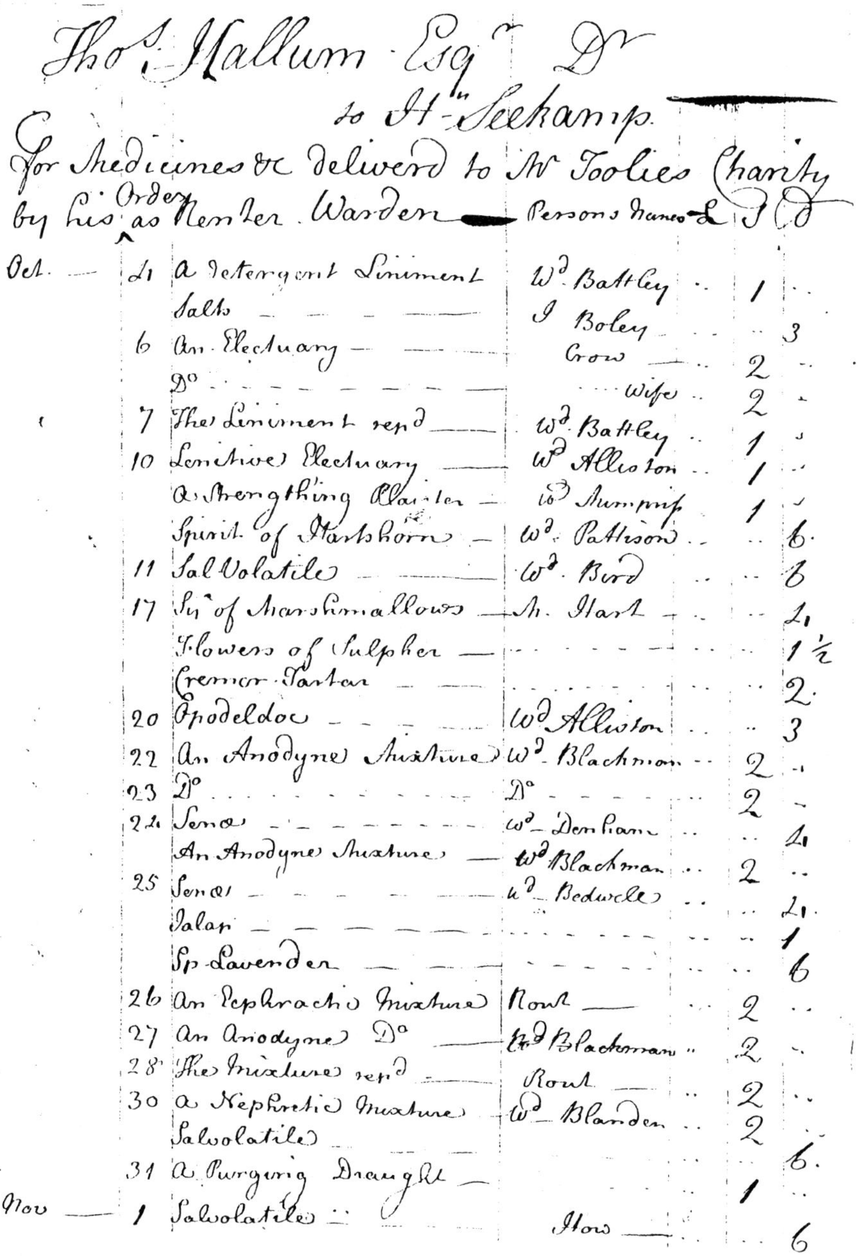

Thos. Hallum Esqr Dr
to H Seekamp.
For Medicines &c delivd to Mr Tooleys Charity
by his Order as Renter Warden —— Persons Names £ s d

Oct.	4	A detergent Liniment	Wd Battley		1
		Salts	J Boley		3
	6	An Electuary	Crow	2	
		Do	wife	2	
	7	The Liniment repd	Wd Battley		1
	10	Lenitive Electuary	Wd Alleston		1
		A Strengthing Plaister	Wd Aumpui		1
		Spirit of Hartshorn	Wd Pattison		6
	11	Sal Volatile	Wd Bird		8
	17	Sy of Marshmallows	M. Hart		4
		Flowers of Sulpher			1½
		Cremor Tartar			2
	20	Opodeldoc	Wd Alleston		3
	22	An Anodyne Mixture	Wd Blackman	2	
	23	Do	Do	2	
	24	Sena	Wd Denham		4
		An Anodyne Mixture	Wd Blackman	2	
	25	Sena	Wd Bedwell		4
		Jalap			1
		Sp Lavender			6
	26	An Pephrachio Mixture	Rout	2	
	27	An Anodyne Do	Wd Blackman	2	
	28	The Mixture repd	Rout	2	
	30	A Nephrotic Mixture	Wd Blanden	2	
		Salvolatile			6
	31	A Purging Draught		1	
Nov	1	Salvolatile	Hows		6

Fig. 21. Bill for medicines supplied to the Tooley almspeople (from the Renterwarden's payment vouchers for 1777–1778, C/5/1/1/8/48)

457

C/5/1/1/8/51   1779–1780
Joseph Clarke, Renterwarden and Receiver
'Payroll' not present
Includes:
— Renterwarden's and Receiver's audited account (vol.), 1779–1780
(81 docs)

C/5/1/1/8/52   1780–1781
John Tyrell, Renterwarden and Receiver
'Payroll' not present
Includes:
— Renterwarden's and Receiver's audited account, 1780–1781
(115 docs)

C/5/1/1/8/53   1781–1782
Henry Seekamp jun., Renterwarden and Receiver
'Payroll' not present
Includes:
— Renterwarden's audited account (Tooley) (vol.), 1781–1782
— Receiver's audited account (Smart) (vol.), 1781–1782
(102 docs)

C/5/1/1/8/54   1782–1783
Charles Norris, Renterwarden and Receiver
'Payroll' not present
(96 docs)

C/5/1/1/8/55   1783–1784
Samuel Wollaston, Renterwarden and Receiver
'Payroll' for the year not present
Includes:
— 'payroll' for 1784–1785
(121 docs)

C/5/1/1/8/56   1785–1786
John Spooner, Renterwarden and Receiver
Includes:
— Renterwarden's audited account (Tooley) (vol.), 1785–1786
— audited account of H. Seekamp, Receiver (Smart) (vol.), 1795–1796
(91 docs)

C/5/1/1/8/57   1786–1787
Christopher Rolfe, Renterwarden and Receiver
(91 docs)

C/5/1/1/8/58   1787–1788
Peter Clarke, Renterwarden and Receiver
Includes:
— Renterwarden's and Receiver's audited account (vol.), 1787–1788
(92 docs)

C/5/1/1/8/59   1788–1789
John Kerridge, Renterwarden and Receiver
Includes:
— Renterwarden's and Receiver's audited account (vol.), 1788–1789
(124 docs)

C/5/1/1/8/60   1790–1791
Samuel Howes sen., Renterwarden
Tooley Foundation only
'Payroll' not present
(83 docs)

C/5/1/1/8/61   1790–1791
Samuel Howes sen., Receiver
Smart's Charity only
'Payroll' not present
(38 docs)

C/5/1/1/8/62   1791–1792
Henry Seekamp, Renterwarden
Tooley Foundation only
'Payroll' not present
(71 docs)

C/5/1/1/8/63   1791–1792
Henry Seekamp, Receiver
Smart's Charity only
'Payroll' not present
(30 docs)

C/5/1/1/8/64   1793–1794
Admiral Thomas Hallum, Renterwarden and Receiver
'Payroll' not present
Includes:
— Renterwarden's and Receiver's audited account (vol.), Oct. 1794–Feb. 1796
(89 docs)

C/5/1/1/8/65   1794–1795
John Kerridge, Renterwarden and Receiver
'Payroll' not present
(90 docs)

C/5/1/1/8/66   1795–1796
Henry Seekamp, Renterwarden and Receiver
Includes:
— Renterwarden's audited account (Tooley only) (vol.), 1795–1796
(140 docs)

C/5/1/1/8/67   1796–1797
Samuel Thorndike, Renterwarden and Receiver
Includes:
— Renterwarden's and Receiver's audited account (vol.), 1796–1797
— survey of timber belonging to Smart's Charity felled and sold on farm in Kirton, Mar.–Jun.
1797 (vol.)
(116 docs)

C/5/1/1/8/68   1797–1798
Admiral Thomas Hallum, Renterwarden and Receiver
Includes:
— Renterwarden's and Receiver's audited account (vol), 1797–1798
(78 docs)

C/5/1/1/8/69   1798–1799
William Norris, Renterwarden and Receiver

459

Includes:
— Renterwarden's audited account (Tooley), 1798–1799
— Receiver's audited account (Smart), 1798–1799
(115 docs)

C/5/1/1/8/70   1799–1800
Peter Clarke, Renterwarden and Receiver
Includes:
— Renterwarden's audited account (Tooley) (vol.), 1799–1800
— Receiver's audited account (Smart) (vol.), 1799–1800
(119 docs)

C/5/1/1/8/71   1800–1801
John Kerridge, Renterwarden and Receiver
'Payroll' marked up for first week of financial year only
Includes:
— Renterwarden's and Receiver's audited account (vol.), 1800–1801
(71 docs)

C/5/1/1/8/72   1801–1802
John Spooner, Renterwarden and Receiver
Includes:
— Renterwarden's audited account (Tooley), 1801–1802
— Receiver's audited account (Smart), 1801–1802
(119 docs)

C/5/1/1/8/73   1802–1803
Samuel Howes, Renterwarden and Receiver
Includes:
— Renterwarden's and Receiver's audited account (vol.), 1802–1803
(88 docs)

C/5/1/1/8/74   1803–1804
Admiral Thomas Hallum (died in office) and John Spooner, Renterwardens and Receivers
2 versions of 'payroll' present: the usual single parchment membrane and a paper book
Includes:
— Renterwarden's and Receiver's audited accounts of the late Admiral Hallum, 29 Sep. 1803–13 Apr. 1804
(104 docs)

C/5/1/1/8/75   1804–1805
John Walford, Renterwarden and Receiver
Includes:
— Renterwarden's audited account (vol.), 1804–1805
— list of almspeople in receipt of coal, Oct. 1804
(118 docs)

C/5/1/1/8/76   1805–1806
Henry Seekamp, Renterwarden and Receiver
Includes:
— Renterwarden's audited account (Tooley), 1805–1806
— Receiver's audited account (Smart), 1805–1806
(138 docs)

C/5/1/1/8/77   1806–1807
Simon Jackaman, Renterwarden
Tooley Foundation only
For 'payroll', see C/5/1/1/8/78

Includes:
— Renterwarden's audited account, 1806–1807
(84 docs)

C/5/1/1/8/78   1806–1807
Simon Jackaman, Receiver
Smart's Charity only
'Payroll' (Tooley and Smart) in book form
Includes:
——Receiver's audited account, 1806–1807
(40 docs)

C/5/1/1/8/79   1807–1808
Frederick F. Seekamp, Renterwarden and Receiver
'Payroll' not present
Includes:
— Renterwarden's and Receiver's audited account, 1807–1808
(130 docs)

C/5/1/1/8/80   1808–1809
James Thorndike, Renterwarden and Receiver
'Payroll' not present
Includes:
— Renterwarden's audited account (Tooley), 1808–1809
— Receiver's audited account (Smart), 1808–1809
(123 docs)

C/5/1/1/8/81   1809–1810
John Spooner, Renterwarden and Receiver
'Payroll' not present
(131 docs)

C/5/1/1/8/82   1811–1812
William Barnard Clarke, Renterwarden
Tooley Foundation only
'Payroll' (Tooley and Smart) in book form
(74 docs)

C/5/1/1/8/83   1811–1812
William Barnard Clarke, Receiver
Smart's Charity only
For 'Payroll', *see* C/5/1/1/8/82
(40 docs)

C/5/1/1/8/84   1812–1813
Samuel Thorndike, Renterwarden and Receiver
'Payroll' not present
(152 docs)

C/5/1/1/8/85   1813–1814
John Forsett, Renterwarden and Receiver
Includes:
— Renterwarden's audited account (Tooley), 1813–1814
— Receiver's audited account (Smart), 1813–1814
(125 docs)

C/5/1/1/8/86   1814–1815
Benjamin Catt, Renterwarden and Receiver
(109 docs)

C/5/1/1/8/87   1815–1816
Benjamin Brame, Renterwarden
Tooley Foundation only
'Payroll' not present
Includes:
— Renterwarden's account (not audited), 1815–1816
(86 docs)

C/5/1/1/8/88   1815–1816
Benjamin Brame, Receiver
Smart's Charity only
'Payroll' not present
Includes:
— Receiver's account (not audited), 1815–1816
(40 docs)

C/5/1/1/8/89   1816–1817
John Denny, Renterwarden and Receiver
'Payroll' not present
(96 docs)

C/5/1/1/8/90   1817–1818
John Spooner, Renterwarden and Receiver
(123 docs)

C/5/1/1/8/91   1818–1819
William Batley, Renterwarden
Tooley Foundation only
Includes:
— valuation of Ulveston Hall Farm in Debenham, Wetheringsett and Mickfield (belonging to
Tooley Foundation), and Camps Green Farm in Debenham (belonging to Christ's Hospital),
18 Sep. 1819
(89 docs)

C/5/1/1/8/92   1818–1819
William Batley, Receiver
Smart's Charity only
For 'payroll', *see* C/5/1/1/8/91
(40 docs)

C/5/1/1/8/93   1819–1820
William Hammond, Renterwarden
Tooley Foundation only
'Payroll' not present
(87 docs)

C/5/1/1/8/94   1819–1820
William Hammond, Receiver
Smart's Charity only
'Payroll' not present
(32 docs)

C/5/1/1/8/95   1820–1821
Samuel Boggis, Renterwarden and Receiver
'Payroll' not present
Includes:
— list of almspeople dying between 24 Dec. 1820 and 16 Aug. 1821, with dates of deaths
(109 docs)

C/5/1/1/8/96   1821–1822
Frederick F. Seekamp, Renterwarden and Receiver
'Payroll' not present
(43 docs)

C/5/1/1/8/97   1822–1823
John E. Sparrow, Renterwarden and Receiver
'Payroll' not present
(101 docs)

C/5/1/1/8/98   1823–1824
William Barnard Clarke, Renterwarden and Receiver
'Payroll' not present
(114 docs)

C/5/1/1/8/99   1824–1825
Richard Bruce, Renterwarden and Receiver
'Payroll' not present
(142 docs)

C/5/1/1/8/100   1825–1826
Benjamin Brame, Renterwarden and Receiver
'Payroll' not present
(124 docs)

C/5/1/1/8/101   1826–1827
Abraham Cook, Receiver
Smart's Charity only
'Payroll' not present
(47 docs)

C/5/1/1/8/102   1827–1828
William Hammond, Renterwarden and Receiver
'Payroll' not present
(91 docs)

C/5/1/1/8/103   1828–1829
William Calver, Renterwarden and Receiver
'Payroll' not present
(144 docs)

C/5/1/1/8/104   1829–1830
F. F. Seekamp, Renterwarden and Receiver
(124 docs)

C/5/1/1/8/105   1830–1831
William Lane, Renterwarden
Tooley Foundation only
'Payroll' not present
(96 docs)

C/5/1/1/8/106   1830–1831
William Lane, Receiver
Smart's Charity only
'Payroll' not present
(39 docs)

C/5/1/1/8/107   1832–1833
Benjamin B. Catt, Renterwarden
Tooley Foundation only

'Payroll' not present
(42 docs, found loose – probably 'strays' from the main voucher file for this year, now missing)

C/5/1/1/8/108   1833–1834
Benjamin Brame, Renterwarden and Receiver
'Payroll' not present
(113 docs)

C/5/1/1/8/109   1833–1834
Benjamin Brame, Renterwarden
Tooley Foundation only
'Payroll' not present
(2 docs, found loose – 'strays' from the main voucher file for this year, C/5/1/1/8/108)

C/5/1/1/8/110   1834–1835
Thomas Dunningham, Renterwarden and Receiver
'Payroll' not present
(109 docs)

C/5/1/1/8/111   1835–1836
Thomas Dunningham, Renterwarden and Receiver
'Payroll' not present
(100 docs)

C/5/1/1/8/112   1835–1836
Thomas Dunningham, Receiver
Smart's Charity only
'Payroll' not present
(10 docs)

C/5/1/1/9   MISCELLANEOUS ACCOUNTS   1569

C/5/1/1/9/1   1569
Account for building work and construction of pump [? at the Foundation]
(2 docs)

C/5/1/2   CHRIST'S HOSPITAL   1583–1836

In 1569 the buildings of the former priory of the Dominicans (Black Friars or Friars Preachers) in what is now Foundation Street were acquired by the Corporation in order to establish a workhouse to complement the work of the nearby Tooley Foundation in relieving the poor. The institution received formal status, as Christ's Hospital, by Elizabeth I's charter of 1572. In addition to providing relief and maintenance for the aged, the sick, and children, and employment and correction for the idle or vicious, from the late 17th century it functioned also as a school, endowed by Nicholas Phillips of Ipswich, merchant, by the bequest of Kersey's Farm in Debenham. The property was conveyed by his executors to the Portmen in 1676 (for the conveyance, see C/3/10/2/5/4/12; see also Canning 1747, 63–65). Though the Tooley Foundation and the Hospital were two separate organisations, each with its own revenues and officials, during Elizabeth's reign their activities were closely linked, and in practice they provided Ipswich with a single centre for indoor relief of the poor. The administration of the Hospital was the responsibility of four Governors (one of whom was nominated Treasurer), elected annually from among the freemen of the town. In practice the governing body was made up of one Portman, two members of the Twenty-four, and one ordinary burgess. The officials in charge of routine administration were appointed by the Corporation, with the advice of the Governors. The Hospital's funding came from the rents of real property both within and outside the town, together with certain petty dues, such as a fee payable by each incoming freeman, and charitable donations and bequests. In the Elizabethan period these sources of income were supplemented from the Common Collection (poor rate). (*See* Webb 1966, 12–14.)

The Hospital eventually abandoned its role as a general poor-house and workhouse, though in addition to its function as a charity school (which it retained until the Endowed Schools Act of 1881) it also maintained a public Bridewell or house of correction until the late 18th century.

C/5/1/2/1   MINUTES   1752–1828
(For Governors' minutes, 1828–1836, *see* Ipswich Record Office, HD 801/1.)

C/5/1/2/1/1   1751–1828
Minute and account book
At front: accounts of receipts (mostly of rents) and payments (mostly for maintenance of the boys, including the costs of binding them as apprentices, and the repair of buildings, etc.), Sep. 1751–12 Feb. 1788
At back: minutes of Governors' meetings, 14 Nov. 1752–16 Oct. 1828
Includes (before the minutes):
— 'rules to be observed for the future for the better government of Christ's Hospital', n.d. [1752]
— articles between the present Governors and the Guide or Keeper, n.d. [1752]
— rules to be observed by the Guide or Keeper, n.d. [1752]
— rules to be observed by the School Master, n.d. [1752]
— rules to be observed by the boys, n.d. [1752]
— general account of rents payable to Christ's Hospital, n.d. [1752]
— inventory of goods and wearing apparel belonging to the Hospital and present children, 1752, audited 1755
— list of boys (names, dates of birth or baptism, dates of admission, home parish), 1752
Includes (interspersed with minutes):
— inventories, 1760, 1761, 1764, 1766, 1768, 1773, 1786, 1787, 1791, 1820
— lists of boys (details as above until 1817, names only thereafter), 1755, 1813, annually 1817–1825, 1828
   (1 vol., with partial index of personal names)

C/5/1/2/2   ACCOUNTS OF THE GOVERNORS AND TREASURER   1583–1807

(For the Treasurer's account book, 1579–1580, *see* Ipswich Record Office, HD 88/3/4; For Treasury warrants, etc,. 1591–1732, *see* HD 88/3/5.)
These are the audited accounts, bearing the signatures of the auditors. Unless otherwise stated, each account is for one full year, beginning and ending at Michaelmas (29 September). The accounts are sometimes in the joint names of the Governors and Treasurer (who was of their number) and sometimes in the name of the Treasurer alone. The chief sources of regular income recorded are the rents of houses and lands appropriated to the Hospital and the fees paid by incoming freemen. Other receipts are from voluntary gifts and legacies. Payments are chiefly for the maintenance of the Hospital buildings and town houses and farm property in its ownership; food, clothing, fuel and medical attention for the inmates; officers' wages; and the expenses of binding apprentices. Many of the volumes have, pinned inside the front cover, receipts for the rent paid to the Crown for the site of the house of the former Friars Preachers. There is a gap in the series of accounts from 1758–59 to 1806–07. For most years after 1779–80 the audited accounts are preserved in the annual files of payment vouchers (C/5/1/2/4). For Hospital accounts covering the years 1751–1788, *see also* the minute book (C/5/1/2/1/1).

C/5/1/2/2/1   1583–1586
Austen Parker, Bailiff, Rauffe Scryvener, gent. and William Smarte, Jan.–Sep. 1583
Rauffe Scryvener, gent., Edward Goodyng, gent., Austen Parker, merchant, and William Smarte, draper, Sep. 1583–Sep. 1584
Edward Goodyng, gent., William Smarte, draper, Thomas Glede and Edward Cage, Sep. 1584–Sep. 1585
Augustin Parker, William Bloyze, Robert Snellinge and John Carnaby, Governors, Sep. 1585–Sep. 1586
Includes, at end:
— account of William Smarte for profit on sale of 8 'foreign' mill stones, 1587
(2 vols, 1 for 1583–1585, the other for 1585–1586, sewn together in reverse chronological order)

C/5/1/2/2/2   Nov. 1586–Sep. 1587
Robert Cutler [?Treasurer]
(1 vol. Front cover annotated, in a later hand, *re* payment of rents to the Master of Mr Felaw's School / the Grammar School, 1596–1703)

C/5/1/2/2/3   1595–1596
John Knappe, Mr Bloyse sen., John Warde and Gilbert Lynkfilld, Governors; John Warde, Treasurer
Includes, inside front cover:
— list of male and female children at present in the Hospital.
(1 vol.)

C/5/1/2/2/4   1596–1597
Mr Goodinge, Mr Mydnall, John Warde and Gilbert Lynkfylld, Governors; John Warde, Treasurer
(1 vol.)

C/5/1/2/2/5   1601–1602
Edward Cage, William Sparrowe, John Warde and George Parkhurste, Governors; John Warde, Treasurer
(1 vol.)

C/5/1/2/2/6   Mar. 1603–Mar. 1604
Matthew Brownrigg, Treasurer
(1 vol.)

C/5/1/2/2/7   Sep.1603–Sep. 1604
Matthew Brownrigg, Treasurer
(1 vol.; found among the series of Town Treasurer's audited accounts)

C/5/1/2/2/8   1606–1607
John Herne, Treasurer
Includes:
— account of money laid out by Herne 'for and abute the Kynges Majestyes Free newe Grammer Schoole', 29 Sep. 1607–1 Jul. 1608
(1 vol.)

C/5/1/2/2/9   1607–1608
James Tillott, Treasurer
(1 vol.)

C/5/1/2/2/10   Mar. 1613–Mar. 1614
Thomas Johnson, Treasurer
(1 vol.)

C/5/1/2/2/11   1614–1615
Matthew Brownbrige, Richard Martine and George Acton [Governors] and Christopher Aldgate,
Treasurer
(1 vol.)

C/5/1/2/2/12   1615–1616
William Clyatt, Treasurer
(1 vol.)

C/5/1/2/2/13   1617–1618
John Bore, Treasurer
Includes, at end:
— inventory of town goods remaining at the Hospital, 25 Feb. 1618
(1 vol.)

C/5/1/2/2/14   1618–1619
John Flicke, Treasurer
(1 vol.)

C/5/1/2/2/15   1620–1621
John Carnabie, Treasurer
(1 vol.)

C/5/1/2/2/16   1623–1624
Richard Pupplet, Treasurer
(1 vol.)

C/5/1/2/2/17   1624–1625
—— Cole, Treasurer
(1 vol.)

C/5/1/2/2/18   1625–1626
Thomas Hayles, Governor, Edmund Humfreye, Governor and Treasurer
(1 vol.)

C/5/1/2/2/19   1626–1627
John Alldus, Treasurer
(1 vol.)

C/5/1/2/2/20   1628–1629
George Acton, Edmund Kene, gent., Isaac Grenewich and Joseph Parkhurst, Governors; Isaac
Grenewich, Treasurer
(1 vol.)

C/5/1/2/2/21   1629–1630
Thomas Seely, Treasurer
(1 vol.)

C/5/1/2/2/22   1630–1631
Robert Sparrowe, John Carnabie, Isaac Daye and Daniel Snowe, Governors;
Daniel Snowe, Treasurer
(1 vol.)

C/5/1/2/2/23   1631–1632
James Tillott, John Aldus, Barnaby Borroughe and John Warner, Governors;
John Warner, Treasurer
(1 vol.)

C/5/1/2/2/24   1633–1634
William Cage, William Moysey, Daniel Snowe and John Alderman, Governors;
Daniel Snowe, Treasurer
(1 vol.)

C/5/1/2/2/25   1634–1635
William Cage, John Aldus, Daniel Snowe and John Warner, Governors;
Daniel Snowe, Treasurer
(1 vol.)

C/5/1/2/2/26   1635–1636
Edmund Keene, Thomas Seely, Thomas Ives and Peter Fisher, Governors;
Peter Fisher, Treasurer
(1 vol.)

C/5/1/2/2/27   1636–1637
John Aldus, Edmund Umphry, Joseph Pemberton and Thomas Knapp, Governors;
Thomas Knapp, Treasurer
(1 vol.)

C/5/1/2/2/28   1637–1638
William Moysey, William Tyler, Richard Denny and William Bull, Governors;
William Bull, Treasurer
(1 vol.)

C/5/1/2/2/29   1639–1640
William Cage, esq., William Tyler, gent., Robert Dunkon and John Bloumfeild, Governors;
Robert Dunkon, Treasurer
(1 vol.)

C/5/1/2/2/30   1640–1641
John Aldus, William Sparrow, gent., Edmund Morgan and Samuel Duncon, Governors;
Samuel Duncon, Treasurer
(1 vol.)

C/5/1/2/2/31   1643–1644
William Sparowe, John Brandling, gent., Jacob Caley and Thomas Wright, Governors; Jacob
Caley, Treasurer
(1 vol.)

C/5/1/2/2/32   1644–1645
Robert Dunckon, gent. (Bailiff), John Sicklemore, gent., Henry Parkehurst and John Blackborne,
Governors; John Blackborne, Treasurer
(1 vol.)

C/5/1/2/2/33   1645–1646
Joseph Pemberton, gent., Edmund Humfrie, John Blyth and Henry Whiting, Governors; Henry
Whiting, Treasurer
(1 vol.)

C/5/1/2/2/34   1646–1647
Richard Haile, gent., Mannuell Sorrell, gent., Benjamin Wade and Benjamin Buttar, Governors; Benjamin Wade, Treasurer
(1 vol.)

C/5/1/2/2/35   1650–1651
John Bradlinge, esq., Jacob Caly, gent., Thomas Newton and Simon Cumberland, Governors;
Simon Cumberland, Treasurer after the death of Thomas Newton
(1 vol.)

C/5/1/2/2/36   1653–1654

Nicholas Phillipps, gent., Richard Jennings, gent., Richard Girlinge and Luke Jowers, Governors; Luke Jowers, Treasurer

(1 vol; back cover endorsed, ? in an early 18c. hand, 'books want from 1672 to 1680', though they are not now missing)

C/5/1/2/2/37   1657–1658

Robert Dunkon, esq., Manuell Sorrell, gent., Simond Cumberland and Thomas Carter, Governors; Thomas Carter, Treasurer

(1 vol.)

C/5/1/2/2/38   1659–1660

John Brandlin, Robert Sparrow, Benjamin Wade and Gilbert Lindfild, Governors; Gilbert Lindfild, Treasurer

Includes:

–inventory of contents of Hospital, 10 Oct. 1659

(1 vol.)

C/5/1/2/2/39   1660–1661

Nicholas Phillipps, Henry Whitinge, Thomas Wright and Thomas Wright Salter, Governors; Thomas Wright Salter, Treasurer

Includes:

— lists of poor children for each quarter

(1 vol.)

C/5/1/2/2/40   1661–1662

John Alldes and Luke Jouers, gents., Richard Haylles and Robert Rednall, Governors; Robert Rednall, Treasurer

(1 vol.)

C/5/1/2/2/41   1662–1663

Thomas Burrough, Robert Sparrow, Luke Jours and Henry Cosin, Governors; Henry Cosin, Treasurer

Includes:

— lists of poor children for three of four quarters

(1 vol.)

C/5/1/2/2/42   1665–1666

John Wright, gent., Luke Jewers, gent., Edward Reynolds and John Sawyer, Governors; John Sawyer, Treasurer

Includes:

— lists of poor children for three of four quarters

(1 vol.)

C/5/1/2/2/43   1666–1667

Nicholas Phillipps, gent., Gilbert Linkfild, gent., John Firmin and Edward Renoldes, Governors; Edward Renoldes, Treasurer

(1 vol.)

C/5/1/2/2/44   1667–1668

Manuell Sorel, gent., —— Wolles, gent., Anthony Appelwhit and John Firman, Governors; John Firman, Treasurer

Includes:

— lists of poor children for each quarter

(1 vol.)

C/5/1/2/2/45   1668–1669

Nicholas Phillips, gent., Thomas Reeve, gent. and Anthony Applewhit, Governors; Anthony Applewhit, Treasurer

Includes:
— lists of poor children for three of four quarters
(1 vol.)

C/5/1/2/2/46   1670–1671
———— Burrough, Treasurer
Includes:
— lists of poor children for each quarter
(1 vol.)

C/5/1/2/2/47   1671–1672
William Cullum, gent., Charles Wright, gent., William Veasey and John Reeve, Governors;
John Reeve, Treasurer
Includes:
— lists of poor children for each quarter
(1 vol.)

C/5/1/2/2/48   1672–1673
William Cullum, gent., John Pemberton, gent., William Vesey and John Reeve, Governors;
John Reeve, Treasurer
Includes:
— lists of poor children for three of four quarters
(1 vol.)

C/5/1/2/2/49   1673–1674
Andrew Sorrell, esq., Lawrence Stistead, gent. and William Vesey, Governors; William Vesey,
Treasurer
Includes:
— on front cover, inventory of goods in Hospital at time of Nicholas Sicklemore's election as
Keeper
— lists of poor children for three of four quarters
(1 vol.)

C/5/1/2/2/50   1674–1675
Henry Gosnold, gent., Richard Phillipes, gent., Samuel Mayle and William Vesey, Governors;
William Vesey, Treasurer
Includes:
— lists of poor children for each quarter
(1 vol.)

C/5/1/2/2/51   1677–1678
John Wright, gent., John Burrough, gent., William Sawyer and Samuel Maile, Governors;
Samuel Maile, Treasurer
(1 vol.)

C/5/1/2/2/52   1678–1679
William Neave, gent., Richard Philips, gent., Thomas Driver and John Camplin, Governors;
John Camplin, Treasurer
(1 vol.)

C/5/1/2/2/53   1679–1680
William Sayer, gent., William Neave, gent., Thomas Bright and John Camplin, Governors;
John Camplin, Treasurer
(1 vol.)

C/5/1/2/2/54   1680–1681
Lawrence Stystead, gent., William Neave, gent., William Tye and John Camplin, Governors;
John Camplin, Treasurer
(1 vol.)

C/5/1/2/2/55   1681–1682
William Neave, gent. (Bailiff), Lawrence Stystead, gent., William Tye and John Camplin,
Governors; John Camplin, Treasurer
(1 vol.)

C/5/1/2/2/56   1682–1683
William Browne, gent., John Wright, gent., Richard Clopton and John Gibbon, Governors;
John Gibbon, Treasurer
(1 vol.)

C/5/1/2/2/57   1683–1684
Richard Phillips, gent., John Blumffild, gent., Henry Sparrow and John Gibbon, Governors,
John Gibbon, Treasurer
(1 vol.)

C/5/1/2/2/58   1684–1685
Lawrence Stisted, gent., John Burrowghs, gent., Israel Barritt and John Gibbon, Governors;
John Gibbon, Treasurer.
Includes:
— list of 21 children bound apprentices out of the Hospital, 1681–1685, with names of masters
and dates of indentures
(1 vol.)

C/5/1/2/2/59   1685–1686
John Lamb, esq., Richard Phillips, gent., John Gibbon and Keble Crosse, Governors; Keble
Crosse, Treasurer
(1 vol.)

C/5/1/2/2/60   1686–1687
Sir Nicholas Bacon and Lawrence Stisted, gent. (Bailiffs), Richard Phillips, gent., John Gibbon
and Keble Crosse, Governors; Keble Crosse, Treasurer
(1 vol.)

C/5/1/2/2/61   1687–1688
Truth Norris, Treasurer
(1 vol.)

C/5/1/2/2/62   1688–1689
Truth Norris, Treasurer
(1 vol.)

C/5/1/2/2/63   1689–1694
Robert Hovell *alias* Smith, Treasurer
(1 vol.)

C/5/1/2/2/64   1694–1698
Henry Skynner, Treasurer
(1 vol.)

C/5/1/2/2/65   1699–1700
Richard Phillips, gent., Samuel Reynolds, gent., Joseph Coleman and Samuel Rudkin, Governors; Samuel Rudkin, Treasurer
(1 vol.)

C/5/1/2/2/66   1700–1703
Joseph Colman, Treasurer. The other Governors are Richard Philips, Samuel Reynolds and
Samuel Rudkin, 1700–1701; Richard Philips and William Neave, 1701–1702; and Richard
Philips, Henry Sparrow and Henry Hill, 1702–1703
(1 vol.)

C/5/1/2/2/67   1717–1721
Cooper Gravenor, Treasurer
(1 vol.)

C/5/1/2/2/68   1721–1725
George Scott, Treasurer
(1 vol.)

C/5/1/2/2/69   1725–1726
John Sparowe, Governor [*sic*]
(1 doc.)

C/5/1/2/2/70   1726–1727
John Sparowe [Treasurer]
(1 doc.)

C/5/1/2/2/71   1727–1728
John Sparowe [Treasurer]
(1 doc.)

C/5/1/2/2/72   1728–1729
John Sparowe [Treasurer]
(1 doc.)

C/5/1/2/2/73   1730–1731
John Goldson, Treasurer
(1 doc.)

C/5/1/2/2/74   1731–1735
Thomas Starling, Treasurer
(1 vol.)

C/5/1/2/2/75   1735–1737
John Sparowe, Treasurer
(1 vol.)

C/5/1/2/2/76   1742–1744
Copy, Treasurer not named
(1 vol.)

C/5/1/2/2/77   1748–1749
Michael Thirkle jun., Treasurer
(1 doc.)

C/5/1/2/2/78   1757–1758
William Truelove, Treasurer
(1 vol.)

C/5/1/2/2/79   1806–1807
William Norris, Treasurer
(1 vol.)

C/5/1/2/3   OTHER ACCOUNTS   1697–1703

C/5/1/2/3/1   1697–1703
Account of Charles Wright for 'Mr Phillips his Gift' [the farm] in Debenham, in the tenure of
George Kersey.
(1 vol; found with the accounts of the Governors and Treasurer)

C/5/1/2/4   VOUCHERS   1754–1836

These consist almost entirely of annual bundles, or, more accurately, rolled files, since most vouchers were found filed on laces; the accounting year ran from Michaelmas (29 September) to Michaelmas. Payments are chiefly for fuel, food and clothing for the Hospital boys; teaching of reading and writing; medical attention; repairs to Hospital buildings and equipment and to town and farm properties in its ownership; and rents due to manorial lords for Hospital lands. For much of the period the Guide's [? or Housekeeper's] quarterly bills for the care of the boys regularly list the names of those who were sick; and the shoemakers' bills frequently name the boys for whom shoes were provided or repaired. Between 1780 and 1808 the files usually include the Treasurer's audited account for the year; these are a continuation of the sequence of audited accounts preserved separately from 1583 to 1758 (C/5/1/2/2/1–79). From 1773 until 1820 the files also include apprenticeship indentures of Hospital boys. Until 1788 these were usually preserved separately (*see* C/5/1/2/5); after 1794 all the surviving indentures are with the vouchers. After 1836, the payment of the Hospital bills was the responsibility of the Trustees of the Ipswich Charities.

C/5/1/2/4/1   1754–1755
William Truelove, Treasurer
Includes:
— notice to Abraham Goldsmith to quit the Hospital's farm in PE, 20 Mar. 1755
(49 docs)

C/5/1/2/4/2   1755–1756
Charles Norris, Treasurer
(54 docs)

C/5/1/2/4/3   1756–1757
Charles Norris, Treasurer
(57 docs)

C/5/1/2/4/4   1757–1758
William Truelove, Treasurer
(50 docs)

C/5/1/2/4/5   1758–1759
William Truelove, Treasurer
(67 docs)

C/5/1/2/4/6   1759–1760
Samuel Hamblin, Treasurer
(48 docs)

C/5/1/2/4/7   1760–1761
James Wilder, Treasurer
(58 docs)

C/5/1/2/4/8   1761–1762
Capt Richard Lockwood, Treasurer
(64 docs)

C/5/1/2/4/9   1762–1763
John Trapnell, Treasurer
Sarah Truelove's account [? as Guide] for quarter 5 Apr.–5 Jul. 1763 includes: 'April 8 – Half a day's liberty for the boys to see Mrs Beddingfield executed, 1s 9d' [Richard Ringe murdered his master, John Beddingfield, by strangling him while asleep, having been importuned by Margery Beddingfield, who promised him marriage as soon as he had killed her husband. Both were executed the same day, he by hanging, she by being strangled and burnt (*Ipswich Journal*, 2 and 9 Apr. 1763)]
(55 docs)

C/5/1/2/4/10   1763–1764
Samuel Hamblin, Treasurer
(61 docs)

C/5/1/2/4/11   1764–1765
Capt Richard Lockwood, Treasurer
(60 docs)

C/5/1/2/4/12   1765–1766
James Wilder, Treasurer
(90 docs)

C/5/1/2/4/13   1766–1767
William Hammond, Treasurer
(64 docs)

C/5/1/2/4/14   1767–1768
William Hammond, Treasurer
(69 docs)

C/5/1/2/4/15   1768–1769
Joseph Clarke, Treasurer
(105 docs)

C/5/1/2/4/16   1769–1770
Joseph Clarke, Treasurer
(105 docs)

C/5/1/2/4/17   1770–1771
Joseph Clarke, Treasurer
(65 docs)

C/5/1/2/4/18   1771–1772
Joseph Clarke, Treasurer
Includes:
— account of Gregory Mulley for 'pulling down the ould armery', 20 Jun. 1770, paid 12 Oct.
1771
(65 docs)

C/5/1/2/4/19   1772–1773
Joseph Clarke, Treasurer
(54 docs)

C/5/1/2/4/20   1773–1774
Joseph Clarke, Treasurer
Includes:
— apprenticeship indenture, James Edwards of Ipswich, singleman, bound to Nathaniel
Saunders sen. of Harwich (Essex), fisherman, 18 Dec. 1773
— apprenticeship indenture, James Cook, singleman, bound to Robert Liveing of Harwich
(Essex), fisherman, 2 Mar. 1774
— apprenticeship indenture, Jonas Howes, singleman, bound to Richard Bloss of Harwich
(Essex), mariner, 25 Aug. 1774
— apprenticeship indenture, Edward Chaplin of Ipswich, singleman, son of Ann Chaplin,
bound to Daniel Whiting of Ipswich, woolcomber, 19 Sep. 1774
— apprenticeship indenture, William Greenleafe of Ipswich, singleman, bound to Francis
Hatch of Harwich (Essex), fisherman, 19 Sep. 1774
(69 docs)

C/5/1/2/4/21   1774–1775
Joseph Clarke, Treasurer
(45 docs)

C/5/1/2/4/22   1775–1776
Joseph Clarke, Treasurer
Includes:
— letter, 15 Nov. 1775, from Thomas Hallum [a Governor] to Clarke, authorising 1 guinea
compensation to John Wade of Ipswich, baker, whose Hospital apprentice, Burke, 'turn'd out
so notorious a thief' that his master was obliged to assign him to the master of a Harwich cod
smack
(75 docs)

C/5/1/2/4/23   1776–1777
Joseph Clarke, Treasurer
(94 docs)

C/5/1/2/4/24   1777–1778
Thomas Hallum, Treasurer
(76 docs)

C/5/1/2/4/25   1778–1779
Thomas Foster Notcutt, Treasurer
(80 docs)

C/5/1/2/4/26   1779–1780
Thomas Foster Notcutt, Treasurer
Includes:
— Treasurer's audited account, 1779–1780, used as wrapper
(80 docs)

C/5/1/2/4/27   1780–1781
Thomas Foster Notcutt, Treasurer
Includes:
— Treasurer's audited account, 1780–1781
— apprenticeship indenture, John Sharpe, singleman, bound to William Sharpe of Ipswich,
mariner, 21 May 1782
— apprenticeship indenture, Benjamin Harvey Smith, singleman, bound to Francis Stevens of
Harwich (Essex), owner of the fishing boat 'Hopewell' 24 Jun. 1782
(102 docs)

C/5/1/2/4/28   1785–1786
John Kerridge, Treasurer
Includes:
— apprenticeship indenture, Thomas Cheese bound to Lazarus Grimwood of Needham
market, cordwainer, 17 Apr.1786
— apprenticeship indenture, George Fuller bound to Henry Johnston Enefer of Harwich
(Essex), fishing smack owner, 19 Apr. 1786
(79 docs)

C/5/1/2/4/29   1786–1787
John Kerridge, Treasurer
Includes:
— apprenticeship indenture, Joseph Easterby bound to Robert Bowman jun. of Ipswich,
glover, 9 Nov. 1786
— apprenticeship indenture, Stebbing Crow, nephew of John Knivett, bound to James Gall of
Wickham Market, tailor, 15 Mar. 1787
(87 docs)

C/5/1/2/4/30   1788–1789
John Kerridge, Treasurer
Includes:
— Treasurer's audited account for 1787–1788

— apprenticeship indenture, Robert Adams bound to Nathaniel Berry of Harwich (Essex), cordwainer, 8 May 1788
— James Stubbin Woods bound to Francis Green of Ipswich, cordwainer, 30 Jun. 1788
— John Wade bound to John Spracklin of Harwich, (Essex), fisherman, 5 Jul. 1788
— William Torvell, son of Sarah Cracknell of Ipswich, bound to David Cracknell of Ipswich, mariner, 5 Sep. 1788
(85 docs)

C/5/1/2/4/31   1790–1791
Capt Thomas Hallum, Treasurer
Includes:
— Treasurer's audited account, 1790–1791 (vol.)
— estimate of annual value of farm and limekiln in Claydon in occupation of Thomas Cooper (lease to expire at Michaelmas 1791), by John Josselyn, 3 Dec. 1789
— itemised bill for medicines supplied by H. Seekamp, Oct. 1790–Aug.1791
— apprenticeship indenture, Isaac Moore of Ipswich, singleman, bound to Benjamin Clover of Ipswich, painter and glazier, 13 Nov. 1790
— apprenticeship indenture, Edward Adams of Ipswich, singleman, bound to Simon Jennings of Ipswich, fisherman, 11 Jun. 1791
— apprenticeship indenture, John Felgate of Ipswich, singleman, bound to Thomas Studd of Ipswich, woolcomber, 15 Jun. 1791
(116 docs)

C/5/1/2/4/32   1791–1792
Capt Thomas Hallum, Treasurer
Includes:
— Treasurer's audited account, 1791–1792
(94 docs)

C/5/1/2/4/33   1792–1793
John Kerridge, Treasurer
Includes:
— Treasurer's audited account, 1792–1793
— apprenticeship indenture, William Wade bound to Robert Pite of Ipswich, baker, 15 Jan. 1793
— John Scott bound to Stephen Buttrum of Hasketon, blacksmith, 21 Mar. 1793
(89 docs)

C/5/1/2/4/34   1793–1794
John Kerridge, Treasurer
Includes:
— apprenticeship indenture, James Thursby bound to William Wall of St Anne's, Soho (Middlesex), hairdresser, 30 Jul. 1794
— apprenticeship indenture, John Broom bound to James Martin of Ipswich, cordwainer, 21 Aug. 1794
(82 docs)

C/5/1/2/4/35   1794–1795
Admiral Thomas Hallum, Treasurer
Includes:
— apprenticeship indenture, Robert Head bound to James Catchpole of Wapping Wall, Shadwell, London, painter and glazier, 10 Oct. 1794
— apprenticeship indenture, William Marshall bound to Tyrell Lambly of Ipswich, mariner, 6 Jun. 1795
— apprenticeship indenture, Edward Woollard bound to Samuel Pooley of Holbrook, cordwainer, 27 Jun. 1795

— apprenticeship indenture, William Orris bound to John London of Woodbridge, hat maker, 1 Jul. 1795
(88 docs)

C/5/1/2/4/36   1795–1796
Admiral Thomas Hallum, Treasurer
Includes:
— Treasurer's audited account, 1795–1796
(104 docs)

C/5/1/2/4/37   1796–1797
Admiral Thomas Hallum, Treasurer
Includes:
— Treasurer's audited account, 1796–1797
— apprenticeship indenture, Robert Hunt bound to William Letch of Stutton, cordwainer, 3 May 1797
— apprenticeship indenture, Samuel Dowsing Hallum bound to James Martin of Ipswich, cordwainer, 31 Jul. 1797
(85 docs)

C/5/1/2/4/38   1797–1798
John Kerridge, Treasurer
Includes:
— Treasurer's audited account, 1797–1798
— apprenticeship indenture, Thomas Harrison jun. bound to John Pratt of Capel St Mary, cordwainer, 9 Oct. 1797
— apprenticeship indenture, John Martin bound to Cuthbert Ranson of Sunderland (Durham), mariner, 13 Mar. 1798
— apprenticeship indenture, Adam Gladdon bound to James Arnold of Henley, cordwainer, 13 Apr. 1798
(89 docs)

C/5/1/2/4/39   1798–1799
John Kerridge, Treasurer
Includes:
— Treasurer's audited account, 1798–1799
— apprenticeship indenture, John Seagrief bound to John Seagrief of St George in the East, London, chairmaker, 11 Sep. 1799
— apprenticeship indenture, William Chambers of Ipswich, singleman, bound to James Butcher of ST, hat manufacturer, 17 Sep. 1799
(105 docs)

C/5/1/2/4/40   1799–1800
Admiral Thomas Hallum, Treasurer
Includes:
— Treasurer's audited account, 1799–1800
— apprenticeship indenture, Joseph Gordon (by consent of his father-in-law [?stepfather] Abraham Jarvis) bound to George Wightman of Grundisburgh, cordwainer, 17 Dec. 1799
— apprenticeship indenture, Robert Frost bound to William Rolfe of Ipswich, cork cutter, 23 Jul. 1800
(108 docs)

C/5/1/2/4/41   1800–1801
John Kerridge, Treasurer
Includes:
— Treasurer's audited account, 1800–1801
— apprenticeship indenture, Benjamin Kimble bound to Samuel Ford of CL, mariner, 19 Jun. 1801

— apprenticeship indenture, William Rogers bound to John Biggs of Ipswich, mariner, 8 Oct. 1801
(81 docs)

C/5/1/2/4/42   1801–1802
John Kerridge, Treasurer
Includes:
— Treasurer's audited account, 1801–1802
(91 docs)

C/5/1/2/4/43   1802–1803
John Kerridge, Treasurer
Includes:
— Treasurer's audited account, 1802–1803
— apprenticeship indenture, James Noble, son of Elizabeth Noble, bound to Samuel Osborn of
CL, basket maker, 10 Jan. 1803
(80 docs)

C/5/1/2/4/44   1803–1804
John Kerridge, Treasurer
Includes:
— Treasurer's audited account, 1803–1804
— apprenticeship indenture, James Emmerson, son of William Emmerson of Ipswich, bricklayer, bound to Joseph Barton of Ipswich, bricklayer, 29 May 1803
— apprenticeship indenture, Thomas Markham, son of Thomas Markham of Deptford (Kent),
mariner, bound to Joseph Hains of St Giles, Camberwell (Surrey), carpenter and joiner, 8 Sep.
1803; with letter from Thomas Markham sen. *re* money due to him from the Hospital School,
19 Sep. 1803
— apprenticeship indenture, Henry Richard Martin bound to John Caston jun. of Ipswich,
mariner, 6 Mar. 1804
— apprenticeship indenture, Job Nunn of Ipswich, singleman, bound to Henry Canham of
Ipswich, butcher, 6 Jun. 1804
— apprenticeship indenture, James Saxby, son of Job Saxby, bound to William Chaplin of PE,
brazier and iron plate worker, 6 Jul. 1804
(84 docs)

C/5/1/2/4/45   1804–1805
William Norris, Treasurer
Includes:
— Treasurer's audited account, 1804–1805
(103 docs)

C/5/1/2/4/46   1805–1806
William Norris, Treasurer
Includes:
— Treasurer's audited account, 1805–1806
— apprenticeship indenture, Richard Hewer bound to Robert Enefer of Harwich (Essex),
fisherman, 15 Nov. 1805
— apprenticeship indenture, John Lacey, a poor child belonging to MW, bound to William
Roberts of St Andrew, Holborn (Middlesex), sawyer and timber dealer, 27 Mar. 1806
(103 docs; stop for file lace formed from season ticket for Mr and Miss Norris to the boxes at
the New Theatre, Ipswich, 1803)

C/5/1/2/4/47   1806–1808
William Norris, Treasurer
Includes:
— apprenticeship indenture, Henry Day bound to Robert Ennefer of Harwich (Essex), fisherman, 23 Jun. 1807
(103 docs)

C/5/1/2/4/48   1807–1808
William Norris, Treasurer
Includes:
— Treasurer's audited account, 1807–1808
— apprenticeship indenture, William Lester bound to Joseph Page sen. and Joseph Page jun. of Manningtree (Essex), fellmongers, 21 Nov. 1807
— apprenticeship indenture, Robert Hamblin, son of Ann Prigg of Ipswich, widow, bound to John Tooke of Somersham, cordwainer, 11 May 1808
— apprenticeship indenture, Samuel Hamblin bound to Robert Bayley of Ipswich, carpenter and joiner, 16 Aug. 1808
— apprenticeship indenture, John Pittock, a poor child of ST, bound to Valentine Evans of Scarborough (Yorkshire), mariner, 28 Sep. 1808
— apprenticeship indenture, William Sargeant, son of William Sargeant of Ipswich, tobacconist, bound to Mark Stockens of Ipswich, tailor, 5 Oct. 1808
— apprenticeship indenture, Joseph Mallett bound to Nathaniel Saunders of Harwich (Essex), fisherman, 27 Oct. 1808
— apprenticeship indenture, Joseph Langley bound to John Woollard of Bradfield (Essex), cordwainer, 27 Dec. 1808
— apprenticeship indenture, Robert Talmash bound to Nathaniel Saunders of Harwich (Essex), fisherman, 3 Feb. 1809
(86 docs)

C/5/1/2/4/49   1808–1809
William Norris, Treasurer
(63 docs)

C/5/1/2/4/50   1809–1810
Edward Bacon, Treasurer
Includes:
— Treasurer's account (unaudited), 1809–1810
— apprenticeship indenture, William Eldridge, a poor boy of MW, bound to William Thurlow of CL, master mariner, 27 Apr. 1810
(93 docs)

C/5/1/2/4/51   1810–1811
William Batley, Treasurer
Includes:
— survey of the Hospital's farm in Debenham in tenure of Mrs Worledge, by Samuel Safford, house and land agent, 24 Sep. 1811
— apprenticeship indenture, Robert Hewes, son of Robert Hewes of Ipswich, woolcomber, bound to James Knighting of Ipswich, cordwainer, 26 Nov. 1810
(89 docs)

C/5/1/2/4/52   1811–1812
Edward Bacon, Treasurer
Includes:
— Mr Safford's audited account as Treasurer of Martin's, Burroughs's, Allen's and Scrivener's Gifts, 1810–1811
— list of persons who received St Thomas's Gift, 1809
 (104 docs)

C/5/1/2/4/53   1812–1813
William Batley, Treasurer
Includes:
— apprenticeship indenture, William Day, son of Henry Day of Harwich (Essex), mariner, bound to Timperly Amner of Harwich, ship owner, 26 Jan. 1813

— apprenticeship indenture, Philip Stevens bound to his father, Philip Stevens of Scole (Norfolk), tailor, 23 Sep. 1813
(85 docs)

C/5/1/2/4/54   1813–1814
William Batley, Treasurer
Includes:
— apprenticeship indenture, Samuel Barber, son of Samuel Barber of Ipswich, mariner, bound to Thomas Shreeve of Ipswich, baker, 22 Jul. 1812
(83 docs)

C/5/1/2/4/55   1814–1815
William Batley, Treasurer
Includes:
— inventory of contents of Hospital rooms, n.d.
— apprenticeship indenture, Samuel Barber, son of Samuel Barber of Ipswich, mariner, bound to Thomas Shreeve of Ipswich, baker, 22 Jul. 1812 (counterpart; endorsed with memo of cancellation by mutual agreement, 18 May 1815)
— apprenticeship indenture, William Rose, son of Mary Rose of Ipswich, singlewoman, bound to Arnold Collett of Ipswich, baker, 15 Dec. 1814
— apprenticeship indenture, Samuel Sharman, son of William Sharman of Ipswich, cordwainer, bound to Robert Borrett of Ipswich, tailor, 9 Feb. 1815
— 12 baptismal certificates of Hospital boys, (1802–1806), 1812–1815
(95 docs)

C/5/1/2/4/56   1815–1816
William Batley, Treasurer
Includes:
— copy apprenticeship indenture, James Boley, son of Michael Boley of Ipswich, gardener, deceased, bound to Peter William Piggott, citizen and merchant tailor of London (4 Dec. 1816), n.d.
(90 docs)

C/5/1/2/4/57   1816–1817
William Batley, Treasurer
(76 docs)

C/5/1/2/4/58   1817–1818
William Batley, Treasurer
Includes:
— letter from the Office of Taxes to Batley *re* Hospital tax allowances, 21 May 1817
— apprenticeship indenture, Philip Rainbird Bannocks, son of Philip Bannocks of Harwich (Essex), mariner, bound to Jesse Candler of Harwich, cordwainer, 4 Dec. 1817
— apprenticeship indenture, Henry Taylor, son of Sarah Taylor of Ipswich, bound to John Brown of Bentley, blacksmith and farrier, 1 Aug. 1818
(84 docs)

C/5/1/2/4/59   1818–1819
Samuel Thorndike, Treasurer
Includes:
— apprenticeship indenture, Thomas Glyde bound to John Singleton of Ipswich, tinman and brazier, 22 Oct. 1818
— apprenticeship indenture, George Page, son of Susan Page of Ipswich, singlewoman, bound to Thomas Robinson of Ipswich, cordwainer, 8 Mar. 1819
— apprenticeship indenture, Henry Harrison, son of Charles Harrison of Ipswich, tailor, bound to William Clarke of ST, cordwainer, 20 May 1819
— apprenticeship indenture, Benjamin Barber, son of Samuel Barber of Ipswich, customs officer, bound to Joseph Pinner of Ipswich, fisherman, 21 May 1819

— apprenticeship indenture, George Sherman, son of William Sherman of Ipswich, cordwainer, bound to Stephen Lambeth of Ipswich, cabinet maker, 27 Jul. 1819
(88 docs)

C/5/1/2/4/60   1819–1820
William Batley, Treasurer
Includes:
— apprenticeship indenture, George Baxter, son of George Baxter of Ipswich, cordwainer, bound to Edmund Bowman of Ipswich, cordwainer, 20 Jan. 1820
— apprenticeship indenture, John South bound to John Caston of Ipswich, master mariner, 14 Feb. 1820
(78 docs)

C/5/1/2/4/61   1820–1821
S. A. Notcutt, Treasurer
(43 docs)

C/5/1/2/4/62   1821–1822
S. A. Notcutt, Treasurer
(85 docs)

C/5/1/2/4/63   1822–1823
S. A. Notcutt, Treasurer
(93 docs)

C/5/1/2/4/64   1824–1825
Joseph Pooley, Treasurer
— account for medical attendance includes charges for vaccinating boys, 2 and 10 Jun. 1825
(62 docs)

C/5/1/2/4/65   1825–1826
Joseph Pooley, Treasurer
(55 docs)

C/5/1/2/4/66   1826–1827
Joseph Pooley, Treasurer
Includes:
— account of John Bransby for surveying an estate in Debenham, 17 Sep. 1819, paid 3 Oct. 1827
(75 docs)

C/5/1/2/4/67   1827–1828
C. Hammond, Treasurer
(89 docs)

C/5/1/2/4/68   1828–1829
James Thorndike, Treasurer
(73 docs)

C/5/1/2/4/69   1830–1831
William Batley, Treasurer
(80 docs)

C/5/1/2/4/70   1831–1832
B. B. Catt, Treasurer
(46 docs)

C/5/1/2/4/71   1833–1834
Henry G. Bristo, Treasurer
(98 docs)

C/5/1/2/4/72   1834–1835
William Calver, Treasurer
(34 docs)

C/5/1/2/4/73   1835–1836
A. B. Cook, Treasurer
(134 docs)

C/5/1/2/5   APPRENTICESHIP INDENTURES   1636–1794

The indentures are all for Christ's Hospital boys. Most boys were apprenticed at the age of
fourteen. The consent of the Governors of the Hospital is either included in the text of the
indenture or mentioned in an endorsement. Virtually all the apprenticeships were for a
seven-year period; shorter terms are mentioned in the catalogue. After 1794 the indentures are
regularly filed with the Hospital Treasurer's payment vouchers for the year in question
(C/5/1/2/4); a few may also be found among the vouchers in the period 1773–1794.

C/5/1/2/5/1   30 Jul. 1636
David Hichbone, son of Thomas Hichbone of Ipswich, sailor, deceased, bound to John Mynnes
of Harwich (Essex), mason
(found loose inside the Hospital account book for 1635–1636, C/5/1/2/2/26)

C/5/1/2/5/2   23 Oct. 1730
Samuel Artis, son of Thomas Artis of Ipswich, bricklayer, bound to William Rowland of
Ipswich, butcher

C/5/1/2/5/3   1 Feb. 1731
Thomas Artis, son of Thomas Artis of Ipswich, bricklayer, bound to John Rodes of Harwich
(Essex), tailor

C/5/1/2/5/4   17 Nov. 1731
Benjamin Hill, son of William Hill of Ipswich, woolcomber, bound to Joseph Boar of Palgrave,
blacksmith

C/5/1/2/5/5   31 Mar. 1732
John Goldsbury, son of John Goldsbury of Ipswich, cordwainer, deceased, bound to Robert
Mimperis of Ipswich, fisherman

C/5/1/2/5/6   20 Apr. 1732
Robert Caston, son of Robert Caston of Ipswich, porter, bound to Richard Davis of Ipswich,
blacksmith

C/5/1/2/5/7   17 Oct. 1732
Thomas Thorne, son of Thomas Thorne of Ipswich, labourer, deceased, bound to John Scott of
Ipswich, mariner

C/5/1/2/5/8   2 Nov. 1732
Samuel Rathbone, son of Samuel Rathbone of Ipswich, maltster, deceased, bound to Samuel
Raymond of Ipswich, fisherman

C/5/1/2/5/9   5 Mar. 1733
Thomas Knevit, son of Thomas Knevit of Ipswich, mariner, deceased, bound to John Lockwood
of Ipswich, tailor

C/5/1/2/5/10   17 Aug. 1733
John Wallage, son of John Wallage of Ipswich, deceased, bound to Richard Fennings of
Harwich (Essex), fisherman

C/5/1/2/5/11   10 Oct. 1733
William Tompson, son of William Tompson of Ipswich, cordwainer, deceased, bound to John
Harwood of Harwich (Essex), baker

C/5/1/2/5/12   5 Aug. 1734
Stephen Gilly, son of John Gilly of Ipswich, woolcomber, bound to Thomas Truelove of Ipswich, woolcomber

C/5/1/2/5/13   17 Aug. 1734
William Trusson, son of Frances Trusson of MW, bound to Richard Fennings of Harwich (Essex), fisherman

C/5/1/2/5/14   29 Jan. 1735
Samuel Brown, son of Samuel Brown of Ipswich, painter, bound to Richard Lockwood of Ipswich, mariner

C/5/1/2/5/15   1 Mar. 1735
William Knapp of Ipswich 'singleman being a Charity Boy in Christ's Hospital', bound to John Hammond of Ipswich, shipmaster and mariner

C/5/1/2/5/16   17 Oct. 1735
Thomas Hopson, son of Edward Hopson of Ipswich, mariner, deceased, bound to John Simpson of Harwich (Essex), fisherman

C/5/1/2/5/17   29 Jun. 1736
George Scott, son of George Scott of Ipswich, baker, bound to Miles Hubbard of Brightlingsea (Essex), bricklayer

C/5/1/2/5/18   9 Sep. 1736
Richard Manning, son of Richard Manning of Ipswich, maltster, deceased, bound to Thomas Harvey of Harwich (Essex), fisherman

C/5/1/2/5/19   28 Oct. 1736
Job Lee, son of Thomas Lee of Ipswich, tailor, deceased, bound to Richard Davies of Ipswich, blacksmith (with counterpart; 2 docs)

C/5/1/2/5/20   16 Jun. 1737
William Palmer, son of John Palmer of Ipswich, cordwainer, deceased, bound to Samuel Rudland of Ipswich, bricklayer (with counterpart; 2 docs)

C/5/1/2/5/21   5 Apr. 1738
Thomas Manning, son of John Manning of Ipswich, bricklayer, deceased, bound to George Bull of Wivenhoe (Essex), cooper

C/5/1/2/5/22   31 Jan. 1739
John Brooke, son of William Brooke of Ipswich, baker, deceased, bound to John Theobald of Wivenhoe (Essex), gardener

C/5/1/2/5/23   15 Mar. 1740
Manuel Jenkins, son of Susan Jenkins of Ipswich, widow, bound to Edmund Warren of Ipswich, mariner (with counterpart; 2 docs)

C/5/1/2/5/24   17 May 1740
Richard Green, son of Martha Green of Ipswich, deceased, bound to Edward Coe of Ipswich, woolcomber (with counterpart; 2 docs)

C/5/1/2/5/25   1 Apr. 1741
Basil Hewett, son of Basil Hewett of Ipswich, labourer, bound to Parker Bradstreet of Ipswich, merchant

C/5/1/2/5/26   4 Nov. 1741
John Southgate, son of Thomas Southgate of Ipswich, husbandman, deceased, bound to William Tyler of Harwich (Essex), fisherman

C/5/1/2/5/27   13 Feb. 1742
William Wright, son of William Wright of Ipswich, gardener, deceased, bound to George
Jessupp of Needham Market, carpenter

C/5/1/2/5/28   6 Oct. 1742
Henry Ide, son of William Ide of Ipswich, butcher, bound to his father by consent of the Governors of Christ's Hospital (with counterpart; 2 docs)

C/5/1/2/5/29   12 Oct. 1742
Nathaniel Chenery, son of Jacob Chenery of Ipswich, woolcomber, deceased, bound to
William Turner of Washbrook, blacksmith

C/5/1/2/5/30   12 Oct. 1743
Holofurius [Holofernes on glass bowl in Town Hall] Freelove, son of Stephen Freelove of
Ipswich, tailor, bound to his father by consent of the Governors of Christ's Hospital (with coun-
terpart; 2 docs)

C/5/1/2/5/31   8 Nov. 1743
William Slythe, bound to Thomas Cock of Ipswich, cordwainer

C/5/1/2/5/32   29 Dec. 1743
Francis Hatch, son of Anne Hatch, 'a poor boy belonging to Christ's Hospital', bound to John
Brook of Harwich (Essex), fisherman

C/5/1/2/5/33   6 Sep. 1744
William Bushaway, son of William Bushaway of Ipswich, locksmith, deceased, bound to
James Bushaway of Ipswich, mariner

C/5/1/2/5/34   8 Oct. 1744
William Burton, son of William Burton of Ipswich, mariner, deceased, bound to Benjamin
Huttiball of Ipswich, mariner

C/5/1/2/5/35   16 Nov. 1747
James Bardoe of MQ, bound to Samuel Street of Ipswich, tailor

C/5/1/2/5/36   15 Jan. 1750
Robert Major, singleman, bound to John Lucy of Kirby (Essex), fisherman

C/5/1/2/5/37   27 Mar. 1750
John Burnes of Christ's Hospital, singleman, bound to Edward Johnson of Bramford, paper
maker

C/5/1/2/5/38   20 Sep. 1750
William Pett, singleman, bound to Richard Fennings of Harwich (Essex), fisherman

C/5/1/2/5/39   28 Sep. 1750
Thomas Taylor bound to Robert Capell of Ipswich, weaver

C/5/1/2/5/40   31 Jan. 1751
John Scott, singleman, bound to William Naunton of Ipswich, baker

C/5/1/2/5/41   9 Mar. 1751
William Avis bound to William Harvey of Ipswich, mariner

C/5/1/2/5/42   9 May 1751
John Brown of Ipswich, singleman, bound to Philip Skinner of Whitby (Yorkshire), mariner

C/5/1/2/5/43   9 Sep. 1751
Richard Watson of Ipswich, singleman, bound to Richard Hunt of Harwich (Essex), fisherman

C/5/1/2/5/44   21 Sep. 1751
Charles Sands, singleman, bound to Zeberdee [sic] Wilson of Greenwich (Kent), fisherman

C/5/1/2/5/45   2 Jul. 1752
Benjamin Gant of Ipswich, singleman, bound to Zeberdee Wilson of Greenwich (Kent), fisherman

C/5/1/2/5/46   28 Sep. 1752
Robert Tokely, singleman, bound to John Turner of Harwich (Essex), fisherman

C/5/1/2/5/47   7 Aug. 1753
Isaac Warner, singleman, bound to John Turner of Harwich (Essex), fisherman

C/5/1/2/5/48   3 Mar. 1755
Henry Green, singleman, bound to George Harvey of Harwich (Essex), fisherman

C/5/1/2/5/49   26 May 1755
Thomas Gusterson, singleman, bound to John Nicholls of Ipswich, lath river

C/5/1/2/5/50   8 Nov. 1755
Bartholomew Taylor, singleman, bound to John Reeve of St Peter, Colchester (Essex), weaver

C/5/1/2/5/51   15 Dec. 1755
James Gislingham, singleman, bound to John Woolford of MW, sackmaker

C/5/1/2/5/52   15 Dec. 1755
Edward Wade, singleman, bound to Thomas Truelove of Ipswich, woolcomber

C/5/1/2/5/53   16 Aug. 1766
Edward Bell, singleman, bound to John Johnson of Norwich (Norfolk), worstead weaver

C/5/1/2/5/54   24 Nov. 1756
John Woods, singleman, bound to James Cook of Harwich (Essex), cooper

C/5/1/2/5/55   30 Sep. 1757
Robert Gislingham, singleman, bound to Philip Haden of St John, Wapping, London, cheesemonger

C/5/1/2/5/56   27 Feb. 1758
John Johnson bound to Joshua Spooner of Ipswich, pipemaker

C/5/1/2/5/57   29 Mar. 1758
Willis King of Ipswich, aged 14 years, bound to Benjamin Thompson of Great Yarmouth (Norfolk), mariner, master of the ship 'Norwich'

C/5/1/2/5/58   10 Apr. 1758
John Verhorselett of Ipswich, aged 14 years, bound to Henry Close of Ipswich, gardener

C/5/1/2/5/59   3 Jul. 1758
Isaac Mullinder, singleman, bound to Joshua Spooner of Ipswich, pipemaker

C/5/1/2/5/60   2 Oct. 1758
William Watkins, singleman, bound to Robert Keys, gentleman gunner on board HMS 'Conqueror'

C/5/1/2/5/61   16 Nov. 1758
Benjamin Wheyman bound to John Barnard of Ipswich, mariner

C/5/1/2/5/62   27 Mar. 1759
William Bardoe, singleman, bound to Thomas Wethrell of South Shields (Durham), master and mariner

C/5/1/2/5/63   27 Mar. 1759
Samuel Taylor, singleman, bound to Thomas Wethrell of South Shields (Durham), master and mariner

C/5/1/2/5/64   3 Apr. 1759
William Parker, singleman, bound to John Selletto of Harwich (Essex), master and mariner

C/5/1/2/5/65   9 Jul. 1759
William Gislingham, singleman, bound to Thomas Ellison of North Shields (Northumberland), master and mariner

C/5/1/2/5/66   15 Oct. 1760
Samuel Smith, singleman, bound to Joshua Spooner of Ipswich, pipemaker

C/5/1/2/5/67   23 Sep. 1760
John Fancett, singleman, bound to James Abadham of Ipswich, cordwainer (counterpart)

C/5/1/2/5/68   19 Mar. 1761
William Barham, singleman, bound to George Brooks of Great Bentley (Essex), bricklayer

C/5/1/2/5/69   24 Mar. 1761
Henry Leach, singleman, bound to Richard Lockwood of Ipswich, master and mariner

C/5/1/2/5/70   21 Jan. 1762
John Mimpress, singleman, bound to William Woods of Ipswich, mariner

C/5/1/2/5/71   19 Apr. 1762
John How, son of John How, bound to John Forcett, owner of the ship 'Nicholas and Anne', to learn the art of mariner

C/5/1/2/5/72   2 Jun. 1763
Robert Denton of Ipswich, singleman, bound to Robert Sickleprise of Harwich (Essex), mariner

C/5/1/2/5/73   21 Sep. 1763
Robert Catt, singleman, bound to Charles Penning of Walton, cooper

C/5/1/2/5/74   13 Feb. 1764
Robert Wilkinson of Ipswich, singleman, son of Robert Wilkinson, deceased, bound to James Cook of Harwich (Essex), cooper

C/5/1/2/5/75   29 Feb. 1764
William Patrick bound to Peter Elphingstone of London (Middlesex), mariner

C/5/1/2/5/76   20 Feb. 1765
Richard Harrison, singleman, bound to William Norris of Ipswich, tinman

C/5/1/2/5/77   8 Apr. 1765
Joseph Host, singleman, bound to Samuel Hamblin of Ipswich, plumber and glazier

C/5/1/2/5/78   7 May 1765
John Chapman, son of Thomas Chapman of Ipswich, maltster, deceased, bound to John Gillchrist, citizen and barber of London

C/5/1/2/5/79   5 Jul. 1765
Thomas Green, singleman, bound to Samuel Crooker of Ipswich, gardener, for 5 years

C/5/1/2/5/80   24 Oct. 1765
Thomas Palmer, singleman, bound to Samuel Truelove of Ipswich, baker

C/5/1/2/5/81   23 Jun. 1766
John Lilly, aged 14 years, bound to Joseph Deane of Harwich (Essex), mariner

C/5/1/2/5/82   15 Jun. 1767
James Sherman bound to Thomas Hobson of Harwich (Essex), fisherman

C/5/1/2/5/83   1 Oct. 1767
Michael Warner, singleman, bound to Thomas Wing of Harwich, fisherman

C/5/1/2/5/84   1 Jun. 1768
John Beech, singleman, belonging to Christ's Hospital, bound to Christopher Prentice of
Ipswich, fisherman

C/5/1/2/5/85   29 Jun. 1768
Francis Fairbrother, singleman, bound to Thomas Alexander of Ipswich, gardener

C/5/1/2/5/86   5 Jul. 1768
William Hubbard, singleman, bound to Christopher Prentice of Ipswich, fisherman

C/5/1/2/5/87   20 Aug. 1768
Joseph Lambert, singleman, bound to Arthur Haggas of Harwich (Essex), fisherman

C/5/1/2/5/88   17 Sep. 1768
Samuel Browne jun. of Ipswich, singleman, bound to John Innols of Chelmondiston, fisherman

C/5/1/2/5/89   26 Oct. 1768
Thomas Parker, singleman belonging to Christ's Hospital, bound to Edmund Smith of Ipswich,
gardener, for 5 years (endorsement indicates sometime use as wrapper for Christ's Hospital
accounts for 1768–1769)

C/5/1/2/5/90   5 Jun. 1769
William Pearson, singleman, bound to Christopher Prentice of Ipswich, fisherman

C/5/1/2/5/91   9 Dec. 1769
William Parker of Ipswich, singleman, bound to Christopher Prentice of Ipswich, fisherman

C/5/1/2/5/92   30 Apr. 1770
James Patrick, singleman, bound to Edward Turner of Woodbridge, fisherman

C/5/1/2/5/93   27 Oct. 1770
James Upson of Ipswich, singleman, bound to Thomas Mitchell of Bucklesham, edge-tool
maker

C/5/1/2/5/94   24 Jun. 1771
Abelener Clarke, singleman, bound to John Scott of Harwich (Essex), fisherman

C/5/1/2/5/95   19 Nov. 1771
Danby Hines of Ipswich, singleman, bound to William West of Ipswich, sawyer

C/5/1/2/5/96   26 Dec. 1771
William Booth, singleman, bound to Richard Watson of Milton next Gravesend (Kent),
fisherman

C/5/1/2/5/97   26 Dec. 1771
Nathaniel Pinner, singleman, bound to Richard Watson of Milton next Gravesend (Kent), fisherman

C/5/1/2/5/98   18 Jun. 1772
John Webb, singleman, bound to Henry Ide of Ipswich, woolcomber

C/5/1/2/5/99   12 Jul. 1773
William Brett, singleman, bound to John Cunningham jun. of Ipswich, ropemaker

C/5/1/2/5/100   26 Oct. 1773
Henry Beeston, singleman, bound to Joseph Bird of Ipswich, staymaker and cordwainer

C/5/1/2/5/101   29 Sep. 1774
Cutler Green, singleman, son of Cutler Green of Ipswich, sawyer, bound to Joseph Jennings of
Ipswich, baker

C/5/1/2/5/102   8 Jun. 1775
William Coe jun. of Ipswich, singleman, son of William Coe sen. of Ipswich, schoolmaster,
bound to Francis Nevill of Greenwich (Kent), fisherman

C/5/1/2/5/103   18 Sep. 1775
James Howes, son of William Howes of Ipswich, sawyer, bound to John Phillips of Harwich
(Essex), baker

C/5/1/2/5/104   2 Oct. 1775
Thomas Thursby, singleman, bound to William Ballard of Harwich (Essex), fisherman

C/5/1/2/5/105   17 Aug. 1776
Archibald Rogers of Ipswich, singleman, bound to Joseph Cole of Ipswich, mariner

C/5/1/2/5/106   9 Dec. 1776
David Haunting of Ipswich, singleman, son of Robert Haunting of Ipswich, house carpenter,
bound to his father

C/5/1/2/5/107   8 Aug. 1777
George Felgate of Ipswich, singleman, bound to John Felgate of Ipswich, tailor

C/5/1/2/5/108   18 Feb. 1782
Thomas Cook, son of James Cook of Harwich (Essex), mariner, bound to Thomas Cook of
Harwich, fisherman

C/5/1/2/5/109   8 Mar. 1784
John Wade jun., singleman, bound to John Wade sen. of Needham, stuff weaver

C/5/1/2/5/110   12 Apr. 1784
Edward Wade jun., singleman, bound to Edward Wade sen. of Ipswich, woolcomber

C/5/1/2/5/111   9 Feb. 1785
William Willoughby, singleman, son of Mark Willoughby of Ipswich, plumber and glazier,
bound to his father

C/5/1/2/5/112   15 Jun. 1785
James Dawson of Ipswich, singleman, bound to John Forsdike of Grundisburgh, baker

C/5/1/2/5/113   21 Jul. 1788
William Foulger, grandson of Mary Foulger, bound to Isaac Smith of Ipswich, cordwainer

C/5/1/2/5/114   13 Feb. 1794
Deed of Assignment. Apprenticeship, 21 Mar. 1793, of John Scott to Stephen Buttrum of
Hasketon, blacksmith (*see* voucher file C/5/1/2/4/33), assigned to Francis Wright of Tuddenham,
blacksmith

C/5/1/2/6   OFFICE HOLDERS   1711

C/5/1/2/6/1   18 May 1711
Bond
In consideration of £40 loan, John Jermyn of Ipswich, wool stapler, bound in £80 to the Bailiffs,
burgesses and commonalty of Ipswich, not to remove from the town or cease his trade, and to
remain Guide of Christ's Hospital, for 5 years

C/5/1/3   OSMOND'S CHARITY   1643–1836

By his will dated 1619, Benjamin Osmond gave £350 to the Corporation, of which £50 was a
contribution towards building a new Market Cross, £100 was for the purchase of houses to be
let, rent free, to four aged poor persons, and £200 was for the purchase of lands, the income
from which was to be used for the maintenance of the almshouses and their inhabitants. The
testator's assets were apparently insufficient to meet the bequest in full, and only £250 was
received. With part of this money a house was purchased on the north side of St Matthew's

Street, next to the Fleece Inn, and divided into four tenements. Two (later three) of these were occupied by the almspeople, and the remaining two (one) let to tenants, the rents being applied towards the maintenance of the almspeople and the property.

In 1695 the Corporation took the remaining portion of the bequest for its own use, mortgaging the Town Marshes to trustees for its repayment at 4 per cent interest. The interest was paid annually by the Town Treasurer to the Receiver of Osmond's Charity until 1795, when it was discontinued, in consideration of the Corporation's having spent more than £200 on putting the four tenements, which had become ruinous, into full repair. *See* Canning 1747, 160–61, and Trustees 1878, 34.

C/5/1/3/1   RECEIVER'S AUDITED ACCOUNTS   1643–1836

These bear the signatures of the auditors; most are for a single financial year. Receipts recorded are for rents, interest payments from the Town Treasurer, and moneys from the Churchwardens of St Matthew's parish. Expenditure is on weekly payments to the poor, provision of coal, Christmas dinners, quit-rents and property repairs.

The accounts from 1715 to 1759 (except for the duplicate for 1756–1757, C/5/1/3/1/21) were found, together with the audited accounts for Tyler's Charity, 1733–1757 (C/5/1/4/1/2–5, 7–10), in a box of loose vouchers for both charities covering the years 1715–1759 (Osmond's) and 1724–1759 (Tyler's), marked 'Vouchers of Mr Richardson as Renterwarden 1718–1755'. As found, all the documents had been removed from the laces on which they were originally filed, and were totally disarranged. The records of the two charities must originally have been filed separately, since until 1748, when John Gravenor served both offices, different Receivers were appointed for each charity. This arrangement has been followed during cataloguing. It is probable that the surviving audited accounts, which are in poor condition, were used as wrappers to the voucher files for their respective financial years, but as this is not certain they were arranged separately when the voucher files were reconstituted.

C/5/1/3/1/1   1643–1650
Richard Pupplett, Governor [*sic*]
A note at the end, in Pupplett's hand, reads, 'These Accomptes being finished, my hope is, to have done with all Towne businesses.'
(1 vol.)

C/5/1/3/1/2   1715–1716
Thomes Osborn, Renterwarden [*sic*]
(1 doc.)

C/5/1/3/1/3   1716–1717
William Melsupp, Receiver
(1 doc.)

C/5/1/3/1/4   1717–1718
Tobias Searson, Receiver
(1 doc.)

C/5/1/3/1/5   1719–1720
Joseph Austin
(1 doc.)

C/5/1/3/1/6   1720–1721
Not audited. [Hugh Wright, Receiver: see account for 1721–1722, C/5/1/3/1/7]
(1 doc.)

C/5/1/3/1/7   1721–1722
Not audited: Hugh Wright, Receiver
(1 doc.)

C/5/1/3/1/8 Daniel Heckford, Receiver (1 doc.)	1722–1723
C/5/1/3/1/9 John Barker, Receiver (1 doc.)	1724–1725
C/5/1/3/1/10 Samuel Hamblin, Treasurer [*sic*] (1 doc.)	1725–1726
C/5/1/3/1/11 William Truelove, Receiver For 3 financial years, 1729–1730, 1730–1731 and 1731–1732 (1 doc.)	1729–1732
C/5/1/3/1/12 William Truelove, Receiver For 2 financial years, 1732–1733 and 1733–1734 (1 doc.)	1732–1734
C/5/1/3/1/13 William Truelove, Receiver (1 doc.)	1734–1735
C/5/1/3/1/14 William Truelove, Receiver (1 doc.)	1735–1736
C/5/1/3/1/15 William Truelove, Receiver For 2 financial years, 1736–1737 and 1737–1738 (1 doc.)	1736–1738
C/5/1/3/1/16 William Truelove, Receiver (1 doc.)	1738–1739
C/5/1/3/1/17 John Firmin, Receiver (1 doc.)	1745–1746
C/5/1/3/1/18 William Truelove jun., Receiver (1 doc.)	1754–1755
C/5/1/3/1/19 William Truelove jun., Receiver (1 doc.)	1755–1756
C/5/1/3/1/20 Richard Batley, Receiver (1 doc.)	1756–1757
C/5/1/3/1/21 Duplicate. Richard Batley, Receiver (1 doc.)	1756–1757
C/5/1/3/1/22 Richard Batley, Receiver (1 doc.)	1757–1758

C/5/1/3/1/23   1757–1758
Duplicate. Richard Batley, Receiver
(1 doc.)

C/5/1/3/1/24   1758–1759
Richard Lockwood, Receiver
(1 doc.)

C/5/1/3/1/25   1760–1761
John Forsett, Receiver
(1 doc.)

C/5/1/3/1/26   1761–1763
Robert Goodwyn, Receiver
For 2 financial years, 1761–1762 and 1762–1763
(1 doc.)

C/5/1/3/1/27   1763–1764
Thomas Amys, Receiver
(1 doc.)

C/5/1/3/1/28   1774–1777
Richard Batley, Receiver
For 3 financial years, 1774–1775, 1775–1776 and 1776–1777
(1 doc.)

C/5/1/3/1/29   1774–1777
Duplicate of C/5/1/3/1/28. Lacking signatures of auditors
(1 doc.)

C/5/1/3/1/30   1833–1836
 Receiver's audited account book. James Thorndike, Receiver
At front: Osmond's Charity, Apr. 1834–Nov. 1836
At back: Tyler's Charity, Dec. 1833–Nov. 1836
(1 vol.; most pages blank)

C/5/1/3/2   RECEIVER'S VOUCHERS   1715–1836

Receipts for rent and interest payments by the Town Treasurer; payments for repairs to the Charity houses in St Matthew's, Ipswich, manorial quit-rents, and coals supplied.
    For the vouchers for the years 1782–1789, 1816–1825 and 1828–1829, *see* Tyler's Charity, C/5/1/4/2/43–45, 70 and 76. For details of the past and present arrangement of some of these documents, *see* the introductory note to the Receiver's audited accounts for this charity (C/5/1/3/1).

C/5/1/3/2/1   1715–1716
[Thomas Osborn, Receiver]
(1 doc.)

C/5/1/3/2/2   1717–1718
[Tobias Searson, Receiver]
(2 docs)

C/5/1/3/2/3   1719–1720
Joseph Austin, Receiver
(7 docs)

C/5/1/3/2/4   1720–1721
Hugh Wright, Receiver
(2 docs)

C/5/1/3/2/5   1721–1722
Hugh Wright, Receiver
(8 docs)

C/5/1/3/2/6   1722–1723
Daniel Heckford, Receiver
(7 docs)

C/5/1/3/2/7   1726–1727
Samuel Hamblin, Receiver
(2 docs)

C/5/1/3/2/8   1729–1730
William Truelove, Receiver
(1 doc.)

C/5/1/3/2/9   1730–1731
William Truelove, Receiver
(7 docs)

C/5/1/3/2/10   1731–1732
William Truelove, Receiver
(4 docs)

C/5/1/3/2/11   1732–1733
William Truelove, Receiver
(2 docs)

C/5/1/3/2/12   1733–1734
William Truelove, Receiver
(8 docs)

C/5/1/3/2/13   1734–1735
William Truelove, Receiver
(8 docs)

C/5/1/3/2/14   1735–1736
William Truelove, Receiver
(2 docs)

C/5/1/3/2/15   1736–1737
William Truelove, Receiver
(8 docs)

C/5/1/3/2/16   1737–1738
William Truelove, Receiver
(11 docs)

C/5/1/3/2/17   1738–1739
William Truelove, Receiver
(3 docs)

C/5/1/3/2/18   1739–1740
William Truelove, Receiver
(5 docs)

C/5/1/3/2/19   1740–1741
William Truelove, Receiver
(7 docs)

C/5/1/3/2/20 John Gardiner, Receiver (3 docs)	1743–1744
C/5/1/3/2/21 John Gardiner, Receiver (5 docs)	1744–1745
C/5/1/3/2/22 John Firmin, Receiver (6 docs)	1746–1747
C/5/1/3/2/23 John Gravenor, Receiver (4 docs)	1747–1748
C/5/1/3/2/24 John Gravenor, Receiver (4 docs)	1748–1749
C/5/1/3/2/25 John Gravenor, Receiver (3 docs)	1749–1750
C/5/1/3/2/26 John Gravenor, Receiver (1 doc.)	1750–1751
C/5/1/3/2/27 Charles Norris, Receiver (5 docs)	1751–1752
C/5/1/3/2/28 Charles Norris, Receiver (11 docs)	1752–1753
C/5/1/3/2/29 Charles Norris, Receiver (6 docs)	1753–1754
C/5/1/3/2/30 William Truelove jun., Receiver (10 docs)	1754–1755
C/5/1/3/2/31 William Truelove jun., Receiver (9 docs)	1755–1756
C/5/1/3/2/32 Richard Batley, Receiver (8 docs)	1756–1757
C/5/1/3/2/33 Richard Batley, Receiver (6 docs)	1757–1758
C/5/1/3/2/34 Richard Lockwood, Receiver (10 docs)	1758–1759

C/5/1/3/2/35   1760–1764
John Forsett, Receiver 1760–1761; Robert Goodwyn, Receiver 1761–1762, 1762–1763; Thomas
Amys, Receiver 1763–1764
For 4 financial years
(18 docs)

C/5/1/3/2/36   1765–1766
James Wilder, Receiver
(12 docs)

C/5/1/3/2/37   1769–1770
James Martin, Receiver
(6 docs)

C/5/1/3/2/38   1771–1772
John Tyrrell, Receiver
(4 docs)

C/5/1/3/2/39   1777–1781
William Norris, Receiver
For 4 financial years, 1777–1778, 1778–1779, 1779–1780, 1780–1781
(10 docs)

C/5/1/3/2/40   1789–1791
John Tyrrell, Receiver
For 2 financial years, 1789–1790 and 1790–1791
(8 docs)

C/5/1/3/2/41   1793–1799
John Tyrrell, Receiver
For 6 financial years, 1793–1794, 1794–1795, 1795–1796, 1796–1797, 1797–1798, 1798–1799
(11 docs, found filed on a single lace)

C/5/1/3/2/42   1800–1804
These appear to be stray items from the voucher files for the years concerned
(7 docs)

C/5/1/3/2/43   1804–1809
Benjamin Catt, Receiver
For 5 financial years, 1804–1805, 1805–1806, 1806–1807, 1807–1808, 1808–1809
(20 docs)

C/5/1/3/2/44   1827–1828
John Gooding, Receiver
(6 docs)

C/5/1/3/2/45   1835–1836
James Thorndike, Receiver
(7 docs)

C/5/1/4 TYLER'S CHARITY   **1697–1835**

In 1643 William Tyler, Portman, gave £300 to the Corporation, in trust to purchase houses or
lands to the yearly value of £15, the rents to be applied towards the 'apparelling, training up and
teaching at school' of as many poor Ipswich children as the money should extend to, and for
binding them apprentices to suitable trades. This £300, supplemented by funds belonging to
Christ's Hospital and Smart's Charity, was used to purchase a farm in Creeting St Peter,
Creeting All Saints and Earl Stonham in 1649. These lands were augmented in 1656 by the
purchase of other land in Creeting with Snow's Gift (the proceeds of the sale of his house in

St Clement's parish). Both properties were owned jointly by Tyler's, Smart's and the Hospital, one-third of the revenues being devoted to each charity.

For many years prior to 1836, the Tyler's Charity share of the income was disbursed as exhibitions to boys on the Foundation at the Free (Grammar) School. Thereafter it was applied to Christ's Hospital School, this being more in accordance with the donor's original intentions.

For further details, *see* Canning 1747, 132–36, and Trustees 1878, 30.

C/5/1/4/1   RECEIVER'S AUDITED ACCOUNTS   1697–1775

These bear the signatures of the auditors; most are for a single financial year. Until 1741 the accounts refer also to Snow's Gift, one-third of the proceeds of which was appropriated to Tyler's Charity. The receipts are for the rents of the Creeting farm; expenditure is on exhibitions for Grammar School boys, contributions to the salaries of the Master and Usher of the School, and property repairs.

The accounts for 1833–1836 will be found with those of Osmond's Charity C/5/1/3/1/ 30.

For details of the past and present arrangement of some of these documents, see the introductory note to the Receiver's audited accounts for Osmond's Charity (C/5/1/3/1).

C/5/1/4/1/1   1697–1702
Receiver not named
(1 vol.)

C/5/1/4/1/2   1733–1735
William Artis, Receiver
For 2 financial years, 1733–1734 and 1734–1735
(1 doc.)

C/5/1/4/1/3   1735–1736
William Artis, Receiver
(1 doc.)

C/5/1/4/1/4   1736–1738
[Henry Bond, Receiver]
For 2 financial years, 1736–1737 and 1737–1738
(1 doc.)

C/5/1/4/1/5   1738–1741
Henry Bond, Receiver
For 3 financial years, 1738–1739, 1739–1740 and 1740–1741
(1 doc.)

C/5/1/4/1/6   1742–1746
Copy. John Firmin, Receiver
(1 vol.)

C/5/1/4/1/7   1750–1751
Thomas Bowell, Receiver
(1 doc.)

C/5/1/4/1/8   1754–1755
William Truelove jun., Receiver
(1 doc.)

C/5/1/4/1/9   1755–1756
William Truelove jun., Receiver
(1 doc.)

C/5/1/4/1/10   1756–1757
Richard Batley, Receiver
(1 doc.)

C/5/1/4/1/11   1756–1757
Duplicate. Richard Batley, Receiver
(1 doc.)

C/5/1/4/1/12   1757–1758
Richard Batley, Receiver
Includes:
— names of exhibitioners at the Grammar School

C/5/1/4/1/13   1757–1758
Duplicate. Richard Batley, Receiver
(1 doc.)

C/5/1/4/1/14   1758–1759
Richard Lockwood, Receiver
(1 doc.)

C/5/1/4/1/15   1760–1761
John Forsett, Receiver
(1 doc.)

C/5/1/4/1/16   1761–1763
Robert Goodwyn, Receiver
For 2 financial years, 1761–1762 and 1762–1763
(1 doc.)

C/5/1/4/1/17   1763–1764
Thomas Amys, Receiver
(1 doc.)

C/5/1/4/1/18   1774–1775
Richard Batley, Receiver
For 3 financial years, 1774–1775, 1775–1776 and 1776–1777
(1 doc.)

C/5/1/4/2   RECEIVER'S VOUCHERS   1724–1835

The majority of these vouchers (almost all of them from 1762) consist of Bailiffs' precepts for
payment of exhibitions to named Grammar School boys on Tyler's foundation. There are also
payments to the Master and Usher of the School in augmentation of their salaries, for teaching
the exhibitioners; for repairs to the Charity farm in Creeting and Earl Stonham; and for Land
Tax. The documents often refer to the Charity as 'Snow and Tyler's Gift'.

The files for the years 1782–1789, 1816–1825 and 1828–1829 include the vouchers for
Osmond's Charity.

For details of the past and present arrangement of some of these documents, see the introductory note to the Receiver's audited accounts of Osmond's Charity, C/5/1/3/1.

C/5/1/4/2/1   1724–1725
Michael Beaumont, Receiver
(15 docs)

C/5/1/4/2/2   1725–1726
Michael Beaumont, Receiver
(9 docs)

C/5/1/4/2/3   1726–1727
Michael Beaumont, Receiver
(2 docs)

C/5/1/4/2/4   1729–1730
William Artis, Receiver
(10 docs)

C/5/1/4/2/5   1730–1731
William Artis, Receiver
(1 doc.)

C/5/1/4/2/6   1733–1734
William Artis, Receiver
(8 docs)

C/5/1/4/2/7   1734–1735
William Artis, Receiver
(10 docs)

C/5/1/4/2/8   1735–1736
William Artis, Receiver
Includes:
— agreement by Treasurers of Tooley's Foundation, Christ's Hospital and Snow and Tyler's
Charity, for allowances to John Gardiner, tenant of the farm in Creeting, for building and repair
work, 26 Jun. 1736
(13 docs)

C/5/1/4/2/9   1736–1737
Henry Bond, Receiver
(14 docs)

C/5/1/4/2/10   1737–1738
Henry Bond, Receiver
(14 docs)

C/5/1/4/2/11   1738–1739
Henry Bond, Receiver
(10 docs)

C/5/1/4/2/12   1739–1740
Henry Bond, Receiver
(10 docs)

C/5/1/4/2/13   1740–1741
Henry Bond, Receiver
(21 docs)

C/5/1/4/2/14   1741–1742
John Firmin, Receiver
(14 docs)

C/5/1/4/2/15   1742–1743
John Firmin, Receiver
(8 docs)

C/5/1/4/2/16   1743–1744
John Firmin, Receiver
(7 docs)

C/5/1/4/2/17   1744–1745
John Firmin, Receiver
(12 docs)

C/5/1/4/2/18   1745–1746
John Firmin, Receiver
(10 docs)

C/5/1/4/2/19   1746–1747
John Gravenor, Receiver
(9 docs)

C/5/1/4/2/20   1747–1748
John Gravenor, Receiver
(14 docs)

C/5/1/4/2/21   1748–1749
John Gravenor, Receiver
(17 docs)

C/5/1/4/2/22   1749–1750
Thomas Bowell, Receiver
(7 docs)

C/5/1/4/2/23   1750–1751
Thomas Bowell, Receiver
(7 docs)

C/5/1/4/2/24   1751–1752
Charles Norris, Receiver
(20 docs)

C/5/1/4/2/25   1752–1753
Charles Norris, Receiver
(5 docs)

C/5/1/4/2/26   1753–1754
Charles Norris, Receiver
(7 docs)

C/5/1/4/2/27   1754–1755
William Truelove jun., Receiver
(8 docs)

C/5/1/4/2/28   1755–1756
William Truelove jun., Receiver
(27 docs)

C/5/1/4/2/29   1756–1757
Richard Batley, Receiver
(19 docs)

C/5/1/4/2/30   1757–1758
Richard Batley, Receiver
(14 docs)

C/5/1/4/2/31   1758–1759
Capt Richard Lockwood, Receiver
(14 docs)

C/5/1/4/2/32   1762–1764
Robert Goodwyn, Receiver 1762–1763; Thomas Amys, Receiver 1763–1764
For 2 financial years
(39 docs)

C/5/1/4/2/33   1764–1766
James Wilder, Receiver
For 2 financial years, 1764–1765 and 1765–1766
(33 docs)

C/5/1/4/2/34   1766–1767
James Wilder, Receiver
(17 docs)

C/5/1/4/2/35   1767–1768
J. Thorndike, Receiver
Includes:
— 2 vouchers for Osmond's Charity
(12 docs)

C/5/1/4/2/36   1768–1769
J. Thorndike, Receiver
Includes:
— 2 vouchers for Osmond's Charity (13 docs)

C/5/1/4/2/37   1769–1770
James Martin, Receiver
(8 docs)

C/5/1/4/2/38   1770–1771
Christopher Rolfe, Receiver
Includes:
— 2 vouchers for Osmond's Charity
(9 docs)

C/5/1/4/2/39   1771–1772
John Tyrrell, Receiver
(9 docs)

C/5/1/4/2/40   1772–1774
Thomas Nuttall, Receiver
For 2 financial years, 1772–1773 and 1773–1774
Includes:
— 4 precepts for payment of exhibitions on Smart's Foundation, 29 Sep. 1773 and 29 Sep.
1774
(40 docs)

C/5/1/4/2/41   1774–1777
R. Batley, Receiver
For 3 financial years, 1774–1775, 1775–1776 and 1776–1777
Includes:
— 2 precepts for payment of exhibitions on Smart's Foundation, 29 Sep. 1776 and 29 Sep.
1777
(25 docs; vouchers for all 3 years found filed on a single lace; wrongly labelled 'Osmond's and
Tyler's')

C/5/1/4/2/42   1777–1782
William Norris, Receiver
For 5 financial years, 1777–1778, 1778–1779, 1779–1780, 1780–1781 and 1781–1782
(31 docs)

C/5/1/4/2/43   1782–1787
John Tyrrell, Receiver
Tyler's and Osmond's Charities
For 5 financial years, 1782–1783, 1783–1784, 1784–1785, 1785–1786 and 1786–1787
(78 docs, 59 for Tyler's and 19 for Osmond's, all found threaded on a single lace)

C/5/1/4/2/44   1787–1788
John Tyrrell, Receiver
Tyler's and Osmond's Charities
(9 docs, 5 for Tyler's and 4 for Osmond's, all found threaded on a single lace)

C/5/1/4/2/45   1788–1789
John Tyrrell, Receiver
Tyler's and Osmond's Charities
(11 docs, 8 for Tyler's and 3 for Osmond's, all found threaded on a single lace)

C/5/1/4/2/46   1789–1790
John Tyrrell, Receiver
(9 docs)

C/5/1/4/2/47   1790–1791
John Tyrrell, Receiver
(12 docs)

C/5/1/4/2/48   1791–1792
John Tyrrell, Receiver
(13 docs)

C/5/1/4/2/49   1792–1799
John Tyrrell, Receiver
For 7 financial years, 1792–1793, 1793–1794, 1794–1795, 1795–1796, 1796–1797, 1797–1798,
1798–1799
(43 docs, found filed on a single lace)

C/5/1/4/2/50   1799–1804
Benjamin Catt, Receiver
For 5 financial years, 1799–1800, 1800–1801, 1801–1802, 1802–1803, 1803–1804
Includes:
— 2 precepts for payment of exhibitions on Smart's Foundation, 29 Sep. 1803
(54 docs)

C/5/1/4/2/51   1804–1805
 Benjamin Catt, Receiver
Includes:
— 2 Bailiffs' precepts for payment of exhibitions on Smart's Foundation
— Town Clerk's warrant for payment of £5 to Robert Lavender Manning, former Grammar
School scholar, towards binding him apprentice to George Joseph Harmer of Ipswich, school-
master
(19 docs)

C/5/1/4/2/52   1806–1807
Benjamin Catt, Receiver
Includes:
— 2 precepts for payment of exhibitions on Smart's Foundation, 29 Sep. 1806
(18 docs)

C/5/1/4/2/53   1807–1808
Benjamin Catt, Receiver
Includes:
— 2 precepts for payment of exhibitions on Smart's Foundation, 29 Sep. 1807

— 'A list of those Free Boys who have been taught writing at the Grammar School', with payments due for each, n.d.
(17 docs)

C/5/1/4/2/54   12 Jul.–28 Nov. 1808
Benjamin Catt, Receiver
Includes:
— precept for payment of exhibition on Smart's Foundation, 29 Sep. 1808
— 'A list of Free Boys who have [been] taught writing at the Grammar School', with payments due for each, 29 Sep. 1808
(30 docs)

C/5/1/4/2/55   11 Mar.–29 Sep. 1809
Benjamin Catt, Receiver
Includes:
— precept for payment of exhibition on Smart's Foundation, 29 Sep. 1809
— 'List of Free Boys who have been taught writing &c at the Grammar School from Michaelmas 1809', with payments due for each, 29 Sep. 1809
(28 docs)

C/5/1/4/2/56   29 Sep. 1810
Benjamin Catt, Receiver
Includes:
— precept for payment of exhibition on Smart's Foundation
— list of Free Boys taught writing at the Grammar School, with payments due for each
(31 docs)

C/5/1/4/2/57   29 Sep. 1811
Benjamin Catt, Receiver
Includes:
— precept for payment of exhibition on Smart's Foundation
(28 docs)

C/5/1/4/2/58   29 Sep. 1812
Benjamin Catt, Receiver
(22 docs)

C/5/1/4/2/59   29 Sep. 1813
Benjamin Catt, Receiver
(29 docs)

C/5/1/4/2/60   29–30 Sep. 1816
[John] Gooding, Receiver
Bailiffs' precepts for payment of exhibitions only
(26 docs. Endorsed: 'No. 1. Grammar School Free Boys — 26. 1816 Michaelmas')

C/5/1/4/2/61   29 Sep. 1817
[John] Gooding, Receiver
Bailiffs' precepts for payment of exhibitions only
(27 docs. Endorsed: 'No. 2. Grammar School Free Boys — 27. 1817 Michaelmas')

C/5/1/4/2/62   29 Sep. 1818
John Gooding, Receiver
Bailiffs' precepts for payment of exhibitions only
(24 docs. Endorsed: 'No. 3. Grammar School Free Boys — 24. 1818 Michaelmas')

C/5/1/4/2/63   29 Sep. 1819
[John] Gooding, Receiver
Bailiffs' precepts for payment of exhibitions only
(28 docs. Endorsed: 'No. 4. Grammar School Free Boys — 27 [sic]. 1819 Michaelmas')

C/5/1/4/2/64   29 Sep. 1820
[John] Gooding, Receiver
Bailiffs' precepts for payment of exhibitions only
(21 docs. Endorsed: 'No. 5. Grammar School Free Boys — 21. 1820 Michaelmas')

C/5/1/4/2/65   29 Sep. 1821
[John] Gooding, Receiver
Bailiffs' precepts for payment of exhibitions only
(18 docs. Endorsed: 'No. 6. Grammar School Free Boys — 18. 1821 — Michaelmas')

C/5/1/4/2/66   29 Sep. 1822
[John] Gooding, Receiver
Bailiffs' precepts for payment of exhibitions
Includes:
— list of boys' names
(23 docs. Endorsed: 'No. 7. 22 Boys. Sept. 30 1822')

C/5/1/4/2/67   29 Sep. 1823
[John] Gooding, Receiver
Bailiffs' precepts for payment of exhibitions
Includes:
— list of boys' names
(25 docs)

C/5/1/4/2/68   29 Sep. 1824
[John] Gooding, Receiver
Bailiffs' precepts for payment of exhibitions
Includes:
— list of boys' names
(26 docs. Endorsed: 'No. 9. Michaelmas 1824. 25 Boys')

C/5/1/4/2/69   29 Sep. 1825
[John] Gooding, Receiver
Bailiffs' precepts for payment of exhibitions
Includes:
— list of boys' names
(16 docs. Endorsed: 'No. 10. Grammar School 1825. Free Boys No. 15')

C/5/1/4/2/70   1816–1825
[John] Gooding, Receiver
Tyler's and Osmond's Charities
For 10 financial years
Contains all vouchers for both charities, except for the precepts for payment of exhibitions
which during John Gooding's Receivership were filed separately (C/5/1/4/2/60–69)
Includes:
— precepts for payment of contributions towards cost of apprenticing former scholars on
Tyler's Foundation, 1817–1825
(51 docs, found wrapped with C/5/1/4/2/60–69 in a parcel labelled 'Mr Gooding's vouchers as
Receiver of Osmond's and Tyler's Charities')

C/5/1/4/2/71   29 Sep. 1826
[John] Gooding, Receiver
Bailiffs' precepts for payment of exhibitions only
(15 docs)

C/5/1/4/2/72   7 Dec. 1826
[John] Gooding, Receiver
Bailiffs' precept for payment of 3 exhibitions
(1 doc.)

C/5/1/4/2/73   29 Sep. 1827
John Gooding, Receiver
Bailiffs' precepts for payment of exhibitions only
(17 docs)

C/5/1/4/2/74   29 Sep. 1828
John Gooding, Receiver
Bailiffs' precepts for payment of exhibitions
Includes:
— list of boys' names
(21 docs; found with Christ's Hospital vouchers)

C/5/1/4/2/75   7 Dec. 1828
[John] Gooding, Receiver
Bailiffs' precept for payment of exhibition to Daniel Alfred Sheppard
(1 doc.)

C/5/1/4/2/76   1828–1829
[John] Gooding, Receiver
Tyler's and Osmond's Charities
Mostly Bailiffs' precepts for payment of exhibitions on Tyler's Foundation, all dated 29 Sep.
1829
Includes:
— list of exhibitioners' names, n.d.
(25 docs)

C/5/1/4/2/77   29 Sep. 1834
[James] Thorndike, Receiver
Bailiffs' precepts for payment of exhibitions only
(8 docs)

C/5/1/4/2/78   29 Sep. 1835
[James] Thorndike, Receiver
Bailiffs' precepts for payment of exhibitions
Includes:
— list of boys, Sep. 1835
(21 docs)

C/5/1/5 THE LENDING CASH CHARITY   **1661–1823**

This originated with Sir Thomas White, who in 1566 endowed a fund to be administered by the
Corporation of Bristol, providing for £104 to be paid annually to twenty-four cities and towns
in rotation. As regards Ipswich, the £104, paid every twenty-fourth year on St Bartholomew's
Day (24 August), was to be lent free of interest to poor Freemen of the town, each loan to be of
£25, for a ten-year period; on repayment the money was to be lent out again in similar manner.

Between 1566 and 1665 seventeen other gifts were made to the Corporation for objects
similar to that of Sir Thomas White (for the details, and also the shortcomings of the charity
administration, *see* Canning 1747, 73–91). In the course of time the various loan charities
became more or less consolidated under the name of the 'Lending Cash Charity', and the
practice eventually prevailed of granting loans of from £10 to £20 each to Freemen of the town
engaged in trade, for varying periods.

See also the separate records of Crane's Charity (C/5/1/6), which was one of those associated
with the Lending Cash.

C/5/1/5/1   REGISTRATION   1661–1816

C/5/1/5/1/1   1661–1816
Clavigers' account book and loan register
At front: accounts, 1754–1816 (audited from 1756); receipts from repayment of loans and
surplus funds transferred from the Receivers of Martin's Charity; payments for loans to poor
Freemen
At back: register of bonds entered into for repayment of loans, 1661–1811, giving date of issue,
length of term, amount lent, names of borrower and sureties, name of Claviger, repayment date
(1 vol.)

C/5/1/5/1/2   26 Nov. 1798
List of persons whose bonds were received from the Clavigers of Ipswich
(1 doc.)

C/5/1/5/2   BORROWERS' BONDS FOR REPAYMENT OF LOANS TO   1666–1823
THE BAILIFFS, BURGESSES AND COMMONALTY

Unless otherwise stated in this list, the sum lent was £25, free of interest, from the fund
endowed by Sir Thomas White, for repayment in 10 years. The much smaller number of
interest-free loans of £20, also for ten years, were from the funds of Crane's Charity; and the
few loans of £20 at 4 per cent interest for 5 years were from the fund endowed by John Hunt, the
interest being spent on the provision of shifts for the poor of St Mary at Elms parish. The single
bond (the earliest now surviving) for repayment of £10 in ten years relates to the endowment of
Thomas Burroughs. Each borrower was required to find 2 sureties, who were parties to the
bond. The borrowers (all of whom had to be resident Ipswich Freemen) and their sureties were,
as usual, bound in a penal sum equal to twice the amount of the loan, which was conditional on
the borrowers' not removing from Ipswich or abandoning their trades during the term. Annexed
to almost every bond is either an order of the Great Court, signed by the Bailiffs, authorising the
loan and signifying approval of the sureties chosen, or simply a signed statement of the Bailiffs'
approval of the sureties.

C/5/1/5/2/1   27 Nov. 1666
William Cole, grocer, obligor; William Feast of Ipswich, grocer and Peter Butcher of
Tattingstone, clerk, sureties
£10 for 10 years

C/5/1/5/2/2   28 Sep. 1719
Samuel Howes, housecarpenter, obligor; John Bumpstead, woolcomber and John Broom,
yeomen, both of Ipswich, sureties
£20 for 5 years

C/5/1/5/2/3   20 May 1728
Benjamin Skeat jun., pipemaker, obligor; Thomas Tye of Washbrook and Thomas Wilder of
Ipswich, maltsters, sureties
£10 for five years

C/5/1/5/2/4   21 Feb. 1756
John Colman, mariner, obligor; Michael Emerson and Turrel Lambley, both of Ipswich,
sureties

C/5/1/5/2/5   6 Oct. 1764
George Curtis jun., butcher, obligor; John Bush of Ipswich, butcher and Edmund Hines of
Walton, yeoman, sureties

C/5/1/5/2/6   23 Dec. 1766
James Ives jun., cordwainer, obligor; John May Dring, woolcomber and James Ives sen.,
yeoman, both of Ipswich, sureties

C/5/1/5/2/7   21 Feb. 1767
Gregory Mulley, carpenter, obligor; William Barthrop, linen draper and Thomas Baker,
innholder, both of Ipswich, sureties

C/5/1/5/2/8   9 Apr. 1767
Jonathan Huggins, cordwainer, obligor; Ann Huggins, widow and John Rolfe, innkeeper, both
of Ipswich, sureties

C/5/1/5/2/9   5 Oct. 1769
Jonathan Bennett, cooper, obligor; Joseph Bennett of Ipswich, labourer and Richard Bennett of
Harwich (Essex), brazier, sureties

C/5/1/5/2/10   4 Oct. 1770
Henry Ide, woolcomber, obligor; Thomas Margetts, woolcomber and John Cunningham sen.,
butcher, both of Ipswich, sureties

C/5/1/5/2/11   25 Dec. 1772
Benjamin Hunt, cordwainer, obligor; Samuel Ruffle, innholder and Matthew Peace, bricklayer,
both of Ipswich, sureties

C/5/1/5/2/12   28 Jan. 1774
Thomas Shave, merchant, obligor; John Shave, stationer and Henry Seekamp jun., apothecary,
both of Ipswich, sureties
£20 for 5 years at 4 per cent

C/5/1/5/2/13   28 Jan. 1774
Charles Squire, gent., John King, maltster, Thomas Turner, carrier and Richard Smith, yeoman,
churchwardens and overseers of ME, obligors
£20 for 5 years at 4 per cent

C/5/1/5/2/14   7 Dec. 1774
William Parkhurst, basket maker, obligor; William Reynolds, porter and Joseph Howard,
chairmaker, both of Ipswich, sureties

C/5/1/5/2/15   16 Jan. 1775
Daniel Waymand, mariner, obligor; Archibald Patrick, innholder and Edmund Warner, shipwright, both of Ipswich, sureties

C/5/1/5/2/16   21 Jun. 1775
Robert Thorndike, baker, obligor; Charles Denny, baker and Richard Slythe, bricklayer, both
of Ipswich, sureties

C/5/1/5/2/17   24 Oct. 1776
John Chenery, staymaker, obligor; William Holmes of Ipswich, baker and Daniel Sheppard of
Rushmere, wheelwright, sureties

C/5/1/5/2/18   24 Jun. 1777
Thomas Blythe, cordwainer, obligor; James Masters, innholder and Joseph Ennew, broker,
both of Ipswich, sureties

C/5/1/5/2/19   16 Sep. 1777
John Harrison, cordwainer, obligor; Samuel Harrison and John Chamberlain, both of Ipswich,
yeomen, sureties

C/5/1/5/2/20   16 Sep. 1777
Joseph Slythe, joiner and cabinetmaker, obligor; John Humphries, sailmaker and John Ungless,
shopkeeper, both of Ipswich, sureties

C/5/1/5/2/21   17 Apr. 1782
Thomas Brame, carpenter, obligor; Joseph Ashpole, baker and Stephen King, cordwainer, both
of Ipswich, sureties

C/5/1/5/2/22   26 Apr. 1782
Christopher Garwood, cabinetmaker, obligor; John Chamberlain, salt officer and William
Burrows, innholder, both of Ipswich, sureties
Annexed:
— promissory note by Chamberlain and Burrows for payment of £8 8s to Garwood in 10 years'
time, 26 Apr. 1782

C/5/1/5/2/23   7 May 1782
William Bennett, cooper, obligor; Richard Prentice, deal merchant and Martin Cole, cooper,
both of Ipswich, sureties

C/5/1/5/2/24   4 Feb. 1784
Christopher Prentice, mariner, obligor; William Prentice, mariner and Thomas Woodward,
coachmaker, sureties

C/5/1/5/2/25   8 May 1784
Lionel Hewitt of Westerfield, cordwainer, obligor; Daniel Fenton, tanner and Henry Cundy,
blacksmith, both of Ipswich, sureties

C/5/1/5/2/26   16 Oct. 1784
William Hewitt of Westerfield, wheelwright, obligor; Richard Prentice, timber merchant and
Henry Chamberlain, innholder, both of Ipswich, sureties

C/5/1/5/2/27   19 Oct. 1784
Thomas Channing, plumber, obligor; Robert Trotman, esq. and Gibson Mann, beer brewer,
both of Ipswich, sureties

C/5/1/5/2/28   22 Feb. 1786
Henry Warren sen., fisherman, obligor; Gibson Mann, beer brewer and Joseph Toosey, brandy
merchant, both of Ipswich, sureties

C/5/1/5/2/29   8 Aug. 1786
Philip Curtis, butcher, obligor; Joseph Ennew, tallow chandler and William Clarke, mariner,
sureties

C/5/1/5/2/30   27 Sep. 1786
Edward Ward, shopkeeper, obligor; Thomas Shave jun., cheese and butter factor and John
Brook, mercer, both of Ipswich, sureties

C/5/1/5/2/31   6 Jan. 1787
Jonathan Cook, twine spinner, obligor; Edward Johnson of Creeting St Mary, paper maker and
Jacob Calver of Newbourne, farmer, sureties

C/5/1/5/2/32   27 Jan. 1787
John King sen., merchant, obligor; John Dobson, mercer and John King jun., baker, both of
Ipswich, sureties
£20 for 5 years at 4 per cent

C/5/1/5/2/33   28 Jan. 1787
James Masters, innholder, William Pennock, yeoman, Stopher Jackson, printer and Edward
Jerrard, chimney sweeper, churchwardens and overseers of ME, obligors
£20 for 5 years at 4 per cent

C/5/1/5/2/34   2 Mar. 1787
Thomas Wilkenson, tailor, obligor; Martin Cole, cooper and John Chamberlain, salt officer,
both of Ipswich, sureties

C/5/1/5/2/35   20 Mar. 1787
Jacob Goldsmith, cordwainer, obligor; Ann Goldsmith, widow and Thomas Podd, innholder, both of Ipswich, sureties

C/5/1/5/2/36   10 Aug. 1787
William Blythe, cordwainer, obligor; Thomas Green sen. and Thomas Green jun., both of Holbrook, farmers, sureties

C/5/1/5/2/37   1 Nov. 1787
Stephen Cook jun., mariner, obligor; Robert Cole, innholder and John Bantoft, maltster, both of Ipswich, sureties

C/5/1/5/2/38   9 Jun. 1788
Edward Caston, mariner, obligor; William Sporle, sailmaker and John Baily, boat builder, both of Ipswich, sureties

C/5/1/5/2/39   22 Sep. 1788
John Folly, mariner, obligor; James Butcher, hatter and Simon Jennings, mariner, both of Ipswich, sureties

C/5/1/5/2/40   27 Sep. 1788
Benjamin Clover, painter, obligor; Henry Chamberlain, innholder and Thomas Gordon, maltster, both of Ipswich, sureties
£20 for 10 years

C/5/1/5/2/41   8 Feb. 1790
John Vince, cordwainer, obligor; Dowsing Steggle, common carter and Thomas Gordon, maltster, both of Ipswich, sureties

C/5/1/5/2/42   7 Apr. 1790
Robert Elliston, cordwainer, obligor; George Cook, innholder and Andrew Raper, yeoman, both of Ipswich, sureties

C/5/1/5/2/43   5 Jul. 1790
William Keyes jun., basket maker, obligor; Thomas Chapman, carpenter and Joseph Evans, fruiterer, both of Ipswich, sureties

C/5/1/5/2/44   26 Aug. 1790
Daniel Batley jun., fisherman, obligor; Charles Lucas of Woolverstone, fisherman and Robert Matthews of Ipswich, innholder, sureties

C/5/1/5/2/45   22 Sep. 1790
Joseph Prigg, jun., tailor, obligor; John Chamberlain, yeoman and Thomas Lamb, breeches maker, both of Ipswich, sureties

C/5/1/5/2/46   13 Oct. 1790
Benjamin Channing, plumber, obligor; Edward Channing of Offton, farmer and John Hunt of Ipswich, mariner, sureties

C/5/1/5/2/47   16 Oct. 1790
William Street, mariner, obligor; William Laws and Thomas Smith, both of Ipswich, innholders, sureties

C/5/1/5/2/48   6 Sep. 1791
James Thompson, cordwainer, obligor; Henry Chamberlain, innholder and William Layman, shopkeeper, both of Ipswich, sureties
£20 for 10 years

C/5/1/5/2/49   22 Nov. 1791
William Brame, baker, obligor; Frederick Penning, miller and Thomas Smith, innholder, both of Ipswich, sureties

C/5/1/5/2/50   22 Nov. 1791
Samuel Smith, carpenter, obligor; Charles Underwood and William Thurlow, both of Ipswich, carpenters, sureties

C/5/1/5/2/51   30 Jun. 1792
William Pack, cordwainer, obligor; Joseph Garwood, innholder and John Louch, carpenter, both of Ipswich, sureties

C/5/1/5/2/52   27 Sep. 1792
William Sharman, cordwainer, obligor; Charles Parker of Somersham, shopkeeper and David Housden of Ipswich, house carpenter, sureties

C/5/1/5/2/53   13 Feb. 1793
John Haunting, bricklayer, obligor; George Baily, boat builder and John Cox, carpenter, both of Ipswich, sureties

C/5/1/5/2/54   30 Apr. 1793
John Giles, peruke maker, obligor; German Stannard, butcher and Lionel Girling, blacksmith, both of Ipswich, sureties

C/5/1/5/2/55   28 May 1793
William Robertson Mulley, carpenter, obligor; Edward Sawyer, innholder and John Revett, carpenter, both of Ipswich, sureties

C/5/1/5/2/56   9 Sep. 1793
John Philips, hairdresser, obligor; William Philips, innholder and Fenn Scoggins, shopkeeper, both of Ipswich, sureties

C/5/1/5/2/57   15 Oct. 1793
William Cook, common carter, obligor; Absalom Blomfield, blacksmith and John Grimwood, carpenter, both of Ipswich, sureties

C/5/1/5/2/58   7 Jan. 1794
Joseph Jobson, fisherman, obligor; William Studd Clackson, pavior and innholder and Enos Page, wherryman, both of Ipswich, sureties

C/5/1/5/2/59   13 Jan. 1794
Robert Cook, innholder, obligor; William Layman, shopkeeper and William Cook, cordwainer, both of Ipswich, sureties

C/5/1/5/2/60   1 Jul. 1794
Isaac Gladding, blacksmith, obligor; James Salmon of Ipswich, gardener and James Lews of Foxhall, yeoman, sureties

C/5/1/5/2/61   30 Aug. 1794
John Artis, tailor, obligor; Thomas Brook, blacksmith and Benjamin Blasby, bricklayer, sureties

C/5/1/5/2/62   6 Jan. 1795
John Scott, butcher, obligor; Joseph Buttermer, butcher and William Cripps, baker, both of Ipswich, sureties
£20 for 10 years

C/5/1/5/2/63   9 Mar. 1795
Samuel Brown jun., patten maker, obligor; Samuel Brown sen. of Sproughton, farmer and Thomas Bickmore of Copdock, wheelwright, sureties
£20 for 10 years

C/5/1/5/2/64   25 Apr. 1795
Robert Bennett jun., cordwainer, obligor; Thomas Gordon, broker and Benjamin Blazby, bricklayer, both of Ipswich, sureties
£20 for 10 years

C/5/1/5/2/65   3 Oct. 1795
Thomas Burrage jun., carpenter, obligor; Thomas Burrage sen. of Ipswich, linen draper and
Robert Welch of Foxhall, yeoman, sureties
£20 for 10 years

C/5/1/5/2/66   4 Apr. 1796
William Blomfield, mariner, obligor; James Stannard, butcher and Robert Fell, blockmaker,
both of Ipswich, sureties
£20 for 10 years

C/5/1/5/2/67   4 Apr. 1796
Jeremiah Cooper, plumber and glazier, obligor; Thomas Alderton and Thomas Baker Cole,
both of Stutton, farmers, sureties
£20 for 10 years

C/5/1/5/2/68   4 Apr. 1796
Charles Jobson, fisherman, obligor; William Garrard, wherryman and Adam Pinner, fisherman, both of Ipswich, sureties
£20 for 10 years

C/5/1/5/2/69   18 Oct. 1796
John Rudland, hairdresser, obligor; Charles Underwood, carpenter and James Rudland, butcher,
both of Ipswich, sureties
£20 for 10 years

C/5/1/5/2/70   15 Nov. 1796
Thomas Cook, hairdresser, obligor; Bridget Deadman, widow and John Stow, bookbinder,
both of Ipswich, sureties
£20 for 10 years

C/5/1/5/2/71   5 Apr. 1797
Robert Hewes, hosier, obligor; Jacob Cole and John Hill, both of Ipswich, carpenters, sureties

C/5/1/5/2/72   27 Feb. 1798
John Mully, bricklayer, obligor; Samuel Tunmer jun., tailor and Richard Jacobs, gardener, both
of Ipswich, sureties
£20 for 10 years

C/5/1/5/2/73   11 Jul. 1798
James Coe, plumber and glazier, obligor; James Mollyner, gent. and Robert Pite, baker, both of
Ipswich, sureties

C/5/1/5/2/74   22 Feb. 1799
Joseph Cooper, merchant, obligor; Lionel Pepper, merchant and William Paxman, innholder,
both of Ipswich, sureties
£20 for 10 years

C/5/1/5/2/75   13 Apr. 1799
John Scarlett, bricklayer, obligor; Nathaniel Chenery Bucke, surgeon, Thomas Severne, cordwainer and Edward Jerard, baker, all of Ipswich, sureties

C/5/1/5/2/76   10 Sep. 1799
Jeremiah Burch, cordwainer, obligor; James Wyard of Somersham, farmer and William
Sheldrake of Ipswich, maltster, sureties

C/5/1/5/2/77   19 Oct. 1799
Jonathan Abbott, tailor, obligor; William Johnson of Freston, wheelwright and James Death of
Ipswich, butcher, sureties

509

C/5/1/5/2/78   19 Mar. 1800
James Gooding, hairdresser, obligor; John Kent, yeoman and William Gooding, innholder, both of Ipswich, sureties
£20 for 10 years

C/5/1/5/2/79   2 Dec. 1801
Stephen Bumpstead jun., plumber and glazier, obligor; John Gray, draper and John Gostling, whitesmith, both of Ipswich, sureties

C/5/1/5/2/80   26 Feb. 1802
William Kettle, plumber and glazier, obligor; Curtis Plumb and Charles Pulfer, both of Ipswich, cordwainers, sureties

C/5/1/5/2/81   14 Mar. 1803
John Lamb, plumber and glazier, obligor; Thomas Lamb, glover and Thomas Pite jun., cabinet maker, both of Ipswich, sureties

C/5/1/5/2/82   22 Mar. 1803
John Burroughs, fisherman, obligor; Jacob Lumbley, master mariner and Squire Ball, musician, both of Ipswich, sureties

C/5/1/5/2/83   3 Oct. 1804
Leaper Robert Wells, grocer, obligor; Edmund Wells and Edmund Clark Wells, both of Ipswich, carpenters, sureties

C/5/1/5/2/84   3 Nov. 1804
Thomas Warren, fisherman, obligor; John Dowsing of Trimley St Martin, miller and William Paine of Walton, carter, sureties

C/5/1/5/2/85   15 Apr. 1805
Richard Caston, house-carpenter, obligor; Charles Galley, cow keeper and Jonathan Hindes, innholder, both of Ipswich, sureties

C/5/1/5/2/86   26 Sep. 1806
Robert Scarlett, whitesmith, obligor; Jospeh Elmey, innholder and Joseph Waspe, butcher, both of Ipswich, sureties

C/5/1/5/2/87   29 Sep. 1806
Jeremiah Howgigo, baker, obligor; Samuel Preston, cheesemonger and Samuel Osborne, basket maker, both of Ipswich, sureties

C/5/1/5/2/88   4 Feb. 1808
Thomas Rannow, brazier, obligor; Edward Chapman, gardener and John Ablitt, watchmaker, both of Ipswich, sureties

C/5/1/5/2/89   16 Aug. 1808
Joseph Beard, painter, obligor; John Brett, cordwainer and James Burgess, grocer, both of Ipswich, sureties

C/5/1/5/2/90   21 Sep. 1808
John Dale, blacksmith, obligor; Willaim Haggar, cooper and Richard Lee, brewer, both of Ipswich, sureties

C/5/1/5/2/91   29 Sep. 1808
Richard Maple, edge-tool maker, obligor; Edward Chapman, gardener and John Maple, tanner, both of Ipswich, sureties

C/5/1/5/2/92   28 Nov. 1808
Benjamin Flory jun., baker, obligor; Rust Brook, innholder and William Taylor, carpenter, both of Ipswich, sureties

C/5/1/5/2/93   14 Dec. 1811
King Garnham, plumber and glazier, obligor; Robert Fenn of Coddenham, farmer and John
Garnham jun. of Nacton, farmer, sureties

C/5/1/5/2/94   30 Apr. 1817
John Finch jun., brazier and tinman, obligor; Robert Finch, cooper and Joseph Moulden, hatter,
both of Ipswich, sureties

C/5/1/5/2/95   27 Jan. 1818
Robert Elliston jun., treenail maker, obligor; Joseph Findell Brady, merchant and Robert
Stannard, carpenter, both of Ipswich, sureties

C/5/1/5/2/96   18 Sep. 1818
Edward Bolton Finch, saddler and harness maker, obligor; John Hardy sen., gent. and John
Hardy jun., gaoler, both of Colchester (Essex) sureties

C/5/1/5/2/97   23 Jan. 1819
Henry Capon, shipwright, obligor; William Klopfer, tanner and William Brown, architect and
builder, both of Ipswich, sureties
Unexecuted

C/5/1/5/2/98   27 Jul. 1819
Thomas Burrage jun., schoolmaster, obligor; John Wilson, turner and Edward Coleman, carpenter, both of Ipswich, sureties

C/5/1/5/2/99   1 Mar. 1820
Samuel Etheridge, blacksmith, obligor; Job Etheridge of Ipswich, carpenter and Thomas
Etheridge of Kirton, schoolmaster, sureties

C/5/1/5/2/100   27 Sep. 1820
Henry Scarlett, bricklayer, obligor; Benjamin Blasby of Ipswich, bricklayer and Jonathan
Stollery of Woodbridge, merchant, sureties

C/5/1/5/2/101   27 Sep. 1823
Emanuel Rands, rope maker, obligor; William Bird and Thomas Smith, both of Ipswich,
innholders, sureties

C/5/1/6 CRANE'S CHARITY   1668–1821

John Crane of Cambridge, by his will dated 26 June 1651, directed his executors to purchase
lands of the yearly value of £62, to be conveyed to trustees, the annual rents to be paid in
rotation to the University of Cambridge and the towns of Wisbech (Cambridgeshire), Cambridge, King's Lynn (Norfolk) and Ipswich. The rents thus payable to Ipswich every fifth year
were, in the first instance, to be used to build up a capital fund of £200, which was to be lent out
to young men setting up in trade, each of whom was to receive £20 for 20 years, interest free.
Once the initial £200 fund (which was one of the gifts that went to form the Lending Cash
Charity) had been built up, future rents were to be applied for the relief of 'honest poor men that
be imprisoned for debt, or old women, or the relief of poor men in want'. By a codicil to his will,
Crane gave 40s to each town to have a commemorative sermon preached each fifth year; the
Ipswich sermon was preached on the second Tuesday in October, in St Matthew's church, the
parish in which the testator's father was born. The property purchased by Crane's executors
was 132 acres in Fleet and Holbeach (Lincolnshire). It was conveyed to ten feoffees, two
appointed by each of the beneficiary corporations. For further details see Canning 1747, 92–98,
and Trustees 1878, 26–28.

C/5/1/6/1 ACCOUNTS 1668–1821

C/5/1/6/1/1 1668–1821
Account book
N.B., there are no entries between 1738 and 1821.
Includes, at front:
— copy clause of will of John Crane of Cambridge, esq., 1657
— memorandum *re* purchase of land in Fleet (Lincolnshire), n.d.
— copy order of Ipswich Great Court *re* appointment of new feoffees, 1717
Found loose inside:
— bill of charges in Chancery suit *re* establishing Charity, 1658
— audited account of Thomas Day as Treasurer for the town bonds, 1703–1709
(1 vol. and 2 docs)

C/5/1/7 MARTIN'S CHARITY AND BURROUGHS'S, SCRIVENER'S 1634–1836 AND ALLEN'S GIFTS

For the period for which the records have survived, down to the end of the old Corporation in 1835 and the establishment of a single board of Trustees for all the Ipswich Charities, these four charities were administered together.

Martin's Charity: On 18 February 1622 Richard Martin, one of the Portmen, conveyed to the Bailiffs and Portmen of Ipswich a farm in Westerfield, in trust to pay every year (after the deaths of certain persons to whom he gave annuities) £20 to two scholars at Cambridge University, resident in one of the Halls or Colleges, who had previously been scholars of the Free School at Ipswich. One scholar, a Bachelor of Arts, was to have £14 p.a., and the other £6, during the pleasure of the Bailiffs and the majority of the Portmen. If no suitable scholars came forward, the Bailiffs and Portmen were empowered to bestow the £20 as they considered appropriate.

Martin also directed that £10 should be bestowed annually in clothing to the poor of Ipswich, those of St Margaret's parish receiving 40s worth. The surplus profits of the farm were to be lent out, free of interest, on good security, to poor Freemen of the town, preference being given to clothiers and shearmen, for terms not exceeding seven years. In practice, this surplus came to be consolidated into the Lending Cash Charity.

The £14 for a Bachelor of Arts was seldom claimed, and it became the practice either to add it to the £10 to be bestowed in clothing, or to use it to augment the income of Burroughs's Gift (*see below*) for distribution on Good Friday. The £10 for clothing was added to Allen's and Scrivener's Gifts (*see below*) to form part of the St Thomas's Day Gift.

Burroughs's Gift: In 1613 John Burroughs of London bequeathed £100 to the Corporation, to be used for the purchase of lands to the yearly value of £5, this income to be distributed annually on Good Friday in St Lawrence's parish church, 2s 6d to each of forty poor men and women. Two pieces of land called Maungers and Swan's Nest in Westerfield were purchased from Richard Martin. The property income increased in course of time, so that it became possible to augment the number of beneficiaries.

Scrivener's Gift: By his will, at the beginning of the 17th century, Ralph Scrivener charged his lands in Blakenham, Bramford and Baylham with the payment of £7 annually to the Corporation, to be laid out in the purchase of gowns, shirts and smocks for poor native residents of Ipswich. In 1609 John Scrivener, in return for £280 and the grant to him of the £7 annuity, assigned to the Corporation an annuity of £26 13s 4d (the 'Brooks Annuity', *see* C/3/10/2/10/4) charged on lands in Ipswich and Bramford, out of which the Corporation covenanted to employ £7 p.a. for the purposes specified by Ralph Scrivener. The £7, along with the £10 from Martin's Charity and the £4 10s of Allen's Gift (*see below*) came eventually to be distributed annually in calico, four yards per person, on St Thomas's Day (21 December).

Allen's Gift: In about 1570 John Allen, Portman, gave to the Corporation £60, the annual income to be used for the purchase of gowns, shirts and smocks for the poor. Allen's capital was used to purchase an annuity of £4 10s, charged on the Bull Inn in St Mary at Quay parish and on lands in Witnesham. The income was consolidated with that of Scrivener's Gift and the £10 from Martin's Charity as described above.

For further details *see* Canning 1747, 98–102, 150, and Trustees 1878, 21–24.

C/5/1/7/1   RECEIVER'S AUDITED ANNUAL ACCOUNTS   1686–1836

Signed by the auditors. The usual receipts recorded are for rents, the Brooks annuity, and the annuity charged on the Bull Inn in St Mary at Quay; the usual payments are for property repairs, supply of coals and clothing, the Good Friday and St Thomas's Day Gifts, and the Cambridge University exhibitions.

Most of the surviving accounts will be found with the Receiver's vouchers (C/5/1/7/2), having been used as wrappers for the voucher files for the financial years concerned. The financial year ran from Michaelmas (29 September) to Michaelmas.

C/5/1/7/1/1   1686–1700
Charles Wright, Receiver
(1 vol.)

C/5/1/7/1/2   1745–1746
Goodchild Clarke, Receiver
(1 vol.)

C/5/1/7/1/3   1803–1804
S. Jackaman, Receiver
(1 doc.)

C/5/1/7/1/4   1785–1836
(1 vol.)

C/5/1/7/2   RECEIVER'S VOUCHERS   1744–1836

For rent and Land Tax on, and repairs to, Charity property; purchase of clothing for the annual distributions (the recipients are sometimes, but not always, named); and exhibitions to named Cambridge University Scholars. Churchwardens' acquittances for money received for disbursement to the poor are also found. The presence of filing holes indicates that the documents making up most of the files were originally threaded on laces. Some files include the audited accounts for the year, originally used as wrappers; these are mentioned in the catalogue where they occur.

C/5/1/7/2/1   1744–1745
Goodchild Clarke, Receiver
(9 docs)

C/5/1/7/2/2   1747–1748
Humphry Rant, Receiver
Includes:
— audited account, 1747–1748
(9 docs)

C/5/1/7/2/3   1749–1750
Michael Thirkle, Receiver
(5 docs)

C/5/1/7/2/4   1750–1752
James Wilder, Receiver
For the 2 financial years 1750–1751 and 1751–1752
(20 docs)

C/5/1/7/2/5   1752–1754
William Hammond, Receiver
For the 2 financial years 1752–1753 and 1753–1754
(19 docs)

C/5/1/7/2/6   1754–1756
James Wilder, Receiver
For the 2 financial years 1754–1755 and 1755–1756
(20 docs)

C/5/1/7/2/7   1756–1758
Lark Tarver, Receiver
For the 2 financial years 1756–1757 and 1757–1758
(25 docs)

C/5/1/7/2/8   1760–1766
James Wilder, Receiver
For the 6 financial years 1760–1761, 1761–1762, 1762–1763, 1763–1764, 1764–1765,
1765–1766
(78 docs)

C/5/1/7/2/9   1766–1767
James Wilder, Receiver
(13 docs)

C/5/1/7/2/10   1768–1769
Miles Wallis, Receiver
(4 docs)

C/5/1/7/2/11   1769–1770
Miles Wallis, Receiver
(4 docs)

C/5/1/7/2/12   1770–1771
Miles Wallis, Receiver
(11 docs)

C/5/1/7/2/13   1771–1772
William Clarke, Receiver
(8 docs)

C/5/1/7/2/14   1772–1773
William Clarke, Receiver
(7 docs)

C/5/1/7/2/15   1773–1774
Miles Wallis, Receiver
(7 docs)

C/5/1/7/2/16   1774–1775
William Clarke, Receiver
Includes:
— vouchers for Land Tax, quit rents and property repairs, 1768–1773
(25 docs)

C/5/1/7/2/17   1775–1776
William Clarke, Receiver
(13 docs)

C/5/1/7/2/18   1776–1777
William Clarke, Receiver
Includes:
— audited account, 1776–1777
(41 docs)

C/5/1/7/2/19   1777–1778
Peter Clarke, Receiver
Includes:
— audited account, 1777–1778
(19 docs)

C/5/1/7/2/20   1778–1779
Peter Clarke, Receiver
Includes:
— audited account, 1778–1779
(20 docs)

C/5/1/7/2/21   1779–1780
Peter Clarke, Receiver
Includes:
— audited account, 1779–1780
(10 docs)

C/5/1/7/2/22   1780–1781
Peter Clarke, Receiver
Includes:
— audited account, 1780–1781
(13 docs)

C/5/1/7/2/23   1781–1782
Peter Clarke, Receiver
Includes:
— audited account, 1781–1782
(17 docs)

C/5/1/7/2/24   1782–1783
Peter Clarke, Receiver
Includes:
— audited account, 1782–1783
(14 docs)

C/5/1/7/2/25   1783–1784
Peter Clarke, Receiver
Includes:
— audited account, 1783–1784
(13 docs)

C/5/1/7/2/26   1784–1785
Peter Clarke, Receiver
Includes:
— audited account, 1784–1785 (incomplete)
(10 docs)

C/5/1/7/2/27   1785–1786
William Middleton, Receiver
Includes:
— audited account, 1785–1786
(29 docs)

C/5/1/7/2/28   1786–1787
C. Squire, Receiver
(16 docs)

C/5/1/7/2/29   1787–1788
William Truelove, Receiver
(16 docs)

C/5/1/7/2/30   1788–1789
William Lynch, Receiver
(12 docs)

C/5/1/7/2/31   1789–1790
William Truelove, Receiver
(14 docs)

C/5/1/7/2/32   1790–1791
Peter Clarke, Receiver
(14 docs)

C/5/1/7/2/33   1791–1792
William Truelove, Receiver
(20 docs)

C/5/1/7/2/34   1792–1793
William Lynch, Receiver
(17 docs)

C/5/1/7/2/35   1793–1794
William Norris, Receiver
(15 docs)

C/5/1/7/2/36   1794–1795
John Walford, Receiver
Includes:
— audited account, 1794–1795
(15 docs)

C/5/1/7/2/37   1795–1796
John Kerridge, Receiver
Includes:
— audited account, 1795–1796
(9 docs)

C/5/1/7/2/38   1796–1797
William Norris, Receiver
(13 docs)

C/5/1/7/2/39   1797–1798
Robert Trotman, Receiver
(12 docs)

C/5/1/7/2/40   1798–1799
Samuel Thorndike, Receiver

Includes:
— audited account, 1798–1799
(10 docs)

C/5/1/7/2/41   1799–1800
John Kerridge, Receiver
(6 docs)

C/5/1/7/2/42   1800–1801
Receiver not named
Includes:
— list of recipients of the Good Friday Gift, 1801
(13 docs)

C/5/1/7/2/43   1801–1802
Samuel Thorndike, Receiver
Includes:
— Treasurer's audited account, 1801–1802
— list of recipients of the Good Friday Gift, 1801–1802
(9 docs)

C/5/1/7/2/44   1802–1803
William Norris, Receiver
Includes:
— list of recipients of the Good Friday Gift, 1803
(10 docs)

C/5/1/7/2/45   1803–1804
 Simon Jackaman, Receiver
Includes:
— alphabetical list of recipients of the Good Friday Gift, n.d.
(8 docs)

C/5/1/7/2/46   1804–1805
Samuel Thorndike, Receiver
Includes:
— audited account, 1804–1805
— list of recipients [of the Good Friday Gift] n.d.
(10 docs)

C/5/1/7/2/47   1805–1806
Simon Jackaman, Receiver
(8 docs)

C/5/1/7/2/48   1806–1807
.... Forsett, Receiver
Includes:
— alphabetical list of recipients of the Good Friday Gift, n.d.
(10 docs)

C/5/1/7/2/49   1807–1808
Simon Jackaman, Receiver
(7 docs)

C/5/1/7/2/50   1808–1809
William Batley, Receiver
Includes:
— alphabetical list of recipients of the Good Friday Gift, 1809
— 'state of the claims' for the Westerfield Green Inclosure, n.d. (printed; addressed to Batley
as Town Clerk)
(14 docs)

517

C/5/1/7/2/51   1809–1810
James Thorndike, Receiver
Includes:
— voucher for payment to John Bransby, surveyor, for mapping the Charity estate in Westerfield,
1810
(5 docs)

C/5/1/7/2/52   1810–1811
(12 docs; found among the records of Christ's Hospital)

C/5/1/7/2/53   1813–1814
James Thorndike, Receiver
(11 docs)

C/5/1/7/2/54   1815–1816
James Thorndike, Receiver
(9 docs)

C/5/1/7/2/55   1816–1817
James Thorndike, Receiver
(10 docs)

C/5/1/7/2/56   1817–1818
J. Sparrow, Receiver
Includes:
— 1 voucher for Osmond's and Tyler's Charities (building repairs), 1777
(12 docs)

C/5/1/7/2/57   1820–1821
William Barnard Clarke, Receiver
Includes:
— Receiver's account (not audited), 1820–1821
(13 docs)

C/5/1/7/2/58   1821–1822
F. F. Seekamp, Receiver
(17 docs)

C/5/1/7/2/59   1822–1823
Benjamin Brame, Receiver
(13 docs)

C/5/1/7/2/60   1823–1824
John Aldrich, Receiver
(8 docs)

C/5/1/7/2/61   1826–1827
John Cobbold, Receiver
Includes:
— agreed estimate for carpenter's work at the Charity farm in Westerfield, 30 Oct. 1826
— 3 small samples of ? calico, presumably that used for shirts and shifts supplied to the Charity
for distribution
(25 docs)

C/5/1/7/2/62   1827–1828
Receiver not named
(14 docs)

C/5/1/7/2/63   1828–1829
W. Lane, Receiver
(4 docs)

C/5/1/7/2/64   1829–1830
J. C. Cobbold, Receiver
(15 docs)

C/5/1/7/2/65   1830–1831
Receiver not named
(7 docs)

C/5/1/7/2/66   1831–1832
Thomas Duningham, Receiver
(12 docs)

C/5/1/7/2/67   1832–1833
R. W. Porter, Receiver
(13 docs)

C/5/1/7/2/68   1833–1834
Thomas Duningham, Receiver
(13 docs)

C/5/1/7/2/69   1833–1836
Henry B. Bristo, Receiver
(18 docs)

C/5/1/7/3   DISTRIBUTION LISTS   1634–1651

These give the numbers of gowns, shirts and smocks distributed each year to each parish, the
sick house and Christ's Hospital; no individual recipients are named.

C/5/1/7/3/1   1634–1651
(18 docs, filed together on a parchment thong)

C/5/1/8   HUNWICK'S CHARITY   **1595–1685**

John Hunwick, Alderman of Colchester (Essex), by his will dated 24 November 1593, gave
£20 to the Bailiffs and Portmen of Ipswich, £10 of which was to be distributed forthwith to the
poor, and £10 to the maintenance of Christ's Hospital and its poor.

Hunwick also bequeathed £300 for the use of 'the poore, lame and impotent persones
inhabitinge and dwellinge within the towne of Colchester and precinctes thereof', subject to the
proviso that the Bailiffs and commonalty of Colchester should bind themselves to the Bailiffs
and Portmen of Ipswich, by indentures of covenant, for the sound administration of the Charity.
In case of failure to carry out the testator's intentions, the Ipswich authorities were empowered
to seize the £300 capital, to retain £100 for the use of Ipswich's poor, and to give £100 each to
the authorities of Sudbury and Maldon (Essex) for poor relief. It was further provided that,
every fifth year, the Colchester authorities should submit their accounts for the previous four
years to the Bailiffs and Portmen of Ipswich. The fifth year's profit (£30) was always to be
divided equally for the use of the poor of Ipswich, Sudbury and Maldon.

The £10 given every fifth year to Ipswich was used to purchase clothes and linen, and distributed to every parish by the Assembly, but because of the negligence of the authorities of both
Colchester and Ipswich it was not paid or claimed after 1725 (*see* Canning 1747, 165–67).

The records listed here relate solely to Ipswich Corporation's audits of the Colchester
accounts. No records of the administration of Hunwick's gift to Ipswich appear to have
survived.

C/5/1/8/1   AUDITED ACCOUNTS   1595–1680

Each account covers a four-year audit period. Except for the earliest, covering the period 1595–1599, they were drawn up in the form of bipartite indentures; the part sealed with the Common Seal of Ipswich was retained by Colchester; that sealed with the Common Seal of Colchester was retained by Ipswich. The accounts contain only summaries of the total sums disbursed annually in each parish. Details of the distribution are contained in the parochial accounts (C/5/1/8/2).

C/5/1/8/1/1   20 Aug. 1600
For the audit period 25 Aug. 1595–26 Aug. 1599
(1 doc.; unsealed)

C/5/1/8/1/2   20 Aug. 1610
For the audit period 25 Aug. 1605–26 Aug. 1609
(1 doc.; Common Seal missing)

C/5/1/8/1/3   20 Aug. 1620
For the audit period 25 Aug. 1615–26 Aug. 1619
(1 doc.; with fragment of Common Seal of Colchester)

C/5/1/8/1/4   20 Aug. 1625
For the audit period 25 Aug. 1620–26 Aug. 1624
(1 doc.; with fragment of Common Seal of Colchester)

C/5/1/8/1/5   20 Aug. 1630
For the audit period 25 Aug. 1625–26 Aug. 1629
(1 doc.; Common Seal missing)

C/5/1/8/1/6   20 Aug. 1635
For the audit period 25 Aug. 1630–26 Aug. 1634
(1 doc.; with Common Seal of Colchester, incomplete)

C/5/1/8/1/7   20 Aug. 1640
For the audit period 25 Aug. 1636–26 Aug. 1639
(1 doc.; with fragment of Common Seal of Colchester)

C/5/1/8/1/8   20 Aug. 1645
For the audit period 25 Aug. 1640–26 Aug. 1644
(1 doc.; damaged by rodent action, part of text missing; with fragment of Common Seal of Colchester)

C/5/1/8/1/9   20 Aug. 1650
For the audit period 25 Aug. 1645–26 Aug. 1649
(1 doc.; Common Seal missing)

C/5/1/8/1/10   21 Aug. 1665
For the audit period 25 Aug. 1661–26 Aug. 1665
(1 doc.; Common Seal missing)

C/5/1/8/1/11   20 Aug. 1670
For the audit period 25 Aug. 1665–26 Aug. 1669
(1 doc.; with Common Seal of Colchester, incomplete)

C/5/1/8/1/12   20 Aug. 1675
For the audit period 25 Aug. 1671–26 Aug. 1675
(1 doc.; with Common Seal of Colchester, almost complete)

C/5/1/8/1/13   20 Aug. 1680
For the audit period 25 Aug. 1675–26 Aug. 1679
(1 doc.; Common Seal missing)

C/5/1/8/2   ANNUAL PAROCHIAL ACCOUNTS   1631–1669

One account for each year for each of the Colchester parishes of All Saints, St Botolph,
St Giles, Greenstead, St James, St Leonard, Lexden, St Mary Magdalene, St Mary at the Walls,
St Martin, St Michael Mile End, St Nicholas, St Peter, St Runwald and Holy Trinity. They
record the distribution by the churchwardens and overseers (whose signatures they bear) of the
income from Hunwick's gift received from the Bailiffs and commonalty, giving the names of
the recipients and the amount paid to each. The accounts for 1631–1639 are in the form of files,
each covering a four-year period corresponding to the audit period, with the documents filed on
leather laces in alphabetical order of parish. The 1669 accounts have become detached from
their file. The accounts presumably served as vouchers for the Ipswich Corporation audit.

C/5/1/8/2/1   1631–1634
(1 file of 60 docs)

C/5/1/8/2/2   1636–1639
(1 file of 60 docs)

C/5/1/8/2/3   20 Dec. 1669
Account for Greenstead missing
(14 docs)

C/5/1/8/3   LETTERS OF ATTORNEY   1599–1685

Appointments by the Bailiffs and commonalty of Colchester, of attorneys to give account to the
Bailiffs, burgesses and commonalty of Ipswich, on 20 Aug., of the yearly distribution of
Hunwick's Gift for the previous four years, and to receive their acquittance

C/5/1/8/3/1   3 Sep. 1599
John Eldred, merchant, attorney
(Common Seal missing)

C/5/1/8/3/2   19 Aug. 1615
13 attorneys named
(with fragment of Common Seal of Colchester)

C/5/1/8/3/3   17 Aug. 1620
13 attorneys named
(with fragment of Common Seal of Colchester)

C/5/1/8/3/4   18 Aug. 1625
13 attorneys named
(with fragment of Common Seal of Colchester)

C/5/1/8/3/5   16 Aug. 1630
11 attorneys named
(with fragment of Common Seal of Colchester)

C/5/1/8/3/6   17 Aug. 1635
13 attorneys named
(Common Seal of Colchester missing)

C/5/1/8/3/7   17 Aug. 1640
13 attorneys named
(with Common Seal of Colchester, complete)

C/5/1/8/3/8   18 Aug. 1645
13 attorneys named
(with fragment of Common Seal of Colchester)

C/5/1/8/3/9   19 Aug. 1650
17 attorneys named
(with Common Seal of Colchester, incomplete)

C/5/1/8/3/10   21 Aug. 1665
18 attorneys named
(Common Seal missing)

C/5/1/8/3/11   2 Aug. 1670
10 attorneys named
(with Common Seal of Colchester, complete)

C/5/1/8/3/12   17 Aug. 1675
5 attorneys named
(with Common Seal of Colchester, almost complete)

C/5/1/8/3/13   17 Aug. 1685
14 attorneys named
(with Common Seal of Colchester, almost complete)

C/5/2   THE GRAMMAR SCHOOL   *c.*1831–1833

The School received its first known endowment by the will of Richard Felaw (d. January 1483),
who bequeathed his two houses in what is now Foundation Street 'to be for ever a commyn
Scole hows and dwellyng place for a convenient scole Master . . . at the nominacion of the
Bayleys of the Town . . . for the tyme beyng'. The School was subsumed by Wolsey's Cardinal's College and narrowly survived its dissolution on its founder's fall. It appears to have
received the status of a royal foundation from Henry VIII, on the recommendation of his
minister Thomas Cromwell, and certainly received at this time a royal annuity for the Master's
and Usher's salaries. By her charter of 1566, Elizabeth I confirmed the annuity and authorised
the Corporation to retain, for its payment, money from the annual fee-farm due to the Crown.
The Bailiffs and Corporation were empowered (with the Bishop of Norwich's approval) to
appoint the Master and (with the Master's agreement) the Usher, and to draw up statutes for the
governance of the School. For the history of the School *see* Gray and Potter 1950; for related
records elsewhere in this catalogue *see* TYLER'S CHARITY (C/5/1/4).

C/5/2/1   n.d. [*c.*1831]
Estimate submitted to the Bailiffs
For repairs to school and Master's house
(watermark dated 1831)

C/5/2/2   1832 and n.d.
Papers *re* endowment of Grammar School
Includes:
— report of committee appointed at Assembly of 19 Dec. 1831 to investigate foundation and
endowments, 11 Jan. 1832
— letter from Revd William Howorth, Master, to Bailiffs, requesting payment of 32 years'
arrears of Felaw's Gift (for himself) and Smart's Gift (for himself and his Usher), to which
[Charity] Commissioners assure him he has a just claim, 12 Apr. 1832
— report of committee appointed to consider Howorth's claims (fragment), n.d. [1832]
(3 docs)

C/5/2/3   29 Sep. 1833
List of scholars on the foundation
Includes:
— names of scholars leaving, 29 Sep. 1832–29 Sep. 1833

— names of those still at school who last year received 40*s* exhibitions
— names of others on the foundation for complete year 29 Sep. 1832–29 Sep. 1833
Certified by J. C. Ebden, Master

C/5/2/4   n.d. [1833]
List of scholars on the foundation, Mar. 1831–Sep. 1833
Certified by J. C. Ebden, Master

C/5/3   POOR RELIEF   1577–1776

C/5/3/1   WEEKLY DISBURSEMENTS   1577–1578

C/5/3/1/1   30 Aug. 1577–29 Aug. 1578
Account of weekly disbursements of poor relief in the town
Arranged by parish; contains the names of the poor and amount of relief given to each (when
the payment is made for the keeping of a child, this is stated), and the weekly total expended.
From 7 Feb. 1578 the residents of the 'Sycke Howse' are listed separately.
Includes:
— Bailiffs' warrant to the Clerk of the Common Collection of the Poor, for weekly payment to
Widow Tompson of MW, 19 Dec. 1577 (loose doc.)
(1 vol., the front cover inscribed: 'Thys booke is for paymentes of a weklye Releyfe to the
poore within the towne of Ypswych 1577'; the last folio, detached, was found elsewhere and
re-united with the volume, apparently in the 1950s)

C/5/3/2   CHURCHWARDENS' AND OVERSEERS' PAROCHIAL   1598–1666
POOR RELIEF ACCOUNT BOOKS

Most of these contain detailed accounts of receipts from the poor rates and disbursements on
relief. They appear to have been drawn up by the parish officers, although the balancing of the
account is sometimes in another hand, which may appear in the accounts of all the parishes for a
period of years; and the signatures of Bailiffs or other Justices have generally been appended.
The accounting year began and ended at Easter, since the Churchwardens and Overseers were
elected at the Easter Vestry.

C/5/3/2/1   ST HELEN'S PARISH   1645–1655

C/5/3/2/1/1   1645–1650
(1 vol., consisting of 4 annual books sewn together in reverse chronological order)

C/5/3/2/1/2   1651–1652
(1 vol.)

C/5/3/2/1/3   1654–1655
(1 vol.)

C/5/3/2/2   ST LAWRENCE PARISH   1598–1645

C/5/3/2/2/1   1598–1645
The accounts for the years 1618–1619, 1636–1637, 1640–1641, 1641–1642, 1642–1643 and
1643–1644 are missing. The account for 1606–1607 has only a summary of the receipts, though
the disbursements are fully itemised.

Includes:

— rate assessment made by the Churchwardens and Overseers by consent of the Bailiffs, 16 Apr. 1615, annexed to the accounts for 1615–1616

— copy court roll of the manor of Illaries in East Bergholt, recording surrender of tenement called Gybrokes by Philip Breton to the use of Robert Rypham and wife Joan, 11 Dec. 1537, found loose in account for 1629–1630

(1 vol., consisting of 41 annual books sewn together in reverse chronological order)

C/5/3/2/3 ST MARY ELMS PARISH   1598–1650

C/5/3/2/3/1   1598–1645
The accounts for the years 1599–1600, 1601–1602, 1614–1615, 1615–1616, 1619–1620, 1622–1623, 1624–1625, 1630–1631, 1635–1636 and 1636–1637 are missing.
(1 vol., consisting of 37 annual books sewn together in reverse chronological order)

C/5/3/2/3/2   1645–1646
(1 vol.; a note in the original catalogue indicates that it was formerly stitched together with the account books for 1646–1647, 1647–1648 and 1648–1649 (C/5/3/2/3/3–5); they were presumably separated when they underwent conservation.)

C/5/3/2/3/3   1646–1647
(1 vol.; see note at C/5/3/2/3/2 above)

C/5/3/2/3/4   1647–1648
(1 vol.; see note at C/5/3/2/3/2 above)

C/5/3/2/3/5   1648–1649
(1 vol.; see note at C/5/3/2/3/2 above)

C/5/3/2/3/6   1649–1650
The payments are arranged on a quarterly basis, a different Overseer being responsible for each quarter
(1 vol.)

C/5/3/2/4 ST MARY AT QUAY PARISH   1598–1654

C/5/3/2/4/1   1598–1645
The accounts for the years 1599–1600, 1602–1603, 1612–1613, 1617–1618, 1623–1624, 1629–1630, 1636–1637, 1641–1642, 1642–1643 and 1643–1644 are missing. The accounts for 1598–1599 are arranged on a monthly basis, and include a list of 'the persones rated to the stock' with the amounts at which they are assessed.
(1 vol. consisting of 37 annual books sewn together in reverse chronological order)

C/5/3/2/4/2   1653–1654
The parish is unnamed, but comparison of the names of the ratepayers with those in the accounts for 1644–1645 (C/5/3/2/4/1) suggests the attribution to MQ.
(2 fols, fragmentary)

C/5/3/2/5 ST MARY STOKE PARISH   1645–1646

C/5/3/2/5/1   1645–1646
The payments are arranged on a quarterly basis, a different Overseer being responsible for each quarter.
(2 fols)

C/5/3/2/6   ST MATTHEW PARISH   1645–1666

C/5/3/2/6/1   1645–1646
(1 vol.)

C/5/3/2/6/2   1647–1648
(1 vol.)

C/5/3/2/6/3   1648–1649
(1 vol.)

C/5/3/2/6/4   1650–1651
(1 vol.)

C/5/3/2/6/5   1651–1652
(1 vol.)

C/5/3/2/6/6   1654–1655
(1 vol.)

C/5/3/2/6/7   1658–1659
The payments are arranged on a quarterly basis, a different Overseer being responsible for each
quarter.
(1 vol.)

C/5/3/2/6/8   1664–1665
The receipts and payments are arranged on a quarterly basis, a different Overseer being responsible for each quarter.
(1 vol., consisting of 4 quarterly books sewn together in chronological order)

C/5/3/2/6/9   1665–1666
The receipts and payments are arranged on a quarterly basis, a different Overseer being responsible for each quarter.
(1 vol., consisting of 4 quarterly books sewn together in reverse chronological order)

C/5/3/2/7   ST NICHOLAS PARISH   1598–1664

C/5/3/2/7/1   1598–1645
The accounts for the years 1599–1600, 1614–1615, 1615–1616, 1617–1618, 1630–1631 and
1639–1640 are missing.
Includes:
— warrant of William Sparrowe and Matthew Brownerigge, Justices of the Peace, for distraint
on goods of 6 named persons for arrears of poor rate, 13 Feb. 1606, annexed to accounts for
1605–1606
(1 vol., consisting of 41 annual books sewn together in reverse chronological order)

C/5/3/2/7/2   1653–1654
(1 vol.)

C/5/3/2/7/3   1660–1661
Receipts and payments on a quarterly basis, a different Overseer being responsible for each
quarter
(1 vol.)

C/5/3/2/7/4   1662–1663
Receipts and payments on a quarterly basis, a different Overseer being responsible for each
quarter
(1 vol., consisting of 4 quarterly books sewn together)

C/5/3/2/7/5   1663–1664
Receipts and payments on a quarterly basis, a different Overseer being responsible for each
quarter
(1 vol., consisting of 4 quarterly books sewn together, the quarters in the order 1, 3, 2, 4)

C/5/3/2/7/6   Jul.–Oct. 1664
For one quarter only
(1 vol.)

C/5/3/2/8   ST PETER'S PARISH   1652–1657

C/5/3/2/8/1   1652–1653
(1 vol.)

C/5/3/2/8/2   1656–1657
Endorsed '1656–1657', though the heading states '1636'. Comparison of the names of the ratepayers with those in C/5/3/2/8/1 suggests that the later date is correct.
(1 vol.)

C/5/3/3   QUARTERLY POOR RATE ASSESSMENTS: INDIVIDUAL   1657–1776
PARISHES

These were made by the Churchwardens and Overseers of the Poor with the consent of the
Bailiffs or Justices of the Peace. Most of the assessments appear to be copies made for preservation by the town authorities. Only those for St Clement, St Margaret and St Peter, and the
earliest for St Mary at Quay, are signed. They give only the names of the ratepayers and the
sums due, except for the two late 18th-century assessments for St Helen, which include descriptions of some properties, e.g. 'mill', 'farm'.

C/5/3/3/1   ST CLEMENT PARISH   1666–1667

C/5/3/3/1/1   15 Apr.–24 Jun. 1666
Six-fold rate for 10 weeks

C/5/3/3/1/2   1 Jan.–7 Apr. 1667
Six-fold rate for 14 weeks

C/5/3/3/2   ST HELEN'S PARISH   1776

C/5/3/3/2/1   7 Apr.–22 Jun. 1776
(1 vol.; front cover bears an engraving of the south prospect of St Helen's church, apparently
printed from one of the plates for John Ogilby's map of Ipswich, surveyed 1674 and engraved
1698)
C/5/3/3/2/2   23 Jun.–28 Sep. 1776
(1 vol.)

C/5/3/3/3   ST MARGARET PARISH   1666

C/5/3/3/3/1   [Jun.]–29 Sep. 1666
Six-fold rate for 12 weeks
(found with the accounts of the Governors and Treasurer of Christ's Hospital)

C/5/3/3/3/2	29 Sep.–[? 25 Dec.] 1666
Five-fold rate for 3 months	

C/5/3/3/4 ST MARY AT QUAY PARISH	1665–1666

C/5/3/3/4/1	[Jun.]–30 Sep. 1665
Seven-fold rate for 14 weeks	

C/5/3/3/4/2	[Apr.]–24 Jun. 1666
Five-fold rate for 10 weeks	

C/5/3/3/4/3	24 Jun.–29 Sep. [? 1666]
Seven-fold rate for 14 weeks	
(slightly damaged; date incomplete)	

C/5/3/3/5 ST MATTHEW PARISH	1666

C/5/3/3/5/1	[Jun.]–28 Sep. 1666
Six-fold rate for 14 weeks	

C/5/3/3/6 ST NICHOLAS PARISH	1657

C/5/3/3/6/1	29 Sep.–25 Dec. 1657
Three-fold rate for 12 weeks	

C/5/3/3/7 ST PETER PARISH	1673

C/5/3/3/7/1	6 May 1673
Valuation of rents of houses and land	
Occupiers as well as owners named	
(1 vol.; front cover marked 'Make the Assessment by this Booke')	

C/5/3/3/8 ST STEPHEN PARISH	1666

C/5/3/3/8/1	21 Apr.–23 Jun. 1666
Six-fold rate for 9 weeks	

C/5/3/3/8/2	24 Jun.–29 Sep. 1666
Five-fold rate for 14 weeks	

(Heading incomplete; the name of the parish is missing, but has been identified by comparison of the names of the ratepayers with those in C/5/3/3/8/1.)

C/5/3/4   REGISTERS OF QUARTERLY POOR RATE ASSESSMENTS: 1714–1722 ALL PARISHES

These are apparently copies of the parochial assessments made by the Churchwardens and Overseers of the Poor of the twelve ancient parishes in the town, with the consent of the Bailiffs or Justices of the Peace, and intended for preservation by the town authorities.

All the assessments for each quarter are normally entered together, but the order in which the parishes appear varies. Details given include the names of the ratepayers and the sums due, and names of inns; brief descriptions of other properties, e.g. 'malting office', 'windmill', 'marsh' and 'orchard' are sometimes given. Contributors are never listed by streets.

The catalogue entries follow the quarterly layout of each volume. The omission of the assessment for any parish for the given quarter is noted, as is the presence of any assessment of uncertain date or for a period other than the given quarter. The dates given in the catalogue for the ending of each quarter are approximate, since they vary from parish to parish and from time to time. The usual quarter days were Lady Day (25 Mar.), Easter (variable), the Nativity of St John the Baptist (24 Jun.), Michaelmas (29 Sep.) and Christmas (25 Dec.).

C/5/3/4/1   1714–1718
Register of assessments
(ff. 1–11)	quarter ending 24 Jun. 1714 CL omitted; HL and MW for ½ year ending 29 Sep. 1714
(ff. 11–19)	quarter ending 29 Sep. 1714 CL, HL, MS and MT omitted
(ff. 19v–26v)	quarter ending 25 Dec. 1714 CL, HL and MS omitted
(ff. 27–35)	quarter ending Easter 1715 CL omitted; MS for ½ year ending Easter 1715
(ff. 35v–45)	quarter ending 24 Jun. 1715 CL, HL and MS omitted
(ff. 45–50v)	quarter ending 29 Sep. 1715 CL, HL, PE and ST omitted; MS for ½ year ending 29 Sep. 1715
(ff. 51–56)	quarter ending 25 Dec. 1715 CL, HL, MG, PE and MS omitted
(ff. 57–65v)	quarter ending Easter 1716 CL and HL omitted
(ff. 66–72v)	quarter ending 24 Jun. 1716 CL, HL and MS omitted
(ff. 73–84v)	quarter ending 29 Sep. 1716 CL omitted; HL and MS for ½ year ending 29 Sep. 1716
(ff. 84v–94v)	quarter ending 25 Dec. 1716 CL, HL and MS omitted
(ff. 94v–105v)	quarter ending Easter 1717 CL omitted; MS for ½ year ending Easter 1717
(ff. 105v–112v)	quarter ending 24 Jun. 1717 CL, HL, MS, NI and PE omitted
(ff. 113–121v)	quarter ending 29 Sep. 1717 CL, PE and ST omitted; HL and MS for ½ year ending 29 Sep. 1717
(ff. 122–131v)	quarter ending 25 Dec. 1717 CL, MS and NI omitted
(ff. 131v–139)	quarter ending Easter 1718 ME and MW omitted; MG and PE for quarter ending 24 Jun. 1718

(1 vol.)

C/5/3/4/2   1718–1720
Register of assessments
(ff. 2v–11)	quarter ending 24 Jun. 1718 CL, HL, MS and MW omitted; NI, PE and ST undated
(ff. 19–29)	quarter ending 25 Dec. 1718 MW, PE and ST undated; CL, LW, MW and NI, totals only
(ff. 29v–36v)	quarter ending Easter 1719 MG, ME, MT, MW, PE and ST undated; LW and NI, totals only
(ff. 36v–51)	quarter ending 24 Jun. 1719 all undated; HL, MS and ST omitted; includes CL, ? for quarter ending Easter 1719

(ff. 51v–64v)   quarter ending 29 Sep. 1719
                 HL and MS for ½ year ending 29 Sep. 1719
(ff. 64v–77v)   quarter ending 25 Dec. 1719
                 HL and MS omitted
(ff. 78–92v)   quarter ending Easter 1720
                 includes: 3 assessments for CL, 26 Dec. 1719–1 Feb. 1720, 1 Feb.–7 Mar.
                 1720, 7 Mar.–Easter 1720; for HL, MS, MW, PE and ST, see continua-
                 tion of this quarter in C/5/3/4/3

(1 vol.)

C/5/3/4/3   1720–1722
Register of assessments
(ff. 1–5)   quarter ending Easter 1720, continued from C/5/3/4/2
                 HL for ½ year ending 25 Mar. 1720; MS for 29 weeks, 29 Sep. 1719–
                 Easter 1720
(ff. 5–15)   quarter ending 24 Jun. 1720
                 HL, MQ and MS omitted
(ff. 15–26)   quarter ending 29 Sep. 1720
                 MG omitted; MS for ½ year, Easter–29 Sep. 1720
(ff. 26–34)   quarter ending 25 Dec. 1720
                 HL, MG, MS and PE omitted
(ff. 34v–45)   quarter ending Easter 1721
                 CL omitted; MS for ½ year 29 Sep. 1720–Easter 1721
(ff. 45–56v)   quarter ending 24 Jun. 1721
                 HL and MS omitted
(ff. 56v–69v)   quarter ending 29 Sep. 1721
                 HL and MS for period Easter–29 Sep. 1721
(ff. 70–82)   quarter ending 25 Dec. 1721
                 HL and MS omitted
(ff. 82v–89)   quarter ending Easter 1722
                 HL, LW, ME, MS, MW, PE and ST omitted

(1 vol.)

C/5/4   ECCLESIASTICAL   1750–1799

C/5/4/1   CHURCH RATE ASSESSMENTS (STIPENDIARY   1749–1761
MINISTERS)

The Ipswich Paving Act of 1571 (13 Eliz., cap. 24), in addition to requiring owners of houses,
lands and tenements within the town to pave the sections of the streets on which their respective
properties fronted, also empowered the Bailiffs and Portmen, in association with the Churchwardens and four leading inhabitants of each parish, to levy an annual rate on all freehold and
copyhold property within the parish, to pay the salary of a suitable stipendiary minister and
meet the cost of repairing nave and chancel, since the Ipswich churches were poorly endowed.

All the surviving assessments give the names of owners, yearly rent or rateable value, and
sum rated. The assessments for St Lawrence and St Mary le Tower give no details of property.
Those for St Mary at Quay and St Peter give brief descriptions, such as 'house', 'malt office',
'shop', 'warehouse' or 'shipyard'; those for St Mary at Quay additionally give the names of
inns or alehouses.

Unless otherwise stated, the assessments bear the signatures of the Bailiffs, Portmen,
Churchwardens and inhabitants. Those which are unsigned are duplicates or copies. As originally found they were grouped by parishes, and this arrangement has been retained.

C/5/4/1/1   ST LAWRENCE   1756–1761

C/5/4/1/1/1   29 Sep. 1756
(1 doc.)

C/5/4/1/1/2   16 Oct. 1758
(1 doc.)

C/5/4/1/1/3   5 Oct. 1759
(1 doc.)

C/5/4/1/1/4   2 Jun. 1760
(1 doc.)

C/5/4/1/1/5   1761
(1 vol., unsigned; day and month left blank; back cover marked 'Duplicate')

C/5/4/1/2   ST MARY AT QUAY   1750–1759

C/5/4/1/2/1   8 Sep. 1750
(1 vol.)

C/5/4/1/2/2   19 Sep. 1752
(1 vol.)

C/5/4/1/2/3   14 Jan. 1757
(1 vol.; certified copy)

C/5/4/1/2/4   16 Oct. 1758
(1 vol.)

C/5/4/1/2/5   5 Oct. 1759
(1 vol., unsigned)

C/5/4/1/3   ST MARY LE TOWER   1749–1759

C/5/4/1/3/1   24 Jun. 1749
(1 vol.)

C/5/4/1/3/2   3 Jul. 1750
(1 vol.)

C/5/4/1/3/3   6 Jul. 1751
(1 vol.)

C/5/4/1/3/4   23 Jun. 1752
(1 vol.)

C/5/4/1/3/5   29 Sep. 1756
(1 vol.)

C/5/4/1/3/6   22 Jun. 1757
(1 vol.)

C/5/4/1/3/7   24 Jun. 1758
(1 vol., unsigned; front cover marked 'copy')

C/5/4/1/3/8   5 Oct. 1759
(1 vol.; back cover marked 'Duplicate of the Minister's Rate')

C/5/4/1/4 ST PETER	1750–1759
C/5/4/1/4/1 (1 vol.)	10 Aug. 1750
C/5/4/1/4/2 (1 vol.)	23 Jun. 1752
C/5/4/1/4/3 (1 vol.)	18 Jul. 1758
C/5/4/1/4/4 (1 vol.)	17 Oct. 1759

C/5/4/2   THE TOWN LIBRARY   1799

The library maintained for the use of the Town Preacher owes its origin to William Smart, Portman, who in 1599 bequeathed 'my latten printed bookes and writen bookes in volume and parchmente . . . towardes one librarye safelie to be keepte in the vestrye of the parishe church of St Mary Tower . . . to be used ther by the common preacher of the . . . Towne for the tyme beinge . . .'. The subsequent history of the library is traced in detail in Blatchly 1989.

C/5/4/2/1   1799
'Numerical Catalogue of the Books in the Town Library under the Public Grammar-School, Ipswich'
(1 vol., 61 pp., printed by William Burrell; signature of S. A. Notcutt on title page)

C/5/4/3   CIVIC CHURCH OF ST MARY LE TOWER   1746–?1747

C/5/4/3/1   19 Nov. 1746
Estimate for restoration of organ, by John Byfield
Details of work to be carried out on Great and Choir organs, including names of some of stops
(1 doc. Found loose inside Memorandum Book of Gifts to the Town of Ipswich, C/3/10/1/1/3)

C/5/4/3/2   n.d. [? 1747]
Schedule of 'work . . . done to the Organ above what was agreed for [in the hand of John Byfield]
Details of alterations and additions to Great, Choir and Swell Organs, including names of some of stops
(1 doc.; found with deeds of Tooley Foundation property in Akenham, Whitton, Bramford, Thurleston and Coddenham)

C/5/5   THE WATER SUPPLY   1615–1833

From 1614 or very shortly afterwards, water was supplied to those householders who were prepared to pay to lease it, from springs on the high ground adjoining Caldwell Hall, near where the old Woodbridge Road used to pass through St Helen's Street, then called Great Wash Lane. The springs were collected into brick conduit-houses before being led into the mains (Clarke 1830, 316). The springs were capable of supplying the whole town, but as there was no reservoir sufficiently large to prevent the water from running to waste at night, many households had an insufficient supply (Glyde 1850, 29). By the early 19th century, great inconvenience was regularly caused to householders by constant tinkering with the mains, which were frequently taken up, and the supply turned off, with the sole object of buying votes at elections by finding regular employment for Freemen, many of whom were to be seen idling about the streets while receiving wages for this unnecessary work (*Municipal Corporations Report* 1835, 2321–22).

C/5/5/1 EVIDENCES OF TITLE TO THE QUAY WATER WORKS   1629–1724

These deeds were found scattered among the Corporation water leases and among the grants of common soil. This private company was acquired by the Corporation *c.*1718, and eventually became part of the Ipswich Water Works Company; *see also* Ipswich Record Office, DD2.

C/5/5/1/1   11 Jul. 1629
Liberty to dig common soil of town, 3ft in breadth, and to lay water pipes from conduit heads in HL through certain named streets
Lease to Tobias Blosse, gent., Edward Mann, gent., Thomas Cleere, gent., John Reynolds, gent., William Inglethorpe, merchant, John Carnaby, mariner, John Blomefeild, ironmonger, Raph Noore, merchant, John Catcher, vintner, Barnabas Burrough, apothecary, John Warner, fishmonger and Edward Hedge, painter, all of Ipswich (who hold a 500-year demise from Samuel Cutler of Ipswich, merchant, of land in HL on which they have built 2 conduit heads), for 500 years for 2*s* 6*d* annual rent

C/5/5/1/2   1 Dec. 1658
Assignor's 5th part of piece of ground with brick conduit head and cistern erected thereon at near end of meadow (3a.) sometime John Clench's in HL, abutting N. on the Wash Lane, with liberty to lay pipes of timber, earth or lead in meadow to draw water to cistern; and his share in pipes laid along the Wash Lane and common street of Ipswich to the Key Water Work
Deed of assignment from Ralph Noare to John Moody, both of Ipswich, merchants, of 469-year term leased to Noare, Manuell Sorrell, gent., Edward Mann sen., gent., Samuel Brandling, gent. and John Blomfeild, merchant, all of Ipswich, by Thomas Clere of Ipswich, gent. and Bennett Clere of Dedham (Essex) clothier, on 14 Oct. 1658, for 10*s*.

C/5/5/1/3   1 Dec. 1658
Assignor's 6th part of piece of ground (10ft x 10ft) used as conduit head or cistern, at near end of the Hop Ground, with liberty to dig for springs and lay 'trees' or water pipes in Hop Ground, Bull Meadow and Conduit Meadow in HL; and his share in pipes laid in the 3 closes
Deed of assignment from Ralph Noare to John Moody, both of Ipswich, merchants, of 469-year term leased to Noare and Manuell Sorrell, gent., Edward Mann, gent., Samuel Brandling, gent. and John Blomfeild, merchant, all of Ipswich, by Gyles Pooley of London, merchant, now deceased, and daughter Elizabeth on 14 Oct. 1658, for 30*s*.

C/5/5/1/4   8 Aug. 1659
Assignor's part of the Quay Water Work, conduit heads, cisterns, cesspools and waterpipes of timber, earth and lead in the closes and streets of Ipswich
Deed of assignment by Robert Clarke of Ipswich, gent., to William Greene of Ipswich, merchant, of 469-year term assigned to him by John Blomfeild on 16 May 1659, for £5

C/5/5/1/5   23 Sep. 1662
Assignor's 5th part of 2 pieces of ground (each 12ft x 12ft), first with a brick cistern, or conduit head erected thereon, at upper end, and second with liberty to build conduit head thereon, at lower ends of close late of Samuel Cutler of Ipswich, gent. abutting N. on Caldwell Brook, in HL, with other 'cesperells' [cesspools], water gutters, pipes of timber, earth or lead in close, and liberty to draw water from close in either cistern and to dig in close for better preservation of springs; and of 5th part of property as in C/5/5/1/2–3
Deed of assignment from Edward Mann sen., of Ipswich, gent. to John Moody of Ipswich, merchant, of 465-year term, for £32

C/5/5/1/6   26 Oct. 1685
4 x 5th parts of: piece of ground (12ft square) at upper end of meadow formerly the inheritance of Samuel Cutler, gent., abutting N. on Caldwell Brook in HL, brick cistern or conduit head

built thereon; piece of ground (12ft square) at lower end of meadow, with liberty to build conduit head thereon; 'cesperills' [cesspools], water gutters and pipes of timber, lead or earth within meadow to carry water into conduit heads; piece of meadow with brick conduit head built thereon at nearest end of meadow (3½a) some time John Clench's in HL, abutting on the Wash Lane commonly called Caldwell Brook; piece of ground (10ft square) near upper end of the Hopground in HL, used for cistern into which several springs are brought, with liberty to dig for springs in Hopground, Bull Meadow and Conduit Meadow and to lay water pipes; and water pipes of timber, earth or lead laid in the Wash Lane and several other streets, known as the Key Water Work, out of which certain rents and profits arise, with liberty to break up streets to lay or repair pipes, on grant of the town of Ipswich for 2s 6d annual rent

Deed of assignment by John Moody of London, merchant, eldest son and executor of John Moody late of Ipswich, esq., deceased, to Thomas Moody, merchant, his younger brother, in consideration of payment of £50 debt owed by John Moody the father to Mary, wife of Richard Moseley, esq.; for 442-year term

Annexed:
— memorandum dated 11 Jul. 1709 that Thomas Moody has assigned remainder of term in waterworks to Samuel Caley for £65; that Caley is to take all the earthen pipes that Moody has spoken to Scott for, not exceeding £500 at 1d a piece; and that Caley is to have all trees that belong to the waterworks, the pump 'woles', the trees buried by the main pipes, the forcer mattock and 'strappet'
— undated note re spring heads and main pipe
(3 docs)

C/5/5/1/7   30 Sep. 1695
£38 life annuity secured on real and personal estate to annual value of £60
Award made by William Hamond as arbitrator of differences between Thomas Moody and John Moody: annuity to be paid by Thomas Moody; on condition that John Moody at his own cost cause satisfaction to be entered upon a judgment obtained against him as executor of his late father John Moody at the suit of Richard Mosely, esq. and wife Mary in Easter Term 1685

C/5/5/1/8   20 Jul. 1709
Bond
From Thomas Moody to Samuel Caley, both of Ipswich, gents, in £130, for performance of covenants contained in indentures of same date

C/5/5/1/9   21 Jul. 1709
4 x 5th parts of several pieces of meadow, conduit heads, cisterns, 'cesperills', watercourses, water gutters, pipes of timber, earth and lead and other premises specified in indenture between Thomas Moody of Ipswich, gent. and Samuel Caley of Ipswich, grocer, dated 20 Jul. 1709, and of all other cisterns and watercourses belonging to the Key Waterworks
Mortgage from Samuel Caley to John Baker of Ipswich, gent., for 442 years, for £65; with bond for performance
(2 docs)

C/5/5/1/10   21 May 1714
Property as in C/5/5/1/9
Deed of further charge from Thomas Wincoll of Ipswich, executor of Samuel Caley deceased, to John Baker of Denton (Norfolk), gent., to whom Caley had mortgaged the property on 21 Jul. 1709, for residue of term of 442 years, for discharge of Caley's outstanding debts

C/5/5/1/11   30 Jun. 1724
Rents for water called Caleys Water alias the Key Water
Letter of attorney from the Bailiffs, burgesses and commonalty to Samuel Hambling of Ipswich, plumber, to collect rents and retain them in his hands towards payment of their debt to him

533

C/5/5/2 CORPORATION WATER LEASES 1615–1766

These are all counterpart leases granted by the Bailiffs, burgesses and commonalty. Where the names of the occupiers are not given in the catalogue, the properties were in the lessees' own occupation. The preambles to the earliest leases recite that the Bailiffs, burgesses and commonalty have lately erected, at their own charge, a new conduit head at the upper end of Caldwell Brook and have laid 'earthen pottes and a great meyne pipe of lead' from it to bring water into the town, and have also erected a cistern near the Moot Hall to receive the water for the general benefit of the town. A lease of 27 Sep. 1622, of a supply to a house in St Peter's parish, further recites that they have laid a lesser pipe of lead from the cistern to convey the water through the common streets leading towards Stoke Bridge. From 1631 the leases refer to the laying of 'bored elms' (later simply described as 'trees') and a main pipe of lead from the conduit head.

Throughout the period covered by the leases it is stipulated that the supply to each property should be by means of a lead 'quill' or pipe of no more than 1 inch bore, and a cock 'of the bigness of a swann's quill and not above'. The supply is to be used only for household purposes and not for the carrying on of any trade. The cock is not to be permitted to run to waste, and no water is to be taken by any person other than a member of the lessee's household. Until the 1680s the lessees were required to keep their wells or pumps, together with the pulleys, ropes, buckets and ironwork, in good repair. In the later 17th century there are provisos against properties being converted into inns, alehouses or starch houses. Until at least 1737 the rents were due annually on the feast of St Bartholomew (24 August). Sometime before 1758 the leases began to be issued from Michaelmas and the rents to be payable quarterly. An interesting lease of 26 Jun. 1718 (C/5/5/2/52), to William Clarke, gent., for the supply of water to messuages in occupation of his tenants in St Mary at Quay parish, waives the customary fine (or connexion charge) 'in consideration of the good services done to the Corporation of Ipswich by [him] in his procuring a lease of the said water of Mr Caley' ['Caley's Water' appears to have been the Quay (or Key) Water Works – *see* C/5/5/1/6–11].

C/5/5/2/1   23 Dec. 1615
Water supply to house in MG
Lease to Joseph Parkhurst of Ipswich, grocer, for 99 years, for £5 fine and 5*s* annual rent

C/5/5/2/2   23 Dec. 1615
Water supply to house in LW
Lease to Bezaliell Sherman of Ipswich, grocer, for 99 years, for £5 fine and 5*s* annual rent

C/5/5/2/3   23 Dec. 1615
Water supply to house in which Rt Hon. Lady Marie Graye dwells in MT and MG
Lease to Dame Elizabeth Felton, widow of Sir Anthony Felton, kt, for 99 years, for £10 fine and 5*s* annual rent

C/5/5/2/4   23 Dec. 1615
Water supply to house in MW
Lease to Edward Dodson of Ipswich, draper, for 99 years, for £5 fine and 5*s* annual rent

C/5/5/2/5   27 Sep. 1622
Water supply to house in PE
Lease to Thomas Seelie of Ipswich, merchant, for 93 years, for 13*s* 4*d* annual rent

C/5/5/2/6   27 Sep. 1622
Water supply to house in MG
Lease to John Smithe of Ipswich, baker, for 93 years, for £5 fine and 5*s* annual rent

C/5/5/2/7   25 Sep. 1624
Water supply to house in MT
Lease to William Tyler of Ipswich, draper, for 90 years, for 5*s* annual rent

C/5/5/2/8   25 Sep. 1624
Water supply to house in which Richard Harle dwells in LW
Lease to Richard Burlingham of Ipswich, mariner, during lessors' pleasure, for 13s 4d annual
rent

C/5/5/2/9   7 Nov. 1625
Water supply to house in which Edward Maynard dwells in MG
Lease to John Aldus of Ipswich, clothier, for 89 years, for £5 fine and 5s annual rent

C/5/5/2/10   7 Apr. 1631
Water supply to house in MG
Lease to Thomas Newton of Ipswich, chandler, for 83 years, for £6 13s 4d fine and 6s 8d annual
rent

C/5/5/2/11   7 Apr. 1631
Water supply to house in which Edward Maynard dwells in MG
Lease to John Bliethe of Ipswich, merchant, for 83 years, for £6 13s 4d fine and 6s 8d annual
rent

C/5/5/2/12   17 Nov. 1632
Water supply to house in which William Doggett, draper, dwells in MT
Lease to Samuel Lane of Ipswich, haberdasher, for 81 years, for £6 13s 4d fine and 6s 8d annual
rent

C/5/5/2/13   11 May 1633
Water supply to house late in occupation of Francis Browne, tailor, in MG
Lease to John Coleman of Sproughton, gent., for 81 years, for £6 13s 4d fine and 6s 8d annual
rent

C/5/5/2/14   8 Jun. 1633
Water supply to house in which Robert Sayer, draper, dwells in MG
Lease to Samuel Aldgate of Ipswich, haberdasher, for 81 years, for £6 13s 4d fine and 6s 8d
annual rent

C/5/5/2/15   27 Sep. 1641
Water supply to house in which Robert Turner, apothecary, dwells in LW
Lease to Stephen Blomefeild of Bentley, yeoman, for 72 years, for £6 13s 4d fine and 6s 8d
annual rent

C/5/5/2/16   1 Sep. 1644
Water supply to house in NI
Lease to Stephen Crashfield of Ipswich, hosier, for 70 years, for £6 13s 4d fine and 6s 8d annual
rent

C/5/5/2/17   13 Jan. 1645
Water supply to house in MT
Lease to Richard Girlinge of Ipswich, grocer, for 69 years, for £6 13s 4d fine and 6s 8d annual
rent

C/5/5/2/18   26 Mar. 1649
Water supply to house in MT
Lease to Tytus Camplyn sen. of Ipswich, cordwainer, for 62 years, for £6 13s 4d fine and 6s 8d
annual rent

C/5/5/2/19   28 Sep. 1657
Water supply to houses in which lessee and Tobias Barker dwell in MT
Lease to John Parker of Ipswich, maltster, for 56 years, for £6 13s 4d fine and 13s 4d annual rent

C/5/5/2/20   29 Sep. 1657
Water supply to house in which widow Dunkon dwells in HL
Lease to Robert Dunkon of Ipswich, gent., for 56 years, for £6 13s 4d fine and 6s 8d annual rent

C/5/5/2/21   26 Nov. 1662
Water supply to house in LW
Lease to John Jolly of Ipswich, apothecary, for 50 years, for £6 13s 4d fine and 6s 8d annual rent

C/5/5/2/22   26 Nov. 1662
Water supply to house in which James Goodinge, draper, dwells in MT
Lease to William Veesey of Ipswich, mercer, for 50 years, for £6 13s 4d fine and 10s annual
rent

C/5/5/2/23   28 Sep. 1670
Water supply to house in which Charles Wyeth, clothier, dwells in HL
Lease to Laurence Mollyner of Bramford, gent., for 43 years, for £6 13s 4d fine and 10s annual
rent

C/5/5/2/24   28 Sep. 1673
Water supply to house in which lessee and Henry Curtice dwell in MT
Lease to Robert Ridnall of Ipswich, haberdasher, for 40 years, for £6 13s 4d fine and £1 6s 8d
annual rent

C/5/5/2/25   28 [Sep.] 1673
Water supply to houses in which lessee, Thomas Seamans and [blank] Fisher dwell in HL
Lease to Simon Cumberland of Ipswich, clothier, for 41 years, for £10 fine and 10s annual rent
(damaged by rodents; text incomplete)

C/5/5/2/26   28 Sep. 1673
Water supply to house in which lessee, James Nicholls and widow Wye dwell in LW
Lease to William Hayle of Ipswich, mercer, for 41 years, for £20 fine and £1 5s annual rent

C/5/5/2/27   28 Sep. 1673
Water supply to house in LW
Lease to William Vesey of Ipswich, woollen draper, for 40 years, for £6 13s 4d fine and 10s
annual rent

C/5/5/2/28   28 Sep. 1673
Water supply to house in which Richard Fulcher and John Ellice dwell in MG
Lease to Thomas Major of Ipswich, dyer, for 40 years, for £6 13s 4d fine and 10s annual rent

C/5/5/2/29   28 Sep. 1673
Water supply to house in MG
Lease to Augustine Pettitt of Ipswich, innholder, for 40 years, for £6 13s 4d fine and 10s annual
rent

C/5/5/2/30   28 Sep. 1673
Water supply to house in which Thomas Paschall, grocer, dwells in LW
Lease to John Reeve of Ipswich, haberdasher, for 41 years, for £6 13s 4d fine and 10s annual
rent

C/5/5/2/31   28 Sep. 1673
Water supply to house in which [blank] Willes and widow Lindfeild dwell in MT
Lease to Robert Palmer of Colchester (Essex), merchant tailor, for 41 years, for £6 13s 4d fine
and 16s 4d annual rent (damaged by rodents; text incomplete)

C/5/5/2/32   28 Sep. 1673
Water supply to house in MT and LW
Lease to Edward Milksopp of Ipswich, ironmonger, for 40 years, for £13 6s 8d fine and £1 6s 8d
annual rent

C/5/5/2/33   28 Sep. 1673
Water supply to house in which lessee and George Joye dwell in LW
Lease to Samuel Male of Ipswich, linen draper, for 40 years, for £6 13s 4d fine and 10s annual
rent

C/5/5/2/34   20 May 1675
Water supply to houses in which Francis Luisse, William Alderman and William Cole dwell in MG
Lease to Anthony Wade of Ipswich, maltster, for 38 years, for £6 13s 4d fine and 20s annual rent

C/5/5/2/35   28 Sep. 1675
Water supply to messuage called the Golden Lion in MW
Lease to John Furman of Ipswich, wine cooper, for 38 years, for £6 13s 4d fine and 10s annual rent

C/5/5/2/36   13 Sep. 1683
Water supply to house in which Edward Reeve and lessee dwell in MG
Lease to Anne Shelvard of Ipswich, widow, for 20 years, for £6 13s 4d fine and 10s annual rent

C/5/5/2/37   6 Jun. 1718
Water supply to house in MT
Lease to John Goldson of Ipswich, gent., for 40 years, for £10 fine and 6s 8d annual rent

C/5/5/2/38   6 Jun. 1718
Water supply to house in which Samuel Baxter dwells in NI
Lease to John Jennings and John Bumpstead on behalf of trustees of property, for 40 years, for £6 13s 4d fine and 10s annual rent

C/5/5/2/39   6 Jun. 1718
Water supply to house in MT
Lease to John Wade of Ipswich, hatter, for 14 years, for £4 fine and 6s 8d annual rent (badly damaged by rodents; text incomplete)

C/5/5/2/40   26 Jun. 1718
Water supply to house in MG
Lease to William Allen of Ipswich, cooper, for 40 years, for £6 13s 4d fine and 6s 8d annual rent

C/5/5/2/41   26 Jun. 1718
Water supply to messuage in tenure of John Smith in LW
Lease to Ann Andrews of Ipswich, widow and Margaret Male of Ipswich, spinster, for 40 years, for £10 fine and 13s 4d annual rent

C/5/5/2/42   26 Jun. 1718
Water supply to messuage in NI
Lease to John Badison of Ipswich, tailor, for 40 years, for £6 13s 4d fine and 6s 8d annual rent

C/5/5/2/43   26 Jun. 1718
Water supply to messuage in LW
Lease to Michael Beaumont of Ipswich, ironmonger, for 40 years, for £10 fine and 6s 8d annual rent

C/5/5/2/44   26 Jun. 1718
Water supply to messuage in NI
Lease to William Beeston of Ipswich, doctor in physick, for 40 years, for £15 fine and 5s annual rent

C/5/5/2/45   26 Jun. 1718
Water supply to messuage and shops in tenure of John Beaumont in LW
Lease to Margaret Blomfeild of Ipswich, widow, for 40 years, for £10 fine and 6s 8d annual rent

C/5/5/2/46   26 Jun. 1718
Water supply to messuage and shops in tenure of John Beaumont in LW
Lease to Margaret Blomfeild of Ipswich, widow, for 40 years, for £10 fine and 6s 8d annual rent

C/5/5/2/47   26 Jun. 1718
Water supply to messuage in ST
Lease to John Bumpstead of Ipswich, woolcomber, for 40 years, for £10 fine and 6s 8d annual
rent (endorsed: 'for Caly's water')

C/5/5/2/48   26 Jun. 1718
Water supply to messuage in LW
Lease to Samuel Burrough of Ipswich, tallow chandler, for 40 years, for £6 13s 4d fine and
13s 4d annual rent

C/5/5/2/49   26 Jun. 1718
Water supply to messuage in which Tobias Searson, goldsmith, dwells in MT
Lease to Sarah Camplin of Hadleigh, widow, for 40 years, for £10 fine and 6s 8d annual rent

C/5/5/2/50   26 Jun. 1718
Water supply to messuage in LW
Lease to John Chaplin of Ipswich, cordwainer, for 40 years, for £6 13s 4d fine and 6s 8d annual
rent

C/5/5/2/51   26 Jun. 1718
Water supply to messuage in which [blank] Cobbold and others dwell in HL
Lease to Joseph Clarke of Ipswich, house carpenter, for 40 years, for £6 13s 4d fine and 10s
annual rent

C/5/5/2/52   26 Jun. 1718
Water supply to messuages in which John Scott, Thomas Sudgwick and [blank] Quintin,
spinster, dwell in MQ
Lease to William Clarke of Ipswich, gent., for 40 years, 'in consideration of the good services
done to the Corporation of Ipswich by [him] in his procuring a lease of the said water of Mr
Caly' for 6s 8d annual rent

C/5/5/2/53   26 Jun. 1718
Water supply to messuage called the Golden Lion in which Robert Hill dwells in MW
Lease to Martha Cole of Ipswich, widow, for 40 years, for £15 fine and 10s annual rent

C/5/5/2/54   26 Jun. 1718
Water supply to messuage in MG
Lease to Joseph Colman of Ipswich, grocer, for 40 years, for £6 13s 4d fine and 10s annual rent
(damaged by rodents; text incomplete)

C/5/5/2/55   26 Jun. 1718
Water supply to messuage in LW
Lease to William Craighton of Ipswich, bookseller, for 40 years, for £6 13s fine and 6s 8d
annual rent

C/5/5/2/56   26 Jun. 1718
Water supply to messuage in which Isaac Alstone, woolcomber, dwells in HL
Lease to Samuel Cumberland of Bury St Edmunds, woolcomber, for 40 years, for £8 fine and
6s 8d annual rent

C/5/5/2/57   26 Jun. 1718
Water supply to messuage in MG
Lease to John Doe of Ipswich, house stone cutter, for 40 years, for £6 13s 4d fine and 6s 8d
annual rent

C/5/5/2/58   26 Jun. 1718
Water supply to messuage in LW
Lease to Edward Duck of Ipswich, brasier, for 40 years, for £10 fine and 6s 8d annual rent

C/5/5/2/59   26 Jun. 1718
Water supply to messuage in NI
Lease to John Flindell of Ipswich, currier, for 40 years, for £6 13s 4d fine and 10s annual rent

C/5/5/2/60   26 Jun. 1718
Water supply to messuage in which Ann Wright, widow, dwells in MG
Lease to John Frohock of Ipswich, esq., for 40 years, for £10 fine and 10s annual rent

C/5/5/2/61   26 Jun. 1718
Water supply to messuage in which Richard Bedingfeild dwells in MG
Lease to Devereux Garwood of Ipswich, maltster and wife Hester, for 40 years, for £6 13s 4d
fine and 6s 8d annual rent

C/5/5/2/62   26 Jun. 1718
Water supply to messuage in which lessee and John Taylor dwell in MG
Lease to John Gaudy of Ipswich, clerk, for 40 years, for 6s 8d annual rent; no fine specified

C/5/5/2/63   26 Jun. 1718
Water supply to messuage in which Alice Nelson, widow, dwells in MG
Lease to James Green of London, merchant, for 40 years, for £6 13s 4d fine and 10s annual rent

C/5/5/2/64   26 Jun. 1718
Water supply to messuages in tenures of lessee, [blank] Collins, John Day and [blank] Carwell,
widow, in MT
Lease to John Grimwood of Ipswich, maltster, for 40 years, for £10 fine and 20s annual rent

C/5/5/2/65   26 Jun. 1718
Water supply to messuages in tenures of lessee and Bridgett Hearn, widow, in NI
Lease to Samuel Hamblin of Ipswich, plumber, for 40 years, for £6 13s 4d fine and 10s annual
rent

C/5/5/2/66   26 Jun. 1718
Water supply to messuage in LW
Lease to Dorcas Hardy of Ipswich, widow, for 40 years, for £6 13s 4d fine and 10s annual rent

C/5/5/2/67   26 Jun. 1718
Water supply to messuage in LW
Lease to John Holborough of Ipswich, salesman, for 40 years, for £10 fine and 10s annual rent

C/5/5/2/68   26 Jun. 1718
Water supply to messuage in LW
Lease to John Jenings of Ipswich, hosier, for 40 years, for £10 fine and 6s 8d annual rent

C/5/5/2/69   26 Jun. 1718
Water supply to messuage in which Thomas Whitehand, tailor dwells in MG
Lease to William Jolly of Ipswich, hosier, for 40 years, for £6 13s 4d fine and 10s annual rent

C/5/5/2/70   26 Jun. 1718
Water supply to messuages in LW
Lease to John Marlow of Ipswich, gent., for 40 years, for £6 13s 4d fine and 5s annual rent

C/5/5/2/71   26 Jun. 1718
Water supply to messuage in tenure of lessee in MT, 2 messuages in tenures of William Tye and
William Cooke and 1 empty messuage in MG
Lease to Robert Marston of Ipswich, confectioner, for 40 years, for £35 fine and 23s 4d annual
rent

C/5/5/2/72   26 Jun. 1718
Water supply to messuages in which lessee, Benjamin Oldroyd and Thomas Booth dwell in MT
and MW
Lease to Thomas May of Ipswich, saddler, for 40 years, for £20 fine and 23s 4d annual rent

C/5/5/2/73   26 Jun. 1718
Water supply to messuages in which lessee and Benjamin Morse dwell in MG
Lease to William Mayhew of Ipswich, maltster, for 40 years, for £10 fine and 6s 8d annual rent

C/5/5/2/74   26 Jun. 1718
Water supply to messuages in LW, MT and MG
Lease to Stephen Melsupp of Ipswich, ironmonger, for 40 years, for £35 fine and 23s 4d annual rent

C/5/5/2/75   26 Jun. 1718
Water supply to messuage in MT
Lease to William Melsupp of Ipswich, grocer, for 40 years, for £10 fine and 6s 8d annual rent

C/5/5/2/76   26 Jun. 1718
Water supply to messuages in tenure of lessee and Ann his mother in LW
Lease to Henry Nash of Ipswich, gent., for 40 years, for £6 13s 4d fine and 5s annual rent

C/5/5/2/77   26 Jun. 1718
Water supply to messuages in which lessee and Edward Wallis dwell in MT
Lease to Mary Newton of Ipswich, widow, for 40 years, for £20 fine and 13s 4d annual rent

C/5/5/2/78   26 Jun. 1718
Water supply to messuage in LW
Lease to Samuel Parish of Ipswich, linen draper, for 40 years, for £15 fine and 5s annual rent

C/5/5/2/79   26 Jun. 1718
Water supply to messuage in MG
Lease to Edward Park of Ipswich, blacksmith, for 40 years, for £6 13s 4d fine and 5s annual rent

C/5/5/2/80   26 Jun. 1718
Water supply to messuage in MT
Lease to Nathaniel Parsey of Ipswich, baker, for 40 years, for £6 13s 4d fine and 6s 8d annual rent

C/5/5/2/81   26 Jun. 1718
Water supply to messuage in MG
Lease to Richard Philipps of Ipswich, esq., for 40 years, for £15 fine and 5s annual rent

C/5/5/2/82   26 Jun. 1718
Water supply to messuage formerly in 2 tenements, now wholly in tenure of lessee, and messuage in tenure of James Osborn, in MG
Lease to Jonathan Quintin of Ipswich, gent., for 40 years, for £15 fine and 5s annual rent

C/5/5/2/83   26 Jun. 1718
Water supply to messuage in which Joseph Clarke, joiner, dwells in MW
Lease to Thomas Scott of Ipswich, butcher, for 40 years, for £6 13s 4d fine and 5s annual rent

C/5/5/2/84   26 Jun. 1718
Water supply to messuage in which Dorcas Richer, widow, dwells in MT
Lease to Daniel Smith sen. of Harwich (Essex), gent. and Margaret Sayer of Ipswich, widow, for 40 years, for £10 fine and 6s 8d annual rent

C/5/5/2/85   2[6] Jun. 1718
Water supply to messuage in LW
Lease to John Sparrow of Ipswich, apothecary, for 40 years, for £15 fine and 5s annual rent (damaged by rodents; text incomplete)

C/5/5/2/86   26 Jun. 1718
Water supply to 2 messuages in tenure of John Cooper and Matthew Whaley in LW
Lease to Thomas Wright Sparrow of Eye, gent., for 40 years, for £16 13s 4d fine and 16s 8d annual rent

540

C/5/5/2/87   26 Jun. 1718
Water supply to messuage in tenure of John Steward in MT
Lease to Thomas Stisted of Ipswich, gent., for 40 years, for £25 fine and 10s annual rent

C/5/5/2/88   26 Jun. 1718
Water supply to messuage in LW
Lease to Thomas Stisted of Ipswich, gent., for 40 years, for £15 fine and 5s annual rent

C/5/5/2/89   26 Jun. 1718
Water supply to messuage in tenure of Thomas Kendall and to 2 messuages with shops, 1 in tenure of Thomas Artis, the other empty, in MG
Lease to Isaac Strutt of Hadleigh, ironmonger and wife Deborah, for 40 years, for £10 fine and 6s 8d annual rent

C/5/5/2/90   26 Jun. 1718
Water supply to messuage in LW
Lease to Priscilla Tastard of Ipswich, widow, for 40 years, for £10 fine and 20s annual rent

C/5/5/2/91   26 Jun. 1718
Water supply to messuage in MG
Lease to John Tayer of Ipswich, bottle maker, for 40 years, for £10 fine and 6s 8d annual rent

C/5/5/2/92   26 Jun. 1718
Water supply to messuage in ST
Lease to Michael Thirkle jun. of Ipswich, joiner, for 40 years, for £6 13s 4d fine and 6s [8d] annual rent

C/5/5/2/93   26 Jun. 1718
Water supply to messuage called the Cross Keys in tenure of John Blomfield in MG
Lease to William Trotman of Ipswich, beer brewer, for 40 years, for £10 fine and 5s annual rent

C/5/5/2/94   26 Jun. 1718
Water supply to messuage in which William Coit, clerk, dwells in ST
Lease to Thomas Ventris of Earl Stonham, clerk, for 40 years, for £6 13s 4d fine and 6s 8d annual rent (endorsed: 'for Calys Water')

C/5/5/2/95   26 Jun. 1718
Water supply to messuages in tenures of John Smith and Henry Simpson in NI
Lease to Shelley Wangford of Stambourne (Essex), gent., for 40 years, for £6 13s 4d fine and 6s 8d annual rent

C/5/5/2/96   26 Jun. 1718
Water supply to messuage in MG
Lease to William Wells of Ipswich, victualler, for 40 years, for £6 13s 4d fine and 6s 8d annual rent

C/5/5/2/97   14 Aug. 1718
Water supply to messuage partly in occupation of Edward Smyth and partly standing empty, abutting N. on the Wash Lane in HL
Lease to Thomas Thurston of Ipswich, gent., for 40 years, for £6 13s 4d fine and 6s 8d annual rent

C/5/5/2/98   26 Aug. 1718
Water supply to messuage in which Thomas Cosins, writing master, dwells in ST
Lease to Barzilla Brame of Ipswich, mariner, for 40 years, for £6 13s 4d fine and 6s 8d annual rent

C/5/5/2/99   1 Mar. 1720
Water supply to messuage in tenure of William Bristow in MT
Lease to Nathaniel Bateman of London, gent., for 40 years from 24 Aug. 1718, for £6 13s 4d fine and 5s annual rent

C/5/5/2/100   1 Mar. 1720
Water supply to messuage in tenure of Elizabeth Fosdike, widow in MT
Lease to William Lynch of Ipswich, esq., for 40 years from 24 Aug. 1718, for £6 13s 4d fine and
6s 8d annual rent

C/5/5/2/101   1 Mar. 1720
Water supply to 3 messuages, 2 in tenure of lessee and Nicholas Du Buck, the 3rd standing
empty, in NI
Lease to Richard Newton of Ipswich, esq., for 39 years, for £6 13s 4d fine and 2 annual rents
of 10s

C/5/5/2/102   15 Jul. 1720
Water supply to that part of messuage lately called the Greyhound in which lessee now dwells
in MG
Lease to Matthew Wealy of Ipswich, ironmonger, for 38 years, for £10 fine and 10s annual rent

C/5/5/2/103   19 Aug. 1720
Water supply to messuage in LW
Lease to Thomas Grimwood of Ipswich, linen draper, for 38 years, for £10 fine and 5s annual
rent

C/5/5/2/104   17 Jan. 1721
Water supply to messuage in tenure of John Beaumont in ST
Lease to Elizabeth Bantoft of Ipswich, spinster, for 38 years, for £6 13s 4d fine and 6s 8d annual
rent (endorsed: 'Caleys Water')

C/5/5/2/105   17 Jan. 1721
Water supply to messuages in occupation of Anne Wright, widow and others, in MQ
Lease to John Beaumont of Ipswich, apothecary, Nehemiah Lodge of Norwich (Norfolk), gent.
and Edward Bass of Norwich, merchant, for 38 years, for £6 13s 4d fine and 10s annual rent
(endorsed: 'Caleys Water')

C/5/5/2/106   17 Jan. 1721
Water supply to messuage in tenure of Joseph Scott, William Smith and Elizabeth Beardwell in
MQ
Lease to Samuel Goldsbury of Ipswich, mariner, for 38 years, for £6 fine and 6s 8d annual rent
(endorsed: 'Caleys Water')

C/5/5/2/107   17 Jan. 1721
Water supply to messuage in MQ
Lease to Joseph Rands of Ipswich, wool comber, for 38 years, for £6 13s 4d fine and 10s annual
rent (endorsed: 'Caleys Water')

C/5/5/2/108   24 Nov. 1722
Water supply to messuage in which lessee and Edward Betts dwell in MQ
Lease to Henry Bowell of Ipswich, mariner, for 35 years, for £6 13s 4d fine and 6s 8d annual
rent

C/5/5/2/109   27 May 1723
Water supply to messuage in MT
Lease to William Chenery of Ipswich, glazier, for 36 years, for £6 13s 4d fine and 6s 8d annual
rent

C/5/5/2/110   27 May 1723
Water supply to 3 cottages, 2 in tenure of Daniel Edgar and Adam Chaplin, the 3rd standing
empty, in MG
Lease to Benjamin Freshfield of Ipswich, house carpenter, for 35 years, for £10 fine and 5s
annual rent

C/5/5/2/111   7 Jun. 1723
Water supply to empty messuage in MT
Lease to John Mathews of Ipswich, gent., for 36 years, for £6 13s 4d fine and 10s annual rent

C/5/5/2/112   10 Jun. 1724
Water supply to messuages called the Stone Houses in occupations of [*blank*] Sare, widow,
John Cage, Christopher Hewett, Samuel Richman, William Holden, Robert Greene, Alice
Nutton and Mary Elliott in Brook Street in HL
Lease to William Allen of Ipswich, cooper, for 34 years, for £5 fine and 6s 8d annual rent

C/5/5/2/113   22 Jul. 1724
Water supply to messuage in which John Copeman lately dwelt, fronting the Cornhill in MT
Lease to William Wilkinson of Ipswich, plumber, for 34 years, for £9 fine and 6s 8d annual rent
(endorsed: 'Towne Water')

C/5/5/2/114   20 Aug. 1724
Water supply to messuage in PE
Lease to Christopher Thorne of Ipswich, merchant, for 34 years, for £5 fine and 6s 8d annual
rent (endorsed: 'Key Water')

C/5/5/2/115   20 Aug. 1726
Water supply to messuage fronting the Butter Market in LW
Lease to John Barker of Ipswich, gent., for 32 years, for £7 10s fine and 5s annual rent
(endorsed: 'Towne Water')

C/5/5/2/116   27 Aug. 1726
Water supply to messuage in the Green Yard in PE
Lease to Thomas Wilder of Ipswich, maltster, for 32 years, for £6 13s 4d fine and 6s 8d annual
rent (endorsed: 'Caleys Water')

C/5/5/2/117   4 Nov. 1726
Water supply to messuage in ME
Lease to Robert Hamby of Ipswich, gent., for 32 years, for £7 fine and 6s 8d annual rent

C/5/5/2/118   10 Nov. 1726
Water supply to messuage in MG
Lease to Amy Farrington of Ipswich, widow, for 32 years, for £4 fine and 5s annual rent
(though the lease is sealed and signed with the lessee's mark, it is endorsed, 'will not agree')

C/5/5/2/119   20 Sep. 1728
Water supply to messuage in LW
Lease to John Wilkinson of Ipswich, haberdasher of small wares, for 30 years, for £7 fine and
6s 8d annual rent

C/5/5/2/120   13 Aug. 1729
Water supply to messuage in which Rebecca Cook, widow, dwells in MT
Lease to Nicholas Cook of Ipswich, grocer, for 29 years, for £8 fine and 6s 8d annual rent

C/5/5/2/121   1 Jul. 1731
Water supply to new-built messuage in ST
Lease to John Groom of Ipswich, gent., for 28 years, for £7 10s fine and 6s 8d annual rent

C/5/5/2/122   3 Apr. 1732
Water supply to messuage lately purchased by lessee from William Allen and wife Priscilla in
HL
Lease to William Burton of the Navy Office, London, gent., for 26 years, for £5 fine and 6s 8d
annual rent

C/5/5/2/123   8 Sep. 1733
Water supply to messuage in which Mrs Anne Edwin dwells in Upper Brook Street in MG
Lease to Devereux Edgar of Ipswich, esq., for 25 years, for £5 5s fine and 10s annual rent

C/5/5/2/124   12 Dec. 1737
Water supply to messuage in HL
Lease to William Reeve of Ipswich, clerk, for 21 years, for 21s fine and 10s annual rent

C/5/5/2/125–181   Water leases granted for 40 years from Michaelmas 1758, expiring in 1798; the contemporary numbering, which is not strictly chronological, is noted.

C/5/5/2/125   25 Aug. 1758
Water supply to messuages in which Ellis Brand, esq., Mrs Harrington and lessee dwell in LW and HL
Lease to Robert Parish of Ipswich, esq., for £15 and £10 fines and £1 annual rent (numbered 1)

C/5/5/2/126   25 Aug. 1758
Water supplies to messuages in which lessee, widow Page, widow Steel and widow Bishop dwell in the Thoroughfare in LW and messuage in occupation of Samuel Gibbon in MW
Lease to Thomas Heming of Ipswich, tinman, for £20 fine and 15s annual rent (numbered 24)

C/5/5/2/127   25 Aug. 1758
Water supply to messuage in which William Truelove jun. dwells in LW
Lease to William Truelove sen. of Ipswich, draper, for £15 fine and 5s annual rent (numbered 27)

C/5/5/2/128   25 Aug. 1758
Water supply to messuage in LW
Lease to John Notcutt of Ipswich, linen draper, for £10 fine and 6s 8d annual rent (numbered 52)

C/5/5/2/129   25 Aug. 1758
Water supply to messuage in which Revd Richard Canning dwells in MG
Lease to Lark Tarver of Ipswich, gent., for £10 fine and 6s 8d annual rent (numbered 53)

C/5/5/2/130   21 Sep. 1758
Water supply to messuage in which widow Catchpole dwells in MT
Lease to Robert Driver of the City of London, surgeon, for £10 fine and 6s 8d annual rent (numbered 29)

C/5/5/2/131   25 Sep. 1758
Water supply to messuage in which Thomas Hallum, gent., dwells in MG
Lease to Lydia Strutt of Ipswich, widow, for £10 fine and 6s 8d annual rent (numbered 2)

C/5/5/2/132   25 Sep. 1758
Water supply to messuage in ST
Lease to Persiana Stisted of Ipswich, widow, for £6 13s 4d fine and 6s 8d annual rent (numbered 6)

C/5/5/2/133   25 Sep. 1758
Water supply to messuage in which George Notcutt dwells in LW
Lease to Bartholomew Wood of Rotherhithe (Surrey [sic], Kent), gent., for £10 fine and 6s 8d annual rent (numbered 7)

C/5/5/2/134   25 Sep. 1758
Water supply to messuage in which Edward Nurse dwells in MT
Lease to Moses Parnell of Ipswich, cabinet maker, for £6 13s 4d fine and 6s 8d annual rent (numbered 11)

C/5/5/2/135   25 Sep. 1758
Water supply to messuage in LW
Lease to Edward Duck of Ipswich, brazier, for £10 fine and 6s 8d annual rent (numbered 13)

C/5/5/2/136   25 Sep. 1758
Water supply to messuage in which Susan Bedwell dwells in ST
Lease to Tyrrell Bird of [blank], yeoman, for £6 13s 4d fine and 6s 8d annual rent (numbered 14)

C/5/5/2/137   25 Sep. 1758
Water supply to messuage in which widow Acton dwells in NI
Lease to Sir Cordel Firebrace of Long Melford, bart, for £10 fine and 6s 8d annual rent
(numbered 21 and endorsed 'Sir Cordell died before this could be executed but the fine is paid
and the lease sealed')

C/5/5/2/138   25 Sep. 1758
Water supply to messuage in LW
Lease to Thomas Alston of Ipswich, linen draper, for £10 fine and 6s 8d annual rent (numbered
22)

C/5/5/2/139   25 Sep. 1758
Water supply to messuage in MT
Lease to John Head of Ipswich, grocer, for £10 fine and 6s 8d annual rent (numbered 23)

C/5/5/2/140   25 Sep. 1758
Water supply to messuage in NI
Lease to Goodchild Clarke of Ipswich, gent., for £10 fine and 6s 8d annual rent (numbered 37)

C/5/5/2/141   25 Sep. 1758
Water supply to messuage in NI
Lease to William Coyte of Ipswich, doctor in physick, for £15 fine and 5s annual rent
(numbered 41)

C/5/5/2/142   25 Sep. 1758
Water supplies to messuages in which lessee and William Alston, esq., dwell in LW
Lease to William Craighton of Ipswich, bookseller, for £10 fine and 13s 4d annual rent
(numbered 43)

C/5/5/2/143   25 Sep. 1758
Water supplies to messuages in which lessee, William Hubbard and Mrs Choice dwell in LW
Lease to John Leggatt of Ipswich, draper, for £15 fine and 18s 4d annual rent (numbered 45)

C/5/5/2/144   25 Sep. 1758
Water supply to messuage in which Thomas Carter dwells in MG
Lease to John May of Ipswich, draper, for £10 fine and 10s annual rent (numbered 46)

C/5/5/2/145   25 Nov. 1758
Water supply to messuage called the Marlborough's Head in which William Fleming dwells in
MT
Lease to James Smith of Ipswich, yeoman, for £6 13s 4d fine and 10s annual rent (numbered 8)

C/5/5/2/146   18 Dec. 1758
Water supply to messuage in which lessee and Robert Boothe dwell in MT
Lease to Thomas Pulford of Ipswich, tallow chandler, for £10 fine and 6s 8d annual rent
(numbered 9)

C/5/5/2/147   18 Dec 1758
Water supply to messuage in MG
Lease to Thomas Bishop of Ipswich, clerk, for £10 fine and 6s 8d annual rent (numbered 10)

C/5/5/2/148   18 Dec. 1758
Water supply to messuage in which Robert Tovell, stonecutter, dwells in MG
Lease to Thomas Singleton of Bury St Edmunds, stonecutter, for £10 fine and 6s 8d annual rent
(numbered 15)

C/5/5/2/149   18 Dec. 1758
Water supply to messuage in ME
Lease to Robert Hamby of Ipswich, esq., for £20 fine and 5s annual rent (numbered 18)

C/5/5/2/150   18 Dec. 1758
Water supply to messuage in ST
Lease to Susanna Reeve of Ipswich, widow, for £6 13s 4d fine and 6s 8d annual rent (numbered 25)

C/5/5/2/151   18 Dec. 1758
Water supplies to messuages in which Thomas Scott and Mrs Holborough dwell in NI
Lease to Thomas Scott and William King, merchant, both of Ipswich, trustees of the property, for £6 13s 4d fine and 10s annual rent (numbered 28)

C/5/5/2/152   18 Dec. 1758
Water supply to messuage in LW
Lease to Samuel Daldy of Ipswich, linen draper, for £6 13s 4d fine and 6s 8d annual rent (numbered 34)

C/5/5/2/153   18 Dec. 1758
Water supply to messuage in NI
Lease to John Flindell of Ipswich, currier, for £6 13s 4d fine and 10s annual rent (numbered 35)

C/5/5/2/154   18 Dec. 1758
Water supply to messuage in which Edward Reeve, Robert Graves and Robert Scrutton dwell in MG
Lease to Robert Tovell of Ipswich, stonecutter, for £6 13s 4d fine and 10s annual rent (numbered 36)

C/5/5/2/155   18 Dec. 1758
Water supply to messuage in ST
Lease to Mary Beaumont of Ipswich, spinster, for £6 13s 4d fine and 6s 8d annual rent (numbered 38)

C/5/5/2/156   18 Dec. 1758
Water supply to messuage in LW
Lease to Thomas Truston of Ipswich, wine merchant, for £8 6s 8d fine and 6s 8d annual rent (numbered 40)

C/5/5/2/157   18 Dec. 1758
Water supply to messuage in LW
Lease to John Wilkenson of Ipswich, haberdasher, for £10 fine and 6s 8d annual rent (numbered 42)

C/5/5/2/158   18 Dec. 1758
Water supplies to messuages in MT
Lease to Nathaniel Bucke, surgeon and Thomas Daldy, ironmonger, both of Ipswich, for £10 fine and 6s 8d annual rent for each house (numbered 47)

C/5/5/2/159   17 Feb. 1759
Water supply to messuage in MG
Lease to John Jackaman of Ipswich, blacksmith, for £6 13s 4d fine and 6s 8d annual rent (numbered 12)

C/5/5/2/160   17 Feb. 1759
Water supply to messuages in which William Folkard, Peter Clarke, gent., and [blank] Skidmore dwell in LW
Lease to William Folkard and John Flindell, both of Ipswich, for £10 fine and 20s annual rent (numbered 16)

C/5/5/2/161   17 Feb. 1759
Water supply to messuage in which Thomas Page, bookbinder, dwells in MT
Lease to Tobias Searson of Hadleigh, gent., for £10 fine and 6s 8d annual rent (numbered 30)

C/5/5/2/162   17 Feb. 1759
Water supplies to messuages in which Richard Dove, coach maker and Peter Pelow dwell in ST
Lease to Thomas Alderson of Ipswich, vintner, for £10 fine and 13s 4d annual rent (numbered 31)

C/5/5/2/163   17 Feb. 1759
Water supply to messuage in ST
Lease to Samuel Pallant of Ipswich, gent., for £6 13s 4d fine and 6s 8d annual rent (numbered 32)

C/5/5/2/164   17 Feb. 1759
Water supply to messuage in MG
Lease to Henry Pegge of Ipswich, tallow chandler, for £6 13s 4d fine and 6s 8d annual rent (numbered 33)

C/5/5/2/165   17 Feb. 1759
Water supplies to messuages in which lessee and William Chinery, carpenter, dwell in MG
Lease to Margaret Humphry of Ipswich, spinster, for £6 13s 4d fine and 6s 8d annual rent (numbered 48)

C/5/5/2/166   17 Feb. 1759
Water supplies to messuages in which lessee, widow Wyley, Hannah Elliston and [blank] Reeder dwell in MG
Lease to Benjamin Rowning of Ipswich, plumber and glazier, for £10 fine and 6s 8d annual rent (numbered 49)

C/5/5/2/167   17 Feb. 1759
Water supply to messuage in which Ann Edwin, spinster, dwells in MG
Lease to Mary Edgar of Ipswich, spinster, for £6 13s 4d fine and 10s annual rent (numbered 50)

C/5/5/2/168   17 Feb. 1759
Water supplies to messuages in which lessee, John May, James Simpson and William Tokely dwell in MG and MT
Lease to Thomas Newton of Ipswich, gent., for £20 fine and 20s annual rent (numbered 51)

C/5/5/2/169   17 Feb. 1759
Water supply to messuage in which John Page, clockmaker, dwells in LW
Lease to Phebe Bond of Weybread, widow, for £6 13s 4d fine and 6s 8d annual rent (numbered 57)

C/5/5/2/170   17 Feb. 1759
Water supplies to messuage in which lessee dwells and messuage in which Richard Davis lately dwelt in MG
Lease to Rebecca Tayer of Ipswich, widow, for £6 13s 4d fine and 10s annual rent (numbered 58)

C/5/5/2/171   17 Feb. 1759
Water supply to messuage in which widow Lilley dwells in MG
Lease to Matthew Brock of Ipswich, innholder, for £6 13s 4d fine and 6s 8d annual rent (numbered 59)

C/5/5/2/172   4 Jun. 1759
Water supply to messuage in which Robert Downing dwells in MW
Lease to Robert Rowning of Ipswich, gent., for £15 fine and 10s annual rent (numbered 4)

C/5/5/2/173   4 Jun. 1759
Water supplies to messuages in which [blank] and Mary Southgate dwell in MQ
Lease to Margaret Harriott Stebbing of Nacton, widow, for £6 13s 4d fine and 10s annual rent (numbered 54)

C/5/5/2/174   4 Jun. 1759
Water supplies to messuages in which lessee, Michael Thirkle jun., Jeremiah Byle, Robert
Faucett and Edmund Haselden dwell in MQ
Lease to Michael Thirkle sen. of Ipswich, gent., for £23 6s 8d fine and £1 6s 8d annual rent
(numbered 55)

C/5/5/2/175   10 Jun. 1759
Water supplies to messuages in which George Almond, Robert Capon, widow Lockwood,
Rose Ledgent and William Trusson dwell in MT, MG and MQ
Lease to William Trotman of Ipswich, gent., for £38 6s 8d fine and £1 16s 8d annual rent
(numbered 3)

C/5/5/2/176   18 Sep. 1759
Water supply to messuages and malting office in occupation of lessee and William Tye, grocer
in MT
Lease to John Grimwood of Ipswich, maltster, for £10 fine and 20s annual rent (numbered 5)

C/5/5/2/177   18 Sep. 1759
Water supply to messuage in which widow Gent dwells in MG
Lease to Edmund Jennings of Ipswich, gent., for £6 13s 4d fine and 6s 8d annual rent
(numbered 17)

C/5/5/2/178   18 Sep. 1759
Water supply to messuage in MQ
Lease to William Lynch of Ipswich, esq., for £6 13s 4d fine and 6s 8d annual rent (numbered
20)

C/5/5/2/179   18 Sep. 1759
Water supply to messuage in ST
Lease to Nicholas Gwyn of Ipswich, doctor of physick, for £10 fine and 6s 8d annual rent
(numbered 56)

C/5/5/2/180   27 Apr. 1762
Water supply to messuage in MG
Lease to Charles Norris of Ipswich, grocer, for 37 years, for £10 fine and 6s 8d annual rent
(numbered 39)

C/5/5/2/181   21 Dec. 1765
Water supply to messuage now rebuilding and adjoining house called the King's Head in MT
Lease to John Shave of Ipswich, stationer, for £12 12s fine and 10s annual rent for each house
(numbered 19)

C/5/5/2/182   25 Jul. 1766
Water supply to messuage in LW
Lease to Samuel Kilderbee of Ipswich, gent., for 32 years, £6 13s 4d fine and 6s 8d annual rent
(numbered 26)

C/5/5/2/183   25 Jul. 1766
Water supplies to messuages in occupation of Richard Canning, clerk, Edmund Newdigate,
doctor in physick, and Catherine Lambert, spinster, and malting office in occupation of John
Fowler, merchant, all in MG
Lease to William Truelove, woollen draper and John Kerridge, surgeon, both of Ipswich, for 33
years, for £10 fine and 10s annual rent for each of the properties (numbered 44)

C/5/5/3   CHAMBERLAINS' ACCOUNT BOOKS OF WATER   **1647–1703**
RENTS RECEIVED

These contain the names of the present (and sometimes the previous) owners and occupiers,
with the amounts of rent paid. Public houses are named, and some other types of property (e.g.
parsonage houses and malting offices) are specified. No parishes are specified in the accounts
for 1647–1648, 1665–1666 or 1678–1679; the later ones cover the parishes of St Helen, St
Margaret, St Lawrence, St Mary le Tower, St Nicholas and St Matthew, in that order.

C/5/5/3/1   1647–1648
Robert Daines, Richard Sheppard, Chamberlains; rents due on St Bartholomew's Day (24 Aug.)
1648
(1 vol.)

C/5/5/3/2   1665–1666
William Neave, William Sayer, Chamberlains; for year ending 24 Aug. 1666
(1 vol.)

C/5/5/3/3   1678–1679
James Page, Benjamin Beaumont, Chamberlains; for year ending 24 Aug. 1679
(1 vol.)

C/5/5/3/4   1679–1680
Henry Skinner, Chamberlain, 'his partner Thomas Hardy being dead'; for year ending 24 Aug.
1680
(1 vol.)

C/5/5/3/5   1680–1681
Miles Wallis and Henry Sparrow, Chamberlains; for year ending 24 Aug. 1681
Includes signatures of auditors
(1 vol.)

C/5/5/3/6   1683–1684
Keble Crosse, Israell Barrell, Chamberlains; for year ending 24 Aug. 1684
(1 vol.)

C/5/5/3/7   1700–1701
Henry Nash and Samuel Smith, Chamberlains; rents due on 24 Aug. 1701
(1 vol.)

C/5/5/3/8   1701–1702
Matthew Goodwin, Lionel Lord, Chamberlains; for year ending 24 Aug. 1702
(1 vol.)

C/5/5/3/9   1702–1703
George Girling, John Clarke, Chamberlains; for year ending 24 Aug. 1703
(1 vol.)

C/5/5/4   ESTREAT ROLLS OF WATER RENTS DUE TO THE   **1705–1758**
CORPORATION

From the financial year 1705–1706 to the year 1714–1715 inclusive these records are kept in
the form of paper books, and thereafter as parchment rolls, with the exception of a paper book
containing a copy of the missing estreat of the 'Key [Quay] Water' rents for 1734–1735. They
contain the names of the present (and sometimes the previous) owners and occupiers, with the
amounts of rent due. Public houses are named, and some other types of property (e.g. parsonage
houses and malting offices) are specified. Until the year 1737–1738 most of the estreats are for
the parishes of St Helen, St Margaret, St Lawrence, St Mary le Tower, St Nicholas and

549

St Matthew only (always listed in that order), and there are seven separate rolls (plus the copy estreat referred to above) for the 'Key Water' only; from 1738–1739 onwards all the rolls cover the Quay Water as well as the six parishes. Most rolls down to 1749–1750 include an instruction to the Chamberlains to make marginal memoranda of the names of the present occupiers, the cocks that are cut off, and the empty houses; such marginalia appear in a number of them, together with occasional notes of unpaid or underpaid rents and poor persons. The accounting year for the water rents began and ended on St Bartholomew's Day (24 August).

C/5/5/4/1   1705–1706
Parishes of HL, MG, LW, MT, NI, MW
(1 vol.)

C/5/5/4/2   1706–1707
Parishes of HL, MG, LW, MT, NI, MW
(1 vol.)

C/5/5/4/3   1707–1708
Parishes of HL, MG, LW, MT, NI, MW
(1 vol.)

C/5/5/4/4   1714–1715
Parishes of HL, MG, LW, MT, NI, MW
Edward Syer and Thomas Grimwood [Chamberlains]
(1 vol.)

C/5/5/4/5   1719–1720
'For the Key Water'
Includes:
— memorandum that leases of various occupiers 'were not sealed till after this year was due, and so you must gather this rental as it is figured notwithstanding any pretence to a lower rent in the lease. R. Love'
(1 membrane)

C/5/5/4/6   1722–1723
Parishes of HL, MG, LW, MT, NI, MW
(1 membrane)

C/5/5/4/7   1720–1721
Parishes of HL, MG, LW, MT, NI, MW
(1 membrane)

C/5/5/4/8   1726–1727
Parishes of HL, MG, LW, MT, NI, MW
(1 membrane)

C/5/5/4/9   1730–1731
Parishes of HL, MG, LW, MT, NI, MW
(2 membranes)

C/5/5/4/10   1731–1732
Parishes of HL, MG, LW, MT, NI, MW
(1 membrane)

C/5/5/4/11   1731–1732
'For the Key Water'
(1 membrane)

C/5/5/4/12   1732–1733
Parishes of HL, MG, LW, MT, NI, MW
(1 membrane)

C/5/5/4/13   1732–1733
'For the Key Water'
(1 membrane)

C/5/5/4/14   1733–1734
Parishes of HL, MG, LW, MT, NI, MW
(1 membrane)

C/5/5/4/15   1733–1734
'For the Key Water'
(1 membrane)

C/5/5/4/16   1734–1735
Parishes of HL, MG, LW, MT, NI, MW; and 'the Kee Water generall'
(2 membranes)

C/5/5/4/17   1734–1735
Copy
'For the Key Water'
Includes, at end:
— memorandum that 'I think this is a trew copy of the Key Water rentrol which is eather lost or
mislayd. John Fowle'
(1 vol.)

C/5/5/4/18   1735–1736
Parishes of HL, MG, LW, MT, NI, MW
(2 membranes)

C/5/5/4/19   1735–1736
'For the Key Water'
(1 membrane)

C/5/5/4/20   1736–1737
Parishes of HL, MG, LW, MT, NI, MW
(2 membranes)

C/5/5/4/21   1736–1737
'For the Key Water'
(1 membrane)

C/5/5/4/22   1737–1738
Parishes of HL, MG, LW, MT, NI, MW
(2 membranes)

C/5/5/4/23   1737–1738
'For the Key Water'
(1 membrane)

C/5/5/4/24   1738–1739
Parishes of HL, MG, LW, MT, NI, MW; and 'the Key Water'
(2 membranes)

C/5/5/4/25   1748–1749
Parishes of HL, MG, LW, MT, NI, MW; and 'the Key Water'
(1 membrane)

C/5/5/4/26   1749–1750
Parishes of HL, MG, LW, MT, NI, MW; and 'the Key Water'
(2 membranes)

C/5/5/4/27   1750–1751
Parishes of HL, MG, LW, MT, NI, MW; and 'the Key Water'
(2 membranes)

C/5/5/4/28   1751–1752
Parishes of HL, MG, LW, MT, NI, MW; and 'the Key Water'
(2 membranes)

C/5/5/4/29   1752–1753
Parishes of HL, MG, LW, MT, NI, MW; and 'the Key Water'
(2 membranes)

C/5/5/4/30   1755–1756
Parishes of HL, MG, LW, MT, NI, MW; and 'the Key Water'
(2 membranes)

C/5/5/4/31   1757–1758
Parishes of HL, MG, LW, MT, NI, MW; and 'the Key Water'
(2 membranes)

C/5/5/5 CHAMBERLAINS' WATER RENTALS   **1758–1796**

These contain the names of owners and occupiers, occasionally (especially in the case of inns)
the names of properties, the amounts of annual rent, and columns recording quarterly payments.
Until *c.*1760 the arrangement is by parish, in the same order as that of the water rent estreat
rolls; from 1761 to 1764 in alphabetical order of owner; and from then onwards by street,
beginning with the route 'from the water head to Major's Corner'. From 1788 the rentals also
distinguish the source of supply – 'Town Water', 'Dairy Lane Water', 'Key Water' and 'St
Nicholas Water'. From 1758 the accounting year, which formerly ran from St Bartholomew's
Day (24 August), was brought into line with that for the Chamberlains' and Treasurers'
accounts, and ran from Michaelmas (29 September) to Michaelmas.

C/5/5/5/1   1758–1759
William Norris and Samuel Howes, Chamberlains
(1 vol.)

C/5/5/5/2   n.d. [? *c.*1760]
(1 vol.)

C/5/5/5/3   1761–1762
(1 vol.)

C/5/5/5/4   1762–1763
(1 vol.)

C/5/5/5/5   1763–1764
(1 vol.)

C/5/5/5/6   1764–1765
(1 vol.)

C/5/5/5/7   ? 1765–1766
(1 vol.)

C/5/5/5/8   ? 1766–1767
(1 vol.)

C/5/5/5/9   ? 1767–1768
(1 vol.)

C/5/5/5/10 (1 vol.)	? 1768–1769
C/5/5/5/11 (1 vol.)	? 1769–1770
C/5/5/5/12 (1 vol.)	? 1770–1771
C/5/5/5/13 B. Brame and W. Goodchild, Chamberlains (1 vol.)	1771–1772
C/5/5/5/14 (1 vol.)	1774–1775
C/5/5/5/15 (1 vol.)	1775–1776
C/5/5/5/16 Robert Small and John Harrison, Chamberlains (1 vol.)	1780–1781
C/5/5/5/17 Robert Batley and Joseph Pooley, Chamberlains (1 vol.)	1783–1784
C/5/5/5/18 Stephen Bumstead [and Barnaby Sheppard], Chamberlains (1 vol.)	1784–1785
C/5/5/5/19 Barlee Garwood and George Durrant, Chamberlains (1 vol.)	1788–1789
C/5/5/5/20 (1 vol.)	1790–1791
C/5/5/5/21 William Downes and T. Raymond, Chamberlains (1 vol.)	1792–1793
C/5/5/5/22 Robert Fuller and Thomas Tayer, Chamberlains (1 vol.)	1793–1794
C/5/5/5/23 William Norris jun. and Charles Batley, Chamberlains (1 vol.)	1795–1796

C/5/5/6   COLLECTOR'S WATER RENTALS   1798–1827

In 1797 or 1798 the responsibility for the collection of the water rents was transferred from the Chamberlains to a Collector. Benjamin Batley Catt, the first Collector of the Water Rents, is also referred to in his audited accounts as 'Water Treasurer to the Corporation of Ipswich'. The arrangement of the rentals, by street, follows that of the latest Chamberlains' water rentals, though the source of the water supply is not given. The accounting year remained unchanged, beginning and ending at Michaelmas (29 September).

C/5/5/6/1 (1 vol.)	1798–1799

C/5/5/6/2   1799–1800
(1 vol.)

C/5/5/6/3   1800–1801
(1 vol.)

C/5/5/6/4   1801–1802
(1 vol.)

C/5/5/6/5   1802–1803
Includes, at front:
— list of applicants for water supply, 1803
(1 vol.)

C/5/5/6/6   1803–1804
Includes, at front:
— list of applicants for water supply, 1804
(1 vol.)

C/5/5/6/7   1805–1806
Renewed by William Batley, Town Clerk, from Michaelmas 1805
(1 vol.)

C/5/5/6/8   1805–1806
Another copy
Renewed by William Batley, Town Clerk, from Michaelmas 1805
(1 vol.)

C/5/5/6/9   1806–1807
Renewed by William Batley, Town Clerk
Includes, at front:
— memorandum of appointment of John Spooner Manning to collect the water rental, 9 Feb.
1807
(1 vol.)

C/5/5/6/10   1807–1808
Signed by William Batley, Town Clerk; despite the memorandum in C/5/5/6/9, Benjamin
Batley Catt's name appears on the title page as Collector
(1 vol.)

C/5/5/6/11   1808–1809
Benjamin Batley Catt, Collector
(1 vol.)

C/5/5/6/12   1809–1810
Benjamin Batley Catt, Collector
(1 vol.)

C/5/5/6/13   1826–1827
(1 vol.)

**C/5/5/7   AUDITED ACCOUNTS OF WILLIAM BATLEY CATT,   1798–1811
VARIOUSLY DESCRIBED AS 'WATER TREASURER TO THE
CORPORATION OF IPSWICH' AND 'COLLECTOR OF THE WATER RENTS'**

C/5/5/7/1   1798–1799
(1 vol.)

C/5/5/7/2   1799–1800
(1 vol.)

C/5/5/7/3	1800–1801
(1 vol.)	
C/5/5/7/4	1801–1803
For the 2 financial years 1801–1802 and 1802–1803; audited together	
(1 vol.)	
C/5/5/7/5	1803–1804
(1 vol.)	
C/5/5/7/6	1804–1805
(1 vol.)	
C/5/5/7/7	1805–1806
(1 vol.)	
C/5/5/7/8	1806–1808
For the 2 financial years 1806–1807 and 1807–1808; audited together	
(1 vol.)	
C/5/5/7/9	1808–1810
For the 2 financial years 1808–1809 and 1809–1810; audited together	
(1 vol.)	
C/5/5/7/10	1810–1811
(1 vol.)	

C/5/5/8   COLLECTOR'S VOUCHERS   1798–1820

The contents of most of these annual files were originally found threaded on a lace. Until the financial year 1810–1811 the vouchers chiefly relate to payments for the maintenance of the supply system, compensation for damage caused to property by the works, and the Town Clerk's administrative charges. From the year 1811–1812 onwards, they consist for the most part of Bailiffs' warrants for payment of the rent receipts to the Corporation Treasurer and for the payment of officers' salaries. Similar vouchers relating to the town water supply may be found among the Treasurer's and Chamberlains' vouchers (C3/4/4 and C/3/3/3).

C/5/5/8/1	1798–1799
Benjamin Batley Catt, Collector	
(27 docs)	
C/5/5/8/2	1799–1800
Benjamin Batley Catt, Collector	
(22 docs)	
C/5/5/8/3	1800–1801
Benjamin Batley Catt, Collector	
(11 docs)	
C/5/5/8/4	1802–1803
Benjamin Batley Catt, Collector	
Includes:	

— agreement between Robert King of Ipswich, plumber, and the Bailiffs and Water Committee, to take up the old Key Main from the stop cock in Lower Brook Street to its end near the sign of the Bull on the Common Quay, to lay a new 1½ in. main and replace all the quills, for £23 and the old materials, 17 Jun. 1803
(40 docs)

C/5/5/8/5   1803–1804
Benjamin Batley Catt, Collector
Town Clerk's itemised bill of administrative charges includes cost of 'Letter to Mrs Frewer to
have a proper cestern to water the cattle to prevent waste of water'
(18 docs)

C/5/5/8/6   1804–1805
Benjamin Batley Catt, Collector
Town Clerk's itemised bill of administrative charges includes cost of letter *re* arrears of water
rent by the management of the Playhouse
(19 docs)

C/5/5/8/7   1805–1806
Benjamin Batley Catt, Collector
(12 docs)

C/5/5/8/8   1806–1808
Benjamin Batley Catt, Collector
Bills of 26 Oct. and 30 Nov. 1807 for freight of pipes show that elm water mains were still being
laid at this time
(46 docs)

C/5/5/8/9   1808–1809
Benjamin Batley Catt, Collector
Includes:
— bill of John Bransby [surveyor and cartographer] for £2 2*s*., for 'taking the level of several
parts of the town and drawing a plan', 18 Sep. 1809
(23 docs)

C/5/5/8/10   1809–1810
Benjamin Batley Catt, Collector
(20 docs)

C/5/5/8/11   1810–1811
Benjamin Batley Catt, Collector
(15 docs)

C/5/5/8/12   1811–1812
Samuel Howes, Collector
Includes:
— water rental for 1811–1812 (made Aug. 1813)
(9 docs)

C/5/5/8/13   1812–1814
Samuel Howes, Collector
(20 docs)

C/5/5/8/14   1814–1815
Samuel Howes, Collector
(5 docs)

C/5/5/8/15   1815–1816
Samuel Howes, Collector
(8 docs)

C/5/5/8/16   1819–1820
Samuel Howes, Collector
(5 docs)

C/5/5/9 WATER COMMITTEE MINUTES 1757–1758

C/5/5/9/1 13 Oct. 1757–5 Jun. 1758
Minute book of 'the Committee for inquiring into the state of the water pursuant to an order of the Great Court'
Includes, at end:
— water rental, much amended, n.d.
(1 vol.)

C/5/5/10 MISCELLANEA 1720–1833

C/5/5/10/1 14 Nov. 1720
List of 'fines and rents settled and agreed upon for Calys Water this 14th of Novr 1720'
(5 loose fols)

C/5/5/10/2 25 May 1833
Report of Committee appointed to consider best means of increasing water supply from Corporation mains to NI and ME
Recommending erection of a reservoir on or near the Cornhill 'where the water (which is now wasted in large quantities during the night) may be collected'; and that the lessees of the water be permitted 'to erect a reservoir in the archway under the Common Councel [*sic*] chamber'
(1 fol.)

C/5/6 PUBLIC HEALTH 1560–1667

C/5/6/1 20 Sep. 1560
Mansion house and houses called St Leonard's or the Lazar House, at S. end of town of Ipswich
Lease from Bailiffs, burgesses and commonalty, 'tendringe the mayntenance and Relife of the poore impotent people of the towne', to John Hall of Ipswich, mariner, from year to year during pleasure; Hall covenants to keep premises in repair, and 'well and discretely to use, order and governe the poore people that are and shalbe appointed to have there abidinge and lyvinge in the same howse in suche wise as becomethe the state and degree of suche people . . . aswell in there meate, drincke and lodginge as otherwise . . .'
Annexed:
— inventory of goods and implements of Lazar House, 20 Sep. 1560
Common Seal missing from tag; endorsed: '. . . Leazar House in Stoake'

C/5/6/2 13 May 1589
Messuage called St Leonard's Hospital or the Lazar House, with adjoining cottage, in Ipswich
Counterpart lease from Bailiffs, burgesses and commonalty to James Sparham of Ipswich, labourer, during pleasure; similar covenants to those in C/5/6/1
Annexed:
— inventory of goods and implements, n.d. [1589]

C/5/6/3 15 Oct. 1635
Messuage called the Sick House with lands and pastures in PE and MS
Letter of attorney from Bailiffs, burgesses and commonalty to Peter Cole, Richard Haile and Richard Dennye to deliver seisin, hand over lease to, and receive counterpart from, Isaac Daye of MS, clothier, to whom property has been leased for 3 years at peppercorn rental

C/5/6/4 1579
Account of money 'layd oute by Thomas Blosse for the provysoninge of the inffektyd houses'
(1 vol., found with Chamberlains' audited accounts for 1561–1583)

C/5/6/5   Apr. 1666–Aug. 1667
Pest account book of Robert Copping
Includes:
— receipts, 23 Apr. 1666–5 Aug. 1667
— disbursements for food and other relief, 23 Apr.–28 Nov. 1666 'on which daye by order
from the Bailiffs I dischardged Mr Sam. Jacob from the Pesthouse'; payments include charges
for conveying families to the Pest House and for burying the dead
— disbursements to parish officers, 22 May 1666–24 Jan. 1667
Unaudited.
(1 vol. found in the series of Treasurers' audited accounts)

C/5/7   PUBLIC CARRIERS   1621

C/5/7/1   25 Oct. 1621
Bond
Thomas Lucas, clothier, Clement Tuttell, haberdasher and Robert Tuttell, surgeon, all of
Ipswich, bound to Bailiffs, burgesses and commonalty in 100 marks each, as security that
Lucas will as town carrier between Ipswich and London observe orders of General Court regulating carriers' charges
Annexed:
— indented copy of orders of General Court: 11 Nov. 1613, setting out authorised scale of
charges for carriers between Ipswich and London; and 4 Jul. 1621, limiting number of weekly
carriers to London to one, present carriers Thomas Lane and Thomas Lucas to alternate their
journeys
(2 docs, joined by 3 seal tags; seals missing)

C/6 ACCIDENTAL ACCUMULATIONS

Under this heading have been brought together records which have no known connexion with the borough's corporate administration or institutions.

C/6/1 COUNTY COURT   1724–1726

C/6/1/1   May 1724–Nov. 1726
Court book of the Sheriff of Suffolk
The courts were held monthly and dealt with pleas of trespass upon the case. Only the names of the parties and occasional brief notes of process are given
(1 vol.)

C/6/2 COUNTY QUARTER SESSIONS   1676–1795

These documents, with the exception of the first, are apparently from the papers of a member of the Notcutt family who was Deputy Clerk of the Peace for the county in the late 18th century. Their presence in the archive is probably explained by the fact that members of this Ipswich firm of solicitors also held offices in the borough, including those of Town Clerk and Clerk of the Peace.

C/6/2/1   n.d. [1676]
Copy order of Suffolk Quarter Sessions
Made 18 Apr. 1670, confirmed 18 Jul. 1676, requiring High and Petty Constables to be diligent in executing laws against vagabonds; with direction to outgoing constables to deliver the order to their successors
(printed broadsheet)

C/6/2/2   5 May 1794
Articles of the Peace
Exhibited by William Taylor sen., William Taylor jun. and Thomas Fitch, all of Great Cornard, farmers, against Jacob Brand of Great Cornard, yeoman, for allegedly threatening to kill them

C/6/2/3   5 May 1794
Articles of the Peace
Exhibited by Robert Carter, constable of Great Cornard, against Jacob Brand of Great Cornard, yeoman, for assault

C/6/2/4   May–Jul. 1794
Record of process
Against Jacob Brand, late of Great Cornard, labourer, at Quarter Sessions at Bury St Edmunds, for assault on Robert Carter

C/6/2/5   13 Oct. 1795
Copy writ to the Sheriff of Suffolk
For appearance of Grand and Trial Juries and prisoners at Quarter Sessions to be held at Beccles, Woodbridge, Ipswich and Bury St Edmunds on 11, 13, 15 and 18 Jan. 1796 respectively

C/6/2/6   13 Oct. 1795
Copy writ to the Sheriff of Suffolk
For appearance of Thomas Emerson, late of Hopton, labourer, accused of misdemeanour, and
Jacob Brand late of Great Cornard, labourer, accused of grand larceny, at the next Quarter
Sessions

C/6/3   TAXATION: OTHER TOWNS   1787–1806

C/6/3/1   24 May 1787
Land Tax Collectors' duplicate assessment
For St Gregory, Sudbury
(1 vol.)

C/6/3/2   24 May 1787
Land Tax Collectors' duplicate assessment
For St Peter, Sudbury
(1 vol.)

C/6/3/3   14 Jun. 1806
Assessment for Window Tax and duties on inhabited houses, male servants and carriages
For Bentley
(1 fol., incomplete)

C/6/4   EXTERNAL OFFICES   1421–1438

C/6/4/1   22 Sep. 1421
Letters testimonial of Edmund, Prior of the Cathedral Church of Ely
Appointing Robert Wode Bailiff of the Liberty of St Etheldreda for the 5½ hundreds of
Winston and Thredling and the leets pertaining to the Liberty
(Latin; seal and tongue missing)

C/6/4/2   6 Oct. 1438
Counterpart lease of office of Marshal of the Admiralty under Lord Huntingdon in Essex
From James Cauncelir of Little Walsingham [Norfolk], Marshal, to John Crawle and William
Smalwode of Colchester (Essex), for 26s 8d p.a.
English; 1 seal on tag, 2nd seal missing

C/6/5   MANORIAL AND ESTATE   1289–1835

C/6/5/1   5 Mar.–3 Jun. 1289, n.d.
Court roll, manor of Tunstall
Includes:
— extent of John de Holebroc at Cransford [? of lands in Cransford], n.d.
Thomas de Weyland, lord of the manor of Tunstall, abjured the realm for felony in 1289, following which the manor was temporarily taken into the King's hands (Copinger 1905–11, V,
110); from 1284 to 1291 Ipswich was also in the King's hands, and it seems likely that this roll
was left behind by the royal officers when the borough's self-government was restored.
(1 membrane)

C/6/5/2   29 Sep. 1398–7 Jul. 1399
Compotus of Robert Moyse, Bailiff of the manor of Claydon
For a 40-week period. Found among the Petty Court and Recognizance Rolls for the reign of
Richard II. The manor was at this time vested in Thomas, Duke of Gloucester (Copinger
1905–11, II, 277), and the presence of the roll in the borough archive is unexplained, though it
is just conceivable that it was among the evidences of title to the farm at Claydon which formed
part of the original endowment of Henry Tooley's Foundation.
(Latin; 4 membranes, stitched together 'Chancery' style)

C/6/5/3   2 Oct. 1469
Rental of Queen Elizabeth [Woodville] for lands in Coddenham
Renewed by William Baldewyn and Thomas Hunne, tenants there
(Latin; 1 membrane)

C/6/5/4   1835
Premises in PE
Printed map by F. Harvey, at scale of 23 feet to 1 inch
'Plan of the freehold and leasehold premises ... in St Peter's, Ipswich, the property of the late
Mr William Calver, to be sold at auction ... September 8th, 1835'
Includes kiln, maltings, houses, garden and paddocks fronting on both sides of Bridge Street
and river Gipping
(uncoloured, paper)

C/6/6   EVIDENCES OF TITLE   1326–1899

These relate to properties which cannot be shown to have belonged to Ipswich Corporation or
to any of its charities.

C/6/6/1   IPSWICH PROPERTIES   1354–1553
See also C/6/6/2/11

C/6/6/1/1   ST LAWRENCE   1354–1553

C/6/6/1/1/1   20 Jun. 1354
Tenements with buildings and curtilages in LW
Feoffment from John Fraunceys of Stoke by Ipswich, chaplain and Seman Merihel of Ipswich,
to Richard Staunpis of Ipswich and wife Margery
Premises were purchased from Alice, widow of Richard le Mercer of Tuddenham, son John,
and John son of Roger le Mercier sen. of Tuddenham
Names of 7 witnesses
Latin; damp-stained and partly illegible; 1 seal on tag, 2nd seal and tag missing

C/6/6/1/1/2   10 Dec. 1368
Messuage with curtilage in LW
Lease from Thomas le Maister of Ipswich to William Wattone and wife Alice, for life of lessor,
at 1 rose annual rent
Premises were purchased from Alice de Cove, daughter and heir of John de Fymbergh
Names of 7 witnesses
Latin; seal and tag missing

C/6/6/1/1/3   1417–1553
Messuage with curtilage in LW and MT
Evidences of title for purchase by Thomas Elyott of Stonham Aspal, husbandman, from Robert

Baron of Ipswich, tailor, 4 Oct. 1553
Premises were known as Kerveres in deeds 1417–1477, and abutted S. on the high street [Tavern Street] and N. on MT churchyard
(17 docs, found among the grants of common soil)

C/6/6/1/2   ST MARGARET   1408–?1478

C/6/6/1/2/1   9 Dec. 1408
Tenement with curtilage in MG
Feoffment from Henry Bunne, chaplain and John Skirwhit of Ipswich to William Lovell of Ipswich, roper and wife Margery; to be void in default of payment of 60s.
Premises lay between messuage formerly of John Jalle on W. and garden formerly of Hugh Hew on E., abutting S. on curtilage formerly of John Jalle and N. on highway; acquired by feoffment of Richard Cardeney
Names of 8 witnesses
Latin; 2 seals on tags

C/6/6/1/2/2   18 May 1460
Messuage in Brookstrete in MG, except shop at S. end, small kitchen, and another house in which Thomas Bast formerly had his stable
Feoffment from Matilda Bast of Ipswich to Thomas Gundolf, clerk, John Balhed, William Dixson and wife Margaret, all of Ipswich
Names of 8 witnesses
Latin; fragment of seal on tag

C/6/6/1/2/3   (1477 or 1478)
Tenement with adjoining garden in MG
Feoffment from Thomas Golyas, Richard Bury, John Berte [? and others] to John Fitzjohn, chaplain, Richard Lytyll, chaplain, John Lytyll [? and others]
Fragment only, cancelled by mutilation; Latin; seal missing from tag

C/6/6/1/3   ST MARY LE TOWER   1387

C/6/6/1/3/1   11 Jun. 1387
Tenement in MT
Feoffment from John Say, chaplain and William Parkyn, executors of will of John Betil of Ipswich, to John Aleyn, John Drewes, Robert Brightwold, Richard Elmham and wife Christiana, all of Ipswich, and heirs of Richard and Christiana; with proviso for re-entry in case of non-payment of £10
Premises lay between tenements of Richard Waleys on both sides, abutting S. on highway and N. on garden of Alice Colman
Names of 5 witnesses
Latin; 5 seals on tags, all incomplete

C/6/6/1/4   ST MILDRED   1399

C/6/6/1/4/1   25 Mar. 1399
Five shops in St Mildred, Ipswich
Feoffment from John Arnald and Robert Lucas to John Lyncolne, clerk, Master Ralph Selby, John Bernard and John Horkeslee of Ipswich
Premises lay between common house on Cornhill on S. and highway on N.; first and second shops abutted E. on way at Tymbermarket and W. on shop lately of Thomas dil Ok; third shop

abutted E. on shop formerly of Geoffrey Starlyng and W. on shop of Prior of St Peter, Ipswich; fourth and fifth shops abutted E. on Prior's shop and W. on Cornhill
Names of 5 witnesses
Latin; both seals missing from tags

C/6/6/1/4/2   29 Mar. 1399
Tenement in St Mildred, Ipswich
Deed of covenant by which John Northerne and Richard Skyrwyt of Ipswich ratify to Master Ralph Selby, Henry Barton and Richard Joye of Ipswich their feoffment of the premises, on condition of payment of £20; feoffment otherwise to be void
Latin; seal missing from tag

C/6/6/1/5   ST NICHOLAS   1445

C/6/6/1/5/1   16 Oct. 1445
Tenement and curtilage in NI
Feoffment from Thomas Busshop, William Pertrich, John Frenssh sen. and John Frenssh jun., all of Ipswich, to Roger Stannard, John Brook, merchant, John Ladyesman, all of Ipswich, and John Talmage of Finborough
Names of ? 8 witnesses
Latin, damp-stained and partly illegible; seals and 2 tags missing

C/6/6/1/6   ST PETER   1468

C/6/6/1/6/1   4 May 1468
18s 4d, part payment for purchase of messuage (no details) in PE
Acquittance from William Merssh of Capel, yeoman, to John Hyll of Claydon
Latin; seal missing from tongue

C/6/6/1/7   PARISH UNKNOWN   1375

C/6/6/1/7/1   28 May 1375
Piece of land in Ipswich, 41 ft x 38 ft
Feoffment from Roger Heynes of Ipswich, weaver and wife Agnes, daughter of late Thomas Mundekyn of Ipswich, to John Sunderlond of Ipswich, skinner and wife Mabel
Premises lay between tenement of Thomas Wade, miller on E. and common ditches of town on W., abutting N. on tenement of Mariot, widow of Richard Jurson and S. on tenement of Thomas Wade
Names of 10 witnesses
Latin; 1 seal, 2nd missing from tag

C/6/6/2   SUFFOLK PROPERTIES   **1324–1899**
In chronological order

C/6/6/2/1   28 Jul. 1324
Cottage with curtilage and adjoining croft in Bradfield
Quitclaim from Isabella and Juliana, daughters of Ralph Rauff of Parve Akle [? Acle, Norfolk], to John son of Alan ate Stonde of Bradfield and wife Godelena; property formerly belonged to Isabella Pelemons, Ralph's sister
Names of 6 witnesses
Latin; 2 seals

C/6/6/2/2   13 Jan. 1333
Piece of meadow in Sproughton
Quitclaim of dower by Joan, widow of Dennis de le Dene, to Alice, daughter of Christina
Rodlond sen. of Stoke by Ipswich
Names of 5 witnesses
Latin; seal on tag

C/6/6/2/3   10 Dec. 1336
Grantor's share of lands which he is to receive on death of his grandfather John de Whatefelde
in WB, WU, Westerfield, Thurleston, Rushmere and Tuddenham; and moiety of third part of
messuage in LW, of messuage in MQ, and of land (20a) in WB, WU, Westerfield, Thurleston
and Tuddenham
Grant from John, son of John de Meleford of Ipswich, to John Goskalk of Ipswich
Premises in MQ lay next to S. step of churchyard
Names of 11 witnesses
Latin; 1 seal on tag

C/6/6/2/4   4 Oct. 1430
Messuage called Mellemores with land and pasture in Mells [hamlet in Wenhaston]
Agreement for avoidance of bond of same date (annexed) in 20 marks from Lawrence Jalcy of
Theberton to Edmund de Ker of Mells, on condition that Alice, daughter and heir of John
Danyell, late of Wenhaston, on reaching 21 years of age, quitclaim premises to Ker and wife
Ellen, in manor court of Mells
2 docs, Latin, each with 1 seal

C/6/6/2/5   23 Apr. 1507
Messuage called Wareynsyerde in Mickfield
Feoffment from Charles Knevett and Thomas Chepherd to John Lokewode, Gilbert Blomvile
and Richard Chepherd
Latin; 2 seals on tags

C/6/6/2/6   10 Oct. 1560
Tenement called Greyscokes with land (49a; field names given) in Thorndon, Occold and
Rishangles
Conveyance by bargain and sale from Robert Brene of Thorndon, husbandman and wife
Agnes, to Richard Short of Thorndon, yeoman

C/6/6/2/7   1 Apr. 1568
Freehold and copyhold messuages and lands (no details) in Troston and Great Livermere
Conveyance by bargain and sale from William Manne of Troston, husbandman, to William
Randall of Westhorpe, yeoman, for £166 13s 4d
Seal on tag

C/6/6/2/8   4 Jun. 1588
Lands, tenements, heaths and marshes called Dingles Walke in Westleton and Dingle [in
Westleton]
Quitclaim from Robert Drurye of Rougham, esq., to William Homberstone, esq.
Latin

C/6/6/2/9   19 Dec. 1616
Messuage called Chapmans with lands in Crowfield
Feoffment from Robert Vigerous of Langham (Essex), gent. to Thomas Rewse of Little
Stonham, yeoman
Latin; found with the deeds of the estate belonging to Smart's and Tyler's charities in Creeting
and Earl Stonham

C/6/6/2/10   (30 Oct. 1640), n.d. [17c]
Manor house called Ricehall *alias* Rysehall with adjoining brick kiln in Akenham and lands
(260a) in Akenham, Claydon, Thurleston and Whitton

Certified copy deed of assignment from John Scrivenor of Sibton, esq. and William Dade of Tannington, esq., to John Hawys jun., son and heir apparent of John Hawys sen. of Ipswich, gent.

Premises were conveyed to Scrivenor and Dade from Sir William Withepole, kt. and others, in trust for John Hawys sen., 12 Jun. 1630

C/6/6/2/11   1747–1899

Public houses and other property in Ipswich, Capel St Mary, Framlingham, Grundisburgh, Hadleigh, Needham Market and Raydon

Evidences of title for purchase by George Ridley of Ipswich, wine merchant, from Henry Ridley of Ipswich, timber merchant, 22 Dec. 1868

Property comprises third part of : former 'Black Boy', warehouse and house in Fore Street, 'Lord Nelson', 'Cow and Pail', 'Earl Grey', house in Duk's Lane, 'White Elm' and 6 adjoining cottages, all in CL; 'Eagle' and 'Cherry Tree' in MG; 'Castle', house adjoining, and bonding warehouse, all in MQ; 'Shipwright's Arms' in MS; 'Leopard' in MT; 'Lord Chancellor' and 'Cardinal's Head' in NI; 'Bluecoat Boy' and adjoining house in PE; brewery (formerly vinegar factory), malting office and 'Pilot' inn adjoining (parish unspecified); all in Ipswich; 'White Horse' and 6 adjacent cottages in Capel St Mary; 'Crown' in Framlingham; 'Dog' and 4 cottages in Grundisburgh; 'White Lion', 'King's Head' chamber, brewhouse, bowling green, hop ground and orchard adjoining 'George', all in Hadleigh; 'George' in Needham Market; and 'Chequers' in Raydon

Deeds, 1747–1813, relate only to Tainters Yard, site of 'Lord Chancellor' in NI

Includes:

— will of Thomas Brahm of Holbrook, yeoman, 1747

— articles of co-partnership between Henry Ridley, George Ridley and William Ridley, all of Ipswich, wine and spirit merchants, brewers, maltsters and coal merchants, 1831

— will of Henry Ridley of Ipswich, wine merchant, 1840

— will of George Ridley of Ipswich, wine and spirit merchant, 1871

— schedule of deeds *re* 5 messuages in Belstead Road in MS, 1899

(23 docs)

C/6/6/3   OUT-COUNTY PROPERTIES   1326–1573

C/6/6/3/1   6 Feb. 1326

Piece of land called le Puchschroneaker in the east field of Effingham [Surrey]

Quitclaim from John son of William Paramours of Effingham to Robert le Broke

Names of 7 witnesses

Latin; seal missing from tag

C/6/6/3/2   15 Apr. 1426

All grantor's goods and chattels in Norfolk, Suffolk or elsewhere

Grant by Thomas Coupere of Norwich, mercer, to John Couteshale, citizen of Norwich, John Sparham of Sparham [Norfolk] and John Mey of Norwich, without power of reclamation

Latin; seal and tag missing

C/6/6/3/3   22 Jul. 1573

Lands, pastures and woods called Martins in Great Clacton (Essex)

Feoffment from John Beanynge of Great Clacton to Thomas Sharpe of Great Clacton, clerk and Edmund Cooke of Creeting All Saints, husbandman; to use of feoffor for life, then to use of his son John and lawful issue

Latin

C/6/7   LEGAL   1327–1826

C/6/7/1   26 Mar. 1327
General release of all actions in respect of the death of Rogier Styward of Hampton Hospital
parish [? in London], or otherwise
From Maud, widow of Rogier, to Simond de Pekham of London, hosier
Names of 6 witnesses
Latin; fragment of seal on tag

C/6/7/2   [*post* 20 Jan. 1378]
Record of proceedings before Barons of Exchequer in Hilary term, ... Ric. II
Re duty owed on wool belonging to various merchants, shipped from Ipswich on board 'le
Nicholas' of Ipswich, William Gerlond master, on 10 Dec. 1372 and arriving at Calais on 2 Jan.
1373
Latin; 2 membranes, attached 'Chancery' style; text badly faded and discoloured by damp,
partly illegible

C/6/7/3   Jan. 1387
Extract of proceedings in Exchequer court
In revenue cause involving the ship 'Le Ingil de Camser', Arnald Papesson master, trading
between Ipswich and Calais in Feb. 1372 with a cargo of wool belonging to various merchants
including Gilbert Boulge [Bailiff of Ipswich 1393–1395] and Richard Haverynlond [Bailiff
1356–1357], on which customs duty was not paid
Latin; 2 membranes, text much faded, parts legible only under ultra-violet light

C/6/7/4   30 Jul. 1450
Certificate of William Lunt, Robert Lunt, John Mors, John Andrew, William Cook, John
Roberd, Robert Halle, Thomas Lunt, John Lunt, Walter Edward, John Templer and Richard
Edward, all of Holbrook
To the Prior and Convent of St Mary of Woodbridge, that Thomas Bryd, late servant of
Geoffrey, Prior of St Peter of Ipswich, on his death-bed at Holbrook, made confession to the
Rector of Holbrook and received the eucharist and extreme unction, avowing that he was not
wounded but died of infirmity of body; certified to relieve Robert Pyt of Woodbridge and wife
Katherine (lately wife of Bryd) from suspicion of having murdered Bryd, such suspicion being
chiefly due to malice of Joan, wife of John Calange and Margaret, wife of Thomas Mours, both
of Woodbridge
Latin; seal and tongue missing

C/6/7/5   24 Oct. 1456
Certificate of Thomas Braunche, clerk, Thomas Bland, gent., John Austyn, Robert Skape, John
Multon, John Beylham, Thomas Songer, John Burgeyn, fuller, Robert Sawkyn, William Semer
and John Lavendeer of St Mary Magdalen, Colchester (Essex)
That 18 seams of malt supplied to Anastase, wife of their neighbour Thomas Edward, by Robert
Brakstret of Wickham Skeith, husbandman, were inferior in quality to 2 seams supplied as a
sample of the 20 seams he had covenanted to sell her
English; 10 seals, all incomplete, on 2 tongues

C/6/7/6   12 Nov. 1457
Certificate of William Baret, Robert Dunche, butcher, Thomas Goodwyn, Robert Dunche,
clerk, Richard Peteman, John Maltwatyr and John Aldous sen. of Mendlesham
That on 19 Sep. 1455 William Morwhyll, late of Mendlesham, removed the goods and
chattels of Master Robert Wylde from Mendlesham vicarage against his will, while he was in
Cambridge
English; 4 seals, one incomplete, on 2 tongues

C/6/7/7   18 Apr. 1621
Exemplification of plea of trespass in Court of Common Pleas
Begun in Hillary term 1621, Daniel Welde v. John Cole, Michael Warde and John Bonde, all
late of Ipswich, tallow chandlers, re 80 lb unwrought tallow taken at Woodbridge; verdict for
defendants
Includes:
— (passed through seal tag) writ for Welde's appearance to make satisfaction of 70s costs,
18 Apr. 1621

C/6/7/8   (27 Apr. 1714), n.d.
Contemporary transcript of proceedings in Chancery
In case brought by Frances, Dowager Countess d'Auverquerque, executrix of William Henry,
late Earl of Bath, v. Grace, Lady Carterett, John, Lord Gower, Henrietta, Duchess of Grafton,
George, Lord Lansdowne and others, re the late Earl of Bath's estate
(16 pp.)

C/6/7/9   Feb.–Apr. 1826
Correspondence re sale of equity of redemption in 2 cottages on Lowestoft Beach
Letters from Samuel Haward, Lowestoft, to John Ward, County Gaol, Ipswich
(3 docs)

C/6/8   TESTAMENTARY   1454–c.1811

C/6/8/1   2 Dec. 1454
Certificate of John Porter and Simond Weyneld of Chelsworth, John Tyler sen., Thomas
Hoberd sen., William Shoppe and William Stannard of Monks Eleigh, and William Hoberd of
Stakewode [sic]
Made to John Buschop of Ipswich, administrator of goods of the late John Moryell of
Chelsworth, re money owed to Thomas Tyler of Monks Eleigh for blue broadcloths purchased
by Moryell during his lifetime
English; 4 seals on 2 tongues, 3 seals missing

C/6/8/2   2 Jun. 1540
Probate copy will of Robert London of Thorndon
Signed, 24 May 1538

C/6/8/3   (17 Sep. 1652), n.d.
Copy will of William Redgrave of Rendlesham, clerk

C/6/8/4   24 Apr. 1693
Probate copy will of Charles Mayhew of Trimley St Mary, yeoman
Signed, 27 Mar. 1693
(found among the Corporation water leases, with which it has no known connexion)

C/6/8/5   n.d. [c.1811]
Account of Mr Bedwell's personal property at the time of his death
(watermark dated 1811)

C/6/9   BUSINESS   1441–1826

C/6/9/1   22 May 1441
Acquittance
By John Smith sen. of Akenham for receipt of 20s from Richard Dallyng of Ipswich
Latin; seal on tongue

C/6/9/2   Feb. 1487
Counterpart indenture
Between John Walworth and William Baker, Bailiffs, and Robert Lee, Thomas Phyllypp and
John Creed, concerning a ship
English, badly discoloured by damp and most of text illegible; 3 seals on tags

C/6/9/3   25 Mar. 1789
Brig 'Draper' of Ipswich
Deed of assignment from William Christie, master and mariner, to John Savage
(fragment only)

C/6/9/4   Oct. 1799–Jan. 1813
Account book of an unidentified coal and corn merchant
The business was probably based in Woodbridge, since the greatest number of its customers
were concentrated there and in neighbouring parishes; though the accounts also record a widespread trade throughout eastern Suffolk
(1 vol.; with index)

C/6/9/5   5 Dec. 1822
Household furniture and goods
Deed of assignment from Edmund Marshall of Ipswich, butcher, to Samuel Newson of
Ipswich, innholder, as security for repayment of £100 loan at 5 per cent interest
Includes:
— inventory

C/6/9/6   1821–1826
Tradesman's account book
Re goods supplied (trade and trader unidentified)
(1 vol.)

C/6/10   TOOLEY FAMILY   1532–1547

Most of the documents were found among the papers of S.A. Notcutt, former Town Clerk of
Ipswich, and subsequently placed in the archive. It is possible that they once formed part of the
papers of Henry Tooley's executors, now included with the records of the Ipswich charity
estates (C/3/10/1/2/1); but having no apparent connexion with the Tooley Foundation estate,
they are treated here as an 'accidental accumulation'.

C/6/10/1   PROPERTY TRANSACTIONS   **1532–1547**

C/6/10/1/1   7 Jun. 1532
Messuage in Thirryngton Street in Stoke-by-Nayland
Mortgage from Thomas Holte of Stoke-by-Nayland, clothmaker, to Henry Tooley of Ipswich,
merchant, for £30
Seal missing from tag

C/6/10/1/2   8 Oct. 1547
Bond
Henry Tooley of Ipswich, merchant, bound to Anthony Coole in £200 for performance of cove-
nants in indentures of even date

C/6/10/2 LEGAL PAPERS   1541–1545

C/6/10/2/1   25 Feb. 1541
Bond
From Richard Ponder of Ipswich, merchant, to Henry Toly, in £100, not to trouble him in any of
King's courts for any cause wherein Toly is bound for appearance of Edward Conyngham,
mariner, to answer a plea of account by Ponder in King's Court of Ipswich or now depending in
any other court
Seal missing from tongue

C/6/10/2/2   1544–1545 and n.d.
Documents in suit brought by Henry Tooley of Ipswich, merchant, against John Downes and
Philip Mason, executors of will of John Armiger, deceased, in Chancery
The case concerned a debt of 1,000 marks allegedly owed to Tooley by Armiger's estate
Includes:
— writs, 16 Oct. 1544, 6 Nov. 1545
— plaintiff's petition to Thomas, Lord Wriothesley, Lord Chancellor, n.d.
— plaintiff's interrogatories, n.d.
— defendants' answer, n.d.
(5 membranes, filed together by tongues of writs)

C/6/10/3 CORRESPONDENCE   1537–?1543

C/6/10/3/1   18 Jan. 1537
Letter from William Rede [son of Henry Tooley's sister Margaret], Barrow, to his aunt [Alice]
Tooley, Ipswich
Details of cloth sales

C/6/10/3/2   Sep.–Dec. 1542
Correspondence *re* cloth sales and other trading activities
Letters from Thomas Copper, Calais and Bordeaux, to his master, Henry Tooley, Ipswich
(3 letters)

C/6/10/3/3   n.d. [? 22 Mar. 1543]
Letter from Johanne Den [Joan Dene], Yarmouth [Norfolk], to her brother Henry Tooley,
Ipswich
Asking advice in her dispute with her stepson William Dene *re* her right of dower
(letter dated simply 'Maundy Thursday'; Ralph Dene, the writer's husband, d. 1543)

C/6/11 APPRENTICESHIP   1448–1659

There is no evidence to suggest that these documents have any connexion with the borough's
activities in binding pauper children as apprentices as part of the provision of poor relief.

C/6/11/1   20 Jun. 1448
Apprenticeship indenture
John Frere of Ipswich binds himself to John Sexteyn of Ipswich, barber, for 7 years
(Latin; seal on tag)

C/6/11/2   15 Sep. 1659
Acquittance
From John Shutter of Ipswich, cordwainer, to John Foord of Ipswich, for 40*s* in discharge of
Foord's apprenticeship

C/6/12 MISCELLANEA 1450–1833

C/6/12/1 22 Apr. 1450
Letters testimonial of Thomas Blewik, Master of Chapel of St Mary in the Sea in Ely diocese
Certifying privileges and special faculties granted by Pope Boniface IX to the brothers and
sisters of the Chapel
(Latin; seal and tag missing)

C/6/12/2 11 May 1799
Ipswich Journal
(4 pp, printed)

C/6/12/3 1833 and n.d.
Papers relating to proposed London and Southampton Railway
Includes:
— prospectus with plan annexed, 5 Dec. 1833 (5 copies, printed)
— address by proprietors of land along proposed route, n.d. (4 copies, printed)
— list of Manchester subscribers with (endorsed) list of Norwich and Yarmouth supporters and
one Ipswich subscriber, Edward Bacon, esq., n.d. (MS)
— comparison of gross returns of various railways with statistics of amount of traffic, n.d.
(MS)
— extract from the *Mirror of Parliament*, 3 Apr. 1833, *re* debate on 3rd reading of London and
Birmingham Railway Bill (4 copies, printed)
(15 docs)

APPENDIX I
Ipswich Borough Correspondence 1529–1815

HD 36/A is an artificial collection of documents purchased by the Ipswich Area Record Office on various occasions between 1951 and 1995 and consisting of letters which originally formed part of the archive of Ipswich Corporation. This correspondence is of great value and interest for historians of 16th- and 17th-century Ipswich, and is particularly rich in material relating to the Civil Wars and the foreign wars in which England was involved in the Commonwealth and Restoration periods.

The letters appear to have gone astray from the archive during the 19th century, probably during the long town-clerkship of William Batley, whose collections for a history of Ipswich, now in the British Library (BL Add MSS 25,334–6), contain a number of documents filched from the town muniment room. Probably with Batley's connivance, the Corporation records were pillaged over a twenty-year period by local antiquarians/collectors, notably his friends John Wodderspoon and William Stevenson Fitch (*see* Martin, 1956, 87–93).

HD 36/A/1   n.d.[early–mid 16c.]
William Rede to his 'Aunt Toly' [Alice Tooley]. *Re* debts owed to his uncle [Henry Tooley, merchant]; his difficulties in raising money

HD 36/A/2   n.d.[early–mid 16c.]
William Forster to the Bailiffs. *Re* debt owed by Harman for which he is in prison; requests that £10 received by one Cowper for sale of wine belonging to Harman be used to discharge debt

HD 36/A/3   n.d.[1529]
Alice Tooley [Ipswich], to Master Semson 'dwelying on London brege'. On business matters, including payment for freight of wood
(Endorsed with memorandum of receipt of £9 16s 8d, 20 May 1529)

HD 36/A/4   13 Jun. 1534
John Sutton, Norwich, to [Henry] Tooley, Bailiff of Ipswich. *Re* business transactions between them

HD 36/A/5   Dec. [c.1535]
Sign Manual of Henry VIII, Richmond, to the Sheriff of Norfolk and Suffolk.
Directing him to elect Anthony Denny 'one of our privie chamber' as burgess for Parliament for Ipswich, to fill the vacancy caused by the death of Thomas Alverd
[Thomas Alverd Jun. d.1535]

HD 36/A/6   13 Nov. 1537
Robert Crampton, goldsmith, London, to Edmund Tolye, draper and tailor, Ipswich
Acquittance for £12 sterling in full payment of £16 for purchase of a house in LW

HD 36/A/7   22 Apr. 1542
——, Boulogne, to Henry Tooley. *Re* various matters of trade (French)

HD 36/A/8   31 Jan. 1543
John Sympson, London, to [Henry] Tooley, Ipswich. He has received all the money due to Tooley. Conveyance of letter to Bordeaux; 'the bordous flytte is taken'

HD 36/A/9   7 Jun. 1545
Harry [Henry] Tooley, Ipswich, to his wife Alice. Instructing her to 'pott aweye alle yowyr workkefolkys bothe the jounars & the massons . . . .'

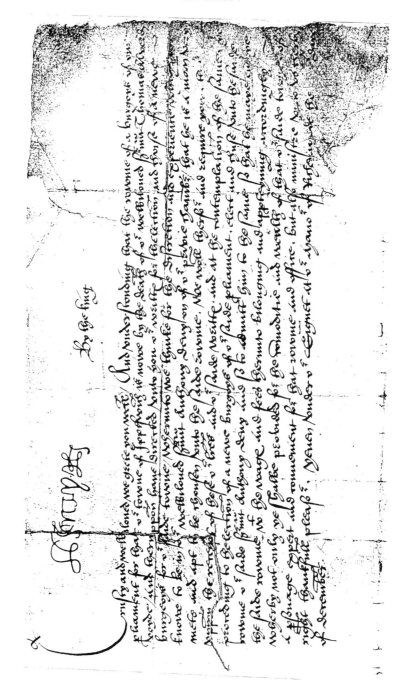

Fig. 22. Royal intervention. Sign Manual of Henry VIII, at Richmond, to the
Sheriff of Norfolk and Suffolk, [probably December 1535], directing him to elect
Anthony Denny 'one of our privie chamber' as burgess for Parliament for Ipswich,
to fill the vacancy caused by the death of Thomas Alverd that year. (HD 36/A/5)

HD 36/A/10   17 Oct. [1545]
[Sir] Humphrey Wingfield, Brantham Hall, to Rauf Goodwyn and William West, Bailiffs.
Requesting postponement of a suit in the Great Court against 'my neighbour Goslying of
Holbrooke' concerning lands in Holbrook. [Rauf Goodwyn and William Best were Bailiffs in
1545, in which year Sir Humphrey Wingfield died]

HD 36/A/11   13 Nov. 1545
William Clyston, Collector of the King's Subsidy for the port of London, to the Customer or his
deputy at Ipswich. Notifying him that John Mason, esq., licensed to import French goods in
allied ships into any English port, has deputed Henry Tooley of Ipswich, merchant, to receive
and sell such goods

HD 36/A/12   1549
Account in Henry Tooley's hand for delivery of wine etc. to 'Master Dandey' and others (total
£44 4s 0d)

HD 36/A/13   n.d.[not later than 1549]
[Sir] Richard Gresham to [Henry] Tooley, Ipswich. Advising him to come [to London] to
answer the Lord Chancellor concerning a bill of complaint by 'serten Dowchemen' re attachment of goods [Sir Richard Gresham d.1549 (DNB)]

HD 36/A/14   22 Oct. [1550]
William Bygott to [Henry] Tooley, Ipswich. Sickness of the Lord Chancellor has prevented
Bygott from moving him in Tooley's suit; requests him to send 'the obligacions [bonds] that ye
have' of Thomas Holton of Nayland, John Deye and Henry Aylmer. (Annotated in Tooley's
hand that bonds were sent to London, 26 Oct. 1550)

HD 36/A/15   6 Jan. 1551
E. Clynton [Edward Fiennes de Clinton, 9th Baron Clinton and Saye, 1st Earl of Lincoln, Lord
High Admiral], Greenwich, to Sir Thomas Woodhows, kt, Vice Admiral in Norfolk and
Suffolk. Ordering him to take a view of all ships and seamen in his area, either at an Admiralty
Court or by letters to officers along the coast, and to give order for arrest of English, Scottish
and other sea rovers and pirates

HD 36/A/16   1 Mar. 1551
John Gosnold, London, to the Bailiffs. Asking for their favour in allowing the butchers to sell
their tallow at a more favourable price

HD 36/A/17   12 Apr. 1551
Richard Purpett, London, to Henry Tooley, merchant, Ipswich. Arrival of their ship with
13 tuns of wine; he has no money to pay freight or customs, but will try to borrow it

HD 36/A/18   n.d.[post Aug. 1551]
John Southwell to [William] Bygot. Re recovery and fine of manors of Ulveston and Sackvilles
[in Debenham] [Southwell was one of Henry Tooley's executors; Tooley d.1551]

HD 36/A/19   6 Oct. 1552
John Southwell, Barham, to [Robert or William] Dandy. Asking him to deliver iron and salt to
Master Bacon, and to acquaint the other executors [of Henry Tooley] with this letter, so that
they may keep tally of goods delivered. [Southwell and Robert and William Dandy were
Tooley's executors]

HD 36/A/20   12 Nov. 1552
William Whetcroft, London, to the Bailiffs. Re delays in hearing a case at Westminster con-
cerning jurisdiction of Ipswich's borough courts; and enrolment of the Borough charter in the
Court of Common Pleas [William Whetcroft was Common Clerk to the Borough]

HD 36/A/21   Nov. [1552]
William Whetcroft [London] to the Bailiffs. *Re* doubt expressed by one of judges that the
wording of the Ipswich borough charter permits conusance of plea to the borough courts in the
action concerned; charges for enrolling the borough charter

HD 36/A/22   16 Jan. 1553
Edward Grymeston, London, to Robert Dundy, William Dundy and Richard Bryde.
In response to their request for relief of the poor, he is content that they shall have all 'the
byllettes' remaining at his house in MT, except 1,000 reserved for his own use. Since Master
Gosnolde, the King's solicitor 'hathe a plasse in the lordes house', requests the borough to elect
William Hanynges as burgess for Parliament

HD 36/A/23   12 Nov. 1553
Mayor and Aldermen of London to the Bailiffs and inhabitants of Ipswich.
Admonishing them for their 'evil and disceytfull doynges' in selling sack cloth (various types
named and sizes given) at short measure, and warning them that any such cloth on sale in
London after the feast of Purification will be seized

HD 36/A/24   n.d.[1550s]
John Southwell, London, to Robert Dawndye, Ipswich. Requesting Dawndye's presence (as
one of Henry Tooley's executors) and that of Mrs Tooley in London for the hearing of the
Tooley will case; many details of the course of the action

HD 36/A/25   16 Jan. [1550s]
Robert Good, 'your proctor', London, to Masters Southwell, Dawndye and Byrde, Ipswich. On
the progress of their lawsuit [*re* Tooley's will]; advising them to come to London as soon as
possible, bringing with them the original depositions of their witnesses [John Southwell,
Robert and William Dundy and Richard Byrde *alias* Bryde were Tooley's executors]

HD 36/A/26   18 Sep. 1560
Copy Signet letter of Queen Elizabeth I, from Windsor, addressed generally to towns and
corporations etc. Explaining the need for the proclamation for withdrawing base coin, offering
3*d* reward for every 20*s* worth brought in to the mint, and ordering justices and ministers to
explain the necessity for the proclamation to 'ignorant people'

HD 36/A/27   21 Jan. [1561]
William Toppesfeld, Westminster, to John Gardyner and Richard Byrd, late Bailiffs. *Re* an
attachment issued in error against the borough in the Exchequer Court [Dated 21 Jan. 'anno
tercio'; Richard Bird was Bailiff 1559–60 and John Gardner in 1560–61]

HD 36/A/28   2 Mar. 1561
[Sir] N[icholas] Bacon, Lord Keeper, from 'my house beside Charing Crosse', to the Bailiffs.
Asking them to procure half a tun of Gascon wine ready for his visit to the country

HD 36/A/29   16 May 1561
[Sir] N[icholas] Bacon, Lord Keeper, 'from my house beside Charring Crosse', to the Bailiffs.
Requesting their assistance to Master Withipoll in preparing his house for the reception of the
Queen during her progress

HD 36/A/30   17 Nov. 1562
[Thomas Howard, Duke of] Norfolk, London, to the Bailiffs, Portmen and Headboroughs.
Recommending Thomas Toose to them for the vacancy of Town Clerk

HD 36/A/31   7 Feb. 1562
Richard Vinyor, Staple Inn [London], to William Hawys, Ipswich. *Re* admission of one Mason
to Hawys's chamber

HD 36/A/32   28 Jun. 1563
[Sir] N[icholas] Bacon, Lord Keeper, 'from my house nighe Charinge Cross', to the Bailiffs,

Portmen and Burgesses. Recommending Thomas Toose to them for the vacancy of Town Clerk (endorsed: 'My Lord Keeper of the Great Seale of England second letter')

HD 36/A/33   17 Aug. 1569
[Sir] N[icholas] Bacon, Lord Keeper [London], to the Bailiffs. Recommending the bearer, a poor townsman, to them as a suitable person to receive relief

HD 36/A/34   1 Oct. 1569
Queen Elizabeth I, Windsor Castle, to the Bailiffs. Writ for reading and posting of a royal proclamation

HD 36/A/35   16 Oct. 1569
Thomas, Lord Wentworth, from Nettlestead, to the Bailiffs. *Re* his visit to Ipswich next Wednesday to examine their book of musters

HD 36/A/36   20 Oct. 1569
[*Signature illegible*], from ? Waphing [? Wapping], to the Bailiffs. Complaining of treatment of his servant, who was stripped and searched at the gaoler's house while in Ipswich

HD 36/A/37   29 Oct. 1569
Robert D[oon] to William Smarte, Bailiff. *Re* suits concerning property in the court of the manor of Ulveston [in Debenham]

HD 36/A/38   31 Oct. 1569
Robert Doon to [? the Bailiffs]. *Re* suit claimed by the Bailiff of the Hundred against Huntinge, a copyholder [? of the manor of Ulveston in Debenham]

HD 36/A/39   3 Nov. 1569
? Nicholas Cock to [William] Smarte, Bailiff. Requesting that Lawrence ? Rey, a poor man 'in the bottom of the jayle' be given the relief of the keeper's house unless he is detained for felony or anything worse

HD 36/A/40   28 Nov. 1569
[Sir] Christopher Heydon [High Sheriff of Norfolk and Suffolk, 1569], Baconsthorpe [Norfolk], to the Bailiffs. Acknowledging receipt of a letter and a little box sent to him and Sir William Butts by Lord Wentworth

HD 36/A/41   4 Dec. 1569
Robert King and William Smarte [Bailiffs], Ipswich, to James Revett, Creeting Green. Asking advice on a case of assault in Ipswich (legal opinion endorsed)

HD 36/A/42   12 Dec. 1569
Thomas [Lord Wentworth] to the Bailiffs. Mr Seckford the customer and others holding the Queen's commission to stay the ship taken by the Frenchman are to arrest the ship accordingly

HD 36/A/43   14 Dec. 1569
Philip Wentworth, Nettlestead, to [William] Smarte and [Robert] King, Bailiffs.
Asking them to recompense the bearer, a poor man, for the apparelling of one who went 'in the place of a Drommer'

HD 36/A/44   n.d.[late 1569 or early 1570]
Robert Doon to [William] Smarte, Bailiff. Memorandum *re* his expenses in surveying the town lands in Claydon and Bramford and the manors of Sackvilles and Ulveston [in Debenham]. [William Smarte was Bailiff in 1569–70, and Doon [Donne] was retained to make a survey of the town lands, 27 Oct. 1569 – *see* Richardson 1884, 284]

HD 36/A/45   9 Jan. 1570
Francis Noone, Martlesham, to the Bailiffs. Asking them to question Richard Rynge of MG and his wife *re* stealing of a sheep about a year ago from Robert Petgrewes of Martlesham; they are not to be charged, in the hope that 'it wold breake the brode of a shrewd company of pyckrs which begynn to swarme rownd abowt' [Francis Noone of Martlesham, reader at Gray's Inn

575

(d.1574), was elected counsel for Ipswich, 22 Mar. 1559/60, and d.1574 – *see* Richardson 1884, 255, 283]

HD 36/A/46   29 Jan. 1570
John Hawis to the Bailiffs. The *quietus est* for Master Dyer's and Master Barker's bailiwick can proceed no further until the enclosed writ is returned to the Exchequer; therefore an inquest is to be empanelled [Hawis was Common Clerk and Clerk of the Peace – *see* Richardson 1884, 284]

HD 36/A/47   29 Jan. 1570
William Whetcroft to the Bailiff. Asking them to appoint Baker, a very honest poor man, as a butcher to kill flesh within the town [Whetcroft was a former Common Clerk to the Borough]

HD 36/A/48   5 Feb. 1570
Thomas, [Lord] Wentworth, 'from my house' [Nettlestead], to the Bailiffs. Asking them to arrest and send to him a purveyor of pease and oats for the Queen's provision, lodging at one Baxter's in Ipswich

HD 36/A/49   8 Feb. 1570
John Ferrrour, 'late servante unto the undre sherif of Suff', Westminster Hall, to [William] Smarte and [Robert] Kyng, Bailiffs. Asking them to execute a writ carried by the bearer

HD 36/A/50   21 Feb. 1570
John ? Forster to [Robert] Kynge and [William] Smarte, Bailiffs. Notifying them that he has examined John Morton, a boy born in Scotland, near kinsman to Peter ? Neryn, under arrest in Ipswich at the suit of William Smyth

HD 36/A/51   2 Mar. 1570
Thomas, [Lord] Wentworth, Nettlestead, to the Bailiffs. He is sending to them a boy who stole 2 gold royals and 6*d* in silver from Thomas Askew of MS, with whom he lodged. Askew will not prosecute. Wentworth thinks he should be 'well whipped', but leaves the punishment to the Bailiffs' discretion

HD 36/A/52   18 Mar. 1570
[Sir] Christopher Heydon, Baconsthorpe [Norfolk], to the Bailiffs. Requesting them to release a ship belonging to the bearer, William Holfoote, a stranger, which has been detained in the port of Ipswich. [Heydon was High Sheriff of Norfolk and Suffolk, 1569–70]

HD 36/A/53   21 Mar. 1570
Owyn Hopton, Cockfield, to [William] Smarte and [Robert] Kinge, Bailiffs. He has received letters from the Earl of Pembroke, Lord Steward, and the Earl of Leicester, in favour of the bearer, Henry Bettes, one of the ordinary officers of the Queen's Pastry, whose marriage suit to the daughter of the widow Braybye, 'a neighbour of yours', the Queen favours; the Bailiffs are to show him their lawful favour touching his appearance at Ipswich Sessions. Bailiffs are to meet Hopton next Thursday, and to order the widow and her daughter to appear, so that the matrimonial cause between them may be examined

HD 36/A/54   3 Apr. 1570
Certificate of Robert Wade and Richard Raynold, constables of Woolpit, and others, that Anne Bernes has been in service there. Endorsed: part of a statement *re* expenses due for performance of various errands, n.d.

HD 36/A/55   28 Apr. 1570
John Hawis [Common Clerk and Clerk of the Peace] to [Robert] Kynge and [William] Smarte, Bailiffs. Notifying them that the hearing of the case between the town and Master Wythepoll has been arranged for the following week

HD 36/A/56   1 May 1570
John Hawis [Common Clerk and Clerk of the Peace] to [Robert] Kynge and [William] Smart, Bailiffs. Requesting them to assemble with some of the town's justices and artificers, to consider the rates of wages for artificers; if they agree with the writer that the present rates are sufficient, they should agree thereon, so that he may certify them next term

HD 36/A/57   3 May 1570
John Hawys [Common Clerk and Clerk of the Peace], London, to [Robert] Kynge and [William] Smarte, Bailiffs. *Re* the date for the hearing of the suit between the town and Master Wythepoll; his reasons for remaining in London; requests deferment of the Town Court

HD 36/A/58   24 Jun. 1570
[Sir] Christopher Heydon [High Sheriff] and [Sir] William Buttes, Saxlingham [Norfolk], to the Bailiffs. Asking them to release from custody Richard Bennet of Ipswich, on bond for his good behaviour

HD 36/A/59   26 Jun. 1570
Thomas, [Lord] Wentworth, London, to the Bailiffs. Requiring them to make enquiries for accomplices of one Whiting, under arrest 'for a wycked conspyracy', and to detain anyone suspected of rebellion

HD 36/A/60   —Jun. 1570
Robert Cole the elder, East Bergholt, to [Robert] Kyng and [William] Smarte, Bailiffs. *Re* alleged vagabondage of Jone Bull and Agnes Barnes; with copies of certificates of their various settlements, 13 Jun. 1570 and n.d.

HD 36/A/61   15 Jul. 1570
[*Signature illegible*], Bury St Edmunds, to [Robert] Kinge and [William] Smarte, Bailiffs. Requesting their favourable consideration of the bearer, George Legate, who has had a suit brought against him in the Ipswich borough court by one Revell

HD 36/A/62   21 Jul. 1570
Henry Woodhowse and [*signature illegible*], Norwich, to the Bailiffs. Ordering them, on the authority of letters from the Privy Council, to stay all ships of 30 tons or more, and all mariners, within the port of Ipswich, for the Queen's service, until further notice. They are to report to the writers the number, names and tonnage of such ships and the number and names of mariners

HD 36/A/63   18 Aug. 1570
By John ?Auker, minister, Norwich. Testimonial in favour of Jasper de ? Muriment, exiled for the word of God, and a member of the French church in Norwich (Latin)

HD 36/A/64   19 Aug. 1570
By N. Drury, Norwich. Open letter recommending Peter de ? Moremounte of ? Audmerye, who has lived in Norwich 'godly and quyetly' for 3 years, and now has occasion to repair with his wife and family to [*illegible*]

HD 36/A/65   30 Aug. 1570
Thomas, [Lord] Wentworth, Nettlestead, to the Bailiffs. Ordering them to levy 3 men, well furnished as footmen arquebusiers, with coats and conduct money, to serve in the Navy, and to send him their names

HD 36/A/66   5 Sep. 1570
Thomas, [Lord] Wentworth, Nettlestead, to the Bailiffs. On the same subject; the 3 footmen arquebusiers are to be ready next Saturday morning

HD 36/A/67   5 Sep. 1570
Francis Noone, Martlesham, to the Bailiffs. Congratulating them on having 'godly and pollytyckly suppressed the ... monstruos hosen' [*sic*] within the town; advising them to choose wise and godly Bailiffs to defend the liberties and customs of the town [On Noone, *see* note at HD 36/A/45 above]

HD 36/A/68   30 Dec. 1570
Lionel Throkmerton, John Edwardes, John Bobright, Robert Smyth, Thomas Curtes and Edward Felld, inhabitants of Bungay, to the Bailiffs. Asking their financial help for Robert Bode, son of a poor widow of Bungay, apprenticed to Philip Horman of Ipswich, barber, who has returned to Bungay with a leg injury received during his apprenticeship

HD 36/A/69   6 Feb. [between 1561 and 1574]
Francis Noone, Martlesham, to the Bailiffs. Interceding for one Kyndersley, 'discharged' along
with other Ipswich victuallers [On Noone, *see* note at HD 36/A/45 above, which explains the
date-span assigned to this letter]

HD 36/A/70   13 May 1575
[Sir] N[icholas] Bacon, Lord Keeper, 'from my house beside Charing Crosse' to the Bailiffs
and commonalty of Ipswich. Recommending favourable consideration to the bearer, his
kinsman, who has a suit before them for his relief

HD 36/A/71   1 Feb. 1584
Deposition of Thomas Moore, servant to Robert Pulham of Ipswich, draper, before William
Bloyse [Bailiff]. Concerning fraudulent sale of silk

HD 36/A/72   26 Aug. 1587
William Smarte and Robert Lymmer, Bailiffs, to Lord Hunsdon, Lord Chamberlain [of the
Household]. [Copy] letter, the original covering a certificate of a view of horses taken within
the liberty of Ipswich in accordance with the Queen's commission of musters

HD 36/A/73   19 Jun. 1593
? Matthew Arundell, Henry ? Trenchard and Raufe Horsey, Clifton, to Sir William Peryam, Kt,
Lord Chief Baron of the Exchequer. On behalf of Richard Miller of Poole [Dorset], who has
been served with process out of the Exchequer Court for non-payment of customs on 2 hogs-
heads of wine, which were corrupt and unsaleable

HD 36/A/74   18 Nov. [between 1569 and 1593]
John Southwell, Barham, to [William] Smarte, Bailiff. Requesting release of a poor man from
Ipswich gaol; Southwell will be bound for payment of the prisoner's debt if it is less than 26s 8d
[Smarte was Bailiff on various occasions between 1569 and 1593]

HD 36/A/75   31 Dec. 1595
William, Lord Burghley, [? Charles, Lord] Howard [of Effingham], W. Cobham, [Thomas
Sackville, Lord] Buckhurst, John Puckering, Robert Cecil and J. Wolley, from the Court at
Richmond, to the Bailiffs and Burgesses of Ipswich. Requesting a charitable contribution
towards work to be carried out at Rye (Sussex), to render the haven safe for shipping

HD 36/A/76   20 Jan. 1596
George Coo, Holbrook, to Master Hawys. Coo's master has taken bail for John Jolley and his
sureties, on condition that the writ be sent today

HD 36/A/77   8 Apr. 1596
Robert Snellinge [Bailiff] to Christopher Ballard, Chamberlain. Warrant for payment of 21s 1d
for his 'horsemeat', horsehire and charges for 3 journeys to Sir Robert Jermyn and Sir John
Heigham, [Deputy] Lieutenants, about the town's business concerning the shipping

HD 36/A/78   24 Jan. 1597
Christopher Ballard [Claviger], to William Mydnall sen., treasurer for the affairs of the 2 ships
which were employed in the Queen's service for the town of Ipswich.
Receipt for 20s assigned to be paid to him by Jefferie Todd out of his wages

HD 36/A/79   — Apr. 1597
Thomas W——, London, to the Bailiffs. The money to be collected in Ipswich is to be sent to
'the knights' as quickly as possible; any who will not pay are to be sent to London 'this terme
tyme while I am here', with details of their names, their ability to pay and the amounts
demanded

HD 36/A/80   n.d.[later 16c.]
Henry Cooke, London, to Master Hawys [? John Hawys, Common Clerk]. *Re* lease of Dr ?
Ferth's farm

HD 36/A/81   14 Jul. [later 16c.]
Edward Sulyard, Wetherden, to [William] Smarte, Bailiff. Requesting an answer within 14 days to his offer to sell lands in Ipswich and Stoke for £3,500

HD 36/A/82   n.d.[later 16c.]
Voucher to the Treasurers for payment of the soldiers' charges for supper, bed and breakfast

HD 36/A/83   n.d.[later 16c.]
William Forster, Copdock, to [William] Smarte, Bailiff. Requests arrest of Christopher Goodwyn, 'a besy felow', and Austen Bird; Bird, at Goodwyn's instigation, has been trying to persuade tenants of a brewhouse in MQ, which Forster purchased 12 years ago, to withold their rent; with draft [in Forster's hand] of an entry for the rolls of the borough court

HD 36/A/84   12 Oct. 1610
Acquittance from Thomas Howard, Earl of Suffolk to Robert Cole, Treasurer of Ipswich, for £10 for his year's fee as Steward of the borough

HD 36/A/85   10 Oct. 1610
Acquittance from Samuel Ward [town preacher] to Master [Robert] Coale [Cole], Town Treasurer, for £18 6s 8d

HD 36/A/86   16 Nov. 1611
Ed[ward] Coke [? Sir Edward Coke, Chief Justice of the Common Pleas], 'Seriantes' [? Serjeants Inn], to Sir Anthony Felton and Sir Edmund Wythypolle, kts and John Lany, esq, or any 2 of them. Order to examine and bind over Roger Wallys and Robert Stewardson of Ipswich, for offences against good government and provision for the poor there

HD 36/A/87   10 Mar. 1612
[Henry Howard, Earl of] Northampton, [Ludovic Stuart, Duke of] Lennox, [Thomas Howard, Earl of] Suffolk, [Gilbert Talbot, Earl of] Shrewsbury, [Edward Somerset, Earl of] Worcester, [William Herbert, Earl of] Pembroke and [Sir] Julius Cesar [Caesar], from the Court of Whitehall, to the Lord Lieutenant of Suffolk. Requiring them to order the Deputy Lieutenants, Justices of the Peace and other ministers to assist Lord Willoughby and others authorised by the King of Denmark to recruit volunteer troops [copy]

HD 36/A/88   16 Mar. 1613–1614
'A coppye of the letters to the towne of Ipswich for theire providing against the day for mustering the soldeires'. Correspondence between the Lord Lieutenant and Deputy Lieutenants of Suffolk and the Bailiffs re equipping of troops and appointment of the Bailiffs as Deputy Lieutenants of the county

HD 36/A/89   10 May 1615
T[homas Howard, Earl of] Suffolk, Northampton House, to [? the Deputy Lieutenants of Suffolk]. The best time to hold musters will be at Whitsuntide, before harvest; they are to arrange this and instruct the High Constables that the service is to be preformed in a more exact manner [copy]

HD 36/A/90   16 Jun. 1617
[George Abbot, Archbishop of] Canterbury, Edward [Earl of] Worcester, Edward [Lord] Zouche, [John, Lord] Stanhope, George Carew and Raphe Winwood [Privy Councillors], Whitehall, to [? the Lord Lieutenant of Suffolk]. Instructions for holding of musters [copy]

HD 36/A/91   27 Jun. 1617
T[homas Howard, Earl of] Suffolk [Lord Lieutenant], Suffolk House, to the Bailiffs and Deputy Lieutenants in Ipswich, Sir Edmund Withypoole, Robert Cutler, William Bloys, Matthew Brownrigg, Robert Snelling and William Cage. Enclosing HD 36/A/90 and requiring them to execute the instructions contained therein

HD 36/A/92   2 Feb. 1619
[The Privy Council] to the Earl of Suffolk, Lord Lieutenant of Cambridgeshire, Suffolk and
Dorset. Commission to cause a general view and muster to be taken of all forces, foot and horse,
to improve training, lay in ammunition and put the beacons in order; amounts of powder and
match to be provided are specified [copy]

HD 36/A/93   19 Mar. 1619
[Sir] George Calvert, [Secretary of State], from the Court at Newmarket, to the Bailiffs.
Instructing them to search the lodgings of one Preudhomme, a Frenchman living in or near
Ipswich, to seize his papers and dispatch them by the bearer, John Brunt, a messenger of the
King's Chamber, who has a warrant for Preudhomme's arrest

HD 36/A/94   18 Dec. 1619
[Sir] Lionel Tallemache and [Sir] Henry Glemham [Deputy Lieutenants], to the Bailiffs.
Informing them that John Wentworth and Jeffery Gilbert have been appointed to confer with
them re safe stowage of powder and match allocated to the town by order of the Privy Council

HD 36/A/95   5 Jul. 1620
James Spens, Robert ? Maxwell, —— Alman and ——— [illegible], to the Bailiffs, Phillipp
Shotbolt, esq. and the Town Clerk. The King has entrusted them in the names of Robert Dixon
and William Almond with a grant of forfeited recognizances of alehousekeepers; informing
them of the policy to be followed in taking action against defaulting alehousekeepers

HD 36/A/96   3 Aug. 1620
T[homas Howard, Earl of] Suffolk [Lord Lieutenant], Audley End [Saffron Walden (Essex)],
to the Bailiffs and Corporation. Their request to nominate their own captain of the town
company was granted conditionally on the mustermaster entering on his rolls the names of
captain, officers and men; the mustermaster is to continue to receive his allowances from the
Corporation

HD 36/A/97   7 Oct. 1622
M[ichael] Gooder [Goodyere] and Robert Sparrow, Bailiffs, to Christopher Alldgat, Town
Treasurer. Warrant to pay £15 to Edmund Deye, to ride to London about the business of the
town 'lector' [lecturer]

HD 36/A/98   1 Nov. 1622
The Mayor and Jurats of Sandwich [Kent], to the Bailiffs and Portmen. Re recovery of a debt of
£100 owed to Robert Mills, mariner, a combaron of Sandwich, by Mary Blomfel alias
Blumfeild, widow and Andrew Leonartson, sailmaker, both late of Ipswich

HD 36/A/99   24 Jun. 1623
Acquittance from Samuel Ward [Town Preacher] to [Christopher] Algatt, Town Treasurer, for
£25

HD 36/A/100   post 25 Dec. 1623
Acquittance from John Lany [Recorder] to [William] Inglethorpe, Town Treasurer, for £10 for
his fee for the half year ended at Christmas 1623

HD 36/A/101   4 Feb. 1624
William Cage and Robert Benham [Bailiffs] to William Inglethorpe [Town Treasurer]. Warrant
for payment of 30s to Phillipp Courtnall for the quarterly exhibition for maintenance of his son
John [at Cambridge University]

HD 36/A/102   10 Apr. 1624
William Cage and Robert Benham [Bailiffs], to William Inglethorpe, Town Treasurer. Warrant
for payment of £6 13s 4d to Frederick Johnson, Town Clerk, for his half year's fee to last Lady
Day

HD 36/A/103   7 Aug. 1624
William Cage and Robert Benham [Bailiffs], to William Inglethorpe, Town Treasurer. Warrant for payment of 30*s* to Phillipp Courtnall for the quarterly exhibition for the maintenance of his son John [at Cambridge University]

HD 36/A/104   7 Aug. 1624
Duplicate of HD 36/A/103

HD 36/A/105   29 Sep. 1624
William Cage and Robert Benham [Bailiffs], to William Inglethorpe, Town Treasurer. Warrant for payment of £6 13*s* 4*d* to Frederick Johnson, Town Clerk, for his half year's fee ended today, and of 4*s* for paper and parchment

HD 36/A/106   30 Sep. 1624
John Sicklemor, John Lany, Thomas Cutler and Tobias Blosse, commissioners for the 2nd subsidy, to Joseph Hubberd, one of the Serjeants at Mace of Ipswich Warrant to order Edmond Daye, Joseph Parkhurst, John Aldus and Thomas Knappe to appear before them on 2 Oct. by 8a.m.

HD 36/A/107   8 Nov. 1624
T[homas, Earl of] Suffolk [Lord Lieutenant of Suffolk], to the Deputy Lieutenants [some of them named]. He has sent them copies of letters from King, Privy Council and Council of War 'touchinge a busines that requiereth greate expedition' (with note of receipt of copies by Bailiff Sicklemore from Sir Henry Glemham's servant, 23 Nov. 1624)

HD 36/A/108   14 Jan. 1625
[Sir] Henry Glemham [Deputy Lieutenant of Suffolk], Glemham, to the Bailiffs. Originally enclosing a copy letter from the Council of War *re* joint certificate of pressed soldiers for the whole county

HD 36/A/109   14 Dec. 1626
Thomas [Earl of] Suffolk, [William Cecil, Earl of] Salisbury, and Robert Naunton, to [? the Bailiffs]. Instructing them to take the outstanding subscriptions to the [forced] loan and return them to the commissioners (enclosed: draft heading for certificate of defaulters, with notes of sums of money due from wards)

HD 36/A/110   18 May 1632
Thomas [Earl of] Suffolk [Lord Lieutenant], Suffolk House, to the Bailiffs and the other Ipswich Deputy Lieutenants. Instructing them to carry out orders contained in [formerly] enclosed letter of the Privy Council *re* musters

HD 36/A/111   16 Jun. 1632
Thomas [Earl of] Suffolk [Lord Lieutenant], from the Court at Greenwich, to the Deputy Lieutenants of Ipswich. Ordering them to pay the town's contribution to the arrears of salary of Captain Woodhouse, the Mustermaster of Suffolk

HD 36/A/112   22 Jun. 1632
Order of the Privy Council. On petition of Henry Church of Ipswich, miller, against the Bailiffs and burgesses, for misconduct [Church was tenant of Horswade Mill, and was being sued by the Corporation for rent arrears and breach of covenant – *see* Richardson 1884, 449]

HD 36/A/113   1 Feb. 1635
W[illiam] Cage [one of the Justices of Ipswich], London, to [Edward] Keene and [Thomas] Seelye, Bailiffs. *Re* raising of further sums of Ship Money, and the difficulties of doing so

HD 36/A/114   8 Apr. 1636
Edmund Poley, Badley, to William Moyses and John Barber, Bailiffs, and William Cadge [Cage] and Robert Sparrowe. *Re* raising of men for the forces

HD 36/A/115   23 Aug., 20 Sep. 1637
Accounts for dinner given by the Corporation to Sir John Brampston, Lord Chief Justice of the
King's Bench, and Mr Justice Crooke, at Ipswich Assizes. With warrants by William Cage and
William Tyler, Bailiffs, to Samuel Donckon and Henry Chaplen, Chamberlains, for payment
(2 docs)

HD 36/A/116   9 Feb. 1638
T[homas] Meautys, Muster-Master General, from the Star Chamber, to the Bailiffs and
Alderman [sic]. Ordering them to pay a pension to James Farr, an old soldier who was
impressed at Ipswich, back-dated to the death of John Clapham, a former pensioner

HD 36/A/117   13 Apr. 1638
John Sicklemor and William Sparowe [Bailiffs], to Robert Clarke and Ellis Coleman, Chamberlains. Warrant for payment of £63 7s 3d to Isaac —— [missing], Peter Fisher, John Warner
and Robert Donckon, for their expenses for entertainment of the judges at the last Lent Assizes

HD 36/A/118   8 Mar. 1639
[? —— Brune], Thomas Glemham, George Le Hunte, Roger North and Edward Poley [Deputy
Lieutenants], Stowmarket, to the Bailiffs. Instructing them to have 45 trained men ready
equipped for military service at York or elsewhere

HD 36/A/119   n.d.[post 11 Oct. 1642]
By [Sir] Francis Bacon [Judge of the King's Bench]. 'Exceptions taken in arrest of judgment in
a cause depending [in the Ipswich Court] between John Barker, plaintiff and Samuel Cake,
defendant'

HD 36/A/120   n.d.[between 1639 and 1642]
Thomas Weekes to the Bailiffs and Peter Fisher and Master Duncon, 2 of the commissioners
for the advance of the Scots. The bearer is to collect the unpaid money levied on Ipswich for the
advance of the Scots, according to the ordinance

HD 36/A/121   13 Jul. 1643
William Cage [one of the Justices of Ipswich], to the Bailiffs and Deputy Lieutenants of
Ipswich. News of movements of the King's and Queen's forces; advice to put the town in a state
of readiness for defence

HD 36/A/122   post 1 Apr. 1644
'A note of such money as John Howell have laid out since Michaelmas last for the weekly
assessments and other taxations for the affairs of the kingdom'

HD 36/A/123   28 Oct. 1644
Richard Pupplet, Joseph Pemberton, William Cage, John Sicklemor, John Aldus, Daniel
Alldred and John Brandlinge [Bailiffs and ? Deputy Lieutenants], to the constables of the East
Ward. Warrant to give notice to all persons [named] appointed to arms to prepare them and
show them on the Cornhill the next Thursday. Twelve additional men are to be appointed and
provided with arms

HD 36/A/124   14 Nov. 1644
William Cage [MP for Ipswich], London, to [Richard] Puplett and [Joseph] Pemberton,
Bailiffs. Re 'the town causes now in suit' and his assistance to Mr Chaplyn [the town's
attorney]

HD 36/A/125   5 Dec. 1644
Edward Tilly, Bury St Edmunds, to the Bailiffs. Asking him to send to him next Tuesday or
Wednesday all money so far collected for the weekly tax, for delivery to Cambridge

HD 36/A/126   6 Dec. 1644
Edward Rede, Henry North, ? W. Springe, W. Bokenham, Thomas Blosse and Thomas Gippes,
Bury St Edmunds, to the Bailiffs and the rest of the Committee for Ipswich. Asking them to
attend a meeting at Bury next Tuesday to consult about the safety of the county

HD 36/A/127   6 Dec. 1644
Lord Grey of Werk, Speaker of the House of Peers, and William Lenthall, Speaker of the
Commons, Westminster, to the Committee in Ipswich appointed by ordinance of Parliament,
18 Oct. 1644, for the assessment to be made there for the relief of the British army in Ireland. *Re*
raising the money for the above purpose

HD 36/A/128   18 Dec. 1644
John Tolye, Mayor of Norwich, from Norwich, to the Bailiffs. Expressing his inability to trace
one Smith in St Andrew's parish; he 'cannot hear of any who sold any such goods as you
mention' elsewhere in the city, but will continue his efforts for the advancement of justice

HD 36/A/129   24 Dec. 1644
[? The Bailiffs] to [Christopher] Glascock. Informing him that he has been 'gladly and freely'
elected Master of the Grammar School; arrangements for his removal to Ipswich [unsigned
copy. Christopher Glascock, MA, St Catherine's College, Cambridge, elected Master 19 Dec.
1644 (*see* Richardson 1884, 539); Master of Felsted School, 1650–90]

HD 36/A/130   8 Jan. 1645
Edmund Harvey, Maurice Barrow, W. Spring, John Rous and Isaac Appleton, Bury St Edmunds,
to the Bailiffs and Deputy Lieutenants of Ipswich. Requesting them to dispatch their ordnance
with all speed and return their lists to the writers

HD 36/A/131   24 Jan. 1645
Edward Lelang, Bury St Edmunds, to the Bailiffs, Recorder and the rest of the Committee of
Ipswich. Asking them to issue their warrants for raising the town's proportion of the first
six months' assessment and of the £500 for maintenance of the garrison of Newport; all
'recovered' soldiers in the town are to be sent back to their colours

HD 36/A/132   17 Feb. 1645
Thomas Rainborowe, Grantham, to the Bailiffs. Asking them to 'lay up' any of his soldiers they
may find; he has had 'nere 200 runn within a month' [On Rainborowe, *see DNB*]

HD 36/A/133   3 Mar. 1645
[Sir] John Meldrum, Scarborough, to the Bailiffs and Burgesses. Requesting the town's assistance in money, victuals or powder, for maintenance of Scarborough for the Parliament; with
an account of his difficulties [Meldrum was killed at Scarborough this year; *see DNB*]

HD 36/A/134   n.d.[Mar. 1645]
[The Bailiffs] to [Sir John Meldrum, Scarborough]. In response to HD 36/A/133, they have
resolved on a speedy collection throughout the town for the troops before Scarborough Castle
[draft]

HD 36/A/135   n.d.[Mar. 1645]
[The Bailiffs] to [Sir John Meldrum, Scarborough]. They have raised £140 to enable his troops
to take Scarborough Castle, and ask how it is to be paid [draft]

HD 36/A/136   15 Mar. 1645
W. Say & Seale [William Fiennes, 1st Viscount Saye and Sele] and [*signature illegible*], Darby
House, in the name of the Committee of both Kingdoms, to the Ipswich Committee for the
assessment for the relief of the army in Ireland. Requesting their speedy accounting for the
money overdue on the town's assessment

HD 36/A/137   4 Apr. 1645
Edmund Harvey, W. Spring, Thomas ——— [*illegible*], Gibson Lucas, John Sudbury and
Thomas Gippes, members of the Committee at Bury St Edmunds, to [? the Bailiffs and Deputy
Lieutenants of Ipswich]. Order for Ipswich soldiers at Stowmarket to come to Bury, where
clothing, pay and conduct money are provided, if they can come at once; if not, they are to
return to Ipswich and come to Bury next Thursday, and in the meantime to receive 6*d* per day
allowance

HD 36/A/138   9 Apr. 1645
(a) William Lenthall, Speaker of the House of Commons, to the Suffolk Committee.
Urging speedy contributions of men, horse and money for the army
(b) Thomas Hodges, John Potts, Thomas Purry, W. Heaveningham, Robert Scawen, Valentine
Wauton and Anthony Bedingfeild, for the Committee for the Army, to the Suffolk Committee.
On the same subject
[2 copy letters, on the same sheet]

HD 36/A/139   *c.*16 Apr. 1645
Account of money received of John Ford (total £332 3*s* 6*d*), 1642–1645

HD 36/A/140   26 Apr. 1645
W. Heveningham, John Sudbury, Samuel Moody, Thomas Chaplin and Thomas Gippes [on
behalf of the Bury Committee], Bury St Edmunds, to the Bailiffs and the rest of the Committee
of Ipswich. Originally enclosing a warrant; they are to send in their proportion for the town at
the same time as other soldiers now in the division

HD 36/A/141   30 Apr. 1645
[Sir] John Meldrum, Scarborough, to Richard Pupplet and Joseph Pemberton, Bailiffs. Asking
for the £140 collected to be sent as quickly as possible, since Scarborough Castle cannot be
taken until the soldiers receive the month's pay promised them when they took the town; with
note of contributions already sent by Lynn and Yarmouth

HD 36/A/142   —— Apr. 1645
W. Heveningham, John Sudbury, Samuel Moody, Thomas Gippes and Thomas Chaplin, on
behalf of the Bury Committee, to the Chief Constables of the Hundreds. Ordering them to issue
warrants to the Petty Constables to levy their proportion of the 400 men charged on the county
for Sir Thomas Fairfax's army, and send them fully equipped to Bury; Petty Constables are to
bring with them 1*s* impress money and 2*s* conduct money for each soldier

HD 36/A/143   1 May 1645
W. Springe, Maurice Barrowe, W. Heveningham, Samuel Moody and Thomas Chaplin, for the
Committee at Bury St Edmunds, to the Chief Constables of Stow, Samford and Bosmere and
Claydon Hundreds. Requesting lists of soldiers in every township, returns *re* enforcement of
'the Church Discipline' and of persons taking the National Covenant, *re* maimed soldiers,
supplies of ammunition, 'posture of defence' and sequestered lands with profits thereon [copy]

HD 36/A/144   8 May 1645
John ? Smythier and Thomas Deye [Town Clerk of Ipswich], London, to the Bailiffs. *Re*
progress of proceedings in a cause brought by the borough in the London courts

HD 36/A/145   13 May 1645
W. Soams, W. Heveningham, Thomas Tirell, Samuel Moody and Thomas Chaplain [for the
Committee at Bury St Edmunds], Bury, to the Bailiffs. Jacob Caley, chosen captain of a foot
company in Ipswich is to be in the regiment of Col Harvey, colonel for Ipswich Division, and is
to choose field officers

HD 36/A/146   19 May 1645
Abraham Chilld, Norwich, to Richard Puplette and Joseph Pembruke [Pemberton], Bailiffs.
Agreeing to pay £140 to Sir John Meldrum [at Scarborough] on their behalf

HD 36/A/147   1 Jun. 1645
P. Wharton and ? F. Houston, for the Committee of both Kingdoms of relief of the British army
in Ireland, from Derby House, to the Ipswich Committee. Requesting additional assessments
and levies, and effective collection of arrears

HD 36/A/148   4 Jun. 1645
Nathaniel Bacon [Recorder of Ipswich], Cambridge, to the Bailiffs and Deputy Lieutenants of
Ipswich. Report on the military situation: troops from the eastern counties are moving into

Cambridgeshire; Royalist assault on Leicester and advance into Rutland; movements of Cromwell and Fairfax

HD 36/A/149   6 Jun. 1645
Thomas Baker, Gibson Lucas, Thomas Bacon, John Sudbury, Thomas Gippes [for the Bury Committee], Bury St Edmunds, to the Bailiffs, Deputy Lieutenants and Committee of Ipswich. The enemy is on the march towards the Association; they are to advance with their horse to Newmarket and send as many foot as possible to rendezvous at Bury

HD 36/A/150   6 Jun. 1645
William Cage [MP for Ipswich], London, to [Richard] Puplett and [Joseph] Pemberton, Bailiffs. *Re* borough business, progress of the borough's lawsuits, and his state of health

HD 36/A/151   7 Jun. 1645
Nathaniel Bacon [Recorder], Cambridge, to the Bailiffs and Deputy Lieutenants.
Advance of the enemy towards Northampton: movements of Parliamentary forces and the Scots. Postcript emphasises gravity of the situation and confidence in Sir Thomas Fairfax

HD 36/A/152   12 Jun. 1645
William Cage, [London], to [Richard] Puplett and [Joseph] Pemberton, Bailiffs. *Re* progress of the borough's lawsuits

HD 36/A/153   13 Jun. 1645
[? the Bailiffs], Ipswich to ? Asking the recipient to return and pay the town's soldiers sent to guard 'the fort' during 'the late suddaine Alarum' in which his regiment was called away [unsigned draft]

HD 36/A/154   14 Jun. 1645
Nathaniel Bacon, Huntingdon, directed first to W. ? Heveningham at Bury St Edmunds, thence to be forwarded to Francis Bacon at Shrubland Hall, then to the Bailiffs of Ipswich. First news of the battle of Naseby

HD 36/A/155   19 Jun. 1645
Thomas Deye [Town Clerk of Ipswich], London, 'late at night', to the Bailiffs. *Re* progress of the borough's 2 lawsuits. Sir Thomas Fairfax has re-taken Leicester, the Scots have reached Nottingham, and Col Massey has gone to relieve Taunton

HD 36/A/156   30 Jun. 1645
P. Wharton and ? F. Houston, for the Committee of both Kingdoms for the relief of the British armies in Ireland, Derby House, to the Ipswich Committee for the same purpose. Asking them to make further levies of money beyond those laid down by the Ordinance of 18 Oct. last

HD 36/A/157   4 Jul. 1645
William Cage [MP for Ipswich], [? London], to 'his son' [*sic*], Thomas Deye [Town Clerk], Ipswich. *Re* recovery of the money contributed to the garrison of Scarborough under Sir John Meldrum, and detained at Hull

HD 36/A/158   4 Jul. 1645
Richard Pupplet and Joseph Pemberton, Bailiffs, to the Mayor of Harwich. Protesting that 2 men infected with the plague have been sent from Harwich to Ipswich (on the excuse that the master of their ship is an Ipswich man) with a Harwich townswoman and her child, at whose house the 2 men lodged; returning all the parties to Harwich herewith

HD 36/A/159   15 Jul. 1645
W. Heveningham, B. Bacon, John Wentworth, Maurice Barrowe, W. Spring, Edmund Harvey, Gibson Lucas, B. Gurdon and Thomas Tirell [for the Bury Committee], Bury St Edmunds, to the Bailiffs. Offence caused by Ipswich's failure to contribute either horse or foot during 'this last alarum'; asking what horse they propose to raise for defence of the county; their proportion of the 500 foot is to be ready on Tuesday

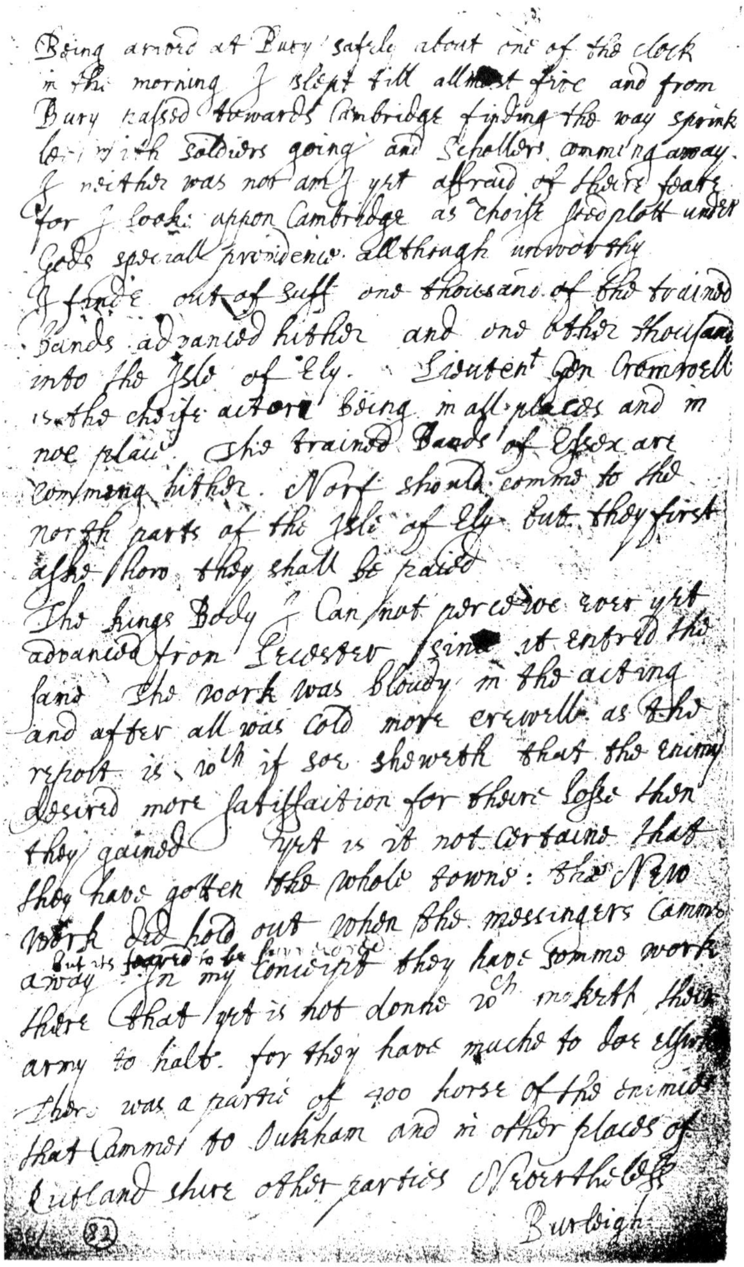

Being arrived at Bury safely about one of the clock
in the morning I slept till allmost five and from
Bury passed towards Cambridge finding the way sprink
led with souldiers going and Schollers comming away.
I neither was nor am I yet affraid of theire feare
for I looke uppon Cambridge as cheife seedplott under
Gods speciall providence allthough unworthy
I finde out of Suff one thousand of the traind
bands advanced hither and one other thousand
into the Isle of Ely. Lieutent Gen Cromwell
is the cheife actor being in all places and in
noe place. The traind Bands of Essex are
comming hither. Norf should comme to the
north parts of the Isle of Ely but they first
aske whoe they shall be paide
The kings Body I can not perceive ever yet
advanced from Leicester since it entred the
same. The worke was bloudy in the acting
and after all was cold more cruell as the
report is, wch if soe sheweth that the enimy
desired more satisfaction for theire losse then
they gained. Yet is it not certaine that
they have gotten the whole towne: the New
worke did hold out when the messingers camme
away. but its feared to be now worse [?] In my conceipt they have somme worke
there that yet is not donne wch maketh their
army to halt. for they have muche to doe elswhere
There was a partie of 400 horse of the enimies
that cammed to Oakham and in other places of
Rutland shire other parties Nevertheless
Burleigh
36/ (82)

Fig. 23. In a letter dated 4 June 1645 from Cambridge to the Bailiffs and Deputy Lieutenants of Ipswich, Nathaniel Bacon [Recorder of Ipswich and Chairman of the Eastern Association Committee], reports on the military situation: troops from the eastern counties moving into Cambridgeshire; Royalist assault on Leicester and advance into Rutland; movements of Cromwell and Fairfax.
(Borough correspondence HD 36/A/148)

HD 36/A/160   25 Jul. [?1645]
Thomas ? Cole, W. Heveningham and Edmund Harvey [for the Bury Committee], Bury St Edmunds, to the Bailiffs. Charging the town with provision of 7 horses and 3 dragoons

HD 36/A/161   31 Jul. [1645]
Peregrine Hoby, MP for Ipswich, Westminster, to the Bailiffs. Certifying good character of the son of a neighbour, and Ipswich man, accused of poisoning wine at Reading; asking them to inform Mr Cage of the surrender of the King's garrison at Bath to Sir Thomas Fairfax

HD 36/A/162   1 Aug. 1645
Edmund Harvey, Bury St Edmunds, to the Bailiffs. Explaining that the 7 horses and 3 dragoons charged on Ipswich by HD 36/A/160 were agreed by the Committee and entered by the book; the circumstances of the decision

HD 36/A/163   25 Aug. 1645
John Sudbury, Samuel Moody and Thomas Chaplin [for the Bury Committee], Bury St Edmunds, 'by one of the clock in the morning', to the Bailiffs, Deputy Lieutenants and Committee of Ipswich. The enemy has advanced this way as far as Huntingdon, driving some of the parliamentary forces before them; they are to send their troop of horse forthwith to Bury, the foot to follow as quickly as possible; 'the alarum holds very strong'

HD 36/A/164   25 Aug. 1645
W. Spring, Maurice Barrowe, Thomas Gippes, Thomas Chaplin and Samuel Moody [for the Bury Committee], to the Bailiffs, 'haste, haste, haste'. Capture of Huntingdon and enemy advance; they are to hasten their foot and horse with all possible speed to prevent the enemy from reaching Cambridge

HD 36/A/165   10 Oct. 1645
Nathaniel Bacon [Recorder] to the Bailiffs. Notifying them of his election as Burgess for the University [of Cambridge]; he will stay at Ipswich for a fortnight on his way to London and hold a court. He has not 'cast off the care of the town' and will continue to serve it. Parliamentary troop movements

HD 36/A/166   9 Nov. 1645
John Maulyverer [Colonel; Parliamentary govenor of Hull, 1646] and N. Denham, Kingston upon Hull, to the Bailiffs. Protesting against the request of Mr Child for repayment of the £140 contributed by Ipswich for the siege of Scarborough, revoked on the death of Sir John Meldrum to whom it was to have been paid

HD 36/A/167   10 Nov. 1645
W. Heveningham and Thomas Chapline [for the Bury Committee], Bury St Edmunds, to the Bailiffs and Committee for Ipswich. Originally enclosing a copy warrant for raising the last 2 months' money for Sir Thomas Fairfax; requesting speedy collection of the money

HD 36/A/168   21 Nov. 1645
William Sparrow and Richard Haile, Bailiffs, to [Col John Mauleverer, Hull]. In reply to HD 36/A/166; requesting repayment of the money in question, in view of 'the great necessities of the inhabitants of this town' [signed draft or copy, unaddressed]

HD 36/A/169   22 Dec. 1645
John Barbur to the Bailiffs. Protesting about his tax assessment, especially in view of the cost of keeping his son at Cambridge and 'parllament charges'

HD 36/A/170   n.d. [? 1645]
Francis Hesilrige, Francis Bacon, John Gurdon, Peter Temple and — [*illegible*] to the Bailiffs and Aldermen [*sic*]. Requesting charitable contributions for the relief of 'the poor town and many of the inhabitants of the county of Leicester' [Leicester Castle was dismantled by the Royalists, 1645]

HD 36/A/171   5 Jan. 1646
Matthew Lawrence, Ipswich, to [? the Bailiffs]. Accepting the post of Public Lecturer at £100 a year, in the place of Samuel Ward

HD 36/A/172   23 Mar. 1646
Edward Lelang, for the Bury Committee, Bury St Edmunds, to the Bailiffs. *Re* collection of money for the poor and distressed town of Leicester

HD 36/A/173   24 Mar. 1646
George Carter, pastor of Elmsett, Richard Glanvile, Edward Salter, John Hayward and John Blosse, Elmsett, to [? the Bailiffs]. Asking them to release Henry Hamond from the 'press', to serve his master Richard Clyfford and maintain his widowed mother

HD 36/A/174   9 Apr. 1646
— Deyy, Edmund Harvey, John Cotton, Maurice Barrowe, W. Spring and Samuel Moody [for the Bury Committee], Bury St Edmunds, to the Bailiffs and Committee for Ipswich. Giving notice of further taxes on the county, and that Thursday 16 Apr. is to be a day of thanksgiving for the great success in the west against Sir Ralph Hopton and the victory over Sir Jacob Ashly and his forces

HD 36/A/175   2 Jun. 1646
W. Heveningham, William Bloys, Thomas Blosse, Edward Pelam, Alderman, and Robert Dunkon, for the Bury Committee, to the Bailiffs. Informing them of the rating of the monthly sum in the county ordered on 15 Feb. last, to be continued until 1 Oct. next; ordering them to appoint parochial collectors; Parliament is now discussing taxation and this is a temporary measure to maintain the army before Oxford

HD 36/A/176   9 Jun. 1646
Matthew Lawrence [Public Lecturer], Ipswich, to the Bailiffs and Assembly. *Re* dispute with the Bailiffs as to whether he should leave Ipswich and return to Lincolnshire; lengthy account of his reasons for wishing to depart

HD 36/A/177   14 Aug. [1646]
Nathaniel Bacon, Grays Inn [London], to the Bailiffs. *Re* debate on dispersal of ordnance from Cambridge; the Eastern Association considers Ipswich a suitable place for it; he asks the Bailiffs for their opinion, and gives an inventory of the ordnance [*see* the Borough Assembly Book for 17 Aug.1646]

HD 36/A/178   15 Aug. 1646
Edward Lelang, ? R Pepys, Samuel Moody, Thomas Gipps and Thomas Chaplin, for the Bury Committee, to the town of Ipswich. By virtue of Parliament's ordinance for demolishing the garrisons of Newport Pagnell, Cambridge, Huntingdon and Bedford and the supplying of the forces in Ireland, the assessment is to be continued for 3 months; money collected is to be paid to Lionel Bacon of Higham

HD 36/A/179   17 Aug. 1646
Edward Lelam, by direction of the Bury Committee, to the Bailiffs and Committee of Ipswich. Originally enclosing a copy warrant for collecting money in Ipswich

HD 36/A/180   20 Aug. 1646
Nathaniel Bacon to the Bailiffs. Promising to do what he can to have the magazine transferred from Cambridge to Ipswich. 'All our endeavour now is to disband the army and get the Scots home'; Scots' requirement for money; this should 'lay all assessments dead but that of Ireland'

HD 36/A/181   24 Aug. 1646
Edward Lelam, ? R. Pepys, Thomas Chaplin, Samuel Moody and Thomas Gippes [for the Bury Committee], Bury St Edmunds, to the Bailiffs and Committee of Ipswich. Letters have been received from the Committee of the Eastern Association for speedy payment of all arrears of money for Newport Pagnell and other garrisons; Ipswich's contribution is to be collected as quickly as possible

HD 36/A/182   10 Feb. 1647
John Rous, ? Thomas Ringham and Edward ? Rede, Halesworth, to the Bailiffs. Asking for the examination of William Hare, now in Ipswich gaol, suspected of being involved with Robert Barker of Halesworth, carrier, in a case of felony

HD 36/A/183   21 Aug. 1649
John Smythier, Ipswich, to ——. Requesting release of officers and seamen imprisoned in Ipswich

HD 36/A/184   19 Sep. 1649
Gilbert Millington, for the Committee for Plundered Ministers. Order, on petition of Robert Devereux, to whom the rectory of Hepworth is sequestered, referring him to the Justices of the Peace for aid in recovering tithes and profits from Robert Shepheard sen., Thomas Abbott, Richard Huffe, Samuel Pett sen. and Nicholas Frost

HD 36/A/185   22 Dec. 1649
Assessment by Lawrence Stisted, Thomas Griggs and Thomas Carter, assessors of MG, by virtue of a warrant from the Bailiffs and Justices, on all householders who brew their own beer

HD 36/A/186   10 Mar. [? later 1640s]
Nathaniel Darell, Melford, to the Town Clerk. Asking him to assist the bearers, his corporals, in execution of their orders

HD 36/A/187   n.d. [? later 1640s]
Thoms Wade, Axe Yard, King Street, Westminster, to Thomas Cullom 'at the sign of the ship, a wooling draper in Tower Street'. *Re* quartering of soldiers from 16 Jan. to 13 Mar.

HD 36/A/188   26 Sep. 1651
Peter Fisher and Robert Dunkon [Bailiffs], to Nicholas Sicklemore and Thomas Griggs, Chamberlains. Warrant for payment of 5*s* to William Hemson for ringing on 4 occasions when the Bailiffs went to Ulveston Hall [Debenham] and the bounds of the town

HD 36/A/189   n.d. [? 1652]
[? The Bailiffs] to the Committee for the Affairs of the Admiralty and Navy and to Lord General C[romwell] or the Council of State. *Re* provision for sick and wounded seamen sent by Admirals Monck and Blake; complaining that the surgeons sent from London wish to use the hospital, thus endangering the poor children and free school if infection should break out (3 draft letters on 1 leaf)

HD 36/A/190   28 May 1653
N. Bourne, Lee [? Leigh (Essex)] to the Bailiffs. By order of the Council of State he has fitted out several ships for sudden service; asks for assistance in pressing able seamen and sending them on board the 'Waymouth' pink, Capt Willkinson commander
[Nehemiah Bourne, major in the Parliamentary army; captain in the Navy on remodelling of the fleet, *c*.1649; rear-admiral, 1652; commissioner for equipment of fleets, 1652; emigrated to America on Restoration. *See DNB*]

HD 36/A/191   5 Jun. 1653
N[ehemiah] Bourne, Harwich, on board the 'Tyger' frigate, to the Bailiffs, 'for the special service of the Commonwealth'. Informing them that he has sent a number of sick men to Ipswich, and is sending a list of them by the lieutenant of the 'Tyger'

HD 36/A/192   Jun. 1653
George Monck [Admiral] and Robert Blake [General at Sea], on board the 'Restoration', to the Chief Magistrate of Yarmouth or any other port. Men wounded in the late engagement with the Dutch are being sent to his town for care

HD 36/A/193   16 Jun. 1653
Nathaniel Bacon, Doctor's Commons, to [?the Bailiffs]. Informing them that he has delivered their letter *re* the cost of providing for [wounded] men to the Commissioners of the Admiralty

HD 36/A/194   17 Jun. 1653
Thomas Smith, Robert Thomson and E. Hopkins, from the Navy Office, to the Mayor [*sic*] and
other magistrates of Ipswich, 7p.m. Sick or wounded men from the fleet arriving at Ipswich are
to be provided for at a rate not exceeding 7*s* a week per man, excluding physick; the magistrates
are to charge bills of exchange payable by the Court of Prize Goods, and send them to the Navy
Office for payment

HD 36/A/195   18 Jun. 1653
Matthew Thomlinson, President of the Council of State, Whitehall, to [? the Bailiffs].
Requesting them to assist the physician and surgeons sent to attend the sick and wounded sent
from the fleet to Ipswich after 'the late fight at sea'; for payment of their expenses they are to
draw a bill of exchange on Richard Hutchinson, Treasurer for the Navy

HD 36/A/196   8 Jul. 1653
George Monck [Admiral], from 'Resolution', at anchor in Southwold Bay, to the Bailiffs. He is
unwilling to overcharge the town with sick men, and is willing for some of them to be quartered
in neighbouring villages, provided that the same care is taken of them

HD 36/A/197   8 Jul. 1653
N[ehemiah] Bourne [Commissioner for equipment of fleets], Ipswich, to the Bailiffs.
Requesting them to arrest all deserters from the fleet, and return their names and ships to him at
Harwich

HD 36/A/198   9 Jul. 1653
Robert Dunkon and Jacob Caley, Westminster, to Richard Pupplet and Nicholas Phillips,
Bailiffs. *Re* reimbursement of money expended for sick and wounded seamen and for
ammunition

HD 36/A/199   9 Jul. 1653
N[ehemiah] Bourne [Commissioner for equipment of fleets], Harwich, to the Bailiffs.
Stating, in reply to their letter, his agreement to the distribution of some of the sick men into
convenient places near Ipswich. He will consider their suggestion of Manningtree as a place
suitable for reception of the sick; thanks for arrest of deserting seamen

HD 36/A/200   14 Jul. 1653
Robert Dunkon [? and Jacob Caley – 2nd signature cut away], London, to Richard Pupplett and
Nicholas Phillips, Bailiffs. *Re* 'the accompt for the sicke and wounded soldiers' and their nego-
tiations with the Commissioners for the Admiralty

HD 36/A/201   15 Jul. 1653
Robert Thomson and E. Hopkins, from the Navy Office, to the Bailiffs and chief magistrates
of Ipswich, 'for the speciall affaires of the State'. At the orders of the Commissioners of
Admiralty they have written to the Commissioners of Prize Goods to provide money for relief
of sick and wounded men discharged from the fleet in and around Ipswich; the Bailiffs should
apply for payment to the Sub-Commissioners of Prize Goods in their area (apparently
despatched on 16 July, since this date appears below the address)

HD 36/A/202   21 Jul. 1653
Robert Dunkon and Jacob Caley, London, to the Bailiffs. *Re* their efforts to obtain money for
the borough from the Committee of Admiralty and Navy

HD 36/A/203   25 Jul. 1653
Robert Dunkon and Jacob Caley, London, to the Bailiffs. On the same subject

HD 36/A/204   25 Jul. 1653
E[dward] Mountagu [afterwards Earl of Sandwich], President, by order of the Council of State,
to the Bailiffs. Order to publish the accompanying declarations of the Parliament of the Commonwealth of England

HD 36/A/205   5 Aug. 1653
George Monck [Admiral], from 'Resolution', Southwold Bay, to the Bailiffs. Requesting them to stop and examine all seamen passing through Ipswich, to secure all except those having an order from Monck, and send them to Major Nehemiah Bourne, one of the Commissioners of the Navy, at Harwich

HD 36/A/206   8 Aug. 1653
N[ehemiah] Bourne, Harwich, to the Bailiffs. *Re* transfer from the fleet to Ipswich of sick and wounded, including the Dutch commander and some eminent officers, to be safely secured as prisoners

HD 36/A/207   16 Aug. 1653
Richard Pupplet and Nicholas Philips [Bailiffs], Ipswich, to 'Colonel Monck, General at Sea'. Informing him that they have almost 1,000 sick and wounded soldiers and seamen in Ipswich, and no more money to relieve them; requesting his order to Mr Weekes, Solicitor for the Assessments of the county, to provide money until further order be taken

HD 36/A/208   18 Aug. 1653
Robert Dunkon and Jacob Caley, from their lodgings in Whitehall, to the Bailiffs. Their efforts to obtain money from the Commissioners of the Admiralty for the care of sick and wounded sailors; they have obtained £500 on account

HD 36/A/209   25 Aug. 1653
Daniel Whisler, Aldborough [Aldeburgh], to the Bailiffs. Requesting them, on behalf of General Monck, to pay the bearer, William Greene, a surgeon sent to take care of sick and wounded men at Ipswich, for a fortnight's attendance at 6*s* per day

HD 36/A/210   26 Aug. 1653
George Monck, from 'Resolution' in Aldeburgh Road, to the Bailiffs. Asking them to send such sick and wounded seamen as are recovered to Major Nehemiah Bourne, a Commissioner of the Navy at Harwich; their expenses are to be repaid by the Collectors for Prize Goods there

HD 36/A/211   27 Aug. 1653
N[ehemiah] Bourne, Harwich, to the Bailiffs. Since 'our men fall sick abord the shipps in the harbour beyond our expectation' and the town is very full, he is sending them 24 sick men; requests that the recovered men may be sent back, 'for we have opertunity to send them away'

HD 36/A/212   19 Sep. 1653
[? the Bailiffs] to the Constables of Ingatestone (Essex) and — . 2 draft letters, asking the recipients to provide one night's quarters for those sick and wounded soldiers and seamen whom the doctors and surgeons consider fit to be sent to the London hospitals

HD 36/A/213   25 Sep. 1653
Account of Mr Haggarth of Ipswich, surgeon, for £27 18*s* for caring for sick and wounded men there (signed Ralph Bathurst, and Thomas Burton and Henry Jackson, surgeons)

HD 36/A/214   5 Oct. 1653
Thomas Peake, Mayor of Colchester, to the Bailiffs. Complaining of the behaviour of the surgeons and waggoners in charge of the sick and wounded [on their way to London] in demanding free quarters; requesting them to let the bearer know if Parliament has ordered free quarters; and requesting a list of the names of any further men who must have free quarters

HD 36/A/215   9 Nov. 1653
N[ehemiah] Bourne [Commissioner of the Navy], Harwich, to Mr Clarke, Ipswich. Requesting that John Ascott of the Malaga merchant ship now in the State's service, sent ashore sick and now in Ipswich, be given the same allowance as other sick and wounded

HD 36/A/216   11 Nov. 1653
N[ehemiah] Bourne, Harwich, to the Bailiffs, 'for the special service of the State'. Many seamen absent from the State's ships at Harwich are being entertained in public houses in Ipswich; offering to send some of his officers to assist in restraining them

HD 36/A/217   15 Nov. 1653
Thomas Vallis, Harwich, to the Bailiffs. Asking them to order the Ipswich constables to search
for John Browne, formerly servant to Henry Robinson of CL, pressed last week by the boat-
swain of the frigate 'Expedition', who escaped by stealing a boat

HD 36/A/218   30 Nov. 1653
Samuel Ward, Joseph Larke, Samuel Cooper and Methuselah Turner, Commissioners for Sick
and Wounded, from Little Britaine, to John Aldus and Emanuel Sorrell, Bailiffs. *Re* transfer
from Ipswich of the sick and wounded from the fleet

HD 36/A/219   1 Dec. 1653
Robert Dunkon and Jacob Caley [London], to [John] Aldus and [Manuel] Sorrell, Bailiffs.
Their continuing efforts to obtain money from the Commissioners of the Admiralty for care of
the sick and wounded of Ipswich

HD 36/A/220   3 Jan. 1654
John Alldous and Manuell Sorrell [Bailiffs], to Mr Cuzings and Mr Coale, Chamberlains.
Warrant for payment of 11*s* 8*d* to Simond Bacon for his wages for cleaning the Cornhill and
Butchery, for quarter ending 25 Dec. 1653

HD 36/A/221   14 Jan. 1654
Humden Hart, Falkenham, to the Bailiffs and Burgesses. *Re* his alleged misdemeanours as a
tenant; offers to justify himself against his accusers (badly discoloured and partly illegible)

HD 36/A/222   3 Feb. 1654
Nicholas Foster, from frigate 'Phoenix', to the Bailiffs. Requesting them to assist the bearer to
press 30 men for service on 'Phoenix', ordered to sea on immediate special service; some of her
crew are sick and not fit to go to sea

HD 36/A/223   7 Feb. 1654
[The Bailiffs] to the constables of Ipswich. Warrant to impress men for service on the 'Phoenix'
frigate (on dorse: scriptural notes, perhaps for a sermon)

HD 36/A/224   21 Feb. 1654
Examination of Edward Hatfield of Shadwell (Middlesex), mariner, taken before R. Brewster
and T. Brewster. *Re* his marriage to Mary Betts of All Hallows the Less, London, and adultery
with Ann Scier of Walberswick

HD 36/A/225   20 Jul. 1654
Joseph Larke and Samuel Cooper [? Commissioners for the sick and wounded], Little Brittaine,
to the Bailiffs. *Re* payments for wounded Dutch seamen at Ipswich, and their repatriation

HD 36/A/226   n.d. [? between 1652 and 1654]
[? Nathaniel Bacon] to 'Your Excellency'. *Re* dispute between some of Captain Gibbons's
troop quartered near Ipswich and the town, concerning 'a misdemeanour committed by four or
five of those troopers in the view of the sessions of the Gaol delivery then assembled' (Draft)

HD 36/A/227   n.d. [? between 1652 and 1654]
[? The Bailiffs] to [? the Commissioners of the Navy]. Stating that since the last engagement
with the Dutch, 320 sick and wounded men have been received; asking that no more be sent.
Many of them have 'pestilential fevers' (Draft)

HD 36/A/228   28 Jun. 1655
John Smythier, Henry Whiting, Richard Pupplet, John Brandlinge, Nicholas Philips, Richard
Jeninges, Manuel Sorrell and Richard Hayle, to Jacob Caley, Receiver of Mr Martin's
Revenues. Warrant for payment of £7 to Robert Noble, a poor scholar, for his stipend for the
half year ended last mid-summer, allowed him out of Martin's Gift

HD 36/A/229   7 Sep. 1655
Henry Lawrence, President, by Order of the Council, Whitehall, to the Bailiffs. Order that
persons arriving from the United Provinces should be prevented from leaving their ships for 20
days, so that those infected with pestilence should not enter the country

HD 36/A/230   13 Sep. 1655
Martin Noell and George Clerke, London, on behalf of Secretary of State Thurloe, to [? the Bailiffs]. On complaint by Jason Grover, postmaster of Ipswich, that the mail was interrupted in Ipswich by pretended constables, for travelling on the sabbath, which the Protector and Council take as an affront to their authority

HD 36/A/231   15 Sep. 1655
[? The Bailiffs] to Nathaniel Bacon, Master of Requests, at his chamber in Grays Inn, London. In response to HD 36/A/230; they know that letters of state should be allowed to pass on the sabbath, but the passage of private letters is a breach of the strict keeping of it; they will submit to a public declaration that the public post is to pass on the Lord's day

HD 36/A/232   6 Oct. 1655
Acquittance by Cave Becke to Mr Feast and Mr Keine, Chamberlains of Ipswich, for £12 3s 4d, for half year's stipend as Master of the Free School, due last Michaelmas. [Beck was Master of the Grammar School, 1650–1657]

HD 36/A/233   26 Oct. 1655
Henry Lawrence, President, by order of His Highness [Cromwell, Lord Protector] and the Council, Whitehall, to the Bailiffs. Originally enclosing printed copies of an order and declaration of Protector and Council, for publication within their jurisdiction

HD 36/A/234   29 Nov. 1655
Henry Lawrence, President, by order of His Highness and the Council, Whitehall, to the Bailiffs. As above

HD 36/A/235   11 Dec. 1655
John Thurloe [Secretary of State], Whitehall, to the Bailiffs and other magistrates
Originally enclosing printed proclamations of peace between the Commonwealth and France, for publication

HD 36/A/236   11 Apr. 1656
H. ? Raynes, Bury St Edmunds, to the Bailiffs and Justices. Re enforcement of rules for licensing of alehouses by the Major-Generals and Justices of the Peace

HD 36/A/237   8 Jul. 1656
John Clerke, Ed Salmon and Edward Hopkins, Whitehall, to the Bailiffs. Ordering them to apprehend seamen impressed by Mr Grassingham, the State's shipwright at Harwich, who have failed to appear for service

HD 36/A/238   25 Sep. 1656
Henry Lawrence, President, by order of the Council, Whitehall, to [? the Bailiffs]. Originally enclosing copies of a declaration by Protector and Parliament for a general fast on 30 Oct., to be published to all parishes and congregations in the town

HD 36/A/239   21 Oct. 1656
Henry Lawrence, President, by order of the Council, Whitehall, to the Bailiffs. Protector and parliament having agreed on 'the narrative herewith sent you', and appointed 5 Nov. as a day of thanksgiving, the copies originally enclosed are to be dispersed to the ministers of the congregations in the town for use as thereby directed

HD 36/A/240   10 Sep. 1657
Henry Lawrence, President, by order of the Council, Whitehall, to the Bailiffs. Originally enclosing several orders of Protector and Council appointing Wednesday 30 Sep. as a day of fasting and humiliation, for distribution to ministers

HD 36/A/241   1 Oct. 1657
John Thurloe [Secretary of State], Whitehall, to the Bailiffs. Requesting them, in the Protector's name, to take care of sick men sent from Mardyke by General Mountagu, until further order, the costs to be repaid

HD 36/A/242   3 Oct. 1657
Ed Salmon, Thomas Kelsey and Robert Beake, Whitehall, to the Bailiffs, 'for the especiall service of his Highnes'. Requesting them to take care of sick and wounded men from Mardyke, who will shortly be put ashore in Ipswich. Expenses not exceeding 12*d* per man per day will be allowed by the Commissioners for Sick and Wounded Seamen in Little Brittaine

HD 36/A/243   n.d. [? 1657]
[? Nathaniel Bacon] to John Thurloe, Secretary of State. Requesting that Ipswich be relieved of the necessity of providing for sick and wounded from Mardyke, since 3 companies of foot and a troop of horse have already been quartered there for more than 10 months [Draft; Mardyke was taken in 1657 and Bacon died in 1660]

HD 36/A/244   n.d. [between 1650 and 1657]
Acquittance by Cave Beck to Miles Wallis, Rent Warden of Ipswich, for 40*s* for his stipend for the half year ended 25 Mar. last

HD 36/A/245   29 Jun. 1658
Acquittance by Robert Woodside to John Pemberton, Chamberlain, for £6 1*s* 8*d* due to the Master of the Grammar School for the quarter ended last Midsummer [Woodside was Usher, 1630–41, Master from 1657; d.1658]

HD 36/A/246   1 Jul. 1658
Acquittance by William Dixon to John Pemberton, Chamberlain, for £3 11*s* 8*d* for his salary as Usher of the Free School, due on 24 Jun. [William Dixon, MA, appointed Usher in Nov. 1651]

HD 36/A/247   28 Sep. 1658
Richard Hayle and Richard Jennings [Bailiffs] to Mr Wright and Mr Pemberton, Chamberlains. Warrant for payment of 15*s* to William Hempson, for the ringers' and trumpeter's services at the proclamation of the Lord Protector [Richard Cromwell]

HD 36/A/248   28 Sep. 1658
Richard Hayle and Richard Jeninges [Bailiffs], to Mr Wright and Mr Pemberton, Chamberlains. Warrant for payment of £12 8*s* 8*d* to William Hamby, according to an order of the Assembly, in repayment of money spent by him on the town's business

HD 36/A/249   20 Nov. 1658
Henry Lawrence, President, by order of the Protector and Council, Whitehall, to the Committee for the Monthly Assessment for the Army in Suffolk. *Re* collection of the Assessment [poor condition; incomplete]

HD 36/A/250   13 Dec. 1658
J. Glynn [? John Glynn, Chief Justice of the Upper Bench], from his chamber in Lincoln's Inn (Middlesex), to the Keeper of Ipswich Gaol. Warrant for release of Richard Tardbucke of St Giles, Cripplegate (Middlesex), inprisoned for bigamy, since he has found sureties for his appearance at the Middlesex Sessions of the Public Peace and General Gaol Delivery

HD 36/A/251   15 Feb. 1659
Examination of several mariners, Henry Gosnold, constable, and others, before Nicholas Phillipps and Robert Sparrowe, Bailiffs. *Re* unlawful press gang activities

HD 36/A/252   n.d. [1650s]
[? The Bailiffs]. 3 draft letters, 1 to Richard Hutchinson, Treasurer of the Navy, the others un-addressed, *re* cost of providing for sick and wounded sailors

HD 36/A/253   7 Sep. 1660
Manuel Sorrell and Thomas Wright [Bailiffs], to Mr Haymer and Mr Wright, Chamberlains. Warrant for payment of £28 1*s* 1*d* to Robert Sparrowe for provisions (itemised) supplied for a feast

HD 36/A/254   10 Sep. 1660
Manuel Sorrell and Thomas Wright [Bailiffs], to Mr Haymor and Mr Wright, Chamberlains.
Warrant for payment of 20s to William Hawkins, to reimburse him for money paid to Sir Henry
Felton's man when Sir Henry presented a buck to the town

HD 36/A/255   25 Oct. 1660
Joseph Harley, London, to Robert Clarke, [Clerk of the Peace], Ipswich. Requesting his help in
obtaining reimbursement of his expenses in a suit on behalf of the town in London

HD 36/A/256   19 Feb. 1661
[George, Duke of] Albemarle, John Buck, William Prynne and Edward Kinge, Commissioners
for disbanding the army and discharging the navy, to the Bailiffs and the rest of the Commissioners for the present six-monthly assessment in Ipswich. Requesting speedy collection and
payment, towards paying off some of HM Ships now in the River [Thames]

HD 36/A/257   21 Feb. 1661
John Steele, London, to Robert Clarke, Ipswich. *Re* settlement on proposed marriage between
Steele's son and Clarke's sister Judeth

HD 36/A/258   4 Mar. 1661
John Hawys to Robert Clarke. Enclosing a pair of gloves and a belt, from the writer's cousin
Samuel Hawys, for his help in obtaining a lease of Handford Hall

HD 36/A/259   7 Mar. 1661
George Reve, Thwaite [Norfolk], to Mr Smythyer and Mr Whitinge, Bailiffs. Requesting them
to release Robert Duncon, committed as a Quaker for refusing to take the Oath of Allegiance,
since the King has ordered the release of all Quakers 'except such as were notorious and
dangerous'; Duncon is to subscribe an engagement to be loyal to the King

HD 36/A/260   9 Mar. 1661
John ? Thrower, Eye, to his kinsman Robert Clarke, Ipswich. He has sent him what turkey eggs
he could get; requesting his help in a personal matter

HD 36/A/261   16 Mar. 1661
Henry Felton to Robert Clarke ('Honest Robin'), Ipswich. Expressing thanks for unspecified
service rendered

HD 36/A/262   23 Mar. 1661
John Thrower, Stonham Pye [? Magpie Inn, Little Stonham], to Robert Clarke, Clerk of the
Peace, at his house by MT Church. On 'the late great purge' of Eye Corporation

HD 36/A/263   1 Apr. 1661
Henry Felton to Robert Clarke, Ipswich. He was with Mr Ward until almost 9 last night, and
found him honest to his party and principles, and resolved to set up his friend if he can

HD 36/A/264   25 Feb. 1662
James Caley, Whitton, to Robert Clarke, Ipswich. *Re* increase in his 'assessment' as to his
personal estate; as Clarke is a Commissioner, he is presumably, with the other Commissioners,
empowered to relieve such as are overcharged

HD 36/A/265   12 Jul. 1662
Thoms —[*signature illegible*] to Mr Clarke [Robert Clarke, Clerk of the Peace]. Originally
enclosing a Commission of the Peace for the county, since 'the Judges in their circuits impute
such blame to the Clerks of the Peace where there are no commissions for them'

HD 36/A/266   8 Sep. 1662
John Brandlinge, Ipswich, to the Bailiffs, burgesses and commonalty assembled in the Great
Court. Requesting to be discharged from holding office in the borough, on the grounds of age
and ill health

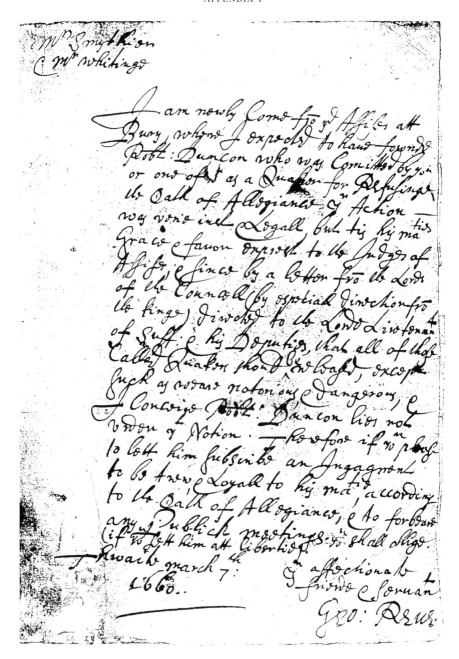

Fig. 24. Letter, dated 7 Mar. 1661, from George Reve of Thwaite [Norfolk], to Mr
Smythyer and Mr Whitinge, Bailiffs, requesting them to release Robert Duncon,
committed as a Quaker for refusing to take the Oath of Allegiance, since the King
has ordered the release of all Quakers 'except such as weare notorious and
dangerous'; Duncon is to subscribe an engagement to be loyal to the King.
(Borough correspondence, HD 36/A/259)

HD 36/A/267   29 Sep. 1662
[Sir] Henry Herbert [Master of the Revels] Lincolne House, Tuttle Street [Westminster], to the
Bailiffs and Town Clerk. Thanking them for their services to the office of the Revels in sup-
pressing persons who obtained undue authority by the 'false actinges' of the writer's servant
James Lyde, now dismissed

HD 36/A/268   ? 4 Feb. 1663
John Sicklemor to — . He has treated with Mr Stone, commended by Mr Thomasin 'our
Bishop's stationer' to be schoolmaster; details of Stone's career; 'I am att a losse in my reputa-
tion concerning your wine licences, the Commissioners will thinke me madd that in ten dayes
time I should give them noe account'

HD 36/A/269   14 Apr. 1663
William Richardson, London, to the Bailiffs. Thanking the Corporation for choosing him as
one of its counsel

HD 36/A/270   6 May 1663
Samuel Duncon, Grundisburgh, to — . He has spoken to his old friend John Reynoulds 'to gitt
me discharged for matters of worshipp and that I might not henceforth be putt into the process';
his difficulties in giving to Caesar the things that are Caesar's [Dated in Quaker style, the 6th of
the 3rd month]

HD 36/A/271   11 May 1663
John Sicklemor, Gray's Inn [Middlesex], to Robert C[?larke], Ipswich. His disapproval of the
Corporation Act as a test for voters

HD 36/A/272   11 May 1633 [recte 1663]
Christopher Glascock, Felsted [Essex], to the Bailiffs. Thanking the town for its hospitality;
regretting that he cannot immediately perform the requested services because of other
obligations

HD 36/A/273   4 Jun. 1663
Francis Widdrington to the Bailiffs. He believes the pink they mention went out last night, but
will make enquiries, and if she has not gone, 'she shall stay or sink'. He does not believe
himself obliged 'to give notice to a jury of men I do not know, it belonging to the civil, not the
martial power'

HD 36/A/274   11 Jul. 1663
[Sir] Henry Herbert [Master of the Revels], Lincoln House, Tutthill Street, Westminster, to the
Recorder and Town Clerk. He formerly requested them to prohibit William Lyde from showing
a blank book at Ipswich, since Lyde had not then submitted to the authority of the King's Office
of the Revels; since he has now submitted, he is to be permitted to enjoy the benefit of his
authority

HD 36/A/275   16 Jul. 1663
Philip Haward to — [torn away], Ipswich. Re arrears of payments towards repairs of Wilford
and Claydon Bridges

HD 36/A/276   22 Aug. 1663
Henry Felton to [Robert] Clarke [Clerk of the Peace], Ipswich. Requesting him to forward a
letter to Sir Edmund Bacon, which 'I doubt not butt it will doe your busines; lett not the messenger be know [sic] to come from any body but me'

HD 36/A/277   10 Sep. 1663
Thomas Lee to Robert Clarke, Ipswich. Requesting him to deliver a commission to Sir Nevill
Catlyn

HD 36/A/278   7 Oct. 1663
T. Southampton [Thomas Wriothesley, 4th Earl of Southampton, Lord High Treasurer] and
Ashley [Anthony Ashley Cooper, Lord Ashley, afterwards 3rd Earl of Shaftesbury],

Southampton House [London], to the Suffolk Justices of the Peace. Ordering application of a new Act of Parliament for collecting the Hearth Tax, and enquiring into delays in the receipt of the money by the Exchequer

HD 36/A/279   13 Nov. 1663
John Arnold, Bernards Inn [London], to Robert Clarke, Town Clerk, Ipswich. If the *Certiorari* is not speedily returned, 'you are like to suffer for it'; reminding him of other legal matters

HD 36/A/280   13 Nov. 1663
William Symons, Registrar to the Commissioners [for Wine Licences], Wine Office [London], to the Bailiffs and burgesses. Requesting payment of half-year's rent for the licence granted to them to sell wine by retail in Ipswich

HD 36/A/281   21 Nov. 1663
Richard Langrishe, London, to his 'loving brother' [unnamed]. *Re* purchase of 'tabels' and 'Rusye lether' [? Russian leather] [*see also* HD 36/A/322]

HD 36/A/282   10 Dec. 1663
Cyrian Coke, Wickham, to [Robert] Clarke [Town Clerk]. *Re* a doe to be sent to Mrs Clarke; requests him to explain to Mr Sheppard that he has not paid him his money this court, because he has been too lame to leave Wickham

HD 36/A/283   15 Jan.1664
Daniel Meadowe, Chattisham, to Robert Clarke, Ipswich. *Re* a suit brought against him by his neighbour Damsell

HD 36/A/284   4 Feb. 1664
? William Harvey, London, to John Sicklemor, Recorder of Ipswich. *Re* the jury's verdict on Mrs Foord's death, whereby her goods are forfeit to the town; other legal matters

HD 36/A/285   4 Feb. 1664
Edmund Poley to [Robert] Clarke [Town Clerk]. On behalf of Mark Williams, a Romish recusant of Stow Hundred, 'a poor fellow, & not worth a groate', starving in Ipswich Gaol

HD 36/A/286   1 Mar. 1664
Acquittance by Edward Sheppard to Robert Clarke, by order of Cirian Coke, for £50 received by Clarke from Coke on 16 Feb. 1664 [*see* HD 36/A/282 above]

HD 36/A/287   23 Mar. 1664
[George Monck, Duke of] Albemarle, [Montague Bertie, Earl of] Lindsey, [Richard Vaughan, Earl of] Carbery, [Anthony Ashley Cooper, Lord] Ashley, J. Seymour, Hugh Pollard, Edward Nicholas and William Morice, Whitehall, to Nicholas Philips and John Robinson, Bailiffs. Commending them for apprehending John Crooke, Thomas Greene and 3 or 4 other Quakers for refusing to take the Oath of Allegiance; they are to be proceeded against according to law

HD 36/A/288   4 Apr. 1664
John Sicklemor [Recorder of Ipswich], London, to Robert Clarke [Town Clerk]. *Re* payment of £25 to Mr Hornigold on Mrs Shawe's account. Postscript: 'Mr Atturney Generall will doe us all the good he cann & we shall [have] many of our desires granted. . . . The Master of the Revells tells me nothing shalbe done by his patent for bowling-alleys and the like but what I shall approve of. I thinke the gagers wilbe quiett.'

HD 36/A/289   30 Apr. 1664
John Robinson, John Sicklemor [Recorder of Ipswich] and William Richardson, London, to Nicholas Philips, Bailiff. *Re* opposition to their efforts to obtain a new borough charter; request that Mr Clarke [Robert Clarke, Town Clerk] be sent to help them. Postcript for Robinson's wife gives his lodging as 'The Naked Boy right against Gray's Inn, the Dog and Ball being full'

HD 36/A/290   2 Jun. 1664
John Moore, 'in Fetter Lane at Mr Darlington's house, a barber against the Flower de Luce Inn', London, to the Bailiffs. *Re* his efforts on their behalf to obtain a new borough charter;

requests the presence of the Borough Recorder, Mr Sicklemore, to discuss proposed additions to the charter with the Attorney General. 'I am now renewing the charter for St Edmunds Bury. The Earl of St Albans is their good friend.'

HD 36/A/291   25 Jun. 1664
John Sicklemor [Recorder of Ipswich], Gray's Inn [London], to Robert Clarke [Town Clerk], Ipswich. *Re* difficulties over grant of a new borough charter: 'Our charter I thinke tis att a full stopp, yet our Lord, our High Steward, is soe zealous as he will not give it over'; addition of Mr Robinson to the Deputy Lieutenancy

HD 36/A/292   — Jun. 1664
? The Bailiffs to Sir Henry Felton, bart, MP at Lady Everett's in Newport Street, 'or leave it with the porter at the Parliament house door'. They have tried to execute his and Mr Sicklemore's warrants for pressing seamen for the King's service, but with little success, 'by reason that they run into the country'; they suggest punishing the refusers and those who hide them

HD 36/A/293   15 Jul. 1664
[Edward Hyde, 1st Earl of] Clarendon [Lord Chancellor], Worcester House [London], to [the Bailiffs]. *Re* dispute between Viscount Hereford and St Peter's parish, Ipswich, *re* curacy of the church; since the curacy is in the King's gift, Clarendon has thought fit to settle Mr Aldus in the position

HD 36/A/294   3 Sep. 1664
? W. Carew, Edward Brooke and William Dickenson to John Sicklemor, Recorder of Ipswich. *Re* their difficulties in Ipswich in implementing their royal grant of the 'Gauging Office' in most of the ports of England and Wales, because of local resistance; appealing for co-operation

HD 36/A/295   12 Sep. 1664
W. Coventry [Commissioner of the Navy and Secretary to the Duke of York (Lord High Admiral)], St James's [Westminster], to the Bailiffs. [Originally enclosing HD 36/A/296]

HD 36/A/296   12 Sep. 1664
James, Duke of York, Lord High Admiral, St James's [Westminster], to the Bailiffs. Warrant to press 150 able mariners and put them on board HMS 'Hound' at Harwich, to be brought into the Thames; each man is to receive 1*s*, which is to be repaid by the Commissioners of the Navy

HD 36/A/297   20 Sep. 1664
H. ? Kearsley, London, to John Robinson, searcher of the customs in the port of Ipswich. Asking him to promote the brief granted by the King to Henry Lisle of Guisborough (York-shire), who has suffered a £4,000 loss by fire

HD 36/A/298   27 Sep. 1664
W. Coventry [Commissioner of the Navy and Secretary to the Lord High Admiral], St James's, to the Bailiffs. The captain of the 'Hound' has informed him that Ipswich has sent only 9 pressed men. 'Hound' will remain at Harwich to receive more men; if the warrant is not executed more effectively, His Royal Highness [the Duke of York] will complain to the King

HD 36/A/299   28 Sep. 1664
Acquittance by H. Gosnold to Robert Clarke [Town Clerk] for £20 disbursed about renewing the charter, and for £130 paid to Mr Sicklemore for the same business

HD 36/A/300   28 Sep. 1664
John Fortiscue, on board HMS 'Hound', Harwich, to the Bailiffs. Requesting them to send him the men they have pressed and to tell him whether there is any order for pressing in the 'out parishes'

HD 36/A/301   29 Sep. 1664
John Fortiscue, HMS 'Hound', Harwich, to the Bailiffs. He has received from them 9 pressed men; he will give an account by express to His Royal Highness concerning 'those men that hide themselves in the country, that there may be an order for impressing them sent down'

HD 36/A/302   1 Oct. 1664
[James Howard, Earl of] Suffolk [Lord Lieutenant], to Lord Cornwallis, for communication to the rest of the Deputy Lieutenants of Suffolk; to be left with the Postmaster at Bury St Edmunds. Requiring their assistance in pressing mariners and seafaring men for the King's service

HD 36/A/303   8 Oct. 1664
James ? Sack, Mayor, and George Coleman, Harwich, to the Bailiffs. A pregnant woman and a young child have been drowned in Ipswich water when their smack capsized in a storm; they will remain upon the water until the Ipswich coroner proceeds according to law

HD 36/A/304   20 Oct. 1664
John Sicklemor [Recorder of Ipswich], Gray's Inn, [London], to the Bailiffs. He will pay the Earl of Suffolk his salary, 'which I have ready in twenty shilling pieces, purchased at a dear rate'; the text of Ipswich's charter has been agreed; it must be engrossed for presentation to the King for a fiat under the Privy Seal, then engrossed again for the Great Seal, which 'I cannot get finished in fourteen days'; much money must be paid, for which he has charged a bill of exchange on Robert Clarke [Town Clerk]. De Ruyter has left Cadiz for Guinea; Prince Rupert is expected tonight in London; 'here no man talks but of the present wars with the Dutch'; 'spotted fever' in Chancery Lane

HD 36/A/305   22 Oct. 1664
John Sicklemor, Gray's Inn, to Robert Clarke [Town Clerk], at his house in MT. On the advantages of the new borough charter; arrangements for payment of costs incurred in obtaining it; the Duke of York 'is suddenly for sea, and without question suddenly the wars will break out'; Prince Rupert's ships are at Portsmouth

HD 36/A/306   18 Nov. 1664
[Edward Hyde, Earl of] Clarendon [Lord Chancellor], [Edward Montagu, Earl of] Manchester, [George Monck, Duke of] Albemarle, [John Granville, Earl of] Bath, [James Annesley, Earl of Anglesey; [John Maitland, Earl of] Lauderdale, Humpfrey [Henchman, Bishop of] London, James Berkeley and [other signatures torn away], from Whitehall, to the Justices of the Peace for Suffolk. Ordering them to give directions to all headboroughs, constables and tithingmen to make exact lists of the names of all seamen residing in their respective parishes, giving their ages; to be sent at once to the writers, with a duplicate to the Vice Admiral of the county or his deputy

HD 36/A/307   3 Dec. 1664
John Sicklemor [Recorder of Ipswich], to Robert Clarke, Town Clerk, Ipswich. *Re* progress in obtaining the borough charter; discussion with the King's Attorney *re* 'our gauging business'. Private postscript: Lord S [? Suffolk] wishes to be informed what persons have money in arrears due to the King, whether poll money, subsidies or other

HD 36/A/308   21 Jan. 1665
[Sir] Jere[miah] Smyth [Admiral], on board HMS 'Mary', Harwich, to the Bailiffs. He has received instructions from HRH [the Duke of York] for pressing able coasters to serve as pilots and masters' mates, and for procuring able seamen; requests their co-operation, 'sparing no persons of what degree or quality you shall judge to be serviceable'; any who absent themselves are to be looked on as legally pressed and proceeded against according to law

HD 36/A/309   31 Jan. 1665
John Sicklemor [Recorder of Ipswich], Gray's Inn, to Robert Clarke, Town Clerk of Ipswich. In response to a query on a point of law *re* killing and eating of flesh in Lent; he and 'cousin

Richardson' intend to bring down the charter; personal matters; rumours of an engagement with the Dutch

HD 36/A/310   2 Feb. 1665
Henry Felton, [? Harwich], to Capt Robert Sparrowe and John Wright, Bailiffs. They will shortly receive from HRH [the Duke of York] instructions for more effectually carrying on 'this great work'; meanwhile they should try to press as many men as possible with the warrant they already have

HD 36/A/311   24 Jun. 1665
John Wingfeld, [? Deputy Lieutenant], to Robert Clarke [Town Clerk], Ipswich. Asking that his friend Mr Humphrey, who is charged in Ipswich with foot arms, be discharged, since he is charged in several companies under the command of the writer's colonel, Sir Philipp Parker; he will reciprocate for any persons they may have charged in Samford Hundred

HD 36/A/312   1 Dec. 1665
Sir Thomas Smyth, Gilbert Thomas, Marshal General, and Robert Clifton, to [? the Bailiffs]. Whereas they have been appointed by George, Duke of Albemarle to search for and seize all goods purloined from the King's prize ships and frigates, they appoint Richard Margerem of Ipswich their deputy

HD 36/A/313   20 Mar. 1666
William Doyly to [Robert] Clarke, Town Clerk, Ipswich. 'The unreasonable demands of the people of Ipswich who quartered the sick and wounded there is the true cause why they are not paid the money'; they shall be paid if they reduce the account from 14s to 7s a week, otherwise the writer must take directions from the King and Council

HD 36/A/314   'Monday night' [? 4 Jun. 1666]
W. Hawkins to —. Informing him, by command of the Bailiffs, of the death of Captain Bacon at sea, in battle with the Dutch; details of the engagement; Sir Nicholas has given Mr Gosnold and his 'consults' full power to manage the solemnity [of the funeral]. [Mounted on the same leaf]: letter, Matthew Cracherode to [Robert] Clarke [Town Clerk of Ipswich] – now that the soldiers of the town are being called together for Captain Bacon's funeral, he is asked to use his endeavours to have them bring in the writer's salary, which is 3 years in arrears [Captain Philemon Bacon, RN, commanding HMS 'Bristol', was killed off the North Foreland, 1 Jun. 1666 – DNB]

HD 36/A/315   1 Feb.–29 Mar. 1668
Bill of receipts for various charges on Ipswich town lands in Kirton and Falkenham, and for purchase of wine and other goods.

HD 36/A/316   8 Jun. 1669
Gilbert Cantuar [Gilbert Sheldon, Archbishop of Canterbury], Lambeth House, to 'Rt Revd and my very good Lord [the Bishop of London]. Re suppression of conventicles in his diocese; the Bishop, as Dean of the Province of Canterbury, is to pass the instructions to the other bishops of the Province. Postscript in Sheldon's hand is not in the undated draft version in the Bodleian (Bodl.Ms Add.c.308, ff.140v–141r) – information from Dr D. L. Wykes, University of Leicester. [badly discoloured by damp and partly illegible]

HD 36/A/317   11 Feb. 1673
Edward Mann, Gray's Inn [London], to Robert Clarke, Town Clerk of Ipswich. He has discussed the business with Mr Aylworth of Lincoln's Inn; the reason for 'the increasing of 3 years' is because of the ruin of Bristol when it was a garrison town in the late wars

HD 36/A/318   May 1673
J[ohn] W[right], G[ilbert] L[indfield] [Bailiffs], and R[obert] C[larke], [Town Clerk], Ipswich, to Nathaniel Dorell, esq., major, etc. Regretting their inability to raise recruits for him, since the several companies of foot and dragoons under command of Sir John Talbot, [Christopher Monck, 2nd] Duke of Albemarle and the Earl of Northampton have been 'up and down amongst us for above these six weeks not only for quarter but recruits' [? draft]

HD 36/A/319   13 Aug. [between 1660 and 1681]
Edmund Hervey, Wickham Skeith, to Mr Clarke, Clerk of the Peace, Ipswich. Asking him to
publish the rates of servants' wages fixed at Easter Sessions; with postscript signed 'G Reve',
approving the letter and stating that the rates should be set up on every market cross [Robert
Clarke was Clerk of the Peace and Town Clerk, 1660–1681

HD 36/A/320   n.d.[between 1660 and 1681]
Charles Gaudy to Robert Clarke, Clerk of the Peace, Woodbridge. Clarke has been mis-
informed concerning a number of named persons alleged to have butchered meat or sold drink
without licence

HD 36/A/321   n.d. [Autumn 1664]
J. Thomas to [Robert] Clarke [Town Clerk and Clerk of the Peace], Ipswich. Reasons for his
failure to visit Ipswich as promised. He hopes 'the school might flourish again, or outshine its
pristine glory', and hopes to serve them in the school in the future

HD 36/A/322   n.d. [between 1660 and 1681]
Richard Langrish to Robert Clarke, Town Clerk of Ipswich. Re purchase of tables and chairs for
the Town Hall [postmark dated 3 Nov.; HD 36/A/281, dated 21 Nov. 1663, appears to be on the
same subject; this letter may reasonably be attributed to 3 Nov. the same year]

HD 36/A/323   14 Apr. [later 17c.]
Certificate by Thomas Hamilton, of discharge of Robert Hicks, a pressed seaman on board the
'Royal Rupert' under Hamilton's command, as unfit for the service

HD 36/A/324   n.d. [? later 17c.]
Inventory of precious stones and jewellery, total value £1,493

HD 36/A/325   n.d. [17c.]
Testimonial by Nicholas Reed and John Lyon in favour of Margaret White of MS, a poor
widow, being allowed to sell cakes to maintain herself and her children

HD 36/A/326   n.d. [17c.]
— [signature torn away] to the Bailiffs. Criticising them for maintaining rogues and vagabonds, in issuing a licence for a man and his wife to pass freely to London, when the woman had
been bound by recognizance to appear at the next assizes in Bury St Edmunds

HD 36/A/327   n.d. [17c.]
Presentment by John Balls, constable of North Cove, before Col Humfrey Brewster, JP, of
Francis Coeman of North Cove, for refusing to serve for reasonable wages

HD 36/A/328   n.d. [? 1650s]
Poor rate assessment for LW, by Anthony Apple[white] and Richard Sparrow, Churchwardens,
and Robert Stebing and Joseph Coleman, Overseers, by consent of [John Aldus and Luke
J[ours] deleted, John Smythier and Henry Whetinge substituted], Bailiffs, from 24 Jun. to
29 Sep. next [According to Richardson 1884, Aldus was Bailiff 1639–40, but with Richard
Pupplet; John Smithier was Bailiff 1640–41 and 1648–49, but with William Cage and Edmund
Humpfrey respectively]

HD 36/A/329   n.d. [? 1650s]
[Poor] rate assessment for MQ, by William Burrough and Christopher Skidmore, Church-
wardens, and Richard Thurston, Daniel Richer and Robert Hall, Overseers, by consent of
Nicholas Phillips and John Robinson, Bailiffs, for 12 weeks ending 25 Mar. next. [According to
Richardson 1884, Phillips was Bailiff 1646–47, but with John Barber; Bacon does not record
Robinson as Bailiff]

HD 36/A/330   n.d. [17c.]
Fragment of an account, signed by Manuell Sorrell, Thomas Wright, John Brandlinge, Richard
Hayle, Richard Jeninges, Thomas Ives, Richard Herne, John ? Ballard, Robert Manning

HD 36/A/331   n.d. [17c.]
'A new remedy for a cancer by M Ruele, a French surgeon'

HD 36/A/332   n.d. [17c.]
Cover only of a letter addressed to the Bailiffs and Recorder, 'and by them to the Assembly and
Town of Ipswich'

HD 36/A/333   9 Sep. 1815
William Snelling jun., Southgate Street, Bury St Edmunds, to Man Bourow [*sic*], Ipswich. *Re*
the Ipswich parliamentary election

APPENDIX II

'Stray' Documents from the Ipswich Borough Archive in Other Suffolk Record Office Collections

This Appendix includes only those items whose origin in the Borough Archive has been estab-lished with reasonable certainty. The Record Office holds other Ipswich documents which *may* be strays; these may be found by means of the place indexes to the Office's holdings. The great majority of the items included are in the Iveagh Collection (HD 1538), which represents Sir Thomas Phillipps's collection of Suffolk manuscripts. Most of Phillipps's Ipswich documents were acquired at William Stevenson Fitch's sale in 1859 (on Fitch's collecting activities, *see* Freeman 1997); the Suffolk collection was purchased *en bloc* by the first Earl of Iveagh in 1914, and acquired for the Suffolk Record Office in 1987. The arrangement of the material listed here duplicates, as nearly as possible, that of the catalogue of the Borough Archive.

PARLIAMENTARY REPRESENTATION

Election Indentures

HD 1538/270/45   16 Nov. 1584
For election of Sir Henry Higham, kt and John Barker, esq.; Sir Charles Framlingham, Sheriff

HD 1538/276/7   21 Apr. 1625
For election of Robert Snellinge, esq. and William Cage, esq.; Geoffrey Pitman, esq., Sheriff, Matthew Brownerigge and John Sicklemore, Bailiffs

HD 1538/276/8   20 Jan. 1626
For election of Robert Snellinge, esq. and William Cage, esq.; Samuel Aylemer, esq., Sheriff, Richard Cocke and Christopher Aldgate, Bailiffs

HD 1538/277/13   3 Mar. 1628
For election of William Cage, esq. and Edmund Daye, gent.; Maurice Barrowe, esq., Sheriff

HD 1538/277/29   20 Mar. 1640
For election of William Cage, esq. and John Gurdon, esq.; Sir Simonds D'Ewes, kt, Sheriff

HD 1538/277/30   6 Apr. 1640
As in HD 1538/277/29

HD 1538/270/55   8 Jan. 1646
For election of Francis Bacon, esq.; John Cotton, esq., Sheriff

LITIGATION CONCERNING THE LIBERTIES

HD 1538/271/20   n.d. [*c.*1567–1568]
'A note of those thinges that Edmund Wythipoll demaundeth of the towne of Ipswyche' (*see* C/1/6/4–6)

TAXATION

Assessed Taxes

HD 1538/277/19   1720
Land Tax assessment duplicate for the town and liberties, giving quarterly and yearly totals for the parishes and hamlets

K 30/2/2   1702–1721
'Copies of the assessments made upon the lands, salaries, vendible stock, monies at interest, annuities, pencions, offices, professions, practizes and persons of the inhabitants of the severall parishes and hambletts within the towne of Ipswich . . . as the same were delivered to the Commissioners . . . by vertue of an Act of Parliament made in the first yeare of . . . Queene Anne, entituled 'An Act for graunting an Aid to her Majestie by diverse Subsidies and a Land Tax'' (vol.)

JUSTICE AND THE COURTS

Portmanmote

HD 1538/277/26   6 Dec. 1615
Bailiffs' precept to Serjeants-at-Mace
In action of recovery, Nicholas Crane and Nicholas Allen *v.* Valentine Bate, of 1 messuage, 2 gardens, 18 acres land and 10 acres pasture in Ipswich

HD 1538/277/35   6 May 1669
Bailiffs' precept to Serjeants-at-Mace
In action concerning right of dower of Susan Richman, widow, in moiety of a messuage in HL

Petty Court

HD 1538/271/14   n.d. [1493–1494]
Bailiffs' precept to Serjeants-at-Mace
For appearance of John Draper to show cause why he should not satisfy Walter Quyntyn, clerk concerning £10, according to his recognizance
(dated by the year of office of Thomas Baldry and Thomas Alvard, Bailiffs)

HD 1538/274/12   20 Apr. 1511
Royal writ to Bailiffs
To proceed in case of breach of covenant between John Skyrwyn and Richard Peyton

HD 1538/274/13   28 Dec. 1530
Royal writ to Bailiffs
To proceed in case of trespass between Christopher Person and Laurence Travers

Sessions

HD 1538/277/4–5   1581–1583
Commissions of Gaol Delivery to the Bailiffs and others
(2 docs)

HD 1538/275/1–16   1570–1681
Commissions of Gaol Delivery to the Bailiffs and others
(16 docs)

HD 1538/275/17   27 Jan. 1758
Gaoler's certified list of prisoners

HD 1538/276/16   29 Sep. 1676
Deed of assignment of (named) prisoners
From William Cullum and Edward Renoldes, outgoing Bailiffs, to their successors John
Wright and John Burrough

FINANCE AND TOWN PROPERTY

Accounts

HD 88/3/5   1591–1732
Treasury payment warrants, vouchers and miscellaneous accounts
(an artificial collection, mounted in vol.)

Town Estate: Evidences of Title

HD 1538/271/8   24 Jan. 1610
Newly-built mills in river-channel W. of Bourne Bridge in MS and Wherstead, and land called
the Channell there
Counterpart feoffment from Bailiffs, burgesses and commonalty to Sir Edward Coke, kt, Chief
Justice of the King's Bench, and Stephen Allen, gent.

Charity Estates: General Surveys and Memoranda

GA 402/1   c. 1820–1828
'An account of the public charities and institutions within the town of Ipswich', compiled by
William Batley
(MS vol.)

Charity Estates: Evidences of Title (Christ's Hospital)

HD 1538/274/11   10 Oct. 1537
Frater house and solar of Friars Preachers of Ipswich
Lease from Prior Edmund and convent to William Golding and William Laurence, both of
Ipswich, gents, for 99 years at 8d p.a.

Charity Estates: Manorial Administration (Tooley's Foundation)

Manor of Sackville's in Debenham
HD 1480/15–16   1626–1708
Court rolls

HD 1480/17, 19, 20   1685–1936
Court books

HD 1480/22–23   1568–1594
Surveys

HD 1480/24–25   1801–1839
Rentals

Manor of Ulveston Hall in Debenham
HD 1480/1–14   1318–1361
Court rolls

HD 1480/16   1703–1708
Court roll

HD 1480/17–18 Court books	1685–1850
HD 1480/21 Extent	n.d. [mid-16c.]
HD 1480/22–23 Surveys	1568–1594
HD 1480/24–25 Rentals	1801–1839

TOWN GOVERNMENT

Custumals

HD 115/1/1   n.d. [? mid-16c.]
Partial transcript of Percyvale's 'Great Domesday'
(Further fragments are in the Borough Archive (C/4/1/5); for details of the contents of HD 115/1/1, *see* the introductory note to C/4/1.)

Other Compilations of Precedents

HD 1538/273   n.d. [? early 18c.]
Book of precedents
Includes:
— partial transcript of James II's Letters Patent, 15 Sep. 1688
— digest of Chamberlains' receipts and payments, 1555–1575
— digest of Treasurers' receipts and payments, 1558–1754

Poll Books for Election of Bailiffs

HD 1538/274/3	8 Sep. 1754
HD 1538/274/4	8 Sep. 1768
HD 1538/274/5	8 Sep. 1769

Qualification for Office

XI/8/1   20 Oct. 1662
Instrument of Commissioners appointed under the 1661 Corporation Act
Removing certain Portmen and members of the Corporation from office for refusal to take the prescribed oaths and renounce the Solemn League and Covenant; nominating their successors; and permitting certain men to postpone their oath-taking and renunciation
Annexed:
— form of renunciation, with subscribers' signatures
(cf. C/4/5/1)

HD 490/1–2   1747–1772, n.d.
Collected correspondence, copy writs of *mandamus* and other legal papers, chiefly *re* election of borough officers and admission of freemen
(2 vols)

TOWN RESPONSIBILITIES AND SERVICES

Christ's Hospital (Minutes)

HD 801/1   1828–1836
Minutes of meetings of Bailiffs and Governors
(vol.)

Christ's Hospital (Accounts)

HD 88/3/4   1579–1580
Treasurer's accounts
(vol.)

Hunwick's Charity

HD 1538/274/30   18 Aug. 1690
Letter of attorney from Bailiffs to Robert Manninge, Robert Smyth, Robert Snellinge, Thomas
Bowle, Thomas Searles and Thomas Kinge
To receive £10 from Corporation of Colchester (Essex), for benefit of the poor of Ipswich

The Water Supply

HD 1538/277/38   24 Aug. 1698
Estreat of water rents

APPENDIX III

'Stray' Documents from the Ipswich Borough Archive in Other Institutions

The arrangement of the material in this Appendix duplicates, as nearly as possible, that of the catalogue of the Borough Archive.

BOUNDARIES

B.L. Add. 25,337   17c.–19c.
Collections relating to the boundaries of Ipswich, compiled by William Batley
Includes:
— some original documents, 17c.
(vol.)

JUSTICE AND THE COURTS

B.L. Add. 30,158   1415–1484
Register of the General Court
Includes:
— admissions of burgesses, trading ordinances, etc.
— copies of charters, leases, etc.
— account of boundaries of the Liberty
(vol.)

B.L. Add. 24,435   1513–1520
Composite register of the borough courts
Chiefly contains pleas of debt and trespass in the Petty Court
Includes:
— enrolments of deeds
— lists of Justices of the Peace, Coroners and other officers
(vol., marked 'No. 8')

B.L. Add. 21,059   1509–1531
Original writs of *certiorari, habeas corpus*, attachment, *procedendo* and *supersedeas*, directed
to the Bailiffs
(vol.)

FINANCE

B.L. Stowe 881   Mar.–Sep. 1588
Original accounts of Edward Cage, Town Treasurer
(included in vol. of antiquarian collections relating to Ipswich, in the hand of Thomas Martin of
Palgrave)

TOWN GOVERNMENT

B.L. Add. 25,012   n.d. [early 14c.]
Custumal

Probably a working copy; the earliest extant version; for discussion, *see* the introductory note
to C/4/1
(vol.)

B.L. Egerton 2,788   n.d. [mid-14c.]
Custumal
Probably a working copy; by the same copyist as the 'White Domesday', C/4/1/2; for discussion, *see* the introductory note to C/4/1
(vol.)

B.L. Add. 25,011   n.d. [15c.]
Custumal
English version; for discussion, *see* the introductory note to C/4/1
(vol.)

CORPORATION CHARITIES

Tooley's Foundation

B.L. Add. 25,343   1566–1595
Annual audited accounts
Includes:
— list of Wardens and other officers
— names, weekly pensions and expenses of the Foundation poor
— (ff. 17v–18v, 23v) 'the chardges of Mr Tolie's tombe' in MQ church
(vol.; from the collections of John Wodderspoon)

Christ's Hospital

B.L. Add. 25,342   1569–1582
Various audited accounts, bound together
Includes:
— Surveyors' accounts 1569–70, 1572–73 (mainly expenses incurred adapting the Blackfriars)
— weekly charges for repairs, maintenance, clothing of inmates
(vol.)

B.L. Add. 31,893   Jan.–Sep. 1574
Account of the 'Weklye paymentes for Chrysts Hospytall'
(vol.)

MISCELLANEA

Bodleian Library, MS Eng. Poet.e.1   15c.
MS song book of an Ipswich minstrel
(vol.; microfilm copy in Suffolk Record Office, Ipswich, ref. J479)

Huntington Library (California), MS HM3   *c*.1538–1540, revised 1560–1563
MS of John Bale's morality play *King Johan*
(vol.; published editions by J. Payne Collier (London, Camden Society, 1838) and J.H.P.
Pafford (Oxford, Malone Society, 1931) in Suffolk Record Office, Ipswich, ref. S822 BAL)

B.L. Add. 25,334–25,336   19c.
Collections for a history of Ipswich, by William Batley
Includes:
— some original documents, 17c.
(3 vols)